INTERFACE OF PSYCHOANALYSIS AND PSYCHOLOGY

INTERFACE OF PSYCHOANALYSIS AND PSYCHOLOGY

Edited by

James W. Barron

Morris N. Eagle

David L. Wolitzky

AMERICAN PSYCHOLOGICAL ASSOCIATION
WASHINGTON, DC

Published by
American Psychological Association
750 First Street, NE
Washington, DC 20002

Copies may be ordered from
APA Order Department
P.O. Box 2710
Hyattsville, MD 20784
Item Number: 431-7270

This book was typeset in Goudy by Scott Photographics, Inc., Riverdale, MD

Printer: Edwards Brothers, Ann Arbor, MI
Cover Designer: Berg Design, Albany, NY
Technical/Production Editor: Christine P. Landry

Library of Congress Cataloging-in-Publication Data

Interface of psychoanalysis and psychology / James W. Barron, Morris
    N. Eagle, David L. Wolitzky, editors.
        p.   cm.
    Includes bibliographical references and index.
    ISBN 1-55798-156-6
    1. Psychoanalysis. 2. Psychology. I. Barron, James W., 1944-
    II. Eagle, Morris N.   III. Wolitzky, David L. (David Leo), 1936-

    [DNLM: 1. Psychoanalytic Theory. 2. Psychological Theory.   WM
    460 I6013]
    RC506.I553   1992
    150.19'5—dc20
    DNLM/DLC
    for Library of Congress   92-10688
                                                                    CIP

Printed in the United States of America
First Edition

In memory of my mother, Jeanette Wedrow Barron,
and my brother, Peter Andrew Barron

J. W. Barron

To my wife, Rita

M. N. Eagle

To my wife, April, and my daughters, Rachel and Sara

D. L. Wolitzky

CONTENTS

FOREWORD

Always thrall to the romantic myth of the lone genius-hero, Sigmund Freud usually denied any influence of contemporary psychology on his theories. His followers have shown a touching ability to subordinate skepticism or curiosity in this matter to filial piety, although that is one of the attitudes most easily subjected to reductionistic deflation by psychoanalytic interpretation as transference. The devout Jones (in the first volume of his *The Life and Work of Sigmund Freud*) did quote the work of Karpinska and Dorer in uncovering evidence of Herbart's influence on Freud's thought, but saw that as favoring the emergence of only a couple of concepts. And an occasional scholar noted Freud's having read Lipps or Taine, or remarked on his having studied with the philosopher-psychologist Brentano without attributing any substantial part of his ideas to any of them. His followers dutifully repeated Freud's claim that the foundation of his work was direct observation of patients and that he had induced his concepts from the residue of his clinical work. Many of them added, in awed tones: *and from his self-analysis.* Contemporary scholarship (from Ellenberger to Kerr) tells a different story: Freud approached his data with as many preconceptions as anyone else, and many of them can be traced to early psychological writers.

From the start, then, psychoanalysis has been motivated to deny or to minimize any influence from psychology. Exaggerating the degree of his rejection and ostracism by the established medical and intellectual communities, Freud and his followers alike deliberately withdrew from the usual means of scientific exchange and remained outside of the community of scholars. They were of course greatly aided by the social situation of their new profession, outside universities. Today we realize that Freud's work was received with no more ambivalence than that of many a scientific discoverer within the university world. It is important to realize that he would have found that situation intolerable even if he had realized that his situation was not unusual. What he wanted from others was not constructive criticism and a stimulating exchange of ideas, giving and taking, but to be hailed as their leader. His self-description as a *conquistador* was quite insightful. Since the part of the scientific world that was concerned with human thoughts, feelings, and behavior—psychology—did not embrace him as its savior and did not enlist as part of his band of disciples, he felt spurned by it.

Nevertheless, he had influential champions within psychology from rather early years. G. Stanley Hall was a considerable figure in the field when he invited Freud to Clark University in 1909 to give the lectures that introduced him to America. In a 1964 monograph, *The Influence of Freud on American Psychology*, Shakow and Rapaport list seven well-known psychologists who wrote in a predominantly approving way about Freud's ideas in the 1920s and the 1930s, including

Gardner Murphy, J. F. Brown, and Else Frenkel-Brunswik. Woodworth (in a 1917 article) is representative of a good many others, in recognizing much that was original and needed saying in Freud's work, while being critical of its excesses and sloppinesses. To the psychoanalysts, balanced assessments like Woodworth's seemed like rejection or misunderstanding motivated by resistance, and they often made things worse by calling it that. Even so fair-minded a pair of observers as Shakow and Rapaport label a good deal of criticism (e.g., that there are elements of vitalism and hedonism in psychoanalytic theory) as misunderstandings that are based on insufficient study of the texts, although today the defense sounds weak and unconvincing. Of course, there was also a great deal of criticism by psychologists that was indeed ill-informed and intemperate.

As Shakow and Rapaport make clear, a major problem in the acceptance of psychoanalytic theory by psychologists was its lack of a clear, definitive statement in a systematic presentation of manageable size. Moreover, they admit that one reason such a source was never written was the many internal inconsistencies in the theory. Most psychologists were not motivated enough to spend the time required to study Freud's scattered works in chronological order; hence, most of them learned what they knew about it from secondary sources, few of which were much good. Moreover, psychologists were justifiably put off by the manifest untestability of large parts of the theory.

In 1940, Gordon Allport assembled nine articles on psychoanalysis by analyzed psychologists and published them in his *Journal of Abnormal and Social Psychology,* the most prestigious journal of its time. The symposium did a good deal to bring Freud's ideas to the attention of American psychologists in a rather persuasive way. The gem of the collection was Henry A. Murray's eloquent "What Should Psychologists Do About Psychoanalysis?"—a ringing call to put relevance to life above methodological nicety.

At this point, Murray had already published, with the staff of the Harvard Psychological Clinic, *Explorations in Personality* (1938), an enormously influential book. It presented the principal results of a four-year group project, an original and frequently copied mixture of multiform personality assessment, experiments, and theoretical work, inspired primarily by Freud (although he shares the dedication with Jung and three others). In the next decade, Murray assembled another talented, multidisciplinary group of co-workers and students for a similar cooperative project, although this time the work was interrupted by Pearl Harbor, and it did not culminate in a single, widely read book.

Aside from showing that psychoanalysis could enormously stimulate good scientific work in several ways (even if few of Freud's dicta were directly tested), Murray contributed a great deal to the fruitful union of psychoanalysis and psychology by training many of the leaders of the emerging field of clinical psychology.

About the same time that Murray was breaking new ground at Harvard, Hull took the initiative to organize a series of seminars at Yale's Institute of Human Relations, with the aim of synthesizing conditioning theory and psychoanalysis. Two of the participants, John Dollard and Neal Miller, discovered that the mechanistic aspects of psychoanalytic theory were pretty congruent with behaviorism. Their 1950 book, *Personality and Psychotherapy,* did a good deal to convince a sector of the hardest-nosed psychologists that psychoanalysis was not some mystical abracadabra but potentially useful to scientific behavior theory. Another member of the seminar, Robert Sears, had a long and distinguished career in which he succeeded in promoting interest in psychological research of psychoanalytic ideas (see especially his 1943 publication, *Survey of Objective Studies of Psychoanalytic Concepts*).

At the end of World War II, when clinical psychology underwent its great growth spurt and came fully into being as a major branch of the discipline, it is safe to say that a large part of its leading figures were more or less following the rising star of psychoanalysis. David Rapaport played an important role in promoting an interest in psychoanalysis among the new generation of clinical psychologists. He was analyzed in Europe but was largely self-trained and was never a practitioner of psychoanalysis until the last few years of his life. By sheer force of intellect, he not only mastered the literatures of psychoanalysis during his first years in this country, but began a lifelong project of clarifying, organizing, and teaching the theory and integrating it with his encyclopedic knowledge of most branches of psychology. At the same time, he and Murray share credit for concretely showing how the clinical theory could greatly deepen and expand psychological testing into the subdiscipline of personality assessment and psychodiagnosis. He left a rich legacy of a psychoanalytic-psychological discipline, which he taught and exemplified at the Menninger Foundation and later at the Austen Riggs Center, integrating clinical practice, a thorough, exegetical study of the theory, and rigorous research. His tradition lives on in the work of his students (now banded together in the Rapaport–Klein Study Group, which meets yearly in Stockbridge, Massachusetts) and in his widely read publications.

I should say a word here about the Research Center for Mental Health (RCMH) at New York University, even though I am too close to it to venture an assessment of its importance in the history of the present topic. My first act on becoming its director in 1953 was to recruit George S. Klein, who had gone with me through the rigors of working under Rapaport at the Menninger Foundation in Topeka. From the start, we decided to follow two paths in our work: to study and clarify psychoanalytic theory in order to make it testable, and to use both the experimental laboratory and the discipline of psychological testing to study theoretically or clinically important problems—ideally, both. Two books (Klein's, 1976, and Holt's, 1989) present the main fruits of our theoretical labors, while the research has been reported in scores of papers, mostly by our colleagues and students. Many of them—including two of the editors of this volume—have become well-known psychoanalytic psychologists.

In the two decades since the RCMH went out of existence, numerous other centers have carried on psychoanalytically informed research, largely on psychotherapy. Well before, however, psychoanalysis had significantly penetrated child and adolescent psychology, particularly in a number of important centers of developmental research. It provided many ideas for empirical investigation and had some influence on method. The numerous findings have had little impact on psychoanalytic theory and practice, however, even when the teams have been led by medical psychoanalysts.

Throughout this century, psychoanalysts continued to show much less interest in psychology than psychologists did in Freud's work. In the 1940s, the gray eminence of the New York Psychoanalytic Institute, Hartmann, argued that psychoanalysis was or could become a general psychology, and his ego psychology seemed to make a place for the sister discipline's findings on perception, thinking, action, and other areas of psychology's strength. The program remained just that, however, and only a few psychoanalytic scholars attempted to learn much of what psychology had to offer.

The very inaccessibility of orthodox psychoanalytic training to all but an elite group of (mostly research) psychologists only increased its desirability to a couple of generations of clinical psychologists. Gradually, the numbers of psychologist–psychoanalysts increased, partly through the work of institutes run by nonmedical analysts, the first of which was Theodor Reik's National Psychological Association for Psychoanalysis, and partly through "bootleg training." Psychiatrist members of institutes of the American Psychoanalytic Association who disagreed with the official exclusion of psychologists ran informal reading seminars and supervised the first efforts of analyzed psychologists.

In 1961, however, Bernard Kalinkowitz and a group of other similarly trained psychologists established the first psychoanalytic institute in the psychology department of a university, New York University, followed very soon by one at Adelphi. A number of the authors of chapters in this book received their psychoanalytic training in these academically based institutes. And, of course, in the past couple of years, a successful lawsuit broke down the doors to the orthodox institutes of "the American" for psychologists.

Having had the good luck to have participated in the Harvard Psychological Clinic, Rapaport's group in Topeka, and the NYU enterprises (the RCMH, and the NYU Postdoctoral Program in Psychotherapy and Psychoanalysis), I may have overemphasized their importance in the process of bringing psychoanalysis and psychology together. As Shakow and Rapaport point out (in their 1964 monograph), only a part of psychology has achieved much integration with psychoanalysis, anyway:

> When clinical psychology followed its own path toward professionalization, it did not signifi-cantly bridge the gap between psychology and psychoanalysis; rather, it tended to add another gap—one between clinical and academic psychology.

The frontier between psychology and psychoanalysis is still partly fortified, although, in parts of it, active commerce in ideas is well-established.

The chapters in this volume take stock of where we are after a century of mutual influence—and do a more thorough and competent job of it than can be found anywhere else. They give impressive evidence that there are indeed many points of useful contact in the complex interface between psychology and psychoanalysis. Although the latter discipline has slipped from the preeminent place it held in the world of the mental health disciplines for over a decade following World War II, and although its theories have seemed to some to have been mortally wounded by a recent generation of informed and sophisticated critics, no reader of this book can come away unconvinced that there is a lot of life in it yet. For all its many faults as a science and its shortcomings as a form of psychotherapy, psychoanalysis can still be enormously suggestive, stimulating, enriching, and enlightening to psychology. I hope that this book will play a large part in encouraging a new generation of psychologists to discover some of the rewards to be found in the interface.

ROBERT R. HOLT
Professor of Psychology Emeritus
New York University

PREFACE

One hundred years have passed since the inception of psychoanalysis and the founding of the American Psychological Association (APA). Although they have not been 100 years of solitude, and although there have been points of contact, the interaction between psychoanalysis and psychology has been less than optimal. Our goal for this book is to explore the interface between psychoanalysis and psychology, contributing to the enrichment of both. Our hope is that this book will make the boundaries more permeable, will encourage psychoanalysts to overcome the relative isolation of clinical thinking and practice from extra-clinical sources of information and knowledge, and will heighten the interest of psychological theorists, students, and researchers in the content and methods that define the psychoanalytic domain.

Two articles that are highly relevant to our topic appeared in the February 1992 special issue of the *American Psychologist* on the history of American psychology. First, Hornstein presented an excellent historical account of the tensions between academic psychology and psychoanalysis.[1] As she notes, "in the 1890s, when this struggle began, there was little sign that it would become another 'Hundred Years' War.' " She cited Buys's (1976) article, which indicated that it was not until two decades ago that psychoanalysis finally began to be portrayed in a positive manner in most introductory psychology texts.[2] Second, Triplet offered an interesting discussion of Henry Murray's experience at Harvard that yields further insights into the relations of psychology and psychoanalysis.[3]

HISTORIC AND CONTEMPORARY OBSTACLES TO DIALOGUE

Nearly 30 years ago, in their 1964 monograph, *The Influence of Freud on American Psychology*, Shakow and Rapaport[4] came to the following conclusion:

---

[1] Her article (Vol. 47, No. 2) is titled "The Return of the Repressed: Psychology's Problematic Relations With Psychoanalysis—1906–1909."

[2] See C. J. Buys (1976), "Freud in Introductory Psychology Texts" in Volume 3 (pp. 160–167) of *Teaching of Psychology*.

[3] His article (Vol. 47, No. 2) is titled "Henry A. Murray: The Making of a Psychologist?"

[4] This article appears in Volume 4, Issue 1, Monograph 13, of *Psychological Issues*.

A separation existed between psychoanalysis and psychology in spite of their common heritage from the Helmholtz tradition—a tradition which permeated the biological and physiological sciences when Freud started his work. It would seem that this gulf actually arose out of the different way in which each viewed its commitment to the Helmholtz program. Psychology did not recognize Freud's serious commitment to the "forces equal in dignity" part of the Helmholtz school oath as parallel to their own concern with the first part of this oath, the part which called for a "reduction to physical–chemical forces." Its own early focus on the "rigor" demanded by the latter led psychology to skip almost entirely the naturalistic stage usual in the development of a science and to identity itself with the "exact" of a hypothetical Science, rather than with the "meaningful" that psychoanalysis had chosen. Since psychology had not come to terms with defining the proper place and time for exact measurement and quantification, there arose confusion in the use and meaning of the terms "good" and "bad" science—"bad" being taken to be that which characterized psychoanalysis. The "naturalistic" method which fitted psychoanalysis so well was derogated as "unscientific."[5]

In a complementary fashion, psychoanalysts have tended to be contemptuous and dismissive of the findings within academic psychology and of research that takes place outside of the dyadic clinical encounter. While focusing on unconscious processes revealed through the lens of the transference, analysts have turned a blind eye to extra-analytic sources of data.

One of us recently reviewed the monograph, "How Does Treatment Help?"[6] One of the questions asked of the monograph's contributors was as follows: How do ideas and data from other than your therapeutic experience influence your conception of therapeutic action? Collectively, the 16 contributing analysts cited almost 200 references, of which only 6 were citations of empirical research—and 5 of those 6 were cited by one author! This recent example illustrates the way in which psychoanalysis has historically insulated itself from developments in psychological research.

Perhaps one reason for the frequent reflexive dismissal of empirical research and extra-analytic sources of data is the belief commonly held by analysts that, in conducting a clinical analysis, they are simultaneously conducting research. In this view, the psychoanalytic situation with its regular and stable features is akin to a research laboratory and, therefore, is a sufficient (or, even, the only) context in which to amass a wealth of rich data *and* to test discoveries, insights, and hypotheses with respect to their clinical utility and theoretical validity.

The belief that the analytic situation is sufficient both for the generation and verification of hypotheses is reflected in Freud's well-known reaction to Rosenzweig's research on repression.[7] Freud wrote,

> I have examined your experimental studies of the verification of the psychoanalytic assertions with interest. I cannot put much value on these confirmations because the wealth of reliable

---

[5]The oath referred to expressed the guiding philosophy of what came to be known as the Helmholtz School of Medicine. Shakow and Rapaport (1964) quote from the 1842 letter of du Bois-Reymond as follows: "Brucke and I pledged a solemn oath to put into power this truth, no other forces than the common physical–chemical ones are active within the organism; that, in those cases which cannot at the time be explained by these forces one has either to find the specific way or form of their action by means of the physical–mathematical method, or to assume new forces equal in dignity to the chemical–physical forces inherent in matter, reducible to the force of attraction and repulsion."

[6]A. Rothstein. (1988). *How Does Treatment Help? On the Modes of Therapeutic Action of Psychoanalytic Psychotherapy.* Madison, CT: International Universities Press. For the review, see D. L. Wolitzky. (1990). "Pathways to Psychoanalytic Care" in Volume 35 of *Contemporary Psychology* (pp. 1154–1155).

[7]See R. Rosenzweig (1934), "An Experimental Study of Memory in Relation to the Theory of Repression" in Volume 24 of the *British Journal of Psychology* (pp. 247–265).

observations (from the clinical situation) on which these assertions rest, make them independent of experimental verification. Still, it can do no harm.[8]

Of course, as Rapaport pointed out, quite often, experimental laboratory research that purportedly tested psychoanalytic hypotheses was based on operational definitions of psychoanalytic concepts that had little to do with essential features of these concepts and, therefore, had little "ecological validity."[9] This was true of much experimental research on repression in which, for example, greater forgetting of associations to emotional words as contrasted with neutral words was taken as evidence of repression.[10] Thus, in many cases perhaps a dismissive attitude on the part of the analyst toward extra-clinical research and theory was justified. However, as many chapters in this volume demonstrate, in view of the flowering of psychological research and theory in many "interface" areas relevant to psychoanalysis, this dismissive attitude is no longer justified. Conversely, the profoundly important "real life" phenomena, concerns, and insights that arise in the clinical psychoanalytic situation need to be addressed by psychological research and theory.

For the sake of brevity, we will merely note the controversies over the years about the extent to which psychoanalysis is, can be, or even should be a science; the ways in which the emphasis on treatment over research (or the assumption that they are synonymous) have retarded the development of psychoanalysis as a science; and the value and limitations of analytic data, as well as the kinds of "truths" at which psychoanalysis can hope to arrive. These are matters long debated inside and outside the psychoanalytic community and discussed in other contexts.[11] Suffice it to say that we believe that the viability of the psychoanalytic enterprise depends on the perspective and attitude animating this current volume.

In more recent years, the competition among analytic theories and the criticism offered by Spence, Grünbaum, and others have made analysts more cautious about the claims and conclusions that can legitimately be drawn from psychoanalytic data alone. Thus, Arlow (1982) cites Glover's observation of the impact of clinical and theoretical pronouncements of analysts with prestige and authority: "Given sufficient enthusiasm and persuasiveness, or even just plain dogmatism on the part of the author, chances are that, without any check, this view or alleged discovery will gain currency, will be quoted and requoted until it attains the status of an accepted conclusion."[12] Arlow observes the excessive reliance on authority and recognizes that we will soon no longer be able to "rely on the memories of bygone heroes" but will require "solid observational data, meticulously gathered in the analytic situation and objectively evaluated. For it is upon this set of procedures that the claim of psychoanalysis to a place among the empirical sciences is based." It is important to note in this context, however, that Arlow does not specifically include extra-clinical sources of evidence or validation.

---

[8]Quoted in D. W. Mackinnon and W. F. Dukes (1964). Repression. In L. Postman (Ed.), *Psychology in the Making*. New York: Knopf.

[9]See D. Rapaport (1942), *Emotions and Memory*. Baltimore, MD: Williams & Wilkins.

[10]See G. Levinger & J. Clark (1961), "Emotional Factors in the Forgetting of Word Associations," in Volume 62 of the *Journal of Abnormal and Social Psychology* (pp. 99–105).

[11]For example, see M. Eagle and D. L. Wolitzky (1985), "The Current Status of Psychoanalytic Theory," in Volume 5 of the *Clinical Psychology Review* (pp. 259–269). Also see M. Eagle & D. L. Wolitzky (1989), "The Idea of Progress in Psychoanalysis," in Volume 12 of *Psychoanalysis and Contemporary Thought* (pp. 27–72).

[12]See J. A. Arlow (1982), "Psychoanalytic Education: A Psychoanalytic Perspective," in Volume 10 of the *Annual of Psychoanalysis* (pp. 5–20). (The original Glover observation can be found in Volume 33 [pp. 403–409] of the *International Journal of Psychoanalysis*.)

TOWARD AN INTEGRATION OF PSYCHOANALYSIS AND PSYCHOLOGY

Although there are signs of a beginning rapprochement between academic psychologists and psychoanalysts (e.g., Masling's 1983 edited volume *Empirical Studies of Psychoanalytic Theories*), their peaceful coexistence has not yet translated into genuine interest and mutual respect. Many analysts and psychodynamic psychotherapists in private practice, as we have indicated, do not read the psychological literature, whether it be studies of infant development or of psychotherapy process and outcome.

In conceptualizing this volume, we start from the position—which we recognize is not universally shared either by academic psychologists or by psychoanalytic practitioners—that psychoanalysis is an integral part of psychology, despite their historical isolation from one another. We believe, to take just one example, that the psychological research on infancy has important implications for psychoanalytic theories of social, cognitive, and emotional development. As another example, psychoanalysis needs longitudinal studies of development to complement its etiological claims derived from the retrospective views of patients and the historical narratives that they construct. Similarly, a psychoanalytic theory of dreams has to be congruent with current knowledge concerning the neurophysiology of sleep and dreams.

Such an attempted integration of psychology and psychoanalysis may not alter the efficacy of psychoanalytic treatment in the near future. However, to the extent that psychoanalysis aspires to be not only a method of observation and treatment, but also a theory of human development and personality functioning, then psychoanalysts must pay attention to the findings of researchers in various disciplines. Thus, at the very least, psychoanalytic theories, derived from the introspective accounts of adult patients, ought not to contradict psychological or neurological findings regarding human functioning.

Our approach was to select authors who would be most likely to contribute to this integrative task by examining the impact of psychoanalysis on psychology, and the influences (actual and potential) of research in academic psychology on psychoanalytic theory and practice. In planning this volume, our aim was to choose authors whose scholarly and research activities, clinical background and training showed them to be exemplars of the scientist/practitioner or scholar/practitioner model. We wanted individuals who felt a genuine respect for both the scientific and clincial aspects of psychoanalysis. Therefore, we sought to assemble a group of psychoanalytically oriented contributors, who were either active themselves in research relevant to psychoanalysis or whose scholarly and intellectual interests and values suggested that they could see the potential mutual enrichment that psychoanalysis and psychology could offer to one another.

In a single volume, we can provide only a limited sampling of work that attempts to embody the integrative theme we have selected for our focus. Nevertheless, we believe that the chapters in this volume, each of which is an original contribution, constitute a representative sample of work that attempts to link psychoanalysis with theory and research within academic psychology.

ORGANIZATION OF THIS BOOK

We have divided this book into five main parts: I. Fundamental Concepts and Assumptions; II. Personality Development and Organization; III. Psychoanalysis and Cognition; IV. Psychopathology; and V. Psychoanalytic Treatment.

In our guidelines to authors, we stressed the need to attempt an integration of the psychoanalytic and psychological research literature in the domain under consideration, to point out areas of convergence and divergence, and to suggest possible directions for future research.

Obviously, some topics lend themselves better to such a focus than others. We deliberately decided not to constrain authors with a specific outline of questions and points to cover. In making this editorial decision, we were aware of both its risks and benefits. Naturally, we hope that the reader will regard the latter as outweighing the former.

In the sections and chapters that follow, we have spanned a broad range of topics in basic areas relevant to psychoanalytic psychology. Each section begins with an editorial introduction aimed at providing an overview of the general area as well as a synopsis of each chapter, along with some integrative commentaries.

ACKNOWLEDGMENTS

As part of the celebration of its centennial, the American Psychological Association (APA) invited the Division of Psychoanalysis to consider editing a volume on psychoanalysis. The Division's Publication Committee, chaired by Robert Marshall, in turn solicited proposals from the membership, and then selected our proposal for the *Interface of Psychoanalysis and Psychology*. As editors, whose names are listed in alphabetical order on the cover, we colloborated closely and contributed equally to this project. We divided the labor for the section introductions as follows: Eagle, Sections I and V; Barron, Section II; Wolitzky, Sections III and IV.

We formed an Advisory Committee consisting of senior psychologists with whom we consulted as we were conceptualizing the project in more detail and who, in some cases, reviewed chapters and provided valuable feedback. The members of the Advisory Committee were Marvin Aronson, Bertram Cohler, Harold Cook, Edward Corrigan, Helen Desmond, Ruth-Jean Eisenbud, Helen Golden, Maurice Green, Bertram Karon, Robert Lane, Zane Liff, Stanton Marlan, Robert Marshall, Murray Meisels, and Joan Trachtman. We thank them for their contributions.

Julia Frank-McNeil, APA Director of Acquisitions and Development, was a strong supporter of this project and was instrumental in its becoming a reality. With coolness and competence, she guided us through the thickets of negotiations with all those individuals and organizations involved. Theodore J. Baroody, APA Development Editor, was exceptionally helpful. We deeply appreciated his thorough understanding of the goals of the project, his prompt and careful readings of the various chapters, and his many helpful suggestions. We would also like to thank Alice J. Rapkin, who functioned in a secretarial and administrative capacity. The fact that we were able to coordinate a project of this size and to meet necessary deadlines was in large measure due to her professionalism and organizational skills.

We are particularly pleased that Robert Holt agreed to write the foreword to this book. He is an incisive critic and distinguished psychologist whose career has helped advance our understanding of psychoanalytic theory and practice.

We hope that this book contributes to the collective efforts of present and future scholars and scientist–practitioners who continue to explore the interface of psychoanalysis and psychology.

Finally, we wish to dedicate this book to our families, whose love and encouragement helped to sustain our efforts.

James W. Barron
Morris N. Eagle
David L. Wolitzky

I

FUNDAMENTAL CONCEPTS
AND ASSUMPTIONS

INTRODUCTION:
FOUNDATIONS OF PSYCHOANALYSIS

What kind of a discipline is psychoanalysis? During the past 30 or 40 years, an intense debate has raged around this question. Although it is perhaps somewhat arbitrary to do so, one can date the beginning of this debate (at least the modern version of it) with the publication of the Hook (1959) symposium on the scientific status of psychoanalysis. The basic question posed in that symposium appeared to be a relatively simple one: Is psychoanalytic theory scientific or is it not? Looking back at that symposium, one can almost view that period as one of relative innocence, at least with regard to the question of whether a theory is scientific. For whatever one's philosophical stance or one's attitude toward psychoanalysis, there would be general consensus today that the question is not a simple one at all. Each of the criteria proposed for distinguishing the scientific from the nonscientific—for example, the verification criterion of Carnap (1936, 1937) and the Vienna Circle or the falsification criterion of Popper (1962)—has been subjected to cogent criticisms and has been found to be wanting.

Since the Hook symposium, debates regarding the status of psychoanalysis have clustered around different specific issues and controversies. For example, at one point, the focus of discussion was the distinction between *reasons* and *causes* (see Davidson, 1963; Toulmin, 1948). Although the reasons-versus-causes debate took place in the broad context of a philosophical theory of action, a particular and narrower focus of the debate was the status of psychoanalysis. One familiar argument was that, whereas the natural sciences deal with causes, psychoanalysis (along with other "human sciences") deals primarily with reasons. The status of psychoanalysis discussion represented a particular version of the old distinction between *Naturwissenschaft und Geisteswissenschaft,* associated with Dilthey (1961) and others, and of the accompanying argument that each kind of knowledge required its own distinctive methods of knowing.

The clinical theory–metapsychology distinction (e.g., Gill, 1976; Klein, 1976) was related both conceptually and historically to the reasons-versus-causes distinction and limited to the psychoanalytic context. Put very briefly and simply, the argument was that the clinical theory represents the heart of psychoanalysis and that the metapsychology is essentially a pseudoscientific and dispensable set of formulations (see Eagle, 1980; & Rubinstein, 1976, for a different point of view). Wakefield presents precisely the opposite view in his chapter in this volume.

The most recent turn that the debate has taken is the argument that, because psychoanalysis is a hermeneutic discipline, the methods it employs and the particular ways that it should be held accountable will differ radically from the methods and forms of accountability of nonhermeneutic disciplines (e.g., Barratt, 1984, 1988; see Grünbaum, 1984, for a devastating critique of the hermeneutic construal of psychoanalysis). A related construal of psychoanalysis can broadly be referred to as *constructivist* or perhaps as *radically constructivist*. Some specific expressions of this position include Spence's (1982) argument that psychoanalytic narratives are possessed of a property that he refers to as *narrative truth* rather than *historical truth* and Geha's (1984) insistence that psychoanalytic narratives, along with other historical accounts, are creative fictions rather than accounts of "what really happened" and, as fictions, are to be judged by aesthetic qualities rather than by concerns with veridicality (see Eagle, 1984a, for a critique of Geha's position, and Eagle, 1984b and Sand, 1984a, 1984b, for a critique of Spence). What we are referring to as a constructivist reading of psychoanalysis is clearly one particular expression of a broad philosophical constructivist trend that includes the writings of, among others, Rorty (1979) and Feyerabend (1975).

In the trends we have very briefly described above, psychoanalysis is generally taken to mean the clinical psychoanalytic situation—that is, psychoanalysis as either treatment or a theory of treatment—rather than psychoanalysis as a broad theory of psychopathology, personality development, and human nature. Thus, it is not entirely clear what a concept such as *narrative truth* would mean in the context of psychoanalysis as a general theory of human nature—unless one wants to argue that the criteria by which a clinical narrative might be evaluated (e.g., coherence, comprehensiveness, persuasiveness) are precisely those by which a general theory is also to be evaluated.

Debates regarding the nature of psychoanalysis have not been limited to its epistemological or scientific status. They have also focused on the content and substantive nature of psychoanalytic theory. For the most part, the chapters in this section concern themselves with these substantive issues. As Greenberg and Mitchell (1983) have observed, recent theoretical developments in psychoanalysis have clustered around a *drive*, as opposed to a *relational*, conception of human nature. In their chapter, Slavin and Kriegman take these two opposing views as a starting point and argue that "a genuine theoretical synthesis" is possible "within the evolutionary (phylogenetic) perspective." From an evolutionary perspective, the mind, or the psyche, would be viewed in a broad adaptive context. That is, over a period of vast evolutionary time, various selection pressures "shaped" the structure and function of the mind. Slavin and Kriegman observe that, because Freud lacked an adequate model of how selection pressures could create the complex design of the mind, he turned to his "phylogenetic fantasies," that is, he turned to the Lamarckian idea of the genetic transmission of acquired characteristics. His basic idea, however—that one must look to past evolutionary time, past environments (what Bowlby, 1969, refers to as our "environment of evolutionary adaptedness," pp. 85–92), and past environmental and social pressures to understand the structure of mind—was, according to Slavin and Kriegman, an eminently sound one.

How does the evolutionary perspective advocated by Slavin and Kriegman serve to integrate the seemingly opposed drive and relational views? Slavin and Kriegman's answer is that, according to a modern conception of adaptiveness, a central measure of which is inclusive fitness, one should expect both overlapping as well as opposing interests between child and parents—that is, one should expect both mutuality and conflict. Slavin and Kriegman present a picture of development as a negotiation process in which the child tries to find ways to guarantee the kind and degree of parental investment necessary for his or her development while protecting his or her "selfish" interests that may conflict with parental interests. They present an intriguing view of repression as a way of sequestering those aims that are incompatible with parental aims and interests and reviving them at a later appropriate time (e.g., during adolescence or during the therapeutic process). From this point of view, repression is largely adaptive insofar as it is "designed" to maximize investment from parents without sacrificing personal aims and interests.

In the picture painted by Slavin and Kriegman, we are inherently and deeply divided between motives "totally dedicated toward the promotion of individual interests" and social motives that stress overlapping interests and relational mutuality. The former set of motives is closely linked to the drives of classical theory, whereas the latter set of motives is interpersonal and relational in nature. In general accord with Rapaport's (1967) discussion of the relationship between the autonomy of the ego from the id and the autonomy of the ego from the environment, it is the existence of drives that, in the final analysis, guarantees us against over-socialization and having our self-interest usurped and our self-identity totally defined by important others (what Eagle, 1987, has referred to as "enslavement by society"). One could add that the existence of overlapping and convergent relational aims guarantees us against developing into creatures unfit to live in a social and interpersonal world. It will be noted that in Slavin and Kriegman's view, neither of these sets of motives is secondary to or derivative of the other. Both are an inherent part of our structure. Furthermore, we are designed, according to Slavin and Kriegman, so that conflicting aims (primarily between convergent mutual aims and aims of self-interest) are an inevitable and inherent feature of the psyche.

Slavin and Kriegman's chapter is a provocative one that undoubtedly will raise many questions in the reader's mind. For example, their rendering of the concept of *repression*, in terms of holding certain "asocial" aims in reserve so that they will not be lost and can be brought forth at the appropriate time, raises the question of the conditions under which repressed material will be brought forth. There is certainly no guarantee that repressed material will be available at a later appropriate time. Nor is there any guarantee that such material will always become available in an adaptive fashion rather than in a maladaptive fashion (e.g., failure of defense and eruptions of anxiety). Furthermore, in those cases where repressed material remains repressed, repression would facilitate rather than work against "oversocialization," insofar as it is the nonsocial that is repressed. One of the important contributions of the Slavin and Kriegman chapter is that it raises many important questions that can occupy us for a long time.

Edelson's fascinating chapter represents nothing less than an attempt to conceptualize the psychoanalytic process. His starting point is the telling and enacting of stories. From a psychoanalytic point of view, Edelson asserts, stories appearing in the psychoanalytic situation begin in childhood, arise from bodily experiences, and involve sexual or hostile wishes. Stories have *antagonist* and *protagonist* (both of whom are the analysand himself or herself), obstacles to be overcome, threats, desires to be fulfilled, and a number of other features. As Edelson conceives of them, stories are essentially unconscious fantasies in which one attempts to gratify wishes through one's imagination. All people have *master stories*, new versions of which appear throughout one's life. Events and features of the external world can be assimilated by unconscious fantasies, with the result that one interprets one's experiences in accord with these fantasies and then acts (often maladaptively) on that basis. The reader will note general parallels and points of convergence between Edelson's discussion of master stories and unconscious fantasies and similar concepts appearing in other chapters—for example, Sampson's *unconscious pathogenic beliefs*, Luborsky's *core conflictual relationship themes*, and Singer and Singer's discussion of the concepts of *schemas* and *scripts*.

According to Edelson, a main task of psychoanalytic treatment is to make unconscious fantasy conscious and "to loosen the grip of a particular master story on the analysand, and, therefore, to reduce the effort allocated to realizing it on the screen of imagination or in relations with external reality." When treatment is successful, there is a gradual change in the unconscious fantasy, in the categories in which the analysand places himself or herself and others, and in the degree of interest in old problems and old desires.

Edelson argues that a focus on the psychoanalytic process, as exemplified by his chapter, rather than on a psychoanalytic theory of mind will be of greater heuristic value to psychoanalytic theory because of the former's emphasis on concepts that are linked to empirical observations available in the psychoanalytic situation. One question that arises here is whether Edelson envisions sources of empirical observation relevant to psychoanalytic theory other than the clinical psychoanalytic situation.

Edelson observes that, although a central concern with narratives has traditionally been associated with hermeneutics, the fact is that cognitive and computer scientists work with *narrative*, *script*, and *scenario* as their key concepts. Edelson believes that an emphasis on narratives and other concepts that are linked to clinical observations in the psychoanalytic process is likely to enhance the possibility of rapprochement between psychoanalysis and other disciplines such as neuroscience, cognitive psychology, developmental psychology, philosophy of mind, and literary studies.

Finally, Edelson notes that the approach taken in his chapter is "part of a detectable convergence among various 'schools' of psychoanalytic theory as well as among those with especially interesting or promising current approaches to psychoanalytic research." According to Edelson, evidence of this convergent trend includes a central emphasis on unconscious fantasy "in both object-relations and instinctual drive depictions of psychoanalytic theory," Weiss and Sampson's (1986) investigation of the "drama of plans and tests," Luborsky and Crits-Christoph's (1990) study of core conflictual relationship themes, and Schafer's (1983) interest in narratives. Although Edelson's emphasis on unconscious fantasy, master stories, and narratives may be part of a convergent trend in psychoanalytic theory and research, his equal emphasis on such factors as the primacy (or even exclusivity) of sexual and hostile wishes would probably not be acceptable to the psychoanalytic "schools" of Fairbairn's (1952) object relations theory and Kohut's (1971, 1977, 1984) self psychology. However, although one might agree or disagree with Edelson's views regarding the particular content of unconscious fantasies, master stories, and narratives, he provides a framework for viewing the psychoanalytic process that is remarkably free of jargon, that is eminently understandable, and that, in accord with the guiding idea underlying this volume, facilitates links between psychoanalysis and psychology as well as other neighboring disciplines.

Consistent with Edelson's emphasis on wishes as the center of unconscious fantasies and master stories, Lichtenberg and Schonbar treat psychoanalysis as essentially a motivational theory. They present a theory of motivation in which five motivational systems are posited along with a concept of self that is understood as an independent center for initiating, organizing, and regulating the different motivational systems. The five motivational systems are as follows: (a) the need for psychic regulation of physiological requirements (e.g., hunger, thirst), (b) the need for attachment and, later, for group affiliation, (c) the need for exploration and assertion, (d) the need to respond aversively through antagonism, withdrawal, or both, and (e) the need for sensual enjoyment and sexual excitement.

As we understand it, in Lichtenberg and Schonbar's view of motivation, all of the motivational systems above, although based on innate needs, are shaped as *psychological* motives in the course of infant–caregiver interactions. For example, hunger is not coincident with the need for nutriment but becomes an internally recognized need through the coordination of infant–mother interactions in which the infant learns to recognize internal sensations and an affect of distress along with the shift in sensations and affect that occurs when the need state is relieved by feeding.

In one section of the chapter dealing with the importance of unconscious motivation, Lichtenberg and Schonbar distinguish between what they refer to as the *fundamental level of the unconscious* and the psychoanalytic *dynamic unconscious.* This distinction is not entirely clear. As we understand it, however, whereas the five motivational systems form the fundamental level of the unconscious prior to the development of symbolic representation, the dynamic unconscious functions at the level of fantasy and symbolic representations of motives.

Finally, we come to Wakefield's illuminating chapter, which deals with the interface between Freudian theory (really, Freudian metatheory) and cognitive psychology. Wakefield's chapter is distinctive in at least two ways: (a) It highlights what Freud has offered and can continue to offer contemporary psychology, particularly cognitive psychology, rather than what contemporary psychology can contribute to psychoanalytic theory. (b) In contrast to what for many in the psychoanalytic community is the received wisdom that although Freud's metapsychology is eminently dispensable, his clinical theory represents his main contribution, Wakefield takes the opposite position and asserts that Freud's importance lies "in the conceptual and metatheoretical framework that he constructed for approaching psychological questions."

Wakefield lists seven points of contact between the conceptual structure of Freudian theory and contemporary cognitive psychology. The most basic of these, it seems to us, lies in Freud's assumption that the mind is composed of and analyzable into intentional states or, equivalently, mental representations in dynamic interaction with each other. Thus, Wakefield points out that, for Freud, "an ultimate understanding of an individual would involve a detailed mapping of the person's intentional system . . . ." One can contrast this conception of what it means to understand a person with some current conceptions in which ultimate understanding appears to consist in empathic resonance or in comprehending another's experiential states.

In accord with contemporary cognitive psychology and philosophy of mind, it should be clear that Wakefield is not using the term *intentional* in its ordinary sense (e.g., "I intend to go to the library"), but in the sense originally developed by Brentano. In that context, mental states are intentional because they are intrinsically directed at a real or an imaginary object or state of affairs. For example, a belief is always a belief *about something,* and a desire is always a desire *for something.*

Having established the primacy of intentional states both in contemporary cognitive psychology and in Freud's metatheory, Wakefield goes on to present with particular lucidity the essential logic of Freud's argument for the meaningfulness of talking about unconscious mental states. If the criterion for the mental is intentionality or representationality (rather than consciousness or awareness) and if representationality is potentially independent of consciousness, then it is meaningful to posit unconscious mental states. Wakefield demonstrates that Freud implicitly appealed to a complex distinction, explicated by both Kripke (1980) and Putnam (1975), between the definition of a term and the essence of the things referred to by that term. Furthermore, determining the essence of a thing is a matter of empirical investigation and discovery. In effect, Freud argued that the essence of the mental could not be decided by semantic definition (i.e., *conscious = mental*), but is a matter of conceptual and theoretical possibility and empirical evidence. With regard to the former, Freud argued, as do contemporary cognitive scientists, that representationality is the essence of the mental. With regard to the latter, Freud presented clinical evidence that he believed empirically supported his conceptual position. In short, although conscious desires, beliefs, and so forth, constitute the model for the mental, their common essence of representationality can operate in conscious and nonconscious states.

In the remaining part of his chapter, Wakefield discusses Freud's conceptualizations of motivation and emotion within a cognitive framework. According to Wakefield, "Freud provided a very modern and still the most elegant solution to the problem of how to conceptualize motivation within a systematic cognitive psychology." The solution is to view desire as a special causal property of representations, even though this property does not appear in the content of the representation itself. A critical source of this special causal property is bodily processes. Wakefield's example is the case in which the motivational significance of the very same idea or representation of water will vary with bodily processes having to do with thirst. As Wakefield points out, for Freud it was the bodily processes having to do with instinctual impulses that lent representations their motivational power. As Wakefield also points out, this general scheme can apply to any set of representational contents, not just sexual and aggressive contents.

As for emotions, Wakefield explicates Freud's implicit view of emotions as a perceptual representation (including a conscious feeling) of what is going on in the body. From this point of view, nausea is as much a representation—albeit a primitive one pertaining to the body rather than to the external world—as the perception of colors and shapes. In short, within Freud's cognitivist framework, emotions consist of ideas, their motivational properties, and corresponding perceptions or representations of bodily states experienced as feelings. Wakefield observes that, for Freud, because emotions include a perceptual (feeling) component and because perception is by nature conscious, emotions cannot be unconscious. He also notes that, given Freud's view of perception as necessarily conscious, he would have to deny the possibility of unconscious perception. There is an interesting irony here. Although some investigators of subliminal perception place their work in the theoretical context of the Freudian concept of the unconscious, if Wakefield's reading of Freud is accurate, Freud would have denied the possibility of subliminal perception.

Wakefield's chapter also includes a discussion linking the psychoanalytic concept of defense to the general process of intentional manipulation of one's own cognitive states and a brilliant exposition of Freud's implicit understanding that a full and ideal account of personality would include a mapping of a person's intentional states, a description of his or her traits, and an evolutionary–biological account of evolutionarily shaped dispositions that were adaptive in the environment in which they involved. (The reader will note that the chapter by Slavin and Kriegman represents an attempt to present such an account.)

Wakefield believes that "interpreted in the right way, psychoanalysis can be seen as an applied ideographic branch of cognitive science, engaged in the intentional mapping of individual minds within a cognitive framework." Although he might not use the same language, this conclusion seems entirely compatible with the spirit of Edelson's chapter. Edelson's dramatistic "master stories" are, it seems to us, one way of construing and carrying out the intentional mapping of an individual's mind. Wakefield ends his chapter with what to many will be the surprising conclusion that "contrary to current wisdom, it may well be that certain of Freud's metapsychological assumptions, understood sympathetically as attempts to incorporate various necessary features into a systematic theory of intentionality, rather than his specific clinical hypotheses, that serve to make Freud a theorist from whom one can still learn." Certainly, Wakefield's particular vision of Freudian metapsychology as a viable and useful cognitivist theory of mind should stimulate much thought and discussion regarding the nature of Freudian theory and metatheory.

There are some basic points of convergence regarding the nature of psychoanalysis among the different chapters in this section. One such fundamental point of convergence is the idea that psychoanalytic theory is, above all, a *motivational* theory. This is seen in Slavin and Kriegman's placement of psychoanalysis in a broad, evolutionary framework, Edelson's emphasis on the role of wishes in the stories people tell and enact, Lichtenberg and Schonbar's explicit depiction of psychoanalysis as a motivational theory and their delineation of five motivational systems, and Wakefield's construal of psychoanalysis as a discipline that is concerned with mapping an individual's intentional states. The point of view expressed in those chapters is entirely compatible with G. S. Klein's (1976) understanding of psychoanalysis as a discipline that is concerned with "reading intentionality." However, although psychoanalysis may be concerned with reading intentionality (particularly, unconscious intentionality), the particular intentions it discerns and "reads" will depend on the content and substance of the particular psychoanalytic theory being formulated. Indeed, the specific content and substance of one's theory will determine whether one is "reading" or "misreading" intentionality. Of course, what we are referring to is the issue of empirical testing of theory. This issue takes one beyond the question of framework—that is, beyond the question of what *kind* of theory psychoanalysis is. It takes one to areas where psychoanalysis *interfaces* (if we may be permitted the use of this awkward term) with other disciplines and research activities. That is, it takes one to the remaining sections of this volume.

REFERENCES

Barratt, B. B. (1984). *Psychic reality and psychoanalytic knowing.* Hillsdale, NJ: Analytic Press.

Barratt, B. B. (1988). Why is psychoanalysis so controversial? Notes from left field! *Psychoanalytic Psychology,* 5(3), 223–239.

Bowlby, J. (1969). *Attachment and loss: Vol. 1. Attachment.* London: Hogarth Press.

Carnap, R. (1936). Testability and meaning. *Philosophy of Science, 3.*

Carnap, R. (1937). Testability and meaning. *Philosophy of Science, 4.*

Davidson, D. (1963). Actions, reasons, and causes. *Journal of Philosophy, 60,* 684–700.

Dilthey, W. (1961). In H. P. Rickman (Ed.), *Meaning in history.* London: Allen & Unwin.

Eagle, M. (1980). A critical examination of motivational explanation in psychoanalysis. *Psychoanalysis and Contemporary Thought, 3,* 329–380. Also in L. Laudan, (Ed.), (1983), *Mind and medicine: Explanation and evaluation in psychiatry and medicine,* (University of Pittsburgh series in philosophy and history of science). Los Angeles and Berkeley: University of California Press.

Eagle, M. (1984a). Geha's vision of psychoanalysis as fiction. *International Forum for Psychoanalysis, 1*(3 & 4), 341–362.

Eagle, M. (1984b). Psychoanalysis and "narrative truth": A reply to Spence. *Psychoanalysis and Contemporary Thought, 7,* 629–640.

Eagle, M. (1987). *Recent developments in psychoanalysis: A critical evaluation.* Cambridge, MA: Harvard University Press.

Fairbairn, W. R. D. (1952). *Psychoanalytic studies of the personality.* London: Tavistock Publications and Routledge & Kegan Paul.

Feyerabend, P. R. (1975). *Against method.* London: NLB Press.

Geha, R. E. (1984). On psychoanalytic history and the "real" story of fictitious lives. *International Forum for Psychoanalysis, 1*(3 & 4), 221–291.

Gill, M. M. (1976). Metapsychology is not psychology. In M. M. Gill & P. S. Holzman (Eds.), *Psychology versus metapsychology: Essays in memory of George S. Klein*. New York: International Universities Press.

Greenberg, J., & Mitchell, S. (1983). *Object relations in psychoanalytic theory*. Cambridge, MA: Harvard University Press.

Grünbaum, A. (1984). *The foundations of psychoanalysis: A philosophical critique*. Berkeley and Los Angeles: University of California Press.

Hook, S. (Ed.). (1959). *Psychoanalysis, scientific method, and philosophy*. New York: New York University Press.

Klein, G. S. (1976). *Psychoanalytic theory: An exploration of essentials*. New York: International Universities Press.

Kohut, H. (1971). *The analysis of the self*. New York: International Universities Press.

Kohut, H. (1977). *The restoration of the self*. New York: International Universities Press.

Kohut, H. (1984). *How does analysis cure?* Chicago: University of Chicago Press.

Kripke, S. (1980). *Naming and necessity*. Oxford: Basil Blackwell.

Luborsky, L., & Crits-Christoph, P. (1990). *Understanding transference: The CCRT method (the Core Conflictual Relationship Theme)*. New York: Basic Books.

Popper, K. R. (1962). *Conjectures and refutations*. New York: Basic Books.

Putnam, H. (1975). The meaning of meaning. In H. Putnam, *Philosophical papers* (Vol. 2, pp. 215–271). Cambridge, England: Cambridge University Press.

Rapaport, D. (1967). The theory of ego autonomy. In M. M. Gill (Ed.), *The collected papers of David Rapaport*. New York: Basic Books.

Rorty, R. (1979). *Philosophy and the mirror of nature*. Princeton, NJ: Princeton University Press.

Rubinstein, B. B. (1976). On the possibility of a strictly clinical psychoanalytic theory: An essay in the philosophy of psychoanalysis. In M. M. Gill & P. S. Holzman (Eds.), *Psychology versus metapsychology: Psychoanalytic essays in memory of George S. Klein*. New York: International Universities Press.

Sand, R. (1984a). Spence's vision of psychoanalysis. *International Forum of Psychoanalysis, 1*, 3–18.

Sand, R. (1984b). Review of Spence's "Historical truth and narrative truth." *Review of Psychoanalytic Books, 2*(3 & 4), 441–467.

Schafer, R. (1983). *The analytic attitude*. New York: Basic Books.

Spence, D. P. (1982). *Historical truth and narrative truth*. New York: Norton.

Toulmin, S. (1948). The logical status of psychoanalysis. *Analysis, 9*(2), 23–29.

Weiss, J., Sampson, H., & the Mount Zion Psychotherapy Research Group (1986). *The psychoanalytic process: Theory, clinical observation, and empirical research*. New York: Guilford Press.

1

MOTIVATION IN PSYCHOLOGY AND PSYCHOANALYSIS

JOSEPH D. LICHTENBERG AND ROSALEA A. SCHONBAR

Motivation is so central a concept in the theories of psychology and psychoanalysis and its manifestations so omnipresently observable in human behavior that one might assume that the best minds would long ago have defined its essential features. Nonetheless, no generally accepted theory has been formulated. Why? We believe that prior efforts have, of necessity, been unsuccessful because of the extreme fragmentation of perspective of the formulators.

A telling example of fragmenting of both information gathering and theorizing developed between academic psychologists and psychoanalysts. Although within academic psychology and psychoanalysis arguments abounded, each group was able to work with a common information base. Between the groups, however, a wall of ignorance or condemnation prevented efforts at a successful integration. One discipline concentrated its efforts on experimental design and statistical evidence, and the other made a clinical appreciation of the dynamic unconscious its sine qua non.

We now see evidence of a current sharing of information and respect among the disciplines of psychoanalysis, academic psychology, ethology, and neurophysiology. When applied to the development of motivation, this confluence provides information used by those who set up observational studies, those who work in clinical settings, those who follow precise experimental designs, and those who study the maturation of the nervous system.

In this chapter we present a contemporary view of five motivational systems (Lichtenberg, 1989). This theory of motivation uses infant observation and research, clinical experience with people at all ages, and neurophysiological data. We discuss the manner in which information and formulations from these varied perspectives can be integrated with our proposal of five motivational systems.

Our working hypothesis is that anything that a human being of any age can be observed to do persistently, consistently, and repeatedly is motivated. Our strategy is to follow motivation through developmental trends that begin in infancy, and then, in subsequent stages of life, both maintain continuities and pass through transformations. We have attempted to discern systems that contain groups of related motives. Each system can be observed in neonates in the form of innate needs and patterns of response to that need. Each system can be observed throughout life in the form of needs altered by the vicissitudes of the age and patterns of response that are added to by learning and maturation.

Using these criteria, Lichtenberg (1989) suggested five motivational systems. One system develops in response to the need for the psychic regulation of physiological requirements: hunger, thirst, elimination, sleep, breathing, equilibrium, tactile and proprioceptive stimulation, health care, and overall stimulus intensity. Another develops in response to the need for attachment to individuals and later affiliation with groups. Another develops in response to the need for exploration and assertion. Another develops in response to the need to respond aversively through antagonism or withdrawal. Another develops in response to the need for sensual enjoyment and later sexual excitement. Each motivational system is quickly responsive to modification (learning) so that the input of caregivers who have the same motivational systems has an immediate effect. The functional patterns of each system trigger affects that give amplification and coloring to the experience involved. At any moment, one of the motivational systems will be dominant and the others either subsets or dormant. In the infant, a predictable cycling of state, alert wakefulness, quiet wakefulness, sleeping, and crying, each with affective amplification, become goals for the infant to re-create. Thus, each motivational system self-organizes and self-stabilizes as a result of three influences: innate and learned response patterns, caregiver ministrations, and an internal inclination to re-create previously experienced affective states. Looked at in this way, a motivational system in infancy involves the infant's innate and learned response patterns (temperament) exerting a regulatory impact on caregivers, whereas caregivers' activities regulate the infant, stimulating some responses, and altering or inhibiting others. The caregivers draw on their own motivational systems for empathic, intuitive, and learned responses. The experiences that ensue recurrently build up infants' expectancies of repetitions (familiarity) that infants strive to repeat—an internal regulation. The self develops as an independent center for initiating, organizing, and integrating experience and motivation. The self ensures that, on the basis of internal and external cuing, motivational dominance shifts, whereas a sense of self-sameness or continuity persists. Within each system and between the systems, dialectic tensions affect moment-to-moment dominance (e.g., between sleep and hunger, or between sleep or hunger and the motive to explore and assert preferences in toy play, or between a continuation of aversive anger and a need for physical closeness and soothing). At different ages and under different conditions, a particular hierarchical arrangement may predominate, such as the pursuit of sensual enjoyment and sexual excitement during times of courting.

We consider the five motivational systems against a background of previous efforts to define and explain motivation by academic psychologists and psychoanalysts. We select from the vast literature of both fields examples that illustrate the complexity of past efforts and their lack of integration. We then consider the topic under three headings: the tower of Babel, the human "animal," and the unconscious.

A TOWER OF BABEL

Anthropologists have noted that Eskimos use a large variety of words to indicate the particular quality of snow and whether it is icy, flaky, dense, windblown, fast- or slow-falling, and the like. Such distinctions reflect the centrality of snow conditions to the lives of these people. Similarly, the number of terms deemed necessary for the understanding of human motivation—drive, instinct, set, wish, will, expectancy, goal, and aim, to name a few—reflects the centrality of motivation to the understanding of human behavior as well as the theoretical preferences and contexts of those attempting to understand human behavior.

To some extent, the proliferation of terms in this area has also risen from attempts at specificity, at differentiating one aspect of the motivational arena from others. Unfortunately, rather than leading to clarification, this multiplicity frequently results in confusing overlap and obsessive overnicety in terminology rather than productive differentiation. In the preferred language of academic psychologists, learning theorists, social psychologists, ethologists, and psychoanalysts of various orientations, similarities and differences result in the same term having different meanings and the same phenomenon bearing the burden of a variety of terms. Thus, although ethologists use the word *instinct* to denote a species-specific, innate, invariant *pattern of behavior,* others mean "a specific motivational tendency that is *inferred* from overt behavior" (Weiner, 1989, p. 28). Freud, for example, used it in the latter sense, as did McDougall (1923), who also postulated cognitive and affective as well as conative characteristics of instincts.

Although McDougall reasoned that human behavior potentials were rooted in an instinct (e.g., a gregarious instinct, an acquisitive instinct, etc.), thus giving rise to a potentially infinite number of instincts, Murray (1938), however, specified only 20 innate bases of behavior that he called "needs" (e.g., succorance, dominance, etc.). Harry Stack Sullivan (1953) posited only two such basic needs—security and intimacy—and, of course, Freud's (1905/1953a) libido and thanatos also fall into the category of instincts, although this aspect of his work is frequently referred to as "drive theory" (cf. Greenberg & Mitchell, 1983). Weiner (1989) pointed out that

> the concepts of drive and need were often used interchangeably. . . . Over time, however, drives became identified with states of deprivation, behaviorism, and research employing infrahuman organisms, while the concept of need became identified with molar personality theorists and signified more stable characteristics of individuals. (p. 180)

To complicate matters further, the humanistic personality theorists, Rogers (1951), and Maslow (1970, 1971), posited a single underlying *drive,* Rogers toward growth, Maslow toward self-enhancement. Maslow did posit five basic *needs,* but these are hierarchical in nature, and he differentiated between the "lower" (biologically rooted) needs and the "higher" (psychologically rooted) needs. In addition, Rogers's growth drive concept may be described as at least partly teleological in nature: Because growth appears inevitable in the absence of deterring conditions, it must be a strong motivating force. This is not wholly unlike the thinking of McDougall and W. James that the very presence of any kind of behavior "proves" that an instinct must exist for that behavior. Fairbairn, Winnicott, Lichtenberg, and others have discussed the "growth" phenomenon under different rubrics and in different languages; we prefer to call it a *principle,* thereby complicating still further the language in this field.

The earliest paradigm in academic psychology for the prediction of behavior was that of S → R, simple stimulus–response. Gradually, it became clear that an intervening consideration was necessary, that of the individual or organism (S → O → R; Woodworth, 1938, 1940). Among the earliest internal variables to be studied was that of *set*; those early studies demonstrated that processes such as perception, learning, and memory could be significantly influenced by an induced expectancy. The classical paradigm for the study of set was to vary the experimental conditions by statements to the subjects such as, "The list of words I will show you contains names of animals; see how many you can remember." Lists of nonsense syllables were then presented tachistoscopically at a speed just at or below the visual threshold. Subjects' "memory" for words was then tested. Those who had been given the instructions "remembered" more animal names than did a control group or than they themselves had when previously shown the same list without instructions. Initially, then, set was studied as a momentary state. However, its effect on longer lasting phenomena such as experimental bias or judgments of intelligence and achievement of children previously labeled as "slow" (Rosenthal, 1966) has been documented. And in more dynamically oriented studies, it has been demonstrated that subjects themselves bring certain sets to tachistoscopic material that determine how certain words are perceived or misperceived in terms of the subjects' previous experience or momentary states; reaction times and psychogalvanic responses also reveal differences in visual thresholds to neutral and "forbidden" words. The commonly held notion that "one sees what one wants to see," consciously or not, received some confirmation in those studies. Moreover, more profound phenomena, such as parataxis, stereotypes, and motivations to respond or behave in certain ways rather than others, are examples of sets. Thus, the concept of perceptual defense was developed as a far broader and yet more specific concept than set.

Klein (1970) used the term *set* synonymously with *interest* to designate a momentary guide to perception. He also defined drive as "a *meaning-inducing* field of activity implemented by *accommodative structures*" (1970, p. 213). The accommodative strategies are cognitive attitudes and styles that, once developed experientially, become relatively constant for an individual and, one might say, become motivation-related determinants of individual differences in perception, memory, and behavior. Witkin, Dyk, Faterson, Goodenough, and Karp (1962) demonstrated the impact of these cognitive styles on many aspects of life; they are, in a sense, broad internalized sets that have been shown to differentiate such complex behaviors as childbirth method choices (Lapidus, 1968), childbearing practices (Lapidus, 1970), career choice (Witkin et al., 1977), and styles of interpersonal relatedness (Witkin & Goodenough, 1979). Shapiro (1965) proposed a personality typology on the basis of these cognitive styles or sets.

This overview of some of the overlapping and inconsistent terminology is in no sense intended to be complete. Rather, we hope to draw attention to some of the difficulties in assuring common referents that are heuristically definitive. This introduction to the Tower of Babel in our field provides the background that influenced the choice of terms and designators for the fresh viewing of motivation we offer.

The strategy used in choosing terms for the theory of motivational systems has been to use designations that resonate with common nontechnical usage (e.g., "attachment"). At the same time, the terms have been chosen to facilitate easy association with major prior contributions, such as Bowlby's (1958) attachment theory. Whenever possible, we have attempted to avoid terms that could be confused with the technical language of drive theory. Because each system is construed as developing in response to a significant innate need, the designator for the system reflects that need.

The psychic regulation of physiological requirements refers to needs such as hunger, thirst, air, elimination of waste, equilibrium, temperature range, tactile and proprioceptive stimulation, health care, and a suitable overall stimulus range. *Physiological* reminds us that many bodily controls are involved, whereas *psychic regulation* reminds us that when speaking of motivation, we are not referring, for example, to lowered blood sugar or to a carbon monoxide build-up but to an affect-laden state of hunger or gasping for breath. We also mean to imply in our choice of *psychic regulation* that innate and quickly learned programs shaping and shaped by the responses of caregivers give precise definition to a pattern of regulation that constitutes hunger and satiety or ordinary breathing for a particular infant. By the choice of the term *psychic regulation of physiological requirements*, we hope to capture a flexible interchange between normal adaptive experiences of hunger and satiety and disturbed experiences present in malnutrition, binge eating, anorexia and bulimia, or breathing without awareness and rasping, wheezing, and asthma.

Historically, this motivational system conjures up years of study of "psychosomatic disorders" as well as Freud's neverending preoccupation with an attempt to define conditions at the border between body and mind without reactivating the confusions of a "body ego" (Lichtenberg, 1978).

The need for *attachment* calls to mind the universal experience of wanting to feel close to, involved with, and intimate with other people. The term carries an immediate association with Bowlby's (1958) observations of seeking, following, and grasping, and Ainsworth and others' descriptions of modes of attachment (secure, ambivalent, and avoidant at 1 year of age). It readily includes the patterns of eye contact and conversational games (Stern, 1985), the extensive world of preverbal and verbal communication between parents and child (Papousek & Papousek, 1986), and the significance of experiences of affirmation, twinlike sharing, and idealization (Kohut, 1971, 1984). *Attachment* as the designator for the motivational system emphasizes the process of engagement with another human being, evoking recognition that from the beginning infants respond differentially to father and mother (Brazelton, 1980) and any other consistent caregiver. The nature of attachments can constantly shift in intensity, opening to a vast dialectic tension of rivalries, jealousy, and possessiveness in pairings and triangles. For the same type of process—the need for intimate engagement—when it involves groups rather than individuals, we have chosen the designation *affiliation*. The need to respond *affiliatively* to family, religious group, school, team, and country draws on studies of group psychology for its explication. We include under both *attachment* and *affiliation* much that has been developed in various theories grouped under the general term *object relations* but have chosen not to use that term because of its multiple meanings.

The need for *exploration and assertion* evokes motivation underlying learning, play, and work. The functioning of this motivational system is best observed when an alert infant's physiological requirements have been met and the infant is disengaged from attachment activity. At these moments, infants scan and grasp whatever objects lie in their perceptual fields. They are guided by inborn and quickly learned preferences for particular stimuli—*assertion* building to agendas to realize preferences. *Exploration* guided by preferences thus builds to a sense of agency or self-assertion, to intentions and planning of agendas in accordance with a strong inborn capacity to track consequences. This development draws on the vast work of cognitive psychologists, especially those who have studied early development (e.g., Piaget) and on learning theories. By using the term *exploration*, we wish to convey the affective elements of interest, curiosity, and surprise weighed against boredom, apathy, or fear of novelty. By using the term *assertion*, we wish to convey the affective elements of a sense of growing efficiency and competence contrasted with frustration, failure, and inadequacy. We prefer to couple *exploration and assertion* rather than mastery because *exploring* can be dominant, as when a drowsy baby is pulled into alertness by accidentally bumping into a rattle, or *assertion* can predominate as when a child repeats inserting a peg into a hole. "Mastery" can be achieved by people who, in their work or hobbies, remain highly *exploratory* and by others who work (*assert*) most energetically in a narrower range to become increasingly efficient and accomplished.

The need to respond *aversively* through antagonism or withdrawal conveys reactions to hunger, physical pain, breaches of expectation, loneliness, and frustrations of every type. It evokes images of the infant's whimpering and crying, frowning and hitting, eye averting and drawing back, going limp or stiff as a board, jolting in startle or cowering in fear or shame. Such images demonstrate the duality of the affective expressions of crying, startle, anger, disgust, contempt, sadness, fear, shame, embarrassment, humiliation, and guilt; each is triggered as part of an innate or learned program (Tomkins, 1962, 1963), and each acts as a means of communicating distress to others. We have selected *aversive* because it is a term that applies equally well to a response that an infant has to the experience of being stuck with a pin and a response that an adult analysand has when urged by an analyst to bring into awareness a thought he or she is ashamed of having about the analyst. The infant's pulling away and crying and the adult's evasiveness and protest are forms of withdrawal at different ages and of vastly different complexity. An infant's pushing out an uncomfortably intrusive nipple and an adult analysand's dream of fighting off a gang of robbers on the day she received her bill are expressions of antagonism. We have selected *antagonism* rather than aggression because antagonism bridges behavior as does aggression but also includes attitude and an affective experience. Likewise, *withdrawal* refers to behavior and an inner sense of being withdrawn (e.g., pulling away as in fear, retreating to within oneself as in a response to shame, embarrassment, guilt, and sadness). The terms *antagonism and withdrawal* are evocative of the ethologists' patterned "fight–flight" reaction. By referring to *antagonism and withdrawal,* we draw attention to a dialectic tension that exists between the two modes of *aversive* responses. Each may be primary at any given moment and the other a shield or cover. This presents the dynamic interplay between the two forms *aversive* motivation is innately patterned to take rather than the narrow view in traditional psychoanalytic "aggressive drive" theory that withdrawal is exclusively a defense against aggression. When one looks ahead in development to the manner by which the "mechanisms" of defense control the flow of information when aversiveness is triggered, one sees the interplay of antagonism and withdrawal. For example, disavowal and denial involve *withdrawing* from information combined with an active *antagonism* to being pressed by chance or others to attend stimuli containing that information.

For the motivational system that deals with *sexuality,* we have chosen two designators. The need for *sensual enjoyment* connotes the pleasurable sensations of stroking, sucking, rocking for a baby and kissing, hugging, touching, listening to music, and other esthetic experiences for an adult. *Sensuality* suggests a two-directional experience. A mother's gentle stroking of her baby soothes and invites sleep just like an adult's warm bath or a back rub. A toddler's stroking his genital area may begin by soothing just like a husband's giving his wife a massage, but the sensation-rich genital area of the child and skin of the adult may then create a tingling mounting of sensation to *sexual excitement.* Thus, *sexual excitement* evokes thoughts of a child's masturbatory arousal and an adult's orgastic experience with intercourse. Included in this *sensual–sexual* motivation is the development of masculinity and femininity from the core gender designation of "It's a boy" or "It's a girl," through all facets of gender identity and functioning. The *sensual–sexual* motivational system would thus suggest all those aspects of life adumbrated as "sexual drive" that involve sensual and sexual sensation—soothing and arousing—the whole erotic aspect of rivalry, loving, and procreating. It would not include other aspects of attachment or curiosity or physiological regulation that did not have these sensation and affective characteristics.

The final main term of our conception, *self,* is suggestive of both person as entity and identity as experience. It necessarily combines the ambiguity of the "I" or agent and the "me" or object. Because of this degree of ambiguity and nonspecificity, we require a definition of this term for use with our theory of motivational systems. The *self* develops as an independent center for initiating, organizing, and integrating motivation and experience. The sense of self reflects that initiating, organizing, and integrating. We refer in our definition to the self *developing* because, unlike the innate programs that are part of the neonate's responses to need in each motivational system, self as defined emerges gradually as the infant develops a sense of agency, of boundaries, of contingent relationships, and of continuity of affective experience. This concept of self is unavoidably circular. The self as a center for initiating, organizing, and integrating motivation develops *from* the regulation of the innate and quickly learned programmed patterns that begin at birth and form each motivational system. Then, subsequently to emergent formation of the self, it becomes the principal source of regulation of each system.

THE HUMAN "ANIMAL"?

A continuing controversy in motivational theory has been the extent to which instincts determine human behavior. As an explanatory concept, based in part on the observation of animals, instinct dates back at least to the ancient Greek philosophers. In the second decade of this century, McDougall (1923) developed his "hormic psychology," in which behavior in and of social entities was attributed to instincts. He and other early instinct theorists were guided, according to Arkes and Garske (1977), by the following paradigm: "if behavior X occurred, instinct X was postulated to account for behavior X. And what was the evidence that instinct X existed? Behavior X, of course" (p. 13). They cited Atkinson (1964) as having reported that by 1924, over 14,000 instincts had been "identified."

Controversy over the instinctual nature of humankind has not been limited to psychology. Before Darwin published *The Origin of Species* in 1859, he was apprehensive about its reception by the religious community because evolution theory violated the biblical account of the creation of the world and of humankind. Linking the evolution of homo sapiens to animal origins threatened the strongly held theological distinction that, although animals were controlled by instincts, human beings were guided by reason and had souls. And, indeed, Darwin's views were denounced, even as they are still opposed by the so-called creationists. A somewhat more moderate view accepts humans' continuity with other animals but identifies their "animal nature" (i.e., instinctual behavior) generally as negative, to be fought against and subdued for the salvation of the soul; true humanity, according to this view, is guided by reason.

The more recent work of ethologists and psychobiologists represents the sole remnant of a view that ascribes human adult behavior to the same kinds of genetically determined instinctual mechanisms as may be seen in certain animals. Lorenz's (1966) work on imprinting and aggression is probably the best known example of this body of work; he saw human aggressiveness, for example, as having been inherited from humans' animal ancestors. Certainly, although the capacity for aversive behavior is innate as a response to safety needs, the work of Harlow and Harlow (1965) on the affectional responses of baby monkeys indicated that, even in infrahuman creatures, aggressive behavior is learned as a response to previous deprivation; Dollard, Doob, Miller, Mowrer, and Sears (1939) have studied human aggression as a response to frustration. Harlow (1965) also demonstrated that species-specific sexual behavior may not develop in adult monkeys who have had less than adequate maternal care.

A number of recent studies reported by Angier (1990) revealed that biologists are finding that patterns of sexual behavior in animals are more complex than had previously been assumed: On the subject of fidelity, for example, Gowaty stated that "it seems that all our old assumptions are incorrect" (cited in Angier, 1990, p. C8). Nevertheless, based on studies of sexual fidelity in chimpanzees and gorillas as a function of testicle size in relation to body size, some biologists offer the observation that human beings have "mid-sized testicles" as "further evidence . . . that our species is basically monogamous, but that there are no guarantees" (Angier, 1990, p. C8). Observing that many species of female birds "cheat" only with dominant or more disease-resistant males, they suggest that women may philander to enlarge or improve the available gene pool for their offspring. Similarly, because the males of many species compete to mate with many females, they are said to be attempting to assure their contribution to the gene pool, particularly if there is a short mating season or a long gestation period, as in humpback whales for example. We find several difficulties both in the interpretations of some of the animal behavior and certainly in their extrapolation to human beings. Observations of evolution-driven behavior in animals are frequently presented as if the animals are aware of and motivated by these considerations. Human beings can make choices and are not so tied to survival strategies. Human beings are also more complex physiologically, psychologically, and socially, and a simplistic extrapolation from less to more complex organisms is, in any event, highly questionable, particularly when these researchers are only now reevaluating even their conclusions on animals because of an underestimation of complexity. Perhaps even more important is that, without being anthropomorphic, researchers cannot assume the same affect in lower animals (e.g., birds) as in humans.

With the exception of this body of work, simple instinct theories to explain human behavior began to wane in the mid-1920s. Pavlov (1927) demonstrated that the simple reflex in dogs of salivating at the sight of food could be evoked by the sound of a bell with which the food had been temporally associated and that the learning and unlearning of such behavior was lawful. Behaviorism, initially based on this phenomenon, has flourished and grown, especially in the United States, reaching perhaps its most interesting and sophisticated development in the work of B. F. Skinner.

Skinner (1938) developed the concept of operant conditioning by observing that hungry pigeons could learn to get food by pressing a lever. Reinforcement contingencies were developed to establish both learning and extinction of these responses. A large body of research by Skinner (1948) and his associates led him to construct the vision of what he thought of as a utopian human society in which all behavior would be developed and controlled through operant conditioning. Interests, desires, goals, affects, expectancies, in fact, all motivational principles except the life-sustaining drives, could thus be differentially developed in people, making the issue of instinct irrelevant. In some sense, even the concept of motivation itself became irrelevant as anything other than a behavioral characteristic that can also be developed and controlled by means of operant conditions. Thus, based initially on animal experimentation, Skinner came down heavily on the side of learning or experience rather than innate, predetermined, instinctual bases of behavior. In so doing, however, Skinner's (1971) ideal view of human society also led him to discard characteristics and values generally considered uniquely human, such as choice, freedom, and dignity.

The nature–nurture dichotomy is basically as arid when applied to motivational development as it is with respect to most other psychological development. The questions raised by motivational development have many other solutions, all of which recognize in various forms the interaction between nature and nurture.

The simplest of these is the one most of us learned in elementary psychology: that the higher a species is on the phylogenetic scale, the less its behavior is governed by instinct and the more by learning. Thus, higher species require longer periods of infancy and a different form of family because of the longer period of dependency. This observation is generally accurate, although it fails to address irregularities among the lower animals themselves necessitated by adaptation to changes in environmental conditions. More important for our purposes, it does not address either the differentiation or the integration of the genetic nature of humans on the one hand and how and what they learn on the other. As indicated, the behaviorists, admitting the drive power of the life-sustaining needs, ascribed all other motives to a single form of learning, namely, conditioning. Other theorists, such as William James and Abraham Maslow have proposed other solutions, congruent with their overall views of human nature derived within their individual foci of interest.

James, for example, asserted that instincts refer to ways of behaving "in such a way as to produce certain ends, without foresight" (1892/1961, p. 258) and without the need for learning. Instincts are the bases for "impulses," which underlie all behavior, but they do not have the imperative quality usually associated with instincts. Rather, they limit what is possible, yet allow for behavioral alternatives. Therefore, because human beings have the capacities for memory and insight, the outcomes of their acts may be remembered, and they are enabled to make choices on the basis of expectancies that they build out of experience. Thus, although instincts underlie behavior, humans can develop habitual "impulses" on the basis of them by inhibiting some and developing preferences, values, and interests on the basis of others.

Moreover, according to James (1892/1961), some instincts are transitory. If, during a critical period, the environment does not offer appropriate opportunity for action or habit formation, or if the individual has or develops competing preferences, those instincts lose their power for motivating learning or behavior and perish. Thus, James integrated instinct and environmental impact, reserving voluntary action as a possibility and opportunity only for organisms with memory and insight, and limiting the power for new learning to quasi-developmental periods in which given instincts are available. He saw instincts as functional correlates of structure, positing no separate sources of energy as did the ethologists and Freud, but also positing no particular learning principles.

An alternative explanation of the uniqueness of human motivation is presented by Maslow's (1971) humanistic self-actualization proposal. Maslow viewed humans as being motivated not only to become as fully human as possible, but to actualize themselves maximally. His fellow humanist, Carl Rogers (1951), proposed a single growth or self-actualization drive that under-girded all human behavior, encompassing such diverse components as security, a need to be unconditionally accepted, internalization, and defenses. By contrast, Maslow (1971) developed a hierarchy of five needs or motives, of which self-actualization is the "highest" or most human.

The five need systems proposed by Maslow are physiological, safety, love, esteem, and self-actualization. The "lower" needs have greater strength than the "higher" needs and must be gratified before the latter can become operative overall or can remain the central focus at any given time. Although, like instincts, these needs are innate and universal, their means of gratification are learned and develop on an individual basis, particularly as one goes from lower to higher. Maslow thus took into account humans' continuity with infrahuman beings, with whom they share the lower and more imperative needs for physiological and safety satisfactions.

Interestingly, what Maslow went on to propose were uniquely human needs that are also considered to be innate. Unlike McDougall's and other early instinct theories, Maslow limited the number of such strivings, while the means of their gratification are learned and may be limited only by genetic endowment and environmental inhibitions and opportunities. There is also an evolutionary concept here, in that the highest or most distinctively human needs are the weakest, yielding at times to the power of ungratified lower needs or developing minimally if the latter are not fulfilled. Although Maslow did not specify his views on how one learns, it is more than unlikely that he would view differential reinforcement as the means by which one becomes fully self-actualizing, especially in view of the fact that Skinner's utopia and Maslow's view of the achievement of full human potential seem diametrically opposed.

Motivation conceived as organized in systems departs totally from the holdovers of a biological–evolutionary instinct theory. Concepts of the human as an upright walking animal or an ape with speech that seemed self-evident to post-Darwinian fin de siecle intellectuals and romanticized in images of the noble savage do not meet the test of infant and child observation. Alternatively, the view of the infant's mind as a tabula rasa on which environment writes is equally at variance with observation. We are today in a better position to face the challenge of a mind–body duality because (a) we can observe the equipment an infant does and does not have, (b) we can follow the stages of development of the nervous system, and (c) we have learned a great deal about the interrelationship of neurophysiology and experience. A discourse on motivation could be written from a neurophysiological dimension, but constant reference to experience in the form of perception, activation, and information-gathering and processing would have to be made. Otherwise, the triggering of affects, the activating of brain centers and sensory and motor tracts, and feedback loops would not be accounted for. Nor could we recognize the increase in neuronal size from the stimuli of experience and the decrease when disuse occurs in the absence of stimuli.

The discourse of motivation we are considering focuses on a psychological dimension while recognizing many neurophysiological and biological correlates. Thus, in considering hunger, we place it not as a drive but as a need that requires psychological regulation. The need can be described biologically in terms of chemical changes such as blood sugar. It can be described neurologically in terms of tracts that transmit sensory information to brain centers and motor information to activate action responses. When described psychologically, hunger refers to a regulation that involves a sensitive reciprocity between caregiver and infant. Infants bring to the reciprocity their inborn rates and rhythms of nutrient need states, nipple responses, and sucking patterns. Caregivers bring their procedural memories and learned techniques (demand feeding or set feeding schedules) and then intuitively respond in a complementary mode, all the while influencing the infants to speed up or slow down, take more during the day, extend the sleep period at night, and so on. The end result of the effectiveness or reciprocal fit of the nutrient response interaction is a psychic regulation that becomes an integral part of the infant's motivational system. We call this *regulation hunger.* Stated differently, hunger is not automatically coincident with nutrient need as an instinct theory would have it; rather, hunger is the developing psychological recognition of an internal sensation and an affect of distress plus the sensation and affect shift that occurs when the need state is relieved by feeding. Hunger, then, refers to an internally recognized state of sensation, an affect of distress that changes to comfort as nutrient is provided. Thus, hunger designates the specific variables of a particular need state and the anticipation of its relief from sucking and later eating. Similarly, satiety designates the specific variables of the state of relief, the anticipation of a cessation of the feeding activity, and the shift to dominance by another motivation, possibly to elimination or attachment or exploration. Just as hunger becomes an internally recognized state of need relief only by the coordination of infant–caregiver activity, so does satiety become an internally recognized state of relief cessation only as a coordinate infant–caregiver activity. A consistent mismatch to either side of the experience may contribute to lifelong problems of nutrient intake as evidenced by the distorted notions of both hunger and satiety in many eating disorders. Looked at this way, both hunger and satiety become well-regulated motivational guides as the result of lived experiences of infant–caregiver coordination, not as a simple unfolding of "instinct." Eating when hungry is not a well-defined motivational guide and bulimic overeating or specific insatiable cravings for sweets or chocolate may be the result of lived experiences of infant–caregiver mismatches and not untamed instinct.

Analytic theoreticians of different schools have turned away from motivation centered on sexual and aggressive drives and have substituted a group of theories loosely referred to as object relations. The core ideas behind this group of theories is that the infant's essential humanness lies in the seeking for relationships with other humans, unfortunately referred to as objects. Many of these theories retain elements of instinctual drive as the characteristic of the relationship itself—for the most part destructive or aggressive. We have opted to regard attachment as one form that human-to-human contact takes throughout life. We see its goal not in the discharge of drive energies or in narrowly fixed instinctlike configurations of stages but as flexible forms of relatedness in which individual and cultural preferences constantly interact with maturational potentialities. For example, in early infancy, baby and parent can and do make meaningful eye and auditory contact. This likelihood is made probable by the finding that the focal gaze of neonates is at 9 to 10 inches, the exact distance from feeding babies and feeders' eyes and the finding that babies respond to high-pitched, slow, sequenced verbalizations such as "Hi, there!" Unlike the hairy primates who attach literally by grasp and hair, the human establishes attachment experiences through more distant receptors of vision and sound. Seeking and scanning plus grasping allow human babies to form attachments to the people who are consistently in their presence to be seen, heard, smelled, and touched. Thus, human babies have both the need for and the equipment to obtain consistent and repetitive patterns of lived experiences specific for their mother and father while also being flexibly able to establish intimacy experiences with a babysitter. The significance of these observations of infants is that a narrow perspective of bonding similar to that of birds or of an inflexible breast-centered instinctual seeking of drive gratification becomes replaced by interactive patterns of attachment as the motivational base for human intimacy. Babies, by their responsiveness to the social contact of parents' eye contact, greetings, speech, hugs, and kisses, and parents by their responsiveness aided in the mother by hormonal preparation and in both mother and father by psychological anticipation meet, share, and enjoy each other. They establish conversational games, patterns of play, and, after the baby has reached 2 months of age, the consistent social smile as the reciprocal come-on to each other. Into this reciprocal world of interaction and emotional intersubjectivity come the idealizing, sponsoring, mentoring, rivaling, and envying that characterize the specific forms the attachment motive take.

Exploration and assertion, with its intimate association with learning, cognition, and intellectual development, appear to be the motivational needs most easily distinguishable from instinct or animalistic limitations. Yet, even with this motivational system, distinctions must be made about the development the system follows, particularly after 18 months of age. The early path taken by the exploratory motivation based on innate givens is to be alert to stimuli, particularly visual and auditory. Interest is triggered and increasing coordination among scanning, grasping, and mouthing occurs. The path taken by exploration is guided by innate and learned preferences. Assertion becomes the infant's way of following preferences, building agendas, and acting in a self-determined, playful manner. These activities, whether with objects, toys, or people, become what is called *play*. The affect that accompanies alerting and exploring is interest, and the affect that accompanies successful assertion is a sense of effectiveness and competence as learning proceeds. Essentially the same process can be observed in other mammals raised in family groups. The big cats learn in their play how to hunt; baby whales, while still being fed by their mothers, learn in their play all of the maneuvers needed to get their nutrients from the sea when weaned. In a number of species, frolicking seems to have the same purpose of expressing exuberance and being endearing to the mature members.

Human children at about 9 months of age become increasingly aware of properties as they explore the world around them. This includes the properties of physical objects (shapes, textures, etc.) and of other humans, particularly their affective states. As a result, humans acquire a way to process information that Lichtenberg (1983) designated *sign–signal communication*. The infant learns to read signs such as an opened toy drawer or a smiling face and to read signals such as a pointing finger or a verbal yes as indicators for exploring. For sign–signal informational exchange to work, that is, for exploratory–assertive motivation to produce a sense of effective and competent agency for human or animal, the environment must provide physical settings and guiding mentors from which and whom reliable indicators can be deduced consistently. Infant humans and animals must learn when exploring and asserting with their teeth is approved of or disapproved of, as indicated by the affect signals of caregivers. It may well be that because humans and animals share a lively, highly adaptive reliance on sign–signal communication that humans and domesticated animals can share habitats. This potential for an empathic sensing between human and animal based on shared motivations (attachment and exploratory–assertive) guided by sign–signal informational exchanges is easily lost when one emphasizes the essential difference created by the human's capacity for symbolic representation in the dual modes of primary and secondary processes. According to Olds (in press), who took a brain-centered, information-processing approach, early mammals have a primitive visualization system in sleep, the rapid eye movement (REM) dream state that allows them to re-represent awake perceptions disconnected from action. This provides an efficient organizer of brain activity. More advanced mammals have, in addition to REM sleep, the capacity to visualize scenes and form strategies ranging from the behavioral map that allows a dog to find its buried bone to a complex strategy that helps a chimpanzee reach a banana by pulling up a table. In the human, awake visualization becomes additionally re-represented through the language function of the dominant cerebral hemisphere. Along with conscious thoughts and actions, Olds noted that words provide a sign system by which the brain talks to itself and the self communicates with others. Stated another way, both human and many animal children form complex agendas designed to solve problems incumbent in exploring their environments, but humans alone, beginning at 18 months of age, have cognitive tools available to simultaneously encode their experiences in complex symbolic representations. Exploration and assertion using words and images comes to be expressed intrapsychically as both linear and logically arranged plans and as conscious and unconscious fantasies in which desires and wishes can be played out. The human alone after 18 months of age is blessed with and burdened by an encoding system that produces inherent contradictions in recording and responding to experience. Humans process information both to know what to do and what meaning to assign. Throughout life, but especially for children, the exploring–assertive person is confronted often with situations of overwhelming ambiguity, and knowing how to respond or what meaning to ascribe becomes impossible. Feelings of helpless confusion, internal conflict, and loss of effective agency are thus as integral to the human state as are the remarkable pragmatic and epistomological solutions that have resulted from successful exploration.

Our conception of the aversive motivational system contrasts strongly with an assumption of an aggressive instinctual drive. We find no evidence that infants are compelled to be destructive. We do, however, see convincing evidence that infants need to respond with antagonism or withdrawal to whatever experiences they find aversive. In the first year of life, a pattern of aversive motivation becomes established in relationships to how caregivers respond to the needs of the other four motivational systems. When needs for physiological requirements, attachment, exploration and assertion, or sensual enjoyment are not met, an aversive response such as crying, startle, anger, fear, distress, and sadness can serve as a signal to caregivers to react affirmatively and empathically to the need or, if that is not possible, to comfort. Infants responded to in this way build an expectation that aversiveness will alert caregivers to ameliorative efforts. Infants not responded to in this way will experience prolonged affect states of anger or avoidance of contact. The persistently antagonistic or withdrawn child may appear to be compelled or driven to destructiveness, and these responses can then be regarded as instinctual without consideration of the empathic failures that have become a dominant characteristic of that child's experience. Likewise, episodic upsurges at 18 months of age, during the second year, and during adolescence of insistence on forming, asserting, and angrily adhering to an agenda give the developing child an appearance of and a sense of being driven. Caregivers and others in the environment must oppose those agendas that endanger the child or others. Thus, a dual aspect of the aversive motivational system plays its part in human culture formation. Developing children must learn that the tools of their culture—knives, stairways, electric plugs, automobiles, medicine bottles—constitute dangers for which they have no innate aversion. They must be "acculturated" for their own safety. Caregivers must build "don'ts," "mustn'ts," and expectations of punishment into autonomous regulations without creating an organization of aversiveness that then dominates other potential experiences, destroying the pleasures of intimacy and converting exploration and assertion into a power–dominance vengeance motive. Theorists have mistakenly assumed that it is an "animal" drive that leads to this all-too-frequent destructive potential in humans, rather than the equally all-too-frequent empathic failures in the experience of children. People are becoming increasingly aware of the staggering statistics of verbal, physical, and sexual abuse children from every socioeconomic status endure as well as the coldness with which their signals of distress are met. Part of the confusion psychoanalytic theoreticians have had lies in the nature of the affects of fear, anger, and sadness. All three affects have strong physiological concomitants so that as their intensity increases, they propel the child or adult into a generalized state of panic, rage, or depression. Once panic, rage, or depression is triggered, the cognitive field is narrowly determined by tendencies for antagonism or withdrawal inherent to those dominated states. Thus, the widely accepted concept that reality is inevitably distorted by ascendant drive must be reconsidered. Misperceptions that indeed are common have their source in two often interrelated human experiences. First, experiences throughout life, but especially in childhood, confront people with more requirements to organize information than they are able to manage. Because infants are extremely dependent for security on building reliable maps of what to expect, breaches in expectancies often trigger fear, anger, or sadness. Once dual-coded symbolic representational processing develops, breaches of expectation and puzzles of every sort—why people die, what is happening in the bedroom, why someone is going to the hospital—threaten at every turn to overwhelm children's intense desire to restore their equilibrium through assigning meanings. Second, experiences, especially for children, with others who are in intense states of fear, anger, or sadness can trigger comparable or even more intense affective states. Once this occurs, because of the cognitive limitation of their own intense affect, children often misperceive the motivation of the other person and of their own as being more dire than it actually is. A child may easily read the fear, anger, or sadness of a parent and of their own as having much greater implication of disaster (danger, murder, suicide) than the parent or self intends.

We believe the motivation that has been referred to as sexual comprises two distinct but often unrelated motivational systems. One develops in response to the need for sensual enjoyment. The manifestations of the sensual system are apparent at birth and present in utero. The other system develops in response to the need for sexual excitement. The manifestations of this system become apparent during the second half of the first year of life. Sensual enjoyment can be observed in the infant's sucking, skin rubbing, rocking, and responses to melodic sounds, being fondled, wiped, and bathed. Sensual enjoyment leads to changes in tension level. The infant can be toned down from an irritable, overexcited, or distress state by the soothing of the sensually enjoyable activity, or the same activity can tone the infant upward into a more lively, fun state of giggles and playfulness. Sexual excitement is an "up" state of increasingly rising tension focused generally on perineal sensations but able to involve other parts and the whole body. A 10-month-old child fondling his or her genitals may gain sensual enjoyment and tone down as a presleep activity along with thumb sucking, or tone up toward a state of sexual excitement, with full vascular engorgement of the penis or perineal area. In adults, the same differentiation can be observed. A warm bath, a back rub, an affectionate hug, or cuddling before sleep can be a soothing calm down, or the same sensual enjoyments can become a component of foreplay building up to orgasmic release. Even in sexual intercourse, one partner may have as the goal sensual enjoyment and the other sexual excitement, and both feel enriched and satisfied.

Why has this separation of sensual enjoyment and sexual excitement as motivational goals not been made? We believe the answer lies in a narrowly focused adherence to an evolutionary concept of ensuring species survival through procreation. The narrowing reading of procreational necessity elevates orgasmic discharge as the essential goal of a sexual drive. Clinically, if one were to find an individual oriented toward only orgasmic discharge, as that theory would suggest, one would regard that individual as being pathologically dissociated from his or her partner—a person pathologically unable to love. The path taken by the developing motivation for sensual enjoyment is intricately involved in the development of attachment and is not gender-specific, although its gender-specific manifestations differ from culture to culture. The path taken by the developing motivation for sexual excitement is intricately involved in the unfolding of gender identity and gender preference. Although traditional instinct theory would posit that the sexual drive for orgasmic release is extremely powerful and is the source of many of humankind's fights with the need for civilizing restraint, observation of the life span indicates otherwise. Clearly, upsurges of sexual excitement seeking occur at different periods—at 18 months of age, at the oedipal period, during the phases of adolescence, and during periods of falling in love. However, unlike the estrous cycles in animals, no reliable hormonal priming pushes humans into sexual excitement states. Humans therefore rely on fantasy as an internal arousal stimulant and have created myth cycles, Bacchanalian festivals, erotic art, erotic literature, and pornography and aphrodesiac potions to reinforce the stimulating effect of self-originated fantasy. Further complications arise when, in childrearing, sensual motives are confused with sexual motives and parents cause children to suffer an unwarranted suppression of bodily and affectionate pleasure and induce excitement in the form of aversive guilt-ridden states.

Because of the ubiquity of tension-arousing exchanges between caregivers and children over sensual–sexual motivations and of an overload of puzzling uncertainties about sexual "mysteries" carried over from childhood, an aversive current becomes inevitably interwoven with sexuality. A sense of overcoming restraint, whether perceived as internal or external, gives an antagonistic power–dominance coloration to sexual excitement fantasies (Stoller, 1975). Thus, in our view, ascribing an "animalistic" sexual nature to men and women is itself an excitement-ensuring myth. Clinical observation suggests that the motive for sexual excitement is often less strong than traditional theory would predict, whereas the motive for sensual enjoyment is much more frequent and intense. Loving is mainly an outgrowth of sensual enjoyment and attachment intimacy. Sexual loving is an outgrowth of the successful combining of sensual enjoyment and gender-directed sexual excitement seeking and consummation, with procreation as one possible augmenting fantasy aim.

Finally, we consider our concept of self in the light of evolutionary–biological drive theory. We define the self as a developing center for initiating, organizing, and integrating experience and motivation. This definition does not distinguish the human self from the self of many mammals. For example, dogs, cats, horses, whales, and primates develop a center for regulating physiological requirements, forming attachments, exploring curiously, asserting preferences, responding aversively through antagonism and withdrawal, and seeking sensual enjoyment and sexual excitement. They initiate, organize, and integrate their experience and motivation in ways that correlate well with our concept of having both an individual and group personality. Within groups, animals react to each other in accordance with traits regarded as personality: friendliness, irritability, and playfulness. Humans are distinguished not by the capacity to initiate, organize, and integrate but by the means and goals used. Animals, it is assumed, form organizational and representational maps of their experiences, but only humans encode (after 18 months of age) their organization and representational maps in the form of dual symbols. The dual-symbol representations of primary and secondary processes provide the human self with plasticity and ambiguity of experience (only humans write and understand poetry), with a communication system discursive from immediate actuality (only humans develop language), and with a need to extend experience and motivation along an extended time line (only humans record history and make long-term predictions). The summary effect of these aspects of symbolic representation is that the human self alone is motivated to be self-reflected and to seek meaning through his or her self-reflectiveness.

THE "UNCONSCIOUS"

As is clear from the preceding discussion, little agreement has been reached previously concerning the development, nature, or dynamics of motivation in human beings. Academic psychologists have generally treated motivation as a concept necessary for understanding other functions in which they were more interested, such as perception, thinking, and learning, rather than as a focus of interest in its own sake. The existence of physiological and life-sustaining drives has been universally acknowledged, although many studies and theories have been unconcerned with them.

The general muddiness that has resulted is nowhere better demonstrated than in the attempt to answer the following question: Other than in psychoanalytic theories, is unconscious motivation acknowledged? The answer to this is another question: What is meant by *unconscious?*

Many psychological phenomena have been discussed as if there were no concept of motivation, conscious or unconscious. As already noted, conditioning is one example, and Piaget's (1954; Piaget & Anhelder, 1969) major acknowledgment of unconscious factors was simply that the structures underlying cognitive development were not conscious (see also Gruber & Voneche, 1977). In addition, like many developmental theorists, Piaget assumed that because he was discussing phenomena that were maturational or invariant, motivational considerations did not have to be considered. King (1990) reviewed evidence that cognition and emotion are generated by separate systems, although there may be interaction between them. King's own research, as well as her review, indicate that although cognitive development is invariant and age related, conflict and affect "may critically constrain the child's conscious access to or expression of his/her cognitive competencies" (1988, p. 10). Moreover, King's research demonstrates that in some instances, children may regress in their ability to access their already-developed cognitive skills when the task is emotionally laden.

On the other hand, Freud's (1905/1953a) theory of psychosexual development also has the characteristics of being maturational and invariant, but it is rife with opportunities for noting the impact of unconscious factors. And Erikson (1963), whose theory is based on Freud's, opened Freud's theory to the impact of socialization while maintaining the characteristic of invariance; L. Mack (1974) and R. Mack (1974) respectively verified that emotional difficulties and cultural environment, although not affecting the invariance of the Eriksonian stages, did nevertheless significantly affect the ages at which they appeared. Moreover, their studies, as well as an earlier one by Elkan (1969), demonstrate that developmental as well as motivational variables can reveal themselves outside of awareness, by using recalled dreams as a basis of study.

The extrapolation from animal to human behavior is another example of failure to recognize the importance of the presence or absence of awareness that is possible in human beings. For example, on the basis of observations of the stickleback fish, Pelkwijk and Tinbergen posited a specific source of energy for each instinct "that is available only for the performance of that particular instinctive act," which is triggered "by some very specific environmental stimulus" (cited in Arkes & Garske, 1977). If no appropriate external stimulus appears, the energy builds until its release is gradually generalized to other stimuli with some similarity to its genetic determinant. Because of the specific energy, its increasing demand for release, and its eventual shift to a new but similar stimulus, an analogy has been made to Freud's (1909/1955b) concept of displacement, despite the facts that for Freud, external stimuli are secondary rather than primary and that displacement is usually an unconsciously motivated process. Our previous discussion of infidelity in birds, primates, and humans is another example. One cannot assume that infrahuman animals have the capacity for awareness of the reasons for their behavior or that they are unconscious of that motivation. Some people may also be unaware of their reasons for their infidelity, but they have the capacity for awareness and may have strong motives of which they are unconscious.

Yet another instance of behavior that resembles displacement or possibly sublimation is Allport's (1937) concept of the functional autonomy of motives. Gordon Allport, a personality theorist, was concerned with the development of traits as personality components and as motives; he was also interested in the individual as the proper unit of study and saw the task of psychology as the understanding of the lawfulness of uniqueness. He therefore denied the existence or importance of universal underlying motives. He did, however, recognize the need for some dynamic force or stress for a trait to be called a motive. He would probably have denied the motive power of the cognitive styles discussed in an earlier section of this chapter. Central to Allport's theory is that behaviors that are instrumental in the service of a given motive may over time or for other reasons develop motive power and operate independent of the original motive: "Activities that earlier in the game were *means* to an end, now become *ends* in themselves" (1937, p. 195). Allport used neuroses and neurotic symptoms as one piece of evidence for this concept: "Like all adult motives, they grow out of antecedent systems, but (are) functionally independent of them. . . . The theory declines to believe that the energies of adult personality are infantile or archaic in nature. Motivation is *always* contemporary" (1937, p. 194). Thus, Allport did away with the need for a dynamic unconscious to account for the development and maintenance of defense mechanisms, especially because Allport believed that most conflicts are essentially conscious.

On the other hand, unconscious contributions to human behavior have long been recognized. For example, the early laboratory studies of set, referred to earlier, amply demonstrated unconscious and semiconscious influences on perception, learning, and memory. Studies of these functions in individuals deprived of food, water, or sex also demonstrated the unconscious effects of deprivation. Perhaps more striking is the finding that water-deprived subjects who dreamed that their thirst had been quenched required less liquid in the morning than subjects who did not have such dreams.

Expectancies and judgments have also been shown to be affected by unconscious factors. Children designated as "slow" are perceived and treated as slow by teachers. Children who can use poker chips to get candy judge poker chips as being larger than do children who received candy without the use of the chips (Lambert & Lambert, 1958). Social psychologists have noted the effects on behavior of prejudice, social attitudes, and stereotypes operating outside of awareness. Bartlett's (1932) research demonstrated that a striving for meaning operated outside of awareness to impose familiar schemata on the perception and memory of narrative material from another culture.

Much of the early academic research on the effects of unconscious factors on other functions was satisfied to demonstrate such effects. On balance, academic psychologists evidenced little curiosity concerning the nature of unconscious functioning itself, even among those who were familiar to varying degrees with the evolving Freudian theory. It must be remembered that early psychology had concerned itself primarily with stimulus–response sequences and that the demonstration of intervening variables was of interest in itself. That these variables could operate outside of awareness was a significant contribution to the psychology of its time. Interest in unconscious processes was strong, but it tended to be in the service of even stronger interests, resulting in a strangely static view of admittedly strong forces.

Before the midcentury, the research or theories developed by academic psychologists interested in the "Freudian unconscious" were frequently fragmentary or shallow, either because their understanding of these concepts was limited or because something important got lost in the translation from theory to laboratory.

Lewin's (1935, 1951) motivational theory, for example, was influenced by Freud and, with his associates, demonstrated that frustration could cause regression in children, just as Dollard et al. (1939) had demonstrated that frustration could lead to aggression. Lewin was also interested in conflict and developed a concept called "leaving the field," an escape mechanism for situations in which the equivalence of conflicting vectors became too painful. On the other hand, much of Lewin's theory is descriptive, set in the context of gestalt field theory; he introduced the concept of life space, which contains external and internal regions that can rise or fall in tension and change valences, thereby motivating behavior either consciously or unconsciously. Much of Lewin's theory is not relevant to our present concerns. He did, however, note that all of the regions interact and that when one is figure, others become ground in a continuously dynamic flow, a notion totally compatible with our view of the relationship of shifting dominance between the motivational systems.

For the most part, only when the work of theorists and researchers also engaged in clinical work or at least influenced substantially by psychoanalysis is examined can one find research and theory that attempt to take into account *dynamically* unconscious factors. The work of George Klein (1970) and his associates is rooted simultaneously in ego psychology and cognitive theory, and focuses precisely on the psychoanalytic concepts of the unconscious through the study of perception and cognition.

Much of Klein's (1970) research focused on perception because he understood perception to epitomize the ego's most direct contact with the environment. Noting that although perception was not simply the sum of its physiological components, it was generally veridical, thereby calling into question an earlier emphasis on the distorting effects of unconscious motivation and supporting a view of the competence of the ego. Witkin et al. (1962) and Witkin and Goodenough (1981), as discussed in an earlier section, had discovered and discussed the development of characteristic styles of perceptual and cognitive responses to the world that then operated automatically and were related to many aspects of functioning. Obviously, with respect to unconscious motivation, for the most part one is not aware of his or her characteristic cognitive–perceptual style or of how it developed, although the reasons might be dynamic in nature. Despite its embeddedness in ego psychology, this approach is also not very dynamic. However, it is congruent with Klein's overall stance that motivation had to be understood within a cognitive context.

It is not possible within the confines of this chapter to outline Klein's (1970) motivational theory in any meaningful detail. Klein made an ambitious attempt to deal with motivation "in terms of a behavioral unit of ideation, affect, and action" (1970, p. 361) rather than drive. He felt it was more meaningful to return to Freud's early notions of "a nonspecific energetic quantity" that had to be directed, and a *repressed idea* (an incompatible cognitive structure) that gave rise to hysterical symptoms (1970, p. 363). According to Klein, "motivation implies direction and intensity of activity" (1970, p. 364) and depends on both internal and external stimuli; its locus is "within the structure of a train of thought" (1970, p. 364). Klein described in intricate detail the activation of a motivational train of thought by a wish, creating an imbalance that can be reduced by gratification, thus terminating that train of thought. If, however, the gratification is associated with unpleasure, a new imbalance occurs and inhibits gratification of the original wish; the new train of thought is toward repression of the original wish. In the service of gratifying the imbalance thus aroused, selective attention or other defense mechanisms are called into play. Klein discussed repression both as a form of memory rather than forgetting, as well as a motivational force in its own right. As previously noted, this theory attempts to integrate aspects of psychoanalytic theory with aspects of cognitive theory. Although, even as inadequately presented here, it does introduce dynamic concepts within the context of cognitive theory, it still seems bland and oversimplified when contrasted with the richness of the "Freudian unconscious."

Recognition of unconscious aspects of motivation and its resultant behavior is historically, then, just the beginning. The difference between unawareness and a dynamic unconscious is a vast one, and a concept of the latter certainly seems to necessitate a grasp of psychoanalytic—although not necessarily only Freudian—theory. As Klein himself concluded, "the intimate links between psychoanalytic clinical theory and the clinical situation, the difficulties of testing the concepts of the clinical theory outside this situation, suggest that any attempt at propositional rigor and validations begin with *the data of the psychoanalytic situation*" (1970, p. 19).

In our attempt to resolve paradoxes in the psychoanalytic concept of the unconscious, we have postulated a fundamental unconscious mentation and an unconscious symbolic mentation (Lichtenberg, 1989; Lichtenberg, Lachmann, & Fosshage, 1991).

In designating a fundamental unconscious mentation, we refer to its formation in the early stage of infancy and to the influence it exerts on the organization of later development. Information present as a component of fundamental unconscious mentation may be encoded as procedural memories or episodic memories or may be pattern regulators that do not receive coding. Fundamental unconscious mentation can be distinguished from unconscious mentation organized by dual modes of symbolic representation by the different means by which information is encoded in each. In appraising any specific clinical entity, we may regard either fundamental unconscious mentation or unconscious symbolic mentation as being more important in contributing to the organization of the phenomenon under consideration.

The hypotheses that bear on fundamental unconscious mentation are as follows:

(a) Motivation organized as five motivational systems (see the boxed display) forms fundamental unconscious mentation.

(b) The five motivational systems shape and are shaped by lived experience prior to the development of dual-coded symbolic representation.

(c) The record of the early lived experience persists, for the most part shaping and being shaped by primary and secondary process modes of symbolic representation but nonetheless contributing its own forms and rules of representation throughout life.

(d) To realize the therapeutic goal of making as full as possible an empathic entry into the state of mind of an analysand, analysts attend not only to the words and categoric affects that are regarded as the ordinary components of free association but also to behaviors, gestures, and affects that reveal links to the deeper layers of experience of unconscious mentation.

(e) From resonating empathically with these behaviors, gestures, and especially categoric and vitalizing affects, analysts can form model scenes (Lachmann & Lichtenberg, 1991; Lichtenberg, 1989), that provide important links to the period of formation of each motivational system and the stability or instability of the contribution of each system to the emergent and core self.

(f) Often the ability to form model scenes indicative of the deeper layers of experience of the unconscious results from the analyst's perusal of his or her own and the analysand's affect-laden role responses and enactments in the intersubjective field of an ongoing analysis.

Unconscious symbolic mentation can be understood through an approach via contents and process. The approach to contents has yielded a richly evocative plethora of organizing fantasies beginning with Freud's (1905/1953a) essays on sexuality. The same approach has yielded an array of defense mechanisms that regulate the path to awareness of these fantasies. Our contribution to an understanding of contents is to suggest that symbolic representations of motives are orga-

Normal or Ordinary Schemas From Infancy

These schemas serve as templates in the
fundamental level of the unconscious for
model scenes of both the presymbolic and symbolic periods.

A need for nutrient intake → the sensation of hunger and the affect of distress (crying) → sucking and intake experience → a sense of enjoyment and a sensation of satiety.

A need for attachment → distress and pursuit behaviors → opportunities for affirmation, sharing, and idealization → a sense of intimacy pleasure, and self-expansiveness.

A need for exploration and assertion → interest and functional activity → a sense of pleasure from efficiency and competence.

A need to react aversively based on pain, violation of preference, mismatch of expectancy → distress and

fear, disgust, sadness	Startle	Anger
→ withdrawal	and/or	antagonistic behaviors

either

self soothing and/or instrumentally effective use of anger → self reliance and competence

or

relief of the source of distress and frustration, restoration of self-expansiveness and intimacy.

A need for sensual enjoyment arising as general distress and irritability and/or a specific sensation in a sensual target zone → soothing, stroking, rhythmic rubbing by self or other →

either

relief or distress and irritability and specific sensations of pleasure with reduced general tension

or

relief of distress and irritability and specific sensations of pleasure with heightened focal and general sensations of sexual excitement.

---

nized during the development of each of the five motivational systems and that these representations bear the stamp of the basic schema of each system (see the display) and the unique and particular shaping of the individual's lived experience. We agree with the authors who suggest that unconscious contents take the form of fantasies (Arlow, 1969a, 1969b), beliefs (Weiss & Sampson, 1986), ambitions and ideals (Kohut, 1977), and goals and values (Gedo, 1979).

The approach to processes of symbolic unconscious mentation requires three perspectives: an intrapsychic, an intersubjective, and an assessment of state. The intrapsychic perspective has been the most studied in traditional psychoanalysis through the concepts of conflict, drive–defense interplay, and compromise formation. Our contribution to the intrapsychic perspective is to recognize the continuous interplay between motives of each system. This interplay often takes the form of a smooth "competition" between motives for the dominance of awareness. To regard these motivational calls for shifts in attention and functional dominance as "conflict" we feel is experientially and conceptually inaccurate. We see this position as being in accord with the attempt by Hartmann (1964) to delineate conflict-free adaptive functioning. We would apply the extensive psychoanalytic knowledge about intrapsychic conflict (Brenner, 1976) to those situations in which the self responds aversively to potential awareness of a motive triggered in any system, including the aversive system. We are then interested in an exploration of the whole experience: the aversive response, its effect, and the motive to which the self is aversive.

The intersubjective perspective adds to the intrapsychic a conceptualization needed to account for the embeddedness of each individual in the ecological world of his or her surround. Each intrapsychic system as it develops is a motivational–*functional* system in that (a) motivation and function are constantly influenced by an informational flow from internal and external sources (see tachistoscopic studies); (b) motivation and function are constantly influenced by the affective ambience perceived to exist internally and externally (see empathy studies [Lichtenberg, Bornstein, & Silver, 1984] and studies of affect [Tomkins, 1962, 1963]; and (c) the call for activation of motivation and functioning can arise internally or externally (Fairbairn's 1952, concept of an exciting object).

Regarding the perspective of an assessment of state, the concept of state refers to an overall organization of the self (or in the neonate to an organization of the emergent self). In infant studies, *state* refers to the innately programmed changes that occur as the neonate passes between crying, alert activity, quiet activity, drowsiness, and sleep (REM and non-REM). In each state, the rules that govern motivations, cognition, affects, and behavior vary predictably. According to Hofer (1990),

in each state, the elements are organized into a particular functional pattern. A change in the state of the system alters the way in which information is processed: things are perceived differently, perceptions are differently integrated, and the nature and intensity of the behaviors likely to result are altered during a state change. (p. 58)

The nonconflictual or ordinary conflictual motivational and functional shifts we have referred to imply a relatively cohesive state of self. The state concept has a long history in psychoanalysis dating from Freud's (1893–1895/1955b) discussion of hypnoid and dissociative states. A central tenet we want to draw attention to is that although we usually speak of altered states of consciousness, altered states affect symbolic *unconscious* mentation as well. What occurs when the state of self is markedly altered? The contemporary clinician is frequently confronted by patients who have suffered the kind of trauma (sexual and physical abuse, concentration camp victims, the alienation of some Vietnam veterans) whose state changes often profoundly affect the organization of their motivation. In more cohesive self states, these patients are able to organize and reveal experiences from their symbolic unconscious with a capacity for self-exploration. However, as these patients attempt to gain access to problems that lie at the heart of their traumatic experiences, they are at risk to revive the fragmented state with an attendant frightening and often paralyzing affective disruption. The intrapsychic and intersubjective perspectives as described ordinarily no longer apply. When a patient is in a toxic state from drugs, from malnutrition as in severe anorexics, or organic disorders, the dysfunction affects the ability of symbolic unconscious mentation to organize motivation in an ordinary manner. Clinicians must reconsider the alignments of motivation arising from symbolic unconscious mentation when parents who were themselves abused as children enter a state of blindly insensitive abuse of their children or various dissociative states, such as suicidal numbness or multiple personality disorganizations. The perspective of a marked alteration of state alerts clinicians to the need to map out the processes of symbolic unconscious mentation that occur in severe disruption–restoration sequences, traumatic states, toxic states, and psychoses.

A multiplicity of factors govern the openness to awareness of the symbolic representations when self-cohesion is intact. At the level of least complexity, the call for an immediate adaptive functioning, say the need to observe a changing traffic signal (an exploratory–assertive motive), may preempt the awareness of a female driver and temporarily force out of awareness a wish to continue to communicate with a passenger (e.g., an attachment motive or a sensual-sexual motive). More complexity is added if the driver is then unable to recall what she intended to say. The previously conscious content is now unconscious and dynamically resistant to will, plan, or intentions. The driver may now be annoyed or embarrassed (conscious aversive motivational state) and now lacks awareness of both the content and the motive for the forgetting (an unconscious aversive motivation). Analysis of the situation could reveal that the driver was unconsciously aversive to a fear state triggered by the driving danger (as in an association to a prior accident) or to a symbolic risk of bodily injury (as in a belief she would be punished for enjoying herself during a period of mourning). Or, analysis could reveal that the driver was unconsciously aversive to the content she was about to reveal, such as a dependent wish for greater closeness or a sensual-sexual desire.

A relationship between fundamental unconscious mentation and symbolic unconscious mentation can be seen in our example of the driver: paying attention to the traffic signal is in direct continuity with the procedural memory from early infancy of the manner in which attention becomes focused in an exploratory-assertive mode. Both infant and mother will instantly interrupt a social sharing to attend to a book that has fallen with a bang from a shelf. Or an infant can be distracted from hunger or sensual sucking by a rattle waved across his or her gaze. The schema of such a procedural memory is an unconscious regulator of how exploratory–assertive motivation may be turned on and how another motivation (e.g., attachment) may be temporarily extinguished. The potentiality for unconscious tension is thus established. The driver's struggle with her forgetting exemplifies not fundamental unconscious mentation but symbolic unconscious mentation. The motives involved are encoded as symbolic representations and are able to be rendered as narrative statements. The defense mechanism of repression is the means by which forgetting results from the aversive motivation triggered by fear of danger, injury, or undesired revelation. Defense mechanisms, like cognitive controls (Gardner, Holzman, Klein, Linton, & Spence, 1959) such as leveling and sharpening, are neither conscious nor capable of encoding. Cognitive regulators often develop early in life as uncoded pattern organizers and thus are both constituents of the fundamental level of the unconscious and active controllers of the dynamic unconscious (see Lichtenberg et al., 1991).

DISCUSSION

Our thesis is that the essential features of motivation have been mapped out piecemeal by academic psychologists of a number of theoretical disciplines and by clinicians, particularly psychoanalysts, who are also splintered into different groups. Neither group has been successful in integrating the work of the other or in integrating remarkable new findings in brain studies and neurophysiology. We have presented Lichtenberg's (1989) theory of five motivational systems and self as an example of a current effort to draw on a wide variety of sources to encompass the complexity of motivation. Lichtenberg based his theory on infant research studies for the core of his development thesis and on psychoanalytic clinical studies, especially those of self psychology. Infant research provides a particularly promising opportunity for integration in that the studies include those with precise experimental design and those using observation based on psychoanalytic postulates. The hypotheses that evolve from these studies can then be compared with findings of neurophysiological development for supportive correlations.

In this chapter we have attempted to illustrate the problems that have confronted motivation researchers and theorists in the past and the manner in which a tentative solution might be approached. To say that this is an enormously large topic is to state the obvious and to offer justification for the many-sided approaches taken in this book.

We have selected three topics to bring into focus the variety of unintegrated approaches that characterize the history of failed attempts to unravel the mystery of human motivation. In the first section we presented a highly selected summary of the terminological confusion that has resulted from relatively isolated attempts by a variety of psychologists and psychoanalysts to use the vocabulary of their respective disciplines to the segment of the problem they chose for study. We attempted to illustrate our belief that a contemporary theory of motivation requires a choice of terms that have ordinary nontechnical meanings in order to maintain an experience–near–affective link even with designations used for categoric purposes. At the same time, we believe wherever possible in the use of terms that evoke associative connections to attempts by diverse contributors in the past. These include students of physiology and bodily experience and its disturbances in "psychosomatic states"; observers of interrelatedness between individuals and between members of groups; researchers into perception, cognition, affect and the realms of play and work; theorists of "man's inhumanity to man" and its permutations in adaptive self-protection or maladaptive destructiveness symptomatology; and pioneer explorers of the unexpectedly far-reaching nature of sensuality and sexuality.

In the second section we presented our account of how early debates over evolutionary theory led to emotion-ridden confusion over instincts and how eventually theorists have sorted out these confusions. On one side, those who have studied animals have increasingly appreciated the oversimplification involved in instinct theories and the necessity of considering motivated patterns of complex behavior involved in relatedness within animal species. With mammals and particularly primates, practices of rearing, communication, and learning are multifaceted. On the other side, those who have studied humans have had to jettison the "commonsense" fallacy of moralistically regarding humans as superior beings who are required by civilization to overcome their animal heritage. We have tried to demonstrate that an essential quality of homo sapiens lies not in having (as do many mammals and all primates) a system of communication but the particular form of dual coding of symbolic representation used in human intrapsychic and intersubjective communication. By focusing on systems built around needs and innate and learned patterns of responses to those needs, we demonstrate the similarities of motivation between animals and humans as well as the differences. We are thus able to regard motivation without the prejudice that arose from viewing animals as organized by primitive destructive aggressiveness and bursts of uncontrolled sexuality. Centering attention on infant and child development, we are able to view human motivation in the light of the empathic potentiality of caregivers and children, who, because they have identical motivational systems, basic needs, and affective responses, are enabled to respond reciprocally to one another. Parenthetically, similar reciprocity can be observed between humans and many animals.

In the last section on the unconscious, we presented our belief that the domains of the "testable" unconscious and the "Freudian" unconscious no longer need to be treated as hostile territories or at best distant neighbors. Academicians must recognize that despite the deficiencies of the Freudian view and the speculative quality of findings derived in the "laboratory" of the clinical setting, motivations that lie outside of awareness are both powerful and extremely varied. Psychoanalytic theoreticians must recognize that despite the limitations of narrowly focused research studies, motivations linked to prior experience cannot be understood without a clear knowledge of the organization of memory and of the means of regulation of cognition and emotion. In postulating fundamental unconscious mentation, we have attempted to remain close to what can be observed in infants and to studies of procedural and episodic memory. We thus reject postulates of psychoanalytic theory that attribute to infants forms of encoding that cannot be demonstrated and are rendered extremely unlikely by studies of brain development. Alternatively, in postulating symbolic unconscious mentation, we draw on years of psychoanalytic clinical experience that demonstrates the enormous plasticity that arises from the dual coding of symbolic representations.

We can point to a contemporary view of dream theory to demonstrate how many of the threads of the differing disciplines intermesh. From evolutionary biology (Winson, 1985) comes the suggestion that the important survival gain from a smaller brain size in mammals came about with the development of the capacity to process information during REM sleep. From infant studies it has been learned that neonates have active REM sleep states, but there is no information about what the experience is like—possibly carryovers of perceptual and sensation flashes. It has also been learned that the first clear evidence of "content" dreams coincides with symbolic play and with the myelinization of the cortices at 18 months of age. Just as the formal structure of event or episodic memory begins at this time (Nelson, 1986), the structure of dream contents takes its basic form concurrently. Event memory organization demonstrates the dominance of secondary process (left hemisphere), whereas dream mentation demonstrates the dominance of primary process (right hemisphere), and dream telling combines both. But what is the function of dreaming? Many psychoanalysts are willing to reevaluate the tortured reasoning required to justify Freud's (1900/1953b) drive energy discharge and wish fulfillment proposal. Information processing (Rosenblatt & Thickstun, 1977) provides the broadest umbrella uniting what is known of dreaming of animals and human infants with that of older children and adults. But information processing is directed toward what end? We believe that dream mentation after 18 months of age has a problem-solving function (Fiss, 1987; Fosshage, 1987). Certainly, then, the psychoanalytic conception of problems with sexuality and aggression would be included in this assessment. We can go further and suggest that unresolved problems triggered by motivations in all five systems and by threats to self-stability and cohesion can be the source of the symbolic representations found in any dream. Unresolved regulation of a physiological requirement, of attachment and affiliative experiences, of exploratory and assertive efforts in play or work, of aversive struggles, and of sensual-sexual seeking can independently or in some combination trigger the largely primary process REM dream representations that attempt to bring a problem into focus (Olds, in press). Communicating one's dream to oneself or others would then be an attempt to frame the imagic experience in the ordering of words, and interpreting a dream by analyst and analysand would be an attempt through reflective consideration to discover the problem being worked on and the status of links in past and present to that effort.

In conclusion, we propose that the framework for a more unified, more coherent, and more clinically useful theory of motivation lies at hand. We hope that through our proposal of five motivational systems and a self organization, we have demonstrated an approach to the problem of integrating findings from the diverse and generally divided fields of psychology and psychoanalysis.

REFERENCES

Ainsworth, M. D. (1979). Attachment as related to mother-infant interaction. In J. B. Rosenblatt, R. A. Hinde, C. Beer, & M. Bushel (Eds.), *Advances in the study of behavior* (pp. 1–51). New York: Academic Press.

Allport, G. W. (1937). *Personality: A psychological interpretation.* New York: Holt, Rinehart & Winston.

Angier, N. (1990, August 21). Mating for life? It's not for the birds or the bees. *New York Times,* pp. C1, C8.

Arkes, H. R., & Garske, J. P. (1977). *Psychological theories of motivation* (2nd ed.). Monterey, CA: Brooks/ Cole.

Arlow, J. (1969a). Unconscious fantasy and disturbances of conscious experiences. *Psychoanalytic Inquiry, 35,* 1–27.

Arlow, J. (1969b). Fantasy, memory, and reality testing. *Psychoanalytic Inquiry, 35,* 28–51.

Atkinson, J. W. (1964). *An introduction to motivation.* New York: Van Nostrand Reinhold.

Bartlett, F. C. (1932). *Remembering.* Cambridge, England: Cambridge University Press.

Bowlby, J. (1958). The nature of a child's tie to his mother. *International Journal of Psychoanalysis, 39,* 350–373.

Brazelton, T. B. (1980, May). *New knowledge about the infant from current research: Implications for psychoanalysis.* Paper presented at the meeting of the American Psychoanalytic Association, San Francisco.

Brenner, C. (1976). *Psychoanalytic technique and psychic conflict.* Madison, CT: International Universities Press.

Darwin, C. (1859). *The origin of species.* London: John Murrey.

Dollard, J., Doob, L. W., Miller, N. E., Mowrer, O. H., & Sears, R. R. (1939). *Frustration and aggression.* New Haven, CT: Yale University Press.

Elkan, B. (1969). *Developmental differences in the manifest content of children's reported dreams.* Unpublished doctoral dissertation, Teachers College, Columbia University.

Erikson, E. H. (1963). *Childhood and society* (2nd ed.). New York: Norton.

Fairbairn, W. R. D. (1952). *An object-relations theory of the personality.* New York: Basic Books.

Fiss, H. (1987, October). *Experimental strategies for the study of the function of dreaming.* Paper presented at 10th Annual Conference on Self Psychology, Chicago.

Fosshage, J. (1987). Dream interpretation revisited. In A. Goldberg (Ed.), *Frontiers in self psychology* (pp. 161–176). Hillsdale, NJ: Analytic Press.

Freud, S. (1953a). Three essays on the theory of sexuality. In J. Strachey (Ed. and Trans.), *The standard edition of the complete psychological works of Sigmund Freud* (Vol. 7, pp. 135–243). London: Hogarth Press. (Original work published 1905)

Freud, S. (1953b). The interpretation of dreams. In J. Strachey (Ed. and Trans.), *The standard edition of the complete psychological works of Sigmund Freud* (Vols. 4 & 5, pp. 1–622). London: Hogarth Press. (Original work published 1900)

Freud, S. (1955a). Studies in hysteria. In J. Strachey (Ed. and Trans.), *The standard edition of the complete psychological works of Sigmund Freud* (Vol. 2, pp. 1–306). London: Hogarth Press. (Original work published 1893–1895)

Freud, S. (1955b). Analysis of a phobia in a five-year-old boy. In J. Strachey (Ed. and Trans.), *The standard edition of the complete psychological works of Sigmund Freud* (Vol. 3, pp. 3–153). London: Hogarth Press. (Original work published 1909)

Gardner, R., Holzman, P. S., Klein, G. S., Linton, H. S., & Spence, D. P. (1959). Cognitive control: A study of individual consistencies in cognitive behavior. *Psychological Issues* (Monograph 4).

Gedo, J. E. (1979). *Beyond interpretation: Toward a revised theory for psychoanalysis.* Madison, CT: International Universities Press.

Greenberg, J., & Mitchell, S. A. (1983). *Object relations in psychoanalytic theory.* Cambridge, MA: Harvard University Press.

Gruber, H., & Voneche, J. (Eds.). (1977). *The essential Piaget.* New York: Basic Books.

Harlow, H. F. (1965). Sexual behavior in the rhesus monkey. In F. A. Beach (Ed.), *Sex and behavior.* New York: Wiley.

Harlow, H. F., & Harlow, M. K. (1965). The affectional system. In A. M. Scjroer, J. F. Harlow, & F. Stollnitz (Eds.), *Behavior of non-human primates.* New York: Academic Press.

Hartmann, H. (1964). *Essays on ego psychology*. Madison, CT: International Universities Press.

Hofer, M. (1990). Early symbiotic processes: Hard evidence from a soft place. In R. A. Glick & S. Bone (Eds.), *Pleasure beyond the pleasure principle*. New Haven, CT: Yale University Press.

James, W. (1961). *Psychology: The briefer course*. New York: Harper. (Original work published 1892)

King, B. E. (1990). *The relationship of object constancy to sorting performance on categorization tasks, psychosexual development, and perceptual differentiation in oedipal-aged children*. Unpublished doctoral dissertation, Teachers College, Columbia University, New York.

Klein, G. S. (1970). *Perception, motives, and personality*. New York: Knopf.

Kohut, H. (1971). *The analysis of the self*. Madison, CT: International Universities Press.

Kohut, H. (1977). *The restoration of the self*. Madison, CT: International Universities Press.

Kohut, H. (1984). *How does analysis cure?* Chicago: University of Chicago Press.

Lachmann, F., & Lichtenberg, J. (in press). Model scenes: Implications for psychoanalytic treatment. *Journal of the American Psychoanalytic Association*.

Lambert, W. W., & Lambert, E. C. (1958). Some indirect effects of reward on children's size estimates. *Journal of Abnormal and Social Psychology, 48*, 507–510.

Lapidus, L. B. (1968). The relation between cognitive control and reactions to stress: A study of mastery in the anticipatory phase of childbirth. *Dissertation Abstracts International, 30*, 384. (University Microfilms, No. 69–11, 818)

Lapidus, L. B. (1970, September). *Cognitive control, parental practices, and contemporary social problems*. Paper presented at 78th Annual Convention of the American Psychological Association, Miami Beach, FL.

Lewin, K. (1935). *A dynamic theory of personality*. New York: McGraw-Hill.

Lewin, K. (1951). *Field theory in social science*. New York: Harper & Row.

Lichtenberg, J. (1978). The testing of reality from the standpoint of the body self. *Journal of the American Psychoanalytic Asssociation, 26*, 357–385.

Lichtenberg, J. (1983). *Psychoanalysis and infant research*. Hillsdale, NJ: Analytic Press.

Lichtenberg, J. (1989). *Psychoanalysis and motivation*. Hillsdale, NJ: Analytic Press.

Lichtenberg, J., Bornstein, M., & Silver, D. (1984). *Empathy I and II*. Hillsdale, NJ: Analytic Press.

Lichtenberg, J., Lachmann, F., & Fosshage, J. (1991). *The unconscious and the path to awareness*. Unpublished manuscript.

Lorenz, K. (1966). *On aggression*. (M. K. Wilson, Trans.). New York: Harcort, Brace & World.

Mack, L. (1974). *Developmental differences in the manifest content of the dreams of normal and disturbed children*. Unpublished doctoral dissertation, Teachers College, Columbia University, New York.

Mack, R. D. (1974). *A comparison of developmental differences in the manifest content of Tunisian and American dreams*. Unpublished doctoral dissertation, Teachers College, Columbia University, New York.

Maslow, A. H. (1970). *Motivation and personality* (2nd ed.). New York: Harper & Row.

Maslow, A. H. (1971). *The farther reaches of human behavior*. New York: Viking Press.

McDougall, W. (1923). *Outline of psychology*. New York: Scribner.

Murray, H. A. (1938). *Exploration in personality*. New York: Oxford University Press.

Nelson, K. (1986). *Event knowledge: Structure and function in development*. Hillsdale, NJ: Erlbaum.

Olds, D. (in press). Consciousness: A brain-centered, informational approach. *Psychoanalytic Inquiry*.

Papousek, H., & Papousek, M. (1986). Intuitive parenting: A didactic counterpart to the infant's precocity in integrative capacities. In J. D. Osofsky (Ed.), *Handbook of infant development* (2nd ed.). New York: Wiley.

Pavlov, I. P. (1927). *Conditioned reflexes* (G. V. Anrep, Trans.). London: Oxford Univeristy Press.

Piaget, J. (1954). *The construction of reality in the child* (M. Cook, Trans.). New York: Basic Books

Piaget, J., & Inhelder, B. (1969). *The psychology of the child* (H. Weaver, Trans.). New York: Basic Books.

Rogers, C. (1951). *Client-centered therapy.* Boston, MA: Houghton Mifflin.

Rosenblatt, A., & Thickstun, J. (1977). Modern psychoanalytic concepts in a general psychology. *Psychological Issues* (Monograph 42/43).

Rosenthal, R. (1966). *Experimenter effects in behavioral research.* New York: Appleton-Century-Crofts.

Shapiro, D. (1965). *Neurotic styles.* New York: Basic Books.

Skinner, B. F. (1938). *The behavior of organisms.* New York: Appleton-Century-Crofts.

Skinner, B. F. (1948). *Walden two.* New York: Macmillan.

Skinner, B. F. (1971). *Beyond freedom and dignity.* New York: Knopf.

Stern, D. (1985). *The interpersonal world of the infant.* New York: Basic Books.

Stoller, R. (1975). *Perversion: The erotic form of hatred.* New York: Pantheon Books.

Sullivan, H. S. (1953). *The interpersonal theory of psychiatry.* New York: Norton.

Tomkins, S. (1962). *Affect, imagery, consciousness: Vol. 1. The positive affects.* New York: Springer.

Tomkins, S. (1963). *Affect, imagery, consciousness: Vol. 2. The negative affects.* New York: Springer.

Weiner, B. (1986). *Human motivation.* Hillsdale, NJ: Erlbaum.

Weiss, J., & Sampson, H. (1968). *The psychoanalytic process.* New York: Guilford Press.

Winson, J. (1985). *Brain and psyche: The biology of the unconscious.* New York: Doubleday.

Witkin, H. A., Dyk, R. B., Faterson, H. F., Goodenough, D. R., & Karp, S. A. (1962). *Psychological differentiation.* New York: Wiley.

Witkin, H. A., & Goodenough, D. R. (1977). Filed dependency and interpersonal behavior. *Psychological Bulletin, 84,* 661–689.

Witkin, H. A., & Goodenough, D. R. (1981). *Cognitive styles, essence and origins: Field dependence and field independence.* New York: International Universities Press.

Witkin, H. A., Goodenough, D. R., Oltman, P. K., Friedman, F., Owen, D., & Raskin, E. (1977). The role of field dependent and field independent cognitive styles in academic evolution: A longitudinal study. *Journal of Educational Psychology, 69,* 197–211.

Woodworth, R. S. (1938). *Experimental psychology.* New York: Holt.

Woodworth, R. S. (1940). *Psychology* (4th ed.). New York: Holt.

2

PSYCHOANALYSIS AS A DARWINIAN DEPTH PSYCHOLOGY: EVOLUTIONARY BIOLOGY AND THE CLASSICAL–RELATIONAL DIALECTIC IN PSYCHOANALYTIC THEORY

MALCOLM OWEN SLAVIN AND DANIEL KRIEGMAN

> With the mention of phylogenesis, however, fresh problems arise, from which one is tempted to draw cautiously back. But there is no help for it, the attempt must be made in spite of a fear that it will lay bare the inadequacy of our whole effort.
>
> (Freud, 1923/1960, pp. 37–38)

> Even in the post-Freudian discussion of metapsychology within psychoanalysis, the antiquated elements in Freud's conceptions of evolutionary biology seem not to have been scrutinized . . . and not, in the light of new knowledge, to have been revised.
>
> (Grubrich-Simitis, 1987, pp. 102–103)

INTRODUCTION

After Freud abandoned the *Project For A Scientific Psychology* (in 1896—the keystone of his initial attempt to make psychoanalysis into a general scientific psychology—he became considerably less oriented toward a reductionistic, physicalistic form of biology and more interested in the historical and social–functional explanations possible in evolutionary thought (Holmes,

We would like to thank the following individuals for their valuable discussions and encouragement during the ongoing development of the thinking involved in this work: Robert Trivers, Jonathan Slavin, Arnold Modell, Arnold Goldberg, Paul Ornstein, Stephen Mitchell, Robert Stolorow, Judith Teicholz, Michael Basch, James Barron, David Edelstein, Marc Fried, Donald Burke, Don Greif, Charles Knight, Virginia DeLuca, and E. Joyce Klein.

1983; Slavin, 1988). He appeared to become increasingly convinced of the validity of studying the biological (i.e., adaptive) reality of psychodynamic structure and process in itself without reducing psychodynamics to neurophysiology (Solms & Saling, 1986). Throughout all of his major subsequent theoretical works (from 1913 to 1939), he persisted in his conviction that various dynamic features of the psyche—such as guilt, signal anxiety, and the superego—comprise an "archaic heritage" that was shaped by ancient, *social* experiences and that served adaptive functions in those ancestral environments (see Gubrich-Simitus, 1987; Ritvo, 1990; Slavin, 1988; Slavin and Kriegman, 1988; Sulloway, 1979).

Although Freud's view of the evolutionary process was in some ways quite crude and quaint (e.g., he drastically abbreviated its time scale and depicted eons of what is now understood to have been essentially random, incremental changes as if they had been one-shot cataclysmic social events), the general thrust of his thinking can be understood as a search for what modern evolutionists (Hamilton, 1964; Mayr, 1983; Tooby & Cosmides, 1990; Trivers, 1985) would call the *social selection pressures* that shaped the intricate, inner design of the psyche.

We shall begin with a critique of Freud's evolutionism as well as the other major attempts to bring the evolutionary dimension into psychoanalytic theory. We shall then go on to illustrate a way of applying contemporary evolutionary theory to psychoanalysis by addressing an issue that, arguably, underlies much controversy in current psychoanalytic thought, namely, the "paradigmatic clash" between the classical tradition of drive theory (including its Kleinian versions and ego psychological revisions) on the one hand, and the relational tradition as represented by Winnicott, Kohut, and various American interpersonalists, on the other (Eagle, 1984; Greenberg & Mitchell, 1983).

THE LOGIC OF FREUD'S SEARCH FOR THE ARCHAIC SOCIAL DETERMINANTS OF PSYCHIC STRUCTURE

Originally envisioned in terms of the prehistoric drama in *Totem and Taboo* (1912–1913/1964a), virtually all of Freud's later references to the evolutionary process illustrate his groping for an understanding of the origins and functions of intrapsychic structure as responses to social or relational dilemmas:

> The Superego, according to our hypothesis, actually originated from the *experiences* that led to totemism . . . it has the most abundant links with [our] phylogenetic acquisition . . . [our] archaic heritage (S. Freud, 1923/1961, p. 38).

For Freud, even features of the psyche that subsequent classical (drive–conflict theory) analysts became accustomed to viewing as endogenous or organically rooted—the drives and the id—could, in principle, be traced back to the shaping effects of ancient external experiences.

> There is . . . nothing to prevent our supposing that the instincts themselves are, at least in part, precipitates of the effects of external stimulation which, in the course of phylogenesis, have brought about modifications in the living substance (S. Freud, 1915, p. 120).

> In the Id, which is capable of being inherited are harbored residues of the existences of countless egos (S. Freud, 1923/1961, p. 38).

Freud's dramatic "primeval tragedies" (Gubrich-Simitus, 1987), the narratives of paternal domination, castration, exile, murder, and mourning in *Totem and Taboo* (1913/1964a) and *The Phylogenetic Phantasy* (1987) represent his vision of the kinds of ancestral social events that necessitated the formation of innate mechanisms like guilt, signal anxiety, and the superego that functioned to channel individual behavior in socially congruent directions. Lacking an accurate conception of natural selection, Freud groped for a way of conceiving the bridge between ancient, interpersonal experiences and the universal, underlying features of existing, internal psychic structure designed to mediate inherent conflict between the individual and others. He intuitively sensed, but could not accurately conceptualize, the fact that, as the modern evolutionists Tooby and Cosmides (1989) pointed out:

> The world is, itself, complex in ways that are not . . . analyzable or deducible without an enormous amount of a priori knowledge: in order to solve a task, you must already know a great deal about the nature of the circumstances in which the task is embedded. (p. 12)

Because he lacked a model that explained how social selection pressures could create a complex, internal psychological design, Freud grasped at one aspect of the Lamarckian model (i.e., that acquired traits can be inherited). He sought to portray the transformation of phylogenetic experience into enduring, inner structures in a fashion that paralleled individual, ontogenetic learning rooted in actual memory traces of events.[1] Yet, contrary to the received wisdom from within psychoanalysis (Rapaport, 1960) and from other fields (e.g., Gould, 1987), the actual theoretical significance of Freud's sweeping Lamarckian metaphors may have been greatly overemphasized. Indeed, it can be argued that Freud made use of these metaphors, the intellectual tropes of his day, as vessels in which to contain a far more significant current of scientific (or proto-scientific) thought (i.e., as heuristic devices in the search for the evolutionary [functional] origins of universal features of the psyche).

It is most revealing that one of Freud's last statements on this topic was one of his most simple and lucid. Still thwarted by his inability to understand what we have come to view as the evolution of behavioral or psychological adaptive strategies, he attempted simply to focus on the underlying logic of applying evolutionary thinking to the human psyche:

> If any explanation is to be found of what are called the instincts of animals which allow them to behave from the first in a new situation in life as though it were an old and familiar one— if any explanation at all is to be found of this instinctive life of animals, it can only be that they bring the experiences of their species with them into their new existence—that is, that they have preserved memories of what was experienced by their ancestors. The position in the human would not at bottom be different. His own archaic heritage corresponds to the instincts of animals even though it is different in its compass and contents. (S. Freud, 1939/1964, p. 100)

Compare the direction of Freud's thought with one of the most sophisticated contemporary versions of evolutionary, or Darwinian, psychology:

> All adaptations evolved in response to the repeating elements of past environments, and their structure reflects in detail the recurrent structure of ancestral environments. Even planning mechanisms (such as "consciousness"), which supposedly deal with novel situations, depend on ancestrally shaped categorization processes and are therefore not free of the past. . . . [E]ach species design functions as an instrument that has registered, weighted, and summed enormous numbers of encounters with the properties of past environments. Species are data recording instruments that have directly "observed" the conditions of the past through direct participation in ancestral environments (Tooby & Cosmides, 1990b, pp. 375, 390).

Freud assumed that certain kinds of links between the experiences of past and present generations of living organisms had to exist in nature to prepare individuals to be capable of executing complex adaptive strategies.[2] Such adaptive strategies can only be possible if there is

---

[1]See Slavin and Kriegman (in press) for a clarification of Lamarckian versus Darwinian thinking, Haeckel's Law, phylogenesis versus ontogenesis, as well as functional versus teleological arguments.

[2]See Slavin and Kriegman (in press) for a clarification of questions of reductionism, determinism, and causation in evolutionary explanations of complex human psychological phenomena.

some way in which the past can be used to evaluate conditions in the present environment and anticipate the future. Such links between experiences throughout the ancestral past and the capacity to evaluate and act in the present became commonplace observations of modern ethology in the 1950s (Lorenz, 1966; Tinbergen, 1953) and have been incorporated into the broader, more powerful theoretical models developed in the past few decades in evolutionary social biology (Hamilton, 1964; Mayr, 1982; Trivers, 1971, 1974, 1985; Williams, 1966).

Thus, we can now recognize that there was much of value and validity in Freud's essentially legitimate Darwinian convictions: that, in many respects, the mind can be understood as an adaptive organ, the basic structure and function of which was shaped over vast evolutionary time (Mayr, 1983; Slavin & Kriegman, 1988; Tooby & Cosmides, 1990b). Freud died long before developments in ethology and the crucial, evolutionary theories of conflict and mutuality in nature that have more recently made possible a sophisticated analysis of motivation in social creatures such as ourselves.[3]

FREUD'S SEARCH EXTENDED, ALTERED, OR DISAVOWED: HARTMANN, BOWLBY, ERIKSON, AND "THOSE WHO DRAW CAUTIOUSLY BACK" FROM BIOLOGY

The subsequent history of psychoanalysis and Darwinism is marked by three major, mainstream attempts at placing analytic concepts in an explicitly evolutionary context.[4] On the other hand, in recent years, we have frequently encountered a pervasive attitude that, as Freud put it,

---

[3]Gould (1980), Mayr (1982), Kitcher (1985), and others have repeatedly emphasized that it is scientifically unsound to take every organismic feature and assume that a specific adaptive evolutionary explanation can be derived to explain its current role and functions. Any given feature may be a part of another feature or larger adaptive organismic system; thus, it may not have been selected because it, in itself, was adaptive. Or, the feature may be an accidental creation (i.e., one that is fortuitously connected to some other adaptive feature) that persists in the genotype because it does not seriously impair the organism's functioning. These are important caveats. However as Mayr (1983) pointed out, the adaptationist question What is the function of a given structure or organ? has been for centuries the basis for every advance in physiology (p. 328).

In other words, it is the source of our most fruitful hypotheses. It has also, of course, been the source of many incorrect hypotheses. What is crucial is that the logical structure of adaptationist hypotheses combined with a dedication to empirical investigation has enabled us to sort out the difference. For this reason, Mayr (1983) concluded that, contrary to what is claimed by its more radical critics, when it is carried out in a fashion that correctly identifies the level of organization on which selection has operated, "it would seem obvious that little is wrong with the adaptationist program as such, contrary to what is claimed by Gould" (p. 332). Mayr went on to argue for the attempt to identify as "adaptations" those structures that truly play a central role in the organization of the individual, not incidental or secondary aspects, of the "whole."

We are in agreement with Mayr, and believe that, in the study of the human psyche, it is psychodynamic structure that represents, precisely, this correct level of organization. Thus, we believe that the concerns of well-intentioned critics such as Gould (1980) are probably far less applicable to a psychoanalytic use of the concept of adaptation than to what is essentially the naive behaviorism of certain proponents of "sociobiology." Indeed, even an outspoken critic of psychobiology such as Kitcher (1987) acknowledged that "the main criticism I level against . . . sociobiology is that it introduces evolutionary considerations in the wrong way by focusing on behavior and not on the underlying mechanisms . . ." (p. 91). All too commonly, sociobiologists isolate specific, discrete behaviors out of the context of the whole organism and its psyche, as the focus of adaptive hypotheses in which specific gene–behavior links are assumed to exist. We, however, are looking at the fundamental structure of the psyche as a "deep structure," so to speak, that underlies myriad specific individual, social, and cultural variations and values. This essential human inner organization and propensity to follow certain developmental paths is not a minor feature that could potentially be accidental. We are examining the basic organization of the psyche and its major psychological components. Certainly such universal features (e.g., the self, major motivational themes, and the mix of certain relational needs with other motivations to pursue narrower individual interests) that seem to underlie human behavior, and often can mean the difference between a successful life and abject failure (even death), are unlikely to be accidental features of the organism that lie outside the ken of the adaptationist hypothesis. Only an antianalytic approach would dismiss these dynamic features as being nonessential aspects of our psychological equipment. Whether or not one wishes to pursue any specific biological analysis of these features, we clearly cannot rule out the effort to understand them from an adaptive perspective. See M. Slavin and Kriegman (in press) for further clarification of these issues.

[4]There are many others—for example, Ferenczi (1924/1968), Leak and Christopher (1982), Winson (1985), Nesse (1990), Lloyd (1984), Badcock (1988), etc. We are, however, restricting this discussion to those that contributed to substantial revisions of the classical paradigm.

"draws cautiously back" from viewing the psyche in a broad, naturalistic context.[5] Both the essentially loyal Freudians (e.g., Hartmann, 1939/1958, in ego psychology) and the more critical relational theorists (e.g., Bowlby, 1969, the tradition of attachment theory, and in systems theory, Peterfreund, 1972; Yankelovitch & Barrett, 1971, Erikson, 1956, 1968) invented interesting, fruitful versions of an "evolutionary" or "adaptive" perspective that may, however, actually limit the scope of an evolutionary approach to psychoanalysis. They may limit the quest for an understanding of the ways in which many of the dynamic structures of the psyche may have evolved as adaptations to universal conflicts, pressures, and dilemmas that are social or relational in nature.

Making use of a biology that was somewhat more updated than Freud's, Hartmann (1939/1958) must be credited with compelling psychoanalysis to appreciate that certain of the ego's adaptive efforts could usefully be understood as built-in biological functions and that the equation of what is "biological" with the id and what is "environmental" with the ego was untenable (Kriegman, 1990). Nevertheless, Hartmann never turned his inquiry around to try to understand the adaptive origins of the id itself—indeed, of the whole realm of the pleasure principle and "conflict-based" or "conflict-born" development and dynamics.

Hartmann (1939/1958) seemed to have recognized the need for an evolutionary analysis of the origins and adaptive design of the drive-defense system when he called natural selection "the reality principle in the broader sense" (p. 44) and went on to acknowledge that this "reality principle in the broader sense would historically precede and hierarchically outrank the pleasure principle" (p. 44). However, he stopped short of even posing the question of how the instinctual drives as forces and the id as a structure could have arisen in, and been designed to function within, a complex relational-environmental context.

At one level, one can see Hartmann (1939/1958) as having fallen victim to what had become (and remains in certain quarters today) an almost doctrinal position articulated by Anna Freud (1936/1966); that there is an "inherent antagonism of the ego toward instinctual drives" and, the parallel assumption of an inherent antagonism between the deepest human motivations and the demands of a realistic, socially appropriate adaptation to the relational environment. In this view, as S. Mitchell (1988) noted, the drives and the id are seen as somehow atavistic relics of an earlier, more elemental animal level of existence upon which adaptive ego processes— although biologically grounded in "primary autonomy" and equipped with the "neutralized energy" of Hartmann's (1939/1958) model—are still overlaid, like a cloak of civilized realism on the "beast."

Thus, ultimately, the larger tradition of ego psychology has served in part to reinforce— indeed to institutionalize—as accepted metapsychological doctrine a certain view of the human organism. Within the context of this institutionalized perspective, we are free to pose questions about adaptation and adaptedness in regard to ego processes and early object relations while we

---

[5]Another psychoanalytic theoretical tradition is, at least superficially, "antibiological." This major contemporary theoretical strategy (i.e., constructing a "pure psychology" [G. Klein, 1976; Kohut, 1982] without reference to biology) was particularly appealing to relational theorists (e.g., Guntrip, Kohut) who, for historical reasons, tended to equate biological reasoning in psychoanalysis with Freud's early physicalistic orientation, particularly with the assumptions about human nature in the classical metapsychology. Equally, many theorists of essentially quite classical sensibility (e.g., Klein, Holt, Schafer) also equated biological perspectives with a positivistic, mechanistic view of mind and reality; their fear was that biological reasoning is incompatible with a proper clinical focus on human subjectivity, personal agency, and narrative (v. objective and absolute) truth.

Yet, as we have argued at greater length elsewhere (Kriegman & Slavin, 1990; Slavin & Kriegman, in press), though this wariness of biology may be well founded in terms of its protection of the unique features of psychoanalytic method and data, the view that biological reasoning is necessarily incompatible with complex experiential data, a clinical appreciation of personal agency, and the individual construction of personal, historical meanings can be overstated. Moreover, as the work of Schafer (1974) and Kohut (1982, 1984) attests, a supposedly non-biological strategy for psychoanalysis still leaves us, on closer examination, with a plethora of assumptions about innate, deep structure and developmental universals that fully qualify as essentially "covert" evolutionary arguments (Kriegman & Slavin, 1989, 1990).

continue to enshrine the presumably immutable, bodily based, animal forces of instinctuality and the pleasure principle as somatic, organic givens. These "organic" forces were exempted from an adaptive analysis and assumed to exist in some kind of primal "antagonism" with autonomous, adapted ego functions. Hartmann's exclusive focus on the ego (as essentially the sole organ that is discussed in terms of its evolved, adaptive functions) essentially short circuited a continued examination of classical assumptions about instinctual drives in evolutionary terms. In effect, Hartmann developed the ego psychological "strategy of accommodation" (Greenberg & Mitchell, 1983); in other words, the stretching of the classical model to include a wider range of presumably innate, adaptive, relational capacities without actually challenging the classical model's most basic drive structure assumptions about human nature (Kriegman, 1990; Slavin, 1990).

Two substantial efforts to introduce an evolutionary perspective with the aim of revising basic psychoanalytic theoretical assumptions are found in the work of Bowlby (1969) and Erikson (1956, 1964, 1968). Both of these theorists were heavily influenced by the "ethological" (Lorenz, 1966; Tinbergen, 1953) and "ecological" thinking that became influential in the 1950s. Both developed new, largely relational, psychoanalytic paradigms in which there is heavy emphasis on the interdependent, mutualistic features of the developmental process wherein individual development is part of a larger, remarkably integrated, reciprocal adaptive system.

Bowlby drew upon aspects of "ethology" to show that a biologically appropriate adaptive explanation (and reformulation) of important universal aspects of attachment and its regulation could not be constructed from the classical drive-defense model—even with the elaborations of ego psychology. He then discarded the theory of instinctual drives in favor of an exclusive focus on attachment and its vicissitudes, substituting the language of information processing for energic, drive-based concepts.

Bowlby's contribution to the ultimate revision of drive theory is of real value, and his approach has ushered in a major area of productive research on early attachment and loss. Yet, in an important sense his model does not directly address the vast realm of inner conflicts and conflictual relationships that, since Freud, have traditionally concerned analytic theorists—and, as we hope to show, has now taken center stage in contemporary evolutionary theory (in contrast to the ethology–ecology of the 1950s). In a word (that we hope to clarify substantially as we go on), Bowlby's model tends to portray the dynamics of attachment as if they operated in a relational world wherein the interests of parents and children predominantly overlap (i.e., a view that omits an appreciation of the inherently competing interests that also characterize the kin environment). The consequences of this conflict for the adaptive challenges faced by the human child—and the inner information processing system, if you will, designed to solve it—is far more complex than has been dealt with by attachment theories.

Alhough Erikson's (1968) "psycho-social" model is portrayed not as an alternative to drive theory but as a complement to it, he supported his new views with a far-reaching critique of what he called "ideological and . . . unbiological [assumptions about] the innate antagonism between the organism and the environment" (p. 221) found in the classical and ego psychological perspective. Rather than a genuine integration of classical drive theory and object relational (and certain self psychological) views, Erikson created the sort of "mixed model" (Greenberg & Mitchell, 1983) that, ultimately, is best viewed as an essentially relational view of the human psyche and development in which the relational world "can only be viewed as the joint endeavor of adult egos to develop and maintain, through joint organization, a maximum of conflict free energy in a mutually supportive psychosocial equilibrium" (p. 223). Although quite arguably the closest approximation to a truly adaptive perspective (Rapaport, 1960) in psychoanalysis, Erikson's ethological–ecological version of an evolutionary model does not incorporate those major aspects of contemporary evolutionary theory that deal with the crucial, universal tensions between mutuality and the inherently biased, competing interests that are part and parcel of even the most intimate, devoted relationships (Trivers, 1985).[6]

Thus, the world of modern evolutionary theory has not only moved dramatically beyond Freud's limited picture of it but has equally superseded the understanding available to Hartmann, Bowlby, and Erikson as well as virtually all other attempts to keep an overt, explicitly evolutionary biological tradition alive within psychoanalysis. Freud's flawed, yet imaginative efforts to deal with the overall structure of the psyche within an adaptive context constitute a task that requires further exploration in light of contemporary evolutionary theory. To engage in such an exploration, we must have a biologically well-grounded perspective on the place and role of conflict and mutuality in the relational world to which our psyche is adapted. We must, somehow, within this perspective, be able to account for some of the fundamental tensions and oppositions that are a major part of our inner, psychic life. To do so, we shall return to the issue that we set for ourselves at the beginning of this chapter: How can we use contemporary evolutionary theory to address some of the basic problems involved in integrating the drive-based, classical model and the relational, social view of human nature that underlie competing psychoanalytic perspectives.

THE PSYCHOANALYTIC DIALECTIC AND THE NEED FOR A NEW PARADIGM

Mixed Models and Pragmatic Combinations

In recent years, a number of theorists have argued that psychoanalytic models tend to coalesce around two divergent paradigms: "drive/structure" and "relational/structure" (Greenberg & Mitchell, 1983), "one-person" and "two-person" psychologies (Modell, 1984), and "instinct" versus "deficit" models (Eagle, 1984). Roughly speaking, these paradigms correspond to the classical/ego psychological traditions on one side and aspects of object relational approaches and self psychology on the other. Moreover, these paradigms are sometimes viewed as resting on "fundamentally incompatible . . . irreconcilable claims concerning the human condition" (Greenberg & Mitchell, 1983, pp. 403–404); or as belonging to "two different conceptual realms . . . two apparently irreconcilable contexts" (Modell, 1984, pp. 257–258; see also S. Cooper, 1989).

Indeed, it has been convincingly shown that most historical attempts at theoretical integration turn out to be either internally inconsistent or heavily tilted toward the basic assumptions of one of these underlying paradigms (Greenberg & Mitchell, 1983; S. Mitchell, 1984). Thus, although they may appear to transcend their origins, attempts to broaden a given perspective sufficiently to embrace the valid insights of the other inevitably remain tied to key underlying assumptions of one of these paradigms. For example, Sandler (1962, 1981), Modell (1968), and Schafer (1976) made significant attempts at various types of integration and expansion that, nevertheless, remained fundamentally loyal to what we shall call "classical" assumptions. On the other side, Stolorow, Brandchaft, and Atwood's (1987) attempt at a "phenomenological" synthesis, as well as aspects of Erikson's (1956) revisions of classical thought, lean heavily toward "relational" premises.

---

[6]The emphasis on ecological systems as stable, interdependent, integrated wholes (prevalent in biological theories from the 1950s until fairly recently) found expression in biologically inspired metaphors that exaggerated how individuals behave in highly mutualistic ways that favor other individuals thus perpetuating and renewing the larger, longer term interests of the system. Newer ecological findings stress the highly limited stability of biological systems, whereas the evolutionary biology of social behavior (Trivers, 1985) has recognized that structures of self-interest and related conflicts of interest play a vital role in the motives and strategies pursued by even highly interdependent individuals.

An acceptance of the incompatibility of these models sometimes finds expression in a "strategy of complementarity" (Kohut, 1977; Modell, 1984; Wallerstein, 1981). This dualistic strategy is used to guide a tactical oscillation between the two perspectives in the clinical context. Frequently, it is implied that such theoretical pragmatism combined with an open, flexible stance in modern clinical practice can achieve, de facto, a perspective that is tantamount to a true integration (Peterfreund, 1983; Pine, 1985). However, in our experience, individual clinicians and sometimes whole clinical settings reveal that their underlying thinking derives from one or the other of these paradigms. In the final analysis, we remain in a historical era in which one or the other vision of the human condition and its related understanding of the true meaning of our patients' communications continues to predominate (Kriegman & Slavin, 1989, 1990, Slavin & Kriegman, 1990).

A Synthesis Grounded in Modern Evolutionary Thought

Despite the persisting difficulties in creating a truly integrative perspective, we question the ultimate conclusion that the deeper philosophical differences that divide these psychoanalytic paradigms are, in fact, ultimately "irreconcilable" (Greenberg & Mitchell, 1983), or must remain in the realm of unresolvable "paradoxes" (Modell, 1984). Moreover, we do not believe that such basic conceptual issues can be adequately addressed and resolved primarily through empirical research (Eagle, 1984).

Rather, we shall try to demonstrate that, indeed, a genuine theoretical synthesis of the two traditions is now possible, but it is only possible if we are able to capture and retain the deeper dialectical tension between the two existing models within a new paradigm. This paradigm must be rooted in a set of assumptions about the mind and the human condition that do not have the same tendency to polarize in the dichotomous way that has characterized analytic thought. Ultimately, to resolve the dialectical tension, this new paradigm must be capable of thoroughly incorporating the crucial and valid elements of both existing psychoanalytic traditions, while simultaneously providing the basis for making the necessary, fundamental alterations in the basic premises of each.

We shall find the basis for such a paradigm within the evolutionary (phylogenetic) perspective. After briefly characterizing the two existing, divergent psychoanalytic paradigms, we shall present a new perspective based on contemporary evolutionary biology. We shall then use this perspective to sketch out a skeletal framework for a truly integrated psychoanalytic paradigm that radically reframes the dichotomies in psychoanalytic thought, a paradigm that is firmly rooted in fundamental realities of the organic world.

THE NATURE OF THE CLASSICAL-RELATIONAL DIALECTIC IN PSYCHOANALYSIS

Two Views of the Nature of Human Psychic Structure and the First Dimensions of the Dialectic

In their examination of psychoanalytic conceptions regarding psychic structure, Greenberg and Mitchell (1983) provided a comprehensive formulation of two key dimensions of the dichotomy between the relational and drive perspectives.

Dimension 1: The Individual Mind Versus the Interpersonal Field as the Basic Unit of Analysis

According to Greenberg and Mitchell (1983), the drive/structure model "takes as its fundamental premise that the individual mind, the psychic apparatus, is the most meaningful unit for the study of mental functioning" (p. 402). In contrast, according to the relational model, the very design of the psyche derives from and can only be understood in the context of the interpersonal field into which human beings are born, and within which they must negotiate a complex web of human relationships.

Dimension 2: Endogenous Forces Versus Relational Experiences in the Development and Structuralization of the Individual Psyche

In the drive/structure tradition, psychic structure is patterned and regulated by the vicissitudes of the discharge of drives. In the relational/structure model, psychic structure derives directly and irreducibly from the vicissitudes of interpersonal experiences.

We believe that in order to capture the full dialectical tension inherent in these dichotomous views of the human mind, we must go beyond the focus on the structure of the psyche to clarify some of our most basic assumptions about the relational world. Indeed, as we hope to show, from an evolutionary point of view, it is not possible to separate one's basic view of psychic structure from one's view of the character and quality of the relational world within which the mind is designed to fit and function. We shall develop this broader view of the "psyche-in-the-world" by elucidating the "narrative structure" that is implicit in the different psychoanalytic accounts of human psychological development. Each theory contains an implicit "developmental narrative" with a presumed universal story of the psychological operations used by the child in the course of development. The notion of the narrative will be carried well beyond where it has been used in the antibiological hermeneutic approach (Schafer, 1983; Spence, 1982). Indeed, this way of "deconstructing" theories into their underlying storylines shall serve as a critical bridge between the psychoanalytic and evolutionary biological paradigm. In the major psychoanalytic narratives we shall find two additional dichotomies beyond those noted by Greenberg and Mitchell (1983). In addition to the different views of psychic structure, these additional dichotomies point to the more basic underlying assumptions about the relational world.

Deeper Within the Dialectical Tension: Two Contrasting Narratives of Human Development

The Classical Narrative of Development

In the classical view, the primary developmental task lies in the need to manage the tensions which derive from the inevitable clash between the endogenous, bodily based, driving forces within the individual and the norms and limits of ordinary social reality. Classical drive theory, Kleinian theory, as well as their innumerable permutations into different versions of modern ego and developmental psychology (e.g., Blos, 1979; A. Freud, 1936; S. Freud, 1930/1961; Hartmann, 1939/1958; Jacobson, 1964; Kernberg, 1976, 1980; Mahler, Pine, & Bergman, 1975) basically start with this conception of an essentially innate "dividedness" and tension at the core of human nature and the human condition.

In the course of development, normal growth entails a reluctant shift of the child's less organized, more selfish and self-centered modes of construing reality away from their central place in the organization of subjective experience. This shift is partially opposed by the child's innate nature. Successful maturation yields a compromise—one that is inevitably somewhat unsatisfactory to the child—between the child's self-centered motivations and the demands of the social world. These motivations and perceptions are, in part, repressed so as not to disrupt the conscious process of subjectively organizing experience and behavior. Such disruption would conflict with the child's adaptation to the realities of the family and after the phase of adolescence to the larger adult social world. On the whole, a significant part of what is repressed can be said to be disguised in a way that is intrinsically deceptive to the individual and others (S. Freud, 1915/1957).

The continued presence, indeed fixation on, repressed contents of the psyche, albeit in deceptively disguised form, represents a continuing threat to the accommodation the child has made to external (largely parental) reality. Moreover, it is assumed in the classical tradition that there is actually an inherent tendency of the repressed to return, to seek expression in ever-changing, deceptive guises. This unbidden return of the repressed is one major form of the "repetition compulsion"—the tenacious, often painful repetition of archaic patterns that lies at the heart of the classical Freudian and Kleinian conceptions of psychopathology (Fenichel, 1945; Segal, 1964) and has been conceptually tailored to fit the altered premises of modern ego psychology.[7] In this view, subjective reality is illusory, prone to distortion and self-deception in the form of various compulsively repetitive defenses, transferences, and resistances. Behind this deceptive facade lies a truer, objective reality.

The Relational Narrative of Development

In contrast, the relational model focuses on a fundamentally different type of tension. On one side lies the child's unique configuration of individual needs, identity elements, or vital experiences of self; on the other side lies a social environment that frequently is insufficiently attuned to, or invested in, the recognition and cultivation of these individual elements. Certain of the "interpersonalist" theorists (e.g., Fromm, 1941; Sullivan, 1953), psychosocial theory (Erikson, 1956), aspects of Winnicott (1965), Guntrip (1971), Fairbairn (1952), and Balint (1968) as well as the self psychologists (Kohut, 1984; Stolorow et al., 1987) have emphasized this relational view of the patterning of inner conflict. They represent a radically different sensibility within psychoanalysis, and they take a different view of the process of selectively altering awareness of defensively reorganizing consciousness and meaning. In this view, a true, spontaneous, or authentic self is hidden from a less than adequate environment. A "hiding" of the self is necessary because the inadequate environment fails to conform to the high degree of mutuality, meshing, and synchrony of individual aims that is assumed to constitute the "good-enough" environment (M. Slavin, 1988, 1990). This hiding constitutes a subjective alteration of meaning and awareness that can be seen as a version of the process of repression.

Repression in the Two Narratives

Each of these two models has its own version of the role and function of repression. Let us define *repression* in a generic, experiential fashion as a state in which a "crucial dimension of meaning" (Greenberg & Mitchell, 1983, p. 15) is not fully in awareness or readily accessible to it. As Freud (1915/1957) put it, it is "in another place"—missing, but not lost. By taking Freud's "other place" absolutely figuratively, without specifying the content of what is "missing" from awareness, one can remain on pretty safe, consensual ground. The task of most analysts from the classical drive theorist, to the object relations theorist, to the self psychologist consists of somehow helping to integrate those "missing dimensions" into the psyche as a whole, thus promoting a reordering of psychic structure into less pathological form.[8] At this point, however,

---

[7]See Kriegman and Slavin (1989) for an extended review and critique of the concept of the repetition compulsion (and the related concept of the negative therapeutic reaction) and Slavin and Kriegman (in press) for an evolutionary conception of repetition.

[8]There is disagreement over whether the phenomenon of diverting awareness is best characterized by the term *repression* (Modell, 1989). We use it because of its very broad connotation of a universal, innate process of regulating awareness. This issue is discussed further in M. Slavin and Kriegman (in press).

the consensus usually breaks down. There is far less agreement over what is missing and why it is missing.

What is critical to the difference between classical and relational models is not that nonclassical models may call these alterations in awareness a split or dissociation in the self or a "disavowing" of aspects of reality; but, rather, that in the relational tradition the process is seen essentially as sheltering, or protecting parts of the self in order to preserve the possibilities for future growth and development. Defenses and transferences are viewed less as a subjective facade that distorts reality and more as developmentally creative efforts to reenvision reality in an attempt to reactivate and reinitiate thwarted growth (Kohut, 1984; Winnicott, 1960a). This is opposed to the classical tradition in which egocentric, forbidden, or dangerous wishes are deceptively disguised to avoid inner conflict and then compulsively repeated (Kriegman & Slavin, 1989).

Two Views of the Relational World and the Additional Dimensions of the Classical–Relational Dialectic

Implicit in these two archetypal narratives are the following two relational dimensions of the classical-relational dichotomy in addition to Greenberg and Mitchell's (1983) two "heuristic dimensions" regarding the nature of *psychic structure.*

Dimension 3: Inherent Conflict Versus Inherent Mutuality in the Relational World

In the classical narrative, from the outset of life, the child's needs and way of viewing reality are seen as clashing with the norms of the environment. Significant amounts of selfishness, rivalry, competition, and aggression are assumed to be part and parcel of relationships within the family. In contrast, in the relational model, family members are motivated by interpersonal needs that contain no inherently conflicting aims.[9]

A corollary of this dichotomy relates to what is assumed to be the normative state of the psyche. In the classical narrative, the psyche is inherently divided and, to some degree, inevitably involved in a degree of inner struggle: The very metaphor of a "tri-partite structure" embodies this sense of normative dividedness. The aims of the id intrinsically diverge from, and conflict with, those of others. This inherent conflict is represented in the struggle between superego and id. Thus, in the classical narrative the metaphor of the divided psyche is a reflection of conflict in the interpersonal world. The relational narrative, on the other hand, shifts the basic metaphor to that of the self, or the equivalently unitary notion of an identity. Cohesion, rather than inevitable struggle, is assumed to be the normative state unless "pathological" distortions have been introduced by destructive or deficient experiences with others.[10]

---

[9]As S. Mitchell (1984) pointed out, certain versions of the relational narrative do not necessarily ignore the existence of conflict, particularly in their clinical appreciation of the tensions between "separateness and merger" and in "competing loyalties" to different objects. However, in virtually no theory that we have termed *relational* is a "genuine clashing" (Goldberg, 1988) of individual aims and goals given a fundamental status as an inherent feature of the basic motives of normal individuals in the good-enough environment. The centrality of this critical theoretical point should become clearer as we proceed. See Kriegman and Slavin (1990) for an extensive discussion of this issue.

[10]On this dimension the interpersonalist theorists fall much less clearly in what we term the *relational tradition.* Sullivan's (1953) concern with "parataxic distortions" of reality and Fromm's (1941) emphasis on "self deception" are, in our view, quite similar to Hartmann's (1939/1958) classically rooted notion that psychoanalysis can be called a science of self-deception. Only Winnicott (in some of his work) and Kohut broke more decisively with the classical emphasis on deception and distortion of reality, diminishing any notion of objective truth and absolute reality in favor of a more relativistic, subjectivist point of view.

Dimension 4: Subjective Experience as Deceptive Distortion Versus Valid Communication

Classical models invariably stress the ways in which subjective experience conceals or misrepresents reality. Defenses, symptoms, and transferences are built around inherently self-deceptive mental operations that, when uncovered, reveal underlying, painful, objective truths. Relational models, on the other hand (including much of the relational/structure tradition, but especially Winnicottian and Kohutian versions), emphasize the ways in which subjective experience often represents crucial, developmentally vital, truths; defenses, symptoms and transferences are seen as inherently valid, self-protective expressions of a personal reality that has been misunderstood by others.

Dialectical Tension and Synthesis

By characterizing the tension between the existing psychoanalytic paradigms in terms of the above four dimensions, which are summarized in Table 1, we hope to portray a fuller sense of the differences between the competing visions of human nature that underlie them. We believe that the tension between these perspectives is best understood as dialectical in nature. We do not intend to discuss the complex philosophical (Hegelian or Marxian) connotations that the term *dialectic* can have. Rather, we mean that it is useful to think of the existing psychoanalytic paradigms as representing a historical tendency for depth psychological thinking to polarize around two, internally coherent sets of assumptions: a classical thesis and a relational antithesis about human nature and the human condition. These assumptions concern the basic nature of the child's mind, the reason that significant conflict is observed in the interaction between parent and child, the meaning of the child's tendency to divert (repress, split off, disavow) awareness of one side of this conflict, and the implications of all this for the process by which the child is transformed into an adult. Calling the distinct paradigms through which we commonly view these processes a *thesis* and an *antithesis* implies mainly that: (a) neither paradigm is complete; (b) although each, in some sense, "calls for" the truths embodied in the other, they are, in their current form, rooted in incompatible premises; and, finally, (c) each will eventually contribute its essential message and then recede as a new synthesis takes form.

THE EVOLUTIONARY PERSPECTIVE

Natural Selection, Adaptation, and Inclusive Fitness

Whenever we call anything about an organism (a physical structure or an aspect of behavior) *adaptive* in contemporary evolutionary theory, we mean that it is organized in a way that maximizes the effective pursuit of ends that are advantageous to its underlying genes (Williams, 1966).[11] Although this may seem somewhat extreme, a moment's reflection will reveal this to be consistent with "survival of the fittest" as the ultimate shaping force (i.e., natural selection). However, there is a new conception of fitness. In 1964, W. D. Hamilton clarified the conception of fitness by introducing the concept of *inclusive fitness*. Inclusive fitness is based on the recognition that survival of copies of an organism's genes in other individuals, and in the resultant future gene pool for the species, is the only measure of evolutionary success or ultimate fitness. The success and survival of the individual is not the ultimate focus of

---

[11] The limits of this adaptationist perspective are addressed in Kriegman and M. Slavin (1989, 1990) and M. Slavin and Kriegman (in press).

TABLE 1
Classical Versus Relational Narratives

Four dichotomies	The classical narrative	The relational narrative
1. **Basic unit of analysis**	**Individual psyche** Emphasis is on intrapsychic dynamics.	**Interpersonal field** The individual can only be understood within an interactive context.
2. **Basic source of patterning (or structure) in the psyche**	**Vicissitudes of endogenous drives** Relational ties are derivative.	**Vicissitudes of interpersonal interactions**
3. **Relation between basic aims of self and other**	**Inherent clash of normal individual aims** Selfishness, rivalry, competition are motivationally primary. (Corollary: The normal [tripartite] psyche is "divided" in a way that reflects the inevitable conflicts between the individual and others.)	**Emphasis on mutual, reciprocal, convergent aims** Significant interpersonal clashes are due to pathology or environmental failure. (Corollary: The psyche [the self] is an essentially "holistic" entity that reflects the possibility of relative harmony between the individual and others.)
4. **Role of deception and self-deception in subjective experience**	**Defense and transference as distortions of reality** Resistance serves to conceal truth. (Corollary: Reception is a means of not knowing; people repeat the acting out of unconscious motivations as a defense for maintaining repression, to preserve ties, or to maintain instinctual fixations.)	**Defense and transference as inherently valid expressions of personal reality** Resistance serves to elicit recognition of individual truth for further growth. (Corollary: repetition is an artifact created as people repeatedly try to elicit a needed response from the relational world to reinitiate thwarted growth and revise the self; people repeat in the process of preserving and protecting a vulnerable self [e.g., by maintaining needed relational ties] so that revision can be tried again in the future.)

Note. The Kleinian model (including the current work of Kernberg) does not fit within the relational tradition if Dichotomies 3 and 4 are used to characterize the dichotomous views of the nature of the relational world. The Kleinian sensibility clearly fits the classical narrative with its emphasis on massive, innate conflict in the relational world as well as the subjective distortions of reality in the mind of the child. This represents one of the most crucial differences between our view of the competing psychoanalytic visions of human nature (including the assumed nature of the relational world) and the view of Greenberg and Mitchell (1983) who put their emphasis on different visions of the structure of "mind" (the psyche). We take a broader, more embracing view of the comparative psychoanalytic field as including normative visions of the environment (relational world) within which particular models of the psyche are assumed to fit and function. In terms of the purely "mental structure" criteria used by Greenberg and Mitchell (Dichotomies 1 and 2), there are elements in Kleinian models that appear "relational." Yet, the deeper implications—especially the clinical implications—of Kleinian narratives are better illuminated by classifying them as lying in the drive or "one-person" (Modell, 1984) tradition. This should become clearer as we proceed.

selective pressures. Natural selection has shaped organisms that maximize their inclusive fitness, not their personal fitness (Hamilton, 1964; Trivers, 1985).[12] While at times these dimensions overlap, there is an important distinction between them.

For example, if we were to define *fitness* in the narrower, personal sense, then behavior that increases another's fitness while decreasing the fitness of the performer would always be self-destructive, and, hence, unfit; it would create a selective pressure toward the removal from the gene pool of any associated genes. However, we can easily see that parental care, which benefits the child often at considerable cost to the parent, fits this definition and would therefore appear to be unfit; a conclusion that is obviously false. It is false because the "cost" to the parent in reduced personal fitness must be diminished by the degree of relatedness to the beneficiary of the parent's behavior (the child) to assess its net adaptive, genetic success. Parental care may reduce a parent's ability to survive and thrive; that is, it may reduce the parent's personal fitness while actually increasing the parent's inclusive fitness given that the beneficiary carries copies of the parent's genes.

Kinship Theory and Parent-Offspring Conflict Theory

The Genetics of Self and Other: The Biological Basis of Self–Other Distinctions

Because of the very close genetic relationship between parents and offspring in all species, there is a large degree of overlap between the individual self-interests of parent and child. They inherently share many of the same aims; in many respects, what is advantageous to one is advantageous to the other. This is particularly obvious from the parents' point of view. We need little biological sophistication to appreciate that the parents' own reproductive success, their "inclusive fitness," is intimately tied to the future reproductive success—the inclusive fitness—of their offspring.

Figure 1 shows a schematic drawing of an individual in relation to others. Humans are inherently social creatures and we can diagram relations as circles in various relationships to each other. The shorter lines indicate close relationships, the longer lines indicate weak ties. On the left is shown the socially observed, or apparent, level of relatedness. The overlapping circles and lines in the diagram on the right show a more accurate and complete picture of relatedness from an evolutionary point of view called here the *gene's eye view*. Parts of the individual genotype are literally shared with others. In a real (evolutionary) sense, self boundaries may well include parts of other individuals! In this sense, the parent-child dyad is a phenotypic illusion, so to speak: Parts of the child's genetic "self" are, literally, included within the parental "self" and vice versa. Although this may appear to be a psychotic version of reality (a fusion or primitive merger of identities), it is, at root, nothing other than the actual biological reality that underlies

---

[12]The pre-Hamilton (1964) evolutionary view explained behavior that was costly to the individual yet benefited others as having evolved for the good of the "group" or, often, for the good of the species as a whole. Thus, penguins control their birthrate, having fewer offspring under overcrowded conditions, because this benefits all penguins. Groups of penguins that do not control their birthrates are less successful than those that do. This is the notion of "group selection" (Wynne-Edwards, 1962).

  Yet, how could the altruist, the innate cooperator, the self-sacrificer, be more successful at replicating his or her genes (surviving and leaving more viable offspring) than other, more selfish competitors? Would not the competitors regularly have the evolutionary advantage? Hamilton (1964) proved that this was not the case when the altruist lived and operated in a largely kin setting. The shared genotypes in such conditions mean that helping related others actually enhances one's own inclusive fitness enough to frequently offset the cost of such actions. Trivers (1971) then went on to demonstrate that, in long-lived, social species, significant amounts of self-sacrifice could also be selected for among unrelated individuals if inner dynamics (including, e.g., memory, a sense of obligation, love, and guilt) had evolved to guarantee that such prosocial behavior was likely to be reciprocated. Using these evolutionary advances (kin altruism and reciprocal altruism) "for the good of the species" explanations have largely been discarded (Kriegman, 1988).

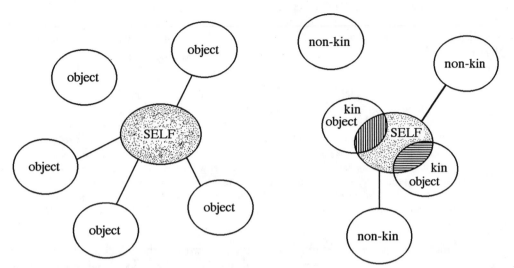

Everyday Phenotypic Perspective   The "Gene's Eye" View

Figure 1. The self: Phenotypic and genotypic perspectives. (From Kriegman & Slavin, 1989. © 1989 by Analytic Press. Adapted by permission.)

Winnicott's (1965) telling aphorism, "there is no such thing as an infant, only a nursing couple." In this important biological sense, the notion of the child's individuality is, in some respects, an illusion based on our conscious overestimation of the phenotypic (overt, observable) physical separateness of the two organisms. At some level, this fundamental biological truth can be seen to underlie the basic metaphors, or vision of human nature, that is found in the relational tradition in psychoanalysis. It is implicit in the notion of the "selfobject" and in Kohut's (1982) description of a parent's deepest joy "being a link in the chain of generations" (p. 403).

However, we must emphasize a second biological fact. Namely, that despite the overlap in their interests, parents and offspring are genetically distinct, unique, separate individuals. Thus, to some degree, from the moment of conception onward, their interests necessarily diverge, compete, and conflict.

The universality of this basic biological matrix has the following major implication. On virtually every crucial psychological issue in the course of development (indeed, of the full life cycle) the parent as a functioning biological organism is likely to have been designed, so to speak, psychologically so as to tend to operate with a subjective interpretation of reality that is consistent with his or her own inclusive fitness (i.e., derived in a self-interested fashion from one's own subjective experience and biased toward those individuals [usually kin] to whom he or she most closely genetically and reciprocally tied). We shall call this the parent's *inclusive self interest;* it is the essence of what, in a biologically consistent fashion, we can also call, borrowing from Erikson's (1956) apt term, the "parental psycho-social identity."

So too, the child will have his or her own unique genetic self and, as a function of it, a distinct, intrinsic self interest that he or she will be geared to maximize in whatever fashion he or she is equipped to do so. Children will seek to know and promote their own inclusive self-interest and to construct, in the course of their own development, their own way of expressing this self-interest in a psychological phenotype that we can call the child's own "psycho-social identity."

Parent–Offspring Conflict Theory: Conflict and Mutuality in Primary Object Relations

The social evolution theorist Robert Trivers was the first to grasp the powerful implications of this biological reality. He used the example of a caribou calf and its mother to illustrate what he called *parent-offspring conflict theory*, a theory applicable to all sexually reproducing species. Note that in this example, as in all evolutionary analyses, the costs and benefits refer to the individual's fitness.

> Consider a newborn (male) caribou calf nursing from his mother. The benefit to him of nursing (measured in terms of his chance of surviving) is large, the cost to his mother (measured in terms of her ability to produce additional offspring) presumably small. As time goes on and the calf becomes increasingly capable of feeding on its own, the benefit to him of nursing decreases while the cost to his mother may increase (as a function, for example, of the calf's size) . . . At some point the cost to the mother will exceed the benefit to her young and the net reproductive success of the mother decreases if she continues to nurse . . . The calf is not expected, so to speak, to view this situation as does his mother, for the calf is completely related to himself but only partially related to his future siblings (Trivers, 1974, p. 251).

The mother is equally related to all of her offspring, whereas the calf clearly is not. Thus, the cost in terms of a decrease in the mother's ability to bear and rear additional young and the benefit to the current suckling have very different meanings to the mother and the calf. The resultant "weaning conflict" has been well documented in many species. Trivers (1974) pointed out that weaning conflict is simply a specific paradigmatic example of the much larger category of conflict over parental investment. This argument holds for all forms of parental investment (e.g., feeding the young, guarding the young, cleaning and grooming the young, carrying the young, teaching the young, etc.). In a similar fashion, Trivers spelled out predictions of parent–offspring conflict over the social behavior of the offspring:

> Parents and offspring are expected to disagree over the behavioral tendencies of the offspring insofar as these tendencies affect related individuals (p. 257) . . . [For example, in interactions among siblings] . . . an individual is only expected to perform an altruistic act towards its full sibling whenever the benefit to the sibling is greater than twice the cost to the altruist (p. 259).

This is so because each sibling carries half of the genetic material of the actor. Thus, if an altruistic act benefits a sibling more than twice the cost to the actor, the actor receives a net benefit to his or her inclusive fitness.

> Likewise, . . . [the actor] is only expected to forego selfish acts when [the cost to their sibling] is greater than [twice the benefit to the self] (where [a] selfish act is defined as one that gives the actor a benefit, while inflicting a cost on some other individual, in this case, on a full sibling). (p. 259)

In our "gene's eye view" (top of Figure 2), we clearly see the overlap between the inclusive fitness of individuals. In other work (Kriegman, 1988, 1990; Kriegman & Slavin 1989, 1990; Slavin 1990; Slavin & Kriegman, in press)—again, following Trivers (1971)—we have noted that there are other kinds of shared interests that can apply even to nonkin relationships. Thus, there is clear support from evolutionary biology for a view of the relational world as containing a good deal of mutuality and sharing of interests. This view of the relational world differs sharply from the classical model in that the boundaries of the individual are far less distinct and that relationships with overlapping interests make the definition of an individual (or self) hard to separate from the relational matrix in which the particular individual exists.

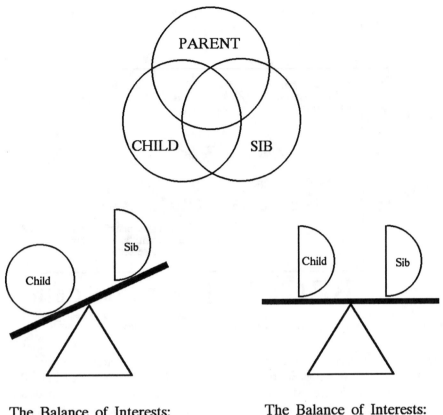

The Balance of Interests:
The CHILD'S Point of View

The Balance of Interests:
The PARENT'S Point of View

Figure 2. Primary conflict in the relational world: The gene's eye view of the balance of interests of subjective realities. (From Slavin & Kriegman, 1990. © 1991 by Analytic Press. Adapted by permission.)

However, there is equally clear evidence from recent infant studies (Beebe & Lachmann, 1988; Lichtenberg, 1989; Stern, 1985) of an extremely early ability to differentiate the skin-bounded self from others. In Figure 2, the "skin boundaries" are represented by the circles that are the child, parent, and sibling, respectively. Note that they do overlap, as emphasized by Ornstein (1989) and Stolorow and Atwood (1989). Also note that the evolutionary biology of parent–offspring conflict theory insists that we recognize that each skin bounded individual is unique. This uniqueness has enormous significance, an example of which is depicted on the bottom of Figure 2.

Viewing the situation from the subjective perspective of the child's self, one sees (on the lower left) that the child values itself twice as much as it values its full sibling. Yet the parent has a subjective view (depicted on the lower right) in which, on average, each child is valued relatively equally (half as much as the parent's self).

So, parents—who are equally related to all of their children—want altruism between their offspring whenever the benefit is greater than the cost, and children only want to act altruistically whenever the benefit is twice the cost. Likewise, parents want their children to forego selfishness whenever the cost exceeds the benefit, and children ought to only be willing to readily forego selfishness when the cost exceeds twice the benefit. In Figure 3, we visually represent this inherent intrafamilial conflict with regard to a child's selfish and altruistic behavior.

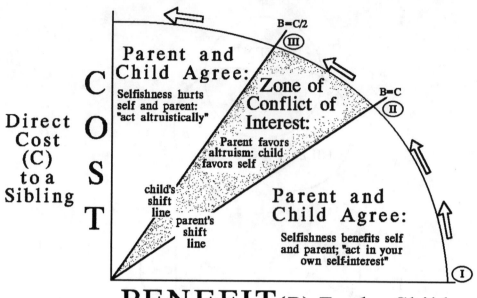

Figure 3. Parent–offspring conflict theory: Intrinsic conflicts of interest between parent and child with regard to sibling's fate. (From Kriegman & Slavin, 1990. © 1990 by Analytic Press. Adapted by permission.)

The vertical axis represents the cost to a sibling of an act, whereas the horizontal axis represents the benefit to the actor. Starting on the horizontal line (at the point labeled I), note that the cost to a sibling is zero, whereas the benefit to the child of such a hypothetical act is great. As we follow the arrow moving counterclockwise up to the shaded area (to II) we pass through a realm in which, because the costs to the sibling is less than the benefit to the actor, the self-interest of both the parent and the child coincide: They agree that the child should act in a self-interested manner.

However, when we enter the shaded region, the situation changes dramatically. Here, in this zone, the cost to the sibling is greater than the benefits to the actor. Thus, the parent who is equally related to both children ceases to find it advantageous for the child to act self-interestedly. But the child does not see it this way until we leave the shaded region (at III), entering, once again, a region of agreement. Here, because the cost to the sibling exceeds twice the benefit to the child, it is in the self-interest of both the parent and the child for the child to forego selfishness and act altruistically. The resultant prediction matches the common observation of intense and ubiquitous sibling rivalry with parents engaged in major struggles with their children over their egoistic impulses. Similar graphic schemes can be presented for behavior among other relatives and behavior with regard to others who are linked in reciprocal ways with one's kin.[13]

The Basic Unit of Analysis Revisited: The Extended (Inclusive) Self

Remember now the first dimension of the classical-relational dichotomy (Table 1): The basic unit of analysis is either the individual or the interpersonal field. The evolutionary perspective thus contains a framework in which our customary notions of individuality and relatedness dissolve. Evolutionarily we expect that there is, simultaneously a unique genetically distinct infant, as well as a nursing couple with its shared overlapping genotype. The overlap

---

[13]This "gene's eye view" of human relationships is developed further in Slavin and Kriegman (in press).

creates a distinct biological reality of its own. Figure 4 presents a schematic contrast between the classical, "individualistic" bias and the equally biased, "mutualistic," picture of self and other in relational theories in which it is implicitly assumed that the normal overlap of interests is far greater than, in fact, it is ever likely to be. Below these is shown the evolutionary perspective. In the evolutionary view, both the fundamental overlap and the inevitable distinctness have clear and powerful implications for all sexually reproducing species. As we shall show, our ways of experiencing reality, our basic motives, and relationships with others have been shaped by this relational matrix.

Primary Relational Conflict and Primary Relational Mutuality

Evolutionary theory tells us that even responsive, attuned, facilitative environments will inevitably be characterized by both a significant degree of conflict as well as a high degree of mutuality. Despite the powerful overlap of interests that make investment in the well-being of others a central feature of human life, we can also expect powerful intersubjective conflicts in which all parties are inherently biased toward seeing reality and dealing with others in terms of their own unique interests. This, the evolutionist tells us, is the normal, natural, universal state of object relations. It must be the fundamental reality of a relational world that is composed of evolved, genetically overlapping yet distinct (i.e., naturally selected) sexually reproducing organisms.

Remember the third dimension of the classical-relational dichotomy: inherent conflict versus inherent mutuality in the interpersonal world. Again, the evolutionary view reframes the issue. A priori, without any clinical or observational data, conflict is expected to be intrinsic to the very nature of human relationships, themselves quite apart from the whole question of drives versus environmental failure as the source of the conflict. At the same time, a significant degree of mutuality and cooperative action must also exist in an equally fundamental way. Over vast

Classical Paradigm

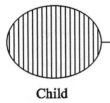

Child   Mother

Relational Paradigm

The Nursing Couple:
Childmother

Evolutionary Paradigm

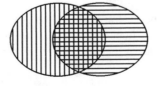

Child/Mother

Figure 4. Classical, relational, and evolutionary assumptions. (From Kriegman & Slavin, 1990. © 1990 by Analytic Press. Adapted by permission.)

evolutionary time, the realities of this "universal relational matrix" represent the chief selection pressures that shaped important aspects of the psychodynamic "deep structure" of the human psyche.[14]

THE EVOLUTIONARY NARRATIVE OF DEVELOPMENT: PSYCHOLOGICAL IMPLICATIONS OF HUMAN PROLONGED CHILDHOOD

Some General Features of Human Adaptation

It is important to keep in mind a few facts concerning human adaptation:

1. Prolonged childhood entails a period of extreme dependency and immaturity in which an enormous amount of innate, hard-wired responsiveness is "sacrificed" in the course of human evolution. Selection replaces fixed action patterns with flexibility in the child's capacity to socially or interactionally construct an identity. This plasticity in the psychosocial representation of the child's own inclusive self-interest— the child's "self" or "identity"—can thus be exquisitely attuned to the complex, unique and changing realities of the family and larger socio-cultural world into which the child is born (La Barre, 1954; Mayr, 1982) as well as to the unique assemblage of traits, strengths, and weaknesses that are part of each individual's biological heritage (Slavin & Kriegman, in press).

2. During the long developmental period of parent–child interaction (as well as the interactions between the child and the wider social environment), most interpersonal transactions are mediated by language and other forms of symbolic communication. Much that is communicated and learned is not rooted in direct observation but, rather, comes through symbolic communication. Thus, the child is able to construct a map of the world that far exceeds (and differs in quality from) anything that could be created from direct experience (Konner, 1982).

3. Yet, as numerous theorists have increasingly noted (e.g., R. Mitchell, 1985; Trivers, 1985), deception is a pervasive, universal intrinsic feature of all animal communication. In the pursuit of their own inclusive fitness, organisms do not simply communicate in order to convey truth to others but, rather, to convey tailored images of both self and environmental realities—to hide certain features and selectively accentuate those that they want others to perceive. Thus, the unique feature of human symbolic communication—its liberation from the need for direct observation— greatly amplifies or potentiates the power both to convey realities accurately *and* to hide them.

Psychological Implications of Human Prolonged Childhood, Language, and the Role of Deception

With prolonged childhood, learning, and language in mind, we will try to formulate the central adaptive dilemma of the human child (i.e., the essence of what he or she must accomplish psychologically to enhance his or her own inclusive fitness). Biologically, we know the child

---

[14]Our term *psychodynamic deep structure* refers to something that closely parallels the complex innate, universal mechanisms that enable individuals to learn and use specific, culturally based languages (Chomsky, 1972). We are referring to those innate, universal psychodynamic structural features (e.g., a self, an ego, repression, primary object attachments) that, similarly, must exist in the psyche in order for it to be capable of processing interactive, developmental experience and using it to build a functioning, adult identity (Tooby & Cosmides, 1989, 1990). This is discussed further in Slavin and Kriegman (in press).

must maximize the amount of investment (time, interest, love, guidance) provided by the parental environment. This is critical to basic survival and any further maximization of fitness. Psychologically, we know that the child must incorporate from his or her parents whatever is in the child's own interest to learn (about self and the world) as this is transmitted through the parents' vision of reality.

The child is almost totally dependent on direct investment from an environment that only partially shares the child's self-interest. More problematic is the fact that the only chance for the child to develop an internalized map of reality, including a well-structured, accurate guide to the relational world, is to have a way of dealing adequately with the inherent, often covert biases in parental views of reality: The child must have some way of correcting or compensating for these biases if he or she is to use the parents' presentation of reality to define and build crucial aspects of his or her own self. In short, the human child is dependent on self-interested parental figures not only to survive, learn, and grow, but also as objects to internalize in the very process of forming a self that includes a well-defined sense of his or her own interest. How, then, is the child able to maintain and promote a sufficiently unbiased sense of his or her own self-interest throughout the developmental process?

The evolutionist asks, "How did the human child evolve the basic structural-dynamic capacity, as it were, to accomplish this task? Given such a universally biased relational environment, how would one "design" a child capable of developing a viable self internalized through interactive relationships while simultaneously looking out for his or her own specific interests? We suggest that the concept of *repression* provides a basic clue as to the nature of the complex solution to this adaptive problem.

THE EVOLUTIONARY ADAPTIVE FUNCTION OF REPRESSION

Repression is a psychological process in which conscious awareness is diverted from certain aims, affects, or images of self and others. Those wishes and aims that are overtly more congruent with the family (including parental identities and views of reality go into the realm of conscious meanings). At the same time, however, the dynamic conception of repression describes a process that ensures that many of the child's aims and views that are less congruent with parental views will not be lost as potential guidelines for the pursuit of the child's own interests. Unlike a nondynamic model in which behavioral responses are learned and unlearned, the process of repression ensures that these aims, as well as being related self and object representations, can be "put away" out of consciousness but held in reserve, as it were, to be retrieved or allowed to return when it is in the child's long-range interest (M. Slavin, 1974, 1985, 1990).

From an evolutionary perspective, what may be the most critical function of repression is not its more obvious diversion of conscious subjective experience[15] but, rather, the way it enables human beings to use such a diversion while simultaneously preserving future access to temporarily unacceptable but potentially vital aims and needs. Indeed, the evolutionary biology of parent–offspring conflict theory predicts, precisely, that such potentially conflictual aims will resurface when (a) conditions of direct parental investment decrease or threaten to decrease (Trivers, 1974) or (b) the parents' control over resources and view of reality are less closely aligned with the child's interests than they were when the repression took place (Slavin, 1985).

---

[15]We are aware that repression functions on a proximal intrapsychic level to maintain psychological equilibrium (e.g., traumatic memories may be repressed by the child's immature psyche). However, we are suggesting that our functional redefinition of repression using evolutionary biology helps to deepen our understanding of how repression may have come to serve complex interpersonal functions. We believe that this broader understanding of repression is compatible with its other subjective functions yet sheds greater light on basic psychoanalytic controversies regarding human nature.

Repression, thus, can be seen as a process that makes possible a certain "innate skepticism"; or a normative resistance to "over-socialization" into the family culture as defined by the parents (M. Slavin, 1985, 1990). This dynamically accessible storage actually permits the child to risk being far more open to, and influenced by, the parental environment. In Winnicott's (1965) sense of "the use of an object" and Kohut's (1984) sense of the "selfobject" (as a means of self-structuralization), the relational world can be "used" far more readily than would otherwise be possible. Thus, the child can avoid the potential costs to fitness incurred by conforming to a psychosocial world biased toward parental as well as other social or group interests. And, given the intrinsic relational conflicts of interest within the family itself, pressures toward such a biased outcome are virtually always part of normative socialization pressures. This, one should remember, is prior to whatever further distortions of a child's ability to pursue his or her own self-interest may be introduced by parental pathology.

Repression thus serves to maximize the investment received initially from parents and other close kin. Its chief functions are to maintain high levels of parental investment in the child, to reduce unproductive levels of interpersonal conflict, and to allow the child to identify with or internalize major components of the parents' psychosocial identities without sacrificing his or her own long-term interests. More significantly, as we shall show, repression permits the child to "plan" for, or to be more fully equipped to deal with, future developmental contingencies—some of which are predictable parts of the life cycle, others of which are not.

DEVELOPMENT AS AN (INTRAPSYCHICALLY REGULATED) NEGOTIATION PROCESS

We are suggesting that the human child is centrally involved in the negotiation of a kind of provisional identity. This provisional psychic structure represents a working compromise between the child's interests and the interests of the kin environment. It allows the child to keep alternative impulses, affects, and narcissistic and creative elements in reserve—out of awareness, perhaps, but not out of the realm of future "renegotiated" possibility (M. Slavin & J. Slavin, 1976).

What are the future events that may require renegotiation? First, there are the common unpredictable changes in parental and kin investment (e.g., the birth of siblings, changes in the health and emotional state of parents, as well as the myriad ways in which family fortunes and dynamics can drastically change over time). We know that there are usually substantial shifts in the quality and attunement of most interpersonal environments at different periods of development (Erikson, 1964).

More significant, however, there are major predictable changes built into every child's life cycle (e.g., adolescence). A prolonged childhood in the context of primarily very close kin relations is an excellent environment in which to develop. Although we have emphasized intra-familial conflicts of interests, it should be clear that "kin altruism"—the motivation to identify with the interests of kin based on highly overlapping self-interests (recall the "zones of harmony" in Figure 3)—is real and indispensable. No one but parents and close kin, whose own inclusive fitness is enhanced by altruistic actions toward the child, could conceivably be counted on in any reliable way to try to make the investments necessary to ensure a human child's development (Kriegman, 1988).

There is, however, a radical shift at adolescence. The biological change that takes place at adolescence is not only the well-known physiological maturation of the body, the brain and the capacity for reproduction. It is also an equally fundamental, equally "biological" shift from an environment composed primarily of interactions between close kin to an environment of close kin, more distant kin, and unrelated individuals who are bound together primarily by ties of reciprocity and exchange. Biologically, there is a vast difference in the meaning of relationships with different degrees of relatedness (Trivers, 1974). We would expect, therefore, that a major developmental mechanism would have to exist by which those elements of individual identity developed in the context of the family can be reevaluated and renegotiated in the context of the drastically different conditions outside the nuclear family.

The ubiquity of regression in adolescence, which has long fascinated psychoanalytic theorists (see Blos, 1979; Erikson, 1964, 1968; A. Freud, 1958), may be understood within the evolutionary framework as an adaptive process—the developmental mechanism that reopens for renegotiation those elements of identity that were originally formulated in the context of the family. This adaptive regression has been "prepared for" by the operation of repression in childhood. In this view, adolescent regression represents a process through which repressed aims and identity elements that did not fit the family environment are retrieved as one enters adolescence. As one leaves the family, the compromise adaptation made there may no longer be beneficial or necessary. The regressive resurgence of the repressed provides a valuable means with which to renegotiate a "new compromise" between individual interests and the new possibilities of the larger environment. Inclusive self-interest as provisionally internalized in a childhood identity is thus reopened and, in the course of interaction and negotiation with new objects, redefined into its adult form (M. Slavin, 1985; M. Slavin & J. Slavin, 1976).[16]

The Compulsion to Repeat Versus the Capacity for Creative Repetition

In the classical tradition, the persistence of symptoms, painful repetitions, transference reenactments, and the like are ultimately described as extended ways of reliving the past without consciously experiencing or knowing it. Most clinically observed forms of repetition are thus regarded not as persistent efforts at accomplishing something new but, rather, as deceptive strategies for maintaining or restoring something old, some prior state of equilibrium, or status quo ante (Bibring, 1943). The emphasis is thus on repetition as signaling self-deception as a way of distorting meanings—of *not* remembering, *not knowing,* and *not* changing. This is the essence of the so-called compulsion to repeat or "repetition compulsion" (Bibring, 1943; Fenichel, 1945; Freud, 1920; Glover, 1955). It is a motivational concept that goes hand in hand with the classical view of repression and invariably plays a central role in the classical and ego psychological understandings of psychological disorder (Kriegman & Slavin, 1989).

From the evolutionary perspective, the repetitive enactment of repressed meanings is only incompletely understood as an effort at restoring a prior state of equilibrium and distorting meaning. It inevitably includes these elements because repression is based, in part, on a functional self-deception that diverts awareness from certain highly conflictual aims. Yet, from the evolutionary perspective, clinically observed repetitions and the whole range of phenomena that are readily referred to as manifestations of "the repetition compulsion" cannot be understood apart from the larger adaptive context in which such repetition occurs (Kriegman & Slavin, 1989).

Specifically, repetitions may be more fully understood as reflecting a striving to retain and make use of certain older, highly subjective meanings for the self-protective and adaptively relevant information they contain (i.e., for their use as renewed developmental guidelines in testing and eliciting responses from the new environment). Encoded in these early "fixations" is a version of reality that contains substantial subjective truth. The acceptance and articulation

---

[16]For a more detailed exposition of the classical-relational dialectic in the theory of adolescent change, see M. Slavin and Kriegman (in press) and M. Slavin (1992).

of the truth in this version of reality is likely to be particularly crucial in the process of redefining self-interest, slowly and cautiously relinquishing no-longer functional fixations, and thus adaptively reorganizing the self. There is always an effort to communicate such meanings in some form and, to the extent that the new environment is reliably different from the old one, to renegotiate their place in the structure of the self.

Repression confers, in effect, a capacity for future repetition—one that may well appear to be (or even to need to operate by means of) a subjectively experienced compulsion. Unlike the "repetition compulsion," such repression does not fundamentally operate in the service of returning to an earlier state or restoring and maintaining an inner "equilibrium" in the sense of a status quo but rather of promoting adaptive change, growth and developmental repair.

Defensive Deception Versus Valid Self Protection

Recall now the fourth dimension of the classical–relational dichotomy (Table 1). Do the highly subjective versions of reality that may be called *defenses* represent deceptive distortions? Or do such self-presentations essentially represent valid personal truths? Classically, defenses such as repression are primarily seen as ways of concealing and distorting reality. Relationally, particularly in Winnicott and Kohut, they are more apt to be interpreted as ways of protecting, maintaining, and ultimately expressing valid, vital aspects of the self to safeguard and promote the process of development. Such self-enhancing and self-protecting views of reality may be particularly important in reinitiating thwarted development.

The evolutionary view suggests that there are strong adaptive reasons why the subjective alterations of experience in a defense such as repression must intrinsically entail both features. The child engages in a completely natural, yet undeniably self-centered quest for advantage even in relation to his or her closest kin. This is the aspect of human action that has been signified by classical views of the id and instinctual drive motivation. Similar to the classical model of defense, repression functions to conceal and distort motives and views that are distinctly biased toward the child's own interest. Simultaneously, the evolutionary model incorporates the relational view: The child is designed to repress aspects of his or her affects, aims, and true identity to sequester them safely—to protect them from the inevitable side of the family system that is geared more closely to its own interests than to those of the child. The biases and self-interested motives of the normal caretaking environment make it necessary for the child to have a way of developing a *subjective* version of his or her needs that remains somewhat independent of the environment. Thus, the evolutionary biological paradigm implicitly suggests the crucial adaptive need for an innate, subjective sense of one's "true" (Winnicott, 1965), "authentic" (Fromm, 1941), or "nuclear" (Kohut, 1984) self. Moreover, it suggests that humans are designed to ensure that such vital configurations of impulses, aims and fantasies are effectively held in reserve to be retrieved and reanimated under altered relational conditions.

Thus, although there is support for the intrinsically deceptive, distorting aspects of defense, the evolutionary perspective is clearly consistent with the views of Winnicott and Kohut that developmental strivings toward the resumption of thwarted growth must play a central, perhaps superordinate, role in the organization of the psyche (Kriegman & Slavin, 1989, 1990).

Repression, Regression, and Transference: A Coordinated Set of Adaptive–Developmental Processes

Repression and regression enable one to reversibly suspend access to parts of one's inner experience—indeed, to vital aspects of the self—and to make use of this "reserve" in negotiations or renegotiations with the environment. This capacity for reversible access to parts of the self serves as a major fulcrum for ongoing adaptation and dynamic change throughout the entire life cycle (Slavin, 1992). As examples, consider any of the times when one's own identity is called upon to complement another's, to compensate for the loss of the other's identity: marriage, divorce, death of a spouse. In all of these normal crises in relationships, one can well make use of that reserve of alternate identity elements and repressed wishes that natural selection has enabled the child to bequeath to the adult (Slavin, 1985).

Normal dynamic functioning entails a fluid, experimental shifting of the line between what is conscious and what is not (Stolorow & Atwood, 1989). In the evolutionary view, this fluidity derives from the fact that humans are designed to synthesize aspects of self structure in a provisional way—a way that always remains highly contingent on the fit between self-interest and the environment. Most important is the continual dissolution and resynthesis of those aspects of self structure that regulate the delicate changing balance between directly selfish and mutualistic aims.

The Psychoanalytic Situation

The psychoanalytic situation itself can be viewed as a human relationship that invites precisely the sort of regressive revival of repressed aspects of the self that were held in reserve for future renegotiation under altered relational conditions. The major reason people are able to mobilize powerful transferences and therapeutic regressions within the analytic situation becomes understandable as a heightened natural phenomenon: Psyches are organized, precisely, to experience new situations as opportunities for the revival of repressed aspects of the self and the reorganization of intrapsychic structure. Indeed, whatever modifications in personality psychoanalysis can achieve may be essentially patterned on this built-in human capacity for regressive renegotiation of identity under altered relational conditions.

Thus, transferences and therapeutic regressions within the analytic situation become understandable not simply in terms of the range of factors typically cited in the analytic literature, namely, as drives pressing for gratification (Fenichel, 1945), as projections of internal objects (Racker, 1954), as the effective activation of a self-selfobject relationship (Kohut, 1984), as the creation of a transitional space (Winnicott, 1965), as the establishment of a sufficient "background of safety" (Weiss & Sampson, 1986), or as simply the ongoing "organizing activity of the psyche" (Stolorow & Lachmann, 1984). These represent essentially descriptive aspects of transference and conditions under which transference is likely to operate and be heightened. More basically, transferences occur as the means by which the psyche is designed to experience new situations as opportunities for the revival and reorganization of intrapsychic structure (see also J. Slavin, 1989). This reorganization is part of a continuing process of redefinition and revision of the complex set of proximal mechanisms (i.e., the structure of the self) that psychologically mediates inclusive fitness.

Thus, repression, regression and transference operate in a coordinated way throughout the life cycle to repeatedly heighten the experienced comparison of the fit between inner needs, old solutions (compromises), and current relational realities. This experiential juxtaposition enables, indeed, compels people (and the objects of their transferences) to engage in the renegotiation/revision process. The centrality of transference as the therapeutic vehicle is thus seen as a way in which psychoanalysis has capitalized on a built-in set of coordinated biological functions designed to maintain and revise inclusive fitness. This conception of transference provides a needed conceptual rationale for Loewald's (1980) notion of "creative repetition" as a force for dynamic change, as well as for recent efforts such as Stolorow and Lachmann's (1984) to increase our basic appreciation of the critical subjective truths entailed in the phenomena of transference and Hoffman's (1983) to recast the meaning of transference in terms of a social exchange. It broadens and lends considerable weight to constructs such as the "curative fantasy" (Ornstein,

1984) in which many of the so-called misperceptions and distortions of reality in the transference are seen as expressions of the patient's overarching effort to generate the interactive conditions in which, for that individual, a cure may be possible.[17]

The Function of Endogenous Drives (and the Drive–Defense System) in the "Negotiation–Renegotiation" Process

If the dynamics of repression do represent a strategy for hiding, preserving, and retrieving those aspects of people's aims and experience that cannot fit within the formative environment—especially the more self-interested aims—we still need to account for those affect states or emotional signals that press them to act in intensely self-interested ways in the first place. From our evolutionary perspective, we ask how a socially or relationally constructed self—one that, to a significant degree, is built out of biased familial–cultural meanings—can be counted on to generate the pursuit of a whole range of passionately individual aims. How can the human child take the enormous historical risk of "sacrificing" a huge amount of innate, hard-wired adaptedness? How can one risk the potential costs of evolving such a long, complex, program of development? Especially, how can one risk relying on a program that is dependent on symbolic, deception-prone interactions with powerful, needed others whose own interests inevitably lead them to try to shape one's identity toward what is beneficial to them?

Enter the notion of endogenous (or instinctual) drives. In the drives there is a mechanism that guarantees access to some types of motivation that arise from non-relational sources and are, in a sense, totally dedicated toward the promotion of our individual interests (M. Slavin, 1986).[18] The single, unique functional feature of endogenous drives conceived as a type of motivation rooted in bodily nature is the way in which they serve as a guarantee against having one's genetic self-interest usurped by the social influence of important others, notably those serving as models for introjection and identification.[19] As Wrong (1963) pointed out, theories that do not adequately address the question of how individuals are equipped with motives that are not entirely social in nature will always present an "oversocialized image of man," an incomplete and absurdly unrealistic picture of human motivation.

This conception of the "balancing" function of the drives echoes Rapaport's (1960) notion of the way in which the drives guarantee a certain "autonomy from the superego"; or, as Eagle (1984) more recently put it, the instincts serve to resist the individual's "enslavement by society." It is critical to note, however, that the evolutionary argument for the adaptive function of the drives differs radically from its ego psychological predecessors (e.g., Rapaport). Beyond any of the modifications introduced by ego psychology, the evolutionary paradigm revises the assumptions of classical theory in several ways: (a) it puts the drives and their role into a clearly subsidiary position in relation to other, superordinate principles of motivation; (b) it acknowledges the existence of fundamental, primary, irreducible social motivations (Kriegman, 1988, 1990); and, (c) it emphasizes the existence of pervasive biases in the motives and aims of normal adults within the thoroughly "good-enough" environment—the essentially nonpathological, yet

---

[17]The evolutionary implications for the psychoanalytic process are taken up in greater detail in M. Slavin and Kriegman (in press).

[18]While all innate (naturally selected) motivations are "endogenous," what distinguishes the classical drives from relational "drives" (i.e., relational needs or motivations) is the asocial nature of the classical drives. We are suggesting that, although it is necessary to correct the extreme classical overemphasis on asocial, selfish drives (Kriegman, 1988, 1990; Kriegman & Knight, 1988), there is an important aspect of such "selfish drivenness" that must not be discarded. When we refer to "endogenous drives" we are referring to this aspect of the classical drive concept.

[19]See Kriegman and Solomon (1985) for a discussion of one of the extremes that such social influence can reach.

profoundly self-interested, environmental influences that the child must be equipped to both internalize and resist in the course of normal development.

Thus, evolutionary theory suggests the need for a type of motivation that, in this function, resembles the instinctual drives of the classical model. The drives provide a unique source of adaptively relevant information (Peterfreund, 1972) operating within the larger functional organization of the aims of the individual (Lloyd, 1984). Yet, simply because such endogenous motives are highly dependent on input from the body (and relatively resistant to social modification) there is no reason to equate them with what is "animal" or "biological" in human nature; nor, certainly, do they exist in basic opposition to something that is, in any basic sense, "nonbiological" or "cultural" in human nature. From an evolutionary perspective, this is a completely false, misleading dichotomy (Mayr, 1974).

Beyond the Endogenous Versus Experiential (Intrapsychic Versus Interpersonal) Dichotomy

Recall now the second dimension of the classical-relational dichotomy (Table 1): endogenous inner forces versus relational experiences in the structuralization of the psyche. From the evolutionary perspective, this dichotomy takes on a completely different meaning. The psyche is seen as an "evolved adaptation" that has been shaped by relational conflict over vast evolutionary time. It is a "fitness optimizing organ" that operates through mechanisms designed to regulate the perception of and response to the conflicting pressures inherent in life within the relational world. Significant, universal aspects of the psyche are, thus, seen as patterned by an "interpersonal field," as Greenberg and Mitchell (1983) have characterized an aspect of the relational perspective. However this field is not equated with the developmental experience of each individual. Rather, it is the relational world of countless life cycles, the world in which hundreds of thousands of generations of our ancestors (and their unsuccessful compatriots) strove to maximize their inclusive fitness. Thus, the psychological precipitate of life within such a relational world— including those parts of the psyche that are traditionally viewed as non-relational, such as endogenous drives—are also seen as having been patterned by the relational field.

We should note that in an evolutionary view of the function of repression, the process of conflict regulation is, simultaneously, both intrapsychic and interpersonal in character. The evolutionary perspective embraces the one-person and two-person psychologies (Modell, 1984), both of which are needed to fully describe this conception of conflict. Countless generations of intrafamilial conflict have equipped the child with a deep structural capacity to apprehend and manage a range of expectable but ambiguous and deceptive tensions between his or her own self-interest and those of closely related others. The particular form, intensity, and to some extent content of these conflicts (as well as the individual's ways of coping with them) will, of course, also be shaped by one's particular interpersonal experience.

There is a "deep structure" to intrapsychic conflict. It is formed in the context of intimate conflictual interactions in the relational world through which a basic tension and division in motives is shaped: Directly self-interested, asocial inner forces are structured into dynamic opposition to equally primary, more mutualistic, prosocial inner aims. This stands in contrast to both the classical tripartite model of intrapsychic conflict and the relational model of conflict derived from environmental failure. All of this is, in the deepest sense, endogenous. Its deep structure is all intrapsychic. It derives from what was interpersonal and social in our evolutionary history. Each individual psyche carries within it the evolutionary history of the interpersonal (Teicholz, 1989).

The capacity to be shaped by a social environment is clearly hard-wired into the human psyche, whereas the content of this influence is variable and open ended. This is similar to the way in which Chomsky (1972) has viewed human capacity to learn language as necessitating an innate structure designed to apprehend complex rules, subtle meanings, and grammatical structures without specifying the actual language itself. In this sense, social selves are as intrinsically built into the human nervous systems as are our drives.[20]

FREUD'S SEARCH RESUMED: TOWARD A PSYCHOANALYTIC EVOLUTIONARY PSYCHOLOGY

Like the proverbial blind men examining an elephant, psychoanalysis has repeatedly focused on parts, or fragments, of human nature. Each analytic tradition has grasped an important aspect of human nature and studied and elaborated it both conceptually and clinically. One is left with all sorts of contradictions, dichotomies, and paradoxes. As in a coin flipping through the air, at one moment we see one face; a moment later we see the other side. Because of the structure of the coin itself, we never see both sides at once. Yet, we know that each implies the other. No one would argue over whether "coin nature" is essentially "headed" or "tailed." In psychoanalytic theory, the heads and tails of the human psyche have been separated from the essential structure of the psyche itself. From the "gene's eye view," the disembodied, dichotomous psychoanalytic "faces" of the human psyche with their paradoxical nature (Modell, 1984) are revealed not as an immutable, transcendent paradox but rather as a historical tension that seeks resolution into a new configuration, a more inclusive paradigm. To be sure, this new, more unified paradigm will inherently entail its own tensions, perhaps eventually breaking down into new dichotomies. Although we still perceive both the social and asocial aspects of human nature, within this new paradigm both become parts composing an intrinsic tension within the same no-longer disembodied and dichotomized psychic "coin." We can, perhaps, step back and obtain a better view of the larger, two-sided structure—complete with its intrinsic tensions—as we observe (and participate in) the experience of the human psyche, which, like the flipping coin, presents first one face, then the other. The conceptual unifying process is a crucial step toward asking newer more fruitful questions. Perhaps it may enable us to move the philosophical grounding of psychoanalysis as a psychological "science of meaning" that is closer to a conceptual framework in which more traditional forms of empirical, psychological research—and integration with other life sciences—can take on more meaningful form.

Table 2 summarizes the way in which the evolutionary paradigm represents a working synthesis of the classical-relational dialectic.

From a philosophical point of view, the evolutionary biology of kinship theory (Hamilton, 1964) and reciprocal altruism (Trivers, 1971) represents what is, arguably, the first major step taken in Western thought to reconceptualize the boundaries of the individual psyche. It does so in a way that expresses the intrinsically social, relational essence of the psyche without omitting those critical features that remain inherently, competitively individual in their aims. Indeed, it is in this regard that our evolutionary perspective most fundamentally validates Kohut's and

---

[20]Let us use a metaphor from the world of artificial intelligence. For simple "closed programs," relatively simple computers with simple information processing instructions can provide standard reflexive responses to differential input. However, for complex "open programs" that try to simulate human intelligence with its interactive flexibility and capacity to learn from experience, a much more powerful computer—with a great deal of additional hardware and more complex sets of a priori instructions for processing information—is necessary. Thus, somewhat paradoxically, we see that greater flexibility and the capacity to learn requires, along with a greater "capacity," a greater amount of "hard-wired" (pre-set) rules for information processing. The same principle can be gleaned from the phylogenetic tree: As one moves from reflexive responses to complex flexibility that is highly dependent on situational nuances and individual history, one does not move away from "hard-wiring" per se. Rather, one moves from simple nervous systems toward greater, more complex and different types of hard-wired rules. It is a mistake to equate hard-wiring (a relatively fixed, predictably reliable "deep structure") with reflexive inflexibility (Mayr, 1974). Humans are "hard-wired" for a relatively invariant deep structure that makes possible adaptive variability and flexibility (Tooby & Cosmides, 1989).

Winnicott's radical revisions of traditional psychoanalytic individualism (the concept of the selfobject and the idea that there is no such thing as an infant); at the same time, it extends and further clarifies the universal nature of the conflict between the narrowly individual aims of the self and its innately social, relational aspects and motives.

In this fashion, our philosophical position differs markedly from both the individualistic (atomist) tradition of 18th-century British philosophy (including 19th-century utilitarian derivatives, e.g., Bentham, Mill) and the social (collectivist) tradition of Continental thought (e.g., Rousseau, Hegel, Marx, Durkheim). Ultimately, the central philosophical difference between Greenberg and Mitchell's (1983) view of the "deeper divergence" between psychoanalytic models and our scheme resides in our view that contemporary evolutionary theory represents a substantive philosophical revision of the individualist–collectivist dichotomy in modern Western thought. Thus, in distinction to Greenberg and Mitchell's conclusion that the "deeper divergence" is inherently unresolvable, the evolutionary perspective may offer a framework that points toward an eventual synthesis of the classical–relational dialectic.

The Psyche as a System of Evolved Adaptations That Has been Structured by Relational Conflict

The basic patterning of the human psyche is ultimately explainable as an evolved, deep structural adaptation that has been shaped over vast evolutionary time as a system of interrelated adaptations working together to optimally represent inclusive self-interest while managing the inevitable conflicting pressures inherent to life within the human relational world.

Intrinsic Relational Conflict in the Expectable, Good-Enough Environment

The evolutionary perspective depicts an environment that universally consists of distinct, unique individuals whose interests (although often overlapping) *necessarily* diverge and, to some degree, inevitably compete. This evolutionarily based conception of conflict is at marked variance with the tendency in existing relational narratives to focus primarily on those dimensions of conflict that can be attributed to inadequacy, pathology, or abnormal lack of attunement in the caregiving environment. In other words, the evolutionary perspective suggests that conflict and its accompanying strategic deceptions and self deceptions are *intrinsic* features of *all* object relational ties and interactions (Kriegman & Slavan, 1990; Modell, 1989; Slavin, 1985). And, this intrinsic relational conflict is given a universal explanation in terms of the genetics of both overlapping and competing interests of self and other (the "gene's eye view," see Figures 1 and 2). In contrast with the "narratives of environmental failure" found in the writings of Winnicott, Kohut, Sullivan, Guntrip, and Fairbairn, from the evolutionary perspective, the conflictual dimension is understood to be absolutely normative in the fully good-enough environment.

This perspective yields a view of inner, intrapsychic struggles that are characterized by primary relational conflict, as distinct from the drive-based conflict depicted in the classical model or the environmentally induced conflict of the relational perspective. In other words, the conflict that exists in human relations is found in the interactive dynamics of interorganismic relations themselves, as opposed to being something that is, in a sense, imposed on them either by drive demands or environmental pathology. To be sure, relational dynamics are influenced by the adaptively relevant information provided by endogenous drives as one source of input on the more selfishly individual side. On the other side, there are the equally primary prosocial motivations. The patterning of the whole is profoundly shaped by the character and reliability of the particular relational world into which people are born. Individuals' "selves" are superordinate structures that include the continuous synthesis of an overarching, relatively unified identity. However, this relative unity is built on a profound dividedness and tension at the core of the

TABLE 2
Classical Versus Relational Narratives, Revisited

Four dichotomies	The classical narrative	The relational narrative	The evolutionary synthesis
1. Basic unit of analysis	**The individual psyche** Emphasis is on intrapsychic dynamics.	**The Interpersonal field** The individual can only be understood within an interactive context.	**The genetically based self— The "gene's eye view"** Individual boundaries are innate and include aspects of related others; the self is intrinsically semisocial.
2. Basic source of patterning (or structure) in the psyche	**Vicissitudes of endogenous drives** Relational ties are derivative.	**Vicissitudes of interpersonal interactions**	**The psyche as an evolved deep structural adaptation** Universal deep structure allows both drive and relational patterning of the psyche to operate; each individual psyche carries within it the evolutionary history of the interpersonal.
3. Relation between basic aims of self and other	**Inherent clash of normal individual aims** Selfishness, rivalry, competition are motivationally primary. (Corollary: The normal [tripartite] psyche is "divided" in a way that reflects the inevitable conflicts between the individual and others.)	**Emphasis on mutual, reciprocal, convergent aims** Significant interpersonal clashes are due to pathology or environmental failure. (Corollary: The psyche [the self] is an essentially "holistic" entity that reflects the possibility of relative harmony between the individual and others.)	**Inherent conflict and inherent mutuality in the good-enough environment** The self interests of genetically distinct yet related individuals necessarily conflict and overlap in the evolved relational world. (Corollary: The normal psyche [the self of inclusive fitness] is designed to operate as an overarching, holistic entity that manages the ongoing negotiation of the inherent tension between selfish and mutualistic aims.)

4. Role of deception and self-deception in subjective experience	Defense and transference as distortions of reality	Defense and transference as inherently valid expressions of personal reality	Defense and transference as adaptive deception (and self-deception) in the promotion of vital individual truths
	Resistance serves to conceal truth. (Corollary: Repetition is a means of not knowing; people repeat the acting out of unconscious motivations as a defense for maintaining repression, to preserve ties, or to maintain instinctual fixations.)	Resistance serves to elicit recognition of individual truth for further growth. (Corollary: repetition is an artifact created as people repeatedly try to elicit a needed response from the relational world to reinitiate thwarted growth and revise the self; people repeat in the process of preserving and protecting a vulnerable self [e.g., by maintaining needed relational ties] so that revision can be tried again in the future.)	Resistance serves to conceal truths while ascertaining whether valid, individual truths can be recognized and used for further growth. (Corollary: Creative repetition; people search for patterns that match past situations in the process of regressive renegotiation; they probe new relational contexts seeking the reasons for maintaining repression and to explore old compromise solutions in the attempt to negotiate a more advantageous fit between their inclusive self-interest and the relational world.)

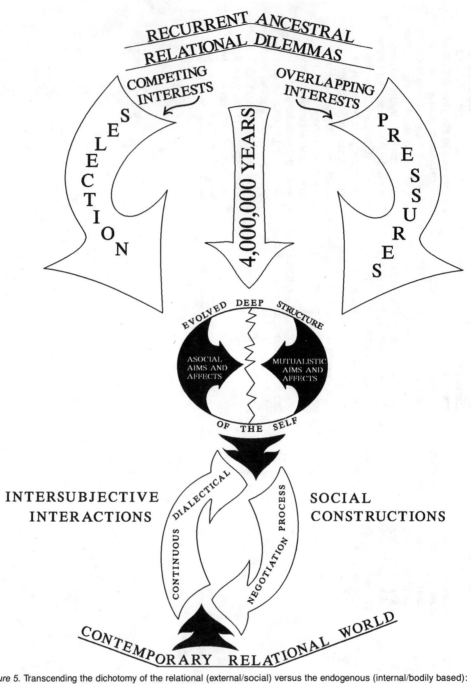

Figure 5. Transcending the dichotomy of the relational (external/social) versus the endogenous (internal/bodily based): The evolution of the divided (semisocial) self.

human psyche. This dividedness is embodied in the fact that primary motivational structure appears to be broadly organized around two simultaneous, yet inherently competing, sets of aims:

1. A relatively altruistic set of "social" aims and related affects that represent adaptations to the realities of our shared, overlapping interests (the realities of the extended

self, see Figures 1 and 2, pages 51 and 53). Such motives (i.e., genuine object love, altruism, and all the "attachment"-based affects) are as real, primary, and innate as the aggressive and libidinal instinctual aims that the classical model views as motivational bedrock. In the classical view, such social motives have been characterized as a complex yet ultimately defensive and reactive overlay on more primary, aggressively self-interested aims (Kriegman, 1988, 1990);

2. A complementary and inevitably conflicting set of more aggressively self-interested, "driven" aims that represent more directly selfish, asocial, uniquely individual needs.[21] Such aims are, in part, sustained and guaranteed to operate in the interests of the individual by virtue of their use of endogenous drives or nonrelationally-based motives as vital, imperative signals of adaptively relevant information. Such peremptory "pushes" effectively counter the powerful, inherently biased forces (of others' self-interests) in the normal relational environment.

Intrapsychic conflict thus represents an "archaic heritage," as Freud (1923/1960) put it, an inherited capacity to organize and cope with the incredibly complex, realities of overlapping and divergent interests in the evolved relational world. The tensions in such a model echo Bakan's (1966) conception of the inherent opposition between "agentic" (individualistic, selfish) aims and "communal" (other-directed, or group-oriented) aims in human motivation as well as Balint's (1956) model in which libido is both pleasure seeking and object seeking. Its emphasis is similar to Klein's (1976) effort to reformulate the universal basis for inner conflict in terms of a clash between inherently opposed, equally primary human aims in preference to the ego psychological notion of an inherent clash between reality based ego and a "biological" id (Eagle, 1984). And, its reinterpretation of instinctual drives as a means subordinate to and operating in the service of broader, relational ends resembles Fairbairn's (1952) attempt to recast the libido theory in an object relational context. Yet, in clear distinction to all such previous attempts at reformulating the nature of inner conflict, the evolutionary model is rooted in a general theory of the inherently conflictual and mutualistic relationship between the individual and the relational environment, and it is supported by a broad conception of the overall functional-adaptive architecture of the psyche viewed in the context of the selective pressures that appear to have shaped it during human evolutionary history.

An evolutionarily based "metapsychology" thus depicts humans as innately individualistic and innately social, as endowed with inherently selfish, aggressively self-promoting aims as well as an equally primary altruistic dispositions. Human beings are, in short, never destined to attain the kind of highly autonomous individuality enshrined in the classical tradition, nor are they the "social animal" of the relational vision. They are essentially "semisocial" beings whose nature or self structure and motivational system is inherently divided between eternally conflicting aims.

---

[21]The aggressive component of these aims is, to be sure, essentially "self-assertive" in nature rather than emanating from a central reservoir of inherently, destructive, or hostile energies, as the Freudian and, particularly the Kleinian metapsychologies would have it. From an evolutionary perspective, the existence of an overriding destructive drive energy that, in some sense, needs continual or periodic discharge would be an unlikely way for natural selection to have designed us (Kriegman & Slavin, 1989). However, our clearly built-in capacity to experience the world in a self-interested manner, and to act on this experience, will lead, in the thoroughly "good enough" environment—from earliest infancy onward—to certain major clashes between our aims and those of even our most intimate objects. The interpersonally adaptive rage (Kriegman & Slavin, 1990) that frequently ensues as a result of conflict within this universal relational matrix could then lend itself readily to interpretation by the outside observer as emanating from a central fund of innate, intrapsychically determined destructive aggression.

Our view may seem to resemble the familiar notion that aggression is a response to frustration or a more contemporary "systems" view (e.g., Lichtenberg, 1989; Stechler & Halton, 1987) that healthy self-assertiveness becomes "contaminated" with destructive rage in an unresponsive environment. However, in the evolutionary perspective, the whole notion of environmental "frustration" and "unresponsiveness" is altered by the recognition that frustrating conflicts of interest and biased responsiveness are thoroughly expectable features encountered by an innately self-interested, self-promoting individual developing in the nonpathological, normally biased object world. Aims that begin simply and benignly enough as self assertion will regularly and inescapably take on significantly destructive and hostile qualities in an environment of inherently competing interests.

Recall the corollary to the classical–relational dichotomy of inherent conflict versus inherent mutuality in the relational world (i.e., that the normative state of the psyche is inherently divided in the classical perspective and unitary—if not subject to pathological distortions—in the relational perspective). Some self psychologists (e.g., Shane & Shane, 1988) have tried to capture aspects of this inherent internal conflict in their formulations (Kriegman & Slavin, 1990). Lichtenberg (1989) attempted to delineate separate and distinct motivational systems that sometimes "compete" for dominance. Yet, he saw an overarching self structure that attempts to organize and prioritize these different motivations. Although our view of the self as a fitness-optimizing, overarching, mental organ (Kriegman & Slavin, 1990) has some similarities, we see aspects of these "competing dominances" not merely as differing motives all striving for expression but in certain cases as *inherently in opposition* to one another. Thus, the evolutionary view presents an overarching self structure with inherent conflict as a design solution for maximizing success in a conflictual relational world—a solution that almost inevitably generates significant developmental problems, some of which will inevitably become intertwined with what we term *psychopathology*.

Freud's Search Revisited: The Evolutionary "Razor" Cuts Both Ways

The evolutionary perspective yields a new, unique paradigm that enables us to steer a conceptual course that avoids the more problematic assumptions of each existing psychoanalytic tradition.

To the extent that we read the classical analytic agenda as synonymous with drive theory, the structural model—and many of its ego psychological revisions with their unsupportable assumptions about the primacy of a limited set of asocial, "animal" drives in human nature (Eagle, 1984; Holt, 1976; Klein, 1976)—the evolutionary perspective clearly does not support it. Drives, and the structural model of drive–defense conflict, assume a subsidiary role within a larger, relationally designed and configured psyche. But, to the extent that we read the classical agenda as a set of metaphors about the innate, evolved structure of driveness and the repression of versions of the self—metaphors that create a "narrative of conflict"—the classical agenda captures certain major, significant features of the relational world and the inherently "divided" way human beings are adapted to it. In the vast range of both analytic perspectives and non-analytic psychologies, only the classical psychoanalytic perspective (and its derivatives), with its metaphors of inner conflict, fully depicts the deep divisions and tensions within the self that are indispensable concomitants of an adaptation to the conflictual relational world.

Freud's vision of the relational world in *Totem and Taboo* (1913/1964a) and *The Phylogenetic Phantasy* (1987) almost exclusively emphasized the conflictual aspects of the ancestral, human environment. Thus, even if he had a better grasp of the workings of natural selection, of social selection pressures, he still might not have been able to modify some of the basic flaws in drive theory. The classical metapsychology is, in effect, a viable model of the psyche of a creature adapted to *one* major facet of relational reality. In skirting the whole issue of Freud's basic assumptions about the (ancestral) relational world and focusing simply on rather neutral adaptive capacities, Hartmann could not make use of the evolutionary perspective any more critically than did Freud.

Conversely, Bowlby and Erikson (and, implicitly the range of other relational theorists) radically altered the picture of social realities, the actual evolutionary relational world to which the psyche is adapted. Yet, by essentially replacing the "narrative of conflict" with a view of the normal relational world as consisting of individuals whose motives essentially converge and mutually harmonize—with its related tendency to downplay the role of endogenously derived, inner conflict in the creation of "psychic reality" (Cooper, 1983; Wallerstein, 1983)—this alternative, embracing vision cannot find validation from the evolutionary perspective (Kriegman

& Slavin, 1990). Instead, one may read the relational tradition as, essentially, a vision of human nature in which the psyche is understood as primarily organized around motives and capacities for conducting social relationships in the service of optimal, authentic self-development. In this way, the relational model finds a strong, clear echo in evolutionary biological thought.

Many aspects of the complexity in human experience have been captured within the diversity of psychoanalytic models and epistomologies—from the relatively experience–distant, reductionist–physicalistic, classical emphasis on individual endogenous drives and presumably "blind" mechanisms to the experience-near, phenomenological–hermeneutic study of intersubjectivity at the forefront of the modern, relational tradition. Unlike the various blind men with the elephant (who, after all, had essentially the same observational methods), we have argued that a new working synthesis for psychoanalysis cannot simply mix or combine these incompatible models and methods. Rather, a meaningful synthesis requires that the models be radically reexamined, essentially "deconstructed" into their underlying meanings, and then altered with reference to a larger, embracing reality. Although limited in his capacity to realize it, this may have been what Freud intended in his quest for the ancestral, phylogenetic, relational meanings and origins of individual, inner human experience (M. Slavin, 1988).

In our view, all psychoanalytic models—implicitly or explicitly, intentionally or disavowedly—are necessarily rooted in complex biological assumptions and are, thus, intrinsically a part of a larger, overarching, and potentially unifying biological reality. Contemporary evolutionary theory thus provides a needed platform, as it were, on which to stand outside of psychoanalytic traditions to view the field as more of a whole and revise it. Without this essentially experience-distant "platform" as a reference point, psychoanalytic hermeneutics risk becoming "hermetic," in the sense of something that is sealed off. Yet, to the extent that such an experience-distant platform—the evolutionary as well as any other—cannot effectively embrace crucial, experiential structures it becomes a kind of "scientism" (i.e., a ritualistic pursuit of "objective" truth that imports methods and concepts that define away the most vital data of human psychological experience and meaning). Therefore, the test of the validity and usefulness of such an outside platform as a vantage point lies in its capacity to help us embrace the crucial experiential data, the structures of inner meaning, elicited within the intersubjective field of the psychoanalytic clinical dialogue.[22]

We believe the evolutionary biological perspective, as we have developed it, enables us to navigate between the methodological Scylla of hermetic hermeneutics and the Charybdis of ritualistic scientism. Substantively, it permits us to embrace elements of both the classical and relational psychoanalytic traditions after we have deconstructed the underlying meanings of the metaphors and narratives that have traditionally defined them. Both existing analytic traditions can be understood as contributing vital parts, indeed complementary, reciprocal parts, to a larger, broader picture of human psychodynamic adaptation. This essay has been an attempt to demonstrate how contemporary evolutionary biology may point the way towards such a psychoanalytic evolutionary psychology.

REFERENCES

Badcock, C. (1988). *Essential Freud*. Oxford, England: Basil Blackwell.

Bakan, D. (1966). *The duality of human existence: An essay on psychology and religion*. Chicago: Rand-McNally.

---

[22]We begin the process of putting the evolutionary perspective to this test in Slavin and Kriegman (in press), where we develop some of the clinical implications of this new perspective.

Balint, M. (1956). Pleasure, object and libido. In *Problems of Human Pleasure and Behavior*. New York: Liveright.

Balint, M. (1968). *The basic fault*. London: Tavistock.

Beebe, B., & Lachmann, F. (1988). Mother-infant mutual influence and precursors of psychic structure. In A. Goldberg (Ed.), *Frontiers in self psychology* (pp. 3–25). Hillsdale, NJ: Analytic Press.

Bibring, E. (1943). The conception of the repetition compulsion. *Psychoanalytic Quarterly, 12*, 486–519.

Blos, P. (1979). *The adolescent passage*. Madison, CT: International Universities Press.

Bowlby, J. (1969). *Attachment*. New York: Basic Books.

Chomsky, N. (1972). *Language and mind*. San Diego, CA: Harcourt Brace Jovanovich.

Cooper, A. (1983). The place of self psychology in the history of depth psychology. In A. Goldberg & P. Stepansky (Eds.), *Kohut's legacy: Contributions to self psychology* (pp. 3–17). Hillsdale, NJ: Analytic Press.

Cooper, S. (1989). Recent contributions to the theory of defense mechanisms. *Journal of the American Psychoanalytic Association, 37*, 865–891.

Eagle, M. (1984). *Recent developments in psychoanalysis*. New York: McGraw-Hill.

Erikson, E. (1956). The problem of ego identity. *Journal of the American Psychoanalytic Association, 4*, 56–121.

Erikson, E. (1964). *Insight and responsibility*. New York: Norton.

Erikson, E. (1968). *Identity, youth and crisis*. New York: Norton.

Fairbairn, W. R. D. (1952). *An object-relations theory of the personality*. New York: Basic Books.

Fenichel, O. (1945). *The psychoanalytic theory of the neurosis*. New York: Norton.

Ferenczi, S. (1968). *Thalassa: A theory of genitality*. In H. A. Bun Kev (Trans.). New York: Norton. (Original work published 1924)

Freud, A. (1966). *The ego and the mechanisms of defense*. Madison, CT: International Universities Press. (Original work published 1936)

Freud, A. (1958). Adolescence. *Psychoanalytic Study of Child, 13*, 255–278.

Freud, S. (1955). Beyond the pleasure principle. In J. Strachey (Ed. and Trans.), *The standard edition of the complete psychological works of Sigmund Freud* (Vol. 18, pp. 3–64). (Original work published 1920)

Freud, S. (1957). Repression. In J. Strachey (Ed. and Trans.), *The standard edition of the complete psychological works of Sigmund Freud* (Vol. 14, pp. 141–158). (Original work published 1915)

Freud, S. (1961). The ego and the id. In J. Strachey (Ed. and Trans.), *The standard edition of the complete psychological works of Sigmund Freud* (Vol. 19, pp. 1–66). (Original work published 1923)

Freud, S. (1961). Civilization and its discontents. In J. Strachey (Ed. and Trans.), *The standard edition of the complete psychological works of Sigmund Freud* (Vol. 21, pp. 59–145). (Original work published 1930)

Freud, S. (1964a). Totem and taboo. In J. Strachey (Ed. and Trans.), *The standard edition of the complete psychological works of Sigmund Freud* (Vol. 13, 1–161). (Original work published 1912–1913)

Freud, S. (1964b). Moses and monotheism. In J. Strachey (Ed. and Trans.), *The standard edition of the complete psychological works of Sigmund Freud* (Vol. 23, 3–137). (Original work published 1939)

Freud, S. (1987). A phylogenetic fantasy. In G. Simitis (Ed.) & P. T. Hoffer (Trans.), *Overview of the transference neuroses*. Cambridge, MA: Belknap and Harvard.

Fromm, E. (1941). *Escape from freedom*. New York: Avon Books.

Goldberg, A. (1988). *A fresh look at psychoanalysis*. Hillsdale, NJ: Analytic Press.

Glover, E. (1955). *The technique of psychoanalysis*. Madison, CT: International Universities Press.

Gould, S. J. (1980). *The panda's thumb*. New York: Norton.

Gould, S. J. (1987). Freud's phylogenetic fantasy. *Natural History, 12*, 10–19.

Greenberg, J., & Mitchell, S. (1983). *Object relations and psychoanalytic theory.* Cambridge, MA: Harvard University Press.

Grubrich-Simitis, I. (1987). Metapsychology and metabiology. In I. Grubrich-Simitis (Ed.), *A phylogenetic fantasy: Overview of the transference neuroses* (pp. 75–107). Cambridge, MA: Harvard University Press.

Guntrip, H. (1971). *Psychoanalytic theory, therapy, and the self.* New York: Basic Books.

Hamilton, W. D. (1964). The genetical evolution of social behavior. *Journal of Theoretical Biology, 7*, 1–52.

Hartmann, H. (1958). *Ego psychology and the problem of adaptation.* Madison, CT: International Universities Press. (Original work published 1939)

Hoffman, I. (1983). The patient as interpreter of the analyst's experience. *Contemporary Psychoanalysis, 19*, 389–442.

Holmes, K. R. (1983). Freud, evolution and the tragedy of man. *Journal of the American Psychoanalytic Association, 31*, 187–210.

Holt, R. (1976). Drive or wish? A reconsideration of the psychoanalytic theory of motivation. *Psychological Issues, 9* (4, Serial No. 36).

Jacobson, E. (1964). *The self and the object world.* Madison, CT: International Universities Press.

Kernberg, O. (1976). *Object relations theory and clinical psychoanalysis.* Northvale, NJ: Jason Aronson.

Kernberg, O. (1980). *Internal world and external reality.* Northvale, NJ: Jason Aronson.

Kitcher, P. (1985). *Vaulting ambition.* Cambridge, MA: MIT Press.

Kitcher, P. (1987). Confessions of a curmudgeon. *Behavioral and Brain Sciences, 10*, 89–99.

King, D. (1945). The meaning of normal. *Yale Journal of Biological Medicine, 17*, 493–501.

Klein, G. (1976). *Psychoanalytic theory.* Madison, CT: International Universities Press.

Kohut, H. (1982). Introspection, empathy and the semicircle of mental health. *International Journal of Psychoanalysis, 63*, 395–407.

Kohut, H. (1977). *The restoration of the self.* New York: International Universities Press.

Kohut, H. (1984). *How does analysis cure?* Chicago: University of Chicago Press.

Konner, M. (1982). *The tangled wing: Biological constraints on the human spirit.* New York: Harper Row.

Kriegman, D. (1988). Self psychology from the perspective of evolutionary biology: Toward a biological foundation for self psychology. In A. Goldberg (Ed.), *Progress in self psychology* (Vol. 3). Hillsdale, NJ: Analytic Press.

Kriegman, D. (1990). Compassion and altruism in psychoanalytic theory: An evolutionary analysis of self psychology. *Journal of the American Academy of Psychoanalysis, 18*, 342–367.

Kriegman, D., & Knight, C. (1988). Social evolution, psychoanalysis, and human nature. *Social Policy, 19*, 49–55.

Kriegman, D., & Slavin, M. (1989). The myth of the repetition compulsion and the negative therapeutic reaction: An evolutionary biological analysis. In A. Goldberg (Ed.), *Progress in self psychology* (Vol. 5, pp. 209–253). Hillsdale, NJ: Analytic Press.

Kriegman, D., & Slavin, M. (1990). On the resistance to self psychology: Clues from evolutionary biology. In A. Goldberg (Ed.), *Progress in self psychology* (Vol. 6, pp. 217–250). Hillsdale, NJ: Analytic Press.

Kriegman, D., & Solomon, L. (1985). Cult groups and the narcissistic personality: The offer to heal defects in the self. *International Journal of Group Psychotherapy, 35*, 239–261.

LaBarre, W. (1954). *The human animal.* Chicago: University of Chicago Press.

Leak, G. K., & Christopher, S. B. (1982). Freudian psychoanalysis and sociobiology. *American Psychologist, 37*, 313–322.

Lichtenberg, J. (1989). *Psychoanalysis and motivation.* Hillsdale, NJ: Analytic Press.

Lloyd, A. (1984). *On the evolution of the instincts: Implications for psychoanalysis.* Unpublished manuscript.

Loewald, H. W. (1980). *Papers on psychoanalysis.* New Haven,CT: Yale University Press.

Lorenz, K. Z. (1966). *On aggression.* London: Methuen.

Mayr, E. (1974). Behavior programs and evolutionary strategies. *American Scientist, 62,* 650–659.

Mayr, E. (1982). *The growth of biological thought.* Cambridge, MA: Belknap Press and Harvard University Press.

Mayr, E. (1983). How to carry out the adaptationist program. *American Naturalist, 121,* 324–334.

Mahler, M., Pine, F., & Bergman, A. (1975). *The psychological birth of the human infant.* New York: Basic Books.

Mitchell, R. (1985). *Deception: Perspectives on human and non-human deceit.* New York: State University of New York Press.

Mitchell, S. (1984). Object relations theories and the developmental tilt. *Contemporary Psychoanalysis, 20,* 473–499.

Mitchell, S. (1988). *Relational concepts in psychoanalysis: An integration.* Cambridge, MA: Harvard University Press.

Modell, A. (1968). *Object love and reality.* New York: International University Press.

Modell, A. (1984). *Psychoanalysis in a new context.* Madison, CT: International Universities Press.

Modell, A. (1989, April). *Discussion of Slavin and Kriegman, "Beyond the Classical-Relational Dialectic in Psychoanalysis: A New Paradigm from Contemporary Evolutionary Biology."* Paper presented at the spring meeting of the Division of Psychoanalysis of the American Psychological Association, Boston.

Nesse, R. N. (1990). The evolutionary functions of repression and the ego defenses. *Journal of the American Academy of Psychoanalysis, 18,* 260–285.

Ornstein, A. (1984). Psychoanalytic psychotherapy: A contemporary perspective. In P. E. Stepansky & A. Goldberg (Eds.). *Kohut's legacy: Contributions to self psychology.* Hillsdale, NJ: Analytic Press.

Ornstein, P. (1989, October). *Why self psychology is not an object relations theory: Clinical and theorectical considerations.* Paper presented at the 12th Annual Conference on the Psychology of the Self, San Francisco.

Peterfreund, E. (1972). Information systems and psychoanalysis: An evolutionary biological approach to psychoanalytic theory. *Psychological Issues* 7(1–2, Serial No. 25–26).

Peterfreund, E. (1983). *The process of psychoanalytic therapy.* Hillsdale, NJ: Analytic Press.

Pine, F. (1985). *Developmental theory and clinical process.* New Haven, CT: Yale University Press.

Racker, H. (1968). Considerations on the theory of transference. In *Transference and countertransference* (pp. 71–78). London: Hogarth Press. (Original work published 1954)

Rapaport, D. (1960). The structure of psychoanalytic theory. *Psychological Issues, 2* (2, Serial No. 6).

Ritvo, L. B. (1990). *Darwin's influence on Freud.* New Haven, CT: Yale University Press.

Sandler, J. (1962). The concept of the representational world. *Psychoanalytic Study of the Child, 17,* 128–145.

Sandler, J. (1981). Unconscious wishes and human relationships. *Contemporary Psychoanalysis, 17,* 180–196.

Sandler, J., & Freud, A. (1985). *The analysis of defence.* Madison, CT: International Universities Press.

Schafer, R. (1974). Freud's psychology of women. *Journal of the American Psychoanalytic Association, 22,* 459–485.

Schafer, R. (1976). *A new language for psychoanalysis.* New Haven, CT: Yale University Press.

Schafer, R. (1983). *The analytic attitude.* New York: Basic Books.

Segal, H. (1964). *Introduction to the work Of Melanie Klein.* New York: Basic Books.

Shane, M., & Shane, E. (1988). Pathways to integration: Adding to the self psychology model. In A. Goldberg (Ed.), *Learning from Kohut: Progress in self psychology* (Vol. 4, pp. 71–78). Hillsdale, NJ: Analytic Press.

Slavin, J. (1989). *On making rules: Towards a reformulation of the dynamics of transference in psychoanalytic treatment.* Paper presented at a meeting of the Appalachian Psychoanalytic Society, Knoxville, TN.

Slavin, M. (1974). *An evolutionary biological view of the mechanism of repression.* Unpublished manuscript.

Slavin, M. (1985). The origins of psychic conflict and the adaptive function of repression: An evolutionary biological view. *Psychoanalysis and Contemporary Thought, 8,* 407–440.

Slavin, M. (1986, February). *A relational model of innate inner conflict: Drives, objects, and the self in evolutionary biological perspective.* Paper presented at the midwinter meeting of the Division of Psychoanalysis of the American Psychological Association, Ixtapa, Mexico.

Slavin, M. (1988, May). *Opening Ferenczi's trunk: A reexamination of Freud's evolutionary thinking on the occasion of his newly discovered "phylogenetic phantasy."* Paper presented at the Massachusetts Association for Psychoanalytic Psychology, Cambridge, MA.

Slavin, M. (1990). The dual meaning of repression and the adaptive design of the human psyche. *Journal of the American Academy of Psychoanalysis, 18,* 307–341.

Slavin, M. (1992). *Adolescence and the problem of human adaptation: The work of Anna Freud, Blos, and Erikson in the perspective of contemporary evolutionary biology.* Manuscript in preparation.

Slavin, M., & Kriegman, D. (1988). Freud, biology, and sociobiology. *American Psychologist, 43,* 658–661.

Slavin, M., & Kriegman, D. (1990). Toward a new paradigm for psychoanalysis: An evolutionary biological perspectives on the classical-relational dialectic. *Psychoanalytic Psychology, 7,* 5–31.

Slavin, M., & Kriegman, D. (in press). *The adaptive design of the human psyche: Psychoanalysis and the therapeutic process.* New York: Guilford Press.

Slavin, M., & Slavin, J. (1976). Two patterns of adaptation in late adolescent borderline personalities. *Psychiatry, 39,* 41–50.

Solms, M., & Saling, M. (1986). On psychoanalysis and neuroscience: Freud's attitude to the localist tradition. *International Journal of Psychoanalysis, 67,* 397–416.

Spence, D. (1982). *Narrative truth and historical truth: Meaning and interpretation in psychoanalysis.* New York: Norton.

Stechler, G., & Halton, A. (1987). The emergence of assertion and aggression during infancy: A psychoanalytic systems approach. *Journal of the American Psychoanalytic Association, 35,* 821–839.

Stern, D. (1985). *The interpersonal world of the infant.* New York: Basic Books.

Stolorow, R., & Atwood, G. (1989). The unconscious and unconscious fantasy: An intersubjective developmental perspective. *Psychoanalytic Inquiry, 9,* 364–374.

Stolorow, R., Brandchaft, B., & Atwood, G. (1987). *Psychoanalytic treatment: An intersubjective approach.* Hillsdale, NJ: Analytic Press.

Stolorow, R., & Lachmann, F. (1984). Transference: The future of an illusion. *Annual of Psychoanalysis, 12–13,* 19–37.

Sullivan, H. S. (1953). *The interpersonal theory of psychiatry.* New York: Norton.

Sulloway, F. (1979). *Freud, biologist of the mind.* New York: Basic Books.

Teicholz, J. (1989, April). *Discussion of Slavin and Kriegman's paper, "Beyond the Classical-Relational Dichotomy in Psychoanalysis."* Paper presented at the spring meeting of Division 39 of the American Psychological Association, Boston.

Tinbergen, N. (1953). *The herring gull's world.* London: Collins.

Tooby, J., & Cosmides, L. (1989). Evolutionary psychology and the generation of culture: I. Theoretical considerations. *Ethology and Sociobiology, 10,* 1–3, 29–51.

Tooby, J., & Cosmides, L. (1990a). On the universality of human nature and the uniqueness of the individual: The role of genetics and adaptation. *Journal of Personality, 58,* 17–67.

Tooby, J., & Cosmides, L. (1990b). The past explains the present: Emotional adaptations and the structure of ancestral environments. *Ethology and Sociobiology, 11,* 375–424.

Trivers, R. (1971). The evolution of reciprocal altruism. *Quarterly Review of Biology, 46,* 35–57.

Trivers, R. (1974). Parent-offspring conflict. *American Zoologist, 14,* 249–264.

Trivers, R. (1985). *Social evolution.* Menlo Park, NJ: Benjamin Cummings.

Wallerstein, R. (1981). The bipolar self: Discussion of alternative perspectives. *Journal of the American Psychoanalytic Association, 29,* 377–394.

Wallerstein, R. (1983). Self psychology and "classical" psychoanalytic psychology: The nature of their relationship. In A. Goldberg (Ed.), *The future of psychoanalysis* (pp. 19–64). Madison, CT: International Universities Press.

Weiss, J., & Sampson, H. (1986). *The psychoanalytic process: Theory, clinical observation, and empirical research.* New York: Guilford Press.

Williams, G. C. (1966). *Adaptation and natural selection.* NJ: Princeton University Press.

Winnicott, D. W. (1965a). The theory of the parent-infant relationship. In *The maturational processes and the facilitating environment* (pp. 37–55). London: Hogarth Press. (Original work published 1960)

Winnicott, D. W. (1965b). Ego distortion in terms of true and false self. In *The maturational processes and the facilitating environment* (pp. 140–152). London: Hogarth Press. (Original work published 1960)

Winnicott, D. W. (1965). *The maturational processes and the facilitating environment.* London: Hogarth Press.

Winson, J. (1985). *Brain and psyche: The biology of the unconscious.* Garden City, NY: Anchor Books.

Wrong, D. (1963). The oversocialized conception of man in modern sociology. In N. Smeltser & W. Smeltser (Eds.), *Personality and social systems.* New York: Wiley.

Wynne-Edwards, V. C. (1962). *Animal dispersion in relation to social behavior.* Edinburgh, Scotland: Oliver & Boyd.

3

FREUD AND COGNITIVE PSYCHOLOGY: THE CONCEPTUAL INTERFACE

JEROME C. WAKEFIELD

It has been a little over a century since psychology was born as an empirical science. It has also been about a century since Freud began writing the articles and books that form the basis for the discipline of psychoanalysis. After a century of parallel and sometimes interwoven development, it is a good time to consider what contemporary nonpsychoanalytic academic psychology owes to Freud, or at least has in common with Freudian theory, and what it can still learn from Freud. In this chapter I focus on the relationship between Freudian theory and cognitive psychology because that is where the most direct and impressive links exist. However, because other areas of psychology have been heavily influenced by cognitive theory, in effect I explore the interface between Freud and contemporary psychology more generally.

The standard account is that Freud's specific clinical and theoretical hypotheses are important contributions, but his metapsychological framework principles are based on outmoded 19th century thinking and have no relevance to modern psychology (Gill, 1976; Holt, 1976; Klein, 1976a, 1976b). I defend an answer that is roughly the opposite of this received wisdom. It is apparent that many of Freud's clinical and theoretical doctrines, including his celebrated explanations of abnormal behavior, are waning in credibility with time, at least in the specific forms in which they were proposed by Freud. Rather, Freud's greatest and most enduring contribution to psychology lies in the conceptual and metatheoretical framework that he constructed for approaching psychological questions. Freud brought together disparate elements from previous systems of psychology and brilliantly elaborated on and integrated them so as to create a comprehensive approach to analyzing the mind. Freud was thus able to provide a remarkably illuminating answer to the all-important question, "What does it take to understand another human being?" Indeed, in my opinion, no later theorist has provided an answer to this question that is conceptually superior to Freud's. This profound metatheoretical contribution is, I think, the reason why, after all of this time and despite all that is new under the psychoanalytic sun (see Eagle, 1984, for a review and analysis of post-Freudian psychoanalytic developments), Freud remains the preeminent psychoanalytic thinker. Freud's framework principles are so much a part of our own intellectual landscape that they often go unnoticed, yet I believe it is this shared conceptual framework that gives Freud's work an engaging sense of familiarity and depth, despite the implausibility of much of its content. Consequently, clarifying the interface between Freud's theory and current approaches is also a way of making more explicit some of the assumptions and challenges of today's psychology. In sum, I argue that it is Freud's proposed framework for psychological inquiry that is his principal legacy and his main point of contact with modern psychology.

I limit myself here to presenting an overview of seven of the most basic points of contact between the conceptual structure of Freud's theory and that of contemporary psychology: (a) the use of intentionality (i.e., mental representation) as the ultimate unit of analysis in psychology and a view of the mind as a system of dynamically interacting intentional states; (b) the argument for the existence of unconscious mental states and the concomitant shift of the focus of psychology from consciousness to conscious and unconscious mental representations; (c) the account of motivation within a cognitivist framework, in which motivation is conceptualized as a causal property of ideas; (d) the account of emotion within a cognitivist framework, in which emotions are conceptualized as cognitions combined with bodily feeling, with the latter being intentionalistically interpreted as perceptual representation of the body; (e) the acceptance of the "modularity of mind" and a rejection of the traditional view of the mind as a unified and inherently integrated entity; (f) the vision of what a complete explanation of a person's behavior must involve, including the integration of intentional, trait, and biological levels of personality explanation; and (g) the emphasis on the importance of intentional self-manipulation of cognitions, as in defense processes. I do not address issues concerning the content of Freud's theory, such as the sexual theory of the neuroses, the theory of sexual component instincts, specific developmental stages including the oedipal stage, the meaning of psychic symbolism, the theory of dreams, and so on. Other recent works have focused on various theoretical doctrines shared by psychoanalysis and cognitive psychology and the empirical evidence for these doctrines (e.g., Erdelyi, 1985; Henle, 1984; Horowitz, 1988; Singer, 1990). The comparison presented in this chapter is distinguished by its greater emphasis on the conceptual level. In looking at the interface between Freud and modern psychology, my concern is for logical connections rather than for demonstrable historical influence. Finally, my goal is to present a summary of some of the results of an ongoing conceptual research program into Freud's theory, the details of which are reported elsewhere (e.g., Wakefield, 1989, 1990b, 1990c, 1991, 1992a, 1992b). I do not attempt to exhaustively argue for the claims made here.

INTENTIONALITY, OR MENTAL REPRESENTATIONS, AS THE ULTIMATE ELEMENTS OF THE MIND

Freud called his new science "psycho-analysis." But what are the units into which the psyche is to be analyzed? Freud's answer, I think, is that the mind is ultimately composed of and is to be analyzed into intentional states or, what is equivalent in Freud's tradition, mental representations, which interact with each other according to associative principles (Wakefield, 1992a, 1992b).

Intentionality refers to the way in which mental states, in virtue of their structure, are intrinsically directed at some real or possible objects or states of affairs (Brentano, 1874/1973; Searle, 1983). For example, a belief is always a belief that something is the case, a desire is always a desire for something, and a fear is always a fear of something. The standard account of how mental states can be directed in this way is that they consist in part of representations of their objects. For example, beliefs, desires, and fears involve mental representations of what is believed to be true, desired, or feared, respectively. Just like cognitive psychologists today, Freud emphasized representations in the form of thoughts and mental images, which represent states of affairs in the world through their pictorial or grammatical structures, respectively, analogous to nonmental pictorial or linguistic representations (Freud, 1923/1957c; Kosslyn, 1980; Paivio, 1986; Rollins, 1989). There presumably are other kinds of mental representational systems in addition to those generating images and thoughts, such as the kinesthetic sensations that represent bodily states and orientations (see the discussion of emotions). However, to whatever degree the brain's representational systems are analogous to the nonmental kinds that are known, it is assumed by the cognitive approach that some form of representation is necessary for a state to be directed at an object.

The representation is said to provide the *content* of the intentional state, and the thing or state of affairs in the outside world at which a mental state is directed via its content is the *object* of the mental state (hence "object relations"). The kind of relationship the person has to the object via the representation, such as one of belief, desire, or fear, is often called the *mode* of the intentional state. Freud's case histories can be conceptualized as analyses of the changing contents, objects, and modes of a person's intentional states over time.

A degree of confusion is engendered by the fact that there are two senses in which *intentionality* is commonly used in the philosophical psychology literature. One use, as discussed earlier, is to refer to a variety of mental states that represent or are directed at states of affairs outside of themselves, including beliefs, desires, and emotions. This is the sense in which I use the term here. A second use is to refer to the intention with which an action is performed, as when one says that a person "intended to do such-and-such." An intention is a specific mental state and is itself an instance of intentionality in the first sense because an intention involves a representation of the goal of the action. However, this more specific sense, in which intentionality refers to the purpose with which an action is performed, should not be confused with the broader notion used in this chapter of intentionality as representationality.

The idea that the mind consists of a system of mental representations is arguably the currently received view in academic psychology and related fields. As a glance at the titles of cognitive science books demonstrates (e.g., Brand & Harnish, 1986; Chomsky, 1980; Fodor, 1981; Paivio, 1986; Putnam, 1988), mental representation is certainly the core concept of that influential discipline. Indeed, Gardner (1985), in his history of cognitive science, stated that "to my mind, the major accomplishment of cognitive science has been the clear demonstration of the validity of positing a level of mental representation" (p. 112). So, in acknowledging the centrality of representationality in any account of the mind, Freud was being thoroughly modern. And, in insisting that an ultimate understanding of an individual would involve a detailed mapping of the person's intentional system, Freud was perhaps ahead of contemporary approaches to idiographic analysis. Freud was also much more clearheaded than his current "hermeneutic" interpreters, who claim that psychoanalysis is about the construction of a useful interpretation of the meanings of a patient's behavior (for a review and critique of hermeneutic approaches to Freud, see Grunbaum, 1984). Like modern cognitivists, Freud was a staunch realist who believed that there is a truth about what representations, and therefore meanings, are in the patient's mind and are causing the patient's behavior. For Freud, the task of the psychologist is not just the construction of something useful but the discovery of the truth about the representations in the mind (Mackay, 1989).

The argument for placing the concept of intentionality at the heart of Freud's account of the mind must be indirect because Freud never explained exactly what he considered to be the essence of the mental. This lack of explicitness in itself is perhaps a reason to attribute to Freud the standard view of his time that mental states are representations because this is the only view that would have been so obvious and natural in Freud's context that Freud would not have felt the need to state it directly. However, there are several other, more positive reasons to agree with the several influential analysts of Freud's theory (e.g., Gill, 1976, 1983; Holt, 1976, 1989; Klein, 1976a, 1976b), who have concluded that Freud's approach is best understood as a theory of the dynamic interaction among intentional states.

For one thing, Freud was a student of the philosopher Franz Brentano (Barclay, 1964; Merlan, 1945, 1949), who systematically formulated the theory of intentionality as a theory of the mental. Moreover, Freud's term *Vorstellung*, translated as "idea," for the type of mental state with which he was mainly concerned, comes directly from the philosophical tradition of which Freud was a part and refers to precisely the kinds of mental representations that the theory of intentionality encompasses. "Idea" does not, however, encompass all mental states; perception and willing, for example, are not types of ideas in Freud's vocabulary. However, all of the kinds of mental states that Freud mentioned, with the possible exception of affects (see the discussion of emotion), clearly involve representations and are intentional; for example, perception involves a perceptual presentation that represents whatever is perceived, and willing involves an intention that represents whatever action is willed (Searle, 1983).

Perhaps the most convincing reason for believing that Freud was an intentionalist is that intentionalism seems to play a critical role in Freud's overall theoretical argument. The most fundamental objection to Freud's theory by the psychologists of his time was that what Freud called "unconscious mental states" are really only nonconscious physiological states that interact with consciousness.[1] Freud could parry this objection most effectively by strictly adhering to an intentional criterion for the mental because there are plausible arguments both that intentional states are mental and that they are capable of being outside of awareness. Briefly, mental representations refer to objects outside themselves and so appear to have meaning, which provides plausibility to the claim that they are mental, and representationality appears to be potentially independent of consciousness because a representational structure can be instantiated in brain tissue even when outside of awareness, just as it is instantiated in other kinds of physical structures outside of awareness, such as a sentence in a book or a painting in a vault. Whether these arguments ultimately succeed, they have strong prima facie appeal and make an arguable case for the possibility of unconscious mental states that has convinced many other intentionality theorists. Moreover, there are few if any other plausible ways to defend the notion of unconscious mentation from the physicalist. So, intentionalism is essential to the plausibility of Freud's project.

Moreover, there are several puzzles about Freud's theory that seem to be resolvable only by an intentionalistic interpretation. The best example is Freud's surprising position that neither instinctual impulses nor affects can be literally unconscious (Freud, 1915/1957b, 1923/1957c; Wakefield, 1990b, 1990c, 1991). As will be seen in later sections, it is possible to make sense of these uncharacteristic concessions to Cartesianism if it is assumed that Freud's criterion for the mental is intentionality. Instinctual impulses and nonconscious emotional processes, as they were understood by Freud, are nonintentional; in this regard, they are unlike nonconscious ideational processes, which are representational and thus were accepted by Freud as unconscious mental states.

There are, of course, dangers and limits in the intentional approach. For one thing, it is easy to erroneously attribute internal representations and meanings to people on the basis of the

---

[1]Note that when I say "physiological," I mean sheerly physiological, that is, physiological and not also mental. Presumably, all mental states are also, at another level of description, physiological, but not all brain physiological states are also mental.

outcomes of their actions, even when in fact the outcomes do not express preexisting intentions. For example, the notion that some women's failure to achieve success shows that they have a fear of success, or the notion that a person's repeated pain and suffering in several marriages shows that he or she has a desire to suffer, are instances in which psychologists are perhaps too facile in attributing intentional states on the basis of outcomes. As Moore (1983) pointed out, Freud sometimes attributed intentions to the person that in reality are probably biological functions, such as his claim that people intentionally dream in order to keep themselves from awakening. (See the section on the components of psychological explanation for a further discussion of the confusion of functionality and intentionality.)

A deeper problem is that much of the working of the mental system is contained in the ways that the representations are connected and processed rather than in the representational contents themselves. The distinction between intentional contents and processing principles is often blurred or left ambiguous, as in talk of defenses (Gillett, 1987). Many phenomenologically oriented thinkers, such as Heidegger (1962), Merleau-Ponty (1962), and Searle (1983), have argued that a large portion of what should be called "meaning" is contained in the background principles by which the mind functions rather than in explicit mental representations, so that the mental might be argued to go beyond the representational (for reviews of these arguments, see Dreyfus & Wakefield, 1988; Wakefield, 1988; Wakefield & Dreyfus, 1991). Rather than entering into these complex issues, suffice it to say that Freud's approach, which heavily emphasizes intentional states as the medium of meaning, remains the one favored by contemporary cognitivists.

THE EXISTENCE OF UNCONSCIOUS MENTAL STATES

Freud accepted the traditional view that intentionality is the essence of the mental. However, Freud deviated from that tradition in one basic way: He insisted that intentional states can be unconscious. Indeed, it is arguable that Freud's greatest contribution to modern psychology is the separation of intentionality from consciousness.

Brentano (1874/1973) also equated intentionality with the mental, but, being a Cartesian, he considered his theory of intentionality to be an account of the essence of consciousness, and so he thought that consciousness and intentionality are identical. He reasoned that, whereas consciousness always involves consciousness "of" something and therefore is intrinsically directed at an object, a purely physical state cannot be intrinsically "about" or "directed at" anything. According to the Cartesian tradition of which Brentano was the culmination, the representational essence of intentional states is realized in the state's conscious phenomenology, that is, in the structure of the experience of images and thoughts that do the representing. So, consciousness, intentionality, and mental representation all come to the same thing in the traditional view. Anything not conscious would, on this account, be a mere brain state and not a mental state or an intentional state, no matter how complex it might be and no matter what its causal influence on mental (i.e., conscious) states.

By contrast, Freud argued for the thesis that has now become routinely accepted in cognitive science, and indeed might be considered the foundation stone on which cognitive psychology rests, that representationality can be realized in nonconscious brain structures and that, therefore, there can be mental states that are not conscious. These states are mental in virtue of their being genuine representations, and they are representational in virtue of their being structured so as to represent and thus refer to outside objects. Just like sentences in a book on the shelf, or paintings stored in a vault, representational states need not be consciously accessed for them to be true representations, according to this line of argument. Contemporary intentionalists follow Freud in rejecting Brentano's (1874/1973) consciousness criterion and assuming that intentional states can be unconscious. They, too, analyze the mind as a system of interacting conscious and unconscious mental representations.

If one puts together the first thesis, that the mental is the representational, and this second thesis, that unconscious mental states exist, one gets the thesis that the mental encompasses conscious and unconscious representations. Indeed, Freud is the pivotal figure in nothing less than the transformation of psychology from a science of consciousness to a science of conscious and unconscious mental representations.

One hundred years ago, psychology was by and large the science of consciousness. Most eminent psychologists, as well as most philosophers, held quite explicitly that "consciousness" and "mental" refer to the same things. Both James (1890) and Brentano (1874/1973), perhaps the greatest philosophical psychologists at the time in America and Europe, respectively, devoted entire chapters in their major works to showing that unconscious mental states are an impossibility and even an absurdity. James (1890) for example, titled a section of his *Principles of Psychology*, "Do Unconscious Mental States Exist," and, after reviewing and rejecting all of the arguments known to him for the existence of such states, answered his question with a resounding no.

It is truly remarkable that, a century later, psychology is hardly at all concerned with consciousness. The focus now, manifested in the "cognitive revolution " (Baars, 1986), is on mental representation (i.e., on the way that internal brain states represent or model external states of affairs and how those representations function to organize behavior, sustain reasoning, trigger affects, etc.). As Mandler (1988) put it, "theoretical cognitive psychology of the past quarter century—in contrast to the psychologies of the nineteenth century—has assumed the dominance of unconscious processes in the explanation of thought and action" (p. 21). Of course, theories change with time, and the concerns of one era may not be the concerns of another. However, the change that has overtaken psychology in the past century, for which Freud argued most persuasively, is of a different magnitude than most changes of theory or focus; it is a change in what is considered to be the basic subject matter of psychology.

Of course, it is now understood that Freud did not "discover" the unconscious (Ellenberger, 1970; Whyte, 1960); rather, he is one in a long line of thinkers who postulated unconscious mental states. Nonetheless, Freud played a critical role in the transformation of psychology from a science of consciousness to a science of mental representations because he offered the most sustained, systematic, and persuasive argument for the change. In fact, I believe that Freud's argument for the existence of unconscious mental states, when suitably reconstructed in modern terms, is exactly the same as the argument that underlies the claims of modern cognitivists that in studying nonconscious representations, they are studying the ultimate constituents of the mind (Wakefield, 1992b).

What is the argument for the existence of unconscious mental states? The full analysis and assessment of that argument requires a book to itself (Wakefield, 1992b). But, briefly, the argument consists of three components. The first is the conceptual point that the definition of the term *mental* does not require that mental states be conscious; that is, *mental* does not mean *conscious*. To show this requires an account of how concepts such as "mental" work. Freud pursued this line of argument in scattered remarks in which he attacked the die-hard Cartesian who would insist that *conscious* is the definition of *mental*. I believe that Freud's critical point here is that the Cartesian must be considered to be putting forward a scientific proposal that consciousness constitutes the essence of the mental and that this essentialistic hypothesis cannot be equated with the meaning of the word *mental*. To understand Freud's point, consider analogous claims such as, say, that "H_2O" is the essence of water or "electron motion" is the essence of electricity. Recent work in the philosophy of language (e.g., Kripke, 1980; Putnam, 1975; Searle, 1983) supports the drawing of a sharp distinction between the meaning of a natural kind term and the essence of the natural kind referred to by the term. As Freud noted, scientists define a theoretical term, such as *water* or *electricity*, by reference to empirical phenomena, usually without knowing the underlying essence of the phenomena. Scientific inquiry often proceeds for years and sometimes for centuries before the essence is discovered; for example, Aristotle, being familiar with rivers, lakes, and so on, understood the meaning of the Greek word for water, even though the essence of water—the molecular structure H_2O—was not known until centuries later. So, the specific essence cannot be part of the meaning of the word. Even today, if scientists found that they had been wrong about the molecular structure of the clear liquid in the rivers and lakes, they would not say that they had discovered that water does not exist, which is what they would have to say if *water* literally meant "H_2O." But they would say that they had discovered that water is not H_2O after all. This shows that, whatever the meaning of water, it is not "H_2O."

The critical distinction between the definition of a scientific term and the essence of the things referred to by the term has only recently been illuminated by philosophers of language (Kripke, 1980; Putnam, 1975; Searle, 1983). Freud never stated the point in so many words, but his arguments and examples show that he implicitly understood this point and argued accordingly. For Freud, *mental* is defined by reference to obvious phenomena such as conscious beliefs, desires, and emotions, and not by reference to a sophisticated theoretical term such as consciousness (or intentionality). He considered himself and the Cartesians to be involved not in a semantic dispute but in the common scientific pursuit of an adequate theory of the essence of the mental, about which there are two hypotheses. Both sides in the dispute agreed on the meaning of mental; the mental encompasses the agreed cases of conscious beliefs, desires, perceptions, emotions, and volitions, as well as any other states that have the same underlying essence as these agreed initial examples of mental states. Thus, the answer to the question of whether mental states can be unconscious depends on the nature of the essence of the mental and whether things with that essence can be unconscious. These are factual, not semantic, issues. Analogously, the fact that the substance term *water* was originally defined relative to the clear liquid in lakes and rivers says nothing about whether water can take the form of a white solid. The substance water consists of the initial agreed example of the clear liquid in the lakes and rivers, plus anything else that possesses the same underlying essence as the intiial agreed example. As it turns out, the same underlying essence can express itself in a form that is white and solid, namely, snow, so water can indeed be a white solid. This is a theoretical discovery about the forms that an essence can take, not a conceptual or semantic decision. Freud could thus successfully fend off the Cartesian who argues that his thesis is conceptually impossible by placing the question back in the scientific theoretical domain where it belongs, as an issue about essences and their manifestations. In taking this essentialist stance, Freud demonstrated a sophistication about the nature of scientific concepts that is thoroughly modern. (For a fuller presentation of the theory of concepts used in the preceding analysis and documentation of Freud's reliance on such a theory, see Wakefield, 1992b.)

Second, if unconscious mentation is not conceptually excluded, then one must establish whether it is theoretically possible. This requires an account of the essence of the mental and an argument that things with that essence can (or cannot) be unconscious. I have already indicated Freud's position here. He thought that the tradition is right that the essence of the mental is representationality of brain states. However, whereas the tradition assumes that it is consciousness itself that confers representationality on the mental, Freud assumed (he did not really present an argument for this point and neither do contemporary cognitive scientists who adopt essentially the same position) that representationality is a property that can apply to nonconscious brain states as well, just as it can to various things such as pictures and sentences. Thus, although the entities that allow one to identify and name the mental in the first place are conscious, the essence of those entities is such that the very same essence can manifest itself in nonconscious brain states as well, which therefore are unconscious mental states.

If Freud were to say that the essence of the mental is representationality and the Cartesian were to say that it is consciousness, then how is one to judge between the two claims? The postulation of an essence is in large part the postulation of an underlying cause of the manifest phenomena by which the category was picked out in the first place. Thus, for example, the motion of electrons is the essence of electricity because the phenomena that were used in naming electricity (e.g., the behavior of cat fur when rubbed, the sparks thrown off by amber, etc.) are ultimately explainable by the underlying phenomenon of electron motion. Once electron motion was established as the essence of the specified phenomena, any further phenomena that happen to have the same essence could be legitimately categorized as electricity. Even when the essence was unknown, a phenomenon could be discovered to belong under the category *electricity* on the basis of indirect evidence that the new phenomenon shares the same essence with the original phenomena; the critical thing is that there be a shared essence, not that the essence be known. For example, Benjamin Franklin was able to provide support for his claim that lightning is a form of electricity without knowing the essence of electricity because his experiments showed that the underlying process that explains lightning is probably the same as the underlying process that explains paradigmatic electrical phenomena. Franklin was right in this conjecture because lightning is indeed essentially electron motion. Similarly, ice has the same molecular structure as liquid water, and so it is the same substance because the molecular structure is the underlying factor that explains the manifest nature of paradigmatic samples of liquid water. However, it was known that ice is the same substance as water long before an understanding of molecular theory because the available evidence (e.g., observations of the processes of freezing and thawing) strongly suggested that ice and liquid water are two forms of the same underlying "stuff."

Analogously, to establish the essence of the mental, one must identify the underlying features that explain the most salient and interesting properties of the phenomena initially labeled *mental*. It was Freud's implicit notion, and it is the explicit notion of most cognitive scientists today, that the relevant explanatory factor is the representational structure of brain states, quite independent of the conscious or nonconscious status of the state. That is, the processing rules that operate on mental states act on the representational structure of the states as realized in brain tissue. Consciousness is just one way that representational structure can be realized (in addition to nonconscious representations in brain tissue), and even then it is the representational content of the conscious state that determines how the state is processed. If something like this argument is correct, then representational structure, and not consciousness, is the essence of the mental, and mental states can perhaps be unconscious. Even though *mental* is defined by reference to conscious states—a state is mental if and only if it is either a conscious belief, desire, emotion, perception, volition, and so forth, or any state that is like these states with respect to their underlying essence, whatever that essence may be—nonetheless, the definition is such that it allows for the theoretical possibility that nonconscious states could be mental, if they have the same representational essence as the conscious states.

Of course, although Freud might have implicitly and provisionally assumed, like cognitivists, that representationality of some sort is the essence of the mental, he understood that a real answer to the question of the essence would require a detailed specification of the nature of the brain's representational system. In that sense, neither Freud nor modern cognitivists really claim to know the essence of the mental.

The essentialistic interpretation of Freud's position that I have just outlined was perhaps most clearly confirmed by Freud at the end of his life, in the following passage:

If someone asks what the psychical really means, it is easy to reply by enumerating its constituents: our perceptions, ideas, memories, feelings, and acts of volition—all these form part of what is psychical. But if the questionner goes further and asks whether there is not some common quality possessed by all these processes which makes it possible to get nearer to the *nature*, or, as people sometimes say, the *essence* of the psychical, then it is harder to give an answer.

If an analogous question had been put to a physicist (as to the nature of electricity, for instance), his reply, until quite recently, would have been: For the purpose of explaining certain phenomena, we assume the existence of electrical forces which are present in things and emanate from them. We study these phenomena, discover the laws that govern them and even put them to practical use. This satisfies us provisionally. We do not know the *nature* of electricity. Perhaps we may discover it later, as our work goes on. It must be admitted that what we are ignorant of is precisely the most important and interesting part of the whole business, but for the moment that does not worry us. It is simply how things happen in the natural sciences.

Psychology, too, is a natural science. (Freud, 1940/1964, p. 282)

In this passage one can see all of the elements of the essentialistic approach that I described earlier. The initial definition of "mental" is in terms of agreed examples, all presumably conscious, of mental states such as perceptions, feelings, ideas, and so on. That allows one to define the class of "the mental" in terms of known agreed examples. However, the specified states are said to form only "part of what is psychical," and one might take this as an indication that the definition of *mental* includes not only the specified known phenomena but also any other phenomena of the same kind, including any that are similar to the specified phenomena in essential nature. Freud sharply distinguished the general definition of *mental* in terms of such examples from the nature or essence of the things that are mental, which is not a matter of semantics but a subject of research and theory. He compared the essence of the mental in these respects to the essence of electricity. Obviously, one cannot pursue research or theory about the mental or the electrical without knowing the meanings of the respective terms, but, as Freud pointed out, one can pursue research and theory without knowing the essence. Freud displayed here a remarkably sophisticated and modern understanding of how science and scientific concepts work, and of the distinction between meaning and essence. No modern cognitivist could improve on this succinct description of the situation with respect to the meaning and essence of the mental.

The third step in the argument for unconscious mental states is to establish that such states are not only conceptually and theoretically possible but actually exist. For Freud, this would involve using the available empirical evidence to show that representationally structured nonconscious brain states are interacting with conscious states. Note that without the conceptual and theoretical arguments, the empirical evidence could be dismissed by opponents as simply showing that there are complex nonconscious and nonmental physiological states that interact with mental (i.e., conscious) states. Thus, the empirical argument, to which Freud devoted the most attention, is only relevant if the conceptual and theoretical points have been established. Freud's case histories constituted long arguments for the necessity of postulating nonconscious representations to explain the manifest thought and behavior of the patient.

Freud reduced the role of consciousness to that of an epistemological tool for knowing about a certain class of one's mental states, removing all ontological implications. This is a momentous choice. The evidence available in Freud's time strongly suggested to many psychologists that some mental states are outside of awareness. To accommodate these data, something in traditional Cartesianism had to be rejected because two fundamental Cartesian principles about consciousness, one ontological and the other epistemological, together imply that all mental states must be conscious. The ontological principle is that consciousness is the essence of, and therefore equivalent to, the mental; the epistemological principle is that all conscious states are accessible to awareness. Freud chose to reject the former principle but he retained the latter. He thus continued to insist that consciousness and awareness are equivalent but that the mental extends beyond the conscious and aware. Other thinkers took the alternative route. For example, James (1890) retained the ontological principle that consciousness is the essence of the mental and that all mental states must therefore be conscious, but, faced with the same data as Freud, James opted to reject the Cartesian epistemological principle that all conscious states are accessible to awareness. Thus, James accommodated the anomalous data via such concepts as split-off, dissociated, or secondary consciousness, that is, by claiming that there are conscious mental states (as opposed to Freud's unconscious mental states) that are nonetheless not accessible to awareness. Freud vigorously rejected the notion of a second consciousness, dismissing his opponents by noting that anyone who objected to the notion of unconscious mental states certainly ought to object to the notion of unconscious (i.e., out of awareness) conscious mental states. Of the two thinkers, it is clearly Freud whose choices represent the path to mainstream modern psychology. However, it is also true that recent work on dissociation (Hilgard, 1977; also see various articles in Singer, 1990) and "split-brain" phenomena (Sperry, 1968) suggests that a compromise between Freud's and James's responses to the anomalies in Cartesianism may yet be forged.

The demotion of consciousness to a purely epistemological role leads to a serious failure, both by Freud and contemporary psychology, to come to grips with the centrality of consciousness for the study of meaning and the mental. If the essence of the mental makes no reference to consciousness, then, in principle, minds could exist without consciousness, and this implication, apparently accepted by Freud, seems to me to be problematic. In the transformation of psychology from a science of consciousness to a science of mental representations, there has certainly been a gain in theoretical power, but there may also have been a loss of something of great value. Psychologists may, in effect, be avoiding the problem that made the mental so puzzling in the first place, the problem of consciousness, and thereby ignoring the mystery that is at the heart of the nature of meaning and mind.

HOW TO INTEGRATE MOTIVATION INTO COGNITIVISM

If the mind is a system of interacting intentional states, then how does motivation come into the picture? The problem of motivation is one that bedevils contemporary cognitive approaches. I argue that Freud provided a very modern and perhaps still the most elegant solution to the problem of how to conceptualize motivation within a systematic cognitive psychology (Wakefield, 1990b, 1990c). It is a solution that, I think, potentially provides a common framework for the formulation of different and even opposed theories of motivation, including those of object relations theorists and others within psychoanalytic theory who reject Freud's instinct theory, as well as nonpsychoanalytic accounts.

Cognitive accounts of the mind tend to focus on the processing of evidential, logical, deductive, inductive, associative, means–end, and other such relationships among representations. Perception and memory can be considered inputs to the flow of mentation that provide additional premises from which the inferential engine that constitutes the mind can derive new propositions. Cognitivists typically link all of this thought to action via Davidson's (1963) account of action as "behavior caused by reasons." That is, cognitions cause people to act to accomplish their goals. However, even on Davidson's account, a belief *and* a desire are necessary to cause action. Each person has many beliefs about what he or she could accomplish by performing various actions; the desire is necessary to explain why the person acts on one belief rather than on another.

However, what is a desire on a cognitivist approach? This question poses a seeming dilemma for the cognitivist. If a desire is held to be just another idea, that would be a thoroughly cognitivist approach, but it would explain nothing because the whole point about desire is that it activates the organism in a way that beliefs alone do not. That is why desires need to be added to beliefs in the standard model. But, if the desire is more than just a cognition, this would seem to imply that there are basic constituents of the mind that are not cognitions, which would undermine the cognitivist vision of the mind as a system of cognitions.

The way out of this dilemma is to interpret desire as some special property of representations. This allows the cognitivist to retain the claim that the mind is a system of representations while also allowing for some difference between desires and other cognitions that do not have the special motivational properties. The problem, then, is to specify the kind of property that makes an idea a desire.

The most obvious way that cognitions differ is in their content; they represent different states of affairs. So, one possible suggestion is that a desire is just a cognition with a certain content. For example, the more harmful a potential outcome is believed to be, the more a person desires to avoid that outcome. Thus, one might identify the intensity of desire with certain features of the representational content of cognitions.

Certainly, the representational content of cognitions is critical in causing desire, but as a systematic account of desire itself, this "content" approach will not work. For one thing, it merely pushes the puzzle back a step; what is it about a certain content that makes it a motivation rather than just another content? The content approach identifies certain contents that are correlated with desire, but it does not capture the nature of the force of desire, nor does it account for the fact that the very same content might be provocative of desire in one context but not in another. For example, the very same belief that there is water nearby might be motivationally activating in a thirsty person, but not in a person whose thirst has been slaked. So, a content account of motivation cannot be adequate.

Cognitions have properties that go beyond whatever is contained in their content. Many of these properties have to do with the causal powers possessed by the cognition as a result of the processing principles that operate on cognitions and are rooted in the structure of the brain. For example, the power of an idea to cause the occurrence of an idea with similar content—that is, the power of the idea to initiate a process of association by similarity—is a property of the idea that goes beyond the sheer content of the idea. Nothing in the content itself can tell one that when the idea becomes activated, it is likely to cause a similar idea to become activated. This causal property of the idea is due to the associative architecture of the brain and the consequent causal laws regulating transitions in ideational activation. Such powers are properties of ideas that are not contained in the content of the idea itself. Analogously, the kinetic force of a moving object is a property of the object, even though it appears nowhere in the material structure of the object.

Given that ideas do have properties that are not reducible to their content, one may suppose that it is just such causal properties (sometimes called "functional" properties) that make a desire a desire and a belief a belief. Obviously, most of the dynamic properties of an idea are sensitive to and constrained by the specific representational content of the idea (e.g., the content determines what logical or means–end reasoning the idea can enter into), but the dynamic transitions themselves involve processing principles that are more than mere features of the representational content. For example, logical transitions from premises to conclusions, means–end reasoning about instrumental action, and associational transitions according to similarity are all sensitive to the representational content of the relevant ideas, but they are all causal processes that go beyond a sheer description of the content because they involve the power possessed by an idea to cause the activation of certain other kinds of ideas.

This way of thinking about associative and inferential dynamics can be generalized to motivational factors. Thus, rather than accounting for motivation by adding noncognitive mental states to the furniture of the mind, the cognitivist instead might try to elaborate on the possible sorts of dynamic interactions in which cognitions are involved. I believe that something very much like this is what Freud (1915/1957a) had in mind in his classic account of instinctual impulses, where he described the "pressure" or "demand for work" of instinctual impulses as "their very essence" (p. 122). Freud's terms can be easily construed to be a description of the causal powers by which the impulse induces various sorts of mental transitions and reactions (Wakefield, 1990b, 1990c). For example, exactly the same idea of water may be more or less active (i.e., may exert more or less pressure and demand more or less work) depending on the bodily state with respect to hydration, so the content of the idea, which is the same, is not what determines the causal powers or the intensity of the activity. Rather, one might argue, the idea takes on new dynamic properties depending on other factors, such as the relation of the idea to bodily processes that make it more or less salient. These new properties include new causal relations of the idea to other ideas, to emotion, and to action. In sum, when one is thirsty, the idea of water takes on entirely new causal properties than when one is not thirsty, and that is the essence of the instinctual impulse of thirst. The acquisition of such causal powers is what Freud had in mind when he wrote of the "cathexis" of an idea by instinct. Seen in this way, the technical concept of cathexis is not, as many have claimed, rooted primarily in outmoded 19th-century biology but is a formalization of the commonsense notion of the intensity of desire. And, the preservation of cathectic energy across transformations is also rooted in a commonsense understanding that motivational powers are communicated from idea to idea under a variety of circumstances; for example, "to desire the end is to desire the means" is a thesis about what is technically an energic transformation.

Freud's strategy for incorporating motivation into a cognitive account of the mind is certainly an elegant solution to the cognitivist's problem. The mind's contents are still considered to be composed sheerly of cognitions, but the cognitivist allows that these cognitions causally interact with each other according to various dynamic properties. The existence of such properties is no challenge to the cognitivist approach because it introduces no mental entities into the mind other than representations. Just as the existence of the force of gravitation in Newtonian mechanics is no counterexample to the thesis that everything in the world is atoms and void, because it is obvious that the atoms must interact according to some "operating principles" that are not themselves additional things in the world, so the existence of changing dynamic properties of ideas due, for example, to changing bodily conditions, does not violate the cognitivist's claim that all mental states are representations. It is a certain class of such changes in the causal properties of ideas that Freud called "instinctual impulses."

The conceptual structure of Freud's account of instinctual impulses can be separated from the theoretical details of his proposals regarding the nature of instincts (e.g., that they constantly build up tension) and his hypotheses regarding their contents (e.g., instincts relevant to psycho-pathology are generally sexual). Once this separation is accomplished, Freud's approach stands as a comprehensive framework within which not only the cognitivist, but also other non-Freudian psychoanalytic theories of motivation such as those presented by object relations theorists, can be incorporated into a thoroughly representational approach to the mind. In his approach to motivation, Freud came closest to being what in modern terminology is called a "functionalist," that is, he conceptualized motivation as consisting sheerly of the functional/causal relationships between mental representations, just as do modern functionalist theoreticians within cognitive science. Thus, his conceptual framework can in principle be applied to any motivational contents that a theory might demand and not just to the bodily sexual tensions that Freud made so basic in his own theory.

There is a strong piece of evidence that Freud did indeed conceptualize motivation as functional causal properties of ideas. In "The Unconscious," Freud (1915/1957b) explicitly asserted that instinctual impulses cannot be unconscious and even that they cannot properly be said to be conscious. This surprising statement makes perfect sense if what Freud meant is that instinctual impulses are not themselves mental contents of any sort, and thus cannot literally be conscious or unconscious, because the latter terms are reserved for the contents of the mind. Freud also noted that if instinctual impulses were not attached to ideas, one would never know of their existence, and this, again, fits well with the view that Freud was asserting that instincts are properties of ideas and not a further noncognitive kind of mental state that can exist independently of ideas.

It can be seen that if this reading of Freud is correct, then the common accusation that Freud "reified" psychic energy into an additional thing in the mind is questionable. It is true that Freud did identify causal chains in which the causal forces of ideas are preserved through various transformations of intentional content and mode, and the causal force that is preserved through those transformations he reasonably enough decided to label *energy*. However, Freud's detractors have claimed to see greater excesses of reification than are actually implied in Freud's most careful theoretical formulations. *Energy* refers to no more than the changing powers of ideas to cause other ideas, emotions, and actions, and to the communication of these powers in mental transformations (Klein, 1967).

EMOTION AS COGNITION PLUS PERCEPTION OF BODILY AROUSAL

Just as motivation is a thorn in the cognitivist's side, so also is emotion because emotion, too, seems to consist of elements that go beyond cognition. Although emotion, like motivation, is commonly "attached" to an idea and is arguably in part a form of motivational energy, the strategy that worked to deal with motivation from a cognitive perspective cannot simply be transferred to emotion. This is because emotion, in addition to its cognitive and motivational elements, also consists of feeling. That is, apart from, say, the belief that there is danger and the desire to avoid it, there is also an experience of a feeling of fear that is not identical to either of the other two components. Understanding this sort of feeling poses the greatest challenge to the cognitivist view of emotion. Here, again, Freud hit on a remarkably contemporary and insightful strategy for incorporating emotion within the cognitive worldview (Wakefield, 1991, 1992a).

The feeling involved in an emotion is not itself just another belief of the kind that typically occurs in an emotional episode, such as the belief that there are snakes nearby or the belief that snakes bite, which occur during an episode of snake phobia. The distinction between such cognitions and the feeling they engender is seen most clearly in cases in which the feeling exists by itself without the cognition, as in cases of free-floating anxiety, a feeling with which both Freud and modern clinical psychologists are much concerned. The problem for the cognitivist is that such anxiety does not seem to be about anything or to be a representation of anything. So, prima facie, emotions are a counterexample to the representationalist account of the mind.

The solution to the cognitivist puzzle of emotion has two steps. First, it can be argued that everything except the feeling in an emotional experience is simply cognition, along with motivational properties of the cognition. Fear involves a belief in impending harm or danger and the motivational properties of such beliefs; guilt involves a belief that one has transgressed and the associated motivational properties; and so on. The rest of an emotion, it might be argued, is bodily feeling and not really mental at all. This approach to the relation between cognition and emotion was taken, for example, by Schachter and Singer (1962) in their classic studies that were instrumental in putting a cognitive spin on emotion for contemporary psychologists. Those studies claimed to show that emotion consists essentially of bodily arousal conjoined with cognition about the cause of the arousal. Similarly, other cognitivists, such as Albert Ellis (1962), who considered negative emotion to consist primarily of irrational belief (a view that goes back to the Stoic philosophers), and Richard Lazarus (see Lazarus, Averill, & Opton, 1970), who asserted that emotion is essentially an evaluative judgment, attempt to explain emotion as essentially a variant of cognition, perhaps conjoined with some other bodily (i.e., nonmental) element. This emphasis on the cognitive component in emotion has become standard in the field (e.g., Ortony, Clore, & Collins, 1988). So, what is mental about emotion is cognition according to this approach.

Freud, too, took the "cognition plus bodily arousal" approach to emotion. However, Freud saw what many other cognitivists did not: that identifying emotions in terms of the cognitions by which they are typically triggered does not fully answer the cognitivist's question about emotion. As noted earlier, some feelings occur without cognitions obviously attached, and feelings are certainly an identifiable and separate component. In addition, the common notion that the feeling component can be dismissed as bodily and therefore as not mental (and, consequently, as not a challenge to cognitivism) is misguided because surely free-floating anxiety is as "mental" as anything can be. Thus, Freud, more explicitly than most cognitive theoreticians, squarely faced the puzzling question of how to account for feeling within a representationalist framework. And he succeeded in giving a remarkably plausible and modern account of why such feelings should be considered representational.

The second step taken by Freud in conceptualizing emotion was to argue that the "bodily" component is best considered a perceptual representation of the body and so is as representational as, say, the perception of a chair. The difference is that the systems that represent the inner and outer worlds are built differently and use somewhat different experiential media (e.g., colors vs. feelings) to represent their objects. However, in principle, there is nothing less representational about the representation of the inside of the body via feelings than there is about the representation of the environment via colors and shapes. For example, nausea is a kind of representation of what is going on in the digestive tract, and pain is a kind of representation of what is going on in the offending area of the body. These are very primitive representations compared with, say, visual representations, but, as Freud (1923/1957c) pointed out, they do take place within a multilocular space containing different qualities at different points in the space, and they do indicate something about the inside of the body that, as Searle (1983) noted, is part of the outside world relative to the mind. So, these experiences do, like all intentional states, refer to something outside of themselves. Emotions, then, consist of ideas, their motivational properties, and corresponding representations of bodily arousal.

The account of Freud's approach to emotion put forward here explains what is otherwise a bewildering fact: that Freud, although arguing vociferously for the existence of unconscious ideas, rejected the notion that unconscious emotions exist. According to Freud, an emotion is typically characterized by a complex of ideas, motivational energies, and bodily feelings. The idea itself can be conscious or unconscious; for example, in cases of displaced emotion, the idea often remains unconscious. But, the idea with its motivational cathexes does not constitute an emotion, which requires feeling as well. So, the question of why emotions cannot be unconscious comes down to why feeling cannot be unconscious. Here, Freud asserted that feelings, being perceptions, cannot be unconscious. It is a historical peculiarity that Freud believed that perception is by nature conscious (he is not alone here; see Searle, 1983, for a similar account of "visual presentations") and virtually never entertained the notion that a perception might literally be unconscious, whereas the exploration of unconscious processing by experimental psychologists has taken place largely within the domain of subliminal perception.

But what if the underlying bodily processes occur without the conscious perceptions of them that constitute feeling? Freud's response was that, if there is no conscious perception of bodily arousal, then there is nothing but a bodily process, so there is nothing that could be distinctively labeled a feeling. A bodily process characteristic of, say, fear, which occurs without the representational experience of the feeling of fear, is by itself no more of a mental phenomenon than, say, reverse peristalsis when it occurs unaccompanied by the feeling of nausea. Such unperceived bodily processes are in no way mental states in the required intentional–representational sense and so are not appropriately labeled as "unconscious" (as opposed to "nonconscious," which applies to all processes outside of consciousness, including sheerly physiological processes).

THE MODULARITY OF MIND

I will be very brief here because the connection between Freud and contemporary psychology in this regard is obvious and has been pointed out by many others. Starting with Socrates, there were those psychologists who argued that the mind is essentially one unified system of rational thought. And, starting with Plato, there were those who, with equal conviction, argued that the mind is a set of subagents and subprocesses that often conflict with each other, some of which can hardly be called rational. Freud stated the case elegantly for the "divided mind" view. He offered careful and persuasive accounts of how individuals who fail to integrate conflicting tendencies of motivational subunits often suffer as a result. Any evolutionist such as Freud will be drawn to the "modularity" thesis (Fodor, 1983) that the mind is composed of many different mental "organs," analogous to the body, the parts of which have evolved to fulfill distinct functions. Freud's vivid clinical accounts, and his simple yet powerful account of the divisions in the mind that can lead to fundamental conflicts, have provided a background to the current move to envision the mind as a set of competing subselves or submechanisms (Elster, 1985) and have made "integration" a central concept in contemporary psychology.

COMPONENTS OF A COMPLETE EXPLANATION OF BEHAVIOR

If one surveys personality theory today, it seems to be more like a set of competing disciplines than one area of scientific inquiry. This is because the field's disputes are not only about specific theories and empirical claims but also about the very nature of an acceptable personological explanation. One might identify at least three main schools of thought on this issue. First, the traditional personality theorist believes that personality is composed of a set of traits and that an adequate account of a person's behavior is achieved when the person is placed correctly within a set of categories or on a set of dimensions representing the person's traits. Trait theorists commonly claim that traits are simply what personality theory is about (e.g., Allport, 1961; Pervin, 1984). Second, an assortment of cognitivists, psychodynamic theorists, hermeneuticists, and action theorists believe that the explanation of a person's behavior must take the form of a specification of the representational states, or reasons, that caused the person to act. To these theorists, the personality is a system of intentional states, and an account of personality would be complete if the entire system of intentional states was specified (e.g., Baars, 1986; Erdelyi, 1985; Searle, 1983). Third, there are those who are attracted to biological explanations (e.g., Buss, 1984, 1991). These theorists point to the fact that humans, like all organisms, have evolved according to the principles of natural selection and that behavior is therefore the result of evolutionarily shaped dispositions that were adaptive in the environment within which they evolved. Thus, the argument goes, an explanation of behavior must be framed in terms of the biological functions of the behavioral mechanisms and dispositions that underlie behavior.

Freud understood that all three approaches are necessary for a full explanation of behavior and, more important, he understood how the three go together in one multilayered logical structure. First, because the mind is a set of intentional states, it stands to reason that any full explanation would include a mapping of the relevant intentional states, such as beliefs and desires and their motivational cathexes, which are involved in giving rise to behaviors targeted for explanation. The specification of such intentional states is more complex than it might seem because the states that are immediately involved in causing the behavior may be caused by yet further intentional states that, in turn, must be specified to obtain a full explanation. In the psychoanalytic literature, this complex layering of the causes of action is often discussed in terms of the layering of defenses and impulses. However, even in simple commonsense explanations of action, the explanation, if pursued in detail, often involves many layers of reasons. For example, Jack Ruby intentionally moved his finger, in order to pull the trigger (i.e., because he desired to pull the trigger and he believed that he could do so by moving his finger), in order to fire the gun, in order to shoot Lee Harvey Oswald, in order to kill Oswald, in order (if one takes him at his word) to exact revenge for the killing of John F. Kennedy. He was motivated to do all of these things, and all of them are actions that he succeeded in performing on the basis of corresponding sets of beliefs and desires, but the ones lower in the means–end hierarchy owe their existence to the ones higher up. There is growing evidence that laypeople—correctly, I think—intuitively think about personality in this layered way.

So, if one tries to explain the initial set of intentional states that explain a target behavior, the explanation can lie in further intentional states. Unfortunately, the mapping eventually becomes too difficult or too cumbersome to complete. However, there fortunately are structures in the mind that provide stable dispositions to experience certain kinds of intentional states (e.g., "talkativeness" implies a stable disposition to experience the desire to talk) and, as a second part of an overall explanation, one can include such traits as summary descriptors of the dispositions of the intentional system when one can no longer penetrate more deeply into the specific intentional states that compose the system. For example, if the person tends to desire to talk but one cannot identify the further intentional states that underlie these desires, then one can simply attribute "talkativeness" to the person as part of the explanation of an action such as talking. All such trait explanations are promissory notes for fuller descriptions in terms of the specific intentional states that make up the dispositional structure. To take another example, if the person's intentional system has a stable structure, whatever it might be, so that the person tends more than most people to perceive his or her rights as being infringed on, then one might attribute the trait "feels entitled" to the person and use that in attempting to explain specific actions in which beliefs about rights are involved, especially if no deeper understanding of the occurrence of these intentional states is available.

Traits such as talkativeness or entitlement might consist of various belief–desire pairs or other stable complexes of intentional states. Let me call traits that can be decomposed in this way "secondary traits." In principle, an explanation of the person's behavior that specified the intentional states of which the secondary trait structures are composed would be superior to an explanation that terminated in trait attributions. The reason that a full intentional mapping would provide a better explanation is that its specificity would provide more understanding and would be more predictive. For example, if a person's talkativeness turned out to be due to the person's belief that he or she is very smart and that everything he or she says is very valuable, then, if the person were to become convinced that this belief is false, that would be likely to affect the person's talkativeness; however, disconfirmation of that particular belief might not affect the trait at all if the trait were composed of other intentional components, such as the belief that talking makes other people like one and the desire to be liked. According to this account, secondary traits are not the ultimate constituents of personality but are simply a shorthand for stable dispositional properties of intentional systems. They specify dispositions of the intentional system and are convenient when one has no understanding of the more specific intentional states that support and compose the trait or when such deeper understanding is not useful. Trait descriptions often tell one little about the workings of the intentional system, but they do tell one enough to sharply narrow the range of explanations of intentional behavior.

No matter how elaborate the specification of the web of intentional states and traits underlying an action, there is eventually a limit that is reached in trying to understand the behavior in terms of intentional states. In following the linked states and traits down the causal chain, one inevitably comes to a point at which no further intentional states can be found to explain the deepest level that has been reached in the explanation of the target behavior. For example, to simplify greatly, a person's talkativeness might be explained by a libidinal tension the person experiences in the mouth and a belief that talking will relieve the tension. However, if an attempt is made to explain the trait of experiencing oral tension, one might find that there is no further mental explanation for it; the person might just possess a high level of tension in the mouth for physiological reasons that are not attributable to further mental states. Or, the tension might have come about initially because of psychological factors, but it may have become functionally autonomous so that the mental states are no longer an active part of the structure that generates the tension. Such traits may be called *basic traits*.

When one confronts a basic trait, one must identify the kinds of intentional states that are being produced by the mechanism in question as the body's basic input to the mind. Freud conceptualized all such biological inputs as "instinctual impulses" that impart energy to ideas, but presumably the types vary more than Freud imagined. Some basic desires, for instance, have nothing to do with bodily zones or component drives of the sort described by Freud; the desire to act altruistically toward children may be an example. Moreover, it is likely that, contrary to Freud's approach to the sexual drives, some motivational mechanisms have the representation of the object of the drive built into the mechanism rather than allowing it to be entirely learned through experience. Certain types of motivationally laden representations (e.g., representations of dangers such as snakes or height) may well be basic and inborn. The kinds of basic mechanisms postulated by Freud are ones in which physiological conditions in bodily erotic zones cause the motivational cathexis of various ideas. Thus, most basic traits for Freud would consist of levels of tension generated in erotic zones and the associated ideation. But whatever their content or nature, basic traits can be incorporated into a full personological explanation by specifying the exact nature of the inputs from the mechanism into the intentional system. In principle, this involves the specification of a disposition of the intentional system, just as in the case of secondary traits, but here there is no further underlying mental explanation of the intentional states that are generated.

In principle, the specification of the relevant intentional states and primary and secondary traits would provide a complete psychological explanation of a target behavior. However, there is another step concerning the basic trait level that is critical for completing the explanation of why the behavior in question occurs; the biological function of the mechanism generating the basic trait must be identified. Freud attempted to provide such functions, albeit very sketchily and in all likelihood incorrectly, through his enumeration of various sexual and ego instincts (or, later, life and death instincts). Only through a specification of the biological function of the mechanism can one understand why the mechanism exists and why it produces the sorts of inputs to the intentional system that it does and thus complete the explanation of the consequent behavior. For example, an inborn fear of snakes cannot be fully understood until one understands the danger that snakes pose and thus the survival function that the fear serves; one does not fully understand sex without understanding that one function of sexual motivation is to produce conception and reproduction; and one does not fully understand tiredness until one understands the biological function of sleep. Although a full explanation of behavior requires this biological functional level, it is also true, as Freud (1915/1957a) observed, that the selective forces that shaped the organism are not, strictly speaking, part of psychology because they involve matters that go beyond the current workings of the intentional system and thus beyond the boundary of the mind.

Freud understood a tricky point about the role of the biological functions in psychological explanation which is often missed by contemporary thinkers. Many psychologists naively move from assumptions about the biological functions of basic mechanisms to conclusions about the nature of psychological motivation. For example, Hogan (1983) moves from premises regarding the function of personality traits as biologically adaptive strategies for improving fitness, to the conclusion that people are self-presenters who are cunningly manipulating their presentation for the purposes of optimizing their payoff. That is, motivational content is modeled on biological function. The tricky point understood by Freud is that, although a full explanation must terminate in biological facts about the functions of basic mechanisms, the biological facts are in themselves not part of psychology because the functions are not intentional states, and psychology is ultimately about intentional states. For example, avoiding predators may be one of the functions of sleep, but the motivational content is just to relieve tiredness, not to avoid predators; and, reproduction may be one of the functions of sexual motivation, but the content of sexual desire in itself is not about reproduction. Functions tell us only about what led to the selection of a mechanism and not about the detailed nature of the mechanism that performs the function, and given that the same function can be accomplished in many different ways via many different kinds of motivational systems, it follows that an understanding of the biological functions of a mechanism does not by itself imply the nature of the motivational contents generated by the mechanism. Hogan (1983), for example, is wrong to assume that the function of optimizing resources available to the self must be pursued via a motivational mechanism that generates motivations to optimize resources available to the self; it might be that, in the environment in which we evolved, a genuinely altruistic motivational mechanism turned out to be better at performing this function than a selfish one.

Freud recognized the true situation with respect to personological explanation better than most contemporary personality psychologists; the three approaches mentioned earlier are all essential complementary parts of a full account of an individual's behavior. Freud wove together these different levels of explanation without ever making the issue explicit. In the same case history, a person's changing intentional states would be mapped, their traits—for example, orderliness and greediness—would be identified (and sometimes, when possible, the interior structure of these traits would be explored), and the instinctual roots of these traits and states in evolved motivational mechanisms would be identified. The vision that guided him is, I think, extraordinarily appealing to this day, and it is one that I have argued for elsewhere (Wakefield, 1989). This model of a full explanation is rarely acknowledged nowadays, except by the most sophisticated methodological thinkers, such as Eysenck (1967, 1984). The fact that a thinker so different from Freud could upon reflection end up with the same vision of what a personological explanation should be is, I think, a testament to the power of the model.

In sum, an account of behavior must ultimately involve a mapping of the person's intentional system, supplemented by identification of critical traits (i.e., stable dispositions of the intentional system) and their explanations, some of which will be in terms of further states and traits, and some of which will be explained at the basic level where the structure of the brain or body impacts the formation of intentional states and their properties; at this point, functional explanations of the existence of the relevant mechanisms and an account of the intentional structures of the states produced by the mechanisms complete the account.

INTENTIONAL SELF-MANIPULATION OF COGNITIONS

A final Freudian contribution to cognitive psychology, about which I will again be quite brief, is related to Freud's theory of defenses, which is often cited as a clear contribution of Freud to substantive psychological theory. However, I believe that an equal or greater contribution lies in a metatheoretical assumption underlying the theory of defenses, namely, that people intentionally manipulate their own cognitive states. This general principle has implications that are much more far-reaching than the theory of defense in the specific form that Freud or his followers developed it, and stands as a major contribution even if the theory of defense, in any specific form, should ultimately fail to be confirmed. Indeed, it may well be that the theory of defense is really just an account of one way of using mechanisms for intentional self-manipulation that have much more general functions.

The metalevel assumption that people are cognitive self-manipulators underlies various literatures that deal both with how people manipulate themselves in order to have desired effects on others, as in the "self-presentation" literature (e.g., Baumeister, 1982), and in how people manipulate their cognitive states in order to have desired effects on their own internal cognitive, affective, and motivational states, as, for example, in the "defensive pessimism" literature (e.g., Norem, 1989). And, intentional self-manipulation of cognitions is at the heart of recent interpretations of Freud's concept of repression (Erdelyi, 1990). The growing emphasis on cognitive self-manipulation both as a matter of normal psychology and as a potentially valuable clinical interventive technique is, I think, indebted to Freud for a general approach to the mind in which such internal self-manipulation makes sense.

CONCLUDING REMARKS

My exploration of the interface between Freudian theory and contemporary cognitive psychology has focused on a few of the most fundamental points of contact between the two traditions. Even in these few cases, I have merely reviewed arguments presented in greater detail elsewhere and pointed in the direction of an analysis without presenting my case in full. But I believe that what I have presented is enough to indicate the remarkable and sometimes hidden conceptual affinity between Freud and cognitive psychology. Interpreted in the right way, psychoanalysis can be seen as an applied idiographic branch of cognitive science, engaged in the intentional mapping of individuals' minds within a cognitivist framework. The growing implausibility of much of the content of Freud's interpretations should not blind us to the enduring plausibility of the very elegant framework within which Freud pursued the construction of such interpretations. Contrary to current wisdom, it may well be certain of Freud's metapsychological assumptions, understood sympathetically as attempts to incorporate various necessary features into a systematic theory of intentionality, rather than his specific clinical hypotheses, that serve to make Freud a theorist from whom one can still learn.

REFERENCES

Allport, G. (1961). *Pattern and growth in personality*. New York: Holt.
Baars, B. J. (1986). *The cognitive revolution in psychology*. New York: Guilford Press.

Barclay, J. (1964). Franz Brentano and Sigmund Freud. *Journal of Existentialism, 5,* 1–35.

Baumeister, R. F. (1982). A self-presentational view of social phenomena. *Psychological Bulletin, 91,* 3–26.

Brand, M., & Harnish, R. M. (1986). *The representation of knowledge and belief.* Tucson: University of Arizona.

Brentano, F. (1973). *Psychology from an empirical standpoint.* New York: Humanities Press. (Original work published 1874)

Buss, D. M. (1984). Evolutionary biology and personality psychology: Toward a conception of human nature and individual differences. *American Psychologist, 39,* 1135–1147.

Buss, D. M. (1991). Evolutionary personality psychology. *Annual Review of Psychology, 42,* 459–491.

Chomsky, N. (1980). *Rules and representations.* New York: Columbia University Press.

Davidson, D. (1963). Actions, reasons, and causes. *Journal of Philosophy, 60,* 684–700.

Dreyfus, H. L., & Wakefield, J. C. (1988). From depth psychology to breadth psychology: A phenomenological approach to psychopathology. In S. Messer, L. Sass, & R. Woolfolk (Eds.), *Hermeneutics and psychological theory: Interpretive approaches to personality, psychotherapy, and psychopathology* (pp. 272–288). New Brunswick, NJ: Rutgers University Press.

Eagle, M. N. (1984). *Recent developments in psychoanalysis: A critical evaluation.* New York: McGraw-Hill.

Ellenberger, H. F. (1970). *The discovery of the unconscious.* New York: Basic Books.

Ellis, A. (1962). *Reason and emotion in psychotherapy.* New York: Lyle Stuart.

Elster, J. (1985). *The multiple self.* Cambridge, England: Cambridge University Press.

Erdelyi, M. H. (1985). *Psychoanalysis: Freud's cognitive psychology.* San Francisco: Freeman.

Erdelyi, M. H. (1990). Repression, reconstruction, and defense: History and integration of the psychoanalytic and experimental frameworks. In J. L. Singer (Ed.), *Repression and dissociation: Implications for personality theory, psychopathology, and health* (pp. 1–32). Chicago: University of Chicago Press.

Eysenck, H. J. (1967). *The biological basis of personality.* Springfield, IL: Charles C Thomas.

Eysenck, H. J. (1984). The place of individual differences in a scientific psychology. *Annals of Theoretical Psychology, 1,* 233–286.

Fodor, J. A. (1981). *Representations: Philosophical essays on the foundations of cognitive science.* Cambridge, MA: MIT Press.

Fodor, J. A. (1983). *The modularity of mind.* Cambridge, MA: MIT Press.

Freud, S. (1957a). Instincts and their vicissitudes. In J. Strachey (Ed. and Trans.), *The standard edition of the complete psychological works of Sigmund Freud* (Vol. 14, pp. 117–140). London: Hogarth Press. (Original work published 1915)

Freud, S. (1957b). The unconscious. In J. Strachey (Ed. and Trans.), *The standard edition of the complete psychological works of Sigmund Freud* (Vol. 14, pp. 166–215). London: Hogarth Press. (Original work published 1915)

Freud, S. (1957c). The ego and the id. In J. Strachey (Ed. and Trans.), *The standard edition of the complete psychological works of Sigmund Freud* (Vol. 19 pp. 12–59). London: Hogarth Press. (Original work published 1923)

Freud, S. (1964). Some elementary lessons in psychoanalysis. In J. Strachey (Ed. and Trans.), *The standard edition of the complete psychological works of Sigmund Freud* (Vol. 23, pp. 281–286). London: Hogarth Press. (Original work published 1940)

Gardner, H. (1985). *The mind's new science: A history of the cognitive revolution.* New York: Basic Books.

Gill, M. (1976). Metapsychology is not psychology. In M. Gill & P. Holzman (Eds.), *Psychology versus metapsychology: Psychoanalytic essays in honor of George S. Klein* (pp. 71–105). Madison, CT: International Universities Press.

Gill, M. (1983). The point of view of psychoanalysis: Energy discharge or person? *Psychoanalysis and Contemporary Thought, 6*, 523–552.

Gillett, E. (1987). Defence mechanisms versus defence contents. *International Journal of Psycho-Analysis, 68*, 261–269.

Grunbaum, A. (1984). *The foundations of psychoanalysis: A philosophical critique.* Berkeley: University of California Press.

Heidegger, M. (1962). *Being and time* (J. Macquarrie & E. Robinson, Trans.). Oxford, England: Basil Blackwell.

Henle, M. (1984). Freud's secret cognitive theories. In J. R. Royce & L. P. Mos (Eds.), *Annals of theoretical psychology* (Vol. 1, pp. 11–134). New York: Plenum Press.

Hilgard, E. R. (1977). *Divided consciousness: Multiple controls in human thought and action.* New York: Wiley-Interscience.

Hogan, R. (1983). A socioanalytic theory of personality. In M. Page & R. Dienstbier (Eds.), *Nebraska Symposium on Motivation* (pp. 55–89). Lincoln: University of Nebraska Press.

Holt, R. (1976). Drive or wish? A reconsideration of the psychoanalytic theory of motivation. In M. Gill & P. Holzman (Eds.), *Psychology versus metapsychology: Psychoanalytic essays in honor of George S. Klein* (pp. 158–197). Madison, CT: International Universities Press.

Holt, R. (1989). *Freud reappraised: A fresh look at psychoanalytic theory.* Madison, CT: International Universities Press.

Horowitz, M. J. (1988). *Psychodynamics and cognition.* Chicago: University of Chicago Press.

James, W. (1890). *The principles of psychology.* New York: Holt.

Klein, G. (1967). Peremptory ideation: Structure and force in motivated ideas. In R. Holt (Ed.), *Motives and thought: Psychoanalytic essays in honor of David Rapaport* (pp. 78–128). Madison, CT: International Universities Press.

Klein, G. (1976a). Freud's two theories of sexuality. In M. Gill & P. Holzman (Eds.), *Psychology versus metapsychology: Psychoanalytic essays in honor of George S. Klein* (pp. 14–70). Madison, CT: International Universities Press.

Klein, G. (1976b). *Psychoanalytic theory: An exploration of essentials.* New York: International Universities Press.

Kosslyn, S. M. (1980). *Image and mind.* Cambridge, MA: Harvard University Press.

Kripke, S. (1980). *Naming and necessity.* Oxford, England: Basil Blackwell.

Lazarus, R. S., Averill, J. R., & Opton, E. (1970). Towards a cognitive theory of emotion. In M. B. Arnold (Ed.), *Feelings and emotions.* New York: Academic Press.

Mackay, N. (1989). *Motivation and explanation: An essay on Freud's philosophy of science.* Madison, CT: International Universities Press.

Mandler, G. (1988). Problems and directions in the study of consciousness. In M. J. Horowitz (Ed.), *Psychodynamics and cognition* (pp. 21–45). Chicago: University of Chicago Press.

Merlan, P. (1945). Brentano and Freud. *Journal of the History of Ideas, 6*, 375–377.

Merlan, P. (1949). Brentano and Freud—A sequel. *Journal of the History of Ideas, 10*, 451.

Merleau-Ponty, M. (1962). *Phenomenology of perception* (Colin Smith, Trans.). London: Routledge & Kegan Paul.

Moore, M. S. (1983). The nature of psychoanalytic explanation. In L. Laudan (Ed.), *Mind and medicine: Problems of explanation and evaluation in psychiatry and the biomedical sciences.* Berkeley: University of California Press.

Norem, J. K. (1989). Cognitive strategies as personality: Effectiveness, specificity, flexibility, and change. In D. M. Buss & N. Cantor (Eds.), *Personality psychology: Recent trends and emerging directions* (pp. 45–60). New York: Springer-Verlag.

Ortony, A., Clore, G. L., & Collins, A. (1988). *The cognitive structure of emotions.* Cambridge, England: Cambridge University Press.

Paivio, A. (1986). *Mental representations: A dual coding approach.* New York: Oxford University Press.

Pervin, L. A. (1984). Persons, situations, interactions, and the future of personality. *Annals of Theoretical Psychology, 2,* 339–344.

Putnam, H. (1975). The meaning of meaning. In H. Putnam, (Ed.), *Philosophical papers* (Vol. 2, pp. 215–271). Cambridge, England: Cambridge University Press.

Putnam, H. (1988). *Representation and reality.* Cambridge, MA: MIT Press.

Rollins, M. (1989). *Mental imagery: On the limits of cognitive science.* New Haven, CT: Yale University Press.

Schachter, S., & Singer, J. (1962). Cognitive, social and physiological determinants of emotional states. *Psychological Review, 69,* 379–399.

Searle, J. (1983). *Intentionality, an essay in the philosophy of mind.* Cambridge, England: Cambridge University Press.

Singer, J. L. (1990). *Repression and dissociation: Implications for personality theory, psychopathology, and health.* Chicago: University of Chicago Press.

Sperry, R. W. (1968). Hemispheric disconnection and unity in conscious awareness. *American Psychologist, 23,* 723–733.

Wakefield, J. C. (1988). Hermeneutics and empiricism: Commentary on Donald Meichenbaum. In S. Messer, L. Sass, & R. Woolfolk (Eds.), *Hermeneutics and psychological theory: Interpretive approaches to personality, psychotherapy, and psychopathology* (pp. 131–148). New Brunswick, NJ: Rutgers University Press.

Wakefield, J. C. (1989). Levels of explanation in personality theory. In D. M. Buss & N. Cantor (Eds.), *Personality psychology: Recent trends and emerging directions* (pp. 333–346). New York: Springer-Verlag.

Wakefield, J. C. (1990a). Expert systems, Socrates, and the philosophy of mind. In W. Reid & L. Videka-Sherman (Eds.), *Empiricism and clinical practice* (pp. 92–100). Silver Spring, MD: NASW Press.

Wakefield, J. C. (1990b). Is Freud's concept of instinct incoherent?: Resolving Strachey's dilemma. *Psychoanalysis and Contemporary Thought, 13,* 241–264.

Wakefield, J. C. (1990c). Why instinctual impulses can't be unconscious: An exploration of Freud's cognitivism. *Psychoanalysis and Contemporary Thought, 13,* 265–288.

Wakefield, J. C. (1991). Why emotions can't be unconscious: An exploration of Freud's essentialism. *Psychoanalysis and Contemporary Thought, 14,* 29–67.

Wakefield, J. C. (1992a). Freud and the intentionality of feeling. *Psychoanalytic Psychology, 9,* 1–23.

Wakefield, J. C. (1992b). *Do unconscious mental states exist? Freud, intentionality, and cognitive science.* Manuscript in preparation.

Wakefield, J. C., & Dreyfus, H. L. (1991). Phenomenology and the intentionality of action. In E. LaPore & R. V. Gulick (Eds.), *John Searle and his critics* (pp. 259–270). Oxford, England: Basil Blackwell.

Whyte, L. L. (1960). *The unconscious before Freud.* New York: Basic Books.

4

TELLING AND ENACTING STORIES IN PSYCHOANALYSIS

MARSHALL EDELSON

In this chapter, I suggest one way of conceptualizing psychoanalytic process—certainly not *the* way and not the *only* way, but a useful way. This conceptualization takes as its point of departure the telling and enacting of stories in the psychoanalytic situation. It features *experience-close concepts*. Such concepts facilitate rapprochement between psychoanalysis and its neighboring disciplines. When observations made in the psychoanalytic situation are couched in these terms, neighboring disciplines should find it easier than is now the case to make use of them. In turn, because this conceptualization is similar to that now used by some cognitive psychologists, computer scientists, and philosophers of mind in their work, psychoanalysts should feel more inclined to draw on that work in clarifying some unresolved issues in psychoanalytic theory.

From the beginning, psychoanalysis and the telling of stories have been linked—although ambivalently. In *Studies on Hysteria*, during the last decade of the 19th century, Freud somewhat ruefully remarked:

> The case histories I write . . . read like short stories. They lack the serious stamp of science. [However,] a detailed description of mental processes such as we are accustomed to find in the works of imaginative writers enables me . . . to obtain at least some kind of insight into the . . . intimate connection between the story of the patient's sufferings and the symptoms of his illness. (Breuer & Freud, 1893–1895/1955, pp. 160–161)

Both the analysand and the psychoanalyst tell stories. The analysand tells and enacts many versions of first one and then another story. (The term *enacts* refers to stories involving analysand and psychoanalyst as principal characters. Enacted stories are not told; the analysand dramatizes them through action in the psychoanalytic situation. Reference to enacted stories is essential, if discussion is to include stories that take place "in the transference.") The psychoanalyst pieces the analysand's stories together from fragments. He guesses at and interpolates missing incidents, characters, and settings.[1]

The analysand may be evasive and often seems to prefer allusiveness, hints, summaries, and generalizations, or a flat telling of what happened. However, for the psychoanalyst, nothing will do but to have the lively particular details of each story, no matter how trivial these details seem. It is these details that make every story the analysand's own story and not some formulaic sequence of events that could have happened to anyone. The psychoanalyst may inquire, even energetically, about these vivid particulars. More often, he patiently waits for them to make their appearance. And they do appear, often casually, as the analysand talks about something else or comes back later to a story line that earlier, frustratingly enough, had been—it turns out temporarily—dropped.

The psychoanalyst serves in part as the analysand's collaborator. In offering an interpretation, he encourages the emergence of, completes, or retells the analysand's story. He calls attention to a beginning, end, or pivotal event that the analysand has held back or has failed to notice in telling or enacting a story. He speculates about unsuspected causal links between seemingly unconnected, isolated, or merely contiguous or coincidental happenings mentioned by the analysand and thereby makes a story where none has yet taken form.

The psychoanalyst identifies a drama taking place in the psychoanalytic situation, in a dream or daydream, or outside of the psychoanalytic situation. The analysand is always the central character in this drama. He is also the author and director. He assigns parts to others, either simply perceiving or thinking of them as playing their parts, or taking action to provoke them into playing their parts.

The psychoanalyst calls attention to the similarities among various stories told by the analysand or enacted by him in the psychoanalytic situation. The psychoanalyst suggests that, even though these stories involve different characters, times, and places, they could be versions or "derivatives" of the same story—frequently a childhood or primal story. In telling this primal story, the psychoanalyst takes care to use as material vivid particulars taken from the analysand's various versions of it. Using such material makes it less likely that the analysand will dismiss the psychoanalyst's tale as merely some theoretical invention. He recognizes the tale and realizes that it exists, although unconsciously, in his own mind.

The psychoanalyst also may make one story out of two kinds of talk, which seem to have nothing to do with one another: the stories the analysand tells about himself and his past and current life, and his seemingly *narrativeless discourse*. Narrativeless discourse refers to the analysand's descriptions of himself, his states of mind, symptoms, and complaints when these do not appear to be part of any story.

THE STORIES TOLD OR ENACTED IN PSYCHOANALYSIS

No single simple definition will cover all of the instances that one might like to include in the category *story*, but a large family of instances have the following features: A protagonist has a problem. He wants to bring about or maintain some state of affairs. By one means or another, he attempts to do so. But, in this attempt, he encounters opposition. An antagonist erects obstacles or imposes constraints that prevent—or threaten to prevent—the protagonist's attaining what he wants. The antagonist may be a person, nature, or a social system. The protagonist overcomes, makes accommodative adjustments in response to, or fails to overcome the antagonist.

---

[1]"He," "his," and "him" are used generically except where the context indicates otherwise in order to avoid awkward locutions such as "he or she," "his or hers," and "him or her."

The story, from beginning to end, forms a trajectory from one state of affairs to another. There is a change for the better (happy ending) or for the worse (unhappy ending) in the protagonist's situation or in himself. Or, despite the protagonist's efforts, there is no change. A change in the protagonist's situation may be a change in his environment, in his body, or in other persons important to him, and a change in the protagonist himself may be a change in his feelings, in what knowledge he has, or in his moral character.

What kind of story does the psychoanalyst listen for? The following is one kind of story a psychoanalyst may listen for. It is not to be read as *the* story or the *only* story. It is an abstraction from many stories told or enacted by analysands. In this story, the analysand is always there and always the protagonist; he may appear as someone or something else, or he may be distributed among many characters.

Wishes

The story begins with a sexual or sensual wish. Or, because desire may have already exposed the analysand to loss or frustration, it begins with a hostile wish. In my view, hostile wishes are intimately related to sexual or sensual wishes—either an expression of them as in anal–sadism or a result of the frustration of them as in occurrences involving loss or deprivation. (The psychoanalyst's commitment to the importance of the body and sexuality in the story he listens for does not necessarily entail a commitment on his part to metapsychological theories of instinctual drive and libido.)

Childhood

Before turning to a consideration of the obstacles to the gratification of the wishes with which these stories begin, let me fill in a bit more just what kind of wishes they are. They are childhood wishes and they are of the body. The sexual or hostile wish has its origin in childhood or is characteristic of childhood. If it is sexual, it is a wish for sensual (i.e., bodily) pleasure. The experience and quality of that pleasure is related to different body parts or zones and different kinds of body activity. These have different degrees of primacy in different stages of development. States of the body, changes in states of the body, different parts and regions of the body, what is done by the child with these parts and what happens to him in these regions, and what he imagines about these parts, places, and happenings provide important "settings," "props," "characters," and "episodes" for childhood or primal stories. In other words, these wishes are constituted by the child's relation to his body; they are, in the deepest sense imaginable, *of* his body.

The Body

The body's early adventures provide the analysand with scenarios for later stories. There are just-so stories of how things came to be as they are—the child's sexual theories. How did I come to be? How did males and females come to be different? Where do babies come from? How did I come to have sexual desire?

There are primal stories of skin, muscle, eye, mouth, anus, womb, and phallus, and all of their later metaphoric derivatives. There are stories of water, wetting and flooding, gushing streams, waterfalls, drooling, and crying; of sucking, ingesting, and spitting out; of tightness and looseness, profligacy, letting go, spending and stinginess, holding back, holding onto, and destruction by dirt, slime, and gas; of tumescence and detumescence, penetration and being penetrated, flight and fall, hardness and softness, bigness and littleness, touching and rubbing;

and of breaking into, sliding inside, being trapped in, or exploring caves and other dark, secret, hidden places.

Lack of appreciation of the marvelous work of the imagination and the complex structures that it is able to build from simple materials is responsible in part for objections to talk of oral, anal, and phallic wishes as simplistic and reductionistic. Such objections do not take sufficiently into consideration the skills and inventiveness of human beings as tellers and enactors of stories—including their ability to forge far-reaching connections and to erect elaborate complex organizations through the exercise of imagination. Any perceptive moviegoer can testify to the variety of ways—and the many levels of sophistication in the ways—derivatives of primal stories can present these explorations of and clashes on the body's terrain.

The philosopher Mark Johnson's (1987) major thesis in his *The Body in the Mind: The Bodily Basis of Meaning, Imagination, and Reason* is relevant here. He argued that image schemata arise in the first place from body experience and are metaphorically extended by processes of imagination to form more abstract themes and the categories and thought-relations of rational cognition.

An analysand's relation to his own body and to his body's states is primal in the sense of "most ancient." It is also primal in the sense that the psychoanalyst listens for a story about it as lying behind and responsible for the various stories the analysand tells and enacts. Psychoanalysts who favor interpersonal themes tend, I think, to neglect the analysand's relation to his body and his attitudes toward and feelings about the wishes he has within the context of this relation. That is not to deny that fairly soon, but probably not from the very beginning, parts of other persons and eventually whole other persons are recognized to be means to the gratification of sensual wishes. Similarly, a person's *own responses* to his wishes and feelings play a larger role in character and symptom pathology than might be guessed from the analysand's preference for telling stories in which the *responses of other persons* to him as well as his response to them are put in the foreground.

Intrapsychic Obstacles

The most salient and crucial obstacle to gratification of a primal wish is intrapsychic. That is to say, the analysand is both protagonist and antagonist of the story the psychoanalyst listens for. The analysand as antagonist erects many kinds of obstacles in the way of the analysand as protagonist, and these obstacles have different sources.

Wishing for the Impossible

The obstacle may have its source in the very nature of the wish itself. Suppose the analysand's wish involves changing a condition or situation that he cannot change and that perhaps no one can change. Here, what is active in producing effects is not an intrinsic feature of the actual world but that the analysand wishes for the impossible. For example, he wishes to be in two places at once, to fly, to be inside his own or another's body, to be perpetually in a state of desire and at the same time to be gratified continuously and without limit, to be with a dead parent, to have had a different childhood.

Rejecting the Wish

The obstacle may have its source in the analysand's own attitude toward or feeling about his wish (Shapiro, 1989). He objects to it. He finds it incompatible with the kind of person he feels he is or wants to be. He rejects it as not-him, is disgusted by it, or fears it will take him over to the exclusion of everything else he values about himself.

Ambivalence

The obstacle may have its source in the analysand's ambivalence toward his wish. He finds himself having two different feelings about the *same* state of affairs. He longs for what he most dreads. For example, he longs for a castration that will enable him to play a role in which passive wishes are fulfilled, despite his terror of losing the penis he values so much. He longs to be warm and safe in a small enclosed space, although he is terrified of being lost or suffocated there.

Conflict

The obstacle may have its source in a conflict within the analysand. He wishes both to bring about one state of affairs and to avoid a second state of affairs that he believes will inevitably follow as a consequence of the first. Or, he has two incompatible wishes. His counterwish opposes his sexual or hostile wish. He wishes to accede to the claims of morality or external reality, but this wish is counter to the gratification of his sexual or hostile wish.

Dilemma

The obstacle may have its source in a dilemma within the analysand. He has two wishes, the second of which competes with the first, although it is not incompatible with it. It is just not possible to gratify both wishes, even though both are acceptable, because the gratification of one involves a loss of what is required for the gratification of the other. For example, the analysand may not have the resources, within or without, to gratify both wishes, or the fulfillment of wishes belonging to one developmental phase involves giving up wishes belonging to an earlier developmental phase. Anton Kris (1982) has been especially clear about the difference, and the technical implications of the difference, between conflict and dilemma.

Wish Fulfillment and Effective Imagination

In part because of the very nature of these obstacles, the analysand gives up on gratifying his wish through instrumental action in the actual world and seeks to fulfill it instead through acts of imagination. The story with its sexual or hostile wish and the intrapsychic obstacles to its fulfillment is dramatized in imagination. It is now, so to speak, a doubly intrapsychic story. First, the obstacles to gratifying the wishes of the analysand-as-protagonist originate most immediately from the analysand-as-antagonist. Second, the entire story comes to be dramatized in imagination.

An imagined wish fulfillment is the psychoanalyst's evidence of the presence of a *wish*. It is an indexical sign of the wish. Hallucinatory wish fulfillment is imagination functioning in its most intense and effective mode, such as in dreams, unconscious fantasy, and some daydreams (Wollheim, 1969, 1974, 1979). In this mode of imagination, wish fulfillment has primacy over any other end. Primal scenes and stories of wish fulfillment are constructed by using pictorialization and iconic symbolization as modes of representation. These modes of representation, together with condensation and displacement, are also characteristic to a greater or lesser extent of the way in which more or less distant derivatives of such primal scenes and stories are constructed. That is, new scenes and stories are made out of primal ones by combinations, deletions, and shifts in emphasis. It is in this sense that the stories the analysand tells or enacts are derivatives of primal scenes and stories.

In effective imagination, the truth of beliefs is not permitted to matter, and the fact that one is merely imagining is suppressed. Effective imagination is dominated by a spatial or (at the most extreme form of imagination) a corporeal concept of mind. The concept of mind as a space makes use of a ubiquitous metaphor in cognition: a nonphysical entity as a container (Johnson,

1987; Lakoff, 1987; Lakoff & Johnson, 1980). The mind is conceived to be a stage, a house, a place where people are and things happen, a body. Fantasies produced by the most extreme effective imagination are not about possible anticipated happenings in the actual world. Rather, they are about the doings of "internal objects"—persons, bodies, body parts, and things that the analysand imagines inhabit his own mind (Edelson, 1988, pp. 180–183). This concept of the mind's processes and contents as physical results in an exaggeration of its powers. Psychic phenomena are overvalued as having the same causal efficacy as physical objects: Thoughts are imagined to be omnipotent and the mind to have magical powers.

Fantasying as Problem Solving

An unconscious fantasy is a story and most probably a primal story or a near-derivative of a primal story. It is characteristic of an unconscious fantasy that it dramatizes in cinematiclike images a story about how a childhood sexual or hostile wish is fulfilled under conditions of threat. It shows the wish being fulfilled.

An analysand's problem is to construct his fantasy in such a way that both a sexual or hostile wish and a wish to mitigate the obstacle to its fulfillment are expressed to some extent. The solution to this problem is precarious. At any time, internal events (e.g., memories, a sequence of thoughts) or external events may intensify the wish, and that intensity, frighteningly enough, interferes with the very thinking and planning required for coping with the obstacle. Or, internal or external events may seem to create and confirm a belief that the obstacle is so formidable that the resources of imagination are irrelevant to any attempt to contain or avoid it. Then, the temptation to abandon the fulfillment of the wish even in imagination may become nearly irresistible.

Contents Become Unconscious

The difficulties the analysand faces are painful. What stands in opposition to his sexual or hostile wish is inescapably within himself, and his solution to his problem in imagination is precarious. Therefore, he seeks in various ways to avoid becoming conscious of his wish, his attempts to gratify it through acts of imagination, his objections to it, his strategies for preventing its gratification, and the fantasy that tells a story about all of these. All become, or are from the first, unconscious.

An analysand's unconscious fantasy might be called his *master story*. Of course, he may have more than one master story or unconscious fantasy. Revisions or variants of a particular master story, evolving through a lifetime, constitute a *fantasy system*. Freud (1919/1955) described such a fantasy system in his paper, " 'A Child Is Being Beaten': A Contribution to the Study of the Origin of Sexual Perversions."

There are analogies between master stories and movies. First, like movie genres—for example, war, western, or women's pictures (Reed, 1989)—various kinds of master stories (e.g., oral, anal, phallic, oedipal) are characterized by typical settings, characters, props, and episodes. (Such a classification of master stories does not commit one to the view that there is a fixed developmental progression from one psychosexual stage to another.)

Second, a master story is an actual earlier story, of which there are many later versions. It is not—as the structuralists would have it—an abstract "platonic" form or structure having many actual manifestations. In creating new versions of a master story through time, the analysand has made use of his increasing competence, the new resources available to him, and the material provided by additional experiences. In the same way, new versions of old movies make use of advances in technology, use recent sociohistorical events as material, and are influenced by responses of past audiences as well as by the expectations of prospective audiences.

Third, some component (prop, kind of character, setting, kind of event) characteristic of one kind of master story (e.g., an oral story) may appear in what appears to be a derivative of a different sort of master story (e.g., an anal story). In the same way, a group of characters confined to the same vehicle and facing dangers together appears in an early western called *Stagecoach* and appears later in a movie of a different genre—a thriller called *Lifeboat*.

This analogy between master stories and movies provides an illustration of the imagination's inventive workings. A movie genre, like a master story, is not simply defined by a category of subject matter (Reed, 1989). It is generative. It passes traits on to other movies.

So, some fragments (episodes, scenes, props, character types) may appear in a movie of any genre. For example, a chase may appear in an action picture or a comedy. A little dog or a baby may appear in almost any kind of movie. Then, again, a movie may be of mixed genre. The musical *Harvey Girls* has many features that belong to the western: the west, the saloon, the dance hall girl versus the domesticating woman. The horror film *American Werewolf in London* is also a comedy. In the same way, a derivative of an oral, anal, or phallic master story may contain fragments typically appearing in another kind of master story. And a new version of a master story may appear to be mixed—oral and anal, anal and phallic. Even when one genre is dominant, many of the features of another genre are also present.

And why not? The imagination is not constrained, as logic is, in what it combines. That condensation and displacement are used in constructing derivatives or new versions of master stories guarantees the production of strange combinations and shifts in emphasis.

EMPIRICAL CLAIMS ABOUT STORIES IN PSYCHOANALYSIS

Apparently Nonsexual Stories

It is an empirical claim of psychoanalysis that the stories an analysand tells or enacts that appear to have nothing to do with any sexual (or hostile) wish, or to have to do only or primarily with "adult" sexual wishes, are "derivatives" of master stories.

The Role of Imagination

It is an empirical claim of psychoanalysis that linkages between a master story and its derivatives are governed by imagination rather than rules of deductive or inductive logic. The stories an analysand tells or enacts are linked to master stories through metaphor, metonymy, image schemata, affect, and symbolic operations such as condensation, displacement, iconic symbolization, and pictorialization. These processes of *category formation* and *content transformation* belonging to imagination play a major role in forming unpredictable connections, unusual combinations, and bizarre substitutions.

The Postulation of Unconscious Contents

It is an empirical claim of psychoanalysis that the stories an analysand tells or enacts are *unwitting* derivatives of master stories that are unconscious. A master story is unconscious. The analysand actively strives to keep himself unaware of it because the wishes fulfilled in it are objectionable or alien, the obstacles to their gratification are frequently terrifying or painful, and the modes of imagination that determine how these wishes and threats are presented seem strange indeed to the adult waking mind. These are also empirical claims of psychoanalysis: that the master story exists in actuality in the analysand's mind, that it can be inferred from its effects (the stories the analysand tells and enacts), and that it can be made accessible to consciousness in the psychoanalytic situation.

Emotion

It is an empirical claim of psychoanalysis that emotion attached to a story told or enacted may have its origin in a master story. Some features of a story told or enacted by the analysand are emotionally charged because they remind him, more or less unconsciously, of something in a master story about an obstacle that interferes with wish fulfillment. Similarly, some features of his story are emotionally charged because they remind him, more or less unconsciously, of the qualities associated with a particular wish and the circumstances under which it is fulfilled in a master story. The reminding is facilitated by vigilant detectors, which the analysand maintains on the lookout through his adventures in external reality for signs of opportunities for, or obstacles to, wish fulfillment.

Changes Throughout Development

It is an empirical claim of psychoanalysis that the stories an analysand tells or enacts are later versions of some master story, which, having undergone revisions through time, is the parent of numerous progeny produced during different developmental epochs.

Each version has its origin in a particular developmental phase, life epoch, or set of circumstances. Each version is a response to and a product of changes in the analysand's cognitive capacities and the "accidental" particular experiences to which he has been exposed or to which in the form of memories he has access. Any one of these changes may determine his more or less unconscious attitudes toward a master story (or its derivatives) and determine as well what material he is able to call on in revising a master story. The analysand, in other words, has worked on the master story as he has grown up. He has fiddled with it, revised it, improved it, and made it over so that it might serve different purposes important to him at different times in his life.

A master story continues to coexist with its later versions, and fragments having their origin in one master story show up in a later version of another master story. One can account for these "impurities," I believe, without having to resort to a technical concept such as "vicissitudes of instinctual drive." Instead, I prefer to remain within the domain of the imagination, which, under special conditions, works inventively with whatever materials are provided by happenings in the environment or the body.

The Master Story and Apparently Narrativeless Discourse

It is an empirical claim of psychoanalysis that there is a causal relation between a master story and the analysand's apparently narrativeless discourse—the symptoms, complaints, sufferings, and states that are described in stretches in the psychoanalysis when the analysand does not appear to be telling any story at all. The analysand describes enigmatic states of mind that are sometimes pervasive, sometimes abruptly intrusive. These states of mind do not make sense because they have no apparent relation to any of his conscious perceptions, beliefs, or wishes. Or, it may be that particular details of a state of mind do not make sense, even after the analysand has done his best to rationalize the state as making sense on the whole.

The analysand also makes generalizations about himself. He attributes characteristics to himself that are divorced from time, place, or specific incident. He repeats more or less stereotyped complaints. All of these are without particulars and seem to constitute a discourse that is not part of any story.

However, such narrativeless discourse can be shown to be causally related to a master story. This talk is often part of an enactment "in the transference" of a master story. It may be a response to some event in the psychoanalysis as that event has been interpreted by the analysand in the terms of a master story. Or, the talk may be intended to affect the psychoanalyst in some particular way, to win from him or evoke in him a particular response, to get him to play his part in the story. Here, there is *similarity* or thematic affinity between enactment and master story.

Such talk may also be a fragment torn out of a master story. Here, there is a part–whole relation between the talk and the master story. The master story is the unconscious context from which the talk has become divorced but in which, if master story and talk were to be reunited, the former could make sense of the latter. For example, an analysand describes a sudden inexplicable mood or emotion. It does not seem to belong to any story but "comes from nowhere." Sometimes the analysand goes on to build a story around it. In the interest of making his experience coherent, he may try, usually with partial success at best, to connect the mood to some circumstances coincident with it. He imposes an interpretation on the circumstances that makes sense of his being in this mood. The consequence of imposing this interpretation, however, is often a "distortion" of reality, which may lead him into further difficulties. As a result of psychoanalytic work, psychoanalyst and analysand may ultimately discover that the mood or emotion actually belonged to another story, a master story that was unconsciously active, and that the mood or emotion was appropriate given what was happening to the protagonist of that master story (Arlow, 1969a).

THE CAUSAL POWERS OF UNCONSCIOUS FANTASY

An Analogy

How does an analysand's unconscious fantasy system affect his conscious mental life? I am going to use some metaphors in what follows as homely models (Edelson, 1988, pp. 328–340), i.e., nonformal or nonmathematical models drawn from everyday experience. Although the metaphors or models involve words such as "attention" and "remind," I do not mean to imply a conscious experience. Rather, I want to suggest that, whatever processes are going on in the mind of the analysand, even if they are outside of awareness, will have some of the properties of the processes exemplified by the model—that something like the conscious experience of shifts in attention or being reminded of is occurring.

I now return to the analogy between master story and movie to suggest the nature of the causal powers of unconscious fantasy. Regard a master story as a movie stored and playing in the mind of the analysand. Like a movie, it has a setting, characters, props, and episodes. It has been created by the analysand, a veritable Orson Welles who writes it, directs it, and acts in it.

This metaphor is a felicitous one because movies share certain phenomenal features with fantasies (e.g., visual imagery; rapid shifts from scene to scene; the use of light that, dimming and brightening, is a means of emphasis and focus). But the metaphor is also problematic, for the analysand has many different relations to his master story. As director, he arranges how the characters will move and interact. As screenwriter, he plans a scenario, monitors and criticizes what he sees, and attempts to revise the script and have it reshot. As audience, he responds with feelings of various kinds to events in the story and also judges himself for taking an interest in such scenes. As actor, he is the protagonist of the story. As a member of the audience, he identifies empathically or sympathetically with the protagonist. (The various possibilities have been elaborated by Wollheim, 1969, 1974, 1979; Edelson, 1988, especially chap. 9, 1990.) Listening to stories told by the analysand, and caught up in his enactments of stories in the psychoanalytic situation, the psychoanalyst sometimes "hears" the director at work, sometimes the screenwriter, sometimes the actor, sometimes the response of the audience, and sometimes all of them together.

Psychoanalysts may consider how what is in a person's mind, including his unconscious fantasies, determines in part at least his response to a movie. However, I use the analogy instead to consider how an unconscious fantasy regarded as being similar to a movie playing in an analysand's mind determines his responses to and interactions with external reality. This way of asking the causal question is similar to asking how movies influence people's attitudes toward their society.

The thoughts and feelings, the attitudes and concerns, the interests and preoccupations, the problems of the director, screenwriter, audience, and actor in imagination influence the analysand's perceptions of, beliefs about, and actions in relation to external reality. For example, in identifying with his protagonist, the analysand takes on the wishes, beliefs, attitudes, and feelings of that protagonist, and he is affected as the protagonist is affected by the favorable and unfavorable reactions of others in the story. Unaware that he is making up, watching, and participating empathically in such a story, he may wonder where conscious wishes, thoughts, and feelings that seem alien to him come from.

A Causal Sequence

The following is a possible sequence of events that exemplifies the causal powers of unconscious fantasy. The world has *intrinsic features*. The perception of such a feature is *relatively* independent of the analysand's wishes. An intrinsic feature may be a characteristic of a social, physical, or cultural object; a body; an event or condition in the actual world; a mental state (including an emotion) that is an appropriate or inevitable response to events or conditions in the actual world; or a mental state arising from an idle train of thought. The following process is wholly or in large part unconscious.

Some intrinsic feature of the actual world resonates with an unconscious fantasy—it is as if it *reminds* the analysand of an unconscious fantasy. It matches a property of or an object in that fantasy. The *capacity* to compare and match, unconsciously, which is manifested in this performance of the analysand's, is an important object of study in cognitive psychology. *Dynamic Memory*, the 1982 work of the computer scientist and cognitive psychologist Roger Schank, contains a theory of reminding that is relevant to and consistent with both the causal account I am giving here and the account emphasizing memory networks rather than fantasy given by Reiser (1984, 1991).

As the analysand is "reminded" of a particular unconscious fantasy by intrinsic features of the actual world, he comes more and more under the sway of that fantasy. It is as if his attention is captured by it. It is as if he directs it, watches it, is involved in it. In so doing, his relation to the actual world is affected. In other words, he assimilates his experience in the actual world to his unconscious fantasy.

A complementary process also occurs. His unconscious fantasy may also be affected. The mental states it produces—his experiences (perceptions, feelings)—confirm and strengthen it. As he responds differently at different times to its derivatives, he changes them and thereby changes the unconscious fantasy to which they are still connected. A sense that features of current reality do not match an unconscious fantasy (they are not what it led him to expect) may revise or weaken it.

The analysand's unconscious thought processes are dominated by analogy and metaphor. From being reminded, he leaps to the conclusion that the problem he now faces in the actual world is the same as the problem he has tried to solve in his unconscious fantasy, that he now has an opportunity to gratify in actuality the wish he has fulfilled in his fantasy and to overcome anew the same obstacle that he has evaded in his fantasy. It is as if he says to himself, "Remembering this familiar fantasy enables me to identify the kind of problem I now face. The fantasy is an old and familiar solution to this problem. It can show me the way."

He wants to believe all of this because he is interested after all in any opportunity to get back to the pleasure associated with the fulfillment of his old wish (and to the relief associated with his evasion of an old threat). Even if the fantasy were no real help in solving his current problem, by immersing himself in it he escapes for a while from the difficulties he faces and is compensated by whatever pleasure he gains from the fantasy for the frustration and difficulties in his current situation. He therefore may immerse himself increasingly in the fantasy.

Some fantasies—conscious or inferred—are full of anxiety, shame, or guilt and do not seem to involve any pleasure. However, it is worthwhile for analysand and psychoanalyst to pursue the possibility that a wish fulfillment lurks in even the most painful fantasy. For example, an analysand dreams of someone dying, an event that, were it actually to occur, would cause the dreamer intense grief. It turns out, however, that the funeral following the imagined tragedy makes possible a longed-for meeting with a lost lover. Obsessive hypochondriacal imaginings often involve unconsciously longed-for invasions and desired changes in the body or conceal the thought, "If I knew I was suffering some dread incapacitating or fatal disease, then I could forego my scruples and gratify this forbidden wish, or allow myself the shameful pleasures of dependency or passivity, for how could it then matter that I took this small objectionable pleasure?" A daydream in which one is forced to participate in consciously objectionable, even disgusting, but unconsciously longed-for acts evades an internal obstacle by the thought, "It is not my doing. I am not to blame. I could not help myself." There are many variants of the stories told or enacted by the sexually frustrated person who is terrified by imaginings of the dark invader, the robber in the night, the rapist under the bed. All of these are strategies that respond to the analysand-as-antagonist's objections to a wish: by disclaiming that the analysand-as-protagonist has any such wish; by picturing the latter as the kind of person who could never have such a wish; by concealing that a wish fulfillment is anywhere around; or by arguing that circumstances justify gratifying such a wish. A fantasy in the mind of the typical analysand that has no pleasure gain may indeed be rare.

Influenced by the unconscious fantasy he has selected, and looking for confirmation of the similarity between it and the state of affairs in the actual world, the analysand begins to *interpret* his experience of this state of affairs. He highlights some of its features and ignores or blurs others. He attributes motives to others on the basis of inevitably incomplete evidence. He anticipates a happy or unhappy ending to the story unfolding in the actual world. He categorizes the story as *this* rather than *that* kind of story. In so doing, he increasingly emphasizes and focuses on analogies between his unconscious fantasy and the actual state of affairs—and suppresses disanalogies.

An unconscious fantasy on a particular occasion thus influences both "input" and "output." An example of input is information that the analysand receives from external reality and that he interprets in his own particular way, influenced among other things by his unconscious fantasy. An example of output is what he feels or how he acts in external reality as a result of the way he has interpreted this information.

To begin generating an output, an analysand does not need input in the form of a stimulus having its origin in external reality. He may bring about or initiate a state of affairs in external reality, influenced by information generated by the spontaneous activity of his own mind. For example, signs or derivatives of an unconscious fantasy take the form of spontaneously appearing feelings, thoughts, daydreams, or a memory, which may lead him to take a certain view of external reality. In other words, influenced by mental contents that are independent of the contingencies of stimuli whose origin is external reality, an analysand may impose an interpretation on external reality and act to confirm it.

Is an unconscious fantasy a mere disposition—like a stick of dynamite that has no effects unless it is set off? Is it, similarly, like a movie merely stored on film and quiescent until particular experiences of the actual world cause the film to be taken off the shelf and played? Or does it play continuously (along with other fantasies)? Is an analysand's conscious mental life always in part the product—does it always bear the marks of the influence—of one or more than one ongoing unconscious fantasy playing at the periphery of his mind? Unconscious fantasy would not then be a mere disposition, a potential cause, but a continuously active causal influence on conscious mental life.

But could all of these fantasies really be playing continuously and simultaneously? What a cacophony! What about the evidence that the analysand's conscious mental life is sometimes influenced primarily by one unconscious fantasy and sometimes primarily by another? Perhaps one might account for this evidence by supposing that the general circumstances of an analysand's life, the particular problems of the developmental phase he is in, or problems persisting from previous developmental phases only precariously resolved will contrive to keep one unconscious story at the center of his mind or to move it from the periphery to the center.

Primary and Secondary Process

Any story told or enacted by an analysand is a product of two kinds of processes. What it is like will depend on the balance between what is contributed by each of them. Each will be responsible primarily for different aspects or features of the story.

Primary process is exemplified in part by special modes of imagination, which operate to give the activity of fantasying its characteristics and a fantasy its form and content. *Secondary process* is exemplified in part by veridical perception of external reality and instrumental cognition.

Instrumental cognition is this kind of thinking: "What do I *want*? What do I *believe* is necessary to get it? What are the *grounds* for my belief? How can I bring about through *actions* in the actual world what is necessary to get what I want?" Instrumental cognition produces instrumental action in reality, whereas special modes of imagination produce fantasies in which wish fulfillment occurs under the shadow of threat. The two processes continuously mingle in the creating of any story but in different degrees from story to story.

The difference between the two processes is not simply a difference in content. Primary process is imagining characterized by an active suspension of concern about the truth of beliefs and governed by a concept of the mind as spatial or corporeal. Secondary process is organized, purposeful thought. Primary process makes use of condensation, displacement, iconic symbolization, and pictorialization. Secondary process makes use of representational rule-governed language (Edelson, 1975). Primary process gives primacy to connections relevant to the immediate gratification of wishes. Secondary process gives primacy to connections formed by means–ends rules. Primary process generates categories by metaphor, metonymy, and mental imagery. Secondary process defines categories as universals or natural kinds according to intersubjectively agreed on, necessary-and-sufficient properties.

Primary and secondary process thus differ in a number of respects: in the state of consciousness in which a story is constructed, in the ways contents of a story are represented, and in the basis for the relation "being reminded of." The basis for that relation is how shared membership in a category formed in a certain way links features in a story or links one story to another. Category formation by processes of imagination is described metapsychologically in the psychoanalytic literature under the rubric "drive-organized or affect-organized memory system" (Rapaport, 1967). The linguist Lakoff (1987), using knowledge from linguistics and anthropology, also described category formation by processes of imagination but in terms especially appropriate to a dramatistic framework. His models of cognition capture the way in which metaphor, metonymy, and mental imagery structure experience. Thus, he provided a possible bridge between work in psychoanalysis, especially that having to do with primary processes, and work in cognitive psychology.

In what follows, a metaphor—someone busy in a room with a television playing a movie in the background, or a television that has a screen capable of showing two programs, a news program and a movie, at the same time—functions as a homely model.

Ordinarily, organized conscious purposes (mainly an expression of secondary process) govern a train of thought along with the memories and feelings appropriately associated with those thoughts. Usually, at the same time, unconscious fantasy (mainly an expression of primary process) is quiet and indistinct, and the influence of purposes associated with it wanes. The analysand is busy at some task. He is purposefully and consciously focused on achieving something, and his mental powers are bent on that achievement. Secondary process is ascendant.

Consider the following case: The analysand is not paying much attention to an unconscious fantasy that intrinsic features of a current state of affairs have evoked. In his mind, the volume of the sound of even this most salient unconscious fantasy is low; the images on the screen of imagination are dim in the bright light of the room in which he strives. Nonetheless, these images have some impact on him. Even under these unfavorable conditions, they peripherally or outside awareness color his interpretations of his purposeful activity or of that which interrupts and disturbs him as he goes about his business.

As he begins to interpret—under the influence of his unconscious fantasy—the state of affairs in which he finds himself, it is as if his experience of that state of affairs as he interprets it rebounds back to turn up the volume and sharpen the image of that particular fantasy. He becomes more interested in and increasingly focuses his attention on its derivatives.

Indeed, perhaps fatigued from his efforts or distracted by interruptions and disturbances, or as he engages in the procedure called "free association" in the psychoanalytic situation, he decides to suspend purposeful activity. His state of mind is as if, while watching a movie on television, he turns off the light, sits back in his chair, and immerses himself in the images on the screen of imagination. These images to which he now gives his whole attention become ever sharper and brighter in the darkness. Their impact on him intensifies. The extent to which they will subsequently or retrospectively influence what he experiences or remembers experiencing increases.

In this case, primary process has become ascendant. The balance between conscious purposes and unconscious purposes has shifted. The analysand's unconscious fantasy increasingly dominates his interpretation of what he experiences. That interpretation, in turn, shifts the fantasy from the periphery and makes it ever more salient on his mind. To the extent that he is immersed in his unconscious fantasy, the network of thoughts and feelings associated with it comes increasingly to dominate, to intrude on, and to infiltrate his conscious mental life.

In the psychoanalytic situation, the interaction of primary and secondary process can be manifested in a number of ways. I can illustrate these interactions by making use of an analogy between unconscious fantasies and watching movies, and an analogy between awareness of reality and watching the news. Imagine that the analysand is simultaneously watching two programs on a screen, one a movie and the other the news of the day. He focuses on one or the other program while being peripherally aware of but not paying much attention to the other, or he divides his attention equally between the two.

The two programs may converge and become one series of images in his mind. Then, the nature of the interaction between primary and secondary processes is suggested by the kind of story the psychoanalyst "hears" the analysand telling. First, that story may, for the most part, take its features from the news (external reality); the movie (unconscious fantasy) is more or less successfully repressed. Second, fragments of the movie may appear jarringly and intrusively in the midst of or periodically throughout a news report ("return of the repressed"). Third, features of the movie (unconscious fantasy) and the news (external reality) are smoothly mixed in a story partly told and partly enacted, and movies and news are no longer perceived as being separate (an effective "secondary revision" or "compromise formation"). Here, as in dreams, the news is used as material in constructing a story that is more or less a disguised depiction of wish fulfillment.

THE THERAPEUTIC ACTION OF PSYCHOANALYSIS

A Comment About Psychopathology

When does the causal process I have been describing eventuate in psychopathology rather than in the texture of everyday life? Under what circumstances does a master story produce symptoms of various kinds as derivatives? Symptoms are stories also, in the same way dreams are, and their relation to master stories is similar to the relation between the manifest and latent content of a dream (Lewin, 1952). The kind of linkages between a symptom and a master story serves to obscure the relation between them; often, the symptom seems to have no narrative properties at all.

Asking the following questions will help illuminate the sources of psychopathology. First, how precarious is the fantasied solution to an analysand's problem? That is, how easily do internal and external events upset whatever balance has been achieved in unconscious fantasy between the protagonist's wish and the antagonist's interference with the fulfillment of that wish? Second, how vehement and implacable are the antagonist's objections? Third, what methods are used by the protagonist to get around these objections, and what are the consequences of these methods for his conception of himself, his psychological functions, and his relation with others? An examination of psychoanalytic process suggests that how an analysand reacts to his own desires and hatreds, what he does about them, and how what he does affects his relation to his inner and outer world have a lot to do with whether psychopathology as symptoms, impaired psychological functions, or character disorder develops.

Perhaps most important in the determination of psychopathology is the power of an unconscious fantasy to dominate how an analysand experiences others (as characters in a master story) and himself (as a protagonist of a master story), and how he experiences his own psychological functions (looking, writing, speaking, thinking) metaphorically, as sexual or hostile acts in a master story. To the extent that an unconscious fantasy dominates how an analysand experiences others and himself, the result may be predominantly but not necessarily exclusively disturbances of love. To the extent that it dominates how he conceives of his own psychological functions—what he imagines he is doing when he looks, writes, speaks, thinks—the result may be predominantly but not necessarily exclusively disturbances of work.

The psychoanalyst repeatedly calls the analysand's attention to currently existing mental states of which he is at the most peripherally aware. "Look here . . . Could it be that . . . ? You sound very much as if. . . ." The psychoanalyst repeatedly intervenes in ways that are designed to make fully accessible to consciousness what the analysand struggles to keep unconscious—namely, an unconscious fantasy and also that fantasy's immediate particular links to external reality (e.g., "The scene you are conveying to me . . . Did you notice this all began when . . . What happened is just like . . .").

"Fully accessible to consciousness" does not mean "access to *knowledge about.*" It means a direct *knowledge of* the phenomenology of a mental state. The phenomenology of a mental state includes its contents, of course, but also what it feels like to be in such a state (e.g., what it is like to be in a state of desire; what it is like to feel hate, love, jealousy, envy, or remorse). A mental state or action once seemed inexplicable to the analysand in the light of his other conscious wishes, beliefs, memories, and perception. Now, he achieves full consciousness of hitherto unconscious mental states. Then, what was previously inexplicable seems to him clearly and evidently the effect of that which, through the work of psychoanalysis, has become conscious (Edelson, 1988, pp. 175, 332–335, 338).

It is not only the contents of an unconscious fantasy that become conscious in psychoanalysis but also the particulars of that fantasy's relation to external reality. How is an unconscious fantasy evoked by a particular event, object, or feature of external reality? How does an analysand make use of the materials provided by external reality to realize an unconscious fantasy through action? How does an analysand exploit aspects of his experience to justify directing feelings aroused by an unconscious fantasy to objects or persons in external reality?

Ideally, the psychoanalyst's repeated interventions make it possible for the analysand increasingly to achieve access in consciousness to his own mental states. He thereby achieves insight: insight into the workings of his own mind; insight into the ways he forges links—and the kind of links he forges—between unconscious fantasy and external reality; insight into how such linkages cause him to confuse what belongs to him and what belongs to others, to distort what he is like and what objects and persons in external reality are like, and to mistake just what he is doing when he carries out some particular psychological function; and insight into how such linkages and their effects produce the symptoms from which he suffers.

Slowly, he changes the categories into which he places himself, others, and his psychological activities, and the metaphors he uses in forming these categories. His responses to himself, to others, and to various psychological functions—how he evaluates and thinks and feels about these—then begin to change. And so the actions based on these responses may change.

These changes open the way to new solutions of old problems of desire. "New solutions" encompasses an outcome in which old problems are not solved but simply fade away. They may continue to be present, but they do not have any charge. The analysand has largely lost interest in them. In the context of the analysand's current life and view of himself, they no longer seem important or relevant. Parallel to these changes, symptoms (as derivatives of master stories grown obsolete) also lose their charge or fade away.

A goal of psychoanalysis is to loosen the grip of a particular master story on the analysand and therefore to reduce the effort allocated to realizing it on the screen of imagination or in relations with external reality. On the other hand, the outcome does not count as a fundamental or "structural" change if the same master story continues to be charged with interest and passion, and the analysand continues to be preoccupied with it, even if as a result of treatment he assigns himself a completely different part to play in it.

Given this conceptualization of psychoanalytic process, what are the properties of a typical intervention by a psychoanalyst? (I do not characterize *every* intervention and do not indicate the interventions that are necessary to prepare the way for those described here.)

A typical intervention is a story or a piece of a story. It always contains reference to vivid particulars; it is about happenings or a sequence of happenings at a particular time and place. It articulates and calls to the analysand's attention those narrative details of which he already is likely to have a peripheral and inadequately articulated awareness. It is not a timeless generalization about an analysand (e.g., "you're rebellious"). It does not classify (e.g., "that thought belongs to your inferiority complex"). It is not diagnostic (e.g., "that's an example of your paranoid attitude").

It describes the nature of the links between unconscious fantasy and some current features of external reality. In other words, it shows the connection between details of an analysand's unconscious fantasy and details of what happens to him or what he does in external reality. It does not describe a disposition or fantasy independent of any current manifestation or derivative of it. It does not confine itself, on the one hand, solely to the contents of the analysand's unconscious fantasy or, on the other hand, solely to a description of what happens to him, or what he does, in external reality (including the reality of the psychoanalytic situation).

The analysand tells stories about the extra-analytic situation, past or present, and tells or enacts stories about the psychoanalyst and analysand. The psychoanalyst must pay attention to, and comment about, both kinds of stories if he is to demonstrate all of the various ways in which an unconscious fantasy system finds expression in symptoms, states, and actions, and infiltrates interactions in many realms of external reality. This is part of the process called *working through* in which both engage.

An intervention of a psychoanalyst is not necessarily always a *transference interpretation* (i.e., an interpretation the focus of which is a story told or enacted by an analysand involving himself and the psychoanalyst, which is a derivative of a master story). It may be true that transference interpretations are especially mutative interpretations (i.e., bring about the kind of changes psychoanalysis aims for). After all, it is in the psychoanalytic situation that the psychoanalyst can most easily observe those inadequately articulated details of which the analysand is only peripherally aware. He can call these to the analysand's attention and (ultimately) link them to his unconscious fantasy. And, most important, when an analysand becomes fully conscious of what he thinks and feels about the psychoanalyst, he has direct knowledge of the causes of that which has hitherto seemed inexplicable to him in the very setting in which those causes are having those effects.

Nevertheless, some of the interventions of the psychoanalyst will arise from his necessary interest in painstakingly obtaining the details of what has happened to the analysand or what the analysand has done *outside of the psychoanalytic situation,* currently or in the past, as the analysand remembers and interprets these happenings. Inferences about the unconscious fantasy that lies behind those stories and inferences about the unconscious fantasy that lies behind stories about the psychoanalyst and analysand converge. That convergence makes credible conjectures about the existence and specific contents of an unconscious fantasy.

For example, the analysand tells a story illustrating how her father dominated her and her secret strategies for defeating him. She also tells a story about her difficulties in completing a school assignment on time. She frequently arrives late at her analytic session and does not remember to tell the psychoanalyst about behavior of which she imagines the psychoanalyst disapproves. Here, there is *similarity* or thematic affinity among (a) stories told about the past and about what is going on currently outside of the psychoanalytic situation and (b) stories enacted in the psychoanalytic situation.

Even more complicated, the two kinds of stories may be part of one scenario that includes them both as causally related episodes—an Episode 1 leading to an Episode 2 leading to an Episode 3, and so forth. Many variations, many oscillations between the two kinds of stories, often having a (vicious) cyclical structure, are possible. The psychoanalyst must be able to follow both kinds of stories in detail, develop his inferences about them, and have the patience to follow the entire scenario through many episodes, so that he can tell the analysand the complete story that the analysand creates both in and out of the psychoanalytic situation.

The following example of how a story about an extra-analytic situation and a story enacted in the psychoanalytic situation may be part of one scenario, which includes both of these stories as causally related episodes, illustrates *causal connection* rather than similarity between stories told and enacted.

A Complex Story

Episode 1: The Analysand Wants Help and Gets It. In one session, a psychoanalyst makes an interpretation. The analysand agrees with it and discusses it calmly and with interest and appreciation.

Episode 2: The Story of a Fight. In the next session, she tells a story about a fight she has just had with a younger brother. It is clear that even before the fight she had been irritable, belligerent, and provocative. She is still fuming in the session, beside herself with rage toward her brother.

Episode 3: A Reproach. The psychoanalyst reminds her of similar episodes. The analysand berates the "psychoanalysis" (not the psychoanalyst) for having done little to change her.

Episode 4: Remorse. However, the analysand in time does become reflective. She cannot understand why she gets so angry and makes life so difficult for herself by behaving this way with others. She has come to recognize that this behavior is usually unwarranted and often self-defeating. Now she is remorseful and wishes that there were some way to make up to her brother for her treatment of him and to undo the bad effects of the quarrel.

Revision of Episode 1: A Response to Humiliation. The psychoanalyst remembers the analysand's reasonableness in the last session and contrasts it with the fulminations and irrationality with which this session began. Knowing the analysand, he wonders if, in the previous session, the analysand had felt humiliated by the psychoanalyst's superior performance (making an interpretation). It turns out that the analysand was peripherally aware of such a feeling: "But, of course, I couldn't express my envy and resentment when you were trying to help me. You would become offended. Then you would really send me away."

A Comment About Displacement. Merely to interpret the analysand's rage as displacement of feeling from the psychoanalyst to her brother would be a poor shortcut—and make a rather lazy use of a formula. The shortcut would miss all of the details of what turned out to be the actual, rather complicated scenario.

A "New" Episode Is Interpolated Between Episodes 1 and 2: A Fantasy of Dominance and Submission. The analysand now tells an additional story. Later in the day following the previous session, the analysand had a conscious fantasy in which she oscillated between scenes in which she was powerful and forcing someone to do what she commanded and scenes in which she was submitting to another. Both psychoanalyst and analysand recognize this conscious fantasy from various details of it as the derivative of a master story lying ready to be activated and used in any circumstances she interprets as humiliating. At this point in the psychoanalysis, various versions of a favorite conscious fantasy were relatively accessible to consciousness, although the analysand, embarrassed, was always reluctant to tell these stories. However, the master story of which the conscious fantasies were derivatives was a still largely unconscious, although increasingly coming into view, sadomasochistic fantasy. The details of this unconscious fantasy were gradually being filled in.

The conscious fantasies were cut off from any contact with—had as far as she was concerned nothing to do with—her everyday life. Why she has such fantasies has been a mystery to her. They make no sense. When having the conscious fantasy this time, the analysand was not aware of any connection between it and her feelings in the previous session and therefore was certainly not aware that in it she was fulfilling a wish in reaction to her feelings in the session—a wish to be superior and powerful like the psychoanalyst and able to humiliate an inferior as she had been humiliated. The connection now became apparent to her.

Additional details emerge. Why could she not stay with a scene in which she tortured her victim? She knows, if she thinks about it, that she is uncomfortable with images of herself as cruel. So she softens the torture and disguises it. She then reverses roles, so she is the one who is gentle and submissive. She is able to recapture some details of the original harsher story and is horrified by them.

Addition to the Episode of the Fight. That anything she does in reality after having a conscious fantasy has to do with her reaction to having had such a fantasy is also outside of awareness. The psychoanalyst wonders whether she had been worried that, after having the dominance–submission fantasy, her submissiveness as she experienced it in her imagined drama might emerge in her real relationships. In response to this intervention, her dread that she will act submissively moves from periphery to center of awareness. Now she remembers just before the fight interpreting something that had happened as indicating that unwittingly she had invited her brother to treat her as an inferior, especially galling given that her brother is younger than she is. It was her desire to cancel this supposed invitation that she now realizes compelled her, as it had on so many other occasions, to be obnoxious and tough.

At the same time, further details of this story about herself and her brother suggest its links to the unconscious sadomasochistic fantasy. It would be inaccurate, therefore, to regard this story as *only* a disguised extra-analytic expression of "the transference."

Episode 6. Putting the Psychoanalyst Down and Making Up. Finally, telling the psychoanalyst the story about her brother is part of an enactment of a story in the psychoanalytic session. For telling this story makes it possible for her to take the psychoanalyst down a peg or two by showing him that the psychoanalysis is not working; she still behaves in the same way she has always behaved. At the same time, her cooperation with the psychoanalyst in doing the analytic work repairs the damage she fears she has done him both by the acts of cruelty in the conscious fantasy and what she feels are ungrateful cruel reproaches about the inefficacy of the psychoanalyst that she makes because of her envy and resentment.

Again, it becomes apparent from various details that there are links between the enacted story in the psychoanalytic situation and the unconscious sadomasochistic fantasy, especially the version of it in which she is submissive. (The submissiveness, among other things, is intended to repair the damage caused by the fulfillment of sadistic wishes.)

Characterizing the Clinical Material or Session

A psychoanalyst's interventions in a particular session are shaped by his sense of what the clinical material is like with respect to six dimensions. One has to do with whether the analysand is telling stories or not. A second has to do with whether what the analysand tells is primarily governed by processes of imagination or instrumental cognition. A third has to do with how involved the analysand is in what he tells. A fourth has to do with how emotionally and expressively he tells his story. A fifth has to do with how spontaneous the analysand is, with whether the story is full of suspense, surprise, unexpected episodes, or is largely predictable. A sixth has to do explicitly with his relationship to the psychoanalyst—with how eager he is to tell the psychoanalyst a story.

1. In a particular session, an analysand may tell stories. Or, he may merely describe himself, his states, his thoughts and feelings, usually repetitively, in general terms and divorced from any specific happening or occasion.

2. His language may be rich with metaphors, symbols, double-entendres, parallels. His words may seem to jump out from their different contexts (different subject matters) to form suggestive clusters or networks (e.g., "spending," "coming," "rubbing," "making a mess"). Or, his language may seem bare, stripped of connotation, without resonance, not evocative. His words seem to cling to their literal meanings and contexts. They do not come together from different contexts to remind either psychoanalyst or analysand of anything other than what each means where it is.

3. The analysand seems very involved in what he talks about, unaware of himself or the situation. His words fall over each other. Or, he seems to be monitoring what he says, reflecting, self-conscious, choosing his words carefully, and constricting his physical motions and gesture.

4. He tells his story emotionally. Or, he speaks with detachment, studied objectivity, or even without much apparent interest in what he is saying.

5. He is eager not simply to speak in front of the psychoanalyst but to tell him all sorts of things. He has been impatiently waiting to come to the session so that he can tell the psychoanalyst what has happened. Or, he has nothing much that he wants to tell him.

6. He moves freely between subjects, between different realms of experience, between different times of his life. He suddenly remembers a dream he had forgotten; something reminds him of it. Both the psychoanalyst and he are surprised by what comes up, by where things lead. Or, what he has to say was thought out ahead of time. He sticks to a topic. The movement from point to point through the session marches like an argument. The connections are evident. All is predictable.

These alternatives describe dimensions. Any session may be characterized by one extreme or another: narratives or generalities; modes of imagination or instrumental cognition; involvement or self-conscious monitoring; emotional expressiveness or detachment and prosaic description; eagerness to tell a story to the psychoanalyst or indifference and reluctance; and spontaneity or sticking to a preplanned agenda. However, sessions may also be characterized by a balance between extremes, by change from one extreme to another, or by oscillations between extremes.

A sudden change or marked oscillation may suggest a path of inquiry or offer a window of opportunity for an interpretative intervention. More often, an analysand's being stuck at one extreme invites an intervention that will break the logjam, and then subsequent change or oscillation on these dimensions influences the psychoanalyst's assessment of the impact of his interpretative intervention.

An analysand's being stuck at one extreme may be an expression of his resentment over what he experiences as interference by the psychoanalyst with his directing, casting, or revising an unconscious fantasy in which he is especially interested. He is determined to prevent the psychoanalyst from interfering with his unconscious strategy for solving a problem that has haunted him for years. However, that an analysand is stuck at an extreme may also be part of quite a different story he is enacting. In that case, it will prove more profitable to get at what that story is than to describe him, however tactfully, as "resisting" or fighting the psychoanalyst or psychoanalysis. (That description, especially if it is repetitive, is very likely to be heard as a scolding.)

Different Ways of Listening to the Clinical Material

Even within the particular way of conceptualizing psychoanalytic process developed in this chapter, psychoanalysts have a wide set of options with respect to what aspects of the clinical material to use in formulating an interpretation. (For a similar list of options, developed in considering varieties of psychoanalytic literary criticism, see Skura, 1981.)

The analysand is telling a story about something that has happened, recently or in the past, in the psychoanalytic situation or outside of the psychoanalytic situation. At the same time—or during another session when the analysand does not appear to be telling any story at all—the psychoanalyst feels that he himself is *in* a story, that something is happening to *him*, that whatever the analysand is doing is affecting him and leading him to respond in particular ways, that some story is being enacted in rather than being told about the psychoanalytic situation.

Content

A psychoanalyst may choose to focus his attention and his interpretative activity on the content of a story an analysand is telling. What other story is it like? Of what other story is it a version? What is the content of the unconscious fantasy of which it is a derivative? The psychoanalyst attends to the content of a story the analysand is telling, without regard to any story the analysand is enacting, and relates it by thematic affinity to or identifies it as an episode in another story the analysand has told.

The relation between the contents of different stories (e.g., similarity) is the path to an unconscious master story. That the analysand tells these similar stories is evidence for an inference to the existence of a master story of which these are all different derivatives.

Function

A psychoanalyst may choose to focus his attention and his interpretative activity on the function a story has with respect to the state of the teller or enactor of it. How does it serve the current purposes of the teller or enactor of it? Why this story *now*? What wish does the analysand imagine is being fulfilled, what obstacle does he imagine is being evaded or mitigated, what inner problem is being solved, if he is, as it were, in this story now? How does engaging in the act of fantasy itself seem to solve the problem?

The fit between a master story and the problem the analysand sees himself as facing in a current situation, and the particular outcome the analysand seems to be working to bring about, lead the psychoanalyst to an inference about what function the analysand's story now has.

Mode of Representation

A psychoanalyst may choose to focus his attention and his interpretative activity on the way a story is constructed, its mode of representation. To what extent is it similar to a dream or a rebus (Edelson, 1975)? To what extent do displacements, condensations, pictorialization, and iconic symbolization enter into the way it is made, told, or enacted?

The psychoanalyst treats the story as he would a manifest dream. (Some stories, notably but not only dreams, invite this approach more than others.) He does not take it at face value. He listens for and reconstructs the actual story—the latent content—that the analysand tells in a disguised form or in a language or mode of representation belonging to imagination. In this reconstruction, however, he pays thoughtful attention to evidence suggesting just what features of the manifest story are a product of reality-accommodated perception and cognition and what features are the product of symbolic operations acting on the contents of the latent story.

By the time condensations have been unpacked, displacements undone, reversals turned around again, symbols decoded, and pictures translated into words, the psychoanalyst and analysand find that they have an entirely different story. Is this the "real" story, the one that is currently causally active? Evidence that it is depends on the cogency of the argument that just this story provides the best explanation for all of the usually hitherto unavailable information the analysand provides to make the unpacking, undoing, turning around, decoding, and translating possible.

The Manner of the Telling

A psychoanalyst may choose to focus his attention and his interpretative activity on the *attitudes* of the analysand toward a story, which is betrayed by *how* he tells it (Shapiro, 1989). The psychoanalyst infers what kind of person tells the story—what ideals, and what conception of himself and beliefs about himself, shape his attitudes toward the story he is telling. In arriving at these inferences, he makes use of observations of the analysand's tone of voice and other paraverbal (and nonverbal) phenomena, his choice of words, emphasis, sentence structure, and figures of speech. His ideals and conception of self often, it turns out, have their origin in an identification with the protagonist of his unconscious fantasy.

Enactment

A psychoanalyst may choose to focus his attention and his interpretative activity on the story an analysand enacts in the psychoanalytic situation and on the story he tells only insofar as his telling it or the way he tells it or the effect he produces by telling it is part of the story he is enacting. The content of the story told and the content of the story enacted may or may not be similar in theme or particulars.

Disagreements Among Psychoanalysts

One possible reason psychoanalysts disagree in their interpretations of clinical material— What is going on in this session?—is that the disputants focus on different aspects of the material or listen to it or approach it in different ways. Theoretical differences are not responsible for every disagreement about how to hear what the analysand is saying.

One source of disagreement is that different approaches involve asking different questions rather than holding different theories. Answers to each of the following kinds of questions may appear to contradict one another, but they do not necessarily constitute rival hypotheses or theories. What is the *content* of the master story that is currently active? What *function* or purpose does fantasying itself, or does having a specific fantasy, serve in this situation? What *materials* and *symbolic operations* did the analysand use to get from the master story to the story he tells or enacts? What *kind of person* tells the story, and what is his response to that story? How does the telling of this story play a part in a story being *enacted*?

A second source of disagreement is the complex nature of a master story. Different approaches may focus on different features or episodes of a master story, which are then taken prematurely and mistakenly to be the whole story. Thus, different psychoanalysts seem to have arrived at different stories when in fact each one has a scene or an episode from the actual whole story. This state of affairs calls for more work of a seeing-how-things-might-fit-together nature.

A third source of disagreement is that different psychoanalysts pay attention to a greater or lesser degree to *particulars* and, then, select different sets of particulars or different stories as a basis for inference. Psychoanalysts have their favorite kinds of stories. Some pay special attention to, and select as a privileged basis for inference, stories about the analysand and psychoanalyst. Some prefer to focus on stories about childhood or interactions with parents or siblings.

A decision to pursue one approach to the clinical material rather than another cannot be called "true" or "false." Such attributes do not belong to decisions. Certain kinds of evidence, however, have bearing on the evaluation of such an approach as tending over time or over cases to be useful or successful in achieving some objective. Such evidence might support the conclusion that choosing this rather than that approach, *as a general policy,* tends to contribute to the occurrence of one or another immediate or remote outcome. What is at issue here has nothing to do with any conjecture about what is actually going on in a particular analysand's mind on a specific occasion.

However, given the same clinical material, one psychoanalyst's assertion that one rather than another master story is the progenitor of a set of told or enacted stories *is* a causal claim about what is going on in the analysand's mind now. The rivalry between this claim and that of another psychoanalyst who reviews the same clinical material can be in principle adjudicated by evidence.

Two kinds of inferences are important here. One is the inference that a particular master story currently exists as a hypothetical entity in the mind of the analysand. That is, he is actually now, although unconsciously, imagining the happenings of the story, identifying with the protagonist, and so forth. The other is the inference that a particular master story influences the analysand's reception and interpretation of information reaching him from his situation (physical and social environment, body).

Here, two sequences need to be distinguished and evidence adduced that has bearing on the conclusion that one rather than the other obtains. The analysand responds, influenced by a master story, to the contingencies of an external situation he may have done nothing to bring about. Or, independently of external stimuli, and influenced by a master story and the mental states to which it has given rise, he may have brought about the external situation that he now perceives and interprets.

CLINICAL THEORY VERSUS METAPSYCHOLOGY

An account of psychoanalytic process in terms of telling and enacting stories, which takes narrative as a central concept, assumes that psychoanalysis is an extension of commonsense or folk psychology in which "dramatistic" concepts such as desires and beliefs play a central role in explanation (Hopkins, 1988). Psychoanalytic metapsychology, in which nonpersonal processes play a central role in explanation, is a rival of this commonsense psychology account. Metapsychological theorizing is not story telling. I have discussed this rivalry extensively in Edelson (1991).

My own view (Edelson, 1989) continues to be that metapsychology is essentially an attempt to replace desire/belief explanation—especially exemplified in psychoanalysis by the explanatory use of mediation by unconscious fantasies—with a nonsemantic theory. Such a nonsemantic theory involves no reference to and assigns no causal role to mental contents (i.e., internal symbolic representations of states of affairs that are part of or the object of desiring or believing).

Metapsychology is, in this sense, similar to the learning theory that tries to formulate laws using concepts such as conditioning, reinforcement, and stimulus generalization without any reference to the content of what is learned. Metapsychology so conceived must fail as a psychoanalytic theory, if psychoanalysis is indeed trying to answer just those questions I have previously described it as trying to answer (Edelson, 1988, 1989). Stoller (1985, pp. 105–106) made the same point.

PSYCHOANALYTIC THEORY AND RESEARCH

In this chapter, I have used a language as free of technical terms from psychoanalytic theory as possible. I have concentrated on conceptualizing the psychoanalytic process rather than the psychoanalytic theory of mind, in part because I believe that psychoanalytic theory will benefit from emphasizing in its core formulations concepts that are closely linked to empirical observations made in the psychoanalytic situation. These will be dramatistic concepts such as wish, defense, conflict, unconscious, fantasy, resistance, and transference, which I have tried to show are necessary for capturing the phenomena observed in the psychoanalytic situation or characterizing the psychoanalytic process. These are, in fact, the concepts most likely to govern the psychoanalyst's way of listening and way of processing what he hears as well as the distinctive interventions he makes in the clinical situation. After *this* set of core concepts has been applied to the domain, however limited, that it is capable of explaining and these explanations success-fully meet challenges to their scientific credibility, then psychoanalytic theory may be plausibly extended to a wider domain.

I believe that this way of proceeding will help to clarify the nature of psychoanalytic theory. I have pointed out elsewhere (Edelson, 1984, 1988, 1989, 1990, 1991) that, despite occasional (largely unsuccessful) efforts to systematize or formalize psychoanalytic theory, it is not a hier-archical pyramidic set of axioms and universal generalizations. It is not a logico-deductive structure. It seems to be, at its center, a narrative form (and narrative in the sense of being about a protagonist's wants, obstacles to satisfying these wants, and means for coping with these obstacles). That is important to any consideration of the problems of establishing its scientific credibility—problems tackled in Edelson (1984, 1988, Part 2, 1989).

I have taken as a principal point of departure *telling and enacting stories* in psychoanalysis. Elsewhere (Edelson, 1992), I have detailed the implications of this paradigm for research and teaching. In choosing this paradigm, I become part of a detectable convergence among various "schools" of psychoanalytic theory as well as among those with especially interesting or promising current approaches to psychoanalytic research.

1. "Unconscious fantasy" has come front and center in both object relations and in-stinctual drive depictions of psychoanalytic theory, and in both the "classical" and "Kleinian" literature (Arlow, 1969a, 1969b; Blum, Kramer, Richards, & Richards, 1988; Segal, 1981).

2. Weiss, Sampson, and the Mount Zion Psychotherapy Research Group (1986), em-bracing the objectives of science, studied dramas of plans and tests.

3. Luborsky and Crits-Christoph (1990), also embracing the objectives of science, studied core conflictual relationship themes as exemplifications of transference.

4. Although Schafer (1983), in work on psychoanalysis, questioned the relevance of science, at least as it is conventionally depicted, he too was interested in narrative.

Luborsky has been especially aware of the convergence of interest among investigators on narrative. He described (Luborsky & Crits-Christoph, 1990, chap. 17) 15 different research measures of "central relationship pattern." What I have written in this chapter raises interesting questions for Luborsky's research program. For example, Is there any way to score for the presence of latent as well as manifest core conflictual relationship themes? How does one go about scoring for the presence of an enactment or, an even more complicated task, for the presence of an enactment that goes over many sessions and includes told stories as part of it?

WORK IN OTHER DISCIPLINES

Although an emphasis on narrative is traditionally the mark of a hermeneutic stance toward psychoanalysis, I do not support abandoning science for hermeneutics. On the contrary. Cognitive and computer scientists such as Schank and Abelson (1977), in the tradition of Piaget's *internal schema*, have chosen to work with *narrative, script,* and *scenario* as key concepts.

Lakoff and Johnson (1988), Lakoff (1987), and Johnson (1987) have put in the foreground the role of imagination and metaphor in studies of reason and category formation. Lakoff (1987, pp. 380–415) exemplified the conceptualizations of feelings within this framework in a case study of *anger*. After an examination of metaphors used to conceptualize anger, which "converge on a certain prototypical model of anger" having a temporal dimension and a number of stages, he formulated the model as a prototypical *scenario*. Similarly, de Sousa (1987, pp. 181–184) referred to paradigm scenarios in his cognitive theory of emotion: "We are made familiar with the vocabulary of emotion by association with *paradigm scenarios*. These are drawn first from our daily life as small children, and later reinforced by the stories, art, and culture to which we are exposed."

Holland, Holyoak, Nisbett, and Thaggard are cognitive scientists also interested—as psychoanalysts are—in dynamic phenomena and problem-solving processes. However, in their immensely impressive book *Induction: Processes of Inference, Learning and Discovery* (Holland et al., 1989), they questioned the value of a conceptual strategy that involves postulating "holistic" internal causal schemata such as scripts. Their skepticism about holistic mental structures arose from evidence in inference, learning, and discovery that subsets of beliefs influence and are influenced by experience independently of other beliefs to which they are logically related. In other words, some beliefs can act discretely to bring about decisions or actions, or be altered by experience, while at the same time other more general or less general but logically related beliefs exert no influence or resist revision.

Nevertheless, even though there is as much ferment and disagreement in neighboring disciplines as in psychoanalysis, it seems to me that an emphasis at this time on psychoanalytic process and concepts closely tied to clinical observations is likely to enhance the possibility of rapprochement between psychoanalysis and neighboring disciplines such as neuroscience, cognitive psychology, developmental psychology, philosophy of mind, and literary studies.

REFERENCES

Arlow, J. (1969a). Unconscious fantasy and disturbances of conscious experience. *Psychoanalytic Quarterly, 38,* 1–27.

Arlow, J. (1969b). Fantasy, memory, and reality testing. *Psychoanalytic Quarterly, 38,* 28–51.

Blum, H., Kramer, Y., Richards, A. K., & Richards, A. D. (Eds.). (1988). *Fantasy, myth, and reality: Essays in honor of Jacob A. Arlow, M.D.* Madison, CT: International Universities Press.

Breuer, J., & Freud, S. (1955). Studies on hysteria. In J. Strachey (Ed. and Trans.), *The standard edition of the complete psychological works of Sigmund Freud* (Vol. 2). London: Hogarth Press. (Original work published 1893–1895)

de Sousa, R. (1987). *The rationality of emotion.* Cambridge, MA: MIT Press.

Edelson, M. (1975). *Language and interpretation in psychoanalysis* (paperback reprint). Chicago: University of Chicago Press, 1984.

Edelson, M. (1984). *Hypothesis and evidence in psychoanalysis* (paperback edition). Chicago: University of Chicago Press, 1986.

Edelson, M. (1988). *Psychoanalysis: A theory in crisis* (paperback edition). Chicago: University of Chicago Press, 1990.

Edelson, M. (1989). The nature of psychoanalytic theory: Implications for psychoanalytic research. *Psychoanalytic Inquiry, 9,* 169–192.

Edelson, M. (1990). Defense in psychoanalytic theory: Computation or fantasy? In J. L. Singer (Ed.), *Repression or dissociation: Implications for personality theory, psychopathology, and health* (pp. 33–60). Chicago: University of Chicago Press.

Edelson, M. (1991). Review of Mind, *psychoanalysis and science.* (P. Clark & C. Wright, Eds.). *Psychoanalytic Quarterly, 60,* 101–108.

Edelson, M. (1992). Can psychotherapy research answer this psychotherapist's questions? *Contemporary Psychoanalysis, 28,* 118–151.

Freud, S. (1955). "A child is being beaten": A contribution to the study of the origin of sexual perversions. In J. Strachey (Ed. and Trans.), *The standard edition of the complete psychological works of Sigmund Freud* (Vol. 17, pp. 179–204). London: Hogarth Press. (Original work published 1919)

Holland, J., Holyoak, K., Nisbett, R., Thaggard, P. (1986). *Induction: Processes of inference, learning, and discovery.* Cambridge, MA: MIT Press.

Hopkins, J. (1988). Epistemology and depth psychology: Critical notes on *The foundations of psychoanalysis.* In P. Clark & C. Wright (Eds.), *Mind, psychoanalysis and science* (pp. 33–60). New York: Basil Blackwell.

Johnson, M. (1987). *The body in the mind: The bodily basis of meaning, imagination, and reason.* Chicago: University of Chicago Press.

Kris, A. (1982). *Free association.* New Haven, CT: Yale University Press.

Lakoff, G. (1987). *Women, fire, and dangerous things: What categories reveal about the mind.* Chicago: University of Chicago Press.

Lakoff, G., & Johnson, M. (1980). *Metaphors we live by.* Chicago: University of Chicago Press.

Lewin, B. (1952). Phobic symptoms and dream interpretation. *Psychoanalytic Quarterly, 21,* 295–322.

Luborsky, L., & Crits-Christoph, P. (1990). *Understanding transference: The core conflictual relationship theme method.* New York: Basic Books.

Rapaport, D. (1967). The collected papers of David Rapaport (edited by M. Gill). New York: Basic Books.

Reed, J. (1989). *American scenarios: The uses of film genre.* Middletown, CT: Wesleyan University Press.

Reiser, M. (1984). *Mind, brain, body: Toward a convergence of psychoanalysis and neurobiology.* New York: Basic Books.

Reiser, M. (1991). *Memory in mind and brain: What dream imagery reveals.* New York: Basic Books.

Schafer, R. (1983). *The analytic attitude.* New York: Basic Books.

Schank, R. (1982). *Dynamic memory: A theory of reminding and learning in computers and people.* New York: Cambridge University Press.

Schank, R., & Abelson, R. (1977). *Scripts plans goals and understanding: An inquiry into human knowledge structures.* Hillsdale, NJ: Erlbaum.

II

PERSONALITY DEVELOPMENT AND ORGANIZATION

INTRODUCTION: PERSONALITY
DEVELOPMENT AND ORGANIZATION

We cannot conceptualize personality development and organization without relying on explicit or implicit theories of human nature and nurture. These theories and their underlying assumptions exert a critical influence on our understanding of the inborn capacities of the infant and of the unfolding of those capacities within a particular relational context. Our understanding of the beginning in turn influences our view of personality development and organization at subsequent stages of the life cycle.

Both within academic psychology and psychoanalysis, there is little agreement about which concepts best describe a *person* or *personality*. These terms, beneath the descriptive surface, take on different meanings for different theorists.

On the basis of the theoretical predispositions that guided the exploration of his own dreams (Freud, 1900), his observations of the behaviors of adult patients and his understanding of their verbal reports, Freud developed the paradigm of the psyche as a more-or-less self-contained apparatus activated by instinctually driven wishes with a variety of aims and objects—what some contemporary critics refer to as a *one-person psychology*. Freud's conception emphasized the primacy of endogenous drives. His early theorizing focused on the sexual (libidinal) drive, and his later theorizing included the aggressive drive. Although drives and their vicissitudes were primary in shaping the personality of the individual, they were not immune to outside influence. Freud (1916–1917, p. 347) described drives as having a complemental relationship with the external environment (i.e., the relational context). In his conceptual system, endogenous and exogenous forces exerted a mutual influence. In addition, there was an implicit, although not fully worked out, theory of object relations.

In Freud's topographic theory, the distinctive features of the individual relate to the complex interplay of systems of the mind (unconscious, preconscious, and conscious), and of drives and defenses. In his structural theory, aspects of personality are described as dynamic relationships among agencies of the mind (id, ego, superego), with special reference to the organizing and synthesizing functions of the ego. Hartmann (1939) and others expanded the role of the ego as the agency of adaptation to the environment and as the container of self-representations.

The concepts of *self-representation* and *self* are not synonymous. Kohut (1977) and his followers have elevated *self* to the status of a supra-ordinate concept and have described personality development as leading toward a *cohesive self*.

Object relations and attachment theorists challenge the premise of sexual and aggressive drives as the basic organizers of personality development. In their view, infants are "object seeking" from the beginning, and the relational field is the key organizer of psychic structure and function.

For theorists such as Mitchell (1988), personality development and organization take place in a "relational matrix" in which there is a dynamic tension between the individual developing and maintaining a sense of self-identity and the individual developing and maintaining a sense of relatedness to others.

VIEWS OF INFANCY

The research examined in this section essentially invalidates the theoretical model of the infant as passive, undifferentiated, and buffeted about by unmodulated psychic forces. Instead, the "new look" at infancy reveals a more sophisticated, complex array of social, perceptual, and cognitive capacities, and discrete affect states than were previously thought to exist. Similarly, the research data do not support the theory that the infant initially travels through an autistic phase of cocoon-like unrelatedness. The opposite appears to be the case, given a biologically healthy infant and a "good enough" environment. Infant and caretaker are engaged in a complicated affective and interactional dance from the beginning.

The data of infant researchers, when considered in the aggregate, are contributing to a paradigm shift. On the basis of observations of the nonverbal behavior of infants both in isolation and in the context of their relational environments, researchers describe an infant capable of engaging in various forms of self-regulation and of participating with others in complex patterns of mutual regulation—a so-called *two-person psychology*, or at least a blend of elements of one and two-person psychologies.

Of course, there is no simple way to extrapolate from observations of infant behaviors to those of older children and adults. Analysis of adolescent and adult patients relies heavily on their capacities (as well as those of their analysts) to split their psychic functioning into self and object. They must be able simultaneously to experience an inner world of thought, feeling and fantasy, and to observe themselves while experiencing. In addition, they need verbal–symbolic capacities to elucidate and elaborate their self-observations, and to enable them to describe their inner experience to another.

Researchers have been highly successful at devising ingenious ways of posing questions and challenges to infants and providing them with meaningful ways of responding. Research suggests that infants are capable of experiencing discrete affect states that, from an adult viewpoint, we might label as *relaxation–contentment, agitation–anxiety, surprise, startle–fear, anger, curiosity,* and so forth. Nonetheless, the methods of data collection and the data themselves are different from those gathered in the analytic situation. We need to be cautious about imposing the template of adult experience onto our understanding of infantile experience, and vice versa.

OVERVIEW OF CHAPTERS

Taking a critical look at the implications of the empirical findings of infant research, Lachmann and Beebe challenge and reformulate psychoanalytic concepts of direct linkages among the domains of early development, psychic structure, and transference. They suggest that mutual and self-regulatory processes provide the basic building blocks in all three domains.

Lachmann and Beebe propose a transformational model that asserts that experiences at each stage of development are reorganized. Intrapsychic changes produce interpersonal changes and vice versa, in continuous interaction between person and environment. Experiences are repeated, but rarely in exactly the same way. The transformational model serves as a counterpoint to the traditional psychoanalytic emphasis on transference as compulsive repetition of infantile prototypes.

They argue that transference phenomena cannot be adequately understood from either a one-person or a two-person perspective, but only from an integration of both, and that from the beginning the infant engages with the caretaker in the construction of both interpersonal and subjective worlds. As Lachmann and Beebe point out, however, despite the discovery of the impressive array of the infant's capacities, future research is needed to determine more precisely what the infant's subjective world is like and what the infant actually "constructs" in terms of mental representations.

Bowlby postulated that infants and young children construct "internal working models" of self and other, and that these working models are acutely responsive to the cumulative interactions between infant and caregiver. His work is particularly important because it relates external and psychic reality, and describes a process in which interactions lead to the formation of psychic structure in the infant.

More than two decades have passed since Bowlby (1969) first described the *attachment behaviors* of infants. His attachment theory has become a major paradigm of the unfolding infant–mother relationship and has greatly influenced infant research. However, his work, which took root in the soil of British object relations, has collided head-on with drive theory and has not been carefully integrated into the larger body of psychoanalytic theory and practice. In their chapter, Aber and Slade take some initial steps toward such an integration. After providing an overview of the findings and concepts of Bowlby and several of his followers, including their own work, Aber and Slade examine convergent and divergent points between psychoanalysis and attachment theory.

One strength of attachment theory so far has been its tendency to be bidirectional, that is, to look carefully at the influence of the caregiver on the infant with particular reference to the formation of the infant's psychic structure, to focus equally on the infant's capacities to shape its environment and to influence the experience of the caregiver. Attachment research examines both sides of the interactional ledger.

In her exploration of object relations, Fast emphasizes the role of interactions in the development of self and in self–other differentiation and integration. Guided philosophically by the constructivist position that asserts that individuals do not perceive the world objectively but rather actively construct the meaning of their experience, Fast maintains that the fundamental psychic unit is not the perception of an object but the construction of a self–other interaction scheme.

She notes the unifying assumption underlying various object relations perspectives, that psychological development occurs from the beginning of life in relationships rather than originating in a self-contained organism. However, she disagrees with those who posit mental representations of objects as the building blocks of psychic structure. Instead, she argues that schemes representing dynamic personally motivated ways of interacting with our worlds are the basic units of psychic organization.

Fast recognizes that object relations, as a loosely connected set of ideas, although attempting to be theoretically comprehensive, has not yet successfully accounted for many psychoanalytic observations already framed in drive theory terms. Attending to convergences in theory and research, and focusing particularly on Piaget's theory of cognitive development (Flavell, 1963), she outlines one approach toward an integrative synthesis of object relations and drive theory perspectives. Fast's work is original and important. However, as infant research data accumulate, Piaget's stage theories are being called into question, posing a challenge to Fast's systematizing efforts.

Demos argues against a stage-like model and for the infant's early competencies and capacities that are elaborated over time. She successfully attempts to integrate recent research findings in developmental psychology with formulations of the self and the early organization of the psyche. Concentrated on early infancy, her work has implications for later personality development and organization. Demos explores such vital areas as the nature and content of the young infant's psychic experiences, as well as the evolution of the infant's capacities for organizing, remembering and acting on those experiences.

Her approach is certainly bidirectional. While acknowledging the importance of environmental variables, she also gives great weight to biologic endowment. She paints a picture of an infant "that is neither buffeted by unstructured energies of the id nor essentially created or activated by the ministrations of the caregiver, but one who arrives in the world with a functioning set of unique organizational capacities and whose developmental course will be influenced as much by these intrinsic characteristics as by experiences with people and inanimate objects."

Demos warns us against the reification of ideas of psychic structure. She prefers to describe the psyche more as a dynamic system whose components can "combine and act in a coordinated manner at one moment in time, and recombine with other components or be inactive at other times." In keeping with the spirit animating this volume, she offers her discussion as "a scientific dialogue in which it is assumed that the more points of view we have available, the richer the debate will be, and the more likely we will be to eventually construct an adequate conceptualization of human psychic processes."

Osofsky examines affective development in the context of early relationships and suggests its clinical implications. In particular, she explores the impact of emotional regulation on disorders of self, mood, and conduct. She describes the role of direct observations of infants and caregivers, although their links to understanding intrapsychic states are not fully elaborated. After citing the evidence for the existence of discrete emotions in infants and describing the major components of a theory of affective development, Osofsky highlights the importance of affective exchanges for the infant–caregiver relationship, referring to the work of Freud, Hartmann, Winnicott, Bowlby, and Ainsworth.

She relates infant–caregiver interactions to the following subjective experiences: basic trust (Erikson, 1964), confidence (Benedek), a secure base (Bowlby, 1969; Ainsworth, 1969), caregiver representations and attunement (Stern, 1985), social referencing (Emde, 1989; Barrett & Campos, 1987), emotional availability (Emde, 1989), affect sharing (Osofsky & Eberhart-Wright, 1988), and empathic mirroring (Kohut, 1977). Finally, Osofsky extrapolates from the research data and suggests their implications for mothers and infants at risk. Psychoanalysis lacks a well-elaborated, coherent theory of affect, and the research of Osofsky and her colleagues is sorely needed and holds much promise for the future.

Coates' chapter on gender identity disorder in a three-year-old boy is an ambitious attempt to set forth a model of personality organization and psychopathology that integrates the perspectives of psychoanalysis, social learning, and cognitive development. The illustrative case history is richly evocative, but as Coates acknowledges, needs to be supplemented by detailed longitudinal and cross-sectional studies. Her review of the literature suggests that gender identity disorder comes about from the interplay of multiple risk factors (biological, familial, environmental-traumatic, and intrapsychic) operating simultaneously. Those who develop gender identity disorder are particularly vulnerable during a critical period of early development. Future research will have to map out the specific interactions and relative etiological contributions of these various factors.

Although stressing that no single discipline or theory provides sufficient explanatory power at this time, Coates argues that the psychoanalytic perspective is uniquely positioned to elucidate psychic structure and the development of pathological behaviors, particularly those such as gender identity disorder, whose essence involves the child's unconscious fantasies.

Levy-Warren examines the relationship between psychoanalytic theory and normal adolescent development, leaving the exploration of adolescent psychopathology to other writers. She states that in the study of adolescence, psychoanalytic theory and psychological research largely complement each other, although different terminology and nonoverlapping theoretical purviews create genuine obstacles to an integration of both perspectives. For example, psychological researchers speak of moral values and expectations and look at variables such as race, class, family constellation, and environmental factors. Psychoanalytic theorists are more likely to speak of aspects of the ego ideal, rather than values and expectations, and would find no meaningful place for the variables that fall outside the intrapsychic sphere.

While pointing out that there is a vast psychological literature on adolescence going all the way back to the work of G. Stanley Hall in 1904, Levy-Warren describes the current models of adolescent development as emanating from the work of two psychoanalytic theorists: Blos's (1962) well-elaborated account of the adolescent passage and Erikson's evocative picture of the adolescent phase of the life cycle. Consistent with those theorists, Levy-Warren defines the major challenges of adolescence as the development of autonomy, competence, and sexual identity. She explores those challenges in four domains: physiological, emotional, cognitive, and social. While looking for overall patterns, she leaves considerable room for individual variation and multiple pathways of development.

She concludes that psychological researchers of adolescent development need to develop a more sophisticated understanding of psychoanalytic theory, and that psychoanalytic theorists need to pay more attention to the relevant psychological research and to grapple with the challenge of developing more refined ways of operationalizing their terms.

In his chapter on adult development and aging, Gutmann echoes some of the concerns of the infant researchers. In the same way that researchers discovered previously unrecognized capacities in newborns and infants, Gutmann believes that researchers are just beginning to discover the strength and resilience of a certain segment of the older population, which he refers to as the *hardy elders*. He contrasts them with the prevailing picture of the older person as "a wasted creature, compounded of irreversible losses in the physical, cognitive, psychological, and social domains." He asserts that, in the face of traumatic losses and narcissistic injuries, moderate doses of psychodynamic psychotherapy can help them maintain self-reliant lives.

Although he draws on his extensive clinical experience, Gutmann's approach in this chapter is largely subjective and anecdotal, and he makes no pretense of providing a comprehensive review of the sizable gerontological literature. He makes interesting use of such Jungian concepts as personal myths and archetypes and the role of the "shadow" in creating areas of vulnerability in the older patient's personality organization. The strength of his approach lies in his insistence on determining the unconscious meanings of the external events, rendering understandable the apparent incongruity of an older person prevailing over major losses while succumbing to seemingly minor injuries. Gutmann's ideas suggest areas for fruitful research that could have an ameliorative impact on many older patients and that could enhance our understanding of the end points of the developmental life cycle.

In sum, all of the authors in this section grapple with fundamental questions of personality development and organization. How much of development is the unfolding of innate capacities? How much is dependent on the roles of key caregivers? What are the interactions between endogenous and exogenous factors? What do we mean by psychic structure? What is the relationship between structure and function? What is the role of repetition in consolidating reliable structures and functions? What is the relationship between repetition/consolidation and transformation into new configurations and modes of organization? How are these dynamic relationships played out over the course of the life cycle? Although they provide partial answers, the authors raise many more questions and, in doing so, suggest many fruitful areas for future research.

REFERENCES

Ainsworth, M. D. S. (1969). Object relations, dependency and attachment: A theoretical review of the infant–mother relationship. *Child Development, 40,* 969–1025.

Barrett, K. J., & Campos, J. (1987). Perspectives on emotional development II: A functionalist approach to emotions. In J. D. Osovsky (Ed.), *Handbook of infant development* (2nd Ed.). New York: Wiley.

Benedek, T. (1970). Parenthood during the life cycle. In E. J. Anthony & T. Benedek (Eds.) *Parenthood: Its psychology and psychopathology.*

Blos, P. (1962). *On adolescence: A psychoanalytic interpretation.* New York: Free Press.

Bowlby, J. (1969). *Attachment and loss. Vol. I: Attachment.* London: Hogarth.

Emde, R. N. (1989). The infant's relationship experience: developmental and affective aspects. In A. Sameroff & R. N. Emde, (Eds.). *Relationship disturbances in early childhood: A developmental approach.* New York: Basic Books.

Erikson, E. H. (1964). *Childhood and society.* New York: Norton.

Flavell, J. H. (1963). *The developmental psychology of Jean Piaget.* Princeton, NJ: Van Nostrand.

Freud, S. (1900/1953). The interpretation of dreams. In J. Strachey (Ed. and Trans.), *The standard edition of the psychological works of Sigmund Freud* (Vols. 4 & 5). London: Hogarth.

Freud, S. (1916–1917/1953). Introductory lectures on psycho-analysis. In J. Strachey (Ed. and Trans.), *The Standard edition of the psychological works of Sigmund Freud* (Vol. 16). London: Hogarth.

Hartmann, H. (1939). *Ego psychology and the problem of adaptation.* New York: International Universities Press.

Kohut, H. (1977). *The restoration of the self.* New York: International Universities Press.

Mitchell, S. (1988). *Relational concepts in psychoanalysis: An integration.* Cambridge, MA: Harvard University Press.

Osofsky, J. D., & Eberhart-Wright, A. (1988). Affective exchanges between high-risk mothers and infants. *International Journal of Psychoanalysis, 69,* 221–231.

Stern, D. (1985). *The interpersonal world of the infant.* New York: Basic Books.

5

REFORMULATIONS OF EARLY DEVELOPMENT AND TRANSFERENCE: IMPLICATIONS FOR PSYCHIC STRUCTURE FORMATION

FRANK M. LACHMANN AND BEATRICE BEEBE

In the practice of psychoanalysis we travel among three domains: transference, early development, and a model of the mind, psychic structure. If we begin our observations in the domain of transference, we may note, for example, that a patient alternates among grievances, rage, and childlike admiration for the analyst. When we account for these observations as, for example, did Mahler (1971), by attributing them to the patient's crucial formative experiences during the separation–individuation phase, we have moved into the domain of early development. Regression, displacement, fixation, and developmental arrest supply the links by which the clinician moves from transference to development. Finally, when we ascribe the observation of grievances, rage, and admiration to the operation of mental mechanisms, we have traveled to the domain of psychic structure. These mechanisms include projection or splitting; a mental agency that has failed to integrate "good" and "bad" images of the mother, or a self-organization that is highly vulnerable to fragmentation. These three domains and the assumptions that link them have been accepted aspects of psychoanalytic formulations. Over the years, both the content of the domains and the concrete manner in which they have been linked have been the subject of a considerable critical literature. The recent empirical studies of early development now add to this challenge.

In this chapter we (a) describe these three domains and the assumptions that link them; (b) summarize recent reformulations of early development based on the empirical infant literature; and (c) present a reformulation of transference and psychic structure that is consistent with our review of the infant literature.

THE THREE DOMAINS AND THE ASSUMPTIONS THAT LINK THEM

In clinical practice, the links among early development, psychic structure, and transference have been widely assumed, justifying direct translations from one domain to another. Direct linkages among the domains are assumed when transference phenomena or various forms of psychopathology are interpreted as though the adult patient resembles a child traversing a particular developmental epoch or psychosexual phase (see Lichtenberg, 1989, and Stern, 1985, for similar arguments). The assumption of these direct links is commonplace in the psychoanalytic literature and practice. We all do it. It is not limited to any particular psychoanalytic persuasion. It may be that the nature of our work and its uncertainties prompts us to gravitate toward concrete and linear translations from one domain to another.

The drive–discharge–conflict model conceptualized the links among the domains of early development, transference, and psychic structure by postulating that the infant was under the sway of his or her id or his or her undifferentiated id–ego matrix. Tension reduction and the need for immediate gratification provided the motivation for attachment to objects. This view of development paralleled its theory of structure formation. Frustration and gratification, with an emphasis on the former, served to replace the inchoate id drives with the more organized ego structure. The same sequence that was used to describe early development was used to describe the formation of psychic structure in psychoanalytic treatment. That is, psychic structure was understood to accrue through intrapsychic conflict, promoted in the transference by the analyst's frustration of the patient's drive derivatives. The patient displaced derivatives of drives, in the form of demands for gratification, onto the analyst. By analyzing rather than gratifying these wishes, the analyst promoted their renunciation and replacement by ego autonomy and frustration tolerance. Although there have been attempts to update this model (see, e.g., Greenspan, 1988; Tyson, 1988), its basic assumptions and its concrete linkage to treatment and structure formation have continued to influence psychoanalytic theory and practice.

Various assumptions about early development contained in the drive–discharge–conflict theory as well as in other psychoanalytic theories are disputed by empirical studies of early development. We propose that the implications of this research could significantly contribute to psychoanalytic theory and practice. To do so, the three domains must be "unhooked" and relinked. Reformulations in any one domain will have reverberations for the others, as well as for the links among them.

THE PROBLEMS WITH CONCRETE LINKS

Inherent in the assumption of direct linkages are problems that can be illustrated by considering the links between (a) transference and psychic structure, (b) early development and psychic structure, and among (c) early development, psychic structure, and transference.

The Link Between Transference and Psychic Structure

The ongoing debate about the organization of the transference has direct bearing on the link between transference and psychic structure. The view that transference is solely a product of the patient's unconscious repetitive strivings, and furthermore, a product of early childhood, has been challenged. We may describe this debate by posing the following questions: Is transference best understood as solely a product of the patient's attempt to divest himself or herself of painful, potentially conflicting feelings by displacing or projecting them onto the analyst? In this instance countertransference is an interference and intrusion into the psychoanalytic process.

This is a one-person psychology perspective. Or, does transference emerge through the interactive contributions of patient and analyst? In this instance countertransference is believed to provide the analyst with an understanding of the patient's transference. This is a two-person psychology perspective (Gill, 1982; Gill & Hoffman, 1982; Racker, 1968). Or is transference best understood as organized by a combination of these two perspectives (Ghent, 1989; Lachmann & Beebe, 1990; Lachmann & Lichtenberg, 1992; Mitchell, 1988; Stolorow, Brandchaft, & Atwood, 1987)? We argue for this integration of the one-person and two-person psychology perspectives.

The Link Between Early Development and Psychic Structure

The ongoing debate about how psychic structure is organized has been restricted by a developmental perspective in which regression and psychosexual fixation are interpreted concretely. Themes seen in the adult are assumed to be in a one-to-one correspondence with childhood configurations. We propose the adoption of a transformational perspective, congruent with numerous analytic theoreticians and developmental psychologists.

From birth on, development is a consequence of the continuous interaction between the person and the environment. Transformational models imply that in order to predict development, the system of interactional exchanges and its regular restructurings must be examined (Osofsky & Eberhart-Wright, 1988; Sameroff, 1976, 1983; Sander, 1983). The contributions of each stage of development are recognized, not just the earliest. Intrapsychic changes produce changes in the environment and vice versa, so that neither the person nor the environment remains static from one point of time to another (Piaget, 1954; Sameroff, 1976).

A transformational model of development asserts that experiences at each stage of development are continually reorganized. The content of these stages differs according to different theorists. For example, Freud (1905/1953) described the psychosexual stages of development. Self psychology addresses the selfobject needs required at various developmental stages and the progressively more sophisticated selfobject functions that are internalized (Kohut, 1984; Lachmann, 1986; Wolf, 1988). In spite of its explicit inclusion in psychoanalytic theories, the implications of the transformational model has not been influential in psychoanalytical clinical discourse.

Infant research describes the transformations in various ways. There is considerable literature documenting the relevance of early patterns of interaction in the first few months for later patterns of attachment and cognition in the second year (see Bretherton, 1985; Isabella & Belsky, 1991; Sroufe, 1979). With the advent of symbolic and other capacities, Stern's (1985) RIGs, representations of interactions that have been generalized, are transformed. They evolve into the more complex scripts (Stern, 1989), internal working models (Ainsworth, Blehar, Waters, & Wall, 1978; Bowlby, 1980; Stern, 1988), and representational configurations of self, other, and self-with-other (Beebe & Lachmann, 1988a, 1988b; Lachmann & Beebe, 1990, in press; Stern, 1983, 1985). Unconscious organizing principles (Stolorow et al., 1987), model scenes (Lichtenberg, 1989; Lachmann & Lichtenberg, in press) and selfobject functions can then be seen as later transformations of earlier interaction structures.

The Links Among Early Development, Transference, and Psychic Structure

Problems in assumption of concrete links among all three domains—early development, transference, and psychic structure—can be illustrated by the controversy over the status of symbiotic longings. Do symbiotic longings predominate for a phase of development (Mahler, Pine, & Bergman, 1975)? If so, adult pathology around separation–individuation issues is derived from that period of life in which symbiosis must yield to separation. According to this view, a specific manifestation in the transference is assumed to be the product of a specific period of development. Or, as has been proposed more recently and as we have argued, do symbiotic longings constitute heightened moments that continue throughout life (Kohut, 1984; Lachmann & Beebe, 1989; Pine, 1985, 1986; Silverman, Lachmann, & Milich, 1982)?

In revisiting oneness fantasies, Lachmann and Beebe (1989) concluded that oneness experiences and a sense of a separate, bounded self constitute a dimension of experience that is optimally characterized by flexibility to span this range. The capacity to span this range may be constituted at numerous phases of development and is extracted from a variety of experiences throughout life. Early experiences that make a relevant contribution to this range, not solely to the "symbiotic" endpoint of the range, include state sharing (Stern, 1985) and matching (Beebe & Lachmann, 1988b; Kronen, 1982; Stern, 1985; Tronick, 1982, 1989), similarities and complementarities (Stern, 1985), alone states (Sander, 1983; Winnicott, 1965), attunements (Stern, 1985), and disruptions and repair of such ruptures in attunements (Gianino & Tronick, 1988; Stechler & Kaplan, 1980). On the basis of both empirical data and clinical theory, Lachmann and Beebe proposed that oneness fantasies can be understood as a product of the postearly childhood mind and that they have a developmental origin that draws from multiple sources across development, not a specific phase.

Our revision of the role of oneness fantasies illustrates our reformulation of the links among development, transference, and psychic structure. Oneness experiences and symbiotic longings do not belong to a specific phase of development. Pathology surrounding oneness, merger, or symbiotic longings is constructed through a variety of phases and experiences, with the possibility of being continuously transformed or rigidified throughout development. Transference involving oneness experiences, and symbiotic longings is not invariably a direct replica of an original symbiotic relationship. It is constructed on the basis of both past relationships from various phases of development as well as from the current patient–analyst interaction. Finally, we do not see difficulties with oneness and symbiotic longings as necessarily indicative of borderline organization (Mahler, 1971), where problems in separation are used as a category of psychic structure. Instead, we view the range of experience from oneness to a separate sense of self as constituting a lifelong theme or configuration.

We have noted the problems inherent in the assumption of direct links among the three domains. We believe that transference does not carry a direct line to a person's childhood. Rather, transference is constructed by both the organizing principles derived from the past as well as the ongoing analyst–patient interaction. Finally, we argue for a model of structure formation that recognizes the transformational contributions from all phases of development.

THE THREE DOMAINS: REVIEW, CHALLENGE, AND REVISIONS

The Preempirical Infant in Psychoanalytic Theory

In *Psychoanalysis of Developmental Arrests* (Stolorow & Lachmann, 1980), in line with the then-current psychoanalytic thinking, assumptions about early development were directly linked to the transference and to psychic structure. Specifically, arrests in the development of the capacity to distinguish self from other (developmental arrests) were linked to the treatment of narcissistic pathology. The model of early development that provided the basis for these formulations was distilled and integrated from the contributions of Spitz (1957, 1965); Mahler et al. (1975); Jacobson (1964); Kernberg (1975); and Kohut (1971). Along with these authors, Stolorow and Lachmann (1980) assumed that the infant was understood to be facing three tasks. As the first developmental task, the infant needed to differentiate or subjectively separate self representations from representations of primary objects and to establish rudimentary boundaries between self and object (Mahler et al., 1975).

A second developmental task facing the infant was the integration of representations with contrasting affects into whole representations of self and object with both positive and negative qualities. This task was derived from the clinical observation of adults who had not accomplished the integration of representations of the "good" and "bad" images of the mother. The accomplishment of this task occupied a major role for Kernberg (1975) in his discussions of early childhood states, "splitting," and "borderline pathology."

The third developmental task entailed the establishment of both self constancy and object constancy. Such constancy would be manifested in the capacity to sustain and relate to an enduring image of another person who is then valued for his or her real qualities and is recognized as a separate individual with needs and feelings of his or her own (Burgner & Edgecumbe, 1972).

Consistent with psychoanalytic tradition, this model of early development paralleled the analysis of transference and was related to a theory of structural pathology. Direct links between early development and transference were assumed. Psychopathology was understood as a consequence of traumatic interferences in the child's ability to negotiate the three developmental tasks. Successful negotiation of these tasks would eventuate in the development of a sense of self with structural cohesion, positive affective coloration, and temporal continuity. Failure to negotiate these tasks would result in an arrest in the subjective separation, differentiation, and integration of self and object representations (i.e., an arrest in development, a structural vulnerability). Such structural vulnerability was considered to be the basis for psychopathology in adults, in that more or less undifferentiated and unintegrated self and object configurations would be prone to be revived. With respect to treatment, it was suggested that developmental progressions set in motion in psychoanalysis would repeat the path of early normal development. The state of nondifferentiation between self and object would develop into separate and constant self and object representations. A fundamental assumption in the three tasks was that development proceeded in a linear way from states of merger, fusion, or nondifferentiation to states of separation, differentiation, individuation, autonomy, and maturity.

The three tasks assumed to characterize early development (i.e., self–object differentiation, affect integration, and self and object constancy) were derived from the writings of a number of psychoanalysts. Later, criticisms were leveled at the perpetuation of this empirically unsubstantiated, mythical infant of psychoanalytic theories (e.g., Eagle, 1984). However, by the time these criticisms were made, the revolution in the infant empirical literature was well under way.

In retrospect, the three tasks attributed to the preempirical infant are relevant for understanding adult psychopathology. However, they cannot be assumed to describe infant development. No doubt the source of the difficulties an adult encounters in dealing with issues in the three tasks may be traced to, but should not be reduced to, early experiences.

Developmental Deficits and Arrests

Kohut (1971, 1977) posited that selfobject needs are the central motivation in human development. As originally formulated, when these needs were thwarted, unmet, or unresponded to by the caretaking surround in early development, deficits in psychic structure were understood to be a consequence. A variety of psychopathologies were understood to be a manifestation of these structural deficits. Kohut also posited that the development of the capacity for self-soothing and self-regulation of affect and arousal in a child is a consequence of the establishment of the requisite selfobject ties. Such a tie is forged when the child's needs for mirroring are recognized, understood, met, and not interfered with by the child's caretakers. The child's experience of having these needs met establishes a sense of cohesion in which affects are integrated into ongoing functioning. The experience of feeling responded to and understood is *one* of the contributors to the capacity to self-regulate affective experience. Failing to have these selfobject needs met may result in an inability to experience a variety of affects within comfortable boundaries. Under such circumstances, affects may appear to become overwhelming or become deadened. These phenomena were understood as deficits in the self-soothing capacity. Treatment could redress this deficit by providing an opportunity to establish the requisite selfobject tie to the analyst. This intact tie would permit the arrested structures to resume their development. The deficit in self-soothing would be replaced by an integrating capacity to regulate affects and arousal and to tolerate and sustain a variety of painful and pleasurable feelings.

The term *developmental arrest* "did not . . . imply that development was completely stopped. Rather [it] meant that the structuralization of the subjective world has been incomplete, uneven, or partially aborted so that more advanced representational structures remain vulnerable to regressive dissolution" (Stolorow & Lachmann, 1980, p. 5). The emphasis was on the extent to which "arrested" configurations of self and object, whether merged or only partially differentiated, were instrumental in determining a variety of psychological states. Deficiencies in the develop-ment, articulation, and elaboration of self and object representations were understood to account for "borderline" states, sexual pathology, and characterological "distortions" such as excessive grandiosity and idealization.

The terms *deficit* and *arrest* belong to a time in the evolution of psychoanalytic thought when the limitations of the drive theory as an explanatory model were being recognized but no compelling alternative source had evolved. The contributions from the empirical infant literature had also not yet made their way into psychoanalytic discourse. The terms *deficit* and *arrest* provided a crude but useful way of articulating pathology that could not be adequately explained on the basis of drive, discharge, and conflict—even when the scope and applicability of that theory were widened (Jacobson, 1954; Stone, 1954).

The "arrest" model posited that derailed experiences created a deficit in structure. A model of normal development drawn from the works of analytic developmentalists (Jacobson, 1964; Mahler, 1968; Spitz, 1957, 1965) provided the standard from which derailments could be evalu-ated. Derailments of normal development were those instances that failed to provide an average expectable environment (Hartmann, 1964). These derailed experiences included "deficiencies in early care as a consequence of psychopathology in the parents . . . an absence of empathic responsiveness to the child's developmental requirements, extreme inconsistencies in behavior toward the child, and frequent exposure of the child to unbearable sexual and aggressive scenes" (Stolorow & Lachmann, 1980, p. 5).

The terms *arrest* and *deficit* were used to describe both functional disabilities as well as the structural organization that accounted for a patient's functional disabilities. For example, the inability to provide oneself with soothing or regulate one's affect was considered to be *both* a functional deficit and to constitute a deficit in structure. Psychoanalytic treatment then needed to investigate the vulnerability and its source, thereby providing for that person the raw materials, in this case the necessary selfobject experiences (Kohut, 1971, 1977), that would be internalized. The internalized experiences would provide the structure that replaced the deficits and promoted the resumption of development.

Kohut's (1971, 1977, 1984) theory has been criticized and expanded by various self psy-chologists (Lichtenberg, 1989; Stolorow et al., 1987). We considered it important to distinguish between deficits in functional capacities (cf. Adler, 1985; Gedo, 1979) and the psychological organization that underlies such functional deficits. This underlying psychological organization is not adequately described as a deficit in structure or as an arrest in development. On the basis of a perspective drawn from the empirical infant literature, we believe that it is better thought of as an organization in and of itself. For example, characteristic expectations of the nature of the interactive regulation, such as expectation of nonresponse or nonmutuality, constitute structure. A model of early development consistent with the empirical research promises to place psychoanalysis as a treatment and as a theory on a firmer foundation.

We illustrate the difference between structural and functional deficit through a clinical example. A patient, a 40-year-old woman, described herself as being unable to cry. She recalled her mother's admonitions against crying and giving in to her feelings. She felt that when she cried it not only hurt, but almost destroyed, her mother. Her feelings profoundly affected her mother's state and vice versa. The inability to cry may be called a functional deficit. She could not regulate her own affects, feel a sense of mastery over painful emotional states and experiences, or mourn losses. The deficit could be understood as derived from an arrest in the capacity to differentiate her own emotional states from those of her mother, which would be considered a deficit in structural organization according to the original theory of developmental deficit. However, closer investigation revealed that the patient expected rebuffs, being shamed (Morrison, 1989), and having to regulate painful affects on her own. She was dominated by rigid self-expectations of control over disruptive states. The patient's tie to her mother led to her organizing her experience so as to maintain tight self-control and to avoid producing distress in another person whom she vitally needed for self-maintenance. The second explanation does not posit the absence of organization as a possibility, as does the deficit model. Rather than seeing this patient as having a deficit in structure, rigid, restrictive expectations structured her experience.

Revisions of Early Development

The research findings reported by the recent generation of "baby watchers" have supported a view of early development that radically alters the assumptions about childhood maintained by a wide spectrum of analysts. According to the findings reported by the infant researchers, the neonate is not a tabula rasa, nor undifferentiated, nor passive, nor initially unrelated to the environment. The infant cannot be described as spending the better part of his or her day struggling with infantile rage or paranoid dangers or escaping from a primary anxiety. Most important, especially with respect to very early development, the full range of capacities at birth with which infants engage their human and nonhuman environments has not been appreciated. The empirical infant literature has detailed an extraordinary array of early social, perceptual, and cognitive capacities. From the beginning of life, the infant engages with the caretaker in an active construction of *both* the interpersonal and subjective world (Beebe, 1985; Beebe & Lachmann, 1988a, 1988b; Demos, 1984; Emde, 1981; Horner, 1985; Lachmann & Beebe, 1989; Lichtenberg, 1983, 1989; Sander, 1983; D. Silverman, 1985; Stern, 1977, 1985).

In former models of early development, the infant was understood to be motivated by drive reduction, which made trauma, anxiety, or loss central motivating factors. There is a realm of the infant's activity, however, that is not accounted for by this model of motivation. Phenomena such as play, curiosity, and exploration decisively contribute to interactive regulations and hence to early representations. A model that recognizes these sources of motivation is therefore necessary. The nature of information itself, novelty, complexity, match, incongruity, or surprise, provides an intrinsic motivation for behavior (Berlyne, 1966; Hunt, 1965; Piaget, 1954). Assuming an intact organism and an adequately responsive environment, the infant is born with various capacities that ensure a highly organized, social relatedness. Inherent in the organism–environment transaction is the construction of a primary nonderivative social relatedness. These sources of motivation have recently been noted by Lichtenberg (1989) in his organization of the empirical infant findings into five motivational systems: regulation of physical requirements, sensuality and sexuality, attachment, exploration or assertion, and reacting aversively with withdrawal and aggression.

Stern (1983) addressed many of the assumptions of early infancy that have been taken for granted in much psychoanalytic theorizing. The notion that adult psychopathology is a revival of normal infantile states (e.g., states of autism, narcissism, a paranoid position, psychosexual phases, etc.) is disputed by him, as is the notion that development proceeds from states of merger to differentiation. In fact, Stern (1985) did not give merger a privileged position with respect to organizing the infant's experience. He suggested that the capacity to have mergerlike experiences depends on an already existing sense of self and other.

In addressing the early basis for the self, Stern (1985) held that the infant is born with the capacity to form separate, distinct schemas of self, other, and self-with-other. However, it is important to note that this "self" is not yet symbolic and not yet subjective in the sense of a capacity for self-reflection. In discussing the early self, he stated that one can no longer contend that

> the infant must differentiate self from other through a laborious, piecemeal process of building up a schema and then representations of self and other . . . from an homogenous array of stimuli and a laborious process of associative learning. (Stern, 1983, p. 52)

Stern's (1985) position is at odds with the previously held formulation that psychological development proceeds from merger to separateness, from an undifferentiated matrix to states of organization, and through a series of stages defined by the prominence of a libidinal zone (i.e., oral, anal, etc.). Furthermore, he held that there are serious problems with using clinical issues such as symbiosis or separation to describe developmental phases, as occurs in a linear model. Using the issues of separation, autonomy, and independence as an illustration, Stern suggested that Erikson (1950) and Freud (1905/1953) placed the decisive encounters that define this phase at about 24 months of age, when the infant achieves independent control of bowel functioning. Spitz (1957), using the child's ability to say no, places the decisive encounters at 15 months of age. Mahler (1968, 1975), using the infant's capacity to walk and to wander away from mother on his or her own initiative, placed the decisive encounters at about 12 months of age. Stern argued that each of the critical encounters contribute to and transform the sense of separateness and autonomy. There are even additional interactions at 4 months of age, such as mutual gazing and the infant's control over the interaction when he or she looks and when he or she looks away that function as contributors to the process of separation.

Mutual and Self-Regulations

In a series of articles (Beebe, 1985; Beebe & Lachmann, 1988a, 1988b; Beebe & Stern, 1977; Lachmann & Beebe, 1989), we spelled out a model of structure formation in early development based on an array of empirical studies of early infancy. We proposed that expectancies of characteristic patterns of mother–infant mutual influences and infant self-regulations contribute to the formation of presymbolic self and object representations. Mother and infant respond to and influence each other on a moment-to-moment basis. By *mutual influence*, we do not mean that infant and caretaker influence each other in equal amount or in like manner. Rather, we mean that each partner's behavior is to some degree predictable from the other's behavior.

The infant is born with his or her own organization and capacity for self-regulation. From birth, the infant has the capacity to regulate arousal and sleep–wake cycles, given an adequate mutual regulation with the caretaker. We suggested that the patterns of mutual and self-regulations, when expected and characteristic, are stored in early presymbolic representations. These interaction structures of expected patterns of mutual and self-regulation are represented over the early months of life and play a major role in the emerging symbolic forms of self and object representations in the second and third years of life. The infant begins to organize a "representational world" in the first half of the first year, prior to the emergence of symbolic capacity. Later, developing symbolic capacities permit defensive processes and fantasy elaborations of one's own experience.

Under conditions of "derailment" or "misattunement," conditions that would result in functional deficits, expectancies of misregulation of attention, affect, and arousal are represented. Furthermore, we reviewed literature (Beebe & Lachmann, 1988b) that documented that variations in early social interactions predict cognitive development and patterns of attachment during the first 2 years of life.

There are several conclusions that emerge from this review that affect propositions about structure formation: (a) The infant arrives with inborn capacities and organization that are the bases for structure formation; (b) the infant is an active contributor to the organization of his or her experience; (c) the cognitive capacities of the infant do not support an original state of nondifferentiation; (d) development proceeds through an interaction between self-regulatory and mutual regulatory processes; (e) structure formation is not only based on a tension-reduction model but also on intrinsic motivation, inherent in information processing; (f) structure formation occurs through continuous processes of transformation brought about through the social interaction between infant and caretaker.

The analyst's model of early development directly influences formulations of the transference, a theory of psychic structure formation, and hence has direct implications for the conduct of an analysis.

TRANSFERENCE

The Linear Model

The link between transference and early development, and the link between transference and psychic structure, has relied on the assumption of various defense mechanisms. For example, when a patient has difficulties with separation–individuation issues in the transference, the assumption is made that these difficulties originated at the time at which such manifestations were normal. Regression to or fixation at the separation–individuation phase is assumed to be the link between early development and transference. In interpreting a patient's projections or splitting, the analyst translates the patient's experience of the treatment into the structures of the patient's mind and their origins. However, when these mechanisms are taken literally, they concretize psychological processes and experience. They lose the essential quality of metaphor and emerge as mechanisms deployed by a disembodied psychic apparatus. The decisive contributions derived from transformations during other developmental phases and later significant influences can be neglected.

Clinical Illustration: Transformation

We illustrate our application of a transformational perspective in a clinical vignette (discussed in detail in Lachmann & Beebe, in press) taken from the first year of the analysis of a 39-year-old divorced woman. She sought treatment because she felt anxious and despondent to the point where she occasionally could not function in her work. After several months of treatment, her symptoms had abated somewhat. Then, over the course of several sessions, she reported dreams and events that led her to describe how resentful she felt about being burdened with chores she performed for her daughter, friends, and clients. On the basis of her associations, the patient's description of herself and her interactions with others, the analyst commented that though she, the patient, might want to be taken care of, she frequently found herself in the position of the caring, self-sacrificing mother.

The patient immediately supplied confirmatory material with respect to her family, her parents, her brother, her ex-husband, and her daughter. However, shortly after the session she became increasingly depressed and confused. She telephoned the analyst in the evening after the session in which the interpretation was offered and asked what she could do because she felt profoundly disorganized. In the brief phone conversation, her disorganized state was connected by the analyst to the session, which she had not done on her own. She was told that an attempt would be made to understand if something occurred in the session that disturbed her so.

From the analyst's perspective, the interpretation attempted to address her masochistic character structure. He suggested that although she might want to be taken care of, she so frequently found herself in the position of the caring, self-sacrificing mother. She was understood as longing for and feeling threatened by her desires to be taken care of, which were defended against through the excessive caretaking of others.

The patient, however, did not share the analyst's perspective. Her sense of cohesion was derived from feeling vitally needed though self-sacrificing and being overburdened. She perceived herself as a caregiver and depicted those under her care as being essentially helpless in the face of a hostile world. She felt effective in helping them. The interpretation undermined this source of efficacy.

In her early years the patient lived in dread of being abandoned by her mother. Her mother's attention was devoted to community affairs and to maintaining her tie with her own parents and sisters. Her father's political activities required frequent moves, so that the family was uprooted several times during her first 8 years. The patient described constraining herself and feeling that any demand on her mother would unduly burden her. She expected to be able to ensure her mother's attention by being undemanding and expecting little from her. Her ability to provide for her mother provided her with a feeling of stability. Although initially derived from her relationship with her mother, her self-organization underwent a crucial transformation during her puberty years with respect to her need to retain her father in an idealized position.

Although the interpretation that she might want to be taken care of but found herself in the position of the self-sacrificing mother did not address the transference per se, it nevertheless had a powerful effect on the patient's experience of the analyst. She felt as if he had said to her, "You are a victim like your mother and I do not need you to sacrifice yourself." She felt implicitly rejected, which contributed to her profound experience of disruption. Exploration of the tie led to the understanding of its organization during her puberty years in relation to her father. At that time, her tie to her father was coupled with an array of newly developing resources and provided the patient with the sense of efficacy and competence that she drew on in much of her later and adult functioning. However, this tie to the father was repeatedly ruptured through disappointments. A combination of unfortunate external circumstances and "bad choices" diminished her father's stature in the family and in his community.

Self-sacrifice established initially to provide stability for her mother and cohesion for herself, was later activated and transformed to restore her father's idealized position and to protect herself against being disappointed by him. She imagined herself as being part of her father's world, which provided her with a sense of vitality and promoted her intellectual curiosity. Her academic work flourished. Her world of skills and interests expanded. Thus, a general masochistic pattern, first organized to retain a connection with her mother, to derive some nurturance through self-abnegation, was later refined and its function transformed. In being activated in relation to her father, she acquired a sense of pride and competence, as well as the feeling that she could be thought of as needed, interesting, and capable.

This case illustrates a transformation of a masochistic pattern at puberty in which, in addition to its pathological features, it became associated with a host of resources. A transformational model recognizes both the continuous construction and potential reorganization of experience at various stages, as well as the repetition of ways of organizing experience shaped by early interactive patterns. Such a model recognizes the constant shifts and transformations that provide a complex texture to ongoing experience and avoids reductionism (see also Mitchell, 1988). It also acknowledges that each transformation generates the possibility that new resources may be acquired as well as providing new ways of organizing past experience (Loewald, 1980).

The Blank Screen Model

In past formulations, transference was understood to emerge solely from the patient. Breuer and Freud (1893–1895/1951) initially called transference a "false connection" made by the patient. Even when transference is considered to be a consequence of a patient's projections, displacements, and regressions, a distortion of a realistic appraisal of the person of the analyst, the "false connection" connotation, remains. This view of transference as emerging entirely from the patient, with the analyst assumed to be a blank screen, is usually formulated as a one-person psychology perspective. It ignores the contributions of the analyst in shaping the transference. This view has been criticized by those to whom countertransference made an indispensable contribution to the treatment process (e.g., Racker, 1968). This latter view illustrates a two-person psychology perspective. When adhered to exclusively, it may overemphasize the purely interactive organization of the transference without sufficient recognition of the contributions brought by the patient.

The Interactive Organization of the Transference

The interactive contributions of analyst and patient in shaping transference have been discussed by Gill (1982), Hoffman (1983), Mitchell (1988), and Stolorow et al. (1987). Stolorow and Lachmann (1984/1985) indicated that the transference is better understood as generated by both patient and analyst as well as reflecting in microcosm the patient's inner life. Through this interaction, rigidly retained structures can be observed, investigated, and transformed, and new experience can organize new themes.

Case Illustration: Interactive Organization

The patient (discussed in greater detail in Lachmann & Lichtenberg, 1992), a woman in her early 30s, sought treatment because of her difficulty in sustaining relationships with men. She felt generally abused, unacknowledged, or shunted aside. She kept her complaints to herself and then, to the surprise of all, would burst forth with rage.

When she was 2 years old, her mother became seriously ill, just after the birth of a sister. When she was 4, her mother died. Her father, an energetic, physically active, successful businessman, then ran the family as a benevolent despot with the aid of a series of housekeepers. During the patient's early teen years, her father married a widow who came with a large family of her own.

The patient had begun analysis with a female analyst who, after 2 years, moved to another city. Thus, the first issue to emerge was her sense of loss and its connections to the loss of her mother.

Toward the end of the first year of analysis, the relationship to her father as well as its consequences for her relationship with other men became central. With this shift in themes, an idealizing transference toward the analyst emerged in which the analyst was seen as one who could manage an ill person. Initially, the analyst (as well as her boyfriend and other people in her life) had been cast as the vulnerable mother whom she had to take care of and treasure during the few precious hours during which they would still be available to her. She now began to experience the analyst as a competent adult who could be expected to relieve her of a precociously felt burden to look after others. She felt "unworthy" and "childish." In particular, she was acutely aware of fearing that she would lose his interest.

The analyst noted in the course of this phase of the analysis that during the sessions with this patient, more frequently than with other patients, humorously phrased interventions would occur to him. He thought of quips and cleverly phrased comments. He noted this reaction and although he generally enjoyed such word play, he thought that he had been able to restrain himself reasonably well.

In a subsequent session, the patient discussed her relationship with her boyfriend and her annoyance that he was always beating her at tennis. By her own admission, she was an excellent tennis player. Further exploration revealed that in the preset warm-up, the patient succeeded in placing the ball in just such a way as to give her boyfriend (and anyone she played with) excellent practice with forehand shots, backhand, net shots, and so forth. He could smash the ball back to her, but she never succeeded in acquiring equal practice for herself. Contained in this interaction was the patient's need to make sure that he would enjoy playing with her and her fear that he might lose interest in her.

The analyst recognized that this vignette provided a perspective for understanding the organization of the transference. The patient was serving beautifully placed straight lines so that the analyst would enjoy smashing them back to her and would thereby want to continue to play with her. She obviously paid a price for maintaining this masochistic pattern. It was not surprising to learn that her first tennis teacher was her father. The patient carefully set up the situation so that her father, her boyfriend, and her analyst would enjoy playing with her and would want to continue to be with her.

In considering the interactive organization of the transference, the patient contributed the propensity to set up masochistic patterns. Specifically, she expertly set up her partners so that they could display and enjoy their prowess. The analyst contributed a capacity to permit himself to enjoy exhibiting his prowess with quips, as well as the capacity to restrain himself from beating the patient with it. The analyst's ability to participate in the interactive pattern of the transference, while maintaining it within analyzable bounds, facilitated the analysis of this transference pattern. This vignette illustrates the interactive contributions of analyst and patient in shaping the transference. In perhaps less obvious ways, such interactions are ubiquitous. Their absence may preclude an analytic engagement, but their contribution to the transference requires constant attention.

REFORMULATING THE LINKS BETWEEN TRANSFERENCE AND DEVELOPMENT: TRANSFORMATIONS IN THE CONCEPT OF THE SELFOBJECT

Within the psychoanalytic tradition, a direct link has been assumed between a patient's early development and subsequent development in the treatment situation. This linear model also influenced Kohut's (1971) initial formulation of the selfobject. Selfobject needs were understood by Kohut to be normal for infancy, but their continuation, maintenance, and persistence in adulthood constituted pathology. When selfobject needs were activated in the transference, they were expected to develop into mature object-related transference configurations (Kohut, 1971; Stolorow & Lachmann, 1980). That is, the transference would evolve from archaic, selfobject configurations to differentiated self and object representations that integrated a spectrum of affective nuances. Selfobject transferences were considered a prestage of the classically described oedipal object-related transferences. Thus, a distinction was made between prestages of transference characterized by selfobject needs and developmentally more mature object-related transferences. Through the establishment of a selfobject transference, early normal paths that had been interrupted or arrested would be opened again and development would be resumed.

A direct connection between pathology in early development and a transference configuration was assumed by Kohut (1971). Linear assumptions can be identified in two aspects of his early formulations. A progression from selfobject to object-related transferences paralleled assumptions about the progression from oneness to separateness and symbiosis to separation–individuation. Second, when selfobject needs emerged in the transference, they were assumed to directly reflect arrested configurations of early development. After 1971, Kohut's understanding of selfobject transferences changed. He proposed that selfobject needs are lifelong (Kohut, 1984). It was furthermore proposed that selfobject functions underwent developmental transformations (Lachmann, 1986; Wolf, 1988).

In the mid-1980s, Stolorow and Lachmann (1984/1985) proposed that selfobject and object-related transferences occupy a figure and ground relationship as *dimensions* of the transference throughout treatment. Furthermore, transference was reformulated as referring to all of the ways (wishfulfilling, defensive, self-punishing, self-maintaining, self-restorative, and adaptive) in which the patient's experience of the analytic relationship is shaped by the patient's psychological structures, as well as by the specific analyst–patient relationship. From this perspective, transference was viewed as an expression of the continuation of organizing principles and imagery derived from the patient's formative experiences, as well as from the current, ongoing, analyst–patient interaction.

We have proposed (Lachmann & Beebe, 1990, in press) a reformulation of the direct link between early development and transference. Our view of transference acknowledges its interactive organization and developmental transformations. The contributions of analyst and patient are neither similar nor equal but, through their interaction, the patient's rigidly retained structures can be engaged, responded to analytically, and transformed. Analysis thereby provides opportunities for new experience and new expectations that can organize new themes.

IMPLICATIONS FOR A MODEL OF PSYCHIC STRUCTURE

Of the various theories of structure formation, Freud's (1923/1961) id–ego–superego partitions as organizers of the mind provided the basis for defining structure in psychoanalytic discourse. The balance among these agencies in conflict and in compromise (Brenner, 1982) provided the metapsychological dynamic to explain psychological motivation. This domain of psychic structure, especially metapsychological propositions and drive theory, has been subjected to critiques from a variety of vantage points (Atwood & Stolorow; 1984; Basch, 1988; Gedo, 1979; Gill, 1982; Holt, 1976; Klein, 1976; Kohut, 1984; Lachmann, 1986; Lichtenberg, 1983, 1989; Rapaport, 1960; Schafer, 1976; Stern, 1985; Stolorow & Lachmann, 1984/1985; Stolorow et al., 1987). Utilizing these contributions, psychic structure has been reformulated in terms of psychological motives, needs, and wishes relying on constructs such as motivational hierarchies, motivational systems, systems of structured motivations, organizing principles, acquisition of functions, and salient themes rather than on biologically rooted impulses or drives.

Infant research provides a further elaboration of the more recent view of psychic structure, particularly its interactive organization. The infant has an extraordinary array of early social, perceptual, and cognitive capacities with which to engage the caretaker in an active construction of *both* the interpersonal and subjective worlds. In our previous discussions of structure formation (Beebe, 1985; Beebe & Lachmann, 1988a, 1988b; Beebe & Stern, 1977; Lachmann & Beebe, 1990, in press), we proposed that mother–infant mutual regulations, interacting with self-regulatory processes, organize a representational world at a presymbolic level. Self-regulations and mutual regulations generate recurrent and characteristic patterns of interaction, "interaction structures," that provide the foundation for early representational structures. This is a dynamic process model of representations based on expectancies of particular patterns of moment-by-moment reciprocal exchanges. These coalesce as self and object representations with the advent of symbolic capacities in the second and third years of life.

Contributions of Mutual and Self-Regulation to Structure Formation

To illustrate the application of our proposals toward a model of psychic structure formation, we offer two illustrations. Mutual influence structures have been demonstrated in the mutual matching of the direction of change of positive facial displays (mother and infant increasingly widening and opening their smiles) and negative displays (mother sobering as infant frowns). We proposed that such matching experiences are crucial ingredients of later symbolized experiences of feeling known, understood, and involved. Such concrete coordination of facial patterns is basic to the coordination of feeling states. As symbolic capacities emerge, the matching experiences might eventually be represented as the following self and object configurations: "I become similar to the way you look at me; I see you look like the way I feel; I feel similar to the way you feel. Our smiles and heads move up and down together; it is both arousing and comfortable. I move at your pace; we are on the same wavelength" (Beebe & Lachmann, 1988b, pp. 327–330). These matching experiences will most likely be represented through the nonverbal representational system rather than through the linguistic representational system (Bucci, 1985).

Such matching experiences might lead to a sense of comfort with affective states and the range of experiences of emotional arousal and quiescence. Neither extreme of this range (Lachmann & Beebe, 1989) threatens to lead to a disruption of the interaction. The entire range of affect and arousal levels can be tolerated. The expectation that affect is mutually regulated within a comfortable range constitutes the structure.

However, if the interaction typical for the dyad is what we describe as "chase and dodge," other expectations would be structured. In the chase-and-dodge interaction, repetitive patterns are described in which the mother tries to engage her baby boy by rapidly looming toward his face. The infant responds by moving his head back and away, losing eye contact. Once the infant has turned away from her, the mother responds by pulling the infant's arm toward her. The infant then pulls his hand right out of hers with such force that he repeatedly looses his balance. With each increased attempt to engage him, the infant moves farther away from the mother with a seeming "veto power" over her efforts. Finally, the infant becomes temporarily limp and unresponsive. Although mother and infant remain mutually responsive to each other moment by moment in the sense that each partner's behavior predicts the other's, the interaction structure is characterized by maternal overstimulation and infant withdrawal. The mother is contingently responsive to the infant's behavior, but the nature of her response is an escalation in the intensity of her stimulation. He may thus experience having to soothe or calm himself by himself. The interaction structures that are eventually represented, should this interaction be characteristic of the dyad, may be described as follows: "When I stay close to you, I feel overaroused and inundated. I feel you are moving in on me. No matter where I move in relation to you, I cannot find a way to feel comfortable. I can neither engage with you nor disengage from you" (Beebe & Lachmann, 1988b, p. 329).

The chase-and-dodge interaction would not give rise to an absence of structure, or a deficit, but to a specific set of delimiting expectations that themselves constitute a structure of experience. The effect would be a functional deficit in the infant's capacity to regulate arousal and affective states, based on the expectation that all of his or her communicative, postural, facial, and temporal signals foreshadow becoming overaroused, out of control, or the necessity to become unresponsive.

CONCLUSIONS: IMPLICATIONS FOR ADULT TREATMENT

The underestimation of the infant's social capacities has had direct consequences for our treatment of adult patients. Our vision of human nature has been biased in two directions. On the one hand, the child has been depicted as being excessively passive and shaped by the environment. On the other hand, the child has been seen as the possessor of a seething cauldron of drive energies pressing for discharge. Both of these positions underestimate the child's own active contributions to the regulation of the interaction and the complexity of early social relatedness. Both biases were extended to conceptualizations of the patient–analyst relationship, prescriptions for the conduct of psychoanalytic treatment, and theories of psychic structure formation.

We have detailed the extensive role that interactive as well as self-regulation plays in constituting psychic structure. Acknowledging that both analyst and patient play active parts in the organization of the transference should not lead to a therapeutic stance whereby the patient may be "blamed" for undermining the analyst or the treatment. Rather, we refer to the mutual construction of the transference as illustrated in the vignette of the patient who sets up the analyst to respond with quips. We proposed that the analyst's participation goes beyond what has traditionally been referred to as countertransference. As an interacting constructor of the treatment situation with the patient, the analyst directly participates in shaping new themes and promoting the transformation of repetitive ones.

The transformational model is a counterpoint to the analytic emphasis on repetition. Transformation directly affects the organization of experience in that the experience is repeated, but rarely in the same way. The changes may be subtle, but the recognition of subtle shifts or transformations is as crucial for the struggling patient as it is for the growing infant. Such recognition will in itself enhance the stability of the transformation. Whereas psychoanalysis has tended to emphasize the repetitive nature of pathology, the analyst has to be cognizant of the way things change as well as the way things remain the same. In our illustration of the patient who shifted her masochistic attachment from her mother to her father at puberty, the analytic recognition of this shift was crucial in consolidating the resources the patient had acquired "in the bargain." To interpret the patient's masochism as solely a manifestation of her tie to her mother would fail to recognize and decisively undermine her subsequent development based on the contributions derived from the transformations at puberty.

Our reformulation of early development and its links to the transference is in line with two decades of psychoanalytic criticism and infant research. Mutual regulatory and self-regulatory processes provide the most basic and pervasive organization of experience in all three domains. They have been observed as salient organizers of early development. Analogously, the transference can also be seen as organized through mutual and self-regulatory processes. Finally, these regulations are represented and symbolically elaborated. We emphasized the continuous transformation of experience to avoid reductionism and linear assumptions.

We recognize the crucial differences between the developmental processes of the infant and therapeutic processes in the adult. We are not proposing a direct translation of the model of structure formation derived from infant study to the adult psychoanalytic situation. Nor do we think that deficits noted in the adult must have been characteristic of a stage of early development or that the therapeutic path requires a belated traversal of early stages. However, we propose that the processes and principles of structuralization in early development can shed light on and contribute to the understanding of the processes in psychoanalytic treatment.

In adults, the capacity for symbolization implies that structure cannot be limited to the organization and representation of interactive behavior. For the child and the adult, structure also refers to the subjective elaboration of experience in the form of fantasies, wishes, defenses, and so forth. Such elaborations require the capacity to symbolize and thus contribute to the themes that define one's experience. From both the analytic dyad and the symbolic capacity to elaborate or restrict one's experience, the analysand "structures" the treatment experiences during all of its phases. In using the interactive contributions of both caretaker with infant and analyst with patient, the mutative factors in the analytic experience can be given broader recognition. Thus, derived from the structures of the patient's past, and the ongoing analyst–patient interaction, the transference can be viewed as being analogous to the mutual and self-regulatory processes that have been reported as organizers of the infant's experience. The treatment prescriptions that follow from our reformulations of the three domains retain a close link between early development, a vision of human nature, and the conduct of an analysis.

Ongoing self- and mutual regulatory processes are intrinsic to the repetitive interactions of the treatment situation. They organize expectations that one *can* affect the other and, in turn, be affected by the other. In psychoanalytic treatment, ongoing regulations range from subtle nonverbal interchanges, posture, and facial expressions to intonations or tone of voice, to greeting and parting rituals, and to the explicit verbal exchanges. They include characteristics of interactions whereby the patient narrates and discloses while the analyst attunes, attends, reflects, describes, and questions. The structuring effect of such interactions are most clearly illustrated in the phase of understanding (Kohut, 1984) and the process of listening (Schwaber, 1984), exploration, and clarification (Greenson, 1967). We believe that these patient–analyst interactions have not been sufficiently recognized as contributing *directly* to the formation of psychic structures. In these phases, repetitive themes of the patient (e.g., expectations of nonresponse, indifference, or rejections) are engaged, disconfirmed (Weiss & Samson, 1986), and woven into the ongoing patient–analyst relationship and recurring themes from the patient's past. Through this process, these themes are altered in that they are assimilated, as a matter of course, with a new context (Loewald, 1980; Modell, 1984). Thus, the ongoing noninterpretive explorations can promote new expectations, that is, new structures of experience.

Another issue in the literature on structure formation is the role of disruption and disequilibrium and whether these are necessary preconditions for structure formation (Behrends & Blatt, 1985; Kohut, 1984). For example, in our discussion of the contributions of matches and nonmatches between caretaker and infant in the chase-and-dodge interaction, we extended the principle of interactive regulations to include the organization of expectations of misregulation, tolerable and intolerable frustrations, and the rupture and repair of the selfobject tie to the analyst. Such interactions structure a range of experience that is noted during phases of explanation (Kohut, 1984) and during the processes of confrontation, working through, and interpretation (Greenson, 1967), as well as during interactions characterized by the analyst's "optimal responsiveness" (Bacal, 1985, 1988). We consider disruption and repair as only *one* avenue of structuralization, not the only one, and as operating during all phases of the treatment. Furthermore, we see disruption and repair as a property of and activity of the patient–analyst interaction (Lachmann, 1990), not solely as a consequence of either the analyst's countertransference or the patient's "resistance." Ruptures and their repair structure a greater flexibility in negotiating disjunctions (Goldberg, 1988) in mutual and self-regulatory processes.

Moments of affect and arousal in the context of the patient–analyst interactions provide opportunities for new experiences in that they promote the integration of newly evolved affectively laden representational configurations. Furthermore, when affective moments are revived, their new context provides a basis for restructuring the traumatic past. Repetitive, inflexible themes can be affectively reexperienced in the ongoing analyst–patient relationship so that new expectations can be established and integrated. The structuring of new themes alters the context in which rigid, archaic themes had dominated a person's experience. These newly organized configurations may then transform the archaic, dominant, rigid themes.

Psychoanalytic discourse relies heavily on analogy, metaphor, and similarities. We search for precursors and origins of adult psychopathology in ever earlier phases of development. It is all too tempting to slip from similarities and analogies to concrete identities and thus to make direct connections and translations between the phenomena of childhood and the phenomena of adulthood. We assume that what is observed now in the adult literally is a direct consequence of specific traumata of childhood. The assumption that what happened earlier explains what happened later offers us a sense of solidity at the price of oversimplification.

In clinical discussions, it is unlikely that anyone would argue in favor of such a reductionistic, linear model of development, one that oversimplifies development by proposing concrete connections between past and present. Yet, in case conferences and published reports, this caution is honored more in the breach than in the observance. We believe that the "leaps from couch to crib" (Lachmann, 1985, p. 17) were partially fueled by misinterpretations of the work of Margaret Mahler.

In our survey of the problems inherent in the assumption of direct links among the three domains, we have argued that transference does not carry a direct line to a person's childhood but that transference must be understood as constructed by both the organizing principles derived from the past as well as from the ongoing analyst–patient interaction. We have argued for a model of structure formation that recognizes the transformational contributions from all phases of development. Finally, we have argued for a conceptualization of early development that recognizes the infant as an active participant in the construction of his or her inner and interpersonal world.

The empirical infant research has been of singular importance in pointing to new directions for psychoanalytic discourse and in recasting the links among the three domains. In psychoanalytic treatment, we recognize the organization and transformation of new themes. In the evolution of psychoanalytic theory, we can avoid reductionism and linear perspectives. The interactive contributions of the three domains affect our vision of human nature and increase our understanding of psychopathology and its cure.

REFERENCES

Adler, G. (1985). *Borderline psychopathology and its treatment.* Northvale, NJ: Jason Aronson.

Ainsworth, M., Blehar, M., Waters, E., & Wall, S. (1978). *Patterns of attachment: A psychological study of the strange situation.* Hillsdale, NJ: Erlbaum.

Atwood, G., & Stolorow, R. (1984). *Structures of subjectivity.* Hillsdale, NJ: Analytic Press.

Bacal, H. (1985). Optimal responsiveness and the therapeutic process. In A. Goldberg (Ed.), *Progress in self psychology* (Vol. 1, pp. 202–226). New York: Guilford Press.

Bacal, H. (1988). Reflections on "optimum frustration." In A. Goldberg (Ed.), *Progress in self psychology* (Vol. 4, pp. 127–131). Hillsdale, NJ: Analytic Press.

Basch, M. (1988). *Understanding psychotherapy.* New York: Basic Books.

Beebe, B. (1985). Mother-infant mutual influence and precursors of self and object representations. In J. Masling (Ed.), *Empirical studies of psychoanalytic theories* (Vol. 2, pp. 27–48). Hillsdale, NJ: Analytic Press.

Beebe, B., & Lachmann, F. (1988a). Mother-infant mutual influence and precursors of psychic structure. In A. Goldberg (Ed.), *Frontiers in self psychology, progress in self psychology* (Vol. 3, pp. 3–25). Hillsdale, NJ: Analytic Press.

Beebe, B., & Lachmann, F. (1988b). The contribution of mother-infant mutual influence to the origins of self- and object representations. *Psychoanalytic Psychology, 5,* 305–337.

Beebe, B., & Stern, D. (1977). Engagement-disengagement and early objective experiences. In N. Freedman & S. Grand (Eds.), *Communicative structures and psychic structures* (pp. 35–55). New York: Plenum Press.

Behrends, R., & Blatt, S. (1985). Internalization and psychological development throughout the life cycle. *Psychoanalytic Study of the Child, 40,* 11–39.

Berlyne, D. (1966). Curiosity and exploration. *Science, 153,* 25–33.

Bowlby, J. (1980). *Attachment and loss* (Vol. 3). New York: Basic Books.

Brenner, C. (1982). *The mind in conflict.* New York: International Universities Press.

Bretherton, I. (1985). Attachment theory: Retrospect and prospect. *Monographs of the Society for Research in Child Development, 50* (1–2, Serial No. 209).

Breuer, J., & Freud, S. (1951). Studies on hysteria. In J. Strachey (Ed. and Trans.), *Standard edition of the complete psychological works of Sigmund Freud* (Vol. 2, pp. 1–309). London: Hogarth Press. (Original work published 1893–1895)

Bucci, W. (1985). Dual coding: A cognitive model for psychoanalytic research. *Journal of the American Psychoanalytic Association, 33,* 571–608.

Burgner, M., & Edgecumbe, R. (1972). Some problems in the conceptualization of early object relationships: Part II. The concept of object constancy. *Psychoanalytic Study of the Child, 27,* 315–333.

Demos, V. (1984). Empathy and affect: Reflections on infant experience. In J. Lichtenberg, M. Bonnstein, & D. Silver (Eds.), *Empathy* (Vol. 2, pp. 9–34). Hillsdale, NJ: Analytic Press.

Eagle, M. (1984). *Recent developments in psychoanalysis.* New York: McGraw-Hill.

Emde, R. (1981). The prerepresentational self and its affective core. *Psychoanalytic Study of the Child, 36,* 165–192.

Erikson, E. (1950). *Childhood and society.* New York: Norton.

Freud, S. (1953). Three essays on the theory of sexuality. In J. Strachey (Ed. and Trans.), *The standard edition of the complete psychological works of Sigmund Freud* (Vol. 1, pp. 125–243). London: Hogarth Press. (Original work published 1905)

Freud, S. (1961). The ego and the id. In J. Strachey (Ed. and Trans.), *The standard edition of the complete psychological works of Sigmund Freud* (Vol. 19, pp. 3–66). London: Hogarth Press. (Original work published 1923)

Gedo, J. (1979). *Beyond interpretation.* New York: International Universities Press.

Ghent, E. (1989). Credo: The dialectics of one-person and two-person psychologies. *Contemporary Psychoanalysis, 25,* 169–211.

Gianino, A., & Tronick, E. (1988). The mutual regulatory model: The infant's self and interactive regulation and coping with defense capacities. In T. Field, P. McCabe, & N. Schneidermann (Eds.), *Stress and coping* (pp. 1–37). Hillsdale, NJ: Erlbaum.

Gill, M. (1982). *Analysis of transference* (Vol. 1). New York: International Universities Press.

Gill, M., & Hoffman, I. (1982). *Analysis of transference* (Vol. 2). New York: International Universities Press.

Goldberg, A. (1988). *A fresh look at psychoanalysis: The view from self psychology.* Hillsdale, NJ: Analytic Press.

Greenson, R. (1967). *The technique and practice of psychoanalysis* (Vol. 1). New York: International Universities Press.

Greenspan, S. (1988). The development of the ego: Insights from clinical work with infants and young children. *Journal of the American Psychoanalytic Association, 36* (Suppl.), 3–56.

Hartmann, H. (1964). *Essays on ego psychology.* New York: International Universities Press.

Hoffman, I. (1983). The patient as interpreter of the analyst's experience. *Contemporary Psychoanalysis, 19,* 389–422.

Holt, R. (1976). Drive or wish? A reconsideration of the psychoanalytic theory of motivation. *Psychological Issues* (Monograph No. 36), 158–197. New York: International Universities Press.

Horner, T. (1985). The psychic life of the young infant: Review and critique of the psychoanalytic concepts of symbiosis and infantile omnipotence. *American Journal of Orthopsychiatry, 55,* 324–344.

Hunt, J. McVickar (1965). Intrinsic motivation and its role in psychological development. In D. Levine (Ed.), *Nebraska Symposium on Motivation* (Vol. 13, pp. 189–282). Lincoln: University of Nebraska Press.

Isabella, R., & Bellsky, J. (1991). Interactional synchrony and the origins of mother-infant attachment: A replication study. *Child Development, 62,* 373–384.

Jacobson, E. (1954). Transference problems in the psychoanalytic treatment of severely depressed patients. *Journal of the American Psychoanalytic Association, 2,* 595–606.

Jacobson, E. (1964). *The self and the object world.* New York: International Universities Press.

Kernberg, O. (1975). *Borderline conditions and pathological narcissism.* Northvale, NJ: Jason Aronson.

Klein, G. (1976). Freud's two theories of sexuality. *Psychological Issues* (Monograph No. 36), 14–70. New York: International Universities Press.

Kohut, H. (1971). *The analysis of the self.* New York: International Universities Press.

Kohut, H. (1977). *The restoration of the self.* Madison, CT: International Universities Press.

Kohut, H. (1984). *How does analysis cure?* Chicago: University of Chicago Press.

Kronen, J. (1982). *Maternal facial mirroring at four months.* Unpublished doctoral dissertation, Yeshiva University, New York.

Lachmann, F. (1985). Discussion of "New Directions in Psychoanalysis" by Michael Franz Basch. *Psychoanalytic Psychology, 2,* 15–19.

Lachmann, F. (1986). Interpretation of psychic conflict and adversarial relationships: A self psychological perspective. *Psychoanalytic Psychology, 3,* 341–355.

Lachmann, F. (1990). On some challenges to clinical theory in the treatment of character pathology. In A. Goldberg (Ed.), *The realities of transference: Progress in self psychology* (Vol. 6, pp. 59–67). Hillsdale, NJ: Analytic Press.

Lachmann, F., & Beebe, B. (1989). Oneness fantasies revisited. *Psychoanalytic Psychology, 6,* 137–149.

Lachmann, F., & Beebe, B. (1990, April). *On the formation of psychic structure: Transference.* Paper presented at the 10th annual spring meeting of the Division of Psychoanalysis of the American Psychological Association, New York:

Lachmann, F., & Beebe, B. (in press). Representational and selfobject transferences: A developmental perspective. In A. Goldberg, *Progress in self psychology* (Vol. 8). Hillsdale, NJ: Analytic Press.

Lachmann, F., & Lichtenberg, J. (1992). Model scenes: Implications for psychoanalytic treatment. *Journal of the American Psychoanalytic Association, 40,* 117–137.

Lichtenberg, J. (1983). *Psychoanalysis and infant research.* Hillsdale, NJ: Analytic Press.

Lichtenberg, J. (1989). *Psychoanalysis and motivation.* Hillsdale, NJ: Analytic Press.

Loewald, H. (1980). *Papers on psychoanalysis.* New Haven, CT: Yale University Press.

Mahler, M. (1968). *On human symbiosis and the vicissitudes of individuation.* New York: International Universities Press.

Mahler, M. (1971). A study of the separation-individuation process and its possible application to borderline phenomena in the psychoanalytic situation. *Psychoanalytic Study of the Child, 26,* 403–424.

Mahler, M., Pine, F., & Bergman, A. (1975). *The psychological birth of the human infant.* New York: Basic Books.

Mitchell, S. (1988). *Relational concepts in psychoanalysis.* Cambridge, MA: Harvard University Press.

Modell, A. (1984). *Psychoanalysis in a new context.* New York: International Universities Press.

Morrison, A. (1989). *Shame: The underside of narcissism.* Hillsdale, NJ: Analytic Press.

Osofsky, J., & Eberhart-Wright, A. (1988). Affective exchanges between high risk mothers and infants. *International Journal of Psycho-Analysis, 69,* 221–232.

Piaget, J. (1954). *The construction of reality in the child.* New York: Basic Books.

Pine, F. (1985). *Developmental theory and clinical process.* New Haven, CT: Yale University Press.

Pine, F. (1986). The "symbiotic phase" in the light of current infancy research. *Bulletin of the Menninger Clinic, 50,* 564–569.

Racker, H. (1968). *Transference and countertransference.* New York: International Universities Press.

Rapaport, D. (1960). The structure of psychoanalytic theory. *Psychological Issues* (Monograph No. 6), 7–158. New York: International Universities Press.

Sameroff, A. (1976). Early influences on development: Fact or fancy? In S. Chess & A. Thomas (Eds.), *Annual progress in child psychiatry and child development* (pp. 3–33). New York: Bruner/Mayel.

Sameroff, A. (1983). Developmental systems: Contexts and evolution. In W. Kessen (Ed.), *Mussen's handbook of child psychology* (Vol. 1, pp. 237–294). New York: Wiley.

Sander, L. (1983). To begin with—Reflections on ontogeny. In J. Lichtenberg & S. Kaplan (Eds.), *Reflections on self psychology* (pp. 85–104). Hillsdale, NJ: Analytic Press.

Schafer, R. (1976). *A new language for psychoanalysis.* New Haven, CT: Yale University Press.

Schwaber, E. (1984). Empathy: A mode of analytic listening. In J. Lichtenberg, M. Bornstein, & D. Silver (Eds.), *Empathy II* (pp. 143–172). Hillsdale, NJ: Analytic Press.

Silverman, D. (1985). Some proposed modifications of psychoanalytic theories of early childhood development. In J. Masling (Ed.), *Empirical studies of psychoanalytic theories* (Vol. 2, pp. 49–72). Hillsdale, NJ: Erlbaum.

Silverman, L., Lachmann, F., & Milich, R. (1982). *The search for oneness.* New York: International Universities Press.

Spitz, R. (1957). *No and yes: On the genesis of human communication.* New York: International Universities Press.

Spitz, R. (1965). *The first year of life.* New York: International Universities Press.

Sroufe, L. A. (1979). The coherence of individual development. *American Psychologist, 34,* 834–841.

Stechler, G., & Kaplan, S. (1980). The development of the self: A psychoanalytic perspective. *Psychoanalytic Study of the Child, 35,* 85–105.

Stern, D. (1977). *The first relationship: Infant and mother.* Cambridge, MA: Harvard University Press.

Stern, D. (1983). The early development of schemas of self, other, and "self with other." In J. Lichtenberg & S. Kaplan (Eds.), *Reflections on self psychology* (pp. 449–484). Hillsdale, NJ: Erlbaum.

Stern, D. (1985). *The interpersonal world of the infant.* New York: Basic Books.

Stern, D. (1988). The dialectic between the "interpersonal" and the "intrapsychic": With particular emphasis on the role of memory and representation. *Psychoanalytic Inquiry, 8,* 505–512.

Stolorow, R., Brandchaft, B., & Atwood, G. (1987). *Psychoanalytic treatment: An intersubjective approach.* Hillsdale, NJ: Analytic Press.

Stolorow, R., & Lachmann, F. (1980). *Psychoanalysis of developmental arrests.* New York: International Universities Press.

Stolorow, R., & Lachmann, F. (1984/1985). Transference: The future of an illusion. *Annual of Psychoanalysis, 12/13,* 19–38.

Stone, L. (1954). The widening scope of indications for psychoanalysis. *Journal of the American Psychoanalytic Association, 2,* 567–594.

Tronick, E. (1982). Affectivity and sharing. In E. Tronick (Ed.), *Social interchange in infancy* (pp. 1–8). Baltimore, MD: University Park Press.

Tronick, E. (1989). Emotions and emotional communication. *American Psychologist, 44,* 112–119.

Tyson, P. (1988). Psychic structure formation: The complementary roles of affects, drives, object relations, and conflict. *Journal of the American Psychoanalytic Association, 36* (Suppl.), 73–100.

Weiss, J., & Sampson, H. (1986). *The psychoanalytic process.* New York: Guilford Press

Winnicott, D. (1965). *The maturational processes and the facilitating environment.* New York: International Universities Press.

Wolf, E. (1988). *Treating the self.* New York: Guilford Press.

6

ATTACHMENTS, DRIVES, AND DEVELOPMENT: CONFLICTS AND CONVERGENCES IN THEORY

ARIETTA SLADE AND J. LAWRENCE ABER

Over the past 10 years, developments in the empirical testing of the fundamental tenets of attachment theory—as delineated by Bowlby (1969)—have led to an abundance of research into the ways the early parent–child relationship affects the child's social and emotional development. The results of these studies provide ample support for the notion that the "success" of the early mother–child relationship serves as a powerful force in shaping later development and facilitating competence. This body of theory and research traces the evolution of these patterns from maternal representations or "internal working models" of their own early parental relationships to child behavior in relationships to child representations of affect and the self. Results reported by numerous investigators indicate that there exists a lawful relation between the nature of a mother's representation of her own childhood experiences, the nature of her behavior with her child, and—ultimately—representational processes in the child. Furthermore, mothers' internal representational models of attachment appear to influence the kinds of feelings they experience and recognize in the relationship with their children. Thus, more and more is being learned about the ways patterns of "being with" significant others are structured and carried forward into new relationships.

The basic theme of these various research efforts is consistent: The quality of early care-giving influences the ways a child experiences emotion, the quality of his or her relationships,

This chapter is dedicated to Dr. Sheldon Bach and Dr. Lawrence O. Brown. An earlier version was presented at a regional scientific meeting of the Childhood and Adolescence Division for Psychoanalysis of the American Psychological Association in January 1987 in New York City.

We wish to thank Drs. Steven Tuber, Marsha Levy-Warren, I. H. Paul, Geoffrey Goodman, and David Wolitzky for their helpful comments on earlier drafts of this chapter.

and the solidity and depth of his or her self-esteem. It also exerts a pivotal influence on an adult's ability to parent. The idea that a mother's thoughts and fantasies about her own childhood influence her behavior with a child, and ultimately the child's own feelings about and representations of the self, is certainly not new to psychoanalysis. In point of fact, such notions are intrinsic to psychoanalytic theory. Nevertheless, despite the great interest generated by John Bowlby's (1969, 1973, 1982) attachment trilogy *Attachment, Separation,* and *Loss,* as it was serially published over the course of the past 20 years, the fundamental tenets of attachment theory have had little impact on clinical psychoanalysis (or on more traditional psychoanalytic theory, for that matter). By contrast, attachment theory and attachment research have dominated virtually all attempts within the empirical child development literature to explain the nature of early social and emotional development.

It is the central aim of this chapter to outline the basic notions of attachment theory and research as they have evolved over the past 15 years and then to examine the ways these advances and theoretical assumptions both converge and diverge with the basic principles of psychoanalytic theory. Insofar as they are distinct and in some ways contradictory theoretical positions, the differences between them should be clarified and understood. Insofar as they are potentially enhancing theoretical positions, the convergences should be considered illuminating and worthy of explication. In essence, this chapter constitutes our effort to understand the standoff between attachment theory and psychoanalysis (see also Bretherton, 1987; Osofsky, 1988; Silverman, 1991).

PATTERNS OF ATTACHMENT IN INFANCY

Attachment theory began with the theoretical work of Bowlby (1969, 1973, 1982), whose views of the origin and nature of the mother–child relationship profoundly influenced the research to be described here. In keeping with object relations theory, Bowlby posited that the infant is predisposed at birth to forming a selective attachment relationship with one or a few caretaking adults. Over the course of phylogeny, humans evolved built-in behavioral systems that enabled such attachments to form. This predisposition toward establishing attachment bonds is manifested in what Bowlby called "attachment behaviors," namely the infant's use of a variety of behaviors—crying, looking, reaching, and so forth—to elicit comforting and caregiving from the other. The goal of what Bowlby called "the attachment behavioral system" is to maintain proximity to the caregiver and to establish what Ainsworth (1969) later called a "feeling of security."

Bowlby viewed the attachment behavioral system as a goal-corrected feedback system. Thus, it operates in such a way that the workings of the system are adjusted once the goal of that system has been achieved. The biological *set goal* of infant attachment behavioral systems was originally conceived by Bowlby as proximity to the parent. Later, the psychological set goal of felt security was added to make the concept of "set goal" relevant to attachment behaviors beyond infancy. Thus, when the infant is feeling safe and secure, by virtue of proximity to mother, or familiarity with the environment, the attachment behavioral system, or need to signal mother to comfort or provide safety, is deactivated. By contrast, when the child feels in need of comfort—by dint of mother's distance from him or her, or the perception of danger from the environment, the attachment system will be activated. When a critical level of felt security has been achieved, the system is deactivated. Simply put, the child will signal his or her need for mother when frightened or feeling himself or herself too far from her, and when the child feels safe in her presence or safe in the knowledge that she will be available should the need arise, the child's expression of these needs will diminish. Although Bowlby orginally viewed the activation of the attachment system as a dichotomous "on–off" condition, Bretherton (1987) proposed that the child's attachment system is always activated but varies along a continuous dimension of activation. Conceptually, the notion that the child always monitors his or her parents' proximity, as well as his or her own felt security has significant implications for how the attachment system is understood. This concept has great heuristic value, for it demonstrates the functional equivalence of different "attachment behaviors" at different stages of early development. Thus, the 6-month-old's cry, the 12-month-old's locomotion to mother, and the 18-month-old's visual and verbal bids for contact over a distance are all behaviors that can be used to increase the child's proximity and felt security and hence are all attachment behaviors.

In infancy and toddlerhood, when not engaged with the parent or caregiver, the most common activity of the child is exploration of the environment. One can think of the attachment and exploratory systems as functioning in a form of dynamic balance. Infants are motivated to explore their environments, but under conditions of perceived danger (a loud noise, a strange adult, a very large distance between mother and child), the attachment system is activated as the exploratory system is deactivated. Then, as the child regains the critical level of felt security, he or she ventures out to explore the environment again. This back-and-forth cycling of attachment and exploratory behaviors are referred to by Ainsworth, Blehar, Waters, and Wall (1978) as *secure base phenomena*. These secure base phenomena are some of the strikingly obvious features of the 1-year-old's behavior in a new environment.

Although Bowlby's theory provided new metaphors for thinking about the phenomena of attachment, separation and loss, it was left to other investigators to realize the empirical potential of these new metaphors. The central empirical breakthrough was made by Mary Ainsworth (Ainsworth et al., 1978). Like so many research breakthroughs, it involved the development of an experimental method or paradigm that could be used to systematically investigate the phenomena of interest. Ainsworth became curious about differences between children in the quality of attachment to the mother and in the nature and workings of the the attachment system. Setting out to explore such differences, Ainsworth developed a now-famous procedure called the Strange Situation.

Following Bowlby, Ainsworth reasoned that differences in maternal sensitivity to infant cues during the first 12 months of life ought to result in differences in the quality of the mother–infant attachment relationship at 1 year. Thus, Ainsworth followed a small group of 23 mother–infant dyads, making detailed home observations and measurements of maternal sensitivity to infant cues every 3–4 weeks over the first year of life. Maternal sensitivity was defined in a variety of ways, including the ways mothers held their babies, responded to their cries, and interacted with them during feeding and play. When the infants were a year old, she assessed the quality of infants' attachment to their mothers.

During the Strange Situation procedure, the infant and his or her mother are brought to a playroom equipped with two chairs and a number of toys. After an initial warm-up and free-play period, a stranger enters the room. Shortly afterward, the mother leaves and the child is left with the stranger. Then, the mother returns. After reuniting with her child, she departs a second time. The child is left alone briefly, at which point the stranger enters and attempts to engage the child. Finally, the mother returns. Each episode of the preseparation play, separation, and reunion lasts 3 minutes and each separation can be terminated by the mother anytime she wishes. Typically, the entire session is recorded on videotape for later analysis. Under these systematic and ecologically valid conditions, Ainsworth reasoned, it should be possible to carefully ascertain whether and how the infant is able to regain a feeling of security after the brief but significant stress of separation from the parent in a strange environment.

Since Ainsworth first devised this paradigm, thousands of Strange Situations have been conducted in this country and increasingly by investigators throughout the world, including

Germany, Israel, and Japan. The newcomer and the veteran of attachment assessments alike are always impressed by the almost infinite variability in how infants organize their attachment and exploratory behaviors under these conditions. Perhaps even more impressive is the orderliness that lies just beyond the apparent infinite variability.

In her original sample of 23 middle-class children and their parents from Baltimore, Ainsworth was able to discern three distinct patterns or organizations of attachment behavior over the series of separation–reunion episodes. We describe each of these major patterns in some detail because of the underlying structure that they reveal and that will serve as the focus of later discussion. To facilitate comparisons across patterns, we describe the preseparation, separation, and reunion behaviors of a prototypical infant demonstrating each major pattern of behavior.

PATTERNS OF INFANT ATTACHMENT

Securely Attached (B) Infants

In Ainsworth's (Ainsworth et al., 1978) original sample and in most "normal" samples in the United States, approximately 65%–70% of the infants assessed in the Strange Situation demonstrate a pattern of attachment and exploratory behaviors over the episodes that Ainsworth believed to be evidence of a "secure" attachment relationship.

Preseparation. On entering the playroom and seeing the stranger, the infant may show a bit of initial wariness. However, by checking in with mother—exhibiting the secure base phenomena—these infants derive sufficient security to explore their environments.

Separation. When mother leaves, secure infants register her departure, perhaps via crying or search behavior, perhaps by diminished quality of exploration and play. The infant will not use the stranger simply as a substitute play partner and will not carry on as before, though he or she may be able to be comforted or distracted a bit by the stranger.

Reunion. When mother returns, infants may signal or greet the mother over a distance or allow themselves to be picked up and comforted by the mother. After clearly deriving comfort and security via mother's return, secure infants are able to return to exploration or play.

Anxious-Avoidant (A) Infants

Children who do not fall into this group are characterized as "insecure" and most often show one of two markedly different "insecure" patterns in the Strange Situation. The largest group of children, approximately 20%–25% in normative U.S. samples, show a pattern Ainsworth describes as "anxious-avoidant attachment," often referred to as the "A" pattern.

Preseparation. Prior to separation, avoidant infants are interested in exploring the environment and are thus somewhat difficult to distinguish from secure infants. However, careful scrutiny of their behavioral protocols indicates that avoidant children do not appear to need a warm-up period to overcome their wariness in a new situation, do not seem to check in much with mother through proximity-seeking or distance interaction, and do not seem very wary of the stranger.

Separation. When mother departs, avoidant children register no protest and very little change in the level or quality of play. Additionally, they may find it relatively easy to "substitute" the stranger for mother as a playmate. Nonetheless, the differences between secure and avoidant infants remain subtle and can easily be missed.

Reunion.   It is upon reunion with the parent that avoidant infants are more easily distinguished from secure infants. As mother approaches and picks the child up, avoidant infants either conspicuously attempt to avoid contact with mother, by turning and walking away or more subtly but nonetheless clearly avert gaze and shift body posture to avoid contact. This stands in clear contrast to the greeting and deriving of comfort characteristic of secure infants' reunion with their caregivers.

As one can tell from this description, many avoidant children appear precociously autonomous and independent. Indeed, such interpretations were common when Ainsworth first described this pattern. However, subsequent research has demonstrated that this is a nonoptimal infant adaptation to a particular style of parenting, at least in U.S. culture. To consider a pattern of infant behavior a "nonoptimal" form of adaptation requires not only longitudinal data indicating that the pattern is predictive of later maladaptation, but more important, a theory of the optimal fit between child and environment. In a pluralistic society, there are many competing theories of optimal fit based on varying value assumptions. Not all cultures or subcultures would agree that the developmental successors to secure attachment are the most valued forms of later adaptation.

Anxious-Resistant (C) Infants

Finally, a very small number (in the United States usually less than 10%) of infants show a pattern of attachment behaviors that is more easily and straightforwardly interpreted as non-optimal/maladaptive. They are called anxious-resistant, or "C," children.

Preseparation.   During the preseparation episode, anxious-resistant children are distressed simply by the novelty of a strange environment. Even after a warm-up period, they demonstrate clinginess to or preoccupation with the mother and are conspicuously unable to explore the environment and become interested and involved in nonsocial play.

Separation.   Resistant babies "fall apart" under the stress of separation. Their cries and protests are more uncontrolled. They seem unable to regulate their distress as well as secure infants, and their cries seem angrier.

Reunion.   On reunion, resistant infants mix proximity-seeking with a high degree of resistance to contact. For this reason, they were originally called anxious-ambivalent. They may bid to be picked up, then angrily hit the parent and squirm to be let down, only to bid for a pickup again. Most important, resistant infants do not derive obvious comfort from reunion with their mothers and hence cannot use her as a secure base to return to play.

This brief overview of the patterns of attachment displayed by 1-year-old infants in the Strange Situation is necessarily condensed and simplified. In fact, there are very important within-pattern differences as well. For instance, some resistant babies are less visibly angry and more passive. Similarly, some secure babies resemble avoidant babies in preseparation behavior and others resemble resistant babies in separation behavior. Consequently, it is very important to keep in mind that it is the pattern, the organization, indeed the *meaning* of behavior that is the key.

As Ainsworth predicted, her own study and subsequent studies by other researchers (Bates, Maslin, & Frankel, 1985; Belsky, Rovine, & Taylor, 1984; Grossman, Grossmann, Spangler, Suess, & Unzner, 1985) confirm that security of attachment at 1 year of age is predicted by quality of caretaking over the first 12 months of life. In the most general of terms, parents of securely attached infants are sensitively and contingently responsive to their infants' cues. Parents of avoidant children are predictably unresponsive and rejecting to bids for comfort and are controlling in free play. Parents of resistant children are unpredictably responsive and inconsistent to bids for comfort and are unresponsive or unavailable in free play. Thus, the quality of the child's attachment—as defined by the secure, anxious-avoidant, and anxious-resistant patterns—essentially provides a measure of the history of the mother–child relationship. Infants who expect their mothers to comfort them in their distress return to them upon reunion and miss them while they are away; infants whose mothers are typically unresponsive to their needs appear to function well in their absence and do not turn to them upon reunion. Infants whose mothers have been inconsistent in their responsiveness find it impossible to function apart from them and to derive comfort from their ministrations, largely because the infants are angry and fussy.

Unsurprisingly, subsequent research has documented that secure attachment in infancy also predicts a range of socioemotional competencies as children move from infancy into the toddler and preschool periods.

LONGITUDINAL FOLLOW-UP STUDIES OF INFANT ATTACHMENT

Numerous longitudinal studies have been conducted to test the predictive validity of the infant attachment classifications. Predictions about the future functioning of secure and insecure infants have been made on a variety of theoretical grounds. For instance, Sroufe has argued that the development of a secure attachment over the infancy period increases a child's ability to cope with later "stage-salient developmental tasks" (Sroufe, 1979, 1983). The ability of infant attachment status to predict a variety of stage-specific competencies from toddlerhood to the early school-age years has been tested independently by a number of laboratories.[1] Results indicate that more securely attached children are (a) freer to sustain high levels of symbolic play under a variety of motivational conditions (Aber, Appel, Baruch, & Morris, 1991; Belsky, Garduque, & Hrncir, 1984 ; Slade, 1987); (b) more persistent and positive in difficult problem-solving tasks (Aber & Baker, 1990; Easterbrooks & Goldberg, 1984; Matas, Arend, & Sroufe, 1978); (c) more competent in early peer relations (Pastor, 1981; Waters, Wippman, & Sroufe, 1979); and (d) more successful in adapting to new relations with teachers in school (Erickson, Sroufe, & Egeland, 1985; Sroufe, 1983).

Similarly, Cicchetti and colleagues (Cicchetti, Cummings, Greenberg, & Marvin, 1990) believed that the development of a secure attachment in infancy can serve as a protective factor against the future development of psychopathology. This does not mean that securely attached infants never develop psychopathology but that their chances are considerably reduced in the face of other relevant risk factors (e.g., secure attachment reduces the probability that early parental loss will result in later depression; Cicchetti & Aber, 1986). Empirical data from several longitudinal studies of early precursors to preschool behavior problems are consistent with this belief (Erickson et al., 1985; Lewis, Feiring, McGuffog, & Jaskir, 1984; Speltz, 1990).

A third approach to predictive validity has been taken by those who believe that a change in family or childrearing conditions should be associated with a change over time in attachment status. In other words, although attachment status is considered increasingly resistant to change over the course of development, it is not considered immutable as children's attachment-relevant life conditions change. Once again, the available evidence from longitudinal studies supports this belief (Egeland & Farber, 1984; Main, Kaplan, & Cassidy, 1985; Waters, 1978).

A variety of issues are raised by this literature on the predictive validity of infant attachment classifications. Perhaps most important to psychoanalytic theories is the question of whether the observed predictability from early attachment to later enhanced competence or risk reduction is due to (a) the child carrying forward internally a set of characteristics that enhances future

---

[1]The findings of studies cited here are illustrations from a rapidly growing literature. Recent reviews of this literature are available in Bretherton (1985) and Cicchetti, Cummings, Greenberg, and Marvin (1990).

functioning or (b) the child simply responding to more sensitive competence-promoting parenting at both early and later stages. The first alternative implies a structured form of internal representations as the cause of continuity over developmental epoch; the latter alternative implies that continuity in child adaptation is epiphenomenal to continuity in parenting abilities. In a major critical review of the attachment literature, Lamb and his colleagues noted that attachment theorists almost invariably interpret their data from the former (child as a source of continuity) perspective without formally testing the latter (parent as a source of continuity) perspective (Lamb, Thompson, Gardner, Charnov, & Estes, 1984). Studies to test these two alternatives require cross-lagged longitudinal designs such as the one displayed in Figure 1.

The question boils down to whether the observed association between C_1 (e.g., infant attachment) and C_2 (e.g., toddler problem-solving ability) (a) is just a reflection of the fact that more sensitive mothers have more secure infants ($P_1 < > C_1$), more competent mothers have more autonomous toddlers ($P_2 < > C_2$), *and* more sensitive mothers of infants are also more likely to be more competent mothers of toddlers ($P_1 > P_2$); or (b) is not fully explained by these other sets of relations. Obviously, analytically oriented theorists as well as attachment theorists sympathetic to Bowlby's and Ainsworth's notions that attachment behavioral patterns are reflections of children's internal representations of relationships are betting that there is a significant residual relation between C_1 and C_2 even after controlling for $P_1 < > C_1$, $P_1 > P_2$, and $P_2 < > C_2$.

The cross-lagged arrows ($P_1 > C_2$, $C_1 > P_2$) add another level of complexity to these issues and raise a third alternative of a modified transactional perspective in which parents and children mutually influence each other over time. The dotted arrow (from $C_1 > P_2$) is meant to signify a weaker causal relation than the solid arrow (from $P_1 > C_2$), suggesting that although the efforts are reciprocal, parents affect children over the course of early development more than the reverse (Belsky & Isabella, 1988).

Few longitudinal studies of the developmental sequelae of infant attachment status have used these research designs, although several studies of the precursors of attachment status have done so (Belsky et al., 1984). The results of these few studies tend to support a transactional model rather than the child or parent as the sole source of continuity.

THE MOVE TO THE LEVEL OF REPRESENTATION

Ainsworth's research did a great deal to bring attachment theory, and particularly the work of Bowlby into the mainstream of child development research. Many consider her discovery of the A, B, and C patterns of attachment to be revolutionary. However, the emphasis within her published work on mother–child behavior diverted attention from what had been her as well as

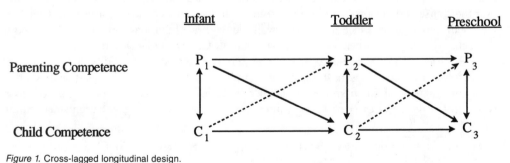

Figure 1. Cross-lagged longitudinal design.

Bowlby's central point, namely, that different patterns of attachment in the Strange Situation derive from different relationship histories and reflect different underlying representations of the relationship. The shift within attachment theory from a behavioral to representational approach was made possible by the work of Main (originally a student of Ainsworth's), who used Bowlby's notion of "internal working models of attachment" to emphasize the fact that individual differences in the organization of attachment behavior reflect individual differences in the *mental representation* of the self in relation to attachment (Main et al., 1985; Main & Goldwyn, in press). Thus, the *behavioral* patterns of attachment just described reflect underlying differences in the ways children think and feel about their caregiver's availability in a stressful situation and reflect the different strategies developed to cope with such affects and cognitions.

Bowlby (1982) believed that infants develop what he called "internal working models" of self and others on the basis of the history of interactions with their primary caregivers. Internal working models are not static but dynamic "working" models. They not only "represent" the nature of past interactional experience, but they also permit the forecasting of future experience and become the prototype for the formation of future relationships. That internal working models represent past interactional experience and become the prototype for the formation of future relationship make them the mechanisms of transference. Indeed, in our opinion, a major reason analytically oriented clinicians would want to follow attachment research is to follow this developing story on the roots of transference (see also Osofsky, 1988). In infancy, the child's internal working models of self and attachment figure (usually the mother) develop in complementary fashion and initially center around the issue of maternal availability. As children's interactional histories with their caregivers progress, children become increasingly able to and motivated to forecast their attachment figure's response to their attachment needs on the basis of prior interactions. Caregivers who are able to accurately read their infant's cues and to respond sensitively and contingently are increasingly "represented" by their infants as "available." By contrast, caretakers who systematically reject their infant's attachment behaviors or respond to them in an unpredictable or insensitive fashion are increasingly represented as "unavailable" to provide protection or felt security. In parallel fashion, the infant comes to represent the self as powerful or powerless to gain felt security and eventually as worthy or unworthy of protection and care. Internal working models are thought to be changeable in early life but to become increasingly resistant to change over the course of development. They typically exist outside of conscious awareness (see Bretherton, 1985, 1987, for a review of Bowlby's and others' notions of internal working models).

In the early 1980s, Main and her colleagues (Main et al., 1985) set out to study the parents of children they had observed 6 years earlier in the Strange Situation. They developed the Adult Attachment Interview (George, Kaplan, & Main, 1985), which asks parents to remember and describe their own responses to childhood situations that might have activated their attachment systems, among them separations, losses, experiences of rejection, and the like. It is an hour-long semistructured interview designed to elicit memories and feelings about attachment relevant experiences and to assess the degree of security implicit in the overall working model of attachment. The interview begins with questions about the circumstances of parents' childhoods, with whom and where they lived, and so forth. Following this introductory phase, they are asked to think of five adjectives that describe their relationship with each parent, and to provide memories supporting such general descriptions. The nature of these relationships is then probed further, via questions concerning memories of early separations, modes of obtaining comfort, feelings about which parent they felt closest to, and memories of being punished and of feeling rejected. Finally, they are asked how they understand their parents' motivations for behaving as they did and to reflect on the ways these experiences might have affected their adult personality and their relationship with their child.

Main et al. (1985) believed that, just as a child's behavior in the Strange Situation *represents* his or her expectations regarding maternal availability, the structure of parental verbalizations would provide clues similar to the quality of an adult's early parenting. According to Main et al. (1985), "internal working models direct not only feelings and behavior, but also attention, memory and cognition, insofar as they relate directly or indirectly to attachment. Individual differences in these internal working models will therefore be related not only to individual patterns in nonverbal behavior but also to patterns of language and structures of mind" (p. 67).

The transcript of the interview is scored as a whole, and both structural and content features of the adult's statements are analyzed. The most critical aspect of scoring is the degree of overall coherence in the narrative. This is defined as fluency of ideation and speech, the absence of contradictions within the narrative, and—perhaps most important—the ability to match semantic generalizations of the relationship (e.g., my mother was loving) with episodic memories that in fact support such generalizations (e.g., a memory of mother responding to the child in ways that seem believably loving). Thus, when parents are asked to provide five adjectives describing the relationship with each of their own parents, they are also asked to provide memories of specific incidents that support their general descriptions. Other variables scored include features such as role reversal, lack of resolution of mourning, and so on, as well as the individual's valuation of attachment relationships and the degree to which he or she is able to recall, integrate, and communicate his or her emotional reactions in attachment relevant situations.

Main and her colleagues found that on the basis of analysis of their interview transcripts, adults can be classified as detached, secure, or enmeshed. These categories are analogous to the "A," "B," and "C" classifications for child attachment. Parents rated as secure tended to value attachment relationships, to regard attachment relationships as influencing personality, and yet to be objective in describing any particular relationship. These parents were easily able to recall early relationships, spoke about attachment in a way that suggested prior reflection and integration, and for the most part did not idealize their parents or past experiences. When asked to describe the relationship with their parents, they were able to provide convincing memories supporting their semantic generalization of the relationship. Parents rated as detached dismissed attachment relationships as being of little concern, value, or influence and often had great difficulty remembering early experiences or describing them with any feeling or insight. They also tended to idealize their parents and in so doing to obscure the reality of rejection and their own subsequent disappointment and hurt. Thus, semantic generalizations were frequently at odds with the apparent reality of the relationship, and episodic memories were not available to serve as evidence for these semantic generalizations. Enmeshed parents still seemed preoccupied with depending on their own parents and still struggled actively to please them. Incoherency in describing early experiences was high in this group. Typically, these individuals seemed flooded with memories for early experience but lacked the structure or semantic generalization to integrate these memories or place them in any perspective.

Thus, the degree of security implicit in adults' working models of attachment is determined not just on the basis of what they say about their childhoods but primarily on the ways they organize memories and feelings about these experiences. For example, the presence within an individual history of neglect, trauma, and insensitive or inconsistent parenting does not necessarily lead to an adult's being classified as insecure; rather, what is most significant for purposes of classification is how these memories and experiences are organized, such that the individual has access to the feelings about these experiences and insight into their effects. Main et al. (1985) suggested that the advent of formal operations during adolescence provides an opportunity to rework representational models, particularly when early experiences have been negative. It is at this time that new abilities make it increasingly possible to gain perspective on the effects and reasons behind such experiences.

In Main's research, the relation between the quality of the adult's internal working model of attachment as assessed from interview transcripts and early infant attachment was quite strong for the mothers. Children of mothers judged to be secure were themselves secure, children of detached mothers were anxious-avoidant, and enmeshed mothers were anxious-resistant. The significance levels for this part of the study were extremely high ($p < .01$). These relationships were also strong for fathers but not as strong as for mothers. Thus, stable relationships were found between mothers' abilities to access feelings, thoughts, and memories of their own attachment experiences and the security implicit in their children's overall working model of attachment. Interestingly, observation and analysis of 6-year-old reunion patterns indicated that there were continuities in the children's internal working models of attachment from ages 1 to 6 as well.

Security of attachment—in adults or children—implies a flexible style of attending to feelings and memories relevant to attachment and to relationships. Flexibility in this sense implies the capacity to balance attention to attachment-relevant phenomena with interest in and exploration of the world. Infants manifest such flexibility in their *behavior* and are able to flexibly check in and interact with their mothers while exploring the environment. In adults, the evidence for such flexibility is manifested in patterns of thoughts, feelings, and memories of childhood attachments: They can support generalized representations of the quality of early relationships with convincing memories of such experiences. Thus, abstract representations of relationships are based on flexible access to memories and feelings about early experience. By contrast, avoidant children and detached adults defensively exclude information that would activate their feelings and longings in relationship to a love object. Because their "internal working models" of attachment allow them to forecast rebuff, avoidant children often pay less attention to mother or seek comfort from her. Detached adults have little access to episodic memories of their childhoods, which would revive feelings of rejection or deprivation. In contrast to avoidant-detached individuals, who *cannot* attend to attachment-relevant phenomena because they are too painful, resistant-enmeshed individuals are preoccupied with them. In the case of infants, they are unable to let the mother out of their sight, or—often—out of clinging range. Enmeshed adults' autonomous functioning is impaired by a preoccupation with familial relationships and with memories and feelings about these experiences. Thus, whereas the avoidant-detached pattern is marked by difficulty attending to experiences or memories concerning attachment, the resistant-enmeshed pattern is characterized by difficulty *not* attending to these experiences or to functioning separately from them.

Main's findings have been replicated by Eichberg (1987), who assessed maternal and child attachment concurrently and reported relationships even stronger than those reported by Main et al. Similarly, Grossmann et al. (1985) reported significant correlations between infant security and ratings of maternal affectivity on the Adult Attachment Interview. Validation of the Adult Attachment Interview has been carried out by Kobak and Sceery (1988), who reported strong relationships between the adult attachment and ego resiliency and control in a sample of college students.

ASSESSING CHILDREN'S ATTACHMENT BEYOND INFANCY: REPRESENTATIONAL AND REGULATORY-STYLE APPROACHES

As attachment theorists increasingly follow their samples of children into the preschool years and beyond, they have begun to develop a number of new approaches to conceptualizing and assessing children's internal working models of self and others in attachment relationships.

As already noted, Bowlby and others have reasoned that the source of continuity is children's internal working models of self and others. If the enhanced ability to cope with future stage-salient tasks is carried forward at least in part by the child (as it would be under either "the child as source" or "transactional models"), how is this accomplished? Two broadly compatible but distinct approaches to conceptualizing internal working models after infancy have been taken to date: representational approaches and regulatory-style approaches. Representational approaches analyze children's verbal responses to attachment-related stories, children's symbolic doll play in response to attachment-related story stems, and children's drawings of themselves and their families. Good examples of these techniques include Bretherton's Attachment Story Completion Task for 3-year-olds (Bretherton, Ridgeway, & Cassidy, 1990) and Cassidy's Puppet Play for 6-year-olds (Cassidy, 1990).

Regulatory-style approaches examine individual differences in how preschool (and older) children regulate affect and behavior in stressful situations such as a mother–child reunion after an hour's separation (Main et al., 1985). Like infant behavioral style in the Strange Situation, preschooler regulatory style is thought to be a reflection of the child's internal working model (IWM); thus the nature of the IWM is inferred from observable differences in style. A comprehensive approach to the behavior assessment of patterns of attachment (what we are calling "regulatory style") from ages 3 to 6 has been developed by the MacArthur Working Group on Attachment (Cassidy, Marvin, et al., 1989).

It will not escape the careful reader that, taken together, the representational and regulatory-style approaches to conceptualizing and assessing IWMs beyond infancy are assessing complex patterns of cognition, attention, affect, and behavior. Most researchers in this area believe that given the increased complexity of preschooler's psychological development, multiple methods will probably be required to accurately assess individual differences in children's IWMs.

Despite the early stage of theoretical and measurement development, this area of research has produced some exciting new insights into how IWMs are organized later in life and are associated with patterns of representations and behavioral–affective functioning (see Bretherton et al., 1990, for a good review of this literature to date). Although the precise content of representations and the specific maneuvers used in regulation change with development, the underlying *organization* of the representation and the underlying *strategy* of the regulatory style appear to be quite consistent. For instance, the avoidant child's idealizing representations of self and other (Cassidy, 1990; Main et al., 1985) and minimizing (Main & Goldwyn, in press) or deactivating regulating styles (Kobak, Cole, Ferenz-Gillies, Fleming, & Gamble, 1991) are discernible across several developmental epochs.

PARENTAL REPRESENTATIONS OF THE CHILD

The work of Main et al. (1985) established the strength of the link between a mother's representation of her relationship with her own parents and the quality of the child's representation of himself or herself and others. More recently, researchers have begun exploring the complement to an adult or child's IWM of the relationship to his or her own parents, namely, the *parent's IWM of his or her relationship with the child*. Reasoning that—in line with Bowlby's assumptions about working models—parents develop representations of the relationship with the child, researchers (Aber & Slade, 1987; Bretherton, Biringen, Ridgeway, Maslin, & Sherman, 1989; George & Solomon, 1989; Slade & Aber, 1986, 1988; Zeanah, Benoit, Hirschberg, Barton, & Regan, 1991) set out to investigate the development of these models by interviewing parents as to the ways they conceived of and understood their attachment to their children. As Bretherton et al. (1989) put it,

> It is not only the infant who keeps tabs on the parent, and who becomes distressed upon separation; parents also tend to keep a watchful eye on their infant, intervene when the infant is getting into a potentially painful or harmful situation, experience feelings of alarm when the infant's whereabouts are not known or the infant's wellbeing is in danger, and relief when the child is found or the danger past. (p. 205)

In this research, the *parental* side of the parent-child attachment bond is at issue.

Although researchers in this area have approached their data in different ways and have used somewhat different terminology to describe overlapping phenomena, the interviews and basic research questions have been quite similar across studies. The questions that have dominated the research to date are whether IWMs of the child are related to an adult's working model of their own parents and whether a parent's IWM of the child influences the quality of child attachment. Both sets of relationships have received preliminary confirmation. Slade and Aber (1986), along with Zeanah et al. (1991), reported that the quality of a parent's working model of his or her child is clearly related to his or her IWM of the relationship with his or her own parents. In a descriptive analysis of interview transcripts, Slade and Aber (1986) compared a small sample of mothers classified as secure in their relationship with their own parents with those classified as anxious; they found that mothers secure in their representation of their own parents were (a) more coherent in their descriptions of their children, (b) more able to acknowledge a wide range of feelings about their children (including anger and anxiety), (c) more able to communicate these to the interviewer directly and meaningfully, and (d) more likely to describe themselves as able to cope directly and openly with their feelings when they did become angry with the child. Zeanah, Benoit, and Barton (1989) developed a system for classifying parental IWMs of the child that is analogous to the Main et al. (1985) system for classifying adult attachment. In this model, parental representations of the child are characterized as balanced, strained, or enmeshed; these correspond to the free/secure, dismissing, and preoccupied classifications described by Main. Zeanah et al. (1991) reported a high concordance between these two forms of adult representation, such that it is highly likely that a mother secure in relation to her own parents will be balanced in her representation of the child, that a mother classified as dismissing will be strained in her representation of the child, and that a mother classified as preoccupied will be enmeshed in her representation of the child.

The question of whether the quality of parental representations will affect the quality of a child's attachment has also been addressed by these researchers. Zeanah et al. (1991) reported a strong relationship between a mother's IWM of her child and the quality of the child's attachment. Thus, babies who are secure in the Strange Situation have mothers who are balanced in their representations of the relationship, babies who are avoidant have mothers whose representations are characterized as strained, and babies who are resistant have mothers whose representations are enmeshed. Bretherton et al. (1989) reported that a single sensitivity rating derived from parental interviews is highly correlated with infant security. Similarly, George and Solomon (1989) reported that two measures derived from parental interviews, one an assessment of the mother's sense of herself as providing a secure base for her child and the second as assessment of the mother's sense of her own competence in caregiving, were likewise related to child security.

One can hope that future research will illuminate the relationships among all three variables: IWMs of the parent, of the child, and infant attachment. Undoubtedly, the relationships are complex, intertwined, and influenced by factors such as the child's gender and birth order and the differential quality of the parent's relationships to her own mother and father; in fact, they may mediate each other's effects. For instance, although the two forms of adult representation may be highly correlated, a child's attachment status may be more strongly related to his or her mother's IWM of her relationship with him or her than to her working model of her relationship with her own parents.

THE ORGANIZATION OF THE ATTACHMENT SYSTEM IN CHILDREN AT RISK

Thus far, we have focused on individual differences in the organization of the attachment system in normal populations of infants and mothers. The avoidant (A) and resistant (C) patterns that we have described are present in any normative subsample of infants in the United States. In this respect, they amount to relatively common infant adaptations to various types of care-taking environments that fall within the range of the normal. This key idea from attachment theory—that infants adapt the organization of their attachment behavior system (and the organization of their IWMs) to the demands of the caretaking environments in which they live—raises an issue of special interest to clinicians. How do infants in especially high-risk environments organize their modes of obtaining comfort and security from their mothers? Are there new, atypical forms of organization of the attachment system which are rarely observed among normal populations but are quite common among at-risk populations?

A series of recent studies have begun to yield answers to these questions. The two types of high-risk infants who have been studied most extensively to date are abused and neglected infants and infants of parents with major affective disorders (both unipolar and bipolar depression). As one would expect, 50%–100% of maltreated children or children of depressed parents are insecurely attached. However, most interesting are the researchers' descriptions of two new "patterns" or "organizations" of attachment that have emerged from these studies as the most common patterns among high-risk children. Some scholars describe high-risk infants who combine moderate-to-high proximity seeking with moderate-to-high avoidance *and* resistance in the Strange Situation. These are now referred to as "A/C attachments" (Crittenden, 1987). Other researchers describe infants who appear disorganized, disoriented, and dazed in the Strange Situation. These are referred to as "D attachments" (Main & Solomon, 1990). In neither case, do these infants meet the criteria for a secure, avoidant, or resistant attachment classification. Formal criteria do exist to code these patterns; they can be coded just as reliably as the "typical" patterns.

Phenotypically, avoidant-resistant and disorganized children behave somewhat differently in the Strange Situation. At another level, however, they share one important characteristic. When compared with "typical" patterns of attachment, each of which reflects a systematic strategy to cope with the stress of separation–reunion, the A/C *and D patterns can be distinguished by their lack of a consistent strategy.* Viewed from the IWM perspective, A/C and D infants do not appear to have constructed consistent, predictable rules to guide cognition, affect, and behavior in attachment-related situations. Even the nonoptimal typical patterns represent a form of organized strategy. For instance, an avoidant child avoids the parent on reunion in order to deactivate the attachment system when proximity seeking is likely to be rebuffed. A/C and D infants do not appear to have the structure required to maintain an organized response, even a nonoptimal organized response. The D, or disorganized, pattern has been clearly linked with forms of severe parental psychopathology and speaks directly to the relationship between parental inconsistency and early failures of structuralization.

Because we believe that the A/C and D patterns are adaptational responses to the inconsistency and unpredictability of abusive and neglectful and depressed caretaking, and because they appear to represent the failure to form early consistent rules and strategies, we suspect that the prognosis for these infants is not as good as for avoidant or resistant infants. Longitudinal studies of these and other high-risk populations (i.e., teenage parents) are needed to flesh out the full implications of these new patterns of attachment for understanding of the etiology of psychopathology in high-risk populations.

PARENT'S UNRESOLVED TRAUMA AS THE SOURCE OF INFANT DISORGANIZATION

The discovery of a fourth major infant attachment classification, the disorganized and disoriented attachment system, has stimulated a search for parental factors that may cause this form of adaptation. Main and Solomon (1990) came on an early lead when they carefully reviewed the Adult Attachment Interviews of the "unclassifiable" (now "D") infants in Main's original middle-class, low-risk Berkeley sample and discovered that most parents of disorganized infants had suffered the loss of a primary attachment figure before completing high school. Because not all parents who had experienced the loss of a primary attachment figure had disorganized infants, they further speculated that only those parents who lacked resolution of mourning had disorganized infants. Subsequent research with middle-class, low-risk families by Main and Goldwyn (in press) on a second Berkeley, California, sample and by Eichberg (1987) on a Charlottesville, Virginia, sample support Main's original hypothesis about lack of resolution of mourning a significant loss.

In the meantime, however, reports of "U" (unclassifiable), combined "A/C" (ambivalent *and* resistant), and "D" (disorganized) infants were emerging from a variety of researchers working with poverty (e.g., Egeland & Sroufe, 1981), high-risk (e.g., Radke-Yarrow, Cummings, Kuczynski & Chapman, 1985; Spieker & Booth, 1985), and maltreatment (Carlson, Cicchetti, Barnett, & Braunwald, 1989; Crittenden, 1985, 1987; Lyons-Ruth, Connell, Zoll, & Stahl, 1987) samples. Recently, Main and her colleagues (Main & Hesse, 1990; Main & Solomon, 1990) have reported a comprehensive review of more than 200 tapes of "disorganized" attachments, half from middle-class, low-risk samples and half from poor, high-risk or maltreatment samples. Through careful behavioral analysis of these tapes, they arrived at coding criteria appropriate to classify disorganized attachments from both low- and high-risk samples (see the section on "D" babies). Of relevance to issues of adult attachment, the review of pathways to disorganization among high-risk and maltreated children has led to a broader notion of the parental factor associated with infant disorganization. Main now believes that the common factor is parental "lack of resolution of trauma" (Main & Hesse, 1990). The trauma could be a traumatic loss of a primary attachment figure (as is common in the low-risk samples) or it could be a parent history of childhood abuse and neglect (as in the maltreatment samples). Consequently, Main now has "lack of resolution of mourning" and "lack of resolution of maltreatment" scales included in her adult attachment interview coding system.

Finally, Main posited as the link between parents' "lack of resolution of trauma" and infants' "disorganized attachments" *frightened or frightening parental behavior.* We do not attempt to capture the richness of her discussion here but refer the reader instead to Main and Hesse (1990) for a full description. Here we emphasize only her bottom line: that frightened or frightening parental behavior puts the attached infant in what she calls an "irresolvable paradox wherein the haven of safety is at once the source of the alarm" (p. 180). Parental working models that represent traumatized and unresolved attachment relationships are a major source of the most serious form of attachment disorder yet identified: the disorganized/disoriented attachment.

THEORETICAL IMPLICATIONS

One of the aims of this chapter is to discuss some of the ways attachment theory—as it has evolved over the past 20 years—is consistent with psychoanalytic theory. Another aim is to delineate some of the essential differences between these two theoretical positions. We believe that an explication of these convergences and divergences in theory will be instructive and clarifying (see also Bretherton, 1987; Silverman, 1991). However, before embarking on this task, it is very important to make several points. First, to use the term *psychoanalytic theory* is in and of itself misleading, as this implies that there is a single, cogent theoretical position that can be contrasted with other theoretical positions. As has been pointed out again and again by psychoanalytic scholars, Freud's own ideas about development, personality, and psychopathology changed many times over the course of his productive career. In addition, each of the schools of psychoanalytic thought that has emerged over the past 50 years (e.g., ego psychology, interpersonal theory, object relations theory, self psychology) has contributed new dimensions and directions to the original, complex, and sometimes contradictory classical or traditional perspectives. A unitary theory it is not (see Eagle, 1987, and Greenberg & Mitchell, 1983, for overviews of historical trends in psychoanalysis). Even a "basic" construct such as drive theory is understood differently by avowedly classical psychoanalysts, such as Loewald (1980) and Brenner (1982). For many latter-day analysts, in fact, what Freud might have termed *drives* are more likely to be referred to as infantile impulses and wishes, and to be considered within the broad framework of developing object relations. In fact, it would be fair to say that the vast majority of today's analysts concern themselves with just this area of overlap: the intersection of personal wishes and concerns with the exigencies and demands of one's primary relationships. And, although few analysts cleave to the notion of drives as Freud originally conceived them, most Freudian psychoanalysts (as variously defined) accept the notion of the infant as moved by libidinous and aggressive strivings that are at once fundamentally antisocial and yet vital to the development of internalized object relationships.

A second issue to consider at this point is the *size* of the theories in question. Relative to attachment theory, psychoanalysis is unquestionably much broader in its scope and domains of inquiry. It is an older theory, having evolved over the course of nearly 100 years. It is a developmental theory, a personality theory, a theory about the etiology and organization of psychopathology, and a theory of mind. It is also a theory about human nature that is deeply rooted in the philosophy and culture of the 20th century. Attachment theory is considerably more modest in its scope. It is a simpler and more parsimonious position, in part because of its continuing tie to empirical study and research. It is concerned primarily with the establishment of significant relationships. Although notions regarding personality functioning and human development can be derived from its principles, it is not fundamentally a theory of personality or development. Similarly, although notions of IWMs contribute significantly to the understanding of how relationships are represented and repeated across generations, attachment theory does not yet offer a broadly based theory of mind. And, despite its obvious applicability to an understanding of clinical situations, the theory itself is not based in or derived primarily from studies of psychopathology. Many attachment researchers have begun to study clinical populations, and Bowlby himself began thinking about these issues while working as a psychoanalyst and while working with delinquent children, yet—in contrast to traditional psychoanalysis—attachment theory came of age in the laboratory rather than in the consulting room. Although it may someday be that attachment theory has a breadth and depth similar to psychoanalytic theory, today it is most accurate to think of attachment theory as being in its infancy and as yet basically and fundamentally tied to the theoretical position from which it derived.

Psychoanalysis and Attachment Theory: Convergences

Over the past 10 years, attachment research has confirmed many of the basic tenets of modern-day psychoanalytic theory. The work of Bowlby, Ainsworth, and Main and their colleagues has documented a strong relationship between (a) the type of care an infant receives and the quality of his or her relationship to significant people in his or her life and (b) the quality of an adult's integration of his or her early experiences and the quality of his or her parenting. These ideas are entirely consistent with the object relations school of psychoanalysis. In fact, attachment theory *is* an object relations theory (Greenberg & Mitchell, 1983); it emphasizes the primacy of a social bond, the direct impact of the quality of the mother–child relationship on internalized object relations, as well as the link between the quality of a parent's internal representations and the nature of their relationships to others (see, however, Osofsky, 1988, for an interesting discussion of the difference between object relations and relational positions vis-à-vis attachment theory). Bowlby was profoundly influenced by early object relations theorists—among them Klein (1932), Fairbairn (1952), and Winnicott (1965)—and developed his ideas in relation and in response to theirs.

Attachment and a wide range of object relations theorists agree that the quality of early caregiving contributes in vital and significant ways to the quality of later relationships and to the coherence and stability of self-feeling. Psychoanalytic thinkers as diverse in their orientation as Mahler (Mahler, Pine, & Bergman, 1975), Kohut (1969), and Winnicott (1965) emphasized the vital importance of the mother's ability to nurture, comfort, and contain her child during the early months and years of life and to link these maternal qualities to the child's later adaptation. Mahler used the term "emotional availability," Kohut "empathy," and Winnicott "the holding environment"; all described the mother's fundamental tolerance and acceptance of her infant's needs and emotions. These are all terms that refer to a mother's ability to recognize, accept, and at the same time contain the child's needs and feelings, and to remain available while supporting autonomous strivings. The corollary in attachment theory is Ainsworth's "sensitive caregiving." Her description speaks for itself: "The optimally sensitive mother is able to see things from her baby's point of view. She is alert to perceive her baby's signals, interprets them accurately, and responds appropriately and promptly, unless no response is the most appropriate under the circumstances. She tends to give the baby what he seems to want, and when she does not she is tactful in acknowledging his communication" (Ainsworth et al., 1978, p. 142). Similarly, Main's "secure" mother is one who is able to remain responsive to a range of her infant's attachment needs and who can accept the wide and conflicting domain of her infant's feelings just as she can remember and access her own.

Although there are certainly differences in the way object relations and attachment theorists define infantile needs, and in the way they define the infant's basic position vis-à-vis human relationships, both recognize that maternal responsiveness and sensitivity contribute in important ways to an infant's ability to make sense of the panoply of internal and interpersonal experiences confronting him or her in daily life. Primary object or attachment relationships make it possible for the child to both experience sustained joy and to manage and integrate negative emotions such as anger, sadness, and anxiety. Following Freud, psychoanalytic theory acknowledges the importance of the pleasure that follows from comfort, need gratification, and contact. This pleasure is intrinsic to the establishment of libidinal bonds and to the establishment of object and self-constancy. The pleasure the infant derives from early nurture leads inevitably to experiences of love and connectedness. Although attachment theory has eschewed terms such as pleasure, even Ainsworth—who largely ignored questions of affect in her writings—acknowledged that the deactivation of the attachment system that follows contact and proximity with the mother leads to feelings of security and comfort that are, by definition, pleasurable. Main, too (Main et al., 1985), noted that infants classify early interactive events on the basis of whether their needs for comfort and security are met; in other words, pleasurable and unpleasurable events are differentially recognized and encoded. Recent work by Kobak (Kobak et al., 1991) and Cassidy (1991) addressed the question of affect more explicitly; both noted that secure and insecure individuals differ in their ability to both acknowledge pleasure in and derive pleasure from significant relationships.

Both object relations and attachment theorists also associate maternal responsiveness, attunement, sensitivity, and acceptance with the child's eventual ability to manage and integrate negative and conflictual emotional experiences. Although the genesis and meaning of such experiences are described differently by these two theories, there is general agreement that the ability to tolerate the experience of negative emotion, to feel comfortable expressing such feelings productively in intimate relationships, and to integrate them into the fabric of self-consciousness is vital to both healthy development and inextricably linked to sensitive parenting. Within the Mahlerian paradigm, the success of the child's resolution of normal "splitting" and ambivalence is directly related to the mother's ability to manage and tolerate the child's rage and aggression such that loving and sensual feelings can be sustained and developed. Winnicott (1965), too, spoke of the mother's containment of the infant's primitive "ruthlessness" as being vital to the infant's integration of these experiences into his or her sense of himself or herself and into the fabric of his or her relationships. Kohut (1969) believed that maternal empathy is of the utmost importance in allowing the child to knit together fragmented and diverse self-experiences into a unified, cohesive self. In the parlance of attachment theory, the "securely attached" child is one who feels free to express the full range of his or her feelings without fear that his or her doing so will disrupt or impede his or her primary attachment relationship (Cassidy, 1991; Cassidy & Kobak, 1988; Kobak et al., 1991). Both Cassidy and Kobak focused on the distortion of negative affect as typifying both dismissing and preoccupied patterns of insecure attachment. Kobak cogently linked the dismissing/avoidant strategy of affect regulation with the infant's perception that any expression of anger, sadness, or anxiety so disrupts his or her relationship with his or her primary caregiver that he or she learns to minimize these feelings. Cassidy speculated that, by contrast, the preoccupied/resistant strategy serves to maximize negative emotions, as this meets the mother's need for closeness via distress.

A mother's ability to respond sensitively to her child is related, of course, to her own childhood history. Although this link is implicit in much of analytic theory, it was Benedek (1959) who first explicitly raised the notion that each phase in the child's development provides the mother with an opportunity to reexperience and perhaps resolve her own early experience during that phase. Confronting her infant's oral needs, for instance, invariably confronts her with the experience of her own intense orality; her success or failure in caring for her infant during this phase will depend both on her own early experiences, as well as on her ability to rework or resolve early deprivations by meeting her infant's needs more effectively and confidently. Mahler also linked the mother's ability to negotiate the conflicts and unconscious memories triggered by her child's progress through development with the success of his or her psychological adaptation (Mahler, Pine, & Bergman, 1970). The relationship between the quality of early parental experience and child adaptation is more explicit in attachment theory; as described earlier, numerous researchers have documented the link between a mother's own childhood experiences and her ability to nurture and care for her child. Main and Goldwyn (in press) took a position similar to Benedek and argued that mothers of insecure infants are insensitive because their infants' experience reawaken intolerable feeling and memories of longing and need. They avoid meeting their infants' needs because to do so would activate their own attachment systems and flood them with feelings they do not have the resources to manage. Using Stern's (1985) attunement paradigm, Haft and Slade (1989) documented that mothers classified as secure are as likely to attune to their infants' negative emotional signals as they are to their positive ones. Mothers who are themselves insecure either ignore or overreact to their children's negative affect. In either case, mothers' difficulties establishing a balanced response to negative affect undoubtedly have a profound effect on the establishment of emotional intimacy. A mother's ability to manage her infant's experiences has much to do with the internal resources she has for managing her own feelings; for both psychoanalytic and attachment theorists, these maternal resources derive directly from the quality of her own early relationship experiences.

Central to both analytic and attachment theory is the notion that infants are guided in their relationships by internal representations that derive from the early parent–child exchange. *Internal representation* refers to the process whereby children's first and most significant relationships become a part of them, shaping the ways they experience themselves and others, and determining the ways they interact in and develop new relationships. Children's internalization of aspects of their relationships with their parents leads to the establishment of internal images that serve a range of developmental and interpersonal functions. Both the psychoanalysts who concern themselves with early infant experience and attachment theorists view these internal representations as deriving directly from experiences in relationships with significant caregivers, and both view these early experiences as providing a template for later relationships. The term to describe these processes varies within psychoanalysis; Mahler used the term "libidinal object constancy," Kohut spoke of "transmuting internalizations," and Stern referred to these as "representations of interactions that have been generalized" (RIGs). Attachment theorists, following Bowlby, use the term "internal working models of attachment." Psychoanalysts and attachment theorists differ in their understanding of how and why such representations develop; they also differ in their understanding of some of the functions of internal representations. Nevertheless, there is wide agreement with the fundamental notion that the development of inner structures and representational models is directly tied to qualitative features of the earliest interactions with the mother and father.

Interestingly, although attachment theory does not have a concept analogous to Freud's (1915/1957) concept of the unconscious, IWMs are thought to operate out of consciousness and to be resistant to change (Bretherton, 1985). This concept carries with it none of the complexity that is intrinsic to Freud's thinking about the unconscious, particularly insofar as drives are concerned. Certainly these two theories differ in their notions of *what* is stored in the unconscious. Nevertheless, the notion that there are unconcious internalizations that guide and influence behavior does imply that important mental and interpersonal operations are unconscious and that memories and feelings about attachment may be stored and encoded in a fashion that is different from less charged, significant memories. Just as psychoanalysis suggests that an individual's access to unconscious material will be determined by the ego's ability to withstand the threat of the repressed, so does attachment theory suggest that access to IWMs—both at an episodic and semantic level—is linked to the nature and quality of the material that is stored out of awareness. And, as Freud believed that unconscious fantasies that threaten the ego must be kept out of consciousness, attachment theorists believe that memories and ideas that threaten the attachment system are stored in such a way as to limit conscious awareness.

These are the most significant and obvious of the convergences between the psychoanalytic position and attachment theory: the role of the mother in providing security and comfort, in modulating positive and negative affect, the significance of maternal history in determining her ability to be sensitively responsive, and the relationship between early history and the development of internalized representations of self and other. One of the less obvious convergences, however, concerns the question of survival. Although the ethological aspects of Bowlby's theory have received a great deal of attention, particularly his emphasis on the attachment system as geared to survival, Freud, too, saw the infant's primitive instincts, as they are manifested in early drive states, as being linked to survival.

> Freudian instinct theory is one of those all-embracing motivational theories of human behavior in which *all* behavior—the cognitive, interpersonal, social, etc.—is seen to be, directly or indirectly, in the service of an an expression of presumably basic or primary drives. In such theories, all behavior either serves to gratify these primary drives or other drives which have secondarily developed in association with the so-called primary drives. I think it can be shown that this formulation derives directly from the quasi-Darwinist assumption that behavior is to be understood in terms of its survival function. This is more apparent in early Freud when he posited essentially self-preservative (e.g., hunger) and species preservative (e.g., sex) instincts. Although later Freud spoke mainly of sexual and aggressive instincts, the essence of the early evolutionary ideal was never relinquished. (Eagle, 1987, pp. 6–7)

These two positions do not differ in their emphasis on survival; as we describe now what distinguishes them is what they define as being critical to survival.

Psychoanalysis and Attachment Theory: Divergences

Historically as well as currently, psychoanalysis' emphasis on the role of drives and their derivatives in motivating relationships, precipitating developmental change, and creating a fundamental set of conflicts between a child and his or her parents is what most clearly and dramatically differentiates it from the work of Bowlby and his followers. For many psychoanalysts, drives are really what makes the theory *psychoanalytic*; from the standpoint of classical psychoanalysis, humans are essentially and ultimately in conflict with those around them, as the demands of social intercourse invariably stand between them and the satisfaction of their most basic wishes. In other words, what the mother wants and what she will try to establish with her child will invariably come into conflict with what the child wants and needs. This is the essence of the Freudian paradigm: the baby, the adult, the individual as—at least to some degree—antisocial. One part of the self—the infantile, demanding, imperious child of the drives—is invariably at odds with the part of the self that longs for and actively seeks relationships.

One of the things that makes discussing some of the differences between psychoanalysis and attachment theory difficult is the fact that psychoanalysts vary considerably in their interpretation of drive theory and in their adherence to its basic principles. Some, such as Klein, took a more extreme position vis-à-vis drives than Freud himself did; others, such as Mahler, embedded an object relations theory within the context of drive development; and some, such as Stern, did not find libidinal and aggressive strivings remotely necessary as explanatory constructs. Nevertheless, most "clinical" theories of development, even the most relationship oriented of the object relations theories, view the child as being locked in a struggle that entails satisfying his or her needs on the one hand and sustaining his or her relationships with his or her primary objects on the other. The differences between attachment and psychoanalysis are most clear when the psychoanalytic theory is, to some extent, a drive-based theory. The less the emphasis on drive, the more subtle the distinctions. Therefore, we use Freud, Mahler, and Winnicott to provide counterpoints to the work of Ainsworth, Main, and their colleagues. Mahler and Winnicott offered theories that specifically address issues of infancy and of internalization and are therefore most directly comparable to attachment theory.

Freud believed that the infant becomes related to his or her parents as a by-product of his or her quest for drive satisfaction. The infant develops a relationship with the mother primarily because she gratifies his or her needs. Relationships ensure survival because they make it most likely that the child's needs for food and—ultimately—procreation will be met. The infant, from the outset, is "pleasure seeking" and only gradually and secondarily becomes object related.

According to some interpreters of Freudian theory (e.g., Eagle, 1987), the child's quest for pleasure is what ensures his or her survival. Although this point of view is most clearly delineated in Freud's (1920/1955) writings, Mahler's description of the "autistic" stage of the separation–individuation process and Winnicott's description of the "true self" likewise describe the baby's quest for instinctual gratification as primary to the establishment of object relatedness. By contrast, the baby of attachment theory is primed from birth to establish attachments (Ainsworth, 1969). The numerous attachment behaviors noted by Bowlby and Ainsworth are manifestations of a complex system that guarantees social interaction and leads to the development of ties that will ensure survival. In contrast to the baby of psychoanalysis, he or she is inherently, basically social. The baby of attachment theory certainly gets pleasure from contact (Eagle, 1987; Wolitzky, personal communication, October 1991), as the baby of psychoanalysis ultimately develops object relationships out of the matrix of drive gratification. Nevertheless, the fundamental motivation behind the establishment of relationships and the formation of internal representations is understood quite differently by these two schools of thought.

Because most psychoanalysts conceptualize the infant's basic needs differently, they differ in their conceptualization of the mother's role in facilitating infant and toddler emotional development. Both Mahler and Winnicott emphasized that, early on, the mother must gratify the infant's needs in order to establish basic homeostasis. Later in development, as the infant and toddler's primitive aggression gains ascendancy, the mother's role includes what is variously termed *holding* and *containment*. These words speak to the degree to which the infant's basic needs are invariably at some odds with the environment; holding allows the infant to experience them as manageable and eventually helps him or her integrate such disruptive (and presumably drive-linked) impulses into his or her experience of himself or herself. For both theorists, the task of containing the infant's experience is invariably challenging for the mother, who must struggle to keep her own needs in check so as not to force the infant into what Winnicott (1965) termed "compliance." It is this containing, gratifying presence that is internalized by the child in the establishment of libidinal object constancy and that allows for separation and individuation.

By contrast, the primary task of the mother of attachment theory is to recognize, affirm, and respond to the infant's bids for contact, comfort, and attachment. As described earlier, such actions certainly bring the infant pleasure and are therefore gratifying in some sense. However, what Bowlby and Ainsworth emphasized was the mother's role in the maintenance of the attachment system; specifically, her ability to respond appropriately when the attachment system is activated and attachment behaviors are increased. She, too, is primed to ensure the infant's survival by responding to his or her bids for contact and proximity. Attachment theorists view the mother's failure to respond sensitively as resulting from efforts to somehow minimize (Kobak et al., 1991) or maximize (Cassidy, 1991) the activation of her own attachment system. The "trouble" caused by the infant's attachment behaviors does not arise from a conflict between the child's wishes and her own but from the mother's need to maintain control over her own feelings in relation to attachment. Certainly, both positions emphasize the importance of the mother's remaining flexibly responsive to her infant's experience and of her being able to circumvent her own early difficulties in doing so. What differentiates them is their definition of infantile experience and the degree to which they see the infant's needs as being invariably pitted against those of the parent and of society.

For psychoanalysts, the quest for pleasure, alongside the need to express intrinsic aggression, operate so as to distort reality, compromise perception, and complicate both the formation of object relationships and the development of internalized representations. Thus, the mother is internalized along with the complex mesh of drive and affect that constitute the infant's interactive history with her; infantile distortions are internalized along with more accurate perceptions of gratification and modulation. Under optimal circumstances, internalization of the mother provides the child with a mode of modulating his or her inner state and with neutralizing his or her aggression. For many psychoanalysts, among them Mahler, one of the steps in the establishment of libidinal object constancy is the unification of the "good" and "bad" aspects of mother; this original separation is thought to serve the developmental purpose of protecting the good parts of the mother (and hence the self) from experiences of rage and disappointment. To the extent that the mother has not gratified the child's basic needs, the establishment of such representations will be compromised by the distorting effects of unmodulated need and rage. Silverman (1991) noted the following:

> Sandler and Sandler (1987) accented the drive-defense underpinnings of fantasy formations. According to their argument, these fantasies get projected onto parents, are reinternalized, and then are transformed into structures that are organized mainly by gratification and defense elements. From this perspective, psychic development stems primarily from young children's manner of organizing experiences rather than from interactions with parents. (p. 170)

For most psychoanalysts, internalizations develop out of a complex matrix of the distorting influence of the drives alongside the mother and baby's actual behaviors; thus, they are in their inception and continue to be over time vulnerable to the press of instinct and wish. Both Mahler and Winnicott viewed the mother's ministrations as providing the child with a sense of reality; her holding and mirroring allows the child to experience himself or herself in an increasingly differentiated, integrated, and whole way.

In attachment theory parlance, compromised (or insecure) representational models arise when the infant is forced to distort the expression of normal attachment behaviors in order to have his or her basic needs for comfort and succor met. Whatever feelings arise from such distortion of his or her attachment expressions must also be regulated; thus, an attachment pattern is both a mode of obtaining gratification and of managing affective experience. Representational models are thus not distortions of reality; rather they are accommodations to reality. They are based on accurate representations of the mother–baby exchange (Main et al., 1985) and serve to regulate the emotion that arises from the mother's success or failure in meeting the baby's attachment needs. Although the experience of pleasure in the interaction contributes in important ways to the establishment of working models, the baby does not split the representation of the mother (or of the self) into "good" and "bad" (Bretherton, 1987). The baby experiences his or her world in a differentiated, integrated fashion from the beginning.

It is these *accurate* perceptions of reality that influence interpersonal behavior and expectations from at least the second half of the first year of life, if not before (see Isabella & Belsky, 1991). The three patterns of attachment described by Ainsworth are understood to be related in a meaningful way to the actual caregiving the child received during the first year of life; the relationship between the quality of care and infant behavior in the Strange Situation is viewed as compelling evidence for the child's ability to accurately assess the actual caregiving he or she received during the first year of life and the caregiver's ability to meet his or her needs for comfort and security. Mothers who are predominantly sensitive and responsive provide a secure base for their children; typically, these children are classified as secure. The children of mothers who are predominantly rejecting when their children seek comfort will be classified as avoidant, although these same mothers may be intrusive in free play contexts (Belsky & Isabella, 1988). Children whose mothers are mixed in their responses to their children's comfort seeking will have children who are classified as resistant. The link between home behavior during the first year and subsequent attachment classification has been documented by numerous researchers (Ainsworth et al., 1978; Bates et al., 1985), although there continues to be debate as to whether avoidant and resistant patterns are the direct result of discrete maternal behavioral patterns or derive from other factors, such as child temperament in conjunction with a complex, less specific pattern of maternal behavior (Belsky & Rovine, 1987; Slade, Director, Huganir, Grunebaum, & Reeves, 1991). Related to this is the question as to whether avoidant and resistant patterns in infancy predict specific patterns of maladaptation in the preschool years (Sroufe, 1983). For attachment researchers, the implication of these findings is clear: The infant perceives the quality of his or her care accurately and forms mental representations in accord with these perceptions. The question of whether the infant is always an accurate decoder of reality is not addressed; rather, the assumption is made that the representations that are formed over the course of the first year are *primarily* based in reality.

As described by Main et al. (1985) and Bretherton (1985, 1987), IWMs derive from accurate perceptions of the relationship; the affects that must be regulated are *sequelae* of the exchange rather than a feature of the infant's makeup that will to a greater or lesser extent compromise his or her perception of reality. For the attachment theorists, the capacity to perceive reality is one that develops in sophistication but that is operative from the very beginning and serves as the dominant force in the establishment of mental representations.

Psychoanalysis has for many years struggled to clarify the relationship between affects and drives in theory as well as in practice (Gaensbauer, 1982). Are affects drive derivatives, as Freud (1915/1957) initially suggested, or are they manifestations of a separate biological system that serves important relational and communicative functions? To what degree are affective expressions conceptualized as manifestations of internal fantasies and impulses that are tied as much to psychosexual development as to reality, and to what extent are they viewed as understandable responses to real situations? Attachment theorists clearly ascribe to the latter position. Stern (1985) combined the two perspectives in an interesting way. His notion of RIGs is very similar to Main's description of IWMs; both assume that representations are directly shaped by real experiences. Stern suggested that they develop across a range of affect situations and are not exclusive to the realm of attachment (1985, p. 114). At the same time, his notions of the mother as a "self-regulating other" have much in common with more traditional psychoanalytic notions of the mother as giving dimension and clarity to a wide range of the infant's emotional experiences. He ascribed to affect rather than drive as a central explanatory concept, however, and omitted any discussion of the conflict between infantile and maternal experience in his formulations.

Many psychoanalysts do not find it necessary to ascribe to one or the other of these opposing views. In fact, some (Silverman, 1991; I. H. Paul, personal communication, June 16, 1990) have suggested that it is probably most meaningful to include drives toward both attachment *as well as* libidinal gratification in conceptualizations of early development. In this view, separating the two aims serves little useful purpose conceptually. Silverman (1991) suggested the following:

> There are two important strands in infant development. The first, which is drive organized, involves bodily experiences. The infants' own emotional feelings, self-experiences, sexual and aggressive wishes, fantasy formations, projections and defenses, and finally compromise solutions orchestrate this drive state. Drive-organized feeling states may occur when alone and/or during interaction with caregivers, but the organization of the experiences is primarily directed toward gratification and is endogenously generated. The second strand, beginning at birth, focusses on attachment—a positive, affective connection to caregivers, which leads eventually to an internalized object relations experience. (p. 170)

Although the drive aspects of psychoanalytic theory have received many challenges over the last 30 years, beginning with Fairbairn and the original object relations theorists, the developmental aspects of psychoanalytic theory have received few challenges from evolving schools of psychoanalytic thought. If anything, the notion of stages and phases has been ampli-fied—by Mahler, Stern, and even Winnicott. Originally, Freud (1905/1953) tied his notions of development to drive development. Psychosexual development referred to patterns of drive orga-nization and expression that characterizes the child's move through the oral, anal, and oedipal phases of development. Mahler added new organizational considerations through her introduction of the subphases of the separation–individuation process. There have been numerous interpre-tations of the term *psychosexual phases* over the course of the long history of psychoanalysis (see Pine, 1985). Nevertheless, however such phases are conceptualized, they are invariably viewed as shaping the way an infant or toddler experiences himself or herself in relationship to those around him or her. The traditional view of phases implies that all experiences are filtered through phase-specific lenses; thus, incorporation is the dominant mode of interaction with the world during the oral phase, all interactions are characterized by a struggle for control during the anal phase, and so forth. Noting that a child can be in more than one phase at any given time, Pine argued that phases are better defined not as the totality of an infant's experience but that they more precisely refer to periods of "peak intensity and peak developmental significance of certain (whatever) phenomena, without prejudgment of their duration" (1985, p. 40). He argued that many phases can take place concomitantly if one thinks of phases as being "affectively super-charged moments," that—for that moment in time—organize experience in ways that are mu-tative and integrative.

Even in modern-day psychoanalytic theory, the phases of psychosexual and separation–individuation development emerge in response to internal maturational pushes. Whereas these pushes are no longer conceptualized strictly in terms of shifts in the libidinization of body zones, all stage theories imply shifts in capacities for organization, differentiation, and symbolization. These shifts dramatically change the way the infant experiences his or her biological urges and continually alters his or her experience of relationships with others. In psychoanalytic thinking, each phase is viewed as a kind of multifaceted opportunity: It provides a chance for new levels of integration and new kinds of relationships; at the same time, the challenges posed by a new phase can stymy development and derail further progress. Failures at earlier levels compromise the resolution of new stages. Thus, for example, a child who enters rapprochement without having had the experiences of delight, elation, and omnipotence that are thought to be critical to resolution of the practicing subphase will presumably be less able to modulate the anger and anxiety of rapprochement with well-established feelings of confidence and self-love.

From the psychoanalytic standpoint, each phase provides the opportunity for reorganization and change. Thus, even when development is proceeding smoothly, the confluence of drive and object relations issues native to a particular phase can be extremely disruptive and potentially maladaptive. The most common example is the failure to resolve the issues central to the oedipal phase, which typically results in neurotic symptomatology or particular sorts of character pa-thology. Within psychoanalysis and most dynamic psychology, in fact, symptomatology, psycho-pathology, and hence diagnosis are related to presumed failures of development. In the most basic and simplistic terms, psychotic disturbances are linked to failures of differentiation (whether biologically or psychologically based), severe character disturbances are linked to failures in the resolution of issues central to the rapprochement subphase, and more neurotic pathology is linked to difficulties resolving anal and oedipal phase issues. Thus, the severity of pathology is tied to the "moment(s)" in development at which things began to unravel.

According to this perspective, internal representations will be modified as development proceeds; in large part, such modifications result from *internal* shifts in organization that in turn alter object relationships. Pine (1985) described the changes in the internalized libidinal object that may follow the establishment of libidinal object constancy:

The internal representation of the libidinal object, once attained, does not remain static any more than does anything else in human development. It is reshaped and extended not only with the growing cognitive capacities of the developing person but also with his encounter with and resolution of the emotional issues of each new stage. Thus, for example, the new view of the parent consequent upon the period of oedipal resolution and school entry, and the further new view at adolescence and even when one reaches parenthood in one's own right, cannot but alter the internal object representation as well. What distinguishes flexible adult functioning is the capacity to evoke, as appropriate, one or another aspect of the object representation, aspects that exist in a hierarchical arrangement shaped to individual need. (p. 107)

Much of attachment research has concerned itself with documenting stability and has, as such, been less concerned with the dynamics of changes in relationships across and as a consequence of development . It might be argued, in fact, that some aspects of attachment theory offer a notion of rigid determinism far more pessimistic than Freud's! Nevertheless, there has been a recent upsurge of interest in the way changes in cognitive development influence the manifestation of attachment patterns (see the section on assessing children's attachment beyond infancy); some researchers have also begun to explore the dynamics underlying instability in attachment patterns (Erickson et al., 1985), particularly the question of why some children shift from secure to insecure or from insecure to secure from infancy to preschool. Such notions of change are quite different from those psychoanalysts have linked to drive development, however. For psychoanalysts, what defines phases are not simply shifts in organization but shifts in the nature of the experience itself. Both the content and form of experience changes across phases. Thus, for instance, changes in bodily sensation and cognitive awareness around 2 years of age trigger struggles for control and autonomy between mother and child. The child of rapprochement is far more tempestuous, moody, irascible, and implacable than the child of practicing. This stems from the child's urge to maintain a more infantile tie to the mother, while exercising his or her autonomy to the hilt, from wishing to express his or her vulnerability while at the same time controlling against such expressions, and from struggling to maintain loving feelings in the face of his or her rage and fear. In psychoanalytic terms, this internal change cannot help but change the relationship; it is in this sense that it provides an opportunity for a new higher level resolution or for the establishment of a layer of unresolved conflict. It is this layering of development, with each phase providing a new set of opportunities for development or regression, that gives psychoanalytic developmental theory its richness.

For attachment theorists, changes in the environment lead to changes in parental behavior that are responsible for changes in IWMs. This was first demonstrated in Sroufe and Waters's (1977) research, which documented that changes in the quality of the mother's life were often related to changes in infant attachment. The links between environmental change and shifts in attachment classification have received further confirmation from later studies by others in the Minnesota group (Egeland & Farber, 1984; Erickson et al., 1985). Main (personal communication, June 25, 1985) reported that it is often the case that changes in child classification from insecure to secure often follow significant environmental changes and reorganization. For instance, a mother whose insecure child developed leukemia was so jolted by his diagnosis that she became vastly more responsive and sensitive, leading to his receiving a secure classification on reassessment at age 6. From the perspective of attachment theory, internal representations derive from actual interpersonal experiences and are changed by actual interpersonal experiences. However, because IWMs are thought to be quite stable and resistant to change (Bretherton, 1985, 1987; Main et al., 1985), modifications in these structures are less likely as the child matures and—in a sense—becomes more inured to environmental influence. Lieberman, Weston, and Paul (1991) noted that when previously unreliable caregivers become more reliable over the course of intervention, it is some time before children view them as trustworthy and treat them accordingly. Main (personal communication, June 25, 1985) suggested that shifts in classification are rare in adulthood, although mutative experiences with a loving partner or therapist can help bring them about.

The significance of these different notions of change for a "clinical" theory of development and psychopathology is considerable. The action of treatment and the dynamics of change are understood differently, as are basic notions of defense, diagnosis, and fantasy. Defense, as defined by psychoanalysis, is understood as the ego's effort to protect itself against disruptive id intrusions and intolerable conflict. The nature and intensity of the conflict, usually defined by its content or psychosexual level, will set in motion the requisite defenses. Defenses are defined by their developmental level; more primitive defenses (denial, projection) are thought to guard against more fundamental and overwhelming feelings, whereas more symbolically based and verbally mediated defenses (repression, rationalization, undoing) are used to guard against a range of more neurotic and higher level conflicts. Thus, an individual's defensive style will have much to do with (a) his or her level of psychosexual development, (b) the nature of the conflict he or she is defending against, and (c) the quality of internalized object relations.

According to attachment theory, defensive style derives more directly from relationship experiences; in essence, what is internalized is the caregiver's response to the child's affect in attachment relevant situations. In the terms of Kobak et al. (1991), the child develops a strategy for regulating affect that is consistent with his or her primary caregiver's response to his or her emotional life. Thus, the child whose mother rejects him or her when he or she is angry or needy will defensively exclude these experiences from his or her own awareness. In this sense, defenses are isomorphic to early interactive experiences. Defensive strategies are not conceptualized in developmental terms, nor are they viewed as fundamentally influenced by organismic development. Defensive exclusion may take different forms over time, but the aim and type of defense remains relatively unchanged. Although attachment theory's view of defense is certainly less complete (derived, as it was, from normative developmental study and not from studies of psychopathology and clinical phenomena), it does, nevertheless, address the critical role played by the mother in establishing a basic attitude toward primary and formative emotional experiences.

One of the most enduring debates within the child development literature concerns the role of temperament in determining the quality of early attachment relationships. This debate has much in common with the (now) age-old debate between object relations and drive theorists, and their struggle to establish the primacy either of relationships or the defining nature of endogenous stimulation. Attachment theorists such as Sroufe (1985) have consistently maintained that biologically based variations in excitability, activity level, fussiness, and soothability cannot be assessed outside the context of the relationship to the mother. In his view, the mother's response to these aspects of the infant's functioning so rapidly shapes the infant's expression that no "pure" measure of temperament is truly possible. The infant's behavior is far more an expression of the history of his or her relationship with mother than it is an expression of his or her own inherited tendencies and inclinations. Temperament researchers argue that there are biological bases to an infant's mode of emotion regulation and that these may significantly influence the development of attachment. The extreme of this position (Kagan, 1989) is that attachment classifications are measurements of temperamental styles rather than of modes of relating. Belsky and Rovine (1987) provided a plausible solution to this standoff, suggesting that temperament does not underlie the security–insecurity dimension but that it may underlie the type of security or insecurity manifested by a child. The concept of temperament has much in common with the concept of drive, insofar as both are ways of thinking about individually varying levels of endogeneous stimulation and are thought to influence the regulation of emotion and of relationships in ways that are intrinsic to the individual and not to the dyad.

Concepts of diagnosis are also inevitably implicated by these underlying differences in the dynamics of change. In essence, a psychoanalytically informed clinical diagnosis is based on certain presumptions regarding the developmental level of an individual's personality organization. Thus, a diagnosis would indicate something important about a person's level of functioning and overall organization. Attachment classification, by contrast, is not a diagnosis and *presumably* says nothing about the overall developmental level of functioning. Most attachment theorists and researchers see the three major classifications as variations along a normative continuum, although there is some consensus that the two insecure patterns are less optimal and more problematic (but nevertheless normal) adaptations. And, security, per se, is not equated with *absence* of neurosis or conflict; rather, it is a pattern of adaptation that allows for more flexible integration and healthier relationships.

Although very few attachment theorists have addressed the question of development directly (although Bowlby, 1969, did introduce the notion of phases of attachment), there are many reasons to assume that there is a latent developmental theory underlying certain of the fundamental tenets and seminal findings of attachment research. Flexible modes of integration and healthier relationships are signs that higher level organization exists and are indicative of more mature and differentiated object relationships. In a recent study, in fact, the level of maternal representation of object relations and quality of both maternal and child attachment were highly correlated (Levine, Tuber, Slade, & Ward, 1991), indicating that security of attachment may actually be strongly related to the quality and developmental level of object relations. Also, it has been our impression in reviewing over 100 adult attachment interview transcripts that dismissing and preoccupied adults are far more likely to manifest severe character disturbances, including narcissistic, schizoid, and borderline personality disorders, than are those classified as secure. Although adults classified as secure are not without character pathology and neurotic symptomatology, there is rarely any evidence of more serious character or personality disorder. This makes a great deal of sense, of course, given the fact that insecure adults are thought to have had extremely frustrating experiences with early attachment figures, with little later opportunity to work through or reintegrate them.

Also, development does more than change the way security and insecurity are manifested. The vicissitudes of the many phases of development will be experienced differently depending on the quality of early parenting. There can be little question that individuals with more basic trust and confidence will be far more able to negotiate these vicissitudes as well as take advantage of the opportunities posed by them than their less secure counterparts. Notions of emotional *development*—as they are variously understood by psychoanalysts and developmental psychologists alike—require further explication and study by attachment theorists. Certain phenomena simply cannot be understood or appreciated fully without such a theory; in part, this is why Freud's theories of psychosexual development have had such remarkable staying power.

Finally, a brief note about the question of fantasy. From the vantage point of psychoanalytic theory, the distorted aspect of a child's fantasies about himself or herself, his or her parents, and about his or her world derive largely from the distorting influence of unconscious wishes and impulses. Many classical psychoanalysts believe that such fantasies are a part of experience from earliest infancy, even before the infant has developed the ability to symbolize. There has been tremendous debate within psychoanalysis (Masson, 1984; Miller, 1981) about the role of reality and real trauma in psychic development; Freud himself eventually saw the bulk of his patients' disclosures of incest, and so forth, as fantasies, although most latter-day analysts would certainly opt for a balance between the role of unconscious and reality factors in determining the content and nature of fantasy. As should be evident from the foregoing discussion, attachment theorists have not addressed the question of fantasy directly. It is quite commonplace for 2- and 3-year-old children to spontaneously offer fantasies that cannot possibly be representations of reality per se. How, for instance, might attachment theorists explain the exclamation made by a secure child immediately prior to his or her brother's birth while playing with a miniature baby and baby carriage: "Baby fall on the floor, smash its head open!!!" (observed by the first author). Clearly, this statement reflects a distortion of reality that must be related to the child's wishes. Although it may, too, be related to reality, the elaboration of his or her fantasy has to be related to something other than real experience. IWMs do not suffice as explanatory constructs in situations such as these. At present, distortion, wish, and fantasy have little place in attachment theory and are still most adequately explained by an adaptation of drive-based psychoanalytic theory.

Similarly, childhood sexuality, both in its fantasized aspects and its emergence over the course of early development, has little place in attachment theory. A single study within the attachment literature examined seductiveness and flirtation in toddlers (Sroufe & Ward, 1980); however, these phenomena were viewed as imitations of pathological adult behavior and not as variations along a continuum of early sexual and sensual development. These, too, are issues for future research, for bodily changes and bodily sensation should be linked to the establishment and maintenance of attachments in a meaningful way.

CONCLUSION

Clearly, there are many points of convergence and divergence between these two theoretical positions. Although certain vital questions remain, the areas of convergence offer compelling evidence for the importance of sensitive parenting in establishing basic and stable modes of interpersonal relatedness. And, as has been true for the past two decades, there continues to be great controversy about the nature of inner experience and its relationship to real environmental events. The data of attachment theory offer compelling evidence that real events, as documented in observable maternal and child behavior and representation, are empirically linked to the development of psychic structure. As research offers new insights into maternal, paternal, and child behavior, theory will be modified even further. We hope that some of the divergences we have described here can be resolved through such efforts, resulting in a more uniform, data-near set of theoretical principles. At the same time, only when theory combines an appreciation of the child's abilities to perceive and integrate reality along with the personal and internally driven aspects of his or her psyche can theorists begin to build a picture of the whole. These kinds of data cannot necessarily be derived from the empirical study but may instead be drawn primarily from naturalistic and clinical investigations.

Attachment theory offers a set of testable hypotheses about the nature of development and, as such, offers a means of systematically evaluating a variety of modes of clinical intervention. Attachment theory clearly provides a new framework for observing preverbal and early representational processes and making valid inferences about the child's subjective experience on the basis of these observables. If the metaphor for sensitive adult clinical work is to really "hear" what a patient means, the metaphor for clinical work with children under 3 is to really "see" what a patient means. Children under 3 do not offer a tremendous amount of symbolic material, nor are they typically able to verbalize their feelings; rather, they *show* what they think and feel. When one learns this language, relatively new forms of treatment suggest themselves. For instance, combining a behavioral perspective with an IWMs perspective, the exquisite complementarity of the parents' representational worlds, the system of parental behaviors, the child's emerging sense of himself or herself in the relationship, and the child's system of attachment behaviors come more clearly into view. Clinicians can now begin to think about both experience and outcome in ways that can be operationalized more explicitly and need rely less and less on speculation and inference. Treatment models that are anchored in actual data can only be revolutionary. Such efforts at consolidation are vital to the establishment of a lively, complete theory of intervention, of development and of relationships, and to helping clinicians, developmentalists, and parents best understand the children before them.

REFERENCES

Aber, J. L., Appel, A., Baruch, C., & Morris, P. (1991). *Toddler symbolic play under stress: Predicted by infant security and parent sensitivity.* Unpublished manuscript.

Aber, J. L., & Baker, A. (1990). Security of attachment in toddlerhood: Modifying assessment procedures for joint clinical and research purposes. In M. T. Greenberg, D. Cicchetti, & E. M. Cummings (Eds.), *Attachment in the preschool years* (pp. 427–463). Chicago: University of Chicago Press.

Aber, J. L., & Slade, A. (1987, January). *Attachment theory and research: A framework for clinical interventions.* Paper presented at the meeting of the Child and Adolescent Division for Psychoanalysis of the American Psychological Association.

Ainsworth, M. D. S. (1969). Object relations, dependency and attachment: A theoretical review of the infant-mother relationship. *Child Development, 40,* 969–1025.

Ainsworth, M. D. S., Blehar, M. C., Waters, E., & Wall, S. (1978). *Patterns of attachment: A psychological study of the strange situation.* Hillsdale, NJ: Erlbaum.

Bates, J. E., Maslin, C. A., & Frankel, K. A. (1985). Attachment security, mother-child interaction, and temperament as predictors of behavior-problem ratings at age three years. *Monographs of the Society for Research in Child Development, 50*(1-2, Serial No. 209).

Belsky, J., Garduque, L., & Hrncir, E. (1984). Assessing performance, competence and executive capacity in infant play: Relations to home environment and security of attachment. *Developmental Psychology, 20,* 406–417.

Belsky, J., & Isabella, R. (1988). Maternal, infant and social-contextual determinants of attachment security. In J. Belsky & T. Nezworski (Eds.), *Clinical implications of attachment* (pp. 41–94). Hillsdale, NJ: Erlbaum.

Belsky, J., & Rovine, M. (1987). Temperament and attachment security in the Strange Situation: An empirical rapprochement. *Child Development, 58,* 787–795.

Belsky, J., Rovine, M., & Taylor, D. (1984). The Pennsylvania Infant and Parent Development Project, III: The origins of individual differences in infant-mother attachment: Maternal and child contribution. *Child Development, 55,* 718–728.

Benedek, T. (1959). Parenthood as a developmental phase. *Journal of the American Psychoanalytic Association, 7,* 389–417.

Bowlby, J. (1969). *Attachment and loss: Vol. 1. Attachment.* New York: Basic Books.

Bowlby, J. (1973). *Attachment and loss: Vol. 2. Separation.* New York: Basic Books.

Bowlby, J. (1982). *Attachment and loss: Vol. 3. Loss.* New York: Basic Books.

Brenner, C. (1982). *The Mind in conflict.* New York: International Universities Press.

Bretherton, I. (1985) Attachment theory: Retrospect and prospect. *Monographs of the Society for Research in Child Development, 50*(1-2 Serial No. 209).

Bretherton, I. (1987). New Perspectives on attachment relations: Security, communication, and internal working models. In J. D. Osofsky (Ed.), *Handbook of infant development* (2nd ed., 1061–1100). New York: Wiley.

Bretherton, I., Ridgeway, D., & Cassidy, J. (1990). Assessing internal working models of the attachment relationship: An attachment story completion task for three-year olds. In M. T. Greenberg, D. Cicchetti, & E. M. Cummings (Eds.), *Attachment in the preschool years* (pp. 273–311). Chicago: University of Chicago Press.

Bretherton, I., Biringen, Z., Ridgeway, D., Maslin, C., & Sherman, M. (1989). Attachment: The parental perspective. *Infant Mental Health Journal, 10,* 203–221.

Carlson, V., Cicchetti, D., Barnett, D., & Braunwald, K. (1989). Finding order in disorganization: Lessons from research in maltreated infants' attachments to their caregivers. In D. Cicchetti & V. Carlson (Eds.), *Child maltreatment: Theory and research on the causes and consequences of child abuse and neglect* (pp. 494–528). New York: Cambridge University Press.

Cassidy, J. (1990). Theoretical and methodological considerations in the study of attachment and the self in young children. In M. T. Greenberg, D. Cicchetti, & E. M. Cummings (Eds.), *Attachment in the preschool years* (pp. 21–87). Chicago: University of Chicago Press.

Cassidy, J. (1991). *Emotion regulation within attachment relationships.* Unpublished manuscript.

Cassidy, J., & Kobak, R. (1988). Avoidance and its relation to other defensive processes. In J. Belsky & T. Nezworski (Eds.), *Clinical implications of attachment* (pp. 300–326). Hillsdale, NJ: Erlbaum.

Cassidy, J., Marvin, R.S., & the MacArthur Working Group on Attachment Network on the Transition from Infancy to Early Childhood. (1989). *Attachment organization in three-and four-year-olds: A classification system.* Unpublished manuscript, University of Virginia, Charlottesville, and Pennsylvania State University, Philadelphia.

Cicchetti, D., & Aber, J. L. (1986). Early precursors to later depression: An organizational perspective. In L. Lipsitt & C. Rovee-Collier (Eds.), *Advances in infancy* (Vol. 4, pp. 87–137). Norwood, NJ: Ablex.

Cicchetti, D., Cummings, E. M., Greenberg, M. T., & Marvin, R. S. (1990). An organizational perspective on attachment beyond infancy: Implications for theory, measurement and research. In M. T. Greenberg, D. Cicchetti, & E. M. Cummings (Eds.), *Attachment in the preschool years* (pp. 3–51). Chicago: University of Chicago Press.

Crittenden, P. M. (1985). Maltreated infants: Vulnerability and resilience. *Journal of Child Psychology and Psychiatry, 26,* 85–96.

Crittenden, P. M. (1987). Relationships at risk. In J. Belsky & T. Nezworski (Eds.), *Clinical implications of attachment* (pp. 136–174). Hillsdale, NJ: Earlbaum.

Eagle, M. (1987). *Recent developments in psychoanalysis.* Cambridge, MA: Harvard University Press.

Easterbrooks, M. A., & Goldberg, W. (1984). Toddler development in the family: Impact of father involvement and parenting characteristics. *Developmental Psychology, 55,* 740–752.

Egeland, B., & Farber, E. A. (1984). Infant-mother attachment: Factors related to its development and changes over time. *Child Development, 55,* 753–771.

Egeland, B., & Sroufe, L. A. (1981). Attachment and early maltreatment. *Child Development, 52,* 44–52.

Eichberg, C. G. (1987, April). *Quality of infant-parent attachment: Related to mother's representation of her own relationship history.* Paper presented at the biennial meeting of the Society for Research in Child Development, Baltimore, MD.

Erickson, M. F., Sroufe, L. A., & Egeland, B. (1985). The relationship between quality of attachment and behavior problems in preschool in a high risk sample. *Monographs of the Society for Research in Child Development, 50*(1-2, Serial No. 209).

Fairbairn, R. (1952). *Psychoanalytic studies of the personality.* London: Routledge & Kegan Paul.

Freud, S. (1953). Three essays on the theory of sexuality. In J. Strachey (Ed. and Trans.), *The standard edition of the complete psychological works of Sigmund Freud* (Vol. 7, pp. 135–243). London: Hogarth Press. (Original work published 1905)

Freud, S. (1957). The unconscious. In J. Strachey (Ed. and Trans.), *The standard edition of the complete psychological work of Sigmund Freud* (Vol. 14, pp. 166–215). London: Hogarth Press. (Original work published 1915)

Freud, S. (1955). Beyond the pleasure principle. In J. Strachey (Ed. and Trans.), *The standard edition of the complete psychological works of Sigmund Freud* (Vol. 18, pp. 7–23). London: Hogarth Press. (Original work published 1920)

Gaensbauer, T. (1982). The differentiation of discrete affects: A case report. *Psychoanalytic Study of the Child, 37,* 29–67.

George, C., Kaplan, N., & Main, M. (1985). *The Berkeley Adult Attachment Interview.* Unpublished manuscript, Department of Psychology, University of California, Berkeley.

George, C., & Solomon, J. (1989). Internal working models of parenting and security of attachment at age six. *Infant Mental Health Journal, 10,* 222–237.

Greenberg, J., & Mitchell, S. (1983). *Object relations in Psychoanalytic Theory.* Cambridge, MA: Harvard University Press.

Grossmann, K., Grossmann, K. E., Spangler, G., Suess, G., & Unzner, L. (1985). Maternal sensitivity and newborns' orientation responses as related to quality of attachment in Northern Germany. *Monographs of the Society for Research in Child Development, 50*(1-2, Serial No. 209).

Haft, W., & Slade, A. (1989). Affect attunement and maternal attachment: A pilot study. *Infant Mental Health Journal, 10,* 157–172.

Isabella, R., & Belsky, J. (1991). Interactional synchrony and the origins of infant-mother attachment : A replication study. *Child Development, 62,* 373–384.

Kagan, J. (1989). *Unstable ideas: Temperament, cognition and the self.* Cambridge, MA: Harvard University Press.

Klein, M. (1932). *The psychoanalysis of children.* London: Hogarth Press.

Kobak, R., Cole, H., Ferenz-Gillies, R., Fleming, W., & Gamble, W. (1991). *A dimensional analysis of adolescent attachment strategies.* Unpublished manuscript.

Kobak, R., & Sceery, A. (1988). Attachment in later adolescence: Working models, affect regulation and representations of self and others. *Child Development, 59,* 135–146.

Kohut, H. (1969). *The analysis of the self.* New York: International Universities Press.

Lamb, M. E., Thompson, R. A., Gardner, W. P., Charnov, E. L., & Estes, D. (1984). Security of infantile attachment as assessed in the "Strange Situation." *Behavioral and Brain Sciences, 7,* 127–171.

Levine, L., Tuber, S., Slade, A., & Ward, M. J. (1991). Mothers' mental representations and their relationship to mother-infant attachment. *Bulletin of the Menninger Clinic, 55,* 454–469.

Lewis, M., Feiring, C., McGuffog, C., & Jaskir, J. (1984). Predicting psychopathology in six-year olds from early social relations. *Child Development, 55,* 123–136.

Lieberman, A., Weston, D., & Paul, J. (1991). Preventive intervention and outcome with anxiously attached dyads. *Child Development, 62,* 199–209.

Loewald, H. (1980). *Papers on psychoanalysis.* New Haven, CT: Yale University Press.

Lyons-Ruth, K., Connell, D., Zoll, D., & Stahl, J. (1987). Infants at social risk: Relations among infant maltreatment, maternal behavior, and infant attachment behavior. *Developmental Psychology, 23,* 223–232.

Mahler, M., Pine, F., & Bergman, A. (1970). The mother's reaction to her toddler's drive for individuation. In E. J. Anthony & T. Benedek (Eds.), *Parenthood: Its psychology and psychopathology* (pp. 257–275). Boston: Little, Brown.

Mahler, M., Pine, F., & Bergman, A. (1975). *The psychological birth of the human infant.* New York: Basic Books.

Main, M., Kaplan, N., & Cassidy, J. (1985). Security in infancy, childhood and adulthood: A move to the level of representation. *Monographs of the Society for Research in Child Development, 50*(1-2, Serial No. 209).

Main, M., & Goldwyn, R. (in press). Interview-based adult attachment classifications: Related to infant–mother and infant–father attachment. *Developmental Psychology*.

Main, M., & Hesse, E. (1990). Parents' unresolved traumatic experiences are related to infant disorganized attachment status: Is frightened and/or frightening parental behavior the linking mechanism? In M. T. Greenberg, D. Cicchetti, & E. M. Cummings (Eds.), *Attachment in the preschool years* (pp. 161–185). Chicago: University of Chicago Press.

Main, M., & Solomon, J. (1990). Procedures for identifying infants as disorganized/disoriented during the Ainsworth strange situation. In M. T. Greenberg, D. Cicchetti, & E. M. Cummings (Eds.), *Attachment in the preschool years* (pp. 121–161). Chicago: University of Chicago Press.

Masson, J. M. (1984). *The assault on truth: Freud's suppression of the seduction theory*. New York: Farrar, Straus & Giroux.

Matas, L., Arend, R. A., & Sroufe, L. A. (1978). Continuity of adaptation in the second year: The relationship between quality of attachment and later competence. *Child Development, 49*, 547–556.

Miller, A. (1981). *The drama of the gifted child*. New York: Basic Books.

Osofsky, J. (1988). Attachment theory and research in the psychoanalytic process. *Psychoanalytic Psychology, 5*, 159–177.

Pastor, D. (1981). The quality of mother–infant attachment and its relationship to toddlers' initial sociability with peers. *Developmental Psychology, 17*, 326–335.

Pine, F. (1985). *Developmental theory and clinical process*. New Haven, CT: Yale University Press.

Radke-Yarrow, M., Cummings, E. M., Kuczynski, L., & Chapman, M. (1985). Patterns of attachment in two-and-three-year olds in normal families and families with parental depression. *Child Development, 56*, 884–893.

Sandler, J., & Sandler, A. M. (1987). The past unconscious, the present unconscious and the vicissitudes of guilt. *International Journal of Psychoanalysis, 68*, 331–342.

Silverman, D. (1991). Attachment patterns and Freudian theory: An integrative proposal. *Psychoanalytic Psychology, 8*, 169–193.

Slade, A. (1987). The quality of attachment and early symbolic play. *Developmental Psychology, 23*, 78–85.

Slade, A., & Aber, J. L. (1986, April). *The internal experience of parenting toddlers: Toward an analysis of individual and developmental differences*. Paper presented at the International Conference of Infant Studies, Los Angeles.

Slade, A., Director, L., Huganir, L., Grunebaum, L., & Reeves, M. (1991, April). *Representational and behavioral correlates of prebirth maternal attachment*. Paper presented at the biennial meeting of the Society for Research in Child Development, Seattle, WA.

Speltz, M. (1990). The treatment of preschool conduct problems: An integration of attachment and behavioral constructs. In M. T. Greenberg, D. Cicchetti, & E. M. Cummings (Eds.), *Attachment in the preschool years* (pp. 399–427). Chicago: University of Chicago Press.

Speiker, S. J., & Booth, C. (1985, April). Family risk typologies and patterns of insecure attachment. In J. O. Osofsky (Chair), *Interventions with infants at risk; Patterns of attachment*. Symposium conducted at the biennial meeting of the Society for Research in Child Development, Toronto, Ontario, Canada.

Sroufe, L. A. (1979). The coherence of individual development. *American Psychologist, 34*, 834–841.

Sroufe, L. A. (1983). Infant-caregiver attachment and patterns of adaptation in preschool: The roots of maladaptations and competence. In M. Permutter (Ed.), *Minnesota Symposium in Child Psychology* (Vol. 16, pp. 41–83). Hillsdale, NJ: Erlbaum.

Sroufe, L. A. (1985). Attachment classification from the perspective of infant-caregiver relationships and infant temperament. *Child Development, 56,* 1–14.

Sroufe, L. A., & Ward, M. J. (1980). Seductive behavior in mothers and toddlers: Occurrences, correlates and family origins. *Child Development, 51,* 1222–1229.

Sroufe, L. A., & Waters, E. (1977). Attachment as an organizational construct. *Child Development, 48,* 1184–1199.

Stern, D. (1985). *The interpersonal world of the infant.* New York: Basic Books.

Waters, E. (1978). The reliability and stability of individual differences in infant attachment. *Child Development, 49,* 971–975.

Waters, E., Wippman, J., & Sroufe, L. A. (1979). Attachment, positive affect, and competence in the peer group: Two studies in construct validation. *Child Development, 50,* 821–829.

Winnicott, D. W. (1965). *Maturational processes and the facilitating environment.* New York: International Universities Press.

Zeanah, C., Benoit, D., & Barton, M. (1989). *The working model of the child interview.* Unpublished manuscript.

Zeanah, C., Benoit, D., Hirschberg, L., Barton, M., & Regan, C. (1991, October). *Classifying mothers' representations of their infants: Results from structured interviews.* Paper presented at the annual meeting of the American Academy of Child and Adolescent Psychiatry, San Francisco.

7

OBJECT RELATIONS: TOWARD A RELATIONAL MODEL OF THE MIND

IRENE FAST

Object relations perspectives are assuming an increasingly dominant place in psycho-analytic psychology. They have led to a number of widely accepted ideas that are incompatible with the drive theory that has historically shaped psychoanalytic thought and observation. It is now generally agreed that infants are not initially oblivious to the environment but are engaged with it from the beginning. Relationships rather than body-derived physical sensations are central to our earliest experiences. Objects (other people) are not merely occasions for drive discharge but are centers of subjectivity reciprocal to the self. Self–world relationships are not products of the infant's turn from exclusively body-centered experience to a cathexis of the external world and the testing of its drive-dominated perceptions against reality. Such relationships develop by processes of differentiation and integration that lead to the establishment of independent, stable self and object organizations in fruitful relationship to one another.

These changes in the view of human development, however, have also raised new theoret-ical questions. As Kuhn (1962) points out, when one theory is increasingly found to be incapable of accounting for relevant observations, new conceptions or part theories are developed that do so more fully. However, for a new theory to take the place of a previously accepted one, it must do more than account for observations that the other did not easily accommodate. It must also deal with those for which the other did account.

For object relations theory, this means, in part, establishing a framework for psychic structure. Freud's conceptions that the infant is initially oblivious to his or her environment, that the mind originates in body-derived physical sensations, that objects are no more than occasions for drive discharge, and that the infant turns to reality and reality testing in the latter half of the second year of life are integral to his ways of formulating widely accepted aspects of

186

mental organization. If object relations perspectives are to replace these conceptions, they must also deal in relational terms with their implications for accepted mental phenomena.

More specifically, if Freud's conception of body-bound experience as prerelational can no longer be accepted, relational frameworks must be found to account for the origins of the mind in the body. Such frameworks must be able to accommodate the primitive experience modes that Freud associated with body boundedness, including experience in which contrary wishes exist side by side without conflict or connection, thought is taken for reality, the self is the arbiter of existence, illusions of omnipotence prevail, and so forth. If objects (object representations) are to be seen as more than occasions for drive discharge, a different way must be found to understand relations between the representational and dynamic aspects of the mind, one that can account for both the distortion of object representations by dynamic forces and, conversely, the influence of object representations on the patterning of dynamic forces. If integration–differentiation processes are to be accepted as central to self–world relatonships, it must be shown how such processes can result in the developments that drive theory attributes to infants' new cathexes of reality in the latter half of the second year of life: reality testing, the emergence of intrapsychic conflict, and the establishment of the reality-oriented ego and the dynamic unconscious.

Significant developments in object relations theory and in other fields within psychology now suggest directions for accomplishing these aims. These developments imply a fundamental change in our conception of the mind. They strike at the heart of the objectivism that lies almost unnoticed at the base of most Western thinking about mental organization. That conception posits that the basic contents of the mind are sensory perceptions and that mental activity consists of organizing these perceptions of external reality.

Objectivism has prevailed in psychology throughout most of the field's history despite contrary views such as those of Piaget (1951) and Werner (1948). Freud also accepted it. In his theory, the basic contents of the mind are objectively accurate representations of objects. To account for the unrealistic in people's experience, he posited drives that in various ways distort these representations. The aim of psychoanalysis, in this view, is to remove the distorting effects of drives and give individuals back the true histories of their lives. (Schimek, 1975, and Feffer, 1988, provide more extended discussions of objectivism and its implications for psychoanalytic theory.)

Ideas congruent with those of Werner (1948) and Piaget (1951) now appear to be emerging from several fields. These ideas suggest that actions, not objects, are primary in human experience. The basic structures of the mind are not representations of objects but schemes representing people's personally motivated ways of interacting with their worlds. They are dynamic rather than representational structures. Individuals' ways of going at things are the basic units of psychic organization. Object representations are secondary, derived from schemes of interaction in the course of development. These views are typically called *constructivist* to emphasize that individuals construct the meaning of their experience rather than receive it as an objective reality.

Quantitative empirical investigators are finding a focus on interaction structures useful in exploring a variety of mental functions in diverse populations. Stern (1985) proposes that such structures are the building blocks of the core self in infancy. Emde (1988) suggests that relational schemes set in infancy are activated in the social engagements of later life. Nelson (1986) explores them as schemes in which children pattern their knowledge of the real world. From the vantage points of cognition and artificial intelligence, researchers are investigating these schemes as mental structures in which adults organize their memories, their understanding of social situations, and their ways of acting in their worlds (Schank, 1982; Schank & Abelson, 1977; Trzebinski, 1989; Tulving, 1972). From their bases in linguistics and philosophy, Lakoff and Johnson (1980) argue that people's modes of interacting with their worlds, represented in metaphor structures, govern the ways in which they perceive and draw inferences from their experiences and set goals.[1]

These notions of ways that interaction structures underlie various aspects of psychic organization converge with clinically derived views. Relational perspectives in psychoanalysis share a fundamental commitment to the proposition that, from the beginning of life, psychological development occurs in relationships. However, they differ in the ways in which they conceive the structure of these relationships and their place in mental organization. Infants may be seen as object seeking (Ainsworth, Blehar, Waters, & Wall, 1978; Bowlby, 1969; Fairbairn, 1952). Rather than this directional focus, theorists may emphasize the two-person relationship as a whole—the mother–child unit rather than the child seeking attachment (Kernberg, 1966; Loewald, 1971; Sandler & Sandler, 1978; Winnicott, 1971). Within this unit, representations of self and other are typically seen as merged in an undifferentiated whole; the relationship modes themselves (e.g., ways of nurturing and being nurtured, trying to achieve goals, being at odds with one another) that structure interactions, historically not the focus of attention, are increasingly being explored as dynamic organizations.

It is this relatively new attention to relationship modes that provides a way to integrate object relations perspectives with constructivist views of the mind. Investigators suggest that beginning with infant–mother relationship modes, interaction schemes, which are registered mentally as dynamic functions, constitute the dynamic aspects of the mind. This way of conceiving relationship structures and their place in mental organization has an honorable history in psychoanalytic psychology. Sullivan (1956) proposes "dynamisms," interpersonal patterns of energy transformation, as the structures by which people understand their experiences. Schilder (1950), similarly, posits dynamic schemes of interaction as the base for all development and as the patterns by which people construe events. More recently, researchers have begun to explore in greater detail how such dynamic interaction structures might be seen as the building blocks from which the id, ego, and superego of Freud's structural model are constructed (Kernberg, 1966; Loewald, 1971; Sandler & Sandler, 1978; Schimek, 1975).

In conceptions focused on interaction modes, object representations have a different place than in Freud's drive theory. They are not perceptual inputs that are passively registered in the mind. Insofar as quantitative empirical investigators concern themselves with the representations' origins and structures, they take a fully constructivist view. Investigators suggest that objects are initially embedded in and defined by events. Only gradually in the course of development do they become stable representational structures.

In object relations theory, questions about how object representations are to be conceived are less fully resolved. Most theorists have not explicitly given up the objectivist view. Implicitly, however, various researchers appear to be leaving it behind. For example, Hartmann's (1939) proposal that the self be seen as a representation in the ego coordinate to object representations inadvertently undercuts it: Self representations are not easily seen as passively registered perceptual inputs; if they are reciprocals of object representations, the objectivist view of object representations is also called in question. The object-relational focus on objects as other people

---

[1]The growing emphasis on interaction structures as basic to various mental functions suggests a convergence of ideas that originate in very diverse areas of inquiry. However, that convergence is by no means complete. In large part, investigators seem to have developed their interactionist perspectives independently of one another. They focus on such diverse interaction aspects as goal characteristics, interaction structures as actions or interactions between self and nonself, the initial nonintegration of differing event structures, the ways such structures might be considered to be dynamic, and so forth. They may be elicited for study in systematic observations of mother–child interactions (Stern, 1985), experimenter-constructed stories (Schank and Abelson, 1977), or subject-generated descriptions of activities (Nelson, 1986). No agreement exists as yet on the defining parameters of interactions or of their mental representations. Indeed, attempts to delineate similarities and differences among the various emphases dictated by particular research interests are in their earliest stages.

who are themselves centers of subjectivity also makes it difficult to conceive object representations in objectivist terms as simple perceptual inputs.

Moreover, although conceptions of development through the differentiation of initially merged self–object representations appear to retain the objectivist perspective, they also suggest that individuals construct their representations of both self and others in interaction processes. Kernberg (1966), for example, suggests that infants' earliest self and object representations are constituted in alternating processes of introjection and projection. However, only Schimek (1975) fully expresses the view (shared with Piaget [Flavell, 1963], Werner, 1948, and researchers engaged in quantitative empirical investigations) that individuals construct their objects as they interact with their worlds.

Object relational models of psychic structure built on constructivist bases may vary considerably. If they are increasingly found to be useful, one can expect lively competition among relational models aimed at accommodating the widest possible range of clinical and developmental observation. In broad strokes, the directions my colleagues and I (Fast, 1985, 1987, 1990) are pursuing suggest, for example, that the fears and wishes whose interplay is central to Freud's view of the mind are interaction structures—ways of loving, being envious, working toward goals, avoiding conflict, or denying reality. The patternings of interaction modes (e.g., ways of loving) have histories that extend to the earliest ways in which people have interacted with others (e.g., taking in food, being comforted, learning to soothe themselves). People's images of self and of others are products of the ways in which they have interacted with others—tenderly, competitively, fearfully, abusively, and so forth—rather than objectively accurate perceptions subsequently distorted by drives.

Unrealistic ways of thinking and feeling can be traced to developmentally early ways in which people have construed their interactions. Such ways persist relatiavely unchanged in adulthood if anxiety results in people excluding them from developmentally appropriate modification. Clinical intervention is not aimed at removing drive-based distortions from basically accurate memories of objects. It is directed at changing the interaction modes that constitute people's minds and govern the ways in which they understand their experiences and act in their worlds.

This chapter outlines the basic parameters of a relational model of mental functioning. We have called it event theory. To illustrate its implications, the chapter elaborates one aspect of the model, the bodily context of early interactions. It suggests ways in which this interactional view of the mind's origins in body experience might account for the phenomena that in Freud's view required the infant to be oblivious to the environment in his or her body-centered experience and for the changes that Freud attributed to the child's new reality cathexis at about 18–24 months of age.

RELATIONSHIP UNITS: THEIR STRUCTURE AND DEVELOPMENT

Interaction Schemes

Event theory proposes that the basic units of experience are interactions between self and nonself. The interactions are called *events* and include all aspects of a particular activity. In the infant's experience, for example, a nursing event includes the infant's own vigorous sucking, the smell of milk, the feel of the mother's body and her various movements, and the creak and motion of the rocker. In Stern's (1985) terms, it is a small but coherent chunk of lived experience.

However, an event is not defined subjectively in terms of its sensory components (e.g., the smell of milk, the feel of the mother's body, the creak of the rocker). It is registered mentally as a scheme of interaction. The sensory-perceptual components of the event contribute to the patterning of the scheme but are at first not separately represented in the mind.

This aspect of relationship modes has not yet been intensively addressed in object relations theory. However, other approaches offer it some support. In his paradigmatic example, Piaget (Flavell, 1963) proposes that the infant's grasping a ring is registered mentally in a grasp scheme (an action scheme), not in a scheme representing the ring or the infant self. Fivush and Slackman (1986) present evidence showing that children's descriptions of an event experienced for the first time (e.g., a trip to the circus, a fire drill, the first day in kindergarten) are not tied to the particulars of the specific event but are organized as general scripts or expectancy sets that represent the flow of the action. Similarly, my colleagues and I (Fast, Marsden, Cohen, Heard, & Kruse, 1992) have found that at the lowest levels of event experience that we can identify in adults, individuals do not focus on the perceptually given realities of an event but on interaction modes that they ascribe to it. In response to a picture stimulus (TAT4, 6BM), for example, subjects identify the situation as "an argument," "a love affair," "getting together," or "mourning." Only at higher levels of event organization do they elaborate the perceptually given aspects of the pictured figures.

Event schemes represent the entire course of a particular activity. In Nelson and Gruendel's (1986) studies, children include in their understanding of an event its beginning, middle, and end. Schank and Abelson's (1977) identification of schemes as scripts implies, similarly, a representation of a particular self–world engagement from beginning to end. Stern (1985) pursues this aspect of events in his analyses of infant–mother interactions in terms of their intensity contours, temporal beats, rhythms, and so forth. Clinicians seem implicitly to accept it in their attention, for example, to the initiation, development, and culmination of a masochistic interchange, or the ways in which an individual elaborates an episode of test anxiety, including its beginning and end. However, the notion that the mental registration of an interacton includes the entire course of an event has not yet become the focus of conceptual attention among object relations theorists.

Event schemes are dynamic. Following Piaget (Flavell, 1963), we propose that interaction schemes constitute the dynamic aspects of the mind. Congruent with this view, Schimek (1975) and Loewald (1971) find in relationship schemes the origins of the id, ego, and superego as conceived in drive theory. If these views are elaborated successfully, one might find in people's ways of engaging masochistically with others or experiencing test anxiety the ways of loving, hating, fearing, and wishing the interplay of which Freud identified as central to the mind.

Interaction schemes are schemes of personal action. This quality of the ways in which people engage in interactions is regularly observed clinically in the personal urgencies of patients' demands, yearnings, and defensive avoidances, although in theoretical discussions the id, ego, and superego are still typically defined as impersonal dynamic organizations. Loewald (1971) emphasizes it in his identification of the dynamic ego with the self, a view that echoes Freud's dual conception of the *ich* as both self and ego. Tulving (1972) appears to note a similar characteristic in his emphasis on the personal aspect of the autobiographical memory system that in his conception is composed of people's representations of their engagements with their worlds. And increasingly Piaget's action schemes are being seen as dynamic self aspects. Piaget (1929) himself suggests that the personal feeling-of-action schemes gives rise to the sense of I. Kegan (1982) elaborates this conception in a neo-Piagetian clinical perspective and Harter (1983) in a developmental one. In our own work, my colleagues and I (Fast et al., 1992) have used it as the base for an object relational conception of the dynamic self and strategies for its quantitative investigation.

Representations of Self and Objects

These dynamic schemes of personally motivated interactions are the bases from which the representational aspects of the mind develop. The conception we propose is fully constructivist. Self and object representations are not fully formed perceptual inputs from the beginning. Rather, they are the initially implicit components of dynamic schemes. The self and mother of early interactions are not two representational entities fused or merged with one another. Like the infant and ring of Piaget's grasp scheme, self and others are not-yet-articulated aspects of interaction modes.

Self and objects are defined by the interaction modes in which they occur. In Piaget's (Flavell, 1963) observations, the ring is no more for the infant than "a graspable" when he or she holds it in his or her hand. If, another time, it is hung over the crib, it is "a seeable." The activity, or mode of interaction, is the organizing principle. Event theory proposes, with Piaget, that this relation of self and object representations to dynamic schemes persists in later life when dynamic schemes are more complexly integrated. Thus, in any situation, an individual's representations of self and of objects are defined by the constellation of schemes then in play.

The notion that a representation or image is structured by a complex of dynamic forces is not foreign to psychoanalytic thought. It is a familiar aspect of Freud's conception of dreams: Dream interpretation relies on the hypothesis that dream images faithfully reflect the interplay of dynamic forces activated in the dreamer's experience. In clinical interchanges too, patients' distorted images of themselves, their therapists, or important people of the past are regularly seen to express dynamic impulse–defense constellations. Our constructivist view extends this conception of dream images and of distorted self and object representations to all representations; it proposes that every representation (image)—accurate or distorted; whether in dream, memory, or present reality—is defined by the dynamic interaction schemes activated in a particular situation.

Initially, when interaction schemes are not yet integrated into complex arrays, self and objects are defined differently in different interaction modes. In Winnicott's (1971) classic example of the holding situation, for example, the good mother and good self of the comfortable mother-holding-baby interaction are not the same for the baby as are the bad mother and bad self of the frustrating or painful interaction. In Piaget's (Flavell, 1963) model, similarly, the ring grasped and the ring tracked visually are not subjectively the same ring. In psychoanalytically familiar terms, self and other are part selves and part objects. Kernberg (1966) most fully elaborates the psychoanalytic view that part selves and part objects are coordinate aspects of discrete interactions (dyads) in early life and in borderline character organizations of adulthood. Although the formulation presented here is not identical to Kernberg's, it appears to be fundamentally congruent with it.

Development by Integration and Differentiation

Congruent with object relations perspectives, event theory proposes that developmental and therapeutic change occurs by processes of integration and differentiation. Dynamic development begins with the establishment of interaction schemes representing a variety of relationship modes. Initially, these schemes are not integrated with one another. This conception is consonant with Kernberg's (1966) suggestion that dyads, not yet integrated with one another, are the basic structures of the mind. It also appears to be congruent with Freud's conception that impulses initially exist in the mind without connection or contradiction.

Event theory proposes that the integration of these schemes with one another and the differentiation of self and other within them occurs by conflict and conflict resolution. Conflict is brought into play when the individual activates two disparate schemes in relation to the same object. In Winnicott's (1971) example, when, at about 3–4 months of age, the frustrated infant is held comfortably by the mother, the infant simultaneously experiences the bad-self–bad-mother relationship and the good-self–good-mother one. Piaget (Flavell, 1963) suggests that at about the same age, the infant begins to activate his or her vision and grasp schemes together in attempts to grasp the ring he or she sees. In a clinical interchange, for example, a young man struggling with his ways of interacting with others in alternately scornful and idealizing ways might allow himself to experience simultaneously both his admiration of his therapist's insight-fulness and his disparagement of her taste in furniture.

In successful conflict resolution, the two dynamic schemes are integrated with and mod-ulated by one another, and the individual's capacity for differentiated interaction with his or her world is enlarged. Winnicott (1971) describes the infant at 3–4 months of age as beginning to integrate positive and negative feelings and be a little more able to adjust his or her ways of interacting to the differing mood states of the other. Piaget (Flavell, 1963) suggests that when the infant has integrated grasp and vision schemes, he or she is more able to deal flexibly with the various objects in the environment. In the hypothetical clinical incident, the young man moves toward a more modulated capacity for engaging in admiring and critical interactions with others and toward greater ability to adapt these interaction modes to the actualities of particular situations.

In the same process, individuals also integrate and differentiate their images of self and others. The good and bad self and mother images of Winnicott's (1971) example begin to be integrated into a self representation with both good and bad aspects and a parallel representation of the mother. The ring of Piaget's (Flavell, 1963) example becomes a seeable–graspable, now defined by both schemes, and the infant self becomes a seer–grasper, defined by this larger number of scheme participations. The young man's images of himself, perhaps as small and insignificant in relation to the awe-inspiring therapist in one interaction mode and assertively superior in relation to the old-fashioned therapist in the other, begin more accurately to reflect his own actual size and bearing and those of the therapist.

These integrations themselves result in increased differentiation of self and other. When self and object representations are defined by more than one scheme, they can no longer be totally undifferentiated components of either one; to that extent, they achieve representation differentiated from the interaction schemes and from each other. Winnicott (1971) suggests that in the integrative processes of the holding situation, the infant also begins to differentiate himself or herself from the mother. Piaget (Flavell, 1963) emphasizes that with the integration of the grasp and vision schemes, the infant begins his or her development beyond egocentrism: The infant begins to establish the ring as an object independent of his or her own actions. And in the clinical situation, we hypothesize, the young man moves toward increased recognition of himself and the therapist as distinct individuals.

Event theory proposes that these processes are central to the development of psychic structure. Increasingly complex constellations of interaction schemes form the dynamic aspects of the mind. Self and object representations, increasingly differentiated and integrated, constitute its nondynamic aspect. The two systems work together in all mental activity: Representations are constructed by and represent dynamic schemes; representations are the stable, nondynamic structures against which dynamic schemes are integrated and differentiated.

Summary

Event theory offers one of many possible bases for a constructivist view of the mind. It suggests that events, episodes of individuals' engagements with their worlds, are registered mentally in dynamic schemes of personally motivated interactions. Schemes representing different interaction modes are initially not integrated with one another; scheme components that will later be ascribed to self and other are initially undifferentiated aspects of schemes.

Both the dynamic and representational aspects of the mind develop in processes of conflict-based integration and differentiation. Conflict occurs when individuals activate two schemes in relation to a single object. In the process of conflict resolution, they integrate their interaction modes into more complex dynamic patterns that increasingly differentiate the self and nonself aspects of interactions. Simultaneously self representations and representations of other people or nonhuman objects specific to the two schemes are integrated into larger wholes and differentiated from one another.

The dynamic and representational aspects of the mind work together in all mental activity. Throughout life, representations of self and objects are constructed by dynamic schemes. Reciprocally, self and object representations are the stable structures in terms of which which dynamic schemes are integrated into the increasingly modulated, internally consistent dynamic constellations by which people understand and act in their worlds.

A RELATIONAL VIEW OF MENTAL ORIGINS IN BODILY EXPERIENCE

Body-Bound Experience

This way of conceiving a relational base for the mind lends itself to a conception of the mind's origins in body experience different from that of Freud's drive theory. Throughout his working life, Freud emphasized that the mind originates in the body and that the body bound-edness of early experience accounts for the unrealistic character of the primitive experience modes he observed clinically: experience in which contrary impulses coexist without connection or contradiction and the self is experienced as arbiter of reality, thought and reality are one, illusions of omnipotence prevail, and objects are without stable meanings and can stand for one another if their dynamic meaning for the individual is the same.

Because he held the objectivist view that perceptions are accurate representations of reality, Freud reasoned that the unreality of primitive beliefs must arise from a developmental period in which the objective realities of the external world have not yet impinged on the infant mind. It appears to have been this objectivist premise that forced him, although doubtfully, to posit the existence of a period of life before the child cathected the world outside his or her own bodily sensations (Freud, 1911/1963, p. 219, n. 4).

Event theory also posits a bodily base for the mind. However, it does so in terms other than Freud's. It proposes, following Piaget (Flavell, 1963), that in their earliest experiences infants do not differentiate the mental and physical aspects of their interactions. In Piaget's terms, their experience is sensorimotor in form. In such experiences, thought is tied absolutely to present bodily action. The infant can "think" or "imagine" only what he or she is presently doing. It is this bodily base for the mind, event theory suggests, that gives rise to the phenomena that Freud attributed to the id.

When infants can "think" only presently occurring events and when interaction schemes are as yet largely unintegrated, their involvements in nursing, grasping, or visual focusing are discrete experiences: One event replaces another without connection to either the previous activity in memory or to the next in anticipation. The vigorously nursing infant, for example, fully involved in the present bodily interaction of the nursing event, cannot recall his or her previous hungry crying, and when the infant's attention shifts to a moving light overhead, the nursing event, for the moment, ceases to exist. Each scheme-specific involvement is a separate "happening." Infants' immersion in their present activity is total: They cannot observe their own action, think about something else, or plan for change. No modulation of the intensity of a present positive or negative experience can be effected by placing it in a time frame or a larger context of experience.

This is a dynamic world. The self, other people, and inanimate objects have no stable existence or meaning. For the nursing infant, the feeding self, the nursing mother, and the rocker come into existence in the context of nursing, subside from existence when a new activity supervenes, and return to reality when nursing occurs again. Moreover, the meanings of self and objects are ephemeral. On the one hand, the self and a particular object are subjectively not the same self and object when they are embedded in different schemes. On the other hand, objectively quite disparate objects may have equivalent meanings if they occur in the same scheme: In sucking activities, for example, a nipple, a parental finger, and a ring may all be no more than suckables for the infant, one able to stand for the other in the context of the particular dynamic scheme.

Such experiences have several characteristics that Freud ascribed to the id:

1. Contrary impulses exist side by side without effect on one another. When schemes are discrete one cannot affect the other.

2. Infants accept uncritically that their own experience is the arbiter of existence. When objects come into existence for them in the context of particular activities and subside from existence when the activity ends, what else could they think?

3. They take their thoughts to be reality. When the mental and physical aspects of schemes are not differentiated and when infants can recognize only that which is actually occurring, their thoughts and reality *are* one.

4. Illusions of omnipotence, the assumption that one's thoughts are realized in actuality, are corollaries of such experience. When the infant cannot think anything beyond what is occurring, its thoughts are indeed unfailingly realized in actual happenings.

5. Infant experience occurs in a timeless present. When schemes are discrete and when the infant cannot connect a present experience with either the previous or the subsequent one, its experience must inevitably be of a timeless succession of present happenings.

6. Objects are without stable meanings and may stand for one another if their dynamic meaning is the same. When objects are defined by the dynamic schemes in which they occur, quite various objects may be equivalent in meaning (e.g., as suckables or graspables) and interchangeable in ways typical of the primary processes (for a more extended discussion of primary process cognition in event terms, see Fast, 1983).

Beyond Body-Bound Experience

In Freud's conception, a major developmental transition occurs at about 18–24 months of age. Freud (1911) attributes it to the infant's new awareness of the external world. Children begin to evaluate body-bound id experience in the light of perception-based, objectively accurate representations of reality. Conflict ensues between body-based understandings and reality-based ones. The triumph of reality-based experience results in the establishment of the ego. Impulses, the reality testing of which the individual cannot tolerate, are consigned to the unconscious and retain their primitive characteristics. In the course of development or in clinical intervention, drive-dominated impulses or ideas can be integrated into the ego by being brought into awareness and tested against reality.

Event theory too posits a major transition at this point in development. As in the drive theory, it is attributed to individuals' developments beyond body-bound thought. Its focus, however, is different than Freud's: It highlights children's newly established differentiation between thought and bodily action. Now, as a result of differentiation–integration processes discussed more fully elsewhere (Fast, 1985, chaps. 1, 2), children become able to evoke events mentally with or without concurrent motor action and whether or not the relevant object is present. Moreover, by this time, images of self and objects have become increasingly stable, not fluctuating with every change in interaction mode. In Piaget's (Flavell, 1963) model, this is the transition from sensorimotor to preoperational thought.

Freud suggested that this is the period in which psychic conflicts first arise. Event theory suggests a possible extension of this conception, namely, that *psychic* conflict arises now but that conflict itself is central to mental functioning from early life. The model suggests that all integrations of dynamic schemes from the earliest coordination of affectively good and bad interactions (Winnicott) or of grasp and vision schemes (Piaget) have the fundamental characteristics of conflict and conflict resolution. In every such integration, two disparate cognitive–affective schemes are expressed toward an object. In the course of that process, incompatibilities are reconciled in ways congruent with the reality of successful interaction (e.g., the successful grasping of objects seen; comfortable interaction with a mother perceived as both good and bad).

This extension invites a new direction of attention to infant development. It suggests that from early periods of development, children establish the patterns by which they deal with conflict. In one home, challenges to conflict resolution may inform much of the infant–caregiver relationship; in another, conflict may be seen as a painful event to be resolved by the caregiver with all possible speed. One child may approach conflicts such as those of integrating grasp and vision schemes with zest and persistence, another with tendencies to frustrated disorganization. One infant may accept the uncertainty inherent in the initial stages of conflict and its resolution with relative equanimity, another as a danger to be accepted only in the reassuring presence of a caregiver. Although there are few data yet to suggest the ways in which such early modes of engaging in conflict are relevant to later ones, it seems likely that such modes may inform people's ways of dealing with conflict when psychic conflict and conflict resolution become possible.

Freud suggests that the proliferation of conflict in this developmental period occurs because children become aware of discrepancies between their id experience and their representations of external reality. Event theory suggests that the proliferation of conflict that Freud observed is made possible by children's new ability for thought free of present bodily activity. When the mental and physical aspects of experience are not yet differentiated, conflict is limited to those schemes that can be evoked together in motor action toward physically present objects. Once thought is freed from the bondage to present physical reality, however, the range of children's thoughts and therefore the possibility of conflict is vastly increased. Thought is then limited only by the power of the individual's imagination. The worlds of memory and anticipation, of pretend, and of the purely hypothetical are opened wide. Any pair of disparate interaction modes can be activated in relation to any object, whether or not they could occur together in physical reality or occur at all in real life. These conflicts and their resolution contribute both to the burgeoning of mental skills and imaginative range widely observed to occur at this time and to such anxieties as those attendant on the recognition of sex differences and the struggles with Oedipal issues to which Freud drew attention.

In both Freud's conception and that of event theory, a major focus of conflict at this period is the primitive experience modes of early development that must be given up. In Freud's view, they must be given up because the child begins to cathect the perceptually based representations of the objectively real world. We suggest, instead, that when children differentiate thought and the physical events to which thoughts refer, the conditions for id experience no longer obtain. Thoughts can no longer safely be taken for reality when they can occur regardless of whether the relevant reality is present. The self can no longer be accepted as the arbiter of reality when objects clearly continue to exist quite independently of one's attention to them. Illusions of omnipotence are clearly seen to be no more than illusions when wishes, no matter how intense, no longer bring with them the relevant realities. When thought can range freely over past and future experience, it no longer occurs in a timeless present. And when objects are increasingly stable structures, they can no longer stand for one another just because their dynamic meaning at a given moment is the same.

At this period, a change also occurs in the criterion for success in the conflict resolution process. When conflict can occur only between physical actions on actual objects, the criterion for conflict resolution is the success of the action (e.g., the ability to grasp the object seen; to accept the comforting mother in the face of one's frustration). However, when altogether imaginary interaction schemes can be tested against fantasied objects, new criteria must be found. Here event theory moves again toward congruence with Freud's conceptions, although again with a difference.

We propose, with Freud, that the external world at this point becomes the criterion for reality. In our view, however, this is not the world of objectively accurate, perceptually given object representations. Rather, it is the world of objects constructed by the child in his or her interactions with the environment. Moreover, this representational world includes self representations as well as object representations. It is against these representational structures that the child now integrates his or her interaction schemes. This criterion for reality is considerably less absolute and reliable than the one Freud posited. Rather than being objectively veridical perceptions, these representations of self and others have typically achieved some stability by the time children are 18–24 months of age, but as Fraiberg (1969) has shown, they still easily succumb to temporary distortion and loss of constancy, particularly when feelings run high.

The event model, finally, suggests that insofar as schemes are excluded from the integration–differentiation processes, they have the characteristics that Freud ascribed to the dynamic unconscious. Event theory adds, however, that they also have the characteristics ascribed in object relations theory to primitive self and object representations. They remain discrete wishes, fears, loves, and hates. Their intensity is not modulated by integration with contrary feelings or aims toward the same object. To the extent that the differentiation of thought and action is incomplete, they retain the characteristics of id experience consequent on body-bound thought. The self and object representations of such relatively undifferentiated and unintegrated schemes are part selves and part objects that are incompletely differentiated from the dynamic schemes and from each other.

The goal of therapy, in this model, is not the removal of drive distortions from original perceptions and the consequent restoration to analysands of the true histories of their lives. It is, instead, the modification of interaction schemes that have been excluded from the normal developmental processes of integration and differentiation. This occurs when patients activate two disparate ways of interacting toward the same object. If they tolerate the resulting conflict and are able to resolve it, they effect changes in both the dynamic and the representational aspects of their minds. The two interaction modes are integrated and modulated by one another and are thereafter more flexibly available to deal with life circumstances. Simultaneously, their self and object representations are deepened and differentiated so that patients are better able to take differentially into account their own and others' characteristics.

SUMMARY

Object relations perspectives are becoming increasingly prominent in psychoanalytic psychology. They have led to a significant number of ideas that are widely accepted but are incompatible with drive theory. However, if object relational views are to take the place of drive theory as the generally accepted framework in which psychoanalytic observations are accommodated, they must also be able to account for observations and conceptions now usefully framed in drive theory terms.

That work is only in its beginning stages. Recent developments emerging from object relations theory; from psychological research in the areas of infancy, development, cognition, and artificial intelligence; and from the related fields of linguistics and philosophy suggest directions for pursuing it. They suggest that the objectivist conception of the mind that has prevailed in these fields (and that underlies Freud's drive theory) be replaced by a constructivist one: Instead of the view that the mind is founded on objective perceptions of external reality, constructivists view self–world interactions as the base from which psychic structure develops.

Event theory, one of the many possible conceptual frameworks compatible with constructivist views has been elaborated here. It suggests that dynamic schemes representing individuals' personally motivated interactions between self and other are the basic units of the mind. Representations of objects and of the self are initially undifferentiated part objects and part selves implicit in interaction schemes. Developmental and therapeutic changes occur through the integration and differentiation of interaction schemes in processes of conflict and conflict resolution. These processes result in both the dynamic organizations of the mind (the id, ego, and superego structures) and representations of self and other increasingly integrated into wholes and differentiated from one another.

To illustrate some implications of this model, a relational conception is elaborated of the origins of the mind in bodily experience. It proposes that the primitive experience modes that Freud attributed to body experience in an infant oblivious to his or her environment (id experience) can be seen to occur in interactional experience the mental and motor aspects of which are not yet differentiated. Such nondifferentiation is shown to account for such id experience as the early occurrence in the mind of contrary impulses without connection or contradiction, the sense that the self is the arbiter of existence, illusions of omnipotence, experience occurring in a timeless present, and objects that are without stable meaning and that can stand for one another if their dynamic meaning is the same.

The developments beyond body boundedness, elaborated by Freud as a function of children's new cathexis of reality, are explored here as a function of the child's new ability for thought independent of motor action: the emergence of psychic conflict, reality testing, the replacement of primitive experience modes with more realistic ones, and the establishment of the unconscious distinct from the reality-oriented ego.

REFERENCES

Ainsworth, M. D. S., Blehar, M. C., Waters, E., & Wall, S. (1978). *Patterns of attachment.* Hillsdale, NJ: Erlbaum.

Bowlby J. (1969). *Attachment and loss: Vol. l. Attachment.* London: Hogarth Press.

Emde, R. B. (1988). Development terminable and interminable. *International Journal of Psycho-Analysis, 69,* 23–42.

Fairbairn, R. D. (1952). *An object-relations theory of the personality.* New York: Basic Books.

Fast, I. (1983). Primary process cognition: A reformulation. *Annual of Psychoanalysis, ll,* 199–225.

Fast, I. (1985). *Event theory: A Piaget–Freud integration.* Hillsdale, NJ: Erlbaum.

Fast, I. (1987, August–September). The relational mind in development and psychotherapeutic change. In A. E. Thompson (Chair), *The relational mind: Implications for the therapeutic process.* Symposium conducted at the 95th Annual Convention of the American Psychological Association, New York.

Fast, I. (1990). Self and ego: A framework for their integration. *Psychoanalytic Inquiry, 10,* 141–162.

Fast, I., Marsden, K. G., Cohen, L., Heard, H., & Kruse, S. (1992). *Self as subject: A formulation and an assessment strategy.* Manuscript in preparation.

Feffer, M. (1988). *Radical constructionism.* New York: New York University Press.

Fivush, R., & Slackman, E. A. (1986). The acquisition and development of scripts. In K. Nelson (Ed.), *Event knowledge: Structure and function in development* (pp. 71–96). Hillsdale, NJ: Erlbaum.

Flavell, J. H. (1963). *The developmental psychology of Jean Piaget.* Princeton, NJ: Van Nostrand.

Fraiberg, S. (1969). Libidinal object constancy and mental representation. *Psychoanalytic Study of the Child, 24,* 9–47.

Freud, S., (1963). Formulations on the two principles of mental functioning. In J. Strachey (Ed. and Trans.), *The standard edition of the complete psychological works of Sigmund Freud* (Vol. 12, pp. 218–226). London: Hogarth Press. (Original work published 1911)

Harter, S. (1983). Developmental perspectives on the self-system. In P. H. Mussen (Ed.), *Handbook of Child Psychology* (Vol. 4, pp. 275–385).

Hartmann, H. (1939). *Ego psychology and the problem of adaptation.* Madison, CT: International Universities Press.

Kegan, R. (1982). *The evolving self.* Cambridge, MA: Harvard University Press.

Kernberg, O. (1966). Structural derivatives of object relationships. *International Journal of Psycho-Analysis, 47,* 236–253.

Kuhn, T. S. (1962). *The structure of scientific revolutions.* Chicago: University of Chicago Press.

Lakoff, G., & Johnson, M. (1980). *Metaphors we live by.* Chicago: University of Chicago Press.

Loewald, H. W. (1971). On motivaton and instinct theory. *Psychoanalytic Study of the Child, 26,* 91–127.

Nelson, K., (Ed.). (1986). *Event knowledge: Structure and function in development.* Hillsdale, NJ: Erlbaum.

Nelson, K., & Gruendel, J. (1986). Children's scripts. In K. Nelson (Ed.), *Event knowledge: Structure and function in development* (pp 21–46). Hillsdale, NJ: Erlbaum.

Piaget, J. (1929). *The child's conception of the world.* Totawa, NJ: Littlefield, Adams.

Piaget, J. (1951). Principal factors determining intellectual evolution from childhood to adult life. In D. Rapaport (Ed.), *Organization and pathology of thought* (pp. 154–175). New York: Columbia University Press.

Sandler, J., & Sandler, A.-M., (1978). On the development of object relations and affects. *International Journal of Psycho-Analysis, 59,* 285–295.

Schank, R. C. (1982). *Dynamic memory: A theory of reminding and learning in computers and people.* Cambridge, England: Cambridge University Press.

Schank, R. C., & Abelson, R. P. (1977). *Scripts, plans, goals, and understanding.* Hillsdale, NJ: Erlbaum.

Schilder, P. (1950). *The image and appearance of the human body.* Madison, CT: International Universities Press.

Schimek, J. G., (1975). A critical re-examination of Freud's concept of unconscious mental representation. *International Review of Psycho-Analysis, 2,* 171–187.

Stern, D. N. (1985). *The interpersonal world of the infant.* New York: Basic Books.

Sullivan, H. S. (1956). *Clinical studies in psychiatry.* New York: Norton.

Trzebinski, J. (1989). The role of goal categories in the representation of social knowledge. In L. A. Pervin (Ed.), *Goal concepts in personality and social psychology* (pp. 363–412). Hillsdale, NJ: Erlbaum.

Tulving, E. (1972). Episodic and semantic memory. In E. Tulving & W. Donaldson (Eds.), *Organization and memory* (pp. 382–403).

Werner, H. (1948). *Comparative psychology of mental development.* Chicago: Follett.

Winnicott, D. W. (1971). Transitional objects and transitional phenomena. In D. W. Winnicott (Ed.), *Playing and reality* (pp. 1–25). Madison, CT: International Universities Press. (Original work published in 1952)

8

THE EARLY ORGANIZATION OF THE PSYCHE

E. VIRGINIA DEMOS

In this chapter I focus on recent research findings in developmental psychology and their implications for formulations of the self and the early organization of the psyche. I concentrate primarily on the period of early infancy, partly because that is where my current interests and energies are most engaged, and partly because I have come to believe that one's understanding of later developmental vicissitudes and processes of change are highly determined and structured by how one conceptualizes the beginning. Therefore, questions about the young infant's capacity for psychic experience, the quality and content of that experience, the capacity for organizing, remembering, and acting on that experience, and what aspects of these capacities and experiences are changing over time will be at the center of this discussion. This chapter, then, represents an attempt to integrate current knowledge of infancy and to present yet another version of how human psychic organization begins and changes over time.

The discussion differs from most available conceptualizations of these processes in many details, but the main differences are in the emphasis on early competence that is continually elaborated over time in lawful and systematic, yet highly idiosyncratic ways, and in the argument against stagelike models or against the necessity for specific progressions in experiences of the self. I present an infant that is neither buffeted by unstructured energies of the id nor essentially created or activated by the ministrations of the caregiver, but one who arrives in the world with a functioning set of unique organizational capacities and whose developmental course will be influenced as much by these intrinsic characteristics as by experiences with people and inanimate objects. This discussion is offered in the spirit of a scientific dialogue in which it is assumed that the more viewpoints there are, the richer the debate will be, and the more likely we will be to eventually construct an adequate conceptualization of human psychic processes.

DEFINITION OF TERMS

Before proceeding, there must be an understanding of the terms *self* and *psyche*. Thus far, it may appear as if I have been using them interchangeably.

What Is Meant by Self?

My assignment for this book was to write about the organization of the self. However, the term *self*, as it is used in this phrase and in the literature, is ambiguous. It may refer to the person as a whole or to self-concepts such as sense of self or self-esteem. For example, object relations theorists such as Fairbairn (1963) and Guntrip (1969) used the term *self* to refer to a unitary or comprehensive psyche, person, or ego that can then become split as a result of frustrating or inadequate caregiving. Winnicott (1969) spoke of a sense of wholeness that can give rise to a true self, versus the frustration of the infant's overall psychic needs that gives rise to a false self. Thus, he seemed to be reserving the term *self* for the later, more structured phase, although this split into a true or false self happens relatively early. Kohut (1977) spoke of the first consolidation of the self occurring in the middle of the second year of life, with earlier experience organized as nuclei of the self. Thus, self-experience is a rather late achievement and seems to carry with it the capacity for self-reflection. Stern (1983, 1985), on the other hand, spoke of self, self–other, and other schemas developing from birth on. In this usage, the term *self* seems to refer to the person or to "an organization that is sensed as a reference point," to an I-ness as differentiated from a we-ness and an otherness; he described the changes in this sense of self as the child develops. George Klein (1976) also wrote of an "I" and a "we" as parts of the self.

As Stechler and Kaplan (1980) pointed out, the term *self* has been used as a hypothetical construct to account for the continuity of experience and for the integrating and organizing function of the psyche. Sutherland (1980) underlined this point when he wondered "why the center of the person should have been so long in becoming the center of our theoretical concern" (p. 852). He went on to argue that we need a conceptualization of the self as a dynamic supraordinate structure that can "contain and organize motives from all the subsystems that have differentiated from it" (p. 857) in order to account for "the person as an agent activated by his own meanings, purposes and goals" (p. 854) rather than as a repository of the turning of libido or aggression toward or away from objects without any notion of what does the turning.

If the continuity of psychic experience and the organizing and integrating of experience are the phenomena that need to be accounted for, is "self" the best conceptual framework to use? These phenomena seem to require an executive function for the self. But an executive self is only one kind of possible self that might be experienced. In actuality there are a plurality of selves that can be delineated, and they may or may not be integrated with each other.

Westen (1990), in an informative discussion of conceptualizations of the self, made a useful distinction between the subjective self and the objective self. The subjective self is defined as the experiential flow of consciousness that can also include an unconscious subjectivity or dissociated consciousness, whereas the objective self involves representations of the self in which the self is the object of reflection, and which can also include conscious or unconscious schemas of the self. Tomkins (1982) has argued that the awareness of self as part of the field can vary from zero to infinity as a salient feature. For example, cultures vary enormously in the degree to which they cultivate the importance of the self as a cultural value and encourage its psychological elaboration, versus cultivating the importance of the group or the family and encouraging the psychological elaboration of group or family goals, events, and so forth, in which an inner awareness of self could be minimal or even absent.

A Working Definition of Psyche

Returning to the context of early infancy, it is a period of life in which the objective self, which involves self-reflection and observing of the self as an object of awareness and interest, is not yet a possibility. The subjective self, involving the experiential flow of consciousness is possible, but I would argue for the use of the term *psyche* for this phenomenon. Indeed, I would argue that psyche is a more inclusive term for any developmental period, which may or may not include representations of the self as a salient feature in the ongoing flow of experience. Thus I see my assignment as writing about the organization of the psyche. The psyche might then be defined as the human capacity for consciously experiencing internal and external events; for actively processing these events in terms of their present, past, and future meanings; and for generating, executing, and evaluating plans and goals related to these meanings. This includes the goal of protecting itself from disorganization and creating defensive strategies, whenever necessary, that can result in keeping some meanings and contents out of awareness or in an unconscious mode. In short, the psyche functions as a control mechanism for the organism and coordinates the use of all of the subsystems of the organism such as the perceptual, cognitive, affective, motoric, and homeostatic systems, and of the components operating at all levels of these systems.

Moving Away From Structures

Such a definition, first of all, views the psyche as a dynamic system in its mode of functioning and *not* as a structure. In dynamic systems, components can combine and act in a coordinated manner at one moment in time, and recombine with other components or be inactive at other times. What we normally call structures would be seen as recurrent organizations that operate as preferential linkages of components, which can occur either because of evolutionary biases or because of well-learned coordinated responses that have emerged under certain conditions. This is not to deny the existence of neuronal and organic structures in the brain and body. Nevertheless, as we are continually learning from neurophysiology, the functioning of any nerve cell is quite variable depending on the chemical substances operating in the cell body and at the synapses at any given moment. Thus to view the psyche as a system is to emphasize its functional variability from moment to moment, its responsiveness to internal and external events, and its complexity, as well as to account for its recurring organizations. This view enables us to focus our attention on organizational processes and their vicissitudes. If it were not so clumsy, I would prefer to use a verb form like "psyching" rather than the noun psyche, because the use of any noun so easily leads to the image of a real object or structure. Instead, I must ask the reader to keep in mind that the noun psyche is referring to the operation of a dynamic system and the "psyching" function of the organism.

The Role of Consciousness

This definition also puts a major emphasis on the role of consciousness in the functioning of the psyche, and is derived primarily from Silvan Tomkins's writings on the theory of the human being (1962, in press). He argued that the study of consciousness has been delayed both by behaviorism and psychoanalysis. Behaviorism, in emphasizing behavior, "submerged the distinctiveness of consciousness as a type of response" (p. 3), whereas psychoanalysis, in emphasizing the role of unconscious, hydraulic-like forces, and the failure of consciousness as a control mechanism in pathological conditions, has "strengthened the notion of consciousness as an epiphenomenon" (p. 4). As Tomkins pointed out, consciousness is a necessary evolutionary adaptation, and must have occurred in the evolutionary timetable when organisms began to move about freely in space. When a species is well adapted to its environment and its environment is unchanging, then much that the species needs to know to survive can be built into the organism. But once a species becomes sufficiently mobile, its environment can change from moment to moment, leading to new encounters with nature and with other species, encounters that cannot be predicted. The information and responses needed to survive cannot be built in. This kind of an organism had to become capable of learning and of making voluntary choices, both of which require an internal context in which the organism can become aware of new information and can actively compare it to old information, construct meanings, devise strategies, monitor responses, and develop new responses and strategies. The state of consciousness is such a context. Tomkins argued that all new learning must take place in a state of consciousness. Once concepts are formulated, meanings are created, plans are generated, behavioral sequences are mastered, and defensive strategies are instituted, these can operate like miniprograms, outside of our awareness, requiring little new input.

In Tomkins's formulation, consciousness is a distinctive kind of knowing that cannot be defined precisely. It shares some characteristics with wakefulness and awareness but is not synonymous with them. We can be asleep and be conscious of our dreams and remember them the next morning. Nor is it exactly the same as awareness because we can be conscious of things that we only later become aware of, thus the focus of our awareness at any given moment is not the totality of our consciousness. Nor does it require self-awareness or the capacity to reflect on one's experience; it is a more basic mode of processing experience and of knowing.

It does not encompass the functioning of the whole person; we cannot become conscious of everything that is going on in our bodies. Many neurological, chemical, and homeostatic processes operate outside of consciousness, such as the regulation of blood-sugar levels. Some of these processes, such as breathing, can be brought under conscious control, but ordinarily operate outside of consciousness. Many of our cognitive, perceptual, and motor processes operate outside of consciousness as well. For example, if we want to telephone a friend, we "remember" the telephone number, but the process by which that bit of information is located and retrieved from the billions of other bits of information stored in our memory is not conscious, nor are the majority of our thought processes. Indeed, if we were to become conscious of everything that was going on, both inside and outside of our bodies, we would be overwhelmed with stimuli. The channel capacity of consciousness is limited. As information theory has determined, that limit is around seven bits of information. Thus, a selection process must be operating; a set of rules must exist that governs the entrance to consciousness.

There are, then, many kinds of phenomena involved in the operation of homeostatic, perceptual, cognitive, motor, and affective mechanisms that are designed to function without the benefit of consciousness. And we can never become conscious of these processes. Thus they are not part of the "psyching" function of the organism, although they may be affected by that function and may affect it. But there are other kinds of phenomena, also involved in the operation of these essential mechanisms, that can be governed by consciousness. It is this latter group of phenomena that exist in the realm of the psyche and that must compete for entrance into the limited channel capacity of consciousness. What are the rules governing this selective process?

Freud articulated some of the rules that operate to keep painful material out of consciousness, by discovering a motivational factor: We become conscious of what we want to know and remain unaware of what we do not want to know. Yet even here there are exceptions, for there are traumatic memories that force their way into consciousness against the individual's wish to know. In *Beyond the Pleasure Principle,* Freud (1920/1955) postulated the existence of a compulsion to repeat in the service of mastery that was even more primary than the pleasure principle to account for such phenomena (although he later tried to tie this to the death instinct). There are undoubtedly several factors, some motivated and some nonmotivated, operating in the competition for the limited channel capacity of consciousness. These factors would produce within the psychic realm, areas of dynamic unconscious material that involves a motivated not knowing, as well as areas of nonconscious material that are simply not urgent enough or important enough to have won out in the competition for entering consciousness, but could become conscious at any time when there is less competition. We do not know enough about all of these factors, nor about the rules that govern their operation. I explore some of these factors further when I discuss infant experience.

A Reevaluation of Integration and of Self

If we return now to the definition of psyche proposed earlier and to its central role in coordinating all of the other subsystems of the organism from moment to moment, there are two additional points to emphasize. Such a definition leaves open the question of whether these moment-to-moment coordinations become integrated with each other over time. And it also leaves open the question of what kinds of conceptual models or representations of these psychic activities the person will eventually develop, with self-concepts comprising only one possible type of concept.

The issue of integration is often discussed as an essential component of healthy psychic functioning, with nonintegration, such as splitting, seen as the result of defensive activities, and thus as motivated failures of integration. There is no question that this formulation has increased our understanding of the dynamic factors involved in creating and maintaining vertical and horizontal barriers to integrating certain kinds of psychic experiences. But it has at the same time made it more difficult to recognize and to explore the nonmotivated instances of nonintegration. For example, the coordinated set of motor, perceptual, cognitive, and motivational components needed to learn to throw a baseball may never become integrated with the coordinated set of motor, perceptual, cognitive, and motivational components used to learn to play the piano. The most likely reason may be that there is very little overlap of specific components between the two sets. Although the motivational component of interest and the wish to succeed may be similar, the specific fine muscle and large muscle patterns, perceptual cues, contexts, and cognitive requirements of the two sets are all different. This lack of overlap of the components will make integration of the two sets less likely, but not impossible. An individual could construct a conceptual framework in which athletic and artistic pursuits could be integrated. By contrast, the experience of throwing a baseball is much more likely to be integrated with the experience of throwing a football, because these two coordinated sets of components have a higher degree of overlap. This rule might be stated as follows: The probability that any two sets of coordinated components will become integrated will increase as the degree of overlap between the specific components within each set increases.

The operation of such a rule, which includes motivational components as well as many other kinds of components, would lead to the lack of integration of coordinated sets of components for reasons other than the activation of defensive barriers. The question of when the integration of psychic functioning occurs becomes an empirical issue. In order to address it we would need much more knowledge about the specific characteristics of the components involved, about how equivalences between components are determined, about how the degree of overlap varies in relation to other variables, and about the kinds of situations or conditions that would facilitate or press for integration. This latter factor raises the question of integration for what purpose. The evolutionary goal of adaptation to one's environment in order to ensure survival must be differentiated from the goal to achieve psychic health in a particular culture at a particular historical moment. The degree and kind of integration required for the latter may not be the same as that required for the former.

Finally, the question of when representations of psychic functioning develop and what forms they take, including conceptualizations about the self, will depend on the familial, social, and cultural settings in which the organism lives. I discuss this in more detail later. At this point in the discussion, it is enough to say the following: Because all human beings possess the capacity for creating symbolic representations of their world, it is assumed that people in all settings will construct representations of their psychic functioning as part of that world; that these representations will vary widely from culture to culture; and that there is no necessity for them to include a conceptualization of the self as a salient part of that world.

THE INFANT PSYCHE

I return now to the questions raised at the beginning of this chapter. What is the young infant's capacity for psychic experience? What is the quality and the content of that experience? What capacities does the young infant possess for organizing, remembering, and acting on that experience? And what aspects of these capacities and experiences are changing over time?

The questions themselves are not new. They have engaged philosophers, psychologists, and psychoanalytic thinkers for decades. But they can now be joined with the new knowledge about infant capacities supplied by psychologists, and thus can be reexamined in the light of this more detailed and specific evidence. Such a union will inevitably produce new formulations about the beginnings of psychic organization and the processes of change.

What follows is an examination of each of these questions in turn. There is some unavoidable overlap in the discussion of each question because the division into psychic capacity, quality and content, and organizational capacities is somewhat artificial. All of these aspects of the psyche are closely related and operate together; it is extremely difficult to discuss one without referring to or making assumptions about the others. Nevertheless, it is important conceptually and highly informative to try to explore each of these aspects separately.

Capacity for Psychic Experience: The Psychoanalytic View

What is the young infant's capacity for psychic experience? In much psychoanalytic writing there is very little explicit discussion of the neonate's capacity for psychic experience. This experience is variously described as possessing unity or wholeness, or as disconnected nuclei (see earlier discussion of self), but these descriptions are vague and often contain the assumption that there is little capacity for organization or form in the beginning, and that these capacities must be supplied by and gradually obtained from the caregiver. Sandler and Sandler (1978) went somewhat further in articulating what this capacity for psychic experience might involve, with their notion of the infant's sensorium on which subjective experiences, predominantly feeling states, are registered. But they also argued that these experiences are chaotic and not under the infant's voluntary control.

Freud's model of the beginnings of psychic life as articulated in *Project for a Scientific Psychology* (1895/1966) is more detailed and allows for some conscious experience and organization at the outset. Freud conceptualized the nervous system as dealing primarily with quantities of excitation and as designed to keep excitations from building up, or if failing that, to rid itself of excitations. He described a variety of mechanisms, operating outside of consciousness, that functioned to reduce or to bring to zero neuronal excitation, mechanisms such as neuronal contact barriers, screens, and dampeners, and direct neuronal connections that facilitated discharge through motor pathways. However, he maintained that the excitation of neurons had a qualitative characteristic as well, and that this quality was experienced in consciousness as unpleasure and also resulted in efforts toward motor discharge. When efforts from all sources, both unconscious and conscious, resulted in the reduction of excitation of neurons, then the quality of pleasure was experienced consciously. Gradually, over time, the effects of all mechanisms were registered automatically in memory. Thus on the occasion of subsequent excitations and experiences of unpleasure, memories of past pleasurable reductions of excitations could be retrieved and experienced consciously (e.g., as hallucinations).

In this formulation Freud is granting to the very young infant a capacity for conscious psychic experience and is assigning to that experience a qualitative and parallel role in the ongoing functioning of the nervous system, a system that is simultaneously dealing with the quantitative aspects of excitation by utilizing unconscious mechanisms. This is the beginning of the pleasure principle in operation and Freud seems to be saying that it operates at least in part in consciousness as qualities of experience from the onset of life. In his later writings, when describing these older primary processes governed by the pleasure principle as residues of a phase of development in which they were the only kind of mental process, Freud (1911/1958) assigns them to the realm of unconscious mental processes. It is not entirely clear whether he means that they were originally conscious and have become unconscious as secondary processes come to dominate mental functioning, or whether this represents an inconsistency in his theorizing. There has been considerable discussion in the psychoanalytic literature about the relationships between unconsciousness and consciousness and primary and secondary processes and about the developmental course of these contents and functions (see Holt, 1967, and Noy, 1969, for extended discussions of this issue). Generally, writers accept that Freud hypothesized that the newborn infant was capable of conscious psychic experience. Leaving aside, for the moment, a discussion of the contents and quality of that experience, one can ask how this formulation fits with current psychological evidence of early infant psychic capacities.

Capacity for Psychic Experience: Developmental Psychology View

Several infant researchers, influenced by psychoanalytic ideas and interested in finding constructs that shed light on the complex connections between the biological level and the psychological level, articulated the centrality of state and state organization in early infancy, (Sander, 1969; Wolff, 1973, 1987). They conceptualized state as any well-defined organizational coherence within the organism that can be recognized when it recurs and that determines how the infant will respond. Thus, they saw state as the psychological manifestation of an integration of multiple physiological subsystems within the infant. Most attention was paid to the cyclical states along the sleep–wake continuum, which were given descriptive labels such as regular sleep, irregular sleep, drowsiness, alert inactivity, waking activity, alert activity, and crying. Sander (1982) argued from his data that the infant's experiences of her own recurrent states represent the focal points around which the infant's inner awareness or consciousness consolidates. He later went on to say that:

> a capacity for inner experience exists at the outset of postnatal life—as an initial level in the organization of consciousness. This initial root of the sense of self does not await the organization of a body image or depend on production effects, or on visual or tactile experience, or the double-tactile experience that through touch begins the differentiation of self and other. The ego begins as a "state ego, rather than a body ego." (Sander, 1985, p. 20)

It follows, then, that "the organization of state governs the quality of inner experience" (Sander, 1985, p. 16).

Other infant researchers, working from different psychological traditions, have demonstrated the neonate's capacity for learning. For example, DeCasper and Carstens (1981) showed that 3-day-old infants could perceive the contingent relationship between their behavior and the experimental stimulus, and quickly learned to space their sucking bursts in order to turn on the sound of a female voice singing. More recently, DeCasper (1990) reported that fetuses in the third trimester of the pregnancy are also capable of learning. Mothers were instructed to read the same brief story, every day, to their fetuses when the mother felt her fetus was in a quiet awake state. Soon after birth, these babies were able to discriminate between the story they had heard in the womb and another story, and between their mother's voice and another female voice.

The evidence from developmental psychology then, clearly supports the hypothesis that the capacity for psychic experience exists at the beginning of extrauterine life, and may even exist before. We may never be able to pinpoint the precise moment of our psychological beginnings, but our increased empirical access to prenatal experience allows us to entertain the possibility of very early beginnings. This possibility makes sense if one views the human fetus as a product of a long evolutionary history. The capacity for psychic experience can then be seen as an integral part of any living organism destined to move about in space, to make voluntary choices, and therefore be ready to learn a great deal about the environment. Thus although Freud postulated the existence of the capacity for psychic experiences of pleasure and unpleasure, these experiences were placed in the context of an organism whose main goal was to reduce all excitation to as little as possible. By contrast, the formulations of the capacity for psychic experience that derive from the data of developmental psychology locate these experiences in an organism that is open to the world and is biologically prepared to interact with it and to learn from it.

Quality and Content of Early Experience: The Psychoanalytic View

The differences between psychoanalytic formulations of early psychic experiences and the descriptions of these phenomena based on findings from infant research become even greater as we examine each of the remaining questions raised at the beginning of this chapter. To move on to the next question, What is the quality and content of these early psychic experiences? The traditional psychoanalytic answer to this question was summarized by Noy (1969):

> In the first weeks of life, the infant shifts between states of sleep and states of tension. Any need (hunger, thirst, cold, etc.) will awaken the infant from his sleep when the tension has mounted to a sufficient degree. This tension is expressed in various somatic ways, such as crying and arm and leg movements. When the specific need is satisfied, the tension is reduced and the infant falls asleep again. In this stage, consciousness is equal to tension, and the only affective qualities that we may assume to exist are pain and pleasure. (p. 167)

What Noy left out is the often added assumption that these experiences of tension and pain are overwhelming and urgent and that the infant is completely dependent on the caregiver for relief. Thus, for example, Anna Freud wrote

> in infantile life instinctive needs are of overwhelming urgency. There is no organized ego, able to postpone wish-fulfillment with the help of the thought processes or other inhibitory functions. Nothing therefore will diminish the painful and distressing tension of the need except immediate satisfaction. Where hungry infants or toddlers are made to wait for their

meals, even for minutes, they suffer acute distress which may prevent them from enjoying the meal when it finally arrives. (1946, p. 123)

These themes are repeated throughout psychoanalytic writings about the quality and content of early experience. To cite only the most prominent writers, Winnicott (1969) and Mahler et al. (1975) described early experience as being directed inward, unintegrated, and alternating between overwhelmingly urgent instinctual tension and relief or quiescence without any control or knowledge of how or why these alternations occur. Both speak of the absolute dependency of the young infant on the caregiver and of the infant's possessing no means of knowing anything about the caregiver. Winnicott's version was slightly different in that he introduced the term "being" to describe the ordinary ups and downs of tension and relief and the term "annihilation anxiety" to describe the results of impingements to which the infant must react and which interrupt "being." Thus, for Winnicott, the only two alternatives for early psychic content were "being" and "annihilation," and too much annihilation prevents the gradual integration of the ego and leads to psychosis.

Divergence of Views: The Nature of Evidence

How do these psychoanalytic formulations fit with current psychological data and formulations about the quality and contents of early psychic experience? There is virtually no fit between these formulations and the evidence and formulations emerging from academic developmental psychology, in spite of the efforts of some to bring about an integration of the two (e.g., Lichtenberg, 1984).

In trying to understand this chasm, at least two things must be kept in mind. First, psychoanalytic formulations are not based on the systematic observation of infants. For example, both Winnicott (1969) and Mahler et al. (1975), although they were in contact with infants and young children, acknowledged that their formulations of the earliest period of life are drawn from their experiences with psychotic children and borderline adults and from metapsychology. Second, the systematic observation of very young infants has only been occurring in academic psychology in the last several decades. Each year brings more and more data on younger and younger infants. Such a radical increase in our knowledge is creating a challenge to traditional academic developmental theories as well (e.g., Piaget & Inhelder, 1969). But because we are interested in understanding the meaning of the infant's psychic experiences, we must ask which of these disciplines is likely to provide us with the best data. Or to phrase the question somewhat differently and to put it in the form in which it is usually asked of infant researchers—of what relevance are the data from infant research for our understanding of the psychological meaning of the infant's early experiences, particularly the quality and contents of those experiences? How can we know what goes on inside an infant?

I would argue that infant researchers are in the best position to discover what goes on inside the infant and that therefore their data are highly relevant for any discipline trying to construct a developmental theory. Psychoanalysis focuses on later reconstructions of early experience, but the success of that enterprise depends to some extent on having an accurate model of early capacities and development. When psychoanalysts insist that one can only discover the meaning of early psychological experience through the transference manifestations in the therapeutic relationship as revealed through verbal descriptions of experience, dreams, and fantasy, they are denying the possibility that the infant's preverbal experience as it is happening is meaningful, that parents (or other adults observing that experience) can understand the inner world of an infant, and that mutually meaningful communications and experiences can occur between them. Such a stance overvalues verbal and symbolic modes of representation and undervalues nonverbal and presymbolic modes. It places language in a privileged position as the only reliable source of information about the inner experience of another. And in emphasizing the uniqueness of the psychoanalytic situation, such a stance also fails to appreciate that although the methods of infant researchers and psychoanalysts appear to be entirely different, they share some important commonalities.

Verbal responses are at a different level of representation than are the infant's responses, but it does not follow that they are therefore a more valid or the only reliable expression of the "true" or "inner" psychological meaning of a person's experience. Language is a symbolic form of representation, but only one of several such possible forms. At best, it can only be a partial representation, and one that has gone through several steps of translation from direct experience to verbal expression. The preverbal infant relies on presymbolic modes of representation, which I describe in more detail later, that are manifested in a variety of behavioral and vocal expressions. As a rule, the young infant is much less able to disguise, falsify, or withhold expressions of its experience, and thus the distance between experience and expression is much shorter in the infant than in the adult. Furthermore, all formulations about psychological meaning are based on inferences derived from observable behaviors. The verbal responses, including tone of voice, pacing, and body movements that occur in the psychoanalytic setting are no less behavioral than the vocal and facial expressions and motor responses of the infant. Also equally important in both methods are the contexts and sequences in which observable behaviors occur. Thus, an infant researcher is in a position to interpret the contemporaneous psychological meaning of the nonverbal expressions of a young infant with the same degree of confidence that a psychoanalyst has in interpreting the psychological meaning of the verbal expressions of a patient. And if a researcher is involved in a longitudinal study of infants, then he or she is in a position to interpret how the meaning of psychological experience continues to change as an infant encounters new events and deals with new experiences.

Many of the same variables operate in the two contexts to increase one's confidence in such interpretations, namely, the frequency of contact with the infant–patient, knowledge of past experiences, the talents and skills of the investigator–therapist, the accuracy of one's short-term predictions, and the adequacy of available methodologies and conceptual models. Given the recent advances in video and computer technologies, and the conceptual and methodological advances in developmental psychology, neurophysiology, biology, and physics, infant researchers are currently in a better position than ever before to obtain an accurate picture of the infant's early psychic experience. What does that picture look like as it emerges from the rapidly expanding data of infant research?

Quality and Content of Experience: Developmental Psychology View

Currently, the quality and content of the young infant's psychic experience is conceptualized as determined partly by the frequency and intensity of the infant's experience of discrete affect states, and partly by the occasions provided by the external environment for the infant's use of preadapted perceptual and cognitive "categories." Let me begin with affect.

Affect: Qualities and Contents

I have argued and presented evidence elsewhere (Demos, 1986, 1988, 1989b) to establish that neonates are capable of experiencing the distinctive quality of each innate affect, in a range of intensities. In other words, the quality of the young infant's psychic experience is neither global nor necessarily overwhelming. This claim is based on Silvan Tomkins's (1962, 1963) theory of affect and on the available evidence on infant affect expressions and behaviors. Tomkins is the only theorist to argue that affect can occur independently of cognition and to focus our attention on the unique characteristics of affect.

Tomkins argued that the human organism has evolved as a "multi-mechanism system in which each mechanism is at once incomplete but essential to the functioning of the system as a whole" (1981, p. 320). Each mechanism is seen as distinct, with its particular components, characteristics, and functions, and capable of acting independently, dependently, and interdependently with any or all of the other mechanisms in this system. The affect mechanism is therefore distinct from the sensory, motor, memory, cognitive, pain, and drive mechanisms, and although it frequently enters into dependent and interdependent relationships with these other mechanisms, it can operate independently of them as well.

What are the distinctive features of the affect mechanism, and what is its distinctive function? Tomkins (1981) differentiated 13 components of the affect system, paying special, but not exclusive, attention to the face as the primary focus of the affect response. He argued that each affect operates as a specific correlated set of responses that includes facial muscles, vocal, respiratory, and blood-flow changes, heightened skin receptor sensitivity, and other autonomic responses. These correlated sets of responses are thought to be innately programmed and to operate involuntarily, but they are at the same time amenable to voluntary control, and thus open to all of the effects of learning. Nevertheless, we never gain complete control over our emotions. Ekman, Friesen, and Levansen (1983) have presented evidence that demonstrates the existence of specific correlated sets of autonomic and facial responses for four distinct affects in adults.

What are these correlated sets of responses designed to do? What is their function in the larger system? In Tomkins's (1962) paradigm, the affect mechanism is the primary motivational system and functions as an amplifier of changing rates and levels of stimulation impinging on the organism. It is activated both innately and through learning by three classes of stimulation change—stimulation increases (surprise, fear, interest), stimulation levels (distress, anger), and stimulation decrease (enjoyment). The correlated sets of responses are designed to replicate by analogous bodily responses these stimulus characteristics. Thus, affect acts as an analogue amplifier of anything that is increasing rapidly, as in fear, or remaining the same at a nonoptimal level, as in distress, or decreasing, as in enjoyment, thereby making bad things worse, and good things better (Tomkins, 1978).

By amplifying stimulus characteristics through bodily responses, affect creates a specific punishing or rewarding qualitative state in the organism that combines urgency, abstractness, and generality, and through this experience motivates the organism to care about what is happening. Thus, for example, a rapid rate of stimulus increase will activate fear, which involves a rapid increase in heart rate, a rapid intake of breath, widening of the eyes, a bilateral pulling back of the corners of the mouth, hair standing on end, and a drop in skin temperature—all combining to create a qualitatively urgent, abstract, general amplified experience of something happening "too fast!" When affect combines with perception and cognition, that urgent, abstract, general something can become quite specific, such as a speeding car heading in this direction, or a charging lion. However, in this example, it is not the verbal labeling of the object, nor one's knowledge of the consequences of being hit or attacked by the object that activates the fear, but rather it is the rate of change in the approach of the object that triggers the fear. Such specific knowledge is not irrelevant, for it may enable one to act in order to escape disaster. Thus although affect supplies the urgency for action, it does not dictate the specific adaptive solution. It must combine with perceptual, cognitive, memory, and motor mechanisms in order to produce an effective response. Nevertheless, it is important to be clear about what is contributed by affect and what is achieved by a coordination of the affect mechanism with other mechanisms.

Tomkins's theory and the facial affect coding manuals derived from it (Ekman & Friesen, 1978; Izard, 1979) allow one to explore this distinction between affect and affect coordinations, or affect complexes as Tomkins described them, with a considerable gain in precision. For if the affect mechanism is governed by innate programs that do not require learning or a cognitive interpretation for their activation, then we can begin to examine the correlated sets of facial, vocal, bodily, and autonomic responses of young infants and conceptualize them as discrete affects, with distinctive experiential qualities. The following patterns have been observed. The interested baby will widen and focus his or her eyes intently on a stimulus, with brows raised or knitted, cheeks raised, and mouth relaxed, holding its limbs relatively quiet, and will tend to scan the stimulus for novelty (Langsdorf, Izard, Rayias, & Hembree, 1983; Oster, 1978; Wolff, 1965). (Wolff, 1973, reported that during the first month of life, this state accounts for 50% of waking time.) The joyful baby will smile and tend to produce relaxed, relatively smooth movements of its limbs, savoring the familiar (Brazelton, Koslowski, & Main, 1974). The angry baby will square its mouth, lower and pull its brows together, cry intensely, holding the cry for a long time, then pause for a long inspiration, its face will redden with increased blood flow, and it will tend to kick and thrash its limbs forcefully or arch its back (Demos, 1986, 1988). By contrast, a distressed infant will produce a rhythmical cry, with the corners of the mouth pulled down and the inner corners of the brows drawn up, and will tend to move its limbs and head around restlessly (Demos, 1986, 1988; Wolff, 1969).

These facial, vocal, and motor responses are *not* random. They are clearly patterned and coordinated with each other. They are also *not* learned. Every healthy neonate knows how to gaze with interest, smile with enjoyment, and cry in distress or in anger. Nor do they operate in a reflexlike manner. They are exquisitely responsive to subtle changes in the environment. We do not yet have a complete picture of the full innate affect program for these affects or of the other innate affects described by Tomkins because no one has done a simultaneous recording of the facial, vocal, motor, skin temperature, and autonomic responses of the neonate's discrete states. But the data we do have is in agreement with the patterns described by Tomkins (1962).

On the strength of this evidence, then, it is possible to assert that these correlated sets of responses observed in the newborn are discrete affects (see Demos, 1988, for a more detailed presentation of the evidence). However, the neonate does not have any cognitive and memory information coassembled with the affect—no memories of prior experiences, no expectations of what is likely to happen next. The young infant's experience of affect, therefore, is as close to pure affect as is possible. The neonate can neither know why he or she is experiencing this qualitative correlated set of responses that is affect, nor what will happen because of it. Nevertheless, I would argue that these experiences are conscious and meaningful because each affect will have a distinct quality. Distress will be experienced as uniquely punishing and as different from the uniquely punishing quality of anger. And the distinctive quality of interest will be experienced as uniquely rewarding and as different from the uniquely rewarding quality of enjoyment. These discrete states will each prime the infant to pay attention to anything that improves or changes the situation in the case of distress or anger, or to anything that prolongs the situation in the case of interest and enjoyment. In other words, these experiences with their unique qualities motivate the infant to care about what happens next, and therefore enhance the infant's capacity for learning at such moments. The rapidity with which the infant learns about the antecedents and consequences of these qualitative experiences is discussed in the next section, "Organizational Capacities."

The quality and content of the young infant's psychic experience therefore, is determined partly by the frequency and intensity of each of these affect states. In a normal full-term infant these states are recognizable both to the infant and to the caregiver when they recur. However, there are individual variations in infants in the clarity or organizational coherence of their states.

This is particularly true of premature infants, or of the more recent phenomenon of crack-addicted babies. These babies have a more difficult time achieving well-organized coherent states of sleep and wakefulness. Sander's statement, quoted earlier, "the organization of state governs the quality of inner experience" is relevant here. The organism needs to be able to achieve a basic level of organizational regularity and stability that can provide the background against which changes in coherent unities can be perceived and recognized. In a well-functioning neonate with a responsive caregiver, this can be achieved in the first week of life (Sander, 1975). Both the baby and the caregiver make contributions to the ease or difficulty of achieving this regularity, which has been conceptualized as a process of reciprocal transactions requiring mutual regulations and adaptations from both partners.

The quality and content of less well-organized infants' experience is more difficult to describe. Their states appear to be less coherent, are often described as mixed, and even where coherent are more fleeting. Thus opportunities for recognizing the recurrence of a prior state, for both the infant and the caregiver, will be less frequent. Also these babies seem less content and less comfortable, suggesting that whatever quality is perceptible to them, it is probably on the negative side. Perhaps the most that can be said, given the current state of our knowledge and methodologies, is that there is less clarity in their psychic experience than is true for well-organized babies and that the process of achieving a basic organizational regularity of coherent states will take longer.

Perceptual and Cognitive Qualities and Contents

Other determinants of the quality and content of the young infant's psychic experiences have to do with the kind of stimuli provided by the external environment. In a normal full-term baby the duration of an alert awake state (which usually occurs after a period of sleep and after a feeding) increases steadily from 5 to 20 minutes in the first few days of life to 30 to 60 minutes by the first month of life. Thus, this alert awake state is likely to recur three to five times a day. At such times the infant is looking at, listening to, touching, smelling, and tasting the world around him or her. Our understanding of the infant's perceptual and cognitive capabilities have radically changed in the last two to three decades. Piaget's (1967) view of the infant who lived in a world of disconnected pieces of reality, with simple, uncoordinated perceptual functions, such as a visual schema and an auditory schema that had to be gradually combined into more complex units, such as a visual–auditory schema, has been overturned by an ever increasing volume of new data.

The current consensus growing out of Gibson's (1969) theoretical ideas and the experimental work of many infant researchers, such as Bower (1977, 1982), and Spelke (1976, 1979), argues that infants begin with a highly complex and unified perceptual system that is designed to detect abstract invariants in stimulation, such as intensities, rates of movement, contours, mass, and so forth, and that operates across modalities. For example, infants can visually recognize the shape of an object that they have previously only explored with their mouth or tongue (Meltzoff & Borton, 1979), and they can match the intensity of a sound with the intensity of a light (Lewkowicz & Turkewitz, 1980). They can recognize the common temporal structure present in auditory and visual events, and will match a sound track to the appropriate film on the basis of temporal synchrony. They can also make categorical judgments about color, musical tones, and phonemes similar to those made by adults. Bower (1982) argued that the newborn lives in a world as close to pure perception as is possible, perceiving the general, abstract stimulus qualities of objects and that over time the infant fills in the details and begins to detect specific features of objects.

This formulation fits well with the latest findings reported by Baillargeon (1990). She discovered that infants can make qualitative judgments about objects before they can make specific quantitative judgments. Using visual tasks with young infants, Baillargeon has seriously challenged Piaget's timetable regarding the infant's understanding of object permanence. She has demonstrated that by 3½ months of age, infants already understand that objects continue to exist when hidden, that they cannot move through the space occupied by other objects, and that they cannot appear at Point A and then at Point B without traveling from Point A to Point B. As this experimental work with infants continues, we should not be surprised to learn that this knowledge is present even earlier.

Other investigators have demonstrated the neonate's responsiveness to human stimuli. The Brazelton Neonatal Behavioral Assessment Scale (NBAS; Brazelton, 1973) was the first scale to focus on the neonate's responsiveness and orientation to the human voice and face, and to demonstrate the neonate's readiness and capacity to interact with a human caregiver. Examiners trained in the administration of the NBAS report being able to elicit smiles from well-organized, alert neonates held in the en face position, (Modansky, personal communication, March 1981). Wolff (1963) reported that the human voice is the single most effective elicitor of neonatal responses, but that the face and voice together are also effective. And Field, Woodson, Greenberg, and Cohen (1982) have demonstrated that neonates are capable of discriminating and imitating three facial expressions (happy, sad, and surprise) modeled by a live adult. This finding illustrates not only the infant's responsiveness to human stimuli, but also the infant's cross-modal capacities discussed earlier, specifically the infant's capacity to match a visual image with a proprioceptive image based on the feedback from its own facial muscles. Martin and Clark (1982) have demonstrated that neonates can discriminate their own distress cry from the distress cry of other neonates, of a chimpanzee, and of an older child.

Summary of Quality and Contents of Psychic Experience

There are many other studies that could be cited illustrating neonatal capacities, and there will be many more to come in the future. Currently, all of these data seem to converge on a picture of a highly competent newborn with an impressive array of preadapted abilities. Although this picture may seem amazing and unbelievable to some and cause others to wonder at how long it has taken us to appreciate and explore systematically the neonate's capabilities, we might stop and ponder the full implications of evolutionary theory. For, as Bower reminded us, earlier formulations arguing for an incompetent infant ignored a basic evolutionary rule, namely that the more capable a species is in adulthood, the more capable is the newborn of the species. We could not possibly learn everything we are capable of as a species if we had to start from scratch. But let us be clear about the implications of these data. They do not support the notion of preformed ideas. What they do strongly indicate is the existence of preadaptive capacities for emotional experience, for human interaction, for recognizing recurrent patterns and detecting invariance in stimuli, and for perceiving certain phenomena. For example, we have already mentioned certain categorical distinctions. Additionally, as a species we can only hear sounds within certain frequencies, we can only see color in certain wavelengths, we can only perceive movement at certain rates, and so forth.

The human infant therefore starts out with a uniquely human nervous system, brain, and body, which in some respects will limit and constrict the range of possible experience, but in the main provides the infant with an enormous head start in adapting to a human world. Thus, the quality and content of the young infant's psychic experience, in combination with the affect states described earlier, is also determined partly by the infant's exposure to objects and people. Questions about rate of exposure, frequency of exposure, and intensity of exposure are all relevant here, for each infant has a characteristic style of taking in stimuli. The caregiver's role is conceptualized as one of titrating the stimulus dose, with the goal of trying to stay within the infant's optimal range without either overstimulating or understimulating the infant's capacities. But here I am quickly getting into issues of the infant's capacities for processing, organizing, and acting on experience that lead directly into the next section.

Organizational Capacities

What capacities does the young infant possess for organizing, remembering, and acting on the qualities and contents of his or her psychic experience? I return to the DeCasper and Carstens (1981) experiment described earlier as an illustration of these capacities. They used 3-day-old infants, who were awake and alert, and had them suck on a nonnutritive nipple that was wired to a computer. During the first 5 minutes, they were able to obtain a baseline rate of sucking and pausing for each infant. In the next 2 minutes they calculated the 70th percentile of the pause, which they used as a criterion. Then, for the next 15 minutes, whenever the duration of the infant's pause between sucking bursts was equal to or greater than the criterion, the experimenters turned on a recording of a female voice singing, which remained on during the ensuing burst of sucking. The infants in this contingency group showed a significant increase in the length of their pauses during the 15-minute phase of the experiment, thereby demonstrating that they perceived the contingency between the length of their pauses and the female voice and that they learned to lengthen their pauses in order to turn on the voice.

A second group of infants was placed in the same situation as the first group for the first 7 minutes of the experiment. Then, for the next 15 minutes, these infants heard a recording of a female voice singing going on and off at random intervals that was not contingent on the infants' pausing and sucking behaviors. The infants in this noncontingent group did not show any significant changes in their patterns of sucking and pausing throughout the 22 minutes of the experiment. Four to 24 hours later, the first group of infants was now placed in the noncontingent condition, and they showed an increase in activity level, facial grimacing, and crying, all signs of becoming upset by the change, or more precisely by the loss of control over the stimulus in this follow-up session. The second group of infants was now placed in the contingent condition, but they showed no signs of detecting the contingency and produced no changes in their sucking patterns.

DeCasper and Carstens (1981) argued that this second group of infants failed to detect the contingency because they had learned in the first noncontingent session that there was no connection between their behavior and the voice, and so in the follow-up session they did not pay attention to the voice. They went on to suggest "that contingencies of stimulation critically affect attention and recognition in newborns" (1981, p. 33) and that memory processes in newborns may be more complex than is usually assumed, in that infants may remember more than just a stimulus, but may remember behavioral interactions with the stimulus as well. They conclude the following:

> The results of this study suggest that newborn humans are sensitive to (can discriminate) contingencies between behavior and a stimulus, and that the nature of the contingency can bias subsequent learning about, attention to, memory of, and emotions elicited by that event. Viewing newborn behavior in the context of contingency theory suggests the human newborn is cognitively competent. . . . and an organism for whom experience has a more pervasive effect on subsequent behavior than previously suspected. (pp. 33–34)

Although the authors stressed the newborn's cognitive competence, I would argue that this study illustrates the coordination of affect, perception, cognition, and motor and memory mechanisms and thereby demonstrates the infant's organizational capacities. For in order for the infant to gain control over the stimulus, all of the following had to occur and had to be coordinated. The infant had to perceive the contingency between his or her own behavior (the length of pausing) and the onset of the singing voice. This connection or event had to be experienced affectively as interesting or enjoyable, thereby producing a motivational tendency to want to repeat or to continue the experience. The infant then had to cognitively generate a plan that involved an understanding of the need to lengthen pausing in order to turn on the singing voice. Then the infant had to be able to execute that plan by voluntarily controlling his or her motor responses so as to produce the effective lengthening of the pause. And in order to continue this response throughout the 15-minute experimental session, the infant had to be able to perceive the effect of his or her efforts, to remember the plan and then compare the outcome with the goal, and to use this information as feedback for planning and executing subsequent responses at each opportunity for repeating this "interesting event."

Early Intentionality

In the second phase of this experiment these same infants became upset when the onset of the singing voice was no longer connected to their own efforts to lengthen their pauses. Such a reaction suggests that the interest and enjoyment experienced by the infants in the first condition was primarily evoked by the contingency between the infant's behavior and the stimulus and not by the stimulus itself. This interpretation is strengthened when we remember that the second group of infants heard the voice as well, but lost interest in it because it was not connected to the pattern of their sucking and pausing. Thus, the experience of being able to control a stimulus or an event appears to be highly motivating and rewarding to a newborn, and as the authors suggested, such experiences have a pervasive effect on subsequent behavior.

Several psychologists, when discussing older infants and children, have used terms such as *effectence motivation* or *sense of agency* (Sander, 1982; White, 1959), but these data reported by DeCasper and Carstens (1981) demonstrate that the organizational capacity to coordinate various psychic mechanisms in order to voluntarily bring about a desired goal is present at birth. The neonates' ability to imitate facial expressions (Field et al., 1982) and to replace reflex sucking with voluntary sucking (Brunner, 1968) are also examples of the infants' intention to do voluntarily what they have experienced involuntarily. Such an intention is not innate. It involves generating the idea that this would be something to do. It is as if the infant thinks "this is nice, but I'd rather do it myself." Where does such an idea come from? Tomkins (1978), in discussing these early phenomena, gave the following answer:

> It represents an extraordinary creative invention conjointly powered by primitive perceptual and cognitive capacities amplified by excitement in the possibility of improving a good actual scene by doing something oneself. These are real phenomena and they appear to be highly probable emergents from the *interaction* of several basic human capacities. This is why I have argued that we have evolved to be born as a human being who will, with a very high probability, very early attempt and succeed in becoming a person. (p. 215)

Arguments for Early Internal–External Discriminations

So far in my discussion of the infant's organizational capacities, I have not mentioned a current controversial issue: the question of whether the infant experiences his or her psychological functioning as separate and distinct from the outside world, or whether the infant lives in an undifferentiated world, unable to distinguish between internal and external events. The DeCasper and Carstens (1981) experiment, although demonstrating many important organizational capacities, including the infant's exquisite ability to detect contingencies, does not help us with this question. But the discussion about the infant's intention to do something and its motivating power suggested by the experiment and elaborated further by Tomkins (1978), places us right in the middle of this issue, for it rests on the premise that the infant is making a distinction between voluntary events and involuntary events and definitely prefers being in voluntary control of events. It is only a very short step further for the infant to realize that voluntary events emanate from the inside and that most involuntary events emanate from the outside.

Stern (1983) made a similar argument when presenting data to support the model of a differentiated, separate infant psyche. In a highly original and creative integration of recent research data on infants, Stern argued that because infants possess predesigned perceptual and cognitive operations (many of which I have already described), they are able to perceive the organizational unity of individuals in terms of their spatial locations and temporal and intensity synchronies, and they can maintain these perceptions in the face of interfering stimuli and changing configurations. Infants are also able to discriminate different schedules of reinforcement and are thus in a position to determine effects that are self-caused and separate them from those that are caused by others. Thus, given an expectable human environment, infants will inevitably construct schemata of at least two separate organizational entities, namely, of their own functioning and of the behaviors of the other. These schemata are not innate but have a high probability of emerging from the integrated functioning of the inherited capacities of the human infant. The remaining question for Stern was "how does the infant 'know' that his organization of behaviors is the one that belongs to him?" (p. 65). It is at this point that Stern stressed the importance of the experience of an intention or motive that accompanies the infant's own behaviors but not those of the other, and the importance of proprioceptive sensations that always and only accompany the infant's behaviors.

I would add to the discussion an explicit acknowledgement of the role of affective experience in enabling the infant to differentiate his or her own experience from the sensations and behaviors emanating from the other. Affect is a powerful source of proprioceptive sensations that occurs in distinctive, qualitative patterns. What evidence do we have that infants can discriminate their own affect from the affect of another? Martin and Clark (1982) reported that calm newborns (18 hours old) cry and that crying newborns continue to cry when they hear the tape-recorded crying of other newborns. However, calm newborns do not respond vocally, and crying newborns stop crying when they hear their own tape-recorded crying. Also, calm neonates do not respond to the cries of a chimpanzee and of an older child, thus they are not simply responding to an aversive sound when responding to the cries of other neonates. The authors conclude that neonates are able to discriminate between the cries of others and their own cries, but they do not offer any explanation for how this might occur.

I would suggest that the infant is making this discrimination on the basis of the presence or absence of internal autonomic and motoric sensations that usually precede and accompany the infant's own crying, combined with the infant's capacity to perceive and recognize the distinctive temporal pattern of own versus other's crying. Thus, the infant cries when it hears another infant cry because of the amplifying function of affect. The rhythmical crying of distress amplifies the original nonoptimal stimulus and produces more distress and more crying in a positive feedback loop. Because of this amplifying function, all affect is to some extent contagious, and perhaps more so for neonates who have fewer resources for breaking into an escalating positive feedback loop. But the neonate stops crying or does not cry when hearing his or her own cry because the infant recognizes the temporal pattern of the crying as its own. However, this pattern is not preceded by the usual proprioceptive stimuli, nor is it accompanied by a matching pattern of autonomic and motor proprioceptive stimuli. Thus, it represents a highly discrepant stimulus, namely, a recognizable sound without any of the other patterned behavior that normally goes with it. Because the experimenters only coded the presence or absence of crying responses to the stimuli, we do not know what the infants did, beyond simply not crying, to the sound of their own cry. My guess is that they became very attentive, experiencing intense interest, if not something akin to perplexity, as they tried to understand this out-of-context event.

If we put all of these data together, it becomes almost impossible to imagine how the infant could *not* discriminate between his or her own behavior and experience and the behavior of others.

Summary of Early Organization

We clearly need more data on newborn functioning, but all of the evidence we do have is consistent with the picture of a highly competent infant, capable of making the distinction between internal events and external events, and capable of coordinating information emanating from affective, perceptual, cognitive, and memory and motor functions in order to try to bring about desired events and to limit or escape from undesired events. Given these organizational capacities of the neonate, the role of the caregiver becomes one of enhancing and supporting these capacities, or interfering with and overriding them, or simply ignoring them. This view represents a shift from earlier views in which it was argued that organization came from the caregiver to the infant and that the infant internalized it. By contrast, I am proposing that the infant already possesses organizational capacities that can be influenced in a variety of ways by the caregiver, but this influence does not amount to creating organization de novo within the infant. A discussion of the fate of these organizational capacities brings us to the final question raised at the beginning of this chapter.

What Changes Over Time?

What aspects of these capacities and experiences are changing over time? We can no longer describe development as going from the global, diffuse, chaotic, and undifferentiated to the discrete, organized, and differentiated. If we begin with a differentiated, organized, infant, equipped with a number of discrete, preadapted, and preorganized functions and human capabilities for learning and integrating experience already in operation, then what is developing and changing over time? What is experience contributing?

Here we are entering new territory. Because this picture of the competent infant has only emerged recently, all of the implications for our understanding of development have not yet been fully explored and conceptualized. What follows then is offered tentatively as one set of possibilities derived from the data on infant capacities. I would suggest there are at least four major kinds of changes going on: (a) The infant is going from being a generalist to becoming a specialist; (b) the infant's sense of being in control of events and thus his or her motivational organization is being determined; (c) the infant's motor strength is increasing and thus his or her instrumental competence is increasing; and (d) the infant is gradually learning to decontextualize his or her knowledge of the world and his or her relation to and place in the world. I discuss each of these briefly. The order of presentation does not indicate an order of importance.

The Infant Becomes a Specialist

The infant begins as a generalist. Earlier when I discussed the infant's perceptual and affective capacities, I described them as operating at a general abstract level. Thus, infants are aware of the intensities, rates, and contours of stimuli, and affects are initially experienced only as general abstract qualities, such as "too much" or "too fast." Over time, through redundant experiences with events that are not exact repetitions but variations on a theme, the infant fills in the specifics. Objects take on specific features. Thus, for example, although a newborn will brighten, gaze, and smile at any human face and voice, one or two months later, if an infant has been cared for by a consistent caregiver, only familiar and specific faces and voices will elicit this reaction. Newborns can discriminate phonemes from any language, but by 5 or 6 months of age, they can only do it for the specific language spoken in their environment. In some respects then, given a redundant predictable environment, the omnipotentiality of any human infant will be lost as the infant becomes more experienced with particular objects and with particular people. The infant quickly becomes a specialist as he or she becomes a member of a particular family, living in a particular place, at a particular moment of historical time.

In the affective realm, the general abstract qualities of affective experience quickly become connected to specific antecedents and specific consequences. Although the hungry, crying neonate neither knows why he or she is crying or that anything can be done about it, by 3 or 4 weeks of age, if the caregiver has responded predictably to the infant's cry, the infant will stop crying at the sight or sound of the caregiver's approach. The infant has already connected the hunger and crying to the approach, comfort, and feeding of the caregiver, has already built up an expectation, and therefore can anticipate that the approach of the caregiver means that comfort and food will soon follow. This expectation allows the infant to stop crying and to wait to be fed.

This process of connecting one's affective experience to specific triggers and to specific aftermaths begins at birth and is ongoing throughout life. It involves a search for the main effect, or in other words, for recognizable invariants in events. Discrete affect states provide one of the major sources of invariance around which experience can be organized. Connecting antecedents and consequences to coherent, recognizable, and recurrent affect states leads to the construction of what Tomkins (1978) called "ideo–affect complexes." Ideo–affect is an abbreviation for ideo–perceptual–memorial–action–affect complexes, which refers to the involvement of all of the critical subsystems that together constitute a human being. Such ideo–affect complexes represent the distilled commonality of a number of discrete events or scenes, with a particular affective quality at their core. This conceptualization has important implications for our understanding of how psychological meaning is constructed, which is discussed later in "Knowledge and Experience Become Decontextualized." For now, I want to emphasize the element of specialization that is involved in this process.

If an infant lives in a sufficiently redundant and predictable environment, his or her affective experiences will become increasingly particularized and elaborated in idiosyncratic ways. The infant will come to know what specific kinds of events or scenes evoke interest-excitement, enjoyment-joy, distress-anguish, anger-rage, fear-terror, shame-humiliation, and so forth, or combinations of these, and what to expect in terms of specific sequelae for each of these kinds of events. Optimally, one would hope to see an ever expanding range of events connected to positive affects, and a relatively small category of events connected to negative affects.

Here we can see how the transactions with the caregiver play an important part in determining the ease or difficulty the infant will have in establishing these connections, and in the specific content and frequency of the connections. For the caregiver is not only engaged in responding to the infant's affective states, which are partially determined by the infant's constitutional and neurological characteristics and partly by the environment, but is also engaged in expressing affects to the infant and in evoking affects in the infant. Thus, the intensity of the affects evoked from all of these sources, the ratio of positive to negative affects, their clarity, their predictability, their frequency, and the rate of change from one affect to another will all be factors that the infant will have to cope with in trying to sort out what goes with what, and what leads to what. For example, an affectively labile parent will make it difficult for an infant and young child to sort out the affective valence of transactional scenes and to predict their consequences, whereas a parent who evokes intense negative affects frequently will focus the infant's efforts on attempts to avoid or limit the punishing quality of these experiences, often limiting the potential scope of the positive affects, and so forth. The interplay of all of these factors, then, not only underscores the complexity of the infant's psychological processes, but emphasizes as well its highly idiosyncratic nature and forces us to acknowledge the magnitude of the variance that can occur in the construction of ideo–affective complexes.

One of the most important consequences of understanding development as moving from the general to the specific is to appreciate that all early learning is deeply embedded in specific contexts. If we want to understand early learning, we must be ready to deal with and to learn from the full range of the details of those specifics and of the individual differences in organizational outcomes that those specific contexts engender. Thus, if we want to understand the infant, we must find ways to evaluate the infant's capacities and organization in contexts that are familiar and meaningful to the infant. And if we want to help our adult patients to understand and to gain some mastery over the present psychological consequences and meanings of their early experiences, we must be able to appreciate the power of the specific details of those experiences in shaping their psychological organization.

The Infant's Motivational Organization Takes Shape

The second major change constituting development involves the determination of the degree to which the infant will feel in control of internal and external events and the determination of the motivational organization of the infant. Earlier we discussed how motivating and rewarding it was for the neonate to be able to voluntarily control an event or an experience. One way to describe this phenomenon is in terms of a sense of agency, namely, the knowledge that one's own efforts are effective in causing something to happen or in recreating and prolonging a positive state, and in limiting, ending, or avoiding a negative state. What role does the caregiving environment play in determining the fate of this rewarding and motivating sense of agency? Sander described this role in the following manner:

> The emergence of infant as agent must be granted by the system because it means a reorganization of the system to admit the newcomer. If the system is such that it can permit the entrance of a new agent within it, it provides the conditions which establish not only the capacity for self-awareness, but conditions which insure the use of such inner awareness by the infant as a frame of reference in organizing his own adaptive behavior, i.e., being in a position that permits him to appreciate what behaviors lead to what state. (Sander, 1982, p. 17)

In this formulation, the family system is conceptualized as facilitating the infant's own efforts at goal realization, and as providing opportunities for the infant to initiate goal-organized behavior. Sander went on to say, "the valence of this inner experience under these conditions of self-initiated goal realization will be felt as the infant's own" (1982, p. 17). Implicit in this statement is its opposite, namely that when self-initiated goals are not realized or facilitated by the family system, then the valence of this inner experience will not be felt as the infant's own, but rather as external to the infant. Under such conditions, the use of inner awareness by the infant as a frame of reference in organizing his or her own adaptive behavior will not be enhanced or supported.

Researchers interested in resiliency and coping strategies of older children have zeroed in on this issue of whether the child perceives the locus of control of events to be inside or outside. They conceptualize this as a central variable in determining the child's ability to persist and to be an effective problem solver. The point I emphasize here is that this issue is pertinent from the beginning of life, and the fate of the infant's initiatives is being determined from birth on. Brazelton (1989) described behaviors manifested by 6-month-old infants that already indicate whether these infants expect to succeed in accomplishing a goal or whether they expect to fail. In previous articles (Demos, 1986, 1988, 1989a, 1989b), I have described several ways in which this issue can be negotiated between infants and caregivers, and many of the variables involved. (What follows is a brief condensation of those ideas; the reader is referred to the above references for a broader discussion.)

I return now to the hungry neonate. This organism is designed so that the hunger, as it gradually increases and becomes perceptible, will innately trigger the affect distress. Distress, at lower intensities, is manifested in the newborn by whimpering, motor restlessness, and a facial pattern that includes some or all of the following: the corners of the lips pulled down, the inner portion of the eyebrows pulled up and together, and eyes opened or closed. At somewhat higher intensities, distress is manifested by a rhythmical cry, an open cry mouth with the corners of the lips pulled down, the same oblique eyebrows, and more vigorous motor restlessness. It is accompanied by a conscious awareness of a general, abstract, urgent negative quality of "too much," which prompts the infant to generate a wish to reduce or end this negative state.

The neonate does not possess the instrumental capabilities to deal with the hunger and possesses only a limited repertoire of behaviors to manage the evoked distress that is amplifying the hunger. Thus, the intervention of the caregiver is necessary both to modulate the infant's distress and to provide food for the infant's hunger. But the timing of the caregiver's intervention has consequences for the infant's sense of agency. If the caregiver responds too early in this sequence of events, for example, at the very first sign of restlessness or vocal whimpering, the infant will receive a remedy before he or she has had the opportunity to become aware of a problem. In this example, the feeding, although providing nutrients for the physical needs of the infant, will bypass the psychological process of becoming aware of a distressed state, wanting it to end, initiating some behaviors to try to achieve that goal, and then receiving comfort and food. There is then an optimal zone of affective experience, which will vary from infant to infant, that is neither too brief and weak, nor too prolonged and intense, that allows enough psychological space for the infant to feel an internal need, to become an active participant in trying to address the need, and therefore to be able to relate subsequent events, such as a feeding, both to the internal need or state and to the plans and efforts to remedy it. Thus, the timing of the caregiver's interventions is a critical variable in determining the fate of the infant's sense of agency.

The contents of the caregiver's interventions are also critical. As an illustration, examine the following sequence. A young infant is gazing intently at and reaching toward a nearby object, thereby manifesting the affective state of interest and the plan to explore the object further; but the infant is unable to fully execute this plan and begins to express fussy sounds of frustration and mild anger. If a caregiver does not understand or believe that young infants are capable of generating plans, becoming affectively engaged in them, and organizing their behaviors toward instrumental goals, but instead perceives infants as helpless and primarily needing comfort, then such a caregiver will be highly unlikely to respond to the infant in a way that will facilitate and enhance the infant's efforts. The infant's fussiness might then be interpreted as fatigue or hunger and responded to accordingly; or as merely inconsequential and simply ignored; or as an irritating intrusion, requiring some punitive response. However, if the caregiver perceives the young infant as an active agent, capable of organized plans and behaviors, then he or she will be far more likely to offer some kind of assistance, such as changing the infant's posture to facilitate the infant's reaching efforts or moving the object closer to the infant, thereby enabling the young infant to remain interested and to persist and hopefully to experience some success in executing plans.

I suggest that from the infant's point of view these events are experienced as affective sequences, such as positive–negative–negative sequences or positive–negative–positive sequences. Thus, the specific kind of caregiver response helps to determine the motivational meaning of the whole sequence for the infant. In this illustration, a positive affective state of interest, with its related plan and instrumental behaviors, leads to a negative affective state of mild anger, which then can lead to any of the following affective states, depending on how the caregiver's responses affect the infant: (a) being put to bed for a nap; (b) being fed or comforted, both of which might lead to an angry protest from the infant or to a giving up of the initial plan, including a decline in interest and investment; (c) being ignored and left to one's own limited resources, which will probably lead to more frustration and perhaps an eventual abandonment of the plan; (d) being yelled at, scolded, or hit, which will lead to distress or anger; or (e) getting help, which will lead to more interest, persistence, and perhaps to the enjoyment of success.

There are many varieties of affective sequences occurring in a young infant's life, each providing meaningful information to the infant about what to expect when he or she experiences interest-excitement and enjoyment-joy and tries to carry out the plans and behaviors generated by these internal states. In the examples just provided, clearly only the last sequence: (e) will facilitate the infant's own efforts at goal realization. But all of these sequences are contributing to the determination of the degree to which an infant will feel in control of internal and external events, and the degree to which an infant will therefore continue to use inner awareness as a frame of reference for organizing adaptive behavior. This aspect of development is central to the construction of the infant's motivational stance toward his or her own inner experience, toward the world, and toward others.

The Infant's Instrumental Competence Increases

The third major kind of change going on in development involves an increase in the infant's muscular strength, which allows the infant to achieve more instrumental competence. The infant begins life with a relatively weak musculature, and therefore is not able to "do" very much. I believe this is one of the main reasons the infant's capacities have been underestimated for so long. It was mistakenly assumed that because the infant could do so little instrumentally, nothing much could be going on inside the infant's mind. Piaget's (1967) theory reinforced this belief by arguing that knowledge had to be obtained by acting on the environment, for example, sucking, looking, touching, and so forth, and painstakingly built up step by step. Thus, muscle weakness became synonymous with a lack of cognitive organization, an absence of preadapted coordinations, and an absence of innate perceptual categories. As this kind of formulation gives way to the accumulation of recent data on infant capabilities, we can begin to understand the development of instrumental behaviors in a new way.

Several preorganized motor patterns are widely acknowledged and documented, for example, the sucking pattern, the walking pattern, the grasping pattern, and the affective expressive patterns on the face. These are often described as reflexes, which were thought to be organized at subcortical levels of the brain, and to disappear as the nerves in the cortex gradually became myelinated and the cortex became more dominant. These behaviors were thought to then reappear at a later date, organized at the higher cortical level as the result of a learning process. However, Thelen (1984; Thelen & Fischer, 1982) provided a different kind of explanation for the apparent disappearance and reappearance of some of these behaviors. She has demonstrated, for example, that the organized walking pattern manifested by newborns does not disappear. Rather its manifestation seems to be controlled by the changing ratio of muscle strength to body fat. In early infancy body fat accumulates more rapidly than muscle strength increases. Thelen speculates that this may occur because temperature regulation has a higher priority than locomotion for the human infant who is not born with a covering of dense hair or fur. Thus, from roughly 1 to 7 months of age, when body fat dominates over muscle strength, the infant appears to lose the organized walking pattern. However, as Thelen has shown, when the infant's lower body is submerged in water at these ages, and the upper torso is supported, the walking pattern is fully evident. In a series of ingenious experiments with treadmills, Thelen demonstrated that the walking pattern continues to be present, but that the onset of bipedal locomotion occurs only when the infant's muscular strength has increased sufficiently to allow the infant to support his or her body weight on one leg (Thelen, 1986; Thelen, Ulrich, & Niles, 1987).

A similar argument can be made about the emergence of the infant's reaching behaviors. These behaviors were thought to be dependent on the infant's having obtained a certain level of cognitive organization, namely the coordination of a visual schema with a tactual schema in order to form a schema of a reachable, graspable object. However, with the aid of slow-motion film, researchers (e.g., Bower, 1977) have been able to show that what seem to be random, swiping motions of very young infants, are in reality quite well-organized reaching and grasping motions directed at objects. The hand moves through a perfectly executed grasping pattern, which reaches its apex just as the hand comes closest to the object. The effort fails not because of a lack of knowledge but because the very young infant does not yet have sufficient muscular strength to support and to guide his or her own arm in an accurate path to the object.

These data suggest that the young infant can imagine and plan goals long before he or she is motorically able to execute them, or in other words, that organization precedes instrumentally successful actions. This may partially explain how an increase in muscular strength can produce such a remarkable investment in instrumental effectiveness. Here I am referring to the intense excitement young infants show when they first produce a "new" behavior, such as rolling over or pulling up to a standing position. They repeat it over and over again as if intoxicated with their new skill. I am suggesting that at least part of this excitement may be due to the feeling that they can now finally do something they have imagined doing for quite a while.

But perhaps the most important implications of this new work involve the need to revise our understanding of the processes of developmental change. In prior formulations, the onset of new behaviors was thought to be part of a master plan, centrally programmed and controlled in the nervous system, unfolding in a regular stage by stage progression and involving a wide range of phenomena, for example, everything changed together, ushering the individual into the next "stage" of development. Piaget's (1967) theory is a prime example of this kind of formulation. However, these data suggest that the onset of new behaviors can occur in quite a localized manner, involving changes in the coordination and constellation of variables that are determined by peripheral and local conditions. Researchers in cognitive development (e.g., Fischer & Pipp, 1984) are also discovering that changes in one content area do not correlate with the level of functioning or changes in other content areas. Thus the case for homogeneous levels of functioning and stagelike reorganizations is becoming less and less viable. Our knowledge of the kinds of variables involved and of the range of mechanisms operating in developmental changes has increased radically, with much yet to be discovered. Perhaps the most that can be said at this point in time is that there is far more complexity and variability within each individual and across individuals than has previously been appreciated, while at the same time it is clear that there are definite constraints operating that ensure that we are recognizable to each other as fellow human beings.

I have highlighted the role of the gradual increase in muscle strength in this discussion because it illustrates several trends in recent developmental thinking. Its importance as a variable in understanding the onset of instrumental behaviors has been underappreciated and misunderstood in the past, and points to the need to broaden our conceptualizations of relevant variables. It is currently receiving more research attention, and has been useful in demonstrating how local changes can occur. And, finally, it represents a continuous variable that changes gradually over a long time span (muscle strength probably continues to increase, at least for some people, well into young adulthood), with no clearly defined stages. It is therefore the example par excellence of the new kind of developmental variable that lends itself to multiple roles in a continually shifting constellation of other variables. There are undoubtedly other such variables, equally important, that we have yet to discover.

Knowledge and Experience Become Decontextualized

The fourth kind of major developmental change is in some respects the counterpoint to the first one discussed. We began by describing how the infant starts as a generalist and quickly becomes a specialist, and how all early learning is deeply embedded in specific contexts. Here we will be describing how the infant begins a lifelong process of decontextualizing knowledge and experience. Both kinds of changes are occurring and they are complementary to each other. What do I mean by decontextualizing knowledge and experience? I have borrowed the term from Margaret Donaldson. Donaldson (1979) used it to describe the learning processes in somewhat older children in her book *Children's Minds*, where she demonstrated, contrary to Piaget's (1967) theory, that the ability to reason logically is present in young children if logical problems are presented in meaningful contexts and that what older children are better at and learn explicitly to do in school is decontextualizing their knowledge. I have extended this idea down to early infancy and expanded her original usage by suggesting that this process begins at birth. Given the preadapted cognitive, perceptual, and organizational capacities of the newborn already described in this chapter, which embody most of the essential human reasoning capacities (e.g., the ability to detect invariance, the ability to detect contingencies, etc.), it follows that one of the major tasks of development is to learn to transfer one's knowledge from one context to another. This process results in the gradual decontextualization of knowledge and experience.

Let me illustrate this process with the following example. Imagine a young infant, lying in a crib and gazing at a blue plastic cup on a table a few feet away. We have learned from studies of early perception (Bower, 1974; Ruff, 1980) and early memory (Rovee-Collier, 1990; Spear, 1990) that infants tend to unitize what they see, or in other words, they see gestalts. As long as the infant and the cup remain immobile, the infant's knowledge of the cup will remain embedded in the total context or unity of cup–table–background (wallpaper), and so forth. Without new information, the infant will have no way of discovering what is essential and what is extraneous to "cupness." Soon, however, a caregiver comes in, picks up the infant, and carries him or her out of, around, or back into the room. The infant now has the opportunity to view the cup from several different angles and perspectives. Bower (1974) demonstrated that very young infants already know that objects have mass and three-dimensionality. So what the infant learns from these different perspectives is more about the specific shape and contours of this particular cup, but the cup still remains largely embedded in its original context of cup–table and now variable backgrounds.

A few weeks or months later, the caregiver picks up the cup and hands it to the infant. Now the infant discovers that the cup is separate from the table, while at the same time discovering its particular texture, weight, and feel. Several months later, when the infant is crawling or walking, the infant carries the cup around, and now discovers that its essential cupness can be transported from room to room. At about this same time the infant is likely to discover that cups come in a variety of colors, shapes, textures, weights, sizes, and have a variety of uses. By now, the infant's image of a cup has transcended any particular cup, context, or usage, but encompasses them all in a distilled version of a cup. Several months later, the infant will learn the word *cup* and will discover that he or she can now take the cup into the past or into the future, or extend its existence in the present by bringing it to mind in a variety of internal contexts. If the child happens to live in a bilingual environment, he or she will discover two words for the same object, yet another step in the decontextualizing of knowledge. And several years later, when the child goes to school and learns how to read, he or she will discover that the essence of cupness can be transported across a wide range of historical and geographical contexts.

This process of decontextualization can in some respects be thought of as a figure and ground problem. In order for the infant to extract the figure from the ground there seems to have to be an optimal ratio between redundancy and variation in repeated presentations of an object. Too much redundancy and the infant will habituate and lose interest; too much variation and the infant will not recognize the object as the same. For example, Rovee-Collier (1990) reported that if she changed too many elements in the second presentation of a mobile, or presented the same mobile but in a different room, or had changed the pattern on the bumper guard around the crib, the infants did not "remember" the mobile or in other words they did not recognize the second presentation as a repetition of the first, but treated it as a new event. It follows, then, that the more experience an infant has with an object, and the more that experience consists of small variations on a theme, the more rapidly the infant will construct a distilled image of the object, an image that is continually becoming more independent of context and therefore more easily evoked in an increasingly wide variety of contexts.

This same process of decontextualization is occurring in relation to the essential people in the infant's life, but is occurring much more rapidly than with inanimate objects because the infant's contact with a caregiver is more frequent and generally involves a much higher density of multimodal redundant patterns optimally blended with minor variations. This blend enables the infant to recognize the caregiver as the same person while at the same time distilling the essence of that sameness from the continually changing internal and external contexts in which his or her transactions are occurring. This formulation raises questions about earlier psychoanalytic assumptions about the infant's incapacities and the derived proposition that the infant *has* to split representations of the mother into the good mother and the bad mother. It also raises questions about current psychological assumptions about the young child's cognitive capacities and the claim that the young child cannot integrate good and bad, or nice and mean behaviors into an image of a single person (Fischer, Shaver, & Carnahan, 1990). This decontextualization formulation would suggest that if the infant's internal positive and negative affective states are generally managed within optimal intensity and duration ranges in relation to the caregiver, and if the external characteristics of the caregiver are sufficiently redundant, then the infant *will* be able to construct a unitary image of the mother that can be transported from context to context.

The crucial variable seems to be the optimal balance between redundancy and variation, both in internal affective states and the external events. This balance is difficult to specify. It will vary from infant to infant and will change with time and experience so that as the infant constructs more elaborate images of people and objects, more variation can be integrated into the images. Other factors, such as the intensity of experience, will affect this balance as well. We know, for example, that in severe cases of trauma and/or abuse in which the young child has experienced intense terror at the hand of a parent, the child often does split off these experiences. In such cases the psyche seems unable to integrate the dense negative affect within the ongoing flow of inner experience, and unable to integrate the image of the abusive parent into a single image of a parent, who might on other occasions provide support and comfort. But these cases represent extreme conditions in which the usual balance between redundancy and variation has been swamped by the intrusion of psychologically toxic levels of negative affect, which require extreme defensive measures in order to preserve the organizational integrity of the psyching function.

In more ordinary, benign childrearing situations it seems highly probable that the young infant can integrate inner experience and will construct a multifaceted, but single image of the mother. Indeed, there are several examples in my videotaped records of mother–infant transactions where the mother is tired or preoccupied and her responsiveness to her infant is somewhat off, or perfunctory, or even contains some irritation, but the infant reacts as if everything is fine. (These examples involve an infant that is in a stable state, e.g., not tired, irritable, or sick.) Winnicott's (1969) phrase the "good enough mother" comes to mind. One way to understand this phenomenon is to argue that the infant is working from an image of "mother" that has been constructed from a multitude of experiences with her and therefore encompasses more than any single experience. As long as the mother's behavior stays within the parameters of this representation, her temporary lapses will not be perceived as being different. At such moments it seems as if the infant's distilled image of the mother is more real to the infant than the actual mother.

Decontextualization of Psychic Experience: Psychological Magnification

I would like to explore one further implication of decontextualization as it relates to the continuing process of organizing psychic experience. I described earlier, when discussing how the infant goes from being a generalist to a specialist, the early construction of ideo–affective complexes. In that context, I stressed the specificity and idiosyncratic nature of these constructions. Here, I want to focus on how these constructions can gradually transcend the details of any single context and be evoked across a variety of contexts. I must return again to the work of Silvan Tomkins for a useful model of how this might occur.

Tomkins (1978) began by assuming that the basic unit of experience is a "scene," which in its simplest form includes at least one affect and at least one object of that affect, which may be the perceived activator of the affect, or the response to the affect or to the activator. It is a happening with a perceived beginning and end, and represents a simple form of an ideo–affect complex. The infant quickly begins to relate one scene to another following one ordering principle of similarity, namely, relating scenes that seem to be variations on a theme, where the central theme, or invariance, or redundancy is provided by the affect. This formulation differs from Stern's (1985) concept of representations of interactions that have been generalized, in that it explicitly places affect at the center of the infant's efforts to organize experience. When the infant connects one affect-laden scene with another affect-laden scene, then what Tomkins called "psychological magnification" occurs. In psychological magnification the meaning of a scene is magnified by its perceived similarity to earlier scenes.

Tomkins (1978) provided an example of how psychological magnification can occur by describing the case of Laura, who was one of the hospitalized children filmed by the Robertsons in their study of the effects on children of separation from parents during a hospitalization. Laura spent a week in the hospital, separated from her parents, undergoing a variety of medical procedures and being filmed by Robertson with a moving picture camera near her crib. She cried a great deal during this week. There is no question then that this experience was upsetting for Laura, but what will be the long-term effect of this experience? Tomkins argued that "the effect of any set of scenes is indeterminate until the future happens and either further magnifies or attenuates such experience," and he states further that "the consequence of any experience is not singular but plural . . . there are *many* effects which change in time" (Tomkins, 1978, p. 219). In another context he stated that "any gratuity must be built upon to reward in the long run; any threat must be elaborated by further action to become traumatic" (Tomkins, 1987, p. 159). The long-term effect for Laura, then, will depend on what happens next. How often will she rehearse these bad scenes? Will the intensity and spacing of these rehearsals be experienced as magnifying or attenuating the negative affects connected with them? Will her parents be able to reassure her, or will they frighten her further with their concerns? Is this the beginning of more medical problems, or an isolated incident in her life?

Laura returned home and after a few days she seemed to be her normal self again, thus initially there appears to be very little magnification of these bad scenes. A few weeks later Robertson visits her home to interview her parents and Laura becomes upset again. An element of the bad scenes has invaded, what was until then, a safe place, and her parents did not prevent it. This event represents a repetition but with a difference, a variation on a theme, and things have now become worse; the family of bad scenes has grown. In a few days Laura once again recovers and all is well for a time. A while later her parents take her to an art museum, place her in a crib (which the museum routinely provides for toddlers), and leave her alone briefly. At first Laura does not cry. She does not seem to perceive the dangerous parallel to her earlier experience of being taken to a strange place, being placed in a crib, and being left by her parents. However, a few minutes later, when a man with a camera approaches and takes her picture, Laura cries. The family of connected scenes has now been enlarged again and magnified. This is not the same man, it is not the same kind of camera, and it is a museum and not a hospital, but it feels the same to Laura and her crying becomes self-validating.

> The scene, whether dangerous or not, has been made punishing by her own crying. Any scene which is sufficiently similar to evoke the same kind of affect is thereby *made* more similar, and increases the degree of connectedness of the whole family of scenes. Just as members of a family are not similar in all respects, yet appear to be recognized as members of the same family, so do connected scenes which are psychologically magnified become more similar as members of a family of scenes. (Tomkins, 1978, p. 220)

As families of scenes are created and the degree of psychological magnification increases, the individual begins to generate a "script" to deal with sets of scenes. In Tomkins's (1978) formulation, scripts are sets of ordering rules for the production, evaluation, interpretation, prediction, and control of a magnified set of scenes. Some of the major components of any script involve specification of quantities, ratios, and directionality of positive and negative affects, for example, how much positive and negative affect is anticipated and enacted? How rapidly does positive affect change to negative affect, or vice versa? Is excitement greater than anger? Does interest lead to distress and shame? They also specify different strategies of relating risks, costs, and benefits so that one can strive for the greatest benefits and least costs at least risks; strive for optimal benefits and costs at a moderate level of risk; or strive for modest benefits with modest costs and modest risks. They operate as if–then propositions. Scripts are selective in the number and types of scenes they order, they are incomplete rules, and they vary in their accuracy. They are therefore continually reordered and changing, and the components of scripts can be combined, recombined, or decomposed. In the early stages of psychological magnification, the set of scenes determines the script. The criteria for connecting scenes can be quite discriminating, the growth of families of scenes gradual, and the degree of flexibility and possibilities for change in the script high. But as magnification increases, the script increasingly determines the scenes.

There are several ways that similarity between affect-laden scenes can be detected and that underlay the process of psychological magnification. In my earlier discussion of how the infant's knowledge of the cup gradually became decontextualized, I relied primarily on the ordering principle of detecting similarity by perceiving variations on a theme. Thus, the infant's knowledge of a cup could be continuously expanded by encountering increasing variations on an underlying core or essence that does not change. Psychological magnification and script generation are also based on this principle of variance, but they rely as well on another more powerful human capacity for detecting similarity, namely the principle of analogue formation. Analogic thinking seems to be a basic mode of human thought. For example, if people are asked to relate the words *mouse* and *elephant* to the words *ping* and *pong*, they do not hesitate to perform this task, and there is nearly universal agreement that *ping* goes with *mouse* and *pong* with *elephant*.

This connection seems to be based on imagined relationships between shared dimensions. These dimensions are part of our basic capacity to perceive abstract properties of stimuli, such as intensities, quantities, rates, contours, and so forth, a capacity that the newborn infant also possesses (see the earlier discussion of innate perceptual capacities).

Psychological magnification and the generation of scripts can occur more rapidly through the human capacity for analogic thinking than by the capacity to perceive variants, because expansion by perceiving variations requires a repetition of at least some of the actual elements of the earlier scenes, whereas expansion by analogue does not. In Laura's case, for example, Dr. Robertson, a member of the original cast of characters in the bad scenes at the hospital, actually had to come to her home in order for her to magnify her earlier experience. But at the museum there was no magnification, even when placed in a similar crib and left alone by her parents, until a strange man with a different kind of camera appeared and the scene was then experienced as an analogue by Laura.

Analogue formation, then, has the potential for generating connections between scenes that are, in most observable respects, quite remote from earlier scenes. It can operate in a highly compressed, abstract manner that results in a rapid scanning of a situation, telling the person all he or she thinks he or she needs to know about the current scene. Because of their power to detect similarity across a wide range of contexts, analogues are particularly likely to be generated when dealing with negative affects. From the beginning of life the human being is designed to try to optimize the ratio of positive and negative affect in his or her life. As the ratio of negative affect increases so too does the urgency to command, understand, predict, and control bad scenes. These conditions will lead to the rapid development of skills to detect danger in current and future scenes, and to the preferred use of analogues over variants as the more powerful tool. It is possible to see how an individual can become a prisoner of his or her own imaginative power to generate analogues and scripts that determine the meaning of scenes, and thereby subject himself or herself to an endless repetition of problematic scenes.

There are several implications of viewing the elaboration of psychological meaning in this way. First of all, it is important to note that not all psychological experience is magnified. There are a variety of trivial scenes in every life that do not evoke sufficient affect to become connected to other scenes and thus are never magnified. There are also a host of habitual scripts, that, although in their initial formation required conscious attention and magnification, once they are mastered cease to continue to be magnified. Regular routines of living, including routine interactions with other people, can fall into this habitual category and evoke little affect or attention.

Psychological magnification continues to occur only when the scripted attempt to deal with a connected family of scenes fails to achieve its goal. This will motivate new efforts to generate a more effective script in order to command, understand, predict, and control this now enlarged family of scenes. It follows, then, that some of the problems that patients bring to psychotherapists represent inadequate scripted solutions that continue to subject the patient to the most current versions of an expanding family of bad scenes. It also follows that in trying to reconstruct a person's history, there is no single point in time to go back to, and no single event on which to focus. To reiterate a point made earlier, in order for any set of scenes to produce an enduring traumatic effect, it must continue to be psychologically magnified by being connected to current and future scenes that are experienced as repetitions and are dealt with in ways that magnify rather than attentuate their punishing aspects.

One final implication of this approach is that it places affect right at the center of psychological organization and it assumes that one of the primary motivating forces is the goal to optimize the ratio of positive to negative affect experienced by the psyche. Closely related goals include the effort to maintain the organizational integrity of the psyche and to retain as much control as is felt to be necessary to achieve these goals. There is much more that could be said about the therapeutic implications of this formulation, which will have to await another opportunity. There is also much more that could be said about scripts, and the process of decontextualizing psychological experience, but I must refer the reader to Tomkins's extensive writings on this subject (Tomkins, 1978, 1991).

Summary of Developmental Changes: The Argument Against Stage Theories

This concludes the discussion of what happens to the organizational capacities of the infant over time. All of the developmental changes discussed, namely, going from a multipotential generalist to a specialist, discovering what opportunities there are for initiative and agency, developing muscle strength and instrumental capacities, and decontextualizing one's knowledge of inanimate objects, people, and one's inner experience, involve gradual continuous processes of change. They do not lend themselves easily to stagelike formulations or to set progressions of skills. Instead, these changes seem to depend on continuous transactions with the environment, whereby the specific characteristics of these transactions and the degree of their particular appropriateness or match with the infant's capabilities at any given developmental moment will determine what skills and at what rate the infant will be able to learn. (See Ruff, 1980, for a similar viewpoint in her discussion of the development of perception.)

It is important to remember that I am talking about psychological organization and changes in psychological organization over time. There is an increasing body of data indicating a multitude of physiological and neurological changes going on in the infant's brain and body, some of which seem to follow an epigenetic model of development and others of which seem to involve discontinuous changes. We still do not yet possess adequate models that would help us understand the relation between these changes and psychological experience and processes, or that would specify with more precision the relationship between experience and changes in the brain. Thus, I am suggesting here that psychological development appears to be different.

There is one developmental change that seems to represent a discontinuous shift in capacities, namely the onset of the use of language or more broadly the onset of the capacity for symbolic thought. This shift ushers in the possibility of self-reflection, the possibility of observing oneself as one functions in the world, the possibility of evocative memory, the possibility of translating one's inner experiences into words, and so forth. The current conceptualizations of these phenomena feature the discontinuities, with vivid pre- and postchange descriptions of capacities, evoking Piaget's (1967) theory and often relating these changes to neurological changes in the brain. I am suggesting that as we learn more about the complex nature of the developmental process and about the large number of variables operating and the precise variables involved, we may discover that even this very dramatic change is the result of a continuous gradual process. For example, it may be that as specific components gradually become more elaborated, and the combinations with other equally elaborated components become more complex, new capacities emerge and that once they emerge they take on a life of their own and continue to elaborate ever new possibilities. Thus, continuous processes may propel the system into new organizations that will appear to be discontinuous, and the timing and rate of these new organizations will vary markedly from individual to individual.

CONCLUDING THOUGHTS

The human infant is born with all of the basic human psychological processes already in place. They exist as discrete mechanisms with an initial organization and an initial capacity to coordinate with each other in changing organizational patterns. Experience with the world results in specific elaborations of these processes and in continual reorganizations. Although biases may exist that result in certain limits or make certain outcomes more probable, nevertheless there remain many degrees of freedom for these elaborations in terms of sequence, particular forms, or even particular endpoints. The developmental course of psychological change will be determined mutually by the infant's own unique set of potentialities and the particular opportunities provided by the people and objects in the infant's environment. It is subject to all of the limitations and biases inherent in the operation of human psychological processes, but within those parameters it is free to develop in any direction experience will take it, for good or for ill.

REFERENCES

Baillargeon, R. (1990, August). *Young infants' physical knowledge.* Paper presented at the 98th Annual Convention of the American Psychological Association Convention, Boston.

Bower, T. G. R. (1974). *Development in infancy.* San Francisco: Freeman.

Bower, T. G. R. (1977). *The perceptual world of the child.* Cambridge, MA: Harvard University Press.

Bower, T. G. R. (1982, March). *The origins of perception and cognition.* Paper presented at the International Conference on Infant Studies, Austin, TX.

Brazelton, T. B. (1973). *Neonatal Behavioral Assessment Scale* (Clinics in Developmental Medicine, No. 50). Philadelphia: Lippincott.

Brazelton, T. B. (1989, December). *Opportunities for identification and intervention in infancy.* Keynote address at the Harvard Graduate School of Education Conference, Cambridge, MA.

Brazelton, T. B., Koslowski, B., & Main, M. (1974). The origins of reciprocity: The early mother-infant interaction. In M. Lewis & L. Rosenblum (Eds.), *The effect of the infant on its caregiver* (pp. 49–76) New York: Wiley.

Brunner, J. (1968). *Processes of cognitive growth: Infancy.* Worcester, MA: Clark University Press.

DeCasper, A. J. (1990, August). *Prenatal influences on newborn's perception and learning.* Paper presented at the 98th Annual Convention of the American Psychological Association Convention, Boston.

DeCasper, A. J., & Carstens, A. A. (1981). Contingencies of stimulation: Effects on learning and emotion in neonates. *Infant Behavior and Development, 4,* 19–35.

Demos, E. V. (1986). Crying in early infancy: An illustration of the motivational function of affect. In T. B. Brazelton & M. Yogman (Eds.), *Affective development in early infancy.* (pp. 39–73). Norwood, NJ: Ablex.

Demos, E. V. (1988). Affect and the development of the self: A new frontier. In A. Goldberg (Ed.), *Frontiers in self psychology: Progress in self psychology* (Vol. 3, pp. 27–53). Hillsdale, NJ: Analytic Press.

Demos, E. V. (1989a). Resiliency in infancy. In T. F. Dugan & R. Coles (Eds.), *The child in our time: Studies in the development of resiliency* (pp. 3–22). New York: Brunner/Mazel.

Demos, E. V. (1989b). A prospective constructionist view of development. *The Annual of Psychoanalysis, 17,* 287–308.

Donaldson, M. (1979). *Children's minds.* New York: Norton.

Ekman, P., & Friesen, W. (1978). *Manual for the facial affect coding system.* Palo Alto, CA: Consulting Psychologists Press.

Ekman, P., Friesen, W., & Levansen, R. W. (1983). Autonomic nervous system activity distinguishes among emotions. *Science, 221,* 1208–1210.

Fairbairn, W. R. D. (1963). Synopsis of an object-relations theory of the personality. *International Journal of Psycho-analysis, 44,* 224–226.

Field, T. M., Woodson, R., Greenberg, R., & Cohen, D. (1982). Discrimination and imitation of facial expressions by neonates. *Science, 218*, 179–181.

Fischer, K. W., & Pipp, S. L. (1984). Processes of cognitive development: optimal level and skill acquisition. In R. J. Sternberg (Ed.), *Mechanisms of cognitive development* (pp. 45–80). New York: Freeman.

Fischer, K. W., Shaver, P. R., & Carnahan, P. (1990). How emotions develop and how they organize development. *Cognition and Emotion, 4*, 81–127.

Freud, S. (1946). The psychoanalytic study of infantile feeding disturbances. In *The psychoanalytic study of the child* (Vol. 2, pp. 119–132). Madison, CT: International Universities Press.

Freud, S. (1955). Beyond the pleasure principle. In J. Strachey (Ed. and Trans.), *The standard edition of the complete psychological works of Sigmund Freud* (Vol. 18, pp. 3–68). London: Hogarth Press. (Original work published 1920)

Freud, S. (1958). Formulation on the two principles of mental functioning. In J. Strachey (Ed. and Trans.), *The standard edition of the complete psychological works of Sigmund Freud* (Vol. 12, pp. 218–226). London: Hogarth Press. (Original work published 1911)

Freud, S. (1966). Project for a scientific psychology. In J. Strachey (Ed. and Trans.), *The standard edition of the complete psychological works of Sigmund Freud* (Vol. 1, pp. 283–387). London: Hogarth Press. (Original work published 1895)

Gibson, E. J. (1969). *Principles of perceptual learning and development.* New York: Appleton-Century-Crofts.

Guntrip, H. (1969). *Schizoid phenomena, object relations and the self.* Madison, CT: International Universities Press.

Holt, R. R. (1967). The development of the primary process: A structural view. In R. R. Holt (Ed.), *Motives and thought: Psychoanalytic essays in honor of David Rapaport* (pp. 344–383). Madison, CT: International Universities Press.

Izard, C. E. (1979). *The maximally discriminative facial movement coding system (MAX).* New York: Plenum Press.

Klein, G. (1976). *Psychoanalytic theory: An exploration of essentials.* Madison, CT: International Universities Press.

Kohut, H. (1977). *The restoration of the self.* Madison, CT: International Universities Press.

Langsdorf, P., Izard, C. E., Rayias, M., & Hembree, E. A. (1983). Interest expression, visual fixation and heart rate changes in 2-8-month-old infants. *Developmental Psychology, 19*(3), 375–386.

Lewkowicz, D. J., & Turkewitz, G. (1980). Cross-modal equivalence in early infancy: Audio-visual intensity matching. *Developmental Psychology, 16*, 597–607.

Lichtenberg, J. (1984). *Psychoanalysis and infant research.* Hillsdale, NJ: Analytic Press.

Mahler, M., Pine, F., & Bergman, A. (1975). *The psychological birth of the human infant.* New York: Basic Books.

Martin, G. B., & Clark, R. D. (1982). Distress crying in neonates: Species and peer specificity. *Developmental Psychology, 18*, 3–9.

Meltzoff, A. N., & Borton, W. (1979). Intermodal matching by human neonates. *Nature, 282*, 403–404.

Noy, P. (1969). A Revision of the psychoanalytic theory of the primary process. *International Journal of Psycho-Analysis, 50*, 155–178.

Oster, H. (1978). Facial expression and affect development. In M. Lewis & L. A. Rosenblum (Eds.), *The development of affect* (pp.43–75). New York: Plenum Press.

Piaget, J. (1967). *Six psychological studies.* New York: Vintage Books.

Piaget, J., & Inhelder, B. (1969). *The psychology of the child.* New York: Basic Books.

Rovee-Collier, C. (1990, August). A conditioning analysis of infant memory. Paper presented at the 98th Annual Convention of the American Psychological Association Convention, Boston.

Ruff, H. (1980). The development of perceptions and recognition of objects. *Child Development, 51*, 981–992.

Sander, L. (1969). Regulation and organization in the early infant-caretaker system. In R. J. Robinson (Ed.), *Brain and early behavior* (Vol. 1, pp. 311–332). New York: Academic Press.

Sander, L. (1975). Infant and caretaking environment: Investigation and conceptualization of adaptive behavior in a system of increasing complexity. In E. J. Anthony (Ed.), *Explorations in Child Psychiatry* (pp. 129–166). New York: Plenum Press.

Sander, L. (1982, May). *The inner experience of the infant: A framework for inference relevant to development of the sense of self.* Paper presented at the 13th Margaret S. Mahler Symposium, Philadelphia.

Sander, L. (1985, January). Toward a logic of organization in psychobiologic development. In H. Klar & L. Siever (Eds.), *Biologic response styles: Clinical implications* (pp. 19–37). Washington, DC: American Psychiatric Press.

Sandler, J., & Sandler, A. (1978). On the development of object relationships and affects. *International Journal of Psycho-Analysis, 59*, 285–296.

Spear, N. E. (1990, August). *What is infantile about the infant rat's memory.* Paper presented at the 98th Annual Convention of the American Psychological Association Convention, Boston.

Spelke, E. S. (1976). Infants' intermodal perception of events. *Cognitive Psychology, 8*, 553–560.

Spelke, E. S. (1979). Perceiving bimodally specified events in infancy. *Developmental Psychology, 15*, 626–636.

Stechler, G., & Kaplan, S. (1980). The development of the self: A psychoanalytic perspective. *Psychoanalystic Study of the Child, 35*, 85–105.

Stern, D. N. (1983). The early development of schemas of self, other, and "self with other." In J. D. Lichtenberg & S. Kaplan (Eds.), *Reflections on self psychology.* (pp. 49–84). Hillsdale, NJ: Analytic Press.

Stern, D. N. (1985). *The interpersonal world of the infant: A view from psychoanalysis and developmental psychology.* New York: Basic Books.

Sutherland, J. D. (1980). The British object relations theorists: Balint, Winnicott, Fairbairn, Guntrip. *Journal of the American Psychoanalytic Association, 28*, 829–859.

Thelen, E. (1984). Learning to walk: Ecological demands and phylogenetic constraints. In L. P. Lipsitt (Ed.), *Advances in infancy research.* (Vol. 3, pp. 213–250). Norwood, NJ: Ablex.

Thelen, E. (1986). Treadmill-elicited stepping in seven-month-old infants. *Child Development, 57*, 1498–1506.

Thelen, E., & Fischer, D. M. (1982). Newborn stepping: An explanation for a "disappearing reflex." *Developmental Psychology, 18*, 760–775.

Thelen, E., Ulrich, B., & Niles, D. (1987). Bilateral coordination in human infants: Stepping on a split-belt treadmill. *Journal of Experimental Psychology: Human Perception and Performance, 13*, 405–410.

Tomkins, S. S. (1962). *Affect, imagery, consciousness: Vol. 1. The positive affects.* New York: Springer.

Tomkins, S. S. (1963). *Affect, imagery, consciousness: Vol. 2. The negative affects.* New York: Springer.

Tomkins, S. S. (1978). Script theory: Differential magnification of affects. In H. E. Howe, Jr., & R. A. Dunstbier (Eds.), *Nebraska Symposium on Motivation* (pp. 201–236). Lincoln: University of Nebraska Press.

Tomkins, S. S. (1981). The quest for primary motives: Biography and autobiography of an idea. *Journal of Personality and Social Psychology, 41*, 306–329.

Tomkins, S. S. (1982, February). *The nature of the self.* Paper presented at Yale University, New Haven, CT.

Tomkins, S. S. (1987). Script theory. In J. Aronoff, A. I. Rabin, & R. A. Zucker (Eds.), *The emergence of personality* (pp. 147–216). New York: Springer.

Tomkins, S. S. (1991). *Affect, imagery, consciousness: Vol. 3. The negative affects anger and fear.* New York: Springer.

Tomkins, S. S. (in press). *Affect, imagery, consciousness: Vol. 4. Cognition.* New York: Springer.

Westen, D. (1990, March). *Cultural, emotional, and unconsious aspects of the self.* Paper presented at Adelphi University Conference, Long Island, New York.

White, R. W. (1959). Motivation reconsidered: The concept of competence. *Psychological Review, 66,* 297–333.

Winnicott, D. W. (1969). The theory of the parent-infant relationship. *International Journal of Psycho-Analysis, 50,* 711–717.

Winnicott, D. W. (1987). *Babies and their mothers.* Edited by C. Winnicott, R. Shepherd, & M. Davis. Reading, MA: Addison-Wesley.

Wolff, P. (1963). Observations on the early development of smiling. In B. M. Foss (Ed.), *Determinants of infant behavior* (Vol. 2, pp. 113–134). London: Methuen.

Wolff, P. (1965). The development of attention in young infants. *Annuals of New York Academic Society, 118,* 815–830.

Wolff, P. (1969). The natural history of crying and other vocalizations in early infancy. In D. M. Foss (Ed.), *Determinants of infant behavior* (Vol. 4, pp. 81–109). London: Methuen.

Wolff, P. (1973). Organization of behavior in the first three months of life. *Association for Research in Nervous and Mental Disorders, 51,* 132–153.

Wolff, P. (1987). *The development of behavioral states and the expression of emotions in early infancy.* Chicago: University of Chicago Press.

9

AFFECTIVE DEVELOPMENT AND EARLY RELATIONSHIPS: CLINICAL IMPLICATIONS

JOY D. OSOFSKY

Clinicians have long used affects as an important part of both understanding and facilitating clinical work. More recently, particularly in the area of infancy, there has been increased interest in the study of emotions as a way to understand what is being communicated in the early parent–infant relationship.[1] In the 19th century, Darwin (1872, 1877) described infant facial, vocal, and gestural expressions, arguing that human expressions of feeling are primarily innate. He noted age-related changes in emotional expressions in infants that have been confirmed by subsequent observers. Darwin's early observations set the stage for our current understanding of emotional expressions.

In this chapter, after reviewing different theoretical perspectives on affect development, two themes will be discussed related to understanding the role of affects or emotions in development. One theme will focus on emotions in the caregiver–infant relationship and as organizers of internal working models of development. A second theme will focus on emotions as the basis for important aspects of reciprocity.

It has been well documented that affects change with age and that certain emotional expressions are present at birth, whereas others develop at a later point (Malatesta, 1989). Discrete emotions theory, emphasizing individual differences in the facial expression of emotions, has focused on emotions such as interest, joy, surprise, sadness, anger, disgust, fear, shame, and guilt (Izard & Malatesta, 1987; Malatesta, 1989). According to this theory, emotions are understood as neurophysiologically based, with much early affective behavior being innate; however,

Some of the research described in this chapter was supported by the Institute of Mental Hygiene, New Orleans, and by Grant MH-39895 from the National Institute of Mental Health, Center for Prevention Programs.

[1]The terms *affect* and *emotion* are used interchangeably in this chapter, as they are for the most part in the literature in this area.

socialization plays a major role in the development of later emotions. The signal properties of the emotions serve as a way for individuals to communicate. These emotions have been recognized cross-culturally and universally, supporting the idea of biological preparedness.

Although not as widely recognized or accepted, another theory of emotional development has been developed by Sroufe (1979), who proposed a differentiation based on early observations of infant affect (see Bridges, 1931; Piaget, 1952; Spitz, 1959). In contrast to discrete emotions theory, Sroufe viewed affects as beginning as undifferentiated precursor states of distress and non-distress and then differentiating into specific emotions over time. Cognition plays an important role in this development, acting as a central mechanism in elaboration and differentiation of the emotions. This theory, although challenging the early differentiation of emotions proposed by discrete emotions theory, does not dramatically change the way in which one can understand the emergence of emotions for the early relationship, a primary concern of this chapter. A very important component of Sroufe's contribution to affect development, however, is its concern with individual differences in personality. Such personality variables relate closely to the concept of attachment (to be discussed later) and influence outcomes in terms of competence and adaptation for the child as well as for the relationship.

The introduction of affectivity as an important influence on the caregiving relationship goes beyond the early observations of Darwin and further elaborations of the work of the discrete emotions theorists to consider a new and broader focus for understanding the development of emotions (Barrett & Campos, 1987; Izard & Malatesta, 1987; Sameroff & Emde, 1989). The infant comes into the world biologically prepared for both self-regulation and interaction (Emde, 1988). Affect is central to this biological preparedness, which is monitored according to pleasure and displeasure and is used to guide caregiver responsiveness. Early theorists viewed affective changes as major indicators of a new level of organization (Spitz, 1959); such shifts have been elaborated by later theorists as providing the incentive for developmental consolidation as well as new ways to engage with caregivers (Emde, Gaensbauer, & Harmon, 1976). Affect is the primary means through which an infant communicates needs and desires to which the caregiver responds empathically or not, the two thus building a relationship. Emde (1983, 1988) has gone further to propose an affective core of self that organizes both meaning and motivation for an infant. This affective core has a central organization that is biological and lends continuity to experience. Emotional signaling provides the basis for the infant's communication of needs and satisfaction, which is very important for both individual development and building relationships.

Trevarthan (1979, 1984), in his careful studies of the expressive behaviors of infants in interaction with their mothers, observed that mother and infant perceived affect in each other and also displayed complementary affective responses in the interaction. Intersubjectivity involves understanding emotions in other people and using emotional expressions to regulate affective interaction. The key function of human emotions, according to Trevarthan, is to regulate the mental representations of interpersonal contacts and relationships. These conceptual ideas, coming out of careful observations of infants in interaction with their mothers, go much further than Darwin's early observations by relating the theory of the evolution of emotions to the role that emotional expression plays both in interaction with others and in building relationships. I review more of the important work that has evolved in this area later in this chapter.

Attachment theory is a good example of how affects can be used to build a relationship. Attachment theory focuses on organizational aspects of behavior, emerging from Bowlby's (1969, 1973, 1980) integration of principles from psychoanalysis and ethology focusing on the infant's attachment to the parent or caregiver. Bowlby proposed that the child's tie to the caregiver is activated by a biologically based, goal-directed motivational system. Attachment behaviors such as crying or smiling are used as signals to the caregiver designed to promote an empathic reciprocal response that leads to a strong "attachment" developing between child and caregiver. More recently, several theorists have gone beyond the initial theoretical propositions to elaborate on the development of internal working models of the caregiver experience that forms the basis for the development of later interpersonal relationships (Bretherton, 1987, 1990).

Much empirical research has been generated by attachment theory following the creative leadership of Mary Ainsworth (1978), who objectified the study of the theory using the "strange situation" paradigm. This structured research method for observing and rating the separations and reunions of the mother and young child has allowed for the categorization of security of attachment into three, and more recently four, categories of behaviors shown by the child. According to the theory and empirical research, a child may be categorized as secure, insecure–avoidant, insecure–resistant, or disorganized (a new distinction coming particularly out of research with high risk samples; see Main & Goldwyn, in press). The attachment process develops as a function of an evolutionary-based preadapted program. The differing emotional profiles have evolved based primarily on the child's responsiveness to the caregiver after experiencing situations of increasing stress (separations). The child's response to separations is assumed to be the result of the quality of the relationship that has developed between the child and the caregiver. More recent research on the attachment relationship has emphasized the importance of not only the earliest emotional relationship but also the mother's past relationships. Main and Goldwyn (in press) have developed an adult attachment interview indicating that there are strong relationships between the mother's reported security of attachment with her mother when she was growing up and her child's current attachment relationship with her. If the mother's earlier relationship was insecure and she did not have the opportunity in her later life to come to a better understanding of that relationship, it appeared to interfere with her ability to build a secure relationship with her child. On the other hand, if she had come to understand the reasons for the insecurity in her earlier relationship, then she was able to facilitate a secure attachment to her child. Thus, there are predictive continuities between a mother's maladaptive experiences with her mother and independently assessed insecure attachment patterns in her own child (Grossman, 1987; Sroufe & Fleeson, 1985). Attachment theory and its variations provide a rich opportunity to understand the importance of affects in the early parent–child relationship.

The role that parents assume in socializing emotions has an effect on the types of affects that the child is capable of expressing, the range and variation of affective expressions, their intensity and duration, the regulation of emotional displays, and the contexts in which emotions are expressed. Furthermore, problems in the socialization of emotions may occur if either the child or the parent experiences problems in their expression of emotions. This is an area of inquiry in need of additional research focusing on precursors and outcomes.

The notion of reframing the infancy experience in terms of the parent–infant relationship harks back to important earlier work based on psychoanalytic object relations theory. Specifically, Winnicott (1965) proposed the idea that "there is no such thing as a baby" referring to the fact that, psychologically, there is only "baby with mother." Classical psychoanalytic theorists have also emphasized the importance of the early parent–infant relationship. Indeed, Freud (1940/1964) referred to the mother-infant relationship as being unique and without parallel, describing it as the prototype of all later love relationships. Hartmann (1950), although continuing to accept classical technique as a primary mode of investigation, believed that for psychoanalysis to be a science, it was crucial that observational methods be used in gathering data and testing theories. Furthermore, he believed that the integration of psychoanalysis with developmental psychology was critical to accomplish these goals. He specifically singled out the earliest periods of development as the ones that are least amenable to standard psychoanalytic modes of inquiry because they are predominantly preverbal, and he again emphasized the importance of observational methods for exploring these periods. The importance of studying affectivity in the relationship, with affects being understood as a primary means of communicating needs and satisfactions as well as providing a sensitive indication of how the relationship was evolving, was added by later theorists.

THE IMPORTANCE OF RECIPROCITY

In reviewing the development of affects for the parent–infant relationship, it is extremely important to consider different theoretical perspectives on the importance of reciprocity in the relationship. Reciprocal relationships between the developing infant and the parent influence both behavioral and affective development. Through the study of affectivity in the early parent–infant relationship, one can understand not only the infant's use of emotions as a primary means of communication but also the degree to which parents exert an influence on infants' overt display, modulation, and control of emotions. In work on emotional matching and mismatching in adolescent mothers and their infants, my colleagues and I observed a changing view of emotional communication and signaling in infancy (Osofsky & Eberhart-Wright, 1988, 1989). Previously, emotions were understood as secondary to drives; however, as has been emphasized above, more recent work has demonstrated their importance for adaptation in the parent–infant relationship (Sameroff & Emde, 1989). Thus, there has been an emphasis on the importance of affective reciprocity for early infant development.

Before reviewing current perspectives on affective reciprocity, it may be instructive to discuss briefly some of the earlier studies. Spitz (1945, 1946), through his clinical observations of infants separated from their mothers in institutions, suggested that a predominance of negative affect and, in severe cases, "anaclitic depression" may accompany disruptions in the early parent–infant relationship. Bowlby (1973) emphasized the importance of early separation and loss as potentially disruptive forces for the development of the relationship. In addition to traumatic events, children may also experience rejecting or overly frustrating events in their families such as abuse or neglect that may lead to defensive exclusion to avoid the pain (Bowlby, 1973, 1980). Both the anaclitically depressed infants whom Spitz has described and the children who have warded off painful affects according to Bowlby's theory have experienced significant problems with the affective reciprocity, which is important for "good enough" psychosocial development. Erikson (1950) wrote of the infant's need to develop "basic trust" in a similar way to the child's need to develop confidence that Benedek (1970) discussed. All of these ideas are closely related to Fraiberg's (1982; Fraiberg & Shapiro, 1975) very sensitive work dealing with disturbed mothers' neurotic patterns of repetitions that occurred as they attempted to parent their infants. She termed these repetitions *ghosts in the nursery*. Similar to Bowlby's observations about the defensive exclusion of painful affects, Fraiberg worked with these mothers psychoanalytically to interrupt the maladaptive patterns.

More recently, several researcher-clinicians have added to the understanding of reciprocity through a combination of empirical work with infants and their families and integration with theory. Stern (1985) discussed the infant forming a representation of a parent–infant relationship that is predictable and dependable. Infants use this "parent representation" to monitor their own behavior in relationship to a parent. As the infant develops more capacities, it is possible to observe a matching of mental states between the infant and the parent as well as both parties' abilities to share feelings. Stern described *affect attunement* as the ability of parents to be resonant with their infants by sharing affectual states. Being able to share emotions is extremely important for affective development because it is the sharing of emotions with the infant that indicates that a feeling state is understood. If the parent is unable to share the infant's affective state, then one may observe a lack of reciprocity in the relationship that can be seen with some frequency in mothers and infants at high psychosocial risk. Over time, this lack of reciprocity in affective sharing may become extremely problematic for the emotional development of the infant.

Another type of reciprocity, *emotional availability*, focuses on the parent's accessibility and capacity for reading the emotional cues and meeting the emotional needs of the infant. Emde (1980) has suggested that emotional availability may be one of the best barometers of how development proceeds in early childhood. Under optimal circumstances, one would expect to see a range of emotions, with a balance of interest and pleasure (positive emotions) between parent and infant. Emotional availability has been illustrated empirically in interesting experiments on social referencing, a form of emotional signaling (Sorce, Emde, Campos, & Klinnert, 1985). In these experiments, an infant encountered through exploration a situation of uncertainty (e.g., a toy robot or an apparent drop-off on a crawling surface). When the infant looked to mother for help in dealing with the uncertainty, he or she signaled fear or anger or signaled joy or interest. In the case of the latter (negative signal), the infant avoided the new situation, whereas in the case of the former (positive signal), the infant approached and explored. Mothers' expressions through either face or voice seemed to have a similar effect on infants' subsequent behavior. Social referencing is an example of a general developmental process that a person uses to gain information from a "significant other" about an uncertain or ambiguous situation. Because uncertainty occurs frequently in the course of development, appropriate emotional signaling may be extremely important to facilitate positive exploration and the development of competent behaviors. A confusing message may, at least temporarily, "derail" this expectable course of development. In risk groups, infants may also show different patterns of social referencing because of differences in the development of an internalized sense of self. They may have difficulty differentiating a healthy sense of self from other because of the unpredictability in their environment (see chapter 8 in this book).

Emde (1990) has emphasized and elaborated the importance of positive emotions for the development of the relationship. Infant affects can serve the dual functions of indicating to an observer the present needs of the infant as well as communicating an understanding of positive and negative features of the parent–infant relationship. With a more responsive, affectively positive parent, greater affective flexibility can be expected in the infant. In contrast, negative or inconsistent affective responses from the parent are more likely to result in fewer positive and more negative affects shown by the infant. Emde (in press) proposed that there is a separate biologically prepared system for positive as compared with negative aspects of the emotional system. Furthermore, he stated that the role of positive affect organization is independent of negative affect organization. This perspective may be important for understanding stress and coping for young mothers and infants in that there is some evidence that positive affective inclinations may be associated with individuals who "steel" or "buffer" themselves during times of stress. The implications for gaining a better understanding of resiliency and invulnerability, especially in risk groups, are important.

Emde (in press) described an interesting phenomenon that occurs toward the end of the first year of life in normative samples that seems to show considerable individual differences. Children of this age tend to look to a significant other and share positive affect (e.g., sharing a smile during exploration or after an accomplishment). Positive affect sharing is a sensitive indicator that all is well with development and the relationship. However, with young mothers and infants in our studies, my colleagues and I (Osofsky & Eberhart-Wright, 1988; Osofsky, Hann, & Peebles, in press) observed less positive and more negative affect than occurred in normative groups. Furthermore, we observed a great deal of nonsharing of affects in the relationship. Thus, the infant may express an affective response to which the mother does not respond—there will not be resonance. Such interactions may place the infant or young child at risk for current and later problems in development and in their developing relationships.

In recent studies, my colleagues and I (Hann, Robinson, Osofsky, & Little, 1990) have examined the influence of the caregiving environment on the display of infant affects. Working with both a risk sample (young mothers and their infants) and a normative sample (older, primiparous married mothers and their infants), we compared affect displays within parent–infant dyads in different environments. The results of these studies are very interesting in light of the theoretical perspective presented above. Infants from the normative sample in a nonstressful situation initially showed a broader range of emotions than did infants from the risk group, with both positive and negative affects occurring with some frequency. In a stressful situation, such as a maternal separation, infants from the normative sample tended to show more positive and fewer negative affects than did infants from the risk sample. The higher incidences of negative affects in the risk group tended to continue even with a decrease in stress. Infants from the risk sample also seemed to show some degree of sadness, which was not observed in the normative group.

In our work with adolescent mothers who tended to react with fewer positive and more negative emotions, my colleagues and I (Osofsky & Eberhart-Wright, 1988, 1992) were concerned about the effect on the relationship. As with problems of affect sharing and attunement, problems in the relationship may develop if one observes limited variability and flexibility in the expression of emotions as well as a dampening of the range of emotions. Concerns for development in this area emerge because of the assumption that important continuities for early and later experience are provided by affective life.

What occurs if a parent is unable to share the infant's affective state, or, even more problematic, if the parent is not only not resonant but contradicts the feelings conveyed by the infant? Sander (1976), based on clinical implications of his work, has emphasized that from a psychoanalytic perspective, a fundamental motivating characteristic of repetition is the seeking of the familiar in a new relationship and the recognition of oneself with the other in that relationship. Through the mechanisms of self-awareness of inner states one recognizes oneself in the context of the other. Thus, one recreates situations for continuity and familiarity with varying degrees of openness to new experiences on the basis of earlier experiences with the parent.

Tronick and colleagues (Tronick, Als, Adamson, Wise, & Brazelton, 1978; Tronick & Granino, 1986) have described a "turning off" phenomenon with a general decreased interest in the environment. In controlled experiments on the short-term effects of depriving the infant of the mother's animated smiling face, they showed that there are profound effects even on the affective displays of 3-month-old infants. When a mother was silent and showed a still face, the infant showed apparent efforts to reengage the mother in animated social interaction. After some time, the experimenters observed more distress in infants with negative affective expressions and withdrawal behaviors. From these data, combined with the Spitz (1945, 1946) and Bowlby (1969) studies on the effects of early deprivation in institutions in which infants suffered severe deficits in social responses, one can conclude that negative emotions and withdrawal appear to be ways that infants cope with discrepant and nonresponsive messages from caregivers. Some recent research findings by my colleagues and me (Carter, Osofsky, & Hann, 1991; Osofsky et al., in press) lend further support to this conclusion. In a sample of 43 adolescent mother–infant dyads evaluated when the infants were 6 and 13 months of age, we hypothesized that reported maternal depression would be negatively related to the intensity of affective signaling behaviors in the infants. The results indicated that infants of depressed mothers showed less intense negative affect than did infants of nondepressed mothers. Infants of mothers who reported more symptoms of depression cried less and showed less anger in a stressful situation. Thus, infants of depressed adolescent mothers may develop maladaptive patterns of affective interaction or a passive coping style as early as the first year of life, becoming less emotionally responsive.

At the extreme, with deprivation or emotionally unavailable parents, infants may display apathy and depression. Recent studies by Wolff and Radke-Yarrow (1987) with children of mothers with a major affective disorder, showed that these mothers were not a source of emotional refueling and enthusiasm (positive emotions) as is characteristic of nondepressed mothers. There were few moments of shared positive affects such as excitement or pleasure; rather, the play proceeded in a boring fashion and eventually petered out. As both researchers and clinicians, psychologists have been concerned about outcomes for infants raised in environments in which there is either no sharing of affects or even disconfirming patterns that contradict some of these important developmental propositions.

Recent investigations of the microinteractions between the infant and parent have begun to elucidate the precise nature of the "dialogue" proposed by Spitz (1964) resulting from the interplay between the psychological structures of infant and parent. On the basis of such observations, Beebe (1986) suggested that the temporal patterning of this "interlocking responsivity" and fine-grained attunement provides the context in which psychic structuralization takes place (see also Stern, 1985). However, similar to Spitz's work, Beebe found that "protodefensive activity" (i.e., withdrawal) occurs when disturbance in this finely tuned reciprocal regulation results in disruptions in the sensorimotor dialogue between infant and parent. Stolorow, Brandchaft, and Atwood (1987) have proposed that

> an absence of steady, attuned responsiveness to the child's affect states leads to minute, but significant, derailments of optimal affect integration and to a propensity to dissociate or disavow affective reactions . . . the child, in other words, becomes vulnerable to self-fragmentation because his [or her] affect states have not been met with the requisite responsiveness for caregiving surround and thus cannot become integrated into the organization of his [or her] self experience. (p. 67)

This agrees with the account of Schwaber (1979).

Affect sharing and affect regulation are also extremely important in the infant's and child's acquisitions of the affective rules inherent to prosocial behaviors, particularly positive affects, empathy, and morality (Emde, 1988). Central to the notion of "good enough" mothering (Bowlby, 1973; Winnicott, 1965) is the ability to be nurturant and emotionally available in response to the cues and needs of the infant. Positive emotions, which are dependent on nurturance in early relationship experiences, are thought to be extremely important mediators of sociability (Demos, 1989; Emde, in press). The smile facilitates bonding and attachment, which add to feelings that all is well with the relationship. Infant affects can serve the dual function of indicating to an observer the present needs of the infant as well as communicating an understanding of positive and negative features of the caregiving relationship. There is now strong evidence that infant affects vary with the quality of the caregiving environment.

For the past 10 years, my colleagues and I have carried out several longitudinal studies of adolescent mothers and their infants, with a focus on the socioemotional development of the infants. Specifically, we have developed observational measures to learn more about the young mothers' uses of emotions in interaction with their infants as well as the infants' display of discrete and reciprocal emotions. Out of these studies, carried out first in the rural midwestern city of Topeka, Kansas (Osofsky, Culp, Eberhart-Wright, & Ware, 1988; Osofsky & Eberhart-Wright, 1988, 1992) and, more recently, in the urban southern city of New Orleans, Louisiana (Osofsky, 1991; Osofsky et al., in press), we have learned and are continuing to learn a great deal about the importance of emotions in early life as well as potential precursors of later problems in development. An example of this work is a recent study (Hann, Robinson, Osofsky, & Little, 1990) comparing affect exchanges of 50 adolescent White, lower socioeconomic status mothers (mean age = 16 years) at psychosocial risk and their 20-month-old infants with 76 adult White, primiparous, lower middle-class and middle-class mothers (mean age = 26 years) at low psychosocial risk and their 20-month-old infants. Significant differences were found between the two groups both in the display of positive and negative affects and in affect sharing. Adult mothers showed significantly higher levels of positive affect and appropriate affect exchanges than did adolescent mothers. In addition, adolescent mothers showed comparably more negative affect and questionable affect exchanges. Variations in socioeconomic status as well as in age accounted for these differences observed between young and older mothers' displays of positive and negative affects and affect exchanges. Nonetheless, we had concerns about the quality of the affective environment provided for the infants of young mothers. The negativity and inconsistency in the affective environment of young mothers increases the risk for their infants' developing difficulties in affect regulation.

There are several other theoretical lines in psychoanalysis that should at least be mentioned in considering affective reciprocity. Kohut (1971, 1977) has postulated that the integration of affect states is crucial for the consolidation of self-esteem and self-confidence. However, a requirement for the child's achievement and consolidation of self–object differentiation is the presence of a "mirroring" parent who, by virtue of having a firmly structured sense of self and other, is able to reliably recognize, affirm, and appreciate the unique qualities and independent striving of the infant or child. Lacan (1977) also discussed "mirroring" in infancy as being important for the normal development of the early parent–infant relationship. Through mirroring, the parent reflects the infant's affective expressions in the context of a caring relationship (e.g., through gesture and emotional expressions as well as vocal "echoing").

Mahler, Pine, and Bergman (1975) have also emphasized parental mirroring of infant behavior as being very important for self-development. When a parent is not secure enough to recognize and affirm central qualities and strivings of the child because they conflict with a need for that child to serve the parent's own needs, then the child may experience disturbances of self as a result of unmirrored grandiosity (Kohut, 1971, 1977). Kohut stressed that disturbances in this area seriously obstruct the process of self–object differentiation because the child may not have the capacity to differentiate and individuate as an independent person. Such integration may be very important in the development of self-soothing capacities that contribute to the development of anxiety tolerance and an overall sense of well-being. The concept of mirroring, however, may not fully take into account the ideas of reciprocity and affect sharing. Mirroring seems to be more of a unidirectional than a bidirectional concept in contrast with the emphasis of the process of affect sharing.

A very recent addition to theory in this area from both research and clinical perspectives is the work of Brazelton and Cramer (1990). Out of their concerns with the "essentials" of early interaction in the parent–infant dialogue, the authors studied the parents' subjective interpretations of their relationships with their children, including imaginary interactions. I review briefly the "essentials" that Brazelton and Cramer identified and how they can lead to the imaginary patterns that are extremely important for the infant's affective development and that my colleagues and I (Osofsky & Eberhart-Wright, 1988; Osofsky et al., in press) have studied in our empirical work. First, Brazelton and Cramer discussed *synchrony*, which involves the parents learning the infant's "language" so that they can synchronize their own states of attention and inattention with those of their infant. Second, they referred to *symmetry*, or the infants' capacity for attention, involving parents' and infants' abilities for both taking in and responding to influence the interaction and their style in doing so. In such a situation, the parent is sensitive to the infant's needs, and both parent and infant are involved in achieving and maintaining a synchronous relationship. Further predictability in the relationship comes from contingency or both the infant's and the parent's abilities to be sensitive to the signaling and timing of the other. The parents' signals are contingent on the infant's state of attention and needs; the infant's capacity to signal is contingent on his or her ability to self-regulate. Finally, after an infant and parent achieve synchrony in their signals and responses, they begin to set up a rhythm with each other to anticipate each others' responses in sequences. This rhythm has been called *entrainment* (Condon & Sander, 1974). To their four interactive dimensions, Brazelton and Cramer have added *play* and *autonomy and flexibility*, both of which involve the appropriate detachment of infant from parent based on the predictability built on the earlier interactive dimensions.

The more mature evolution of the interactive process and relationship building is more problematic in parent–infant pairs for whom there is little emotional predictability. In these cases, the subjective meaning of the infant for the parent may interfere with both the infant's emotional development and the building of the parent–infant relationship. Brazelton and Cramer's (1990) discussion of imaginary interactions includes the infant as "ghost." In these cases, the infant represents for the parent an important person from the past, the relationship reenacts past modes of relationships, and the infant represents a part of the parent's own unconscious. Brazelton and Carmer provided vivid clinical cases illustrating the concerns for these infants at psychosocial risk in problematic relationships similar to those that my colleagues and I (Osofsky & Eberhart-Wright, 1988, 1992; Osofsky et al., in press) have observed in our empirical research. They go beyond the earlier, more unidirectional perspectives of Lacan (1977; mirroring) and the less developmental but related approach of Kohut (1971, 1977) and his colleagues dealing with the importance of empathy in relationships and in the treatment process.

Currently, there have been important developments in the use of this new clinical approach in our field. Cramer and Stern (1988) discussed a single case designed to illustrate how one can objectify interactional variables that may correspond behaviorally with underlying maternal mental representations during the course of representation-oriented brief psychotherapy with mother–infant dyads. They found that in the course of the psychotherapy, changes in the mother's representations affected both the mother–infant relationship and the infant's functioning. Watanabe (1988), following Cramer and Stern's model for mother–infant psychotherapy, has illustrated in a very sensitive presentation such an approach with a Japanese mother–infant dyad. The important cross-cultural parallels and applications of this approach for treating mother–infant dyads are evident in this work.

What does the theoretical and empirical work discussed above mean in terms of early affect development, the development of empathy, and the risk for psychopathology? How can children accomplish the important tasks of emotional development if they do not have the presence of parents who can reliably distinguish, tolerate, and respond appropriately to the child's intense and shifting affect states? Through the parents' responsiveness, the child gradually learns to modulate and contain strong affects. This parent function is similar to Winnicott's (1965) "holding environment" and Bion's (1962) concept of the mother as "container." Identifying correctly and verbalizing the child's early affects is important both to help the child put feelings into words and to integrate affective and cognitive abilities (Stolorow et al., 1987).

Developmental clinicians are often faced with very serious dilemmas when they observe differences from what would be considered to be optimal patterns of interaction. More longitudinal studies are needed with good follow-up data to answer obvious questions about the potential for later psychopathology. However, it is also apparent that researchers need to find ways to institute effective, comprehensive early intervention programs to help these parents and infants "get back on track" as early as possible during the course of development.

REFERENCES

Ainsworth, M. D. S., Blehar, M., Waters, E., & Wall, S. (1978). *Patterns of attachment.* Hillsdale, NJ: Erlbaum.

Barrett, K. J., & Campos, J. (1987). Perspectives on emotional development: II. A functionalist approach to emotions. In J. D. Osofsky (Ed.), *Handbook of infant development* (2nd ed., pp. 555–578). New York: Wiley.

Beebe, B. (1986). Mother-infant mutual influence and the precursors of self and object representations. In J. Masling (Ed.), *Empirical studies of psychoanalytic theories* (Vol. 2, pp. 27–48). Hillsdale, NJ: Analytic Press.

Benedek, T. (1970). Parenthood during the life cycle. In E. J. Anthony & T. Benedek (Eds.), *Parenthood: Its psychology and psychopathology* (pp. 185–206). Boston: Little, Brown.

Bion, W. R. (1962). *Learning from experience.* New York: Basic Books.

Bowlby, J. (1969). *Attachment and loss* (Vol. 1). New York: Basic Books.

Bowlby, J. (1973). *Attachment and loss* (Vol. 2). New York: Basic Books.

Bowlby, J. (1980). *Attachment and loss* (Vol. 3). New York: Basic Books.

Brazelton, T. B., & Cramer, B. G. (1990). *The earliest relationship.* Reading, MA: Addison-Wesley.

Bretherton, I. (1987). New Perspectives on attachment relations: Security, communication and internal working models. In J. D. Osofsky (Ed.), *Handbook of infant development* (2nd ed., pp. 1061–1100). New York: Wiley.

Bretherton, I. (1990). Communication patterns, internal working models and the intergenerational transmission of attachment relationships. *Infant Mental Health Journal, 11,* 237–252.

Bridges, K. M. B. (1931). *The social and emotional development of the preschool child.* London: Kegan Paul, Trench, & Trubner.

Carter, S., Osofsky, J. D., & Hann, D. M. (1991, April). *Maternal depression and affect in adolescent mothers and their infants.* Paper presented at the biennial meeting of the Society for Research in Child Development, Seattle, WA.

Condon, W., & Sander, L. (1974). Synchrony demonstrated between movements of the neonate and adult speech. *Child Development, 45,* 456–462.

Cramer, B., & Stern, D. (1988). Evaluation of changes in mother-infant brief psychotherapy. *Infant Mental Health Journal, 9,* 20–45.

Darwin, C. (1872). *The expression of emotion in animals and man.* London: Methuen.

Darwin, C. (1877). The biographical sketch of an infant. *Mind, 2,* 285–294.

Demos, E. V. (1989). A prospective constructionist view of development. *The Annual of Psychoanalysis, 27,* 287–308.

Emde, R. N. (1980). Emotional availability: A reciprocal reward system for infants and parents with implications for prevention of psychosocial disorders. In P. M. Taylor (Ed.), *Parent-infant relationships* (pp. 87–115). New York: Grune & Stratton.

Emde, R. N. (1983). The prerepresentational self and its affective core. *Psychoanalytic Study of the Child, 38,* 165–192.

Emde, R. N. (1988). Development terminable and interminable: I. Innate and motivational factors from infancy. *International Journal of Psychoanalysis, 69,* 23–42.

Emde, R. N. (1990). Lessons from infancy: New beginnings in a changing world and morality for health. *Infant Mental Health Journal, 11,* 196–212.

Emde, R. N. (in press). Positive emotions for psychoanalytic theory. *Journal of the American Psychoanalytic Association.*

Emde, R. N., Gaensbauer, T., & Harmon, R. J. (1976). Emotional expression in infancy: A biobehavioral study. *Psychological Issues, 10* (37, whole issue).

Erikson, E. (1950). *Childhood and society.* New York: Norton.

Fraiberg, S. (1982). Pathological defenses in infancy. *Psychoanalytic Quarterly, 51,* 612–635.

Fraiberg, S., & Shapiro, V. (1975). Ghosts in the nursery: A psychoanalytic approach to the problems of impaired infant-mother relationships. *Journal of The American Academy of Child Psychiatry, 14*, 387–421.

Freud, S. (1964). An outline of psychoanalysis. In J. Strachey (Ed. and Trans.), *The standard edition of the complete psychological works of Sigmund Freud* (Vol. 23, pp. 141–205). London: Hogarth Press. (Original work published 1940)

Grossman, K. (1987). Maternal attachment representations as related to child-mother attachment patterns and maternal sensitivity and acceptance of her infant. In R. A. Hinde & J. Stevenson-Hinde (Eds.), *Relations between relationships within families* (pp. 241–260). London: Oxford University Press.

Hann, D. M., Robinson, J. D., Osofsky, J. D., & Little, C. (1990, April). *A comparison of emotional availability in two caregiving environments.* Paper presented at the meeting of the International Society of Infant Studies, Montreal, Quebec, Canada.

Hartmann, H. (1950). Psychoanalysis and developmental psychology. *Psychoanalytic Study of the Child, 5,* 7–17.

Izard, C., Malatesta, C. (1987). Perspectives on emotional development: I. Differential emotions theory of early emotional development. In J. D. Osofsky (Ed.), *Handbook of infant development* (2nd ed., pp. 494–554). New York: Wiley.

Kohut, H. (1971). *The analysis of the self.* Madison, CT: International Universities Press.

Kohut, H. (1977). *The restoration of the self.* Madison, CT: International Universities Press.

Lacan, J. (1977). *Ecrits.* New York: Norton.

Mahler, M., Pine, R., & Bergman, A. (1975). *The psychological birth of the human infant: Symbiosis and individuation.* New York: Basic Books.

Main, M., & Goldwyn, R. (in press). Adult attachment classification system. In M. Main (Ed.), *A typology of human attachment organization: Assessed in discourse, drawings, and interviews.* Cambridge, England: Cambridge University Press.

Malatesta, C. Z. (1989). The development of emotion expression during the first two years of life. *Monographs of the Society for Research in Child Development, 54,* (1–2, Serial No. 219).

Osofsky, J. D., Culp, A. M., Eberhart-Wright, A., & Ware, L. M. (1988). *Final report to the Kenworthy Foundation.* Menninger Clinic and Louisiana State University Medical Center.

Osofsky, J. D. (1991). *A preventive intervention program for adolescent mothers and their infants.* Final report to the Institute of Mental Hygiene, New Orleans.

Osofsky, J. D., & Eberhart-Wright, A. (1988). Affective exchanges between high risk mothers and infants. *International Journal of Psychoanalysis, 69,* 221–231.

Osofsky, J. D., & Eberhart-Wright, A. (1992). Risk and protective factors for parents and infants. In G. J. Suci & S. S. Robertson (Eds.), *Future directions in infant development research* (pp. 25–39). New York: Springer-Verlag.

Osofsky, J. D., Hann, D. M., & Peebles, C. D. (in press). Adolescent parenthood: Risks and opportunities for mothers and infants. In C. Zeanah (Ed.), *Handbook of infant mental health.* New York: Guilford Press.

Piaget, J. (1952). *Origins of intelligence in children.* Madison, CT: International Universities Press.

Sameroff, A., & Emde, R. N. (Eds.). (1989). *Relationship disturbances in early childhood: A Developmental Approach.* New York: Basic Books.

Sander, L. (1976). Issues in early mother-infant interaction. In E. Rexford, L. Sander, & T. Shapiro (Eds.), *Infant psychiatry: A new synthesis. (pp. 127–147).* New Haven, CT: Yale University Press.

Schwaber, E. (1979). On the self within the matrix of analytic theory—Some clinical reflections and reconsiderations. *International Journal of Psychoanalysis, 60,* 467–479.

Sorce, J., Emde, R. N., Campos, J., & Klinnert, M. D. (1985). Maternal emotional signaling: Its effect on the visual cliff behavior of 1-year-olds. *Developmental Psychology, 21,* 337–341.

Spitz, R. (1945). Hospitalism: An inquiry into the genesis of psychiatric conditions in early childhood. *Psychoanalytic Study of the Child, 1,* 53–74.

Spitz, R. (1946). Anaclitic depression: An inquiry into the genesis of psychiatric conditions in early childhood II. *Psychoanalytic Study of the Child, 2,* 313–342.

Spitz, R. (1959). A genetic field theory of ego formation: Its implications for pathology. Madison, CT: International Universities Press.

Spitz, R. (1964). The derailment of dialogue: Stimulus overload, action cycles, and the completion gradient. *Journal of the American Psychoanalytic Association, 12,* 752–775.

Sroufe, L. A. (1979). Socioemotional development. In J. D. Osofsky (Ed.), *Handbook of infant development* (pp. 462–516). New York: Wiley.

Sroufe, L. A., & Fleeson, J. (1985). Attachment and the construction of relationships. In W. Hartup & Z. Rubin (Eds.), *The nature and development of relationships.* (pp. 51–71). Hillsdale, NJ: Erlbaum.

Stern, D. (1985). *The interpersonal world of the infant.* New York: Basic Books.

Stolorow, R. D., Brandchaft, B., & Atwood, G. E. (1987). *Psychoanalytic treatment: An intersubjective approach.* Hillsdale, NJ: Analytic Press.

Trevarthan, C. (1979). Communication and cooperation in early infancy: A description of primary inter-subjectivity. In M. Bullowa (Ed.), *Before speech: The beginnings of human communication* (pp. 371–347). Cambridge, England: Cambridge University Press.

Trevarthan, C. (1984). Emotions in infancy: Regulators of contact and relationships with persons. In K. R. Scherer & P. Ekman (Eds.), *Approaches to emotion* (pp. 129–162). Hillsdale, NJ: Erlbaum.

Tronick, E. Z., Als, H., Adamson, L., Wise, S., & Brazelton, T. B. (1978). The infant's response to entrapment between contradictory messages in face to face interaction. *Journal of the American Academy of Child Psychiatry, 17,* 1–13.

Tronick, E. Z., & Gianino, A. F. (1986). The transmission of maternal disturbance to the infant. In E. Z. Tronick & T. M. Field (Eds.), *Maternal depression and infant disturbance* (pp. 5–11). New York: Wiley.

Watanabe, H. (1988, March). *Mother-infant psychotherapy.* Paper presented at the World Association of Infant Psychiatry Pacific Rim Congress, Honolulu, HI.

Winnicott, D. (1965). *The maturational processes and the facilitating environment.* Madison, CT: International Universities Press.

Wolff, D., & Radke-Yarrow, M. (1987). *Play in children of depressed mothers.* Unpublished manuscript, National Institute of Mental Health, Bethesda, MD.

10

THE ETIOLOGY OF BOYHOOD GENDER IDENTITY DISORDER: AN INTEGRATIVE MODEL

SUSAN COATES

Colin is the 3-year-old only son of an upper-middle-class couple who are heavily invested in his creativity and beauty. Colin is an attractive, physically delicate child with blonde hair and blue eyes. He is an intelligent boy, consistently testing in the superior range of intellectual functioning. He is also very sensitive to his surroundings, and he is highly reactive to the affect of others. He does not like rough-and-tumble play, and in new situations he shows none of the boldness that other boys his age often manifest. When Colin was an infant his mother nicknamed him "Peach" because he was "the softest thing I've ever held."

Colin's problem is that he hates himself, wants to be somebody else, and specifically wants to be a girl. Since the age of 2½, Colin has frequently dressed in his mother's clothes, has developed a keen interest in makeup and jewelry, and has spent long periods of time observing himself cross-dressed in front of a mirror. Colin has a strong preference for playing with dolls, his favorite stories are "Snow White," "Rapunzel," and "Alice in Wonderland," and he prefers girls as playmates. He overtly dislikes being a boy; he states emphatically that he was born a girl and that "if you wore girls' clothes you could *really* become a girl."

A diagnostic evaluation revealed that Colin suffered from a *gender identity disorder* (GID), separation anxiety, and symptoms of depression. These latter symptoms were etiologically linked to his cross-gender wishes.

GID in boys represents the extreme end point of a continuum involving imitative behavior; the midpoint would involve the ability to put oneself in the other gender's shoes, so to speak,

---

I am very grateful to John Kerr, Emmanuel Ghent, and Neil Altman for numerous helpful suggestions on an earlier draft of this chapter.

through trial imitations; the opposite extreme endpoint would involve an equally rigid disavowal of any and all such imitation of the behavior of the opposite gender. Boys with GID manifest a predominant interest in behaviors and activities that are typical of girls. The wish to be a girl is enacted in their behavior by a persistent interest in and preference for stereotypically female activities, such as dressing up in girls' clothes, playing with dolls, and taking the role of a woman in play-acting. In a variety of ways, boys with GID express feelings of self-hatred that are sometimes expressed in an overt dislike of and wish to be rid of their penis. The syndrome is defined by its intensiveness, pervasiveness, and duration.

In prospective studies, about two thirds of boys with childhood GID grow up to be homosexual (Green, 1987a; Money & Russo, 1979; Zuger, 1984). Although most homosexual men report gender-role nonconforming behavior as children, only a small subgroup have had a boyhood GID (Friedman, 1988; Saghir & Robins, 1973). Given the present lack of knowledge about the specific multiple factors that predict homosexuality or heterosexuality, for any individual child clinicians are unable to predict sexual orientation on the basis of their knowledge of the individual's early childhood behavior.

In this chapter, I explore the question of how the perspective of psychoanalytic psychology helps to understand the origin of GID in boys. How does GID look through the lens of social learning theory and cognitive developmental theory in contrast to psychoanalytic theory? Is there an area of overlap and is there room for an integration?

BOYHOOD GENDER IDENTITY DISORDER

The following characteristics have been repeatedly observed by systematic observers of boyhood GID.

1. It emerges in a limited time frame during development.

2. It often emerges and consolidates very rapidly, particularly in the context of a traumatic experience.

3. In some cases, it does not appear to emerge in the context of trauma.

4. It is usually associated with other psychopathology such as separation anxiety and symptoms of depression.

5. It typically emerges in the context of family psychopathology.

6. It usually occurs in boys with temperamental characteristics that are similar, such as the avoidance of rough-and-tumble play.

Any theory attempting to understand this disorder must be able to account for these six observations. There have been three theories that have been advanced in the past for explaining the origin of this disorder: the blissful symbiosis imprinting theory of Stoller (1966); the social learning theory of Green (1974); the trauma theory of Bloch (1978), Coates (1985), and Meyer and Dupkin (1985). All three theories of the etiology of boyhood GID were developed before a consensus had emerged on the associated features of this disorder so that when the theories were developed, the authors did not try to account for all six of the features noted above.

All observers of this disorder believe that a biological predisposition lowers the threshold for the disorder, but individual researchers have placed different emphases on the role that this putative biological predisposition plays and on what specific characteristics are involved.

The study of gender disorders began in the late 1950s with the ground-breaking work on hermaphroditism by Money, Hampson, and Hampson (1957) and Money and Ehrhardt (1972) at Johns Hopkins in which it was discovered that parental gender assignment far outweighed biological factors in determining gender identity. This work subsequently became integrated into psychoanalysis through the pioneering work of Stoller on gender disorders and the paraphilias. Much of Stoller's work has been devoted not only to understanding the intrapsychic meanings of these disorders but also to understanding their etiology as well.

STOLLER'S BLISSFUL SYMBIOSIS IMPRINTING THEORY

In 1968, Stoller put forth the first comprehensive theory of the etiology of boyhood gender identity disorder. The term *gender identity disorder* was not yet used and Stoller referred to the boys as having "extreme femininity" (Stoller, 1966, 1968a, 1968b, 1975, 1985a, 1985b). Despite the fact that Stoller was a psychoanalyst, his theory has many similarities to social learning theory in that he viewed the central mutative forces as involving conditioning or imprinting. Stoller (1975) explicitly stated that "extreme femininity" in boys is brought about by "non-traumatic forces" (p. 38). Rather, Stoller (1975) believed that this disorder comes about when a rare coincidence of four factors come together: a bisexual mother, a physically and psychologically absent father who permits the excessive symbiosis to develop and then does not interrupt it, a period of several years in which mother and son can keep up their blissful symbiosis, and a special beauty in the boy (p. 55).

Stoller also believed that the boy does "not seek femininity but rather receives it passively via excessive impingement of the too-loving bodies of their mothers" (1975, p. 54). According to Stoller, this does not involve an active process of identification but a more primitive process such as "conditioning" or "imprinting."

Stoller believed that the disorder emerges in a particular kind of disturbed family in which the mother's wish for a phallus is enacted in creating a blissful symbiosis and in which the father is psychologically unavailable to rescue the boy from the symbiosis. He believed that this wish occurred in women who, as children, wanted for many years to be a boy. As girls, they dressed in boys' clothes, would only play with boys, and avoided contact with female peers. So, although Stoller did not believe that the boy's dynamics are causal in consolidating the disorder, he did think that maternal dynamics play a central role in the way the mother shapes her son.

In Stoller's thinking, such boys do not have a disturbance in ego functioning or even in body ego except in regard to their sense of femaleness. None of the boys show "the slightest evidence of psychosis or precursors of psychosis" (Stoller, 1975, p. 54). Stoller implied that they are well functioning and are "creative, charming, outgoing children . . . whose mothers permit them unhampered opportunity for separation and individuation except around the area of attachment to their mothers' femaleness and femininity" (1975, p. 54).

In Stoller's (1975) theory, the cross-gender wish is not a symptom in that it is not a compromise formation. Stoller's specific developmental thesis is that the bedrock of masculinity is femininity. By this, he meant that the boy first identifies with the mother and with her femininity and must subsequently "dis-identify" with her (Greenson, 1966) and switch his identification to the father in order to develop a masculine identity. In this developmental framework GID is said to occur because of an intensification of an early developmental process ("blissful symbiosis") and a failure of another developmental process to take place (switch of the identification to the father).

Stoller believed that the contribution of biological factors to the disorder involves the son's beauty and his gentle nature, both of which make him vulnerable to the family dynamics that he described.

This theory can encompass the following:

- Cases of gradual onset of the disorder.

- Family psychopathology.

- Its emergence during a limited period during development.

- A role of biology in the risk for developing the disorder.

    This theory does not account for the following:

- Rapid onset in the face of trauma.

- Associated psychopathology in the child.

GREEN'S REINFORCEMENT THEORY

The first systematic prospective controlled study of boys with atypical gender identity was launched by Green (1974). His studies led him to conclude that "femininity" in boys is caused by a succession of interlocking social reinforcing events that he describes as follows: The mother spends time with her son and he begins to imitate her and becomes interested in her possessions as inherently more interesting than the father's possessions. She feels it is cute. She laughs and reinforces it. The father does not object. When the father begins to try to have a relationship with his son, his son rejects him. The boy's early socialization of female skills makes it very difficult for him to become integrated with his peers. He is teased and alienated from his peer group, which further interferes with the consolidation of his masculine identity. Green (1974, p. 238) thought that the one necessary variable to produce this disorder is the absence of any discouragement of feminine behavior by the child's principal caretakers.

The heart of Green's (1974) theory is that reinforcement and lack of discouragement of feminine behavior both causes and perpetuates the disorder. In his system, the cross-gender wish is not a symptom in the sense of a compromise formation. It is not a wish to avoid something else. Green believed that the boy's negative feelings about himself are acquired later on when the boy is rejected by his peers and are not inherently associated with the disorder.

Green (1974) identified an important factor that all observers of this disorder confirm: Once the behavior emerges, it is usually not discouraged, at least initially, by the child's caretaker. Parental acquiescence in the child's behavior undoubtedly plays a major role in perpetuating the disorder but does not indicate why it emerged in the first place. Many boys are raised in single-parent families without developing a GID, and it is not uncommon for mothers of boys, with or without spouses, to have wished that they had had a girl instead of a boy. Furthermore, in the early years of life, most children imitate the behavior of their mothers as well as of their fathers and siblings. Moreover, not only is the phenomena of boys' imitating their mothers common, but it is often responded to with amusement; yet, in most cases, this does not lead to a GID. From Green's perspective, one would have to argue that the reinforcement was more intense and more persistent to bring about the disorder or else that the child was unusually sensitive to it.

In Green's (1987b) most recent communication on etiology, he clarified the case for selective reinforcement by suggesting that the mothers of gender-disordered boys harbor strong wishes that their sons be girls. Such a strong wish in the mother would, of course, differentiate her from an ordinary mother who responded to their son's feminine behavior positively but less strongly. Yet, for the mother's wish to play a major role in precipitating the disorder, one would have to suppose further that she had spent a great deal of time with her child, enough time so that her selective reinforcement could shape his behavioral repertoire. In this respect, Green's latest formulations begin to approximate that of Stoller's (1975) in emphasizing maternal dynamics and in supposing that these affect the child through an intensified interaction of mother and son. Interestingly, however, Green's data seem to run in the opposite direction. Specifically, he found that the mothers of gender-disordered reported spending *less* time with their sons than did mothers of "masculine" boys. This important finding has serious negative implications both for the theory of blissful symbiosis and for Green's (1974) own reinforcement theory insofar as it is used to account for the genesis of the disorder as opposed to its perpetuation.

As for the role of predisposing biological factors, Green (1974), like all observers of this syndrome, found that "feminine" boys avoided rough-and-tumble play. His research findings also confirmed Stoller's (1968a, 1975) observations that the mothers of more feminine boys experienced their sons as more beautiful than the mothers of more masculine boys. In terms of his specific theory, the putative biological factors would lower the threshold for the parental reinforcement to become determinative for the child.

This theory can accommodate the following:

- Why the disorder may arise in cases not involving trauma.

- The role of biological factors in the risk of developing this disorder.

This theory does not account for the following:

- Why the disorder occurs in a limited time span during development.

- Why it is associated with other forms of psychopathology such as separation anxiety and symptoms of depression.

- Why it emerges and consolidates very rapidly in the context of trauma.

- Why it typically emerges in the context of family psychopathology.

TRAUMA THEORY

There are many clinical case reports in which childhood traumata have been reported along with the presence of boyhood GID. The watershed contribution was Bloch's (1978) formulation, developed during her clinical work with 4 children (2 boys and 2 girls), that such traumas were dynamically instrumental in precipitating the disorder. Prior to Bloch (1978), case reports describing traumatic experiences in the child had not explicitly identified such traumata as being critical to the disorder; subsequently, Coates (1985, 1990) and Meyer and Dupkin (1985), in larger, more systematic studies, have also described and elaborated on the etiological role of trauma in the development of GID. Those researchers viewed the onset of GID as often being directly linked to traumatic events and as occurring in the context of severe family psychopathology (Marantz & Coates, 1991; Meyer & Dupkin, 1985). Bloch's (1978) specific thesis in regard to children who insisted that they belonged to the opposite sex was that the trauma involved threats of violence:

> In each instance the child had commenced acting out the fantasy when a specific incident jeopardized his already precarious situation and convinced him that his life was endangered. . . . In all instances, they had been exposed to the actual violence of one parent, so that they had to defend themselves, not merely against the fear, but against the threat of infanticide. (Bloch, 1978, p. 50)

In elaborating on her view of the determining forces, Bloch (1978) argued that the gender-disordered child (a) typically experiences his or her parents as not loving one another, (b) perceives that he or she is actually preferred by the opposite-sex parent, and (c) the same-sex parent is murderously jealous. In the face of the "violent rejecting" same-sex parent, and to save himself or herself from being the target of that parent's "jealous retaliation," the child develops the GID (Bloch, 1978, p. 51). Bloch (1978) believed that the children felt that "the only way to save their lives was to change their sex" (p. 51).

> By creating the fantasy that they really belonged to the sex that they felt was preferred by the threatening parent, they hoped not only to allay that parent's jealous fears, but to transform violence into love. The acted out fantasy of a sexual reversal thus provided a refuge against the fear of being killed by supplying a framework within which it was possible to maintain the hope of eventually being loved (Bloch, 1978, p. 51).

Bloch (1978) further believed that the onset of the symptoms occurred when an "already charged situation was further exacerbated" (p. 51) by an event such as the birth of a sibling or a sexual seduction.

In 1985, Meyer (Meyer & Dupkin, 1985) and Coates (Coates, 1985; Coates & Person, 1985), working in separate units, simultaneously reported on larger samples of boys with GID. Meyer reported on 12 children, 10 of whom were boys, and concluded that in all cases, GID occurred in children who came from disturbed family settings, that the cross-gender behavior occurred in the context of trauma, and that the children showed signs of other psychopathology in addition to atypical gender behavior.

In Coates's (1985) first study of mothers of boys with GID, 45% spontaneously reported that they had had a traumatic experience themselves during the child's first 3 years of life. A subsequent study in which this information was directly elicited in a new sample of 22 mothers showed that 78% of the mothers reported traumatic experiences during the first 3 years of their sons' lives (Coates, Friedman, & Wolfe, 1991). These traumata coincided in most cases with the onset of intense cross-gender behavior in the child and the consolidation of a GID. The following is a list of the traumata that were most frequently reported:

1. Death of the mother.

2. Death of a sibling, especially a female sibling.

3. Miscarriages and abortions.

4. Severe life-threatening illness in the boy.

5. Severe physical illness in a sibling.

6. Physical assault to the mother, including rape.

7. Severe physical injury to a father or close male relative.

8. Life threats to the father.

These traumata led to severe depression, rage, and withdrawal on the part of the mothers. Coates (1985, 1990) put forth the hypothesis that the mothers' withdrawal and rage had a cascade effect on her son, traumatically inducing severe separation anxiety. Coates and Person (1985) argued that, in the face of the mother's precipitous depression, withdrawal, and rage, and in the grip of his own traumatically intensified separation anxiety, the child attempted to restore a tie to the mother in fantasy by imitating mother, in the process "confusing having Mommy with being Mommy."

CHILD AND FAMILY PSYCHOPATHOLOGY

Beginning in the 1970s, Bates and his colleagues (Bates, Bentler, & Thompson, 1973, 1979; Bates, Skilbeck, Smith, & Bentler, 1974) at UCLA studied gender-referred boys and found that they were as behaviorally disturbed as other clinic-referred boys. When compared with other clinic-referred boys, they were rated as being more inhibited and more fearful and their families were described as inhibiting and protective. The Clarke group in Toronto (Bradley, Doering, Zucker, Finegan, & Gonda, 1980) also found that gender-referred children did not differ from psychiatric controls on their scores on the Behavioral Symptoms of the Child Behavior Checklist (CBCL). Using the CBCL, Coates and Person (1985) similarly found that 84% of a sample of 25 boys with GID were as behaviorally disturbed as other children referred to psychiatric clinics. In addition, they found that 60% met the criteria for a diagnosis of a *DSM–III* separation anxiety disorder and that over 50% had symptoms of depression. On projective tests, when compared with normal controls, the boys with GID showed impairments in object relations with representations of women as overpowering, intrusive, and destructive (Coates & Tuber, 1988; Tuber & Coates, 1985, 1989).

Coates (1985) also described disturbances in the mothers of boys with GID. These mothers were more depressed and had more borderline psychopathology, separation anxiety, and depression than mothers of normal controls. Marantz and Coates (1991) subsequently confirmed those observations using systematic measures. Overall, the mothers had difficulties with affect regulation (i.e., in modulating affect and controlling impulses), with interpersonal relations, and in their patterns of mothering, where they were found to discourage autonomy, separation, and individuation. These findings have been further amplified by the systematic research of Wolfe (1990), who found that a preponderance of mothers of boys with GID had anxiety and mood disorders.

Bradley (1985) and Coates (1985) observed that most fathers as well as mothers of boys with GID typically had problems in affect regulation and were often either remote or violent. Bradley, in particular, noted that they had problems with substance abuse. Coates (1985) observed that fathers were unable, in the face of the trauma to the mother, to move in and make up for this loss to the son. The first systematic study of psychopathology in fathers of boys with GID was carried out by Wolfe and Coates (1991). These findings supported previous observations that fathers have difficulties with affect regulation and significant problems with substance abuse.

The concurrent psychopathology in the father observed in the foregoing studies suggests that there may be significant, chronic dysfunction in the family system of boys with GID. Such familial dysfunction can be assimilated to a theory of traumatic etiology for the syndrome in that a dysfunctional family system will be unable to provide a protective factor that might minimize or alleviate the impact of trauma for both the mother and the child. In this regard, Coates (1985) specifically suggested that if the fathers in her sample had been capable of playing a more effective role either as husbands to their wives or as fathers to their son, the specific set of intrapsychic and interpersonal forces subtending the GID syndrome might never have been consolidated.

In evaluating the trauma theory of the ontogenesis of boyhood GID, one should also note the role attributed to the biological predisposition. Coates et al. (1991) assumed that susceptibility both to parental psychopathology and to childhood trauma can be significantly affected by inborn biological factors such as a vulnerability to anxiety, separation, and loss, and unusual sensory sensitivities. However, research has also shown that the presence of early trauma can have a significant effect on temperament in the direction of fostering increased basic fearfulness, withdrawal, and other traits generally thought of as being constitutional (van der Kolk, 1987). In the absence of longitudinal and comparative studies, it remains unclear how much weight to attribute to the two factors, trauma and susceptibility, and it remains equally unclear whether trauma is best conceptualized as reinforcing a basic biological disposition or whether it should be seen, at least in some cases, as instigating a shift in basic disposition.

The trauma theory can account for the following:

- The rapid onset of the disorder.

- Its association with other psychopathology in the child such as separation anxiety.

- Its emergence in the context of family psychopathology (although each of the theorists places a different emphasis on the role of family psychopathology).

- The role of biology in developing this disorder.

It cannot account for the following:

- Why the disorder emerges during a limited time frame during development.

- Why the disorder emerges gradually in some cases.

To summarize, the trauma theory provides a convincing explanation for the rapid onset of the disorder, associated psychopathology in the child, parental psychopathology, and aspects of temperament reflecting a greater vulnerability to the experience of trauma. It does not account for the emergence of the disorder during a limited time frame or for putative cases of a nontraumatic and gradual onset.

Green's (1974) reinforcement theory convincingly takes into account factors perpetuating the disorder in that Green emphasized the parents' lack of discouragement of the boy's cross-gender behavior; his theory also takes into account the gradual onset of the disorder as observed in some cases. His theory cannot explain cases of rapid onset in the face of trauma—in my experience this is the more usual pattern—nor can it explain its emergence in a limited time frame developmentally, for the the associated psychopathology in the child, and the accompanying familial psychopathology.

Stoller's (1975) blissful symbiosis theory can explain the gradual nontraumatic emergence of the disorder, its emergence in the context of family psychopathology, and its onset in a limited developmental time frame. It cannot explain the cases of rapid onset, the emergence of the syndrome on the heels of trauma, or the associated psychopathology in the child.

The fact that each of these theories can account for some of the characteristics of the disorder and not for others suggests that each may be partly correct about etiological forces or partly correct in some cases. This suggests the need for a more comprehensive view of GID in boys that would permit the integration of aspects of these theories into a more detailed and perhaps transformed explanation. Research in this area has proceeded to a point where old paradigms can no longer account for the accumulation of observations that are now available and a paradigm shift (Kuhn, 1962) is necessary for us to account for the complexity of the phenomena observed.

DEVELOPMENTALLY SENSITIVE PERIODS IN COGNITIVE MENTAL REPRESENTATION ABILITIES

Two further considerations deserve attention. The first of these is the element of timing. All observers of this disorder agree that it usually emerges in a limited time frame during the first 3 years of the child's life (Coates, 1985, 1990; Green, 1974; Meyer & Dupkin, 1985; Stoller, 1968a). This raises the question of what is unique about this period as it might relate to gender identity. As I noted earlier, several investigators operating from completely different theoretical frames have observed that the acquisition of gender identity involves a sensitive period during the early years of life (Mahler, Pine, & Bergman, 1975; Kohlberg, 1966; Money et al., 1957). On the embryological level, there is no question that prenatal structuralization of the male and female brain develops during specific critical periods (McEwen, 1983). The question here is whether there is an analogous critical period for the consolidation of the psychic structures governing gender identity.

Studies of the development of gender identity in both biologically normal (Fagot & Leinbach, 1985; Kohlberg, 1966) and in hermaphroditic children (Money & Ehrhardt, 1972) have demonstrated that children's ability to categorize themselves and others in gender terms first emerges at about age 2. Before this age, children are able to differentiate differences in gender, but these differences do not become important to them until they are able to categorize themselves and others by gender. The acquisition of this ability to categorize the self by gender has a significant effect on children's motivation and behavior. Once this differentiation is established, children show a marked increase in a preference for same-sex activities and a preference for same-sex-peers. Fast (1984) persuasively argued that before this age, children's gender identity is undifferentiated despite their ability to observe differences in gender behavior. Children are interested in all activities, both those that are considered stereotypically male and those that are considered female, and it is only after self-categorization by gender has occurred that each gender experiences a loss of the capacity potentially to do or potentially to be everything.

Although children can assign themselves to the correct gender by about 2½ years of age, it will take a few years before gender stability and gender constancy are established. *Gender stability* refers to an understanding that one's gender at birth will remain the same throughout life, that boys start out as boys and grow up to be men. A boy lacking gender stability might believe that he was a female when he was born or that he might grow up to be a woman. *Gender constancy* is a technical term that followers of Piaget use to refer to the child's understanding that external changes in appearance or activity do not change one's gender identity. For example, a boy must learn that even if he changes his physical appearance by putting on a dress or growing long hair, he will still be a boy. A boy lacking in gender constancy might believe that through some external change in appearance or activity he may actually become a girl, not just in fantasy.

Although the achievement of gender constancy and stability usually occur in sequence, they can overlap in development or occur simultaneously. In most children, these differentiations have developed by age 6 (Fagot & Leinbach, 1985). I suggest that the age of 2–3 is a sensitive period for boys at risk to develop GID because they have begun to develop a capacity to categorize by gender (albeit in an overgeneralized and therefore inevitably stereotyped manner) but have not yet developed either gender constancy or gender stability and, accordingly, do not yet possess a stable internalized and differentiated sense of gender.

A further cognitive–developmental contribution to the risk of developing a GID derives from the fact that in the late sensorimotor period of cognitive representational development, the child's thinking is dominated by imitation. For the young child, action or imitation is equivalent to the thought (Piaget, 1962). Thus, for developmental reasons as well as in some cases a temperamental predisposition, imitative capacity is readily available for defensive use.

BIOLOGICAL PREDISPOSITION

The second consideration that must be taken up is the role of biological factors in predisposing certain children to develop a GID. There is now substantial research on the role of prenatal psychoneuroendocrine influences on the development of sexual and nonsexual behavior (Ehrhardt & Meyer-Bahlburg, 1981; Hines, 1982; McEwen, 1983; Ward, 1984). Both human and animal research has shown that prenatal hormones exert an effect on the structural organization of the brain that can influence aspects of temperament but not on gender identity directly. The role of temperament must be understood as predisposing children to respond to environmental stimuli in predictable ways and also to influence their caretakers' behaviors toward them.

Boys with GID have thus far not been identified as having any specific biological marker in that they do not differ from normal boys in hormone levels, in structural morphology, or in karyotyping of sex chromosomes (Green, 1976; Rekers, Crandall, Rosen, & Bentler, 1979). Yet, the suspicion that biological factors play a role in the disorder persists due to certain common behavioral traits found in boys with GID. Specifically, they are timid and fearful, particularly in new situations in which other boys are bold (Green, 1987a; Zuger, 1988); all observers of this disorder believe boys with GID are avoidant of rough-and-tumble play. Other observations have been less consistent. Stoller (1975) noted that they are more physically beautiful. Coates (1990) observed several additional characteristics in a sample of over 130 boys that she has studied in the past decade. They are as follows:

1. A sense of body fragility and vulnerability that expresses itself in avoidance of rough-and-tumble play.

2. Anxiety that expresses itself as timidity and fearfulness in the face of new situations.

3. Strong affiliative needs/intense orientation to people.

4. Extreme sensitivity to affect.

5. A vulnerability to separation and loss.

6. A remarkable ability to imitate.

7. Sensory sensitivities to sound, color, texture, odor, temperature, and pain.

CUMULATIVE RISK FACTORS

I believe that for a GID in boys to consolidate, multiple cumulative risk factors must converge during a critical period of development. In my experience, a critical mass is most often reached after a traumatic event that suddenly renders the mother emotionally unavailable in a household in which the father is also emotionally unavailable. The precipitating event, however, has usually been preceded by chronic family dysfunction and patterns of parenting that have interfered with the child's development of autonomy. The child's heightened sensory sensitivities make him particularly vulnerable to his parents' chronic difficulties in affect regulation, particularly to their withdrawal and rage. The traumatic event exaggerates these difficulties in the child's relations to his parents even further.

Another factor must be taken into account. The critical period for the development of gender constancy fatefully coincides with rapprochement period, during which children are first experimenting with an identity separate from the mother and therefore are particularly vulnerable to experiences of loss and trauma in general.

To summarize, the boy who is likely to develop a GID must be exposed to a critical mass of risk factors converging during a sensitive time frame. In children at older ages who already have an internally structured representation of gender, exposure to the same risk factors may result in a passing cross-gender fantasy, but this does not consolidate into a disorder.

CASE ILLUSTRATION

I attempt to demonstrate with an illustrative case presentation a way of integrating the following five risk factors as a means of understanding the ontogenesis of this disorder in an individual boy. I chose this case because of its clinical presentation as well as the fact that the family associated psychopathology and psychodynamics are typical of the majority of cases that are referred for treatment. The five risk factors are as follows:

- Biological predisposition.

- A sensitive period in the development of mental representations.

- Chronic family psychopathology, including the parents' psychodynamics.

- Trauma.

- The child's psychodynamics.

In any individual child, the relative weight of one of these factors may outweigh the others in bringing about the disorder and therefore lead to a pathway that is somewhat different; these are accordingly multiple pathways whereby different children develop this disorder, although certain commonalities across cases can nonetheless be detected.

Colin's parents, both of whom work for the media in creative capacities, described during intake how Colin's arrival had given them great pleasure. Colin's mother was surprised to discover that she liked being a mother and she particularly enjoyed breastfeeding the baby. Colin was easily drawn to people even as an infant; as Mrs. S. put it, he would just "drink in" the world around him. Indeed, so satisfying was the early relationship between mother and son that when Colin was weaned at 8 months of age—he had begun to bite his mother's nipples—Mrs. S. felt that while he was ready to stop nursing, *she* was not.

Colin's arrival significantly altered the dynamics of the family. During the immediate postpartum phase, Mr. S., who had been involved during the pregnancy, began to feel unimportant and withdrew. Mr. S. was a man who had chronic anxieties about his own sense of masculinity, dating back to childhood and adolescence, and he was surprised to discover how left out he felt while Colin was breastfeeding. Moreover, he now began to experience episodes of intense and seemingly inexplicable rage, during which he would become destructive of property; these episodes continued at the rate of about four or five episodes a year right up to the time Colin was referred for treatment.

Mrs. S., meanwhile, was having significant troubles of her own. Her own mother, an embittered woman who had never fully recovered psychologically from a miscarriage she had had when Mrs. S. was 2 years old, moved into the same apartment building, ostensibly to assist in Colin's care. But Mrs. S. experienced her mother's assistance as hypercritical, intrusive, and undermining, and there were daily explosions between the two women. Underneath the turmoil lay interlocking unconscious dynamics between the two women dating back to the miscarriage. It centered around issues of who had damaged whom and who owed the other reparation. At the same time, Mrs. S. also felt abandoned by her husband. She had married him because she felt he was a "nurturant" man—this image as well as a contrasting image of men as aggressive and potentially violent stemmed from her childhood experiences with her own father—and now that he withdrew, she felt angry and abandoned.

For his part, Mr. S. distanced himself not only from his wife but from his son as well. His chief preoccupation as a parent, which was in line with his preexisting anxieties about being masculine, was that Colin should develop a sense of his own "power." What this meant in practice, however, was that Mr. S. would not interfere in Colin's activities even when these began to become troubled.

Despite the turmoil in the household, Colin seemed to develop normally during the first year of life. He had many of the sensory sensitivities that are typical of gifted children but have also been noted in children with emotional disturbances (Bergman & Escalona, 1949; Weil,

1970). For example, he would cry when he heard loud sounds such as the door bell. His sensitivity, however, gave him pleasure as well. He enjoyed music and pretty colors and was very attentive to even small visual changes in his environment. Mrs. S. remembers Colin at age 1 as a "laughing baby" who was loving and "always happy." At age 2, when Colin was interviewed for a nursery school program for mothers and children, Mrs. S. remembers how emotionally connected he was to the interviewer and how much he seemed to enjoy the teacher's attention.

Thus far, two of the known risk factors that can produce a GID were present in Colin's case: a temperamental disposition in the child and parental psychopathology. Concerning the latter, it should be noted that key issues for the parents were feelings of loss and abandonment on the one hand and seemingly uncontrollable anger and aggression on the other. Moreover, although I cannot describe these dynamics in any greater depth here, both these themes were organized around issues of gender for both parents.

Although one does not see the great dynamic specificity that Bloch (1978) postulated here (i.e., jealous, murderous rage from the opposite-sex parent against which the child defends himself by magically changing his gender), it is not difficult to imagine that as Colin became more difficult to manage, his parents' difficulties in managing anger, his and their own, were subliminally colored by fantasies having to do with gender. One should also note Mrs. S.'s reaction to the first 8 months of life, when breastfeeding gave her pleasure, comfort, and a sense of having repaired both herself and, magically, her mother too. (Colin's role in this regard continued unabated thereafter. During the initial intake, Mrs. S. spoke of how Colin had filled a void in his grandmother's life: "She has nothing to live for. Colin is her only reason for living.") Although one might argue that Mrs. S.'s feelings during these first 8 months, and possibly Colin's as well, could be described as "blissful," Stoller (1975) was very explicit in making the point that he was not talking about an early blissful stage during the first 6 months of life that occurs with many mothers and babies, but a protracted "blissful symbiosis" that goes on for several years uninterrupted. That said, one should also note that in Colin's case, the early "blissful" period had been successfully if ambivalently terminated without any apparent sequellae.

Colin's GID developed only in the context of three additional risk factors. One of these was developmental in nature. Although I lack specific data on this from the parents, it can be assumed in light of Colin's intelligence and general precocity that by his second birthday, he had reached the stage where he was able to classify himself and others by gender. However, he was still too young to have developed gender constancy and stability. This period fatefully coincides with the height of the rapprochement crisis during which children are very sensitive to the issue of loss. This sensitivity can be further aggravated by the blow to the child's omnipotence that occurs when a child realizes that he or she belongs to one gender category and therefore can no longer be all things (Fast, 1984). Significantly, this was also a time when Colin first seemed to have become sensitized to issues of loss and abandonment due to an external event. Shortly after Colin's second birthday, his father and his grandmother both left for a trip abroad. During their absence, as mother reported, "Colin became inconsolable and cried until his father and grandmother returned." Mother, too, became angry and depressed, although later these feelings were suppressed and could be elicited from her only with detailed questioning.

Both parents agree that Colin's behavior changed at this point in time: He became both more anxious and extremely sensitive to all separations. The change became magnified when he began attending nursery school the following fall. Mrs. S. remembers that Colin seemed very shy and had difficulty adapting. He did not get along with the other children and would hit them if he did not get his way, or else he would scowl, cross his arms, and turn his face to the wall.

At this time, he also began to have temper tantrums at home, a new behavior for him and one that exacerbated parental anxieties about controlling anger and aggression.

The change in Colin's behavior shortly after he turned 2 deserves further comment. First, it should be noted that the temporary absence of his father and grandmother, coupled with his mother's own sense of having been abandoned, constituted a trauma for Colin, one that specifically sensitized him in the direction of greatly increasing his separation anxiety. This traumatically induced anxiety, in turn, seems to have exacerbated certain innate trends toward sensitivity that were part of his basic endowment. Colin had moved from being an unusually sensitive child to being an unusually oversensitive one. Then, too, one should note that as one consequence, Colin began to develop significant difficulties in relating to his peers. He would not play unless he totally got his way. He did not know how to take turns and had to be the boss of the game. In fact, it was those difficulties in adjusting to the nursery school environment that ultimately led to Colin's being evaluated. What needs to be noted here, however, is that Colin's social difficulties both reflected his having been initially traumatized and preceded any sign of his GID. In Colin, the difficulties with self-esteem and peer relations were not the effect of his GID, as Green (1974) supposed, but existed prior to it and reflected the precariousness of his overall adjustment.

In short, at the age of $2\frac{1}{4}$ years, the fourth risk factor, emotional disorder, was present. Colin was already a child in trouble, even if he had not yet developed a focal disorder based around gender. For that to happen, a fifth risk factor was also required, an additional trauma, one that would massively increase his already heightened separation anxiety. It came in the wake of his difficulties in nursery school.

His mother, concerned that Colin was too isolated from his peers, decided to have a second child "to provide Colin with companionship." Mrs. S. also remembered her pleasure when Colin was an infant and was eager to repeat that experience. However, this time her pregnancy went quite differently. It ended in tragedy: amniocentesis led to the fetal diagnosis of Down's syndrome. With her husband's agreement, Mrs. S. decided to abort the pregnancy, but on medical advice, she delayed the abortion for 3 weeks. Having also discovered through the amniocentesis that the child was a girl, Mrs. S. named the fetus "Miriam" after a revered teacher and she felt elated when she thought she experienced the fetus kicking. Ever after, she felt grateful for the 3-week delay before the abortion because this allowed her "to get to know 'Miriam.'" Notably, although her husband experienced a grief reaction following the abortion, Mrs. S. did not. Thus, while he wept relating the experience during intake, she related to the tragedy without any sign of affect. Although she has felt chronically depressed and anxious ever since, Mrs. S. did not connect these feelings to the loss of "Miriam," whose ashes continued to reside in an urn in her bedroom closet.

Colin's cross-gender behavior began within weeks after the abortion, and it rapidly assumed the driven quality characteristic of children with the full syndrome of GID. Both parents had artistic interests and viewed his cross-gender interests as part of his artistic and creative nature and did not make any efforts to limit the behavior. Mr. S. did feel somewhat uneasy about his son's preference for female attire and activities, but he did not redirect it because he believed that it was temporary and that Colin would outgrow it. In keeping with his general policy of nonintervention, he saw it as a creative expression and he did not want to thwart Colin's sense of his own "power." For her part, Mrs. S. did not identify Colin's gender preferences as a matter of concern in any way. Neither parent was aware of any possible "cause" of Colin's behavior. It appeared to emerge de novo.

The reactions of Colin's parents were typical for the syndrome. The parents implicitly supported Colin's symptomatic behavior, with the mother being more bland and complacent in her denial than the father, and conversely they did nothing to interfere with it. Indeed, they did not even see it as a problem; Colin's referral to treatment had been predicated on his difficulties adjusting at nursery school, not his cross-gender behavior. In this respect, both parents did indeed conform to Green's social learning hypothesis, although that is far from the whole story. Indeed, were the parents' account taken at face value, not only would the interfamilial dynamics have been completely obscured, but the pattern of onset would have been misrepresented. Colin was initially described by his parents as having been one of those relatively infrequent cases in whom the GID arose only gradually when in fact the disorder had arisen quite rapidly and in response to a clear precipitant. In effect, Mrs. S.'s denial of her own trauma, coupled with her husband's emotional detachment from her suffering, had created a lacuna in both parents' perception of what was happening in their child. This lacuna, moreover, extended not only to the onset of the condition but also, more profoundly, to the terrible distress that Colin was suffering as a result. His cross-gender behavior was not an ego-syntonic or conflict-free activity, even less was it an "artistic" expression; in fact, it was quickly evident after viewing the family videotapes and from Colin's behavior in treatment that it represented a defensive organization that was exhausting his creative capacities in a repetitive, compulsive, and altogether joyless attempt to escape intolerable anxiety.

Some of the idea of the depth of Colin's pain—it would be almost 2 years before he could reveal it more fully in his therapy—can be gleaned from his behavior in his initial interview. Colin was eager to talk, was uninterested in toys, and despite being only 3 years old behaved like a compliant adult eager to be interviewed. Throughout the interview, he seemed riveted to our faces as if he were intensely studying every expression. Of particular note was his expressed preoccupation with "ladies with angry eyes." He talked about how afraid he was of a girl in his class who had angry eyes and, with obvious emotional pressure informing the performance, he proceeded to imitate her for us. In studying the family's home videotapes, we also discovered that he would cross-dress in front of a mirror and make the same "angry eyes" that he demonstrated to us in our initial interview. Before the mirror, he would pause and study his own angry face as if he were trying to metabolize something he could not comprehend (Ghent, 1990).

Just as the blissful symbiosis theory fails to capture Colin's emotional turmoil, it also does not accurately reflect the ongoing struggle between mother and son. At approximately the same time as the GID emerged, Colin began having intensified temper tantrums at home, but these only exacerbated his mother's sense that aggressive impulses were both difficult to control and, in males, a precursor of abandonment. She viewed Colin's tantrums in terms of his abandoning her, as a loss of his previously adoring behavior, which, in turn, was reminiscent of how she had experienced his biting her nipples at the age of 8 months. It was only after years of therapy that she was able to remember how strongly she would censure these outbursts by the boy. She would shake Colin and yell at him full-face. In therapy she recalled that while shaking him she would "look into his eyes and realize that he was afraid that I might kill him." She began to feel threatened that her rage was turning both her son and herself into "monsters" and she feared that she might "destroy" Colin.

In short, here is a boy and his mother in the grip of intense anger, hatred, and fear, the emotional residue of which was visibly leaking out from behind the mask of Colin's seemingly unconflicted cross-gender behavior. As well, here is a boy who is otherwise manifestly symptomatic, with temper tantrums, immaturity, and poor peer relations. I must return again to Stoller's (1975) thesis of blissful symbiosis. At the time Colin's gender disorder began, he and his mother were anything but blissfully symbiotic. And, as with Colin, so with all other boys observed so far; the fact is that no other researcher has been able to confirm the blissful symbiosis theory. The reason for emphasizing this fact is not so much to criticize Stoller, but because, only partly because of his work, there has come into currency a widespread misconception about GID children that they are basically okay and that their relations with their mothers are not troubled. It is this misconception that needs to be changed.

How did the "blissful symbiosis" theory originate if it cannot be confirmed? Stoller's (1968a) theory was based on his treatment of three mothers of boys with GID. He was not a child psychiatrist and other therapists treated the children. It is possible, indeed likely, that what Stoller observed was the revival of the mothers' fantasies about their relationships with their sons, fantasies that may have reflected an earlier developmental period while being replete with other meanings and that were then enforced on the son via projective identification. Certainly, such a formulation would have applied to Colin's mother. After her abortion, she became determined not only to keep her fantasized daughter "Miriam" alive but to do so in a way that both restored her sense of herself as a mother and repaired her inner sense of her own damaged mother. Indeed, in moments she experienced Colin as the idealized nurturant mother for whom she longed. This involved not only a revival of the period before weaning when he had been nick-named "Peach" because he was "the softest thing I ever held," but also an adaptation of that relationship to her own needs of the moment, as she attempted to manage her feelings following the abortion. Thus, Mrs. S. now came to experience Colin's general sensitivity as selectively attuned to herself: "He was always tuned into my feelings. He always knew how I felt." She began to call him by a new name, "Lovey," and took a new delight in his "artistic" talents, which now included cross-dressing.

Three points need to be stressed here. First, Mrs. S.'s selective reinforcement of Colin's new cross-gender identity reflected her own internal splits as they applied to gender. Thus, she sought to transform him subtly into the nurturant mother–Miriam figure she felt she had lost while negatively reinforcing aspects of his masculine assertive and aggressive behavior. Intrapsychically, she developed a fantasy fusion with a nurturant, maternal "Lovey" as a means of reclaiming her lost internal tie to her mother. Simultaneously, she restored her internal tie to the sensitive aspects of her father. By preventing her son from becoming "too rambunctious" or too aggressive, she avoided reexperiencing the dissociated rage that she felt toward her father for his physical abuse and his subsequent abandonment of her. In all this, Mrs. S. was exerting a tremendously powerful influence on her son.

Second, by means of this impact on her son, Mrs. S. was managing her own enormous depression in the wake of the abortion. In this sense, Colin's becoming a little girl "worked" for her—it mitigated her anxiety and depression, which indeed could now go unfelt. Conversely, Colin's being a little boy did not "work" for Mrs. S. Insofar as he might resist her attributions, she was thrown back on to her turmoil, for which she lacked the inner resources to manage and from which her husband had already distanced himself. But that situation for Colin was even more intolerable; already highly sensitized to the threat of separation, Colin simply could not tolerate losing his mother to her own withdrawn depression.

Third, Colin's vulnerability to his mother's projection identification was predicated on his special interpersonal sensitivity and his traumatically heightened fear of abandonment. His need to keep his mother available to himself was the organizing motivation for his self-fusion fantasy. It is important to bear in mind here that such traumatically increased separation anxiety occurring during the rapprochement crisis when both the child's self-representation and sense of emotional object constancy are still quite fragile constitutes the most dire of psychological threats. In essence, the child is faced with a fear that can best be described as annihilation panic. Psychologically, it is an emergency situation, like being caught in a burning house or having an abyss open beneath one's feet; the child must take immediate steps or face annihilation. Moreover, thereafter the child will need to take precautions to avoid any and all situations that threaten a recurrence of this degree of anxiety. In point of fact, in the initial stage of his treatment, Colin was far more concerned with issues of object permanence than with gender themes. At the beginning of each session, he would study the room to see what had changed and whether everything was still in place. When his concerns in this area were aroused, he would then respond by initiating doll play—ritually stroking Barbie's hair was one recurrent device—in an attempt to soothe himself. Issues concerning loss and aggression were problematic for Colin, and when they arose, he would typically respond by intensifying his feminine identification. For example, when confronted with a separation, at the end of sessions, he would destroy clay figures of boys that he had constructed during the session and would replace them with one of a girl. For Colin, as for his mother, aggression was functionally equivalent to abandonment (for a more detailed account of this case, see Coates et al., 1991).

The fact that Colin's GID and his mother's unfaced trauma were inextricably linked with one another has important therapeutic ramifications. Although I do not discuss Colin's treatment here (but see Coates & Wolfe, 1992), it is worth noting that a key feature in his treatment was that in addition to initiating therapy with Colin, it was also possible, with a separate therapist, to engage the mother around issues relating to her own trauma. By providing a protective, therapeutic space for the mother that would contain her own pain, it became possible both to engage her directly at a deep emotional level and to send an important signal to Colin that he had space to begin to individuate in his own treatment and that someone else would be taking care of his mother. I mention this here because in so many cases of boyhood GID, it is difficult to keep the case in treatment long enough to have a significant impact. It took almost 2 years before Colin could fully symbolize for himself the dynamics involved in his disorder and thus begin to handle the issues in fantasy as opposed to overt behavior. I and my colleagues have found that engaging the traumatized parent in collateral treatment directly around his or her own issues that are fueling the boy's GID can significantly help reduce the frequency of premature termination as well as facilitate the treatment of the child. Conversely, when the traumatized parent is the mother, excluding her from treatment in an effort to get the father more involved is likely to be counterproductive because it will only heighten the child's anxiety about separation.

In summary, in Colin's case, one sees each of the five identified risk factors: (a) biological predisposition, (b) a sensitive period developmentally, (c) trauma, (d) parental psychopathology and psychodynamics, and (e) child's psychodynamics. Colin's case is typical in terms of the etiology of many cases of boyhood GID, and both he and his parents exhibit a great number of correlative features including many that have previously been discussed in the literature. Indeed, perhaps the only feature of Colin's case that was atypical, putting to one side those cases in which the syndrome does indeed emerge gradually, is that he did not show an aversive reaction to his penis; most boys with GID do. This was perhaps due to the fact that his treatment began when he was still only 3 years old and therefore had not yet begun to think of his penis as an emblem of his gender identity.

THE UNIQUE CONTRIBUTION OF A PSYCHOANALYTIC PERSPECTIVE

I have tried to demonstrate that a disorder as complex as a GID comes about when a critical mass is reached involving the interplay of multiple risk factors operating simultaneously during a sensitive period in development. No single explanatory hypothesis, neither temperament, nor reinforcement, nor trauma, nor cognitive developmental level, can by itself adequately account for the complexity of the clinical phenomena that are presented in this disorder. Rather, it is only by combining and integrating findings culled from a variety of researchers working in different disciplines that one begins to approach a satisfactory etiological model. Here I should mention that the model presented in this chapter is incomplete in at least one important respect:

I have not discussed cases in which the disorder does indeed arise gradually. I should also note that much remains to be clarified about the specific ways that the multiple factors interlock both additively and synergistically. I believe that there are multiple roots to the development of this disorder that will depend on the relative weights of the risk factors in combination with each other. When there is less of one factor, there will need to be more of another factor to bring about the disorder. The specification of these multiple pathways is part of the task of future researchers.

Is one left, then, with the familiar scientific moral that interdisciplinary approaches are usually best? In a sense, the answer is yes. However, I would make a special plea for the potentially pivotal role of psychoanalytic theory in the construction of such multidisciplinary etiological models. For in understanding a phenomenon, it is not sufficient merely to list risk factors and hope that the reader can somehow compound them into an explanation through some sort of rudimentary and largely unconscious factor analysis of her or his own devising. To the contrary, it is necessary to show how the different risk factors fit together, to see what comes first, what second, and so forth, and how they all interact in highly specific ways. And, for this, one must necessarily have some theory of personality structure and how it evolves. Ultimately, it is only through the medium of the personality structure that the risk factors become organized in an enduring pattern of behavior.

Psychoanalytic theory, with its focus on how people create meanings, potentially offers a uniquely valuable window on the development of pathological behaviors, most especially those such as GID, which involve fantasy enactments and fantasy solutions. In this respect, psychoanalytic theory has the advantage over other personality theories inasmuch as it focuses directly on the point of transition from the external to the internal world and on the mechanisms that govern how pathological beliefs encode aspects of lived interpersonal experience and are then used to construct psychic reality. Moreover, the accompanying emphasis on the patient as both actor and inventor of his or her own universe of meaning is no mere theoretical nicety, no fine point that, although true, can be safely disregarded for practical purposes. To the contrary, as I now attempt to show, just this point of departure is necessary for understanding two of the central aspects of GID: its relative intractability and its resistance to a behavioral form of treatment.

To summarize the case that I have presented here from a psychoanalytic perspective, many factors had to come together in a sensitive time frame to create the fertile ground for Colin to develop a fantasized fusion of himself with his mother that then led to his enacting the wish to become a girl. First his temperament made him more vulnerable to separation anxiety and more reactive to his parents' difficulty in managing their aggression. When it was compounded by the significant stress created by his dysfunctional family, his temperament led further to his developing an anxious attachment to his mother. This pattern of anxious attachment was in place before the trauma occurred that precipitated his GID. The fact that his mother's withdrawal and rage occurred during the height of the rapprochement crisis before gender constancy had been established compounded the problem further. First, it added fuel to a developmental crisis that usually creates a period of separation anxiety even in children of families that are not dysfunctional. Second, cross-gender fantasies were more readily available to Colin because he had not yet established gender constancy. Upon his mother's precipitous withdrawal following her abortion, the intensity of his separation anxiety reached traumatic levels. He was experiencing emergency emotions and needed to create emergency defenses to alleviate his impending sense of panic.

Colin's cross-gender behavior should first be understood as his attempt to manage his overwhelming anxiety. Specifically, by becoming a girl at a time when both his self-representation as a separate person and his sense of gender were still quite fragile, he was in effect instituting a fantasy of being fused with his mother. By being mommy, he no longer needed to fear losing her. However, the cross-gender behavior was also successful in yet another direction as well. For the mother's oscillation between withdrawal in the face of Colin's spontaneous expression of his own needs and wishes and her rageful attempts to enforce her own expectations on him when she did interact with him had created an altogether unworkable mother–child relationship. In this context, the emergence of Colin's cross-gender behavior was like a balm on troubled waters. In his own way, Colin had correctly assessed what was troubling his mother and had taken steps to alleviate the problem. To be sure, his solution was in some ways forced on him. That is to say, his mother's oscillation between withdrawal and angry attempts to force her own expectations on Colin had given this unusually sensitive child little choice but to become even more attuned to her desires; the interpersonal field was ripe for him to become vulnerable to her projective identifications. Yet, one must also take into account the delicacy and the accuracy of Colin's judgment. He had come to sense that he had lost his mother as a "good enough" mother in Winnicott's (1956/1975) sense because she had lost her daughter, but he also may have sensed in moments that she wished he was a girl. Accordingly, as was eventually revealed in his treatment, Colin's cross-gender behavior was imbued with the additional meaning of giving his mother the girl she longed for and thus repairing her depression.

The invented compromise formation of "becoming a girl" lowered Colin's own anxiety and protected his mother from having to face her own trauma full force. Thus, he both protected himself and altruistically sacrificed his needs and strivings to protect his mother. In developing his cross-gender behavior, he drew on the cognitive skills available to him and on his experience to make inferences that led him to believe that if his mother had a girl, she would no longer be depressed and would emotionally return to him. Ultimately, it was *his* invention to become a girl. Once he enacted the fantasy, it decreased his anxiety as well as his mother's. Thus, the behavioral enactments of the self-fusion fantasy with the mother became powerfully self-reinforcing because they succeeded in internally reducing his anxiety while simultaneously repairing his mother. Now Colin could better tolerate his separation anxiety without resorting to external reassurances from his mother or another caretaker to lower his anxiety. To a certain degree, he could now "manage" his anxiety on his own while simultaneously reassuring himself that his mother was more stabilized. The contribution that the cross-gender fantasy makes to the child's ability to manage traumatic levels of anxiety, I believe, is the major reason why GID seems to be so entrenched once it has developed, not simply because it is reinforced by the child's parents.

The foregoing analysis also explains why any simple behavioral treatment of this disorder cannot succeed. By the time children have been referred to me and my colleagues, therapists and parents have often tried to eliminate cross-gender behavior with behavioral interventions. Although such interventions often succeed in extinguishing the child's overt cross-gender behavior, the determined effort to be a girl most often continues in the boy's fantasy life. In my experience, not until both the child and the parents are able to work through the traumatic experiences that fueled the symptom in the first place can alternative, more flexible, and age-appropriate defenses be developed for handling separation anxiety.

I believe that the goal of treatment should be the restoration of the child's right to be and not the elimination of cross-gender fantasies per se. Our goal is to help the child out of an obligatory identification and compliance and to create psychological space for his own authentic individual development. We do not view cross-gender fantasies as a problem when they are not relied upon in a compulsive and addictive way. These fantasies can be useful in helping one to empathically understand the point of view of the other gender.

Let me close by saying that we have found that successful treatment of GID must address each of the etiological threads that are involved in both precipitating and perpetuating the disorder. Thus it is not surprising that the treatment is lengthy, difficult, and fraught with complications. The intricate interconnections between family pathology and the child's dynamics require a treatment strategy that is sophisticated, flexible, and highly individualized and for this reason it is important that therapists who treat these children have specific preparation in the treatment of this disorder. In this chapter, I have concentrated on presenting an integrated model of the etiology of the syndrome of GID; elsewhere (see Coates & Wolfe, 1992), I report on its treatment.

The case of Colin illustrates the multiple cumulative risk factors involved in the development of a typical case of GID. One of the important next steps in research on GID is to integrate this work with research on the development of attachment. An adequate understanding of this disorder will only be possible by combining systematic developmental longitudinal research that includes cognitive and social reinforcement models, knowledge of the biological roots of temperament, and an in-depth understanding of the meaning-making system of the child and parents that emerges from psychoanalytic psychotherapy. These different approaches are ultimately complementary to one another. Only with an integrative model can a truly comprehensive and specific understanding of this disorder become possible.

Finally, an understanding of GID at this level of complexity will provide us with the knowledge that can create a specific and effective psychotherapeutic intervention that will restore the damaged self of both the child and his parents.

REFERENCES

Bates, J. E., Bentler, P. M., & Thompson, S. K. (1973). Measurement of deviant gender development in boys. *Child Development, 44,* 591–598.

Bates, J. E., Bentler, P. M., & Thompson, S. K. (1979). Gender deviant boys compared with normal and clinical control boys. *Journal of Abnormal Child Psychology, 7,* 243–259.

Bates, J. E., Skilbeck, W. M., Smith, K. V. R., & Bentler, P. M. (1974). Gender role abnormalities in boys: An analysis of clinical ratings. *Journal of Abnormal Child Psychology, 2,* 1–16.

Bergman, P., & Escalona, S. K. (1949). Unusual sensitivities in very young children. *Psychoanalytic Study of the Child, 3–4,* 333–352.

Bloch, D. (1978). Four children who insisted they belonged to the opposite sex. In: *"So the witch won't eat me": Fantasy and the child's fear of infanticide* (pp. 50–70). Boston: Houghton Mifflin.

Bradley, S. J. (1985). Gender disorders in childhood: A formulation. In B. W. Steiner (Ed.), *Gender dysphoria: Development, research, management* (pp. 175–188). New York: Plenum Press.

Bradley, S. J., Doering, R. W., Zucker, K. J., Finegan, J. K., & Gonda, G. M. (1980). Assessment of the gender/disturbed child: A comparison to sibling and psychiatric controls. In J. Sampson (Ed.), *Childhood and sexuality* (pp. 554–568). Montreal, Quebec, Canada: Editions Etudes Vivantes.

Coates, S. (1985). Extreme boyhood femininity: Overview and new research findings. In Z. Defries, R. Friedman, & R. Corn (Eds.), *Sexuality: New perspectives* (pp. 101–124). Westport, CT: Greenwood.

Coates, S. (1990). The ontogenesis of gender identity disorder in boys. *Journal of the American Academy of Psychoanalysis, 18,* 414–438.

Coates, S., Friedman, R. C., & Wolfe, S. (1991). The etiology of boyhood gender identity disorder: A model for integrating psychodynamics, temperament and development. *Psychoanalytic Dialogues: A Journal of Relational Perspectives, 1,* 341–383.

Coates, S., & Person, E. (1985). Extreme boyhood femininity: Isolated finding or pervasive disorder? *Journal of the American Academy of Child Psychiatry, 24,* 702–709.

Coates, S., & Tuber, S. (1988). Self-other representations in the Rorschachs of extremely feminine boys. In H. Lerner & P. Lerner (Eds.), *Primitive mental states and the Rorschach* (pp. 647–654). Madison, CT: International Universities Press.

Coates S., & Wolfe, S. (1992). *Psychotherapy of boys with gender identity disorder.* Manuscript in preparation.

Ehrhardt, A. A., & Meyer-Bahlburg, H. F. L. (1981). Effects of prenatal sex hormones on gender-related behavior. *Science, 211,* 1312–1318.

Fagot, B. I., & Leinbach, B. (1985). Gender identity: Some thoughts on an old concept. *Journal of the American Academy of Child Psychiatry, 24,* 684–688.

Fast, I. (1984). *Gender identity: A differentiation model.* Hillsdale, NJ: Analytic Press.

Friedman, R. C. (1988). *Male homosexuality: A contemporary psychoanalytic perspective.* New Haven, CT: Yale University Press.

Ghent, E. (1990). Masochism, submission, surrender: Masochism as a perversion of surrender. *Contemporary Psychoanalysis, 26,* 108–136.

Green, R. (1974). *Sexual identity conflicts in children and adults.* Baltimore, MD: Penguin Books.

Green, R. (1976). One hundred ten masculine and feminine boys: Behavioral contrasts and demographic similarities. *Archives of Sexual Behavior, 55,* 425–446.

Green, R. (1987a). Gender identity in childhood and later sexual orientation: Follow-up of 78 males. *American Journal of Psychiatry, 142,* 339–341.

Green, R. (1987b). *The "sissy boy syndrome" and the development of homosexuality.* New Haven, CT: Yale University Press.

Greenson, R. (1966). A transvestite boy and a hypothesis. *International Journal of Psychoanalysis, 47,* 396–403.

Hines, M. (1982). Prenatal gonadal hormones and sex differences in human behavior. *Psychological Bulletin, 92,* 56–80.

Kohlberg, L. A. (1966). A cognitive-developmental analysis of children's sex-role concepts and attitudes. In E. E. Maccoby (Ed.), *The development of sex differences* (pp. 82–172). Stanford, CA: Stanford University Press.

Kuhn, T. S. (1962). *The structure of scientific revolutions.* Chicago: University of Chicago Press.

Mahler, M., Pine, F., & Bergman, A. (1975). *The psychological birth of the human infant: Symbiosis and individuation.* New York: Basic Books.

Marantz, S., & Coates, S. (1991). Mothers of boys with gender identity disorder: A comparison to normal controls. *Journal of the American Academy of Child and Adolescent Psychiatry, 30,* 136–143.

McEwen, B. S. (1983). Gonadal steroid influences on brain development and sexual differentiation. In R. O. Greep (Ed.), *Reproductive physiology* (Vol. 4, pp. 99–145). Baltimore, MD: University Park Press.

Meyer, J., & Dupkin, C. (1985). Gender disturbance in children. *Bulletin of the Menninger Clinic, 49,* 236–269.

Money, J., & Ehrhardt, A. A. (1972). *Man and woman, boy and girl: The differentiation and dimorphism of gender identity from conception to maturity.* Baltimore, MD: Johns Hopkins University Press.

Money, J., Hampson, J. G., & Hampson J. L. (1957). Imprinting and the establishment of gender role. *Archives of Neurology and Psychiatry, 77,* 333–336.

Money, J., & Russo, A. J. (1979). Homosexual outcome of discordant gender identity/role in childhood: Longitudinal follow-up. *Journal of Pediatric Psychology, 4,* 29–41.

Piaget, J. (1962). *Play, dreams and imitation in childhood.* New York: Norton.

Rekers, G. A., Crandall, B. F., Rosen, A. C., & Bentler, P. M. (1979). Genetic and physical studies of male children with psychological gender disturbances. *Psychological Medicine, 90,* 373–375.

Saghir, M. T., & Robins, E. (1973). *Male and female homosexuality: A comprehensive investigation.* Baltimore, MD: Williams & Wilkins.

Stoller, R. J. (1966). The mother's contribution to infantile transvestic behavior. *International Journal of Psychoanalysis, 47,* 384–394.

Stoller, R. J. (1968a). *Sex and gender: Vol. 1. The development of masculinity and femininity.* New York: Science House.

Stoller, R. J. (1968b). A further contribution to the study of gender identity. *International Journal of Psychoanalysis, 49,* 364–368.

Stoller, R. J. (1975). *Sex and gender: Vol. 2. The transsexual experiment.* New York: Science House.

Stoller, R. J. (1985a). *Presentations of gender.* New Haven, CT: Yale University Press.

Stoller, R. J. (1985b). Gender identity disorders in children and adults. In H. I. Kaplan & B. J. Sadock (Eds.), *Comprehensive textbook of psychiatry* (4th ed., pp. 1034–1041). Baltimore, MD: Williams & Wilkins.

Tuber, S., & Coates, S. (1985). Interpersonal phenomena in the Rorschachs of extremely feminine boys. *Psychoanalytic Psychology, 2,* 251–265.

Tuber, S., & Coates, S. (1989). Indices of psychopathology in the Rorschachs of boys with severe gender identity disorder: A comparison with normal controls. *Journal of Personality Assessment, 53,* 100–112.

van der Kolk, B. A. (1987). *Psychological trauma.* Washington, DC: American Psychiatric Press.

Ward, I. C. (1984). The prenatal stress syndrome: Current status. *Psychoneuroendocrinology, 9,* 3–13.

Weil, A. P. (1970). The basic core. *Psychoanalytic Study of the Child, 25,* 442–460.

Winnicott, D. W. (1975). Primary maternal preoccupation. In *Through pediatrics to psychoanalysis.* London: Hogarth Press. (Original work published 1956)

Wolfe, S. (1990). *Psychopathology and psychodynamics of parents of boys with a gender identity disorder of childhood.* Unpublished doctoral dissertation, City University of New York, New York.

Wolfe, S., & Coates, S. (1991, August). *Psychopathology in fathers of boys with gender identity disorder.* Paper presented at the International Academy of Sex Research, Barrie, Ontario, Canada.

Zuger, B. (1984). Early effeminate behavior in boys: Outcome and significance for homosexuality. *Journal of Nervous and Mental Diseases. 172,* 90–97.

Zuger, B. (1988). Is early effeminate behavior in boys early homosexuality? *Comprehensive Psychiatry, 29,* 509–519.

11

ADOLESCENT DEVELOPMENT

MARSHA H. LEVY-WARREN

Adolescence is a developmental phase with issues that have repercussions throughout adult life. It is a period of vast change, more aptly described as a series of phases that mark the transition from childhood to adulthood. It is also a period of life in which several forms of sociopathy and psychopathology often appear.

It would be impossible to address all of these issues with any degree of thoroughness in the space of one chapter. This chapter thus focuses on a subset of the topic. It examines the relation between psychoanalytic theory and psychological research on aspects of normal adolescent development in the United States. The discussion of adolescent pathology such as delinquency, eating disorders, or imposture will be left to others (e.g., Aichhorn, 1925; Allen, Leadbeater, & Aber, 1990; Battle, 1980; Donovan, Jessor, & Costa, 1985, 1988; Eissler, 1950; Glover, 1956; Kaplan, 1984; Kratcoski & Kratcoski, 1975; Plaut & Hutchinson, 1986; Rutter, 1980; Weiner, 1980; D. J. West, 1982).

Much of the literature on adolescence is conceptually limited or methodologically unsystematic. Few studies use comparable research populations and measures. For example, some samples are middle class, some suburban, some urban; in each case, large portions of the adolescent population are left out. Similarly, many of the theorists' conclusions have been drawn from clinical observation of adolescents, based on a tacit assumption that normal development can be extrapolated from the clinical population. This chapter will attempt to work around these limitations by examining some of the more commonly assumed notions about adolescence and relevant research in these areas.

In adolescent development, psychoanalytic theory and psychological research primarily amplify one another—there are only a few areas in which they conflict. The terms used by each often differ, but the concepts are consonant. For example, psychoanalysts such as Lampl-de Groot (1962), Blos (1962, 1972, 1974), and Jacobson (1964) have written about the importance of the "ego ideal" during adolescence; researchers in psychology such as Kohlberg (1969) and Gilligan

(1982) have reported their work on adolescents' "moral values." Their language is different, but both the psychoanalysts and the researchers are well aware of the need for adolescents to question the values with which they were raised and to formulate values of their own. As a group, psychological researchers tend to be more aware of psychoanalytic theory than are psychoanalytic theorists of psychological research. Psychological researchers often refine the sweeping notions that psychoanalytic theorists develop.

It was the recipient of the first psychology PhD in the United States, G. Stanley Hall, who put adolescence on the intellectual map. In 1904, he published a two-volume tome on the subject titled *Adolescence: Its Psychology and Its Relation to Physiology, Anthroplogy, Sociology, Sex, Crime, Religion, and Education.* Hall wrote about adolescence as a unique developmental phase, one that recapitulated both the experiences of early childhood in an individual's life (a notion reiterated by psychoanalyst Ernest Jones, 1922/1948) and, in the Darwinian tradition, recapitulated an earlier time in history. Hall described this as a transitional time, post-cave-dwelling and precivilization. He further characterized it as a period of *sturm und drang* (storm and stress), in which social relations are structured and moral values formed. These are concepts on which many adolescent theorists and researchers have elaborated in the past few decades (e.g., Blos, 1962; Erikson, 1959; A. Freud, 1958; S. Freud, 1905/1953; Kohlberg, 1969; Lewin, 1939; Spiegel, 1951).

The major current theories of adolescent development come from two writers in the psychoanalytic tradition: Peter Blos (1962) and Erik Erikson (1959). Both of these theorists have extrapolated, to some degree, from clinical populations to formulate their ideas. Blos' work focuses exclusively on the adolescent passage; Erikson's looks at adolescence as one of several developmental phases through which people pass in going through the life cycle.

In general, psychological researchers tend to look in a more detailed manner than do the psychoanalytic theorists at important factors that mediate both normal and pathological development. These include factors such as adolescents' expectations and values, race, class, and family constellation (e.g., Allen, Leadbeater, & Aber, 1990; Bell, 1986; Elliot & Ageton, 1980; Hanson, Henggler, Haefele, Rodick, & Douglas, 1984; Loeber, 1982; Rees & Wilborn, 1983; Simmons, Rosenberg, & Rosenberg, 1973). Many of these, such as the environmental factors, fall outside of the traditional purview of psychoanalytic theory.

What is considered fundamental to adolescent development in psychoanalytic theory also is of primary significance in psychological research. These fundamentals include a "second individuation" or identity formation process, some kind of "turmoil," an examination and redefinition of values (i.e., maturation of the ego ideal), and a special significance for both the peer group and social world.

There is agreement in substance, if not terminology, that adolescent development requires change in three major areas: autonomy, competence, and sexual identity. Certain historic points of conflict are now points of agreement: when adolescence starts and ends, the fact of its existence, and its variability within and between adolescents. There is disagreement about the degree to which adolescence recapitulates earlier (childhood) experience versus forming its own experience; the degree to which there is turmoil—and, if there is, of what type (internal or external, conscious or unconscious); and the role of environmental factors. (Psychological research assumes that there are significant environmental factors; psychoanalytic theory mentions such factors but offers no way to understand their inner workings, for example, what form they take or how prominent they are in identity formation.)

Adolescence takes place, roughly speaking, between the ages of 10–12 and 20–22 years. It begins with the physiological changes of puberty and ends with a psychological sense of consolidation, an integration in the sense of self. The achievement of this sense of self is difficult to ascertain. Thus, some feel that adolescence should be defined more strictly by the biological changes. However, these are not easily determined either because they vary according to cycles, nutritional intake, stress levels, sleep levels, activity level, and so on; thus, accurate measurement is extremely difficult (Doering, Fraemer, Brodie, & Hamburg, 1975; Resko & Eik-Nes, 1966; Santen & Bardin, 1973; Seyler & Reichlin, 1974; C. D. West, Mahajan, Chavre, Nabors, & Tyler, 1973). It is with these difficulties in mind that I will proceed with the more agreed-on definition of adolescence: that which begins with the physiological and ends with the psychological. This psychological consolidation includes an integration of the fact and meaning of the physiological changes, one's changed appearance, and one's new role and status in the family and sociocultural world.

Most who write about adolescence no longer conceptualize it as a unitary developmental period. It is divided into (at least) three subphases: early, middle, and late. Early adolescence focuses on a relative turning away from the parents and a move toward the peer group in the wake of vast physiological changes. In middle adolescence, parents are deidealized at the same time as intimate relationships (including a sexual component) are pursued within the peer group. Late adolescence brings an integration of identity and consequent focus on developing personal standards and goals (Blos, 1962; Kaplan, 1984; Schonfeld, 1971).

In this chapter, I will discuss adolescent development from four points of view. First, it is a time in which a child's body transforms into the body of an adult (the physiological sphere). Second, it is a period of major identity formation (the emotional sphere). Third, it is a phase in which there is a change from concrete to abstract reasoning (the cognitive sphere). Fourth, it is a period of transition from childhood into adulthood (the social sphere). I will allude to the ways in which these different spheres interact as the chapter proceeds, but I will discuss them more fully in the conclusion.

I will also examine each of these points of view in terms of the three major tasks of adolescence: the exploration of competencies, the development of autonomy, and the determination of a sexual life. The exploration of competencies involves the development of a realistic appraisal of capacities—both what they are and how they work in the social world. The development of autonomy concerns the evolution of a sense of separateness and individuality, as well as personal moral and ethical standards with which one can gauge self-esteem and maturity. The determination of a sexual life is defined in the broadest sense, that is, the development of the capacity for intimacy, including that which exists in friendships, and the capacity for shared physical pleasure. These three tasks are interrelated—with each other in the present, with earlier life experiences, and with environmental opportunities. They constitute a framework within which one can look at adolescent development from the dual perspectives of psychoanalytic theory and psychological research.

THE PHYSIOLOGICAL SPHERE

This chapter on adolescent development begins as adolescence begins, with the physiological changes of puberty. The timing and nature of these pubertal changes are determined by genetic potentials. Once begun, the pubertal process unfolds with the hypothalamus secreting hormones that stimulate the pituitary. The pituitary then produces both growth hormones (which lead to a growth spurt) and gonadotrophins (which stimulate the gonads). When the gonads are stimulated, they in turn stimulate genital growth. These also lead to the development of secondary sex characteristics (e.g., pubic and axillary hair; deepening of the voice; facial, chest, leg, and forearm hair in boys; widening of girls' hips and growth of their breasts). These changes bring with them the physiological capacity to produce children: Boys begin to produce live sperm, and girls experience the onset of menarche (Ford & Beach, 1951; Katchadourian, 1977;

Stoltz & Stoltz, 1951). Concurrent with these physiological changes are sexual sensations, surges of energy, and sudden changes in mood. The adolescent's body, once so familiar, may now seem quite unfamiliar. There may even be a sense that one's identity is separate from one's body (Stone & Church, 1957).

All of these physiological changes are involved in the three tasks of adolescent development. The youth must come to recognize and integrate these bodily changes to be autonomous and develop a clear sexual identity. He or she must learn how the new bodily parts and sensations work to feel competent in this "new" body (Brooks-Gunn, 1987; Jones, 1965; Malina, 1974).

Adolescents must come to understand the meaning of having both sexually mature bodies and bodies that are capable of much greater physical strength and energy. For psychoanalytic theorists Moses Laufer and M. Egle Laufer, the importance of this cannot be overemphasized. They claimed that it is the unconscious awareness of an adolescent's actual body, when it compares unsatisfactorily with the adolescent's fantasied body, that ushers in adolescent breakdown at puberty (Laufer, 1986; Laufer & Laufer, 1984).

One of the ways in which the adolescent comes to know his or her body—what it is and how it works—is through masturbation, a subject psychoanalytic theorists elaborate on more than do psychological researchers. Kinsey, Pomeroy, and Martin (1948, 1953) reported masturbatory activity during adolescence, but it is the psychoanalytic theorists who have described the function of masturbation in adolescents' lives (Blos, 1962; Borowitz, 1973; Clower, 1975; Francis & Marcus, 1975; Lampl-de Groot, 1950; Laufer, 1968, 1976; Reich, 1951). There is a strong emphasis on the need for adolescent masturbation (and accompanying fantasy) as a transitional activity through which adolescents come to be more familiar with their bodies and sexual feelings, thus preparing them for the world of intimate sexual relations with others.

Psychoanalytic theorists such as Freud (1905/1953) himself, his daughter Anna Freud (1936, 1958), and the foremost adolescent theorist, Peter Blos (1962, 1967), assumed that a large portion of the psychological upheaval and reintegration that takes place during this developmental period stems directly from the vast physiological changes. A. Freud saw these as requiring a major shift away from the family because of the surge of sexual feeling that the adolescent feels and the necessity to find ways of relieving the resultant tension (that do not violate the incest taboo) by turning to interactions outside the family. A. Freud wrote about a relatively strong id confronting a relatively weak ego, which leaves the adolescent with the task of strengthening the ego enough to find ways to relieve instinctual anxiety and to control impulse expression, strong affect, and urges to regress behaviorally. Blos based his theory on the premise that the pubertal changes require an adolescent to change the relationship to his or her body, parents, peers, and sense of self (i.e., that a second individuation is called forth by these changes).

Research in the area emphasizes the importance of both the rate and magnitude of change during adolescence (e.g., Bock et al., 1973; Horst, Bartsch, & Dirksen-Thedens, 1977; Marcus & Korenman, 1976; Petersen & Taylor, 1980). The experience of this change is different from the vast changes of infancy and early childhood because of adolescents' greater capacity to understand these changes, including their role in the social world (e.g., Tanner, 1972). Much of the other physiological research has focused on how puberty actually evolves, such as the factors involved in the onset of puberty (summary in Grumbach, Grave, & Mayer, 1974) and the details of how it progresses (e.g., Eichorn, 1975; Faust, 1977; Tanner, 1962, 1969, 1974).

There are two basic approaches to studying the psychological effects of puberty. One looks at the direct effects of physiological changes on psychological development; the other looks at variables (e.g., self-esteem, bodily concerns, attitudes toward adulthood) that intervene between the physiological and psychological changes. By virtue of their not specifying such intervening variables, psychoanalytic theorists are assumed to use a direct effects model (Petersen & Taylor,

1980). Among the psychoanalytic theorists, however, it is only Kestenberg (1967a, 1967b, 1968) who is specific in her assumptions about this matter (i.e., she posits direct hormone/mood changes). Others do not expressly discuss the issue (e.g., Blos, 1962; A. Freud, 1936, 1958; S. Freud, 1905/1953).

The fact that theorists do not expressly discuss variables that intervene between physiological and psychological development does not mean that they are thought not to exist. In fact, certain of these factors are implicit in the psychoanalytic theory of development. For example, one's fantasies play a critical role in behavior and attitude—and "fantasy" is an example of an intervening variable (Petersen & Taylor, 1980). Other mediating factors will be noted in later sections of this chapter (i.e., emotional, cognitive, and social factors).

How physiological changes are integrated into the adolescent's sense of self (his or her identity) leads to the next aspect of adolescent development, the emotional sphere.

THE EMOTIONAL SPHERE

The integration of the sense of self that takes place at the end of adolescence is described in a number of different ways. One major theorist in this area is Erikson (1956, 1959), who wrote about the establishment of "ego identity." He saw this as "experienced preconsciously as a sense of psychosocial well-being" (1959, p. 118). The process through which this ego identity is formed includes both a "normative crisis" and a "psychosocial moratorium." A normative crisis is both a period of increased conflict, with shifts in ego strength, and a time of potential high growth. Erikson also regarded this as a period in which society permits adolescents to experiment relatively freely for the purpose of finding a personal niche; this is what he defined as the psychosocial moratorium.

Researchers such as Douvan and Adelson (1966), Marcia (1966), Offer and Offer (1975), Offer, Ostrov, and Howard (1981), and Waterman (1982) have further delineated this identity formation process. Marcia, for example, has delved into adolescents' attitudes, types of decision making, and commitments in the areas of occupation and ideology. He developed an identity status interview, which establishes four different levels of identity formation: foreclosure, diffusion, moratorium, and achievement.

Psychoanalytic theorists Gitelson (1948) and Blos (1968) have regarded adolescence as the primary period for the formation of character. In fact, Gitelson regarded the most important role that the therapist has in adolescent treatment as that of a catalyst in the synthesis of character. Blos (1967) further posited that adolescence involves a second individuation process that resembles the earlier separation/individuation process, ending in the attainment of object constancy that is described by Mahler, Pine, and Bergman (1975), but has its own particular characteristics. Both the earlier and later processes involve a heightened vulnerability in personality organization, an urgency for change in the psychic structure, and a potential for deviant development. The second individuation is resolved through the achievement of constancy in self-esteem and mood and disengagement from internalized infantile objects.

The necessity for an adaptive regression during adolescence is emphasized by Blos (1967) and Geleerd (1961, 1964). Their position is that without the regression, there cannot be sufficient energy for the disengagement and requisite forward movement. Erikson's (1959) "normative crisis" makes a similar assumption. The adolescent uses the regressive process to become familiar with the real needs of the present in contrast to what was needed in the past.

This disengagement process has also been discussed by a number of other theorists (e.g., A. Freud, 1958; Jacobson, 1961, 1964; Katan, 1937; Schafer, 1973). A. Freud and Katan emphasized the unidirectionality of the process (which Katan referred to as *object removal*; i.e., leaving outmoded aspects of self and object representations behind). In Jacobson's (1964) schema, a "self" and an "identity" develop. These are specifically defined in the context of the ego and superego, primary and secondary autonomy, identifications, and the internalized self and object (mental) representations of Freudian object relations theory. Schafer stressed the importance of making careful distinctions and using precise definitions among terms such as *self, identity,* and *individuation.* He further asserted that these terms are often used in a manner that makes comparisons among them unclear and incorrect. This is a point that is well taken when an attempt such as this is made to speak generally about the adolescent developmental process.

All of these theorists describe a process by which adolescents become more autonomous from their parents, their friends, and their sociocultural worlds. Adolescents become more aware both of their unique, identifying characteristics and the social groups with which they feel a sense of belonging. The fact of their greater independence from their families is related to their need to form relationships with these other social groups (a subject that will be explored in greater depth in the section of this chapter titled The Social Sphere).

There are clearly many agreements and disagreements about the nature of self and identity, and the quality and quantity of integration that takes place at the end of adolescence in these structures. Substantial controversies have developed over the degree to which adolescent integration is a recapitulation of an earlier identity formation in childhood and whether turmoil is an inevitable part of this consolidation process. These are controversies among theorists, among researchers, and between the two groups.

Theorists who regard adolescence as a separate developmental phase, with unique characteristics, include Erikson (1959), Furman (1973), Jacobson (1961, 1964), Kaplan (1984), Katan (1937), Lewin (1951), and Spiegel (1951). Those who argue that adolescence recapitulates early childhood include Hall (1904), Jones (1922/1948), and Blos (1962), although Blos sees the "second individuation" of adolescence as resembling the first individuation process rather than recapitulating it.

The issue of whether there is or is not adolescent turmoil is one that has raised a good deal of turmoil in the field. In her seminal paper "Adolescence," A. Freud (1958) argued that adolescent upset is inevitable. Indeed, it is her position that it is an absence of upheaval that is indicative of psychological disturbance at this time. Prominent writers about adolescence such as Blos (1962), Deutsch (1967), Geleerd (1961), Jacobson (1961, 1964), Josselyn (1952, 1967), Kiell (1964), Laufer (1966), and Pearson (1958) also describe this as a period of enormous change, disruption, turmoil, and turbulence.

Whether there really is turbulence—and, if so, how and when it takes place—is a question that Offer (1969a, 1969b; Offer & Offer, 1975) and others have attempted to answer through extensive research. There are others who have described adolescents who are not obviously in turmoil (e.g., Ausubel, 1954; Douvan & Adelson, 1966; Elkin & Westley, 1955; Friedenberg, 1963; Gesell, Ilg, & Ames, 1956; Hsu, 1961; Keniston, 1962; Stone & Church, 1957). Within this group, Douvan and Adelson, Friedenberg, and Keniston seem to be in agreement with A. Freud when they describe the relative peacefulness of the adolescents that they observed as a potentially troublesome sign.

In the Offer studies (e.g., Baittle & Offer, 1971; Offer, 1969a, 1969b; Offer & Offer, 1975; Offer et al., 1981), the greatest turmoil was evident during early adolescence (ages 12 to 14 years). After that time, adolescents appeared to be relatively stable. This was taken as evidence that A. Freud was wrong, although it is clear from her 1958 article that A. Freud expected the upheaval of adolescence to take place at approximately this same time. In that article, she made specific reference to those adolescents who "as late as the ages of 14, 15, or 16 show no such outer evidence of inner unrest" (p. 149). The clear implication is that she would have expected the unrest to have taken place during the early years of the adolescent period.

Offer and his associates, however, made a much more general point. They took issue with the use of a term such as *turmoil* to describe what is regarded as normal in the developmental process of adolescence. They found no real evidence in their studies of very large normal populations that significant disruption occurs in the behavior of these adolescents. They concluded that the characterization of adolescence as a time of turbulence is exaggerated. They have made a significant contribution by carefully delineating the types and degrees of turmoil or disruption that occur. The psychoanalytic theorists are far less specific in their use of terms such as *turmoil* and *disruption*. The conclusions of the Offer studies should, at the very least, lead psychoanalytic writers to be more clear about the timing and nature of the adolescent turmoil that they observe. It does seem, however, that the psychoanalytic use of *turmoil* is one that is comparable to the use of *calm* to describe latency. That is to say, there is calm in latency relative to the stormy Oedipal period, as there is turbulence in adolescence relative to the greater stability of both latency and adulthood.

The source of adolescent turbulence is important as well. The psychoanalytic theorists describe the vast number of physiological and psychic shifts that take place; psychological researchers point to these and other factors. Simmons et al. (1973), for example, studied a very large sample of innercity adolescents. Consistent with the Offer studies and the writings of A. Freud (1936, 1958), the most significant degree of upset was found in the early adolescents. This was attributed both to the effects of puberty and the environmental circumstance of moving from elementary to junior high school. These researchers and others have pointed out that the arrival of puberty puts adolescents in a state of heightened vulnerability to environmental stress.

In a similar vein, Nesselroade and Baltes (1974) annually tested the personality stability of a large sample of adolescents for 3 years, from 1970 to 1972. They found that the year in which the testing occurred was more significant than chronological age, although both were important variables in the relative stability of the population. A study comparing prominent problems for adolescents in the years 1936, 1959, 1961, and 1968 showed significant changes among these even longer time intervals (Chabassol & Thomas, 1969). These studies suggest that the historical time period in which adolescent development occurs is a substantial factor in each adolescent's development.

There is clearly much for the adolescent to integrate both intrapsychically and interpersonally. The development of autonomy and the development of a sexual identity, two major components of this integration, involve the recognition of bodily changes and their sociocultural ramifications. What is involved is the adolescent's awareness and acceptance of sex, sex role, and gender (Block, 1973).

Dreyer (1975) asserted that children arrive at adolescence with an awareness of both their (biological) gender and the fact that gender is an important social and cultural construct. During adolescence, this awareness grows and becomes far more complex. There is evidence that sex differences that exist prior to the age of 12 years become more marked at this time (Nesselroade & Baltes, 1974). The integration of the bodily changes, their social signficance, and their personal meaning is critical. Laufer (1986) richly summarized this aspect of adolescent development:

> To talk of the adolescent means that we must address ourselves to the meaning of having a sexually mature body; impregnating and becoming pregnant; incest and incestuous fantasies; the destructive violence which is now possible through the use of one's own body; the near inescapable need to face the fact, in spite of one's fantasies or efforts to change the external world, of being either male or female. (p. 368)

It is the subject of meaning that introduces the next aspect of adolescent development: that which involves cognitive process.

THE COGNITIVE SPHERE

Adolescence is a time in which cognitive process is ever expanding, reminiscent of the child's shift from being a nonreader to being a reader. Suddenly, the world opens up to that child. What once appeared as jumbles of letters now appears as words: messages, directions, communications of all kinds. For adolescents, it is the abstract world that is now open: the world of ideas and concepts. Adolescents can think about thinking, think through hypotheses, think ahead. This is what allows them to use the defense of intellectualization, which A. Freud (1958) identified in "Adolescence." Adolescents can think instead of taking action as a way to discharge energy and reduce conflict.

With the development of the capacity for abstract thinking, adolescents can think beyond the present; they can conceptualize a past. This is how they can leave "childhood," an abstraction, behind while they live in the present and, eventually, begin to contemplate a future. In her 1937 article, Katan described "object removal" as a process that involves a directional change for adolescents wherein they leave old ways of looking at important people behind. This takes place in the context of an adolescent's ability to conceptualize a "past."

When analytic thinking develops, the social, political, aesthetic, and religious spheres open up for the adolescent's exploration. Adolescents develop theories about how these spheres should be and then try to validate their theories by looking at the world around them (Leadbeater & Dione, 1981; Piaget, 1947, 1972). According to Inhelder and Piaget (1958), this represents an important change in the direction of thinking: Children look at the world and develop hypotheses to explain what they see; adolescents think about what is possible and then look out to see whether they are correct. Reality is secondary to possibility. This is described as the change from concrete to formal operations.

Kohlberg and Gilligan (1971) have explored the relation between cognitive and moral development. They looked at whether the Piagetian stages of cognitive development corresponded to Kohlberg's six stages of moral development. They found correspondence in childhood and established that it was only with the attainment of formal operations that Kohlberg's last stages of moral development could be achieved.

Adolescents delight especially in consideration of that which is not, a capacity that develops in the move from concrete to formal operations. They show a marked preference for abstraction (Peel, 1975). This may be what permits adolescents to deidealize their parents, a necessary component of the second individuation process that takes place at this time (Blos, 1967). Early adolescents can see that other parents are different from theirs; by midadolescence, they are able to criticize their parents for things that they have not done or ways that they have not been. Both of these serve the adolescent disengagement process.

Esman (1975) wrote about the state of anomie in which adolescents find themselves once the deidealization of their parents takes place. They go through a mourning process in which they may search for alternative "gods" in politics, religion, or ideology. This process may also simply serve to motivate a search for values, political and religious beliefs, or ethics. This search often brings the adolescent into contact with different groups. The group involvement diminishes some of the anomie that results from the disengagement from the family of origin.

That to which people aspire is denoted as their *ego ideal* (Blos, 1962, 1967; Esman, 1975; Jacobson, 1964; Lampl-de Groot, 1962; Milrod, 1990). As people approach this ego ideal, self-esteem rises. Blos posited that there is a maturation of the ego ideal during adolescence given that adolescents develop the capacity and the motivation to formulate values and goals that are different from those of their parents. It is the move toward autonomy that permits goals and values to be examined and reformulated. Adolescents look to the world around them for both people and ideas that may be transiently used to aid them in forming these new goals and values.

Thinking about, through, ahead, and beyond are all forms of exercising new potential and gaining mastery over both internal and external reality. These contribute to the adolescent's achievement of greater competence. An adolescent does not have to look to others for explanations of that which is not immediately comprehensible; hypotheses can be generated and tested (Ausubel & Ausubel, 1966; Manaster, Saddler, & Wukasch, 1977). This contributes to the adolescent's sense of greater autonomy.

Researchers on the development of a concept of self during adolescence note that there is more differentiation evident over time (Mullener & Laird, 1971). This is seen as a direct result of adolescents' increasing cognitive ability. The components of their self-concept become more and more complex, both quantitatively and qualitatively (Marsh & Shavelson, 1985; Shavelson, Hubner, & Stanton, 1976). This is very much in keeping with the second individuation theory of Blos (1967), which posits that adolescents have an increased capacity to see and define themselves.

In their major study of sex differences, Maccoby and Jacklin (1974) established that the effect of children's cognitive skill is greater than the influence of their parents' attitudes and behavior on the development of sex roles. This suggests that it is the greater cognitive skill of adolescents that leads them to be more aware of and responsive to sex differences, as noted by Nesselroade and Baltes (1974).

A major psychoanalytic characterization of self or identity is that people form mental pictures or representations of themselves. The representations of adolescents must include images of their now more mature bodies. This gives them a sense of ownership of their bodies. It is no longer the caretaker of bodily needs from childhood who is responsible for "seeing to" the body; it is the adolescent (Laufer, 1976). These mental representations of the body must include images of the genitals as functioning organs for the adolescent to feel identified as male or female, or potential father or mother (S. Freud, 1905/1953; Laufer, 1986; Ritvo, 1984).

The individuation process in which an adolescent is engaged involves the forming of these mental representations for all aspects of the adolescent's person, which Jacobson (1964) described as constituting a "self." The representations include those that constitute an adolescent's sense of cultural or ethnic identity as well: Adolescents come to see themselves as being part of various larger groups, which have personal and social meaning, through the forming of images and identifications (Levy-Warren, 1987; Settlage, 1972). I address the necessity for forming these cultural or ethnic identifications, as well as the adolescent's general involvement in the social world, in the next section.

THE SOCIAL SPHERE

In the developmental movement toward greater autonomy, adolescents shift their primary attention from their families of origin to the sociocultural world, with particular focus on their contemporaries and adults who are not their parents. They use this turn outward to provide them with ideas, models, and experiences to establish personal traits, values, and goals.

It is not simply a turn away from families that takes place at this time; it is a turn toward the outside world that is in keeping with adolescents' developmental needs and capacities. What is meant by greater autonomy in adolescence is the capacity to be independent enough from those who were most significant in childhood that the adolescent can, through personal knowledge and experience, have the (internal) freedom to make decisions and act. This requires that the adolescent have other bases for comparison; other people with whom to compare experiences;

and other people who can offer advice, direction, or models for behavior. Adolescents' experiences in school and in the community provide them with new information about themselves, by virtue of how people outside the family react to them and how they see others interacting with each other. These experiences permit the forming of the new identifications that lead to the development of a mature ego ideal.

The adolescent needs to find a way of fitting into the sociocultural world. This is a major aspect of the identity formation process that takes place at this time (Erikson, 1956, 1959; Lewin, 1939; Ritvo, 1971). At the very least, the sociocultural context provides adolescents with opportunities for testing new physical, sexual, and social capacities that aid in the development of a sense of competence. There are, however, theorists and researchers who regard the sociocultural context as even more important than this. They see the context as determining the actual nature of adolescence: the form it takes and its duration (Baltes & Nesselroade, 1972; Benedict, 1938; Dunphy, 1963; Elder, 1974; Mead, 1928; Ritvo, 1971; Spiegel, 1958).

Baltes and Nesselroade (1972), for example, conducted a large sample study of adolescent personality trait development in subjects aged 12½–16½ years old. They found that relative stability grew over time, but that the patterns of social change in the environments in which their subjects lived were actually the most significant influence on changes in personality traits.

Psychological research is rich with data on the influence of the adolescent peer group and the importance of environmental factors in the lives of adolescents (e.g., Allen, Aber, & Leadbeater, 1990; Berger, 1963; Coleman, 1980; Lewin, 1939). Much of the research has focused on whether youth subcultures exist and whether these subcultures are good or bad for adolescents and society (Berger, 1963; Coleman et al., 1974; Eve, 1975; McClintock, 1979; Niles, 1981; Smith, 1976; Timpane, Abramowitz, Bobrow, & Pascal, 1976). Most of the studies concluded that adolescents tend to influence each other in matters of taste, such as dress and manners, and other issues related to social status among their contemporaries. However, they tend to look to their parents for guidance about major life issues such as career, marriage, and moral values (Bandura & Walters, 1963; Chand, Crider, & Willets, 1975; Douvan & Adelson, 1966; Eve, 1975; Kandel, Lesser, Roberts, & Weiss, 1970; Niles, 1981; Sherif, 1966).

Adolescence is known generally as a period of transition from childhood to adulthood. The world outside the family, however, does not provide the adolescent with any clear indication of when adulthood is reached (Friedenberg, 1963; Hill, 1973; Hotaling, Atwell, & Linsky, 1978). This ambiguity is amply demonstrated in the varied legal ages for drinking, voting, driving, legal liability, financial emancipation, and marriage and medical treatment without parental consent. What is expected of adolescents as they move from childhood to adulthood also varies by geographic location, ethnic group, socioeconomic class, and sex (Epstein & McPartland, 1976; Group for the Advancement of Psychiatry, 1968).

Psychoanalytic theorists are aware that the outside world is very significant but note that they do not yet understand the impact on adolescent psychic structure (e.g., Ritvo, 1971). (Psychological researchers tend not to address psychic structure; they usually look from the vantage point of variables that account for portions of the statistical variance in the behaviors or attitudes of groups of adolescents.) A partial response to the question of how sociocultural context becomes part of the adolescent's psychic structure might be found in a further examination of the development of the capacity for abstraction during adolescence. It is with this capacity that an abstraction such as a thematic group identification can be internally represented and thus integrated into the adolescent's identity. That is, adolescents can affectively experience themselves as members of groups of people or see themselves as adherents to beliefs (e.g., "punk rockers," "Deadheads," "conservatives," or "feminists"). These group identifications are both emotionally and intellectually integrated; that is, they are seen as part of the adolescent's self.

This adolescent capacity derives from earlier experiences of context, which can be looked at developmentally (Levy-Warren, 1987).

Lewin (1939), an experimental psychologist, developed "field theory" as a method for analyzing causal relations and building scientific constructs. He used topology theory (in geometry) to establish an equation for defining "life space," which focuses on the interdependence of relevant contemporaneous forces as a person interacts with the environment. Adolescence was his test case: Lewin saw it as a time in which there is a lack of cognitive clarity about the nature of the more adult world that the adolescent is entering that leaves the adolescent in a state of uncertainty. He also portrayed adolescence as a period that involves a shift in group belongingness (i.e., from that of a child to that of an adult). Lewin recognized the necessity for grappling with the history, developmental characteristics, and current forces emanating from the environment.

Friendships that are both transient and permanent form during adolescence. The transient, intense relationships are seen to stem particularly from the need to connect, restitutively, following the relative withdrawal of emotional energy from the significant people of childhood (A. Freud, 1958; Spiegel, 1958). This withdrawal follows the reactivation of Oedipal interest that comes with puberty and the subsequent need (because of the incest taboo) for the more sexual early adolescent to turn away from the members of the family of origin and toward the social world (Loewald, 1979; Ritvo, 1984). This mirrors the shift from preoccupation with internal to external reality that Deutsch (1944) so aptly described in girls during this period.

This theoretical perspective on transient relationships may well explain some of the data described earlier about the influence of peers on adolescents' attitudes and behavior. It may be because of the nature of these relationships that peers only influence each other on such transient matters as dress and manners.

There are also shifts in narcissism and object relations during adolescence. Both the physical changes and the move away from the family of origin leave the adolescent feeling somewhat estranged, weakened, and unsupported. These feelings usher in a strong attraction to those of the same sex, a need to connect with those who are similar in body and position. It is after the building up of some pride, strength, and self-awareness that adolescents venture out into the heterosexual world for friendship and, often, sexual contact. These reflect changes from (familial) object to narcissistic to (peer-oriented) object relations (Fenichel, 1938; A. Freud, 1936; Kohut, 1971). It is often the early, more narcissistic relations that are fleeting; the later relationships tend to be more permanent.

Much of what takes place in the social sphere involves the redefining of adolescents' sense of belonging. Newly refined capacities for observation permit adolescents to make choices in these areas. When they use these capacities to make independent choices, adolescents are developing both their competence and autonomy. Finding ways of interacting in the social world as young women and men aids them in defining their sexual identities.

CONCLUSION

Adolescence is a period of tremendous growth in all spheres: physiological, emotional, cognitive, and social. The vast physiological growth has great meaning both to adolescents themselves and to the world in which they live. They must use the significant developments in their cognitive capacities to make sense of these changes.

Their once sexually undifferentiated bodies begin to change, leaving them with no (rational) option other than to accept their gender and physical form. It is no longer as possible to imagine themselves as different adult body types, with different physical features. This is emotionally difficult for adolescents, because it implies a need to accept what are sometimes painful realities about physical limitations.

The pubertal changes arrive, initiating a need for preadolescents to look for sources of affection and recognition outside the family. The social world becomes even more significant during early adolescence as the need to achieve a sense of belonging in a group other than the family of origin comes to the fore. Sex differences, including both their sociocultural meanings and significance, become more evident. It becomes necessary to form personal resolutions about sex-role and gender. Same-sex relationships, which provide bases for comparison for adolescents in the throes of forming these resolutions, are particularly important.

With the refining of formal operations during middle adolescence, adolescents see both their bodies and their parents more clearly. This leads to the further understanding and acceptance of their bodies and how they work and to the de-idealization of their parents. With the development of the capacity for abstraction, new beliefs and values are formulated. Middle adolescents are thus far more able to explore all kinds of relationships in the social and intellectual worlds.

The final consolidations and integrations of adolescence are achieved in the last subphase of this developmental period. It is these late adolescents who must accept the relative slowdown or halt in their physical growth. They must clearly define values and goals for themselves and become more autonomous in the regulation of their moods and self-esteem. Having established that they have a past and a present, they are then able to look toward the future. Without the cognitive and emotional growth that has taken place, adolescents would not be able to look ahead in this manner.

The theory and research on adolescence forms a largely cohesive entity, although problems and issues are often approached from different vantage points. The theory looks at the intricacies of the individual's experience; the research looks at variations in large groups. Much of the theory derives from observations made when normal development has gone awry; the research tends to look at populations that are regarded as normal.

The theory is usually described in quite general terms, despite the fact that it is often an attempt to look at individuals microscopically. Those researchers who are better versed in theory look at more refined versions of the terms that the theorists use. In general, the psychological researchers evidence more knowledge of psychoanalytic theory than do the psychoanalysts of the relevant research. However, the researchers who refer to psychoanalytic theory rarely do so in a manner that conveys a complex understanding of the material.

There is no question that it would serve the theorists well to look more carefully at what has been achieved by the psychologists who do research in the relevant areas. In looking at adolescent development, researchers have refined concepts such as "turmoil," established the importance of environmental variables such as class and race, and demonstrated the significance of historical time periods. In contrast, psychoanalytic theorists have barely begun to refine their concepts or fully define the process of development with an appreciation of the significance of the sociocultural world.

Similarly, psychological researchers seemingly fail to take into account many of the complex sources and interactions of motivation, thought, fantasy, and action that the psychoanalytic theorists discuss as a matter of course. Researchers tend to examine one of these dimensions at a time (i.e., they explore adolescents' attitudes toward their peers, adolescent self-concept, or adolescent sexual behavior without being able to give an adequate account of the overall complexity of adolescent development).

It is hoped that this chapter marks the beginning of what can be a very valuable exchange between psychoanalytic theorists and researchers. If this does prove to be such a beginning, the next exploration of this kind will surely show a greatly enriched understanding of adolescence.

REFERENCES

Aichhorn, A. (1925). *Wayward youth*. New York: Viking Press.

Allen, J. P., Aber, J. L., & Leadbeater, B. J. (1990). Adolescent problem behavior: The influence of attachment and autonomy. *Psychiatric Clinics Of North America, 13*, 455–467.

Allen, J. P., Leadbeater, B. J., & Aber, J. L. (1990). The relationship of adolescents' expectations and values to delinquency, hard drug use and unprotected sexual intercourse. *Development and Psychopathology, 2*, 85–98.

Ausubel, D. P. (1954). *Theory and problems of adolescent development*. New York: Grune & Stratton.

Ausubel, D., & Ausubel, P. (1966). Cognitive development in adolescence. *Review of Educational Research, 36*, 403–413.

Baittle, B., & Offer, D. (1971). On the nature of adolescent rebellion. *Adolescent Psychiatry, 1*, 139–160.

Baltes, P. B., & Nesselroade, J. R. (1972). Cultural change and adolescent personality development: An application of longitudinal sequences. *Developmental Psychology, 7*, 244–256.

Bandura, A., & Walters, R. H. (1963). *Social learning and personality development*. New York: Holt.

Battle, J. (1980). Relationship between self-esteem and depression among high school students. *Perceptual and Motor Skills, 51*, 157–158.

Bell, R. Q. (1986). Age-specific manifestations in changing psycho-social risk. In D. C. Farran & J. D. McKinney (Eds.), *The concept of risk in intellectual and psychosocial development* (pp. 169–185). San Diego, CA: Academic Press.

Benedict, R. (1938). Continuities and discontinuities in cultural conditioning. *Psychiatry, 1*, 161–167.

Berger, B. M. (1963). On the youthfulness of youth culture. *Social Research, 30*, 319–342.

Block, J. H. (1973). Conceptions of sex-roles: Cross-cultural and longitudinal perspectives. *American Psychologist, 28*, 512–526.

Blos, P. (1962). *On adolescence: A psychoanalytic interpretation*. New York: Free Press.

Blos, P. (1967). The second individuation process of adolescence. *Psychoanalytic Study of the Child, 27*, 162–186.

Blos, P. (1968). Character formation in adolescence. *Psychoanalytic Study of the Child, 23*, 245–263.

Blos, P. (1972). The functions of the ego ideal in adolescence. *Psychoanalytic Study of the Child, 27*, 93–97.

Blos, P. (1974). The genealogy of the ego ideal. *Psychoanalytic Study of the Child, 29*, 43–88.

Bock, R. D., Wainer, H., Petersen, A., Thissen, D., Murray, J., & Roche, A. F. (1973). A parameterization for individual human growth curves. *Human Biology, 45*, 63–80.

Borowitz, G. H. (1973). The capacity to masturbate alone in adolescence. *Adolescent Psychiatry, 3*, 130–143.

Brooks-Gunn, J. (1987). Pubertal processes: Their relevance for developmental research. In V. B. Hasselt & M. Hersen (Eds.), *Handbook of adolescent psychology* (pp. 111–130). New York: Pergamon Press.

Chabassol, D. J., & Thomas, D. C. (1969). Sex and age differences in problems and interests of adolescents. *Journal of Experimental Education, 38*, 16–23.

Chand, I., Crider, D., & Willets, F. (1975). Parent–youth disagreement as perceived by youth: A longitudinal study. *Youth and Society, 6*, 365–375.

Clower, V. L. (1975). Significance of masturbation in female sexual development and function. In I. M. Marcus & J. J. Francis (Eds.), *Masturbation* (pp. 107–143). Madison, CT: International Universities Press.

Coleman, J. C. (1980). Friendship and the peer group in adolescence. In J. Adelson (Ed.), *Handbook of adolescent psychology* (pp. 408–431). New York: Wiley.

Coleman, J., Bremner, R., Clark, B., David, J., Eichorn, D., Griliches, Z., Keet, J., Ryder, N., Doering, Z., & Mays, J. (1974). *Youth: Transition to adulthood* (Report of the Panel on Youth of the President's Science and Advisory Committee). Chicago: University of Chicago Press.

Deutsch, H. (1944). *The psychology of women.* New York: Grune & Stratton.

Deutsch, H. (1967). *Selected problems of adolescence.* Madison, CT: International Universities Press.

Doering, C. H., Fraemer, H. C., Brodie, H. K. H., & Hamburg, D. A. (1975). A cycle of plasma testosterone in the human male. *Journal of Clinical Endocrinology and Metabolism, 40,* 492–500.

Donovan, J. E., Jessor, R., & Costa, F. M. (1985). Structure of problem behavior in adolescence and young adulthood. *Journal of Consulting and Clinical Psychology, 53,* 890–904.

Donovan, J. E., Jessor, R., & Costa, F. M. (1988). Syndrome of problem behavior in adolescence: A replication. *Journal of Consulting and Clinical Psychology, 56,* 762–765.

Douvan, E., & Adelson, J. (1966). *The adolescent experience.* New York: Wiley.

Dreyer, P. H. (1975). Sex, sex-roles and marriage among youth in the 1970's. In E. J. Havighurst & P. H. Dreyer (Eds.), *Youth: The 74th yearbook of the National Society for the Study of Education. Part I.* Chicago: University of Chicago Press.

Dunphy, D. C. (1963). The social structure of urban adolescent peer groups. *Sociometry, 26,* 230–246.

Eichorn, D. (1975). Asynchronizations in adolescent development. In S. Dragastin & G. H. Elder, Jr. (Eds.), *Adolescence in the life cycle* (pp. 81–96). New York: Wiley.

Eissler, K. R. (1950). Ego-psychological implications of the psychoanalytic treatment of delinquency. *Psychoanalytic Study of the Child, 5,* 97–121.

Elder, G. (1974). *Children of the great depression.* Chicago: University of Chicago Press.

Elkin, F., & Westley, W. A. (1955). The myth of adolescent culture. *American Sociological Review, 20,* 680–684.

Elliott, D. S., & Ageton, S. S. (1980). Reconciling race and class differences in self-reported and official estimates of delinquency. *American Sociological Review, 45,* 95–110.

Epstein, J., & McPartland, J. (1976). The effects of open school organization on student outcomes. *American Educational Research Journal, 113,* 15–30.

Erikson, E. H. (1956). The problem of ego identity. *Journal of the American Psychoanalytic Association, 4,* 56–121.

Erikson, E. H. (1959). Identity and the life cycle. *Psychological Issues, 1,* 680–684.

Esman, A. H. (1975). Consolidation of the ego ideal in contemporary adolescence. In A. H. Esman (Ed.), *The psychology of adolescence* (pp. 211–218). Madison, CT: International Universities Press.

Eve, R. (1975). Adolescent culture, convenient myth or reality? A comparison of students and their teachers. *Sociology of Education, 48,* 152–162.

Faust, M. S. (1977). Somatic development of adolescent girls. *Monographs of the Society for Research in Child Development, 1,* Serial No. 169.

Fenichel, O. (1938). [Review of *The ego and the mechanisms of defense*]. *International Journal of Psychoanalysis, 19,* 116–136.

Ford, C., & Beach, F. (1951). *Patterns of sexual behavior.* New York: Harper.

Francis, J. J., & Marcus, I. M. (1975). Masturbation: A developmental view. In I. M. Marcus & J. J. Francis (Eds.), *Masturbation.* Madison, CT: International Universities Press.

Freud, A. (1936). *The ego and the mechanisms of defense.* Madison, CT: International Universities Press.

Freud, A. (1958). Adolescence. *Psychoanalytic Study of the Child, 13,* 255–278.

Freud, S. (1953). Three essays on the theory of sexuality. In J. Strachey (Ed. and Trans.), *The standard edition of the complete psychological works of Sigmund Freud* (Vol. 7, pp. 125–243). London: Hogarth Press. (Original work published 1905)

Friedenberg, E. (1963). *Coming of age in America: Growth and a acquiescence.* New York: Knopf-Vantage.

Furman, E. (1973). A contribution to assessing the role of infantile separation–individuation in adolescent development. *Psychoanalytic Study of the Child, 28,* 193–207.

Geleerd, E. R. (1961). Some aspects of ego vicissitudes in adolescence. *Journal of the American Psychoanalytic Association, 9,* 394–405.

Geleerd, E. R. (1964). Adolescence and adaptive regression. *Bulletin of Menninger Clinic, 28,* 302–308.

Gesell, A. L., Ilg, F. L., & Ames, L. B. (1956). *Youth: The years from ten to sixteen.* New York: Harper.

Gilligan, C. (1982). *In a different voice: Psychological theory and women's development.* Cambridge, MA: Harvard University Press.

Gitelson, M. (1948). Character synthesis and the psychotherapeutic problem in adolescence. *American Journal of Orthopsychiatry, 18,* 422–431.

Glover, E. (1956). Psychoanalysis and crimonology: A political survey. *International Journal of Psycho-Analysis, 37,* 311–317.

Group for the Advancement of Psychiatry. (1968). *Normal adolescence: Its dynamics and impact.* New York: Scribner.

Grumbach, M. M., Grave, G. D., & Mayer, F. E. (Eds.). (1974). *Control of the onset of puberty.* New York: Wiley.

Hall, G. S. (1904). *Adolescence: Its psychology and its relation to physiology, anthropology, sociology, sex, crime, religion, and education.* New York: Appleton-Century-Crofts.

Hanson, C. L., Henggler, S. W., Haefele, W. F., Rodick, J. D., & Douglas, J. (1984). Demographic, individual, and family relationship correlates of serious and repeated crime among adolescents and their siblings. *Journal of Consulting and Clinical Psychology, 52,* 528–538.

Hill, J. (1973). *Some perspectives on adolescence in American society.* Washington, DC: Office of Child Development, U.S. Department of Health, Education and Welfare.

Horst, H. J., Bartsch, W., & Dirksen-Thedens, I. (1977). Plasma testosterone, sex hormone binding, globulin binding capacity, and percent binding of testosterone and 5a-dihydrotesterone in prepubertal, pubertal, and adult males. *Journal of Clinical Endocrinology and Metabolism, 95,* 522–527.

Hotaling, G. T., Atwell, S. G., & Linsky, A. S. (1978). Adolescent life changes and illness: A comparison of three models. *Journal of Youth and Adolescence, 7,* 393–403.

Hsu, F. L. K. (1961). Culture patterns and adolescent behavior. *International Journal of Social Psychiatry, 7,* 33–53.

Inhelder, B., & Piaget, J. (1958). *The growth of logical thinking from childhood to adolescence.* New York: Basic Books.

Jacobson, E. (1961). Adolescent moods and the remodelling of psychic structures in adolescence. *Psychoanalytic Study of the Child, 16,* 164–183.

Jacobson, E. (1964). *The self and object world.* Madison, CT: International Universities Press.

Jones, E. (1948). Some problems of adolescence. In *Papers on psychoanalysis* (5th ed., pp. 389–406). London: Bailliere, Tindall, & Cox. (Original work published 1922)

Jones, M. C. (1965). Psychological correlates of somatic development. *Child Development, 36,* 899–911.

Josselyn, I. (1952). *The adolescent and his world.* New York: Family Services Association of America.

Josselyn, I. (1967). The adolescent today. *Smith College Studies in Social Work, 38,* 1–15.

Kandel, D., Lesser, G., Roberts, G., & Weiss, R. (1970). The concept of the adolescent subculture. In R. E. F. Purnell (Ed.), *Adolescents and the American high school* (pp. 194–205). New York: Holt, Rinehart & Winston.

Kaplan, L. J. (1984). *Adolescence: The farewell to childhood.* New York: Simon & Schuster.

Katan, A. (1937). The role of displacement in agoraphobia. *International Journal of Psycho-Analysis, 32,* 41–50.

Katchadourian, H. (1977). *The biology of adolescence.* San Francisco: Freeman.

Keniston, K. (1962). Social change and youth in America. *Daedalus, 91,* 53–74.

Kestenberg, J. (1967a). Phases of adolescence with suggestions for a correlation of psychic and hormonal organization: 1. Antecedents of adolescent organizations in childhood. *Journal of the American Academy of Child Psychiatry, 6,* 426–463.

Kestenberg, J. (1967b). Phases of adolescence with suggestions for a correlation of psychic and hormonal organization: 2. Prepuberty, diffusion, and reintegration. *Journal of the American Academy of Child Psychiatry, 6,* 577–614.

Kestenberg, J. (1968). Phases of adolescence with suggestions for a correlation of psychic and hormonal organization: 3. Puberty, growth, differentiation, and consolidation. *Journal of the American Academy of Child Psychiatry, 7,* 108–151.

Kiell, N. (1964). *The universal experience of adolescence.* Madison, CT: International Universities Press.

Kinsey, A., Pomeroy, W. B., & Martin, C.E. (1948). *Sexual behavior in the human male.* Philadelphia: Saunders.

Kinsey, A., Pomeroy, W. B., & Martin, C. E. (1953). *Sexual behavior in the human female.* Philadelphia: Saunders.

Kohlberg, L. (1969). Stage and sequence: The cognitive developmental approach to socialization. In D. A. Goslin (Ed.), *Handbook of socialization theory and practice* (pp. 347–480). Chicago: Rand McNally.

Kohlberg, L., & Gilligan, C. (1971). The adolescent as philosopher: The discovery of the self in a post-conventional world. *Daedalus, 100,* 1051–1086.

Kohut, H. (1971). *The analysis of the self.* Madison, CT: International Universities Press.

Kratcoski, P. C., & Kratcoski, J. E. (1975). Changing patterns in the delinquent activities of boys and girls: A self-reported delinquency analysis. *Adolescence, 10,* 83–95.

Lampl-de Groot, J. (1950). On masturbation and its influence on general development. *Psychoanalytic Study of the Child, 5,* 153–174.

Lampl-de Groot, J. (1962). Ego ideal and superego. *Psychoanalytic Study of the Child, 17,* 94–106.

Laufer, M. (1966). Object loss and mourning during adolescence. *Psychoanalytic Study of the Child, 21,* 269–294.

Laufer, M. (1968). The body image, the function of masturbation, and adolescence: Problems of ownership of the body. *Psychoanalytic Study of the Child, 23,* 114–137.

Laufer, M. (1976). The central masturbation fantasy, the final sexual organization, and adolescence. *Psychoanalytic Study of the Child, 31,* 297–316.

Laufer, M. (1986). Adolescence and psychosis. *International Journal of Psychoanalysis, 67,* 367–372.

Laufer, M., & Laufer, M. E. (1984). *Adolescence and developmental breakdown.* New Haven, CT: Yale University Press.

Leadbeater, B. J., & Dione, J. P. (1981). The adolescent's use of formal operations thinking in solving problems related to identity formation. *Adolescence, 16,* 111–121.

Levy-Warren, M. H. (1987). Moving to a new culture: Cultural identity, loss, and mourning. In J. Bloom-Feshbach, S. Bloom-Feshbach & Associates, (Eds.), *The psychology of separation and loss* (pp. 300–315). San Francisco: Jossey-Bass.

Lewin, K. (1939). Field theory in social psychology: Concepts and methods. *American Journal of Sociology, 44,* 868–896.

Lewin, K. (1951). *Field theory in social science.* New York: Harper.

Loeber, R. (1982). The stability of antisocial and delinquency child behavior: A review. *Child Development, 53,* 1431–1446.

Loewald, H. (1979). The waning of the Oedipus complex. *Journal of the American Psychoanalytic Association, 27,* 751–775.

Maccoby, E. E., & Jacklin, C. N. (1974). *The psychology of sex differences.* Stanford, CA: Stanford University Press.

Mahler, M. S., Pine, F., & Bergman, A. (1975). *The psychological birth of the human infant.* New York: Basic Books.

Malina, R. M. (1974). Adolescent changes in size, build, composition and performance. *Human Biology, 46,* 117–131.

Manaster, G. J., Saddler, C. D., & Wukasch, L. (1977). The ideal self and cognitive development in adolescence. *Adolescence, 7,* 547–558.

Marcia, J. E. (1966). Development and validation of ego identity status. *Journal of Personality and Social Psychology, 3,* 551–558.

Marcus, R., & Korenman, S. G. (1976). Estrogens and the human male. *Annual Review of Medicine, 27,* 357–370.

Marsh, H. W., & Shavelson, R. (1985). Self concept: Its multifaceted, hierarchial structure. *Educational Psychology, 20,* 107–123.

McClintock, E. (1979). Adolescent socialization and the high school: A selective review of literature. In J. Kelly (Ed.), *Adolescent boys in high school* (pp. 35–58). Hillsdale, NJ: Erlbaum.

Mead, M. (1928). *Coming of age in Samoa.* New York: New American Library.

Milrod, D. (1990). The ego ideal. *Psychoanalytic Study of the Child, 45,* 43–60.

Mullener, N., & Laird, J. D. (1971). Some developmental changes in the organization of self-evaluations. *Developmental Psychology, 5,* 233–236.

Nesselroade, J. R., & Baltes, P. B. (1974). Adolescent personality development and historical change: 1970–1972. *Monographs of the Society for Research in Child Development, 39*(1, Serial No. 154).

Niles, S. (1981). The youth culture controversy: An evaluation. *Journal of Early Adolescence, 1,* 265–271.

Offer, D. (1969a). *The psychological world of the teenager.* New York: Basic Books.

Offer, D. (1969b). Adolescent turmoil. In A. Esman (Ed.), *The psychology of adolescence* (pp. 141–154). Madison, CT: International Universities Press.

Offer, D., & Offer, J. (1975). *From teenager to young manhood.* New York: Basic Books.

Offer, D., Ostrov, E., & Howard, K. I. (1981). *The adolescent: A psychological self-portrait.* New York: Basic Books.

Pearson, G. H. J. (1958). *Adolescence and the conflict of generations.* New York: Norton.

Peel, E. A. (1975). Predilection for generalizing and abstracting. *British Journal of Educational Psychology, 45,* 177–188.

Petersen, A. C., & Taylor, B. (1980). The biological approach to adolescence. In J. Adelson (Ed.), *Handbook of adolescent psychology* (pp. 117–155). New York: Wiley.

Piaget, J. (1947). *The psychology of intelligence.* New York: Harcourt.

Piaget, J. (1972). Intellectual evaluation from adolescence to adulthood. *Human Development, 15,* 1–12.

Plaut, E. A., & Hutchinson, F. L. (1986). The role of puberty in female psychosexual development. *International Review of Psycho-Analysis, 13,* 417–432.

Rees, C. D., & Wilborn, B. L. (1983). Correlates of drug abuse in adolescents: A comparison of families of drug abusers with families of non-drug abusers. *Journal of Youth and Adolescence, 12,* 55–64.

Reich, A. (1951). The discussion of 1912 on masturbation and our present-day views. *Psychoanalytic Study of the Child, 6,* 80–91.

Resko, J. A., & Eik-Nes, K. B. (1966). Diurnal testosterone levels in peripheral plasma of human male subjects. *Journal of Clinical Endocrinology and Metabolism, 26,* 573–576.

Ritvo, S. (1971). Late adolescence: Developmental and clinical considerations. *Psychoanalytic Study of the Child, 26,* 241–263.

Ritvo, S. (1984). The image and uses of the body in psychic conflict. *Psychoanalytic Study of the Child, 39,* 449–469.

Rutter, M. (1980). *Changing youth in a changing society.* Cambridge, MA: Harvard University Press.

Santen, R. J., & Bardin, C. W. (1973). Episodic luteinizing hormone secretion in man. *Journal of Clinical Investigation, 52,* 2617–2628.

Schafer, R. (1973). Concepts of self and identity and the experience of separation–individuation in adolescence. *Psychoanalytic Quarterly, 42,* 42–59.

Schonfeld, W. A. (1971). Adolescent development: Biological, psychological, and sociological determinants. *Adolescent Psychiatry, 1,* 296–323.

Settlage, C. S. (1972). Cultural values and the superego in late adolescence. *Psychoanalytic Study of the Child, 27,* 74–92.

Seyler, L. E., & Reichlin, S. (1974). Episodic secretion of luteinizing hormone-releasing facter (LRF) in the human. *Journal of Clinical Endocrinology and Metabolism, 39,* 471–498.

Shavelson, R., Hubner, J. J., & Stanton, G. C. (1976). Validation of construct interpretations. *Review of Educational Research, 46,* 407–441.

Sherif, C. W. (1966). Adolescence: Motivational, attitudinal and personality factors. *Review of Educational Research, 36,* 437–449.

Simmons, R. G., Rosenberg, F., & Rosenberg, H. (1973). Disturbance in the self-image at adolescence. *American Sociological Review, 38,* 553–568.

Smith, D. (1976). The concept of youth: A re-evaluation. *Youth and Society, 7,* 347–365.

Spiegel, L. A. (1951). A review of contributions to a psychoanalytic theory of adolescence. *Psychoanalytic Study of the Child, 6,* 375–393.

Spiegel, L. A. (1958). Comments on the psychoanalytic psychology of adolescence. *Psychoanalytic Study of the Child, 13,* 296–308.

Stoltz, H. R., & Stoltz, L. M. (1951). *Somatic development in adolescence.* New York: Macmillan.

Stone, L. J., & Church, J. (1957). Pubescence, puberty, and physical development. In A. H. Esman (Ed.), *The psychology of adolescence* (pp. 75–85). Madison, CT: International Universities Press.

Tanner, J. M. (1962). *Growth at adolescence.* Springfield, IL: Charles C Thomas.

Tanner, J. M. (1969). Growth and endocrinology of the adolescent. In L. I. Gardner (Ed.), *Endocrine and genetic diseases of childhood* (pp. 19–60). Philadelphia: Saunders.

Tanner, J. M. (1972). Sequence, tempo, and individual variation in growth and development of boys and girls aged twelve to sixteen. In J. Kagan & R. Coles (Eds.), *Twelve to sixteen: Early adolescence* (pp. 1–24). New York: Norton.

Tanner, J. M. (1974). Sequence and tempo in the somatic changes in puberty. In M. M. Grumbach, G. D. Grave, & F. E. Mayer (Eds.), *Control of the onset of puberty* (pp. 448–470). New York: Wiley.

Timpane, M., Abramowitz, S., Bobrow, S., & Pascal, A. (1976). *Youth policy in transition.* Santa Monica, CA: Rand Corporation.

Waterman, A. (1982). Identity development from adolescence to adulthood: An extension of theory and a review of research. *Developmental Psychology, 18,* 341–358.

Weiner, I. B. (1980). Psychopathology in adolescence. In J. Adelson (Ed.), *Handbook of adolescent psychology* (pp. 447–471). New York: Wiley.

West, C. D., Mahajan, D. K., Chavre, V. J., Nabors, C. J., & Tyler, F. H. (1973). Simultaneous measurement of multiple plasma steroids by radio-immunoassay demonstrating episodic secretion. *Journal of Clinical Endocrinology and Metabolism, 36,* 1230–1236.

West, D. J. (1982). *Delinquency: Its roots, careers and prospects.* Cambridge, MA: Harvard University Press.

12

TOWARD A DYNAMIC GEROPSYCHOLOGY

DAVID L. GUTMANN

INTRODUCTION: THE UNKNOWN ELDERS

In this chapter I report on psychodynamically informed observations, made during the past 13 years in the course of diagnosing and treating older patients with late-onset psychopathology, and in the course of supervising graduate students preparing for a psychogeriatric specialty. Before we consider the material from the older, patient population, we should attend to a revealing finding from the younger, trainee population: Namely, that few promising graduate students are attracted to clinical geropsychology. Instead, once matriculated, they concentrate their efforts at the other end of the life cycle. They rarely want to treat the aged; they do want to treat children, adolescents, young adults, and young families. Some part of our graduate students' evident gerophobia comes from our common culture; but it is also a reasonable reaction to the dismal picture of aging routinely propagated by academic and clinical geropsychology. Typically, the older person is pictured as a wasted creature, compounded of irreversible losses in the physical, cognitive, psychological, and social domains. Older patients particularly are depicted as frail victims of cultural gerophobia, elder abuse, incontinence, and dementia. Typically, the treatment prescribed for these unfortunates is some version of long-term care, to be provided by nursing institutions or by "overburdened" caretakers. So defined, this senescent patient population is not likely to capture the imagination or concern of smart, spirited graduate students, charged high with therapeutic ambition. Small wonder that they turn their attention to younger patients, who appear to require "real" therapy, and trained expertise, rather than well-meaning hand-holding, or some equivalent of hospice care. Inevitably, once abandoned by clinical psychology, the field of geriatrics is taken over by those professionals committed to providing long-term care—nurses and social workers.

However, despite their bad press, there is a largely overlooked, silent majority of elders whose major goal is to avoid long-term, custodial care. Even when frail, they shun dependency and institutional care up to the last moment of possibility. This cohort still preserves, as a reality of the inner mind, the ethic of work and self-responsibility that used to be the keynote of our common culture. Certainly, this majority has its own psychological fragilities, and their stubborn pride can itself become—particularly in later life—a potent pathogen; but a growing percentage are slowly discovering that moderate doses of psychotherapy can help them achieve their unsurrendered goal of preserving a self-reliant life. Because we are beginning to see them as patients in psychotherapy, dynamically inclined psychologists are discovering the special virtues and vulnerabilities of this unique population, the hardy elders overlooked by academic psychology and by victim-centered politics.

In the body of this chapter, I discuss some specific patterns, some regularities that are becoming apparent as researchers explore, via psychodynamic tools, the special vulnerabilities, strengths, and sensitivities of this unexamined breed, the late-onset older patient.

CONVENTIONAL THERAPY AND PRACTICE: THE FORGOTTEN PATIENT

I start by considering, with greater specificity, the theoretical and practical shortcomings of the conventional, or "mass-effect" sighting on late pathogenesis. This rather actuarial, even bureaucratic, set of ideas, which dominates practice in geropsychiatry and clinical geropsychology, puts the major weight on the "exopathogens," the expectable physical and social stressors that pile up in later life. The older patient is presumably undone, overwhelmed by a barrage of stressors, external in origin. Presumably, these insults cannot be compensated by a personality system already weakened from prior depletions, particularly in the cognitive realm. When, in this view, the psyche cannot hold its emergency reactions to subclinical levels, then we get the late-onset psychiatric disorders: depressions, paranoias (in later life, the paraphrenias), anxiety states, and suicidal preoccupations that afflict the aged, and that swell to the point of social crisis with the proportional increase in the elderly population. Besides expressing the derogatory and catastrophic view of aging, such mass-effect conceptions lack the specificity that is necessary to any useful view of pathogenesis. Mass-effect theories are in effect "last straw" theories. Any one of an avalanche of stressors can be the undistinguished straw that finally breaks the camel's back.

Mass-effect ideas are contrary to the strong impressions gleaned from clinical observation of elder late-onset patients. One finds that they can deal heroically with major threats but routinely become unbalanced in response to stressors that do not loom very large on any objective scale. They can shrug off a potentially lethal cancer but become severely depressed in response to arthritic conditions, illnesses that at the worst threaten their motility rather than their life. The devastating effects of such—objectively speaking—minor insults attest to the subjectivity of stress. Thus, there are times when minor and seemingly innocuous events can appear, to patients with specific vulnerabilities, as though they were not the last straw but the whole bale.

Clinical geropsychologists have been profoundly influenced by the actuarial bias of the social sciences. Like the academic geropsychologists, they count things, and in assessing pathogenesis, they count straws and forget to examine the condition of the camel's back. The practices of academia, when translated to clinical practice, bring research rather than clinical criteria into the consulting room. Driven by the researcher's need for accuracy in measurement, clinical attention retreats from the combinatorial complexities of the historic *person*, the predisposed host, to the pseudospecificity provided by the standard, quantifiable features of the disease, the countable stressors and disease symptoms (e.g., the number and severity of depressive signs). In this externalized view, the febrile symptoms of depression become confounded with the total disease process. When the symptoms are reduced, again through some "external" means such as antidepressant or electroconvulsive (ECT) therapy, then the total disease has presumably been cured. A comparison with standard medical practice quickly reveals the inadequacy, even the danger, of such thinking. A leukemia, for example, is not "cured" when the fevers that attend its later stages have been suppressed; the bone marrow must be treated before it kills the host, even when the disordered material is not producing fever symptoms.

To be useful, and to be attractive to talented young recruits, clinical geropsychology has to become less defensively academic, and more truly clinical, more open to the complexities— but also the possibilities—that are introduced by the forgotten factor, the phenomenology of the individual older patient.

REDISCOVERING THE ELDERLY PATIENT

Paradoxically, virologists rather than psychologists are developing the new conceptions, including restoring the host as a vital element in the pathogenic drama, that are needed in geropsychiatry.

Before improved imaging and biochemical technology clarified matters, the virus, as a pathogenic element, was considered to be the sole cause of the infection. Like an invader, the virus presumably violated the host cell, forcing its rude way through the cell membrane and into the vulnerable interior nucleus. The cell was an innocent bystander and the pathology was the criminal act of the virus alone. However, improved instruments and techniques showed that the typical virus does not act unilaterally; instead, the cell in effect collaborates with the virus in bringing about the pathogenic outcome. In the modern view, the *locus* of pathology shifts away from the virus alone to the virus–cell interface and to the crucial interaction that is set in train by the conjunction of the particle and *specific* parts of the cell membrane.

Admittedly, the modern picture has become complex. Virologists can no longer be satisfied with the simple moral vision of a "bad," invasive virus that must be blocked from reaching the passive but innocent cell. However, when the disease is understood as a total process, one in which the "victim" cell is equally implicated, then specificity of diagnosis is gained, and the therapeutic options are greatly expanded. Internists now intervene against the virus, against the cell membrane, and against the pathogenic sequences that are set off by their mutual contact.

But, as I have indicated, the kind of sophisticated thinking that may conquer even the dreaded AIDS (acquired immunodeficiency syndrome) virus is not found among those who study, diagnose, and treat the late-onset functional psychiatric disorders. Conventional geropsychiatry and clinical geropsychology have not generated models of late-onset psychopathology that capture the complex interactions, among them the isomorphism between host and pathogen, that are found in advanced biological thinking. Returning to the viral analogy, it is as if the geropsychiatrists are still stuck with the "virus-as-invader" model that was dominant before the pivotal contribution of the host cell to the pathogenic process had been recognized. In conventional geropsychiatry, the pathogenic role, equivalent to that of the all-powerful virus, is played by the avalanche of stressors—the multiple losses in the somatic, cognitive, social, and economic realms—that supposedly swamp the typical elder.

As a consequence, the study and treatment of the late-onset disorders retreats to the *externals*, the stressful transitions, the incidental losses of aging, while ignoring the personal vulnerabilities and sensitivities that give particular losses their catastrophic weight for late-onset patients. Neglecting the predisposed individual is similar to investigating forest fires by studying only sparks or matches while disregarding the forest floor—the conditions of aridity and dead-wood clutter that render forests particularly vulnerable to the action of incendiary agents.

Psychodynamic perspectives are particularly useful at this point, as we turn to consider the predisposed, specifically vulnerable patient. Academic psychology urges one to consider the peripherals of the disease process, the stressors, and the symptoms; however, the historic patient, who mediates between stress and symptom, can best be grasped through the application of psychodynamic methods and conceptions. These are particularly useful in helping us to understand the contribution of historic trauma, and the defenses against them, to the current vulnerabilities of the predisposed patient.

TRAUMA, MYTH, NICHE: TRACING THE PREDISPOSITIONS

Our clinical studies, conducted under the auspices of the Older Adult Program (Northwestern University Medical School), have led to a model of life span development for those individuals who show some capacity for love and work in their young adult years but who are vulnerable to late-onset psychopathology. Consistent with life span developmental doctrine, we trace the origins of elderly distress to its beginnings in childhood. Our working model holds that the bases of the patient's lifelong vulnerability are laid down in early childhood, following some trauma or loss. That same vulnerability is brought to crisis in later life, when the defensive, compensatory structures that buffered the survivor against the original trauma are compromised. Whatever its nature, the early trauma—usually having to do with the loss of primary caretakers—underscores for the child its "natural" condition, its passive, shameful impotence before the awful blows of fate. Many children so stricken may not, in the psychic sense, survive such insults, but our text has to do with those hardier souls who do manage, by dint of their own psychological resources, to give themselves a compensatory, restorative experience. Defying their disconfirming situation, they generate fantasies—in actuality, origin myths of the self—that replace the numbing reality of their true condition of helplessness and vulnerability. As Erik Erikson (personal communication, circa 1962) put it, the child who lacks trustworthy caretakers might "find his thumb, and damn the world." In this manner a disappointed child, bereft of reliable nurture by others, might transfer the sense of trust from the disappointing parents to itself, or more precisely, to a grandiose, narcissistic myth about the self. Such fantasies depict the child, *to itself*, as totally self-sufficient, as holding all the resources necessary for survival. During early development, when reality and fantasy are still confounded, this myth, this dream about the self can have the tonus of immediacy and truth. Like the baby's thumb, it can be soothing and restorative. However, as developing children form self–other boundaries, they become aware of the crucial distinction between subjective fantasy, which is internal to the person, and objective reality, which is shared with others and external to the person. When this inner–outer distinction is reliably established, the fusion of fantasy and reality is undone, and the personal myth, now recognized as a piece of fantasy, loses the *tonus* of reality and much of its power to soothe. If it is to be again believable, the myth must be recombined with reality, which is now external and consensual. In this transformation, the fantasy can no longer be self-accredited; rather, it must be confirmed by those external others who have become significant to the self. Peers and elders must be found who will acknowledge the myth and deal with the person as though he or she were, in actuality, a true representation of the myth. The growing child must also find those who confirm the myth through paradox, by representing its contradiction: *They*, out there, are the Mama's boys, the cowards, or the savage brutes.

These roles in the mythic drama become essential, invariant elements of the personal *niches*, the psychosocial ecologies that vulnerable individuals construct from the raw materials of their shared psychosocial *habitats*. Defined by their objective properties, such habitats range from those formed around parents in childhood to those formed around peers and organizations in adulthood. In the course of development, they become more complex, more communal, and more abstract. However, in each new habitat the essential niche, the structure that confirms and defends the myth, has to be reconstituted.

This distinction, between habitat and niche, registers a split within the development of the at-risk individual. Normal development guides the search for and the adaptation to new *habitats*, but the essential niche and its contents evade normal development. The niche is the ecology of childish thinking; the arena in which development is retarded in the service of irrational defenses and grandiose legends. Thus, the personal integrity of the older patient is guarded by a niche that is, owing to the primitive logic of its construction, chronically at risk, particularly so in later life. The vulnerability of the primary niche is most apt to be revealed as the processes of aging degrade the capacity for adaptation to new habitats, reduce the potential niche population, and demonstrate, as in childhood, the tragic discrepancy between the personal myth and the patient's real situation. In short, as the niche deconstructs, the myth is unprotected, laid bare for comparison against the standards of impersonal "habitat" reality. No fantasy is ever finally lost, but the protective myth is revealed to be no more than a fantasy: "I am not what I pretended; I have lived a lie." In this regression, the myth loses its compensatory power, and the at-risk person is left with equally intolerable choices: To defend the myth in delusional ways, abandoning reality in favor of the myth; or to reexperience the *stranger*, the terror and isolation of the abandoned infant. Ultimately, the loss of the vital niche leaves at-risk elders alone with the stranger, alone with their bad internal objects. Much current theorizing in the gerontology literature (see Atchley, 1976) emphasizes the importance of self-continuity and the disabling consequences for the aging personality when the depletions of later life bring about, through mass effect, the loss of self-continuity. My contention is that the vital experience of self-continuity is finally compromised not by external losses but by the discovery of the bad internal presence, the *stranger* embedded at the core of self.

Those psychodynamic theorists who study late-onset pathology agree with the position stated here in that they reject mass-effect thinking, instead analyzing the *specific* effect of pathogenic stressors. Generally they propose that losses in later life are emotionally disabling insofar as they reverberate with a personal history of traumatic early loss. For them, the precipitant losses of later life are metaphors of early, still unhealed wounds.

I do not completely reject this view and find it useful in some instances. But, unlike these theorists, I do not propose that current precipitants are pathogenic only because they call up the early loss in some concrete, one-to-one fashion. In my view, the truly pathogenic stress does not directly invoke the original loss. Instead, it attacks and brings about the loss of the intervening, compensatory structures, niche and myth, that fended off the traumatic experience of, for example, early loss. In short, where other psychodynamic theorists have elaborated the equivalent of a *germ* theory, my and my colleagues' theory of pathogenesis deals with the psychoimmune system and its fate in the later years. The primary lesion in psychopathogenesis (as in pathogenesis generally) is the loss of the psychoimmune system; after that, a variety of specific traumas can more easily reverberate with early loss to bring on an opportunistic pathology.

POSTPARENTAL TRANSITIONS AS PATHOGENIC STRESSORS

Late-life threats to the vital niche are imposed from two sources: the internal, developmental transitions of the young–old (postparental) period and the external losses of the old–old (postproductive) period. I first discuss the transitions imposed by normal, postparental development and then use clinical material to identify the personality and niche factors that render certain men and women pathologically vulnerable to changes that normally bring about some growth, some expansion of self for the majority of their same-age peers.

My studies of older men and women in various cultures have led to this conclusion: Late development and late-onset pathology are often fueled by the same forces. They are driven by energies, released in men and women, in the course of the postparental transition toward androgyny. This tendency on the part of older individuals to become androgynous, to take on appetites, attitudes, and even behaviors characteristic of the opposite sex (e.g., the *contrasexual* transition) was first identified by Carl Jung (1933) on the basis of clinical evidence and was first studied empirically, in nonclinical and non-Western populations by Gutmann (1987). Confirmatory findings have been reported by a number of independent investigators: Atchley (1976); Brenneis (1975); Brown (1985); Feldman, Biringen, and Nash (1981); Galler (1977); Gold (1969); Hurlbert (1962); Jaslow (1976); Leonard (1967); Lewis (1965); Lowenthal, Thurnker, and Chiriboga (1975); Ripley (1984); Tachibana (1962); and Van Arsdale (1981).

Men discover a hitherto unsuspected vein of nurturance and aesthetic sensibility; women discover tough, managerial, and competitive qualities that they can apply in a first career or in a career change, as from social worker to lawyer. Bear in mind that the postparental transition, although it inevitably entails some stress, does not in itself constitute a crisis. Clinical observation of first-time casualties is required to help us identify the specific predispositions distinguishing the vulnerable individuals who convert potential development into clinical crisis.

The Postparental Male Patient: Fear of the Anima

In brief, my and my colleagues' clinical investigations reveal that late-onset male patients become victims of their own special sensitivity to assertive women, a tendency that has its roots in early experience: As they saw it, in their families of orientation, a passive father was domineered and "castrated" by a powerful mother. Their private myth is that they are not really the sons of such degraded men and that they will avoid or perhaps, through elevating themselves, redeem their fathers' fate. This myth is successively enacted in niches formed out of all the habitats that normal masculine development can sequentially provide: home, schoolyard, playing field, battlefield, shop, office. In each of these settings, these men had found ways of demonstrating to others—and through others, to themselves—that they are *not* the clones of their craven fathers; unlike their fathers, they are without fear, not to be trifled with. The niche that they establish within marriage is also organized to serve their myth. They marry quiet, biddable, even *adoring* women. As long as niche and myth are maintained, these men can appear as paragons of civic and psychological health; however, the postparental appearance of "passive" tendencies (Jung's *anima*) within themselves, and aggressive, competitive strivings in the wife, disrupt the niche—and usually at that time of life when they are too old to seek a new and properly passive woman. Lacking a "womanly" mate who will "hold," for them, their own contrasexual aspect, these men are forced to recognize that their sexual bimodality is located within themselves and not conveniently distributed between themselves and their wives. In their eyes, within the family of procreation they are reentering the traumatic situation of their family of origin: The wife is turning into the frightening mother, and they themselves are turning into their passive, compliant fathers. The Damoclean doom that they have spent their lives avoiding will now finally announce itself.

Ernest Hemingway, who committed suicide at age 62, was a prime example of the patterns identified here. Thus, his mother was formidable, particularly toward Ernest's father, who was disparaged in the home. (During his first 2 years of life, the mother also dressed Ernest as a girl and sometimes referred to him as a daughter.) Ernest, however, tugged strongly against the golden cord, and at the age of 3 announced, "Ain't afraid of nothin'!" This was his lifelong, pilot myth, and he sought out those habitats—battlefield, jungle, boxing ring, bull ring, and barroom—in which he could demonstrate and protect this myth. Adoring women, who looked to Hemingway to guide them through the African and urban jungles, were essential embellishments of his niche. *They* were the "daughters," the opposite of his ascendant mother, and they held in escrow for him the shadow side, the negation of his myth: *They*, not he, were the daughters, the frightened ones. Through these "daughters," Papa Hemingway could stay in touch with his contramythic side, protecting and even cherishing it in its outward form.

But internal change and external depletion made it more and more difficult for Hemingway to stock his niche with the requisite women. Internal shifts rendered him more dependent, more ready to trade submission for a woman's nurture. In addition, changes in his body brought on by alcoholism and wounds made him more needful of a woman's care but less capable of being a potent lover. Declaring him to be a phony, Martha Gellhorn (his third wife) left him, and ethereal young women, the usual daughters, although flattered by his attentions, no longer took him seriously as a lover. Hemingway's devastated response to these abandonments has now been made available to us in his posthumously published book, *The Garden of Eden* (1986). This is a chilling portrait of Katherine, a psychotic young woman who wills herself to become a man while requiring that her husband become her androgynous twin, even her "female" lover. Hemingway's twin-mother, barely disguised as Katherine and ready to turn him back into a "daughter," had returned.

Standard psychiatric discussions of Hemingway's late psychosis and final suicide have usually cited brain damage brought on by alcoholism and body damage brought on by his rugged life as sufficient causes for his terminal decline. They point, as is the psychiatric convention, to the exopathogens: the irreversible, organic contributions to Hemingway's suicidal depression. However, the functional, *reversible* predispositions had an equal if not greater effect—even though these were not addressed in his treatment—in bringing about the alcoholism that provoked the organic damage and his final coup de grace. Hemingway's alcoholism and its psychological preconditions, although potentially reversible, were left untreated. Treatment was instead concentrated on the irreversible somatic consequences of Hemingway's alcoholism, but by then it was too late.

The Postparental Female Patient: Fear of Power

A minority of postparental women become casualties of their own crescent aggression. Again, although most women adapt to and even enjoy their new infusion of aggressive spirit, a minority are terrified of this endowment and respond as though it were a profound depletion rather than a potential gain. This is an important group of patients because, owing to their self-abasing presentation, they are very commonly misdiagnosed. Afraid of their cresting anger, they deny it through outward postures of weakness, exhaustion, and handwringing despair. They present themselves as victims of avalanching losses rather than as potential attackers. Mental health workers too often collude with their denial and agree with these women that they are indeed hapless victims of losses and insults over which they had little or no control. As a consequence, they are treated in palliative ways that, although they may reduce symptoms, do not get at fundamental conflicts. The patient is left vulnerable to later episodes.

Again, in treating these patients, my colleagues and I concentrate not on symptoms but on the predispositions that lead these women to break down, for the first time, following the normal transition toward a more combative nature. Like the male casualties of the postparental period, these women also report a destructive mother, but where the male patients defend against their identification with a weak father, these women defend against their identification with the destructively strong witch-mother. For them, to become aggressive means that they are turning into their own "bad" mothers; they will be hated by their children and husbands just as the mother had once been hated by their fathers and by themselves. Women of this complexion are inordinately sensitive to the postparental transition, the emptying of the nest. For them, the home is the habitat out of which they craft their special niche, peopled with their gratified mate and children. Their adoring dependents prove their myth: "I am a loving, not a hateful, mother." These twin events, their rising assertion and their loss of niche, render these women very vulnerable to the sealed-off stranger and to the traumatic idea: "*I am a destructive, hence hated, mother.*"

Predisposing vulnerabilities of the sort outlined here can interact with other "normal" precipitant circumstances—for example, the husband's illness and her own widowhood—of the young–old period. Widows who show pathological depression rather than normal grief are particularly worthy of attention from our viewpoint. Conventional practitioners regularly view them as inadequate creatures, without resources of their own, when bereft of the protection of loving husbands; overlooked in this rather sexist calculus is that the widow, while genuinely grieving her loss, may bring on depression by guilt rather than by grief: She blames her newfound anger for her husband's death. Feelings of guilt and depletion are mingled in widowhood, but practitioners too often focus on the irreversible element, loss, while ignoring the reversible element, irrational guilt.

As a case example, consider the life history and treatment history of an "empty nest" woman who came to us for outpatient treatment so evidently devastated and needful that she frightened her student therapist. "She will eat me up," the trainee told the supervisor. The projective test protocols showed that the blighted presentation represented a defensive posture, designed to provoke "niche" responses in the therapist, and not a true decompensation. Thus, the Rorschach responses were not at all depressive in content but full of combative—albeit destructive—energy: "two bulls charging each other, head-on, with blood splattering" and "an erupting volcano, with a phoenix coming out of the ashes" were typical. Clearly, this woman was not a victim of the empty nest. Instead, she was terrified of the aggressive energies released by normal postparental development and by the loss of the "motherhood" niche within which she could anchor her defenses against such dangerous promptings. In the course of a treatment that dealt with rage rather than loss as a focal issue, this woman reviewed her anger, as well as the historic roots of her irrational fears around such lively motives. In so doing, she was able to "normalize" her assertive feelings, split them from their dangerous meanings, turn their sign from completely negative to qualifiedly positive, and even come to enjoy them.

DISORDERS OF THE OLD–OLD: IMPOSED LOSS AS A PRECIPITANT

The conventional wisdom, as expressed in the mass-effect model, has it that all disorders of the later years, whether among the young–old or the old–old, have external losses as their precipitant. However, my colleagues and I hold that such exopathogens are the major precipitants of disease only among the old–old, after the developmental transitions and endopathogens of the young–old period have subsided. Nevertheless, although imposed losses rather than developmental transitions fuel the disorders of the old–old, our basic diagnostic questions and analytic scheme remain unchanged. Given that most elders endure the usual attritions of later life without developing significant emotional disorders, researchers must study the predisposing elements in the psyches of those who do succumb. Indeed, the analysis of predisposing elements is particularly relevant for the late-onset old–old patients: Until their breakdowns, they have endured many blows of fate without becoming ill. What, then, are the predisposing factors that have remained latent for so long and that render them particularly sensitive to the special losses and transitions of senescence?

Clinicians need to consider three classes of old–old casualties: those prompted by public and social losses (e.g., retirement); those prompted by losses in the intimate domain (e.g., losses of kin, widowhood, etc.); and those prompted by losses in the physical domain (e.g., losses of vision, audition, and motility; life-threatening illness). I begin with the social transitions, such as retirement, that aged patients experience as catastrophic losses.

Men predisposed to suffer from retirement are troubled for a variety of reasons: Their valued competence is no longer confirmed, they are no longer demonstrably powerful, they have lost a milieu stocked with "male allies," or retirement has brought about their long-delayed reentry into the domain of the now-empowered wife. Chronically dependent men—in particular those who derive their self-esteem from the alliance with some powerful boss or corporation—may feel empty after retirement and vulnerable to attrition from all quarters, including their ascendant wives.

A female casualty of retirement defended against her latent identification with a masochistic, victimized mother by forging a compensatory alliance with the father and later with men in general. Such women have special reason to value their careers, and in her case, retirement meant a loss of her "masculine" myth, the niche that protected it, and entry into the feared, negative identity of the "weak mother." Finally, through retirement from the men's world, she had been "feminized," castrated, turned into the abhorred mother, the silly creature that the adored father would despise.

Therapy interventions with this patient led her to recontact her established "masculine" strengths; having found her way back to a trusted constancy, she could endure change: She could begin to explore and come to terms with her "weak" feminine side.

PHYSICAL ILLNESS AS THE PRECIPITANT OF LATE-ONSET DISORDER

The physical pathogens present a paradox: The life-threatening illnesses—cardiac disorders, cancers—are less likely to sponsor emotional disorders in the old than the objectively more benign disorders, those that attack mobility and independence, rather than life itself. Such findings demonstrate the specificity of stress: It is the subjective implications of the stress—its antagonism to some vital niche—rather than its objective magnitude, that determines the degree of pathogenic effect.

Thus, the "niche" model helps to resolve the paradox of subjective stress. Clinicians know, for example, that nonlethal losses of motility can bring about psychologically lethal depressions and paraphrenias. This is because free, self-directed movement is very important to those counterdependent elders who deal heroically with a cancer but who break down when crippled by severe arthritis. These people, men and women alike, share predisposing experiences of loss, desolation, and abandonment from early childhood, and such trauma left them without much trust in others. For them, to walk meant to take charge of their own bodies, to render *them* under control, trustworthy. Walking meant that they could stride away from a worried mother, instead of waiting passively and fearfully for her to return after she had walked away from them. For these patients, the body is a kind of primary niche, guarding their necessary myth, of complete self-sufficiency. When their executive capacities—walking, hearing, seeing—are compromised, they lose more than specific skills; they lose the assurance of a reliable body, their confirmation as self-sufficient beings. They lose, in effect, the reality of their private myth. When myth loses the tonus of reality and regresses to the status of fantasy, its protective power is lost along with its credibility. The patients are left alone with the internal "stranger": Once again, they experience themselves as the hapless child, abandoned by the untrustworthy caretaker, on the verge of destruction.

Typical is the case of a 73-year-old childless widow, living alone in public housing. After suffering a partially disabling hip fracture, she developed paranoid delusions concerning her neighbors and housing project supervisor: They were conspiring to squirt a disabling gas under her door. This delusion protected the patient's unrelinquished myth, of a completely trustworthy body: She could protest that her motility was not compromised by irreversible bone damage, but by a *reversible* cause, the ill will of her neighbors. If only the police or mayor would intervene, her legend of complete, untarnished body integrity would be restored. The remedial approach with such patients is to help them build trust in the therapist so that they are less dependent on their own "body myth," and less devastated by the untrustworthiness of their own senescent bodies.

Mild organic losses, whether brought on by early dementia or by stroke, can serve as the precipitant for a severe though reversible *functional* disorder. Thus, one sees patients whose organic brain disease is not in itself disabling; rather, they are disabled by the intensity of their own catastrophic reaction to mild memory losses. In these cases, the anxious or depressive reaction can itself have disabling (reversible) effects on cognition, maintaining and even worsening the precipitating dementia. Under such circumstances, too many therapists diagnose the dementia, and overlook the treatable aspect, the depression.

EXISTENTIAL CRISES AND LATE-ONSET DISORDERS

My colleagues and I encounter patients who are disabled by the more fateful, inexorable concomitants of later life: aging per se, and mortality, the end of existence. The fear of aging and death is felt most keenly by particularly narcissistic individuals, those "addicted" to a cosmetic vision of themselves or to a myth of their own complete invulnerability. The greatest sensitivity to the threat of death is often found among women who have not lived a full life cycle (e.g., those who have never raised children). The fear of losing others through death is often strongest among those older childless women whom we call "mother's daughters": Women who have never become mothers because they themselves never ceased to be *daughters*. Always tied to their mothers or to a succession of maternal figures (aunts, older sisters, or even the mother's physical domicile), these women tend to fall apart when the last of such "mothers" dies or goes into a nursing home. At this point, such patients are catapulted by fate into the separate existence that they have spent their life avoiding. For them, the psychiatric hospital and its corps of attendant nurses can be the final "mother figure"; they are even willing to lose reality via psychosis in order to secure this continuity of "maternal" care. Other childless women are troubled by the looming prospect of their own deaths. Never having had children, they have not undergone the major transformations of adult narcissism that routinely result in the mother valuing the life of the offspring above his or her own. They have never, through their own maturation as parents, come to terms with their own mortality; in the later years, particularly with the onset of illness, they experience a kind of "life-cycle shock"—one strong enough to precipitate a depression or even a psychosis.

However, some childless patients have reached their disordered state by a different route: They are "father's daughters" rather than "mother's daughters," and their vulnerability to the existential terrors of later life also has its own unique history. As children, these women were profoundly attracted to their fathers, but they avoided the oedipal rivalry with their mothers by altering, in fantasy, their gender: Instead of being the father's daughter, their myth holds that they are his best son. They ally themselves with the father as achiever, they develop their own careers, and they join the father in disparaging the "silly," feminine mother. They may marry, but they avoid like the plague any experiences that would irreversibly stamp them "woman." Although they did not let their mature, fertile bodies turn them into women, they cannot stop their aging bodies from demonstrating their "feminine" weakness. Like the other victim groups, the loss of their masculine myth leaves them alone with their bad object, the stranger that—because it memorializes the despised mother—is also the most intimate part of themselves. Again, the task of psychodynamic treatment is to acquaint patients with this most intimate stranger, so that they can finally own it, without the need for a vulnerable superstructure of buffering myths (and the equally vulnerable niches that rationalize those myths).

TREATING THE OLDER PATIENT

In our therapeutic work we give special emphasis to the new perspectives on later-life treatment that are suggested by the foregoing analyses. These notions, already tested in practice, include the analysis of niche–myth relationships; the identification of focal, treatable concerns; the use of the therapeutic situation as an alternate niche; the usefulness (and limitations) of reminiscence therapies; and the particular value of the young therapist (as a metaphor of the patient's younger self).

In later life, the vital sense of self-continuity is particularly threatened, and the resulting pathologies can be effectively and specifically treated by the process of guided reminiscence, a therapeutic technique that sponsors the recall, even the reliving, of crucial memories. For the young adult patient, the memories elicited in therapy tend to cluster around their formative years, but for the older patient, the recovered memories call up the time when the niche was intact, the time when the patient had in effect formed, or "parented," an adult self. Such accounts reconstitute for the therapist, and for the patient, a vivid sense of what the client once was, and in important respects, still is.

The reminiscing patient becomes, for the therapist, a *historic* person, one who relates the past to the present via a consistent personal theme, the expression of the personal legend. Sensitized to the patient's "founding" theme, the therapist deals now with the patient in terms of that legend, becoming a counterplayer in the patient's personal drama.

This form of empathy does not condemn the therapist to long-term hand-holding. Quite the contrary: When dealing with elderly survivors, one should avoid, particularly in the early stages of treatment, the temptation to be "soothers" and rescuers. The rigidly self-sufficient, late-onset patient often feels patronized—ultimately, infantilized—by a demonstrably "soft," supportive approach on the part of the therapist. Such patients are more apt to feel respected and confirmed by a therapist who mixes warmth with confrontation and who credits the older patient with "street smarts" or tough-mindedness.

Late-onset patients frequently present themselves as mavericks, as life members of the opposition, and the therapist should acknowledge and even relish this stance. In addition, the therapist should become the dedicated opponent, an opponent who is not defeated by the patient, who does not defeat the patient, and who does not leave the patient. In effect, the therapist's voice replaces the voices that have been lost, irretrievably, from the patient's niche: The voices of those who—whether as enemies or "fighting friends"—once dealt with the patient as a serious contender. Thus, the therapist deals with the older patient *now* as he or she used to be, back *then;* the therapist takes over the function of relating the past to the present which the patient had previously entrusted to members of the now-defunct niche. As a consequence, the patient begins to reestablish, via the therapist, the lost experience of historic depth, of being a *recognized* self, marked by a continuous and distinctive theme. In effect, the patient is self-restored as a constant, familiar psychological *object.*

Again, this is more than supportive treatment. The restoration of self-continuity is a necessary precondition for an uncovering therapy. Any passage in human development—including the experience of psychotherapy—calls up a dialectic between constancy and change, and the older patient can provoke change, can open the hidden bays and reaches of the psyche, once he or she has reestablished the lost constancy of the self. When the patient is convinced that the therapist will "hold" the self-myth, the patient can temporarily depart from that familiar station to explore the strange, contramythic parts of self. When self-continuity is lost, the elderly patient is assaulted by bad objects, by the internal strangers; however, when myth and constancy are restored, the elderly patient can seek out, *explore* the internal strangers, resolve the tension between them and the myth, and bring them into the precincts of the familiar self.

Feeling rooted, constant, the patient is more able to risk change: the exploration of the toxic essence, the contralegendary aspects of self. The therapist accepts and even relishes these once lost, reemerging parts of the self, thereby "normalizing" them as acceptable contents of the personality. In this fashion, the therapist portrays a new integration of the legendary and contralegendary aspects of the patient's personality. The patient can identify with this integration and take it in to form a more expansive, less vulnerable version of self.

In sum, by applying principles and concepts generic to psychodynamic practice, my colleagues and I have come up with some guidelines for the diagnosis and treatment of a population that has been underserved by practitioners of this discipline. The psychodynamic perspective has helped us to identify *specific,* reversible features of the individual case, and it has helped us to craft specific, hence useful, interventions.

REFERENCES

Atchley, R. (1976). Selected social and psychological differences between men and women in later life. *Journal of Gerontology, 31,* 204–211.

Brenneis, C. R. (1975). Developmental aspects of aging in women. *Archives of General Psychiatry, 32,* 429–435.

Brown, J. (1985). *In her prime, a new view of middle-aged women.* South Hadley, MA: Bergin & Garvey.

Feldman, S., Biringen, C., & Nash, S. (1981). Fluctuations of sexual-related self-attributions as a function of stage of family life cycle. *Developmental Psychology, 17,* 24–25.

Galler, S. (1977). *Women graduate student returnees and their husbands: A study of the effects of the professional and academic graduate school experience on sex-role perceptions, marital relationships, and family concepts.* Unpublished doctoral dissertation, Northwestern University, Evanston, IL.

Gold, S. (1969). Cross-cultural comparisons of role change with aging. *Student Journal of Human Development, 1,* 11–15.

Gutmann, D. (1987). *Reclaimed powers: Toward a new psychology of men and women in later life.* New York: Basic Books.

Hemingway, E. (1986). *The garden of eden.* New York: Scribner.

Hurlbert, J. (1962). *Age as a factor in the social organization of the Hare Indiana of Fort Good Hope, Northwest Territories.* Ottawa, Ontario, Canada: Northern Coordination and Research Centre, Department of Northern Affairs and National Resources.

Jaslow, P. (1976). Employment, retirement and morale among older women. *Journal of Gerontology, 31,* 212–218.

Jung, C. (1933). *Modern man in search of a soul.* New York: Harcourt, Brace.

Leonard, O. (1967). The older Spanish-speaking people of the Southwest. In E. Youmans (Ed.), *The older rural Americans* (pp. 239–261). Lexington: University of Kentucky Press.

Lewis, O. (1965). *Life in a Mexican village: Tepoztlan restudied.* Urbana-Champaign: University of Illinois Press.

Lowenthal, M., Thurnher, M., & Chiriboga, D. (1975). *Four stages of life.* San Francisco: Jossey-Bass.

Ripley, D. (1984). *Parental status, sex roles, and gender mastery style in working class fathers.* Unpublished doctoral dissertation, Illinois Institute of Technology, Chicago.

Tachibana, K. (1962). A study of introversion-extraversion in the aged. In C. Tibbitts & W. Donahue (Eds.), *Social and psychological aspects of aging: Aging around the world* (pp. 655–656). New York: Columbia University Press.

Van Arsdale, P. W. (1981). The elderly Asmat of New Guinea. In P. T. Amoss & S. Harrel (Eds.), *Other ways of growing old: Anthropological Perspectives.* Stanford, CA: Stanford University Press.

III

RESEARCH APPROACHES TO COGNITIVE PROCESSES

INTRODUCTION: PSYCHOANALYSIS AND COGNITIVE PSYCHOLOGY

Psychoanalysis has aspired to be a general theory of human development and behavior. As such, it has aimed to understand and explain both the mechanisms and the meanings of normal and pathological behavior. Naturally, in the consulting room, the primary emphasis was on the purposes and the meanings of the patient's pathology, whereas, on the level of theory the focus was broadened to include explanations of the processes and mechanisms underlying behaviors. Initially, there was a reductionistic tendency in the theory. If one could account for behavior in physical/chemical terms, one could feel that the explanation of meaning and experience had also been achieved. Although Freud abandoned this goal as unrealistic, some of his later writings still reflected this bias. As George Klein (1976) correctly noted, the metapsychology was designed to explain the clinical theory, and in that sense was regarded as the more fundamental level of explanation. In more recent years, especially with the hermeneutic turn in psychoanalysis and the demise of Freud's metapsychology (Holt, 1981), the realm of purposeful strivings, meanings, and intentions increasingly has come to be seen as a realm in its own right and one that requires clinical theories appropriate to the psychological domain (Klein, 1976).

As suggested above, Freud was always concerned with both meanings and mechanisms (Holt, 1972). With respect to repression, for example, Freud was interested in both the motives and purposes it served as well as how such a process operated. From an interest in how the mind worked in defending itself against unpleasure Freud developed a more general interest in cognition, an interest that was already evident in his monograph *On Aphasia* and that pervaded much of his subsequent writings. The variety of cognitive aspects of behavior addressed by Freud included the nature of mental representation; the distinction between conscious and unconscious mentation and the functional significance of awareness; the differences between primary and secondary process thought, the mechanisms, selectivity, and limits of attention; the relationship of cognition to altered states of consciousness (e.g., the differences in verbal and imagistic representation of thought and the model presented in Chapter 7 of *The Interpretation of Dreams*); and the nature of memory and perception. Of course, one of Freud's central interests was the manner in which unconscious wishes and conflicts influenced conscious thought.

Several key features of Freud's theory of cognition already appeared on his *Project for a Scientific Psychology* (Freud, 1885/1966) and were further elaborated in Chapter 7 of *The Interpretation of Dreams* (Freud, 1900/1953). Cognition is used here in a broad sense to include perception, learning, thinking, memory, and attention as well as defensive processes. The concepts of primary and secondary process thinking and their relation to hallucinatory wish fulfillment and the development of reality-oriented thinking, the mechanisms of condensation, displacement, and symbolism, and the distinction between "word representations" and "thing representations" are a few of the concepts that Freud used to explain a variety of conscious and unconscious mental activities ranging from dreams, symptoms, jokes, and parapraxes to myths and rituals.

Concern with the neurophysiological mechanisms underlying cognition and other psychological processes was evident in Freud's posthumously published *Project for a Scientific Psychology*. Although Freud abandoned the *Project* in favor of a psychological level of explanation, he believed that eventually it would be possible to explain psychological phenomena on a neurophysiological level. In fact, the model developed in the *Project* turned out to be a fairly sophisticated one, given contemporary knowledge in the neurosciences (Pribram & Gill, 1976). In recent years, there have been a few attempts to study brain–behavior relationships from the perspective of psychoanalytic theory (e.g., Galin, 1974; Shevrin & Fritzler, 1968a, 1968b; Shevrin & Dickman, 1980; Reiser, 1984). Three of the contributions in this section (Shevrin, Winson, and Ellman) reflect this approach.

Several of Freud's subsequent writings indicate his abiding interest in the nature of cognition. A *Note Upon a "Mystic Writing Pad"* (Freud, 1925/1961) and *Formulations Regarding the Two Principles of Mental Functioning* (Freud, 1911/1958) are but two examples of this concern. Of course, Freud was drawn to the issue of cognitive functioning in connection with his focus on how the ego mediates between the demands of the drives and the dictates of reality. Central to Freud's account of cognition and, more broadly, ego functioning are the concepts of intentionality and mental representation. As Wakefield clearly points out in chapter 3, Freud's interest in intentionality and in mental representations are an important link to the recent work in cognitive science.

The subsequent development of ego psychology (Freud, 1926/1959; Hartmann, 1939, 1964; Arlow & Brenner, 1964), with its concepts of primary and secondary autonomy, conflict-free spheres of ego functioning, and the elaboration of the ego's role in adaptation and in reality-oriented thinking, led to a renewed interest in cognition. For example, Gill (1967) and Holt (1967) presented important theoretical clarifications of problematic aspects of the concept of primary process thinking. Wolff (1960) attempted to compare and integrate Piaget's and Freud's views of cognitive development.

At the time of Freud's death, the influence of psychoanalytic theory on academic psychology was nil. Nor did analytic writers turn to the psychological literature for contributions to their theoretical efforts. Psychological research in the area of cognition was concerned with the establishment of general laws. Individual differences generally were regarded as troublesome "error" variance. The typical study of cognitive functioning involved a subject in an alert state of consciousness, set to make a reality-oriented, intentional response to emotionally neutral stimuli. Such conditions virtually assured that the contribution of personal motives would be minimal. Laboratory efforts to incorporate emotional material in purported tests of Freud's view of repression were oversimplified and irrelevant tests of repression, as Rapaport (1960) showed in his review of research on psychoanalytic theory.

In the 1940s, a small cadre of psychoanalytically informed academic psychologists began conducting research in perception and cognition. The distinguishing features of this psychoanalytically oriented approach were its emphasis on (a) the motivational dynamics of cognition, (b) individual differences in cognitive structures, (c) the various experiential modes of cognition (e.g., dreams, fantasies, images), and (d) the functional significance of awareness (i.e., cognition with and without awareness). Detailed accounts of these early efforts can be found in Rapaport (1960), Sears (1943), Klein (1970), and Wolitzky and Wachtel (1973).

MOTIVATIONAL DYNAMICS OF COGNITION

The postwar emergence of the New Look in perception was a forceful corrective to the prior neglect accorded motivational influences on behavior. A multitude of studies in the past four decades have provided evidence that perception and cognition can be influenced by bodily needs (e.g., hunger), rewards and punishments, variations in stimulus emotionality, and the personality characteristics of the perceiver. These variables were shown to influence judgments of size, weight, and brightness, thresholds for perceptual recognition, and response latency and content. It was found, for example, that poor, compared with rich, children were more prone to overestimate the size of coins (Bruner & Goodman, 1947), that the number of food responses to ambiguous pictures increased as a function of hunger (Sanford, 1937), and that emotionally disturbing or so-called taboo words, compared with neutral ones, had higher *or* lower recognition thresholds (called *perceptual defense* and *perceptual vigilance*, respectively).

Many of the early New Look studies suffered from a simplistic application of Freud's concept of wish-fulfillment, in which it was assumed that the stronger the need or motive, the greater would be its impact on cognition. It was soon realized that an adaptive view of perception required a theory in accord with the fact that cognition was responsive to both reality and to wishes and needs. Task, stimulus, and subject variables interacted to determine the impact of motive and need. Contradictory and equivocal findings made this evident. For instance, replication of the original coin estimation study indicated that the overestimation of size was obtained when the judgments were made from memory but not when the stimuli were physically present (Carter & Schooler, 1949). Similarly, it was found that the influence of hunger on responses to ambiguous stimuli was not a monotonic function of hours since last eating and was more apparent in open-ended tasks (e.g., imagery) with many degrees of freedom for response as compared with more structured tasks (e.g., word completion).[1]

COGNITIVE CONTROL AND COGNITIVE STYLE

In posing the question, Where is the perceiver in perceptual theory?, Klein and Schlesinger (1949) called attention to individual differences in "perceptual attitudes," later called "cognitive styles" and "cognitive controls," as reflecting basic dispositions that mediated the impact of needs and motives. Klein (1954) demonstrated, for example, that the same need (thirst) had *opposite* effects in subjects with contrasting perceptual attitudes. This perspective made sense of findings

---

[1]See Wolitzky (1968) for a discussion of these issues. For a review and discussion of the numerous studies of perceptual defense see Eagle and Wolitzky (1977).

regarding perceptual defense and perceptual vigilance. It was shown, for example, that defense versus vigilance effects were predictable from independent assessments of subjects' defensive styles. Thus, "repressors" (who used avoidant defenses) had raised perceptual thresholds for emotionally charged stimuli, whereas "sensitizers" (i.e., those who manifested more intellectualized defenses) had lowered thresholds for the critical stimuli (Erdelyi, 1974; Eagle & Wolitzky, 1977).

It should be noted that the idea of perceptual defense was from the start a subject of considerable controversy. Many psychologists were unwilling to believe that there could be an active inhibition of perceptual processing on the basis of "discrimination without awareness." Such a notion seemed like a contradiction in terms because it implies preperceiving homunculi or "unconscious mannequins." Presumably more parsimonious hypotheses (word frequency, response suppression, response bias, partial cues) were advanced to account for the effects.[2]

The work on cognitive controls and cognitive style (the patterning of cognitive controls) was linked by Klein and his coworkers (Gardner, Holzman, Klein, Linton, & Spence, 1959) to the ego-psychological concepts of secondary autonomy and conflict-free spheres of ego functioning. The central notion guiding this work was that a relatively few basic individual consistencies in preferred modes of perceiving and thinking (measured mostly by performance on simple psychophysical tasks) could account for behavior in a wide variety of situations and that these basic dispositions formed the prototype for different forms of defense. To cite one example, tendencies toward the cognitive control of "leveling," which referred to the tendency not to notice subtle, but progressive changes in stimuli, were found to be correlated with a repressive style of defense (Holzman & Gardner, 1959).

STATES OF CONSCIOUSNESS AND LEVELS OF AWARENESS

Inspired by psychoanalytic theory, some psychologists attempted to conduct laboratory studies aimed at demonstrating that stimuli outside focal awareness could influence the nature and content of conscious thought and that these effects could differ as a function of different states of consciousness. Obviously, we cannot review this vast body of literature here. These studies went beyond the perceptual defense studies in that they sought to demonstrate delayed effects of subliminal stimuli on various aspects of conscious thought and behavior. Wolitzky and Wachtel (1973) presented a comprehensive overview of this work.

The original impetus for this work came from Poetzl's (1917) study, which showed that unreported (and presumably unconsciously processed) aspects of a stimulus presented in the waking state found a way into the subject's dream, thereby giving credence to Freud's thinking about the "day residue." Fisher (1954, 1956) picked up on Poetzl's work and stimulated much further work in this area. As with the perceptual defense studies, there was heated controversy about whether the reported effects could really occur in the absence of awareness, and many methodological controls and differing criteria of awareness were set forth in an attempt to pin down the phenomenon of subliminal perception.

Perhaps the most ambitious program of research that went beyond attempts to demonstrate cognition without awareness to the investigation of specific psychoanalytic hypotheses was conducted by Silverman and his coworkers (Silverman, 1983). The subliminal stimulus used most

---

[2]For an account of this long and heated controversy see Erdelyi (1974) and Eagle and Wolitzky (1977).

frequently by Silverman was "Mommy-and-I-are-one," a message designed to activate an uncon-scious fantasy of merging. The aim was to determine the kinds of subjects for whom such a stimulus would temporarily intensify or lessen pathological thinking and behavior.[3]

ATTENTION AND LEARNING

In his 1960 review of the status of psychoanalytic theory, Rapaport observed that an important gap in the comprehensiveness of the theory was its relative silence regarding the processes of learning, perception, concept formation, and other aspects of normal cognitive functioning. This is one area in which, with a few exceptions, psychologists still have not applied psychoanalytic concepts to their empirical work. On the other hand, analysts have been quite interested in the work on early cognitive development and the infant's cognitive capacities as it bears on their theories of personality development and psychopathology. These concerns are well represented in this book in Section II.

PRIMARY AND SECONDARY PROCESS THINKING

This is an area in the psychoanalytic theory of cognition that has received a considerable amount of empirical study, although most of it has been the contribution of one person—Robert Holt (1966). As is well known, Freud (1911/1958) spelled out the distinction of primary and secondary process thinking. Briefly stated, primary process thinking is characterized by the immediate discharge of drive energy through the mechanisms of symbolization, displacement, and condensation. This kind of thinking is based on a "drive organization" of memories and is most clearly observed in dreams, hallucinations, and fantasies. Secondary process thinking is dominated more by the reality principle than by the pleasure principle. It is reality-oriented, nonperemptory, and is based on a "conceptual organization" of memories. This quality of thinking reflects structuralized delay involving experimentation in thought with small amounts of cathectic energy (Rapaport, 1960). The energic aspects of this conceptualization have been soundly criticized. Nonetheless, its descriptive accounts have guided research.

Holt's research program on primary process thinking (Holt, 1966; Holt & Havel, 1960) focused on the operationalization of the concept in the form of a highly elaborate, complex Rorschach scoring system that, by now, has been translated into several languages. Individual differences in formal and content aspect of primary process thinking have been related to several aspects of personality functioning, to behavior in experimentally induced special states (e.g., LSD, sensory deprivation), and to particular phenomena (e.g., regression in the service of the ego). Other noteworthy efforts relevant to a psychoanalytic theory of thinking include the work of Blatt and Wild (1976), and Johnston and Holzman (1979).

We should also note that the chapters in Section II reflect many efforts inspired by psychoanalytic conceptions of early infancy to map the cognitive capacities of the neonate. This body of work has important implications for a psychoanalytic theory of thinking.[4]

---

[3]For reviews of this body of work and its related methodological issues see Silverman (1983), Balay & Shevrin (1988), and Cheeseman and Merikle (1986).

[4]See also Wolff's (1960) attempt to explore the similarities between Freud's and Piaget's theories of cognition.

EGO DEFENSES

This aspect of Freud's theory has stimulated a vast body of research by academic psychologists. Cooper's chapter in book volume summarizes a good deal of the more recent work, particularly with pathological populations. It might be noted that, beginning with the work on perceptual defense discussed above, there have been continual efforts to measure Freudian descriptions of defense and to relate them to other behaviors. Actually, as we noted in the Preface, Rosenzweig (1934) had made a very early attempt to study defenses, dismissed by Freud as unnecessary but harmless (Mackinnon & Dukes, 1964).

Nonetheless, the past four decades have seen a multitude of empirical studies influenced more or less directly by the psychoanalytic concept of defense. A good deal of the early work in this area was done in the laboratory. Unfortunately, the manner in which most of these studies were carried out was such that the requirements of measurement and control changed the meaning and nature of the phenomena to the point that they could hardly be seen as relevant tests of Freudian hypotheses. In fact, as indicated earlier, Rapaport (1960), in his appraisal of the research evidence for or against psychoanalytic theory, concluded that almost all of it was irrelevant because it violated the terms and conditions of the theory. Holmes (1990), for example, reviewed the laboratory evidence for repression and concluded that it was negative. In line with Rapaport's (1960) point, however, an examination of these studies indicates that few, if any of them, were meaningful tests of the Freudian hypothesis of repression.[5]

THE CHAPTERS IN THIS SECTION

We have presented a brief overview of psychological research in cognition relevant to psychoanalysis in order to provide an historical context for the appreciation of the chapters in this section. The chapters to follow are examples of efforts currently underway that can contribute to a comprehensive psychoanalytically based theory of cognitive processes. Central to such a theory is an account that integrates what is known about motivation, affect, and cognition and their interaction in adaptive and maladaptive behavior.

According to Westen, cognitive theories have finally come to the realization that conscious awareness is not necessary for the processing of even complex information and that social-cognitive psychology has become increasingly interested in mental representations and in the interaction of cognition and affect. The moment would appear to be at hand for the potentially mutually enriching contributions that the psychoanalytic and the social-cognitive model can offer one another. Westen states that ". . . any comprehensive theory of the role of cognition and affect in interpersonal functioning will have to integrate aspects of these two approaches." However, Westen argues, that the path to such an integration is blocked by untenable assumptions in each model.

He begins by noting that Jacobson, Sandler, Bowlby, Mahler, and Kernberg each have developed concepts that describe the child's construction of an inner world in which the self and objects are represented mentally. Integral to these models are the role of affect, motivation, and unconscious processes in relation to cognition, conflict, and the person's developmental history. The problematic features of many of these models include nine assumptions that Westen

---

[5]However, see Wolitzky, Klein, and Dworkin (1975) for an experimental demonstration of repression that has more ecological validity. The interested reader should also see the experimental studies of stress and defense by Lazarus and his coworkers (e.g., Lazarus & Folkman, 1984), the literature on repressive coping style (Weinberger, 1990), hypnosis (Spiegel, 1990; Bowers, 1990; Kihlstrom & Hoyt, 1990) and other contributions in Singer's (1990) recently edited volume, *Repression and Dissociation*.

spells out—for example, "(1) A continuum of development is isomorphic with a continuum of pathology . . . (2) The origin of severe character pathology lies in the first three years of life. . . .", and so forth. In each instance, he offers logical or empirical reasons (or both) to show that these assumptions are incorrect.

Westen then proceeds to a critique of social-cognitive theories. He notes that social-cognitive psychologists now are interested in unconscious processes (e.g., as in "priming" studies of chronically activated schemas) and in the interaction of cognition and affect (e.g., the influence of emotion or judgment). Most of these studies are well-designed empirical investigation that benefit from reasonably sophisticated measures of cognitive structures, strengths not always present in psychoanalytic approaches. However, social-cognitive research shows several failings. Most notably, the treatment of motivation, affect, defenses, and consciousness is inadequate, and the work often has little ecological validity. In short, the strengths of one model are the weaknesses of the other model.

In his own studies of object relations, Westen has attempted to draw on the best of both approaches. He also points to other phenomena of analytic interest that can both benefit from a social-cognitive perspective and inform social-cognitive theory. The concept of transference is one such example (see the Singers' chapter in this book).

As an introduction to Shevrin's chapter, we should note that despite the experimental demonstration of subliminal perception over a century ago (Pierce & Jastrow, 1884), cognitive psychologists were slow to investigate the proposition that a considerable amount of cognitive processing can and does take place outside of conscious awareness. However, in the past two decades, there has been an explosion of research that offers clear evidence that information not accessible to conscious awareness influences memory, perception, and thinking. Kihlstrom (1990) presents an extensive review of this work, which includes studies of "automatic" processing of information, and "implicit" perception, memory, and learning. The idea that there are unconscious cognitive structures and that human behavior is based on a considerable storehouse of tacit knowledge is now readily accepted by cognitive psychologists. However, cognitive psychologists still have difficulty accepting the notion of the dynamic unconscious. Kihlstrom (1990, p. 447), for example, claims that demonstrations of ". . . preconscious (and even unconscious) mental life while having its origins in neo-Freudian psychoanalysis does not thereby support the essential propositions of psychoanalytic theory." He argues that cognitive theories offer the same propositions and that they have ". . . evolved independently of, and owe no intellectual allegiance to, the psychoanalytic tradition" (p. 447). Instead, he sees the idea of unconscious processes as evolving from the Helmoltzian tradition and urges that the methods and strategies used to study what he terms *implicit cognition* be extended to the domains of motivation and emotion. Without debating here the issues raised by Kihlstrom, we can agree that a comprehensive theory of the structure and function of unconscious processing and unconscious mental contents would have to integrate the findings from cognitive psychology with those generated from the study of the kinds of unconscious influences posited by psychoanalytic psychology. However, as Westen observed, virtually none of the work by cognitive psychologists included a focus on the motivational and emotional factors central to the psychoanalytic conception of a dynamic unconscious. The points of congruence and dissimilarity between cognitive and a dynamic view has received some attention recently (Eagle, 1987).

Shevrin's chapter is concerned with the phenomenon of unconscious processing of information and the links between psychoanalytic conceptions of the unconscious and those advanced by cognitive science. He reminds us that Freud, in his 1915 paper, *The Unconscious*, stated that, although the "repressed is part of the unconscious . . . the repressed does not cover everything that is unconscious." As he points out, cognitive scientists have been actively exploring this other nonrepressed realm of the unconscious (i.e., the cognitive rather than the dynamic unconscious). Shevrin seeks to help us understand the similarities and the differences between the two.

To set the stage for this task, Shevrin gives careful, detailed definitions of some key terms (including *mental, experience, unconscious* and *preconscious*). He then points out that both analysts and cognitive scientists have used the terms *conscious* and *consciousness* in a confusing manner by having them refer to "a particular psychological state and at the same time to consciousness as an immediate subjective given." That is, we are conscious in a dream and also in the waking state, but the principles of the organization of these experiences are different.

Shevrin next reviews some of his own work and that of Libet. It turns out that, following the registration of a stimulus there is a time interval of about 500 milliseconds that is required for the emergence of a conscious experience. What, then, is the function of consciousness? He suggests that it is to "fix" the "*quality* of a given experience."

Libet also found that a time interval of 300–500 milliseconds occurs between the decision to perform a voluntary action and the actual action. This time interval is regarded as a "readiness potential" and, as Shevrin notes, is comparable to the time interval between the registration of a stimulus and its appearance in consciousness. Shevrin interprets Libet's "readiness potential" as a physiological index of preconscious choice. So far, these phenomena may be regarded as neurophysiological markers for conscious experience and preconscious choice in the realm of the unconscious that is not repressed (i.e., what can be called the *cognitive unconscious*).

We begin to address the dynamic unconscious if there is evidence that the time interval between registration of a stimulus and its appearance in consciousness is altered when the content of the stimulus is relevant to a subject's conflicts, or defensive style or both. In fact, Shevrin found that (a) individual differences in repressiveness were related to variations in the length of time that it took for a subject to become conscious of a stimulus, (b) obsessional, compared to nonobsessional, subjects showed a longer time interval between the beginning of the "readiness potential" and their "awareness of the intention to act," and (c) subliminal, but not supraliminal, presentations of words related to subjects' unconscious conflicts evoke distinctive brain responses. These findings constitute clear evidence of the operation of the dynamic unconscious.

Shevrin concludes that cognitive science and psychoanalysis are alike "[i]n the broad sense of a descriptive, relatively conflict-free organization of nonconscious experience. . . ." Like Westen, he finds conflict, affect, and motives absent in cognitive science research but thinks that theories of unconscious attention deployment might facilitate a better integration of cognitive science and psychoanalysis.

Dreams, considered by Freud to be the "royal road to the unconscious" have of course been central to psychoanalytic work. As an introduction to the chapters by Winson and Ellman, we remind the reader that in the preface to the third (revised) English edition, which appeared 31 years after the original publication, Freud proudly tells us that The Interpretation of Dreams "contains . . . the most valuable of all the discoveries it has been my good fortune to make. Insight such as this falls to one's lot but once in a lifetime." (Freud, 1900/1953, p. xxxii).

For the first half century following the original publication of the Interpretation of Dreams (Freud, 1900/1953), there was relatively little empirical investigation of dreams. Rapaport (1951), in his volume The Organization and Pathology of Thought, includes some of the few studies that attempted to explore aspects of Freud's views of dream formation (e.g., symbolism).

It was, however, the discovery of REM sleep (Aserinsky & Kleitman, 1953) that ushered in the modern era of research on dreams and sleep. In the past three decades a small cadre of psychoanalytically oriented investigators, starting with Fisher (1965), have attempted to test specific aspects of Freud's dream theory (e.g., Fisher & Dement, 1960) as well as to use the empirical knowledge regarding REM and REM deprivation to investigate other implications of

Freudian theory. Levin (1990) recently summarized the burgeoning literature on dream research relevant to psychoanalytic theory. He reviewed studies of the meaningfulness of the manifest contents of dreams, the effects of external stimuli on dream content, the effects of REM deprivation, and the adaptive function of dreams. The next two authors whose chapters we summarize, Winson and Ellman, are among the contributors to the sleep and dream literature cited by Levin in his review.

On the basis of his neurophysiological studies of animals and his evolutionary perspective, Winson offers the hypothesis that dreams express individual survival strategies. It is in this context that he discusses Cartwright's study of dream reports of REM awakenings in subjects going through the personal crisis of marital separation and divorce. Cartwright (1986, 1991) had found that women whose preexisting personality characteristic would make them less effective in coping with stress showed greater disturbances in REM sleep patterns (e.g., decreased REM latency) than women with more adaptive coping styles.

Winson does not view dreams as the guardian of sleep or the failure to recall dreams as the result of repression, but as a form of memory processing influenced by early, critical periods of brain development. He focuses particular attention on animal studies of theta rhythm in support of his contention that REM sleep allows for the activation, processing, and consolidation of early emotionally laden memories that have important survival value. In the course of his argument, Winson also critically evaluates the Hobson–McCarley and Crick–Mitchison hypotheses concerning the meaning and function of dreams and he concludes that there is indeed a "deep psychological core" to dreaming. This view, of course, is reassuring to psychoanalytic practitioners.

As noted above, Winson feels that theta rhythm is essential to understanding the function of REM sleep and the meaning of dreams. This brain wave that appears in the hippocampus when animals show increases in arousal in the waking state is also present throughout REM sleep. The hippocampus plays an essential role in memory functioning, including long-term storage. Winson hypothesizes that, during REM sleep, information from current experiences is processed again and is integrated with memories of past experiences in ways that promote survival.

Ellman is one of a small cadre of psychoanalytically oriented investigators, following the pioneering work by Fisher (1965), who have attempted to study aspects of Freud's dream theory and, more broadly, some implications of Freud's theory of motivation. For Ellman, a major focus of interest is Freud's writings concerning endogenous stimulation as the biological substrate of "drives." In a series of studies with animals, Ellman located certain brain sites that can be stimulated in a manner that compensates for the experimental reduction in REM sleep. Specifically, intracranial self-stimulation during the waking state greatly reduced the amount of time spent in REM sleep and eliminated the typical rebound effect following REM deprivation. Similarly, REM deprivation led to increased intracranial self-stimulation. These findings, in which the relevant brain sites are central to feeding, sexual, and aggressive behavior, lead Ellman to suggest that REM sleep is a manifestation of an endogenous, cyclical "drive" system. Ellman believes that the overall evidence indicates that, although wishes do not instigate dreams, they are a vehicle for the expression of drive derivatives and related memories and, thereby, constitute adaptive efforts relevant to "essential gratifications and dangers."

In developing the other pieces in a complex puzzle, Ellman turns to a discussion of his research with humans, particularly the study of the nature of self-representations in dreams and the likely developmental precursors of stable, well-differentiated self-representations. A central thesis in these studies is that there is a decrease in the degree of reflective self-representation following REM awakenings (i.e., a greater absorption in the dream), that individual differences in this tendency are correlated with defensive styles, and that the mentation reports elicited after

REM deprivation show a decrease in degree of self-representation. Extrapolating from these findings, Ellman offers the hypothesis that the failure to contain phasic events in waking life is likely to be associated with greater difficulties in establishing and maintaining self–other boundaries, because periods of alert inactivity will be more apt to be invaded by "drive" phenomena.

In the latter part of the chapter, Ellman puts forth some intriguing developmental hypotheses: (a) REM systems are activated during wakefulness, (b) there are individual differences in the extent of this activation and in the degree to which it interferes with periods of quiet wakefulness, (c) the greater the interference, the less likely it is that the infant will perceive its mother as an external source of adequate satisfaction, and the less likely it is to develop clearly delineated intrapsychic boundaries. Thus, Ellman sees a high level of REM system activation during wakefulness as potentially interfering with the development of reflective self-awareness, of clear self–other differentiation, and of stable self-representations. It is in this context that Ellman believes that the study of the representation of the self in dreams will offer important insights into how we deal with endogenous stimulation.

Ellman's work also has interesting implications for theories of personality development. Linking his findings to the writings of Stern, Winnicott, Mahler, Jacobson, and other developmental theorists, Ellman offers a persuasive account of how findings from REM studies can inform our understanding of the complex interactions of maternal behavior, infant arousal level, regulation of endogenous stimulation in relation to qualities of the mother–infant dyad and the infant's progressive development of a differentiated, separate sense of self.

The combination of neurophysiological and psychological investigations such as is reflected in the work of Winson and of Ellman appears to be a fertile area in which a scientifically based, psychoanalytically informed theory of sleep and dreams will continue to take shape.[6]

The chapter by Cooper provides a useful overview of differences in psychoanalytic conceptions of defense and a thoughtful, selective review of the burgeoning empirical literature on defenses.

Cooper begins his informative exposition with a brief review of the conceptualizations of Freud, Brenner, Schafer, Winnicott, Modell, Kohut, and Kernberg. He notes the differences among these theorists with respect to "the referent points for defenses, the types of patients for whom the concepts of defense are most useful, and types of defense interpretations." For traditional Freudians (e.g., Brenner) defense is viewed primarily as an intrapsychic phenomenon and related mainly to oedipal-level conflicts, whereas those who view pathology mainly in pre-oedipal terms think of defenses in relation to the preservation of views of the self or the object are more likely to think in terms of developmental arrest and are less inclined to view defense as resistances to be interpreted and overcome.

Cooper then turns his attention to a review of research on defenses, covering the early experimental analogues of repression, clinical methods of assessing defenses based on interview and biographical data, and self-report measures of defense. These sections include accounts and critiques of Haan's longitudinal studies of defense and coping, Vaillant's efforts to develop a hierarchy of defenses with respect to their level of "maturity" and to relate these assessments to long-term studies of quality of life adaptation, and Horowitz's method for evaluating "control processes" relevant to posttraumatic stress reactions.

In the past several decades, there have been numerous efforts to devise Rorschach indices of defense, using formal measures, content measures, or a combination of the two. Two of the notable efforts in this research area are the defense scales devised by Lerner and Lerner focused

---

[6]Although this is not the place to extend our discussion, it is worth noting how often the theme of self-regulation of tension states appears at least implicitly not only in several of the chapters in this section but throughout this book (e.g., see the chapters in Section IV on psychoanalysis and psychopathology).

only on responses involving human figures. They found that borderline patients, compared to neurotics, showed greater evidence of projective identification, splitting, idealization, and devaluation. In Cooper's work, all Rorschach responses are rated. Similar results were obtained. In addition, *splitting*, as measured on the Rorschach, was correlated with ratings of splitting that were based on diagnostic interviews.

Cooper concludes his chapter with an account of the conceptual and methodological problems that must be addressed in the next generation of the quantitative study of defenses. Defenses may be included as an axis in the forthcoming *DSM-IV,* and Cooper believes that this should add an important dimension to the study of diagnosis, psychotherapy process, and treatment outcome.

In summary, this sampling of work in the area of cognition, broadly defined, suggests that our knowledge of unconscious processes in both the waking (Shevrin) and sleeping (Ellman, Winson) state, the beginning cross fertilization of the social-cognitive and the psychoanalytic approach to clinical phenomena (Westen), and the increasingly rigorous, systematic study of defenses (Cooper), taken together, and combined with the rich clinical insights generated in the consulting room, can point the way toward a more sophisticated, comprehensive psychoanalytic theory of cognitive/affective/motivational processes.

REFERENCES

Arlow, J. A., & Brenner, C. (1964). *Psychoanalytic concepts and the structural theory.* Madison, CT: International Universities Press.

Aserinsky, E., & Kleitman, N. (1953). Regularly occurring periods of eye motility and concomitant phenomena during sleep. *Science, 118,* 273.

Balay, J., & Shevrin, H. (1988). The subliminal psychodynamic activation method: A critical review. *American Psychologist, 43*(3), 161–174.

Blatt, S. J., & Wild, C. M. (1976). *Schizophrenia—A developmental analysis.* New York: Academic Press.

Bowers, K. S. (1990). Unconscious influences and hypnosis. In J. L. Singer (Ed.), *Repression and dissociation* (pp. 143–180). Chicago: Chicago University Press.

Bruner, J., & Goodman, C. (1947). Value and need as organizing factors in perception. *Journal of Abnormal and Social Psychology, 42,* 33–44.

Carter, L., & Schooler, E. (1949). Value, need, and other factors in perception. *Psychological Review, 56,* 200–208.

Cartwright, R. (1986). Affect and dream work from an information processing point of view. *Journal of Mind and Behavior, 7,* 411–427.

Cartwright, R. (1991). Dreams that work: The relation of dream incorporation to adaptation to stressful events. *Journal of Dreaming, 1,* 3–9.

Cheesman, J., & Merikle, P. M. (1986). Distinguishing conscious from unconscious processes. *Canadian Journal of Psychology, 40,* 343–367.

Eagle, M. (1984). *Recent developments in psychoanalysis.* New York: McGraw-Hill.

Eagle, M. (1987). The psychoanalytic and the cognitive unconscious. In R. Stern (Ed.), *Theories of the unconscious and theories of the self.* Hillsdale, NJ: Analytic Press.

Eagle, M., & Wolitzky, D. L. (1977). Perceptual defense. In B. Wolman (Ed.), *International encyclopedia of psychiatry, psychology, psychoanalysis, and neurology* (Vol. 8, pp. 260–265). New York: Van Nostrand Reinhold.

Eagle, M. N., & Wolitzky, D. L. (1985). The current status of psychoanalysis. *Clinical Psychology Review, 5,* 259–269.

Erdelyi, M. H. (1974). A new look at the new look: Perceptual defense and vigilance. *Psychological Review,* *81,* 1–25.

Fairbairn, W. R. D. (1952). *An object-relations theory of the personality.* New York: Basic Books.

Fisher, C. (1954). Dreams and perception: The role of preconscious and primary modes of perception in dream formation. *Journal of the American Psychoanalytic Association, 2,* 389–445.

Fisher, C. (1956). Dreams, images, and perception: A study of unconscious–preconscious relationships. *Journal of the American Psychoanalytic Association, 4,* 5–48.

Fisher, C. (1965). Psychoanalytic implications of recent research on sleep and dreams. *Journal of the American Psychoanalytic Association, 13,* 197–303.

Freud, S. (1953). The interpretation of dreams. In J. Strachey (Ed.), *The standard edition of the complete psychological works of Sigmund Freud* (Vol. 4, pp. 1–338; Vol. 5, pp. 339–627). London: Hogarth Press. (Original work published 1900)

Freud, S. (1958). Formulations regarding the two principles of mental functioning. In J. Strachey (Ed.), *The standard edition of the complete psychological works of Sigmund Freud* (Vol. 12, pp. 218–226). London: Hogarth Press. (Original work published 1911)

Freud, S. (1959). Inhibitions, symptoms, and anxiety. In J. Strachey (Ed.), *The standard edition of the complete psychological works of Sigmund Freud* (Vol. 20, pp. 87–172). London: Hogarth Press. (Original work published 1926)

Freud, S. (1961). A note upon the "Mystic Writing-Pad." In J. Strachey (Ed.), *The standard edition of the complete psychological works of Sigmund Freud* (Vol. 19, pp. 227–232). London: Hogarth Press. (Original work published 1925)

Freud, S. (1966). Project for a scientific psychology. In J. Strachey (Ed.), *The standard edition of the complete psychological works of Sigmund Freud* (Vol. 1, pp. 295–391). London: Hogarth Press. (Original work published 1895)

Galin, D. (1974). Implications for psychiatry of left and right cerebral specialization: A neurophysiological context for unconscious processes. *Archives of General Psychiatry, 31,* 572–583.

Gardner, R. W., Holzman, P. S., Klein, G. S., Linton, H. B., & Spence, D. P. (1959). Cognitive control: A study of individual consistencies in cognitive behaviors. *Psychological Issues, 2*(4) Monograph 8.

Gill, M. M. (1967). *The collected papers of David Rapaport.* New York: Basic Books.

Gill, M. M. (1967). The primary process. In R. R. Holt (Ed.), *Motives and thought: Psychoanalytic essays in honor of David Rapaport. Psychological Issues, 5,* 260–298.

Hartmann, H. (1958). *Ego psychology and the problem of adaptation.* Madison, CT: International Universities Press. (Original work published 1939)

Hartmann, H. (1964). *Essays on ego psychology: Selected problems in psychoanalytic theory.* Madison, CT: International Universities Press.

Holmes, D. S. (1990). The evidence for repression: An examination of sixty years of research. In J. L. Singer (Ed.), *Repression and dissociation* (pp. 85–102). Chicago: Chicago University Press.

Holt, R. R. (1966). Measuring libidinal and aggressive motives and their controls by means of the Rorschach test. In D. Levine (Ed.), *Nebraska Symposium on Motivation* (Vol. 14, pp. 1–47). Lincoln: University of Nebraska Press.

Holt, R. R. (1967). The development of the primary process: A structural view. In R. R. Holt (Ed.), *Motives and thought: Psychoanalytic essays in honor of David Rapaport. Psychological Issues, 5,* 345–383.

Holt, R. R. (1972). Freud's mechanistic and humanistic images of man. *Psychoanalysis and contemporary science, 1,* 3–24.

Holt, R. R. (1981). The death and transfiguration of metapsychology. *International Review of Psychoanalysis, 8,* 129–143.

Holt, R. R., & Havel, J. (1960). A method for assessing primary and secondary process in the Rorschach. In M. A. Richers-Ovsiankana (Ed.), *Rorschach psychology* (pp. 263–315). New York: Wiley.

Holzman, P. S., & Gardner, R. W. (1959). Leveling and repression. *Journal of Abnormal and Social Psychology, 59,* 151–155.

Johnston, M. H., & Holzman, P. S. (1979). *Assessing schizophrenic thinking.* San Francisco: Jossey-Bass.

Kihlstrom, J. F. (1990). The psychological unconscious. In L. A. Pervin, *Handbook of personality: theory and research* (pp. 445–464). New York: Guilford Press.

Kihlstrom, J. F., & Hoyt, I. P. (1990). Repression, dissociation, and hypnosis. In J. L. Singer (Ed.), *Repression and dissociation* (pp. 181–208). Chicago: University of Chicago Press.

Klein, G. S. (1954). Need and regulation. In M. R. Jones (Ed.), *Nebraska Symposium on Motivation* (pp. 224–274). Lincoln: University of Nebraska Press.

Klein, G. S. (1970). *Perception, motives, and personality.* New York: Knopf.

Klein, G. S. (1976). *Psychoanalytic theory: An exploration of essentials.* Madison, CT: International Universities Press.

Klein, G. S., & Schlesinger, H. J. (1949). Where is the perceives in perceptual theory? *Journal of Personality, 18,* 32–47.

Lazarus, R. S., & Folkman, S. (1984). *Stress, appraisal, and coping.* New York: Springer.

Levin, R. (1990)). Psychoanalytic theories of the function of dreaming: A review of empirical dream research. In J. Masling (Ed.), *Empirical studies of psychoanalytic theories* (Vol. 3). Hillsdale, NJ: Analytic Press.

Mackinnon, D. W., & Dukes, W. F. (1964). Repression. In L. Postman (Ed.), *Psychology in the making.* New York: Knopf.

Mitchell, S. A. (1988). *Relational concepts in psychoanalysis.* Cambridge, MA: Harvard University Press.

Pierce, C. S., & Jastrow, J. (1984). On small differences in sensation. *Memorials of the National Academy of Sciences, 3,* 73–83.

Poetzl, O. (1960). The relationship between experimentally induced dream images and indirect vision. *Psychological Issues, 2,*(7), 41–120. (Original work published in 1917)

Pribram, K. H., & Gill, M. M. (1976). *Freud's "Project" Reassessed.* New York: Basic Books.

Rapaport, D. (1942). *Emotions and memory.* Baltimore, MD: Williams & Wilkins.

Rapaport, D. (1951). *Organization and pathology of thought.* New York: Columbia University Press.

Rapaport, D. (1960). The structure of psychoanalytic theory: A systematizing attempt. *Psychological Issues, 6.*

Reiser, M. (1984). *Mind, brain, body: Toward a convergence of psychoanalysis and neurobiology.* New York: Basic Books.

Rosenzweig, S. (1934). An experimental study of memory in relation to the theory of repression. *British Journal of Psychology, 24,* 247–265.

Sanford, R. N. (1937). The effects of abstinence from food on imaginal processes: A further experiment. *Journal of Psychology, 3,* 145–159.

Sears, R. R. (1943). Survey of objective studies in psychoanalytic concepts. *Social Science Research Council Bulletin,* No. 52.

Shevrin, H., & Dickman. (1980). The psychological unconscious: A necessary assumption for all psychological theory? *American Psychologist, 35,* 421–434.

Shevrin, H., & Fritzler, D. (1968a). Visual evoked response correlates of unconscious mental processes. *Science, 161,* 295–298.

Shevrin, H., & Fritzler, D. (1968b). Brain correlates of repressiveness. *Psychological Reports, 23,* 887–892.

Silverman, L. H. (1983). The subliminal psychodynamic activation method: Overview and comprehensive listing of studies. In J. Masling (Ed.), *Empirical studies of psychoanalytic theory* (Vol. 1, pp. 69–100). Hillsdale, NJ: Erlbaum.

Singer, J. L. (Ed.) (1990). *Repression and dissociation.* Chicago: Chicago University Press.

Spiegel, D. (1990). Hypnosis, dissociation, and trauma: Hidden and overt observers. In J. L. Singer (Ed.), *Repression and dissociation* (pp. 121–142). Chicago: Chicago University Press.

Wallerstein, R. S. (1983). Self psychology and "classical" psychoanalytic psychology: The nature of theory relationship. In A. Goldberg (Ed.), *The future of psychoanalysis* (pp. 19–63). Madison, CT: International Universities Press.

Weinberger, D. A. (1990). The construct validity of the repressive coping style. In J. L. Singer (Ed.), *Repression and dissociation* (pp. 337–386). Chicago: University of Chicago Press.

Wolff, P. H. (1960). The developmental psychologies of Jean Piaget and psychoanalysis. *Psychological Issues, 2.*

Wolitzky, D. L. (1968). Effect of food deprivation on perception–cognition: A comment. *Psychological Bulletin, 68,* 342–344.

Wolitzky, D. L., & Wachtel, P. L. (1973). Perception and personality. In B. Wolman (Ed.), *Handbook of general psychology.* Englewood Cliffs, NJ: Prentice-Hall.

Wolitzky, D. L., Klein, G. S., & Dworkin, S. F. (1975). An experimental approach to the study of repression: Effects of a hypnotically induced fantasy. *Psychoanalysis and Contemporary Science, 4,* 211–233.

13

THE FREUDIAN UNCONSCIOUS AND THE COGNITIVE UNCONSCIOUS: IDENTICAL OR FRATERNAL TWINS?

HOWARD SHEVRIN

We have learnt from psychoanalysis that the essence of the process of repression lies, not in putting an end to, in annihilating, the idea which represents an instinct, but in preventing it from becoming conscious. When this happens we say of the idea that it is in a state of being "unconscious," and we can produce good evidence to show that even when it is unconscious it can produce effects, even including some which finally reach consciousness. Everything that is repressed must remain unconscious; but let us state at the very outset that the repressed does not cover everything that is unconscious. The unconscious has the wider compass: the repressed is a part of the unconscious. (Freud, 1915/1957a, p. 166)

These words were written by Freud in 1915 and constituted the opening paragraph of his paper, "The Unconscious," one of five essays generally referred to as the "Papers on Metapsychology." Strachey (1957) tells us in his editor's introduction to the series of papers that Freud apparently wrote seven additional papers on metapsychology, all within a space of 6 months. The additional seven papers were never published, which may be a source of relief to those who look on metapsychology as an embarrassment.

In this opening paragraph, Freud announces the major themes in the thesis he will subsequently elaborate: (a) the centrality of repression in understanding unconscious processes; (b) the persistence of the repressed and its impact on consciousness; and (c) the broader domain of the unconscious than is determined by repression; repression may be the cornerstone of the unconscious, but there is much more to the building.

It has been more than 75 years since the publication of Freud's paper on the unconscious. What has happened in the interim? Within psychoanalysis the concept of the unconscious has maintained its rock-ribbed permanence. Although new and diverse clinical theories have been

313

developed (e.g., various object relations theories, self-psychology, etc.) to address clinical phenomena of interest, surprisingly little continuous attention has been paid to the nature of unconscious processes in their own right. With the exception of a handful of ego psychologists, Hartmann (1964) and Rapaport (1967) most notably, the problems addressed by Freud in his metapsychology papers have not been pursued. By and large, psychoanalysts, with a few significant exceptions, have concentrated on assuming and using the centrality of the unconscious, but have not addressed the nature of the assumption itself and the role it plays in practice and theory. Thus, object relations theories have stipulated the existence of so-called primitive defenses, such as splitting and projective identification, but have said nothing about how these more primitive defenses might in fact bear on our understanding of unconscious processes and how they work. Ironically, the situation has been quite different in contemporary cognitive science, and at least in a little, but significant, corner of neurophysiology. In recent years cognitive scientists have become more and more intrigued with the necessity of assuming the existence of unconscious processes and to accord to them a primary role in understanding how the mind works (Kihlstrom, 1987; Shevrin & Dickman, 1980). Cognitive scientists have, often without realizing it, taken Freud at his word, that the unconscious has a "wider compass" than the repressed. They have been actively exploring the extensive region beyond the repressed with some interesting consequences for understanding the unconscious. The very questions that contemporary psychoanalysts by and large ignore are now being addressed by cognitive scientists and to a lesser extent by some neurophysiologists. We may ask, With what import for both psychoanalysis and the sciences of the mind? Will we discover that the versions of the unconscious developed by psychoanalysis and currently being explored by cognitive science will ultimately be identical, or will they form a distant, if fraternal, twinship? Bear in mind that the Bible warns us that fraternal twins may also be fratricidal. There is no guarantee that family resemblance results in family harmony. So we must also be alert to the potential dangers—theoretical, clinical, and empirical—of concepts that may be descriptively similar but may, in fact, be in conceptual enmity. In what follows I examine the conditions for one or another outcome.

In the opening section of his paper on the unconscious, Freud makes it clear that the notion of a psychological unconscious is a fundamental assumption. He considers the assumption necessary, legitimate, and mainly of a clinical nature (for which there is considerable proof). In citing what he considers to be clinical proof, Freud uses what Grünbaum (1984) has called the "tally" argument, based on Freud's claim that the success of the psychoanalytic method in producing cure by discovering the unconscious roots of the disorder constitutes, in Freud's terms, "incontrovertible proof of the existence of what we have assumed" (Freud, 1915a/1957a, p. 167). Unfortunately, one cannot be as sanguine in this respect as Freud was.

The psychological unconscious is necessary, argues Freud, because of the gaps and discontinuities in consciousness. An obsessive thought or unexplained fear will appear seemingly out of nowhere, or an individual will experience a puzzling jump from one idea to another. Both clinical and daily observations of this nature force us, Freud continues, to assume that there are indeed causes for these gaps of a psychological nature that are inaccessible to the person.

Freud insisted that the unconscious is mental in nature and thus fully psychological; indeed, he asserted that all psychological events known to us (with one exception) were capable of being unconscious. The one exception was affect, which he viewed not as a psychological event such as an idea, but as a discharge process. Freud categorically denied that we can have introspective access to the physiological processes that were concomitants of unconscious processes, or that any "physiological concept or chemical process [can] give us any notion of their nature" (1915a/1957a, p. 108). Quite otherwise, we can only learn about these unconscious processes through their "points of contact" with conscious processes, that is, by inference from consciously available events. (I cite evidence later in this chapter to challenge this assertion.) Neurophysiological processes can at least tell us of the *presence* of unconscious processes and may in time tell us something of their nature.

Cognitive science shares some of Freud's uneasiness with the role of the neurophysiological. Kihlstrom (1984), in an article dealing with the cognitive science view of the unconscious, states in words entirely congenial to Freud, "Psychological concepts demand psychological reference. . . . Subjective report and overt behavior . . . will serve as windows of the mind" (p. 154). Psychoanalysts and cognitive scientists are uneasy about invoking neurophysiology because it might give birth to a hybrid monster—part neurophysiological unconscious and part psychological consciousness—as some have in fact proposed (e.g., Hobson & McCarley, 1977).

At another point in his paper on the unconscious, Freud tells us that, "To have heard something and to have experienced something are in their psychological nature two quite different things, even though the content of both is the same" (1915a/1957a, p. 176). Freud made this statement while debating with himself about the nature of the transformations affecting an idea as it changed from being unconscious to being conscious. Once you assume a psychological unconscious, you have to explain the conditions under which an idea remains unconscious and the complementary conditions under which an idea becomes conscious. The problem has clinical relevance insofar as psychoanalysts ever since Freud have asserted that when ideas are unconscious, especially if repressed (which generally means that they have once been conscious), that they are more likely to cause trouble than when they are conscious, although this bare statement is not altogether correct. Cognitive psychologists, who are concerned with how something unconscious becomes conscious and the reverse, have arrived at different solutions. Before discussing the different solutions to the problem of transformation as I shall call it, let me define several terms that have been defined variously and confusingly both within psychoanalysis and psychology at large.

DEFINITIONS

The terms I will define are mental, experience, presentation, unconscious, preconscious, conscious, principles of organization, and level of categorization or abstraction.

Mental

Insofar as we are in need of a superordinate term under which we can cluster a variety of psychological events from the repressed unconscious to higher level reflective awareness, the term mental would seem to be a likely candidate. It is theoretically neutral and intuitively understandable. So, in using the term *mental*, I will refer to all those psychological events—perceptions, judgments, affects, motives, and impulses—that constitute our life experiences, and in addition, those organizing principles and levels of categorization and abstraction that comprise the framework or structure of the mental and its operation. Mental stands in contradistinction to physiological, but not in opposition to it. The mental and the physiological require different languages of description and explanation, which can in principle be coordinate.

Experience

If mental is the superordinate category, then *experience* is the term by which to refer to the substantive nature of what is mental. In the language I propose, we experience the mental. We can have no direct experience of the physiological.

Presentation

A necessary-and-sufficient condition for an experience is that a given event be organized in such a way that it forms a presentation. In traditional terms, this presentation can be an idea, an affect, an image, a memory, and so forth. Presentations are to experience as food is to eating; we cannot eat in the true sense of that word without food, nor can we be said to experience without presentations. I would like to avoid a content–process division. Presentations can either be static contents as in perceptions, or images, or a process extended in time as is true of affects. Both are presentations capable of being experienced and are equally mental in nature. Presentations can exist at different levels of categorization or abstraction and can be structured on the basis of different principles of organization (both terms are defined later). Thus, a *representation* is a presentation at a higher level of categorization and abstraction. In these terms, when Freud talks about the "psychic-representative" of an instinct (Freud, 1915b/1957b), it might best be understood as a "psychic-presentation" because it is likely meant to be taken as an experience at a low level of categorization and abstraction. On the other hand, when Freud talks about a "thing-presentation" in the unconscious, his usage is in keeping with the definition offered here. Not so, however, with his counterpart notion of the "word-presentation" in the preconscious, for here we are talking about a *representation*, an experience at a higher level of organization.

Unconscious

By *unconscious* I refer to those experiences that are not conscious by reason of inhibition of one kind or another. Notice that the unconscious is not defined as a "locus" or "receptacle" in which inhibited experiences are to be found. To my mind that would be confusing the use of the term *unconscious* as a concept referring to a class of events (in which case it is in a metaphoric sense a conceptual container) with the actual unconscious, which is simply the totality of inhibited experiences that may be organized, grouped, or integrated in various ways that require other descriptive and explanatory terms. Simply put, the unconscious refers to inhibited experiences. I leave as an open question how these inhibitions occur. The dynamic unconscious refers to the motivated inhibition of experience and to such defenses as repression, isolation, and so forth. But conceivably, inhibition can occur because of dissociation, which some argue is not necessarily defensive in the dynamic sense (Kihlstrom, 1984). Or, inhibition may occur on the basis of the incompatibility of some forms of experience with the usual nature of conscious experience in one particular state. This incompatibility may be a function of different modes of thought or contradictory views of the self that may also play a vital role in repression. I refer to a point made by Gill (1963) about ideas remaining unconscious because they are too primitive or organized in primary process ways so that they are not compatible with more rational, conscious experiences.

Preconscious

By *preconscious* I refer to all experiences readily available to consciousness as a consequence of voluntary choice. Note that I have added to the usual psychoanalytic definition of the preconscious the condition of "voluntary choice," which I believe to be implicit in the term *readily*. Otherwise we would need to include recurrent obsessional thoughts that are in fact too readily available to consciousness as belonging to the preconscious when clearly they are in large measure eruptions of unconscious experiences. In traditional psychological terms, preconscious experiences are subject to voluntary control, that is, they are customarily available on the basis of consciously experienced choice, whereas obsessional ideas are not. There is an interesting implication of this definition with respect to such altered states of consciousness as dreams, which are not experienced as being readily available on the basis of a conscious choice. Dreams *happen* to us. Thus, by my definition there is no preconscious experience in dreaming, although previously available preconscious experience, as in the case of day residues, may play an important role. By introducing the requirement of voluntary choice, the preconscious as defined here must be distinguished from the "automatic" unconscious processes of some cognitive psychologists (Shiffrin & Schneider, 1977).

Conscious

This is the first and only term that must be considered as a primitive given. All of the other terms are either derivative or are constructions. But the term *conscious* refers to an irreducible and irreplaceable phenomenon, no matter what the name. Such terms as *awareness, reflective awareness, phenomenal awareness,* and *phenomenal representation* have been used to refer to the same thing. Each of these terms has its own problems. Awareness, for example, has been used to refer not only to what we mean when we say we are at the moment conscious of something, but also to refer to a latent knowledge of something. The term *conscious,* unless burdened with additional meanings (which unfortunately it often is), can serve very well as the primitive term for what is immediately, subjectively, and introspectively given in experience. Thus, we can be conscious of a rational, abstract idea, an obsessional preoccupation, or a hallucination. The condition of being conscious *says nothing* about the origin or nature of the experience. We are conscious in psychosis, states of intoxication, dreams, fugue states, and so forth. Each of these represents a quite different mental organization of experiences obeying different principles of organization and existing on different levels of categorization and abstraction.

Principles of Organization

Although it is conceivable that experiences can exist solely as individual instances and remain unrelated to any other experiences, it is highly unlikely that this would be the case. Both psychology and psychoanalysis have described various principles of organization on the basis of which experiences are ordered. Classically, psychology has formulated the laws of association— frequency, contiguity, similarity, saliency, recency, primacy, and so forth. Another important principle of organization not formally identified in psychology as such but more recently investigated under the name of categorization or classification is what I will refer to later as level of categorization or abstraction, by which I mean the extent to which experiences are formalized, simplified, and treated as *representations* of other experiences. The most obvious instance of such a formalized, simplified, experience is a concept, but these formalizations and simplifications exist at many intermediate levels. In cognition these are referred to as schemas following Bartlett's (1932) theory of memory formation. What I want to stress here is that experiences are organized in levels or hierarchies of abstraction in the sense just defined. Psychoanalysis has to an extent incorporated some of the laws of association, in particular contiguity and similarity, as well as levels of categorization and abstraction in the form of primary and secondary processes, but has also added several of its own—the pleasure and reality principles and, most importantly, the stages of psychosexual development. Take note of the fact that I place the primary and secondary processes in the category of principles of organization of experience rather than individual experience. For example, an obsessional thought may not be any different in content from an ordinary thought; what makes it different is its intrusiveness and insistent repetitiveness and, in particular, the nature of its relationship to other experiences that may in fact be unconscious or conscious. Freud's patient Lorenz reported the obsessional thought of expecting his father to appear. There is nothing odd about this content, but when we learn that his father is dead, it assumes a different character by virtue of its contradictory relationship to other experiences, in this instance a memory of his father as no longer alive. On the other hand, it is possible to entertain the wildest and most primitive idea and for it still to be in the bounds of the secondary process because it may simply be an imaginative exercise or something learned from another source. We often encounter this on the Rorschach, where we take great pains to determine if a particularly bizarre response is drawn from some other available experience or is the product of the patient's own experiential organization. If, for example, a patient were to see on the Rorschach a monster with leafy arms and legs, we would think one way about this response if he then described that he had recently read a science fiction tale in which a monster of this prodigious nature appeared, as compared to the possibility that it was the momentary product of his own mentation. Primary and secondary processes refer to principles of organization applying to experiences similar in function to the laws of association and to levels of categorization and abstraction. Freud felt that association by contiguity played an important role in the primary process. We can be conscious of experiences ordered on the basis of quite different principles; the condition of being conscious of an experience is not inextricably tied to a given organization of experience. Thus, we can be conscious of more or less primary process organizations of experience as in dreams or psychotic states.

Level of Categorization and Abstraction

Having already talked about the difference between presentation and representation, let me now be more specific about the basis for this distinction. It is self-evident that adaptation in the broadest sense requires the operation of some selection principles to determine what stimuli we will respond to out of an incredible array of possible stimuli. Our sensory organs thus institute the first level of categorization in our contact with the world. If we are so inclined, we can put it in terms of sampling and data reduction. In any case, the sheer number and variety of stimuli from within and from without necessitate means for "transducing" these stimuli so that we can apprehend them. Selective attention is another example of the operation of levels of categorization and abstraction. We can imagine a series of levels of increasing abstractness of categorization so that finally language approaches the most abstract level insofar as a word can stand for and refer to a multiplicity of events. In clinical terms, symptoms can appear at different levels of categorization and abstraction so that a conversion reaction may in fact be a concrete somatic representation at a high level of abstraction having reference to incestuous wishes and feelings of a quite low level of abstraction and categorization, whereas schizophrenic thought disorder may appear in the apparent form of language, which, however, has lost its representational function.

THEORETICAL IMPLICATIONS

Now let us use these terms to clarify, or at least restate, some fundamental issues bearing on the transformation of unconscious experiences into consciousness and the reverse. We are now in a position to dispel a persistent terminological and conceptual confusion that dogged Freud's own thinking and continues to confound the thinking of contemporary cognitive psychologists. Over the years, Freud struggled with what one could call the adjectival and substantive uses of the terms conscious, preconscious, and unconscious. The adjectival use, as when we say a *conscious* idea, simply describes an immediate condition of the idea, meaning that the idea is directly, subjectively given and capable of being introspected, although it need not be.[1] I would like to use the primitive term, *consciousness*, or simply *conscious*, to refer to this form of experience. However, the experience can be conscious in a variety of different states—a waking alert state, a dream state, a psychotic state, and so on. Is the experience conscious in the same way in each state? Clearly not. And yet in one sense, the adjectival sense, it is. Consciousness as a subjective, introspective given is in fact indivisible and the same no matter what the particular state of consciousness. But the principles of organization and the level of categorization and abstraction effecting or producing that experience may, in fact, be quite different. In a dream we are conscious of odd, sometimes bizarre conjunctions and combinations (a person or a place can be two different things at the same time), and yet we are as conscious of these oddities as we are of the most mundane perception of waking life. But the processes of transformation by which the previously unconscious experiences become conscious are entirely different in these two states. Dream experiences are organized on a totally different basis and at an entirely different level of categorization and abstraction from that prevailing in waking perception. Yet, consciousness as that primitive experience is the same. We are as conscious of the dream as we are of a waking perception. In the term *state of consciousness*, consciousness is actually being used mainly in its substantive meaning as referring to differences in levels of organization and abstraction rather than simply to the primitive condition of being conscious of something. On these grounds, one can object to the use of the term *state of consciousness* because of the ambiguity in the usage of the term *conscious*. It would be better to refer to these normally recurring changes in state as *psychological states*, so that the confusion described is avoided. A psychological state would be a relatively stable organization of experiences—conscious, preconscious, and unconscious—that differs in terms of its organizing principles and levels of categorization and abstraction.

Cognitive science has not been immune from confusing and ambiguous uses of the terms *conscious* and *consciousness*. The confusion is compounded by efforts to incorporate such neo-dissociationist concepts as the subconscious and co-consciousness (Kihlstrom, 1984). Even a cursory reading of the cognitive literature reveals that most, if not all, cognitive scientists are referring to a particular psychological state and at the same time to consciousness as an immediate subjective given when they use the term *conscious*. The particular psychological state is the normal waking state of most (not all) subjects in psychological experiments. Mandler (1975), in an article entitled "Consciousness: Respectable, Useful, and Probably Necessary," assigned to consciousness the function of choice and the transfer of information to long-term storage, among other talents. Posner and Snyder (1975) ascribed to consciousness one distinguishing attribute—that of serial order or single channel capacity: Only one "item" can enter consciousness at any one time, while processes can proceed along many pathways simultaneously and unconsciously, the so-called parallel processes of an "automatic" nature. Aside from the great difficulty in defining an "item," we can see that cognitive scientists have confused a mode of organization of experience with consciousness as a subjective given. It may be that in the psychological state characterizing normal waking consciousness of subjects in cognitive experiments, only one item at a time can enter consciousness; but that may be because consciousness in this state is regulated by rational secondary process modes of organization at a high level of abstraction and constrained by the highly specific and abstract task defined by the experimenter. Contrast this state with that of a patient lying on a couch in a quasi-restful position and given no other task than to say

---

[1]Most conscious experiences are present only fleetingly, are seldom reflected on, and even less often communicated. Consciousness in the adjectival sense should not be confused with reflection, introspection, or communication of what is present in consciousness. These all require additional acts while also involving consciousness in the adjectival sense and thus paradoxically we may also be only fleetingly aware of our reflections, introspections, and communications. However, these additional acts may in turn be reflected on, and so forth, so that one can imagine a lengthening series of recursive conscious events. The obsessive is most often bound to this recursively turning wheel of consciousness, whereas the hysteric seeks constantly to brake it.

whatever comes to mind. The more undefended the patient becomes, the more consciousness is characterized by multiple items entering simultaneously as more irrational, primary process modes of organization at lower levels of abstraction now begin to prevail. But the experimental subject and the analytic patient are each still conscious in the primitive meaning of that term. However, when psychoanalysts have talked about making the unconscious conscious, or where id was there shall ego be, or the difference between experiencing something and simply hearing about it, there is the clear implication that unconscious experience has not only become conscious in the adjectival sense, but also that it has been raised to a higher level of organization. Similarly, when cognitive scientists talk about consciousness as involving a single channel as opposed to the parallel processing of the unconscious, they are again talking in systematic terms and thus introducing a different principle of organization.

Once we free the word *conscious* of its systematic meaning and restore its concrete meaning, a new problem emerges hitherto obscured behind verbal ambiguities: If to be conscious can occur in a variety of psychological states, and it is always the same indivisible experience of being conscious regardless of the particular principles of organization, what purpose does being conscious serve, and furthermore, what special conditions are necessary for consciousness as such to occur? What role does simply being conscious play in our mental life apart from the operation of different principles of organization and levels of abstraction?

Freud exclaimed after stripping our conscious life of most of its power and influence, "But what part is then left to be played in our scheme by consciousness which was once so omnipotent and hid all else from view? Only that of a sense organ for the perceptions of psychical qualities" (1900/1953, p. 615). Freud ascribed to consciousness the capacity to transform into experienced qualities the purely quantitative activity of the unconscious, parallel to the way in which the physical pulsations of light are transformed into the perceptions of qualities of color, and perhaps parallel to the cognitive science conception of the unconscious as the purely quantitative computational processes subserving all psychological events. In particular, Freud argued that the psychic sense organ, consciousness, transformed quantities of unconscious excitation into the qualitative experiences of pleasure and unpleasure. Moreover, consciousness could in part play some organizing and inhibiting role in permitting thoughts to become conscious, not on the basis of their strength of pleasurable excitation but because of their reality relevance. Again we see how systematic considerations have crept into Freud's account of consciousness. In psychotic states or states of intoxication would it be true that consciousness exercises this control over thoughts, and yet consciousness as a primitive given exists in these states as well? Intuitively we balk at the notion that consciousness as such may have no function because it sounds as if we would be reduced to automatons, but that is because we intuitively equate being conscious with a higher level organization linked in particular to voluntary action. But our wills are not necessarily indissolubly linked to the experience of consciousness. To my knowledge, all efforts to define the function of consciousness have stipulated characteristics of a system or organization and have thus not dealt with the experience of consciousness as such, which occurs in every psychological state.

If the experience of being conscious must be distinguished from its organizational attributes, then it should be possible to distinguish special conditions for that experience quite apart from organizational considerations. I have attempted elsewhere to identify what special function might be attributed to consciousness as a subjective given (Shevrin, 1986; Shevrin, Ghannam, & Libet, 1992). Drawing on subliminal research, research on source amnesia, and observations from clinical psychoanalysis, I suggested that consciousness taken in the adjectival sense may serve the purpose of "fixing" the *quality* of a given experience where quality is defined ostensively as referring to the commonly identified varieties of experience, such as percepts, memories, thoughts, images, dreams, and so forth. When, for example, a stimulus is *never* in consciousness but registers unconsciously as in subliminal perception, and is retrieved (i.e., in an image, dream, free association, etc.), the person has no awareness of its true source although what is retrieved may be a faithful version of the subliminal stimulus. The person can have no memory of a percept because the stimulus was never in consciousness as a percept and, thus, was not "fixed" as such in subjective consciousness. The same occurs in the retrieval of information by organic amnesics who have no memory of the source of the retrieved information. In psychoanalytic patients, repression may undue the "fixing" process so that what was previously in consciousness as a percept, thought, or memory may return as a "derivative," that is, as some other percept, thought, or memory whose content may relate to what is repressed but is not recognized as such. It is as if repression does to the conscious "fixing" process what subliminality accomplishes mechanically and organicity accomplishes in the case of source amnesics.

Of special interest in understanding the experience of consciousness is the research of the neurophysiologist Benjamin Libet. In a series of studies employing direct cortical activation, he has demonstrated that before a stimulus can become conscious, a certain period of cortical recruitment, lasting an average of 500 msec, needs to occur (Libet, 1965, 1966). When this recruitment does not take place, it can still be shown that the brain has been activated by the stimulus but without conscious experience. Libet's and my own findings on the electrophysiology of subliminal stimuli (Shevrin, 1988; Shevrin & Rennick, 1967; Shevrin et al., 1988; Wong, Shevrin, Williams, & Marshall, 1988) amply demonstrate that higher level cortical activity involved in the sorting of complex meanings can go on without benefit of conscious experience and is consistent with the assumption of a psychological unconscious. Beyond that, however, Libet's (1965, 1966) research has shown that for the experience of consciousness in its adjectival sense to occur, an additional train of cortical activation is necessary, which lasts by electrophysiological standards a rather long time—one half of a second. To my knowledge, this is the only work investigating the actual conditions for the emergence of an experience of consciousness rather than the investigation of the principles of organization of conscious experience.

Libet's (1965, 1966) research, however, leaves unanswered the question concerning the function of the experience of consciousness as such once we strip it of its systematic properties. Our introspections tell us that this experience counts; Libet's research tells us there is a separate cortical process of some sort associated with the experience of consciousness. Perhaps this cortical process is the brain instantiation of the "fixing" function of consciousness described previously.

Let me cite another intriguing piece of research by Libet, Wright, and Gleason (1982, 1983) that bears on the role of will or voluntary action and its relationship, on the one hand, to conscious experience, and on the other, to the level of organization of unconscious experience. Libet asked his subjects to initiate a voluntary action, quickly flexing the wrist, whenever they wanted to do it. The only condition he placed on his subjects was that they should not plan in advance when they would perform the action. At the very moment they decided to perform the action, they were to note the position of a moving light on a clock and report its position to fix the moment at which they experienced the urge to act. Two physiological measures were obtained, one of a so-called readiness potential detected by scalp electrodes, and the other of a myographic response measured at the time the wrist was flexed. The readiness potential has been identified as the brain event occurring at the time a subject is preparing to perform a self-paced task. Libet collected the brain measurements for the readiness potential backward from the moment the subject flexed his wrist, which provided an electromyographic response serving as a time-locked marker for the recording of the readiness potential. He found that the readiness potential preceded the conscious decision to act by approximately 300-500 msec and that the conscious decision to act preceded the myographic response by some 200 msec. I will not go into the various controls introduced by Libet. The method itself is impressive and the findings provocative. Libet interprets the presence of the readiness potential as the unconscious precursor of a consciously experienced decision to act. Interestingly, the time lag between the onset of the readiness potential and the conscious experience was of the same order as he had previously discovered to be the time necessary for consciousness itself to develop.

How can we interpret this result? Is the subject deceiving himself when he thinks that it is his conscious decision that causes the act? Or is there some unconscious impulse within him which will out and all he can do is give it full rein? This line of reasoning is patently specious. Why identify the person solely with the experience of conscious choice? The experience of conscious choice may be one important phase of a person's total psychological state. The readiness potential tells us that the will to act begins to form unconsciously, increases over a 500-msec time interval, and finally reaches a point at which we become conscious of the urge and we act. Previously, I suggested that the preconscious should be defined so as to include voluntary choice. I suggest that Libet's readiness potential is a physiological marker for that preconscious choice, in this instance the choice to perform a motor act.

But what of the experience of consciousness itself? Will Libet help us out by identifying a function for this experience? He does suggest that the experience of consciousness permits the subject to nullify the decision to act, as if consciousness of the choice already made gives the person a second chance. There is a problem with this hypothesis because presumably the decision to nullify is itself a willed act with its own readiness potential emerging from the preconscious and requiring a certain length of time to attain consciousness. Libet is aware of this objection and tries to get around it by further hypothesizing that once the experience of consciousness is aroused at a certain complex level no readiness potential is necessary. This has the ring of an ad hoc hypothesis that requires further testing.

Libet's findings are important and may have clinical implications with respect to our understanding of conscious and unconscious experiences. First, it is important to recognize that what Libet has investigated would fit best within the preconscious organization of experience rather than within the dynamic organization of unconscious experiences. However, as Fisher (1957) pointed out, the preconscious is the meeting ground of conflict-free and potentially conflictual unconscious experiences. Fisher suggested that all external stimuli enter the psychic apparatus by way of the preconscious where contact is made with long-term memory for purposes of recognition and where the influences of unconscious experiences may be exercised. The preconscious is the soil out of which conscious derivatives or compromise formations spring. Fisher developed this hypothesis in order to account for the findings of subliminal perception, but generalized it to account for all perception and for the formation of dream imagery. Thus, the organization of preconscious experience is pivotal in understanding conflict-free perception and thought, on the one hand, and such repressive conflict-laden compromise formations as dreams, on the other. Contemporary cognitive science is in substantial accord with one half of this formulation, the half dealing with the conflict-free organization of perception and thought; it ignores the other conflict-laden half because it thus far has developed little interest in affect, motive, anxiety, and conflict.

Perhaps the method developed by Libet can be put to another use once we realize, following Fisher, that preconscious processes may in fact give us a point of entry into the interaction of conflict-free and conflict-laden forces, between normality and pathology. For example, the length of time—some 500 msec on average—apparently necessary for conscious experience to emerge might vary as a function of defensive organization and of the meaning of stimuli employed. Might we find that people with a repressive disposition have a longer latency for conscious experience than people with an isolating, intellectualizing disposition? Or, might individual variations in the latency for conscious experience be a built-in dispositional factor that might contribute to developing a defensive style? It is also conceivable that within a given individual the latency for conscious experience might vary as a function of the conflict relevance of the material and we thus might discover a nonclinical, laboratory-based method for identifying individual acts of repression, so far a most elusive goal. In collaboration with Libet, Ghannam and I have made a tentative beginning in exploring these possibilities. We found that repressiveness, as measured by the Rorschach and HOQ, was indeed correlated with individual variations in the length of time for consciousness to develop in subjects tested previously by Libet (Shevrin, Ghannam, & Libet, 1992).

Turning next to Libet's method for identifying what we might call a preconscious experience of willing prior to the conscious experience of willing, we might hypothesize that in certain disorders of choice as in obsessional neurosis and impulse disorders that we might again discover dispositional factors as well as variations as a function of conflict related content. When, in fact, the Libet method was applied to obsessional and nonobsessional subjects, it was found that for obsessionals the awareness of the intention to act occurred significantly closer in time to the movement than for the nonobsessional subjects and that the length of time elapsed between the onset of the readiness potential and the awareness of the intention to act is greater for the obsessional subjects. These findings might be interpreted to mean that the actual obsessional process as such occurs between the onset of the readiness potential and the conscious intention to act (Wong, Shevrin, Williams, & Marshall, 1988).

In our own work on electrophysiological indexes of unconscious conflict, we have become convinced that one can select meanings on a clinical basis that are quite individually related to particular conflicts and obtain electrophysiological indicators that differ as a function of consciousness (Shevrin, 1988; Shevrin et al., 1988). Our method combines (a) a clinical assessment of patients suffering from symptoms such as phobias; (b) the subliminal and supraliminal exposure of words used by the patient that clinicians have selected as reflecting the patient's conscious experience of the symptom and the underlying hypothesized unconscious conflict; and (c) a signal analysis of brain responses obtained each time a word is flashed subliminally or supraliminally. We have found that certain frequency features of the brain responses allow us to show that when the words related to the unconscious conflict are presented subliminally, it is possible to group them together on the basis of their brain responses, whereas when the same words are presented supraliminally, the brain responses no longer appear to group them together, as if the relationship among the words is no longer recognized when the subject is consciously aware of them. Libet's and our work, in my judgment, amply attest to the promise of neurophysiological indexes for the study of unconscious experiences when investigated in an appropriate theoretical context. Freud may not have anticipated the development of methods of the kind just discussed.

In the light of Libet's work and Fisher's reformulation, the preconscious turns out to be of some special interest and not simply as a way station between the dynamic unconscious and consciousness. Psychoanalysis and cognitive science are probably closest to being identical in their views on the preconscious, although by no means entirely so. In the broad sense of a descriptive, relatively conflict-free organization of nonconscious experience, psychoanalysis and cognitive science indeed do see eye to eye. There is also an important congruence with respect to the role of attention, in particular as developed in the hands of Rapaport (1967), who developed a theory of attention deployment having normal, pathological, and structure building, or learning, implications. Cognitive science has not as yet gone this far, although it is likely that it will be through the further development of attention theory that psychoanalysis and cognitive science might continue to converge in their investigations of unconscious experience. For example, Kahneman (1973), a cognitive attention theorist who spent a summer as Rapaport's research assistant, has introduced into cognitive theory the concept of unconscious attention deployment and the concept of a limited reservoir of attention, the latter central to Rapaport's efforts to explain the limiting effects of conflict and dynamic forces on conflict-free functioning. There is some parallel between the psychoanalytic notion of cathexis (psychic energy) and

Kahneman's cognitive science concept of effort. This equivalence cannot quite work because Rapaport posits, in following Freud, that a hypercathexis (an increased quota of psychic energy) of attention is involved when an experience passes from a preconscious state to a conscious state; a shift in level of organization as well as the emergence of conscious experience is involved. Rapaport never quite solved theoretically the mystery as to how a sheer increase in psychic energy in the form of cathexis resulted in a shift to a higher level of organization. We see once again how the two different meanings of consciousness—adjectival and substantive—are at the heart of the problem. However, Kahneman does not do much better with the notion of effort. Aside from Kahneman, most cognitive scientists seem to prefer the quasi-physiological concept of activation to explain how a cognitive system or network passes from a latent to an active state.

By and large, cognitive scientists employ a vague "information processing" metaphor rather than the "hydraulic" metaphor characterizing much of Freud's thinking. Neither metaphor is particularly generative in the sense that one can independently draw inferences from the metaphors that lead to new expectations. Both metaphors are closer to being languages of description rather than explanation. One speaks English because one has learned English and one's friends and colleagues also speak English. "Information processing" is the English for cognitive scientists because it permits a neutral, computerlike lingo, divisible into manageable cognitive units, with reasonably clear levels of abstraction. The hydraulic metaphor has been until recently the English for most psychoanalysts because for historical reasons Freud was trying to talk to the physiologists and physicists of his time, and in part because it fit with the phenomenology of clinical experience. The recent shift by some psychoanalysts to an "information" metaphor, therefore, does not in my judgment represent a theoretical advance, although it may make it possible for psychoanalysts to talk to different people about their mutually unsolved problems. The main problem, however, remains: We do not have a comprehensive generative metaphor for the relationships between conscious and unconscious experience. To replace, as it were, the German of the hydraulic metaphor with the English of the information metaphor is no advance.

CONCLUSIONS

Whether the psychoanalytic and cognitive science views of the unconscious are fraternal or identical twins, they were certainly reared apart from one another. The psychoanalytic twin was raised in the consulting room, exposed to primal scenes, intrapsychic conflict, and the risky improvisations of clinical practice, while the cognitive science twin was raised in a laboratory where order, predictability, calm, and cooperation prevailed. The psychoanalytic view of the unconscious has been forged on the front lines of the psyche as it were, although the cognitive science view has been formed in the rear echelons. It should be no surprise that there are substantial differences in these views raised so differently and out of different traditions. As a result, there is a clear and almost totally unchallenged emphasis in cognitive science on the purely cognitive to the detriment of affect, motive, and conflict, whereas in psychoanalysis, the pressures of clinical work rivet attention to what is conflictual, personal, and away from a concern with the fundamental underlying psychological processes. However, what is surprising is that there are in fact convergences between these two so different views; we are reminded of the recent studies that show twins reared apart somehow manage to marry people by the same names and show other remarkable parallels in their life courses. The reasons for these convergences are not hard to find. They follow from the similarity in the nature of the problems addressed, even though at first blush they may seem far apart.

As I have suggested, I believe that theories of attention will provide the bridge across which psychoanalysts and cognitive scientists will cross over to each other's side of the river. Already,

Kahneman has developed a theory that has thrown several provisional pontoons across the river to the other side. On the psychoanalytic side, we need to pick up the burden put down prematurely by Rapaport and develop further the psychodynamic attention theory he started to bring into being. The joint exploitation of the preconscious from both directions will yield exciting results. Also, the newly developing field in cognitive science dealing with categorization and an understanding of judgmental processes will be of value in investigating the hierarchical relationship structuring the organization of the mind, and in particular the interactions between unconscious and conscious experiences. New methods of exploration that can also bridge the gap between the laboratory and the consulting room are now available. I refer to the use of subliminal stimuli of clinical import and to the electrophysiological techniques used by Shevrin and coworkers and explored so ingeniously by Libet. We are now in a position to broaden and deepen the scientific investigation of the unconscious in a way never before possible. We need only apply our imaginations and goodwill.

REFERENCES

Bartlett, R. C. (1932). *Remembering: A study in experimental and social psychology*. Cambridge, England: Cambridge University Press.

Fisher, C. (1957). A study of the preliminary stages of the construction of dreams and images. *Journal of the Psychoanalytic Association, 5,* 60.

Freud, S. (1953). The interpretation of dreams. In J. Strachey (Ed. and Trans.), *The standard edition of the complete psychological works of Sigmund Freud* (Vols. 4 & 5). London: Hogarth Press. (Original work published 1900)

Freud, S. (1957a). The unconscious. In J. Strachey (Ed. and Trans.), *The standard edition of the complete psychological works of Sigmund Freud* (Vol. 14, pp. 166–204). London: Hogarth Press. (Original work published 1915)

Freud, S. (1957b). Instincts and their vicissitudes. In J. Strachey (Ed. and Trans.), *The standard edition of the complete psychological works of Sigmund Freud* (Vol. 14, pp. 109–140). London: Hogarth Press. (Original work published 1915)

Gill, M. M. (1963). Topography and systems in psychoanalytic theory. *Psychological Issues,* Monograph 10.

Grünbaum, A. (1984). *The foundations of psychoanalysis: A philosophical critique*. Berkeley: University of California Press.

Hartmann, H. (1964). *Essays on ego psychology: Selected problems in psychoanalytic theory*. Madison, CT: International Universities Press.

Hobson, J. A., & McCarley, R. W. (1977). The brain as a dream state generator: An activation-synthesis hypothesis of the dream process. *American Journal of Psychiatry, 134,* 1335–1348

Kahneman, D. (1973). *Attention and effort*. Englewood Cliffs, NJ: Prentice-Hall.

Kihlstrom, J. F. (1984). Conscious, subconscious, unconscious: A cognitive perspective. In K. S. Bowers & D. Meichenbaum (Eds.), *The unconscious reconsidered* (pp. 149–211). New York: Wiley.

Kihlstrom, J. F. (1987). The cognitive unconscious. *Science, 237,* 1445–1452.

Libet, B. (1965). Cortical activation in conscious and unconscious experience. *Perspectives in Biology and Medicine, 9,* 77–86.

Libet, B. (1966). Brain stimulation and the threshold of conscious experience. In J. C. Eccles (Ed.), *Brain and conscious experience* (pp. 165–181). New York: Springer-Verlag.

Libet, B., Wright, E. W. Jr., & Gleason, C. A. (1982). Readiness-potentials preceding unrestricted "spontaneous" vs. preplanned voluntary acts. *Electroencephalography and Clinical Neurophysiology, 54,* 322–335.

Libet, B., Wright, E. W. Jr., & Gleason, C. A. (1983). Preparation—or intention—to act in relation to pre-event potentials recorded at the vertex. *Electroencephalography and Clinical Neurophysiology, 56,* 367–372.

Mandler, G. (1975). Consciousness: Respectable, useful and probably necessary. In R. Solsos (Ed.), *Information processing and cognition: The Loyola Symposium* (pp. 229–254). Hillsdale, NJ: Erlbaum.

Posner, M., & Snyder, C. (1975). Attention and cognitive control. In R. Solsos (Ed.), *Information processing and cognition: The Loyola Symposium* (pp. 55–85). Hillsdale, NJ: Erlbaum.

Rapaport, D. (1967). The theory of attention cathexis: An economic and structural attempt at the explanation of cognitive processes. In M. M. Gill (Ed.), *The collected papers of David Rapaport* (pp. 778–794). New York: Basic Books.

Shevrin, H. (1973). Brain wave correlates of subliminal stimulation, unconscious attention, primary-process and secondary-process thinking, and repressiveness. *Psychological Issues, 8*(2), Monograph 30, 56–87.

Shevrin, H. (1986, August). *A proposed function of consciousness relevant to theory and practice.* Paper presented at the meeting of Division 39 of the American Psychological Association, Washington, DC.

Shevrin, H. (1988). Unconscious conflict: A convergent psychodynamic and electrophysiological approach. In M.J. Horowitz (Ed.), *Psychodynamics and cognition* (pp. 117–167). Chicago: University of Chicago Press.

Shevrin, H., & Dickman, S. (1980). The psychological unconscious: A necessary assumption for all psychological theory? *American Psychologist, 35,* 421–434.

Shevrin, H., Ghannam, J. H., & Libet, B. (1992). *Electrophysiological correlates of unconscious mental processes: Implications for hemispheric specialization and psychoanalytic theory.* Manuscript in preparation.

Shevrin, H., & Rennick, P. (1967). Cortical response to a tactile stimulus during attention, mental arithmetic, and free associations. *Psychophysiology, 3,* 381–388.

Shevrin, H., Williams, J. J., Marshall, R. E., Hertel, R. K., Bond, J. A., & Brakel, L. A. (1988, September). *Event-related potential indicators of the dynamic unconscious.* Paper presented at the Fourth International Conference on Psychophysiology, Prague, Czechoslovakia.

Shiffrin, R., & Schneider, W. (1977). Controlled and automatic human information processing: II. Perceptual learning, automatic attending, and a general theory. *Psychological Review, 84,* 127–190.

Strachey, J. (Ed.). (1957). Introduction. In *The standard edition of the complete psychological works of Sigmund Freud* (Vol. 14, pp. 105–107). London: Hogarth Press. (Original work published 1915)

Wong, P. S., Shevrin, H., Williams, W. J., & Marshall, R. E. (1988, October). *The psychophysiology of voluntary movement: Awareness of the intention to act and the obsessional personality.* Paper presented at the 28th annual meeting of the Society for Psychophysiological Research, San Francisco.

14

THE EMPIRICAL STUDY OF DEFENSIVE PROCESSES: A REVIEW

STEVEN H. COOPER

In Freud's (1894) first paper on the subject of defense, he termed the study of psychological defenses or defense mechanisms "the cornerstone on which the whole structure of psychoanalysis rests." Freud's (1894) notion of defense followed from a statement of the "fundamental hypothesis" involving a sum of excitation and the theory of cathexis. He conceptualized defense as counter-cathexis, a counterforce struggling to achieve the diminution of a drive or a drive derivative, or depressive affect. Since Freud's first description, there has been significant interest in elaborating the understanding of defense both within intrapsychic and object relational contexts. Broadly speaking, these elaborations of defense have helped to delineate the role that defenses play in the individual's adaptation to conflict, the maintenance of psychopathology, and the role of defense as one aspect of ego functioning among others such as reality testing, judgment, and other adaptive functions.

In this chapter, I focus on the vast and burgeoning literature related to the empirical psychoanalytic study of defense mechanisms. Note that contemporary defense research has gone well outside of the domain of psychoanalytic research to include information-processing approaches and the study of the psychophysiology of defense. Due to the complexity and scope of the entire body of empirical defense research and the focus of this overall book dedicated to psychoanalysis, my focus is restricted to studies that have examined defense from either a psychoanalytic theoretical framework or that have used psychotherapy, interviews, or the Rorschach as research instruments.

The psychoanalytically informed literature includes a number of varying methodological approaches as well as differing study questions involving defense. Some investigators have attempted to use clinical rating methods in order to refine assessment methods for determining the presence of defenses; others have been interested in the relationship between defenses and

327

diagnostic categorization; and still others have studied the relationship between defenses and more global psychosocial functioning. A variety of instruments have been used in studying defense mechanisms including videotaped interview rating methods (Horowitz, Markman, Stinson, Fridhandler, & Ghannam, 1990; Perry & Cooper, 1986a, 1989), self-report instruments (e.g., Bond, Gardner, Christian, & Sigel, 1983; Gleser & Ihlevich, 1969), and Rorschach research instruments (Cooper, Perry, & Arnow, 1988; P. Lerner & Lerner, 1980). Although most studies of defenses have been heavily influenced by psychoanalytic theories of defense, more recently some investigators have begun empirical attempts to integrate psychoanalytic and cognitive psychology approaches to the study of defense (e.g., Horowitz, 1988; Horowitz et al., 1991).

The theoretical and clinical study of defense has undergone vast changes since Freud's original contributions. In the last 20 years in particular, the concepts of defense and adaptation have been expanded in ways that have been clinically illuminating, even if, at times, theoretically confusing. I begin this chapter with a brief sketch of developments in the body of theory related to defense in order to provide a theoretical backdrop for the emergence and proliferation of the empirical study of defense.

SOME THEORETICAL PROPOSITIONS AND CONTROVERSIES RELATED TO DEFENSE

Freud's (1894/1962) earliest discussion of defense revolved around the notion of defense as countercathexis—a force struggling against a counterforce, usually involving undesirable (anxiety-producing) content. Freud (1926/1959) articulated a theory of signal anxiety in which defenses were viewed as a general process functioning within the ego to maintain the unconscious status of forbidden impulses, thereby attempting to mitigate anxiety. Over the course of his writing, Freud moved from the use of the term *defense* as being synonymous with repression, to the articulation of a series of defenses including isolation, regression, reaction formation, undoing, and splitting of the ego as special methods of defense. Anna Freud (1936) subdivided the larger concept of defense even further, citing a number of examples of other defenses not proposed by Freud. She suggested a classification or taxonomy of defenses according to the source of anxiety (e.g., superego, external world, strength of instinctual pressures) that gives rise to them.

Brenner (1955, 1982) emphasized a "functional approach" (Cooper, 1989) to defense, focusing on the ego's breadth in accomplishing the reduction of anxiety or depressive affect associated with drive derivatives or superego functions. In Brenner's view, anything is usefully regarded as defensive that functions to reduce anxiety or drive tensions. Brenner's work is highly related to the work of Hartmann, Kris, and Loewenstein (1964), who emphasized the ego as an organ of adaptation and accommodation that had access to the use of defense, among a variety of ego functions, to cope with exigencies of the external world as well as drive demands.

Schafer (1968) also built on the work of Hartmann et al. (1964). Schafer attempted to delineate the dynamic properties of the ego, emphasizing that defenses are never simply neutral countercathexes. Instead, Schafer argued that although defenses always attempt to block expression of undesirable content, at the same time, they express undesirable impulses, thereby allowing for gratification. Thus, Schafer described defenses as "double agents" and justified the unconscious status of defenses (i.e., defenses must remain unconscious because defenses gratify as well as defend).

In many ways, Winnicott was a transitional figure between theorists who focused on defense as ego function and theorists who tried to understand defensive processes within the context of object relations. Winnicott (1965, p. 147) differentiated between "ego defense organized against id impulse" and more traumatic environmental failures leading to massive defensive efforts such as "false self" adaptations. Winnicott emphasized that the infant's expression of need must be met with an object's accepting response (at least a good part of the time) as a prerequisite for the capacity to use the ego to organize against id tensions. He suggested that id excitements (experience of and expression of impulses) can be traumatic when the ego is not able to incorporate those excitements that occur when the caretaking other communicates to the child that id excitement is injurious. Thus, for Winnicott (1965) the good-enough maternal response to the child's id excitement is a precondition for "ego defense organized against id impulse" (p. 143).

Modell (1975) and Kohut (1984) were influenced by similar concerns stressed by Winnicott (1965). Modell (1975) suggested that defense is not always organized against impulses, but in instances of massive empathic failure, defense is organized against object failure. In these instances, Modell described a defensive organization involving a falling back on the self and the avoidance of expressed needs toward others that he termed "self-sufficiency as a defense against affect." In so doing, Modell (1984) emphasized what he termed a "two-person" theory of defense.

Kohut outlined how defenses are often organized against empathic failures of disappointing "selfobjects" from childhood. Kohut (1984, p. 132) defined defensive structures as attempts to safeguard an enfeebled self. Kohut noted the presence of what he termed "the innately present vigor of the self" that he defined as the "nuclear self's resistiveness to disintegration and capacity to fight noxious influences." Self psychology views the expression of drives primarily as an attempt to remedy a besieged self, in contrast to a view of unneutralized drives as indicative of drive fixations and regression from later forms of conflict (Cooper, 1989). Paralleling this theoretical position, Kohut stated that defense and resistance interpretations may at times interfere with transferences related to reactivated needs for mirroring of the "enfeebled self."

Kohut's formulations are to some extent consistent with those of Fairbairn, Winnicott, Guntrip, and Modell in terms of the emphasis on the degree to which the self may need to be safeguarded in its state of vulnerability. Guntrip's (1969) notion of the "schizoid citadel" and Modell's (1975) analogy of the self's "cocoon state" are defensive positions invoked to protect equivalents of Kohut's "enfeebled self" (Cooper, 1989). As Newman (1980), among others, pointed out, Kohut's notion of the vertical split-off part of the psyche largely overlaps with Winnicott's (1965) description of the defensively motivated "false self," which involves compliance with an empathically faulty object. However, one of Kohut's points of divergence with Modell, in particular, lies in the former's relative minimization of instinctual processes and instinctual derivatives. As stated earlier, the notion of wish, from the self psychological perspective, is conceptualized primarily as an expression of motives to complete development and "thereby realize the nuclear program of the self" (Kohut, 1984, p. 148).

Kernberg (1975, 1983) made a number of contributions to the understanding of defense mechanisms. Kernberg straddled extensions of the defense mechanism concept from both the intrapsychic and the object relational field. He viewed the defense mechanism concept as an intrapsychic phenomenon but broadened the components of intrapsychic conflict to include the object representation concept. Kernberg suggested that all character defenses represent a defensive constellation of self and other object representations directed against an opposite, anxiety-producing, repressed self and object representation. Kernberg emphasized that a particular type of defensive organization may be helpful in diagnosing borderline personality organization. For example, Kernberg (1975) suggested that the predominance of splitting and subsidiary defenses of projective identification, denial, primitive idealization, and devaluation were usually indicative of borderline personality organization. Kernberg's propositions regarding the diagnostic significance of defensive organization have been particularly conducive to empirical study.

This cursory review does little justice to the nuances of theoretical controversy among psychoanalysts related to defense and defense interpretation since Freud's 1894 paper. However, some of these theory developments allow for a brief delineation of some of the repeated controversies that have accompanied the evolution of varying theoretical approaches to defense.

Controversies within defense theory may be seen as a series of splits or bifurcations (Cooper, 1989). These bifurcations in theory relate to varying ideas about the referent points for defenses, the types of patients for whom the concepts of defense are most useful, and the types of defense interpretations. One type of bifurcation involves theorists who discussed the referent of defense (that which defense defends against) as impulse or drive derivative (e.g., Brenner, 1955; Kernberg, 1975; Kris, 1982; Schafer, 1968) whereas another group of theorists (e.g., Kohut, 1984; Modell, 1975; Stolorow & Lachmann, 1980) emphasized that the function of some defenses is to defend against object loss, environmental failure, or an "enfeebled self" (Kohut, 1984). For the former group, defense was conceptualized within a strictly intrapsychic context. By contrast, Modell, Kohut, and Stolorow, and Lachmann extended the "field" to include the self and the other. For this group of theorists, defense mechanisms may serve to maintain or preserve a view of the self or the object that, without it, would signify overriding anxiety.

Another area of controversy or tension in theory of defense is related to the application of psychoanalysis to the "preoedipal" world or the widening scope of patients. Some theorists such as Stolorow and Lachmann (1980), as Balint (1950) had done earlier, suggested that this bifurcation in the referent point of defense relates to the fact that there are different types of patients, some for whom it is meaningful to discuss defense and others for whom it is more meaningful to discuss developmental arrest (i.e., the failure of the development of defense).

Finally, a major area of dispute among psychoanalysts over the last 20 years has involved the technical handling of defense interpretation in the analytic situation. Kohut (1971, 1979) suggested that some forms of idealization and other defenses are not usefully regarded as resistances to be overcome. A major debate has ensued about whether the protection of the self as it manifests itself in the analytic situation is a phenomenon that is beneficially interpreted or allowed more fully to unfold.

REVIEW OF METHODS OF EMPIRICAL STUDIES OF DEFENSE MECHANISMS

Early Experimental Research

A number of postwar clinical investigators, including Ernst Kris, George Engel, David Hamburg, Irving Janis, Percival Symonds, and Karl Menninger, emphasized the need to define a hierarchy of defenses. However, each of these authors presented clinical examples and anecdotes rather than seeking mutually exclusive definitions of defense or empirical evidence including interrater reliability. At the same time, after the war an experimental literature studying defenses began to develop. These studies generally used psychology laboratories rather than psychotherapy sessions or clinics for conducting research.

Because of the vastness of the body of empirical research on defense and the presence of several exhaustive and excellent reviews of experimental research (e.g., Erdelyi, 1985; Paulhaus, Fridhandler, & Hayes, in press), I only briefly summarize the experimental findings related to defense. Most early experimental research related to defense focused on experimental analogues to repression. The research on repression may be broadly divided into studies of memory and studies of perception. Perceptual research (e.g., Holmes, 1974) on repression has generally shown that the emotional loading for a stimulus influenced the way in which that stimulus was processed. This research also suggested that negative emotional loading for a stimulus was causally related to the disruption of perception. As Holmes (1974) and Paulhaus et al. (in press) have suggested, it is unclear to what degree evidence of perceptual disruption may be equated with perceptual avoidance as is the case for defense.

Memory studies of repression sought to demonstrate that memories associated with unpleasant feelings are more difficult to recall than memories associated with pleasant feelings. Such studies argued that studies that used sensory hedonic tones (unpleasantness) had little relation to repression because these studies failed to assess feelings associated with the subject's own wishes. Holmes (1974), in his review of experimental investigations of repression, questioned whether sufficient laboratory evidence for repression had been found. Many have questioned the positive findings, however, on the basis of the questionable relevance of experimental analogues to repression proper. Interestingly, Freud himself wrote to Saul Rosenzweig in the early 1930s questioning the value of empirical research as an avenue for validation for psychoanalysis (Rosenzweig, personal communication, May 1973), instead arguing that clinical analysis was the necessary laboratory for such validation.

Clinical Methods

A number of authors have studied defense by developing explicit definitions of defense, often with accompanying scales to rate clinical data. Generally, these scales are rated on the basis of psychodynamically informed interviews. In an early such study, Weintraub and Aronson (1963) rated formal aspects of speech obtained from a recording of 10 minutes of continuous speech from each subject. Although those authors were able to obtain good reliability, it was unclear to what extent they were measuring defense as opposed to more formal aspects of cognitive style or the interpenetration of cognitive and defensive functioning.

Haan's (1963) longitudinal studies provided an important advance both in the study of defense and the value of the longitudinal method. Haan explicitly described 20 adaptive styles or "ego actions" that were divided into two groups: 10 described as coping (healthy) and 10 described as defending (pathological). Coping styles were characterized by conscious, purposeful, and timely decisions that were said by Haan to be more reality bound and at higher levels of moral development. Within her taxonomy, defensive styles were characterized as rigid and distorted behaviors. She described fragmentation as the result of failure of coping or defensive styles: Essentially fragmentation is equivalent to symptom or "impulse" breakthrough. On the basis of interview notes derived from an average of 12 hours of interview data, two raters judged the two coping and defending styles. Haan's work has stimulated a number of subsequent investigations using these and related scales. Haan also developed a self-report version of the ego-process scales by administering the California Psychological Inventory and the Minnesota Multiphasic Personality Inventory, although, as Morrissey (1977) noted, she never cross-validated her various methods.

Haan's contributions to the study of defense were quite significant. She explicitly defined a hierarchy of defenses according to pathological impact, which was highly unusual at that point in empirical research (Vaillant, Bond, & Vaillant, 1986). Not only did she try to develop mutually exclusive definitions of defensive and coping styles, but she subsequently tried to validate her scales through correlations with other longitudinally derived measures of mental health. Her methodology fostered further empirical interest in developing Anna Freud's clinical interest in the notion of a hierarchy of defenses—this research was to be most thoroughly developed by George Vaillant. It is worth noting, as many have suggested (e.g., Perry & Cooper, 1987; Vaillant et al., 1986) that Haan's studies were also flawed. First, Haan's definitions of defenses were sometimes quite idiosyncratic. Although some investigators (e.g., Paulhus et al., in press) have noted Haan's attempt to expand and elaborate on the more narrow focus of defense by including "coping, defense, and fragmentation," this expansion has led to a terminological and methodological confusion in studying the overlapping concepts of defense, symptom, and compromise formation. Haan's longitudinal sample also was composed of members of the Oakland Growth Studies, a unique longitudinal study with questionable generalizability. Finally, as many have pointed out (e.g., Perry & Cooper, 1987; Vaillant et al., 1986), Haan's interrater reliability for the 20 styles was quite uneven.

Bellak, Hurvich, and Gediman (1973) rated the overall effectiveness of defensive functioning as part of their Ego Function Assessment Scales. Bellak et al. studied schizophrenic patients. The reliability between raters for this scale was originally reported as quite high but problematic in a subsequent report. This scale has never been empirically validated. Semrad, Grinspoon, and Feinberg (1973) also studied defenses in a developmental longitudinal context. Semrad attempted to study and outline the process of recovery in acute schizophrenic patients. He and his co-workers devised the 45-item Ego Profile Scale to measure nine defenses based on observation of inpatients. Although the reliability and factor structure of the instrument were found to be favorable, the rating scale was never sufficiently validated.

Despite these significant early contributions, as Vaillant et al. (1986, p. xiii) cogently stated, "by the mid-1970s the empirical understanding of defense mechanism remained in semantic and conceptual disarray." In their view, it was partly the status of this disarray that led to the complex decision to not include defenses as a possible axis for the third edition of the *Diagnostic and Statistical Manual of Mental Disorders* (DSM–III). Since the mid-1970s, largely because of Vaillant's seminal contributions, research has been moving in the direction of augmented empirical and conceptual clarity.

Vaillant has been interested in the naturalistic study of defenses, which involves studying subjects over long spans of time with regard to their "adaptation to life." Vaillant's approach to defense has been explicitly developmental: He has described defenses in terms of their "maturity." The components of maturity involve the degree to which a defensive style or mechanism adheres to reality and reflects adaptiveness. Vaillant (1971) first proposed a theoretical hierarchy, grouping individual defenses into four categories from least to most adaptive: psychotic, immature, neurotic, and mature. This categorization did not include the so-called borderline level defenses proposed by Kernberg (1975). Vaillant used a broad base of information over the course of many years within an individual's life for assessing defenses. Using a variety of biographical materials, he composed vignettes for each subject prior to coding defenses. The vignettes show the subject's methods for resolving and managing a variety of problems and life conflicts. Vaillant (1971, 1976, 1977) devised a glossary of 18 defenses ranging from the mature to psychotic, which he applied to the life vignette data reported by subjects. In Vaillant's studies, pairs of raters categorized each vignette according to Vaillant's hierarchy of defenses. Vaillant's reliability results have been generally among the highest of empirical defense researchers. However, his method for determining reliability differs from researchers who directly rate interview data. Vaillant's coding procedure involves an intermediate step in which he categorizes the life historical material. This method reduces the "noise" but does not allow for an assessment of the degree to which reliable defense ratings may be made from direct life historical data.

Vaillant studied two large samples of subjects in particular: a sample of 95 college men and a second sample of inner-city boys. In the sample of college men, Vaillant (1971) found that "mature" defenses correlated positively and "immature" defenses correlated negatively with a 32-item scale measuring objective success in loving and working. Vaillant and Drake (1985) replicated these findings studying an inner-city sample of 307 47-year-old men. They demonstrated that maturity of defensive style correlated with adjustment and mental health cross-sectionally. Vaillant (1976) reported evidence to suggest that defensive style increases in maturity over the life span. Vaillant et al. (1986) reported that levels of defense maturity increase among adults particularly for subjects with traumatic or depriving childhood environments.

Five studies have examined Vaillant's hierarchy of defense (Battista, 1982; Jacobson et al., 1986; Perry & Cooper, 1989; Vaillant, 1976; Vaillant & Drake, 1985). These researchers have used different assessment methods of defense and global psychological functioning, different psychiatric samples, and different time frames. Yet, it is striking that there is a fairly strong similarity in the pattern of findings lending support to the hierarchical model (Perry, in press). Defenses can be grouped on the basis of empirical association or clustering, conceptual relationship, or the ability of a group of defenses to predict a specified area of functioning such as treatment outcome or general functioning. Despite the promising results yielded by the hierarchical model, there is need for more empirical study relating to both individual defenses and overall defensive organization before researchers can be more certain about the most valid grouping method for defenses.

Hauser and his co-investigators have been interested in evaluating defense mechanisms from clinical interview material with an overall aim of studying coping patterns during adolescence. In particular, Hauser, Jacobson, and Noam (1983) studied the developmental processes of adolescent self-images, self-esteem, and ego development. Jacobson et al. (1986) devised rating scales and definitions for 12 defenses and for overall defense effectiveness, which they applied to interviews of adolescents. Reliability results for most of the defense scales were quite acceptable and are promising in their clarity for both teaching and research purposes.

Perry and Cooper (1986b, 1986c, 1989), using videotaped interviews, have longitudinally studied defenses among subjects diagnosed with personality disorders. They devised definitions and rating scales anchored with examples for 30 defenses. They have explored the relationship between individual defenses and overall defense summary scores, the degree to which defenses predict longitudinal functioning, and the relationship between defense and overall diagnosis. They found with regard to reliability that group consensus ratings were more reliable than individual ratings and that reliability was also higher when applied to life vignette data rather than to videotaped interviews.

Horowitz and his colleagues have introduced a groundbreaking theoretical and empirical method for the study of defense using ratings from psychoanalytic psychotherapy sessions. Horowitz (1988) and Horowitz et al. (1990) have incorporated principles of cognitive psychology into a psychodynamic framework for studying "control processes." Horowitz began with the assumption that control processes operate unconsciously and govern what is represented in conscious awareness and what form this awareness takes (Paulhus et al., in press). Thus, Horowitz regarded traditional defenses as outcomes of more basic or rudimentary cognitive processes. Although Horowitz retained the idea that researchers can determine and delineate defense mechanisms, he did not regard them as fundamental processes. Instead, defenses are viewed as being the result or outcome of more elemental cognitive processes. Each defense mechanism, within this view, may be broken down into a series of cognitive processes that accomplish the final outcome. Horowitz retained the idea that control processes and defenses function to mitigate awareness or altogether avoid ideas or feelings that would threaten the individual.

Horowitz developed a set of processes and, applying Haan's (1963) model, proposed that any one of the control processes may be manifested at adaptive, maladaptive, or dysregulatory levels. Horowitz (1988) studied videotaped psychotherapy sessions of subjects with unresolved posttraumatic reactions. In studying psychological coping strategies following traumatic stress, he found that therapists helped these individuals to change various regulatory and control operations. From these observations, he developed a list of three levels of regulation: regulation of person schemas, regulation of mental set, and regulation of conscious representations and sequencing (Horowitz, 1988). Obviously, certain traditional defense mechanisms tend to cluster within certain levels of regulation, although they do not appear to be highly overlapping measures. Horowitz and his colleagues are currently doing single case studies involving the refinement of scoring methods of the control processes rated from ongoing intensive psychotherapy sessions. Horowitz et al. (1991) have recently used the control process approach for describing the emergence of control processes within a single psychotherapy session and related these descriptions to more traditional classifications of defense mechanisms.

Self-Report Instruments

Several investigators have developed paper-and-pencil tests to assess defense mechanisms. The merits and debits of this approach have long been debated among defense researchers. An obvious advantage to such an approach is that it saves the clinician's time, avoids subjective inference in coding and scoring, and is generally highly reliable. However, it is a matter of empirical and theoretical debate to what degree such instruments are valid measures of defense. Although by definition defenses are unconscious, self-reports of defenses may be thought to measure something akin to a conscious derivative of defense or defense derivative—a conscious report about the presence or absence of defense. Thus, it is necessary to demonstrate that self-report measures correlate highly with other clinical measures of defense in order to determine the relevance of research findings.

Gleser and Ihlevich (1969) constructed the Defense Mechanism Inventory to assess five aspects of defensive functioning. After subjects read a series of stories, they noted their most and least likely responses on a forced-choice questionnaire. The choices or dimensions rated subjects included turning against objects, projection, prinicipalization (encompassing isolation of affect, intellectualization, rationalization), reversal (reaction formation, repression), and turning against the self. Gleser and Ihlevich (1969) found quite good immediate and short-term stability of the scales. Unfortunately, the relationship of these scales to clinical measures of defenses is unknown.

Bond et al. (1983) developed a self-report questionnaire—the Defense Style Questionnaire (DSQ)—in order to assess conscious derivatives of 24 defense mechanisms. A factor analysis revealed four stable defense styles. The first factor involved the "immature defenses" (Vaillant, 1976) and included regression, withdrawal, acting-out, projection, passive aggression, and inhibition. Bond et al. referred to this style as a maladaptive reaction pattern. The second style was referred to as the image-distorting defenses and included defenses of primitive idealization, splitting, omnipotence, and devaluation. The third style, termed a self-sacrificing neurotic style, consisted of pseudoaltruism and reaction formation. Finally, the fourth style consisted of humor, suppression, and sublimation constituting an adaptive or mature style. Bond et al. found that the maladaptive action pattern style correlated most negatively with interdependent measures of ego strength and ego development, whereas the second and third styles correlated somewhat negatively and the adaptive style correlated positively. Importantly, Bond et al. noted that these findings were consistent with the defense constructs that the questionnaire attempts to assess. Bond and Vaillant (1986) reported that maladaptive, image-distorting, and neurotic defense styles were more associated with psychiatric patients than with normal controls. However, they failed to find a clear relationship between any style and particular diagnostic groups. Bond and Vaillant concluded that defensive functioning appears to be independent of Axis I, Axis II, and Axis IV of the *DSM–III*. Thus, they argued that defensive functioning should be considered for its independent contribution to patient diagnosis.

Vaillant et al. (1986) studied Vaillant and Drake's (1985) sample of inner-city men and compared DSQ ratings at age 54 with clinical ratings of defenses at age 47. Approximately 50%

of the DSQ items were correlated with the defensive style that they were intended to represent.

Several researchers have studied the stability of Bond's factor structure in the DSQ. Andrews, Pollock, and Stewart (1989) administered the 88-item revised DSQ (Bond & Vaillant, 1986) to a sample of outpatients and nonpsychiatric controls. They found a three-factor solution in which defenses such as splitting and projective identification ("image distorting") loaded either with the "immature" defenses or the "neurotic" defenses. Andrews et al. (1989) also found, as expected, negative correlations between mature defense style and scores on the SCL-90 and Eysenck's Neuroticism measure; the neurotic defense style correlated more highly with these measures, and the maladaptive style correlated quite highly with the measures. Flannery and Perry (1990) studied normal adults and found that only the maladaptive style resembled Bond's factor structure. The maladaptive defense style was highly correlated with reports of life stress, anxiety, and depressive symptoms. Perry (in press) concluded that among the styles, the maladaptive style is the most valid and stable on the DSQ relative to the adaptive or mature style.

A SUMMARY OF EMPIRICAL RORSCHACH DEFENSE METHODS AND RESEARCH

Despite the widespread reliance on the Rorschach for collaborating clinical diagnosis, there have been relatively few empirical studies of defense mechanisms as manifested on the Rorschach test. I summarize the basic research strategies and important findings in this area, focusing on work since around 1950.

There have been three general strategies for assessing Rorschach manifestations of defenses. The first involves an exclusive focus on "formal" scoring including dimensions such as the location of a percept and determinants of perception (e.g., the shape, color, or shading of the blot that led to a particular perception). A second approach analyzes the thematic content of percepts using psychodynamic principles of interpretation. Finally, a third research strategy involves a combination of formal scoring and verbal, thematic content.

For the most part, studies that have relied exclusively on formal scores have provided limited information about the nature of defensive functioning in both clinical and nonclinical populations. Haan (1963) examined the relationship between a large number of formal scores and her voluminous data related to coping and defense mechanisms (interview-derived data). The results of these correlations were not impressive, but led her to develop, post hoc, a more promising set of criteria that included the phenomenology of the Rorschach situation (e.g., enjoyment of the test and level of attention focused on the task). In another study focusing on formal scores, Bahnson and Bahnson (1966) devised a 16-item index of repression that included various determinant ratios, reaction times, and card rejections in order to study the role of repression in the etiology of malignant neoplasm. Inadequate control groups impeded their ability to draw definitive conclusions about the validity of their measure of repression.

Schafer's (1954) seminal monograph on the psychoanalytic interpretation of the Rorschach strongly affected content-oriented measures of defense. For example, Cooper et al. (1988), in developing the Rorschach Defense Scales, used many of Schafer's clinical formulations of the classical defenses in composing an empirical manual. Levine and Spivack (1964) developed a thorough research manual for assessing repressive style. A potentially confounding issue for Levine and Spivack's manual as well as other content approaches is their reliance on verbal expressive style in assessing repression. For example, Perry and Cooper (1987) noted that other factors than repression such as depression, guardedness, or low level of intellectual functioning may influence verbal expression. Finally, Baxter, Becker, and Hooks (1963) developed content criteria for scoring projection, undoing, displacement, denial, and isolation in a study comparing defensive styles between parents of good versus bad premorbid schizophrenics. These criteria were based on factors such as test-taking attitudes, response dynamics, card rejections, and characteristic imagery. Baxter et al. found significant differences between parents of good versus bad premorbid schizophrenics but not between these groups and the parents of neurotics.

Only a few Rorschach researchers have examined defense scoring using both content and formal scoring. Gardner, Holzman, Klein, Linton, and Spence (1959) examined the relationships between the defenses of repression and isolation and their cognitive correlates or counterparts, referred to as cognitive styles of leveling and sharpening. Gardner et al. included among the content variables of repression such phenomena as childlike Rorschach content, constriction in the variety of Rorschach content, and poor integrative effort. Using these criteria, they selected protocols reflecting extreme reliance on either repression or isolation. They found interesting correlations between particular defenses and perceptual styles. Along similar lines, Luborsky, Blinder, and Schimek (1965) found significant correlations between repression and venturing to look around less (as measured by eye fixation photography) and between defensive isolation and venturing to look around more. Finally, several investigators (e.g., Appelbaum, 1977; Bellak et al., 1973) have used the intuitive judgment of experienced Rorschach clinicians without recourse to objectively determined criteria. For example, Bellak et al. developed global criteria to study ego functioning among normal, neurotic, and schizophrenic individuals. Rorschach clinicians then rated the presence of defensive failure and pathological interference by certain defenses such as projection and repression along with adaptive behavior. Similarly, Appelbaum (1977) used expert Rorschach clinicians in the Menninger Psychotherapy Outcome Study.

Since 1980, two Rorschach defense scales (Cooper et al., 1988; P. Lerner & Lerner, 1980) have been designed. Lerner and Lerner developed a scoring manual in order to assess five defense mechanisms related to borderline personality organization as described by Kernberg (1975). The Lerner Defense Scales (LDS) are divided into sections on the basis of the specific defenses of splitting, denial, devaluation, idealization, and projective identification. The defenses of devaluation, idealization, and denial are also ranked on a continuum of high versus low order. The LDS limit themselves to examination of human figure responses in keeping with Blatt's earlier scales examining qualitative and formal properties of object relations (Blatt, Brennis, Schimek, & Glick, 1976) and Kernberg's proposals that these defenses both organize as well as reflect the internalized object world (H. Lerner, Albert, & Walsh, 1987).

Comparing neurotic and borderline samples, P. Lerner and Lerner (1980) found that the borderline sample used significantly more projective identification, splitting, and lower level denial on the Rorschach. They found that borderline patients tended to use more devaluation and idealization. Interestingly, although the latter two defenses were also used among neurotic patients, the neurotic group tended to use these defenses accompanied by higher level denial in contrast to the borderline group. In a related study, H. Lerner, Sugarman, and Gaughran (1981) compared the Rorschachs of a hospitalized schizophrenic and hospitalized borderline patients. They found that the borderline patients manifested instances of splitting significantly more than did the schizophrenic patients. Projective identification was manifested exclusively in the borderline group. Four of five scale measures of devaluation were observed significantly more often among the borderline patients. As P. Lerner (1990) summarized, the results of P. Lerner and Lerner (1980) supported Kernberg's (1975) contention that borderline and neurotic patients may be differentiated by their levels of defensive organization. However, the study conducted by H. Lerner et al. (1981) failed to support Kernberg's suggestion that borderline and schizophrenic patients share a common "primitive" defensive constellation.

Cooper and colleagues (Cooper & Arnow, 1986; Cooper et al., 1988) developed the Rorschach Defense Scales (RDS), which measure 15 defenses across the range of psychotic, borderline, and neurotic defenses. Cooper's system draws on theoretical propositions of Winnicott (1965), Kernberg (1975), Kohut (1977), and Stolorow and Lachmann (1980). In contrast to the Lerner Defense Scales, which focus exclusively on human figure responses, Cooper et al. sought to examine all Rorschach responses. This aspect of the manual attempted to take into account Ames's (1966) empirical findings that with increased development there is an increase in the frequency of the human figure response. The manual was constructed, partly, to assess a broad range of patients, including patients described as having "structural deficiencies" (Stolorow & Lachmann, 1980), in which well-consolidated object representations are presumably less prominent. The RDS includes approximately 132 scoring criteria and combines a video interview with scored Rorschach data. The instrument primarily uses verbal content but secondarily includes aspects both of formal scoring and of the subject–examiner relationship.

Cooper et al. (1988) examined the relationship between specific dimensions of psychopathology and defenses in comparing borderline, antisocial, and bipolar type II adults. Borderline psychopathology was positively associated with manifestations of devaluation, projection, splitting, and hypomanic denial but was negatively associated with intellectualization and isolation. Interestingly, no significant relationships were found between specific defenses and antisocial psychopathology. Cooper et al. found concurrent evidence for the external validity of splitting. Splitting on the Rorschach correlated significantly with clinical ratings of splitting from independently obtained diagnostic interviews.

H. Lerner et al. (1987) compared the LDS and the RDS among four psychiatric groups including neurotics, outpatient borderlines, inpatient borderlines, and schizophrenic patients. To assess the discriminatory power of each defense, an analysis of differences among the four experimental groups was carried out separately for each scale. Lerner et al. found that both scales were able to distinguish borderline patients from other diagnostic groups. In general, the LDS was more effective in differentiating poorer functioning patients and the RDS was more effective in distinguishing among higher functioning outpatients.

Finally, Cooper, Perry, and O'Connell (1991) examined the ability of the RDS to longitudinally predict global functioning. They found that two defenses in particular—devaluation and projection—were quite highly predictive of impaired global functioning and that intellectualization and isolation of affect were predictive of higher levels of global functioning.

In general, Rorschach defense scoring systems that have relied exclusively on formal scoring have provided more information about cognitive style than defensive functioning per se. Most scoring systems have focused on a narrow range of defense mechanisms, regardless of whether the scales have predominantly used content, formal scoring, or a combination of the two approaches. Although the use of the Rorschach for empirical research has the disadvantage of requiring highly specific training for its administration and interpretation, it has the advantage that it is less influenced by the examiner's technique than is true for a clinical interview. Perry and Cooper (1987, p. 15), using both videotaped interview and Rorschach methods for studying defense, concluded that "to date, it [the Rorschach] has been over-valued as an aid to descriptive diagnosis, while in fact there is no evidence that it provides more valid data than a clinical interview. It has, perhaps, been undervalued as a method to provide a profile of defensive functioning." Future studies using the RDS and the LDS should attempt to study further what defenses predict about functioning both within and outside psychoanalytic psychotherapy. Above all, it is necessary to attempt to compare Rorschach and videotaped interview methods to determine the relative utility of each approach.

Diagnostic Findings

A number of investigators have examined the degree of association between defense mechanisms and diagnostic groups, particularly Axis II diagnostic groups. Axis II tends to focus more on personality traits than on symptoms, and because defenses are generally studied as dynamic traits, this has generated more work studying the relationship between Axis II and defenses.

Regarding Axis I disorders, Ablon, Carlson, and Goodwin (1974) studied the course of improvement in hospitalized patients with unipolar and bipolar affective disorders. Using the Ego Profile Scale, developed by Semrad et al. (1973), they serially examined the changes in defensive functioning. Ablon et al. found that nearly two thirds of the patients demonstrated a shift away from using defenses such as projection, denial, and distortion as they improved clinically. Manic patients showed an increase in hypochondriasis and somatization immediately prior to switching out of manic episodes.

Perry and Cooper (1989), assessing defenses through ratings of videotaped interviews, studied the association of defensive functioning and Axis I episodes in the follow-up of a sample of individuals with personality and affective disorders. Perry found that action and major image-distorting defenses (which he termed *borderline*) predicted increases in depressive symptoms and gradual recurrences of major depressive episodes. Perry also found that major image-distorting defenses also predicted the occurrence of psychotic and psychoticlike symptoms over the follow-up.

Many researchers have examined the relationship between defensive functioning and Axis II disorders. Dahl (1984), using the Bellak Ego Function Assessment, examined differences between hospitalized patients with borderline personality and other disorders. The borderline diagnostic group demonstrated significantly higher defensive functioning than the schizophrenic group but did not differ from the group with affective psychoses. In agreement with Kernberg's (1975) original observations, Dahl found that borderline patients scored lower than other personality disorders and neuroses. Goldsmith, Charles, and Feiner (1984) also used the Bellak Ego Function Assessment and found that defensive functioning and level of object relations were the two ego functions that most differentiated borderline from neurotic patients.

Vaillant and Drake (1985) independently rated their follow-up sample of inner-city men for the presence of a personality disorder at age 47 and for the defenses they displayed in their independently gathered life vignettes over the previous 10 years. Sixty-six percent of those men with any Axis II diagnosis used mostly immature defenses (dissociation, acting-out, fantasy, projection, hypochondriasis, passive-aggression), in contrast to 10% of those with no Axis II disorder. Conversely, the use of particular mature defenses such as suppression and humor was negatively correlated with the presence of any type of personality disorder. Vaillant and Drake also found that the overall defense maturity correlated highly with the Health–Sickness Rating Scale. They found that certain personality disorders were highly associated with certain defenses. For example, paranoid disorder with projection and acting-out; antisocial disorder with acting-out and dissociation; narcissistic disorder with dissociation, acting-out, and projection; schizoid disorder with fantasy; and dependent disorder with dissociation and denial.

Perry and Cooper (1986b) assessed the relationship between groups of defenses and diagnosis in their study of personality disorders. They found that borderline psychopathology was associated with the defenses of splitting, projective identification, and action defenses including acting-out, hypochondriasis, and passive-aggression. Antisocial psychopathology correlated with defenses such as omnipotence, idealization, and devaluation and with disavowal defenses (denial, projection, and rationalization). The presence of bipolar type II affective disorder was associated with obsessional defenses such as isolation, intellectualization, and undoing. Multivariate analyses were not able to separate study diagnoses on the basis of each subject's defenses alone. Thus, Perry and Cooper concluded that defenses were not powerful discriminators of the study diagnoses. An interesting finding and one that replicated an earlier finding from Vaillant and Drake (1985) was the discovered relationship between antisocial and narcissistic psychopathology; this finding is particularly noteworthy in that antisocial disorder is generally composed of diagnostic criteria that are more descriptively oriented in contrast to the criteria for narcissistic disorder.

Perry and Cooper (1986b) also tested the hypothesis that the group of "borderline defenses" suggested by Kernberg (1975) actually represented two independent dimensions. A factor analysis of defense ratings within their sample revealed two factors: (a) a "borderline" factor consisting of splitting of self and object images and projective identification and (b) a "narcissistic" factor consisting of omnipotence, devaluation, and idealization.

The data related to diagnostic studies suggest that there are a number of associations between defenses (which are dynamic) and descriptive personality diagnosis, although very few of these associations are specific. There are findings that suggest that borderline patients have lower defensive functioning than other nonpsychotic disorders that have been studied. The so-called immature defenses (Vaillant, 1977) and major and minor image-distorting defenses (e.g., splitting, devaluation, idealization) have been generally found to be associated with personality disorders, whereas the "mature" defenses are negatively associated with personality disorders. In agreement with Vaillant (1977), Perry and Cooper (1989) found that denial was the most commonly used (or rated) defense in response to life events among a group of patients diagnosed as having personality disorder. Perry (in press) concluded that this suggests that the factors that produce denial appear to be generic to what produces personality disorders. Finally, there appears to be little evidence thus far to be able to assess whether disorders that share defenses in common actually share some common dynamic etiological factors as Perry (in press) has suggested. This is an area of exciting possible future research because several studies (Perry & Cooper, 1986a; Vaillant & Drake, 1985) have found a common defensive clustering among differing diagnostic groups (narcissistic personality disorder and antisocial personality disorder).

Clinical, Nondiagnostic Studies

There has been a large sample of studies examining the clinical correlates of defense mechanisms and the correlates associated with changes in defense mechanisms. For example, Haan (1963) reported that IQ was positively correlated with coping mechanisms (mature defenses) and negatively correlated with nonmature defense mechanisms. In a prospective study, Haan (1963) found that the coping mechanisms were correlated with particular aspects of increased intellectual functioning.

Using the same sample as Haan (1963), Weinstock (1967) correlated defenses in adulthood with ratings of the subject's families that were made during childhood and adolescence. Weinstock reported that family conflict during early childhood was correlated with individuals' later use of denial, repression, regression, and doubt. Weinstock proposed that individuals learn these defenses through imitation of their parents' methods for dealing with conflict. The more adaptive coping mechanisms, such as tolerance of ambiguity, suppression, regression in the service of the ego, and sublimation, were correlated with increased stability in childhood and the emergence of family conflict during the subject's adolescence. Weinstock argued that the relationship between coping mechanisms and family environmental variables was more complex than the imitation model proposed for defense mechanisms.

Vaillant (1983) examined the relationship between childhood variables and the maturity level of defenses. Interestingly, Vaillant found that areas of childhood strength such as feelings of adequacy, IQ, and even environmental strengths were only weakly associated with the maturity of defenses during adulthood. Snarey and Vaillant (1985) found that the defenses of intellectualization, altruism, and anticipation were associated with upward mobility in Vaillant's inner-city male sample. Snarey and Vaillant argued that these defenses assist the individual in a number of tasks such as problem solving, which in turn affect career success.

A number of subsequent studies have indicated that maturity of defenses is not synonymous with adult mental health. In a study examining the relationship between maturity of adult defenses and three adult measures (social competence, adult global functioning, and psychosocial maturity), Vaillant et al. (1986) found that the correlations were strongest among those who had the most difficult childhoods. They concluded that maturity of defenses may have more of a causal influence on subsequent adult mental health, particularly among individuals with bleak childhoods. Any conclusions regarding such work must be tempered with the caveat that defenses were not measured during or even close to childhood. Vaillant et al. prospectively examined some of these relationships in his sample of college men and found that maturity of defenses among men at age 20–47 was correlated strongly with psychosocial adjustment and physical health.

Using Vaillant's method for assessing defenses, Ellsworth et al. (1986) found that patients with temporary weight loss had lower maturity levels of defenses than patients who were able to sustain weight loss at 18 months. Patients who sustained weight loss tended to use more altruism and less passive-aggression than the patients who were less successful in the weight-loss program.

Using the Defense Mechanism Rating Inventory, Schwilk and Kachele (1989) examined the relationship between defenses and overall adjustment within a group of survivors of leukemia who had been given bone-marrow transplantation treatment. The defense ratings were accomplished retrospectively for periods before, during, and following recovery from treatment. A cluster analysis divided the patients into two groups: one group of patients, using more projection and omnipotence, were more able to cope with the life-threatening illness and subsequent treatment; the second group of patients tended to use resignation and avoidance, which resulted in a depressive attitude during treatment and recovery. Interestingly, these findings underscore that defenses that are generally regarded as less adaptive, in certain circumstances may be even more useful or have special importance in particular life-threatening circumstances.

The nondiagnostic studies examining defenses suggest that defenses are only a component of a complex mixture of past and present variables that are a part of mental health. An important and interesting finding is that the overall maturity of defense mechanisms correlates with mental health, but differentially, depending on the nature and quality of one's childhood. Thus, by no means does empirical work suggest that defense and mental health are synonymous or even highly overlapping. Like every other aspect of empirical studies of defense, these studies would benefit from as much prospectively oriented research in the future as possible.

CONCLUSIONS

As is clear, the empirical study of defense has become a significant area of clinical research spawning numerous methods and applications to a wide variety of clinical populations. There are also a number of problems that plague empirical defense research. These problems include the problem of conceptual clarity regarding definitions of defense, specificity of defenses, the degree to which defenses can be differentiated from other clinical phenomena such as symptoms, and problems of interrater reliability and clinical validity.

Anna Freud (1936) began to develop a taxonomy of defense, thereby lending some clarity to concepts used in highly overlapping and confusing fashion. However, despite these efforts, Anna Freud's taxonomy often lacked specificity regarding her own definitions of defense. For example, many of the defenses mentioned in her classic text, *The Ego and the Mechanisms of Defense* (20 by Vaillant's, 1976, count), lack mutually exclusive definitions. A problem related to that of specificity regarding particular mechanisms of defense is that of carefully distinguishing between defense and symptom. This problem pervades diagnostic-defense research, where it is not always clear whether and to what extent what is being studied is defense per se or clinical manifestations of the disorder under investigation. Still another problem involves the ability for empirical investigators to differentiate and detect instances of defense from characteristic defense patterns.

Psychoanalysts have long been interested in the possibility of a hierarchy of defenses. As Vaillant et al. (1986) pointed out, a number of contributors from ego psychology such as Glover, Brenner, Gill, and Rapaport addressed the likelihood of a hierarchically arranged continuum of defenses from the least pathological to the most pathological. However, none of these authors mapped or sketched the possible theoretical terrain. Thus, in many ways despite their significant clinical contributions to psychoanalytic theory and therapy, their contributions did not really lay the groundwork for subsequent empirical defense work. Anna Freud was keenly interested in the importance of, even if skeptical about the possible problems, in developing a chronology of defenses. She stated the following:

> Defenses have their own chronology . . . they are more apt to have pathological results if they come into use before the appropriate age or are kept up too long after it. Examples are denial and projection, which are "normal" in early childhood and lead to pathology in later years; or repression and reaction formation which cripple the child's personality if used too early. (A. Freud, 1936, p. 177)

A. Freud (1936, p. 42) acknowledged that the chronology of defenses would not be easily determined: "The chronology of psychic processes (defenses) is still one of the most obscure fields of analytic theory."

Although empirical researchers have much further work to accomplish regarding developmental studies of defense and defense hierarchies, the delineation of a hierarchical pattern for the study of defenses has borne much fruit. Hauser (1986) cogently set forth several questions related to the relationship between defense and lines of child, adolescent, and adult development. Hauser asked whether the presence of certain defenses necessitates the accomplishment of particular levels of cognitive or emotional development. He also posed the opposite question of whether advances in cognitive or psychosexual development involve requisite changes in defensive repertoire. Hauser and his collaborators have made substantial contributions to the study of such questions (e.g., Hauser, Jacobson, & Noam, 1983). One of the aspects of their research that has been exciting and valuable has been their determination to empirically study developmental evidence for grouping defenses rather than collapsing defenses into groups such as "mature" or "immature."

An extremely important area for future defense research involves the study of questions related to resiliency and coping with stress. Defenses offer one aspect of coping mechanisms that are probably quite important for the successful adaptation to stress. For example, Beardslee et al. (1985) attempted to study adaptive processes among adolescents, identifying specific coping and defense patterns. An important and fascinating study by Snarey and Vaillant (1985), cited earlier, provides an example of how investigators can isolate particular defense mechanisms that are associated with resilience and adaptive capacities.

Much research has been conducted within the last 15 years regarding the relationship between defense and diagnosis and course of illness. Here the thorniest methodological problem has involved the degree to which investigators can be certain that they have distinguished between symptom and defense. As Hauser et al. (1983) instructed, only if independent measures of these constructs are taken at certain intervals such as at time of diagnosis and at regular intervals during the duration of the study can researchers study the relationship between defense and psychopathology (symptom). For example, if there are problems in discriminant validity between symptom and defense, it would be surprising to not find high correlations between defense and diagnosis. The problem of discriminant validity is not unique to that between defense and symptom. The trend in recent research toward studying the relationship between defense and global psychosocial impairment also requires clear and distinguishable definitions for each construct so that meaningful relationships or lack thereof can be discerned.

In my view, the hazard of studies that examine the relationship between diagnosis and defense is one of making global and general statements regarding enormously complex psychodynamic and diagnostic phenomena. For example, clinicians know quite well that the presence of certain defenses in and of itself is rarely pathonomic; rather, it is an overall defensive organization and the other personality factors that accompany it that determine one's adaptation in life. Another hazard is the importance of determining the context in which defenses manifest themselves: generalizations to one's outside life are difficult to make based on the presentation of defenses within psychodynamic therapy—the latter context is one that is often laden with transferential valence and intense conflict and is not necessarily representative of an individual's overall defensive functioning. On the other hand, the benefits of including defenses as an axis for the fourth edition of the DSM (DSM–IV) far outweigh the disadvantages. Currently, a task force including Horowitz, Perry, Fridhandler, Bond, Vaillant, and Cooper are conducting empirical studies investigating the value of including such an axis for DSM–IV. Although the DSM–III and DSM–III–R have been successful in lending high degrees of reliability to diagnosis and clarity to descriptive diagnosis, there is little trace of a psychodynamic perspective that might be helpful in illuminating the nature of treatment for a variety of patients, once diagnosed. Because a large proportion of clinicians conduct psychodynamically informed psychotherapy, a diagnostic method that contains more psychodynamic referents would be useful. For example, does a "borderline" patient seem to have many more adaptive capacities such as sublimatory channels, humor, or defensive intellectualization that may be used or developed over the course of psychotherapy? One can hope that the defense axis and other aspects of psychodynamically oriented observation will find their place in DSM–IV.

The establishment of quantitative procedures for assessing defense offers some new and very exciting ways of investigating both psychotherapy process and outcome. These methods offer the possibility of studying in a moment-to-moment fashion changes in defense over the course of a particular session, particularly in response to therapist interventions. This work may also provide the opportunity to study changes in characteristic modes of defense over the course of psychotherapy. Still other possibilities include developing methodologies for studying the nature of therapist interventions that focus on patients' defensive styles. Among such ongoing research efforts, in my view the most outstanding is the psychotherapy process research currently being conducted by Horowitz, Fridhandler, and their associates. Their work is oriented toward studying nuances of control processes (processes that underlie or describe how defenses operate and manifest themselves) over the course of psychotherapy sessions and in response to particular therapist interventions. This type of research may allow the study of a variety of interesting questions such as discovering the best ways for therapists to address particular defenses with a patient; discovering how to help a patient develop or use a broader repertoire of defenses or "higher" level defenses; helping patients to develop flexibility within the use of their repertoire of defenses; and helping therapists to assess which interpretations facilitate an individual being able to extend changes in defensive functioning within a session to stressful situations outside therapy or analysis.

REFERENCES

Ablon, S., Carlson, G., & Goodwin, F. (1974). Ego defense patterns in manic-depressive illness. *American Journal of Psychiatry, 131,* 803–807.

Ames, L. (1966). Longitudinal survey of child Rorschach responses: Older subjects aged 10–16 years. *Genetic Psychology Monographs, 62,* 185–229.

Andrews, G., Pollock, C., & Stewart, G. (1989). The determination of defense style by questionnaire. *Archives of General Psychiatry, 46,* 455–460.

Appelbaum, S. (1977). *Anatomy of change.* New York: Plenum Press.

Bahnson, J., & Bahnson, T. (1966). The role of ego defenses: Denial and repression in the etiology of malignant neoplasm. *Annual of the New York Academy of Science, 125,* 826–844.

Balint, M. (1950). Changing therapeutic aims and techniques in psycho-analysis. *International Journal of Psychoanalysis, 31,* 117–124.

Battista, J. (1982). Empirical test of Vaillant's hierarchy of ego functions. *American Journal of Psychiatry, 139,* 356–357.

Baxter, J., Becker, J., & Hooks, W. (1963). Defensive style in the families of schizophrenics and controls. *Journal of Abnormal Social Psychology, 5,* 512–518.

Beardsley, W., Jacobson, A., & Hauser, S. (1985). An approach to evaluating adolescent adaptive processes: Scale development and reliability. *Journal of the American Academy of Child Psychology, 24,* 637–642.

Bellak, L., Hurvich, M., & Gediman, H. (1973). *Ego functions in schizophrenics, neurotics and normals.* New York: Wiley.

Blatt, S., Brenneis, C., Schimek, J., & Glick, M. (1976). Normal development and psychopathological impairment of the concept of the object on the Rorschach. *Journal of Abnormal Psychology, 85,* 364–373.

Bond, M., Gardner, S., Christian, J., & Sigel, J. (1983). Empirical study of self-rated defense styles. *Archives of General Psychiatry, 40,* 333–338.

Bond, M., & Vaillant, G. (1986). An empirical study of the relationship between diagnosis and defense style. *Archives of General Psychiatry, 43,* 285–288.

Brenner, C. (1955). *An elementary textbook of psychoanalyis.* Madison, CT: International Universities Press.

Brenner, C. (1982). *The mind in conflict.* Madison, CT: International Universities Press.

Cooper, S. (1989). Recent contributions to the theory of defense mechanisms. *Journal of the American Psychoanalytic Association, 37,* 865–891.

Cooper, S., & Arnow, D. (1986). An object relations view of the borderline defenses: A review. In M. Kissen (Ed.), *Assessing object relations phenomena* (pp. 143–171). Madison, CT: International Universities Press.

Cooper, S., Perry, J., & Arnow, D. (1988). An empirical approach to the study of defense mechanisms: I. Reliability and preliminary validity of the Rorschach Defense Scales. *Journal of Personality Assessment, 52,* 187–203.

Cooper, S., Perry, J., & O'Connell, M. (1991). The Rorschach Defense Scales: II. Longitudinal perspectives. *Journal of Personality Assessment, 56,* 191–201.

Dahl, A. (1984). A study of agreement among raters of Bellak's Ego Function Assessment test. In L. Bellak & L. Goldsmith (Eds.), *The broad scope of ego function assessment* (pp. 16–176). New York: Wiley.

Ellsworth, G., Strain, G., Strain, J., Vaillant, G., Knittle, J., & Zumoff, B. (1986). Defensive maturity ratings and sustained weight loss in obesity. *Psychosomatics, 27,* 772–781.

Erdelyi, M. (1985). *Psychoanalysis: Freud's cognitive psychology.* New York: Freeman.

Flannery, R., & Perry, J. (1990). Self-rated defense style, life stress, and health status: An empirical assessment. *Psychosomatics, 31,* 313–320.

Freud, A. (1936). *The ego and the mechanisms of defense.* New York: International Universities Press.

Freud, S. (1959). Inhibitions, symptoms and anxiety. In J. Strachey (Ed. and Trans.), *The standard edition of the complete psychological works of Sigmund Freud* (Vol. 20, 87–174). London: Hogarth Press. (Original work published 1926)

Freud, S. (1962). The neurospychoses of defense. In J. Strachey (Ed. and Trans.), *The standard edition of the complete psychological works of Sigmund Freud* (Vol. 3, 45–70). London: Hogarth Press. (Original work published 1894)

Gardner, R., Holzman, P., Klein, G., Linton, H., & Spence, D. (1959). Cognitive controls: A study of individual consistencies in cognitive behaviors. *Psychological Issues, 2*(4), Monograph 8.

Gleser, G., & Ihlevich, D. (1969). An objective instrument for measuring defense mechanisms. *Journal of Consulting and Clinical Psychology, 33,* 51–60.

Goldsmith, L., Charles, E., & Feiner, K. (1984). The use of EFA in the assessment of borderline pathology. In L. Bellak & L. Goldsmith (Eds.), *The broad scope of ego function assessment* (pp. 340–361). New York: Wiley.

Guntrip, H. (1969). *Schizoid phenomena, object relations and the self.* Madison, CT: International Universities Press.

Haan, N. (1963). Proposed model for ego functioning: Coping and defense mechanisms in relationship to IQ change. *Psychological Monographs, 77,* 1–23.

Hartmann, H., Kris, E., & Loewenstein, R. M. (1964). Papers on psychoanalytic psychology. *Psychological Issues,* Monograph 14.

Hauser, S., Jacobson, A., & Noam, G. (1983). Ego development and self-image complexity in early adolescence, longitudinal studies of psychiatric and diabetic patients. *Archives of General Psychiatry, 40,* 32–33.

Holmes, D. (1974). The evidence for repression: An examination of material experientially or naturally associated with ego threat. *Psychological Bulletin, 81,* 632–653.

Horowitz, M. (1988). *Introduction to psychodynamics: A new synthesis.* New York: Basic Books.

Horowitz, M., Cooper, S., Fridhandler, B., Bond, M., Perry, J., & Vaillant G. (1991). *Control processes and defense mechanisms: A theory to phenomena linkage.* Unpublished manuscript.

Horowitz, M., Markman, H., Stinson, C., Fridhandler, B., & Ghannam, J. (1990). A classification theory of defense. In J. L. Singer (Ed.), *Repression and dissociation: Defense mechanisms and personality styles: Current theory and research.* Chicago: University of Chicago Press.

Jacobson, A., Beardslee, W., Hauser, S., Noam, G., Powers, S., Houlihan, J., & Rider, E. (1986). Evaluating ego defense mechanisms using clinical interviews: An empirical study of adolescent diabetic and psychiatric patients. *Journal of Adolescence, 9,* 303–319.

Kernberg, O. (1975). *Borderline conditions and pathological narcissism.* New York: Jason Aronson.

Kernberg, O. (1983). Object relations and character analysis. *Journal of the American Psychoanalytic Association, 31,* 247–271.

Kohut, H. (1971). *The analysis of the self.* Madison, CT: International Universities Press.

Kohut, H. (1979). The two analyses of Mr. Z. *International Journal of Psychoanalysis, 60,* 3–27.

Kohut, H. (1984). *How does analysis cure?* Chicago: University of Chicago Press.

Kris, A. O. (1982). *Free association: Method and process.* New Haven, CT: Yale University Press.

Lerner, H., Albert, C., & Walsh, M. (1987). The Rorschach assessment of borderline defense: A concurrent validity study. *Journal of Personality Assessment, 51,* 334–348.

Lerner, H., Sugarman, A., & Gaughran, J. (1981). Borderline and schizophrenic patients: A comparative study of defensive structure. *Journal of Nervous and Mental Disease, 169,* 705–711.

Lerner, P. (1990). Rorschach assessment of primitive defenses: A review. *Journal of Personality Assessment, 54,* 30–46.

Lerner, P., & Lerner, H. (1980). Rorschach assessment of primitive defenses in borderline personality structure. In J. Kwawer, H. Lerner, P. Lerner, & A. Sugarman (Eds.), *Borderline phenomena and the Rorschach Test* (pp. 257–274). Madison, CT: International Universities Press.

Levine, M., & Spivack, G. (1964). *The Rorschach Index of Repressive Style*. Springfield, IL: Charles C Thomas.

Luborsky, L., Blinder, B., & Schimek, J. (1965). Looking, recalling, and GSR as a function of defense. *Journal of Abnormal Psychology, 70*, 270–280.

Modell, A. (1975). A narcissistic defense against affects and the illusion of self-sufficiency. *International Journal of Psychoanalysis, 56*, 275–282.

Modell, A. (1984). *Psychoanalysis in a new context*. Madison, CT: International Universities Press.

Morrissey, R. (1977). The Haan model of ego functioning: An assessment of empirical research. In N. Haan (Ed.), *Coping and defending: Processes of self-environment organization*. New York: Academic Press.

Newman, K. (1980). Defense analysis in self psychology. In A. Goldberg (Ed.), *Advances in self psychology* (pp. 263–278). Madison, CT: International Universities Press.

Paulhus, D., Fridhandler, B., & Hayes, S. (in press). Psychological defenses: Contemporary theory and research. In S. Briggs, R. Hogan, & W. Jones (Eds.), *Handbook of personality psychology*. New York: Academic Press.

Perry, J. (in press). The study of defense mechanisms and their effects. In N. Miller, L. Luborsky, & L. Docherty (Eds.), *Psychodynamic treatment research*. New York: Basic Books.

Perry, J., & Cooper, S. (1986a). A preliminary report on defenses and conflicts associated with borderline personality disorder. *Journal of the American Psychoanalytic Association, 34*, 865–895.

Perry, J., & Cooper, S. (1986b). What do cross-sectional measures of defenses predict? In G. Vaillant (Ed.), *Empirical studies of the ego mechanisms of defense*. Washington, DC: American Psychiatric Press.

Perry, J., & Cooper, S. (1986c). Psychodynamics symptoms and outcomes in borderline and antisocial personality disorders and bipolar type II affective disorder. In T. McGlashan (Ed.), *The borderline: Current empirical research* (pp. 63–78). Washington, DC: American Psychiatric Press.

Perry, J., & Cooper, S. (1987). Empirical studies of psychological defense mechanisms. In R. Michels & J. Cavenar (Eds.), *Psychiatry* (Vol. 1, pp. 1–19). Philadelphia: Lippincott.

Perry, J., & Cooper, S. (1989). An empirical study of defense mechanisms: I. Clinical interview and life vignette ratings. *Archives of General Psychiatry, 46*, 444–452.

Schafer, R. (1954). *Psychoanalytic interpretation in Rorschach testing*. New York: Grune & Stratton.

Schafer, R. (1968). The mechanisms of defense. *International Journal of Psychoanalysis, 49*, 49–62.

Schwilk, C., & Kachele, H. (1989, September). *Defense mechanisms during severe illness*. Paper presented at the Third European Conference on Psychotherapy Research, Berne, Switzerland.

Semrad, E., Grinspoon, L., & Feinberg, S. (1973). Development of an Ego Profile Scale. *Archives of General Psychiatry, 28*, 70–77.

Snarey, J., & Vaillant, G. (1985). How lower- and working-class youth become middle-class adults: The association between ego defense mechanisms and upward social mobility. *Child Development, 56*, 899–910.

Stolorow, R., & Lachmann, F. (1980). *Psychoanalysis of developmental arrests*. New York: International Universities Press.

Vaillant, G. (1971). Theoretical hierarchy of adaptive ego mechanisms: A 30-year follow-up of 30 men selected for psychological health. *Archives of General Psychiatry, 24*, 107–118.

Vaillant, G. (1976). Natural history of male psychological health: The relation of choice of ego mechanisms of defense to adult adjustment. *Archives of General Psychiatry, 33*, 535–545.

Vaillant, G. (1977). *Adaptation to life*. Boston: Little, Brown.

Vaillant, G. (1983). Childhood environment and maturity of defense mechanisms. In D. Magnusson & V. Allen (Eds.), *Human development: An interactional perspective* (pp. 343–352). New York: Academic Press.

Vaillant, G., Bond, M., & Vaillant, C. (1986). An empirically valid hierarchy of defense mechanisms. *Archives of General Psychiatry, 43,* 786–794.

Vaillant, G., & Drake, R. (1985). Maturity of ego defenses in relation to DSM-III Axis II personality disorder. *Archives of General Psychiatry, 42,* 597–601.

Weinstock, A. (1967). Family environment and the development of defense and coping mechanisms. *Journal of Personality and Social Psychology, 5,* 67–75.

Weintraub, W., & Aronson, H. (1963). The application of verbal behavior analysis to the study of psychological defense mechanisms: Methodology and preliminary report. *Journal of Nervous and Mental Disease, 134,* 169–181.

Winnicott, D. (1965). Ego distortion in terms of true and false self. In D. Winnicott (Ed.), *The maturational processes and the facilitating environment* (pp. 140–152). Madison, CT: International Universities Press.

15

THE FUNCTION OF REM SLEEP AND THE MEANING OF DREAMS

JONATHAN WINSON

This chapter presents a series of neuroscientific findings from my laboratory and, based on these findings and other supporting data, a new hypothesis concerning the function of rapid eye movement (REM) sleep and the meaning of dreams. It is divided into three parts. In the first, I review certain of the major results obtained by neuroscientific and sleep researchers during the modern era of sleep research, from 1953 to the present. In the second, I summarize three prior theories of the meaning of dreams: the psychological theory set forth by Freud (1900/1953) in "The Interpretation of Dreams" and two related neuroscientifically based hypotheses, the activation–synthesis hypothesis of Hobson and McCarley (1977) and the theory of reverse learning of Crick and Mitchison (1983). In the final section, I describe the findings of my own laboratory, develop my hypothesis, and relate it to the three previous theories.

CHARACTERISTICS OF SLEEP

Human sleep begins with the hypnogogic state. The neocortical electroencephalographic (EEG) recording is low level and irregular, similar to that seen during waking. There are thoughts during this stage, but in contrast with the coherent thinking present just before drifting off to sleep, hypnogogic thoughts consist of fragmented images or minidramas. The hypnogogic state persists for several minutes. For the next 90 minutes or so, sleep continues in the slow-wave phase, named for the low-frequency, high-amplitude waves that appear in the EEG. Slow-wave sleep proceeds through three descending stages, 2, 3, and 4, the demarcation being made according to the progressive pattern of lower frequency, higher amplitude waves that appear in the EEG. The stages of slow-wave sleep then reverse rapidly through ascending stages 4, 3, and

2 and finally reach the first REM period of the night. The EEG then reverts to a low-amplitude, irregular signal that characterizes the waking state, and there are clusters of rapid eye movements. (The sleeper's eyes move together under closed lids in rapid, jerky motions of relatively short arc.) There is no gross body movement, but very fine distal limb and finger movements are present. Heart rate increases, and breathing becomes rapid and uneven. And, of central interest here, REM sleep is accompanied by dreams.

The first REM period of the night is about 10 minutes long. As sleep continues, the cycle of slow-wave and REM sleep is repeated three or four additional times, the episodes of slow-wave sleep growing progressively shorter and the REM periods progressively longer. The final REM period of the night is approximately 20–30 minutes long and is followed by awakening. If a dream is remembered at all, it is generally the dream that occurs in the final REM period.

The sleep cycle, alternating slow-wave and REM sleep, appears to be present in all placental and marsupial mammals. It has been identified in diverse species ranging from human to opossum and bat. Slow-wave sleep, but not REM sleep, is present in the echidna (spiny anteater), the one monotreme (egg-laying mammal) that has been tested. Thus, REM sleep seems to have evolved some 140 million years ago in a common ancestor of marsupial and placental mammals after this common ancestor split off from the monotreme evolutionary line and seems to have been retained by nature since that time.

The various behavioral manifestations of REM sleep are all observed in animals. In the cat, for example, there are rapid eye movements, irregular breathing and twitching of vibrissae, ears, paws, and tail. By direct recording in the neocortex of animals, it has been verified that neurons in visual and associational neocortical areas are as active during REM sleep as they are in waking; hence, the similarity in the EEG signal during the two states. Animals dream during REM sleep. A direct demonstration of this has been provided by researchers who have destroyed neurons in the brain stems of cats, the function of which is to prevent movement during sleep. These animals rise and attack or appear to be startled by invisible objects, acting out their dreams—all while still in REM sleep as evidenced by closed inner eyelids and other physiological indicators.

The detailed manner in which the brain controls sleep has not yet been fully elucidated and is a subject of active investigation. It is known, however, that neural control of REM sleep is centered in the brain stem. Brain stem neurons have been shown to produce the following effects during REM sleep:

1. The inhibition of spinal motor neurons, thus preventing significant gross motor activity. Movement is reduced to the fine finger and limb tremors noted earlier.

2. The generation of both rapid eye movements and, associated with them, PGO (pontine–geniculate–occipital cortex) spikes—neural signals proceeding from brain stem to visual cortex.

3. The generation of theta rhythm in the hippocampus. The hippocampus is a forebrain structure closely associated with memory. (The hippocampus and theta rhythm are central to my own research and are described later.)

The net result is a most dramatic and intriguing aspect of brain function. Embedded in a night's sleep are REM periods in which the brain is isolated from the environment—there is no input and no motor output. While so isolated, the neocortex is as active as during the waking state, that activity being reflected in dreams. By all evolutionary criteria, a complex brain process such as REM sleep, having been maintained by nature for 140 million years, might be expected to serve a function important for the survival of mammalian species.

THE MEANING AND FUNCTION OF DREAMS: THREE THEORIES

> In the following pages, I shall bring forward proof that there is a psychological technique which makes it possible to interpret dreams, and that, if that procedure is employed, every dream reveals itself as a psychological structure which has a meaning and which can be inserted at an assigned point in the mental activities of waking life. (Freud, 1900/1953, p. 1)

With this opening statement in "The Interpretation of Dreams," Freud introduced his theory of the meaning and function of dreams. To briefly summarize, Freud posited the existence in each individual of an unconscious, a series of primitive thoughts and wishes repressed in the waking state, kept from conscious awareness by a censor of the mind. During sleep, repression is relaxed, and unconscious wishes are expressed in dreams—specifically, their "latent" content. Although relaxed, repression is not entirely absent during sleep. An unconscious censor disguises the unconscious wishes, transforming latent content to "manifest" content, the actual dream narrative. In this less disturbing form, primitive wishes can be expressed without disrupting sleep. There are two consequences. Of intellectual importance, Freud could assign a function to dreams—the guardian of sleep. And of overriding importance in treating his patients and in understanding human personality, dreams were the royal road to the unconscious. Thus, dream interpretation during psychoanalysis would reveal the deepest elements of an individual's inner life.

In the light of later developments, the elements of psychoanalytic theory have been modified in the following way. REM sleep and accompanying dreams are part of a biologically determined sleep cycle—the function of dreams is not to preserve sleep. By no means are all dreams expressions of unconscious wishes. (Freud had difficulty with dreams that were clearly negative in content.) Other aspects of the theory appear to stand. In particular, dreams are considered to give direct access to the unconscious.

In 1977, Hobson and McCarley of Harvard Medical School published an article titled "The Brain as a Dream State Generator: An Activation–Synthesis Hypothesis of the Dream Process" in the *American Journal of Psychiatry*. The hypothesis was based on the neurophysiological findings regarding brain stem control of REM sleep. In this theory, dreaming consists of associations and memories elicited from the forebrain (neocortex and associated structures) in response to random inputs from the brain stem such as PGO spikes. The authors stated that "the forebrain may be making the best of a bad job in producing even partially coherent dream imagery from the relatively noisy signals sent up to it from the brainstem" (p. 1347). They agreed that dream content may at times have psychological content. Such material is, however, without inherent meaning; it is simply the "best fit" the forebrain can provide to random bombardment by brain stem stimuli.

A revision was provided by Hobson in 1989:

> Thus I would like to retain the emphasis of psychoanalysis upon the power of dreams to reveal deep aspects of ourselves, but without recourse to the concept of disguise and censorship or to the now famous Freudian symbols. My tendency, then, is to ascribe the nonsense [in dreams] to brain–mind dysfunction and the sense to its compensatory effort to create order out of chaos. That order is a function of our own personal view of the world, our current preoccupations, our remote memories, our feelings, and our beliefs. That's all. (p. 166)

Although Hobson and McCarley (1977) proposed an explanation of dream content, the basic function of the entire REM sleep process remained admittedly unknown. Such a function, a process termed *reverse learning*, was proposed by Crick of the Salk Institute in La Jolla,

California, and Mitchison of the University of Cambridge, England, in a commentary in *Nature* titled "The Function of Dream Sleep" in 1983. Working from the Hobson and McCarley assumption of random neocortical bombardment by PGO waves during REM sleep and from their own knowledge of the behavior of simulated neural networks, Crick and Mitchison postulated that a complex, associational neural network such as the neocortex, exposed as it is to vast amounts of incoming information, might become overloaded and develop "parasitic" modes of behavior that would jeopardize orderly memory storage. It would therefore be essential for such a network that a mechanism exist to erase such parasitic associations on a regular basis. This task is accomplished during REM sleep. Random brain stem stimuli (the PGO waves), impinging on the neocortex, tend to excite parasitic associations that are inappropriate compared with associations produced by true information transmitted to the neocortex by the senses during the waking state. Excitation of these parasitic associations in the absence of sensory input during REM sleep weakens these associations, thereby actively producing reverse learning. Reverse learning serves an essential function in all marsupial and placental mammals: It clears false or parasitic associations and thereby allows the orderly processing of memory. In humans, dreams are a running record of these parasitic thoughts (i.e., material to be erased from memory). This is expressed in the phrase "we dream to forget."

Crick and Mitchison provided a revision to their theory in 1986. Erasure of parasitic thoughts accounted only for bizarre dream content. Nothing could be said about a dream narrative. Furthermore, dreaming to forget was better expressed as dreaming to reduce fantasy or obsession.

THE SIGNIFICANCE OF THETA RHYTHM

I turn now to the work of my own laboratory. The key to my own work in determining function of REM sleep and the meaning of dreams has been theta rhythm. Theta rhythm was discovered in 1954 by Green and Arduini, neuroscientists at the University of California, Los Angeles. They reported that a regular sinusoidal signal with a frequency of approximately 6 cycles per second appeared in the hippocampus of freely moving rabbits whenever the animals were aroused by any stimulus in their environment. Green and Arduini (1954) called the signal *theta rhythm* in keeping with the term *theta* applied earlier to the 6-cycles-per-second component of the multifrequency neocortical EEG. Theta rhythm is unique in its regularity, different from the EEG or any other signal recorded in the brain. Theta rhythm has been subsequently recorded in diverse species ranging from the tree shrew to the mole, and its behavioral correlates have been studied in some detail in the cat, the rabbit, and the rat (Winson, 1972, 1975). The waking correlates were different in each of these species. For example, in marked contrast with the rabbit, environmental stimuli, regardless of how startling they might be, did not induce theta rhythm in the rat. Theta rhythm was present only during movement, typically when the rat explored its environment. The behavioral correlates in the cat were different again from those in the rabbit and the rat. There was, however, one behavioral correlate in all three species: Theta rhythm was present in the hippocampus throughout REM sleep (first discovered in the rat by Vanderwolf (1969) at the University of Western Ontario in 1969). In 1972, I published a commentary pointing out that the different behavioral correlates could be understood ethologically. Theta rhythm appeared in behaviors that were most important for the survival of each species, namely, predatory behavior in the cat, prey behavior in the rabbit (behavior characterized by sensitivity to any stimulus in the environment to escape from predators), and exploration in the rat. (Theta rhythm was also present during exploration in the cat and the rabbit. Knowledge of the environment is essential for the survival of all animals.) Moreover, as noted above, theta rhythm was present in the hippocampus throughout REM sleep in all three species. The hippocampus is known to be essential for memory processing. Theta rhythm might therefore reflect a neural process whereby information essential to the survival of a species, gathered during the day, is reprocessed into memory during REM sleep.

To begin the investigation of this hypothesis, I recorded signals from the hippocampus of freely moving rats and rabbits to ascertain the source of theta rhythm (Winson, 1974, 1976). The hippocampus is a sequential structure. Information from all sensory and association areas of the neocortex converge to a neocortical area called the *entorhinal cortex*. From the entorhinal cortex, this information is transmitted to the hippocampus and is processed in that structure through three successive neuronal populations—the granule cells of the dentate gyrus, the CA3 pyramidal cells, and the pyramidal cells of CA1. Processed information is then transmitted back to the entorhinal cortex and from there to the neocortical areas from which the entorhinal cortex received its initial input. This neocortical–hippocampal network is believed to provide the neural basis for memory.

In 1974, I reported that theta rhythm is generated from two sources within the hippocampus, the dentate gyrus and the CA1 field. The rhythm in the two fields is synchronous. A third synchronous generator was identified in the entorhinal cortex in 1980 by Mitchell and Ranck, of the State University of New York's Health Science Center at Brooklyn. It was clear that theta rhythm paces the entire hippocampus. Is the pacing in any way related to memory? To study this question, I made small electrolytic lesions in the rat septum, a forebrain structure projecting to the hippocampus, the pacemaker cells of which, firing in periodic bursts, are responsible for the generation of the hippocampal theta rhythm (Winson, 1978). These lesions eliminated theta rhythm. Rats that had previously learned, using spatial cues, to locate a particular position in a maze from which a reward could be obtained were no longer able to do so. Without theta rhythm, spatial memory was destroyed. Control rats with similar septal lesions that did not eliminate theta rhythm had intact memory.

As mentioned earlier, the neural control of the various components of REM sleep is centered in the brain stem. In 1977, Vertes of Wayne State University, recording in the reticular formation of the brain stems of freely moving rats, discovered the neurons that control theta rhythm. The output of these cells, transmitted to the septum, activates theta rhythm in the hippocampus during both waking and REM sleep. Thus, in both of these states, the brain stem activates the neocortex and the hippocampus, that is, the core memory system of the brain.

Could anything be said about the mechanism of memory at the cellular level, and if so, is there any relation between this mechanism and theta rhythm? An understanding of the cellular basis of memory has been a long-sought goal of neuroscience. In 1973, Bliss and Lomo of the National Institute of Medical Research, London, and the University of Oslo, respectively, provided a clue. If one stimulates the perforant pathway, the pathway from the entorhinal cortex to the (first stage) granule cells of the hippocampus, with a single electrical pulse, the response of the granule cells can be measured with an indwelling electrode. Bliss and Lomo measured this response and then applied tetanic stimulus (a long train of high-frequency pulses) to the perforant pathway. Subsequent responses of the granule cells to single pulses were markedly greater. The effect persisted for up to 3 days. This phenomenon, termed *long-term potentiation* (LTP), was precisely the sort of long-term increase in synaptic efficacy that would be capable of sustaining memory. Intensive study of LTP in a number of laboratories followed the Bliss and Lomo report. A major development has been the elucidation of the NMDA (*N*-methyl-dextro-aspartate) receptor. The NMDA receptor is a molecule imbedded in the dendrites of granule cells (as well as in CA1 cells of the hippocampus and neurons throughout the neocortex). Like other neural receptors, it is activated by a neurotransmitter, glutamate in this case, which momentarily opens a non-NMDA channel in the granule cell dendrite, allowing the influx of sodium from the extracellular space, resulting in depolarization of the granule cell. If the depolarization is sufficient, the granule cell fires an action potential that transmits information to target cells. However, the NMDA receptor possesses an additional property. Depolarization of the granule cell produces a transient modification of the NMDA receptor. Should a second activation by glutamate occur while the cell is depolarized, a second channel linked to the NMDA receptor is opened allowing the passage of calcium into the granule cell. Calcium is believed to act as a second messenger, initiating a cascade of intracellular events that culminates in long-lasting synaptic change that is evidenced as LTP. It is this mechanism that is triggered by tetanic stimulation. (The description given is simplified. Presynaptic changes also occur. The subject is under widespread investigation.)

An important problem remained. The tetanic stimulation that produced LTP was not physiologic; it did not occur naturally in the brain. In 1986, Larsen and Lynch of the University of California, Irvine, and Rose and Dunwiddie of the University of Colorado suggested that the answer to the inconsistency was theta rhythm. They applied a small number of stimulus pulses within the physiological range to CA1 cells. LTP was produced but only when the pulses were separated by the normal time that elapses between two theta waves, approximately 200 msec. Theta rhythm was apparently the natural means by which the NMDA receptor is activated in the hippocampus. In 1988, in my own laboratory, Pavlides, Greenstein, Grudman, and I confirmed this finding in the granule cells in which LTP was originally found by Bliss and Lomo (1973). We further demonstrated that with theta rhythm present in the granule cell field, low-amplitude pulses applied at the peak of theta waves induced LTP, whereas the same pulses, if applied at the trough of the waves or in the absence of theta rhythm, did not.

A coherent picture emerged from these findings. As a rat explores, brain stem neurons activate theta rhythm. Olfactory information (sampled by inhalation synchronized with theta rhythm) and other sensory input converges on the entorhinal cortex and the hippocampus and is partitioned into 200-msec segments by theta rhythm. Theta rhythm, acting in conjunction with the NMDA receptor, allows for long-lasting storage of this information. A similar process occurs during REM sleep. During REM sleep, there is no incoming information and movement is prevented. However, the neocortical–hippocampal associational network is once again paced by theta rhythm, which is capable of producing long-lasting changes in memory storage. (Theta rhythm has not yet been demonstrated in primates. Because vision replaced olfaction as the dominant sensory input, an equivalent mechanism may have evolved to periodically activate the NMDA receptor in the primate hippocampus.)

In 1989, Pavlides and I performed one additional experiment. As a result of the discovery by O'Keefe and Dostrovsky (1971) of the University College of London, it was known that individual CA1 neurons in the rat hippocampus fired when the rat was in a particular area of the environment termed the neuron's *place field*. The strong implication was that CA1 neurons are involved in representing the environment in memory (i.e., in mapping space). We located two CA1 neurons in the rat hippocampus that had different place fields, and we recorded the cells simultaneously. After determining baseline firing rates in waking and sleeping states, the rat was positioned in the place field of one of the neurons. The neuron fired vigorously, mapping that location. The second cell fired only sporadically; it was not coding space. The recording of both neurons was continued as the rat moved about and then entered several sleep cycles. Six pairs of neurons were recorded in this manner. The results were the following. Neurons that had coded space fired at their normally low rate as the animal moved about prior to sleep. In sleep, however, they fired at a significantly higher rate than their previous sleeping baseline. Furthermore, the neurons fired in high-frequency bursts previously shown to be most likely to induce LTP. There was no such increase in firing rate during sleep in neurons that did not map space.

The experiment suggests that reprocessing of waking information occurs in sleep at the level of the individual neuron involved in coding that waking information.

Recall that the echidna, the monotreme antecedent of the marsupial and placental mammals, exhibits slow-wave but no REM sleep. The echidna has a well-developed hippocampus, and theta rhythm is present when the animal burrows for food. However, without REM sleep, there is no theta rhythm during sleep. Coincident with the occurrence of REM sleep in marsupial and placental mammals is a remarkable change in the anatomy of the mammalian brain. The echidna has a large convoluted prefrontal cortex, larger in relation to the rest of the brain than that of any other mammal, including humans. With the occurrence of REM sleep, the prefrontal cortex is reduced dramatically in size. Why does the echidna, a simple insectivore, require this large prefrontal cortex? I suggest that it is because the prefrontal cortex performs a dual function, both reacting to incoming information in an appropriate manner based on past experience and evaluating and storing the new information to aid future survival. This line of evolution has been limited—additional brain tissue that would be required for advanced capabilities could not be accommodated within the echidna skull. At this point, evolution provided a new brain mechanism, REM sleep. Far less prefrontal cortex was then required. Brain capacity could then grow to provide the advanced perceptual and cognitive abilities of higher species.

What is the body of information dealt with during REM sleep? It is information that is most important for the survival of each species—the location of food, the means of predation, or the escape from predators. These are the experiences during which theta rhythm is present and provides the mechanism by which memory can be encoded. During REM sleep, this information is accessed again and integrated with past experience to provide an ongoing behavioral strategy. However, the reprocessing of the information that is gathered during waking experience is not easily dissociated from the locomotion and eye movements that normally accompany this experience. (Such disassociation might be expecting too much of a revision in the logic of brain circuitry.) To maintain sleep, therefore, locomotion has to be suppressed. This is accomplished by motor neuron inhibition. (Recall that lesions removing this inhibition led to cats acting out their dreams.) It is not necessary to suppress eye movements because they do not disturb sleep. Eye movement potentials, similar to PGO spikes, accompany rapid eye movements in the waking state. Their function has not been established, but they may serve to alert the visual cortex to incoming information. Similarly, PGO spikes may reflect the reprocessing of this information during REM sleep. In any case, PGO spikes do not disturb sleep and do not have to be suppressed.

THE NATURE OF DREAMS

I now turn to dreams in humans and first note that dreams are sensory, primarily visual (i.e., their content is not expressed as a verbal narrative). I suggest that this again is a result of the evolutionary origin of dreams. Animals do not possess language—the information processed during REM sleep is necessarily sensory.

What information is processed in human dreams? In keeping with evolution and evidence derived from dream reports, I suggest that dreams reflect each individual's strategy for survival. The ideas are broad ranging, including self-image, insecurities as well as secure areas and grandiose ideas, sexual orientation and desires, and jealousy and love. They are biased strongly toward early experience because of the early critical periods of learning in the mammalian brain. (For details, see Winson, 1985). Furthermore, these concepts are unconscious; that is, they are not readily available to conscious introspection. This is because REM sleep processing is an integral part of memory processing in animals and remains so in humans. There is no functional necessity for this material to become conscious, nor is there an absolute bar to it—dreams are remembered most readily if awakening occurs during or shortly after a REM period.

The evidence from dream reports can be evaluated as follows. There is a deep psychological core. This has been reported by psychoanalysts since Freud and is clearly illustrated by the work of Cartwright (1986, 1991) of Rush-Presbyterian-St. Luke's Hospital in Chicago. Cartwright is in the process of studying a series of 90 subjects during marital separation leading to a divorce and for 1 year thereafter. The subjects are evaluated clinically to ascertain their attitudes and affective responses to this personal crisis. They are also awakened from REM sleep to report their dreams. The dreams are interpreted by the subjects themselves without subjective questioning that might contaminate meaning. In the 70 subjects studied to date, Cartwright has found that dream content conveys the person's unconscious thoughts, insecurities, and strengths and is strongly correlated to the manner in which the crisis is being dealt with in the real world.

The subject chosen for consideration during a given night's dreams is unpredictable. Certain of life's crises, as in the case of Cartwright's subjects, so engage psychological survival as to be selected for REM processing. In the ordinary course of events, and depending on individual personality, the subjects chosen may be freewheeling. Coupled with the intricate associations that are an intrinsic part of REM processing, the dream's statement may be obscure. Nevertheless, there is every reason to believe that the same cognitive process takes place as is seen in Cartwright's subjects and that a coherent statement is being made. Interpretation of that statement depends on the individual's tracing of the relevant associations.

There is one further aspect of REM sleep I have not yet discussed. Newborn infants spend 8 hours a day in REM sleep. The sleep cycle is disorganized at this point. Sleep occurs in 50–60 minute bouts and begins with REM rather than with slow-wave sleep. By the age of 2 years, REM sleep is reduced to 3 hours a day, and the adult pattern of alternating slow-wave and REM sleep is established. Thereafter, the time spent in REM sleep gradually diminishes to a little under 2 hours a night in adults. What is the reason for the greater amount of REM sleep in infants and children than in adults? REM sleep may perform a special function in infants. A leading theory proposes that it may serve to stimulate neural growth (Roffwarg, Muzio, & Dement, 1966). Whatever the function in infants may be, I suggest that at about the age of 2 years, when the hippocampus (still in the process of neural development at birth) becomes functional, REM sleep takes on the memory processing function I have hypothesized here. The waking information to be integrated at this point in development constitutes the basic cognitive substrate for memory—the characteristics of the real world to which later experiences must be related. The organization in memory of this extensive infrastructure requires the additional REM sleep time.

For reasons he could not possibly have known, Freud (1900/1953) set forth a profound truth in "The Interpretation of Dreams." There is an unconscious, and dreams are the royal road to its understanding. However, the characteristics of the unconscious and associated processes derived here from brain function are quite different from those postulated by Freud. Rather than a cauldron of untamed passions and destructive wishes, the unconscious is a cohesive, continually active mental structure that takes note of life's experiences and reacts according to its own scheme of interpretation and responses. The scheme of interpretation is strongly influenced by early experience as the result of the critical period of brain development. Repression does exist under certain conditions to block stressful thoughts from conscious awareness, but it is not the operative mechanism preventing the conscious accessibility of dream material. This is the normal result of the operation of memory. Furthermore, dreams are not disguised as consequences of repression. Their usual character is due to the complex associations that are called from memory to most succinctly express the meaning of the dream. Finally, of course, dreams are not the guardians of sleep but are the products of a brain-based cognitive process.

Recall that in the original Hobson and McCarley (1977) activation hypothesis, dreams are merely the "best fit" associations that the neocortex can provide to random bombardment from the brain stem. Hobson's (1989) recent comments have acknowledged the deep psychological significance of dreams as set forth by psychoanalysis and sleep research. As a consequence, in the revised theory, random brain stem bombardment is responsible for only the nonsense elements of the dream, not its narrative content. In a further retraction of the original theory, Hobson has suggested that brain stem activation may merely serve to switch from one dream episode to another. In its present truncated form, the activation hypothesis appears to have little explanatory or predictive power. The Crick and Mitchison (1983) hypothesis provided a function for REM sleep, namely, reverse learning. However, as noted earlier, an important modification is introduced in its updated version (Crick & Mitchison, 1986). The revised theory excluded the narrative of a dream and restricted reverse learning to bizarre dream content. The implication of this restriction with regard to REM sleep processing in lower animals must be specified before further evaluating the theory's ramifications. However, one finding may be relevant at this point. In the experiment in my laboratory related earlier in which hippocampal neurons that coded spatial information in the rat were recorded in waking and sleeping states, the neurons that coded space fired at an elevated rate during the REM sleep that followed, whereas the neurons that did not code space did not increase their firing rate (Pavlides & Winson, 1989). This suggests the orderly reprocessing of waking information during REM sleep. The reverse learning hypothesis, as applied to the hippocampus, would predict that randomly selected neurons would increase their firing rate during REM sleep. This was not the case.

I look forward to experiments that will further understanding of REM sleep and dreaming. Crucial to my hypothesis would be the demonstration of a memory deficit following prolonged interference with REM sleep processing. Experimentation is required to determine the mechanism by which the NMDA receptor is activated in the primate hippocampus. Expanded versions of my laboratory's individual neuron recording experiment should yield additional data on the neuronal network level regarding the reprocessing of waking information during REM sleep. Finally, I believe that the question of combined nonsense and meaningful dream content versus a coherent dream statement can be resolved by sophisticated sleep research. These experiments and others to come will probe basic aspects of memory and human psychological structure.

REFERENCES

Bliss, T. V. P., & Lomo, T. (1973). Long-lasting potentiation of synaptic transmission in the dentate area of the anesthetized rabbit following stimulation of the perforant path. *Journal of Physiology, 232,* 331.

Cartwright, R. (1986). Affect and dream work from an information processing point of view. *Journal of Mind and Behavior, 7,* 411–427.

Cartwright, R. (1991). Dreams that work: The relation of dream incorporation to adaptation to stressful events. *Journal of Dreaming, 1,* 3–9.

Crick, F., & Mitchison, G. (1983). The function of dream sleep. *Nature, 304,* 111–114.

Crick, F., & Mitchison, G. (1986). REM sleep and neural nets. *Journal of Mind and Behavior, 7,* 229–249.

Freud, S. (1953). The interpretation of dreams. In J. Strachey (Ed. and Trans.), *The standard edition of the complete psychological works of Sigmund Freud* (Vol. 4, p. 1). London: Hogarth Press. (Original work published 1900)

Green, J. D., & Arduini, A. (1954). Hippocampal electrical activity in arousal. *Journal of Neurophysiology, 17*, 533–557.

Greenstein, Y. J., Pavlides, C., & Winson, J. (1988). Long-term potentiation in the dentate gyrus is preferentially induced at theta rhythm peridicity. *Brain Research, 438*, 331.

Hobson, J. A. (1989). *Sleep.* San Francisco: Freeman.

Hobson, J. A., & McCarley, R. W. (1977). The brain as a dream state generator: An activation–synthesis hypothesis of the dream process. *American Journal of Psychiatry, 134*, 1335–1348.

Larson, J., & Lynch, G. (1986). Multiple events involved in the induction of hippocampal long-term synaptic potentiation. *Science, 232*, 985–988.

Mitchell, S., & Ranck, J. B., Jr. (1980). Generation of theta rhythm in medical entorhinal cortex of freely moving rats. *Brain Research, 189*, 49–66.

O'Keefe, J., & Dostrovsky, J. (1971). The hippocampus as a spatial map: Preliminary evidence from unit activity in the freely moving rat. *Brain Research, 34*, 171–175.

Pavlides, C., Greenstein, Y., Grudman, M., & Winson, J. (1988). Long-term potentiation in the dentate gyrus is induced preferentially on the positive phase of theta rhythm. *Brain Research, 439*, 383–387.

Pavlides, C., & Winson, J. (1989). Influences of hippocampal place cells firing in the awake state on the activity of these cells during subsequent sleep episodes. *Journal of Neuroscience, 9*, 2907–2918.

Roffwarg, H. P., Muzio, J. N., & Dement, W. C. (1966). Ontogenetic development of the human sleep–dream cycle. *Science, 152*, 604–611.

Rose, G. M., & Dunwiddie, T. V. (1986). Induction of hippocampal long-term potentiation using physiologically patterned stimulation. *Neuroscience Letters, 69*, 244–248.

Vanderwolf, C. H. (1969). Hippocampal electrical activity and voluntary movement in the rat. *Electroencephalography and Clinical Neurophysiology, 26*, 407–418.

Vertes, R. P. (1977). Selective firing of rat pontine gigantocellular neurons during movement and REM sleep. *Brain Research, 128*, 146–152.

Winson, J. (1972). Interspecies differences in the occurrence of theta. *Behavioral Biology, 7*, 479–487.

Winson, J. (1974). Patterns of hippocampal theta rhythm in the freely-moving rat. *Electroencephalography and Clinical Neurophysiology, 36*, 291–301.

Winson, J. (1975). The theta mode of hippocampal function. In R. Isaacson & K. Pribram (Eds.), *The hippocampus* (pp. 169–183). New York: Plenum Press.

Winson, J. (1976). Hippocampal theta rhythm: II. Depth profiles in the freely moving rabbit. *Brain Research, 103*, 71–79.

Winson, J. (1978). Loss of theta rhythm results in spatial memory deficit in the rat. *Science, 201*, 160–163.

Winson, J. (1986). *Brain and psyche: The biology of the unconscious.* New York: Doubleday.

16

PSYCHOANALYTIC THEORY, DREAM FORMATION, AND REM SLEEP

STEVEN J. ELLMAN

Shortly after rapid eye movement (REM) sleep[1] was discovered (Aserinsky & Kleitman, 1953), Dement and Kleitman (1957) found that dreaming occurred during this stage of sleep.[2] Subsequently, a number of studies demonstrated that many parts of the central nervous system (CNS) fire at high rates during this state (rates equivalent to that during active waking). On first consideration, it seems paradoxical[3] that during sleep so many aspects of the CNS are activated.[4] This seeming paradox and the lure of the dream together created a tremendous interest in the REM state. Psychoanalysts were among the first REM investigators; it was Dement, working in Charles Fisher's[5] laboratory, who discovered that if humans are deprived of REM

---

[1]Because Winson (see chapter 15 in this book) gives an overview of some aspects of REM sleep, I will not repeat many of the descriptive characteristics that he details (see, however, Ellman & Antrobus, 1991, for a recent review of the sleep mentation literature). The focus of this chapter will be to present some of the results from our laboratory, and as importantly to show how my work derives from and has implications for Freudian and current psychoanalytic theory.

[2]This early discovery was met with a number of methodological criticisms. The history of sleep mentation begins with this early claim and various responses to this finding (see Pivik, 1991, for a good review of this literature). Recently, my colleagues and I (Weinstein, Schwartz, & Ellman, 1988) have shown that REM mentation is discriminably different from all other sleep mentation.

[3]Jouvet (1967) originally called REM sleep *paradoxical sleep*.

[4]These systems are by no means limited to the brain stem and the hippocampus. In fact, many parts of the CNS display equally dramatic activity during this state. I mention this because Winson (chapter 15 of this book) focuses on hippocampal activity during REM sleep.

[5]Fisher was a well-known analyst and analytic investigator. He wrote the first review of the modern sleep literature in a psychoanalytic publication (Fisher, 1965).

sleep, they will attempt to make up this sleep on subsequent occasions (REM rebound). The discovery of REM rebound, or a need for REM sleep, was a crucial finding in the history of sleep research. Many investigators used REM deprivation (REMD) to test a variety of hypotheses about the function of REM sleep (Ellman, Spielman, & Lipschutz-Brach, 1991; Ellman, Spielman, Luck, Steiner, & Halperin, 1991).

Fisher and Dement (Dement, 1960) performed such an experiment to test Freud's (1900) idea of the dream as safety valve. Thus, one can say that one of the first experiments in REM research was stimulated by a Freudian hypothesis. In 1968, the first experiments were influenced not only by Freud's ideas but by the findings of Dement and Fisher in their pioneering REMD studies.

A MOTIVATIONAL HYPOTHESIS: ANIMAL STUDIES

In a previous publication Weinstein and I (Ellman & Weinstein, 1991) divided theories of REM sleep into four categories.[6] The motivational theory is only one that attempts to explain the function of REM sleep.[7] This chapter will not present reviews of other theories of REM sleep. Rather, it will briefly retrace some of Freud's ideas to show the relation between these and other experiments and Freudian thought. Interestingly, Freud's (1900/1953) views on dreams are not the only, or perhaps even the main, writings that form the basis for the motivational theory. Rather, it is Freud's views on endogenous stimulation or drive that have been most influential in forming our hypotheses. For Freud, drive implied an internal force or source of stimulation. To paraphrase, the drives maintain a constant and unavoidable flow of stimulation (Freud, 1915/1957). Freud asserted that an essential component in his conception of drive was that (periodically) there is an unavoidable amount of internal or endogenous stimulation that provides some motivational impetus for the organism. Freud assumed that this stimulation could occur in varying intensities (differences in force) and had a physiological source (biochemical, neurochemical, neurophysiological, etc.) about which he could only speculate. Although it is true that the concept of drive is virtually taboo in much modern psychoanalytic theorizing (Ellman & Moskowitz, 1980), as I have mentioned, it is Freud's version of drive and the concept of the dream as a "safety valve" that led to the first REMD studies.

It was reasoned that if one eliminated REM sleep (thus, ostensibly eliminating the dream) there would be noteworthy psychological effects. Although Dement's initial reports were striking,[8] very few of the psychological results were replicated (except for REM rebound).[9] Despite this, Fisher (1965) postulated that REM sleep might be the neurophysiological manifestation of what Freud called drive. Fisher's ideas were speculative, but they led him to study sexuality in the REM process and to discover the fact that penile erections typically occur during REM sleep. Although Fisher's work did not form the basis of an empirically testable theory, I believe that he was a source from which other investigators drew. When my colleagues and I (Ellman, Spielman, Luck, et al., 1991; Ellman, Spielman, & Lipschutz-Brach, 1991) began our series of studies, the phenomenon of REM rebound had been studied in both human and animal species. Although

---

[6]The categories are learning–memory consolidation, neural nets, CNS stimulation, and motivational theories of REM sleep.

[7]At least two other authors (Dement, 1965, 1969; Vogel, 1979) have put forward motivational hypotheses. Winson's chapter 15 contains another point of view.

[8]Dement reported that some subjects displayed psychotic manifestations; others began to overeat following REMD. In general, he reported results that indicate that if REMD takes place, there will be adverse psychological consequences.

[9]REM rebound is not really a psychological effect but rather a physiological effect of REMD.

REM rebound had become a well-established fact, the psychological consequences of REMD remained a puzzle. Given the experimental evidence, the idea of REM as a safety valve was no longer a viable concept.[10] Despite this, my colleagues and I began to think of REM as a source of endogenous stimulation, and in wondering what neurophysiological system could mediate what Freud had called drive, we postulated that the positive reward or intracranial self-stimulation (ICSS) could be such a system.

Olds (1962) demonstrated that animals will reliably press a bar to stimulate parts of the brain that are primarily located in the limbic system. Olds, and many investigators after him, showed that ICSS sites are typically in midbrain areas that are also implicated in such behaviors as eating, drinking, sex, and aggression. My colleagues and I (Ellman & Weinstein, 1991) speculated that REM sleep provides endogenous stimulation through an ICSS neural network. This line of reasoning led us to the following ideas: (a) During REM sleep, an ICSS neural network is fired; the firing of this ICSS system is an essential component of the biological function of REM sleep; (b) this REM–ICSS network is fired periodically throughout the 24-hour cycle, during wakefulness and sleep (although during wakefulness, the manifestations of REM may be masked); and (c) the ICSS network has sites in the pons, not only in the midbrain (as was thought to be the case in 1968 when we began this research). This third hypothesis was included because Jouvet (1967) demonstrated that REM sleep is initiated by pontine nuclei. From these ideas, we concluded that there can be an experimentally demonstrated reciprocal relation between the ICSS network and REM sleep. In our first experiments, my colleagues and I (Steiner & Ellman, 1972) found that (a) REMD lowers ICSS thresholds and raises ICSS response rates and (b) as few as 1½ hours of ICSS can reduce 24 hours of REMD by 50%.

After these initial results, my colleagues and I (Bodnar, Ellman, Coons, Achermann, & Steiner, 1979) began to explore new ICSS sites (C). More specifically, this line of research involved ICSS experiments that were conducted to substantiate the view that there are ICSS sites in the pons. At the time we began conducting these experiments, most sleep researchers felt that there was substantial evidence that implicated the locus coeruleus (LC) in the initiation and control of REM sleep.[11] We found the LC to be an ICSS site, and we went on to study the relation of LC ICSS with midbrain sites (Bodner et al., 1979; Ellman, Ackermann, Bodner, Jackler, & Steiner, 1975). Our finding that the LC is an ICSS site was surprising in itself given that investigators to that point had conceived of ICSS as a midbrain phenomenon. The interactions that we found between LC ICSS and midbrain ICSS led us to a model that posits the LC[12] as a controlling site for the activation and/or modulation of midbrain ICSS and forebrain ICSS areas. Essentially, we found that certain ICSS sites are influenced by and in turn influence the LC, whereas other ICSS locations are influenced by but do not influence the LC.

To review my and my colleagues' interaction data more fully would be beyond the scope of this chapter, but perhaps one related experiment will give an indication of our thinking. Based on the interaction studies between the LC and a variety of other sites, we predicted that lesions in the LC should eliminate or reduce ICSS in some areas and facilitate it in other areas. This

---

[10]I will not deal with issues that involve methodology and replicability here. In other places I have dealt with these issues extensively (see Ellman, Spielman, & Lipschutz-Brach, 1991; Ellman, Spielman, Luck, et al., 1991; Ellman & Weinstein, 1991).

[11]Today, one can certainly say that the situation is more complicated but that thus far some experimenters (e.g., Hobson, Lydic, & Baghdoyan, 1986; Hobson & McCarley, 1977) think that the role of the LC is to cease firing at the onset of REM and that this in turn triggers cells (FTG cells) that are responsible for at least the phasic activation of REM sleep. Almost all investigators agree that the subcoeruleus is responsible for components of motor inhibition present in REM. It is a matter of dispute as to the role of the LC in activating phasic components of REM sleep. However, there is a reasonable amount of evidence that still implicates the LC in triggering aspects of REM phasic activity (see Jones, 1985; Sakai, 1985).

[12]As well as pontine areas surrounding it and perhaps adjoining pathways.

was a precarious prediction because lesions involving ICSS have never been successful in producing such results in previous experiments. ICSS was thought of as a phenomenon that had redundant pathways that maintained this behavior. Our lesion data showed that lesions in the LC virtually eliminated ICSS in several distant midbrain sites (e.g., fields of forel, crux cerebri, etc.). These were the sites that were facilitated by but did not facilitate LC ICSS. There were other areas that were facilitated by LC lesions. Thus, we concluded that a function of LC ICSS is to modulate, facilitate, or act as one factor in the control of midbrain and forebrain ICSS and "drive" behavior thresholds.

It is important to emphasize that there can be different effects of a lesion on ICSS depending on the ICSS site tested. The same is true in terms of reaction to pharmacological interventions, as many laboratories, including mine and my colleagues' have shown. It may be that REMD has differential effects on certain ICSS sites. Thus, it is important to take into account the ICSS site in determining the effect of REMD on ICSS.

Having established that the LC is an ICSS site, that it interacts in specific ways with midbrain ICSS sites, and that the LC can exert both facilitating and inhibiting influences on ICSS, my colleagues and I (Spielman & Ellman, 1991; Spielman, Ellman, & Steiner, 1973) again considered the interaction of ICSS and REM sleep. In these experiments, we studied the effect of ICSS on the animal's normal sleep cycle.[13] In these experiments, we considered essentially two paradigms: (a) Animals are allowed varying amounts of ICSS at fixed times of the day, and (b) animals are allowed free access to ICSS.

In the latter, the amount of ICSS, as well as the time spent in sleep, were under the animal's control. In the former, there were several variations: Animals were given 2 hours of ICSS every 24-hour period or 2 hours of ICSS every 6-hour period (8 hours of ICSS per 24-hour period). In this paradigm, animals received lateral hypothalamic ICSS.

If one considers the experiments using the first paradigm, a simple, straightforward prediction would be that the more ICSS, the greater the amount of REM reduction. In fact, this is what occurred. A related prediction would be that ICSS should eliminate REM rebound (i.e., if there is a reciprocal relation between REM sleep and ICSS, then one should see ICSS completely substitute for REM without a subsequent REM rebound). Following this paradigm, all animals that demonstrated a REM reduction also showed a subsequent REM rebound. These results failed to support our theoretical position. At the same time that my colleagues and I were performing these experiments, we were also performing ICSS studies (Ellman et al., 1975). We reasoned that an ICSS site might be crucial in determining the extent of reciprocity between REM and ICSS. We decided to change the ICSS site from the lateral hypothalamus to the LC, while at the same time allowing unlimited ICSS. Obviously, by changing both site of stimulation and access to ICSS, we could not compare the results from the two paradigms and thus could not tell which factor accounted for the different results. In the second paradigm (unlimited ICSS), we were concerned with providing what we considered to be a crucial test for our hypothesis. Our results were interesting in several ways: (a) Animals chose ICSS for virtually the first 17 hours of the experiment; (b) after this 17-hour period, animals had very small amounts of REM sleep; and (c) in recovery, animals displayed no REM rebound, although they were significantly REM deprived (their REM sleep was reduced by about 90%). These results strongly support our position and we now intend to study other sites using this paradigm. Our prediction is that other sites will not yield the same results as we obtained with LC ICSS.

I have of necessity been brief in describing our animal studies, but I believe that my colleagues and I have compiled sufficient evidence to conclude that there are ICSS nuclei (or

---

[13]Non-REMD would be a better term than *normal* because once the animal is allowed ICSS, it no longer has a normal sleep cycle.

pathways) in the pons that can substitute for REM sleep. Moreover, we have evidence that these sites interact with and control midbrain ICSS sites. These midbrain ICSS sites are involved in behaviors that include sex, aggression, and eating.[14] The conclusion is that the LC–midbrain interaction forms a source that is similar to the one that Freud (1915/1957) postulated in his concepts about the importance of endogenous stimulation. To end this section, I specify a prediction that one can make from my theoretical position. Rechtschaffen, Gilliland, Bergmann, and Winter (1983) have performed a number of sleep deprivation and REMD experiments that indicate that if an animal is deprived of REM sleep, it will die. These deprivation periods are of long duration (as long as 30–40 days), but given the controls that they used, one can conclude that prolonged REMD has lethal effects. I predict that if animals were deprived of REM while they were receiving LC ICSS, they would survive significantly longer than when they only receive REMD. This prediction is in line with my hypothesis that REM sleep is an ICSS system. If one activates the system by providing ICSS, it should ameliorate the lethal effects of REMD.

LITERATURE REVIEW: REM SLEEP AND PSYCHOPATHOLOGY

To fully understand REM human studies, it is necessary to briefly review some of the REM sleep literature. Dement concluded from a series of animal studies that REM phasic events can be displaced into non-REM (NREM) sleep and under some conditions even into the waking state. There are several lines of research that relate to these findings. Gillin and Wyatt (1975) reported that actively ill schizophrenic patients do not show REM rebound following REMD, whereas chronic schizophrenic patients do show REM rebound following REMD. On the basis of these studies and his pharmacological data, Dement (1965) concluded that actively ill schizophrenic patients are not able to contain phasic events within REM sleep. He maintained that the symptoms of acute schizophrenia are partially related to phasic events intruding directly into the waking state. Despite the fact that some methodological questions remain, these results would be striking if validated.

Vogel, in a series of studies (Vogel, McAbee, & Barker, 1975; Vogel, Vogel, McAbee, Barker, & Thurmond, 1980), has looked at the effect of REMD on depression. Essentially, Vogel found that REMD leads to clinical improvement in subjects with endogenous depression and that this improvement is at least comparable to those resulting from pharmacological treatment. He has related his findings to the previously discussed ICSS studies and has articulated his own version of a REM–drive theoretical model (Vogel et al., 1980). His findings can be explained by my and my colleagues' animal model in that REMD activates reward sites, and it is precisely the type of functions mediated at those reward sites with which subjects with endogenous depression have difficulty; more specifically, such subjects often have difficulty in eating, sleeping, and sexual activities and in general have a low activity level (psychomotor retardation). I maintain that through the ICSS network, all these functions are activated by REMD.

I conclude that operation of the ICSS during REM is part of what is generated by phasic activation during REM sleep. It follows that intense firing of the REM phasic system may cause dramatic changes in a person's perception of reality. I have implied a model that assumes that individuals, to be appropriately interested in and motivated toward external events, need some optimum level of internally generated stimuli. If there is too much internally generated stimuli, the world becomes difficult to perceive; if too little, thresholds for interest in external stimuli are elevated. One may consider acute schizophrenic patients to be pathologically concerned with

---

[14]I have not reviewed the effects of REMD on these behaviors but believe this literature to be consistent with our hypotheses (for a review, see Ellman, Spielman & Lipschutz-Brach, 1991; Ellman, Spielman, Luck, et al., 1991).

internally generated events and endogenously depressed patients to be unmotivated because of a paucity of internally generated events. Thus, REMD helps depressed patients by increasing internally generated events and making them more receptive to various drive-related stimuli. Acute schizophrenic patients have such intense internal stimuli that external events are to a large extend obscured. Of course, this does not offer ideas approaching a complete explanation for either acute schizophrenia or endogenous depression; rather, I think that some of the factors that I have mentioned may be involved in these disorders.

Given that various REMD studies have pointed to the possibility that REM phasic events can be displaced into other sleep stages as well as waking, it may be that individuals differ in terms of their propensity for displacement. Several authors (Cartwright, Monroe, & Palmer, 1967; Cartwright & Ratzel, 1972; Nakasawa, Kotorii, Kotorii, Tachibana, & Nakano, 1975) have suggested this possibility as well as offered evidence that this may be the case. There may be characteristic individual differences in how easily people displace phasic events and also characteristic individual differences in absolute and proportional amounts of REM sleep. (By *proportional*, I mean the amount of phasic events per unit of REM time.)

HUMAN STUDIES

My and my colleagues' (Weinstein, Schwartz, & Ellman, 1991) recent human studies were to a reasonable extent based on the animal studies that I have outlined. In this section, I wish to integrate these findings more fully into our theoretical model. Although it is true that sleep mentation is not limited to REM sleep, it is also true that the most vivid, most absorbing mentation during sleep occurs in REM sleep, particularly during times of phasic activity (Pivik, 1991; Weinstein et al., 1991). Freud (1900/1953) thought that the dream was instigated by the (system) unconscious; most modern sleep researchers have maintained that dreams are in part influenced by the underlying neurophysiology of REM sleep. I postulate that during REM sleep, the firing of the ICSS system is one factor that is involved in the instigation of dreaming. The firing of this reward system is a way of increasing the probability of activating the neurophysiological substratum of drive systems (i.e., neural networks involved with eating, sex, aggression, etc.). When these systems fire, there is also an increased probability of activating memories and representations that Freud characterized as wishes.[15]

I have mentioned that the LC is responsible for triggering a substantial portion of phasic events during REM sleep and that phasic events are a compelling form of endogenous stimulation (Pivik, 1991; Weinstein et al., 1991).[16] Operationally, I maintain that when phasic events are fired during REM, the dreamer tends to experience accompanying mentation as real, absorbing, and occurring in the external world. This would be true even if one compared points in REM sleep (i.e., occasions on which there are many phasic events [REM phasic]) with ones on which phasic events are relatively absent (REM tonic). To test this hypothesis, my colleagues and I

---

[15]This hypothesis does not presume an isomorphic relation between activating the REM–ICSS network and activating a wish. This lack of a one-to-one relation could be true for many reasons. To cite one relatively simple example, firing ICSS sites at high intensities is aversive (Steiner, Beer, & Schaffer, 1969). One might say that the ICSS firing at high rates would increase the probability of aversive elements appearing in dream content. Whether these dreams should be characterized as instigated by wishes depends on one's theoretical predilections, but at least it can be maintained that the intensity of firing increases the probability that dream content is experienced as aversive.

[16]The idea that phasic events are a compelling form of stimulation is not by any means restricted to our theoretical position. Dement originally maintained that REMD is accomplished by depriving a subject of phasic events; he contended that tonic aspects of REM sleep were not important in REM rebound. There are a variety of neurophysiological studies that have separated tonic and phasic aspects of REM sleep.

(Weinstein, Schwartz, & Ellman, 1988, 1991) developed several scales that measure aspects of what we have termed a person's *absorption in mentation* (AIM). We reasoned that a crucial aspect of what makes an experience absorbing is the temporary suspension of self-observation. Thus, the AIM scales were designed to measure transient suspensions in self-reflection. These scales were successful at discriminating reports from REM phasic awakenings as compared with reports of REM tonic awakenings. In addition, in a comparison study these scales were more discriminating than were any other sleep mentation scales.

After my colleagues and I (Weinstein et al., 1991) had developed the AIM scales, we used them to look at the effect of REMD on mentation. Following some early findings (Dement, 1965, 1969), we assumed that REMD causes some displacement of REM phasic activity into NREM sleep. Thus, we expected that NREM mentation following REMD would be experienced as more absorbing or, in our terms, more like REM phasic mentation. This increased absorption should be apparent only on those scales that can discriminate REM phasic from REM tonic awakenings. This hypothesis was confirmed, and this result was the first one to demonstrate that REMD has an effect on mentation.

After our main hypothesis was confirmed, we looked at the effect of REMD on REM mentation. We did not expect to find a significant effect given that REM mentation scores on the AIM scales were quite high even without REMD. To look at some aspect of individual differences, we performed a post-hoc analysis, dividing subjects into two groups; this division was based on a test that measured the likelihood of their reporting anxiety-producing thoughts.[17] Subjects who were more willing to report anxiety-producing percepts were considered to be less anxious about internally generated fantasy material. The REM mentation of these subjects did not change following REMD. This was not surprising given that on baseline nights, these subjects demonstrated responses that were virtually at the top of the AIM scales. REMD for these subjects did not alter REM mentation because they already showed a ceiling effect. The other group of subjects, who tended to avoid thinking about (or perhaps reporting) anxiety-producing thoughts, had significantly less absorbing REM mentation following REMD. Thus, on recovery nights following REMD, these subjects had less absorbing mentation from REM phasic awakenings. That this was not simply a response to stress was shown by their failure to show a similar response during NREM deprivation. That it was specifically a response to the patterning and intensity of REM phasic activation following REMD was shown by the fact that the effect was only significant with the scales that were good discriminators of REM phasic and REM tonic activity.

We expected that subjects whose REM phasic mentation was virtually at the top of all scales during baseline nights would not, indeed could not, show a REMD effect. Our prediction that NREM mentation should become more REM-like following REMD was confirmed. This is what one would expect if one assumes that following REMD, REM phasic activity occurs more often in NREM sleep. The result that was not predicted until our post-hoc analysis was that subjects who found fantasy material anxiety provoking, or at least difficult to admit, showed decreased absorption in REM mentation following REMD. Our hypothesis was that increased intensity following REMD caused these subjects to attempt to distance themselves from their dream experiences. This characteristic defensive style was intensified by REMD. In these mentation studies, we demonstrated that REM stimulation affects mentation, particularly the manner in which the self is experienced in the dream. In addition, we are beginning to examine in experimental settings something analogous to defensive style. This attempt, of course, lacks the

---

[17]The subject's willingness to report anxiety-producing thought was measured by their responses to the guilt daydreaming scale of the Imaginal Processes Inventory. An analysis of the responses to the individual items on the scale showed that subjects who tended to score higher on this scale were more willing to focus on or report their inner experiences, even if these experiences were not socially acceptable.

type of sophistication possible in the clinical situation. Our findings in mentation studies and in our animal studies have encouraged us to speculate on the developmental importance of REM sleep.

DEVELOPMENTAL ASSUMPTIONS[18]

Phylogeny and Ontegeny

I have already mentioned that one sees large amounts of REM sleep in infants both in absolute and relative terms (Petre-Quadens, 1974). I agree with Roffwarg, Muzio, and Dement (1966) that REM sleep is a likely candidate to provide endogenous stimuli to the infant at a time when exogenous stimuli is not available. Jouvet (1967) previously postulated that the large amounts of REM sleep in infants are available for survival mechanisms. What I understand this to mean is that the function of REM sleep in infancy is the facilitation of responses that the infant will need when he or she begins to ambulate fully and independently. Crick and Mitchison (1986) have criticized this notion, claiming that another mechanism exists for this purpose, namely play. It is hard to see how in some species one can invoke play, because for a few hours to many months, some mammalian infants are unable to ambulate, much less play. I would hypothesize that total and relative amounts of REM sleep would drop in those species that ambulate more rapidly. Thus, large amounts of REM would not be needed to facilitate survival mechanisms, because in these species, a mechanism such as play could be utilized.

It is important to say more about what I mean by survival mechanisms. Clearly, I am talking about mechanisms that underlie food seeking, mating, and aggressive behavior and in the human (probably in all primates) various social behaviors that bond infant and mother. It is my assumption that infant primate survival is dependent on mutual gratification occurring between infant and mother. However, in each species different abilities come into play; in the cat, visual tracking is extremely important for food seeking; in the rat, olfactory mechanisms are essential. I would predict that in different species the factors that are used characteristically in survival behaviors would be facilitated by REM. Our prediction is that if animals were not allowed to have REM sleep, then one would see effects similar to the effects Heubel and Wiesel (1963) obtained in their pioneering studies of the visual system. They found deterioration of the visual system without visual stimulation in infancy. Correspondingly, lack of REM would mean that mechanisms that are used by the animal in drive- or species-specific behavior would be involved in maturational deficits. In the rat aspects of the olfactory system, in the cat the visual system, and in all mammalian species aspects of the positive reward system would be impaired.

Human Development

How might these views be specifically relevant to the development of the human infant? To begin, I sketch out an aspect of my view of "normal" or ideal development in relation to the development of REM sleep. During the first month or few months of life, REM sleep is not a unified state (Petre-Quadens, 1974; Roffwarg et al., 1966). During this period of time there is neither motor inhibition (or atonia) that is characteristic of adult REM sleep, nor are phasic

---

[18]What follows in this section is largely speculative but I believe logically connected to the body of experimental research that we have accumulated. At times I realize that I am writing as if some of these points were established facts and I wish to remind the reader and myself that this is a theoretical section of the present chapter. I, of course, believe that a variety of authors are guilty of the same tendency that I find myself falling into in this section.

events restricted to REM periods. In ontogenetic terms, it appears to be a maturational and perhaps a developmental landmark to fully unite phasic and tonic aspects of REM sleep. Given the high percentage of time the infant spends in vegetative activities (eating and sleeping), it is my view that in the first month the infant is forming what might be termed *passive and active bonding precursors*. These might be considered elements of, as well as precursors to, various kinds of object relationships. Winnicott's (1960) term of absolute dependence seems to me an appropriate concept in describing this period. Jacobson (1964) similarly viewed the infant as living a psychophysiological life and developing a psychophysiological self organization. This view does not exclude other important events in the infant's life; it is only that early on the infant spends a great deal of time involved in vegetative functions, and for most babies the psychological organization that Jacobson highlights is the main factor in early infancy. Parenthetically, one might note that when Stern (1985) wrote about the infant, he presented a view that seemed to underplay the vast amount of sleep and feeding that are present during early infancy. I believe this to be true even though recent research (Brazelton & Cramer, 1990; Stern, 1985) has demonstrated that the infant is capable of learning even in the first day of life.

REM Containment and Quantitative Factors

Given that the infant does not have unified REM states, what are the developmental implications? In adult life when REM periodically fires during waking life it is possible to inhibit REM mechanisms or at the very least divert one's attention to other aspects of the external environment (because this form of stimulation tends to restrict attention to drive derivatives). I assume that when REM mechanisms fire during waking, the infant has far less capacity than the adult to redirect attention. In the normal infant after a short time REM firing becomes periodic during waking as well as sleeping. When this occurs phenomena such as sucking and erection cycles occur in organized periodic cycles. Most mothers will quickly learn that during these "REM" cycles the baby is activated and responsive to only a limited range of stimuli. As the infant develops there will be increasing amounts of what Wolf (1966) described as quiet wakefulness. At these times the baby will be responsive to a wider range of stimuli. Our hypothesis is that during quiet waking, or what Brazelton and Cramer (1990) have called alert waking, REM mechanisms are not firing or are firing at low rates. These quiescent times, between feedings, when the baby is alert and not extremely active, are the times when considerably more learning can take place. The infant can attend more easily to external stimuli because endogenous sources are relatively quiescent. (This follows a form of Freud's, 1900/1953, views on attention cathexis.) The oscillation of alert and active waking periods depends to some extent on the containment of REM phenomena. By *containment*, I mean the organization of waking or even sleeping REM phenomena into a relatively unified state. This reduces aspects of REM present in other parts of the infant's waking life. In other terms, without containment it is assumed that REM activation spills over into other states.

In (minor) support of the relationship of REM containment and infant bonding and learning, there is evidence (Anders, 1974; Emde & Metcalf, 1970; Petre-Quadens, 1974) of major changes in the organization of REM sleep at 3 months of age. This involves the dropping out of undifferentiated REM states (waking, fussing, and drowsy REM) and the coalescing of random eye movements into burst patterns (the beginning phases of containment). These changes are temporally correlated with a marked increase in behaviors that demonstrate the infant's enhanced capacity for interactively bonding with the mother, namely social smiling, mutual looking, and mutual vocalizing (Brazelton & Cramer, 1990). We would hypothesize that if REM phenomena are not restricted to a unified period in a given infant, then quiet or alert wakefulness will be disrupted. We are then postulating that in the infant (as in some REM-deprived adults), when

REM phenomena are not restricted to a single unified period, there is a greater likelihood that internal events will interfere with external perception. Such an infant would have more difficulty perceiving a separate mothering object, or being able to see satisfaction as fully originating outside of himself or herself (both critical developmental tasks). Thus, I consider the amount of REM organization or containment as an important factor in the development of object relations in infants.

A second factor in this developmental picture is the total amount of phasic phenomena that a given infant produces. We are assuming that this is a maturational phenomenon, as is REM restriction. Infants with large amounts of phasic activity will tend to be absorbed more intensely in rudimentary drive behaviors. This intensity will spread to other states if the infant is not able to contain his or her REM sleep. Thus, an infant with high endogenous amounts of REM and poor containment will be most likely to have his or her quiet (alert) wakefulness disrupted. This infant will have greater difficulty in attending to and then internalizing the external world.

The Mother–Infant Dyad

In this rudimentary model we have so far left out the role of the mother. It is clear that some mothers may be able to gauge their baby's sensitivities quite well and help the infant to overcome these tendencies. In fact, we can imagine that under some developmental conditions, high endogenous (REM) stimulation and poor REM containment may enhance certain cognitive and interpersonal functions. I am, however, assuming that a baby who has relatively little quiet wakefulness will be perceived as being more difficult by most mothers. More specifically, it will be hard for the mother to understand her child's restricted range of reactions as well as the infants' relative sensitivity.[19] In this context, let us remember that the greater the firing of the REM-phasic-ICSS system, the lower the threshold for drive behaviors that can include a tendency toward aggression. Thus, the high-phasic event, poorly contained infant would have a lowered threshold for a variety of drive reactions including aggression.[20] There is another characteristic that is related to aggression: a tendency to experience "normal" levels of stimulation as aversive (see footnote 19) while at the same time displaying a restricted range of reactions toward the mother.

I would maintain that a high-drive, poorly contained baby is, on the whole, less reinforcing for the mother than is an average infant. I have mentioned three (related) factors that may be difficult for the mother to understand: (a) the baby's intensity, (b) the baby's ability to respond to only a restricted range of stimuli, and (c) the infant's rapid shifts from positive to negative affect when experiencing what the mother might consider to be normal stimulation.

Of course, I am assuming or fantasizing the normal or average maternal response. I believe we know that there are some mothers who would thrive with a high-drive, and even a high-drive poorly contained, baby. These mothers may produce extraordinary individuals. At any rate, when contemporary researchers talk about the reinforcing aspects of the baby, I believe that endogenous stimulation level is one factor that will determine how reinforcing the infant is for a

---

[19]In this model positive reinforcement is seen as following an inverted U function. Thus, as intensity increases the reinforcing value increases up to a particular point. At intense-enough values of stimulation, the stimulation actually becomes aversive (Steiner, Beer, & Schaffer, 1969). The high-drive infant has lower thresholds for positive reinforcement, but stimulation also becomes negative at lower intensities. Thus, what may be a pleasurable interchange for normal-drive infants may be aversive for high-drive infants. This has the potential to be confusing for mothers interacting with sensitive babies.

[20]By *aggression*, I mean only a tendency toward aggression because I believe a full aggressive response occurs later than in the initial phases of infancy.

given caretaker. I also am assuming that the matching of "temperaments" is a function of matching endogenous stimulation levels.

Although our discussion of the infant may seem to be some distance from our dream research, conceptually we can bridge the gap in terms of the development of the reflective self-representation (RSR). Our theoretical position is that the child's awareness of himself or herself as a separate entity or object develops originally within the matrix of the mother–child unit and coalesces as the child gradually emerges from that bond. If an infant is presented with either a great deal of exogenous or endogenous stimulation, it will be difficult for the infant to develop or clearly delineate intrapsychic boundaries. From our theoretical position, large amounts and lack of containment or restriction of REM phasic events are factors that can retard the development of the RSR. This idea is similar to the conceptualization in our dream research; given a great deal of activation it is difficult, at times impossible, to represent oneself except in terms of action or activity.[21] This would mean that the RSR develops optimally when there is some diminution of both internal and external stimulation. If there is a continuous flow of either or both (internal and external stimulation), then it is more difficult to coalesce a stable representation of the self.

In summary, if the infant is experiencing a great deal of inner stimulation, this reduces thresholds for certain kinds of stimuli, makes other types of stimuli irrelevant, and makes the delineation between mother and infant more difficult by hampering the development of RSR. This will be particularly true if the mother responds to such an infant with a great deal of stimulation. We recognize, of course, that mothers (or fathers) do not respond to children in terms of stimulation but in terms of actions and meanings, but in this context we are trying to point out the importance of different levels of endogenous (and exogenous) stimulation to the infant. The level of stimulation (endogenous or exogenous) can be an important factor in shaping meaning between mother and infant.

Comparing Theoretical Views

I want to briefly mention some implications for defense and psychic structure (or structural precursors) from an endogenous stimulation perspective. Again, I use the high-drive infant as an example. If the mother provides a high level of stimulation, then I would assume that at least the precursors of primitive defenses would be formed. The world would be more likely to be divided or split and defenses such as projection and projective identification would be more likely to be used on a permanent basis. A maxim of Stern's (1985) is to provide stimulation just slightly under the level of excitation the baby is exhibiting; this level is one in which he sees the mother as being attuned or providing the correct amount of stimulation. In my view, this might interact with a high-drive baby in a way that is experienced as aversive by the infant. A homeostatic endogenous stimulation model, such as the one stated by Jacobson (1964), would offer a different concept of attunement. My interpretation of such a model is that for many infants (children and adults), Stern's ideas would be entirely appropriate, but as one begins to approach the extremes, his ideas do not reflect what is optimal for the child. Thus, the present endogenous stimulation model makes predictions that are contrary to those that Stern would make. I believe that the present model is compatible with Jacobson's restatement of Freud's ideas (i.e., the movement from a hydraulic to a homeostatic model).

One might ask whether these models are substantively different. To answer this question it might be instructive to look again at various theorists of early development: Stern (1985), Melanie Klein and Jacobson (1964). Stern viewed the child as entering the world with a sense

---

[21]That is, if the self at the point is represented at all.

of self (and presumably other) and certainly not in the type of state that a theorist such as Klein postulated in her views of early development. The types of internal dramas that are taking place in Klein's views are unlike anything that Stern conjured up in his ideas about early learning in the infant. Jacobson, on the other hand, gave another type of view of the infant's first few months. Interestingly, both Stern and Klein saw the young infant as an active processor of the environment. Both saw the infant as having some rudimentary sense(s) of self, and Klein obviously believed in an extensive network of both connotative and denotative symbols that are available to the child. Jacobson, on the other hand, saw the first month of life in terms of the infant gaining psychophysiological equilibrium; she also conceived of the first month of life as consolidating the child's psychophysiological sense of self. Active cognitive processing by the infant is certainly not highlighted in her theoretical writings. The mother is there to help the child make psychophysiological adjustments to the world (really as a physiological provider, regulator, and comforter).

Is it possible to reconcile these very different pictures of the child's first few months of life? In my view, Stern (1985) was talking about infant capacities that are certainly present but that are not in the forefront of the infant's world. One again has to remember that a 1-day-old infant may spend up to and beyond 18 hours a day in sleep (10–12 of those hours are in REM sleep or some version of REM sleep). One way of reconciling Jacobson's (1964) emphasis and Stern's is to simply say that they are talking about the infant in different states and that their theoretical positions lead them to accentuate one aspect of the infant's experience over another. I would add that the extent to which we are impressed with a given infant's development depends on a variety of factors, and obviously the factor that I have stressed is what Freud called the quantitative factor. High-drive infants do not impress us with their social attunement and early learning; more typically we are impressed with their passion and their needs. Some mothers delight in these needs (I do not want to overplay the delight) and do not feel depleted by this type of child. Others long for the type of infant experience that Stern frequently depicted.

One possibility is to think of each theorist describing different states; another possibility is to think about different theorists describing different infants and different infant–mother interactions. Stern (1985), it seems to me, was talking about the average or midrange infant and the mother–infant interaction during special points of socializing and learning. He was describing infants at points of low intensity, and we may say that Stern was presenting a theoretical view of midrange infants. Low or high endogenous stimulation infants may affect typical mother–infant interactions in ways, it seems to me, that Stern did not consider. When Pine (1985) wrote about moments, he was talking about moments of intensity that midrange infants will experience. What I am trying to explain are infants whose "moments" are those points of rare quiet alert wakefulness. Or, for the low-drive infant, the rare moments when there is a strongly gratifying mother–infant relationship.

I interpret Klein (1975) as talking about infants who are not only high-drive infants and partly because of this experience the external world as aversive. She is talking about particular types of mother–infant interaction in which the mother impinges on (and frequently overstimulates) the infant. The phase of absolute dependence that Winnicott (1960) and Jacobson (1964) described is never satisfactorily attained, and the infant has entered the world with a tendency to split and project the world in an attempt to rid himself or herself of a world that is experienced as repellent, frustrating, and terrifying.

I have so far taken what I regard as two extremes in viewing the world of the infant (Stern and Klein). When Freud wrote about early development, he suggested that we look at three polarities of mental life: ego (self)–object, pleasure–unpleasure, and active–passive. In Winnicott's (1960) and Jacobson's (1964) views of early development, self and object are not clearly distinguished. The infant is clearly in a passive state with respect to his or her eventual maturation and his or her life is strongly rooted in the pleasure–unpleasure series.[22] The pleasure–unpleasure series can be seen as more complicated than we expected from the infant side, and I believe that we now understand the pleasure–unpleasure sequence in at least three ways: (a) from the infant's point of view (Freud's and Klein's sole focus); (b) from the mother's point of view (a focus that Winnicott drew to our attention); and (c) the interaction between the two (a focus that both Stern and Winnicott have accented in different ways).

It is the interaction where relatively complicated contingencies can occur. It is by far the most intriguing aspect of the puzzle, and the one that is, I believe, crucial to understand in terms of endogenous tendencies of the infant, as well as maternal proclivities in terms of sensitivities, intensity level, and consistency.

Because I have mentioned Winnicott implicitly or explicitly a number of times, I end this section with an example of how I view Winnicott in terms of some of the issues I have raised. Let me begin by paraphrasing: Winnicott (1960) postulated that after a phase of absolute dependence, the infant achieves what might be called unit status. The infant is becoming a person in his or her own right. Associated with this attainment is the infant's psychosomatic existence, which begins to take in a personal pattern; Winnicott called this the psyche indwelling in the soma. The basis for this indwelling is a linkage of motor and sensory and functional experiences with the infant's new state of being a person. As a subsequent development there comes into being what he called a limiting membrane, which to some extent (if the baby is healthy) is equated with the surface of the skin and has a position between the infant's "me" and his or her "not-me" representations. So, the infant comes to have an inside and an outside and a body scheme. In this way meaning comes to the function of intake and output; moreover, after a period of time it gradually makes sense to postulate a personal or inner psychic reality for the infant. I would add to this that the strength of the drives and how well the drives unite into a consolidated state (waking and sleeping) will be a powerful determinant of how well formed this membrane will become in the infant's developing body ego. If the mother is not able to understand the intensity and the restrictive range of certain high-drive infants, then this membrane will at best be a highly permeable one or, alternatively, one that is so impermeable as to render object relations as giving little life or sustenance to the child. I believe we are at a point in being able to study this process. In a similar vein, I would say that the analyst who encounters such a patient in adult life has to wait until the patient can use the analyst and then has confidence that the analyst will not break through (or impinge on) this membrane. It is here that we respect the analysand's sense of self and fragility of ego until the patient can own his or her own drive states, fantasies, and object relationships.

CONCLUDING COMMENTS

Many of the issues that I have raised implicitly or explicitly point to the problems of mind–body interaction. A derivative of this type of issue occurs in the modern dispute about the nature of the dream. Various writers (e.g., Hobson & McCarley, 1977; Crick & Mitchison, 1986) have seen the dream as epiphenomenal, stimulated only by the neurophysiology of REM sleep. These authors have received a good deal of attention in the popular press. My colleagues and I (e.g., Vogel et al., 1980) have provided at least some answers that have come from the laboratory. For the purposes of this chapter, I will sidestep these controversies and relate some of the theorizing to issues that have emerged from these findings. One alternative theoretical position that attempts

---

[22]Winnicott's genius helps us understand the infant's mental life during this phase of development. He contended (1960) that the infant is experiencing an actual feeling of omnipotence if "good-enough" mothering is present.

to explain the function of REM sleep is the learning–memory consolidation point of view (Ellman & Weinstein, 1991). One of the main experimental findings that bolsters this theory is the phenomenon of REM augmentation.[23] In what follows, I explain the REM augmentation phenomena within my hypotheses. To do this, I will introduce one more hypothesis.

Various authors involved in learning research have made a distinction between incentive rewards and consummatory rewards (e.g., Osgood, 1953). Incentives are those stimuli that activate the subject toward a particular goal object, whereas consummatory responses are those responses that lead to the consumption of the goal object (e.g., eating food, sexual orgasm, attack, etc.). For example, one might distinguish between searching for or gathering food as one type of behavior and consuming food as another type of behavior. In the model put forth by my colleagues and me (Ellman & Weinstein, 1991), the incentive system continues to be active until the consumption system turns it off and says, in effect, "You can stop pursuing a given goal, we've had enough." The ICSS system that fires during REM sleep is considered an incentive system in this model. It is a system that fires and influences the threshold of various consummatory centers; in turn, the system thresholds are changed when consummatory centers fire.

I maintain that under normal conditions in REM, when the REM phasic–ICSS system fires, there will be regular consummatory feedback so that during REM, the ICSS system is continuously attenuated until a given REM period ends. If in the period of wakefulness before the animal sleeps, there has been an event or series of events that activates the ICSS system, there will be a tendency toward increased REM. This tendency will be activated only if there is at least a small amount of consummatory reinforcement that follows the activation of the ICSS network. If there is no consummatory reinforcement after ICSS activation, then there will be a different prediction. This will lead to little or no consummatory centers firing during REM sleep; the ICSS system then will fire at high enough rates so that at some point it will become aversive during sleep and arouse the organism.

This furnishes an explanation for the REM augmentation phenomenon. During an avoidance paradigm, for example, the animal is put in a situation that is potentially life threatening. This activates the ICSS incentive system; if the animal is given one reinforcement, this will lead to a small amount of consummatory firing and subsequent large amounts of REM sleep. If the animal is given many trials of consummatory reinforcement, there will be a normal amount of REM sleep. If the reinforcement is completely withheld, then the animal has little or no REM sleep. This would be true because the ICSS system would fire at high rates and arouse the organism. Thus, I also predict that if the animal is completely starved, there would be little or no REM sleep.

Coming back to the dream state, I hypothesize that dreams are originally mental representations of the activation of (or activity motivated by) incentive and consummatory centers. Dreams are initially adaptive attempts to represent both an approach (incentive network) and a consummation (consummatory network) of a sequence of behaviors or thoughts. I assume that infants begin to have this type of mental imagery with the onset of intentional (incentive and

---

[23]*Augmentation* is defined as an increase in REM sleep following a given learning task. Thus, when an animal (usually a mouse, cat, or rat) is successful in a newly learned two-way avoidance task, this position predicts an increase in REM sleep so that the animal can consolidate this new learning experience. A variety of experiments have reported REM augmentation, and it is perhaps the most powerful experimental evidence for the learning–memory consolidation theoretical perspective. This augmentation occurs only in the beginning or acquisition of learning tasks. In addition, the learning must involve some important reward.

Pearlman (1979), in reviewing various studies, stated that REMD disrupts animal learning when the tasks to be learned are complex and require integrative skills. Some authors have maintained that REMD affects memory consolidation if it comes within 3 hr of learning, whereas REMD after 3 hr of learning does not disrupt consolidation. Thus, according to this position, REM sleep is necessary for memory consolidation.

consummatory) actions.[24] In adults or older children, recent "drive" behaviors, thoughts, or fantasies are automatically compared with older or past sequences. In each dream, an attempt is made to reconcile past and present sequences.

Here, I differ from Freud's (1900/1953) account of dreams. To begin with, I see REM mechanisms and dreaming as originally serving an adaptive function. My view is that although wishes are certainly represented in dreams, it is not theoretically useful to maintain that a wish is the instigator of dreaming.[25] Freud saw the wish as serving only primary process functions. I contend that the content that is represented in dreams has to do with essential gratifications and dangers that are attached to and represent the underlying REM neural mechanisms. Dreams depict important life-threatening or life-enhancing themes. These themes frequently (probably always) in the adult involve some degree of wish (in the Freudian sense of the term) and conflict. Conflicts are depicted as those ideas or tendencies that the dreamer sees as making it difficult to approach a goal or, in psychoanalytic terms, to obtain drive gratification. This may involve incompatible motives (i.e., as superego prohibitions) and defenses. When the conflict is strong enough, it will be difficult to even symbolically represent a consummatory response. In this event, there will be either anxiety or awakening from the dream. Dreams representing traumatic events are instances of the incentive system being mobilized without any consummatory response ever having been possible. Thus, the organism is helpless to respond satisfactorily to an activating signal. When this sequence is repeated, bringing up former memories is useless because there have been no adequate consummatory responses in the past. As past memories are brought to consciousness, the organism is increasingly activated while at the same time developing increasing anxiety because no consummatory response is seen as adequate. Because the REM phasic–ICSS system gives the dreamer a powerful feeling of reality, the dream with no dampening consummatory response is particularly real and activating. From this point, the consummatory response has two related effects: First, dampening the REM phasic–ICSS system allows the dream to continue by making the dream slightly less intense and therefore less absorbing; second, this dampening and diminution of the absorbing qualities of the dream says to the dreamer "You can continue to sleep; this is only a memory and you currently are not in danger or in need." To make this last point clearer, I assume that if the dreamer's incentive system is highly aroused when he or she enters sleep,[26] then the dream has an increased probability of being so absorbing that it awakes or at least creates anxiety for the dreamer. When a symbolic or actual consummatory response occurs, the dreamer is able to reflect and in effect remember that it is only a dream. This recognition is normally not at a conscious level.[27]

To repeat, from this perspective, dreams in later childhood and adulthood contain wishes and frequently represent conflict. However, the original impetus for a dream is to represent drive behaviors so they may be facilitated in waking life. Large amounts of REM sleep in the infant enable drive networks to be facilitated before the infant is able to ambulate.[28] When the organism is able to make a range of approach and consummatory responses, REM levels diminish and

---

[24]This may be a meaningless statement given that infants may have rudimentary intentional behavior in the first days of life.

[25]Perhaps it would be more precise to change Freud's concept of the wish. This, however, would lead to a discussion of the nature of primary and secondary process that would last longer than the present chapter.

[26]This arousal necessarily implies that during waking there has not been a satisfactory consummatory response (either actually or symbolically).

[27]In fact, when recognition is at an overt conscious level, defense processes are needed to the extent that even the dream is derealized to some extent.

[28]I assume this facilitation takes place both on a neurophysiological as well as a representation or experiential level.

muscle atonia appears. At the point of early volitional behaviors (purposeful signaling, etc.), drive issues begin to be represented mentally and the manner in which drive-related issues have been handled in the past are reviewed in the dream. In this respect, I agree with the learning–memory position that memories are reviewed in REM sleep. However, I maintain the type of memories that are reviewed are related to drives or drive derivatives. Clearly, what an adult may consider life sustaining or life threatening may be very far from the biological roots that I have postulated. In addition, these issues almost always undergo some primal repression and therefore are necessarily involved in conflict. Thus, while I may be on the way to changing my ideas about the nature of a wish and the role of primary process in development, I still postulate that these issues are best understood in terms of drive and drive derivatives.

It can be discerned from the research I have discussed that the way someone represents himself or herself in a dream is quite important in the process of dream formation. The beginning of coalescence of the infant's sense of self and eventually reflective self or RSR are, in my view, both extremely important developmental achievements. Once these achievements occur, the dream can be seen as a process of oscillating between relative loss of RSR (absorption in dreaming) and a relatively strong representation of the RSR. Unless defensive processes intervene, this oscillation will correspond to the absence or presence of phasic events in the REM period. At times in the dream, the dreamer is the actor; at other times, the dreamer reflects on his or her actions and consolidates the implications of these actions. This oscillation is by no means a perfect correlation to the waxing and waning of phasic activation. I fully expect that, even taking defensive processes into account, individuals will differ as to how they represent themselves and the extent to which they become absorbed in their dreams or fantasy lives. These differences may be important in understanding how individuals process what I have called *drive material* and what others have called *matters of emotion or temperament.*

Clearly, the representation of the self in the dream is a topic that holds some of the answers to the riddle of dream formation. How the self is represented gives important clues to a person's responses to his or her internal promptings or endogenous stimulation. One of the current research issues is the role of defensive processes in dream formation (as well as in dream reporting). To attempt to spell out my thinking in this area would constitute an attempt to develop a theory of the self. This, however, in my opinion, is where a psychoanalytic theory of drive has to develop to be a truly explanatory theory. To accomplish this would be to bridge some of the gaps in psychoanalytic theory. It is my hope that my schematic theorizing is a beginning in this direction.

REFERENCES

Anders, T. F. (1974). An overview of recent sleep and dream research. In L. Goldberger & Rosen (Eds.), *Psychoanalysis and contemporary science* (Vol. 3). Madison, CT: International Universities Press.

Aserinsky, E., & Kleitman, N. (1953). Regularly occuring periods of eye motility and concomitant phenomena during sleep. *Science, 118,* 273–274.

Bodnar, R. J., Ellman, S. J., Coons, E. E., Ackermann, R. R., & Steiner, S. S. (1979). Differential locus coeruleus and hypothalamic self stimulation loci. *Physiological Psychology, 6,* 48–52.

Brazelton, T. B., & Cramer, B. G. (1990). *The earliest relationship.* Reading, MA: Addison-Wesley.

Cartwright, R. D., Monroe, L. J., & Palmer, C. (1967). Individual differences in response to REM deprivation. *Archives of General Psychiatry, 16,* 297–303.

Cartwright, R. D., & Ratzel, R. (1972). Effects of dream loss on waking behaviors. *Archives of General Psychiatry, 27,* 277–280.

Crick, F., & Mitchison, G. (1986). REM sleep and neural nets. *Journal of Mind and Behavior, 7,* 229–250.

Dement, W. C. (1960). The effect of dream deprivation. *Science, 131,* 1705–1707.

Dement, W. C. (1965). Recent studies in the biological role of REM sleep. *American Journal of Psychiatry, 122,* 404–408.

Dement, W. C. (1969). The biological role of REM sleep. In A. Kales (Ed.), *Sleep: Physiology and pathology.* Philadelphia: Lippincott.

Dement, W. C., & Kleitman, N. (1957). Cyclic variations in EEG during sleep and their relation to eye movements, bodily motility and dreaming. *Electroencephalography and Clinical Neurophysiology, 9,* 673–690.

Ellman, S. J., Ackermann, R. R., Bodnar, R. J., Jackler, F., & Steiner, S. S. (1975). Comparisons of behavior elicited by electrical brain stimulation in dorsal brainstem and hypothalmus of rats. *Journal of Comparative and Physiological Psychology, 88,* 816–828.

Ellman, S. J., & Antrobus, J. S. (1991). *The mind in sleep.* New York: Wiley.

Ellman, S. J., & Moskowitz, M. (1980). Examination of some recent criticisms of psychoanalytic "metapsychology." *Pschoanalytic Quarterly, 4,* 631–662.

Ellman, S. J., Spielman, A. J., & Lipschutz-Brach, L. (1991). REM deprivation update. In S. J. Ellman & J. S. Antrobus (Eds.), *The mind in sleep.* New York: Wiley.

Ellman, S. J., Spielman, A. J., Luck, D., Steiner, S. S., & Halperin, R. (1991). REM deprivation: A review. In S. J. Ellman & J. S. Antrobus (Eds.), *The mind in sleep* (pp. 329–368). New York: Wiley.

Ellman, S. J., & Weinstein, L. (1991). REM sleep and dream formation: A theoretical intergration. In S. J. Ellman & J. S. Antrobus (Eds.), *The mind in sleep.* New York: Wiley.

Emde, R., & Metcalf, D. R. (1970). An electroencephalographic study of behavioral rapid eye movement states in the human newborn. *Journal of Nervous and Mental Disease, 159,* 376–385.

Fisher, C. (1965). Psychoanalytic implications of recent research on sleep and dreaming: Part 1. Empirical findings; Part 2. Implications for psychoanalytic theory. *Journal of the American Psychoanalytic Association, 13,* 197–303.

Freud, S. (1953). The interpretation of dreams. In J. Strachey (Ed. and Trans.), *The standard edition of the complete psychological works of Sigmund Freud* (Vol. 5, pp. 588–604). London: Hogarth Press. (Original work published 1900)

Freud, S. (1957). Instincts and their vicissitudes. In J. Strachey (Ed. and Trans.), *The standard edition of the complete psychological works of Sigmund Freud* (Vol. 14, pp. 117–140). London: Hogarth Press. (Original work published 1915)

Gillin, J. C., & Wyatt, R. J. (1975). Schizophrenia: Perchance a dream? *International Review of Neurobiology, 17,* 297–342.

Heubel, D. H., & Wiesel, T. N. (1963). Receptive fields and functional architecture of monkey striate cortex. *Journal of Physiology, 195,* 215–243.

Hobson, J. A., Lydic, R., & Baghdoyan, H. A. (1986). Evolving concepts of sleep cycle generation: From brain centers to neuronal populations. *Behavioral and Brain Sciences, 9,* 371–448.

Hobson, J. A., & McCarley, R. W. (1977). The brain as a dream state-generator: An activation–synthesis hypothesis of the dream process. *American Journal of Psychiatry, 134,* 1335–1348.

Jacobson, E. (1964). *The self and the object world.* Madison, CT: International Universities Press.

Jones, B. E. (1985). Neuroanatomical and neurochemical substrates of mechanisms underlying paradoxical sleep. In D. J. McGinty (Ed.), *Brain mechanisms of sleep* (pp. 139–156). New York: Raven Press.

Jouvet, M. (1967). Neurophysiology of the status of sleep. *Psysiological Reviews, 47,* 117–177.

Klein, M. (1975). *Envy and gratitude and other works, 1946–1963.* New York: Free Press.

Nakasawa, Y., Kotorii, M., Kotorii, T., Tachibana, H., & Nakano, T. (1975). Individual differences in compensatory rebound of REM sleep, with particular reference to their relationship to personality and behavioral characteristics. *Journal of Nervous and Mental Disease, 161,* 18–25.

Olds, J. (1962). Hypothalamic substrates of reward. *Physiological Reviews, 42,* 554–604.

Osgood, C. E. (1953). *Method and theory in experimental psychology.* New York: Oxford University Press.

Pearlman, C. (1979). REM sleep and information processing: Evidence from animal studies. *Neuroscience and Biobehavioral Reviews, 3,* 57–68.

Petre-Quadens, O. (1974). Sleep in the human newborn. In O. Petre-Quadens & J. Schlag (Eds.), *Basic sleep mechanisms* (pp. 355–380). San Diego, CA: Academic Press.

Pine, F. (1985). *Developmental theory and clinical process.* New Haven, CT: Yale University Press.

Pivik, R. T. (1991). Tonic states and phasic events in relation to sleep. In S. J. Ellman & J. S. Antrobus (Eds.), *The mind in sleep* (pp. 214–248). New York: Wiley.

Rechtschaffen, A., Gilliland, M. A., Bergmann, B., & Winter, J. B. (1983). Physiological correlates of prolonged sleep deprivation in rats. *Science, 221,* 182–184.

Roffwarg, H., Muzio, J., & Dement, W. C. (1966). The ontogenetic development of the human sleep–dream cycle. *Science, 152.* 604–619.

Sakai, K. (1985). Anatomical and physiological basis of paradoxical sleep. In D. J. McGinty (Ed.), *Brain mechanisms of sleep* (pp. 111–137). New York: Raven Press.

Spielman, A. J., & Ellman, S. J. (1991). *The effects of ICSS on the normal sleep cycle.* Manuscript in preparation.

Spielman, A. J., Ellman, S. J., & Steiner, S. S. (1973). The effects of varying amounts of intracranial self-stimulation on the normal sleep cycle of the rat. *Psychophysiology, 11,* 171–174.

Steiner, S. S., Beer, B., & Schaffer, M. M. (1969). Escape from self produced rates of brain stimulation. *Science, 163,* 98–99.

Steiner, S. S., & Ellman, S. J. (1972). Relation between REM sleep and intracranial self stimulation. *Science, 177,* 1122–1124.

Stern, D. (1985). *The interpersonal world of the infant.* New York: Basic Books.

Vogel, G. (1979). A motivational theory of REM sleep. In R. Drucker-Colin, M. Shkurovich, & M. B. Sherman (Eds.), *The functions of sleep* (pp. 233–251). San Diego, CA: Academic Press.

Vogel, G. W., McAbee, R., & Barker, R. (1975). Endogenous depression improvement and REM pressure. *Archives of General Psychiatry, 32,* 765–777.

Vogel, G. W., Vogel, F., McAbee, R., Barker, R., & Thurmond, A. J. (1980). Improvement of depression by REM sleep deprivation: New findings and a theory. *Archives of General Psychiatry, 37,* 247–253.

Weinstein, L., Schwartz, D., & Ellman, S. J. (1988). The development of scales to measure the experience of self participation in sleep. *Sleep, 11,* 437–447.

Weinstein, L., Schwartz, D., & Ellman, S. J. (1991). Sleep mentation as affected by REM deprivation: A new look. In S. J. Ellman & J. S. Antrobus (Eds.), *The mind in sleep* (pp. 377–395). New York: Wiley.

Winnicott, D. W. (1960). The theory of the parent-infant relationship. *International Journal of Psycho-Analysis, 41,* 585–595.

Wolf, P. (1966). The causes, controls, and organization of behavior in the neonate. *Psychological Issues,* Monograph 5, 1–104.

17

SOCIAL COGNITION AND SOCIAL AFFECT IN PSYCHOANALYSIS AND COGNITIVE PSYCHOLOGY: FROM REGRESSION ANALYSIS TO ANALYSIS OF REGRESSION

DREW WESTEN

It is tempting to begin a chapter in this book on interactions of cognition, affect, and interpersonal functioning with a statement to the effect that these are exciting times. Indeed, in one sense they are: Intellectually, the gulf between psychoanalysis and the rest of psychology appears narrower than it ever has been. Psychology has rediscovered emotion, and numerous research programs are devoted to the experience, expression, and physiology of affect. In cognitive science, the notion that complex cognitive processing requires conscious attention is all but abandoned. In personality psychology, the major alternative perspective on personality structure, social–cognitive theory, is now concerned with cognitive–affective interactions, unconscious processes, and mental representations of the self and others; major social–cognitive theorists even occasionally cite object–relations theorists (Cantor & Zirkel, 1990; Markus & Cross, 1990). In developmental psychology, attachment research has begun to document links between early experience of relationships and later social adjustment (George & Solomon, 1989; Main, Kaplan, & Cassidy, 1985; Sroufe & Fleeson, 1986; Zeanah & Zeanah, 1989). In clinical psychology, cognitive therapists are beginning to address interpersonal processes (Safran, 1990) and the patient–therapist relationship (Goldfried & Hayes 1989).

If we have learned anything from the behavior therapists, let alone our patients, however, it is that insight and action are not always closely linked. Ironically, research methodologies and theoretical perspectives have evolved in academic psychology that permit a focus on many of the concerns that were once exclusive to psychoanalysis just as the last generation of psychoanalytic psychologists is beginning to retire from psychology departments (and be routed out of psychiatry departments). Psychoanalytic thinking is flourishing in the humanities, but in psychology, the preference for quantity and quickness over quality of research, and the lure of a lucrative private practice over an academic life that rarely approximates the scholarly life of eras past, have virtually shut off the flow of dynamically informed young psychologists into academia. From the perspective of psychoanalysis at psychology's centennial, then, these are the best of times, these are the worst of times.

This chapter tells the tale of two models, psychoanalysis and cognitive psychology, focusing on the understanding of affect and cognition in social functioning.[1] Contemporary psychoanalysis is, in its multiple variants, a theory that focuses on affective and interpersonal processes but that also presupposes notions about cognition. Cognitive psychology is a theory of cognition that has expanded to address questions of cognitive–affective interaction and cognition in the social realm. In this chapter I argue that both approaches need to address a series of untenable assumptions deeply engrained in the respective models and metaphors.

PSYCHOANALYTIC VIEWS OF COGNITION AND AFFECT IN INTERPERSONAL FUNCTIONING

Although ego psychology and object–relations theory at first had somewhat separate trajectories, with ego psychology focusing more on the nature of cognition in development and psychopathology (Hartmann, 1939; Rapaport, 1967), representational processes and cognitive–affective interactions have been a persistent focus of object–relations theories. Jacobson (1964) described the development of representations of self and others and the way disruptions in early differentiation could lead to later disturbances. Sandler and his colleagues (Sandler, 1987; Sandler & Rosenblatt, 1962) described the structure and function of the "representational world" and the interaction of affective and representational processes with a clarity unparalleled in object–relations theories. Bowlby (1969, 1973, 1982) integrated psychoanalytic theory with ethology to provide a recasting of psychoanalytic notions of motivation and object-seeking. Like Sandler, Bowlby focused on interpersonal motivation (in Bowlby's case, attachment), affect as a motivational force, and the role of internal working models or relationship representations in mediating interpersonal behavior and psychopathology.

Mahler, Pine, and Bergman (1975) described the way young children walk a tightrope between relatedness and autonomy and ultimately land on their feet as individuated beings capable of seeing people realistically and investing in relationships despite momentary anger or disappointment. Kernberg (1976, 1984) developed a theory of the normal and pathlogical development of representational structures, arguing for the role of failures in differentiation and integration of representations of self and others in object–relational disturbance. In his view, whereas psychotics fail to differentiate self and others, patients with borderline pathology master that developmental achievement but fail in the next: the ability to integrate representations of different affective valence. Kohut (1971, 1977) proposed a theory of the normal and pathological development of what he called the "self." The Kohutian self is the repository of a person's ambitions and ideals, which regulates a person's strivings, self-esteem, and ways of experiencing other people. Many other theorists have contributed as well to the understanding of the cognitive, affective, and motivational processes that underlie interpersonal functioning in intimate relationships—that is, to the understanding of object relations (for a review, see Greenberg & Mitchell, 1983.)

---

[1]For broader discussions of possible links between psychoanalysis and cognitive science, see Erdelyi, 1985; Horowitz, 1987, 1988; Peterfreund, 1971; Pribram and Gill, 1976; Westen, 1985.

The strengths of psychoanalytic theories in this domain, particularly in comparison with cognitive theories, are numerous. Unconscious processes, affect, motivation, development, and cognitive–affective interaction were built into these theories from the start, rather than grafted onto models based on metaphors from artificial intelligence. Since these theories developed from clinical work with people engaged in meaningful and emotionally significant life situations, psychoanalytic approaches to cognition and emotion in interpersonal functioning have had an obvious ecological validity as well as sophistication in conceptualizing the interaction of complex variables.

Key points on which most theorists agree and which will likely be building blocks for any integrated approach to the role of affect and cognition in social functioning include the following:

1. Affective and cognitive processes can occur unconsciously, and these unconscious processes influence behavior.

2. Representations are almost always, if not always affective as well as cognitive. People think about things that are meaningful to them, that is, objects of their needs, interests, wishes, and fears, so that very few representations are likely to be neutral. Most representations are ambivalent, that is, include both positive and negative affective features.

3. Developmentally, representations of the self and others are initially poorly differentiated from each other, minimally integrated and transitory, unidimensional, and dominated by affect.

4. Many, if not most, cognitive representations of the self and others are motiviated, that is, reflect compromises among various wishes, fears, and defenses (see Brenner, 1982).

5. Thought, feeling, and behavior can be strongly influenced by, wished for, feared, and fantasied representations of the self, others, and relationships.

6. Adult cognitive structures about the self, others, and relationships have a long history and must always be understood in their developmental context.

7. Pathological representational processes at different developmental junctures play a key role in various forms of psychopathology.

PROBLEMATIC ASSUMPTIONS OF PSYCHOANALYTIC THEORIES OF COGNITION AND AFFECT IN SOCIAL FUNCTIONING

Despite a number of important strengths, psychoanalytic theorizing in this domain suffers from several problems, including a series of assumptions that are in certain respects problematic in the light of empirical data. Following, I describe briefly these assumptions and some of their difficulties; elsewhere (Westen, 1989, 1990a, 1990b, 1991a, 1992) I have described these issues and some of the relevant empirical evidence in more detail (as well as similar difficulties in cognitive models), as have others (Holt, 1985; Lichtenberg, 1981; Peterfreund, 1978; Stern, 1985). One should note, as well, that the disarray characterizing much of the psychoanalytic literature on affect and drive (and their interaction) render the psychoanalytic treatment of interpersonal affect and motivation more problematic still.

1. *A continuum of development is isomorphic with a continuum of pathology.* The object relations of patients with a borderline level of personality organization are often described as

"primitive," but our language, and its underlying assumptions, has prevented us from discriminating two very different meanings of primitive: primitive as developmentally early and primitive as grossly pathological. The direct mapping of level of personality disturbance from the borderline to the neurotic range onto a developmental timetable of preoedipal to oedipal has been useful heuristically but now needs to be reconsidered as a global theory of pathological object relations. Some aspects of the pathological object relations of character-disordered patients do appear to reflect developmental arrests, but others, such as malevolent expectations of relationships in borderline patients, are off the beaten track of normal development (for empirical evidence, see Westen, Lohr, Silk, Gold, & Kerber, 1990). Issues become even more complex when one places psychosis and psychotic forms of personality organization on the same continuum, since psychosis may not fit a developmental model at all (see Willick, 1990).

2. *The origin of severe character pathology lies in the first 3 years of life.* In many cases this hypothesis is likely to be correct, but it is a very difficult assumption to evaluate because the same child and the same caretakers typically interact, often in manifestly pathological ways, well beyond the preoedipal years. Unempathic preoedipal mothers are often unempathic oedipal and latency mothers, and one cannot simply assume that the damage is done only or primarily during a critical period, or that good-enough parenting during the latency years could not substantially alter an incipient disordered character structure. Biological abnormalities, and the fears, fantasies, wishes, and expectations resulting from the severe sexual abuse (often in latency) that has been found in the developmental histories of a substantial proportion of borderline subjects in several recent studies (Herman, Perry, & van der Kolk, 1989; Ogata et al., 1990; Westen, Ludolph, Misle, Ruffins, & Block, 1990; Zanarini, Gunderson, Marino, Schwartz, & Frankenberg, 1989) are likely implicated in many cases of severe object relations disturbance as well.

3. *Certain phenomena indicative of severe character pathology (such as splitting, poorly integrated self-structure, and narcissism) are normatively transcended by the oedipal period.* Several researchers have challenged many aspects of the psychoanalytic account of infancy on empirical grounds (e.g., Horner, 1985; Lichtenberg, 1981; Peterfreund, 1978; Stern, 1985). Less well known is a body of literature in developmental psychology on the development of social cognition that has examined phenomena such as the development of representations of self and others in childhood and adolescence. By and large, research on the development of children's conceptions of friendship, morality, authority, the self, and significant others supports basic psychoanalytic assertions about the development of object relations—such as the view that representations become more differentiated, complex, integrated, and inclusive of subrepresentations with opposing affective valence—but suggests considerable revisions in the relevant timetables. Self-serving modes of relatedness, a tendency to split representations, and an inability to form cohesive and multidimensional representations of the self and objects persist throughout much of childhood and are not specifically associated with the preoedipal period. If this is the case, theories of borderline object relations that link such phenomena in pathological adults to developmental disturbances in the preoedipal period are highly problematic. Many of the phenomena we call preoedipal in character-disordered adults are normatively preadolescent.

4. *Object relations refers to a unitary phenomenon or developmental line.* Diagnosis of a patient's global level of object-relational capacity is clinically useful, but, both clinically and theoretically, this heuristic may lead to a failure to consider several interdependent but distinct phenomena and developmental lines subsumed under the rubric of object relations. In concrete terms, "object relations" refers to the enduring cognitive, affective, motivational, and behavioral processes underlying interpersonal functioning in close relationships. As such, it includes self- and object-representations, understanding of social causality (that is, what causes people to think, feel, and act as they do), capacity for mature cathexis or emotional investment in the self and others, capacity to take the perspectives of others, self-observation, superego development,

empathy, interpersonal wishes, dominant interpersonal concerns and conflicts (such as struggles around trust or autonomy), and affective quality of the object world. These are distinct developmental lines, and there is no reason to assume that a patient's level of maturity in one is a good predictor of maturity or developmental level in another.

5. *Object–relational stages are culturally invariant.* When theorists write about the subjective experience of "the toddler" or "the oedipal age child," they seldom consider the role of cultural factors, such as whether the toddler has spent much of his or her life tied to the mother's back while she works in the field, or whether the oedipal-age child is developing in a society that places a premium on autonomy and individuation. In most cultures in human history, self, for example, has been understood in its social context, not as a property of individuals (see Roland, 1988; Shweder & Bourne, 1984; Westen, 1985, 1992).

6. *Clinical data from pathological adults are necessary and largely sufficient for constructing and evaluating theories of object relations.* When psychoanalytic theorists offer theories of normal development, they do so almost exclusively from their work with adults. Seldom do analytic theorists cite any child observation other than Mahler's work, which is one of hundreds of relevant sources. The purpose of proposing theories of normal object-relational development is to locate the junctures at which things have gone wrong with personality-disordered patients. This procedure is only valid to the extent that one assumes what one must first document empirically, that pathology and development occupy exactly the same continuum.

7. *Motivational explanations are to be preferred over cognitive explanations.* Psychoanalytic theorists typically prefer motivational to cognitive or social learning explanations as a matter of course. If a borderline patient has malevolent representations, this is viewed as a projection of aggressive impulses. An alternative explanation that must at least be considered is that a borderline patient may have malevolent representations because he or she was abused as a child or had so much difficulty regulating affects that minor parental failures were experienced as abandonments or deliberate injuries. In reality, cognitive–social learning and motivational processes typically interact, as when children who are abused not only expect abuse because they have experienced it but also become rageful, project that rage onto others, and consequently elicit precisely what they expect. The use of concepts such as "projection" needs to be carefully examined in specific instances to determine the extent to which a motivational process is really operative (seeing something in someone else instead of in oneself to avoid a feared self-representation and consequent aversive affect) rather than a schematic process (seeing something in someone else because one has observed or inferred that in significant others, generalized it, and become sensitized to anything that might resemble it).

8. *Intrapsychic mechanisms are to be preferred over interpersonal mechanisms in explaining psychopathology.* Systems theorists generally skirt the question of why people repeat pathological family processes in the systems into which they voluntarily enter as adults, which requires intrapsychic motivational and cognitive explanations. Psychoanalytic theorists, by contrast, often fail to examine the interpersonal processes that maintain and exacerbate dynamically instigated patterns (Wachtel, 1987). In the rageful borderline patient, for example, a key link in the maintenance of the pathology may be that the patient projects his or her own aggresssion and expects aggression from significant others, which in turn produces hostility and abandonment. These interpersonal reactions then confirm dysfunctioanl relationship representations and hence make the patient more wary of anyone (such as a therapist) who does not appear to fit the pattern. Research by Swann (1989) documents the lengths to which people will go to get others to confirm their views of themselves, even negative views. Similarly, as Wachtel (1977, 1987) argues, interpersonal avoidance patterns (as in socially phobic or schizoidal patients) will rarely extinguish spontaneously because to escape anxiety the person avoids potentially frightening interpersonal experiences that could disconfirm the expectation.

9. *Social motivation must be understood as either libidinal or object-relational.* A chronic tension in psychoanalysis since the emergence of object relations theories has been, as Fairbairn (1954) put it, between those who view people as pleasure-seeking versus those who view people as object-seeking. In other words, some theorists consider the tendency to enter into relationships a primary motivation *sui generis*, whereas others see social motivation as derivative of the sexual drive. This is actually a false antinomy, based on Freud's confounding of a theory of pleasure-seeking with a theory of sexual pleasure-seeking, both of which are called "libidinal" (see Westen, 1990b). Social object-seeking and libidinal object-seeking are both mediated by affect, that is, by the desire for pleasurable, and avoidance of unpleasurable, feelings. Proximity-seeking behavior in infants (and adults) can be instigated by separation distress (Bowlby, 1969), just as sexual behavior can be instigated by lust or affect-laden fantasies. In both cases an underlying system of needs, partially learned and partially innate, gives rise to feelings; these feelings motivate, and are in turn modulated, by behavior as well as by intrapsychic mechanisms. Just as sexual fantasies become linked to motivation through the affects they engender, representations of "being held by mother" become motivationally significant through repeated associative link-ages of those representations with pleasure or reduction of distress, producing a wish that is both instinctively and environmentally determined.

INFORMATION-PROCESSING VIEWS OF COGNITION AND AFFECT IN SOCIAL FUNCTIONING

As the cognitive revolution gradually deposed the behaviorist regime over the past 2 decades, cognitive methods and metaphors have come to dominate nearly every area of psychology. The study of social functioning is no exception, with much of contemporary social psychology thoroughly cognitive (Markus & Zajonc, 1985). The field of social cognition, now one of the major research domains in social psychology, has applied concepts and methods from cognitive science to the understanding of social thinking and cognitive–affective interaction (for a review, see Higgins & Bargh, 1987).

The metaphor underlying the cognitive or information-processing approach to social cognition and affect is the computer: The mind, like the computer, is an information-processing machine that transforms environmental inputs into codeable units that can be stored, brought on line, transformed, and manipulated to produce useful output. Typical methods imported to social cognition research from cognitive science include asking subjects to memorize paragraphs, traits, vignettes, or word pairs; manipulating variables such as prior or subsequent information, order of information presented, or interval between encoding and retrieval; and assessing the impact of various manipulations on dependent variables such as reaction time or the quantity or type of information retrieved.

Two recent developments in the social–cognitive literature should be of particular interest to psychoanalytic psychologists. The first is a growing interest in unconscious processes. Al-though, as will be discussed later, the "cognitive unconscious" (Kihlstrom, 1987) is only a fraction of the Freudian descriptive unconscious and excludes entirely the dynamic unconscious, research on unconscious information processing has been methodologically creative and in many respects illuminating (see Bowers & Meichenbaum, 1984; Lewicki, 1986; Nisbett & Wilson, 1977; Uleman & Bargh, 1989). Research by Higgins, Bargh, and colleagues (see Bargh, 1989; Higgins, 1990; Higgins & Bargh, 1987), for example, demonstrates the impact of momentarily and chronically activated schemata or constructs on ongoing social information processing. Exposing subjects subliminally or supraliminally to a word like "lazy" will make them more likely to use that construct in assessing or describing people in an unrelated task because the construct has been primed; this occurs even though the person is unaware of the activation of the schema. Chronically activated schemata have been shown to operate similarly: A person who is characterologically "primed" to see people as lazy or to evaluate people on this dimension is likely to have such judgments operate even when they are inappropriate or distracting. In essence, research on chronic schema accessibility has confirmed the projective hypothesis, that in ambiguous situations enduring interests, concerns, needs, and ways of experiencing reality are likely to be expressed.

A second area of research of considerable interest from a psychoanalytic perspective is on cognitive–affective interactions. Most of these investigations focus on the way emotion or mood influences memory and judgment (see Gilligan & Bower, 1984; Isen, 1984). For example, if a person is encoding information about a character from a vignette after induction of a positive mood, he or she is likely to elaborate or focus more on positive attributes, leading to superior recall for positive aspects of the character on retrieval. Mood at retrieval also influences information processing: Subjects in a happy mood are more likely to remember positive childhood memories or positive words presented in a word list a week earlier, to think flexibly, and to anticipate positive events in the future. These findings are less robust with negative affects, apparently because the automatic information processing effect that maximizes congruence between mood and cognitive contents encoded or retrieved is counterbalanced by an affect-regulatory process that preferentially selects positive information (in most subjects) in order to avoid distress.

Cognitive models of social cognition and social affect have several strengths: (a) They are grounded in replicable and carefully designed empirical investigtions. (b) They attend to specific mechanisms rather than to broad constucts that cannot be operationalized and hence are seldom refined (i.e., social–cognitive investigators have systematically examined the effects of affect on encoding, retrieval, decision making, judgment, and problem solving). They have also delineated several distinct types of unconscious processes (Bargh, 1989). (c) They have applied relevant cognitive notions of categorization, hierarchical storage of information, schemata, and priming to the processing of information about social objects.

PROBLEMATIC ASSUMPTIONS OF SOCIAL–COGNITIVE THEORIES OF COGNITION AND AFFECT IN SOCIAL FUNCTIONING

Despite these strengths, which tend to correspond to deficiencies of psychoanalytic models, cognitive approaches are problematic in a number of respects. The cognitive model evolved for 20 years before anyone began to raise questions about where consciousness, affect, and motivatation fit in. The attempt to graft these domains of functioning onto a model based on a computer metaphor has, not surprisingly, led to what often looks like skin grafts pasted onto an inanimate object.

1. *The treatment of consciousness is inadequate.* Consciousness in cognitive science was for years largely equated with "working memory," that is, with informational units currently active and being manipulated "on line." The obvious problem with this conceptualization is that many more ideas, images, and memories are active at any time than can possibly be conscious. The expanding literature on unconscious information processing allows for active unconscious processes, accepting the proposition that most cognition is unconscious and that what becomes conscious are the products of processes that are not, by and large, accessible to consciousness. Indeed, parallel distributed processing (PDP) models in cognitive science (Rumelhart, Mc-Clelland, et al., 1984) assert that processing occurs in parallel, with the simultaneous activation of multiple neural networks leading ultimately to a unified conscious experience. This conscious

experience may or may not be necessary for the regulation of behavior in various situations. These models can account for phenomena that can only be convincingly explained using a model in which both bottom-up and top-down processes occur simultaneously. For example, when a person is reading the words "stop rape" scrawled in chalk on the subway wall, in which the straight part of the letter "p" has eroded away, letter representations that include a round part are activated (e.g., b, p, and d) simultaneously with representations of words of the form "ra_e" and slogans of the form "stop ____." Activation from representations at each of these levels spreads to compatible representations at the other levels and inhibits processing of letters, words, or slogans that are incompatible with the parameters at each level. The person seemingly effortlessly reads the phrase correctly despite its imperfect presentation, and the message may influence later thoughts through a priming effect even if the person does not consciously notice it.

This kind of parallel processing model is certainly compatible with psychoanalytic ideas about the way multiple and potentially conflicting mental processes can be activated simultaneously and generate conscious experience. Social cognition researchers, however, have continued to use words like "activation" and "working memory" to describe cognitive processes without specifying whether these words refer to conscious or preconscious cognitive processes and contents, and have by and large ignored the implications of parallel processing models for affect and motivation. Instead, they apply notions of parallel and unconscious processing to cognition but posit serial processing models of motivation, in which goals come in and out of consciousness one at a time to direct behavior.

A striking example is provided by a recent collection of chapters on unconscious social information processing (Uleman & Bargh, 1989). The name of the book, *Unintended Thought*, reflects an assumption that people can only intend consciously, which is particularly peculiar in light of one of the editors' very impressive arguments against assuming that attention, awareness, intention, and control always co-occur and distinguish automatic from nonautomatic thought. Bargh (1989) in his chapter carefully delineates different kinds of unconscious cognitive processes, describing some that are initiated by conscious goals; however, he never reflects on whether consciously active goals could have been elicited or synthesized unconsciously, how goals are selected for conscious attention in the first place, or why a stage of consciousness is so crucial for motives when it does not appear so necessary for cognition. Psychoanalytic ideas are only mentioned five times in the entire volume, and usually with a brief disclaimer that "this is very different from the Freudian notion of 'unconscious' . . ." (Bargh, 1989, p. 26). Given the accessibility of psychoanalytic writing and the substantial basis now even in *experimental* work for the existence of unconscious motivational and affective processes (see LeDoux, 1989; McClelland, Koestner, & Weinberger, 1989; Westen, 1990b), the fact that a book on unconscious processes such as this could be crafted without considering or citing what clinicians have been writing about for 100 years is probably as impressive an empirical demonstration of the existence of unconscious motivation as one could desire. Indeed, it exemplifies the point made by object–relations theorists that behavior can be influenced by feared and wished-for representations because so much of the avoidance of psychoanalytic ideas in this literature probably reflects a fear of being associated with a tradition that was totally vilified throughout the training of most of these researchers, beginning with condescending and usually grossly inaccurate coverage of psychoanalysis in introductory psychology classes.

2. *The understanding of affect and motivation is inadequate.* As suggested earlier, motivation and affect were transplanted to social–cognitive models quite recently, and the new organs have often been rejected. Motivational constructs have remained simplistic, with people seen as pursuing only conscious and rational life tasks, goals, or personal projects; the implicit model for these analyses is the idealized academic life, without the intrigue, politics, and neurotic foibles

that always seem to accompany this noble pursuit of knowledge. One could also read much of the social–cognitive literature on affect without ever knowning that people *feel*, and that emotion is not just another node in a network but is in fact a powerful motivator. Once again the problem lies in the computer metaphor: How does one program a computer to model what it feels like to experience guilt or to grieve for the loss of a loved one?

3. *Defensive processes are left unexplained.* Although social–cognitive researchers know of self-serving biases such as tendencies to view oneself positively (Greenwald & Pratkanis, 1984; Taylor & Brown, 1988), which imply defensive functioning, their formal models cannot account for them. Self-serving biases are sometimes studied in the social–cognitive literature, but nowhere are they explained, probably because this would require examination of the notion that cognitions cannot be accepted at face value and can be motivated. This would undermine both the computer metaphor and the form of data most congenial to many researchers—self-report— that relies on the assumption that people can and will largely report on their attributes accurately. The failure to incorporate defensive processes into cognitive models is particularly problematic when considering clinical material. For example, narcissistic patients are usually at their most grandiose when they are feeling most deflated; both grandiose and deflated representations are active in "working memory," even though only the former are conscious. Only an explicit theory of defense can explain the relation between activated unconscious representations that generate the conscious experience of their opposites.

4. *Cognitive theories assume a preference for cognitive over motivational explanations.* In this respect cognitive science and psychoanalysis are mirror images of each other. The extent to which social psychologists, for example, search for cognitive explanations for obviously motivated processes is as perplexing as the failure for years of theorists of borderline personality disorder to consider the possibility that malevolent representations may in part reflect a history of abuse (see Nigg et al., in press; Westen, Ludolph, Block, Wixom, & Wiss, 1990). Contributors to the literature on self-serving biases often perform the most astounding intellectual acrobatics to explain away the obvious fact that people see themselves more positively than reality supports because to do otherwise would be unpleasant. By contrast, the fact that many depressed people repeatedly prefer to view themselves negatively is unlikely to reflect the simple unmotivated automatic information processing that most cognitive theorists propose, because thinking negative thoughts about oneself is so aversive that the act of doing so would readily be conditioned away were the person not motivated to do so. An alternative explanation would suggest that negative representations of the self are compromise formations—motivated cognitive processes— that at one point in a person's developmental history may not only have appeared accurate to the child but may also have seemed to be the best available solution to a dilemma. For example, seeing oneself as a failure may beat someone else to the punch, deactivate or temper potential wishes that one expects will not come true, allow identification with a parent who is perceived as critical, assuage guilt at being happier or more successful than a depressed or somehow inadequate parent, or allow a sense of virtuousness in the face of one's misdeeds.

5. *Seldom do social–cognitive accounts demonstrate a link between cognitive processes and meaningful social behavior.* To date, most research in social cognition has demonstrated few links to social behavior, raising considerable questions about ecological validity. Usually the only behavior measured is the same behavior that serves as an index of the occurrence of some cognitive process.

6. *Social–cognitive models are largely inapplicable to complex representational processes that are the norm outside the laboratory.* Methodologically, experimental researchers who ignore clinical theory and discount clinical observation assume that a molecular approach can eventually generalize to a molar view (i.e., by examining hundreds of pieces of a puzzle, one will eventually get the big picture). In the field of social cognition, experimentalists have thus assumed that if

they start with relatively trivial events that can be managed in a brief experimental session with a college freshman, such as presenting subjects with lists of trait adjectives or three-sentence vignettes about a fictional character, then what they learn from dozens of these studies will generalize to the way people think about people more generally. My guess is that this is a bad strategy. Experimental evidence is beginning to accumulate to suggest that information processing about acquaintances and people who a person does not know well may have little resemblance to information processing about significant others (Andersen & Cole, in press; Leigh, Westen, Barends, & Mendel, in press). Perhaps more importantly, one observes numerous properties of social cognition with significant others clinically and in meaningful social interactions that one simply does not observe in a laboratory, and to the extent that models are generated from laboratory experience, these models will be misleading.

For example, social–cognitive models now often assume that a schema can be "tagged" with affect of one valence or another; however, matters are for more complex. A person's schema of her or his mother, for example, may include dozens of specific and generalized representations, which may not only have conflicting affective qualities among them but also within them. These encoded affective valuations will influence information processing and behavior in complex and interactive ways. An everyday event, in which a mother and her adult daughter are at a dinner party together, serves as a simple example. Suppose the mother responds inappropriately to some question or comment in a way that is relatively obvious but not altogether unusual for her. For the daughter, this may simultaneously activate an experience of shame that she tries to defend against by denying the inappropriateness of her mother's remark as well as anger and sadness at her mother's inappropriateness that has associative links to many similar experiences in the past. The representation of her mother's inappropriateness may in turn be associated with guilt and remorse for devaluing and feeling superior to the mother, as well as pride and oedipal enjoyment of the perceived superiority. The resulting conscious representation of the social situation may be that "people were just angry because my mother was saying what other people think and don't say," with a corresponding effort to come to the mother's defense. The anger at the mother is thus deflected onto other people and projected onto them, the representation of the mother is left relatively untarnished (and is in fact exalted), and the shame and guilt are overridden by a conscious experience of anger at everyone but the mother. This leads as well to a representation of self as "coming to the aid of the downtrodden" that could potentially be a chronically activated schema for other reasons as well.

What is crucial about this example is that it is *commonplace*, yet it is beyond what any current social–cognitive model could accommodate. It relies heavily on cognitive notions such as spreading activation, parallel processing, and construct accessibility, but it builds in from the start the idea that what leads a representation to become conscious includes both affective–motivational and more strictly cognitive, often automatic processes. It also does not assume that the representation that becomes conscious is the one that receives the most activation, because a strongly activated representation may be too painful to acknowledge and may thus leave its mark through a defensively transformed derivative. What determined the nature of the conscious representations of mother, the self, and the episode in this example, as in many in real life, is a combination of amount of activation, efforts to regulate aversive affect, and efforts to perceive the situation relatively accurately, most of which are unconscious.

7. *Cognitive models do not account adequately for the role of culture in shaping information processing about the self and others.* In this respect the computer metaphor again has led researchers astray: Computers do not have families, tribes, or nations, so their thought processes are not constrained or influenced by cultural or familiar patterns of thought and feeling, often described by anthropologists with terms such as ethos, eidos, world view, value systems, belief

systems, and so forth. People are not individual information processing systems independent of one another; cultural constructions of the self, personality, and the like shape the way schemata and attributional processes develop.

CONCLUSION

Having traced the tale of two models, perhaps it is to be expected that some heads would roll. The psychoanalytic and cognitive models of social cognition and social affect each have features that lead both to psychological understanding and to blind alleys. As should be clear, simply integrating the two models is not likely to be a productive strategy because the integration of two faulty models will probably produce a bigger, faultier one. Perhaps even more problematic is the disinclination many cognitive psychologists have for psychoanalytic thinking and clinical data and the corresponding disinterest in cognition and experimental data among many psychoanalytic psychologists.

Where, then, does one go from here? The path to developing a more comprehensive theory of social cognition and social affect that draws on the obvious virtues of these two approaches must begin in two places: from a thorough understanding of the assumptions of each approach and their limits, and from an examination of concepts that the two approaches share (such as associational networks, parallel processing, certain ideas about mental representation, spreading activation, and some forms of automaticity involving automatic activation or priming of associatively linked representational units). Some integrative efforts of this sort have already begun to appear (Epstein, 1990; Horowitz, 1987, 1988; Singer & Salovey, 1991; Westen, 1985, 1988, 1990a, 1990b, 1991a, 1992). Such models will need to describe interactions of associative processes with efforts to regulate feeling-states through manipulation of representations and their consciousness.

Any efforts at integration will also need to respect the validity, and understand the parameters for utility of both experimental and clinical data. As psychology enters its second century, perhaps the most important task ahead is the development of a philosophy of science that allows some rapprochement between experimentalists and clinicians, whose philosophical and methodological differences are typically little more than rationalizations of characterological dispositions toward styles of thinking and objects of thought (i.e., atomism vs. holism, prediction and control vs. interpretation, empiricism vs. rationalism, reason vs. passion, and a host of other antinomies that predate psychology by at least 2 millenia). Short of that, we are likely to witness the continued erosion of psychoanalytic thinking in the academies, the appropriation of eviscerated pseudoanalytic concepts by patchwork cognitive models, and the training of competent clinicians (who will have minimal appreciation for research) only in the professional schools. It would be a far, far better thing to keep one eye on cognition, one on affect, motivation, and psychodynamics, and to stop severing the hemispheres so we can get a more integrated picture.

REFERENCES

Andersen, S. M., & Cole, S. W. (in press). "Do I know you?": The role of significant others in general social perception. *Journal of Personality and Social Psychology.*

Bargh, J. A. (1989). Conditional automaticity: Varieties of automatic influence in social perception and cognition. In J. S. Uleman & J. A. Bargh (Eds.), *Unintended thought* (pp. 3–51). New York: Guilford Press.

Bowers, K., & Meichenbaum, D. (Eds.). (1984). *The unconscious reconsidered.* New York: Wiley.

Bowlby, J. (1969). *Attachment and loss: Vol. 1. Attachment.* New York: Basic Books.

Bowlby, J. (1973). *Attachment and loss: Vol. 2. Separation.* New York: Basic Books.

Bowlby, J. (1982). Attachment and loss: Retrospect and prospect. *American Journal of Orthopsychiatry, 52,* 664–678.

Brenner, C. (1982). *The mind in conflict.* Madison, CT: International Universities Press.

Cantor, N., & Zirkel, S. (1990). Personality, cognition, and purposive behavior. In L. A. Pervin (Ed.), *Handbook of personality: Theory and research* (pp. 135–164). New York: Guilford Press.

Epstein, S. (1990). Cognitive-experimental self-theory. In L. A. Pervin (Ed.), *Handbook of personality: Theory and research* (pp. 165–192). New York: Guilford Press.

Erdelyi, M. (1985). *Psychoanalysis: Freud's cognitive psychology.* San Francisco: Freeman.

Fairbairn, W. R. D. (1954). *An object-relations theory of the personality.* New York: Basic Books.

George, C., & Solomon, J. (1989). Internal working models of caregiving and security of attachment at age six. *Infant Mental Health Journal, 10, 222–237.*

Gilligan, S. G., & Bower, G. H. (1984). Cognitive consequences of emotional arousal. In C. E. Izard, J. Kagan, & R. H. Zajonc (Eds.), *Emotions, cognition, and behavior* (pp. 547–588). New York: Cambridge University Press.

Goldfried, M., & Hayes, A. (1989). Can contributions from other orientations complement behavior therapy? *Behavior Therapist, 12,* 57–60.

Greenberg, J. R., & Mitchell, S. A. (1983). *Object relations in psychoanalytic theory.* Cambridge, MA: Harvard University Press.

Greenwald, A. G., & Pratkanis, A. R. (1984). The self. In R. S. Wyer & T. K. Srull (Eds.), *Handbook of social cognition* (Vol. 3, pp. 129–178). Hillsdale, NJ: Erlbaum.

Hartmann, H. (1939). *Ego psychology and the problem of adaptation.* Madison, CT: International Universities Press.

Herman, J., Perry, J. C., & van der Kolk, B. A. (1989). Childhood trauma in borderline personality disorder. *American Journal of Psychiatry, 146,* 490–495.

Higgins, E. T. (1990). Personality, social psychology, and person–situation relations: Standards and knowledge activism as a common language. In L. A. Pervin (Ed.), *Handbook of personality: Theory and research* (pp. 301–338). New York: Guilford Press.

Higgins, E. T., & Bargh, J. A. (1987). Social cognition and social perception. *Annual Review of Psychology, 38,* 369–425.

Holt, R. R. (1985). The current status of psychoanalytic theory. *Psychoanalytic Psychology, 2,* 289–315.

Horner, T. (1985). The psychic life of the young infant: Review and critique of the psychoanalytic concepts of symbiosis and infantile omnipotence. *American Journal of Orthopsychiatry, 55,* 324–343.

Horowitz, M. J. (1987). *States of mind: Configurational analysis of individual psychology* (2nd ed.). New York: Plenum Press.

Horowitz, M. (1988). *Introduction to psychodynamics: A synthesis.* New York: Basic Books.

Isen, A. M. (1984). Toward understanding the role of affect in cognition. In R. S. Wyer, Jr., & T. K. Srull (Eds.), *Handbook of social cognition* (Vol. 3, pp. 179–236). Hillsdale, NJ: Erlbaum.

Jacobson, E. (1964). *The self and the object world.* Madison, CT: International Universities Press.

Kernberg, O. (1976). *Object relations theory and clinical psychoanalysis.* Northvale, NJ: Jason Aronson.

Kernberg, O. (1984). *Severe personality disorders: Psychotherapeutic strategies.* New Haven, CT: Yale University Press.

Kihlstrom, J. F. (1987). The cognitive unconscious. *Science, 237,* 1445–1452.

Kohut, H. (1971). *The analysis of the self: A systematic approach to the treatment of narcissistic personality disorders*. Madison, CT: International Universities Press.

Kohut, H. (1977). *The restoration of the self*. Madison, CT: International Universities Press.

LeDoux, J. E. (1989). Cognitive–emotional interactions in the brain. *Cognition and Emotion, 3*, 267–289.

Leigh, J., Westen, D., Barends, A., & Mendel, M. (in press). Assessing complexity of representations of people from TAT and interview data. *Journal of Personality*.

Lewicki, P. (1986). *Nonconscious social information processing*. New York: Academic Press.

Lichtenberg, J. D. (1981). Implications for psychoanalytic theory of research on the neonate. *International Review of Psycho-Analysis, 8*, 35–52.

Mahler, M., Pine, F., & Bergman, A. (1975). *The psychological birth of the human infant: Symbiosis and individuation*. New York: Basic Books.

Main, M., Kaplan, N., & Cassidy, J. (1985). Security in infancy, childhood, and adulthood: A move to the level of representation. *Monographs of the Society for Research in Child Development, 50*(1–2).

Markus, H., & Cross, S. (1990). The interpersonal self. In L. Pervin (Ed.), *Handbook of personality: Theory and research* (pp. 576–608). New York: Guilford Press.

Markus, H., & Zajonc, R. (1985). The cognitive perspective in social psychology. In G. Lindzey & E. Aronson (Eds.), *Handbook of social psychology* (3rd ed., pp. 137–320).

McClelland, D. C., Koestner, R., & Weinberger, J. (1989). How do self-attributed and implicit motives differ? *Psychological Review, 96*, 690–702.

Nigg, J. T., Silk, K. R., Westen, D., Lohr, N. E., Gold, L. J., Ogata, S., & Goodrich, S. (1991). Object representations in the early memories of sexually abused borderline patients. *American Journal of Psychiatry, 148*, 864–869.

Nisbett, R., & Wilson, T. (1977). Telling more than we can know: Verbal reports on mental processes. *Psychological Review, 84*, 250–256.

Ogata, S., Silk, K. R., Goodrich, S., Lohr, N. E., Westen, D., & Hill, E. (1990). Childhood abuse and clinical symptoms in borderline personality disorder. *American Journal of Psychiatry, 147*, 1008–1013.

Peterfreund, E. (1971). Information, systems, and psychoanalyses: An evolutionary biological approach to psychoanalytic theory. *Psychological Issues* (Monograph No. 25–26.).

Peterfreund, E. (1978). Some critical comments on the psychoanalytic conceptualization of infancy. *International Journal of Psychoanalysis, 59*, 427–441.

Pribram, K. H., & Gill, M. M. (1976). *Freud's "Project" reassessed: Preface to contemporary cognitive theory and neuropsychology*. New York: Basic Books.

Rapaport, D. (1967). The scientific methodology of psychoanalysis. In M. Gill (Ed.), *The collected papers of David Rapaport*. New York: Basic Books.

Robbins, M. (1989). Private personality organization as an interpersonally adaptive modification of cognition and affect. *International Journal of Psycho-Analysis, 70*, 443–459.

Roland, A. (1988). *In search of self in India and Japan: Toward a cross-cultural psychology*. Princeton, NJ: Princeton University Press.

Rumelhart, D. E., McClelland, J. L., & the PDP Research Group. (1986). *Parallel distribution processing: Explorations in the microstructures of cognition* (2 vols.). Cambridge, MA: MIT Press.

Safran, J. (1990). Toward a refinement of cognitive therapy in light of interpersonal theory: I. Theory. *Clinical Psychology Review, 10*, 87–105.

Sandler, J. (1987). *From safety to the superego: Selected papers of Joseph Sandler*. New York: Guilford Press.

Sandler, J., & Rosenblatt, B. (1962). The concept of the representational world. *Psychoanalytic Study of the Child, 17*, 128–145.

Shweder, R. A., & Bourne, E. J. (1984). Does the concept of the person vary cross-culturally? In R. A. Shweder & R. LeVine (Eds.), *Culture theory: Essays on mind, self, and emotion* (pp. 158–199). New York: Cambridge University Press.

Singer, J., & Salovey, D. (1991). Organized knowledge structures and personality: Person schemas, self-schemas, prototypes, and scripts. In M. Horowitz (Ed.), *Person schemas and recurrent maladaptive interpersonal patterns.* Chicago: University of Chicago Press.

Sroufe, L. A., & Fleeson, J. (1986). Attachment and the construction of relationships. In W. W. Hartup & Z. Rubin (Eds.), *Relationships and development.* Hillsdale, NJ: Erlbaum.

Stern, D. N. (1985). *The interpersonal world of the infant: A view from psychoanalysis and developmental psychology.* New York: Basic Books.

Swann, W. B. (1989). Identity negotiation: Where two roads meet. *Journal of Personality and Social Psychology, 53,* 1038–1051.

Taylor, S. E., & Brown, J. D. (1988). Illusion and well-being: A social psychological perspective on mental health. *Psychological Bulletin, 103,* 193–210.

Uleman, J. S., & Bargh, J. A. (1989). *Unintended thought.* New York: Guilford Press.

Wachtel, P. (1977). *Psychoanalysis and behavior therapy: Toward an integration.* New York: Basic Books.

Wachtel, P. (1987). *Action and insight.* New York: Guilford Press.

Westen, D. (1985). *Self and society: Narcissism, collectivism, and the development of morals.* New York: Cambridge University Press.

Westen, D. (1988). Transference and information processing. *Clinical Psychology Review, 8,* 161–179.

Westen, D. (1989). Are "primitive" object relations really preoedipal? *American Journal of Orthopsychiatry, 59,* 331–345.

Westen, D. (1990a). Psychoanalytic approaches to personality. In L. Pervin (Ed.), *Handbook of personality: Theory and research* (pp. 21–65). New York: Guilford Press.

Westen, D. (1990b). The relations among narcissism, egocentrism, self-concept, and self-esteem. *Psychoanalysis and Contemporeary Thought, 13,* 185–241.

Westen, D. (1991a). Social cognition and object relations. *Psychological Bulletin, 109,* 429–455.

Westen, D. (1991b). Toward a revised theory of borderline object relations: Implications of empirical research. *International Journal of Psycho-Analysis, 71,* 661–666.

Westen, D. (1992). The cognitive self and the psychoanalytic self: Can we put ourselves together? *Psychological Inquiry, 3,* 1–13.

Westen, D., Lohr, N., Silk, K., Gold, L., & Kerber, K. (1990). Object relations and social cognition in borderlines, major depressives, and normals: A TAT analysis. *Psychological Assessment: A Journal of Consulting and Clinical Psychology, 2,* 355–364.

Westen, D., Ludolph, P., Block, J., Wixom, J., Wiss, F. C. (1990). Developmental history and object relations in psychiatrically disturbed adolescent girls. *American Journal of Psychiatry, 147,* 1061–1068.

Westen, D., Ludolph, P., Misle, B., Ruffins, S., & Block, M. J. (1990). Physical and sexual abuse in female adolescents with borderline personality disorder. *American Journal of Orthopsychiatry, 60,* 55–66.

Willick, M. S. (1990). Psychoanalytic concepts of the etiology of severe mental illness. *Journal of the American Psychoanalytic Association, 38,* 1049–1081.

Zanarini, M. C., Gunderson, J. G., Marino, M. F., Schwartz, E. D., & Frankenburg, F. R. (1989). Childhood experiences of borderline patients. *Comprehensive Psychiatry, 30,* 18–25.

Zeanah, C. H., & Zeanah, P. D. (1989). Intergenerational transmission of maltreatment: Insights from attachment theory and research. *Psychiatry, 52,* 177–196.

IV

PSYCHOPATHOLOGY: CLINICAL AND EXPERIMENTAL RESEARCH

INTRODUCTION: PSYCHOANALYSIS AND PSYCHOPATHOLOGY

If Freud's psychology can be characterized as the era of the Oedipus complex based on the unconscious conflicts of the young boy, the current dominant psychoanalytic theoretical prototype is the experiential qualities of the mother–child dyad and their impact on the preoedipal child. This theoretical shift has progressively taken hold in the years since Freud's death in 1939. Psychopathology has increasingly come to be viewed as having its main roots in disturbances in the earliest experiences of the infant in relation to its mother. Concurrent with this changed theoretical emphasis has been the shift from the so-called drive discharge model to a so-called relational model (Greenberg & Mitchell, 1982; Mitchell, 1988) in which Freudian instinct theory is replaced by the proposition that we are inherently and primarily motivated by the desire for object relatedness, as reflected in Fairbairn's (1952) by now oft-repeated dictum that "libido is object-seeking not pleasure-seeking" (p. 82).

The idea that it is not compromise drive gratifications that are the primary motivational thrust of the organism but the development and maintenance of a firm, cohesive sense of self in the context of the interpersonal relatedness provided by a supportive, empathic "holding environment" that includes the availability of mirroring and idealized so-called selfobjects is the object relational and self-psychological underpinning of much current psychoanalytic theory and practice. A correlate of this central notion is that developmental arrests and deficits, rather than conflicts concerning sexual and aggressive wishes, are the significant element in psychopathology. A main implication for treatment is that the undoing of arrested development requires the availability of a "good object" more so than insight. That is, if it is assumed that the major "cause" of psychopathology is trauma rather than unconscious fantasy and conflict, then, it is assumed that the amelioration of the damage to the self is best achieved through a therapeutic "holding environment." Although some theorists have attempted to incorporate the importance of the environment and of selfhood with certain emendations and elaborations of Freudian theory (e.g., Loewald), the British object relation theorists (particularly Fairbairn), and Kohut (in his self psychology), evidenced a more radical departure from traditional Freudian theory.[1]

One possibility to consider is that the nature of psychopathology has changed over the years and that clinicians are no longer seeing primarily classical neurotic patients with "structural conflicts" but, instead, are encountering many more borderline and narcissistic patients. To what extent this is so or to what degree it is changes in theory that are altering our views of psychopathology—or some mixture of the two—is unclear. Also worthy of consideration in trying to understand the historical shifts in theoretical emphases are the issues of the growing dissatisfaction with aspects of traditional Freudian theory (particularly the metapsychology), the increasing disillusionment with insight as the key curative agent in treatment, and the personal resonance of object relations and self psychological concepts to issues of selfhood and relatedness in contemporary American culture.[2]

Given these changes, it is no longer accurate to speak of the psychoanalytic theory of psychopathology, as was the case until about two decades ago when psychoanalytic ego psychology was the dominant paradigm. The development of self psychology by Kohut and the strong appeal of the British object relations theorists have ushered in an era of theoretical pluralism in American psychoanalysis. Some writers (e.g. Silverman, 1986; Pine, 1990) claim that the phenomena emphasized by traditional Freudian theory, ego psychology, object relations theories, and self psychology all have an essential place in understanding clinical phenomena and in the conduct of psychoanalysis. These theories point to different classes of phenomena and subjective experience, thereby enabling us to view the same clinical material from different theoretical vantage points. However, they make basic theoretical assumptions that are incompatible with one another. Whether the consistent clinical use of one or another of these theoretical models, as opposed to the use of all of them, makes for a measurable difference in therapeutic efficacy is an open empirical question. To what extent the pathology of patient or the stage of treatment is relevant to the simultaneous, alternating, or sequential therapeutically efficacious use of these multiple perspectives also remains to be determined. Perhaps the use of multiple perspectives allows the analyst to maintain an optimal balance in focusing both on what has been done to the child and what the adult patient does with what has been done to him or her.

On the level of theory, it is fair to say that none of the three main paradigms (traditional Freudian theory with its ego-psychological extensions, object relations theory, self psychology) has been articulated in a sufficiently formal or systematic manner as to allow meaningful, comparative empirically based evaluations within or outside the clinical situation. We are at a stage where we realize more than ever that theory shapes how we process clinical data (e.g., Pulver, 1987). Therefore, we probably will need to rely more on extraclinical data in seeking to validate different conceptions of psychopathology. In fact, the work reported in this volume by Taylor, Horowitz, Lerner, and Blatt and Blass are examples of theoretical efforts that are based primarily on data obtained outside the therapeutic context.

When we look beyond the competition among rival psychoanalytic schools to the broader context of different approaches to psychopathology, psychoanalytic thinking clearly has lost ground. For example, advances in biological psychiatry and the efforts to establish a more reliable, descriptive taxonomy of psychiatric disorders free of a psychoanalytic cast have seriously challenged the prior dominance of the psychoanalytic perspective. Yet, once the DSM diagnosis is made and the biological diathesis is stated, clinicians will often feel at a loss without a psycho-

---

[1]See Eagle (1991) and Friedman (1988) for accounts of why the views of the object relations theorists enjoy the popularity they currently do in North American psychoanalysis.

[2]See Kirschner (1990) and Eagle (1991) for a discussion of these matters.

dynamic perspective to guide them (Perry, Cooper, & Michels, 1987). Empirical studies guided by a psychoanalytic perspective should enable us to arrive at an increasingly comprehensive and valid psychoanalytic conception of psychopathology.

The chapters in this section reflect some of the trends and issues outlined earlier. They are not intended to cover all theories and phenomena relevant to a psychoanalytic theory of psychopathology. Thus, no attempt was made to include material on all important clinical entities (e.g., schizophrenia, affective disorders), nor were we able to have separate chapters representing all the major theoretical orientations (e.g., Sullivanian, object relations theory, etc.).

THE CHAPTERS IN THIS SECTION

In the past two decades, Kohut's (1971, 1977, 1984) self psychology has come to occupy an increasingly prominent place in the psychoanalytic world. A recent survey (Strauss, Yager, & Strauss, 1984) of leading psychiatrists confirms our everyday impression of Kohut's pervasive influence. As Kohut's views were becoming increasingly influential, the psychology of the self shifted from a narrow conception in which the self was a content of the mental apparatus to a broader view in which the self was regarded as the superordinate, central concept relevant to all forms of psychopathology. In this conceptualization, drive manifestations are regarded as so-called breakdown or disintegration products of a self struggling to avoid fragmentation and preserve some measure of cohesion. For Kohut, the core factor of psychopathology is the degree of cohesiveness of the self. As Kohut (1977, p.279) put it, disorders of the self are "the dominant pathology of our time."

Ornstein (1978, 1981) is one of many analysts who have hailed Kohut's theory as the "revolutionary" third paradigm (following drive psychology and ego psychology). There has been considerable controversy over whether Kohut's main contribution is one of an enormously enriching clinical perspective or whether it constitutes a new, improved conception of personality (see Wallerstein, 1983, for a discussion of this point).

Cohler and Galatzer-Levy offer an appreciative overview of Kohut's self psychology, including its implications for development throughout the life cycle and its emergence in a cultural climate in which issues of meaning and personal integrity are prominent. Within psychoanalysis, the limitation of traditional therapeutic approaches, particularly with the nonclassical patient, the demise of Freud's metapsychology and the corresponding renewed interest in the clinical theory are among the factors that they believe contributed to the receptivity to Kohut's ideas.

The authors begin by tracing the transition of the concept of self in psychoanalytic theory from an aspect of ego functioning in traditional Freudian theory to its superordinate status in Kohut's self psychology. Important to this transition, according to Cohler and Galatzer-Levy, were poor therapeutic results with some patients treated along traditional Freudian lines and the writings of Gill, G. S. Klein, Schafer, and others (e.g., Winnicott) urging a clinical theory that focuses on meanings and motives and is concerned with "the origins and treatment of deficits in realizing personal cohesion and intimacy."

In addition, Kohut's emphasis on empathic understanding enabled him to observe selfobject transferences. These observations, which the authors consider his "central contribution to clinical psychoanalysis," led him to view the personal distress of neurosis in terms of the failure of selfobject functions. For example, Kohut did not regard the analysand's idealization of the analyst as a defensive resistance to the acknowledgment of competition and envy but as a needed means of strengthening the self. The "idealizing transferences" together with the "mirror transferences" generally operate silently and, in this phase of treatment, "provide the analysand with missing functions necessary in order to sustain the self."

Cohler and Galatzer-Levy stress repeatedly the importance of "the analyst's ordinary empathy and courtesy toward the analysand" in promoting and sustaining the therapeutic alliance. They warn that adherence to traditional technique may foster an iatrogenic traumatization, and they alert us to other technical implication of a self-psychological approach to treatment. In this connection, Cohler and Galatzer-Levy describe the common countertransference issues that may cause analysts to fail in their selfobject function for the patient.

In the last section of their chapter, the authors go beyond the clinical situation to articulate a developmental perspective. Here they refer to the importance of affect attunement and of selfobjects throughout the life course. They introduce the term *essential other* to indicate that, as development proceeds, the person who performs the selfobject function is also part of an increasingly multifaceted relationship.

Because Kohut's theory is a relatively recent development, we have not yet seen its impact on psychological research, nor has the theory yet attempted to incorporate previous, related theories or psychological research. Kohut himself consciously and deliberately did not want to attempt to make links to related conceptualizations. Yet aspects of Kohut's theory and treatment approach seem to have a important similarity to the work of others (e.g., Carl Rogers). It remains a task for the future to see if there can be a mutual enrichment of self psychology and empirical research in psychology. One obvious area of importance would be to investigate the etiological claims made by Kohut regarding the genesis of disorders of the self through longitudinal studies that incorporate the variables relevant to Kohut's claims concerning failures in parental empathy. As we shall see, some of the empirical work reported in Taylor's chapter and aspects of his conceptualization of it fit nicely with Kohut's ideas about selfobjects as regulators of psychological functioning. Similarly, some of the empirical research literature on parental disturbances as risk factors in psychopathology seems to dovetail with Kohutian formulations regarding failures in parental empathy, but the issues here are exceedingly complex and require a lot of further study.

Clinical psychological testing has played an important historical role in the psychoanalytic assessment of psychopathology, primarily because of the pioneering work of Rapaport, Gill, and Schafer in the mid-1940s. Over the years, psychological testing has been increasingly used in research that is relevant to psychoanalytic theories.

Basing himself primarily on studies using the Rorschach test, Lerner's chapter focuses on borderline psychopathology, particularly on Kernberg's formulations of borderline personality organization. Lerner begins with a brief historical overview of the borderline concept, emphasizing Kernberg's classification of levels of personality organization. He then proceeds to review research findings that are relevant to borderline functioning. Rorschach studies of internalized object relations, ego weakness, and defensive structure generally support Kernberg's formulations. For example, compared with normals and with other patient groups, borderline patients show ego weaknesses such as difficulties in impulse control, frustration tolerance, and in separating reality and fantasy. In most studies, they also show more evidence of splitting than do relevant comparison groups. Lerner points out that findings form such studies lead to refinements in the construction of Rorschach scales. In the final section of the chapter, Lerner discusses the treatment implications of this body of research.

The work reported by Lerner is an instance in which a psychoanalytic conceptualization has spawned a considerable amount of empirical research. It appears that we now have the assessment tools necessary to conduct studies comparing different theoretical views of borderline pathology and different approaches to treatment. It also remains to be seen to what extent hypotheses regarding the etiology of borderline (and other forms of) psychopathology will be supported by empirical tests.

As Blatt and Blass note, there have been several personality theories that focus on self-definition and interpersonal relatedness as two fundamental dialectic processes of personality development. A balance and integration of these two developmental lines is considered necessary for normal development and functioning. As Blatt and Blass put it, "recognition of the role of attachment in the development of identity and the understanding of the dialectic between the development of attachment and separateness necessitate the postulation of two distinct but interactive lines of development."

In the first part of their chapter, they demonstrate the frequency with which the emphasis on these two fundamental dimensions appear in the literature. They are seen in the theories of Angyal (*autonomy* and *homomimy*), Bakan (*agency* and *communion*), Freud (*work* and *love, ego libido* and *object libido*), Balint (*philobatic* and *oncophilic*), Adler (*self-perfection* and *overall interest*), Rank (*self-* and *other-directedness*), McAdams (*achievement* and *affiliation*), and Spiegel and Spiegel (*differentiation* and *fusion*). The relative emphasis on individuality and attachment differs in different theories (e.g., Mahler's focus on separation and individuation versus the British object relations theorists' emphasis on relatedness and object seeking). Other theorists stress the importance of a balance between autonomy and connectedness (e.g., Angyal and G. Klein). Infant researchers (e.g., Stern and Emde) have made contributions that fit well with Blatt's and Blass's articulation of these two main aspects of human development.

In the second part of their chapter, the authors reformulate Erikson's well-known epigenetic psychosocial model to make a clear and equal place for both self-definition and relatedness and their integration. This convincing framework, which includes a stage of "cooperation/collaboration versus alienation," serves to broaden Erikson's emphasis on identity and allows us to see generativity and integrity as "expressions of self in a relational context." This reformulation also is consistent with some feminist contributions to developmental theory.

In the third part, the authors advance the argument that these two broad dimensions of development describe "two basic personality configurations" that have implications for corresponding cognitive styles, defensive strategies, and modes of adaptation. Different forms of psychopathology are to be seen as reflecting the relative emphasis on either autonomy or interpersonal relatedness. Blatt uses the terms *anaclitic* and *introjective* to refer to personality styles focused on interpersonal relatedness versus self-definition, respectively. When anaclitically organized individuals reach a point in the life cycle when development goes awry, they are likely to show evidence of infantile or hysterical character styles and to suffer from depression concerning loss of the love object or the object's love. Pathological difficulties in those with an introjective style would be more likely to take the form of paranoia, guilt-ridden depression, and obsessive–compulsive symptoms and defenses because these qualities reflect preoccupation with self-control and self-definition. Thus, Blatt and Blass tell us that "different types of psychopathology are considered as distorted exaggerations of either the anaclitic or the introjective developmental line," although they recognize that some patients show aspects of both basic configurations. A conceptual advantage of this scheme, according to the authors, is that one goes beyond an atheoretical classification scheme that is based on manifest symptomatology to one in which "the various forms of psychopathology are considered no longer as isolated, independent disease entities, but rather as interrelated modes of adaptation, organized at different developmental levels within two basic configurations that focus on either interpersonal relations or self-definition."

In the final section of their chapter, Blatt and Blass turn to the empirical research literature on depression and on psychotherapy to demonstrate the predictive and heuristic value of organizing the extensive literature in these areas in terms of their basic conceptualization. For example, dependent and self-critical subjects respond differently to themes of loss/rejection and failure/criticism and show evidence of anaclitic versus introjective forms of depression that are consistent with their general personality style. Likewise, initial changes in psychotherapy differ for anaclitic versus introjective patients in ways predicted from knowledge of their basic styles of conflict and defense. The impressive array of empirical findings relevant to Blatt's theoretical model constitutes an excellent example of the reciprocal influences of theory and research.

Taylor's contribution focuses on the importance of self-regulation as a central factor related to bodily illness and disease. His major thesis, elaborated in his excellent 1987 book, is that interpersonal relationships and the manner in which they are represented mentally serve a vital homeostatic, regulating function with respect to basic biological processes. Taylor assembles an impressive array of research evidence from both animal and human studies that supports a "new psychosomatic model which views illnesses and diseases as disorders of regulation."

As Taylor notes, most of Freud's followers had little use for the notion of actual neuroses and concentrated on the emotional conflicts presumed to contribute to the development of the "classical" psychosomatic diseases (e.g., peptic ulcer, essential hypertension, ulcerative colitis, etc.).

In more recent years, the psychological significance of interpersonal relationships and stressful life events was accorded greater attention. As Taylor notes, the influential work of Engel and Schmale on helplessness and hopelessness and the "giving up/given up complex" and its implications for immunological changes set the stage for further research on the relationships between object loss and disease.

Taylor next turns his attention to a review of research on the psychobiology of attachment and separation, linking the famous Harlow studies and other research on the mother–infant interactional matrix (particularly the work of Hofer) to object relations and self-psychological concepts. He cites the growing evidence of "hidden" biological regulatory mechanisms of early mother–infant interactions in animals (e.g., thermoregulatory disturbances induced by means of maternal deprivation) and reinterprets the Spitz findings within this framework. Taylor believes that the interactions of mutual regulatory and self-regulatory processes are not consistent with Freud's drive-discharge model and fit better with object relations theories and self psychology. These theories are preferred because they offer a better account of how the infant moves from a dependent state in which the mother provides psychobiological regulation to a state in which the developing infant, under optimal conditions, progressively becomes a self-regulating organism. In this context, Taylor invokes Kohut's idea that optimal failures of the selfobject function of the mother facilitate "psychic structure building" and notes Kohut's point regarding the importance of selfobjects for the mature and healthy functioning of adults. Winnicott's concept of the transitional object is also relevant in this context. Although not explicitly mentioned by Taylor in his contribution here, Winnicott's conception of the "holding environment" and his account of the capacity to be alone would also seem to be central to the idea of the transition to increasing self-regulation. In this context, it is tempting to note that Adler's (1985, p. 4) central thesis regarding the key defect in borderline pathology is that there is "a relative developmental failure in formation of introjects that provide to the self a function of holding-soothing security."

In the next section, Taylor presents a discussion of alexithymia and its relation to vulnerability to psychosomatic illness and disease that is based on the notion of self-regulating cybernetic systems. In this view, the various interactive subsystems of the organism (e.g., the neuroendocrine system and the immune system), including psychic structure, regulate psychobiological adaptation. From this holistic perspective, the traditional distinction between "organic" and "functional" disorders is eliminated and the distinction between physical and psychiatric disorders is now seen "psychosomatically." That is, problems in self-regulation can be contributing causes to any physical illness or disease process.

As Taylor recognizes, the disregulation model he has articulated requires much more empirical testing. At the present time, it strikes us as a powerful, organizing concept for a variety of psychological research endeavors (e.g., the work on social support or bereavement reactions and, more generally, on the role of personality factors in health and disease).

One of the many interesting implications of Taylor's conceptualization is that excessive reliance on others for homeostatic regulation of psychobiological functioning is a risk factor for illness. We think it is fair to say that the thrust in much of psychoanalytic theorizing emphasizes the adaptive advantage of a more autonomous, self-regulatory trend following a developmental line from dependence to independence. For example, Mahler's account of the separation–individuation process has that quality, as does Erikson's conception of ego-identity. In fact, Blatt and Blass attempt to modify Erikson's scheme to give it more of a relational emphasis. If we compare this formulation with Blatt's and Blass's account of the two basic personality configurations of autonomy and affiliation, we may ask under what conditions psychological adaptation and physical well-being are facilitated by a more autonomous, self-regulatory style and when it might be less adaptive.

In recent years, there has been a greater acknowledgment of posttraumatic stress reactions and of the variety of stress response syndromes. The 1980 *DSM–III* established posttraumatic stress disorder as an official diagnostic category, partly on the basis of the remarkably productive series of research programs conducted by Horowitz and his colleagues. In his contribution to this volume, Horowitz presents an account of the psychological manifestations of traumatic events and the phases of response to trauma.

According to Horowitz, psychic trauma influences states of mind, schemas, and what he calls *control processes*. For example, with respect to states of mind, memories may emerge into awareness in an unbidden, intrusive manner, or, they may be conspicuously absent. The absence of schemas to process unanticipated events (e.g., violence, sexual abuse) contributes to the traumatic nature of the event and accounts, in part, for the signs and symptoms seen in the denial and intrusion phases of stress response syndromes. As Horowitz puts it, "perceptions of a traumatic event seem to be inscribed in a special form of memory" and require a working through. Control processes function as a means of coping with the unintegrated memories and affects associated with the trauma.

There are, of course, significant individual differences in personality style and psychopathology that will influence the degree and nature of the impact of unusual traumatic events as well as common traumas (e.g., death of a loved one). In regard to the latter, Horowitz outlines the characteristics of normal and pathological grief reactions.

In the final portion of the chapter, Horowitz illustrates his ideas with reference to the trauma of childhood sexual abuse. In this context, he refers to work in cognitive science which is relevant to the concept of schemas. This emphasis is similar to that of some other contributors to this volume who believe that a psychodynamic combined with a cognitive science perspective should inform research on clinical phenomena (e.g., Singer and Singer).

In the research on trauma, we have a fertile area for the study of several, important, related issues: (a) premorbid personality factors as predictors of response to trauma, (b) individual differences in the long-range effects of childhood trauma, (c) the relationship of traumatic experiences to developmental arrests and the shaping of intrapsychic conflict, (d) the effects of parental availability and empathy in mediating the effects of childhood trauma, (e) the relationship of acute trauma to cumulative trauma (Khan, 1963) in influencing subsequent development, and, (f) the determinants of the extent to which external events are experienced as traumatic in the first place. Of course, the literature already contains studies of these questions (e.g., the relation of childhood trauma to borderline personality functioning in adulthood), although often not from a psychoanalytically informed position.

As a concluding observation about the chapters in this section, it appears that at least implicit in some of the chapters in this section and throughout the book is the theme of self-regulation. Taylor, basing himself largely on attachment research, is most explicit in offering us a valuable articulation of the process and of the adaptive significance of self-regulatory processes, particularly with respect to psychosomatic problems. The selfobject concept, the process of coping with trauma, the relative emphasis on self-definition versus interpersonal relatedness, and the difficulties that borderline patients have can all be seen from the perspective of problems in the self-regulation of tension states. As this work becomes increasingly integrated with the burgeoning empirical literature on personality development, we should be in the position to formulate even better theories concerning the causes and forms of psychopathology.

Taken together, then, these chapters offer us excellent examples of the enriching effect on psychoanalytic theorizing of psychoanalytically informed empirical research as well as research that was not undertaken with any psychoanalytic interest in mind but that, nonetheless, has interesting implications for a comprehensive psychoanalytic theory of psychopathology.

REFERENCES

Adler, G. (1985). *Borderline psychopathology and its treatment.* Northvale, NJ: Jason Aronson.

Eagle, M. (1991). *The dynamics of theory change in psychoanalysis.* Paper presented at a conference on the future of psychoanalysis, Bologna, Italy, June 24–28.

Fairbairn, W. R. D. (1952). *An object-relations theory of the personality.* New York: Basic Books.

Friedman, L. (1988). The clinical popularity of object relations concepts. *Psychoanalytic Quarterly, 57,* 667–691.

Greenberg, J., & Mitchell, S. A. (1983). *Object relations in psychoanalytic theory.* Cambridge, MA: Harvard University Press.

Khan, M. M. R. (1963). The concept of cumulative trauma. *Psychoanalytic Study of the Child, 18,* 286–306.

Kirschner, S. (1990). The assenting echo: Anglo-American values in contemporary psychoanalytic developmental psychology. *Social Research, 57,* 821–857.

Kohut, H. (1971). *The analysis of the self.* Madison, CT: International Universities Press.

Kohut, H. (1977). *The restoration of the self.* Madison, CT: International Universities Press.

Kohut, H. (1984). *How does analysis cure?* Chicago: University of Chicago Press.

Mitchell, S. A. (1988). *Relational concepts in psychoanalysis.* Cambridge, MA: Harvard University Press.

Ornstein, P. H. (1978). Introduction. In P. H. Ornstein (Ed.), *The search for the self* (pp. 1–106). Madison, CT: International Universities Press.

Ornstein, P. H. (1981). The bipolar self in the psychoanalytic treatment process: Clinical-theoretical considerations. *Journal of the American Psychoanalytic Association, 29,* 353–375.

Pine, F. (1990). *Drive, ego, object, and self.* New York: Basic Books.

Perry, S., Cooper, A. M., & Michels, R. (1987). The psychodynamic formulation: Its purpose, structure, and clinical applications. *American Journal of Psychiatry, 144,* 543–550.

Pulver, S. (1987). Epilogue. *Psychoanalytic Inquiry, 7(2),* 289–299.

Silverman, D. (1986). A multi-model approach: Looking at clinical data from three theoretical perspectives. *Psychoanalytic Psychology, 3,* 121–132.

Strauss, G. D., Yager, J., & Strauss, G. E. (1984). The cutting edge in psychiatry. *American Journal of Psychiatry, 141,* 38–43.

Taylor, G. (1987). *Psychosomatic medicine and contemporary psychoanalysis.* Madison, CT: International Universities Press.

Wallerstein, R. S. (1983). Self psychology and "classical" psychoanalytic psychology: The nature of their relationship. In A. Goldberg (Ed.), *The future of psychoanalysis* (pp. 19–63). Madison, CT: International Universities Press.

18

RELATEDNESS AND SELF-DEFINITION: TWO PRIMARY DIMENSIONS IN PERSONALITY DEVELOPMENT, PSYCHOPATHOLOGY, AND PSYCHOTHERAPY

SIDNEY J. BLATT AND RACHEL B. BLASS

In this chapter we present a theoretical model that considers personality development as proceeding through the simultaneous development of two basic capacities: the ability to establish increasingly mature and satisfying interpersonal relationships (relatedness) and the development of an increasingly differentiated, integrated, essentially positive concept of the self (self-definition). We demonstrate how this theoretical model of personality development provides an effective way of conceptualizing various forms of psychopathology as disruptions of normal developmental processes and how these psychoanalytic formulations of personality development and psychopathology facilitate research on depression and the study of psychotherapy change.

THEORETICAL PERSPECTIVES

Personality development is the result of a complex transaction of two fundamental developmental lines: the development of increasingly mature, reciprocal, and satisfying interpersonal relationships, and the development of a consolidated, realistic, essentially positive, increasingly integrated self-definition or identity. These two developmental lines normally evolve throughout the life cycle in a complex dialectical process. The development of an increasingly differentiated, integrated, and mature sense of self is contingent upon establishing satisfying interpersonal experiences and, conversely, the development of increasingly mature and satisfying interpersonal relationships depends on the development of more mature self-definition and identity. In normal personality development, these two developmental processes evolve in an interactive, reciprocally balanced, mutually facilitating fashion from birth through senescence (Blatt, 1990; Blatt & Shichman, 1983).

Numerous personality theorists, using a variety of terms, discuss interpersonal relatedness and self-definition as two central processes in personality development. Angyal (1941, 1951), for example, discusses surrender and autonomy as two basic personality dispositions. Surrender for Angyal (1951) is the desire to seek a home, to become part of something greater than oneself; while autonomy represents a "striving basically to assert and to expand . . . self-determination, [to be] an autonomous being, a self-governing entity that asserts itself actively instead of reacting passively. . . . This tendency . . . expresses itself in spontaneity, self-assertiveness, striving for freedom and for mastery" (pp. 131–132). Bakan (1966), in a conceptualization similar to Angyal, defines "communion" and "agency" as two fundamental dimensions in personality development. Communion for Bakan is a loss of self and self-consciousness in a merging and blending with others and the world. It involves feeling a part of and participating in a larger social entity, of being at one with others, of feeling in contact or union and experiencing a sense of openness, cooperation, love, and eros. Agency, in contrast, defines a pressure toward individuation that Bakan believed permeates all living matter. It emphasizes being a separate individual and being able to tolerate isolation, alienation, and aloneness. The predominant themes in agency are self-protection, self-assertion, self-expansion and an urge to master the environment and make it one's own. The basic issues are separation and mastery.

Bakan's communion and Angyal's surrender both define a fundamental desire for union in which the person seeks to merge or join with other people and with the inanimate environment in order to achieve a greater sense of participation and belonging. Communion and surrender refer to a stable dimension of personality organization directed toward interdependent relationships with others. Themes of dependency, mutuality, and unity define this basic dimension in life.

Agency (Bakan) and autonomy (Angyal) both define a basic striving toward individuation—a seeking of separation from others and from an attachment to the physical environment as well as a fuller differentiation within oneself. Agency and autonomy both refer to a stable dimension of functioning that emphasizes separation, individuation, control, self-definition, and autonomous achievement—the striving for uniqueness and the expression of one's own capacities and self-interests (Friedman & Booth-Kewley, 1987).

Freud articulated a distinction similar to this emphasis on relatedness and self-definition in his often-quoted statement that the two major goals in life are to be able to love and to work. Freud (1914/1957, 1926/1959) also distinguished between object and ego libido, and between libidinal instincts in the service of attachment and aggressive instincts necessary for autonomy, mastery, and self-definition. Freud (1930/1961) distinguished between "the man who is predominantly erotic" and gives "first preference to his emotional relationships to other people . . . [and] the narcissistic man, who inclines to be self-sufficient . . . [and] seek[s] his main satisfactions in his internal mental processes" (pp. 83–84). Freud (1930/1961) noted that these "two urges, the one towards personal happiness and the other towards union with other human beings must struggle with each other in every individual; and so, also, the two processes of individual and of cultural development must stand in hostile opposition to each other and mutually dispute the ground" (p. 141). He contrasted on "egotistic" urge with the urge toward union with others in the community. Freud extended this contrast by distinguishing anxiety and guilt due to aggression and the internalization of authority in the superego, both of which are related to the ego instincts and issues of mastery, from social anxiety that involves primarily the fear of the loss of love and contact with others. Loewald (1962) discussed how Freud identified a fundamental polarity inherent in human existence: "the polarity of individuation and primary narcissistic union—a polarity which Freud attempted to conceptualize by various approaches but which he recognized and insisted upon from the beginning to the end by his dualistic conception of instincts, of human nature and of life itself" (pp. 490–491).

Other psychoanalytic investigators articulated similar distinctions. Bowlby (1969, 1973), for example, explored libido and aggression as emotional substrates for the human personality that are expressed in striving for attachment and separation. Balint (1959), from an object relations perspective, also discussed two fundamental dimensions in personality development— a tendency for clinging or connectedness ("ocnophilic") and toward self-sufficiency ("philo-batic"). Shor and Sanville (1978), based on Balint's formulations, discuss psychological development as an oscillation between "necessary connectedness" and "inevitable separations"— between "intimacy and autonomy". Adler (1951) discussed social interest and self-perfection. He viewed neurosis as the consequence of a distorted overemphasis on self-enhancement in the absence of sufficient social interest. Pampering (overprotection, overindulgence, and overdomi-nation) or rejection lead to feelings of inadequacy and selfishness and a lack of independence. Rank (1929) also discussed self and other-directedness and their relation to creative and adaptive personality styles. Horney (1945, 1950) characterized personality as either moving toward, against, or away from interpersonal contact.

Research investigators in personality development have also discussed similar dimensions. Gilligan (1982), for example, stresses the importance of including interpersonal responsibility as well as investment in individual rights and principles of justice as two dimensions in moral development. McAdams (1980) discusses motives for affiliation (or intimacy) as well as achieve-ment (e.g., McClelland, 1986; McClelland, Atkinson, Clark, & Lowell, 1953) or power (Winter, 1973) as central dimensions in personality organization. In a series of studies of life narratives, McAdams (1985) identified power and intimacy as two central themes or dominant clusters. Individuals high on motivation for intimacy speak frequently of reciprocal harmonious interper-sonal interactions and participation in social groups and express a "recurrent preference or readiness for experiences of warmth, closeness, and communicative exchange" (p. 76). They often portrayed themselves as a helper, lover, counselor, caregiver, and friend. In contrast, people high on motivation for power spoke frequently of self-protection, self-assertion, and self-expan-sion; they separate themselves from the social context and express needs for mastery, achievement, movement, force, and action. McAdams (1985) defined this power motive as "a recurrent preference or readiness for experiences of having impact and feeling strong and potent vis-a-vis the environment" (p. 84). Individuals high on the power motive often spoke of themselves as a traveler, master, father, authority, or sage. Spiegel and Spiegel (1978) also discuss these two fundamental dimensions of relatedness and separation and draw a parallel between these two personality dimensions and two fundamental physical or biological forces—fusion and fission or integration and differentiation (Blatt, 1990).

Although many personality theories consider to some degree the dimensions of both relatedness and self-definition, most theories of psychological development usually emphasize primarily one or the other of these two dimensions: either separation and individuation or attachment and interpersonal relatedness. Theories focusing on separation attempt to understand the development of the individual as a self-contained unit, striving toward individuation, differ-entiation, autonomy, and identity. Development is viewed as a process by which innate capacities find optimal expression in the attainment of various levels of self and of ego functioning. Emphasis is on the experience of the self as separate and independent and on its evolvement in the course of the life cycle (Blatt & Blass, 1990).

Within psychoanalytic theory, an emphasis on separation is best exemplified by the con-tributions of Mahler, Settlage, Anna Freud, and Blos, who focus on the processes of separation–

individuation. Mahler (1971) describes the separation–individuation process as a gradual distancing from the mother, a transition from the dependency of infancy to independent functioning: "One could regard the entire life cycle as constituting a more or less successful process of distancing from the introjection of the lost symbiotic mother" (p. 130). Blos (1979), emphasizing the importance of separation throughout development, contends that the process in infancy of "hatching from the symbiotic membrane to become an individuated toddler (Mahler, 1963) becomes in adolescence the shedding of family dependencies [and] the loosening of infantile object ties. . . . [which] render the constancy of self-esteem and of mood increasingly independent from external sources" (pp. 142–143). Settlage (1980) stressed these aspects as well: "The separation–individuation process results in the formation of the psychic structures or functions underlying the sense of self and enabling a beginning capacity for self regulation and for object relations across a new established psychic boundary of separateness" (p. 527). This emphasis on separation in psychological development is consonant with S. Freud's emphasis on drive and ego maturation and A. Freud's (1965a, 1974) description of individual development as a series of progressive moves toward emotional and physical independence and self-reliance. S. Freud (1905/1953), in fact, described adolescent development as involving "*detachment* from parental authority," which he viewed as one of the "most significant, but also one of the most painful, psychical achievements of the pubertal period . . . a process which alone makes possible the opposition, which is so important for the progress of civilization, between the new generation and the old" (p. 227, emphasis added). "The dominance of the pleasure principle can really come to an end only when a child has achieved a complete psychological detachment from its parents . . ." (Freud, 1911/1951, p. 220). Throughout his work, Freud (e.g., 1930/1961) stressed the importance of separation in personal as well as societal development: "Detaching himself from his family becomes a task that faces every young person, and society often helps him in the solution of it by means of puberty and initiation rites" (p. 103).

Psychological development in separation focused theories occurs in relationships with significant others, such as in learning, imitation, and internalization, but the establishment and maintenance of relationships are not viewed as developmental goals in their own right. Rather, the disengagement from relationships is seen as resulting in a concomitant enrichment of the self and an increasing independence—the hallmark of maturation. According to Mahler (1974b), in

> the *normal individual* the sociobiological utilization of the mother, of the "outer half of the self" (Spitz, 1965), and later on, the emotional availability of the love object—the post-symbiotic partner—are the necessary conditions for an *intrapsychic* separation–individuation process. This is, in fact, synonymous with the *second*, the psychological birth experience: a rather slow and very gradual *hatching out process*, as it were. (p. 151)

In contrast to theories that emphasize separation, other psychoanalytic theories focus primarily on attachment and view the development of the individual as a unit in interaction. The definition, integrity, and continuity of the self are maintained by the gestalt of past and present interpersonal relationships. The individual is viewed as predominantly object seeking; development is defined not by what occurs within the individual per se, but by the quality of his or her relationships. Intimacy, dependency, care, and affection are the topics of study. Emphasis is on the individual's perception of and experiences with the other, rather than on the self.

Proponents of attachment or relatedness theories come primarily from the British object relations theorists (e.g., Balint, 1934/1952a, 1937/1952b; Fairbairn, 1952, 1953, 1963; Guntrip, 1969, 1971; Winnicott, 1958b, 1971), who emphasized the development of interpersonal relationships and themes of dependency, care, affection, mutuality, reciprocity, and intimacy. The primary criterion of psychological development is the maturation of relationships; the development of a positive, clearly demarcated, and independent sense of self is viewed as a by-product. Guntrip (1969, 1971), for example, noted that in object relations theory psychological development is no longer discussed in terms of maturation of internal psychic structures, but relatedness becomes the major dimension of the developmental process—"the emotional dynamics of the infant's growth in experiencing himself as 'becoming a person' in meaningful relationships, first with the mother, then the family, and finally with the ever enlarging world outside" (1969, p. 243). Although Guntrip (1969) did not completely neglect the development of the individual as a separate entity, his focus is on attachment and relatedness: "Meaningful relationships are those which enable the infant to find himself as a person through experiencing his own significance for other people and their significance for him, thus endowing his existence with those values of human relationship which make life purposeful and worth living" (p. 243).

Sullivan's (1940, 1953) interpersonal theory also views personality development as involving increasing capacity for interpersonal relatedness. Sullivan's theories of interpersonal relations, with their theoretical antecedents partly in social psychology and social philosophy (e.g., Baldwin, 1902; Cooley, 1902; Mead, 1934), consider personality development as the consequence of exchanges between the person and the significant others on whom the person depends for satisfaction and security. Personality development evolves through increasingly mature interactions with significant others. Intimate relationships in infancy are established through "emotional contagion" in the shared experience between parent and child. The experiences of trust and mistrust described by Erikson develop in this context of affective sharing. The next level of interpersonal relatedness, according to Sullivan (1940, 1953), occurs in the preschool child who becomes increasingly aware of his relationships with others and begins to learn to accommodate his needs to the needs of others. The child learns the rudiments of compromise in the oedipal phase. Sullivan (1940, 1953) also described the child's transition from primary involvement with parents within the family unit to an involvement with peers during the early primary school years from kindergarten through second grade (ages 5–8). At this time, the child begins to generalize the rudiments of cooperation and compromise first learned with authority figures to his or her relationships with peers (Selman & Schultz, 1990).

This capacity for cooperation and accommodation is initially relatively egocentric (Sullivan, 1940, 1953; see also Piaget, 1954/1970) and is expressed primarily toward significant others who are essential sources of gratification. Around the age of 8, however, the child begins to transcend this egocentrism and develops the capacity to appreciate the perspectives of others (Feffer, 1969, 1970; Piaget, 1945/1962). And, at this time, the child's social needs become increasingly more important than the satisfaction of his or her biological needs (Selman & Schultz, 1990). During later latency and preadolescence (approximately ages 8–12), the capacity for cooperation with authority figures and peers is transformed into a more mature capacity called collaboration. According to Sullivan, the primary interpersonal mechanism for the transition from cooperation to collaboration involves a shift from a general participation with a number of equally important peers to a close and special friendship with a particular peer or chum. With the emergence of this "chumship," the satisfaction of the needs of the other becomes as important as the satisfaction of one's own needs. Sullivan, like Piaget, viewed this transcendence of the egocentrism of childhood—what Sullivan called the "quiet miracle of preadolescence"—as a major developmental achievement and milestone in the child's growth toward interpersonal maturity and of the capacity for mutuality and reciprocity. The relinquishing of childhood egocentrism is essential for the development of both formal operational thought (Inhelder & Piaget, 1955) and interpersonal maturity (Sullivan, 1940, 1953). The development of a chumship in early adolescence is an essential step in the eventual development of the intimacy and reciprocity of a mature sexual relationship in which there is a little need to dominate or be dominated by another.

Sullivan specified particular milestones and qualities (e.g., emotional contagion, accommodation and cooperation, and collaboration) in the development of interpersonal maturity, but he also stressed that there is no particular endpoint, ideal goal, or telos to this process. Rather, interpersonal maturity is characterized by an open-ended capacity for collaboration and reciprocity in a wide range of relationships. Sullivan considered this entire developmental progression to depend on the quality of the shared experiences with significant others, from the satisfaction of biological needs to more symbolic or psychological needs—from relationships that are reflexive or reactive to those that are more reflective (Werner, 1948). More mature levels of interpersonal relatedness require a communicative competence that develops primarily during latency and the preadolescent period when the child begins to be able to transcend his or her egocentrism and to assume the perspective of the other (Inhelder & Piaget, 1955; Piaget, 1954/1970). Communicative competence requires not only the capacity to be reflectively aware of one's own thoughts and feelings in order to put them into suitable language, but also to be able to assume the role of the other in order to appreciate how the other may be perceiving one's communication. Language becomes a tool for interpersonal communication—for the sharing of experiences in social intercourse. The sharing of bodily experiences that occurred in the emotional contagion of infancy and in the shared action and play patterns of early and midchildhood (ages 5–8), now continue on a more symbolic and conceptual level in preadolescence and beyond. Language is essential for experiencing consensual validation and for establishing enduring interpersonal relationships. Personal experiences are enriched and extended through a mutual sharing of experiences with an other (Selman & Schultz, 1990).

The role of attachment and relatedness in personality development is also stressed in the works of investigators of infant development, most notably Bowlby (1969, 1973, 1988), who regarded the propensity to establish strong emotional attachments as a basic, biologically based, motivational system that is active from the earliest moments of infancy through adulthood into senescence. The vicissitudes of attachment throughout the life cycle are expressed in pervasive intense desires to form bonds, "sometimes in the care-seeking role and sometimes in a caregiving one" (Bowlby, 1988, p. 3). The autonomous sense of self that emerges in the course of development is viewed not as a goal, but as a necessary byproduct in the process of development toward increasingly mature relationships. As Winnicott (1958a) concluded based on extensive clinical experience, "the basis of the capacity to be alone is the experience of being alone in the presence of someone" (p. 36).

Although S. Freud viewed separation as a major dimension of psychological development, he was also aware of the importance of love and attachment. S. Freud, for example, in a 1926 letter to Romain Rolland wrote that "our inborn instincts and the world around us being what they are, I could not but regard love as no less essential for the survival of the human race than such things as technology" (cited in Erikson, 1982, pp. 27–28), "a mature sense of identity means a sense of being at one with oneself as one grows and develops; and it means, at the same time, a sense of affinity with a community's sense of being at one with its future as well as its history—or mythology." Freud (1914/1957a) noted that "we must begin to love in order not to fall ill, and we are bound to fall ill if, in the consequence of frustration, we are unable to love" (p. 85). He (1930/1961) also described a

> way of life which makes love the center of everything, which looks for all satisfaction in loving and being loved. A psychical attitude of this sort comes naturally enough to all of us; one of the forms in which love manifests itself—sexual love—has given us our most intense experience of an overwhelming sensation of pleasure and has thus furnished us with a pattern for our search for happiness. (p. 82)

Freud considered it essential to recognize "love as one of the foundations of civilization" (p. 101). Egoism, self-preservation, is important but insufficient. "One of the major endeavours of civilization is to bring people together into larger unities" (p. 103). One of the primary characteristics of civilization according to Freud is the "manner in which relationships of men to one another, their social relationships, are regulated—relationships which affect a person as a neighbour, as a source of help, as another person's sexual object, as a member of a family and of a State" (p. 95); "civilization depends on relationships between a considerable number of individuals . . . [and, therefore] aims at binding the members of a community together in a libidinal way" (p. 108). Freud (1930/1961), in fact, noted that "the development of the individual seems . . . to be the product of the interaction between two urges. The urge toward happiness which we usually call 'egotistic,' and the urge towards union with others in the community, which we call 'altruistic' " (p. 140).

Although a number of theories emphasize either separation or relatedness as the primary dimension of psychological development, or view these processes as developing in parallel, other theories explore the importance of the integration of these two dimensions as central to personality development and psychological well-being. Modell (1968), for example, stated, "with the painful acceptance of the limitations of other persons and an acceptance of separateness, there is established a capacity for a more mature form of loving, that is, a love relationship that can be maintained in the face of privation and ambivalence" (p. 60). Bowlby (1969, 1973) spoke of the complementary development of connectedness and autonomy (of attachment and separation); Schafer (1968) discussed the importance of maintaining a balance between dependency and self-sufficiency for the attainment of optimal personal development, and according to Erikson (1982), "a mature sense of identity means a sense of being at one with oneself as one grows and develops; and it means, at the same time, a sense of affinity with a community's sense of being at one with its future as well as its history—or mythology" (pp. 27–28).

A number of theoretical perspectives stress that normal personality organization involves an integration of these two basic dimensions: the capacity for interpersonal relatedness and the development of self-definition (Steward & Malley, 1987). Angyal (1951), like Bakan, stressed that the major task in life is to achieve a compromise and balance between these two "autonomous" forces so that both are represented fully in one's experiences. Increased autonomy, mastery, and a capacity to govern one's life and environment are best done not by force or violence, but by understanding and by respect for laws and rules of the social matrix. Similarly, a loving relationship not only requires relinquishing one's autonomy and agency to some degree, but it also requires a capacity for mastery of one's environment, resourcefulness, and self-reliance, without which a relationship is in danger of deteriorating into helpless dependency, exploitation, and possessiveness. Both Angyal and Bakan emphasized the need for differentiation as well as for integration—for the emergence of each of these dimensions and the constructive resolution of these polarities. Kobassa (1979) discussed the importance of a blend of communion and agency, of intimacy and power, as central to the development of psychological well-being and hardiness. McAdams (1985) found that an integration of power and intimacy motivation in TAT stories was correlated with a capacity to portray constructive action scripts that are future oriented and high on generativity. Power and intimacy are integrated by establishing a clear agentive sense of self and by establishing intimate exchange with others. A mature identity for McAdams (1985) is one based on a sense of "sameness and continuity which provides unity and purpose" (p. 28). This requires both individuation and connectedness, an integration of identity formation and interdependence, a continuity with as well as a separation from one's past and one's current environment, and a sense of the future and the capacity to establish new connections.

As suggested by these various authors, relatedness and self-definition are basic dimensions essential for psychological maturity. These two dimensions constitute two developmental lines and the relationship between these two developmental lines. However, it goes well beyond parallel processes or a simple interaction or integration but rather involves a complex dialectical process throughout the life cycle in which progress in each developmental line is essential for progress in the other (Blatt, 1990; Blatt & Blass, 1990; Blatt & Shichman, 1983). Bakan (1966), for example, discusses the importance of a "dynamic tension" between agency and communion, between surrender and autonomy. Shor and Sanville (1978) similarly discuss personality development as "oscillating between a necessary connectedness and the inevitable separateness. The pace and style of oscillation and the transitions between these two axes will vary for each person and map his particular life history, his individual spiral of growth" (p. 121). Shor and Sanville view personality development "as a dialectical spiral or helix which interweaves the two dimensions of development, intimacy and autonomy" (p. 121). The capacity for adult intimacy and love is a product of an "intense search . . . to formulate one's individual identity and, . . . once having formed it, [to] risk to suspend concern with oneself while focussing on the qualities of a potential mate" (p. 126).

Klein (1976) was among the earliest psychoanalytic theorists to develop a detailed conceptual framework that could emcompass this dialectic process between the experience of the self as separate and the experience of attachment. He notes, "the terminology of subject and object has contributed to misleading conceptualizations of selfhood and especially to obscuring its 'we' aspect. The traditional view of man as becoming gradually aware of himself as 'subject' confronting others as objects may be applicable *morphologically* but it does not describe dynamic wholes" (pp. 178–179). Klein went on to describe how individuals can experience deprivation in relation to feeling autonomous or in feeling needed by another. Needs for autonomy may be manifest as ambition, competitiveness, or aggression. Affiliative needs

> may be expressed through familial and societal bonds; or the person may crave surrender to the higher entities of god and cosmos. . . . Affiliative needs can also be reflected in *esprit de corps* or clannishness, in loyalty and devotion . . . or in contagious mob behavior and group violence. . . . Separateness and independence . . . [and] cooperation and dependence . . . may be served by motives and emotional commitments that run the gamut from constructiveness to destructiveness, good to evil. (p. 179)

Klein was especially interested in the development and maintenance of an identity as a basic principle of psychological development: "a sensibility for identity may be inborn, but the identity structure itself—its contents—is not inborn; it is an artifact, a creation which emerges. . . . Loss of identity is a specifically human danger; maintenance of identity is a specifically human necessity" (p. 177). Klein, like Erikson, was particularly interested in the structural development of self-identity that is "shaped according to the instrumentalities and sociocultural conditions of each period of life" (p. 177). The motives and aims in relation to a sense of self-integration or identity are a central concern for psychoanalysis as a general psychological theory. But Klein emphasized that there are two aspects of identity: an autonomous distinction from others as a locus of action and decision, and a "we-ness" which is a necessary part of the self that transcends one's autonomous actions—the *we* is as an important part of the self as the *I*. Thus, for Klein "identity must always be defined as having aspects of both separateness and membership in a more encompassing entity. The person can experience deprivation in relation to either or both aspects" (p. 179). Thus, Klein called for the development of a psychoanalytic theory of "we-go" to correspond to its theory of ego—a theory that would account for a concept of *we* emerging from the dialectic between the sense of self and the sense of relationship to the other.

Klein, in part derived from Erikson, stressed the need for an integration of autonomy and affiliation: One must feel "both separate and a part of an entity beyond itself . . . . Identity must always be defined as having aspects of both separateness and membership in a more encompassing entity, and as developing functions that reflect one's role in a relationship with a larger entity" (pp. 178–179). Klein (1976) viewed psychoanalysis, as well as much of psychology, as having been predominantly concerned with a concept of self as a separate, autonomous unit and as not involving a sense of "belonging to" or of we-ness:

> This [latter] aspect of identity—"we-ness"—has its earliest prototype in the mother–infant unit. The infant *Unwelt* can be considered as a kind of prolongation of the mother–child symbiosis; the mother "pole" is the surrounding total organism, and the infant is an organic "part" within this totality. The actions of the infant occur within this mother–child sphere. From this symbiosis emerges a feeling of being part of a larger identity. (p. 179)

This desire to be part of a larger unit serves as a "continuing presence and a molding factor" in the development of the self (p. 179). Thus, Klein forcefully argued for the need in psychoanalysis to incorporate this sense of we that emerges from the dialectic between the development of a sense of self and a sense of relatedness to the other.

Investigators, coming mainly from the field of infant research, recently have begun to elaborate further the conceptualization of this dialectic developmental process. Lichtenberg (1983), integrating empirical infant studies with psychoanalytic theory, concluded that it

> may be that psychoanalysis overstates our separateness, our degree of independence from our animate and inanimate surround. Rather than simply eliminating the interactional concept with an intrapsychic model, we need to retain a view of the interactional context as an explanatory concept with considerable validity throughout the life cycle. (p. 35)

Stern (1977, 1983, 1985, 1988) systematically studied this interactional context by examining the infant's capacity to create not only schemata of self and of other but of "self-with-other." According to Stern (1983), there are three types of relationships of self-with-other: self–other complementing, state-sharing, and state-transforming. Although these relationships can be characterized by the degree of attachment or separateness they imply, it is their contribution to the structuralization of the self through the schematization of interpersonal experiences that interested Stern. He took the concept of relationship beyond the meaning ascribed to it by separation theories that view self–other relationships as a means toward the development of a sense of self as separate, as well as beyond the meaning ascribed to the relationship by attachment theories that consider the relationship a goal. Stern (1983) stated that these relationships

> are also the stuff that human connectedness, as well as normal intimacy and basic trust, are made of at all points in development. The ability to engage in them is among the most needed and healthy of capacities. The point of view I am taking proposes to take the being with experience (in normally developing infants) beyond their primarily problematic role in the differentiation of self and other and establish them as positive human capacities, the development of which is best understood against a background of intact schemata of self and other. (pp. 80–81)

Emde (1988), discussing the work of Stern and others who have begun to consider the dialectic between the development of a sense of self and of relatedness, believed that the emergence of this dual emphasis is reflective of an important theoretical development:

> It is perhaps ironic that in our age, so preoccupied with narcissism and self, we are beginning to see a different aspect of psychology, a "we" psychology in addition to a "self" psychology. I draw our attention to the fact that this represents a profound change in our world view. (p. 36)

The profound change of which Emde spoke involves an expansion of our notion of the self-system to include the we dimension. Emde discussed three dynamic aspects of the self system: the experience of self, the experience of the other (e.g., attachment figure), and the experience of the self with other or we.

These formulations from a psychoanalytic perspective are consistent with the recent emphasis of feminist theorists (e.g., Chodorow, 1978, 1989; Gilligan, 1982, 1989; Miller, 1976; Surrey, 1985) on the importance of the development of a "self-in-relation" and Sampson's (1985, 1988) distinction between "self-contained" and "ensembled individualism." The complex interactive process in the development of self-definition and of interpersonal relatedness should, in normal development, lead to a sense of we (e.g., Klein, 1976), ensembled individualism (e.g., Sampson, 1988), and of self-in-relation (e.g., Gilligan, 1982, 1989). Personality development and psychopathology might be more effectively conceptualized by considering the complex interactive dialectic between relatedness and self definition throughout the life cycle.

TWO PRIMARY DIMENSIONS OF PERSONALITY DEVELOPMENT

A reformulation of Erikson's psychosocial, epigenetic model of psychological development provides an opportunity to articulate more fully the relative contributions that the evolving capacities for relatedness and self-definition each makes to psychological development. Erikson's formulations also provide an opportunity to consider how aspects of these two developmental lines are eventually integrated, beginning in late adolescence, in the development of we system (Klein, 1976), in a sense of self-in-relation (e.g., Surrey, 1985), and of ensembled individualism (e.g., Sampson, 1988).

Through a linear series of hierarchical stages, Erikson (1950, 1959, 1963, 1964, 1968, 1977, 1982) described the individual's progress from infantile dependency toward increasing individuation through processes of identification and socialization. Although Erikson stressed the importance of social agents for the facilitation of psychological development and for the ongoing articulation of the individual development, his emphasis was consistently on the antecedents and consequences of the attainment of a separate self-identity. Such statements as "true 'engagement' with others is the result and the test of firm self delineation" (1968, p. 167) reflect the special status that Erikson assigned to the stage of identity formation and what he considered to be its associated tasks—separation and individuation. Erikson's overriding emphasis on individuation, to what appears at times to be a neglect of the attachment task of development, has recently been discussed as a limitation of Erikson's epigenetic model (Blatt & Shichman, 1983; Franz & White 1985). Franz and White (1985) called for the addition of an attachment or relatedness developmental line to broaden Erikson's emphasis on individuation and identity. Blatt and Shichman's (1983) proposal of adding a stage of cooperation versus alienation between the phallic of age of initiation—guilt and the latency stage of identity—inferiority more clearly defined a relatedness developmental line within Erikson's formulations. The inclusion of a developmental dimension of relatedness (i.e., attachment, trust, cooperation, and intimacy) as an integral aspect of personality development to complement the more usual emphasis on individuation, self-definition, and identity is consistent with the observations of feminist theorists (e.g., Chodorow, 1978, 1989; Gilligan, 1982, 1989; Miller, 1984) who stressed the failure in most theories of personality development to give equal status to the development of interpersonal relatedness. This call for the recognition of the importance of attachment and relatedness is also consistent with the extensive research and theory of the past 2 decades that demonstrate the importance of attachment (e.g., Ainsworth, 1969; Bowlby, 1969, 1973) and of the development of mutuality and empathy (e.g., Beebe & Lachmann, 1988; Stern, 1985) in personality development.

Although we agree that the attachment task has not received sufficient consideration in Erikson's formulations, it is important to note that Erikson's model is not exclusively a separation or an identity theory of personality development. Attachment and relationship tasks are, in fact, embedded in his model. Segments of Erikson's formulations implicitly and explicitly call attention to the importance of issues of relatedness. In discussing identity formation in one of his later statements, Erikson (1982), for example, noted the following:

> epigenetically speaking, of course, nobody can quite "know" who he or she "is" until promising partners in work and love have been encountered and tested. Yet, the basic patterns of identity must emerge from (1) the selective affirmation and repudiation of an individual's childhood identifications; and (2) the way in which the social process of the times identifies young individuals—at best recognizing them as persons who had to become the way they are and who, being the way they are, can be trusted." . . . In summary, the process of identity formation emerges as an evolving configuration—a configuration that gradually integrates constitutional givens, *idiosyncratic libidinal ties* [italics added], favored capacities, significant identifications, effective defenses, successful sublimations, and consistent roles. All these, however, can only emerge from a mutual adaptation of individual potentials, technological world views, and religious or political ideologies. (pp. 72–74)

Erikson (1982) also discussed the development of the "I" and the "we," but in many ways he viewed the development of the "we" with awe, as a mystical process:

> Freud put the self-observing "I" and the shared "we" into the exclusive service of the study of the unconscious . . . a more systematic study of "I" and "we" would seem to be not only necessary for an understanding of psychosocial phenomena, but also elemental for a truly comprehensive psychoanalytic psychology. I am, of course, aware of the linguistic difficulty of speaking of *the* "I" as we do of *the* ego or *the* self; and yet, it does take a sense of "I" to be aware of a "myself" or, indeed, of a series of myselves, while all the variations of self-experience have in common . . . the conscious continuity of the "I" that experienced and can become aware of them all. Thus, the "I", after all, is the ground for the simple verbal assurance that each person is the center of awareness in a universe of communicable experience, a center so numinous that it amounts to a sense of being alive and, more, of being the vital condition of existence. At the same time, only two or more persons who share a corresponding world image and can bridge their languages may merge their "I's" into a "we." It could, of course, be of great significance to sketch the developmental context in which the pronouns—from "I" to "we" to "they"—take on their full meaning in relation to the organ modes, the postural and sensory modalities, and the space-time characteristics of world views. (pp. 87–88)

Erikson relies primarily on Freud's (1921) analysis in *Group Psychology and the Analysis of the Ego* of the individual's relationship to primal groups and to the charismatic leader to understand the development of the sense of "we." Erikson (1982) stressed the importance of mutual relationships with others:

> It must be remembered that children must continue to learn to use other selected adults, be they grandparents or neighbors, doctors, or teachers, for much-needed extraparental encounters. Thus, what is sometimes monotonously referred to as the child patient's search for "*object-relations*" (that is, for a fully deserving and responding recipient of one's love) must come to include that clarified *mutuality of involvement* on which the life of generations depends. (p. 100)

But Erikson (1982) acknowledged the limitations of his theory in fully articulating the development of the "we": "the overall theory seemed to be working toward and yet stopping short of a systematic attention to the ego's role in the relationship of *individuality* and *communality*" (pp. 15–16).

The importance of attachment tasks is underplayed in Erikson in part because of his unidimensional linear schematization of development. Erikson's emphasis on self-identity places the consolidation of a separate identity as the central goal or result of normal development. Within such a context, attachment and interpersonal relatedness appear to play secondary roles, those of facilitating, and as by-products of, identity development. Attachment tasks in the Erikson model are intermediary links in the process of development toward individuation. Mature relationships are what occur in the attainment of individuation. Although the term *identity* has been used somewhat ambiguously by many authors, for Erikson (1959) the development of identity stresses the individual as a separate and autonomous agent. Although separateness implies an ability to recognize similarity as well as differences with others and autonomy implies the ability to see oneself in relation to others, relationships are not commonly emphasized in Erikson's concept of identity, which stresses the "integration of perceptions of oneself as separate and distinct from the other" (Mussen, Conger, & Kegan, 1979, p. 495).

It would be valuable, however, to consider self-identity as emerging through an ongoing dialectic between the self as separate and the self as experienced in its attachments to objects. Recognition of the role of attachment in the development of identity and the understanding of the dialectic between the development of attachment and of separateness necessitate the postulation of two distinct but interactive lines of development. These assumptions provide the basis for our modification of Erikson's psychosocial developmental model. A reformulation of Erikson's psychosocial model enables us to emphasize the two fundamental developmental lines of self-definition and interpersonal relatedness, as well as their eventual integration. Erikson's (1950) epigenetic model of psychosocial development, although presented basically as a linear developmental process, provides implicit support for the view that normal personality development involves the simultaneous and mutually facilitating development of interpersonal relatedness and self-definition. Blatt and his colleagues (Blatt, 1990; Blatt & Blass, 1990; Blatt & Shichman, 1983) noted that if one includes in Erikson's model an additional stage of cooperation and collaboration versus alienation (occurring around the time of the development of cooperative peer play and the initial resolution of the oedipal crisis at the age of about 4–6), and places this stage at the appropriate point in the developmental sequence between "initiative versus guilt" and "industry versus inferiority," then the complex transaction between interpersonal relatedness and self-definition throughout the life cycle becomes apparent in Erikson's epigenetic model of psychosocial development.

Erikson initially emphasized interpersonal relatedness in his discussion of trust versus mistrust, followed by two stages of self-definition, autonomy versus shame, and initiative versus guilt. This is then followed by another stage of interpersonal relatedness, cooperation versus alienation, and then by two stages of self-definition—industry versus inferiority, and identity versus role diffusion. The following stage, intimacy versus isolation, is again a stage of interpersonal relatedness, followed by two more stages of self-definition, generativity versus stagnation and integrity versus despair (Blatt & Shichman, 1983). Although we have placed identity and integrity in the self-definitional line, subsequently we discuss how these two advanced stages of psychological development are also really stages of integration and consolidation.

The interactive dialectic process of development, and the place of the relatedness developmental line within it, is consistent with concepts from Sullivan's interpersonal theory, which can be integrated in the basic Eriksonian model. In one developmental line, individuality, we include Erikson's stages of autonomy versus shame, initiative versus guilt, industry versus inferiority, generativity versus stagnation and integrity versus despair. In the other developmental line, relatedness, we include the stages of trust versus mistrust, cooperation/collaboration versus alienation, and intimacy versus isolation. The addition of concepts from Sullivan of an early stage of emotional contagion and an intermediate stage of cooperation/collaboration in the relatedness developmental line allows us to delineate several different stages in the progression of each of these developmental lines and to consider their coordinated development (see Figure 1). This reformulation of Erikson's model (Blatt, 1990; Blatt & Blass, 1990; Blatt & Shichman, 1983) corrects to some extent the deficiency observed by Franz and White (1985) that Erikson's model neglects to an important degree the development of intimacy and interpersonal attachment.

Relatedness and individuality (attachment and separation) both evolve through a complex interactive developmental process. The evolving capacities for *autonomy, initiative,* and *industry* in the individuality developmental line develop in parallel with the development of a capacity for relatedness—to *engage* with and *trust* another, to *cooperate* and *collaborate* in group activities (e.g., play), to develop a close friendship with a same-sex *chum,* and to eventually experience and express feelings of *mutuality, intimacy,* and *reciprocity* in an intimate, mature relationship. In normal development, there is a high degree of coordination between the evolving capacities along the two lines. For example, one needs a sense of basic trust to venture in opposition to the significant, need-gratifying other in asserting ones' autonomy and independence, and, later, one needs a sense of autonomy and initiative to establish cooperative and collaborative relationships. Though these two developmental lines interact throughout the life cycle, they remain relatively independent of each other through the early developmental years, until adolescence, at which time the developmental task is to integrate these two developmental lines into a comprehensive core of "self-identity."

Self-identity, although partly a stage in the development of self-definition, is also a cumulative, integrative stage in which the capacity to cooperate and share with others is coordinated with a sense of individuality that has emerged from a capacity for autonomy, initiative, and industry—the capacity for sustained goal-directed, task-oriented activity (Blatt & Blass,

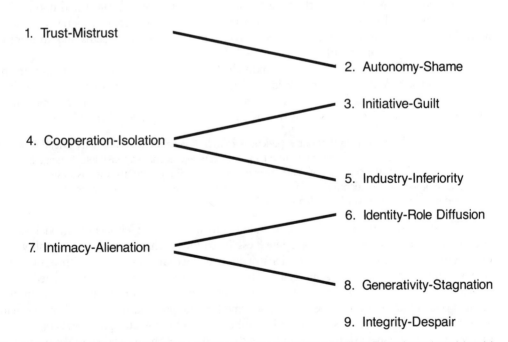

Interpersonal Relatedness	Self-Definition

1. Trust-Mistrust

2. Autonomy-Shame

3. Initiative-Guilt

4. Cooperation-Isolation

5. Industry-Inferiority

6. Identity-Role Diffusion

7. Intimacy-Alienation

8. Generativity-Stagnation

9. Integrity-Despair

Figure 1. The dialectic interaction of interpersonal relatedness and self definition implicit in Erikson's psychosocial model. (Adapted from Blatt, 1990. Used by permission.)

1990). Identity involves a synthesis and integration of individuality and relatedness—the internality and intentionality that develops as part of autonomy, initiative, and industry as well as the capacity and desire to participate in a social group with an appreciation of what one has to contribute to, and gain from, participating in the collective, without losing one's individuality within the collective or the relationship. Thus, in this sense, Erikson's more advanced stages of identity versus role diffusion and integrity versus despair can be viewed as periods of integration of the relatedness and self-definitional developmental lines. These later two stages involve the individual's formation of a new and more complete synthesis of mature expressions of both individuality and relatedness (Blatt & Blass, 1990).

Thus, a marked change occurs in the developmental process in adolescence. Earlier in development, the various components of the two developmental lines are internalized primarily as independent components. Beginning in adolescence, these various components are integrated and coordinated in a new gestalt or synthesis. This shift in the mechanisms of development from internalization to integration in late adolescence is in accord with Erikson's (1968) description of the identity stage at adolescence as one of the integration of the identity elements ascribed . . . to the childhood stages" (p. 128). "*Identity formation,* finally, begins when the usefulness of identification ends. It arises from the selective repudiation and mutual assimilation of childhood identifications and their absorption in a new configuration . . . [into] a new, unique gestalt which is more than the sum of its parts" (p. 158–159). The successful outcome of the establishment of a new configuration is an integrated sense of self-identity.

The stage of identity, this period of integration and consolidation, is also characterized by self-awareness and self-reflectivity—what Baumeister (1986) called self-knowledge, as well as a recognition of and an appreciation for the integrity of others (Waterman, 1981). Identity is a process of self-discovery and a self-reflective awareness of one's intentions, values, and goals that result from the internalization of the attitudes of the generalized other (Mead, 1934) and of role relations in the social context (Parsons, 1958). The capacity for intentionality, self-reflectivity, and evaluation derive, at least partly, from the internalization of social values and norms. The attainment of identity, therefore, is not just a product of the development along the line of individuality but involves an integration of individuality with social concerns and an identification with communal standards.

Erikson (1974) noted this duality of individuality and relatedness (or community) in the attainment of self-identity: "A sense of identity means a sense of being at one with oneself as one grows and develops; and it means, at the same time, a sense of affinity with a community's sense of being at one with its future as well as its history—or mythology" (p. 27–28).

> A sense of identity implies that one experiences an overall sameness and continuity extending from the personal past (now internalized in introjects and identifications) into a tangible future; and from the community's past (now existing in traditions and institutions sustaining a communal sense of identity) into foreseeable or imaginable realities of work accomplishment and role satisfaction. (Erikson, 1954, p. 53)

The synthesis of these two developmental lines in an integrated self-identity in adolescence leads to more mature expression of relatedness in intimacy characterized by mutuality and reciprocity, as well as in fuller expressions of individuality in generativity with a sustained commitment to enduring values and goals. The integration of individuality and relatedness in self-identity results in a capacity to establish a mutual and reciprocal relationship with another because one is now aware that he or she has something unique and special to offer and share with the other. This capacity is in part derived from a sense of self-worth, pride, and competence that has previously emerged during the various earlier stages of the individuality developmental line as well as from a sense of appreciation of the unique needs of the other. The capacity for intimacy also derives from a growing recognition of one's own needs and limitations, not only in what one has to offer the other, but also of the enrichment one can gain from the other and the pleasures in sharing and the advantages of reciprocity. Likewise, generativity is not just a goal or task-oriented expression of individuality but, as formulated by Erikson, it also involves a concern about extending beyond one's own self-interest and dedicating oneself to broader goals, values, and principles, including contributing to others and society. Thus, Erikson's stages of intimacy and generativity—the capacity to form a unique, mutual, and reciprocal relationship with another and to dedicate oneself to long-term principles and goals, which extend beyond one's self-interest—are expressions of an integration of earlier developmental levels of individuality and relatedness that have been consolidated in a mature self-identity.

The articulation of two primary developmental lines of relatedness and individuality enables us to identify different development levels inherent in both relatedness and individuality. Erikson formulated in considerable detail the development of a sense of individuality as it proceeds from an early sense of autonomy and separation from the control of another, to initiative with the capacity to take action not only in opposition to the other but also as internally determined as a proactive rather than as a reactive action, to industry with its implications for sustained, goal-directed activity that has an inherent direction and purpose. The developmental achievements of these three early stages in the development of individuality provide important attributes and qualities that enter into the eventual attainment of self-identity.

The articulation of the two primary developmental lines of relatedness and individuality also allows us to consider a sequence in the development of the capacity for relatedness, extending from an initial emotional contagion (Sullivan, 1940, 1953) or sharing of affective experiences between mother and infant as documented in the infant research of Stern (1985) and Beebe and Lachmann (1988); to the sense of trust between infant and parent described by Erikson (1950); to a capacity for cooperation and collaboration and the evolution of a close friendship with a same-sex chum as discussed by Sullivan (1940, 1953); to the development of an enduring, intimate, mutual, reciprocal relationship. The formulations of this relatedness developmental sequence allows us to identify various developmental levels of relatedness and to distinguish dependency at a lower developmental level from a more mature reciprocal relatedness in which one gains pleasure from giving as well as receiving care and affection. Although feminist contributions to developmental theory have stressed the importance of including the relatedness developmental line in theories of personality development, some of these theorists (e.g., Gilligan, 1982, 1989; Surrey, 1985) use the term *dependency* to designate this entire developmental sequence of relatedness. It would be more precise to view dependency as an early form of relatedness and to distinguish it from more mature forms of relatedness in which there is a clear and well-articulated sense of self as a separate and effective agent, but one who participates in mature, reciprocal, mutual, satisfying relationships with others.

The articulation of various levels in the development of relatedness and individuality also serve to clarify further the important distinction of self-contained and ensembled individualism discussed by Sampson (1985, 1988). Sampson discussed "self-contained" and "ensembled" individualism as two different types of individuality, but this distinction can also be useful in conceptualizing two broad phases in the development of individuality. Self-contained individualism describes an earlier developmental period in which the qualities of individuality develop with relatively little recognition and appreciation of others and of the social collective, such as during the development of autonomy, initiative, and industry. Ensembled individuality, by contrast, describes an individuality that develops later in the life cycle in which the sense of self is defined in relation to others and the collective, such as in later developmental stages of identity, generativity, and integrity. Sampson also discussed the intimacy of the infant–mother relationship as a form of ensembled individualism. But it is important to distinguish this early reflexive type of relatedness from a more mature ensembled individualism that is based on oneself in relation to another. A separate sense of self is an essential component of more mature levels of relatedness.

Lykes (1985) pointed out that segments of the feminist movement have accepted the culture's predominant value of self-contained individualism with its overvaluation of characteristics such as autonomy, initiative, and industry (achievement) and have sought to apply this model of autonomous or self-contained individualism to women. Other feminist theorists, however, describe a "social individuality" based on an understanding and appreciation of "the person and the interaction of autonomous individuals in a co-acting network of relationships embedded in an intricate system of social exchange and obligations" (Lykes, 1985, p. 362). Numerous femininist theorists (e.g., Noddings, 1984; Chodorow, 1978, 1989; Miller, 1976) have discussed ensembled individualism as an important alternative to the predominant contemporary emphasis on self-contained individualism. Lykes (1985) noted that it is often people from the less powerful and prestigious segments of society that emphasize social individualism or ensembled individuality. But as Freud (1930/1961) noted, the "replacement of power of the individual by the power of the community constitutes the decisive step in civilization" (p. 95). The "readiness for a universal love of mankind and the world represents the highest standpoint which man can reach" (p. 102).

Ensembled individualism involves feeling that one is part of a social order and that one seeks to establish and sustain harmony with that society. This more mature proactive form of ensembled individualism—the reflective, intentional, explicit decision to adhere to, participate in, and contribute to the activities of a social collective and the well-being of others requires an established sense of one's individuality—a self-identity and a differentiated conception of what one can uniquely contribute to the collective as well as an appreciation of how one's own experiences are enriched by such participation. Although the antecedents of this mature form of ensembled individualism emerges from, and has continuity with, the earlier more passive and less reflective form of relatedness that occurs in the mother–infant matrix (Klein, 1976), the more mature form of ensembled individualism is a very different phenomena, based in part, on a clear sense of identity and purpose that can only occur at a much later developmental stage. The more mature form of ensembled individualism is not only a later developmental stage but also an expression of the integration of relatedness and a concern for others with the development of a sense of individuality. It is the consequence of the integration of the products of maturation along the two developmental lines. This integration of self-definition and relatedness, in what Erikson called self-identity, enables the individual to participate in experiences of intimacy, generativity, and integrity, which are self-expressions in a relational context.

TWO PRIMARY CONFIGURATIONS OF PSYCHOPATHOLOGY

The consideration of personality development from the perspective of the coordinated and integrated development of a capacity for relatedness and of a sense of self or individuality also provides a basis for considering various forms of psychopathology from a developmental perspective. Although normality can be defined ideally as an integration of interpersonal relatedness and self-definition, within the normal range individuals usually place relatively greater emphasis on one developmental line over the other. The relative emphasis on either interpersonal relatedness or self-definition delineates two basic personality configurations, each with a particular experiential mode and preferred forms of cognition, defense, and modes of adaptation (Blatt, 1990; Blatt & Shichman, 1983). Which of these two tendencies receives priority (Maddi, 1980) defines important differences in personality style and motivational dispositions (Bakan, 1966).

Individuals who place a relatively greater emphasis on interpersonal relatedness are generally more figurative in their thinking and usually focus primarily on affects and visual images.

Their thinking is characterized as more simultaneous than sequential, and they emphasize reconciliation, synthesis, and integration of elements rather than the critical analysis of separate elements and details. In terms of cognitive style, these individuals tend to be repressors and levelers, and are primarily field dependent. They seek fusion, harmony, integration, and synthesis and are interested more in feelings, affects, and personal reactions rather than facts, figures, and details. Their primary instinctual mode is libidinal rather than aggressive, and they value affectionate feelings and the establishment of close, intimate relationships (Blatt & Shichman, 1983).

Thinking in individuals primarily focused on self-definition is more literal, sequential, linguistic, and critical. Overt behavior, manifest form, logic, consistency, and causality are attended to rather than feelings and relationships. Emphasis is on analysis rather than synthesis, on the critical dissection of details and part properties rather than on achieving integration and synthesis. These individuals would tend to be sensitizers or sharpeners and field independent (Witkin, 1965; Witkin, Dyk, Faterson, Goodenough, & Karp, 1962). Their primary goal is self-assertion, control, autonomy, power, and prestige and their primary instinctual mode involves assertion and aggression in the service of differentiation and self-definition rather than affection and intimacy (Blatt, 1990; Blatt & Shichman, 1983).

Blatt (1974, 1990) and Blatt and Shichman (1983), in discussing these two primary personality configurations, utilized the term *anaclitic* to define the personality organization that focuses predominantly on interpersonal relatedness. The term anaclitic was used by Freud (1905/1963, 1915/1957b), (taken from the Greek "anklitas"—to rest or lean on) to characterize all interpersonal relatedness derived from dependency experienced in satisfying nonsexual drives such as hunger or from dependency experienced initially with a pregenital love object such as the mother (Laplanche & Pontalis, 1974; Webster, 1960). Blatt (1974) and Blatt and Shichman (1983) used the term *introjective* to define the personality organization primarily focused on self-definition. The term *introjective* was used by Freud (1917/1957c) to describe the processes whereby values, patterns of culture, motives, and restraints are assimilated into the self (e.g., made subjective), consciously or unconsciously, as guiding personal principles, through learning and socialization (Webster, 1960).

Spiegel and Spiegel (1978), deriving in part from Kant, presented a similar distinction in their formulation of Dionysian and Apollonian personality styles. They described Dionysians as sensitive to interpersonal issues, more distractable, intuitive, passive, dependent, emotionally naive, trusting, and focused more on feelings than ideas. They are open to and easily influenced by new ideas and others, place greater value on tactile and kinesthetic experiences, and are more action-oriented. They tend to suspend critical judgment, live primarily in the present rather than in the past or the future, and value affiliation and interpersonal relationships.

Apollonians, by contrast, are described as very cognitive, organized, and critical; they value control and reason over emotions. They are very steady, responsible, reliable, unemotional, and highly organized individuals who use critical reason to plan for the future. Apollonians value their own ideas, use them as a primary reference point, and seek to influence others to accept and confirm their ideas. They dominate interpersonal relationships, seek to be in control, and are often very critical about the ideas of others. They are very cautious and methodological, comparing and contrasting alternatives and evaluating ideas and situations piece by piece before they arrive at a final decision and take action. They often pride themselves on being extremely responsible and are hesitant about making commitments, which, once made, they feel obligated by. They are highly reliable and steadfast, often able to stick to a decision, and are relatively uninfluenced by others. They seek to make sure that things are carried out correctly and precisely, and they plan logically and systematically. Spiegel and Spiegel (1978) succinctly summarized the differences between these two personalities or character styles by noting that Dionysians are oriented to and influenced by the heart whereas Apollonians are organized and influenced by the head.

A similar but somewhat more limited distinction was made by Jung (1928) about extraverted and introverted personalities styles. Extraverts seek contact with others and derive gratification and meaning from relationships, whereas introverts give priority to their own thoughts and experiences and maintain a clear sense of self-definition, identity, and uniqueness. Jung, like Spiegel and Spiegel (1978), Blatt (1974), and Blatt and Shichman (1983), viewed these character types as independent of, but related to, concepts of psychopathology (e.g., hysteric and obsessive; Shapiro, 1965). Eysenck (1960), however, extended the Jungian topology to discuss neuroticism in terms of both the hysteric and the obsessive. Research with the Myers-Briggs Personality Inventory (e.g., Myers, 1962; McCaully, 1981) and the Eysenck (1960) Neuroticism Scale provides empirical support for the importance of this differentiation of two basic character types and their relations to neurotic psychopathology.

Relatedness and self-definition evolve in normal development in an integrated form leading to the development of a capacity for reciprocal interpersonal relatedness and of a viable sense of self. Biological predispositions and disruptive environmental events can, however, disturb this integrated developmental process in complex ways and lead to exaggerated emphasis on one mode at the expense of the other. Mild deviations result in unique character styles, such as introverted–extraverted and Appollonian–Dionysian, that are within the normal range. More extensive deviations, markedly exaggerated emphasis on one developmental line at the expense of the other, however, occur in psychopathology.

On occasion, severe and repeated untoward events disrupt the complex, normal, dialectic developmental process. Depending on biological predispositions, cultural factors, gender, basic capacities and vulnerabilities, and cultural and family patterns, individuals attempt to compensate for serious developmental disruptions by exaggerating one developmental line at the expense of the other. In distorted ways, individuals establish excessive preoccupation with issues of relatedness or with the sense of self, at the expense of the other developmental line. The normal developmental process is disrupted and, if there are no subsequent ameliorating circumstances and experiences, these distorted preoccupations are repeated over and over again in various stages of the life cycle and become consolidated as distorted modes of adaptation. The earlier in the developmental process these disruptions occur and the more extreme the distortions, the more severe the psychopathology. Thus, as a consequence of developmental deviations, individuals develop particular character types that emphasize one developmental line over the other. Some individuals become increasingly preoccupied with issues about relatedness and others become increasingly preoccupied about their self-definition, integrity, and prerogatives. In the extreme, an exaggerated preoccupation with interpersonal relatedness at the expense of developing important aspects of the sense of self—or conversely, preoccupations about preserving and protecting the sense of self at the expense of developing adequate forms of interpersonal relatedness—defines two primary configurations of psychopathology.

As a consequence of major disruption of the normal developmental, dialectic processes of relatedness and self-definition, some individuals, most often women, become excessively preoccupied with relatedness at the expense of development of the sense of self. If this developmental disruption occurs early in the life cycle, it can lead to the development of an infantile (or borderline) character, someone exclusively preoccupied with wanting to be held, cared for, fed, and attended to (Blatt, 1974). If the disruption of the developmental process occurs later in the life cycle, a more organized kind of hysterical disorder can develop in which the person is concerned not only with being held, cared for, and loved but also with being able to express as well as receive love. Patients at the infantile level tend to use denial as their primary defense; their concerns are primarily dyadic in structure and they strive to be accepted and cared for, like the young child with its mother. Patients at a developmentally higher hysterical level, in contrast, use repression as their primary defense; their primary concerns involve triadic configurations and oedipal themes such as striving for the attention and love of one parent in competition with the other. At both the infantile level and the developmentally more advanced hysterical level, the issues focus primarily on libidinal attachment—concerns about being loved, intimate, and close. Denial and repression are generically the same type of defense—they are avoidant defenses.

Infantile and hysteric disorders can occur in relatively pure form, but they are not isolated disorders or diseases. Rather, they represent relative end-points on a continuum of a configuration of anaclitic psychopathology and many patients combine features of both levels of functioning, and their level of organization will vary depending on environmental circumstances and psychological stress. These formulations are consistent with Zetzel's (1968) discussion of the differences between the so called "good hysteric" and the lower level hysterical characters.

Some individuals, more often men, deal with severe disruption of the normal dialectic developmental process by exaggerated attempts to consolidate a sense of self. In the extreme, this is expressed in paranoia, obsession–compulsion, guilt-ridden (introjective) depression, and phallic narcissism. These disorders all express preoccupations about the self ranging from primitive concerns in paranoia to more integrated concerns about the self in introjective depression and phallic narcissism. The paranoid patient is preoccupied with maintaining a rigid definition of self as distinct and separate from others. Paranoid patients struggle to prove that they are a separate and independent entity and that they are not merged and fused in a symbiotic relationship with another (Blatt & Wild, 1976). They struggle to establish a sense of self in a primitive form—all bad is placed onto the other, all good is attributed to the self, and an isolated and embattled distance is maintained from others. Obsessive–compulsive disorders, in contrast, express somewhat higher concerns about the self—concerns about mastery, autonomy, control, prerogatives, and possessions. At a still somewhat higher developmental level, individuals are more concerned about issues of self-worth than about autonomy and mastery. In introjective depression, the predominant concerns are about one's worth in comparison to an idealized value system with the belief and feeling that one has failed or transgressed. Phallic narcissism is the reversal of introjective depression in which, through counteraction, the individual seeks to exhibit himself or herself and win endless accolades and approval in order to defend against intense feelings of guilt and shame, worthlessness, and humiliation (Blatt & Shichman, 1983).

The dynamics, conflicts, defenses, and the cognitive–affective and interpersonal style of the various forms of psychopathology of the introjective configuration share a fundamental similarity. Paranoia, obsession–compulsion, introjective depression, and phallic narcissism all involve issues of self-definition expressed in self-reproach, guilt, and preoccupations with self-worth and self-control. Interest is directed primarily toward things rather than people, and there is a heightened emphasis on thoughts, ideas, activities, and accomplishments (deeds) rather than on feelings and interpersonal relationships. In all the psychopathologies of the introjective configuration, defenses are essentially counteractive rather than avoidant. Projection, reversal, intellectualization, doing and undoing, reaction formation, introjection (or identification with the aggressor), and overcompensation, with varying degrees of effectiveness, all attempt to alter or transform impulses and conflicts rather than to avoid (deny and/or repress) them. Each of the disorders in the introjective configuration can be viewed as independent and separate, but they are really interrelated disorders, and most often individual patients present a complex admixture of these various disorders.

In these formulations, different types of psychopathology are considered as distorted exaggerations of either the anaclitic or the introjective developmental line. Thus, as illustrated in Figure 2, there are two primary configurations of psychopathology, each defined primarily by exaggerations of the tasks of each of the two fundamental developmental lines. Exaggerated and

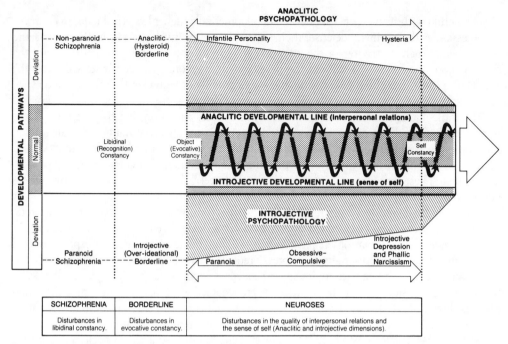

Non-paranoid — — — Anaclitic — — — Infantile Personality — — — — — — — — — — — — — — Hysteria
Schizophrenia   (Hysteroid)
                       Borderline

Deviation

DEVELOPMENTAL   PATHWAYS

Normal

ANACLITIC DEVELOPMENTAL LINE (interpersonal relations)

Libidinal   Object   Self
(Recognition)   (Evocative)   Constancy
Constancy   Constancy

INTROJECTIVE DEVELOPMENTAL LINE (sense of self)

INTROJECTIVE
PSYCHOPATHOLOGY

Deviation

                                                                    Introjective
                     Introjective   Depression
                     (Over-ideational)   and Phallic
Paranoid — — — — — — Borderline — — — Paranoia   Obsessive—   Narcissism
Schizophrenia   Compulsive

SCHIZOPHRENIA	BORDERLINE	NEUROSES
Disturbances in libidinal constancy.	Disturbances in evocative constancy.	Disturbances in the quality of interpersonal relations and the sense of self (Anaclitic and introjective dimensions).

Figure 2. A model of normal and psychopathological development. (Adapted from Blatt & Schichman, 1983. Used by permission.)

distorted preoccupation about satisfying interpersonal relations, to the neglect of the development of concepts of self, defines the psychopathologies of the anaclitic configuration—infantile and hysterical disorders. Exaggerated and distorted concerns about the integrity of the self, at the expense of establishing meaningful interpersonal relations, defines the psychopathologies of the introjective configuration—paranoid, obsessive–compulsive, introjective depressive, and phallic narcissistic disorders.

In each of these two configurations of psychopathology, there are several evolving levels of organization ranging from more primitive to more integrated attempts to establish meaningful interpersonal relationships and a consolidated self-concept. The various levels of psychopathology within the anaclitic and the introjective configurations define lines along which patients progress or regress. Thus, an individual's difficulties can be specified as being predominantly in one or the other personality configuration, at a particular developmental level, and with a differential potential to regress or progress to other developmental levels within the configuration. In this conceptualization, the various forms of psychopathology are considered no longer as isolated, independent, disease entities but rather as interrelated modes of adaptation, organized at different developmental levels in two basic configurations that focus on either interpersonal relationships or self-definition. Psychopathologies within the anaclitic configuration share a basic preoccupation with libidinal issues such as closeness and intimacy. There is a greater emphasis on affective bonding and greater potential for the development of meaningful interpersonal relationships. Psychopathologies within the anaclitic configuration also have a similar defense style with a predominant use of avoidant defenses such as denial, repression, and displacement. Psychopathologies in the introjective configuration share a basic focus on anger, aggression, and themes of self-definition, self-control, and self-worth. They also share a similarity in defensive style with the use of counteractive defenses such as isolation, doing and undoing, intellectualization, reaction formation, introjection, identification with the aggressor, and overcompensation. Cognitive processes are more fully developed, and there is greater potential for the development of logical, abstract thought. Although most forms of psychopathology are organized primarily around one configuration or the other, there also may be some patients who have features from both the anaclitic and the introjective dimensions and whose psychopathology derives from both configurations.[1]

RELATEDNESS AND SELF-DEFINITION IN RESEARCH ON DEPRESSION AND THE THERAPEUTIC PROCESS

The importance of the distinction between an emphasis on interpersonal relatedness and self-definition in personality development and psychopathology is supported by recent research on depression and psychotherapeutic change.

Studies of Depression

The distinction between patients who focus on issues of relatedness as compared to those who focus on issues of self-definition has had considerable impact in recent research on depression. A number of clinical investigators, dissatisfied with difficulties in establishing meaningful subtypes of depression based on differences in clinical symptoms, have proposed differentiating between subtypes of depression based on the phenomenology of the experiences or the issues that lead individuals to become depressed. Three independent groups of psychoanalytic theorists have stressed the importance of differentiating two basic types of depression. Bowlby (1969, 1973, 1977, 1980, 1988) from an ethological and object relations point of view, and Arieti and Bemporad (1978, 1980), from a Sullivanian interpersonal orientation and Blatt and his colleagues (Blatt, 1974; Blatt, D'Afflitti, & Quinlan, 1976; Blatt, Quinlan, Cheveron, McDonald, & Zuroff, 1982), from a psychoanalytic and a cognitive developmental perspective have all stressed the importance of differentiating between a depression focused on interpersonal issues such as dependency, helplessness, and feelings of loss and abandonment, and a depression focused on issues of self-definition, such as autonomy, self-criticism, and feelings of failure and guilt. Beck (1983), from a cognitive–behavioral orientation, also proposed a similar distinction (Blatt & Maroudas, in press).

Arieti and Bemporad (1978, 1980) discussed a dominant-other and a dominant-goal type of depression in which depression can focus on issues of being passively gratified by a dominant other or of being reassured of one's worth and being free of guilt. In the dominant-other type of depression, the child reacts to the experience of a sudden withdrawal of love and approval by developing a clinging, demanding, dependent, and infantile relationship with the dominant other. In the dominant-goal type of depression, the child reacts to the experience of sudden withdrawal of love and approval by feeling that he or she must submit to the parents' expectations. The child seeks to regain love and approval not only by being compliant but also by directing one's entire effort toward a dominant goal that becomes an end in itself. When the dominant other is lost or the dominant goal is not achieved, depression results. The person feels dependent on others for support, direction, and a sense of well-being and feels that he or she lacks the resources to establish a sense of meaning and purpose of life. Arieti and Bemporad (1978) discussed two intense wishes in depression: "to be passively gratified by the dominant other . . . [and] to be reassured of one's own worth, and to be free of the burden of guilt" (p. 167).

---

[1]Fuller discussion of the various forms of psychopathology and their interrelationships in the anaclitic and introjective configuration is available in Blatt and Shichman (1983).

Beck (1983) also recently discussed a socially dependent (sociotropic) and an autonomous type of depression. Sociotropy (social dependency)

> refers to the person's investment in positive interchange with other people. This cluster includes passive–receptive wishes (acceptance, intimacy, understanding, support, guidance); and "narcissistic wishes" (admiration, prestige, status). . . . Individuality (autonomy) refers to the person's investment in preserving and increasing his independence, mobility, and personal rights; freedom of choice, action, and expression; protection of his domain;—and attaining meaningful goals (p. 272).

Beck postulated that disruption of personal relationships in socially dependent individuals, and a failure to meet personal goals or standards in autonomous individuals, can precipitate a depression. In addition, recent factor-analytic studies of the Dysfunctional Attitude Scale developed by Weissman and Beck (1978) to assess attitudes presumed to predispose an individual to depression, reveal two major factors that have been labeled concerns about "approval by others" and "performance evaluation" (or self-worth; Cane, Olinger, Gotlib, & Kuiper, 1986) or "a need for approval" and "perfectionism" (Oliver & Baumgart, 1985).

Bowlby (1969, 1973, 1977, 1980, 1988) differentiated between several groups of patients and discussed how compulsively self-reliant and anxiously attached individuals are predisposed toward depression. Compulsively self-reliant individuals avoid relationships and are scornful of people who seek close, intimate, interpersonal relationships. Bowlby viewed this excessive autonomy as a defense against reexperiencing early childhood frustrations in caring relationships or as an expression of having been a "parentified child" who prematurely assumed caretaker responsibilities in his or her family, often for his or her own parents. Anxiously detached individuals, by contrast, eagerly seek interpersonal contacts and are excessively dependent on others.

Blatt (1974) distinguished between an anaclitic (dependent) and an introjective (self-critical) depression. Anaclitic depression is characterized by feelings of loneliness, helplessness, and weakness; the individual has intense and chronic fears of being abandoned, uncared for, and unprotected. These individuals have a desperate need to keep in close physical contact with need-gratifying others because they have not fully internalized the experiences of gratification or the qualities of the individuals who provided satisfaction. They experience deep longings to be loved, cared for, nurtured, and protected; others are valued primarily for the care, comfort, and satisfaction they provide. Others are needed in order to maintain a sense of well-being and therefore these individuals have great difficulty expressing anger for fear of destroying the need gratification others can provide. Separation from others and loss are sources of considerable fear and apprehension, and are often dealt with by primitive means such as denial and/or a desperate search for immediate substitutes. Introjective depression, by contrast, is characterized by self-criticism and feelings of unworthiness, inferiority, failure, and guilt. An extremely punitive and critical superego results in constant and harsh self-scrutiny and evaluation. These individuals have a chronic fear of criticism and loss of approval and acceptance; they constantly strive for excessive achievement and perfection, are often highly competitive and work hard, make many demands on themselves, and often achieve a great deal, but with little lasting satisfaction. They can be critical and aggressive toward others because of their intense competitiveness. Their primary defenses are overcompensation and introjection, through which they seek to maintain approval and a positive sense of self-esteem.

Both Beck and his colleagues (Beck, 1983) and Blatt and his colleagues (Blatt, D'Afflitti, & Quinlan, 1976; Blatt, Quinlan, Cheveron, McDonald, & Zuroff, 1982) developed methods for systematically assessing these two types of depression and have demonstrated the validity of these distinctions. A wide range of clinical research indicates that the distinction between an exaggerated preoccupation with issues of interpersonal relatedness or with self-definition identifies two major types of depression and this distinction appears to have considerable reliability and validity, more so than traditional diagnostic categories or subtypes of depression based on differences in manifest symptoms.

Research with both clinical and nonclinical samples indicates that the distinction between an exaggerated preoccupation with relatedness and with self-definition identifies two major types of depression that provides important leads into some of the mechanisms about how personality predispositions and current stressful life events interact to create depression. The distinction between dependent and self-critical personality characteristics—the difference in emphasis on interpersonal relatedness (e.g., dependency) and self-definition (e.g., self-criticism)—have made possible a wide range of investigations that have explained ways in which environmental events interact with personality and/or cognitive styles and how they reciprocally influence one another. This interactive perspective has the potential for establishing a fuller integration of cognitive and interpersonal approaches in the study of personality dimensions, especially depression.

Studies using both experimental and longitudinal designs indicate that dependent subjects are especially vulnerable to negative interpersonal events (Hammen, Marks, Mayo, & deMayo, 1985; Mongrain & Zuroff, 1989; Segal, Vella, & Shaw, 1987; Zuroff & Mongrain, 1987). Self-critical subjects, on the other hand, appear to be vulnerable to a wider range of events, to both failure as well as to interpersonal loss. It is possible that dependent individuals are at a lower developmental level (Blatt, 1974) and therefore are vulnerable primarily to one major concern, while self-critical individuals may interpret rejection and interpersonal loss as a failure and as having implications for their feelings of self-worth. It would be of interest in subsequent research to explore the meanings attributed to rejection and failure by both dependent and self-critical individuals. Recent findings by Smith, O'Keefe, and Jenkins (1988) suggested that gender may also influence the relation between specific classes of events and anaclitic and introjective personality styles. They found that an interaction of dependency and life events predicted depression scores for men whereas the interaction of self-criticism and life events predicted depression for women. These data suggest that individuals with gender-incongruent personality types (e.g., dependent males and self-critical females) may be especially vulnerable to depression initiated by interpersonal and achievement issues, respectively. The differential sensitivity of highly dependent and highly self-critical subjects to themes of abandonment, loss and rejection or themes of failure and criticism may also result in different coping or defensive styles in response to these different types of stressors. Individuals who are high on dependency are likely to seek compromise in order to avoid direct conflict and confrontation, whereas individuals who are high on self-criticism and are more responsive to issues of self-definition, power, control, autonomy, and mastery (themes of separation–individuation) are more likely to react to these stressors with heightened counterreactive responses (Blatt & Shichman, 1983).[2]

Studies of Therapeutic Change

The distinction between disruptions of relatedness and self-definition has been important not only in the study of depression, but also in providing a valuable differentiation in two studies of therapeutic change. Data from two studies (Blatt, in press; Blatt, Ford, Berman, Cook, & Meyer, 1988) indicate that patients who are excessively preoccupied with issues of interpersonal relatedness (anaclitic patients) and those who are excessively preoccupied with self-definition (e.g. autonomy, control, and individual prerogatives; introjective patients) change in different ways in the treatment process and are differently responsive to different forms of therapy.

---

[2]See Blatt and Zuroff (in press) for a fuller discussion of the research on dependent and self-critical depression.

Seriously disturbed anaclitic and introjective patients appear to change in different ways in long-term, intensive, psychoanalytically oriented psychotherapy. Clinical change in anaclitic patients occurs primarily in the quality of their interpersonal relationships with other patients and with the clinical staff including the therapist, paralleled by changes in the quality of their representation of the human figure and of interpersonal interactions on the Rorschach. Introjective patients change primarily in the degree to which they manifest symptoms of psychosis, neurosis, and affect disturbances, paralleled by changes in quality of their cognitive processes as measured by the Wechsler Intelligence Test and thought disorder on the Rorschach. Changes in the manifest symptoms and the aspects of cognitive functioning appear to be consistent measures of therapeutic change primarily in introjective patients (Blatt, Ford, Berman, Cook, & Meyer, 1988).

It seems quite consistent that anaclitic patients, with their preoccupations about the quality of their interpersonal relationships, should demonstrate therapeutic change primarily in interpersonal behavior as reported in clinical case records and in their conception of the human figure on the Rorschach. Likewise, it seems quite consistent that the more ideational introjective patients, with their preoccupations about issues of self-definition, should demonstrate change primarily in reports of manifest symptoms in their clinical behavior and on psychological test measures of cognitive functioning and thought disorder. Patients appear to change primarily along the dimensions most salient in their personality organization.

A reanalysis of the data of the Menninger Psychotherapy Research Project (Blatt, in press) provided an opportunity to examine the differential impact of two forms of treatment, supportive–expressive psychotherapy and psychoanalysis, on anaclitic and introjective patients. In the original Menninger study, 33 patients were assessed with psychological tests both prior to and subsequent to treatment. The various analyses of the Menninger data indicate that both forms of treatment were equally effective and that there was no differential advantage of one form of treatment over the other. A reanalysis of these data, however, based on a reliable independent differentiation between anaclitic and introjective patients, indicates that there are differential treatment effects for the two types of treatment and that this differential effect depends on the character structure of the patient.

On the basis of independent ratings of case history records established at intake, 21 of the patients were considered to be predominantly anaclitic (8 males and 15 females) and 12 predominately introjective (6 males and 6 females). Of the 21 anaclitic patients, 9 were treated in psychoanalysis and 12 in psychotherapy. Of the 12 introjective patients, 6 were seen in psychoanalysis and 6 in psychotherapy. Independent analysis of Rorschach protocols at intake and again at termination clearly indicates significant differential effect of the two types of treatment, depending on the character structure of the patient. This highly significant Treatment × Patient interaction indicates that anaclitic patients, those patients predominately concerned about issues of interpersonal relatedness, had more constructive change if they were in face-to-face, supported–expressive psychotherapy. Introjective patients, those predominately concerned with issues of self-definition, power, and autonomy, were more constructively responsive if they were in psychoanalysis (Blatt, in press).

Thus, both in the study of depression and in the study of psychotherapy change, it has been very useful to distinguish between individuals who place an exaggerated emphasis on issues of interpersonal relationships from those who place an exaggerated emphasis on aspects of self-definition and individuation. The distinction between anaclitic and introjective patients has provided important insight into the different types of early and current life experiences that can lead to a differential vulnerability to two types of depression. Also, these two different types of patients change in different ways in psychotherapy and they are differentially responsive to psychotherapy and psychoanalysis. All patients do not change along the same dimensions, but they change along the dimensions most salient to their predominant character structure. And all patients are not equally responsive to the same form of therapy but are differentially responsive depending on the congruence of the form of treatment with their character style.

SUMMARY

In this chapter we presented a theoretical model of personality development and of psychopathology based on a formulation of personality development as involving a complex dialectic transaction between the development of the capacity to establish increasingly mature and satisfying interpersonal relationships and the development of a consolidated, realistic, essentially positive, differentiated, and integrated self-definition and identity. Normal variations in character or personality style occur as a consequence of a relative emphasis on one or the other of these two developmental lines. In the extreme, however, exaggerated emphasis on one developmental line at the neglect of the other defines two major configurations of psychopathology. This formulation enables us to consider various forms of psychopathology, not as separate and independent diseases distinguished primarily by differences in manifest symptoms, but as distorted modes of adaptation that emerge out of disruptions of basic psychological development (Blatt, 1991). This formulation not only enables us to begin to specify linkages between normality and pathology, but it enables us to identify some of the interrelationships between different types of psychopathology. One set of disturbances (e.g., the infantile and hysterical characters) appears to be expressions of exaggerated investment in interpersonal relatedness, at the expense of self-definition. These disorders not only share this libidinal focus, but they also have similarity in their use of avoidant defenses (e.g., denial and repression). Another set of disturbances (e.g., paranoia, obsessive–compulsive disorders, and guilty depression) involve an exaggerated emphasis on issues of self-definition at the expense of relatedness. These disorders also share a common focus on anger and aggression directed at others and/or the self, and the use of counteractive defenses (e.g., isolation, intellectualization, reaction formation, and overcompensation).

In this chapter we reviewed research findings and clinical evidence that demonstrate the value of these distinctions in defining subtypes of depression and exploring the clinical characteristics and etiology of these subtypes of depression, as well as in the study of aspects of the psychotherapeutic process. These research findings provide support for the validity of our psychodynamic formulations of personality development and psychopathology and suggest that there is much to be gained by redirecting efforts from differentiations among types of diseases based on clusters of manifest symptoms to beginning to consider various forms of psychopathology as distortions and disruptions of normal psychological processes (Blatt, 1991) that involve the development of a capacity for interpersonal relatedness and of an effective, realistic, and essentially positive sense of self.

REFERENCES

Adler, A. (1951). *The practice and theory of individual psychology* (P. Radin, Trans.). New York: Humanities Press.

Ainsworth, M. D. S. (1969). Object relations, dependency, and attachment: A theoretical review of the mother–infant relationship. *Child Development, 40,* 969–1025.

Angyal, A. (1941). *Foundations for a science of personality.* New York: Viking Press.

Angyal, A. (1951). *Neuroses and treatment: A holistic theory.* (Edited posthumously by E. Hanfmann & R. M. Jones). New York: Wiley.

Arieti, S., & Bemporad, J. (1978). *Severe and mild depression: The psychotherapeutic approach*. New York: Basic Books.

Arieti, S., & Bemporad, J. (1980). The psychological organization of depression. *American Journal of Psychiatry, 136*, 1365–1369.

Bakan, D. (1966). *The duality of human existence: An essay on psychology and religion*. Chicago: Rand McNally.

Baldwin, J. (1902). *Social and ethical interpretations in mental development: A study in social psychology*. New York: Macmillan.

Balint, M. (1952a). The final goal of psychoanalytic treatment. In M. Balint (Ed.), *Primary love and psychoanalytic technique* (pp. 178–189). London: Hogarth Press. (Original work published 1934)

Balint, M. (1952b). Early developmental states of the ego: Primary object-love. In M. Balint (Ed.), *Primary love and psychoanalytic technique* (pp. 90–108). London: Hogarth Press. (Original work published 1937)

Balint, M. (1959). *Thrills and regressions*. Madison, CT: International Universities Press.

Baumeister, R. F. (1986). *Identity: Cultural change and the struggle for self*. New York: Oxford University Press.

Beck, A. T. (1983). Cognitive therapy of depression: New perspectives. In P. J. Clayton & J. E. Barrett (Eds.), *Treatment of depression: Old controversies and new approaches* (pp. 265–290). New York: Raven.

Beebe, B., & Lachmann, F. M. (1988). The contributions of mother infant mutual influence to the origins of self and object representations. *Psychoanalytic Psychology, 5*, 305–337.

Blatt, S. J. (1974). Levels of object representation in anaclitic and introjective depression. *Psychoanalytic Study of the Child, 24*, 107–157.

Blatt, S. J. (1990). Interpersonal relatedness and self-definition: Two personality configurations and their implication for psychopathology and psychotherapy. In J. Singer (Ed.), *Repression and dissociation: Implications for personality theory, psychopathology and health* (pp. 299–335). Chicago: University of Chicago Press.

Blatt, S. J. (1991). A cognitive morphology of psychopathology. *Journal of Nervous and Mental Disease, 179*, 449–458.

Blatt, S. J. (in press). The differential effect of psychotherapy and psychoanalysis with anaclitic and introjective patients: The Menninger Psychotherapy Research Project revisited. *Journal of the American Psychoanalytic Association*.

Blatt, S. J., & Blass, R. B. (1990). Attachment and separateness: A dialectic model of the products and processes of psychological development. *Psychoanalytic Study of the Child, 45*, 107–127.

Blatt, S. J., D'Afflitti, J. P., & Quinlan, D. M. (1976). Experiences of depression in normal young adults. *Journal of Abnormal Psychology, 85*, 383–389.

Blatt, S. J., Ford, R. Q., Berman, W., Cook, B., & Meyer, R. (1988). The assessment of therapeutic change in schizophrenic and borderline young adults. *Psychoanalytic Psychology, 5*, 127–158.

Blatt, S. J., & Maroudas, C. (in press). Convergence of psychoanalytic and cognitive behavior theories of depression. *Psychoanalytic Psychology*.

Blatt, S. J., Quinlan, D. M., Chevron, E. S., McDonald, C., & Zuroff, D. (1982). Dependency and self-criticism: Psychological dimensions of depression. *Journal of Consulting and Clinical Psychology, 150*, 113–124.

Blatt, S. J., & Shichman, S. (1983). Two primary configurations of psychopathology. *Psychoanalysis and Contemporary Thought, 6*, 187–254.

Blatt, S. J., & Wild, C. M. (1976). *Schizophrenia: A developmental analysis*. New York: Academic Press.

Blatt, S. J., & Zuroff, D. C. (in press). Interpersonal relatedness and self-definition: Two prototypes for depression. *Clinical Psychology Review*.

Blos, P. (1979). *The adolescent passage*. Madison, CT: International Universities Press.

Bowlby, J. (1969). *Attachment and loss: Vol. 1. Attachment.* New York: Basic Books.

Bowlby, J. (1973). *Attachment and loss: Vol. 2. Separation, anxiety, and anger.* New York: Basic Books.

Bowlby, J. (1977). The making and breaking of affectional bonds: 1. Etiology and psychopathology in light of attachment theory. *British Journal of Psychiatry, 130,* 201–210.

Bowlby, J. (1980). *Attachment and loss: Vol. 3. Loss, separation and depression.* New York: Basic Books.

Bowlby, J. (1988). Developmental psychology comes of age. *American Journal of Psychiatry, 145,* 1–10.

Cane, D. B., Olinger, L. J., Gotlib, I. H., & Kuiper, N. A. (1986). Factor structure of the dysfunctional attitude scale in a student population. *Journal of Clinical Psychology, 42,* 307–309.

Chodorow, N. (1978). *The reproduction of mothering: Psychoanalysis and the sociology of gender.* Berkeley: University of California Press.

Chodorow, N. (1989). *Feminism and psychoanalytic theory.* New York: Random House.

Cooley, C. H. (1902). *Human nature and the social order.* New York: Scribner.

Emde, R. N. (1988). Development terminable and interminable. *International Journal of Psycho-Analysis, 69,* 23–42.

Erikson, E. H. (1950). *Childhood and society.* New York: Norton.

Erikson, E. H. (1954). The dream specimen of psychoanalysis. *Journal of the American Psychoanalytic Association, 2,* 5–56.

Erikson, E. H. (1959). *Identity and the life cycle.* Madison, CT: International Universities Press.

Erikson, E. H. (1963). *Childhood and society* (2nd ed.). New York: Norton.

Erikson, E. H. (1964). *Insight and responsibility.* New York: Norton.

Erikson, E. H. (1968). *Identity, youth and crisis.* New York: Norton.

Erikson, E. H. (1974). *Dimensions of a new identity.* New York: Norton.

Erikson, E. H. (1977). *Toys and reasons.* New York: Norton.

Erikson, E. H. (1982). *The life cycle completed.* New York: Norton.

Eysenck, H. J. (1960). *Behaviour therapy and the neuroses.* Oxford, England: Pergamon Press.

Fairbairn, W. R. D. (1952). *Psychoanalytic studies of the personality.* London: Tavistock.

Fairbairn, W. R. D. (1953). *An object relation theory of the personality.* New York: Basic Books.

Fairbairn, W. R. D. (1963). Synopsis of an object relations theory of the personality. *International Journal of Psychoanalysis, 44,* 224–225.

Feffer, M. (1969). The cognitive implications of role-taking behavior. *Journal of Personality, 27,* 152–168.

Feffer, M. (1970). Developmental analysis of interpersonal behavior. *Psychology Review, 77,* 177–214.

Franz, C. E., & White, K. M. (1985). Individuation and attachment in personality development: Extending Erikson's theory. *Journal of Personality, 53,* 224–256.

Freud, A. (1965a). The concept of development lines. In A. Freud (Ed.), *Normality and pathology of childhood: Assessments of development* (pp. 62–92). Madison, CT: International Universities Press.

Freud, A. (1965b). Assessment of pathology in childhood. In A. Freud (Ed.), *The writings of Anna Freud* (Vol. 5, pp. 26–59). Madison, CT: International Universities Press.

Freud, A. (1974). A psychoanalytic view of developmental psychopathology. In A. Freud (Ed.), *The writings of Anna Freud* (Vol. 8, pp. 57–74). Madison, CT: International Universities Press.

Freud, S. (1951). Formulations of the two principles of mental functioning. In J. Strachey (Ed. and Trans.), *The standard edition of the complete psychological works of Sigmund Freud* (Vol. 12, pp. 218–226). London: Hogarth Press. (Original work published in 1911)

Freud, S. (1953). *Three essays on sexuality.* In J. Strachey (Ed. & Trans.), *The standard edition of the complete works of Sigmund Freud* (Vol. 20, pp. 135–243). London: Hogarth Press. (Original work published 1905)

Freud, S. (1955). Group psychology and the analysis of the ego. In J. Strachey (Ed. and Trans.), *The standard edition of the complete works of Sigmund Freud* (Vol. 18, pp. 69–143). London: Hogarth Press. (Original work published 1921)

Freud, S. (1957a). On narcissism: An introduction. In J. Strachey (Ed. and Trans.), *The standard edition of the complete psychological works of Sigmund Freud* (Vol. 14, pp. 73–102). London: Hogarth Press. (Original work published 1914)

Freud, S. (1957b). Repression. In J. Strachey (Ed. and Trans.), *The standard edition of the complete psychological works of Sigmund Freud* (Vol. 14, pp. 146–158). London: Hogarth Press. (Original work published 1915)

Freud, S. (1957c). Mourning and melancholia. In J. Strachey (Ed. and Trans.), *The standard edition of the complete psychological works of Sigmund Freud* (Vol. 14, pp. 243–258). London: Hogarth Press. (Original work published 1917)

Freud, S. (1959). Inhibitions, symptoms and anxiety. In J. Strachey (Ed. and Trans.), *The standard edition of the complete psychological works of Sigmund Freud* (Vol. 20, pp. 87–174). London: Hogarth Press. (Original work published 1926)

Freud, S. (1961). Civilization and its discontents. In J. Strachey (Ed. and Trans.), *The standard edition of the complete psychological works of Sigmund Freud* (Vol. 21, pp. 64–145). London: Hogarth Press. (Original work published 1930)

Friedman, H. S., & Booth-Kewley, S. (1987). The disease-prone personality: A meta-analytic view of the construct. *American Psychologist, 42,* 539–555.

Gilligan, C. (1982). *In a different voice.* Cambridge, MA: Harvard University Press.

Gilligan, C. (1989). Remapping the moral domain. In C. Gilligan, J. V. Ward, & J. M. Taylor (Eds.), *Mapping moral domain* (pp. 3–19). Cambridge, MA: Harvard University Press.

Guntrip, H. (1969). *Schizoid phenomena, object relations and the self.* Madison, CT: International Universities Press.

Guntrip, H. (1971). *Psychoanalytic theory, therapy and the self.* London: Karnac.

Hammen, C., Marks, T., Mayo, A., & deMayo, R. (1985). Depressive self-schemas, life stress, and vulnerability to depression. *Journal of Abnormal Psychology, 94,* 308–319.

Horney, K. (1945). *Our inner conflicts.* New York: Norton.

Horney, K. (1950). *Neurosis and human growth.* New York: Norton.

Inhelder, B., & Piaget, J. (1955). *The growth of logical thinking from childhood to adolescence: An essay on the construction of formal operational structures.* New York: Basic Books.

Jung, C. G. (1928). *Contributions to analytic psychology.* London: Routledge & Kegan Paul.

Klein, G. S. (1976). *Psychoanalytic theory.* Madison, CT: International Universities Press.

Kobassa, S. C. (1979). Stressful life events, personality, and health: An inquiry into hardiness. *Journal of Personality and Social Psychology, 37,* 1–11.

Laplanche, J., & Pontalis, J. B. (1974). *The language of psychoanalysis* (D. Nicholson-Smith, Trans.). New York: Norton.

Lichtenberg, J. D. (1983). *Psychoanalysis and infant research.* Hillsdale, NJ: Analytic Press.

Loewald, H. W. (1962). Internalization, separation, mourning and the superego. *Psychoanalytic Quarterly, 31,* 483–504.

Lykes, M. B. (1985). Gender and individualistic vs collectivistic notions about the self. In A. T. Stewart & M. B. Lykes (Eds.), *Gender and personality: Current perspectives on theory and research* (pp. 268–295). Durham, NC: Duke University Press.

Maddi, S. (1980). *Personality theories: A comparative analysis* (4th ed.). Homewood, IL: Dorsey.

Mahler, M. S. (1963). Thoughts about development and individuation. *Psychoanalytic Study of the Child, 18,* 307–324.

Mahler, M. S. (1971). A study of the separation–individuation process and its possible application to borderline phenomena in the psychoanalytic situation. *Psychoanalytic Study of the Child, 26,* 403–424.

Mahler, M. S. (1974a). Individuation: The psychological birth of the human infant. *Psychoanalytic Study of the Child, 29,* 89–106.

Mahler, M. S. (1974b). Symbiosis and individuation. In M. S. Mahler (Ed.). *Selected papers of Margaret S. Mahler* (Vol. 2, pp. 149–165). Northvale, NJ: Jason Aronson.

McAdams, D. P. (1980). A thematic coding system for the intimacy motive. *Journal of Research in Personality, 14,* 413–432.

McAdams, D. P. (1985). *Power, intimacy, and the life story: Personological inquiries into identity.* Homewood, IL: Dorsey.

McCaully, M. H. (1981). Jung's theory of psychological types and the Myers-Briggs Indicator. In P. McReynolds (Ed.), *Advances in psychological assessment* (Vol. 5, pp. 294–352). San Francisco: Jossey-Bass.

McClelland, D. C. (1986). Some reflections on the two psychologies of love. *Journal of Personality, 54,* 334–353.

McClelland, D. C., Atkinson, J. W., Clark, R. A., & Lowell, E. L. (1953). *The achievement motive.* New York: Appleton-Century-Crofts.

Mead, G. H. (1934). *Mind, self, and society.* Chicago: University of Chicago Press.

Miller, J. B. (1976). *Toward a new psychology of women.* Boston: Beacon Press.

Miller, J. B. (1984). The development of women's sense of self. *Work in Progress* (No. 84-01). Wellesley, MA: Wellesley College, The Stone Center.

Modell, A. H. (1968). *Object love and reality.* Madison, CT: International Universities Press.

Mograin, M., & Zuroff, D. C. (1989). Cognitive vulnerability to depressed affect in dependent and self-critical college women. *Journal of Personality Disorders, 3,* 240–251.

Mussen, P. H., Conger, J. F., & Kagan, J. (1979). *Child development and personality.* New York: Harper & Row.

Myers, I. B. (1962). *Manual: The Myers-Briggs Type Indicator.* Palo Alto, CA: Consulting Psychologists Press.

Noddings, N. (1984). *Caring: A feminine approach to ethics and moral education.* Berkeley: University of California Press.

Oliver, J. M., & Baumgart, B. P. (1985). The Dysfunctional Attitude Scale: Psychometric properties in an unselected adult population. *Cognitive Theory and Research, 9,* 161–169.

Parsons, T. (1958). Social structure and the development of personality. In T. Parsons (Ed.), *Social structure and personality* (pp. 78–111). New York: Free Press.

Piaget, J. (1962). *Play, dreams and imitation in childhood.* New York: Norton. (Original work published 1945)

Piaget, J. (1970). *The construction of reality in the child* (M. Cook, Trans.). New York: Basic Books. (Original work published 1954)

Rank, O. (1929). *Truth and reality* (J. Taft, Trans.). New York: Knopf.

Sampson, E. E. (1985). Redecentralization of identity: Toward a revised concept of personal and social order. *American Psychologist, 40,* 1203–1211.

Sampson, E. E. (1988). The debate on individualism: Indigenous psychologies of the individual and their role in personal and societal functioning. *American Psychologist, 43,* 15–22.

Schafer, R. (1968). *Aspects of internalization.* Madison, CT: International Universities Press.

Segal, Z. V., Vella, D. D., & Shaw, B. F. (1987, August–September). *Life stress and depression: Does personality subtyping improve prediction of recurrence?* Paper presented at the 95th Annual Convention of the American Psychological Association, New York.

Selman, R. L., & Schultz, L. H. (1990). *Making a friend in youth: Developmental theory and pair theory.* Chicago: University of Chicago Press.

Settlage, C. F. (1980). The psychoanalytic theory and understanding of psychic development during the second and third years of life. In S. I. Greenspan & G. H. Pollock (Eds.), *The course of life* (pp. 523–539). Washington, DC: National Institute of Mental Health.

Shapiro, D. (1965). *Neurotic styles.* New York: Basic Books.

Shor, J., & Sanville, J. (1978). *Illusions in loving: A psychoanalytic approach to intimacy and autonomy.* Los Angeles: Double Helix.

Smith, T. W., O'Keefe, J. C., & Jenkins, M. (1988). Dependency and self-criticism: Correlates of depression or moderators of the effects of stressful events. *Journal of Personality Disorders, 2,* 160–169.

Spiegel, H., & Spiegel, D. (1978). *Trance and treatment: Clinical uses of hypnosis.* New York: Basic Books.

Spitz, R. A. (1965). *The first year of life.* Madison, CT: International Universities Press.

Stern, D. N. (1977). *The first relationship.* Cambridge, MA: Harvard University Press.

Stern, D. N. (1983). The early development of schemas of self, of other, and of various experiences of "self with other." In J. D. Lichtenberg & S. Kaplan (Eds.), *Reflections of self psychology* (pp. 49–84). Hillsdale, NJ: Analytic Press.

Stern, D. N. (1985). *The psychological world of the infant.* New York: Basic Books.

Stern, D. N. (1988). Affect in the context of the infant's experience. *International Journal of Psycho-Analysis, 69,* 233–238.

Steward A. S., & Malley, J. E. (1987). Role combination in women in early adult years: Mitigating agency and communion. In F. Crosby (Ed.), *Spouse, parent, worker: On gender and multiple roles* (pp. 44–62). New Haven, CT: Yale University Press.

Sullivan, H. S. (1940). *Concepts of modern psychiatry.* New York: Norton.

Sullivan, H. S. (1953). *The interpersonal theory of psychiatry.* New York: Norton.

Surrey, J. L. (1985). The "self-in-relation": A theory of women's development. *Work in Progress* (No. 85-02). Wellesley, MA: Stone Center Working Papers.

Waterman, A. S. (1981). Individualism and interdependence. *American Psychologist, 36,* 762–773.

Webster. (1960). *Third new international dictionary.* Springfield, MA: Merriam.

Weissman, A. N., & Beck, A. T. (1978, August–September). *Developmental and validation of the Dysfunctional Attitudes Scale: A preliminary investigation.* Paper presented at the 86th Annual Convention of the American Psychological Association, Toronto, Ontario, Canada.

Werner, H. (1948). *Comparative psychology of mental development.* Madison, CT: International Universities Press.

Winnicott, D. W. (1958a). The capacity to be alone. In D. Winnicott (Ed.), *The maturational processes and the facilitating environment* (pp. 29–36). London: Hogarth Press.

Winnicott, D. W. (1958b). *Collected papers: From pediatrics to psychoanalysis.* New York: Basic Books.

Winnicott, D. W. (1971). *Playing and reality.* London: Tavistock.

Winter, D. (1973). *The power motive.* New York: Free Press.

Witkin, A. H. (1965). Psychological differentiation and forms of pathology. *Journal of Abnormal Psychology, 70,* 317–336.

Witkin, A. H., Dyk, R. B., Faterson, H. I., Goodenough D. R., & Karp, S. A. (1962). *Psychological differentiation.* New York: Wiley.

Zetzel, E. (1968). The so-called good hysteric. *International Journal of Psycho-Analysis, 49,* 256–260.

Zuroff, D. C., & Mongrain, M. (1987). Dependency and self-criticism: Vulnerability factors for depressive affective states. *Journal of Abnormal Psychology, 96,* 14–22.

19

PSYCHOANALYSIS, PSYCHOLOGY, AND THE SELF

BERTRAM J. COHLER AND ROBERT M. GALATZER-LEVY

Across the past 3 decades, psychology and psychoanalysis have shown increased interest in study of the self, returning to earlier concern with the means by which people maintain sense of personal coherence and integrity: From William James to contemporary psychoanalysis, study of the self has been regarded as central in understanding the psychology of wish and intent. This renewed interest in self and personal integrity has been accompanied by critical examination of the positive philosophy of science that has guided much psychological inquiry across this time from the 19th century to the past decade.

Just as 19th-century study of the self was part of an effort to make sense of modernity, late 20th-century study of the self addresses the impact of postmodern culture on person and life course. Contemporary study of the self and the maintenance of personal integrity has been additionally informed by recent contributions from critical theory, other human sciences, including history, anthropology, and the humanities. The psychoanalytic concept of relational reenactment (Mitchell, 1988) may be of particular significance as a means for studying the emergence and maintenance of a sense of personal coherence within lives over time. Clinical and developmental psychoanalytic study of the self has provided new means for understanding the psychology of meaning and motive from early childhood through oldest age. This study has also led to clinical innovations that are of particular significance for those persons previously believed to be too psychologically fragile to be able to benefit from psychoanalysis.

THE CONTRIBUTIONS OF PSYCHOANALYSIS TO STUDY OF THE SELF

Within the sciences of humans, attempts to incorporate the universal experience of self into coherent theory led to wide ranging theoretical and empirical investigations. Contemporary psychoanalysis, in particular, has been troubled by the incapacity of drive and ego theories to meaningfully address this central aspect of experience. On the basis of clinical experience, informal observation, and logical reconstructions, Sullivan (1962) posited a developmental line of the self across the life course that contrasted with other psychoanalytic perspectives by stressing the permanence of self as an entity evolving, at least through young adulthood.[1]

Despite the limitations of their analyst's theories, analysands repeatedly call attention to issues of personal integrity. These issues, often expressed as feelings of personal disorganization, depletion, or "emptiness," seemed incomprehensible or intractable from other psychoanalytic perspectives and became more tractable when conceptualized as disorders of the self. Some analysands who had responded poorly to psychoanalysis understood in terms of conflicts between drives and internalized social prohibitions, benefited to a greater extent from psychoanalysis understood in terms of problems maintaining sense of self-integrity, together with the experience of others as a source of solace and comfort. These several levels of study of the self—broad cultural trends, social science investigations, and theoretical-clinical psychoanalytic study—reciprocally interact in determining present understandings of self and society.

Freud developed two distinct and somewhat contradictory psychological perspectives, metapsychology and clinical theory (Cohler, 1987; Gill, 1976; G. Klein, 1976). Metapsychology reflected Freud's attempt to continue his mentor Brucke's effort to extend physicalistic physiology to the study of mind (Cohler, 1987; Sulloway, 1979). Mental phenomena were to be reduced to the interaction of knowable forces and energies. Metapsychology, in its several forms, attempts a mechanistic description of mental functioning. In contrast, the clinical theory of psychoanalysis describes human psychology in terms of meanings and motives. The latter approach is a specific hermeneutic method. We believe it is this method that results in the continued value of psychoanalysis.

Review of the contemporary status of metapsychology shows that is an incomplete, mechanistic description of mind that returns to the functional psychology that Freud initially sought to revise (Cohler & Galatzer-Levy, 1990).[2] These problems were amplified in the ego-psychology emerging from Freud's (1923/1961, 1932–1933/1964) reformulation of his topographic theory of mental functioning as a theory of psychic conflict. Ego-psychology reorganized the fundamental psychoanalytic model of the mind, stressing the significance of conflict between drive, ideals, and reality. It increased attention to the ego as the psychic agency responsible for reconciling conflicting demands of drive and reality. Efforts at elaborating this model (Hartmann, Kris, & Lowenstein, 1946), led to inquiry little different from experimental psychological study of such ego functions as attention and memory that are better explored using the concepts and methods of learning and physiological psychology (Gill, 1976; G. Klein, 1976). Ego psychology reflected Freud's (1895/1966, 1940/1964) metapsychological project, to which Freud repeatedly returned over the course of 50 years of writing and study, ambivalently regarding it as a curse preoccupying but eluding him (Freud, 1937/1964). The same ambivalent status has been accorded to ego-psychology within contemporary psychoanalysis; although Meissner (1976, 1981, 1986) and Holzman (1985) believed that concern with issues of psychic structure advances our thinking,

---

[1] One of the tragic consequences of the split between Freud and Jung was that the latter's concept of centrality of the self in psychology, the role of community and tradition in self-experience, and the idea of life course development of the self, all pioneered by Jung (1933) had little effect on non-Jungian psychoanalysts (Satinover, 1986; Ticho, 1982). Only lately have other analysts begun to appreciate these contributions.

[2] It is conceivable that a theory of mental function based on brain physiology will emerge. In fact, there are interesting attempts to develop such theories. Freudian metapsychology, emphasizing energies, corresponding to no known physical quantities, based on the analogy with structures only roughly corresponding to brain anatomy, is only a candidate for such a theory by way of generous readings informed by modern neuroscience (Pribram & Gill, 1976).

Gill (1976) and G. Klein (1976) questioned the value of understanding psychoanalysis in terms of psychological functions and mechanisms.

Gill and G. Klein called for renewed attention to the experientially near clinical theory rather than the scientism characteristic of the metapsychology. Gill (1976) urged renewed attention to the clinical theory, focusing on the study of conflict and defense enacted within the transference—a subject uniquely addressed by psychoanalysis. The sole value of metapsychology may be its metaphoric use within clinical theory. For example, "psychic energy," analogous to physical energy, is not a viable concept; however, the concept of intensity of wish may be more clinically and experientially relevant. The potential confusion arising from metaphoric use of physicalistic terms within metapsychology led George Klein (1976) and Schafer (1976, 1978) to recommend a shift in psychoanalysis from the study of function and mechanism (metapsychology) to the study of person and experience (clinical theory). G. Klein was particularly insistent in the view that, although Freud had tried to integrate mid-19th century mechanistic psychology with a psychology founded on personal experience, his metapsychology ultimately had resulted in a psychoanalysis specifically and actively alienated from the experience-near realm that represents the unique contribution of the psychoanalytic approach.

Problems inherent in the elaboration of ego-psychology emerged at about the same time as significant changes in the postwar world, pointing to the importance of renewed attention to issues of wish and intent that had initially inspired Freud's careful study of mental life (Galatzer-Levy & Cohler, 1990). Postmodernism in fields as disparate as criticism, history, anthropology, and experimental psychological study of memory, required renewed attention to the experiential perspective that provides the foundation for psychoanalysis as a discipline. The empathic method of psychoanalysis is uniquely able to observe wish and intent through reenactment of wishes expressed over a lifetime, and has played an increasingly prominent role within both the humanities and the human sciences (Cohler, 1989; Habermas, 1968/1971; Ricouer, 1970, 1977). In turn many psychoanalysts have returned to the study of person or self that is so evident in Freud's (1900/1958) study of dreams, and in his case studies of Dora (Freud, 1905) and the "Rat-Man" (Freud, 1909/1955).

Contrasting Concepts of Self Within Psychoanalysis

Hartmann (1950), LaPlanche and Pontalis (1973), Kernberg (1982), and Bettelheim (1983) all maintained that Freud never intended a sharp distinction between the terms *ego* and *self*. They observed that translating the German *ich* as *ego* overemphasized Freud's concept of system. The editors of the *Standard Edition* (Strachey & Editors, 1961) noted this problem but translated the text according to what they believed to be Freud's intent in the original German. Although Kernberg claimed the translation was faithful to Freud's intent, Bettelheim (1983) asserted that the inflected meaning of ich is the reflective or introspective "I." Schafer (1976, 1980, 1983) believed that Freud had an active self in mind to a greater extent than is evident to readers of the *Standard Edition*. Regardless of Freud's intent, he believed that an active self is central to psychoanalytic study of lives.

Contemporary discussion of the term *self* in psychoanalysis begins with the Hartmann et al. (1946) paper on the theory of psychic structure, and Hartmann's (1950) paper on the theory of the ego. Hartmann suggested that the term *ego* be replaced by the term *self*, because self is more congruent with clinical phenomena. He used self as equivalent to person, and contrasted it both with objects (including other persons) and ego. Following Hartmann's studies of the self as its adaptation to reality, Jacobson (1964) focused on a theme initially posed by James (1890/1959)—the objective and subjective self. Jacobson posed a distinction between the subjective world and both ego processes or such structures as identifications fostering drive regulation, and identity, the sense of differentiation from others. Jacobson was particularly concerned with those factors determining self-representation and personal coherence in the midst of life changes, emphasizing the importance of emotionally laden images of experience shaping self-representation.

The concept of self used in psychoanalysis is readily confused with psychosocial or interpersonal constructs. The difference between interpersonal and intrapsychic was central to the emergence of ego-psychology, as portrayed in the work of Hartmann (1950), Jacobson (1964), and, somewhat later, Richards (1982) and Meissner (1986). Much of this discussion includes the ego, the sense of being the subject (vs. the object) of experience, the bodily self and sense of being a whole person as aspects of the self. Hartmann's equation of self and person may be problematic because "person" is a social, not an intrapsychic concept (Meissner, 1986). Jacobson's (1964) formulation of self may be internally inconsistent (Gedo, 1979, 1981; Meissner, 1986); she viewed the self both as an intrapsychic function resulting from experience or representation of others, as opposed to actual experiences with others (Sandler & Rosenblatt, 1962), and also as an active agent.

George Klein (1976) provided the most incisive discussion to date of the self in psychoanalysis. He maintained that the concept of self is more inclusive and experientially relevant than Hartmann's (1939) "synthetic function of the ego" as a means for portraying emerging sense of personal regulation. He also maintained that lives are best understood as active, motivated efforts to master wish and experience, observing that the motivational aspects of mastery are "a by-product of efforts to make the unfamiliar familiar and comfortable" (G. Klein, 1976, p. 267). The motivational aspect of the self reflects concern with maintenance of integrity as a person, together with realization of a continued sense of sameness and oneness, and continuity of experience over time rather than arousal of a need for mastery. Mastery is an expression and consequence of this integrative tendency in which first the body and then self-conception are the reference points for organizing experience. Extending a point of view first elaborated by Kohut (1977), Goldberg's (1982, 1988) clinically informed discussion supports G. Klein's (1976) discussion of self and the emergence of a sense of vitality in personal experience. Goldberg affirmed the importance of retaining an intrapsychological perspective, observing that the self-concept must include a sense of continuity of experience and of the body and bodily function. Concern with subjectively construed or intrapersonal experience of regulation, and confidence in the capacity to realize goals (Basch, 1983) also differentiates psychoanalytic perspectives on the self from interpersonal approaches to the self that are more common in American psychology.

Developmental psychologists, psychoanalysts, and personality theorists share an interest in the two selves, originally distinguished by James (1890/1959) in *Principles of Psychology,* between the subjective self, concerned with coherence and continuity, and the objective (or categorical self) concerned with differentiation of self from others. Mahler and her associates (Mahler, Pine, & Bergman, 1975; Pine, 1985, 1989) focused primarily on the objective self, whereas Klein (1976), Stechler and Kaplan (1980), Atwood and Stolorow (1984), Stern (1985), and the Chicago school of self psychology (Kohut, 1959/1978, 1971, 1977, 1984) focused primarily on the subjective self emerging as a consequence of the experience of others from earliest childhood or intersubjectivity. Of particular significance among these clinical and developmental formulations of the subjective self is this concern with the experienced other as essential for maintenance of personal integrity and sense of continuity over time.

Consistent with G. Klein's (1976) call for study of the self as "a single apparatus of control which exhibits a variety of dynamic tendencies, the focus of which is either an integration experienced in terms of a sense of continuity, coherence, and integrity, or its impairment, as cleavages or dissonance" (p. 8), Stechler and Kaplan (1980) observed the following:

> The capacity to function in accordance with an internal self-regulating organization is a developmental acquisition originating in innumerable attempts to resolve experienced breaches of expectancy. That is the external facet of the experience. Internally, it may be viewed as an experienced breach of integration. The growing child's manifest behavior, viewed from within this perspective, can thus be understood as reflecting efforts to deal with incompatible tendencies that result in crises of integration. (pp. 86–87)

Clinical and clinical–theoretical contributions by Winnicott (1945/1958, 1953), Khan (1963/1974), and, most recently, Bacal (1989) and Bacal and Newman (1990), similarly address the centrality of the self for understanding lives over time and for intervening in personal distress.

Kohut and the "Chicago School" of Psychoanalytic Self Psychology

Heinz Kohut and his associates, principally in Chicago, have pioneered in the psychoanalytic study of the person and experience focusing on origin, course, and intervention in personal distress that interferes with sense of well-being or personal integrity, and with capacity for intimacy. The work of Kohut and his associates must be understood in terms of the shift away from drive and instinct within contemporary psychoanalysis toward a psychology of self and experienced other. Self psychology, as portrayed by Kohut and his associates, is too readily misunderstood as an idiosyncratic and completely unique statement of the importance of the self. It is too easy to overlook the continuity of the contributions of Kohut and his associates with those of other contributions within contemporary psychoanalysis, psychology, and philosophy of mind, all of which point toward the construction of a relational psychology (Bacal & Newman, 1990). "Self psychology," as elaborated by the Chicago group over the past 2 decades, is consistent with earlier contributions of Melanie Klein emphasizing the importance of studying subjectivity and meaning, and with more recent contributions by Winnicott, Khan, George Klein, Schafer, Gedo, and others. Each of these theorists of development and clinical process has been concerned with the origins and treatment of deficits in realizing personal coherence and intimacy (Cohler, 1980).[3]

Self psychology, as psychoanalysis more generally, has benefited from recent studies of ordinary development including the emergence of intersubjectivity as reported by Sander (1975) and Trevarthan (1989), together with reformulations of child development, ranging from Kagan's (1981) account of the emergence of self-awareness over the second year of life, to the developmental psychoanalytically informed conceptualizations of Stechler and Kaplan (1980) and Stern (1985). Self psychology has also been influenced by reformulations within the human sciences (Habermas, 1968/1971; Toulmin, 1981), emphasizing the role of empathy as an intrinsic element not only of the clinical process but, more generally, as a way of studying subjectivity within the human sciences.

Kohut explicitly avoided defining the self, maintaining that such a definition would only serve to reify complex concepts. He expected readers to understand the term from its contexts

---

[3]Self psychology's problems with its relation to related investigations seems to go beyond the usual problems arising from the "narcissism of small differences" and wishes for priority and recognition. Kohut seems to have been personally reluctant to credit other investigators with ideas like his own. In Kohut's (1971) *The Analysis of the Self*, he is at pains to demonstrate how his work differs qualitatively from that of Mahler, Winnicott, and Sullivan. In 1977 Kohut introduced the term "bipolar self," which he uses, without attribution, in a way very similar to Baldwin's use of the same term 80 years earlier. Whatever Kohut's personal motives in this matter, he set a precedent in which self-psychologists have been "splitters" rather than "lumpers" when considering their relation to other, similar, psychological investigations.

and their own experiences. As a result, just as earlier in the extension of Erikson's work, Kohut's preference for ambiguity in the definition of the concept of self in self psychology has led to an extensive literature devoted to explicating the meaning of Kohut's concept of self and its relation to the wide range of uses of the term both inside and outside of psychoanalysis. Much of the discussion centers on the relation between mental representation and the represented object. Kohut sometimes refers to the self as agent, sometimes as a mental content. Adequate development of the self as an agent requires that the representation of self develop appropriately. Conversely, the developing representation of the self is significantly determined by the manner in which the self functions as agent.

Several interrelated concepts have been included in Kohut's concept of self, which continues the tradition in American psychology, since James's (1890/1959) initial discussion, between subjective and objective self. Kohut has used the term self in several ways, sometimes in order to refer to an experience-near sense of effectiveness, vitality, and vigor, sometimes in order to refer to the sense of coherence and continuity in space and time, and sometimes in order to portray the experience of personal differentiation from others in early and middle childhood, which leads to increased psychological autonomy and to enhanced use of capacities first acquired by internalization of attributes of essential others (Schafer, 1968; Stern, 1985).

Self psychology differs from other psychoanalytic perspectives in assuming that these others ordinarily remain potentially available as a psychological resource leading to a continuing sense of solace and comfort across the course of life. Consistent with common sense understanding, albeit inconsistent with much of ego psychology, and the separation–individuation theories of Mahler (Mahler et al., 1975), Kohut has maintained that persons characteristically continue to experience others as a source of vitality and comfort throughout life: memories of being with others and, often, aspects of physical presence as well, may also be used in order to provide solace and comfort at times of distress (Greenson, 1971) or in later life, with the death of consociates, as a survivor of a generation or cohort (Cohler & Galatzer-Levy, 1990; Galatzer-Levy & Cohler, 1990).

Freud (1911/1958) and Federn (1934) addressed the issue of self in relation to psychopathology. However, Freud (1911/1958, 1914b/1958) believed that issues of "narcissistic neurosis," or deficit in capacity for maintaining sense of personal integrity, could not be investigated within psychoanalysis, because they are qualitatively different from transference or psychoneuroses. Freud (1914a/1958) maintained that transference, the core of the psychoanalytic process, required disguised reawakening of interest in archaic sources of satisfaction. Because issues regarding self seemed to focus interest on the self rather than on others, concern with issues of solace and maintenance of sense of continuity could not be the center of feeling about another person, and could not become the focus of the analytic work. Erikson's (1959) recognition that apparently malignant psychopathology first appearing in late adolescence often reflected an "identity crisis" rather than schizophrenia, was a first step in the revision of this position. Further revision came from refinements in psychiatric and psychoanalytic diagnosis. Manifestly neurotic pathology was observed to reflect profoundly disorganized personalities (Zetzel, 1958). Psychopathology, which appeared to be the early stages of psychotic deterioration, was considered as a stable configuration.

Several analysts (Kernberg, 1975; Modell, 1990; Winnicott, 1945/1958) have reported positive outcomes among analysands showing severe disturbance in sense of self in intensive psychotherapy or psychoanalysis. However, although this work focused on reenactment of archaic experiences in personality development through distinctively psychoanalytic study and interpretation of transference and transference-like enactments, this pioneering psychoanalytic study was less successful in providing a coherent theory of development and psychopathology of the self across the course of life. First steps in the development of such a theory of self may be found in the work of Kohut and his associates, identifying and interpreting a group of archaic transference-like enactments emerging in the psychoanalytic process, known as "selfobject" transferences.

Kohut's study of self was founded in a reconsideration in the clinical psychoanalytic method similar in many respects to that urged by Gill (1976), G. Klein (1976), Schafer (1980, 1983), and Gedo (1984). The traditional, "received method" of psychoanalytic investigation assumes a positivistic, experience-distant view of the analytic process in which the analysand's own understanding of self and experience merely informs the analyst regarding the particular ways in which the analysand represents necessarily disguised, unconscious wishes. By contrast, the analyst's understanding of the analysand's life-world, based on empathy or vicarious introspection, through an effort to experience self and others in the manner of the analysand, is believed to inform rather than to mislead the analyst. Kohut has explicitly rejected the theory of technique positing the analyst as an observing scientist who must put aside personal resonance with the analysand's thoughts and feelings in the service of therapeutic neutrality making possible the reenactment of unconscious striving within the transference without being misled by the analysand's surreptitious efforts at gratification through displacement of these wishes out of awareness.

Kohut (1959/1978, 1971) characterized the analytic situation quite differently from this traditional perspective, asserting that empathic understanding is the essential psychoanalytic method. The analyst should allow a prolonged period of empathic immersion in the analysand's psychological world in order to best provide understanding of the meanings and motives of the analysands thoughts, actions, and feelings. This view of understanding the subjective or experiential world is consistent with G. Klein's (1976) view that the central contribution of psychoanalysis is in the clinical theory rather than the metapsychology. Kohut's interest in self, intentions, and motives, rather than drives, offers alternative functions and mechanisms and reflects a departure from the received analytic view.[4] Many analysts continue to regard empathy as a poor guide to understanding the analysand's psychology, and regard Kohut's methods as not distinctively psychoanalytic (Reed, 1987; Wallerstein, 1986). Others (Atwood & Stolorow, 1984; Goldberg, 1988; Lichtenberg, 1981; Lichtenberg, Bornstein, & Silver, 1984; Schwaber, 1983) have attempted to characterize the empathic stance more precisely. Problems with an empathic position range from inevitable challenge to naive visions of an absolute reality, to strains realized through the analyst's efforts to experience the analysand's subjectivity through the transference.

THE SELF, PERSONAL DISTRESS, AND PSYCHOANALYTIC INTERVENTION

Kohut's understanding of disorders of the self suggests that the analysand's enactment of important wishes and intents are repeated anew within the psychoanalytic interview. Although his view of the analytic mode of listening extends understanding of the analyst's contribution to the analytic process, Kohut extended the range of enactments that may be observed within the transference. Explication of these additional enactments, in turn, was largely the consequence of Kohut's critique of metapsychology. He was particularly critical that Freud's insistence on an experience-distant and a priori approach to development, founded principally through analogy with Freud's prepsychoanalytic study of developmental neurobiology (Galatzer-Levy & Cohler,

---

[4]There were certainly empathically gifted and intuitive therapists before Kohut. Many analysts appreciated the central role of empathy in support in the analytic process (Gitelson, 1962; Loewald, 1960). Other analysts appreciated that the specifically human qualities of the analyst could contribute to understanding the patient but these modalities were quite different from empathy. Reik (1948), for example, described a process of creative association on the part of the analyst, whose greater access to unconscious mental processes allowed him to better understand the patient's unconscious. Racker (1968), among others, recommended the systematic exploration of countertransference as a way to understand the patient's unconscious.

1990; Sulloway, 1979) was not consistent with Freud's own accounts of clinical process. Disorders of the self, or narcissistic personality disorders, as Kohut (1966, 1971) initially referred to them, are characterized by the danger of loss of coherence or vitality of self. Clinical presentation includes fairly direct expressions of an endangered or damaged self, such as the experience of emptiness, triviality, fears of disorganization, and hypochondriasis. Alternatively, the analysand may be involved in such desperate attempts to maintain a sense of self, as perverse sexual activity, substance abuse, or driven perfectionism (Kohut & Wolf, 1978). Kohut differentiated between persons with major psychopathology for whom psychoanalysis was an inappropriate psychotherapeutic modality, persons reporting an impaired sense of personal integrity or cohesion, experiencing chronic feelings of fragmentation or personal depletion, and persons experiencing intrapsychic conflicts not threatening self-cohesiveness or vitality (Kohut, 1971).[5]

On the basis of empathic observation within the psychoanalytic setting, Kohut provided an additional point of view for understanding psychological phenomena that complemented that of traditional clinical psychoanalysis. He did not assume that wishes and intents must express biological urges but, rather, emphasized their foundations in the maintenance of the self. Kohut portrayed the self as composed of three elements: a sense of grandiosity, concern with maintaining ideals, and supporting skills and talents.[6] These aspects of the self are supported, throughout the course of life, by experiences with others serving as selfobjects. Grandiose aspects of the self, at various times, require merger into a single entity, a sense of sameness with similar individuals (alter-ego states), and the appreciative response of the environment (mirroring). Ideals emerge from the experience of idealization of others. Skills and talents emerge as a consequence of others' appreciation and support of fledgling abilities. Kohut (1971) maintained that these selfobject functions continue across the course of life, with both immature and mature expressions. However, much of the interest in self-psychology has focused on the immature forms of experiencing others characteristically associated with psychopathology. One perspective on selfobject experience portrays the expression of continuing need for selfobjects as a reflection of a continuing deficit in psychological development first experienced in early life (Tolpin & Kohut, 1980/1989). Recently, Basch (personal communication, October 1990) has recommended limiting use of the term selfobject to the reenactment of these modes of experiencing others, which is ordinarily characteristic of the caregiver across the first years of life.

An alternative perspective suggests that others are experienced throughout life in terms of functions continuing to enhance sense of personal cohesion and integrity. Inevitable, tolerable disruptions of these functions joined with the child's ability to temporarily provide the function for oneself, foster increasing capacity for providing functions in the absence of the person experienced as the selfobject. Characteristically, parents are experienced as "good enough" (Winnicott, 1960) and sufficiently available for the child to experience caregiving as sustaining. Expression of these functions varies across the course of life, but is always present. The need for solace and comfort, and for assistance in maintaining sense of coherence and vitality, may vary in terms of place in the course of life but is never absent. From this perspective, disorders of the

---

[5]Subsequently, the area of interest of self psychology has enlarged in both directions. Malin (1988) and Stolorow, Brandchaft, and Atwood (1987) have applied self psychology to work with psychotic patients; Galatzer-Levy (1987) has described work with manic-depressive individuals from this point of view, and Tolpin (1980) has applied self psychology to the understanding of borderline states. Kohut (1984) and many of his co-workers (Wolf, 1988) came to regard oedipal neurosis as a special form of self-pathology.

[6]In the unfortunate metaphor of the "bipolar self," Kohut (1977) likened the integration of these three elements to the electric poles and lines of force between them. Although the metaphor captures the notion of the unity of the self (for there is no such thing as a negative pole without a positive pole), concepts of force, tension, and energy introduce extraneous images and pose metapsychological problems, such as those related to the economic point of view, which have already been resolved in psychoanalysis (Applegarth, 1977; Galatzer-Levy, 1976; Swanson, 1977; Wallerstein, 1977).

self result from disturbances of selfobject function, not only in infancy, but at any time across the course of life (Galatzer-Levy & Cohler, 1990; Wolf, 1988). Some find it difficult to let themselves make use of others, psychologically, during times of distress. Some persons are unable to obtain solace from the memory of the past experience of others. Particularly adverse life changes may lead to transformations in sense of self and others, which is of such a magnitude as to interfere with existing abilities to experience solace. However, most adults are able to rely on others for selfobject functions and that interdependence is expectable across the course of life, even though its expression may be shaped by present circumstances. The curative factor in psychoanalysis involves restoration of the capacity to appropriately use others to maintain a sense of personal integrity and vitality and to enlarge the capacity for these functions through interpretation of enactment in response to experienced disappointments and frustrations within the analytic setting.

Self psychology has reconsidered the origins and course of personal distress in terms of the self and selfobject functions. For example, Wolf (1988) understood neurosis not as the result of conflicted wishes of the oedipal period but as the consequence of failures of the experienced other of the preschool years to modulate the conflict associated with this developmental epoch. This view is consistent with Kohut's (1975, 1984) observation that the oedipal period is not inevitably conflictual, but only becomes so as a result of the failure of selfobjects to support expectable the assertiveness and sexuality of the preschool and early school-aged child. According to Kohut, the primary source of personal distress lies in the inability to provide adequate means for supporting the self. The struggles and difficulties arise anew within the analytic process. This view contrasts with ego and drive psychological formulations assuming inevitable conflict between wish, sense of reality, and internalized social values as the foundation of psychopathology.

This perspective assumes that the primary goal of pathology is disguise of wish and intent while providing gratification (A. Freud, 1936/1966). From this perspective, the goal of analysis is to bring these conflicts into awareness with their full emotional intensity in order that they may be reworked and the accompanying distortions stemming from early childhood repression made consistent with the present reality. The analysand is assumed to resist recognition of wish and intent in order to ensure continued partial satisfaction of repressed wishes. Understood in terms of this traditional perspective, the analytic process reflects continuing struggle between the analyst and the analysand's mature ego, on one hand, and, on the other, the forces of repression and disguised infantile gratification. Within this traditional perspective, ambiance in the analytic setting may be best characterized as respectful warfare. In contrast, the ambiance of psychoanalysis, understood from the perspective of self psychology, is characterized as self-psychology-oriented analysis and may be best characterized as constant attention to the legitimacy of analysand's expressed needs. Intentions are understood as reflecting the analysand's best current effort at maintaining an enhanced sense of personal integrity and vitality. Psychological symptoms may be best characterized as a response to a world experienced as overwhelming and as failing to provide support for a distressed self.[7]

Analytic Setting and Selfobject Transference

Kohut's central contribution to clinical psychoanalysis was his realization that, in contrast both with Freud's original formulation and much of earlier so-called "object relations" psychology

---

[7]These considerations are commonly misunderstood to mean that self psychologists believe that being kind to patients is curative. From the point of view of ego psychology, the assumption that the patient means something close to what he or she says would simply be an error. This is not at all the point of view of self psychology. Rather, the two distinctive assumptions about the underlying motives of human psychology predict different kinds of psychological operations on the part of the patient. These different understandings of the patient naturally engender different attitudes and responses in the analyst.

(Balint, 1935/1965), persons showing disorders of self commonly form very intense attachments and a wide range of transference-like enactments portrayed by Kohut (1971, 1977) as "self-object" transferences.[8] These selfobject transferences are characterized by the analyst as experienced as necessary to the cohesiveness and/or vigor of the analysand's self. The analyst's significance for the analysand is in realizing enhanced self-coherence and solace rather than with being the object of love or hate. In contrast with Kernberg (1976), who, following Melanie Klein (1948/1975), posited inherent rage in response to inevitable thwarting of the search for intimacy, Kohut maintained that this rage is reactive to a feeling of not being understood and of not being assisted in dealing with the analysand's developmentally determined deficit in the capacity to maintain sense of personal coherence.

Many of the phenomena that Kohut described had been observed by other analysts. However, others understood these phenomena in terms of defensive operations. For example, the analysand's obvious idealization of the analyst may be understood as an unconscious attempt to deny intense competitive and derogatory attitudes toward the analyst. Interpretations prematurely portraying these transferencelike enactments as manifestations of resistance derail their elaboration and interpretation in the analysis. Kohut permitted these transferences to emerge without interpretation as resistance, observing that when he did not interfere with the spontaneous emergence of transferencelike enactments among analysands with disorders of the self, these intense enactments shared the common feature of unusual sensitivity to the analyst's psychological presence. This concern was most often evident accompanying disruption in the analytic schedule, problems in the analyst's own life, or countertransference responses interfering with the analyst's maintenance of an empathic listening to the analysand.

The analysand typically responds to these interruptions with symptoms initially experienced in relation to the external world, now expressed within the analytic setting, ranging from sense of fragmentation or depletion, to rage, hypochondriasis, and increased dependence on the analyst in a desperate effort to provide a missing selfobject function. The curative aspect of psychoanalysis requires that these symptoms, initially experienced in regard to the external world, become integral to the analytic relationship itself. This analytic reenactment, facilitating interpretation of the analysand's efforts at maintaining sense of personal integrity evoked in response to feelings of failure of experienced others as a means fostering enhanced personal integrity, reflects an important therapeutic achievement and a necessary first step in the realization of the analytic "cure" (Kohut, 1984). From the perspective of self psychology, psychoanalysis is directed at the effort to restore the capacity to obtain solace from currently available selfobjects and evocation of others from memory. The analysis is directed at interpretive activity aimed at understanding the source of problems in being to use appropriately sources of comfort offered by others that characteristically are important in maintaining a continued sense of personal integrity at points of personal crisis. It is not the use of the evoked other that requires psychoanalytic intervention but, rather, interference in the capacity to obtain solace and support from the evoked other. This interference may appear as arrogant indifference to others, a variety of forms of asocial or antisocial activity, or sense of chronic depression and lowered morale.

The selfobject transferences provide the same intimate view of self-pathology as the transference neurosis provide within classical psychoanalysis. However, in contrast to conflict-centered reenactments, selfobject transferences, believed to reflect unresolved nuclear conflict of the preschool years, reflect a more archaic failure to realize sense of integrity and solace at times of

---

[8]Kohut used the term *transference* in the clinical sense meaning the analyst has become of central emotional importance to the patient. His usage differs from that of other analysts who reserve the term for the reexperiencing in the present of repressed memories or what is conceptualized as the same thing, making the analyst the object of repressed unacceptable desires or the embodiment of a projected superego. Selfobject transference need not reflect unconscious wishes or be reenactments of past experiences.

distress, which reflects a stable, vigorous, and cohesive self.[9] The analyst is not experienced as an autonomous person, but as an aspect of the self whose capacity for solace and for enhancing sense of personal integrity is believed to be essential for the analysand's continued psychological existence. This reliance on the analyst remains out of awareness and is defended against, both because of the fear of yet another selfobject failure and because of potential interference with whatever means the analysand has found for realizing stability of the self.[10] Usually denial, splitting, and, particularly, disavowal, are the principal defenses employed in the service of providing protection against awareness of this vulnerability.

Kohut (1971) divided the selfobject transferences into two major groups: mirror transferences, involving stabilization of the grandiose self; and idealizing transferences, involving the selfobject functioning as part of an ideal self. Generally, when functioning effectively, the selfobject transferences are silent. In this silent phase they provide the analysand with missing functions necessary to sustain the self. This silence contrasts with the fully engaged transference neurosis in which ever more explicit transference longings lead to increasingly intense distress. For the analysand whose psychopathology is primarily related to disorder of self, distress is only felt when the selfobject fails. Two such failures most commonly observed are those in reaction to disruptions in continuity (e.g., weekend or vacation interruption) or in reaction to experienced breaks in empathy (e.g., the analyst's inevitable failure to appreciate the significance of a particular external event). Kohut's initial distinction between the various selfobject transferences may have been conceptually useful but are not always consistent with clinical observations. Selfobject transferences tend to blend with one or another aspect most significant at a particular time. To be an adequate mirror of grandiosity the mirroring person must be admirable. Similarly, merger with an idealized object results in feelings of grandeur. Appreciation of the nondefensive idealizing transference is an instance of the expanded possibilities associated with self psychology theory. Analysts who believe that all transferences are aspects of the nuclear neurosis, are bound to interpret manifest idealization as a disguise for underlying competition. Self psychological perspectives point to the possibilities.

It is important to recognize that selfobject transferences (like other transferences) enacted over time within the analytic setting, are fostered simply by the analyst's ordinary empathy and courtesy toward the analysand. As acknowledged by Zetzel (1958, 1966–1969), Stone (1961), and Greenson (1967), the therapeutic alliance represents a critical element in the therapeutic process. Major contributions of self psychology to the theory of technique have been to emphasize anew the significance of the therapeutic alliance and to explore the significance of this alliance for the process of analytic cure. Particularly when working with disorders of the self, iatrogenic traumatization may be a consequence of reliance on the antiseptic, model technique recommended by Eissler (1953). Remaining silent in response to the analysand's questions, refusing to

---

[9]The difference between selfobject transference (expressing current needs) and neurotic transference (reenactments of infantile experience) becomes particularly important when the transference is used to reconstruct childhood experience. If transferences in the neuroses are indeed the product of current happenings and unconsciously motivated ways of perceiving, then it should be possible, by factoring out the current external reality, to discover the unconscious processes at work. In so far as these are continuations of infantile experience, it is possible then to reconstruct those experiences from the transference. This theoretical possibility does not apply to selfobject transferences. All that we can say is that infantile needs are revivified, but on the basis of these central transferences we can say little about the attempts to meet them. This is because, as discussed previously, the self is capable of meeting its needs in many ways. The fact that patients in treatment can find good solutions to these needs says nothing about the normal mechanisms a developing infant or child might use.

[10]The term *need* (as opposed to a wish) is used here in three related senses, a need is something essential to continued normal development, something essential to the continued cohesion and vitality of the self, a subjective experience of need. Neurotic patients frequently describe their wishes and defensive maneuvers as needs, thereby both indicating the urgency of the underlying wish and denying that it is a wish. Therefore, accepting the patient's view that something is a need may be collusion with the patient's defensive operations. As discussed later, it is not the patient's avowal of need but the nature of the transference manifestations that differentiate selfobject from object-related transferences.

look at photographs, or interpreting socially appropriate greetings, may make the analysand more vulnerable to disorders of the self to experience the analyst's silence and apparent neutrality as another traumatic selfobject failure and may interfere in the effort to interpret selfobject transferences.

Just as with other transference and transferencelike enactments emerging over the course of psychoanalysis, selfobject transferences emerge against great resistance. It is important to distinguish between rapidly emerging, expectable bids for understanding and support across the first weeks and months of analysis and evidence of serious problems in being able to use others as a source of comfort and support, which reflects disturbance of self and maintenance of personal integrity. Because use of selfobjects is ubiquitous across the entire course of life, intermittent use of the analyst as a selfobject is expectable. Although this use of the analyst needs to be understood and appreciated by the analyst, it may be best to reserve the term *selfobject transference* for situations in which the central configuration of the treatment involves analysand's recurrent effort to use the analyst as a selfobject in order to seek restoration of deficits in maintaining sense of personal coherence and integrity.

Idealizing and Mirror Transferences and Countertransferences

In the idealizing transference, the analyst is viewed as the incarnation of strength, goodness, and power. Through his relationship with the idealized analyst, the analysand feels vigorous, good, and whole. Conscious wishes to be like the analyst are common. Initially idealization tends to be coarse. Aspects of the analyst, such as appearance, manner of speech, and office decor, may be included in the idealization. As a result, working through the idealization becomes increasingly specific and related to the analysand's specific needs. Idealizing transferences may be less than optimally managed when the analyst fails to recognize idealizing transferences. Overstimulated by idealization, some analysts confront analysands with reality or question the need to idealize.[11] Idealizations may be mistakenly and prematurely interpreted, usually as a resistance against recognizing the analysand's hostility. These efforts impede emergence and resolution of the transference, and may lead to interruption of treatment as the analysand is forced to search elsewhere for idealizable objects.

Another major error is to use the idealizations to make oneself a model for the analysand, sometimes believed to foster an enhanced sense of congruence for the analysand.[12] Some analysts find the analysand's idealization ego syntonic and believe that they actually possess the marvelous qualities ascribed to them (e.g., empathy of a quality the analysand can find nowhere else or wisdom about leading the good life, derived from analytic insights or personal experience). However, fostering idealization may also interfere with recognition and resolution of idealizing transferences. Analysts who familiarize themselves with their own responses to idealization can often recognize its presence through responses to the analysand's material.

The mirror transferences, the other major group of selfobject transferences, include three overlapping mirror transference enactments—merger transference, alter-ego transference, and

---

[11]Problems in tolerating idealizations may be observed not only in the consulting room, but also in the classroom. Apprentices, from high school through professional training, find that idealizing their mentors and their chosen field of study is of assistance in mastering the curriculum. Confrontation with teachers, made uncomfortable with this idealization because it stimulates the teacher's unresolved grandiosity, leads students to feel criticized, unappreciated in their efforts to learn, and interferes in optimal learning.

[12]That this is not an uncommon outcome of unresolved idealizing transferences is apparent in the psychoanalytic community, where inadequately analyzed idealizations of the training analyst and analysis itself lead to irrationally doctrinaire positions about technique and theory or alternatively to wholesale rejections of analytic ideas. When such idealizations are more adequately analyzed, analysands are able to develop ideas beyond those of their analysts and teachers without wholesale rejection of their ideas.

mirror transference proper. In the merger transference the analysand's grandiose self is supported by the idea of a single entity, the analyst-analysand. The alter-ego transference reflects the analysand's effort to maintain enhanced feelings of personal integrity through assumed similarity of ideals and intention. In the mirror transference proper, the analysand feels well because of the analyst's appreciative response to his grandiosity. Commonly, analysts respond to mirror transferences with discomfort at being treated as a part of another's self, without independent will. Boredom and fatigue are common when chronically (and, often, coercively) treated as though one's purpose of being is satisfaction of the analysand's selfobject needs. Analysts often deal with the distress of being treated as an extension of the analysand through increased therapeutic activism (e.g., elaborate interpretation, confrontations, or suggestions) that demonstrate to the analyst that he is still alive. It is common for the analyst, with the conscious motive of improving the analysand's interpersonal relations, to sermonize about the importance of treating others as people in their own right. Pejorative diagnostic labels, such as "borderline" or "primitive object relations," may be attached to analysands who are particularly strident in their demand that the analyst function as a selfobject.

Another group of countertransference responses involves manifest fears that the analysand's grandiosity will become unmanageable or intolerable. Interpretations are replaced with emergency educational measures or prohibitions designed to protect the analysand from damaging himself or herself and others. Generally, such measures only lead the analysand to feel out of control and evoke increased disorganization.[13] The most effective therapeutic strategy at such times may be recognition and acceptance of the analysand's need for mirroring. This understanding leads analysands to a stabilized sense of self and, as a consequence, both increases the capacity to better understand the manner in which others may be psychologically used in order to provide enhanced stability of self and decreases the urgency of action. The analyst's own incompletely analyzed grandiosity may be stimulated to such an extent that he or she is likely to try to convince the analysand that the analyst appreciates external reality better then the analysand.

A third group of responses, which we regard as distortions, based on reenactment of the analysts's own problems in maintenance of sense of self, but which such clinical theorists as Ferenczi, Winnicott, and Bettelheim regard as essential elements of work with such analysands, involves efforts to directly satisfy the analysand's transference needs, in their infantile forms, within the analytic situation. Such activities as literally holding (Little, 1981), feeding (Sechehaye, 1951), and providing "appropriate presents" to child analysands, are intended to provide supplies that it is believed the analysand had missed earlier in life. The better that the analyst can provide "reparenting" reflects the analyst's wish, often determined by a fantasy that his or her own defective development can be remedied in similar fashion, of undoing past deprivations.[14]

Selfobject transferences pose particular challenge to the analyst, possibly evoking overstimulation and lack of mirroring responses. As in the analysis of drives and conflicts, where countertransference responses arise, based on evocation of the analysts's own unresolved nuclear neurosis, it is essential that the analyst has adequately worked through these problems in order that countertransference responses do not continue to interfere with the maintenance of an

---

[13]There is a group of patients whose psychological state might be likened to a chronic tantrum, who indeed need to be firmly and calmly held psychologically because they continue to create escalating difficulties for themselves. It sometimes brings these patients considerable relief to be forbidden self-destructive enactments. The therapist position differs from the countertransference–determined response described here in that the patient usually has a long history of genuinely dangerous behavior and the therapist does not experience a pressing urgency when making these interventions.

[14]Our experience with therapists who become sexually involved with patients suggests that such activities are often attempts to magically and concretely provide for narcissistic needs of the patient. At the same time they reflect the therapist's rage at the patient that leads to enactment taking a destructive form and a sexualized attempt to reassert the vigor of the therapist's self in a context where (the often seriously narcissistically depleted therapist) feels particularly unresponded to.

empathic stance toward the analysand. The curative elements of psychoanalysis are understood differently in self psychology than in more traditional psychoanalytic approaches. Analysts have long maintained that new psychological structure is laid down through internalization of psychological functions in response to object loss (Freud, 1914a/1958; Schafer, 1968). Kohut believed that the cure process of disorders of the self occurred as new psychological structure was realized through nontraumatic interruption of the analysand's disrupted capacity for using others as selfobject function. This intensified search for archaic selfobjects, in turn, was believed to arise from traumatic failures in early childhood selfobject functioning, which did not permit the analysand to make these functions his own. Growing to adulthood, the analysand continued a disparate, continually frustrating, and unsatisfying search for a source of solace and comfort.

When, as they inevitably do, the analysts fail in their selfobject function for the analysand, supported by the analysts' empathic comprehension of this failure (Goldberg, 1988), the analysand develops increasing capacity for managing this experienced failure without the loss of spontaneity and vigor of the self, which formerly characterized such disappointments. This capacity for resolving disappointments more effectively than prior to beginning analysis results in what Kohut (1971) had termed a "transmuting internalization," in which functions previously performed by the external selfobject are now taken on by the analysand. When this process goes well, persons are able to make use of the psychological attributes of others as a source of self-regulation. However, when one is unable to realize effective sense of coherence and vitality, others may be used in a desperate effort at realizing enhanced personal cohesiveness and vitality. In treatment, often after working through considerable resistance to awareness of the analyst's significance, the analysand begins to use the analyst more effectively and with lessened disavowal, as a selfobject, leading to increased capacity for self-regulation and enhanced sense of personal cohesion.

SELF PSYCHOLOGY AND LIFE COURSE

The conceptual shift from a psychology of drives and defenses to the direction of a psychology of the self required a new approach to understanding the developmental process. Starting with the work of Spitz (1945) and Winnicott (1945/1958), and continuing with the contributions of Bowlby (1973/1979, 1988) and Mahler (Mahler et al., 1975), psychoanalysis and child development have increasingly attended to those aspects of development involving the formation of ties to others and the emergence of intersubjectivity. Much of this study has focused on the development of the self, and what in psychoanalysis might be viewed as the selfobject function. Findings from infant study have been used within psychoanalysis to correct, complement, and extend a view of early development of self and selfobjects obtained from the study of the transference within clinical psychoanalysis. This study has replaced semimystical images of empathy with descriptions of the particular means used by the child and the caregiver in the realization of reciprocity leading to the child's increasing sense of self-regulation and self-understanding. Findings from infant studies across the first years of life have suggested important relationships between emergence of sense of personal integrity and observed processes of social and psychological development (Beebe & Lachmann, 1988; Lichtenberg, 1983; Stern, 1985).

On the basis of the clinical experience that increased sense of personal congruity results from the feeling of being understood (i.e., being the object of accurate empathy) Kohut and his coworkers posited the centrality of adequate empathy for the development of the cohesive self (Tolpin, 1971; Tolpin & Kohut, 1980/1989). Earlier, Winnicott (1960) had proposed similar views. However, the question of how infants perceive empathy, other than through the simple fulfillment of biological wishes, remained obscure until explorations of affectivity of child and parents (Brazelton & Youngman, 1986) suggested the means by which increasing affective attunement between infant and caretakers leads to enhanced intersubjectivity. Split-screen videotaping of infants and caretakers illustrated the dynamic complementarity between affective states and conversational interchange of very young infants and their caretakers (Demos, 1988).

The presence of cardinal affective expressions observed in neonates (Tomkins, 1968) does not necessarily indicate similarity between psychological states of mother and child. Nonetheless, caretakers respond to these cardinal affective expressions as though they represent true affectivity. It is still not clear how much facial affective expressions, associated physiological responses, and associated subjective states are biologically linked, the extent to which aspects of these states are learned, or the extent to which support is required for emergence of particular affective expression. The fact of alexithymic patients who do not associate facial and physiological aspects of affect and who may lack the motivation necessary to act consistent with subjective experience of affect, suggests that appropriate experience of affect may require the experience of accurate environmental responsiveness.

Appropriate response to the infant suggests that the internal state may be accurately understood. More promising than simple similarity of primary affect, is the demonstration of empathy in the tempo of affective change and cross modal expression (Stern, 1985). For instance, when the infant reaches toward an object and the mother grunts as though stretching for the object herself, this verbal expression, which is coincident with the infant's muscular activity, may communicate convincingly to the infant that the mother comprehends the infant's internal experience.[15] However promising this infant study has been, it remains problematic for clinical psychoanalytic study because the confirmatory tool of empathic understanding is not available in work with infants.

Different kinds of selfobjects are needed during different eras of life. For example, college students require teachers who they can admire and who can employ that admiration in the service of the student's intellectual development, whereas among older adults, a rich stock of memories and anecdotes of both present and past serve selfobject functions (Cohler & Galatzer-Levy, 1990). The characterization of these different forms of selfobject function remains an important area for study. The wide range of developmental issues beyond infancy relating to the self and selfobjects has only begun to be explored in terms of self psychology. Kagan's (1981) extremely suggestive work regarding the emergence of self-experience during the second year of life has yet to be integrated with self psychological concepts. Furthermore, aside from scattered observations, characteristic selfobject functioning during the preschool period has not been systematically investigated. Although Wolf (1988) suggested that alter-ego selfobject functioning is characteristic of the school-aged child, details of selfobject functioning during childhood remain to be elucidated.

The selfobjects of adolescence have been reviewed in terms of the child's need for people who serve a parental function while separating from the family (Wolf, Gedo, & Terman, 1978). These formulations are consistent with Blos's (1989) view that adolescence is a process of separation from preoedipal parental attachments. Sexuality and sexual relations play an important role in the adolescent self-experience. Sklansky (1977) suggested that sex is normatively narcissistic at the beginning of adolescence and progresses to greater intimacy with the transition to young adulthood. Selfobject functions during adolescence have also been explored in terms of creativity and friendship (Galatzer-Levy & Cohler, 1989; Wolf, 1980, 1982).

---

[15]A more mature version of this phenomenon may be seen in individuals who are deeply moved when a therapist restates the experience not in the patient's words but in words specific to the therapist. Computer programs such as Eliza, which syntactically transform fragments of the patient's discourse into requests for further information or restatements of the patient's position, are generally experienced as annoying and unresponsive after a brief time. Their failure to indicate a process that transforms the patient's experience into a reality of the therapist produces a sense of vacuity.

Expectable selfobject functioning in adulthood has received little attention in self psychology. Although intended to be profoundly respectful of the analysand's world view, Kohut's work continued to be a pathology orientation view of dependence. People are thought to need selfobjects less as they mature. Basch (personal communication, October 1990) recommends that the term *selfobject* be limited to those situations in which the experience of another is essential for the maintenance of a cohesive and invigorated self in the same way that it is psychologically significant across the first years of life. Kohut and his associates have been most concerned with psychological development across the time from birth through the preschool age, which continues to be the major focus of developmental study most influenced by self psychology, and the fundamental purpose of relating to other people is assumed to be the maintenance of the self.

Recently, we reviewed these models of expectable adult self and selfobject development (Cohler & Galatzer-Levy, 1990; Galatzer-Levy & Cohler, 1990, in press), we found that more mature selfobject functioning is closely interrelated with other functions served by the same person who may be a selfobject and who performs an adaptive function and we introduced the term *essential other* to reflect this multifaceted experience that includes selfobject functioning. With maturity the richness of the experience of the essential other increases. Across the course of life, selfobject functions are successively integrated into increasingly complex contexts. The caretaker of infancy is experienced predominantly in terms of the role in regulating the child's self-states; a colleague in middle age serves not only significant selfobject functions but is also the object of rivalry, a partner in realistic collaboration, and object of affection among adults in midlife.

The selfobject concept describes a psychological rather than material reality. Selfobjects need not be physically present to serve their function. With increased maturity the physical presence of the selfobject commonly becomes less important. Selfobject functions are no less important but the means in which they are used in order to provide solace may change. The selfobject world usually enlarges across the course of life, with lessened threat to the self caused by the loss of a particular selfobject. Rather than viewing development as a lessened need for self-object functions, there is a lessened vulnerability to the loss of any particular selfobject or a person in whom that function is embodied. Whether there ever is a time when self-experiences are so solidly laid down as to be immutable to psychological stress is not clear. Massive psychological trauma (Krystal, 1976) may undo the most cohesively organized self, while configurations of experience and biological endowment may foster enhanced resilience of self (Cohler, 1987). Certainly, the centrality of anxiety regarding disillusion and coherence, or lack of vigor of the self, shows marked variation. It is less likely that the self reaches a point of ultimate stability than that experience of personal coherence at any point across the course of life is a function of experienced solace obtained from selfobjects across the life history, together with present circumstances. Experience of coherence and integrity is always vulnerable as a result of loss of essential others, illness or other personal adversity, and more global misfortune. For example, Alzheimer's disease affects memory itself. An important aspect of the depression associated with early to midphase Alzheimer's disease, is the loss of the capacity to evoke the experiences of others and accompanying loss of memory, which may lead to terrifying states of an endangered self (Lazarus, Newton, Cohler, Lesser, & Schweon, 1987).

The study of selfobject transference has shown that the report of despair and depletion associated with disorders of the self is a consequence of experienced meaninglessness and emptiness rather than a sense of attack on the self, which has been reported for the major depressive disorders (Goldberg, 1975). Rage among analysands showing disorders of the self is usually intense in ways not reported for the rage of a depressive disorder. Furthermore, although rage might be manifest toward particular persons or things, it was characteristically noninstrumental (Kohut,

1972). Symptoms designed to restore the self-experience ranged from driven, often perverse, sexual enactments to search for the needed function in the environment, to vigorous attempts at demonstrating personal worth through such means as athletic activities or professional productivity.

Depleted, fragmented, and overstimulated states of the self, together with the relation to the missing selfobject function, are often manifest in dreams (Kohut, 1971). Self psychology views these "self state" dreams differently from traditional psychoanalytic perspectives. Freud (1900/1958) viewed dreams as disguised compromise formation between impulses and prohibiting forces. Self psychology views dreams as metaphoric expressions of self states. For example, a distressing dream of flying out of control might be understood by a classical analyst as a disguised representation of sexual arousal combined with the dangers of being so aroused. A self psychologist would likely understand the dream as representing danger of loss of relatedness, resulting in overstimulated grandiosity. Flying would not be understood as an attempt to disguise the underlying wish but as the best concrete representation available to portray the dreamer's state. The technique of dream interpretation in self psychology is also somewhat different from that in more traditional psychoanalysis. In traditional analysis, the analysand's associations to the elements of the dream, combined with the analyst's understanding of the operation of unconscious processes that transform unconscious fantasies into dream representations, provide the means for dream interpretation. However, self psychological interpretation is based on the analyst's empathic understanding of the overall sense of integrity as communicated through report of the dream (Fosshage, 1988).

CONCLUSION

Self psychology is the natural outgrowth of increased concern with personal integrity and meaning characterizing the modern era across the past century. In psychoanalysis several factors, including a renewed appreciation of clinical theory, therapeutic limitation of traditional approaches, and cultural awareness of the problematic self, converged to make the self an urgent subject for investigation. Kohut's insight that the self could be studied in analysis through the exploration of selfobject transferencelike enactments fostered systematic exploration of disorders of the self that, in turn, led to reformulation of traditional psychoanalytic and developmental concepts. Advances in self psychology across the past decade, joined with life course developmental psychology, have produced new understandings regarding self in relation to others across the course of life. Emergence of self psychology has opened new frontiers for study, ranging from therapeutics to theory.

REFERENCES

Applegarth, A. (1977). Psychic energy reconsidered: A critique. *Journal of the American Psychoanalytic Association, 25,* 599–602.

Atwood, G., & Stolorow, R. (1984). *Structure of subjectivity: Explorations in psychoanalytic phenomenology.* Hillsdale, NJ: Analytic Press.

Bacal, H. (1989). Winnicott and self-psychology: Remarkable reflections. In D. Detrick & S. Detrick (Eds.), *Self-psychology: Comparisons and contrasts* (pp. 259–274). Hillsdale, NJ: Analytic Press.

Bacal, H., & Newman, K. (1990). *Theories of object relations: Bridges to self psychology.* New York: Columbia University Press.

Basch, M. (1983). The concept of "self": An operational definition. In B. Lee & G. Noam (Eds.), *Developmental approaches to the self* (pp. 7–58). New York: Plenum Press.

Balint, M. (1935/1965). Clinical notes on the theory of the pregenital organizations of the libido. In M. Balint (Ed.), *Primary love and psychoanalytic technique* (pp. 37–58). New York: Liveright.

Beebe, B., & Lachmann, F. (1988). Mother–infant mutual influence and precursors of psychic structure. In A. Goldberg (Ed.), *Frontiers in self psychology* (pp. 3–26). Hillsdale, NJ: Analytic Press.

Bettelheim, B. (1983). *Freud and man's soul.* New York: Knopf.

Blos, P. (1989). The place of the adolescent process in the analysis of the adult. *Psychoanalytic Study of the Child, 44,* 3–18.

Bowlby, J. (1973/1979). Self-reliance and some conditions that promote it. In J. Bowlby (Ed.), *The making and breaking of affectional bonds* (pp. 102–125). London: Tavistock Press.

Bowlby, J. (1988). Developmental psychiatry comes of age. *American Journal of Psychiatry, 145,* 1–10.

Brazelton, T., & Youngman, M. (Eds.). (1986). *Affective development in infancy.* Norwood, NJ: Ablex.

Cohler, B. (1980). Developmental perspectives on the psychology of self in early childhood. In A. Goldberg (Ed.), *Advances in self psychology* (pp. 69–115). Madison, CT: International Universities Press.

Cohler, B. (1987). Approaches to the study of development in psychiatric education. In S. Weissman & R. Thurnblad (Eds.), *The role of psychoanalysis in psychiatric education: Past, present and future* (pp. 225–270). Madison, CT: International Universities Press.

Cohler, B. (1989). The human studies and the course of life. *Social Service Review, 62,* 552–576.

Cohler, B., & Galatzer-Levy, R. (1990). Self, meaning and morale across the second-half of life. In R. Nemiroff & C. Colarusso (Eds.), *New dimensions in adult development* (pp. 214–259). New York: Basic Books.

Demos, V. (1988). Affect and the development of the self: A new frontier. In A. Goldberg (Ed.), *Frontiers in self psychology* (pp. 27–54). Hillsdale, NJ: Analytic Press.

Eissler, K. R. (1953). Effect of the structure of the ego on psychoanalytic technique. *Journal of the American Psychoanalytic Association, 1,* 104–143.

Erikson, E. (1959). *Identity and the life cycle: Selected papers.* Madison, CT: International Universities Press.

Federn, P. (1934). The analysis of psychotics. *International Journal of Psychoanalysis, 15,* 209.

Fosshage, J. (1988). Dream interpretation revisited. In A. Goldberg (Ed.), *Frontiers in self psychology* (pp. 161–175). Hillsdale, NJ: Analytic Press.

Freud, A. (1936/1966). *The ego and the mechanism of defense* (rev. ed.). Madison, CT: International Universities Press.

Freud, S. (1895/1966). Project for a scientific psychology. In J. Strachey (Ed. and Trans.), *The standard edition of the complete psychological works of Sigmund Freud* (Vol. 1, pp. 295–387). London: Hogarth Press.

Freud, S. (1900/1958). The interpretation of dreams. In J. Strachey (Ed. and Trans.), *The standard edition of the complete psychological works of Sigmund Freud* (Vols. 4–5). London: Hogarth Press.

Freud, S. (1905/1953). Fragment of an analysis of a case of hysteria. In J. Strachey (Ed. and Trans.), *The standard edition of the complete psychological works of Sigmund Freud* (Vol. 7, pp. 1–122). London: Hogarth Press.

Freud, S. (1909/1955). Notes upon a case of obsessional neurosis. In J. Strachey (Ed. and Trans.), *The standard edition of the complete psychological works of Sigmund Freud* (Vol. 11, pp. 63–138). London: Hogarth Press.

Freud, S. (1911/1958). Formulations regarding the two principles of mental functioning. In J. Strachey (Ed. and Trans.), *The standard edition of the complete psychological works of Sigmund Freud* (Vol. 12, pp. 215–226). London: Hogarth Press.

Freud, S. (1914a/1958). Remembering, repeating, and working-through (further recommendations on the technique of psychoanalysis, II). In J. Strachey (Ed. and Trans.), *The standard edition of the complete psychological works of Sigmund Freud* (Vol. 14, pp. 145–156). London: Hogarth Press.

Freud, S. (1914b/1958). On narcissism: An introduction. In J. Strachey (Ed. and Trans.), *The standard edition of the complete psychological works of Sigmund Freud* (Vol. 14, pp. 73–102). London: Hogarth Press.

Freud, S. (1923/1961). The ego and the id. In J. Strachey (Ed. and Trans.), *The standard edition of the complete psychological works of Sigmund Freud* (Vol. 9, pp. 12–59). London: Hogarth Press.

Freud, S. (1932–1933/1964). The new introductory lectures. In J. Strachey (Ed. and Trans.), *The standard edition of the complete psychological works of Sigmund Freud* (Vol. 22, pp. 5–184). London: Hogarth Press.

Freud, S. (1937/1964). Analysis terminable and interminable. In J. Strachey (Ed. and Trans.), *The standard edition of the complete psychological works of Sigmund Freud* (Vol. 23, pp. 216–253). London: Hogarth Press.

Freud, S. (1940/1964). An outline of psychoanalysis. In J. Strachey (Ed. and Trans.), *The standard edition of the complete psychological works of Sigmund Freud* (Vol. 23, pp. 141–207). London: Hogarth Press.

Galatzer-Levy, R. (1976). Psychic energy: A historical perspective. *Annual of Psychoanalysis, 4,* 41–64.

Galatzer-Levy, R. (1987). Analytic experiences with manic-depressive patients. In A. Goldberg (Ed.), *Progress in self psychology* (Vol. 3, pp. 87–102). Hillsdale, NJ: Analytic Press.

Galatzer-Levy, R., & Cohler, B. (1989). The selfobjects of the second half of life: An introduction. In A. Goldberg (Ed.), *The realities of the transference: Progress in self-psychology* (Vol. 6, pp. 93–112). Hillsdale, NJ: Analytic Press.

Galatzer-Levy, R., & Cohler, B., (1990). The developmental psychology of the self and the changing worldview of psychoanalysis. *Annual Review of Psychoanalysis, 17,* 1–44.

Galatzer-Levy, R., & Cohler, B. (in press). *The essential other.* New York: Basic Books.

Gedo, J. (1979). *Beyond interpretation: Toward a revised theory of psychoanalysis.* Madison, CT: International Universities Press.

Gedo, J. (1981). *Advances in clinical psychoanalysis.* Madison, CT: International Universities Press.

Gedo, J. (1984). *Psychoanalysis and its discontent.* New York: Guilford Press.

Gill M. (1976). Metapsychology is not psychology. In M. M. Gill & P. S. Holzman (Eds.), *Psychology versus metapsychology: Psychoanalytic essays in memory of George S. Klein* (pp. 71–105). Madison, CT: International Universities Press.

Gitelson, M. (1962). The curative factors in psychoanalysis: I. The first phase of psychoanalysis. *International Journal of Psychoanalysis, 43,* 194–205.

Goldberg, A. (1975). A fresh look at perverse behavior. *International Journal of Psychoanalysis, 56,* 335–342.

Goldberg, A. (1982). The self of psychoanalysis. In B. Lee (Ed.), *Psychosocial theories of the self* (pp. 9–22). New York: Plenum Press.

Goldberg, A. (1988). *A fresh look at psychoanalysis.* Hillsdale, NJ: Analytic Press.

Greenson, R. (1967). *The technique and practice of psychoanalysis.* Madison, CT: International Universities Press.

Greenson, R. (1971). A dream while drowning. In J. McDevitt & C. Settlage (Eds.), *Separation–individuation: Essays in honor of Margaret S. Mahler* (pp. 377–384). Madison, CT: International Universities Press.

Habermas, J. (1968/1971). *Knowledge and human interests* (J. Shapiro, Trans.). Boston: Beacon Press.

Hartmann, H. (1939). *Ego psychology and the problem of adaptation.* Madison, CT: International Universities Press.

Hartmann, H. (1950). Comments on the psychoanalytic theory of the ego. In H. Hartmann (Ed.), *Essays on ego psychology* (pp. 113–141). Madison, CT: International Universities Press.

Hartmann, H., Kris, E., & Lowenstein, R., (1946). Comments on the formation of psychic structure. In H. Hartmann, E. Kris, & R. Lowenstein (Eds.), *Papers on psychoanalytic psychology* (pp. 27–55). Madison, CT: International Universities Press.

Holzman, P. (1985). Psychoanalysis: Is the therapy destroying the science? *Journal of the American Psychoanalytic Association, 33,* 725–770.

Jacobson, E. (1964). *The self and the object world.* Madison, CT: International Universities Press.

James, W. (1890/1959). *Principles of psychology* (2 volumes). New York: Dover Publications.

Jung, C. C. (1933). *Modern man in search of a soul.* New York: Harcourt, Brace.

Kagan, J. (1981). *The second year: The emergence of self-awareness.* Cambridge, MA: Harvard University Press.

Kernberg, O. F. (1975). Further contributions to the treatment of narcissistic personalities: A reply to the discussion by Paul H. Ornstein. *International Journal of Psychoanalysis, 56,* 245–247.

Kernberg, O. (1976). *Object relations and clinical psychoanalysis.* Northvale, NJ: Jason Aronson.

Kernberg, O. (1982). Self, ego, and drives. *Journal of the American Psychoanalytic Association, 30,* 893–917.

Klein, G. (1976). *Psychoanalytic theory: An exploration of essentials.* Madison, CT: International Universities Press.

Klein, M. (1948/1975). On the theory of anxiety and guilt. In M. Klein (Ed.), *Envy and gratitude and other works 1946–1963* (pp. 25–47). London: Hogarth Press.

Kohut, H. (1959/1978). Introspection, empathy and psychoanalysis: An examination of the relationship between mode of observation and theory. In P. Ornstein (Ed.), *The search for the self: Selected writings of Heinz Kohut, 1950–1978* (pp. 205–232). Madison, CT: International Universities Press.

Kohut, H. (1966). Forms and transformations of narcissism. *Journal of the American Psychoanalytic Association, 14,* 243–272.

Kohut, H. (1971). *The analysis of the self: A systematic approach to the psychoanalytic treatment of narcissistic personality disorders.* Madison, CT: International Universities Press.

Kohut, H. (1972). On the adolescent process as a transformation of the self. In. E. S. Wolf, J. E. Gedo, D. M. Terman, & P. Ornstein (Eds.), *The search for the self* (Vol. 2, pp. 659–662). Madison, CT: International Universities Press.

Kohut, H. (1975). A note on female sexuality. In P. Ornstein (Ed.), *The search for the self: Selected writings of Heinz Kohut, 1950–1978* (Vol. 2, pp. 783–792). Madison, CT: International Universities Press.

Kohut H. (1977). *The restoration of the self.* Madison, CT: International Universities Press.

Kohut, H. (1984). *How does psychoanalysis cure.* Chicago: University of Chicago Press.

Kohut, H., & Wolf, E. (1978). The disorders of the self and their treatment: An outline. *International Journal of Psychoanalysis, 59,* 413–425.

Krystal, H. (Ed.). (1976). *Massive psychic trauma.* Madison, CT: International Universities Press.

LaPlanche, J., & Pontalis, J. B. (1973). *The language of psychoanalysis.* New York: Norton.

Lazarus, L., Newton, N., Cohler, B., Lesser, J., & Schweon, C. (1987). Frequency and presentation of depressive symptoms among inpatients with primary degenerative dementia. *American Journal of Psychiatry, 144,* 41–45.

Lichtenberg, J. (1981). The empathic mode of perception and alternative vantage points of psychoanalytic work. *Psychoanalytic Inquiry 1,* 329–356.

Lichtenberg, J. (1983). *Psychoanalysis and infant research.* Hillsdale, NJ: Analytic Press.

Lichtenberg, J., Bornstein, M., & Silver, D., (1984). *Empathy* (2 volumes). Hillsdale, NJ: Analytic Press.

Little, M. (1981). *Transference neurosis and transference psychosis: Toward basic unity.* Northvale, NJ: Jason Aronson.

Loewald, H. (1960). On the therapeutic action of psychoanalysis. In H. Loewald (Ed.), *Papers on psychoanalysis* (pp. 221–256). New Haven, CT: Yale University Press.

Mahler, M., Pine, F., & Bergman, A. (1975). *The psychological birth of the human infant.* New York: Basic Books.

Malin, A. (1988). A short history of the psychoanalytic approach to the treatment of psychotic disorders. In A. Goldberg (Ed.), *Frontiers in self psychology: Progress in self psychology* (Vol. 3, pp. 81–86). Hillsdale, NJ: Analytic Press.

Meissner, W. (1976). New horizons in metapsychology: View and review. *Journal of the American Psychoanalytic Association, 24,* 329.

Meissner, W. (1981). Metapsychology: Who needs it? *Journal of the American Psychoanalytic Association, 29,* 291.

Meissner, W. W. (1986). Can psychoanalysis find its self? *Journal of the American Psychoanalytic Association, 34,* 379–400.

Mitchell, S. A. (1988). *Relational concepts in psychoanalysis: An integration.* Cambridge, MA: Harvard University Press.

Modell, A. (1990). *Other times, other realities.* Cambridge, MA: Harvard University Press.

Pine, F. (1985). *Developmental theory and clinical process.* New Haven, CT: Yale University Press.

Pine, F. (1990). *Drive, ego and self: A synthesis for clinical work.* New York: Basic Books.

Pribram, K., & Gill, M. (1976). *Freud's "Project" re-assessed: Preface to contemporary cognitive theory and neuropsychology.* New York: Basic Books.

Racker, H. (1968). *Transference and countertransference.* Madison, CT: International Universities Press.

Reed, G. S. (1987). Rules of clinical understanding in classical psychoanalysis and in self psychology: A comparison. *Journal of the American Psychoanalytic Association, 35,* 421–446.

Reik, T. (1948). *Listening with the third ear: The inner experience of a psychoanalyst.* New York: Farrar Strauss.

Richards, A. D. (1982). The superordinate self in psychoanalytic theory and in the self psychologies. *Journal of the American Psychoanalytic Association, 30,* 939–957.

Ricoeur, P. (1970). *Freud and philosophy: An essay on interpretation.* New Haven, CT: Yale University Press.

Ricoeur, P. (1977). The question of proof in Freud's psychoanalytic writings. *Journal of the American Psychoanalytic Association, 25,* 835–872.

Sander, L. (1975). Infant and caretaking environment: Investigation and conceptualization of adaptive behavior in a system of increasing complexity. In E. J. Anthony (Ed.), *Explorations in child psychiatry* (pp. 129–166). New York: Plenum Press.

Sandler, J., & Rosenblatt, B. (1962). The concept of the representational world. *Psychoanalytic Study of the Child, 17,* 128–145.

Satinover, J. (1986). Jung's lost contribution to the dilemma of narcissism. *Journal of the American Psychoanalytic Association, 34,* 401–438.

Schafer, R. (1968). *Aspects of internalization.* Madison, CT: International Universities Press.

Schafer, R. (1976). *A new language for psychoanalysis.* New Haven, CT: Yale University Press.

Schafer, R. (1978). *Language and insight.* New Haven, CT: Yale University press.

Schafer, R. (1980). Narration in the psychoanalytic dialogue. *Critical Inquiry, 7,* 29–53.

Schafer, R. (1983). *The analytic attitude.* New York: Basic Books.

Schwaber, E. (1983). A particular perspective on analytic listening. *Psychoanalytic Study of the Child, 38,* 519–546.

Sechehaye, M. (1951). *Symbolic realization*. Madison, CT: International Universities Press.

Sklansky, M. (1977). The alchemy of love: Transmutation of the elements in adolescents and young adults. *Annual of Psychoanalysis, 5*.

Spitz, R. (1945). Hospitalism: An inquiry into the genesis of psychiatric conditions in early childhood. *Psychoanalytic Study of the Child, 1*, 53–72.

Stechler, G., & Kaplan, S. (1980). The development of the self. *Psychoanalytic Study of the Child, 35*, 85–105.

Stern, D. (1985). *The interpersonal world of the infant*. New York: Basic Books.

Stolorow, R., Brandchaft, B., & Atwood, G. (1987). *Psychoanalytic treatment: An intersubjective approach*. Hillsdale, NJ: Analytic Press.

Stone L. (1961). *The psychoanalytic situation*. Madison, CT: International Universities Press.

Strachey, J., & Editors. (1961). Editor's annotation, remarks on the theory and practice of dream interpretation. In J. Strachey (Ed. and Trans.), *The standard edition of the complete psychological works of Sigmund Freud* (Vol. 19, p. 133). London: Hogarth Press.

Sullivan, H. S. (1962). *Schizophrenia as a human process*. New York: Norton.

Sulloway, F. (1979). *Freud: Biologist of the mind*. New York: Basic Books.

Swanson, D. (1977). On force, energy, entropy, and the assumptions of metapsychology. *Psychoanalysis and Contemporary Science, 5*, 137–153.

Ticho, E. A. (1982). The alternate schools and the self. *Journal of the American Psychoanalytic Association, 30*, 849–862.

Tolpin, M. (1971). On the beginnings of a cohesive self: An application of the concept of transmuting internalization to the study of the transitional object and signal anxiety. *Psychoanalytic Study of the Child, 26*, 316–352.

Tolpin, P. (1980). The borderline personality: Its makeup and analyzability. In A. Goldberg (Ed.), *Advances in self psychology* (pp. 299–316). Madison, CT: International Universities Press.

Tolpin, M., & Kohut, H. (1980/1989). The disorders of the self. In S. Greenspan & G. Pollock (Eds.), *The course of life: II. Early childhood* (pp. 229–254). Madison, CT: International Universities Press.

Tomkins, S. S. (1968) Affects: Primary motives of man. *Humanities, 3*(3), 321–345.

Toulmin, S. (1981). On knowing our own minds. *Annual of Psychoanalysis, 9*, 207–221.

Trevarthan, C. (1989, Autumn). Origins and directions for the concept of infant intersubjectivity. *SRCD Newsletter*, 1–4.

Wallerstein, R. (1977). Psychic energy reconsidered: Introduction. *Journal of the American Psychoanalytic Association, 25*, 529–536.

Wallerstein, R. (1986). Psychoanalysis as a science: Response to new challenges. *Psychoanalytic Quarterly, 55*, 414.

Winnicott, D. (1945/1958). Primitive emotional development. In D. W. Winnicott (Ed.), *Collected papers: Through pediatrics to psychoanalysis* (pp. 145–156). New York: Basic Books.

Winnicott, D. W. (1953). Transitional objects and transitional phenomena. In D. W. Winnicott (Ed.), *Collected papers: Through pediatrics to psychoanalysis* (pp. 229–242). New York: Basic Books.

Winnicott, D. W. (1960). The theory of the parent-infant relationship. *International Journal of Psychoanalysis, 41*, 585–595.

Wolf, E. (1980). Tomorrow's self: Heinz Kohut's contribution to adolescent psychiatry. *Adolescent Psychiatry, 8*, 41–50.

Wolf, E. (1982). Adolescence: Psychology of the self and selfobjects. *Adolescent Psychiatry, 10*, 171–181.

Wolf, E. (1988). *Treating the self: Elements of clinical self-psychology*. New York: Guilford Press.

Wolf, E., Gedo, J., & Terman, D. (1978). On the adolescent process as a transformation of the self. *Journal of Youth and Adolescence, 1,* 257–272.

Zetzel, E. (1958). Therapeutic alliance in the analysis of hysteria. In *The capacity for emotional growth* (pp. 182–196). Madison, CT: International Universities Press.

Zetzel, E. (1966–1969). The analytic situation and the analytic process. In *The capacity for emotional growth* (pp. 197–215). Madison, CT: International Universities Press.

20

THE *BORDERLINE* CONCEPT: CROSSROADS OF THEORY AND RESEARCH

PAUL LERNER

Rapaport envisioned the relation between psychoanalytic theory and psychological tests as a two-way street. In one direction, he saw theory as providing the clinical examiner with an array of concepts and propositions that could remarkably broaden the range and clinical relevance of test derived inferences. In the other direction, and to be emphasized in this chapter, he saw how the tests themselves provided a means for operationalizing and measuring concepts that were hazy and elusive; how this would then permit the testing of key psychoanalytic formulations; and then, in time, how this could add to the evolving scope of psychoanalytic theory.

The borderline concept has provided an especially fruitful area for observing the interplay between theory and testing (i.e., method) as described by Rapaport. Based particularly on the conceptual groundwork laid by Kernberg (1975), the past decade has witnessed a host of empirical studies, employing various psychological tests, especially the Rorschach, that have sought to bring greater clarity and precision to the borderline concept.

In this chapter I first provide a historical review of psychoanalytic contributions to the borderline concept. I then use Kernberg's (1975) conceptual and diagnostic model as an organizational framework for reviewing and integrating these various studies that have employed psychological assessment. Finally, I discuss the implications of this body of theory and research for psychoanalytic theory.

Before beginning this review, it is important to recognize that despite the increasing number of empirical studies, the controversy surrounding the borderline concept has not abated. Indeed, by contrast, more recent theoretical and empirical writings have tended to add to the number of unresolved conceptual issues. Excellent comprehensive reviews of the broad array of vexing questions stirred by the borderline concept have been offered by Lerner (1990) and Westen (1990).

452

HISTORICAL REVIEW

The borderline concept, as Sugarman and Lerner (1980) have noted, "has a long, uneven and particularly controversial history in both psychiatry and psychoanalysis" (p. 11). The term *borderline,* as these authors go on to point out

> has been referred to as a "wastebasket" diagnosis for patients who could not be classified as neurotic or psychotic (Knight, 1953), as an "unwanted category" traceable to Bleuler's (1924) attempts to classify patients whose conventional behavior masked an underlying schizophrenia (Gunderson & Singer, 1975), and more recently as a "star word"—seeming to illuminate a great deal (Pruyser, 1975). (p. 11)

The borderline concept as well as its delineation as a pathological entity has arisen from the convergence of two streams of conceptual development within psychiatry—descriptive psychiatry with its emphases on discrete and observable phenomena and exclusive nosological categories and psychoanalysis with its view of attempting to establish structural, dynamic, and developmental roots of the disorder.

The origins of the psychoanalytic stream are found in Reich's work on character and character analysis. In his 1925 book *The Impulsive Character,* he not only used the term borderline, but also described the pregenital conflicts, ego and superego defects, immature defenses, and narcissistic orientation of the impulsive personality in a way that Sugarman and Lerner (1980) refer to as having a "remarkably contemporary cast" (p. 13).

Following Reich, several investigators have contributed to the psychoanalytic literature on borderline pathology. Alexander (1930) coined the term "neurotic character" to describe a group of patients who presented with "an irrational style of life" as contrasted with discrete symptoms. Stern (1938, 1945, 1948) extended Alexander's concept of the neurotic character to the "borderline group." Stern (1938) also delineated 10 critical factors in assigning the borderline diagnosis, five of which—narcissism, negative therapeutic reaction, masochism, use of projective mechanisms, and impairments in reality testing—have significant contemporary relevance.

Zilboorg (1941) used the term "ambulatory schizophrenic" to characterize those patients who maintained a social facade amid unrealistic thinking, related to others in a highly superficial manner, and presented as aimless. Deutsch (1942) wrote of the "as if" personality, an individual who manifested impoverished object relations, feelings of inner emptiness, intact reality testing, fleeting feelings of depersonalization, and narcissistic identifications. Schmideberg (1947, 1959) provided the evocative phrase "stable in their instability" to characterize a group of patients who were unreliable, were intolerant of rules, had difficulty free associating in psychoanalysis, were poorly motivated for treatment, were unable to make use of insight, and failed to establish meaningful emotional contact with others.

Although Deutsch (1942) described the "as if" patient's unstable and diffuse sense of identity, movement within the psychoanalytical stream from a more descriptive to a structural point of view is found in the work of Knight (1953) and in his emphases on the severe ego weaknesses that underlay the borderline patient's seeming adaptation to environmental demands and superficial object relations. These patients, according to Knight, were more disturbed than they appeared. Speaking to the issue of differential diagnosis, he identified three basic aspects of the syndrome: (a) the use of compensatory defenses and symptoms to cover over the underlying defects; (b) a lack of awareness of psychoticlike expressions; and (c) an inability to maintain reality-bound functioning in unstructured situations such as projective tests.

Beginning in 1966 with a reexamination of the borderline concept and the spectrum of disorders of character from the perspective of structural derivatives, the work of Kernberg (1975, 1976) has had an enormous impact on the field. By integrating the British school of object relations with the structural theories of ego psychology, he has been able to develop a unitary process conceptualization of psychopathology and demonstrate that a descriptive clarification of borderline disturbances contains only "presumptive diagnostic elements."

KERNBERG'S DIAGNOSTIC SCHEME

Insistent that a descriptive characterological diagnosis is necessary but not sufficient, Kernberg (1970) devised a system for classifying level of personality organization based upon a systematic appraisal of underlying psychological structures. The system calls for a placing of each structure on a three level continuum ranging from higher level to intermediate level to lower level. Patients at the lower level, according to Kernberg, present a borderline personality organization.

Level of Instinctual Development

This category involves the predominant level of instinctual attainment and fixation. In contrast with previous psychoanalytic systems that classify character on the basis of the stages of libidinal development (oral, anal, phallic, etc.), here, a major distinction is drawn between genital and pregenital instinctual strivings.

Manifestations of Ego Weaknesses

By ego weaknesses, Kernberg was referring to the nature and quality of ego functions including impulse control, tolerance of frustration, and anxiety, reality testing, and effectiveness of defenses. Also included is the nature and extent of expressions of primary process thinking.

Level of Defensive Organization

Kernberg proposes two overall levels of defensive organization. At the lower level, primitive dissociation or splitting is the crucial defense bolstered by the related defenses of denial, primitive idealization, primitive devaluation, and projective identification. At the higher level, repression supplants splitting as the major defense and is accompanied by the related defensive operations of intellectualization, rationalization, undoing, and higher forms of projection and denial.

Level of Internalized Object Relations

In keeping with formulation arising from the British school of object relations, Kernberg views the defensive organization and the level of internalized object relations as intimately related. More specifically, defenses organize the inner object world and are reflected in external object relations.

Level of Superego Development

The internalization of object relations constitutes a major organizing factor for superego development. Failure to integrate all good and all bad object and self images interferes with superego integration by creating an excessively demanding ego ideal that insists on ideals of power, greatness, and perfection. Sadistic superego forerunners, maintained through projective and introjective processes, are not toned down or integrated with idealized superego components. For Kernberg (1976),

> the development of a level of integration within the ego creates the precondition for the integration of the sadistically determined superego forerunners with the ego ideal and the subsequent capacity to internalize the realistic, demanding, and prohibitive aspects of the parents. (p. 150)

Attainment of Ego Identity

Also related to the internalization of object relations is the attainment of ego identity. Only with the synthesis of good and bad self images is the basis laid for the development of ego identity. Kernberg (1976) put it this way," when "good" and "bad" internalized object relations (involving self-images, object-images, ideal self-images and ideal object-images) are so integrated that an integrated self concept and a related "representational world" develops, a stable ego identity is achieved" (p. 150).

In summary, in contrast with more descriptive diagnostic systems that place borderline disturbances along the same dimension as other personality types or disorders (i.e., narcissistic disorder, hysterical reaction, etc.), Kernberg devised a second dimension, referred to as level of personality organization, and then placed borderline disturbances along this axis. More specifically, the lower level of personality organization comprises the borderline disorders. By conceptualizing borderline functioning and organization in this way, the system takes into account the clinical and research finding that patients with varying character structures can manifest borderline pathology.

RESEARCH FINDINGS

Using Kernberg's conceptual and diagnostic model as an organizational framework, in this section I review a host of research studies that have used psychological tests for assessing the borderline patient. Although the empirical literature related to the borderline concept is far broader, I confine this review to the testing literature so as to demonstrate the mutually enhancing relation between testing and psychoanalytic theory as originally envisioned by Rapaport. In addition to reporting the essential test findings, I also point out the reciprocal effects the investigation of borderline patients has had on the use of tests, note certain theoretical and methodological issues raised by this research, and review select studies in greater detail that I believe are of particular importance. It is important to note that in general, the testing literature has focused on structural aspects of the borderline patient's personality rather than on factors related to drive development. In terms of Kernberg's model, the specific structural features investigated have included manifest ego weaknesses, nature and level of defense, and level of internalized object relations.

With respect to manifest ego weaknesses, the combined results of studies regarding reality testing (Berg, 1990; Exner, 1986; Hymowitz, Hunt, Carr, Hurt, & Spear 1983); thought disorder (Edell, 1987b; Exner, 1986; Hymowitz et al., 1983; Lerner, Sugarman & Barbour, 1985), boundary disturbance (Lerner, Sugarman & Barbour, 1985; Wilson, 1985), and impulse control (Edell, 1987a; Evans, Ruff, Braff, & Ainsworth, 1984; Exner, 1986; Gustin et al., 1983; Kroll et al., 1981; Kroll, Carey, Sines, & Roth, 1982; Lloyd, Overall, Kimsey, & Glick, 1983; Snyder, Pitts, Goodpaster, Sajadi, & Gustin, 1982) indicate that borderline patients do exhibit ego weaknesses that are identifiable and that distinguish them from other patient groups and from normal controls. They have considerable difficulty maintaining the distinctions between reality and fantasy, the internal and the external, and between past and present object relationships. Their hold on reality is tenuous and too readily fantasy elaborations encroach on and become a replacement for reality. In addition, they exhibit poor impulse control and limited frustration tolerance.

Conceptually and methodologically, the studies regarding thought disorder, especially those regarding differences in disturbed thinking between borderline and schizophrenics (Lerner, Sugarman, & Barbour, 1985), are important in that they demonstrate that viewing thought disorder as a unitary dimension and investigating it purely quantitatively is insufficient. Beginning with Watkins and Stauffacher (1952) and their attempts to order thought disorder along a single continuum of severity, subsequent investigators have followed this line and in the process have obscured possible qualitative differences among differing types of thought disorders. It should be remembered that Rapaport's indexes of deviant verbalizations represented an attempt to find Rorschach counterparts to what Freud (1900/1953) had initially described as the mechanisms of dream work. Thus, the contamination response on the Rorschach was considered equivalent to Freud's mechanism of condensation and, in a similar way, the confabulatory response was equated to the mechanism of displacement. Therefore, although Rapaport's indexes likely vary in level of severity and may be collectively grouped under the broad umbrella "primary process," it is quite likely that they are tapping different processes. If this be the case, then investigators when exploring differences in thought disorder among various diagnostic groups, need to look at kind of disorder and not just amount.

Although based on Kernberg's theory, investigations of defense organization have yielded impressive and consistent findings in support of his formulations. In a series of studies (Berg, 1990; Collins, 1983; Cooper, Perry, & Arnow, 1988; Farris, 1988; Lerner, Albert, & Walsh, 1987; Lerner & Lerner, 1980; Lerner, Sugarman, & Gaughran, 1981), it has been demonstrated that patients organized at a borderline level manifest a discernable defensive structure different in kind from those of psychotic, neurotic, and narcissistic patients. Although the specific pattern of defenses among groups of borderline patients may vary, in most studies the centrality accorded splitting has been supported.

Studies related to borderline defenses, in a reciprocal way, have contributed meaningfully to the testing literature. More specifically, attempts to investigate borderline defenses have spawned the development of several innovative conceptually based Rorschach scales.

Based on Kernberg's theoretical formulations and the test work of Mayman (1967), Pruitt and Spilka (1964/1975), Holt (1970), and Peebles (1975), Lerner and Lerner (1980) devised a scoring system designed to assess the borderline defenses. The scoring manual is divided into sections on the basis of the specific defenses of splitting, devaluation, idealization, projective identification, and denial. Within each section the defense is defined, Rorschach indexes of the defense are presented, and clinical illustrations are offered. The sections on devaluation, idealization, and denial call for an identification of the defense as well as the ranking of the defense on a continuum of high versus low order. In keeping with Kernberg's contention that these defenses organize and reflect the internal object world and with the empirical relation found between human responses on the Rorschach and the quality of object relating (Blatt & Lerner, 1983), the system involves a systematic appraisal of the human figure response.

A second scoring system was developed by Cooper, Perry, and Arnow (1988). Rooted in the theoretical contributions of Kernberg (1975) and the Stolorow and Lachmann (1980) and the test work of Schafer (1954), Holt (1970), and Lerner and Lerner (1980), these authors devised a content based scoring system for assessing 15 defenses including the borderline defenses of devaluation, omnipotence, primitive idealization, projection, projective identification, and splitting. Broader in scope than the Lerner and Lerner scale, here, the scoring criteria are applied to all Rorschach content rather than just the human figure response. A comprehensive comparison of both scales was conducted by Lerner, Albert, and Walsh (1987).

Efforts to assess the concept internalized object relations have involved the study of impairments in object representations and the study of developmental arrest in the separation–individuation process. Results from several studies (Blatt & Lerner, 1983; Farris, 1988; Lerner & St. Peter, 1984; Spear, 1980; Spear & Sugarman, 1984) indicate that the object representations of borderline patients are more impaired and less developmentally advanced than are those of less severely disturbed patients and of normal controls.

Representative of this line of investigation is the work of Lerner and St. Peter (1984). These authors applied the Concept of the Object Scale (Blatt, Brenneis, Schimek, & Glick, 1976) to a sample of four groups including outpatient neurotic patients, outpatient borderline patients, hospitalized borderline patients, and hospitalized schizophrenic patients. Overall, strong support was found for the general proposition that impairments in level of object representation, as indicated by assessing developmental–structural properties of human responses given on the Rorschach, show distinct patterns for groups differing in type and severity of psychopathology. In addition, several other informative and unexpected findings were also obtained.

Subdividing the responses into those accurately perceived and those inaccurately perceived, the investigators found a direct relation between developmental level of the concept of the object and lessening degrees of psychopathology. That is, the less severe the psychopathology the higher the developmental level of the object. The direct inverse relation, however, did not hold for the inaccurately perceived responses. Here, quite surprisingly, the hospitalized borderline group achieved the highest levels of human differentiation, articulation, and integration for inaccurately perceived responses. Because response accuracy is taken as an indication of quality of reality testing, this finding prompted the authors to question the relation between reality testing and object relations.

Therefore, the investigators then compared the protocols of the two borderline groups. They found that although the outpatient borderlines produced more accurate human responses than did their hospitalized counterparts, their responses tended to involve quasi-human rather than whole human figures. In other words, although the outpatient borderlines were able to perceive objects accurately (intact reality testing), it was accompanied by distancing and dehumanizing the object. The hospitalized borderlines, by contrast, were unable to distance their objects and as a consequence, their reality testing suffered. If one conceptualizes the tendency to distance and devalue objects as reflective of the defenses of splitting and primitive devaluation and the inability to distance and devalue objects as indicative of the failure of these defenses, then the findings may be interpreted as supporting Kernberg's (1975) contention regarding the intimate relation among quality of reality testing, nature of the defensive structure, and the organization of internalized object relations.

Finally, in reviewing the thematic content of the human responses, the investigators found that the hospitalized borderline patients, in comparison with all of the other groups, offered the most malevolent content and was the only group to produce inaccurately perceived malevolent responses. As such, these patients seem unable to defend against or escape from internal malevolent objects.

Other studies (Gold, 1988; Nigg, Lohr, Westen, Gold, & Silk, 1989; Stuart, et al., 1990; Westen, 1990; Westen, Lohr, Silk, Gold, & Kerber, 1989; Westen, Ludolph, Lerner, Ruffins, & Wiss, in press) of object representations in borderline patients indicate that such patients view relationships in need-gratifying ways; attribute the causes of people's behavior, thought, and feelings idiosyncratically; tend to represent the self and others pathologically, which at times involves infusing their representations with fantasy elaborations resulting in representations that are hyper complex and distorted; and experience their object world as highly malevolent.

Two recent empirical studies Westen, Moses, et al., 1989; Wixon, 1988) support Kernberg's (1975) contention that the depressive affect of the borderline patient has a distinct quality characterized by a sense of inner badness, feelings of emptiness, and concerns about abandonment. For Kernberg, underlying this depressive affect are failures in establishing a stable ego-identity and the lack of attainment of object constancy. According to Mahler (Mahler, Pine, & Bergman, 1975), the attainment of ego-identity and object constancy are the end results of a complex process involving the infant's gradual separation and individuation from the mother.

Because of the relevance of Mahler's work for an understanding of specific borderline phenomena, her theory has served as a conceptual base for a second line of investigation aimed at elucidating the object relations of borderline patients.

Using the descriptions of Mahler et al. (1975) as a guideline, Coonerty (1986) devised a scale for identifying and categorizing Rorschach responses reflective of concerns and issues associated with the preseparation stage and each of the phases of the separation–individuation process. She applied the scale to the Rorschach protocols of 50 borderline patients and 50 schizophrenic patients. As predicted, the borderline group attained more separation–individuation themes than the schizophrenic group, whereas the schizophrenics showed more preseparation themes.

As part of an attempt to study early disturbances in the object relations of borderline patients, Kwawer (1980) developed a Rorschach scale consisting of various points (e.g., narcissistic mirroring, symbiotic merger, separation and division, metamorphosis and transformation) in the unfolding of selfhood through differentiation from a primary maternal figure. Underlying the scale is the notion that borderline pathology recapitulates stages of symbiotic relatedness and other primitive modes of unity and disharmony. In pilot work, Kwawer (1980) found that the Rorschachs of borderline patients could be significantly distinguished from those of a matched normal control group on the basis of the scoring categories. More specifically, each of the borderline patients offered at least one scoreable response and this was not the case with the controls.

In summary, research using psychological tests to study the borderline patient has focused on structural aspects of the patient's personality. Specific aspects studied have included manifest ego weaknesses, nature of the defensive structure, and level of internalized object relations. Overall, the findings have supported several of Kernberg's theoretical formulations and clinical observations. At the same time, this work has contributed to the testing literature in that it has stimulated the development of several innovative Rorschach scales, especially in the areas of defense and developmental object relations.

IMPLICATIONS FOR PSYCHOANALYTIC THEORY

As noted previously, research regarding the borderline patient has focused on structural features. This emphasis is in keeping with a broader shift in psychoanalysis; namely, a decrease in interest in drives, drive defense interplay, and conflict, and an increase in interest in structures and structure formation. With increasing emphasis on the process of structure formation has come a reexamination of the complex interactions among early object relations, the development and level of psychological structures including thought processes, defensive functioning, and the internal representational world, and ongoing object relations and the ways these units of experience are internalized and become part of the personality.

From a conceptual perspective, contributions to the borderline concept have prompted a rethinking of core psychoanalytic concepts including defense, transference, regression, countertransference, thinking, and affects.

The concept of defense has been a cornerstone of psychoanalytic theory and technique. Beginning with Freud, defense referred to a way of managing instincts and drive derivatives. It denoted the individual's attempt to keep painful and unendurable ideas and affects out of awareness. With the emergence of the British school of object relations, however, contemporary theorists such as Kernberg and Modell are suggesting that defenses are also intimately related to the experience, internalization, and organization of object relations.

Work with borderline and other difficult patients (i.e., narcissistic) has also led to a broadening understanding of transference. Kohut (1971, 1977), for example, attempted to identify transference paradigms unique to the narcissistic patient and to distinguish these paradigms from the classical transference neurosis. In a classical transference neurosis, the analyst is experienced as a phase-determined (i.e., oral, anal, oedipal) new edition of parents as objects of libidinal and aggressive urges. By contrast, in the so-called "selfobject" transferences the analyst is not experienced as separate and distinct but as an extension of the self and as needed to correct or carry out functions that are normally managed intrapsychically. In addition to describing these patterns, Kohut and his colleagues have also suggested innovative ways in which such configurations should be therapeutically managed. As a result of these efforts, not only have our notions of transference been altered, but analysts and therapists are now able to effectively treat a growing group of patients who, in the past, were considered essentially untreatable.

With the identification and understanding of atypical transference configurations has come a renewed interest in more primitive regressive states and in therapeutic ways of responding to these states (Loewald, 1979; Ornstein & Ornstein, 1980). Regression, in its broadest sense, as Ornstein and Ornstein (1980) noted, involves "a return to, or a revival of genetically earlier modes of thought, behavior and object relations" (p. 12). Regression in treatment has classically meant the unfolding of the patient's psychopathology. Although retaining these earlier meanings, current theorists, especially Loewald (1979) have highlighted a second aspect of regression—its restorative function. This is to say that regression also implies a state in which, through conflict resolution or belated structure building, arrested development may again proceed.

These newer views of transference and regression have had major treatment implications. For example, in classical analysis regressive states were permitted to develop and then dealt with through interpretation. By contrast, in selfobject transferences the regressed patient repeatedly expresses the wish that the analyst "be there," accompany the patient on the regressive journey, and remain in empathic contact with the patient and thereby confirm, rather than question the patient's psychic reality (Ornstein & Ornstein, 1980). What is being suggested here, then, is that the working through process is enhanced not through pure interpretation but by the analyst's acceptance and optimal participation in the regressive experience and through the analyst's empathic presence and empathic responsiveness.

Another psychoanalytic concept that is being reexamined is that of affects. More recent psychoanalytic conceptions of affects have tended to draw attention to their relation not to drives but to object relations. Representative of this line of theorizing is the work of Modell (1975, 1976) and his formulation that affects are object-seeking. He noted that although the sharing and communication of affects affords closeness and intimacy, defenses against affects are also defenses against object relations. Modell reminds us that those individuals who are emotionally constricted tend to be self-sufficient as well. Believing that nothing is needed from others and that they alone can provide their own emotional sustenance, these individuals use self-sufficiency to ward off dangers associated with need and closeness. Winnicott (1961), in this same conceptual vein, noted that one can keep himself or herself hidden by not sharing genuine feelings.

Beyond a reconsideration of basic psychoanalytic concepts, work with borderline patients and research into borderline phenomena has been a major part of changing psychoanalytic conceptualizations of psychopathology and psychoanalytic treatment. Concepts of psychopathology based on the more traditional foundations of psychic conflict and unconscious strivings drew attention to the drives and their vicissitudes, the prevailing modes of defense, and the interaction between the two as manifest in character traits and neurotic symptoms. Concepts of psychopathology predicated on impairments in psychic structure formation, by contrast, draw attention to the nature and quality of the structures themselves (i.e., self system, internalized object relations, etc.), the degree to which they have been internalized, and their genetic roots.

With the emergence of new models of psychopathology has also come important treatment implications. As Michaels (1983) noted,

> concepts of pathology as the product of psychic conflict and unconscious wishes and fears invite models of treatment that emphasize interpretation and insight, with therapy being seen as a special kind of education, and the therapeutic relationship as a unique laboratory for exploring and demonstrating the critical dynamic configurations as they emerge in the transference. Concepts of pathology as the product of developmental arrest and deviance with the resulting formation of abnormal psychic structures invite models of treatment that emphasize the psychological substrate and nutrients necessary for growth and development, with therapy being seen as a second chance for development with a special kind of parenting, the interpretive process as a model of growth promoting interaction, and the therapeutic relationship as a substitute for the nuclear family as a matrix for individuation and growth. (p. 5)

In summary, it was David Rapaport who first envisioned the reciprocal and enhancing impact psychoanalytic theory and psychological tests could have on one another. The borderline concept, especially as formulated by Kernberg, has provided a highly useful arena for observing this interplay. In this chapter I have reviewed psychoanalytic contributions to the borderline concept, briefly outlined Kernberg's diagnostic and structural model of borderline pathology, used the model as an organizational framework for discussing a group of studies that have employed psychological assessment and suggested the broad implications of this body of theory and research for psychoanalytic theory.

REFERENCES

Alexander, F. (1930). The neurotic character. *International Journal of Psychoanalysis, 11,* 292–311.

Berg, J. (1990). *Differentiating ego functions of borderline and narcissistic personalities.* Unpublished manuscript.

Blatt, S., Brenneis, B., Schimek, J., & Glick, M. (1976). Normal development and psychopathological impairment of the concept of the object on the Rorschach. *Journal of Abnormal Psychology, 85,* 364–373.

Blatt, S., & Lerner, H. (1983). The psychological assessment of object representations. *Journal of Personality Assessment, 47,* 7–28.

Bleuler, E. (1924). *Textbook of psychiatry.* New York: Dover.

Collins, R. (1983). *Rorschach correlates of borderline personality.* Unpublished doctoral dissertation, University of Toronto, Toronto, Ontario, Canada.

Coonerty, S. (1986). An exploration of separation-individuation themes in the borderline personality disorder. *Journal of Personality Assessment, 50,* 501–511.

Cooper, S., Perry, J., & Arnow, D. (1988). An empirical approach to the study of defense mechanisms: I. Reliability and preliminary validity of the Rorschach defense scale. *Journal of Personality Assessment, 52,* 187–203.

Deutsch, H. (1942). Some forms of emotional disturbance and their relationship to schizophrenia. *Psychoanalytic Quarterly, 11,* 301–321.

Edell, W. (1987a). Relationship of borderline syndrome disorders to early schizophrenia on the MMPI. *Journal of Clinical Psychology, 43,* 163–176.

Edell, W. (1987b). Role of structure in disordered thinking in borderline and schizophrenic disorders. *Journal of Personality Assessment, 51,* 23–41.

Evans, R., Ruff, R., Braff, D., & Ainsworth, T. (1984). MMPI characteristics of borderline personality inpatients. *Journal of Nervous and Mental Disease, 172,* 742–748.

Exner, J. (1986). Some Rorschach data comparing schizophrenics with borderline and schizotypal personality disorders. *Journal of Personality Assessment, 50,* 455–471.

Farris, M. (1988). Differential diagnosis of borderline and narcissistic personality disorders. In H. Lerner & P. Lerner (Eds.), *Primitive mental states and the Rorschach* (pp. 299–338). Madison, CT: International Universities Press.

Freud, S. (1953). The interpretation of dreams. In J. Strachey (Ed. and Trans.), *The standard edition of the complete psychological works of Sigmund Freud* (Vol. 4, pp. 1–338). London: Hogarth Press. (Original work published 1900)

Gold, L. (1988). *Moral experience in borderline personality and major depressive disorders.* Unpublished doctoral dissertation, University of Michigan, Ann Arbor.

Gunderson, J., & Singer, M. (1975). Defining borderline patients: An overview. *American Journal of Psychiatry, 132,* 1–10.

Gustin, Q., Goodpaster, W., Sajadi, C., Pitts, W., La Basse, D., & Snyder, S. (1983). MMPI characteristics of the DSM-III borderline personality disorder. *Journal of Personality Assessment, 47,* 50–59.

Holt, R. (1970). *Manual for the scoring of primary process manifestations and their controls in Rorschach responses.* New York: Research Center for Mental Health.

Hymowitz, P., Hunt, H., Carr, A., Hurt, S., & Spear, W. (1983). The WAIS and the Rorschach in diagnosing borderline personality. *Journal of Personality Assessment, 47,* 588–596.

Kernberg, O. (1970). A psychoanalytic classification of character pathology. *Journal of the American Psychoanalytic Association, 18,* 800–822.

Kernberg, O. (1975). *Borderline conditions and pathological narcissism.* Northvale, NJ: Jason Aronson.

Kernberg, O. (1976). *Object relations theory and clinical psychoanalysis.* Northvale, NJ: Jason Aronson.

Knight, R. (1953). Borderline states. In R. Knight & C. Friedman (Eds.), *Psychoanalytic psychiatry and psychology* (pp. 97–109). Madison, CT: International Universities Press.

Kohut, H. (1971). *The analysis of the self.* Madison, CT: International Universities Press.

Kohut, H. (1977). *The restoration of the self.* Madison, CT: International Universities Press.

Kroll, J., Sines, L., Martin, K., Lari, S., Pyle, R., & Zander, J. (1981). Borderline personality disorder. Construct validity of the concept. *Archives of General Psychiatry, 38,* 1021–1026.

Kroll, J., Carey, K., Sines, L., & Roth, M. (1982). Are there borderlines in Britain? *Archives of General Psychiatry, 38,* 1021–1026.

Kwawer, J. (1980). Primitive interpersonal modes, borderline phenomena and Rorschach content. In J. Kwawer, H. Lerner, P. Lerner, & A. Sugarman (Eds.), *Borderline phenomena and the Rorschach test* (pp. 89–106). Madison CT: International Universities Press.

Lerner, H. (1990). *The current state of the borderline concept in psychoanalysis.* Unpublished manuscript.

Lerner, H., Albert, C., & Walsh, M. (1987). The Rorschach assessment of borderline defenses. *Journal of Personality Assessment, 51,* 344–354.

Lerner H., & St. Peter, S. (1984). Patterns of object relations in neurotic, borderline, and schizophrenic patients. *Psychiatry, 37,* 77–91.

Lerner, H., Sugarman, A., & Barbour, C. (1985). Patterns of ego boundary disturbances in neurotic, borderline and schizophrenic patients. *Psychoanalytic Psychology, 2,* 47–66.

Lerner, H., Sugarman, A., & Gaughran, J. (1981). Borderline and schizophrenic patients: A comparative study of defensive structure. *Journal of Nervous and Mental Disease, 169,* 705–711.

Lerner, P., & Lerner, H. (1980). Rorschach assessment of primitive defenses in borderline personality structure. In J. Kwawer, H. Lerner, P. Lerner, & A. Sugarman (Eds.), *Borderline phenomena and the Rorschach test* (pp. 257–274). Madison, CT: International Universities Press.

Lloyd, C., Overall, J., Kimsey, M., & Glick, M. (1983). Screening for borderline personality disorders with the MMPI-168. *Journal of Clinical Psychology, 39,* 722–726.

Loewald, H. (1979). Reflections on the psychoanalytic process and its therapeutic potential. *Psychoanalytic Study of the Child, 34,* 155–168.

Mahler, M., Pine, F., & Bergman, A. (1975). *The psychological birth of the human infant.* New York: Basic Books.

Mayman, M. (1967). Object representations and object relationships in Rorschach responses. *Journal of Projective Techniques and Personality Assessment, 31,* 17–24.

Michaels, R. (1983, February). *Plenary address.* Paper presented at the Distortions of Personality Development and Their Management Symposium. Toronto, Ontario, Canada.

Modell, A. (1975). A narcissistic defense against affects and the illusion of self sufficiency. *International Journal of Psychoanalysis, 56,* 275–282.

Modell, A. (1976). The holding environment and the therapeutic action of psychoanalysis. *Journal of the American Psychoanalytic Association, 24,* 285–307.

Nigg, J., Lohr, N., Westen, D., Gold, L., & Silk, K. (1989). *Affective quality of object relations in the early memories of borderline patients.* Unpublished manuscript, University of Michigan, Department of Psychiatry.

Ornstein, P., & Ornstein, A. (1980, April). *Self psychology and the process of regression.* Paper presented at the Toronto Psychoanalytic Society, Toronto, Ontario, Canada.

Peebles, R. (1975). Rorschach as self-system in the telophasic theory of personality development. In P. Lerner (Ed.), *Handbook of Rorschach scales* (pp. 71–136). Madison, CT: International Universities Press.

Pruitt, W., & Spilka, B. (1975). Rorschach empathy—object relationship scale. In P. Lerner (Ed.), *Handbook of Rorschach scales* (pp. 315–323). Madison, CT: International Universities Press. (Original work published 1964)

Pruyser, P. (1975). What splits in splitting. *Bulletin of the Menninger Clinic, 39,* 1–46.

Reich, W. (1974). *The impulsive character and other writings.* New York: New American Library. (Original work published 1925)

Schafer, R. (1954). *Psychoanalytic interpretation in Rorschach testing.* New York: Grune & Stratton.

Schmideberg, M. (1947). The treatment of psychopathic and borderline patients. *American Journal of Psychotherapy, 1,* 47–71.

Schmideberg, M. (1959). The borderline patient. In S. Arieti (Ed.), *American handbook of psychiatry, Vol. 1* (pp. 398–416). New York: Basic Books.

Snyder, S., Pitts, W., Goodpaster, W., Sajadi, C., & Gustin, Q. (1982). MMPI profile of DSM-III borderline personality disorder. *American Journal of Psychiatry, 39,* 1046–1048.

Spear, W. (1980). The psychological assessment of structural and thematic object representations in borderline and schizophrenic patients. In J. Kwawer, H. Lerner, P. Lerner, & A. Sugarman (Eds.), *Borderline phenomena and the Rorschach test* (pp. 321–342). Madison, CT: International Universities Press.

Spear, W., & Sugarman, A. (1984). Dimensions of internalized object relations in borderline and schizophrenic patients. *Psychoanalytic Psychology, 1,* 113–130.

Stern, A. (1938). Psychoanalytic investigation of therapy in the borderline neuroses. *Psychoanalytic Quarterly, 7,* 467–489.

Stern, A. (1945). Psychoanalytic therapy in the borderline neuroses. *Psychoanalytic Quarterly, 14,* 190–198.

Stern, A. (1948). Transference in borderline neuroses. *Psychoanalytic Quarterly, 17,* 527–528.

Stolorow, R., & Lachmann, F. (1980). *Psychoanalysis of developmental arrest.* Madison, CT: International Universities Press.

Stuart, J., Westen, D., Lohr, N., Benjamin, J., Becker, S., Vorus, N., & Silk, K. (1990). Object relations in borderlines, depressives, and normals: An examination of human responses on the Rorschach. *Journal of Personality Assessment, 55,* 296–318.

Sugarman, A., & Lerner, H. (1980). Reflections on the current state of the borderline concept. In J. Kwawer, H. Lerner, P. Lerner, & A. Sugarman (Eds.), *Borderline phenomena and the Rorschach test* (pp. 11–38). Madison, CT: International Universities Press.

Watkins, J., & Stauffacher, J. (1952). An index of pathological thinking in the Rorschach. *Journal of Projective Techniques, 16,* 276–286.

Westen, D. (1990). Toward a revised theory of borderline object relations: Contributions of empirical research. *International Journal of Psychoanalysis, 71,* 661–693.

Westen, D., Lohr, N., Silk, K., Gold, L., & Kerber, K. (1989). *Object relations and social cognition in borderlines, major depressives and normals: A TAT analysis.* Unpublished manuscript, University of Michigan, Department of Psychology, Ann Arbor.

Westen, D., Ludolph, P., Lerner, H., Ruffins, S., & Wiss, C. (in press). *Journal of the American Academy of Child and Adolescent Psychiatry.*

Westen, D., Moses, M., Silk, K., Lohr, N., Cohen, R., & Segal, H. (1989). *Quality of depressive experience in borderline personality disorder and major depression: When depression is not just depression.* Unpublished manuscript, University of Michigan, Department of Psychology, Ann Arbor.

Wilson, A. (1985). Boundary disturbance in borderline and psychotic states. *Journal of Personality Assessment, 49,* 346–355.

Winnicott, D. (1961). Ego distortion in terms of true and false self. In D. Winnicott (Ed.), *The maturational processes and the facilitating environment* (pp. 140–152). Madison, CT: International Universities Press.

Wixom, J. (1988). *The depressive experience of adolescents with borderline personality disorder.* Unpublished doctoral dissertation, University of Michigan.

Zilboorg, G. (1941). Ambulatory schizophrenia. *Psychiatry, 4,* 149–155.

21

PSYCHOSOMATICS AND SELF-REGULATION

GRAEME J. TAYLOR

Psychosomatic medicine is the branch of medicine that is concerned primarily with the interrelationships among biological, psychological, and social factors in health, illness, and disease. Psychoanalysis and psychology have both contributed extensively to the exploration of these relations, in particular through their attempts to identify personality variables that protect against, or contribute to the predisposition to, initiation of, and maintenance of disease; and devise and evaluate psychological treatments for physically ill patients. In this chapter I focus mainly on psychosomatic models of disease derived from psychoanalysis and show how these are currently being revised in light of findings from research in psychology as well as from the biological sciences that are pointing toward a view of humans as self-regulating cybernetic systems.

CONTRIBUTIONS FROM CLASSICAL PSYCHOANALYSIS

The psychoanalytic approach to physical illness has its roots in the longstanding and widely held belief that people's health can be influenced by their emotions. During the 19th century, many physicians attempted to evaluate this belief scientifically by investigating the direct effects of various emotions on different bodily functions (Stainbrook, 1952). Beaumont (1833), for example, demonstrated that fear and anger reduce secretion from the gastric mucosa. The emergence of psychoanalysis at the beginning of the 20th century led to a very different approach, as it inspired several psychoanalysts to begin to study the personality traits and psychological conflicts that were assumed to be responsible for the emotional states contributing to the development of disease.

Although Freud was intensely curious about the mental processes that underly the somatic symptoms of hysteria, he showed little interest in organic bodily diseases. In fact, he encouraged his followers to "resist the temptation to flirt with endocrinology and the autonomic nervous system" (Freud, 1927/1959b, p. 257). Freud (1898/1962a) did, however, make an important distinction between hysterical symptoms, which he categorized as "psychoneurotic" and attributed to psychic conflict over unconscious impulses and fantasies from childhood, and symptoms of the "actual neuroses," which he regarded as somatic in origin and therefore without primary psychological meaning.

This distinction was almost completely discarded after Freud replaced his first theory of anxiety by his theory of signal anxiety (1926/1959a), as his followers concluded that patients suffering from actual neuroses (anxiety neurosis, neurasthenia, and hypochondriasis) would ultimately reveal evidence of intrapsychic conflict (Waelder, 1967). Apart from Glover (1939) and MacAlpine (1954), who emphasized that psychosomatic disorders have no primary psychic content and are therefore different from psychoneuroses, the early psychosomaticists adopted Freud's drive-conflict-defense model of psychopathology and enthusiastically applied this model to patients with somatic diseases. They gave little attention to hypochondriasis and neurasthenia and other so-called "functional" somatic illnesses that showed no structural tissue changes, and instead focused their investigations mainly on a group of seven diseases (bronchial asthma, peptic ulcer, ulcerative colitis, essential hypertension, rheumatoid arthritis, thyrotoxicosis, and neurodermatitis), which were then of uncertain etiology and subsequently came to be referred to as the "classical" psychosomatic diseases.

The efforts of Alexander (1950), Deutsch (1959), and several other psychoanalysts led to the development, during the 1940s and early 1950s, of a variety of psychosomatic models of disease, which I have described in detail in a book (Taylor, 1987). These were mostly multifactor models that included important roles for biological variables and stressful life events, but the preoccupation of the early psychosomaticists was with the psychogenesis of disease, that is, "the mysterious leap from the mind to the body" (Deutsch, 1959). Consequently, they used linear theories of causality in which intrapsychic conflicts were assumed to evoke intense emotions that produce arousal in the autonomic nervous system leading eventually to pathological changes in the function and structure of vulnerable organs of the body. Although there was disagreement as to whether the physical symptoms of disease have primary symbolic meaning, comparable to the symptoms of conversion hysteria, the different theoretical disease models that were devised were all based on the notion that intrapsychic conflicts, and the emotions associated with them, play a central role in the pathogenesis of disease. In that classical psychoanalysis generally views emotions as derivatives of instinctual drives that need to be discharged or "tamed" (Sandler, 1972), the early psychosomaticists emphasized a therapeutic approach that attempted to release "strangulated" affects and resolve conflicts over drive-related wishes.

The idea that neurotic psychopathology might be a risk factor for disease has played a useful role in the evolution of psychosomatic theory. However, the limitations of the early psychosomatic disease models were already apparent by the late 1950s when the anticipated efficacy of psychoanalytic therapy for physically ill patients failed to materialize (Lipowski, 1977), and as critical examinations of the models revealed certain inconsistencies and a dearth of validational data (Mendelson, Hirsch, & Webber, 1956). Research using psychological assessments, or physiological data, or both, subsequently provided some empirical support for a conflict-based psychosomatic disease model (Alexander, French, & Pollock, 1968; Weiner, Thaler, Reiser, & Mirsky, 1957), but recent advances in statistical techniques and methodology (Friedman & Booth-Kewley, 1987; Holroyd & Coyne, 1987), and the realization that many of the diseases that were investigated are heterogeneous (Weiner, 1977), have seriously weakened this support. For example, without objective measures of physical health, the association between high scores on measures of neuroticism and reports of somatic complaints may reflect an increased concern and reporting bias, as Costa and McCrae (1987) have demonstrated, rather than a direct relation between neuroticism and disease. Nonetheless, a recent meta-analytic report of published studies on the personality correlates of five diseases (bronchial asthma, peptic ulcer, headache, rheumatoid arthritis, and coronary heart disease) found moderate support for the construct of a "disease-prone personality" that involves the affects of depression, anger/hostility, and anxiety (Friedman & Booth-Kewley, 1987). Whether these affects are necessarily associated with intrapsychic conflicts remains uncertain. For example, high levels of anger and hostility, which are now regarded as the critical components of the Type A (coronary-prone) behavior pattern (Dembroski, MacDougall, Williams, Haney, & Blumenthal, 1985), might be explained by an impaired ego capacity for containing and modulating narcissistic rage and for tolerating frustration rather than by conflicts over unconscious drive-related wishes. Type A behavior would then be reconceptualized as a disorder of self-regulation (Grotstein, 1986), a concept that was implicit in Freud's (1895/1962a, 1898/1962b) model of the actual neuroses that he simplistically attributed to sexual habits that produced either an excessive accumulation of libido (as in anxiety neurosis) or a marked depletion of libido (as in neurasthenia). I elaborate on the concept of disorders of self-regulation later in this chapter.

HUMAN RELATIONSHIPS IN ILLNESS AND DISEASE

As the limitations of the classical psychoanalytic approach to physical illness and disease became apparent, several psychoanalytically trained physicians shifted their investigative focus from the intrapsychic worlds of their patients to the life setting in which the disease process commences. This led to an increasing understanding of the role of stressful life events in the development of disease, and to a greater recognition of the influence of human relationships on bodily processes. Extensive investigations by Engel (1955) and his associates (Greene & Miller, 1958; Schmale, 1958) during the 1950s and 1960s led to the discovery that the onset or exacerbation of disease is frequently associated with the affects of helplessness and hopelessness evoked by a recent separation or loss of an important relationship. Although there was no evidence of a direct causal relation between object loss and the development of disease, Engel (1968) and Schmale (1972) postulated that there is a heightened susceptibility to disease in individuals who adapt poorly to separations and other object losses. Such individuals appear to develop the specific depressive affects of helplessness and/or hopelessness, attitudes of "giving up" and "given up," and a conservation–withdrawal physiological response (Engel & Schmale, 1972). Engel and Schmale called this intervening psychobiological state the "giving up/given up complex." They postulated that once the complex develops it initiates autonomic, endocrinological, and immunological changes that might lead to the emergence of disease if the necessary constitutional and/or environmental factors are also present.

Empirical support for the validity of Engel and Schmale's (1972) psychobiological model was provided by a number of investigations including studies that predicted (a) the frequency of illness in first-year nursing students living in residence, on the basis of their responses to separation from home (Parens, McConville, & Kaplan, 1966); and (b) the outcome of cone biopsy in women with suspicious cervical cytology, on the basis of ratings for depression and hopelessness (Schmale & Iker, 1966). Research examining the effects of bereavement on health also provided evidence that the loss of a close relationship can lead to increased morbidity and mortality (Klerman & Izen, 1977; Parkes, Benjamin, & Fitzgerald, 1969). However, the mediating mechanisms between bereavement and a decline in health remain unknown. As several authors (Jacobs & Ostfeld, 1977; Weiner, 1987) have asked, is it grief, the loss of specific interactions between the survivor and the departed person, alcohol abuse and changes in the health practices of the survivor, or a combination of these factors that leads to a decline in health?

Although not all investigators have assessed whether their subjects developed a giving up/given up complex following the major losses they experienced, several prospective longitudinal studies have supported Engel and Schmale's (1972) proposal that there may be physiological changes associated with object loss. For example, in a pioneering study, Wolff, Friedman, Hofer, and Mason (1964) demonstrated that the levels of 17-hydroxycorticosteroids in parents of children dying from leukemia could be predicted by the effectiveness of the parents' psychological defenses. More recently, Schleifer, Keller, Camerino, Thornton, and Stein (1983) demonstrated a suppression of lymphocyte function in men during the first 2 months following the deaths of their wives from breast cancer. It remains to be determined, however, whether those physiological changes are related to the onset or course of disease.

In addition to demonstrating an association between attachment disruptions and the onset or exacerbation of disease, Engel (1955, 1958) observed, as did several other psychoanalysts (Jessner et al., 1955; Mushatt, 1975, 1989; Sperling, 1978), that many physically ill patients (children as well as adults) manifest developmental arrests and remain excessively dependent on symbiotic relationships (with a parent, spouse, or friend) to compensate for certain ego deficits. The nature of these deficits was not fully explored, but it seemed that this excessive dependency rendered such patients more vulnerable to illness relapses or remissions in response to the vicissitudes of their interpersonal relationships, including the transference relationships they established with doctors. An in-depth study of patients with chronic ulcerative colitis showed that improvement of the illness was more likely to occur in those patients who could move from symbiotic attachments to more individuated and self-sufficient ones (Karush, Flood, & O'Connor, 1977).

Despite their interest in the interpersonal relationships of physically ill patients, none of the analysts engaged in this research attempted to integrate their observations and formulations with the psychoanalytic theories of object relations that were emerging during the 1950s and 1960s as alternatives to Freud's drive theory. The results of their clinical research helped shift psychosomatic theory from the earlier linear causality and one-person orientation to a two-person interactional model. However, committed as they were to instinct theory, these analysts, and some of their present-day followers (see, e.g., Savitt, 1977; Wilson & Mintz, 1989), continued to emphasize a role for conflicts over libidinal and aggressive impulses in the pathogenesis of disease. Consequently, they failed to appreciate adequately other functional aspects of human relationships and to conceptualize object loss as involving not only the disruption of an emotional bond, but also a withdrawal of homeostatic regulating functions. These functional aspects of human relationships have become better understood during the past 15 years, mainly as a result of research on the psychobiology of attachment and separation in early life (Reite & Field, 1985; Weiner, 1987).

THE PSYCHOBIOLOGY OF ATTACHMENT AND SEPARATION

Classical psychoanalytic drive theory conceptualizes the infant's attachment to the mother as motivated primarily by the need to discharge tension and satisfy oral instinctual impulses (Freud, 1905/1953). This view of attachment was initially challenged in the 1950s by Harlow's (1959) classic studies of rhesus monkey infants raised with surrogate mothers. The monkey infants spent most of their time clinging to the soft terrycloth "mothers" even when nursing bottles containing milk were attached to the wire "mothers," thus demonstrating that body contact plays an important role in the attachment process and that infants need more than the mere satisfaction of oral instinctual needs. But despite experiencing tactile stimulation similar to that obtained within the normal mother–infant relationship, Harlow's monkeys turned out to be strikingly abnormal in their behavior. While growing up they developed stereotyped body rocking and as adults had difficulty mating, were fearful of social encounters, and mistreated their offspring (Jolly, 1985). Quite clearly, much more needed to be learned about the physiology and dynamic properties of the early mother–infant relationship.

Psychologists' knowledge of these aspects of the mother–infant relationship has now increased considerably as a result of recent human and animal infant research. By studying the relational field between mother and infant, developmental psychologists have demonstrated that the mother–infant relationship functions as an *interactional system* that organizes and regulates much of the infant's behavior from birth (Emde & Robinson, 1979; Stern, 1977, 1985). Indeed, the findings from human infant research support the viewpoint of Fairbairn (1952) and other early object relations theorists who contended that libido is primarily object-seeking rather than pleasure-seeking and that compulsive tension-relieving behavior implies some failure of object relationships. Many studies have shown that the newborn infant is actively engaged in object-relating behavior from the start of life (Lichtenberg, 1983). Furthermore, there is mutual regulation within the early dyad—what the infant does changes how the mother responds. Careful observations reveal that both infant and mother use repertoires of behavior to initiate, reinforce, and regulate the other's behavior much like a dancing couple (Sander, 1980; Stern, 1977). Even the rhythm of the infant's limb movements is synchronized with the rhythm of the mother's speech (Condon & Sander, 1974).

In addition to the observable reciprocal regulatory behaviors within the mother–infant relationship, it appears that there are probably also several "hidden" sensorimotor processes whereby the mother can regulate aspects of the infant's biology until self-regulating mechanisms mature. Researchers still know very little about the physiology of the human mother–infant relationship, but research with rodents and primates has identified various "hidden" nutritional, olfactory, tactile, thermal, and vestibular processes whereby the mother "serves as an external regulator of the infant's behavior, its autonomic physiology, and even the neurochemistry of its maturing brain" (Hofer, 1983a, p. 199). By altering specific components of the animal mother–infant relationship, developmental biologists have been able to modify the infant's responses to separation, thereby showing that the responses reflect the withdrawal of multiple external regulatory processes rather than the loss of a single mechanism. For example, Mason and Berkson (1974) discovered the importance of vestibular stimulation by finding that the self-rocking behavior of maternally deprived infant monkeys could be prevented by providing them with mobile surrogate mothers rather than stationary ones.

The need for tactile stimulation is not confined to rhesus monkey infants; Hofer and Shair (1978) demonstrated that the distress-signaling ultrasonic vocalizations of 2-week-old rats separated from their mothers could be reduced by providing body contact with surrogates or by placing a piece of synthetic fur on the cage floor. Body contact and tactile stimulation provided by the mother licking the back of the necks of infant rats also regulate the level of growth hormone and the level of the enzyme ornithine decarboxylase in the brain and heart, both of which fall following separation (Evoniuk, Kuhn, & Schanberg, 1979). A 30% reduction of heart rate following separation can be prevented only by providing the infant rats with graded amounts of feedings by stomach tube (Hofer & Weiner, 1975). This effect is mediated by the autonomic and central nervous systems and not via the circulatory system. The milk has to be delivered intermittently in a pattern mimicking the rhythmicity of the normal mother–infant feeding relationship to prevent the profound sleep disturbance that infant rats develop following premature separation. Furthermore, the body temperature of infant rats, which is determined largely by the body temperature of the mother, has been shown to regulate levels of brain protein, nucleic acids, and catecholamines, all of which are reduced when infants are separated prematurely from their mothers (Stone, Bonnet & Hofer, 1976).

There is evidence also that crucial components in the attachment behavior of infant rats are regulated by olfactory stimuli (Hofer, 1978). For example, infant rats are unable to locate and become attached to the nipple in the absence of a pheromone secreted from the mother's areolar glands. The emission of this substance is regulated by the hormone oxytocin (not by its action on milk letdown), which, in turn, is released in the mother rat by suckling. At a certain age, infant rats are attracted to their own mother at a distance in response to another olfactory cue, that is, a substance called "cecotrophe," which is excreted in sufficient quantity in the feces of the mother at a time corresponding to the days postpartum when the infants are most responsive to it. As Hofer (1978) noted, this is "an example of exquisite synchrony in the early parent–infant relationship" (p. 141).

These and other animal studies provide evidence that the infant's homeostatic organization is a relatively open system, rather than a closed system as previously thought, and that some of the infant animal's responses to separation (especially the more slowly developing responses) are biological release phenomena (i.e., the manifestations of biological subsystems released from normal interactional regulation) rather than "part of the acute emotional response to disruption of attachment" (Hofer, 1983a, p. 199). Although caution must be taken in extrapolating from one species to another, developmental biologists suspect that "hidden" regulatory processes are present also in the human mother–infant relationship. The human infant definitely regulates the flow of the lactating mother's milk because suckling stimulates the release of oxytocin. Maternal regulation of the infant's attachment behavior is suggested by the discovery that, within several days after birth, breast-feeding infants respond preferentially to the breast odor from their own mother when paired with the breast odor from an unfamiliar lactating woman (Porter, Balogh, & Makin, 1988). It has also been shown that premature babies grow faster if they receive regular tactile stimulation (White & La Barba, 1976).

Many of the human infant's biological systems are relatively stable at birth and probably unaffected by interactions with the mother, but the mother certainly plays an important role in the entrainment of such biological rhythms as the sleep–wake cycle and the oral instinctual (feeding) cycle (Emde & Robinson, 1979). It appears likely that future research will identify specific stimuli and types of interaction within the human mother–infant relationship that regulate or "fine tune" a variety of other physiological and behavioral systems in the infant. If this is so, then the symbiotic stage of human development would need to be reconceptualized as serving not only psychological needs of infant and mother, but also certain biological needs, at least while their individual homeostatic systems are linked in a superordinate organization (Hofer, 1987). Furthermore, the long duration of the symbiotic stage of human development might, as Hofer (1983b) suggests, "allow the environment to modify gene expression in the infant through variations in the mother's contribution to the infant's developing [biological and] behavioral systems" (p. 62). The human infant's responses to prolonged separation would be due not simply to the breaking of an attachment bond, but also to withdrawal of the previous biological and behavioral regulation supplied by the mother. The ensuing disregulation of biological systems might precipitate the immediate onset of a somatic disorder. Alternatively, the withdrawal of these hidden regulatory processes in early life might alter an individual's homeostatic organization and thereby influence susceptibility to disease later in life (Hofer, 1983b). This has been demonstrated in animals by Ackerman, Hofer, and Weiner (1978), who investigated the effects of early experience on immobilization-induced gastric lesions in rats. They found that the greater vulnerability of maternally deprived rats occurs not because they are more stressed by the confinement of immobilization, but because early separation from the mother induces a thermoregulatory disturbance that is made manifest when the rats are immobilized several weeks later.

The importance of biological regulatory processes in the human mother–infant relationship is suggested by the observations on institutionalized infants that were reported by Spitz (1945; Spitz & Wolf, 1946) during the 1940s. Following prolonged separations from their mothers, these infants developed anaclitic depressions resembling the conservation–withdrawal response described many years later by Engel and Schmale (1972); they showed an increased susceptibility to infections and other diseases, a failure to thrive, and a high mortality. Using the conceptual framework of classical psychoanalysis, Spitz (1960) attributed these harmful consequences of maternal separation to the damming up of libidinal and aggressive drives. It now seems probable that the apathy and slowed maturation of these infants' bodies and brains, and their high incidence of infections, were due to physiological disturbances, such as thermoregulatory disturbances and impaired febrile and immune responses, consequent to the withdrawal of regulatory processes that were present in the preexisting relationships with their mothers (Stone et al., 1976).

Although the extreme condition of prolonged premature separation invariably results in behavioral and physiological disorganization, research findings suggest that the infant's physiological development may be modified even in the presence of the mother if she and the infant are not well attuned and fail to provide for each other optimal levels of stimulation and arousal modulation (Field, 1985). For example, a depressed or highly anxious mother who is out of tune with her infant will be less involved in developing the reciprocal regulatory interactions mentioned earlier. Temperamental differences might also influence the way a mother relates to her infant. In other words, it is the quality of attachment, not just the presence or strength of attachment, that is important in the maturation of the infant's self-regulatory capacities; characteristics in both mother and infant help determine the "goodness of fit" between them (Thomas & Chess, 1977).

INTERACTIONAL REGULATION, SELF-REGULATION, AND PSYCHOANALYTIC THEORY

The findings from infancy research and developmental biology, especially the discovery of the dynamic interplay between self-regulatory and mutual regulatory processes, have important implications for both psychoanalysis and psychosomatic medicine. Not only is Freud's drive-discharge model of attachment and other infant behavior rendered obsolete, but Bowlby's (1969) attachment theory is also being revised to incorporate the regulation of diverse physiological and behavioral systems along with social bonding and protection from predators (Field, 1985; Hofer, 1983a; Hofer, 1987; Pipp & Harmon, 1987). These advances can be integrated, however, with many of the conceptualizations of psychoanalytic object relations theories, including self psychology, which focus on the interpersonal and intrapsychic aspects of relationships rather than on how individuals discharge libidinal and aggressive drives (Eagle, 1984; Hamilton, 1989; Mitchell, 1988). Indeed, the conceptualizations of the various object relations theories help in developing an explanatory model for how the infant normally progresses from a state of initial dependency on the mother, as an external psychobiological regulator, to a state of relative independence and autonomous functioning.

Like developmental psychologists, most contemporary object relations theorists conceptualize the mother–infant relationship as an interactive system that organizes and promotes the formation of psychic structure in the infant (Greenberg & Mitchell, 1983). Although some of these psychoanalytic theorists retain modified versions of drive psychology, they employ a dyadic view of early development and have outlined epigenetic sequences of early object relations that parallel the emergence and maturation of self-regulatory mechanisms in the infant (Sander, 1983). Mahler (1968), for example, describes initial autistic and symbiotic phases that are followed by four subphases of separation–individuation before the infant is fully differentiated from the mother. The unfolding of object relations is accompanied by the maturation of cognitive and affective processes and the infant's early images of good and bad objects are gradually transformed into stable mental representations of self, of object, and of the pattern of interactions that have developed between them. These internal representations correspond to the internal working models described by Bowlby (1969, 1988) and are presumed to provide important self-regulatory functions including affect regulation (which I will discuss later), self-esteem regulation, and self-stimulation (deLissovoy, 1971; Schafer, 1968; Stierlin, 1970). Hofer (1984) has speculated that internal representations may also function as biological regulators, much the way the actual sensorimotor interactions with the mother regulate aspects of the infant's physiology and behavior.

A parallel view of early object relations was proposed by Kohut (1977, 1984) who introduced the concept of *selfobjects* to refer to the child's initial experience of the parents as though they are part of the self. Self psychologists conceptualize the symbiotic mother–infant pair as a *self–selfobject unit* in which mother and infant function as regulatory selfobjects for one another (Wolf, 1980). According to Kohut (1977), it is the infant's repeated experience of merger with the empathically attuned maternal selfobject, along with optimum (nontraumatic, phase-appropriate) failures of the selfobject that lead to psychic structure building and the internal representation of the self–selfobject unit. The infant's experience with the parental selfobjects, and the formation of mental representations, gradually lead to the maturation and development of self-regulatory functions in the child, who is then able to reduce his or her reliance on the mother as an external regulator.

As several authors have noted (Greenberg & Mitchell, 1983; Grotstein, 1989; Mitchell, 1988; Smith, 1989), Kohut's theory of early healthy development resembles Winnicott's earlier concept that the infant's sense of self emerges within the "facilitating" environment provided by the mother. But unlike Kohut, who gave little attention to the role of the body in early development, Winnicott (1949) emphasized the nature of the mother's involvement with her infant's body; he considered this involvement critical for the development of a sense of self located in the body. Indeed, Winnicott (1949, 1966) believed that the failure to achieve an integration of mind and body during early development predisposed a person to becoming psychosomatically ill at some later time. This mind–body splitting is most evident clinically in patients suffering from somatization disorders or other so-called "functional" somatic disorders but has remained a poorly understood phenomenon. With their chronic complaints of bodily symptoms such patients are clearly ill; however, they generally show no evidence of physical lesions, and there is usually an absence of underlying mental content to provide psychological meanings for their symptoms. As I discuss later, such disorders correspond, in certain respects, to Freud's actual neuroses and can also be conceptualized as disorders of self-regulation.

Also of importance to both psychosomatic theory and the understanding of normal development was Winnicott's (1953) recognition that the process of internalization, and the emergence and maturation of self-regulatory capacities in the child, are facilitated by the *transitional object*. Like the parental selfobjects, the transitional object functions as an external regulator of anxiety and other distressing emotional states. Winnicott conceptualized the transitional object as a "not-me" possession arising in the intermediate area ("potential space") between the infant's illusion of oneness with the mother and the awareness of separateness from her, although careful observations of infants and young children by Gaddini (1978) and Tustin (1981) have revealed that transitional objects evolve from precursor objects that are either provided by the mother (e.g., bottle, pacifier) or are a part of the infant's body (e.g., thumb, fist, fingers, tongue), or part of the mother's body or clothing (e.g., hair, ear lobes, buttons). These precursor objects, or "sensation objects" as Tustin (1981) called them, are experienced as an extension of the infant's body and evoke sensations similar to those experienced within the nursing situation, thus preserving the illusion of oneness with the mother. Like the terrycloth "mothers" preferred by Harlow's monkey infants, a sensation object, or a rhythmically handled transitional object (usually a soft blanket, diaper, or stuffed toy animal), provides tactile and kinesthetic sensations that are reminiscent of early body contact with the mother. In addition to receiving tactile stimulation, the infant brings such an object to his face, smells it, and places parts of it inside his mouth, suggesting that it may regulate separation anxiety by means of olfactory pathways as well. These tactile and olfactory sensorimotor mechanisms are comparable to the hidden regulatory processes that have been discovered within animal mother–infant relationships. Interestingly, the incidence of transitional object usage appears to be related inversely to the amount of physical contact between mother and infant (breast-feeding, rocking, etc.) (Gaddini & Gaddini, 1970; Hong & Townes, 1976). This finding supports the notion that the transitional object fulfills some of the regulatory functions initially provided by the mother and that it becomes a more necessary creation of the infant when the mother withdraws prematurely.

In the course of normal development, there is a gradual transition from interactional regulatory processes that use sensorimotor pathways to self-regulatory processes that are primarily psychological (Hofer, 1978; Peters, 1971). For example, the texture and smell of the transitional object are initially essential for its functioning. But, as the child's cognitive capacities mature, transitional objects and phenomena come to reduce anxiety and tension by symbolically evoking a reunion with the absent mother. In addition, the early and simple cognitive schemata of the self and attachment figure are replaced by more complex and sophisticated internal working models that reflect the child's changing perception and increasing cognitive and affective understanding of relationships (Beebe & Lachmann, 1988; Bowlby, 1988; Brown, 1984–1985; Emde, 1988a; Fraiberg, 1969; Stern, 1983). Developmental research suggests that the child who has established adequate attunement with parents and experienced an optimal level of responsive care will have constructed a stabilizing internal working model that includes an enthusiastic and confident sense of self, a capacity to be self-solacing and generally self-reliant, and a capacity for establishing intimate nonsymbiotic relationships throughout life (Bowlby, 1988; Bretherton, 1985; Main, Kaplan, & Cassidy, 1985). Once organized, these working models tend to operate largely outside of awareness and resist dramatic change (Bowlby, 1988).

With the attainment of self-regulating capacities, the child is able to discard his or her cuddly blanket or stuffed toy animal and to replace these transitional objects with fantasies, dreams, play, and other creative interests that evoke a similar illusory state whereby the individual can transcend the experience of aloneness (Horton, 1981). This may fail to occur, however, when there has been an absence of secure attachment or other deficiencies in the early parent–child relationship. Tustin (1981), for instance, observed that when there has been a catastrophic disruption of the early infant–mother relationship, there is often a persistent use of sensation objects by the infant, seemingly in an attempt to restore the lost comforting sensations and to deny bodily separateness. These sensation objects do not evolve into transitional objects, and the capacity for thinking, feeling, playing, and imagining do not develop in the normal way. The pathological use of sensation objects also forms a barrier between the infant and the mother and the usual mutual regulatory interactions therefore do not occur. Such disturbances in the mother–infant regulatory system have been associated with the emergence of behavioral and somatic disorders in early life. These have been conceptualized as "disorders of regulation"

(Taylor, 1987) and include body rocking, sleep disturbances, feeding difficulties, rumination (merycism), colic, and bronchial asthma (Gaddini, 1978; Kreisler, 1984).

Although self-regulation generally replaces regulatory interactions with the mother as a means of maintaining homeostasis, self-regulation itself operates through a large number of individually distinct and hierarchically arranged mechanisms, some of which rely on social relationships and other environmental feedback (Hofer, 1984; Peters, 1971). In other words, it appears that people are never completely independent of others, a view shared by Kohut (1984) when he emphasized the regulatory function of selfobject relationships throughout the entire life cycle. By drawing attention to experiments on sensory deprivation and work in the field of chronobiology, Hofer (1984) showed the extent to which external stimulation, especially regularly occurring social interactions, is important for self-regulation. When deprived of environmental stimulation and *Zeitgebers* (which synchronize or entrain biological rhythms), the organism quickly becomes disregulated and symptomatic, as in the "jet lag" syndrome experienced by travelers who cross time zones. Under normal circumstances, the brain uses environmental stimulation as feedback to make adjustments in its regulation of all of the major systems in the body (Schwartz, 1979).

Further evidence that the biological systems of adults can be regulated to a certain degree by human relationships comes from the observation that young women who live together soon menstruate in synchrony (Graham & McGrew, 1980; McClintock, 1971). This phenomenon is thought to be mediated by a pheromone (Preti, Cutler, Garcia, Huggins, & Lawley, 1986), as McClintock (1978) found with other species. There is also preliminary evidence that women who are exposed regularly to pheromones from men have more regular menstrual cycles and a higher rate of ovulation than women who do not have regular physical contact with men (Cutler et al., 1986; Veith, Buck, Getzlaf, van Dalfsen, & Slade, 1983). And although the mediating mechanisms remain unknown, research has shown that frequent social interaction among elderly people living in the same apartment building can effect several favorable endocrine and metabolic changes that do not occur in elderly tenants who remain socially isolated (Arnetz, Theorell, Levi, Kallner, & Eneroth, 1983). Thus, although healthy individuals are essentially self-regulating, some of their biological functions may be more finely tuned by interactional regulatory processes.

Weiner (1982) and Hofer (1984) suggested that some individuals fail to achieve the usual and proper level of self-regulation. Like the infant, they continue to rely excessively on another person to maintain their homeostatic equilibrium. It is likely that these dependent people have suffered deficiencies in their earliest object relationships that are reflected in the quality of their inner self and object representations. Consequently, they have failed to acquire self-regulatory functions that normally would substitute for the regulatory functions provided by the external mother in a healthy early nurturant relationship. As noted earlier, these individuals may compensate partly for their deficits by maintaining symbiotic selfobject relationships with other people, but they are at greater risk for developing illness or disease following separation and object loss.

AFFECT REGULATION AND THE ALEXITHYMIA CONSTRUCT

Another major way in which psychoanalysis and psychology are informing psychosomatic theory (as well as one another) is through their contributions to our understanding of affect development and affect regulation. Prior to the 1970s, psychosomatic medicine largely ignored the theoretical problems involved in emotions. As noted earlier, emotions were regarded as drive derivatives that create bodily tensions and adverse physiological changes unless they are discharged regularly; intrapsychic conflicts were thought to interfere with this normal model of drive and affect regulation.

Although prolonged states of emotional arousal are still thought to increase people's vulnerability to illness and disease, clinical observations during the past 2 decades, together with new knowledge about affect development in infancy and early childhood, have led several psychoanalysts and psychologists to propose that these pathogenic emotional states are a consequence, at least in part, of deficits in the cognitive processing and regulation of emotions (Krystal, 1988; Lane & Schwartz, 1987; McDougall, 1974; Taylor, 1987). Such deficits are manifested clinically as a cluster of cognitive and affective characteristics that have come to be referred to collectively as the "alexithymia construct" (Taylor, Bagby, & Parker, 1991).

The salient features of the alexithymia construct are (a) difficulty identifying and describing feelings; (b) difficulty distinguishing between feelings and the bodily sensations of emotional arousal; (c) constricted imaginative processes, as evidenced by a paucity of fantasies; and (d) an externally oriented cognitive style (Taylor et al., 1991). The construct was explicated by Nemiah and Sifneos (1970; Nemiah, Freyberger, & Sifneos, 1976) during the 1970s on the basis of systematic investigations of the communicative style of patients with "classical" psychosomatic diseases. However, as I have detailed in previous work (Parker, Taylor, & Bagby, 1989; Taylor, 1987), similar cognitive and affective characteristics had been occasionally reported among groups of medical patients during the previous 2 decades. More recently, alexithymic characteristics have been reported among patients with certain psychiatric disorders including somatization disorders (Shipko, 1982), eating disorders (Bourke, Taylor, & Crisp, 1985; Bourke, Taylor, Parker, & Bagby, in press), psychoactive substance use disorders (Krystal, 1982; Taylor, Parker, & Bagby, 1990), and posttraumatic stress disorders (Hyer, Woods, Summers, Boudewyns, & Harrison, 1990).

Like other new personality constructs, the alexithymia construct has encountered considerable criticism (Ahrens & Deffner, 1986; Kirmayer, 1987; Knapp, 1989; Lesser & Lesser, 1983). Initially much of this criticism was warranted, especially when many of the early proponents of alexithymia speculated about its role in somatic symptom formation with insufficient supporting data and before adequate attempts at verifying the construct were made. However, recent research using measurement-based construct validational methodologies (Acklin & Alexander, 1988; Acklin & Bernat, 1987; Taylor, Bagby, Ryan, & Parker, 1990) has provided considerable empirical support for the construct. The development of reliable and valid measures of alexithymia have led also to investigations that have provided preliminary empirical evidence supporting the theoretical formulation and clinical impression of an association between alexithymia and somatic illness (Acklin & Alexander, 1988; Fernandez, Sriram, Rajkumar, & Chandrasekar, 1989; Sriram, Chaturvedi, Gopinath, & Shanmugam, 1987). However, prospective longitudinal studies have yet to be conducted to determine whether alexithymia is in fact a predisposing risk factor or merely a consequence of having a chronic medical disorder.

Developmental research and advances in the psychoanalytic theory of affect are also generating an increasing interest in the alexithymia construct and in the nature of emotional processing in illness and health. Although most contemporary theorists in psychology and psychoanalysis (Buck, 1984; Knapp, 1983; Krystal, 1988; Schwartz, 1987; Thompson, 1988) agree with Freud's (and Darwin's) premise that emotions are biological phenomena that play a vital role in the existence and survival of living organisms, they have replaced his mechanistic discharge model of affect regulation with a model that firmly locates the development and regulation of affects within the context of early relationships. Developmental psychologists have demonstrated that an important component of the early mother–infant regulatory system is an emotional signaling and communication subsystem. This is based initially on the reciprocal responses of mother and infant to facial and vocal expressions and other spontaneous motor behaviors that signify different emotional states (Emde, 1988a, 1988b; Stern, 1984, 1985).

Several studies have shown that the capacity to recognize and express several basic emotions (including joy, anger, disgust, surprise, fear, and sadness) is universal and present in early infancy (Ekman & Friesen, 1982; Izard, 1971). Through her attunement to these emotional expressions in the infant, the mother is guided to respond with appropriate caregiving and emotional expressions that, in turn, help organize and regulate the emotional life of the infant (Stern, 1984). During this phase in their relationship, infant and mother display periodic runs of affective synchrony as they regulate and adapt to each other's behaviors and changing needs. Once the child develops the capacity for symbolization and language, his or her level of emotional awareness gradually increases as the mother teaches words and meanings for her child's somatic emotional expressions and other bodily experiences (Edgcumbe, 1984; Emde, 1984; Furman, 1978). The subjective experiencing and increasing verbalization of affects allows the child to think about and organize his or her feelings and needs, and to begin to contain and tolerate the tensions they generate without always having to rely on parents. In addition, the cognitive processing of emotions and mental representation of affective experiences of the self interacting with others provide raw data for the creation of memories, fantasies, and dreams, which further help in containing and modulating states of emotional arousal.

There appear to be individual differences, however, in the level of awareness of inner states and in the ability to communicate emotions symbolically. Such differences are presumed to reflect variations in the complexity of the cognitive schemata and linguistic and other symbolic representations of emotions. Indeed, by integrating concepts of symbol formation with Piaget's stages of cognitive development, Lane and Schwartz (1987) recently conceptualized a developmental sequence of five levels of emotional awareness ranging from a simple awareness of undifferentiated bodily sensations only (Level 1) to an awareness of complex blends of feelings and a capacity to appreciate the emotional experience of others (Level 5). In so doing, Lane and Schwartz elaborated the dimensional (as opposed to categorical) nature of the alexithymia construct and extended earlier conceptions of Schur (1955) and Krystal (1974), who conceptualized an epigenetic sequence for affect development involving a progressive desomatization, verbalization, and differentiation of emotions as cognitive capacities mature. By linking the capacity to form mental representations of emotions and the ability to experience subjective feelings with ego development and ego functioning, these theorists departed from the earlier view that emotions are simply drive-related discharge phenomena. Like Freud's (1915/1957) concept of instinct, affects are still viewed as arising at "the frontier between the mental and the somatic," but contemporary psychoanalytic theories emphasize the signal, integrative, and communicative functions of affects as well as the cognitive mechanisms involved in their regulation and modulation (Basch, 1976; Emde, 1988b; Gedo, 1988; Krystal, 1988; Lichtenberg, 1983). These functions and mechanisms appear to be absent or impaired in alexithymic individuals, who consequently appear vulnerable to mounting tension from undifferentiated states of emotional arousal. Although such states are comparable to the "dammed-up" state in Freud's (1895/1962a) original description of anxiety as an actual neurosis, they cannot be attributed simply to a blockage of libidinal satisfactions as he proposed. Intrapsychic conflicts may be one source of intense emotional arousal, as Alexander (1950) and other early psychosomaticists claimed, but the alexithymic individual's vulnerability to illness is attributed primarily to deficits in the cognitive processing of emotions, independent of their source.

It has been hypothesized that the failure to process emotions cognitively so that they are experienced as conscious feeling states leads to a focusing on and amplification of the somatic component of emotional arousal; this is thought to contribute to the development of hypochondriasis and somatization disorders (Barsky & Klerman, 1983; Lane & Schwartz, 1987). Similarly, the inability to modulate emotions through cognitive processes is thought to contribute to compulsive behaviors aimed at reducing unpleasant emotional tension, such as binge-eating, psychoactive substance abuse, and the self-starvation of anorexia nervosa. In addition, several authors have proposed that the failure to regulate and modulate distressing emotions at the cognitive level might result in exacerbated physiological responses to stressful situations, thereby producing conditions conducive to the development of somatic disease (MacLean, 1949; Martin & Pihl, 1985; Papciak, Feuerstein & Spiegel, 1985). The particular disease that might emerge when general susceptibility is increased is presumed to be determined by constitutional risk factors, possibly transmitted genetically, and environmental agents (Holroyd & Coyne, 1987).

Although multiple factors are thought to play a role in the etiology of alexithymia, including neurobiological deficits and sociocultural influences (Nemiah, 1977; Taylor, 1984), psychoanalysts have mostly emphasized the contribution of early developmental deficiencies (Krystal, 1988; McDougall, 1980, 1982; Taylor, 1987). Their speculations are supported by observational studies of infants and children demonstrating that when the primary caregiver is emotionally unavailable, or when the child is repeatedly subjected to inconsistent responses because of parental "misattunements," the child is likely to manifest abnormalities in affect development (Edgcumbe, 1984; Emde, 1984, 1988a, 1988b; Furman, 1978; Osofsky & Eberhart-Wright, 1988; Stern, 1984, 1985). These abnormalities include emotional constriction, reduced playfulness, and a failure to acquire the sense of an "affective self." As the individual progresses from infancy to childhood, the consistently faulty patterns of affective interchange with the caregiver are presumed to be internalized and to produce faulty internal working models that reduce the ability to self-regulate states of emotional arousal (Emde, 1988a, 1988b). To compensate for these deficits and to help modulate dysphoric states, alexithymic individuals often use pathological symbiotic relationships adaptively (Robbins, 1989).

As I indicated earlier, psychosomaticists have long known that many physically ill patients are excessively dependent on symbiotic relationships and prone to exacerbations of their illnesses when these relationships are disrupted. An alexithymic inability to self-regulate distressing affects following an attachment disruption, including the affects of helplessness and hopelessness described by Engel and Schmale, might partly account for these illness exacerbations. Indeed, a retrospective examination of the clinical descriptions of the ulcerative colitis patients in the study by Karush et al. (1977), which I referred to earlier, suggested a high prevalence of alexithymia among patients categorized as symbiotic (Nemiah, 1982).

A DYSREGULATION MODEL OF ILLNESS AND DISEASE

Although research in developmental psychobiology, and concepts and observations from self psychology and object relations psychology, have led to an awareness of the regulating functions of interpersonal relationships and their mental representations, advances in the biomedical sciences have also led to an increasingly accepted view that living organisms are self-regulating cybernetic systems (Schwartz, 1989; Weiner, 1989). This view evolved from the gradual realization that virtually all biological systems function in a rhythmic manner over time (Glass & Mackey, 1988), and from the discovery of a host of neuropeptides and other chemical messengers that provide positive and negative feedback to regulate these rhythms (Dinarello & Mier, 1987; Pert, Ruff, Weber, & Herkenham, 1985).

In addition, there is evidence that the various subsystems that comprise the organism regulate each other's activities as well as their own. Recent research, for instance, has shown that not only can the neuroendocrine system regulate immunologic functions, but also the immune system can regulate neuroendocrine functions (Blalock, 1989). The regulatory mechanisms seem to include peptide hormones that are produced by both systems and interact with receptors that are common to the two systems (Smith & Blalock, 1986). These findings are consistent with general systems theory, which regards every naturally occuring system as a hierarchical arrangement of reciprocally regulating subsystems (Schwartz, 1989; von Bertalanffy, 1968).

The bidirectional communication between the various subsystems of the body involves specialized chemical and electrical signals, although Weiner (1989) reminds us that language and emotional behavior are also communication signals that perform functions analogous to those of peptide hormones and neurotransmitters. By providing information exchange between the human organism and the social and physical environment, verbal and emotional behavior may contribute to the self-regulation of biological systems as well as to the regulation of psychological states (such as mood and self-esteem) and aspects of the person's environment. This conception of the living system is supported by the research I reviewed previously showing that social relationships can serve regulatory functions and that homeostatic organization is an open, rather than a closed, system. In addition, Weiner (1989) suggested that the notion of feedback systems using a wide variety of coded communication signals, ranging from ions to words, allows psychosomaticists to surmount the dualistic mind–body problem that has impeded progress in their field. In other words, the concept of self-regulation overarches the realms of mind and body and articulates with the closely related concept of interactional regulation (Grotstein, 1990).

In recent years, several psychosomatic investigators have used the concept of the human organism as a self-regulating cybernetic system to develop a new psychosomatic model of illness and disease (Schwartz, 1983, 1989; Taylor, 1987; Weiner, 1989). The basis for this model, as outlined by Weiner (1989), is that perturbations in one or more components of the feedback loops of a self-regulating living system lead to changes over time in the rhythmic function of a biological subsystem. Perturbations can arise at any level in the system, from the cellular or subcellular level (as with viral infections, sensitivity to allergens, and variations in the expression of genes) to the psychological or social level (as with intrapsychic conflicts, attachment disruptions, and loss of self-esteem). Through complex feedback loops, these initial perturbations may trigger perturbations at other levels; if the ensuing dysregulation is sustained it may initiate a transition from health to illness and disease.

An advantage of this new model over the prevailing biomedical model and previous psychosomatic models is that it eliminates the distinction between organic diseases and functional disorders (Weiner, 1989). With the emphasis on the functioning of biological systems rather than the structure of cells and organs, many illnesses and diseases can be reconceptualized as "disorders of regulation," which may or may not be associated with actual structural changes (Schwartz, 1989; Taylor, 1987). The new model also eliminates the traditional distinction between physical disorders and psychiatric disorders, which can now all be viewed psychosomatically. Indeed, Grotstein (1986) recently proposed a new paradigm for psychiatry and psychoanalysis in which all psychopathology is reformulated as disorders of self-regulation or interactional regulation involving "the failure of inherent internal control-regulators and/or external object and selfobject modulators" (p. 104). Thus, panic disorder, for example, which is the DSM–III–R term for actual anxiety neurosis, may be initiated by object loss, as recent life events research has demonstrated (Faravelli & Pallanti, 1989); however, there is evidence also for a genetic predisposition for this disorder involving a brain stem mechanism that can be dysregulated by ingestion of yohimbine or caffeine, infusion of sodium lactate, and inhalation of carbon dioxide (Crowe, 1988; Gorman, Liebowitz, Fyer, & Stein, 1989). Similarly, loss of a close relationship or loss of self-esteem are well-known triggering events for major affective disorders, but there is accumulating evidence for a trait vulnerability involving an instability in one or more neurotransmitter homeostatic regulatory mechanisms (Siever & Davis, 1985).

Although the new psychosomatic model includes neurotic conflict as one factor that might initiate the dysregulation of psychobiological systems, it is more akin to Freud's conception of the actual neuroses in which the symptoms have biological but not psychological meaning. This is especially evident with the so-called functional somatic disorders, such as the irritable bowel syndrome, fibromyalgia, and the chronic fatigue syndrome (a modern term for neurasthenia). These medical disorders overlap with the psychiatric diagnostic categories of somatization disorder and somatoform pain disorder and are often associated with anxiety or depression (Hickie, Lloyd, Wakefield, & Parker, 1990; Tilbe & Sullivan, 1990). But, although the symptoms in all of these disorders are sometimes somatic manifestations of anxiety or depression (Kellner, 1990; Lipowski, 1988), many of the patients manifest an alexithymic deficit in the mental representation and regulation of affect or evidence of dysregulated biological systems. For instance, Sriram et al. (1987) found a group of patients with somatoform pain disorders to be significantly more alexithymic than a healthy control group matched for age, sex, education, and marital status. Patients with fibromyalgia or chronic fatigue syndrome typically show an abnormal alpha–delta sleep rhythm and associated changes in the immune system (Klimas, Salvato, Morgan, & Fletcher, 1990; Moldofsky, 1989). These physiological abnormalities seem to be initiated by a viral illness in some patients (Komaroff & Goldenberg, 1989). There is also accumulating evidence that patients with the irritable bowel syndrome have a disordered motility of the intestinal tract, which may be due to a diffuse disorder of smooth muscle or its autonomic regulation (Tilbe & Sullivan, 1990). Ongoing research in chronobiology, neuroimmunoendocrinology, and other biomedical sciences is likely to identify alterations in the regulation of other physiological systems that will help to further explain the puzzling chronic bodily symptoms of so-called somatizing patients (Blalock, 1989; Mathias, Ferguson,. & Clench, 1989; Pert et al., 1985; Weiner, 1989).

The concepts of self-regulation and dysregulation obviously provide a way of integrating many of the recent discoveries in the biomedical sciences with the theories and research from the fields of psychology and contemporary psychoanalysis that I have reviewed in this chapter. Through their exploration of attachment and separation behavior in early life, developmental psychology and developmental biology have identified many of the variables in the early social environment that can influence the maturation of self-regulatory capacities and thereby increase an individual's resilience or vulnerability to illness and disease. Psychoanalysis, with its contemporary emphasis on object relations and the development of the self (Eagle, 1984), has increased the understanding of the homeostatic regulatory functions of stable self and object representations; it also provides a way of conceptualizing the apparently greater risk for illness and disease in individuals who rely excessively on external relationships to compensate for deficits in their self-regulating capacities. The psychoanalytic construct of alexithymia, and its recent validation using a measurement-based method from the field of personality psychology (Taylor, Bagby, Ryan, & Parker, 1990), has focused attention on deficits in affect representation and regulation and generated renewed efforts to investigate the extent to which unmodulated emotions are risk factors for illness and disease.

Although the dysregulation model of illness and disease has yet to be subjected to rigorous empirical testing, research examining the interrelations among life stress, social support, and health is providing mounting evidence that actual health outcomes are influenced by the availability and quality of interpersonal relationships (Cohen & Syme, 1985; House, Landis, & Umberson, 1988). Berkman and Syme (1979), for instance, found that people who lacked social and community ties had a higher mortality (from all causes) than those who were not socially isolated, and that the more intimate ties of marriage and close contact with friends and relatives were more protective than belonging to churches or other organized groups. In a 5-year prospective study of the development of new angina pectoris among almost 10,000 Israeli men, Medalie and Goldbourt (1976) found that the incidence of heart disease was significantly reduced in men who experienced their wives' love and support even in the presence of other high-risk factors such as hypertension and high blood levels of cholesterol.

The mental representation of human relationships (i.e., the internal working model) is more difficult to operationalize than the availability and quality of social support. The development of the Rorschach Interaction Scale, however, and its application in a long-term prospective study of medical students, has provided preliminary evidence of an association between mental representations that reflect unstable patterns of attachment and poor affect modulation and the subsequent development of cancer (Graves, Mead, & Pearson, 1986; Graves & Thomas, 1981).

Psychological treatments based on the dysregulation model are aimed at enhancing patients' self-regulating capacities. Such treatments include autogenic training and biofeedback, which produce a heightened awareness of bodily processes and sensations and increase a patient's ability to self-regulate various physiological functions that are under the control of the autonomic nervous system (Taylor, 1987). The ability to self-regulate affects may be improved by specialized psychotherapeutic techniques that address alexithymic deficits and attempt to elevate emotions from a primitive sensorimotor level of experience to a mature representational level (Krystal, 1988; Robbins, 1989; Taylor, 1984; Taylor et al., 1991). Psychoanalytic therapy promotes increasing self-regulation by facilitating separation–individuation and the formation of stable mental representations. This requires a careful analysis of the patient's unconscious internal object relations as these are externalized in the transference relationship. The resolution of interpersonal and intrapsychic conflicts, and the unification of split "good" and "bad" representations of self and object, also enhance the quality of the patient's intimate and social relationships that potentially provide mature selfobject and other interactive experiences that complement his or her self-regulatory capacities. Although there is now considerable evidence supporting the application of biofeedback and other behavioral techniques to the treatment of medical disorders (see, e.g., Achmon, Granek, Golomb, & Hart, 1989; Blanchard et al., 1982; Lehnert, Kaluza, Vetter, Losse, & Dorst, 1987), much research is needed to evaluate the extent to which contemporary psychoanalytic and psychotherapeutic approaches can modify susceptibility to disease and the course of existing illness.

CONCLUSIONS

The usefulness of psychoanalysis to psychosomatic medicine has been limited by the long-standing assumption that intrapsychic conflicts, and their associated affects, play a central role in the pathogenesis of physical illness and disease. Alternative models which linked the onset of disease to environmental stress, including separation and object loss, were too simplistic in their conceptualization of the psychobiological mediating mechanisms. During the past decade, however, new knowledge from the rich field of infant research and a paradigm shift in psychoanalysis from drive theory to relational-model theories (Mitchell, 1988) have afforded an opportunity for a new and active involvement of psychoanalysis with physically ill patients. In addition, advances in the biomedical sciences have led to a greater emphasis on alterations in function, as opposed to changes in structure, as explanations of disease, and to the realization that such alterations can be produced by multiple rather than single causes (Weiner, 1989). The overarching concept of self-regulation permits an integration of theories and research from developmental psychology, developmental biology, personality psychology, psychoanalysis, and several of the biomedical sciences. This synthesis has led to the emergence of a new psychosomatic model which views illnesses and diseases as disorders of regulation. Continuing collaboration between psychoanalysis and academic psychology, and cross-fertilization with the biological sciences, should result in rigorous testing and refinement of this model and bring us closer to having a comprehensive theory of health, illness, and disease.

REFERENCES

Achmon, J., Granek, M., Golomb, M., & Hart, J. (1989). Behavioral treatment of essential hypertension: A comparison between cognitive therapy and biofeedback of heart rate. *Psychosomatic Medicine, 51*, 152–164.

Ackerman, S. H., Hofer, M. A., & Weiner, H. (1978). Early maternal separation increases gastric ulcer risk in rats by producing latent thermoregulatory disturbance. *Science, 201*, 373–376.

Acklin, M. W., & Alexander, G. (1988). Alexithymia and somatization. *Journal of Nervous and Mental Disease, 176*, 343–350.

Acklin, M. W., & Bernat, E. (1987). Depression, alexithymia, and pain prone disorder: A Rorschach study. *Journal of Personality Assessment, 51*, 462–479.

Ahrens, S., & Deffner, G. (1986). Empirical study of alexithymia: Methodology and results. *American Journal of Psychotherapy, 40*, 430–447.

Alexander, F. (1950). *Psychosomatic medicine: Its principles and applications.* New York: Norton.

Alexander, F., French, T. M., & Pollock, G. H. (1968). *Psychosomatic specificity, Vol. 1: Experimental study and results.* Chicago: University of Chicago Press.

Arnetz, B. B., Theorell, T., Levi, L., Kallner, A., & Eneroth, P. (1983). An experimental study of social isolation of elderly people: Psychoendocrine and metabolic effects. *Psychosomatic Medicine, 45*, 395–406.

Barsky, A. J., & Klerman, G. L. (1983). Overview: Hypochondriasis, bodily complaints, and somatic styles. *American Journal of Psychiatry, 140*, 273–283.

Basch, M. F. (1976). The concept of affect: A re-examination. *Journal of the American Psychoanalytic Association, 24*, 759–777.

Beaumont, W. (1833). *Experiments and observations on the gastric juice and the physiology of digestion.* Plattsburg, NY: F. P. Allen.

Beebe, B., & Lachmann, F. M. (1988). The contribution of mother–infant mutual influence to the origins of self- and object representations. *Psychoanalytic Psychology, 5*, 305–337.

Berkman, L. F., & Syme, L. (1979). Social networks, host resistance, and mortality: A nine-year follow-up study of Alameda county residents. *American Journal of Epidemiology, 109*, 186–204.

Blalock, J. E. (1989). A molecular basis for bidirectional communication between the immune and neuroendocrine systems. *Physiological Reviews, 69*, 1–32.

Blanchard, E. B., Andrasik, F., Neff, D. F., Teders, S. J., Pallmeyer, T. P., Arena, J. G., Jurish, S. E., Saunders, N. L., & Ahles, T. A. (1982). Sequential comparisons of relaxation training and biofeedback in the treatment of three kinds of chronic headache or, the machines may be necessary some of the time. *Behavior, Research and Therapy, 20*, 469–481.

Bourke, M., Taylor, G., & Crisp, A. (1985). Symbolic functioning in anorexia nervosa. *Journal of Psychiatric Research, 19*, 273–278.

Bourke, M. P., Taylor, G. J., Parker, J. D. A., & Bagby, R. M. (in press). Alexithymia in women with anorexia nervosa: A preliminary investigation. *British Journal of Psychiatry.*

Bowlby, J. (1969). *Attachment and loss, Vol. 1: Attachment.* New York: Basic Books.

Bowlby, J. (1988). Developmental psychiatry comes of age. *American Journal of Psychiatry, 145*, 1–10.

Bretherton, I. (1985). I. Attachment theory: Retrospect and prospect. In I. Bretherton & E. Waters (Eds.), *Growing points in attachment theory and research. Monographs of the Society for Research in Child Development, 50*(Serial No. 299).

Brown, L. J. (1984–1985). Levels of mental representation and communicative modes of the bipersonal field. *International Journal of Psychoanalytic Psychotherapy, 10,* 403–428.

Buck, P. (1984). *The communication of emotion.* New York: Guilford Press.

Cohen, S., & Syme, S. L. (Eds).(1985). *Social support and health.* New York: Academic Press.

Condon, W. S., & Sander, L. W. (1974). Neonate movement is synchronized with adult speech: Interactional participation and language acquisition. *Science, 183,* 99–101.

Costa, P. T., & McCrae, R. R. (1987). Neuroticism, somatic complaints, and disease: Is the bark worse than the bite? *Journal of Personality, 55,* 299–316.

Crowe, R. R. (1988). Family and twin studies of panic disorders and agoraphobia. In M. Roth, R. Noyes, Jr., & G. D. Burrows (Eds.), *Handbook of anxiety, Vol. 1: Biological, clinical, and cultural perspectives.* (pp. 101–114). New York: Elsevier.

Cutler, W. B., Preti, G., Krieger, A., Huggins, G. R., Garcia, C. R., & Lawley, H. J. (1986). Human axillary secretions influence women's menstrual cycles: The role of donor extract from men, *Hormones and Behavior, 20,* 463–473.

Dembroski, T. M., MacDougall, J. M., Williams, R. B., Haney, T., & Blumenthal, J. A. (1985). Components of Type A, hostility and anger-in. Relationship to angiographic findings. *Psychosomatic Medicine, 47,* 219–233.

deLissovoy, V. (1971). Foreword. In D. N. Walcher & D. L. Peters (Eds.), *The development of self-regulatory mechanisms.* New York: Academic Press.

Deutsch, F. (1959). *On the mysterious leap from the mind to the body: A study on the theory of conversion.* Madison, CT: International Universities Press.

Dinarello, C. A., & Mier, J. W. (1987). Lymphokines. *New England Journal of Medicine, 317,* 940–945.

Eagle, M. N. (1984). *Recent developments in psychoanalysis.* New York: McGraw-Hill.

Edgcumbe, R. M. (1984). Modes of communication: The differentiation of somatic and verbal expression. *Psychoanalytic Study of the Child, 39,* 137–154.

Ekman, P., & Friesen, W. V. (1982). *Emotion in the human face* (2nd ed.). Cambridge, England: Cambridge University Press.

Emde, R. N. (1984). The affective self: Continuities and transformations from infancy. In J. D. Call, E. Galenson, & R. L. Tyson (Eds.), *Frontiers of infant psychiatry* (pp. 38–54). New York: Basic Books.

Emde, R. N. (1988a). Development terminable and interminable. 1. Innate and motivational factors from infancy. *International Journal of Psycho-Analysis, 69,* 23–42.

Emde, R. N. (1988b). Development terminable and interminable. 2. Recent psychoanalytic theory and therapeutic considerations. *International Journal of Psycho-Analysis, 69,* 283–296.

Emde, R. N., & Robinson, J. (1979). The first two months: Recent research in developmental psychobiology and the changing view of the newborn. In J. D. Noshpitz (Ed.), *Basic handbook of child psychiatry, Vol. I* (pp. 72–105). New York: Basic Books.

Engel, G. L. (1955). Studies of ulcerative colitis: III. The nature of the psychologic process. *American Journal of Medicine, 19,* 231–256.

Engel, G. L. (1958). Studies of ulcerative colitis: V. Psychological aspects and their implications for treatment. *American Journal of Digestive Diseases, 3,* 315–337.

Engel, G. L. (1968). A life setting conducive to illness: The giving up-given up complex. *Annals of Internal Medicine, 69,* 293–300.

Engel, G. L., & Schmale, A. H. (1972). Conservation-withdrawal: A primary regulatory process for organismic homeostasis. In *Physiology, emotion and psychosomatic illness. Ciba Foundation Symposium 8* (pp. 57–75). Amsterdam, the Netherlands: Elsevier.

Evoniuk, G. E., Kuhn, C. M., & Schanberg, S. M. (1979). The effect of tactile stimulation on serum growth hormone and tissue ornithine decarboxylase activity during maternal deprivation in rat pups. *Communications in Psychopharmacology, 3,* 363–370.

Fairbairn, W. R. D. (1952). *An object relations theory of the personality.* New York: Basic Books.

Faravelli, C., & Pallanti, S. (1989). Recent life events and panic disorder. *American Journal of Psychiatry, 146,* 622–626.

Fernandez, A., Sriram, T. G., Rajkumar, S., & Chandrasekar, A. N. (1989). Alexithymic characteristics in rheumatoid arthritis: A controlled study. *Psychotherapy and Psychosomatics, 51,* 45–50.

Field, T. (1985). Attachment as psychobiological attunement: Being on the same wavelength. In M. Reite & T. Field (Eds.), *The psychobiology of attachment and separation* (pp. 415–454). Orlando, FL: Academic Press.

Fraiberg, S. (1969). Libidinal object constancy and mental representation. *Psychoanalytic Study of the Child, 24,* 9–47.

Freud, S. (1953). Three essays on the theory of sexuality. In J. Strachey (Ed. and Trans.), *The standard edition of the complete psychological works of Sigmund Freud* (Vol. 7, pp. 123–245). London: Hogarth Press. (Original work published 1905)

Freud, S. (1957). Instincts and their vicissitudes. In J. Strachey (Ed. and Trans.), *The standard edition of the complete psychological works of Sigmund Freud* (Vol. 14, pp. 117–140). London: Hogarth Press. (Original work published 1915)

Freud, S. (1959a). Inhibitions, symptoms, and anxiety. In J. Strachey (Ed. and Trans.), *The standard edition of the complete psychological works of Sigmund Freud* (Vol. 20, pp. 87–156). London: Hogarth Press. (Original work published 1926)

Freud, S. (1959b). The question of lay analysis. In J. Strachey (Ed. and Trans.), *The standard edition of the complete psychological works of Sigmund Freud* (Vol. 20, pp. 251–258). London: Hogarth Press. (Original work published 1927)

Freud, S. (1962a). On the grounds for detaching a particular syndrome from neurasthenia under the description 'anxiety neurosis.' In J. Strachey (Ed. and Trans.), *The standard edition of the complete psychological works of Sigmund Freud* (Vol. 3, pp. 90–115). London: Hogarth Press. (Original work published 1895)

Freud, S. (1962b). Sexuality in the aetiology of the neuroses. In J. Strachey (Ed. and Trans.), *The standard edition of the complete psychological works of Sigmund Freud* (Vol. 3, pp. 263–285). London: Hogarth Press. (Original work published 1898)

Friedman, H. S., & Booth-Kewley, S. (1987). The "disease-prone personality." A meta-analytic view of the construct. *American Psychologist, 42,* 539–555.

Furman, R. A. (1978). Some developmental aspects of the verbalization of affects. *Psychoanalytic Study of the Child, 33,* 187–211.

Gaddini, R. (1978). Transitional object origins and the psychosomatic symptom. In S. A. Grolnick, L. Barkin, & W. Muensterberger (Eds.), *Between reality and fantasy: Transitional objects and phenomena* (pp. 111–131). Northvale, NJ: Jason Aronson.

Gaddini, E., & Gaddini, R. (1970). Transitional objects and the process of individuation: A study in three different social groups. *Journal of the American Academy of Child Psychiatry, 9,* 347–365.

Gedo, J. (1988). *The mind in disorder: Psychoanalytic models of pathology.* Hillsdale, NJ: Analytic Press.

Glass, G., & Mackey, M. C. (1988). *From clocks to chaos. The rhythms of life.* Princeton: Princeton University Press.

Glover, E. (1939). *Psychoanalysis.* London: Staples.

Gorman, J. M., Liebowitz, M. R., Fyer, A. J., & Stein, J. (1989). A neuroanatomical hypothesis for panic disorder. *American Journal of Psychiatry, 146,* 148–161.

Graham, C. A., & McGrew, W. C. (1980). Menstrual synchrony in female undergraduates living on a co-educational campus. *Psychoneuroendocrinology, 5,* 245–252.

Graves, P. L., Mead, L. A., & Pearson, T. A. (1986). The Rorschach interaction scale as a potential predictor of cancer, *Psychosomatic Medicine, 48,* 549–563.

Graves, P. L., & Thomas, C. B. (1981). Themes of interaction in medical students' Rorschach responses as predictors of midlife health or disease. *Psychosomatic Medicine, 43,* 215–225.

Greenberg, J. R., & Mitchell, S. A. (1983). *Object relations in psychoanalytic theory.* Cambridge, MA: Harvard University Press.

Greene, W. A., & Miller, G. (1958). Psychological factors and reticuloendothelial disease: IV. Observations on a group of children and adolescents with leukemia: An interpretation of disease development in terms of the mother–child unit. *Psychosomatic Medicine, 20,* 124–144.

Grotstein, J. S. (1986). The psychology of powerlessness: Disorders of self-regulation and interactional regulation as a newer paradigm for psychopathology. *Psychoanalytic Inquiry, 6,* 93–118.

Grotstein, J. S. (1989). Winnicott's importance in psychoanalysis. In M. G. Fromm & B. L. Smith (Eds.), *The facilitating environment* (pp. 130–155). Madison, CT: International Universities Press.

Grotstein, J. S. (1990). Nothingness, meaninglessness, chaos, and the "black hole." III: Self- and inter-actional regulation and the background presence of primary identification. *Contemporary Psychoanalysis, 26,* 377–407.

Hamilton, N. G. (1989). A critical review of object relations theory. *American Journal of Psychiatry, 146,* 1552–1560.

Harlow, H. F. (1959). Love in infant monkeys. *Scientific American, 200,* 68–74.

Hickie, I., Lloyd, A., Wakefield, D., & Parker, G. (1990). The psychiatric status of patients with the chronic fatigue syndrome. *British Journal of Psychiatry, 156,* 534–540.

Hofer, M. A. (1978). Hidden regulatory processes in early social relationships. In P. G. Bateson & P. H. Klopfer (Eds.), *Perspectives in ethology* Vol. 3, (pp. 135–165). New York: Plenum Press.

Hofer, M. A. (1983a). On the relationship between attachment and separation processes in infancy. In R. Plutchik (Ed.), *Emotion: Theory, research and experience: Vol. II. Emotions in early development* (pp. 199–219). New York: Academic Press.

Hofer, M. A. (1983b). The mother–infant interaction as a regulator of infant physiology and behavior. In L. Rosenblum & H. Moltz (Eds.), *Symbiosis in parent–offspring interactions* (pp. 61–75). New York: Plenum Press.

Hofer, M. A. (1984). Relationships as regulators: A psychobiologic perspective on bereavement. *Psychosomatic Medicine, 46,* 183–197.

Hofer, M. A. (1987). Early social relationships: A psychobiologist's view. *Child Development, 58,* 633–647.

Hofer, M. A., & Shair, H. (1978). Ultrasonic vocalizations during social interaction and isolation in two week old rats. *Developmental Psychobiology, 11,* 495–504.

Hofer, M. A., & Weiner, H. (1975). Physiological mechanisms for cardiac control by nutritional intake after early separation in the young rat. *Psychosomatic Medicine, 33,* 353–363.

Holroyd, K. A., & Coyne, J. (1987). Personality and health in the 1980s: Psychosomatic medicine revisited? *Journal of Personality, 55,* 359–375.

Hong, K. M., & Townes, B. D. (1976). Infants' attachment to inanimate objects: A cross-cultural study. *Journal of the American Academy of Child Psychiatry, 15,* 49–61.

Horton, P. C. (1981). *Solace: The missing dimension in psychiatry.* Chicago: University of Chicago Press.

House, J. S., Landis, K. R., & Umberson, D. (1988). Social relationships and health. *Science, 241,* 540–545.

Hyer, L., Woods, M. G., Summers, M. N., Boudewyns, P., & Harrison, W. R. (1990). Alexithymia among Vietnam veterans with posttraumatic stress disorder. *Journal of Clinical Psychiatry, 51,* 243–247.

Izard, C. E. (1971). *The face of emotion*. New York: Meredith/Appleton-Century-Crofts.

Jacobs, S., & Ostfeld, A. (1977). An epidemiological review of the mortality of bereavement. *Psychosomatic Medicine, 39,* 344–357.

Jessner, L., Lamont, J., Long, R., Rollins, N., Whipple, B., & Prentice, N. (1955). Emotional impact of nearness and separation for the asthmatic child and his mother. *Psychoanalytic Study of the Child, 10,* 353–375.

Jolly, A. (1985). *The evolution of primate behavior* (2nd ed.). New York: MacMillan.

Karush, A., Flood, C., & O'Connor, J. F. (1977). *Psychotherapy in ulcerative colitis.* Philadelphia: W. B. Saunders.

Kellner, R. (1990). Somatization: Theories and research. *Journal of Nervous and Mental Disease, 178,* 150–160.

Kirmeyer, L. J. (1987). Languages of suffering and healing: Alexithymia as a social and cultural process. *Transcultural Psychiatric Research Review, 24,* 119–136.

Klerman, G. L., & Izen, J. E. (1977). The effects of bereavement and grief on physical health and general well-being. *Advances in Psychosomatic Medicine, 9,* 63–104.

Klimas, N. G., Salvato, F. R., Morgan, R., & Fletcher, M. A. (1990). Immunologic abnormalities in chronic fatigue syndrome. *Journal of Clinical Microbiology, 28,* 1403–1410.

Knapp, P. H. (1983). Emotions and bodily changes: A reassessment. In L. Temoshok, C. Van Dyke, & L. S. Zegans (Eds.), *Emotions in health and illness: Theoretical and research foundations* (pp. 15–27). New York: Grune & Stratton.

Knapp, P. H. (1989). Psychodynamic psychotherapy for somatizing disorders. In S. Cheren (Ed.), *Psychosomatic medicine: Theory, physiology, and practice* (Vol. 2, pp. 813–839). Madison, CT: International Universities Press.

Kohut, H. (1977). *The restoration of the self.* Madison, CT: International Universities Press.

Kohut, H. (1984). *How does analysis cure?* Chicago: University of Chicago Press.

Komaroff, A. L., & Goldenberg, D. (1989). The chronic fatigue syndrome: Definition, current studies and lessons for fibromyalgia research. *Journal of Rheumatology, 16* (Suppl. 19), 23–27.

Kreisler, L. (1984). Pediatric to psychosomatic economy: Fundamentals for a psychosomatic pathology of infants. In J. D. Call, E. Galenson, & R. L. Tyson (Eds.), *Frontiers of infant psychiatry* (Vol. 2, pp. 447–454). New York: Basic Books.

Krystal, H. (1974). The genetic development of affects and affect regression. *Annual of Psychoanalysis, 2,* 98–126.

Krystal, H. (1982). Adolescence and the tendencies to develop substance dependence. *Psychoanalytic Inquiry, 2,* 581–617.

Krystal, H. (1988). *Integration and self-healing: Affect, trauma, alexithymia.* Hillsdale, NJ: Analytic Press.

Lane, R. D., & Schwartz, G. E. (1987). Levels of emotional awareness: A cognitive-developmental theory and its application to psychopathology. *American Journal of Psychiatry, 144,* 133–143.

Lehnert, H., Kaluza, K., Vetter, H., Losse, H., & Dorst, K. (1987). Long-term effects of a complex behavioral treatment of essential hypertension. *Psychosomatic Medicine, 49,* 422–430.

Lesser, I. M., & Lesser, B. Z. (1983). Alexithymia: Examining the development of a psychological concept. *American Journal of Psychiatry, 140,* 1305–1308.

Lichtenberg, J. D. (1983). *Psychoanalysis and infant research.* Hillsdale, NJ: Analytic Press.

Lipowski, Z. J. (1977). Psychosomatic medicine in the seventies: An overview. *American Journal of Psychiatry, 134,* 233–244.

Lipowski, Z. J. (1988). Somatization: The concept and its clinical application. *American Journal of Psychiatry, 145,* 1358–1368.

MacAlpine, I. (1954). Psychosomatic symptom formation. *Lancet, 1,* 278–282.

MacLean, P. D. (1949). Psychosomatic disease and the "visceral brain." *Psychosomatic Medicine, 11,* 338–353.

Mahler, M. S. (1968). *On human symbiosis and the vicissitudes of individuation.* Madison, CT: International Universities Press.

Main, M, Kaplan, N., & Cassidy, J. (1985). III. Security in infancy, childhood, and adulthood: A move to the level of representation. In I. Bretherton & E. Waters (Eds.), *Growing points in attachment theory and research. Monographs of the Society for Research in Child Development, 50*(Serial No. 299), 66–104.

Martin, J. B., & Pihl, R. O. (1985). The stress-alexithymia hypothesis. Theoretical and empirical considerations. *Psychotherapy and Psychosomatics, 43,* 169–176.

Mason, M. A., & Berkson, G. (1974). Effects of maternal mobility on the development of rocking and other behaviors in rhesus monkeys. *Developmental Psychobiology, 8,* 197–211.

Mathias, J. R., Ferguson, K. L., & Clench, M. H. (1989). Debilitating "functional" bowel disease controlled by leuprolide acetate, gonadotropin-releasing hormone (GnRH) analog. *Digestive Diseases and Sciences, 34,* 761–766.

McClintock, M. K. (1971). Menstrual synchrony and suppression. *Nature, 229,* 244–245.

McClintock, M. K. (1978). Estrous synchrony and its mediation by airborne chemical communication (Rattus norvegicus). *Hormones and Behavior, 10,* 264–276.

McDougall, J. (1974). The psychosoma and the psychoanalytic process. *International Review of Psycho-Analysis, 1,* 437–459.

McDougall, J. (1980). *Plea for a measure of abnormality.* Madison, CT: International Universities Press.

McDougall, J. (1982). Alexithymia: A psychoanalytic viewpoint. *Psychotherapy and Psychosomatics, 38,* 81–90.

Medalie, J. H., & Goldbourt, U. (1976). Angina pectoris among 10,000 men: II. Psychosocial and other risk factors as evidenced by a multivariate analysis of a five year incidence study. *American Journal of Medicine, 60,* 910–921.

Mendelson, M., Hirsch, S., Webber, C. S. (1956). A critical examination of some recent theoretical models in psychosomatic medicine. *Psychosomatic Medicine, 28,* 363–373.

Mitchell, S. A. (1988). *Relational concepts in psychoanalysis: An integration.* Cambridge, MA: Harvard University Press.

Moldofsky. H. (1989). Nonrestorative sleep and symptoms after a febrile illness in patients with fibrositis and chronic fatigue syndromes. *Journal of Rheumatology, 16,*(Suppl. 19), 150–153.

Mushatt, C. (1975). Mind–body-environment: Toward understanding the impact of loss on psyche and soma. *Psychoanalytic Quarterly, 44,* 81–106.

Mushatt, C. (1989). Loss, separation, and psychosomatic illness. In C. P. Wilson & I. L. Mintz (Eds.), *Psychosomatic symptoms: Psychodynamic treatment of the underlying personality disorder* (pp. 33–61). Northvale, NJ: Jason Aronson.

Nemiah, J. C. (1977). Alexithymia: Theoretical considerations. *Psychotherapy and Psychosomatics, 28,* 199–206.

Nemiah, J. C. (1982). A reconsideration of psychological specificity in psychosomatic disorders. *Psychotherapy and Psychosomatics, 38,* 39–45.

Nemiah, J. C., Freyberger, H., & Sifneos, P. E. (1976). Alexithymia: A view of the psychosomatic process. In O. W. Hill (Ed.), *Modern trends in psychosomatic medicine* (Vol. 3, pp. 430–439). London: Butterworths.

Nemiah, J. C., & Sifneos, P. E. (1970). Affect and fantasy in patients with psychosomatic disorders. In O. W. Hill (Ed.), *Modern trends in psychosomatic medicine* (Vol. 2, pp. 26–34). London: Butterworths.

Osofsky, J. D., & Eberhart-Wright, A. (1988). Affective exchanges between high risk mothers and infants. *International Journal of Psycho-Analysis, 69,* 221–231.

Papciak, A. S., Feuerstein, M., & Spiegel, J. A. (1985). Stress reactivity in alexithymia: Decoupling of physiological and cognitive responses. *Journal of Human Stress, 11*, 135–142.

Parens, H., McConville, B. J., & Kaplan, S. M. (1966). The prediction of frequency of illness from the response to separation. *Psychosomatic Medicine, 28*, 162–176.

Parker, J. D. A., Taylor, G. J., & Bagby, R. M. (1989). The alexithymia construct: Relationship with sociodemographic variables and intelligence. *Comprehensive Psychiatry, 30*, 434–441.

Parkes, C. M., Benjamin, B., & Fitzgerald, R. G. (1969). "Broken heart": A statistical study of increased mortality among widowers. *British Medical Journal, 1*, 740–743.

Pert, C. B., Ruff, M. R., Weber, R. J., & Herkenham, M. (1985). Neuropeptides and their receptors: A psychosomatic network. *Journal of Immunology, 135*, 820S–825S.

Peters, D. L. (1971). Epilog. In D. N. Walcher & D. L. Peters (Eds.), *The development of self-regulatory mechanisms*. New York: Academic Press.

Pipp, S., & Harmon, R. J. (1987). Attachment as regulation. *Child Development, 58*, 648–652.

Porter, R. H., Balogh, R. D., & Makin, J. W. (1988). Olfactory influences on mother–infant interactions. In C. Rovee-Collier & L. Lipsitt (Eds.), *Advances in infancy research* (Vol. 5, pp. 39–68). Norwood, NJ: Ablex.

Preti, G., Cutler, W. B., Garcia, C. R., Huggins, G. R., & Lawley, H. J. (1986). Human axillary secretions influence women's menstrual cycles: The role of donor extract of females. *Hormones and Behavior, 20*, 474–482.

Reite, M., & Field, T. (Eds.). (1985). *The psychobiology of attachment and separation*. Orlando, FL: Academic Press.

Robbins, M. (1989). Primitive personality organization as an interpersonally adaptive modification of cognition and affect. *International Journal of Psychoanalysis, 70*, 443–459.

Sander, L. W. (1980). New knowledge about the infant from current research: Implications for psychoanalysis. *Journal of the American Psychoanalytic Association, 28*, 181–198.

Sander, L. W. (1983). Polarity, paradox, and the organizing process in development. In J. D. Call, E. Galenson, & R. L. Tyson (Eds.), *Frontiers of infant psychiatry* (Vol. 1, pp. 333–346). New York: Basic Books.

Sandler, J. (1972). The role of affects in psychoanalytic theory. In *Physiology, emotion and psychosomatic illness. Ciba Foundation Symposium 8*, (pp. 31–56). Amsterdam, the Netherlands: Elsevier.

Savitt, R. A. (1977). Conflict and somatization: Psychoanalytic treatment of the psychophysiologic response in the digestive tract. *Psychoanalytic Quarterly, 46*, 605–622.

Schafer, R. (1968). *Aspects of internalization*. Madison, CT: International Universities Press.

Schleifer, S. L., Keller, S. E., Camerino, M., Thornton, J. C. & Stein, M. (1983). Suppression of lymphocyte stimulation following bereavement. *Journal of the American Medical Association, 250*, 374–377.

Schmale, A. H. (1958). Relationship of separation and depression to disease. *Psychosomatic Medicine, 20*, 259–277.

Schmale, A. H. (1972). Giving up as a final common pathway to changes in health. *Advances in Psychosomatic Medicine, 8*, 21–40.

Schmale, A. H., & Iker, H. P. (1966). The affect of hopelessness and the development of cancer. *Psychosomatic Medicine, 28*, 714–721.

Schur, M. (1955). Comments on the metapsychology of somatization. *Psychoanalytic Study of the Child, 10*, 110–164.

Schwartz, A. (1987). Drives, affects, behavior and learning: Approaches to a psychobiology of emotion and to an integration of psychoanalytic and neurobiologic thought. *Journal of the American Psychoanalytic Association, 35*, 467–506.

Schwartz, G. E. (1979). The brain as a health care system. In G. C. Stone, F. Cohen, & N. E. Adler (Eds.), *Health psychology: A handbook* (pp. 549–571). San Francisco: Jossey-Bass.

Schwartz, G. E. (1983). Disregulation theory and disease: Applications to the repression/cerebral disconnection/cardiovascular disorder hypothesis. *International Review of Applied Psychology, 32*, 95–118.

Schwartz, G. E. (1989). Disregulation theory and disease: Toward a general model for psychosomatic medicine. In S. Cheren (Ed.), *Psychosomatic medicine: Theory, physiology, and practice* (Vol. 1, pp. 91–117). Madison, CT: International Universities Press.

Shipko, S. (1982). Alexithymia and somatization. *Psychotherapy and Psychosomatics, 37*, 193–201.

Siever, L. J., & Davis, K. L. (1985). Overview: Toward a dysregulation hypothesis of depression. *American Journal of Psychiatry, 142*, 1017–1031.

Smith, B. L. (1989). Winnicott and self psychology. In M. G. Fromm & B. L. Smith (Eds.), *The facilitating environment* (pp. 52–87). Madison, CT: International Universities Press.

Smith, E. M., & Blalock, J. E. (1986). A complete regulatory loop between the immune and neuroendocrine systems operates through common signal molecules (hormones) and receptors. In N. P. Plotnikoff, R. E. Faith, A. J. Murgo, & R. A. Good (Eds.), *Enkephalins and endorphins: Stress and the immune system* (pp. 119–127). New York: Plenum Press.

Sperling, M. (1978). *Psychosomatic disorders in childhood.* Northvale, NJ: Jason Aronson.

Spitz, R. A. (1945). Hospitalism: An inquiry into the genesis of psychiatric conditions in early childhood. *Psychoanalytic Study of the Child, 1*, 53–74.

Spitz, R. A. (1960). Discussion of Dr. Bowlby's paper. *Psychoanalytic Study of the Child, 15*, 85–94.

Spitz, R. A., & Wolf, K. M. (1946). Anaclitic depression. *Psychoanalytic Study of the Child, 2*, 313–342.

Sriram, T. G., Chaturvedi, S. K., Gopinath, P. S., & Shanmugam, V. (1987). Controlled study of alexithymic characteristics in patients with psychogenic pain disorder. *Psychotherapy and Psychosomatics, 47*, 11–17.

Stainbrook, E. (1952). Psychosomatic medicine in the nineteenth century. *Psychosomatic Medicine, 14*, 531–543.

Stern, D. N. (1977). *The first relationship.* Cambridge, MA: Harvard University Press.

Stern, D. N. (1983). The early development of schemas of self, other, and "self with other." In J. D. Lichtenberg & S. Kaplan (Eds.), *Reflections on self psychology* (pp. 49–84). Hillsdale, NJ: Analytic Press.

Stern, D. N. (1984). Affect attunement. In J. D. Call, E. Galenson, & R. L. Tyson (Eds.), *Frontiers in infant psychiatry* (Vol. 2, pp. 3–14). New York: Basic Books.

Stern, D. N. (1985). *The interpersonal world of the infant: A view from psychoanalysis and developmental psychology.* New York: Basic Books.

Stierlin, H. (1970). The functions of "inner objects." *International Journal of Psycho-Analysis, 51*, 321–329.

Stone, E. A., Bonnet, K. A., & Hofer, M. A. (1976). Survival and development of maternally deprived rats: Role of body temperature. *Psychosomatic Medicine, 38*, 242–249.

Taylor, G. J. (1984). Alexithymia: Concept, measurement, and implications for treatment. *American Journal of Psychiatry, 141*, 725–732.

Taylor, G. J.(1987). *Psychosomatic medicine and contemporary psychoanalysis.* Madison, CT: International Universities Press.

Taylor, G. J., Bagby, R. M., & Parker, J. D. A. (1991). The alexithymia construct: A potential paradigm for psychosomatic medicine. *Psychosomatics, 32*, 153–164.

Taylor, G. J., Bagby, R. M., Ryan, D. P., & Parker, J. D. A. (1990). Validation of the alexithymia construct: A measurement-based approach. *Canadian Journal of Psychiatry, 35*, 290–297.

Taylor, G. J., Parker, J. D. A., & Bagby, R. M. (1990). A preliminary investigation of alexithymia in men with psychoactive substance dependence. *American Journal of Psychiatry, 147*, 1228–1230.

Thomas, A., & Chess, S. (1977). *Temperament and development.* New York: Brunner/Mazel.

Thompson, J. G. (1988). *The psychobiology of emotions.* New York: Plenum Press.

Tilbe, K., & Sullivan, S. (1990). The extracolonic manifestations of the irritable bowel syndrome. *Canadian Medical Association Journal, 142,* 539–540.

Tustin, F. (1981). *Autistic states in children.* London: Routledge & Kegan Paul.

Veith, J. L., Buck, M., Getzlaf, S., van Dalfsen, P., & Slade, S. (1983). Exposure to men influences the occurrence of ovulation in women. *Physiology and Behavior, 31,* 313–315.

von Bertalanffy, L. (1968). *General systems theory.* New York: Braziller.

Waelder, R. (1967). Inhibitions, symptoms, and anxiety: Forty years later. *Psychoanalytic Quarterly, 36,* 1–36.

Weiner, H. (1977). *Psychobiology and human disease.* New York: Elsevier.

Weiner, H. (1982). The prospects for psychosomatic medicine: Selected topics. *Psychosomatic Medicine, 44,* 491–517.

Weiner, H. (1987). Human relationships in health, illness, and disease. In D. Magnusson & A. Ohman (Eds.), *Psychopathology: An interactional perspective* (pp. 305–323). Orlando, FL: Academic Press.

Weiner, H. (1989). The dynamics of the organism: Implications of recent biological thought for psychosomatic theory and research. *Psychosomatic Medicine, 51,* 608–635.

Weiner, H., Thaler, M., Reiser, M. F., & Mirsky, I. A. (1957). Etiology of duodenal ulcer: I. Relation of specific psychological characteristics to rate of gastric secretion (serum pepsinogen). *Psychosomatic Medicine, 19,* 1–10.

White, G. L., & La Barba, R. C. (1976). The effects of tactile and kinesthetic stimulation on neonatal development in the premature infant. *Journal of Developmental Psychobiology, 9,* 569–577.

Wilson, C. P., & Mintz, I. L. (Eds.). (1989). *Psychosomatic symptoms: Psychodynamic treatment of the underlying personality disorder.* Northvale, NJ: Jason Aronson.

Winnicott, D. W. (1975). Mind and its relation to the psyche-soma. In *Collected papers: Through pediatrics to psychoanalysis* (pp. 243–254). London: Hogarth Press. (Original work published 1949)

Winnicott, D. W. (1953). Transitional objects and transitional phenomena. *International Journal of Psycho-Analysis, 34,* 89–97.

Winnicott, D. W. (1966). Psychosomatic illness in its positive and negative aspects. *International Journal of Psychoanalysis, 47,* 510–516.

Wolf, E. S. (1980). On the developmental line of selfobject relations. In A. Goldberg (Ed.), *Advances in self psychology* (pp. 117–130). Madison, CT: International Universities Press.

Wolff, C. T., Friedman, S. B., Hofer, M. A., & Mason, J. W. (1964). Relationship between psychological defenses and mean urinary 17-hydroxycorticosteroid excretion rates. *Psychosomatic Medicine, 26,* 576–591.

22

THE EFFECTS OF PSYCHIC TRAUMA ON MIND: STRUCTURE AND PROCESSING OF MEANING

MARDI J. HOROWITZ

Psychological trauma is an exception to the way in which information is usually processed in the mind. A serious life event can become traumatic because it leads to mental states that differ from ordinary experiences of consciousness. These mental states may occur or recur after the intensity of external events and/or the stressful perceptual stimuli that they generate have subsided.

Memories of the traumatic events are retained and are difficult to integrate with the preexisting meaning structure of the mind. Unusual regulatory processes may occur, ranging from failures of defense to atypically high levels of inhibition. These properties of psychic trauma will be reviewed in terms of states of mind, schemas, and control processes that affect memories and schemas.

STATES OF MIND

Psychic trauma affects the quality of mental activity, manifest as states of mind that deflect from usual conscious experience in normal states. In highly stressed states there are phases of both more intrusive experiences and unusual omissions of memory and thinking from conscious representation. These unbidden states of mind during intrusive phases and numb, constricted states of mind during denial phases are primary signs of traumatic stress.

States of mind are not exactly the same as states of consciousness. "States of consciousness" is a term usually used to describe the variety of alternative experiences that range from hallucinatory deliria, through waking, to absorption, hypnotic trance, dreaming and nondreaming

489

sleep, and coma. "States of mind" is a term whose meaning is usually confined to waking consciousness. The term is close to "mood," but states of mind may include little felt or displayed emotion. States of mind include recognizable styles and patterns of awareness, action, relating, emoting, and controlling ideas and feelings.

A state of mind is a pattern of experience and behavior that includes verbal and nonverbal characteristics. When the features of a state occur simultaneously, an observer (or the observing self) can recognize the change into that state. Shifts in emotionality are prominent features observed in describing a transition from one state of mind into another. So, too, is the degree of apparent self-control, as in over-, well-, or undermodulated experiences and behaviors. Sometimes the person is shimmering, exhibiting the features of under- and overmodulation, as when a person sobs but tries not to cry, or grinds teeth while verbally disclaiming anger (Horowitz, 1979, 1987).

Early psychoanalytic theories about the effects of psychic trauma emphasized the state of consciousness that might be produced by high-impact life events and have strange impacts on memory, thinking, and feeling. Breuer and Freud (1895/1955) described a "hypnoid state" during frightening events as part of the etiology of the subsequent strangely intrusive states of mind in patients with hysteria. Some of the special peremptory effects of memories of traumas were thought to be due to perceptions that were registered during such hypnoid states. The hypnoid states were believed to be due to an overload of stimuli, an amount of excitation exceeding the barrier of the perceptual apparatus.

The special state theory of psychic trauma continued, especially in the work of Janet as reviewed by van der Kolk, Brown, and van der Hart (1989), and Putnam (1989), and Ellenberger (1970). Freud (1914/1958), however, dropped the theory of the hypnoid state, and developed his theory of repression, a barrier against recollection of painful memories caught up in current psychic conflict. That is, a barrier of inhibition was not only imposed against incoming arousing stimuli (Krystal, 1985), it was also imposed against the repetition of memories of the traumatic event and the drives that might relate to such memories (Freud, 1926/1950).

The traumatic memories tended toward repetition just as the actual events pressed on the person. Defenses countered the repetition. The result was a dynamic that could lead to symptom formation, as in unbidden image repetitions of traumatic perceptions. The earliest form of trauma cure was to undo the repressive barrier, to face memories in full consciousness in a context of emotional support (Freud, 1914/1958).

Another milestone in the states theory of psychic trauma was advanced by Lindemann (1944) in his paper on normal and pathological grief. In pathological grief there were extreme states, either overwhelming feeling and preoccupation with the memory and meaning of the traumatic events and the traumatic perceptions themselves, or states that might be called "frozen grief," in which the expectable memories and emotions were strangely absent from conscious representation or communication to others. In one kind of state persons might tell the traumatic story again and again; in another kind of state they might have a dialogue as if they were oblivious to their recent losses.

From these and other observations it was possible to put together a general model of the phases of response to stressful life events and the states of mind that occurred in each phase (Horowitz, 1973, 1976, 1986). Unlike some theories of phases, which emphasized specific emotions and mental contents such as fear, pining, and angry response, this phase theory had to do with the form of consciousness in stress-induced states of mind. The main differentiations were between states that were unusual in that they contained many intrusive ideas, images, and pangs of feeling, and states that had the opposite characteristics, ones in which there were conspicuous omissions of ideas, images, and emotions and signs of warding-off reminders (Horowitz, 1988).

These phases and some signs and symptoms are shown in Figures 1–3.

By establishing a context for systematic report of thought content and thought form, it was possible to set up experiments that used films as stimuli with various population groups and varied demand characteristics. A content analysis manual for the form and quality of reported thought permitted independent judges to reach reliability in scoring the recorded experiences of subjects. Experimental support for the intrusion-heightening effects of stressful events was obtained (Horowitz, 1969, 1975).

The operational definitions used in the experimental content analysis manual had been derived from clinical studies of people exposed to real life traumas. These descriptions also led to scales such as the Impact of Event Scale (Horowitz, Wilner, & Alvarez, 1979), which could be used in field and epidemiological studies of groups of disaster victims or bereaved survivors. The intrusion and avoidance scales showed the validity of the intrusive and denial phases or states of mind that increase systematically in frequency and intensity with exposure to very stressful life events.

Traumatic neuroses were noted in all major wars and after disasters such as railway wrecks. But controversy raged around various diagnoses such as combat neuroses, combat fatigue, and gross stress reaction. The signs and symptoms of heightened intrusion and, in denial phases, warding-off, having been clinically, experimentally, and epidemiologically validated in a quantitative manner, it was finally possible to establish an official diagnosis of posttraumatic stress disorder during the transition from *DSM–II* to *DSM–III* (Horowitz, Wilner, Kaltreider, & Alvarez, 1980). The long psychoanalytic recognition of traumatic neuroses reached a wider audience.

These official diagnostic descriptions are made by committees. They include the recognition that a constellation of traumatic memories can be reexperienced intrusively or excessively warded off, leading to prolongation, delay, or chronicity of response.

The memory of traumas are processed differently in different states of mind. In some states of mind the traumatic story is recounted with neutral emotion, in others, emotions pour out in an overwhelming torrent of jumbled ideas. In one state of mind the person may convey the story

Stress Response States   ## Pathologic States

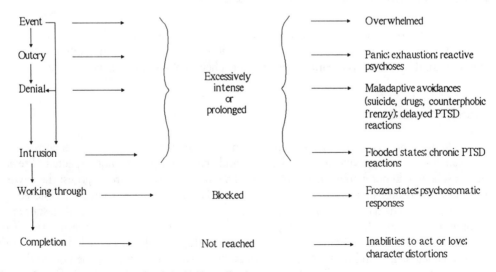

Figure 1. Stress response states and pathological intensification.

Perception and attention	Daze. Selective inattention. Inability to appreciate significance of stimuli.
Consciousness	Amnesia (complete or partial). Nonexperience.
Ideational processing	Disavowal of meanings of stimuli. Loss of reality appropriateness of thought by use of disavowal. Inflexibility of organization of thought. Fantasies to counteract reality.
Emotional manifestations	Numbness.
Somatic manifestations	Tension-inhibition-type symptoms.
Actions	Frantic overactivity to withdrawal.

Figure 2. Some signs and symptoms of denial phase of stress response syndromes.

in a way that evokes emotions in the companion but not the self, in another state, the self may be flooded with feeling. The meaning of a specific traumatic memory may differ in different states of mind because it is organized by different schemas of self and others.

PERSON SCHEMAS

Human traumas are often events that do not fit the way a person has schematized interpersonal transactions: sexual abuse, violence, and malevolence were not expected. Previous person schemas do not match what happened. Many natural disasters are surprises: the environment destroys people in a way one has not expected. People are weaker than once believed.

A person schema is an organized meaning or knowledge structure, an overall gestalt of self or of another person. In the schema are the traits, roles, attributes, and characteristics of the person. Complex person schemas such as role-relationship models might include not only the roles, characteristics, and traits of self and other, but a schematic script of the potential transactions and communications of emotion between them (Horowitz, 1991; Singer & Salovey, 1991; Stinson & Palmer, 1991). Many, but not all, traumatic events are traumatic because the victim

Perception and attention	Hypervigilance and startle reactions. Sleep and dream disturbances.
Consciousness	Intrusive-repetitive thoughts, images, and behaviors (illusions, pseudohallucinations, nightmares, ruminations, and repetitions).
Ideational processing	Overgeneralization. Inability to concentrate on other topics; preoccupation; obsession. Confusion and disorganization.
Emotional manifestations	Emotional attacks or "pangs."
Somatic manifestations	Symptomatic sequelae of chronic "fight or flight" readiness (or of exhaustion).
Actions	Search for lost persons and situations; compulsive repetitions.

Figure 3. Some signs and symptoms of intrusion phase of stress response syndromes.

has no ready route of response to cope with the event. For example, a postdisaster rescue worker who has not developed schemas for his or her task may have a posttraumatic stress disorder after he or she confronts and picks up dismembered human bodies.

When stressful events and memories that repeat them do not match with enduring schemas and expectations, emotional reactions become more intense; they are alarm reactions (Horowitz, 1986; Horowitz, Fridhandler, & Stinson, in press; Mandler, 1975). These emotions, alarms, and startle reactions continue, with episodic repetitions, until the schematic discrepancies are resolved and the new information is schematically integrated.

Memory is rapid; schematic change is slow. Active memory, the tendency of important stressful experiences to be recorded and repeatedly represented, may lead to intrusion of the topic into other foci of conscious attention. Nightmare repetitions may occur. Each repetition may lead to contemplation, and the information processing may lead to schematic change. This schematic change, exemplified by the process of mourning a loss may lead to relative completion. That is, a working-through process gradually reduces states of intrusion or excessive warding-off, as in denial phases.

Not infrequently, children are traumatized by events that are forced on them for which they do not have adequate schemas. Children are very vulnerable to traumas because of their limited prior experience and their dependency. A "trauma schema" may be developed after an overwhelming life event. In later life, persons may be traumatized by events that activate the early trauma schemas related to the childhood events and memories. (This does not mean that all adult psychic traumas are based on childhood traumas. It is possible to traumatize an adult with experiences that are unlike anything heretofore known or ones that far exceed schematized coping capacities.)

To recapitulate: Once experienced, the perceptions of a traumatic event seem to be inscribed in a special form of memory. These memories have a tendency to unusually vivid, repeated imagistic representation in conscious thought. The traumatic event tends to persist in the mind not only in the form of unintegrated and active memories, but in schemas in which the self is relatively vulnerable to threats of death, dismemberment, loss, insult, degradation, or torture.

Working through a traumatic memory to the point that intrusive states of mind are no longer likely requires not only the memories of the event, but confrontation with the schemas that may have been built up as a consequence of the event. Even with working through, the person may be vulnerable to regressive states of mind in which memories related to the trauma are once again organized by role-relationship models such as those in which the self is a severely harmed victim and others are either helpless to prevent it or aggressors who bring forth the harm on the self.

The transition from one state of mind to another is assumed to be due to a change in the relative activity level of particular schemas, ones from a repertoire of many schemas. This assumes that each person may have a repertoire of self-schemas and role-relationship models. A memory of a trauma can be reorganized according to the meaning structure of various elements in this repertoire. The state of mind produced during that process of working through may vary according to not only the qualities in the traumatic memories but qualities in the schemas. Control processes may affect not only which topics or memories become the focus of conscious attention but which schemas organize thinking, feeling, communicating, and acting during the recollection.

CONTROL PROCESSES

From Freud's theory of repression, subsequent psychoanalytic investigations have developed more complex understandings of unconscious mental processes and conscious goals. Now we assume that a person has a very extensive repertoire of memories, and of self-concepts and role-relationship models, and that each element in this repertoire may be inhibited or facilitated by control processes. Shifts in set points of various mental activities by these control processes can accomplish a change in state of mind. Some states may be more adaptive than others.

The negative discrepancy between current conditions and memories and enduring schemas that occurs after traumatic events can lead to alarming and distressingly emotional states of mind. The person dreads the recurrence of both memory and these states. Some control processes may be activated as a result of unconscious anticipation of a dreaded state of mind. The interaction of several control processes can result in defensive operations (Horowitz, Markman, Stinson, Fridhandler, & Ghannam, 1990).

This is psychoanalytic theory only partially changed from Freud's (1926/1959) theory of signal anxiety. Freud described how, in order to ward off the consequences of consciousness of a traumatic memory, the person might interrupt the processes that form conscious representation. A traumatic memory may be repressed rather than represented to ward off too much affect. Some fear (of the dreaded state) occurs as a signal of the danger of recollection. Highly important, this theory is concordant with cognitive theories of Janis (1969) and Lazarus and Folkman (1984). In addition, the theories of emotionality as related to person schemas converge nicely with the most recent and advanced psychological theories of emotion and adaptation (Lazarus, 1991).

The tendency to facilitate recollection to achieve schematic integration is opposed by the tendency to inhibit conscious representation to avoid dreaded states. The person cycles between warding off and intrusion. As reschematization occurs there is less tendency to either extreme, and working through to a point of relative completion. Maladaptive results of control processes also occur, leading to various types of psychopathology.

TRAUMA-RELATED PSYCHOPATHOLOGY

Various forms of psychopathology may occur as a consequence of the psychological trauma, how its meanings intersect with prior psychic structure, and the sequelae in terms of biological, psychological, and social interactions. It is important to distinguish between the signs and symptoms of stressed states of mind and the occurrence of psychopathological states. Grief, for example, is not an illness, but pathological grief may be a mental disorder (Horowitz, 1990; Parkes & Weiss, 1983; Raphael, 1983).

The person may go through phases of intrusion and denial in an adaptive way, working through the traumatic event and reaching a stage of relative completion. In such instances memories of the event are integrated with the previous world of the subject. This may be best understood in person schematic terms: the person now has a schema that has assimilated and accommodated the new meanings. This means that he or she has differentiated reality from fantasy, and has not exaggerated the degrading or impairing effects of the trauma on the self.

On the other hand, any of the normal phases of a passage through a period of stress can be accentuated to the point that the person can be said to have a form of psychopathology. The clearest forms of such psychopathology are the posttraumatic stress disorders, but there has been considerable argument about nosology since these disorders were introduced into the third edition of the *Diagnostic and Statistical Manual of Mental Disorders* (American Psychiatric Association, 1980). Research and understanding of conscious and unconscious mental processes as a consequence of psychic trauma continues, and it is likely that future diagnostic systems will be further differentiated in terms of the varieties of stress response syndromes.

One of the debates concerning the posttraumatic stress disorders concerns chronicity, inhibition, or maladaptive impairment with intrusive thinking and feeling. The clearest form of the disorder is continuation of intrusive signs and symptoms to the point where the person senses that he or she is not working through the event, and others can observe him or her as being impaired by unnecessary prolongation of reactions to it. On the other hand, there may be persons with a variety of characterological limitations that represent avoidance of reaction to the event. Memories are repressed to the point that the person cannot integrate aspects of the event into an altered world circumstance.

A variety of arguments about the effects of trauma occur in legal contexts. There have been decades of debate as to how much of symptom formation is a result of the person's experience with the traumatic event, and how much was due to preexisting personality styles, dispositions, conflicts, or psychopathology of personality. It seems clear from intensive case studies that a traumatic event always combines with preexisting meaning structure of the person to produce the consequences. The person has developed psychopathology; not only because he or she had preevent morbid characteristics, but also because he or she had the experience of the particular life event. This does not mean that the event has not been a major cause in the formation of the psychopathology, only that there is no *tabula rasa* upon which experience writes.

Because of the legal issues of responsibility of some people for the trauma of others, there have also been arguments about how stressful an event must be in terms of its external characteristics. Even in the diagnostic nomenclature, there was inclusion of a criterion that the event had to be outside the usual realm of experience of people. This was left very ambiguous, and so argument emerged as to whether a pathological grief reaction could be a posttraumatic stress disorder. All people expect to be confronted by the death of a loved one at some time in their lives. On the other hand, such deaths could be outside their ordinary realm of experience, or the deaths could be of a traumatic nature and, so, even more outside the realm of usual experience.

Pathological grief experiences are an especially important type of event with reference to psychic trauma. Any of the normal phases of grief can be exaggerated or prolonged to the point that the person has a pathological grief reaction, as shown in Table 1.

TREATMENT ISSUES

The treatment for psychic trauma depends on the particular variant noted. If the person is having pathological denial leading to rigid avoidances of confrontation with traumatic memories, more exploratory treatments are indicated. If the person is having intrusion of unbidden images of the traumatic event, a period of more supportive treatment may be indicated before

TABLE 1
Common Experiences During Grief and Their Pathological Intensification

Phase	Normal response	Pathological intensification
Outcry	Outcry of emotions	Panic; dissociative reactions; reactive psychoses
Denial	Avoidance of reminders, social withdrawal, focusing elsewhere, emotional numbing, not thinking of implications to self of certain themes	Maladaptive avoidances of confronting the implications; drug or alcohol abuse, counterphobic frenzy, promiscuity, fugue states, phobic avoidance, feeling dead or unreal
Intrusion	Intrusive experiences, bad dreams, reduced concentration, compulsive enactments	Flooding with negative images and emotions, uncontrolled ideation; self-impairing compulsive reenactments; night terrors, recurrent nightmares, distraught from intrusion of anger, anxiety, despair, shame, or guilt themes; physiological exhaustion from hyperarousal
Working-through	Recollections and contemplations with reduced intrusiveness of memories and fantasies, increased rational acceptance, reduced numbness and avoidance	Sense that one cannot integrate loss with a sense of continued life. Persistent warded-off themes may manifest as anxious, depressed, enraged, shame-filled, or guilty moods, and psychophysiological syndromes
Completion	Reduction in emotional swings with a sense of self-coherence and readiness for new relationships; able to experience positive states of mind	Failure to complete mourning may be associated with inability to work, create, feel emotion, or positive states of mind

Note. Table derived from Horowitz (1990). Copyright © 1990 by International Universities Press. Reprinted from the *Journal of the American Psychoanalytic Association*, Volume 38, page 302. Reprinted by permission of the publisher.

exploration of the more extended meanings of the life event. By defining phase-oriented treatment strategies, it has been possible to develop brief psychoanalytic–cognitive approaches to psychotherapy for traumatic events (Horowitz, 1976, 1986). Using some of the quantitative procedures mentioned previously, it has been possible to quantify the effects of such treatment, and to show its effects on both symptom reduction and improved personality functioning (Horowitz, Marmar, Krupnick, Wilner, Kaltreider, & Wallerstein, 1984; Horowitz, Marmar, Weiss, DeWitt, & Rosenbaum, 1984; Horowitz, Marmar, Weiss, Kaltreider, & Wilner, 1986).

A focus in such therapeutics is often the meaning to the self of the life event. Because people may have a repertoire of multiple self schemas, this means exploring memories and fantasies linked associatively to the traumatic event in relation to various views of self as weak or strong, good or bad, self-centered, or protective of others. In the most extreme cases this may lead to confrontation with usually warded-off or usually unconscious self-schemas, such as the self-as-wishing-harm-to-others and feeling guilty as a consequence of a belief in the magical properties of these wishes. Since traumatic events involve loss, frustration, pain, and severe fright, they also tend to occasion a kind of diffuse rage. This rage may activate any type of primitive memories of rage, and so irrational fantasies may be added to the terror of the real memories. Differentiation of the reality and fantasy has been found in a variety of psychoanalytic studies to be key to the treatment and resolution of these disorders.

CHILDHOOD SEXUAL TRAUMAS

A long-standing theme in psychoanalysis concerns the traumatic sexual abuse of children and its effect on character development. Suppose the trauma in question is the sexual abuse by a parent of a vulnerable child. The child may schematize the role of the parent as the sexual aggressor, and the self as the sexual victim of such abuse. At the same time, the child has schematized for the self both roles, and may occupy in fantasy and real action (play or interpersonal behaviors) the role of the abusing, aggressive, and stronger person. Such schemas can guide future behavior and mental processes. A person who was the childhood victim of sexual abuse may compulsively reenact not only the victim role, but also the aggressor role. Thus, unless there are corrective factors, child abuse tends to run in families and across generations. He or she who was abused as a child may tend to misinterpret current situations as leading toward abuse; he or she may also provoke abuse, or abuse others.

In children, schemas are recorded on a groundwork that is not as complex and differentiated as that of an adult; supraordinate forms that can merge diverse schemas are less developed. Thus, the child may develop dissociations in instances of traumatic interaction with parents, and may maintain a good, loving, and caretaking relationship with the same parent who, in other states of mind, is viewed as an abusing aggressor. The child develops a repertoire that seems contradictory but permits continued attachment.

Schemas developed from traumatic events that occur in childhood or in adulthood influence formation of schemas about how to avoid such events. If the child believes that certain traits of self have led into the occurrence of the traumatic life events, he or she may preserve a self-schema as having such partially provocative traits. He or she may also be motivated to practice some counteraction to such traits in order to avoid reentry into the dreaded state of traumatization. If the child has come to believe, magically or otherwise, that a trait of wide-eyed staring at persons of the opposite sex has led to sexual abuse, then that trait can be counteracted by developing a trait of hooding the eyes and always averting the gaze. That person might become habitually vulnerable to states of wide-eyed staring associated with fearful emotional arousals, and states of hooded gaze aversion, experienced as wooden and overcontrolled.

A child abused by a father who performed sexually traumatic acts when he was drunk might fear the father when he was in the drunken state. The father in a sober state may have been a loving caretaker, sought after and loved by the child. The seemingly incompatible role-relationship models of father and self may be held in dissociated rather than integrated forms. Their extreme, contradictory features make it difficult for the child to develop integrated and supraordinate schemas during later stages of development when such integrations and supraordinate forms might otherwise be possible.

This type of cleavage leads to dissociation of self-schemas. The self may be characterized critically as *strong and bad*, in some way magically instigating the abuse scenario; as *degraded and weak* for having had to submit to it; and as *good and attractive* because of interactions with the beloved parent in other situations.

Childhood traumas have long-lasting waves of impact. The trauma itself tends to be retained as special memory in repeated unbidden images. The fact of the trauma, and its repetition and play, including attempts to undo it, may lead to a variety of schematizations. These schematizations have their own intrinsic emotional effects. In addition, trauma may increase the tendency to dissociation, or may decrease the likelihood of being able to integrate schemas and to avoid dissociations. In all these ways childhood traumas may interfere with development of self-organization.

Because of the many direct and indirect effects of childhood traumas, the treatment of the adult who has been traumatized in childhood becomes complex. That is why long-term psychoanalytic psychotherapy, or psychoanalysis, is recommended. The properties of memory, fantasy, and repetition in relationship are such that direct conscious approaches toward clarification and insight are insufficient. Instead, reenactments in the form of developing transferences, developing concurrent therapeutic alliances, and differentiating realities from projections are important routes to learning new meaning structures.

These new meaning structures never erase the memories and schemas that were based on the traumatic event. The development of new knowledge structures does lead to states of mind of a new sort, ones with more control and self-efficacy. These new states of mind, and the schemas upon which they are based, themselves serve to control and ward-off the etched-in trauma schemas.

Because traumatic events are often known to other members in the family, and because they are often real events, their effect on the lifetime development of the individual can be traced. Intensive studies of psychoanalytic cases to unravel the effects of trauma are still an important route to understanding the core structure of the human personality. Such studies could usefully examine the meaning structures used to organize memories and fantasies of childhood and other past developmental phases; patterns in recurrent interpersonal situations; and patterns observed through transference, that is, patterns enacted in the here-and-now relationship of analysand and analyst.

The concordances across patterns—the repetitiousness that is based on enduring and slowly changing structures of intrapsychic meaning—is indicative of person schemas. Psychic trauma in childhood, or any later phase, can lead to dissociations in such schemas. In the absence of integrative reschematization processes such as mourning, the dissociated schemas are reenacted without as much self-regulation as would be desirable for maximum adaptive functioning. These neurotic repetitions are the central focus of most analyses. The person schemas and motivations upon which they are based are current topics of high interest in cognitive science (e.g., Rumelhart & Ortony, 1977; Singer & Salovey, 1991; Stinson & Palmer, 1991). The time for a psychodynamic and cognitive science convergence is now at hand, and the enjoined theory can elucidate further the potential lifelong effects of psychic trauma on the mind.

REFERENCES

American Psychiatric Association. (1980). *Diagnostic and statistical manual of mental disorders* (3rd ed.). Washington, DC: Author.

Breuer, J., & Freud, S. (1955). Studies on hysteria. In J. Strachey (Ed. and Trans.), *The standard edition of the complete psychological works of Sigmund Freud* (Vol. 2, pp. 3–319). London: Hogarth Press. (Original work published 1895)

Ellenberger, H. F. (1970). *Discovery of the unconscious: The history and evolution of dynamic psychiatry.* New York: Basic Books.

Freud, S. (1958). Remembering, repeating and working through. In J. Strachey (Ed. and Trans.), *The standard edition of the complete psychological works of Sigmund Freud* (Vol. 12, pp. 145–156). London: Hogarth Press. (Original work published 1914)

Freud, S. (1959). Inhibitions, symptoms, and anxiety. In J. Strachey (Ed. and Trans.), *The standard edition of the complete psychological works of Sigmund Freud* (Vol. 20, pp. 87–156). London: Hogarth Press. (Original work published 1926)

Horowitz, M. J. (1969). Psychic trauma: Return of images after a stress film. *Archives of General Psychiatry, 20,* 552–559.

Horowitz, M. J. (1973). Phase-oriented treatment of stress response syndromes. *American Journal of Psychotherapy, 27,* 506–515.

Horowitz, M. J. (1975). Intrusive and repetitive thoughts after experimental stress. *Archives of General Psychiatry, 32,* 1457–1463.

Horowitz, M. J. (1976). *Stress response syndromes* (1st ed.). Northvale, NJ: Jason Aronson.

Horowitz, M. J. (1979). *States of mind* (1st ed.). New York: Plenum Press.

Horowitz, M. J. (1986). *Stress response syndromes* (2nd ed.). Northvale, NJ: Jason Aronson.

Horowitz, M. J. (1987). *States of mind* (2nd ed.). New York: Plenum Press.

Horowitz, M. J. (1988). *Introduction to psychodynamics: A new synthesis.* New York: Basic Books.

Horowitz, M. J. (1990). A model of mourning: Change in schemas of self and others. *Journal of the American Psychoanalytic Association, 38,* 297–324.

Horowitz, M. J. (Ed.). (1991). *Person schemas and maladaptive interpersonal patterns.* Chicago: University of Chicago Press.

Horowitz, M. J., Fridhandler, B., & Stinson, C. H. (in press). Person schemas and emotion. *Journal of the American Psychoanalytic Association.*

Horowitz, M. J., Markman, H. C., Stinson, C. H., Fridhandler, B., & Ghannam, J. H. (1990). A classification theory of defense. In J. L. Singer (Ed.), *Repression and dissociation: Implications for personality theory, psychopathology, and health* (pp. 61–84). Chicago: University of Chicago Press.

Horowitz, M. J., Marmar, C., Krupnick, J., Wilner, N., Kaltreider, N., & Wallerstein, R. (1984). *Personality styles and brief psychotherapy.* New York: Basic Books.

Horowitz, M. J., Marmar, C., Weiss, D. S., DeWitt, K., & Rosenbaum, R. (1984). Brief psychotherapy of bereavement reactions: The relationship of process to outcome. *Archives of General Psychiatry, 41,* 438–448.

Horowitz, M. J., Marmar, C., Weiss, D. S., Kaltreider, N., & Wilner, N. (1986). Comprehensive analysis of change after brief dynamic psychotherapy. *American Journal of Psychiatry, 143,* 582–589.

Horowitz, M. J., Wilner, N., & Alvarez, W. (1979). The impact of event scale: A measure of subjective stress. *Psychosomatic Medicine, 41,* 209–218.

Horowitz, M. J., Wilner, N., Kaltreider, N., & Alvarez, W. (1980). Signs and symptoms of post-traumatic stress disorder. *Archives of General Psychiatry, 37,* 85–92.

Janis, I. L. (1969). *Stress and frustration*. New York: Harcourt Brace Jovanovich.

Krystal, H. (1985). *Trauma and the stimulus barrier: Psychoanalytic inquiry* (Vol. 5). Hillsdale, NJ: Analytic Press.

Lazarus, R. S. (1991). *Emotion and adaptation*. New York: Basic Books.

Lazarus, R. S., & Folkman, S. K. (1984). *Stress, appraisal and coping*. New York: Springer.

Lindemann, E. (1944). Symptomatology and management of acute grief. *American Journal of Psychiatry, 161,* 141–148.

Mandler, G. A. (1975). *Mind and emotion*. New York: Wiley.

Parkes, C. M., & Weiss, R. S. (1983). *Recovery from bereavement*. New York: Basic Books.

Putnam, F. (1989). Pierre Janet and modern views of dissociation. *Journal of Traumatic Stress, 2,* 397–449.

Raphael, B. (1983). *The anatomy of bereavement*. New York: Basic Books.

Rumelhart, D. E., & Ortony, A. (1977). The representation of knowledge in memory. In R. C. Anderson, R. J. Spiro, & W. E. Montague (Eds.), *Schooling and the acquisition of knowledge* (pp. 99–135). Hillsdale, NJ: Erlbaum.

Singer, J. L., & Salovey, P. (1991). Organized knowledge structures and personality. In M. J. Horowitz (Ed.), *Person schemas and maladaptive interpersonal patterns* (pp. 33–79). Chicago: University of Chicago Press.

Stinson, C. H., & Palmer, S. (1991). Parallel distributed processing models of person schemas and psychopathologies. In M. J. Horowitz (Ed.), *Person schemas and maladaptive interpersonal patterns* (pp. 339–377). Chicago: University of Chicago Press.

van der Kolk, B., Brown, P., & van der Hart, O. (1989). Pierre Janet on post-traumatic stress. *Journal of Traumatic Stress, 2,* 365–395.

V

RESEARCH ON TREATMENT PROCESS AND OUTCOME

INTRODUCTION: THE TREATMENT PROCESS

Section 5 deals with issues and concepts arising out of the treatment process, particularly, of course, psychoanalytically oriented treatment. As is well known, there is an enormous research literature on psychotherapy process and outcome. There is also an enormous *psychoanalytic* literature on the psychotherapy process, but it is less of a research literature. With the exception of a limited number of researchers, some of whom are represented in this volume, the psychoanalytic literature on the psychotherapy process consists mainly of formulations taken from various psychoanalytic theories of treatment and from a general sense of the "received wisdom," usually buttressed with clinical case material.[1] In a recent book titled *How does treatment help?* (Rothstein, 1988), the contributors were asked "How do ideas and data from other than your therapeutic experience influence your conception of therapeutic action?" Wolitzky (1990) reported that of the total of 200 references cited by the sixteen analysts contributing to the book, only 6 were citations of empirical research, and 5 of these 6 references were cited by one contributing author. This is not really surprising. Analysts tend to read and to present their work in the form of clinical cases and in psychoanalytic journals rather than journals with broader content and interests. Furthermore, as Gedo (1984) observes, analysts tend to be more influenced by "compelling ideas" rather than by research evidence.

In contrast to this tendency in the psychoanalytic literature to eschew systematic empirical research and to ignore the general body of research on psychotherapy process and outcome, most of the contributors in Part 5 report their own research (as well as their own theoretical formulations) or refer to research and theory in the psychological literature that is relevant to understanding the psychotherapy process.

If one takes a broad view of major changes in a psychoanalytic theory of treatment, perhaps the most evident shift is an alteration of an early model of treatment in which the therapist is a

---

[1] For exceptions to this general trend see, e.g., the work of Kantrowitz and her coworkers (1986; 1987; 1989; 1990a, 1990b, 1990c) and a recent survey by Bachrach et al. (1991) of research on the outcome of psychoanalytic treatment.

"blank screen" on whom the patient projects infantile wishes and conflicts and who offers interpretations to patients that, if successful, facilitate insight and resolution of conflict. Over a period of time, there has been increasing recognition that the therapist is not and cannot be a blank screen. Rather, the therapist presents various cues to the patient, who interprets these cues in a variety of ways (Gill, 1982). More and more, treatment came to be seen as an *interactional* process (a point of view already enunciated by Sullivan, 1953). Consistent with this perspective, from a near exclusive emphasis on interpretation and insight as the "curative" factors in treatment, the therapeutic role of relationship factors in the treatment came to be increasingly recognized and stressed. Of course, as was noted by Eagle and Wolitzky (1981), there was never any inherent incompatibility between the two sets of factors, insofar as the making of an accurate and empathic insight-facilitating interpretation is part of what constitutes a therapeutic relationship.

One expression of the newer perspective of treatment as an interactional process and the increased emphasis on relationship factors was a correspondingly greater interest in, as well as a reconceptualization of, the concepts of *transference* and *countertransference* (see Eagle & Wolitzky, 1989, for a description of this reconceptualization). These developments are well represented in this volume. Singer and Singer's chapter considers a broadened conception of transference that is linked to research and theory in social cognition. Tansey's chapter traces the reconceptualization of countertransference since Freud and describes a number of studies that are relevant to a consideration of the role of countertransference in psychotherapy. Another expression of the perspective of treatment as an interactional process and of the increased emphasis on relationship factors is a renewed interest in the concept of the *helping alliance*. This emphasis is well represented in Luborsky, Barber, and Crits-Christoph's chapter. From a somewhat different angle, Sampson's chapter also conveys an understanding of psychotherapy as an interactional process in which the patient actively presents tests that can either be failed or passed by the therapist. Spence's chapter, although it concerns itself with interpretation, ends with a call for an "ideal interpretive model [that] will indicate how the classic forms of mother–infant sharing can be simulated in language when the patient is on the couch." Finally, although Binder, Strupp, and Rock focus on psychoanalytic technique (which has often been pitted against relationship factors), it is clear that an essential aspect of what they mean by good psychoanalytic or psychotherapeutic technique include a sensitivity to relationship factors, such as maintaining "an attitude toward the patient that is neither indulgent nor critical."

As one would expect in a volume such as this, another common theme is the need for empirical research on psychotherapy process and outcome as well as on training for doing psychotherapy and the appropriateness of an attitude of open-minded skepticism toward the time-honored assumptions and the received wisdom found in the psychoanalytic literature until adequate evidence is available. Thus, for example, Singer and Singer question a number of cherished assumptions about transference; Luborsky, Barber, and Crits-Christoph present evidence that, contrary to the traditional assumptions, patients' wishes may not be relinquished or radically altered in the course of successful therapy; and Sampson presents evidence for a new theory of psychotherapy that is quite different, in important respects, from traditional theory. Tansey finds evidence supporting a therapeutic role for countertransference that is very different from the role assigned to it by Freud. Spence presents a devastating critique of the traditional psychoanalytic theory of the role of interpretation in treatment and suggests directions for a more adequate theory; and Binder, Strupp, and Rock present an equally devastating critique of the status of theory and practice in understanding and providing training in the techniques required for doing effective psychoanalysis and psychotherapy and make important suggestions for change.

As is the other sections in this book, the chapters in this section are not intended to provide a complete and exhaustive account of all the key issues and concepts that pertain to the psychoanalytic theory of treatment. Thus, for example, there are no chapters on important psychoanalytic concepts such as *insight, resistance,* and *working through.* Coverage is, as it needs must be, selective, then, and not exhaustive.

Of all the psychoanalytic concepts dealing with the treatment process, the concept of *transference* has received the greatest attention in the current psychoanalytic literature. Indeed, some psychoanalytic writers maintain that only transference interpretations are therapeutically useful (Gill, 1982). The chapter by Singer and Singer deals with this central concept of transference and relates transference to current research in memory and social cognition. Singer and Singer's rich chapter serves as a model of the mutual enrichment that obtains when one relates an appropriate psychoanalytic concept to relevant psychological research.

Singer and Singer believe that Freud's identification of the phenomenon of transference represents a major discovery that is likely to endure. Furthermore, they note that some recent research findings and theoretical developments in person memory and social cognition have begun to confirm the ubiquitousness of transference phenomena beyond the analytic or psychotherapy session. They go on to describe transference phenomena in terms of *schemas, scripts,* and *metascripts,* concepts that have proved heuristic in the area of social cognition.

A *schema* may be thought of as an organized knowledge structure that helps organize memories and experiences and that operates, to borrow from Piaget (1926), in an assimilative manner. That is, new experiences are "fit" or assimilated into preexisting schemas. The term *script,* originated by Tomkins (1970, 1979, 1987), is defined as a construct that organizes one's understanding of sequence of events. Thus, the phrase "going to a restaurant" functions as a script insofar as it immediately establishes a set of event sequences and expectations. People also have personal scripts about interpersonal interactions, such as being married or being in an intimate relationship. Scripts, particularly self-referential scripts, can be emotion-laden, egocentric, and resistant to change, even in the face of conflicting information. A central thesis in the Singer and Singer chapter is that transference phenomena "can be understood as highly evolved and complex versions of these cognitive structures."

The Singers point out that these conservative and assimilative structures are normally adaptive, insofar as they reduce cognitive complexity and help one predict and anticipate future events. These adaptive advantages, at least partly, account for their resistance to change—perhaps obviating the need to posit a special compulsion to repeat.

As to how schemas and scripts develop, Singer and Singer refer to the proposal of theorists such as Tomkins (1987), Abelson (1981), and others that, starting with particularly important "nuclear scenes," the individual "begins an abstracting process that matches new experiences with the nuclear scene and extracts their common properties of affect, plot, setting, and participants." This abstracting process results in a template or prototype, or *metascript,* that no longer retains specific episodic memory details but begins to function as an unconscious rule or command (e.g., "trying to get close to someone will inevitably lead to getting hurt").

Singer and Singer present some fascinating work suggesting that, although positive scripts grow through experiencing nuances and variations in new experiences, negative scripts develop by taking new experiences and pulling them back into preexisting structures. One way of putting this is to say that negative scripts operate mainly by assimilation—that is, by primarily finding similarities between the old and the new—whereas positive scripts operate both by assimilation and accommodation—that is, by finding not only similarities between the old and the new, but also embellishments, variations, and different nuances in the new. As the authors point out, this suggests that positive and negative transference operate in very different ways. That positive scripts operate by sensitivity to variation (i.e., to subtle differences between the old and the new) seems to be incongruent with Freud's (1900/1953) basic conception of a wish as an urge to reestablish earlier conditions of satisfaction and perceptual identity.

One can note the parallels between these concepts and formulations taken from social cognition and similar ones found in the psychoanalytic literature. Thus, the "unconscious pathogenic beliefs" discussed by Sampson in his chapter parallel the generalized metascripts discussed by social cognitive theorists. One can point to other examples in the psychoanalytic and related literature. For example, Stern's (1985) concept of *Response Interactions Generalized* (RIGs) is understood as an abstracted or prototype structure that represents the common and invariant features of repeated interactions—a concept, it will be noted, that is very similar to the concepts of schemas, scripts, and metascripts. This is also true of Beebe and Lachmann's (1988) concept of *interactional structures*. Bowlby's (1973) *internal working model* can also be understood as a particular version of the general idea that individuals develop generalized and schematic representations of self, others, and self–other interactions that then serve to guide subsequent interpersonal interactions as well as conceptions of self and others. In general, one finds an increasing emphasis in the psychoanalytic literature on the developmental and etiological role of self, other, and interactional representations (e.g., Kernberg, 1976). Indeed, for better or worse, the unconscious of contemporary psychoanalytic theories has been increasingly transformed from a "dynamic unconscious" of instinctual wishes, urges, and drives to an unconscious of representations, schemas, belief systems, and cognitive–affective structures that guide behavior in particular adaptive and maladaptive directions (Eagle, 1987). This has meant that it has become increasingly possible to find the kinds of points of contact between psychology and psychoanalysis that are highlighted in Singer and Singer's chapter. Exploiting this possibility should enrich both fields.

Finally, another important contribution of the Singers' chapter is to remind us that some of our cherished assumptions regarding transference still await systematic empirical support. Thus, despite claims in the psychoanalytic literature, there is no firm evidence that interpretations of transference toward the therapist are necessarily more therapeutically effective than interpretations of transference reactions toward other significant figures. They also question the assumption that all "faulty or ineffective schemas, which emerge as transference, can be reduced to early childhood origins." Perhaps, they suggest, experiences and memories from other periods of life (e.g., adolescence) may be equally important in establishing and influencing subsequent relationship patterns. A similar question arises in the attachment literature. We do not know the extent to which patterns of attachment (and accompanying internal working models) formed early in life remain stable and are determinative of later patterns versus the extent to which they are susceptible to change as a function of changed conditions and life circumstances.[2]

Sampson's chapter deals with a number of issues very similar to the ones discussed by Singer and Singer. In his chapter, Sampson presents an overview of the research program carried out by the San Francisco Psychotherapy Research Group and the "control-mastery" theory developed by Weiss on which that research is based.

Along with a relatively few others (including Luborsky and his colleagues, and Strupp and his colleagues, whose chapters appear in this volume), Sampson, Weiss, and their colleagues have carried out systematic and rigorous empirical research on a number of psychoanalytic hypotheses, using clinical data from the therapeutic situation. Relatively rare in psychoanalytic (as well as other) research, Sampson and his colleagues have employed clinical data to test directly two opposing theories regarding the treatment process and the patient's functioning in that process.

According to traditional Freudian theory, repressed contents such as wishes can become conscious only with interpretative help from the analyst or if the repressed material is sufficiently intensified so that it erupts into consciousness. In the latter case, such eruptions would be

---

[2]For a discussion of this and related issues, see Thompson, 1991.

accompanied or followed by anxiety, continuing conflict, and attempts at re-repression. In the traditional view, the entire psychoanalytic situation, including the ubiquitous presence of transference, the use of the couch, and the neutrality of the analyst, work toward intensifying repressed wishes, thereby making it more likely that at least derivatives of those wishes will emerge into consciousness. Furthermore, given the traditional conception of transference, it is expected that the patient will unconsciously push for the analyst to gratify his or her repressed infantile wishes—that is, the patient repeats rather than remembers.

In contrast to this view, Weiss and Sampson (1986) believe that patients come to treatment, not to gratify infantile wishes, but with an *unconscious plan* to lift their repressions and to disconfirm their *unconscious pathogenic beliefs*, the primary source of their suffering and distress. According to control-mastery theory, at the core of much pathology are these unconscious pathogenic beliefs, which are based primarily on early traumatic experiences with parents and which are generally characterized by the conviction that the pursuit of certain normal developmental goals (e.g., to separate and lead an independent life; to have outside friendships; to have ambitions and to succeed) will seriously harm one's parents, disrupt one's ties to them, or both. In treatment, patients make unconscious assessments of safety and danger and lift repressions when their appraisals indicate that it is safe to do so. Of critical importance, patients present *unconscious tests* to the therapist in the hope of experiencing in their interactions with the therapist disconfirmations of their pathogenic beliefs. When the therapist passes a test, the patient is more likely to lift defenses, to become aware of hitherto warded off material, and to make therapeutic progress. Test failures—of which the essence is that they constitute confirmations of the patient's pathogenic beliefs—are more likely to be followed by increased defensiveness and lack of therapeutic progress or even by therapeutic regression and failure.

As Sampson makes clear in this chapter, in their program of research, Weiss, Sampson, and their colleagues have presented impressive empirical evidence that supports these hypotheses. As Sampson also makes clear, a number of findings have been reported that are not easily explained by, and indeed appear to be incompatible with, traditional theory, but that are predictable from control-mastery theory: the emergence of warded off material without interpretation and without increased anxiety; positive correlations between test-passing and certain patient behaviors such as increased depth of experiencing, increased boldness, and increased relaxation; significant positive relationships between the plan compatibility of therapist interpretations and increased insight, increased depth of experiencing, and positive outcome; and, most impressively, greater predictability when patient–therapist interactions are understood in terms of test-passing rather than in terms of frustration of the patient's unconscious wishes.

Weiss and Sampson's emphasis on unconscious pathogenic beliefs as the core of psychopathology suggests parallels and points of convergence, not only with the research and theory on social cognition discussed in the Singer and Singer chapter, but also specifically with cognitive behavior theory and therapy, where the focus is also on the role of maladaptive belief systems in symptomatology and psychopathology. As has been pointed out elsewhere (Eagle, 1987), the pathogenic beliefs discussed by Weiss and Sampson "are similar, in important respects, to the schemata and 'rules of living' invoked by Beck and his colleagues (e.g., Beck, Rush, Shaw, & Emery, 1979) to account for the cognitive distortions associated with depression. Both involve implicit assumptions and belief systems that are dysfunctional and are associated with maladaptive behaviors and dysphoric affects (above all, anxiety and depression)." (p. 168) However, there are also important differences between Weiss and Sampson's control-mastery theory and cognitive–behavior theory. In the latter, little attention is given to developmental issues and to the object-relational context in which pathogenic beliefs are acquired. Moreover, whereas Beck, for example, discusses a *general* set of dysfunctional beliefs (i.e., his "cognitive triad" of negative concepts about oneself, the future, and the external world), Weiss and Sampson focus on *idiosyncratic* pathogenic beliefs that grow out of early personal experiences that take on unconscious meanings in relation to parental figures and that are pathogenic to the extent that they conflict with normal developmental goals and aims (e.g., separating and achieving some degree of autonomy). Finally, and of great importance, because their perspective is psychoanalytic, according to Weiss and Sampson, pathogenic beliefs are both *enacted* in the transference relationship with the therapist and, under favorable conditions, are *disconfirmed* in the therapeutic relationship. By contrast, in cognitive–behavior therapy, the focus is on pointing out and "correcting" dysfunctional beliefs rather than identifying them as they are enacted in the therapeutic relationship and transforming them in the context of that relationship. With regard to this last point, Safran (1984), himself a cognitive behavior therapist and theorist, has noted that cognitive–behavior therapists typically neglect the information available from their interactions with the patient and suggests that the cognitive behavior therapist should actively "use the therapeutic relationship to disconfirm the client's dysfunctional expectations about interpersonal relationships." The incorporation of Safran's comments and suggestions into the theory and practice of cognitive behavior therapy would, of course, narrow the differences mentioned above between Weiss and Sampson's control-mastery theory and cognitive behavior theory and practice.

Although it is not emphasized in Sampson's chapter, the fact is that Weiss and Sampson's conception of transference is radically different, in important respects, from the classical Freudian conception. According to the latter, the essence of transference lies in the patient's attempt to gratify unconscious instinctual wishes. That is, the transference reflects the patient's drive to repeat rather than remember and, in that sense, constitutes a primary expression of resistance. Thus, by analyzing the patient's transference, the therapist is at the same time analyzing the patient's resistances. In contrast to this traditional view, Weiss and Sampson propose that the patient repeats, or, more accurately, enacts, core relationship themes, not in order to gratify infantile instinctual wishes but in order to disconfirm early pathogenic beliefs and to master early anxieties and conflicts. Singer and Singer would make the additional point that people repeat relationship patterns because the schemas and scripts that they have developed help order their experience of the world and render it familiar, understandable, and predictable.

Finally, in both the relatively rigorous methods that they use and in the content of the theoretical formulations and hypotheses that they have developed, Weiss, Sampson, and colleagues have helped forge closer links between psychoanalysis and psychology and, as Sampson notes at the end of his chapter, have helped "bring psychoanalysis into the mainstream of contemporary science, making it part of a larger scientific enterprise."

The chapter by Binder, Strupp, and Rock deals with a topic about which little is written in the psychoanalytic literature, namely, explicit and specific discussions of therapeutic technique. As they point out, the psychoanalytic theory of treatment provides only general principles, such as the importance of lifting repressions, rather than specific and practical guidelines on technique. As they also point out, there is often a very tenuous connection between psychoanalytic theories of mental functioning and therapeutic technique.[3] Furthermore, in much clinical case material published in psychoanalytic journals, one gets relatively little detailed information about what the analyst actually and specifically *does* in the treatment situation.

The authors demonstrate the vagueness of the psychoanalytic literature in accounting for the commonly recognized components of therapeutic skill, including the comprehension and organization of clinical data, the recognition of thematic patterns, the use of clinical supervision, and the application of theoretical knowledge to clinical work. The authors maintain that, in all of these areas, in the psychoanalytic literature, there is not an adequate identification of the complex perceptual and cognitive processes that are necessary for competent therapeutic work.

---

[3]See Berger, 1985, for an extended discussion of the lack of a clear relationship between theory and practice in psychoanalysis.

The authors further suggest that those interested in understanding and improving psychoanalytic technique can profitably look to the cognitive psychology literature on the acquisition of skills and the nature of expert performance in various domains. They proceed to examine a number of skills that are involved in expert performance, including pattern recognition, the capacity to combine declarative knowledge (*knowing that*) and procedural knowledge (*knowing how*) in a smoothly spontaneous performance, and the capacity to engage in self-monitoring and self-regulating in the course of performing.

One of the challenges involved in becoming a competent performer or an expert is the ability to transform declarative knowledge (i.e., propositional knowledge of facts, concepts, etc.) into procedural, "use-oriented" knowledge. When an individual cannot do that well, he or she might be said to be possessed of "inert" knowledge, that is, knowledge that is not integrated with and spontaneously accessible to the learner at the appropriate performance time. According to the authors, much of current training in psychotherapy (e.g., didactic courses unintegrated with practical experience) encourages the development of inert knowledge. They suggest changes in the training of therapists, and they point to a skills theory of psychoanalytic technique that would focus on the generic perceptual and cognitive functions necessary for competent performance in any knowledge domain, the discrete technical acts that are part of a skillful psychoanalytic psychotherapy, and the strategies for implementing combinations and sequences of these technical acts.

This chapter has important implications for clinical training in psychotherapy—psychoanalytic or otherwise—and those involved in clinical psychology training programs would do well to consider it seriously. Given the relatively closed nature of traditional psychoanalytic training institutes, one wonders about the likelihood of their instituting the kinds of changes in training suggested in this chapter. In conjunction with Division 39 chapters, a number of psychoanalytic training institutes have been and will continue to be established. Will these training institutes mirror the traditional psychoanalytic institutes or will they be more open to the kinds of concerns and procedures highlighted in this chapter?

Finally, Binder, Strupp, and Rock call for research on the effectiveness of training procedures in teaching practitioners a variety of therapeutic skills and competencies. There is an implicit assumption in the chapter that increased skill and improved technique is lawfully and intrinsically linked to better therapeutic outcome. But this issue would need to be addressed explicitly. Thus, the research program that the authors call for would need to study the relationship among the variables of instructional methods, degree and kind of competence achieved as revealed in the specific techniques employed, and therapeutic outcome. The linking of technique to therapeutic outcome is especially important in view of the frequent claim (see Tansey's chapter) that the personal qualities of the therapist that are expressed and translated into an attitude of warmth, respect, and support and into forging a helping alliance (see Luborsky, Barber, & Crits-Christoph's chapter) are perhaps more important than technique in achieving positive therapeutic outcome.[4] Given Binder, Strupp, and Rock's emphasis on technique in their chapter, it is ironic that, in his chapter, Tansey mildly takes Strupp to task for stressing relationship over technique factors. We would expect that Strupp would not sharply demarcate between these two sets of factors but would tend to view the establishment of a helping alliance as a critical aspect of good technique.

In Tansey's chapter on countertransference, the author acknowledges that, prior to researching and writing it, he had been exceedingly skeptical regarding the value of systematic

---

[4]Luborsky, Barber, and Crits-Christoph present evidence that accuracy of interpretation—surely as aspect of technique—is related to good outcome. They also refer to Sach's (1983) study reporting that errors in technique were related to poorer outcome. However, Tansey points out that Luborsky et al. (1988) rank technique last among curative factors in psychotherapy.

empirical (particularly quantitative) research for understanding clinical issues. Obviously opting for the value of countertransference disclosure, he describes his experience as one of a new respect for research and for researchers dealing with the psychotherapy process. (The editors certainly hope that Tansey's experience will be prototypical of the analytically oriented reader's response to this volume.)

Tansey presents a brief overview of different perspectives on the concept of countertransference, from Freud's position that countertransference always represents an impediment to treatment to the later "totalist" view, in which all emotional reactions to the patient are considered part of the countertransference and are examined to provide information on what is going on in the patient. According to at least some versions of this latter view, rather than constituting an impediment to treatment, countertransference represents a useful tool for determining the inner state of the patient. Tansey ends up favoring a balanced position, associated with Racker (1957), that is somewhere between the two extremes. According to this position, countertransference, like transference, can represent both the greatest danger and the greatest tool in treatment.

Tansey next reviews a selective sample of psychotherapy research (the work of Orlinsky and Howard, Strupp and his colleagues, Luborsky and his colleagues, and Wallerstein) that he believes is relevant to understanding the nature and role of countertransference. The conclusion warranted by the research evidence, according to the author, is that the therapist's attitudes and feelings toward the patient are perhaps the most important factors, in the outcome of psychotherapy. This is seen in a number of findings pointing to the role of the helping alliance and the therapist's responsiveness and supportiveness in positive therapeutic outcome. Tansey links these findings to the issue of countertransference by observing that it is difficult to be supportive and forge a helping alliance unless the therapist can manage his or her countertransference reactions and place them in the service of the treatment. Tansey discusses sexual contact between therapist and patient as a blatant and destructive example of the therapist's inability to manage countertransference reactions. He also observes that there are remarkably few papers (perhaps none at all) in the literature on countertransference sexual feelings.

Tansey's overall conclusion is that "the consistent and unanimous message across all four studies . . . cited is that the quality of the relationship reigns supreme as a curative factor." Contrastingly, he finds that the curative role of accurate interpretations is not as clear and conclusive.[5] He then observes that the studies he has summarized support the developmental arrest and relational-conflict models of psychoanalysis. Although one can understand that an emphasis on the importance of the therapeutic relationship in treatment would be especially compatible with a relational-conflict model, its link to a developmental arrest model is not as apparent. Because the development of a therapeutic alliance and the provision of support are especially helpful in treatment does not appear to constitute evidence that the patients helped are suffering from developmental arrests or that psychopathology is best understood in terms of developmental arrests. These are, however, highly significant questions that merit further investigation and thought.

The chapter by Luborsky, Barber, and Crits-Christoph reviews six central psychoanalytic propositions about change in psychodynamic psychotherapy and the empirical research bearing on them. Furthermore, the authors present their views on the kind of future research that would be useful in this area. The propositions that they examine were taken from a representative sample of research on the technique of psychodynamic psychotherapy.

The first proposition is that a therapeutic alliance must develop if the patient is to benefit

---

[5]See the chapter by Luborsky, Barber, and Crits-Christoph for evidence that accuracy of interpretations is related to positive outcome.

from psychodynamic psychotherapy. The authors briefly review the different operational measures of the therapeutic alliance and point to the general finding from a number of studies that measures of therapeutic alliance significantly predict outcome (e.g., the mean correlation from eight studies was .5).

The second proposition is that patients display a central relationship theme (the transference pattern). One of the breakthroughs in the reliable measurement of transference patterns was Luborsky's (1984) development of the Core Conflictual Relationship Theme (CCRT) method. Patients' narratives about their interactions with people, including the therapist, are scored on three components: the wishes toward others, the responses of the others, and the responses of the self. A series of studies using the CCRT method generated findings consistent with the proposition that a central relationship theme is expressed in interaction with other people as well as with the therapist. As in the Singer and Singer chapter, these authors relate the transference pattern to the *schema* concept in cognitive psychology and note the general finding that, once a schema has been established, new information tends to be assimilated into that schema.

The third proposition is that the therapists' interpretations of the patients' transference pattern will be especially beneficial in treatment. Their brief review of the research relevant to this proposition indicates inconclusive results, with some studies providing support for the proposition and others failing to do so.

The fourth proposition states that accurate interpretations will be especially beneficial in treatment. One of the thorny problems in this area has been the unavailability of reliable and independent criteria for accuracy of interpretation. Obviously, unless one has such criteria, it is difficult to evaluate the proposition. One of the interesting and important developments in this area is the availability of reliable and independently assessed measures of accuracy of interpretation. One such measure is the degree of compatibility between the therapists' interpretations and the patients' unconscious plan—each measure assessed independently of the other (Weiss & Sampson, 1986; also, see Sampson's chapter in this volume). Another recent measure is the degree of convergence between the therapists' interpretations and the patients' independently assessed CCRT (Crits-Christoph, Cooper, & Luborsky, 1988).

A number of studies in which each of these measures was used suggests a positive relationship between accuracy of interpretations (in specified areas such as interpretations related to the patients' wish and the response from the other) and good outcome. This is an important area about which there has been much, perhaps unnecessary, controversy (e.g., interpretation vs. the therapeutic relationship). Perhaps the controversy will yield to empirical findings. Clearly, more work needs to be done in this area.

The fifth proposition discussed in this chapter is that patients gain self-understanding during psychodynamic treatment and that such understanding leads to better outcome. Although the concept of *insight* (obviously, a synonym for *self-understanding*) plays a central role in theoretical formulations of psychodynamic treatment, there is little systematic empirical evidence related to it. As the authors observe, this may (in part, at least) be due to the unavailability of useful and reliable measures of self-understanding. Although the authors do not make this point, one can speculate that the findings noted above on the relationship between accuracy of interpretations and good outcome may indirectly support the proposition that self-understanding is positively related to good outcome. These findings are not definitive, insofar as it is possible that the main reason that accuracy of interpretations is related to positive outcome is that the patient *feels understood* (Kohut, 1984) rather than that he or she has gained self-understanding and insight. Hence, as the authors observe, the discipline really needs reliable measures of self-understanding and studies of the relationship between these measures and therapeutic outcome.

The sixth and final proposition is that improved patients will show a greater change in their transference patterns than unimproved patients. Although they have limited data, the authors present the fascinating finding that although the wish component of the CCRT tended to remain unchanged, the patients' expectations of others and responses from self became less negative in the course of treatment. Furthermore, these changes were significantly correlated with overall improvement in the patients' mental health.

In the final section of their chapter, Luborsky, Barber, and Crits-Christoph discuss areas in which future research on psychodynamic psychotherapy should focus. These include: capacity for internalization as a factor in maintaining therapy gains; resistance; working through; greater awareness and understanding of unconscious conflictual material; and the relation between the therapists' adherence to recommendations regarding technique and outcome (see the chapter by Binder, Strupp, and Rock). They also observe that research on psychodynamic psychotherapy constitutes a good basis for rapprochement between psychoanalysis and psychology. Their specific examples of such rapprochement include links between studies on the helping alliance and the broader area of research on attachment in children and adults; between relationship interactions in psychotherapy and the work on schemas in cognitive psychology (as noted earlier, Singer and Singer's chapter thoroughly investigates these links) and between investigations of accuracy of interpretations and the broader work on the sources and nature of empathy in children and adults. Surely, this chapter, along with many other chapters in this volume, makes it clear that the rapprochement between psychoanalysis and psychology is a natural and desirable development that would benefit both fields.

Finally, we come to Spence's chapter on interpretation in psychoanalytic theory and practice. Spence takes Strachey's (1934) classic paper, "The Nature of Therapeutic Action in Psychoanalysis" as his model for psychoanalytic thinking about interpretation. According to Spence, the psychoanalytic approach to interpretation is similar in many respects to medieval reasoning, a system of reasoning in which many things in the world are looked at as a system of outward signatures and signs of buried similarities. Relating two items by analogy would be an example of such a system. Thus, in Spence's specific example of interpretation by analogy, the therapist may interpret the vigorous house-cleaning activity of a patient planning termination of therapy as symbolic of that termination. According to Spence, although the Newtonian revolution put an end to medieval reasoning in science, it still predominates in psychoanalytic interpretation and clinical practice.

This kind of reasoning by "signatures" and the general tendency to "find" clinical evidence supporting one's theoretical preconceptions are rooted, according to Spence, in a number of cognitive tendencies that are elucidated by experimental studies of clinical judgment and memory. These studies suggest that, in the absence of systematic records, therapists will overestimate events predicted by their preferred theory and tend to minimize or overlook phenomena incompatible with that theory. These tendencies have obvious implications regarding the evidential value of the typical case report and, according to Spence, help account for the persistence of claims unsupported by adequate evidence.

One such claim, Spence suggests, is that a "well-crafted interpretation, because of its form and content, can bring about a significant clinical effect."[6] Spence presents a number of "specimen interpretations" found in the literature, most of which are found wanting, and some of which serve as examples of valid interpretations. An important feature, distinguishing the two sets of examples is that the latter provide information on the patients' response and the clinical changes brought about by the interpretation (e.g., remembering something long forgotten; an

---

[6]The work on accuracy of interpretation and therapeutic outcome reported by Luborsky, Barber, and Crits-Christoph represents an attempt to test this claim empirically.

abrupt change of emotional mood, whereas the former do not. Here Spence seems to equate the clinical effectiveness of an interpretation with its veridicality and seems to endorse a version of Freud's insistence that only interpretations that "tally with what is real" in the patient will have a therapeutic impact (see Grünbaum, 1984, for a further discussion of this issue).

In the next section of the chapter, however, Spence makes clear his view that the clinical effectiveness of an interpretation is a complex function of such factors as the developmental level of the patient and the state of the transference. Thus, some so-called pre-oedipal patients may not be able to benefit from any verbal interpretation for a long period of time. Moreover, generally speaking, the sense as well as the clinical effect of an interpretation may depend on the state of the transference. Thus, if the transference is very positive, a wide range of interpretations may be endowed with clinical and persuasive power. It follows from all this, Spence concludes, that without information on the developmental phase being re-enacted by the patient and the state of the transference we cannot tell why an interpretation failed or succeeded. Spence's suggestion is that every clinical specimen include information on the re-enacted developmental period, the state of the transference, and other surrounding clinical features. Although more contextual information is always useful in understanding clinical specimens, we would expect that there would be enormous problems with the reliability of judgments regarding the particular developmental period being re-enacted, the state of the transference, and other matters. Many of the same problems afflicting case reports that Spence highlights in this chapter—for example, the degree to which one's theoretical predilections influence what one observes and "sees" in the patient—would apply at least equally to reports of the developmental period re-enacted by the patient and of the state of the transference. In these areas, too, the issue of reliability arises, and, in general, there appears to be no substitute for the use of the kinds of quasi-experimental designs (e.g., blind and independent judges; the use of some sort of control) typified by, for example, the work of Luborsky and his colleagues and of Sampson and his colleagues.

Spence's overall conclusion is that the theory of interpretation in psychoanalysis is seriously out of touch with clinical practice and that, perhaps, "verbal interpretations are significantly overrated as a therapeutic tool." Spence's point here, as we understand it, is that the effects of an interpretation are always a function of the "developmental surround" and the nature and state of the relationship between patient and therapist. Hence, it would be relatively meaningless to study the effects of interpretations without taking these contextual factors into account. We would add to this point the observation that there is probably an ongoing dialectic between the nature of interpretations and the patient–therapist relationship, so that an accurate and empathic interpretation in which the patient *feels understood* (Kohut, 1984) helps in forging a positive relationship and in which a positive relationship, in turn, makes it more likely that the interpretation will be received in a way that renders it clinically effective. This bidirectional interaction probably characterizes the nature of communication in all relationships, not just the therapeutic one.

Spence's chapter is chock full of stimulating ideas and constitutes the outlines of a veritable research program dealing with a psychoanalytic theory of interpretation. There are enough implicit suggestions here to keep a large number of researchers meaningfully occupied for a long time.

Indeed, all the chapters in this section are filled with implicit and explicit suggestions for future research. They also vividly demonstrate the propelling idea underlying this volume: the interface between psychoanalysis and psychology. Although the chapters focus explicitly on what psychology (.e.g., cognitive psychology, research methods) can offer psychoanalysis, there are also implicit suggestions regarding what psychoanalysis offers psychology. Psychoanalysis brings to psychology a set of vital insights, phenomena, and concerns—such as the nature of transference and countertransference, and the nature of psychoanalytic and psychotherapy technique, including the role of interpretation—and it challenges psychology to incorporate these insights, phenomena, and concerns into its theories and research.

REFERENCES

Abelson, R. P. (1981). Psychological status of the script concept. *American Psychologist, 36*, 715–729.

Bachrach, H. M., Galatzer-Levy, R., Skolnikoff, A., & Waldron Jr., S. (1991). *Journal of the American Psychoanalytic Association, 39*(4), 871–916.

Beebe, B., & Lachmann, F. (1988). *The contribution of mother–infant mutual influence to the origins of self- and object representations. Psychoanalytic Psychology, 5*(4), 305–337.

Beck, A. T., Rush, A. J., Shaw, B. F., & Emery C. (1979). *Cognitive theory of depression.* New York: Guilford Press.

Berger, L. S. (1985). *Psychoanalytic theory and clinical relevance: What makes a theory consequential for practice?* Hillsdale, NJ: Erlbaum.

Bowlby, J. (1973). *Attachment and loss: Vol. 2. Separation.* New York: Basic Books.

Crits-Christoph, P., Cooper, A., & Luborsky, L. (1988). The accuracy of therapists' interpretations and the outcome of dynamic psychotherapy. *Journal of Consulting and Clinical Psychology, 56*, 490–495.

Eagle, M. (1987). The psychoanalytic and the cognitive unconscious. In R. Stern (Ed.), *Theories of the unconscious and theories of the self* (pp. 155–189). Hillsdale, NJ: Analytic Press.

Eagle, M., & Wolitzky, D. L. (1981). Therapeutic influences in psychoanalytic treatment. In S. Slipp (Ed.), *Curative factors in psychodynamic therapy* (pp. 349–378). New York: McGraw-Hill.

Eagle, M., & Wolitzky, D. L. (1989). The idea of progress in psychoanalysis. *Psychoanalysis and Contemporary Thought, 12*, 27–72.

Freud, S. (1953). The interpretation of dreams. In J. Strachey (Ed.), *The standard edition of the psychological works of Sigmund Freud* (Vol. 5). London: Hogarth Press. (Original work published 1900)

Gedo, J. (1984). Letter to the Editor. *Review of Psychoanalytic Books, 3*, 511–515.

Gill, M. M. (1982). *Analysis of transference: Vol 1. Theory and technique.* Madison, CT: International Universities Press.

Grünbaum, A. (1984). *The foundations of psychoanalysis: A philosophical critique.* Berkeley & Los Angeles: University of California Press.

Kantrowitz, J. L., Paolitto, F., Sashin, J., Solomon, L., & Katz, A. L. (1986). Affect availability, tolerance, complexity, and modulation in psychoanalysis: Followup of a longitudinal, prospective study. *Journal of the American Psychoanalytic Association, 34*(3), 529–559.

Kantrowitz, J., Katz, A. L., Paolitto, F., Sashin, J., & Solomon, L. (1987). Changes in the level and quality of object relations in psychoanalysis: Follow-up of a longitudinal prospective study. *Journal of the American Psychoanalytic Association, 35*(1), 23–46.

Kantrowitz, J. L., Katz, A. L., Greenman, D. A., Morris, H., Paolitto, F., Sashin, J., & Solomon, L. (1989). The patient–analyst match and the outcome of psychoanalysis: A pilot study. *Journal of the American Psychoanalytic Association, 37*(4), 893–920.

Kantrowitz, J. L., Katz, A. L., & Paolitto, F. (1990a). Follow-up of psychoanalysis five to ten years after termination: I. Stability of change. *Journal of the American Psychoanalytic Association, 38*(2), 471–496.

Kantrowitz, J. L., Katz, A. L., & Paolitto, F. (1990b). Follow-up of psychoanalysis five to ten years after termination: II. Development of the self-analytic function. *Journal of the American Psychoanalytic Association, 38*(3), 637–650.

Kantrowitz, J. L., Katz, A. L., & Paolitto, F. (1990c). Follow-up of psychoanalysis five to ten years after termination: III. The relation between the resolution of the transference and the patient–analyst match. *Journal of the American Psychoanalytic Association, 38*(3), 651–678.

Kernberg, O. F. (1976). *Object relations theory and clinical psychoanalysis.* New York: Jason Aronson.

Kohut, H. (1984). *How does analysis cure?* Chicago: University of Chicago Press.

Luborsky, L. (1984). *Principles of psychoanalytic psychotherapy: A manual for supportive–expressive (SE) treatment.* New York: Basic Books.

Luborsky, L., Crits-Christoph, P., Mintz, J., & Auerbach, A. (1988). *Who will benefit from psychotherapy? Predicting therapeutic outcomes.* New York: Basic Books.

Piaget, J. (1926/1955). *The language and thought of the child.* Cleveland, OH: Worth.

Racker, H. (1957). The meanings and uses of countertransference. *Psychoanalytic Quarterly, 26,* 303–357.

Rothstein, A. (Ed.) (1988). *How does treatment help?* Madison, CT: International Universities Press.

Sachs, J. (1983). Negative factors in brief psychotherapy: An important assessment. *Journal of Consulting and Clinical Psychology, 51,* 557–564.

Safran, J. (1984). Some implications of Sullivan's interpersonal theory for cognitive therapy. In M. A. Reda & M. J. Mahoney (Eds.), *Cognitive psychotherapies: Recent developments in theory, research, and practice* (pp. 251–272). Cambridge, MA: Ballinger.

Stern, D. (1985). *The interpersonal world of the infant.* New York: Basic Books.

Strachey, J. (1934). The nature of the therapeutic action of psychoanalysis. *International Journal of Psychoanalysis, 15,* 127–159.

Sullivan, H. S. (1953). *The interpersonal theory of psychiatry.* New York: Norton.

Thompson, R. A. (1991). Construction and reconstruction of early attachments: Taking perspective on attachment theory and research. In D. P. Keating & H. Rosen (Eds.), *Constructionist perspectives on developmental psychopathology and atypical development.* Hillsdale, NJ: Erlbaum.

Tomkins, S. S. (1970). A theory of memory. In J. S. Antrobus (Ed.), *Cognition and affect* (pp. 59–130). New York: Little Brown.

Tomkins, S. S. (1979). Script theory: Differential magnification of affects. In H. E. Howe, Jr., & M. M. Page (Eds.), *Nebraska symposium on motivation* (Vol. 27, pp. 201–236). Lincoln, NE: University of Nebraska Press.

Tomkins, S. S. (1987). Script theory. In J. Aronoff, A. I. Rabin, & R. A. Zucker (Eds.), *The emergence of personality* (pp. 147–216). New York: Springer.

Weiss, J., Sampson, H., & the Mount Zion Psychotherapy Research Group (1986). *The psychoanalytic process: Theory, clinical observation, and empirical research.* New York: Guilford Press.

Wolitzky, D. L. (1990). Pathways to psychoanalytic cure. *Contemporary Psychology, 35*(12), 1154–1155.

23

TRANSFERENCE IN PSYCHOTHERAPY AND DAILY LIFE: IMPLICATIONS OF CURRENT MEMORY AND SOCIAL COGNITION RESEARCH

JEFFERSON A. SINGER AND JEROME L. SINGER

He who does not make the experiment . . . will scarcely believe how much a few hours take from certainty of knowledge and distinctiveness of imagery; how the succession of objects will be broken, how separate parts will be confused, and how many particular features and discriminations will be compressed and conglobated into one gross and general idea. (Johnson, 1775/1985, p. 122)

The phenomenon of transference is one of the contributions of Freud that is likely to endure as a major discovery in behavioral science. At first observed by Freud as a specific feature of the psychoanalytic process, he soon came to realize that transferences, the hidden agendas based on childhood experience, which we all bring to each new social encounter, are an intrinsic feature of human interaction. This conception has deeply enriched our understanding of the complexity of even relatively minor social relations; it helps us to grasp what often seems puzzling in ongoing intimate relationships as well as in more casual encounters. Although Freud regarded the transference "as both the greatest danger and the greatest tool for analytic work" (Racker, 1988, p. 158), he also made clear his recognition of the importance of the phenomenon outside of the treatment process. He came to see transferences as a general human experience in which individuals bring longstanding wishes and conflicts into new adult interactions with spouses, co-workers, or authorities (Freud, 1912/1958, 1925/1959a, 1937/1959b).

Some of the research by the authors described in this chapter was conducted in connection with the Program on Conscious and Unconscious Mental Processes, University of California, San Francisco, School of Medicine and was funded by a grant from the John D. and Catherine T. MacArthur Foundation.

Recent developments in the study of person memory, and of social cognition more generally, have begun to confirm Freud's observation about the presence of transference beyond the boundaries of the analytic session. In fact, transference may be an inherent property of much of social information processing (J. L. Singer, 1985, J. L. Singer, Sincoff, & Kolligian, 1989). In this chapter, we examine some of the relevant theory and research from cognitive and social–personality psychology that can help us articulate this broader perspective on the transference phenomenon. We also examine the status of research support for the use of transference analysis in psychotherapy.

Although one of psychoanalysis's defining characteristics has always been the analysis of the transference between patient and therapist (Bird, 1972; Chrzanowski, 1979; Gill, 1982; Kernberg, 1987; Langs, 1989; Schimek, 1983), an almost exclusive focus on the patient–therapist interaction, early suggested by Sullivan (1953) and Ruesch (1961), has been more and more stressed by psychoanalysts like Gill (1982; 1984), Langs (1989), and Schafer (1977; 1983). We therefore address the question of whether an exclusive focus on the patient–therapist transference is critical for psychotherapeutic progress or whether a more general emphasis on identifying maladaptive person schemas[1] (Horowitz, 1991) or "pathogenic beliefs" about others (Weiss & Sampson, 1986) may be as effective in promoting personality change. Psychotherapies using Kelly's personal construct orientation (Kelly, 1955) or a cognitive–behavioral orientation (Salovey & J. A. Singer, 1991) also depend heavily on examination of patterns of thought that may or may not involve the therapist but may be self-defeating in interpersonal interactions.

In this chapter, we hope to provide an initial attempt to utilize relevant social cognition and memory data to outline a conception of how transferences may operate both in therapy and in daily life. We also hope to forge links between not only the experimental literature and psychodynamic therapy, but also between psychodynamic and cognitive therapies. We begin with a case study in which the transference phenomenon seems clearly manifest, perhaps even to the eyes of an "objective" cognitive researcher.

CASE STUDY OF TOM

Tom was a 26-year-old, diabetic, single, White man who was self-employed as a house-cleaner. He was seen twice weekly for a 2-year period in individual psychotherapy. His presenting problems were dissatisfaction with both his work and his relationships. Although he held a BA in economics and had aspirations to attend graduate school to become an accountant, he was unable to give up his work cleaning private homes. Similarly, though he had had a series of relationships, he had still not married or felt genuinely fulfilled or respected by any of the women with whom he had been involved.

Tom's father had come from a relatively well-off family, but had ended up working in the post office, while the father's sister had become a physician. Tom's father drank excessively and was verbally abusive and mockingly critical of Tom as he grew up. Tom's mother did not work and was dominated by his father. She doted on Tom and was often a source of comfort for him.

In the first session and again in the 22nd session, Tom described an early emotional memory that encapsulated many of the major themes of the therapy:

> It was in first grade. I was given a green pencil along with the other children. I wanted to bend it to see how far it would go. It broke. Then the teacher asked us all to write and I asked for a new pencil. She held up the brown pencil she was about to give me to replace the broken

[1]Although we recognize that the classical plural of *schema* is *schemata*, we prefer to follow George Mandler's usage of the simple English plural.

one. She said, " 'B' is for 'Brown' and for 'Baby'." She held me in front of the class and showed them the broken pencil. Each time I tried to turn away from the eyes of the class, the teacher yanked my head back. Finally, she punished me by putting me at the back of the room in the clothes closet. It had a window and supplies and I started to feel pretty safe in there, less depressed.

In discussion of the importance of the memory to Tom, the following meanings emerged. Tom was being exploratory and playful by bending the pencil. Though his experiment failed, he was not too upset by this setback. However, a teacher and caregiver misinterpreted his initiative and condemned it, evoking feelings of failure in Tom. Furthermore, she humiliated him in front of his peers, leaving him both angry at authorities and ashamed. As the crowning defeat, he was judged unfit to be in the company of his fellow students and banished to isolation. Once in the coat closet, he found solace in his removal from a hostile society, but also sensed he was not worthy to rejoin his peers.

The themes of failed initiatives, hostile authorities, and rejecting peers with resulting shame, low self-esteem, and finally comfort in a protective marginality formed the core of Tom's depression and were the foci of the dynamic therapy. Not surprisingly, this complicated pattern of emotions, behaviors, and cognitions telescoped in his first-grade memory was recreated in his relationship with the therapist.

Through the initial sessions, Tom maintained a highly controlled and distant air. He referred to the therapist as "cold" and "professional"—the "automatic hug machine." He often came five minutes late and expressed indifference to the therapist's vacations. He repeatedly spoke of jaw and neck pain, while condemning supposed healers, who withheld the comfort and cure he desired.

Throughout this first year of treatment, Tom's depression persisted at a mild-to-moderate level. He linked his continued dysphoria to the therapist's withholding of advice or treatment strategies that would elevate his mood. In response to repeated requests by Tom, an antidepressant trial was initiated. Tom elected to stop the trial after 3 weeks, concluding that his depression was not grave enough to warrant the side effects of the medication.

Still convinced that the therapist was not giving him what he needed, Tom then requested that cognitive–behavioral methods be attempted. After several weeks of efforts in this regard with some behavioral progress toward his goal of entering graduate school, he decided to set aside this approach as well.

At this point, Tom had reached a critical crossroads in his therapy. He had portrayed the therapist for the first 1½ years of treatment as a distant, withholding figure. He had focused on poor caretaking by others as the key to his chronic setbacks rather than look at his own fear of taking risks or making changes. Now after he had received two interventions based on his own requests and had voluntarily given them up, he was forced to look at his own defensive structure and his intense feelings of fear and anger toward the therapist. In a number of emotional sessions continuing over several weeks, he slowly articulated his fear that he would be criticized and rejected by the therapist. He spoke about unconsciously hurting himself after feeling slighted in therapy rather than revealing his hurt or anger. Afraid to show weakness, he equally feared appearing healthy based on the belief that the therapist would no longer be interested in him or would expect too much of him.

As the patient identified his fear of rejection by the therapist, he also grasped the power and breadth of his defenses. He felt embarrassment that he painted the therapist as a machine and made a renewed effort to check his tendencies toward abstraction and overcontrolling behavior. His affect became much less restricted and his interpersonal warmth increased markedly. Although he experienced appropriate sadness and anger as termination neared (due to the therapist's relocation), his overall depression resolved. The clarification of this powerful transference appeared to have ramifications in Tom's life outside of therapy. After 5 years of procrastination, he had entered and successfully completed his first quarter of an accountancy program. He had also found a satisfying relationship and was due to be married 3 weeks after the termination of therapy.

Tom's transference onto the therapist of a critical, withholding father, who shamed and humiliated him, emerged in innumerable exchanges and behavioral patterns over the course of the treatment. Almost 3 months into the therapy, Tom came late to a session and placed a half-eaten apple down on the table by his chair. When asked about the apple, he indicated that he assumed he was not supposed to eat during the hour, but would need to finish eating after the session due to his diabetic condition. He denied that the apple or his lateness held any meaning or communicative value concerning his feelings toward the therapy or the therapist. He called the therapist, "a still voice in a dark room" and explained his display of the unfinished apple as only "a question of logistics." The therapist pointed out that Tom had assumed he would be forbidden from eating his apple without confirming that this would indeed be the case. Tom then responded that it was also his assumption that if he asked for anything from the therapist he would not get it and that if he revealed himself too nakedly to the therapist, the therapist would not like him. Tom and the therapist were then able to explore the passive–aggressive pattern that the apple embodied. Assuming rejection, Tom deprived himself of his necessary nourishment; yet at the same time, he placed the browning apple provocatively between the therapist and himself. Failing to make his needs and his consequent vulnerability known, he could secretly harbor resentment against an authority that deprived him of an opportunity to meet those needs. Through avoiding any inquiry about the apple, he both avoided being hurt by another person and was able to maintain a safe (albeit resentful) distance from a dangerous authority. Additionally, he could "soil" the therapist's office as indirect retribution for the therapist's imagined denial of his request.

The self-defeating pattern expressed in the patient–therapist transference was acted out in many aspects of his life. He became a housecleaner after leaving a fairly successful position as an assistant manager of a sporting goods store. He had developed a highly conflicted relationship with the manager of the store in which he alternately tried to please him and then provoke him by challenging his authority. He had chosen the housekeeping work precisely because he did not have to answer to authorities and could perform his work in solitude away from social exchanges. Yet, at the same time, he felt demeaned by cleaning up other people's messes and by the low status of his work. He described the passive–aggressive combination of shame and pleasure he would experience when asked at a cocktail party about what type of work he did. Although embarrassed to answer, he also took relish in the awkward silence of the questioner on hearing his reply.

Tom's relationships with women also repeated a similar emotional pattern. Prior to and for the first year of his therapy, he was exclusively involved with women who had come from alcoholic families and for whom he played a caretaking and parental role. These relationships protected him from self-exposure and the potential of being judged inadequate. Yet, with each relationship he would eventually feel that his own needs had become secondary and that he was not known by his partner. At the beginning of therapy, he was living with a woman, but the two were sleeping in separate rooms and growing increasingly unwilling to share emotionally with each other. Although this woman's stoicism in the face of her own alcoholic family had initially appealed to him as a safe retreat from intimate intensity, he had begun to feel isolated and humiliated by her coldness and inaccessibility.

In his therapeutic encounters, his vocational choices, and his romantic relationships, Tom seemed doomed to repeat the painful self-defeating resolution of his first grade memory. Experiencing himself as unworthy and in danger from a hostile world, he sought a haven at the margin of each encounter. From this edge, he looked ruefully outward, exiled from true satisfaction, but momentarily protected from open humiliation. It was at best a crippling compromise that led to dysthymia, somatic complaints, and hopelessness.

SCHEMAS AND SCRIPTS IN CURRENT PSYCHOLOGY RESEARCH

Our case vignette demonstrates the transference phenomenon as it emerges from an early memory of an experience of humiliation by a trusted authority following an innocent childish exploration, the bending of a pencil. The adult patient shows a pattern of distrust and feared humiliation toward a therapist and also reflects this memory and its impact in relation to significant persons outside the therapy situation. If we are to understand transference from the standpoint of current research in cognitive and social psychology, we must first look at the fundamental memory constructs that have emerged from research in the past 30 years.

Schemas

In the shift away from a pure associationist stimulus–response psychology that characterized the so-called "cognitive revolution" of the 1960s, investigators of human information processing found it increasingly necessary to devise constructs to account for the special advantages in human memory of organized and verbally meaningful material. The term *schema* introduced by the neurologist, Head (1926), and in psychology by the classic memory studies of Bartlett (1932), seemed useful as representing an organized cluster of correlated and meaningfully associated experiences or words that possessed special advantages for retention, retrieval, and anticipation of new experiences. Schemas have become the generic constructs that reflect the research on plans (Miller, Galanter, & Pribram, 1960), expectancies (Feather, 1966), personal constructs (Kelly, 1955), and scripts (Schank & Abelson, 1977). For a fuller review of the various strains of theory and research and of the research-based operational definitions of schemas, scripts, and prototypes that relate to the construct of organized memory structures, see J. L. Singer and Salovey (1991).

A schema may be considered a general knowledge structure about a domain including a specification of its principal attributes, the relation among these attributes, as well as specific examples or instances (Taylor & Crocker, 1981). Schemas afford us selection criteria for regulating attention and provide both focus and structure to encoding, storage and retrieval of information in a specific domain (e.g., "fathers, father figures, and authorities" or "dining room sets, furniture, and home furnishings").

Evidence for the utility of schemas for cognitive processing can be found in numerous experimental studies summarized by Alba and Hasher (1983), Fiske and Taylor (1984), Graesser and Nakamura (1982), or Hastie (1981). Fiske and Linville (1980) outlined the advantages of the construct in studies of accurate recall, intruded recall, recognition confidence, recall clustering, and resistance to disconfirmation.

Schemas are also evident in the situations where individuals show inaccuracies of recall when information is schema consistent. When shown words or pictures that had not been previously displayed, but that are consistent with a preestablished schema, individuals will show false-positive responses, asserting with confidence that they had seen these earlier. The power of schemas can be shown by presenting lists of words briefly to people who are then asked to recall as many as possible. Usually, only about 15%–20% of a list can be retrieved but when information is provided that the words fall into schematic categories such as tools, locations, foods, or sporting activities, recall may be tremendously enhanced.

Schemas can be classified further for clinical purposes as person schemas, which might include self and other schemas. The unfortunate term *object relations* that has become so much a part of psychoanalytic discourse may perhaps be better reflected in the form of what Horowitz (1988, 1990) called role relationship models. These represent self-schemas in particular domains (e.g., "father," "mother," "husband," "wife," "student") and significant other schemas (e.g., "parent," "spouse," "teacher," "friend") with the subjective script relations between these two sets of schemas sketched out.

Scripts

Script, a term originated by Tomkins (1970, 1979, 1987), has been generalized and refined for use in studies of artificial intelligence and social cognition by Schank and Abelson (1977). Abelson (1981) has defined the script as a construct that organizes one's understanding of sequences of events. It is not only a grouping of inferences about clusters of events related to nonevent schemas, but may also establish expectations about the specific sequences in which events occur as well as their specific form. Using the phrases "going to the hair salon" or "attending a ballgame" establishes at once for the reader a rather detailed set of specific event sequences and expectancies. From a clinical standpoint, scripts determine our expectancies of the order and specificity of events when we go out on a date, enter into an intimate relationship or a marriage, or start to see a therapist. Experiments show that our personal scripts as well as more generally accepted social scripts often lead to erroneous gap-filling or misremembering of actual experiences when such experiences were not actually part of one's dominant script for a given situation (Bower, Black, & Turner, 1979; Fiske & Taylor, 1984). Termed the "ghost effect" in cognitive research, it appears that when variations of the same script occur, the "ghost" of a general case from the dominant script hovers above related scripts and results in irrelevant gap-filling (Fiske & Taylor, 1984). From this perspective, Tom's transference to the therapist or to his girlfriend of the expected sequence of events drawn from his first grade memory and subsequent memories of rejection or humiliation can be understood as a more complex manifestation of the same ghost effect demonstrated in simple experiments of word or picture recognition. Yet, rather than the mere repetition of perceptual effects, one would expect Tom to be haunted by powerful emotions and meaning distortions inherited from these earlier experiences.

For Tomkins (1979, 1987), as well as for Berne (1964), the script becomes a major unit of human social interaction. Tomkins identified emotion-laden scripts originating in childhood, although, one might add, there is no reason theoretically that they could not develop at any stage of life. They would simply require a series of subsequent experiences that repeated the major sequence of events found in the original formative scene. Using a study in which subjects wrote brief fictional scenarios that indirectly drew on their own personal scripts, Carlson and Carlson (1984) demonstrated that subjects' scripts were organized around powerful emotions such as joy, shame, anger, and fear.

Biases of Scriptal and Schematic Processing

Of special relevance to understanding transference is the consistent research evidence of the biasing effects of self-referential schemas and scripts. Termed "beneffectance, egocentricity, and cognitive conservatism," these consequences of schemas and scripts lead to a tendency to shift one's thoughts or new information to more positive affective directions, an overemphasis on the self-reference of external events, or difficulty in giving up established schemas and scripts even in the face of new or conflicting information (Greenwald, 1980; Greenwald & Pratkanis, 1984; Salovey & J. A. Singer, 1989; J. L. Singer & Salovey, 1991). The power of self-focus is manifest in studies of thought-sampling and on-going consciousness (Klos & J. L. Singer, 1981; J. L. Singer & Bonanno, 1990) and in experiments on memory and incidental recall (Klein & Kihlstrom, 1986; Kreitler & J. L. Singer, 1991; J. A. Singer, 1990). Finally, cognitive conservatism, which leads to a sticking to one's schemas, sometimes at all costs, accounts often not only for the emergence of transferences in therapy, but to their persistence in the face of contrary evidence and, indeed, even after much therapeutic effort has been expended, as Freud noted to his sadness in his paper, "Analysis Terminable and Interminable" (Freud, 1937/1959b). This conservatism in self-schemas was also noticed by Sullivan (1956) in his recognition that early self-concepts proved especially resistant to change in psychotherapy. More recently, it has been proposed that even forms of countertransference reflect the normal biasing properties of schematic structures (J. L. Singer, Sincoff, & Kolligian, 1989).

A SOCIAL COGNITIVE PERSPECTIVE ON TRANSFERENCE

Given this emphasis on the assimilative and biasing properties of schemas and scripts in ongoing information processing, it would appear that transference phenomena detected in psychotherapy can be understood as highly evolved and complex versions of these cognitive structures. Let us examine this possibility by reconceptualizing transference into the language of social cognition and personality psychology.

Motivational Origins of Transference

Although social cognition has tended to avoid reliance on motivational variables, at least until recently (Showers & Cantor, 1985), there is an underlying implicit motive of cognitive organization and clarity that pervades this research. Individuals as information processors seek to reduce the overwhelming complexity of both internal (i.e., thoughts, sensations, emotions, etc.) and external stimuli (Kreitler & Kreitler, 1976; Singer & Bonanno, 1990; White, 1960). From the earliest ages, infants are already using their limited cognitive and imagery skills to shape seemingly random events into schemas that group together sensory experiences, verbal associations, and interactions. These schemas make for efficient retrieval of accumulated experience and for expectation and anticipation as one confronts new situations (Flavell, 1963; Mandler, 1984; Piaget, 1926/1955, 1962). Although Piaget emphasized the cognitive operations involved, the pioneering analyses of Tomkins (1962, 1963, 1991) have also pointed to the link of cognition to emotion. Schemas are used to anticipate future environments and when new experiences cannot be readily assimilated into established schemas, the affects of fear, terror, or surprise are aroused. Scripts are also composed of affective sequences, in which there is usually a sharp change from one affect to another (i.e., fear to sadness to anger, interest to joy to pride, anger to shame to guilt, etc.).

If grouping experiences into organized meaning structures is an overarching human motivation, we should not minimize two other powerful needs that frame the human condition. We seek to attach ourselves physically, socially, and cognitively to intimate others as well as to larger groups (e.g., family, neighborhood, religious and ethnic groups, or nationality). At the same time, we also strive to sustain a central core of individuality, a sense of privacy in thought or autonomy in will, a feeling of agency in our development of unique skills and vocations. This tension between attachment and individuation becomes a central dialectic of the human life course and along with the need for formation of meaning structures probably defines the major dimensions of what it is to be human (Bakan, 1966; Blatt, 1990; D. G. Singer & J. L. Singer, 1990; J. L. Singer & Bonanno, 1990). Transference reflects both the tension between attachment and individuation and the attempt to create meaning from experience. As we engage with a new individual, we struggle to achieve a fresh and unique relationship with this other person. At the same time, the influence of past relationships, and our investment in maintaining these relationships, sway this new encounter to certain familiar patterns, forcing its meaning into a set of previous feelings and understandings. Simultaneously, the therapist brings an entirely different set of uniquely formed feelings and understandings about relationships. In successful relationships, each individual learns over time to compromise these personal agendas to achieve a secure and mutual attachment with another person.

The Development of Specific Transference Patterns

How do transferences take shape? One possibility is they begin with specific episodes, or, to use Tomkins's (1979) term, "nuclear scenes"—experiences that surprise, intrigue, or frighten a child and that are then the subject of repeated reminiscence or fantasy as a part of the stream of consciousness (J. L. Singer, 1985; J. L. Singer & Bonanno, 1990). Such episodes may recur in consciousness as the child (or adult, for that matter) may gradually seek to assimilate the information from an established schema or script or to reshape both old and new experiences into a new schematic structure. Indeed, at this point, the veridical experience may become the basis for a fantasized possible future event or "possible self" (Markus & Nurius, 1986; Markus & Wurf, 1987) so that, in effect, a new personal truth is formed. Sullivan (1953) spoke long ago of parataxic distortions, his concept of transference, as the outcome of a childish association of two disparate events into a presumed causal sequence.

We have already provided some definitions and examples of schemas and scripts and of their properties as memory or anticipatory structures. Now we will focus on how specific nuclear scenes gradually form into scripts through ongoing thought. Tomkins (1979) has proposed that beginning with the nuclear scene, the individual begins an abstracting process that matches new experiences with the nuclear scene and extracts their common properties of affect, plot, setting, and participants. Thus, there are both an increasing set of connected episodes and an emerging abstracted template that organizes these events. Such evolving organization parallels Rumelhart and Ortony's (1977) view of a schema as a data structure for representing generic contents stored in memory; it contains the network of intercorrelations among the constituents of the concept in question. Such a network might operate for storage and retrieval in keeping with a cognitive model of associational structures (Andersen, 1983) or the more recent parallel-distributed models of Rumelhart, McClelland, and the PDP Research Group (1987). The individual nuclear scene begins to serve as a "prototype," in the terminology of Cantor and Mischel (1977) or Rosch and Mervis (1975) in which categories are organized around focal stimuli (or one might say, episodic memories) with less prototypical or "fuzzier" members forming a continuum away from the central prototypic exemplars.

Tomkins (1979) has suggested that scripts that convey positive affect experiences are assembled differently from negatively toned scripts. Negative nuclear scripts grow through the identification of analogous new experiences that highlight similarities to the original nuclear scene. For example, one may meet a new boss and immediately detect a resemblance to one's authoritarian and overly demanding father, setting off a series of nuclear memories about resistance, struggle, and resignation.

On the other hand, positive nuclear scripts grow through the identification of new experiences that resemble the original positive nuclear scene, but vary from it in important ways. Confronted with a new, untested ski slope, one recalls the pride of conquering a first downhill run and now repeats these feelings with a new sensation of challenge and novelty. Positive scenes are magnified in an expansive way; they are variations on a theme. Negative scenes take the new and pull it back into the constricted structure of the past. Although Tomkins does not provide an analysis of why this assembling process should differ based on hedonic value of the scenes, one might propose the following rationale.

Harking back to Freud's concern with the compulsion to repeat in the form of traumatic memories, nightmares, and self-defeating behavioral patterns (Freud, 1920/1959c), these repetitions all involve, we propose, a need to master and work out an unresolved or conflicted experience. Left powerless by a lack of resolution or paralyzed by conflicting wishes, one unconsciously makes an effort to regain control by incorporating the dilemma into the individual's ongoing thoughts and behaviors. The individual assumes ownership of the problem and thereby reduces one aspect of the sense of powerlessness. As long as the individual repetitively raises the conflict or suffers anew the consequence of the self-defeating pattern, the possibility of working through and mastering the dilemma remains. The individual (operating most likely at an unconscious level) forces a new event into the existing structure of a negative script in order to gain yet another opportunity to change the outcome of this script that has ended badly. On the other hand, positive scripts would present the individual with a different agenda, the embellishment of a basic positive experience with new nuances and variants. Rather than seeking resolution, the individual increases the number of cues that will provide access to the positive script. Through variation, the script remains vibrant, interesting, and reinforcing for future activation.

Using Script Theory to Understand Transference Interpretation

Given this conception of differences in magnification of positive and negative scripts, the familiar psychoanalytic dictum—interpret negative transference, but leave positive transference alone—makes sense. By bringing the compulsive repetition of the negative scene to consciousness, the therapist offers the patient exactly the opportunity for mastery that he or she unconsciously seeks. The patient, working with the therapist, can examine an in vivo example of the negative nuclear script in action. This examination can lead to identification of the repetitive affective pattern—the specific sequence of emotions—played out in the role relationship pattern (Horowitz, 1991) with the therapist. Patient and therapist can work to locate "core conflicts" that organize both the affective and relationship patterns (Luborsky & Crits-Christoph, 1990). Armed with an awareness of the nuclear script's imposition onto new relationships and interactions, the patient may slowly gain mastery over the self-defeating effects of this overlearned pattern.

On the other hand, positive transference that grows out of a positive nuclear scene brings to the therapy the energy and excitement that the patient feels in finding a new person to confide in and trust, who, though possessing many of their best qualities, is not mother, father, or spouse. As long as this positive transference is not the overidealizing distortion one might find in a borderline or histrionic patient, the patient will feel enriched by the opportunity to begin anew an intimacy not known since childhood. As the therapy progresses, the patient may detect further variations or nuances around a basic core of trust (C. R. Rogers, 1951), and pleasing affective states (e.g., interest, joy, pride, warmth, empathy, and affection) will continue to emerge.

Empirical Support for Mechanisms of Script Theory

McAdams, Lensky, Daple, and Allen (1988) have recently provided some experimental evidence for this conception of positive and negative scene magnification. Depressed and nondepressed subjects were asked to generate both positive and negative memories and then to group the memories by common features or themes. According to Tomkins's theory, it was predicted that nondepressed subjects would use more categories to describe their positive memories than their negative memories (identifying more variation in positive vs. negative experiences), while depressed subjects would show less ability to see nuances in positive experiences. The results confirmed this hypothesis. Although depressed subjects used roughly the same or more categories to describe negative memories than the nondepressed subjects, the number of categories they generated for positive memories was smaller than the number identified by the nondepressed subjects. This study suggests that nondepressed individuals may seek to expand positive experience through variation, while one mechanism of depression may be the inability to extract nuance and variation from positive experience.

Williams and colleagues, in a series of studies (Moore, Watts, & Williams, 1988; Williams & Broadbent, 1986; Williams & Dritschel, 1988) and using different measures, have also demonstrated the depressed individual's inability to locate and describe specific positive experiences. In fact, the overidealizing positive transference alluded to previously may also reflect an individual's imposition of diffuse or global positive categories on the therapist or their interaction. Such overgeneralized categories are likely to prove ill-fitting when the individual begins to confront the actual specifics of the therapist and the therapeutic relationship. Additionally, these vague categorizations may be prone to distortion and superficiality, lacking an anchor to actual feelings within the self (Shapiro, 1965).

Memory Specificity and Generality: Implications for Transference

The distinction between the specificity or generality of information stored in memory has attracted a great deal of attention in the past 20 years of memory research. Tulving's (1972, 1983) work on semantic and episodic memory has excited the most interest and debate, though cognitive science researchers (Reiser, 1983; Reiser, Black, & Kalamarides, 1986; Schank, 1982) have also presented a hierarchical model of memory in which specific events are indexed within more general categories of recall ("times I have eaten at Italian restaurants" would be subsumed by a larger memory category of "eating at restaurants").

Robinson and Swanson (1990) and Brewer (1986) have both pointed to the need to distinguish summarized or "generic" memories from memories of specific events, identifiably tied to a single date or time period. Barsalou (1988), in a free recall study of how individuals remembered events from their summer vacations, found evidence for the existence of these summarized memories. In a recent series of experiments involving both written and spoken memories of personally significant events, J. A. Singer and Moffitt (1991–1992) demonstrated over a combined sample of approximately 500 subjects, roughly an 80/20 split in single event versus summary memories.

If transference phenomena may be understood as highly elaborated and abstracted summary of memories drawn from a series of single event memories, how might the transition from specific scene to script be characterized? Abelson (1981) early proposed that event schemas or scripts develop through three stages—specific memories, followed by a categorical stage, and finally, a level of abstraction or metascripts. Figure 1 reflects this conception; a single episode (Tom's first-grade memory), becomes part of a series of analogue memories that gradually are integrated into a script. These then form the basis for summary memories that take on properties that are broader and more generalized than the original episodes. At a later stage, a superscript or schema may form, which becomes more semantic in character. It no longer involves an imagistic rendering of the events that comprise the script. Rather, it is a rule or command that captures the essential meaning or theme of the script. In Tom's case, it might be: "Any attempt to join my peers will be met with ridicule or shame" or "Never trust authorities, they will always disappoint you." As

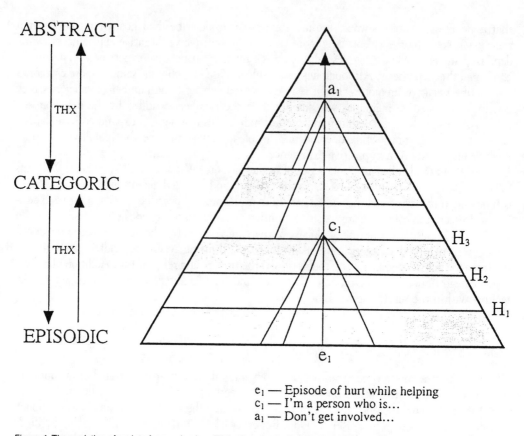

ABSTRACT

CATEGORIC

EPISODIC

THX

THX

e_1 — Episode of hurt while helping
c_1 — I'm a person who is...
a_1 — Don't get involved...

Figure 1. The evolution of scripts from episodes. (This diagram, a visualization of a verbal analysis derived from Abelson, 1981, suggests how a series of comparable memory episodes, for example, "I was trying to help X when she attacked me" gradually merge into a categorical belief, "I'm a person who is often hurt when I try to help," and, finally, becomes an abstract script that governs an array of possible events, "Don't get involved." [The assistance of Charles Stinson in preparation of this figure is gratefully acknowledged.])

Figure 1 makes clear, these metascripts exist at a higher level than summary memories; they operate like overlearned rules that may not even be in our awareness.

Drawing again on memory research on automatic and controlled processing (Schneider & Shiffrin, 1977), and what has been recently described as implicit and explicit memory (Roediger, 1990), once the transference script reaches the level of a metascript, it may pass out of the conscious control of memory. We may transfer highly complex patterns of affective and interpersonal reactions onto new individuals and new relationships with little awareness that these metascripts have been instantiated. The goal of the therapist in working through the transference with the patient would be to return the overlearned automatic metascript to the control of conscious memory and ongoing thought, thereby allowing for relearning and revision.

Other Personality Influences on the Transference Phenomenon

Given the many intense and emotional experiences the child and later the adult encounter, one may wonder how some affective scenes become nuclear and others do not. One key influence we have already discussed in depth is the process of repetition and magnification. Yet, it would also seem that other structures within the personality may contribute to the saliency and pervading influence of certain affective memories. Specifically, there may be aspects of the self-concept that would interact with memory to promote certain scenes to a nuclear quality. In turn, there would be a reciprocal effect on the self through the repetition of and ongoing rumination about these events. Higgins (1987) demonstrated that individuals possess certain beliefs about the self in the form of "what I am" (actual self), "what I might become" (future self), and "how I am perceived by others" (ought self). Discrepancies within or among these self-beliefs can both produce changes in affect and motivate behavior to repair the discrepant self-concept. These self-concept discrepancies have even been correlated with physiological changes in skin conductance and heart rate (Strauman & Higgins, 1987).

As the personality assembles certain nuclear scenes, these actual, future, and ought selves may reinforce and give additional affective intensity to a given scene. If an individual holds the future self belief that "I can become a great person," then a memory that reflects discrepancies ("I was not selected for that special award") or reinforces a different ought self-belief ("my parents told me that being a nice person is more important than winning") may hold particular affective significance.

Along similar lines, J. A. Singer (1990) has demonstrated that longstanding goals within an individual's personality play an important and differentiated role for the affective intensity of autobiographical memories. Subjects were asked to rate the desirability of long-term goals, similar to the personal strivings examined by Emmons (1986, 1989), and to recall a series of autobiographical memories. It was found that affective responses to the memories could be predicted from the memories' relevance to the attainment or nonattainment of the subjects' goals. These findings suggest the possibility that an individual's thoughts and fantasies about important self-beliefs and personal goals may interact with their ongoing recollection of affective memories to help shape a set of nuclear scripts. These scripts, triggered by resemblances in new experiences, invest these experiences with immediacy, emotionality, and personal significance. As this emphasis on thoughts and fantasies suggests, it is not only memory that might lead to the emergence of transference scripts. The stream of consciousness provides an ongoing commentary of imagery, daydreams, and self-questioning that all serve to amplify, challenge, and reshape self-beliefs, goals, and memories themselves (J. L. Singer & Bonanno, 1990). From this crucible of conscious and unconscious mentation, the nuclear script and its transferences may emerge.

Social Cognition Research Evidence for Transference Itself

It is the working assumption of this chapter that the kind of nuclear scripts elaborated thus far are an inevitable part of all of our interpersonal interactions, not only the heightened reactions that emerge in response to the psychoanalytic therapist. As we have attempted to demonstrate, social–cognitive and personality research have provided a growing body of evidence that might account for how components of transference are embedded within the course of more general cognitive and personality development. Yet, what evidence is there in social cognition research for the actual phenomenon of transference itself?

Andersen and Cole (1990) have produced the first set of experimental findings that point to the ways in which one's schemas about "significant others" are more influential and organizing in information-processing than schemas about "nonsignificant others." Such significant other person schemas are richer, more distinctive, and cognitively accessible and also more conducive of "false positive" errors in recognition tests, that is, they seem more likely to be transferred onto new targets that bear some resemblance to them. These errors involve *feeling* attributions as well as cognitive ascriptions. Andersen and Cole's work has opened the way for an intriguing series of studies that may tease out more precisely the process by which transferences occur in ordinary life situations outside of therapy.

SOCIAL COGNITION, TRANSFERENCE, AND THE CASE OF TOM

How does a social cognitive framework help us to conceptualize transference phenomena in both Tom's life and his psychotherapy? (It might help at this point to reread the specifics of Tom's case.) Tom's first-grade memory may be understood as an excellent example of Tomkins' nuclear scene. Figure 2 depicts the metascript and affective sequence that can be extracted from the events of the memory. It should be noted that in the course of therapy, Tom described several more memories in detail that could be considered analogue memories to the first nuclear one. We would presume the process of analogue magnification for the negatively toned script had been at work to link these memories to the original nuclear scene. These other memories included an episode in which his father humiliated him in front of a group of men at the Shriners' hall or a vague memory of sexual advances by a male teenage babysitter. In these memories and in others, the same pattern of humiliation by authorities or peers, followed by shame and withdrawal could be detected.

Over time, the original nuclear scene and its analogue memories became linked in an emotionally laden interconnected schema or set of nodes (using Anderson's associative network language), such that retrieval of one of these episodes would activate the connected memories and prime them for retrieval as well. The overall effect of this network would be to infuse the memory with greater availability, intensity, and immediacy. Through the influences of both egocentric and conservative effects of the scripts (Greenwald, 1980), Tom would begin to construe more and more events in terms of his core conflict (Luborsky & Crits-Christoph, 1990) surrounding humiliation and marginality. Here we would see the beginning of the distortion and overgeneralization associated with classical transference phenomena.

As Tom collected enough separate analogues of his original nuclear scene, he would slowly move to the categoric phase depicted in Figure 1. Rather than recall each individual memory, he would develop a summary memory such as "the whole time growing up I was picked on or rejected." In actual fact, Tom explained in his first session:

> I was an angry kid. I was always picked on. I matured late and was the class scapegoat. I picked up from my parents that I wasn't O.K., that most other people were better than me. I didn't have any friends in school, only kids in the neighborhood.

This kind of summarized recollection is an example of what was meant earlier by a generic memory. It blends many events across many different occasions into a single conglomerate, in this case, of rejection and despair. Connecting to the emergence of these categorical memories might be the parallel emergence of self-beliefs ("I am no good") and long-term goals ("I want to avoid rejection and humiliation"). From categoric memories, the next step would be to the metascript or abstraction. It cannot be assumed that Tom has conscious access to the metascript

Initiative $\longrightarrow$ Interest

Failure $\longrightarrow$ Mild Disappointment, Fear

Discovery of Failure by Authority $\longrightarrow$ Fear, Embarrassment

Ridicule and Humiliation by Authority $\longrightarrow$ Shame, Sorrow, Anger

Banishment from Peers and Isolation $\longrightarrow$ Anger, Shame, Relief

Figure 2. Tom's nuclear script

that connects his network of nuclear memories. The repetitive and overlearned aspect of the metascript has rendered it automatic, loosening any need for attentional resources. Furthermore, the nuclear script is so widely interconnected and dense in semantic memory that only the slightest cues (perhaps not even noticeable unless given specific directed attention) are necessary to activate its schematic processing. The automatic processing of an interaction may begin, activating the metascript and its concomitant transference reaction, before Tom can become aware of the impetus for his feelings, thoughts, or behavior.

Within the therapy, Tom would attempt to move closer to the therapist, only to detect with a sudden chilling effect that the therapist appeared to be looking at his watch, stifling a yawn, or laughing at him instead of with him. Such therapist behaviors, what Gill (1982, 1984) has called "actual clues," may not necessarily always reflect attitudes toward the patient, but can easily be so interpreted without conscious awareness by the patient. Tom's painful observations, spurred on by the automaticity of his nuclear script, would result in a subsequent withdrawal from the relationship with the therapist and a renewed complaint that he could not trust any caregiver. It is worth noting that the strength of the nuclear script as it guides the individual's behavior in interpersonal interactions is that it can induce the expected patterns of response in the other member or members of the interaction. Some aspects of countertransference reactions in therapists and others in general may be seen as just this kind of inadvertent collusion (J. L. Singer, Sincoff, & Kolligian, 1989; see also Ogden, 1982, on the topic of projective identification).

Thus, a patient whose nuclear script involves ingratiation with an authority followed by a later test for expected betrayal may recount an incident or dream that has a strong oedipal or other classic psychosexual theory implication and then notice a "knowing nod" or even a smile or smug "mm-hmm" from the usually poker-faced therapist. By eliciting the approval of the therapist, the patient has now created a scenario that will lead to a later test of presumed betrayal. It is highly possible that this entire sequence of behavior between patient and therapist will be played out without awareness on either participant's part.

Tom's tendency to fall for women who had come from alcoholic families and their attraction to him could be understood in part as a complex instantiation of this metascript. His role as a vulnerable caretaker for these women repeated a familial dynamic that they had known intimately—the overcontrolling parent who is extremely needy underneath his caretaking stance. The mutual attraction shared by Tom and each new girlfriend could be linked to the automatic and unarticulated nature of both his and their metascripts.

Given the relative inaccessibility to Tom of his metascript regarding his transference responses both to his therapist and in his romantic and work relationships, it is important to examine how he finally gained more conscious control over his transference. This leads us to the last major theme of this chapter: Is the analysis of the transference relationship between the therapist and client the crucial curative element in psychodynamic therapy or is this relationship only one of several important transferences that collectively lead to change through their analysis and understanding?

TRANSFERENCE ANALYSIS IN PSYCHODYNAMIC THERAPY

As indicated at the outset, a group of influential psychoanalysts propose that the key to psychoanalytic effectiveness as a treatment lies in treating each patient communication as a reflection of the transference process transpiring within the therapeutic dyad. Whatever the persuasive attraction of clinicians like Gill or Langs, we ought not necessarily accept their argument without any supporting research data.

Our case of Tom provides instances in which his self-defeating schemas and scripts were played out both in therapy and in incidents involving work and intimacy with women. The ineffective script about authority figures that was detected by the therapist in Tom's reactions to the treatment situation certainly was important in helping him. Within the safe atmosphere of the sessions, he was able to explore his expectations, their links to early memories and their "outmoded" or socially ineffective import. Yet therapy also included much review of Tom's use of similar nuclear scripts in other settings. Treatment took time because the sheer identification of a self-defeating schema often had to be followed by observation of its operation both within and outside therapy. In effect, the psychodynamic "working through" could also be viewed as a gradual extinction process not unlike desensitization in cognitive behavior therapy.

A case like this points up how transferences can be useful, but it cannot resolve the empirical questions raised. Luborsky and Crits-Christoph (1990) and Luborsky, Barber, and Crits-Christoph (1990) have sought to identify researchable features of the transference phenomenon and to relate these to therapy process and outcome. They used as a measure the Core Conflictual Relationship Theme (CCRT), derived by extracting relationship episodes narrated in therapy transcripts and scoring these in terms of the patients' expressed desire in the situation, the response of the other and the patient's subsequent reaction.

By showing that core (or frequently occurring) discrepancies between patient wishes and responses of others are evident not only for persons outside, but for the therapist they propose to support Freud's identification of the transference in its pristine form. By taking 22 statements made by Freud about transference, they sought through using the CCRT to support these from therapy protocols. Their data clearly support 7, and marginally, 8 additional of these presumed manifestations of transference. Of special relevance for our purposes is their report that accurate interpretations (as operationally defined) correlate with more benefits of treatment and also that some changes over treatment in the CCRT reflect presumably beneficial effects. What is less clear from their work is whether the therapist–patient dyad interpretations are more critical for a good outcome than other dyad or script identifications. And what of interpretations of pure self-schemas (e.g., "I'm doomed to being a lonely person"), which may not get picked up by the relationship episodes that are used to score the CCRT?

Some of the shorter term psychodynamic therapies of the past 15 years have sought to speed up the therapeutic process by more quickly identifying patient-therapist responses and their linkages to parents and to significant others (Davenloo, 1980, Horowitz, 1988; Malan, 1976, 1979). Some data from such short-term treatment indicate support for at least the fact that specific therapist–patient–parent (or significant other) linkage intepretations do correlate with measures of good outcome in therapy (Malan, 1976; Marziali, 1984; McCullough, Winston, Laikin, & Vitolo, 1989). Other studies have either found no clear support for the positive effects of transference interpretations (Piper, Debbane, Bienvenu, deCarufel, & Garanti, 1986; Silberschatz, Fretter, & Curtis, 1986) or yield indications that transference interpretations produce positive effects in therapy chiefly if they are followed by a visible affective response in the patient or if the patient has already shown more mature patterns of object relations (Azim, Piper, McCallum, & Joyce, 1988; McCullough 1987). None of the studies cited is of sufficient complexity or in some cases has been reviewed extensively or replicated so as to permit strong statements regarding their support for the value of transference interpretations in psychotherapy.

We cannot, therefore, answer (as yet) questions about transference analysis of the therapeutic dyad from research findings despite the importance attributed to it in clinical lore or in case anecdotes such as our own. We cannot say for certain that an emphasis on the transference to the therapist per se is a crucial, if not the crucial, ingredient of therapeutic change. We also cannot assert, in keeping with some of the more classically oriented theories that transferential reactions, whether to therapist or others, are invariably linked to early childhood scenes or recurrent experiences and to specific conflicts about the psychosexual stages or the even earlier phases of object-relation formation, so emphasized in current theorizing (Mitchell, 1989). Finally, we cannot be certain that helping the patient to identify transferential responses to others as well as to the therapist are effective in producing change. These are all eventually researchable questions, however. The thrust of our argument in this chapter may be summarized as proposing that if we integrate clinical descriptions with conceptions of memories, schemas, and scripts from the behavioral sciences, we can find support for some clinical propositions in a large body of experimental work and we can also identify more precise operations for evaluating the clinical value of transference intepretations in ongoing therapy.

INTEGRATING COGNITIVE–BEHAVIORAL AND PSYCHODYNAMIC THERAPIES

We have already mentioned in passing that recent extensive clinical psychoanalytic research, such as that of Weiss and Sampson and the Mount Zion Group or of Horowitz and the Program on Conscious and Unconscious Mental Processes at the Langley Porter Psychiatric Institute, has focused increasingly on "pathogenic belief systems" (Weiss & Sampson, 1986) or "person-schemata and recurrent maladaptive behavior patterns" (Horowitz, 1988, 1991). Such concepts appear to bring psychoanalysis closer to the cognitive–behavioral emphasis on Beck's (1976) "cognitive distortions," Kelly's (1955) early emphasis on "personal constructs" and "role repertories" and Meichenbaum and Gilmore's (1984) "core organizing principles." Messer (1986) in a valuable examination of psychoanalytic and cognitive–behavior therapy practice has outlined a series of practical implications for both groups of therapists. These boil down, we believe, to recognizing that one must systematically identify the patient's self-defeating or irrational belief systems as well as those that are consensually valid for our society and effective in social interaction. We need to determine both through direct inquiry and by investigation of patients' images, fantasies, memories, or even dreams sets of consistent relationship themes or role relationship models that are hierarchically and structurally organized into adaptive, wishful, consciously problematic or dreaded (often these are out of awareness) formats that guide the patient's behavior (Horowitz, 1991).

Behavior therapists need to be more prepared to tolerate the often wildly irrational nature of some schemas and scripts reflecting early rejection, humiliation, or undersocialization. Psychoanalytic therapists need to be more willing to confront the necessity for practice by the patient in reshaping overlearned role relationship models, some of it very likely by direct patient–therapist interaction, but much of it, undoubtedly, by planning, trying out, and then reporting on "new initiatives" with key significant others outside the consulting room. The use of cognitive–behavioral homework assignments with Tom allowed him to see in vivo both his capacity for following through and competently reaching his goal of entering graduate school, but equally his older pattern of pulling back from these successes to avoid the risk of failure and further rejection.

Collaborative relationships between therapist and patient encouraged by cognitive–behavioral techniques (Salovey & J. A. Singer, 1991) are a perfect arena for analysis of the patient's ability to trust others, to negotiate authority, and to explore both dependency and autonomy. Ultimately, it was Tom's failure to make full use of the cognitive–behavioral intervention, which he himself requested, that forced him into a pivotal exploration of his self-defeating relationship to authority as personified most powerfully in his therapist.

At a more cognitive and less behavioral level, as Tom accrued more success experiences both within and outside of therapy, he had begun to build a new set of specific memories that, on retrieval, provide new images and felt emotions to challenge the older summary memories' diffuse anxiety-based quality. In time these memories may have helped to reshape Tom's familiar script and open up the possibility of replacing its humiliating ending with a more self-affirming and positive image.

A CAVEAT REGARDING THE NOTION OF TRANSFERENCE AS REGRESSIVE

Although we have in our case history and research review put a good deal of emphasis on some early memories and childhood nuclear conflicts, there is a real danger for the therapist in assuming, even in the face an apparent patient's transference response to therapist or to others, that this reflects a childlike or "regressive" behavior. In a telling analysis of the dangers in tilting all interpersonal problems back to preoedipal stages or infancy (a practice common in object relations therapists especially of a Kleinian persuasion), Mitchell (1984, 1989) has shown how therapists can often demean their patients. Patients who show yearning for attention, for physical fondling, for proofs that they will not be rejected, and so forth should not be confronted with these as "babylike" responses related to early object relations formations. They are appropriate to adult roles and needs and should be so respected even if experiences in adolescence or adult life have led to their manifestation in schemas or scripts that are somewhat or extremely inappropriate for a given social setting or relationship.

At one point during his therapy, Tom's cat, his pet for 10 years, died. Normally formal and highly intellectual in his presentation, Tom was inconsolable regarding this loss and openly wept for large portions of several sessions as he discussed the illness, death, and burial of his pet. Although one could easily link his intense reaction to a need for unconditional acceptance and intimate bonds that dates back to the earliest formative episodes of his life, one would risk missing the immediacy and seriousness of his tangible loss in the present. In one sense, the cat served as a "selfobject" (Kohut, 1971), to fill Tom's painful need for acceptance, it also was an obedient, affectionate animal that had entered Tom's adult life, and whose death left Tom without his decade-long companion.

As yet, there is no systematic evidence that all "faulty" or ineffective schemas, which emerge as transference, can be reduced to early childhood origins. Indeed, an analysis (J. A. Singer, 1988) of a series of memories reported by a patient suffering from an aggravated grief reaction indicated that young adult memories and adolescent memories were perhaps even more telling in role relationship models formed than childhood memories. The cognitive scientist concerned with script formation needs to be responsive to the anecdotal accounts of psychoanalysts that emphasize such early memories, but analysts as well need to be sensitive to the demand characteristics of their procedures (e.g., the use of the couch or the call for childhood associations), which may put too great an emphasis on such early material (J. L. Singer, 1974; J. L. Singer, Sincoff, & Kolligian, 1989).

CONCLUDING REMARKS

In keeping with the theme of this volume, our exploration of the transference phenomenon first described in psychoanalysis has important implications for the psychology of cognition, personality, and social process. At the same time, the expanding research on schemas, memories, ongoing consciousness, and script formation in psychological research can increasingly inform psychoanalytic conceptions by helping make our analytic understanding more precise and our interventions more telling. We have tried to show, for example, in the case of Tom, that his summary memories in (to quote Johnson, 1775/1985, again) their "compressed and conglobated" form could by encouragement be differentiated into a series of memories linked to strong affective responses. In their summary form, his affect was of distress and anxiety. As a new narrative is formed and new experiences assembled in an effort to reshape old scripts, new memories, and new affective sequences lead to the altering of Tom's overall life story (McAdams, 1990). This new life story relates to an emergent new set of self-schemas and beliefs that, in his case, were correlated with more productive work and more satisfying interpersonal relationships.

The transference phenomenon need not be viewed as a mystery or as a childhood phantasmagoria projected into adult social relations. Our transferential responses may in extreme cases seem as if we are indeed under a spell of enchantment (induced by rejecting parents, humiliating teachers, or seductive relatives), but in actuality these hidden agendas are an intrinsic feature of human information processing and emotionality. Transference reactions conform to basic cognitive principles of organization, economy, conservatism, and self-reference. Transference is rooted in the building blocks of a script theory or a life-narrative theory of personality. From this perspective, transference is the inevitable result of the linkage of emotions and memory as they reflect the significant events and relationships of our lives. Although psychotherapy, dynamic or cognitive–behavioral, offers a powerful vehicle for the identification and reexamination of transference patterns in our lives, one should not overemphasize the transference relationship of therapist and patient to the exclusion of these other manifestations of transference. To do so limits the amount of learning and exploration that can take place in therapy. To make the therapist–patient dyad, the preemptive concern of the therapy may distract the patient from relationship patterns that are not easily assimilable by the therapist–patient relationship. What might sometimes be interpreted as the patient's resistance to transference interpretations by the therapist may actually reflect the patient's genuine frustration that important self-defeating behaviors outside of the domain of their dyad are not being discussed and analyzed.

Whether considering transference analysis or the role of early experience, we have taken a position in this chapter against reductionist explanations of the transference phenomenon. Advances in the psychology of cognition and emotion continue to point to the complexity of human information processing and emotionality (Ekman & Friesen, 1975; Rumelhart, 1980), as opposed to a reliance on a simple set of motives or mechanisms. When Freud observed the transference in psychoanalysis, but then went further to remark on its manifestations in other relationships, he provided an exciting and profound new way in which psychology could study not simply a psychotherapeutic phenomenon, but the subtle confluence of memory, emotion, and personality in our daily lives.

REFERENCES

Abelson, R. P. (1981). Psychological status of the script concept. *American Psychologist, 36,* 715–729.

Alba, J. W., & Hasher, L. (1983). Is memory schematic? *Psychological Bulletin, 93,* 203–231.

Anderson, J. R. (1983). *The architecture of cognition.* Cambridge, MA: Harvard University Press.

Andersen, S., & Cole, S. W. (1990). "Do I know you?" The role of significant others in general social perception. *Journal of Personality and Social Psychology, 59,* 384–399.

Bakan, D. (1966). The duality of human existence: *Isolation and communion in western man.* Boston: Beacon Press.

Barsalou, L. W. (1988). The content and organization of autobiographical memories. In U. Neisser & E. Winograd (Eds.), *Remembering reconsidered: Ecological and traditional approaches to the study of memory* (pp. 193–243). Cambridge, England: Cambridge University Press.

Bartlett, F. C. (1932). *Remembering: A study in experimental and social psychology.* Cambridge, England: Cambridge University Press.

Beck, A. T. (1976). *Cognitive therapy and the emotional disorders.* Madison, CT: International Universities Press.

Bird, B. (1972). Notes on transference: Universal phenomenon and hardest part of analysis. *Journal of the American Psychoanalytic Association, 20,* 267–301.

Blatt, S. (1990). Interpersonal relatedness and self-definition: Two personality configurations and their implications for psychopathology and psychotherapy. In J. L. Singer (Ed.), *Repression and dissociation: Implications for personality theory, psychotherapy, and health* (pp. 299–335). Chicago: University of Chicago Press.

Bower, G., Black, J. B., & Turner, T. J. (1979). Scripts in memory for text. *Cognitive Psychology, 11,* 177–220.

Brewer, W. F. (1986). What is autobiographical memory? In D. C. Rubin (Ed.), *Autobiographical memory* (pp. 25–49). New York: Cambridge University Press.

Cantor, N., & Mischel, W. (1977). Traits as prototypes: Effects on recognition memory. *Journal of Personality and Social Psychology, 35,* 38–48.

Carlson, L., & Carlson, R. (1984). Affect and psychological magnification: Derivation from Tomkins' script theory. *Journal of Personality, 52,* 36–45.

Chrzanowski, G. (1979). The transference-countertransference transaction. *Contemporary Psychoanalysis, 15,* 458–471.

Davanloo, H. (1980). *Short-term psychodynamic therapy.* Northvale, NJ: Jason Aronson.

Ekman, P., & Friesen, W. V. (1975). *Unmasking the face.* Englewood Cliffs, NJ: Prentice-Hall.

Emmons, R. A. (1986). Personal striving: An approach to personality and subjective well-being. *Journal of Personality and Social Psychology, 51,* 1058–1068.

Emmons, R. A. (1989). The personal striving approach to personality. In L. A. Pervin (Ed.), *Goal concepts in personality and social psychology* (pp. 87–126). Hillsdale, NJ: Erlbaum.

Feather, N. J. (1966). Effects of prior success and failure on expectations of success and subsequent performance. *Journal of Personality and Social Psychology, 3,* 287–298.

Fiske, S. T., & Linville, P. W. (1980). What does the schema concept buy us? *Personality and Social Psychology Bulletin, 6,* 543–557.

Fiske, S. T., & Taylor, S. E. (1984). *Social cognition.* Reading, MA: Addison-Wesley.

Flavell, J. (1963). *The developmental psychology of Jean Piaget.* Princeton, NJ: Van Nostrand.

Freud, S. (1958). The dynamics of transference. In J. Strachey (Ed. and Trans.), *The standard edition of the complete psychological works of Sigmund Freud* (Vol. 12, pp. 99–108). London: Hogarth Press. (Original work published 1912)

Freud, S. (1959a). An autobiographical study. In J. Strachey (Ed. and Trans.), *The standard edition of the complete psychological works of Sigmund Freud* (Vol. 20, pp. 7–74). London: Hogarth Press. (Original work published 1925)

Freud, S. (1959b). Analyses terminable and interminable. In J. Strachey (Ed. and Trans.), *The standard edition of the complete psychological works of Sigmund Freud* (Vol. 23, pp. 147–207). London: Hogarth Press. (Original work published 1937)

Freud, S. (1959c). Beyond the pleasure principle. In J. Strachey (Ed. and Trans.), *The standard edition of the complete psychological works of Sigmund Freud* (Vol. 18, pp. 7–64). London: Hogarth Press. (Original work published 1920)

Gill, M. (1982). *Analysis of transference: I. Theory and technique.* Madison, CT: International Universities Press.

Gill, M. (1984). Psychoanalysis and psychotherapy: A revision. *International Review of Psychoanalysis, 11,* 161–179.

Graesser, A. C., & Nakamura, G. V. (1982). The impact of schemata on comprehension and memory. In G. Bower (Ed.), *The psychology of learning and memory* (Vol. 16, pp. 59–109). New York: Academic Press.

Greenwald, A. G. (1980). The totalitarian ego: Fabrication and revision of personal history. *American Psychologist, 35,* 603–618.

Greenwald, A. G., & Pratkanis, A. R. (1984). The self. In R. S. Wyer & J. K. Scrull (Eds.), *Handbook of social cognition* (pp. 129–178). Hillsdale, NJ: Erlbaum.

Hastie, R. (1981). Schematic principles in human memory. In E. T. Higgins, P. Herman, & M. P. Zanna (Eds.), *Social cognition: The Ontario Symposium* (pp. 39–88). Hillsdale, NJ: Erlbaum.

Head, H. (1926) *Aphasia and kindred disorders of speech.* London: Macmillan.

Higgins, E. T. (1987). Self-discrepancy: A theory relating self and affect. *Psychological Review, 94,* 319–340.

Horowitz, M. J. (1988). *Introduction to psychodynamics.* New York: Basic Books.

Horowitz, M. J. (1990). A model of mourning: Change in schemas of self and other. *Journal of the American Psychoanalytic Association, 38,* 297–324.

Horowitz, M. (1991). *Person schemas and maladaptive interpersonal patterns.* Chicago: University of Chicago Press.

Johnson, S. (1985). *Journey to the western islands of Scotland.* Oxford, England: Clarendon Press. (Original work published 1775)

Kelly, G. A. (1955). *The psychology of personal constructs.* New York: Norton.

Kernberg, O. F. (1987). An ego psychology object relations theory approach to the transference. *Psychoanalytic Quarterly, 56,* 197–221.

Klein, S. B., & Kihlstrom, J. F. (1986). Elaboratory organization and the self-reference effect in memory. *Journal of Experimental Psychology: General, 115,* 26–38.

Klos, D. S., & Singer, J. L. (1981). Determinants of adolescents' ongoing thought following a simulated parental confrontation. *Journal of Personality and Social Psychology, 41,* 975–987.

Kohut, H. (1971). *The analysis of the self.* Madison, CT: International Universities Press.

Kreitler, N., & Kreitler, S. (1976). *Cognitive orientation and behavior.* New York: Springer.

Kreitler, S., & Singer, J. L. (1991). The self-reference effect in incidental memory: Elaboratory, organization, rehearsal and self-complexity. *Imagination, Cognition, and Personality, 10,* 167–194.

Langs, R. (1989). Models, theory, and research strategies: Toward the evolution of new paradigms. *Psychoanalytic Inquiry, 9,* 305–331.

Luborsky, L., Barber, J., & Crits-Christoph, P. (1990). Theory-based research for understanding the process of dynamic psychotherapy. *Journal of Consulting and Clinical Psychology, 58,* 281–287.

Luborsky, L., & Crits-Christoph, P. (1990). *Understanding transference: The CCRT method (the core conflictual relationship theme).* New York: Basic Books.

Malan, M. (1976). *Toward the validation of dynamic psychotherapy.* New York: Plenum Press.

Malan, D. M. (1979). *Individual psychotherapy and the science of psychodynamics.* London: Butterworths.

Mandler, G. (1984). *Mind and body: Psychology of emotion and stress.* New York: Norton.

Markus, H., & Nurius, P. (1986). Possible selves. *American Psychologist, 41,* 954–969.

Markus, H., & Wurf, E. (1987). The dynamic self-concept: A social psychological perspective. *Annual Review of Psychology, 38,* 299–337.

Marziali, E. A. (1984). Prediction of outcome of brief psychotherapy from therapist interpretive interventions. *Archives of General Psychiatry, 41,* 301–304.

McAdams, D. P. (1990). Unity and purpose in human lives: The emergence of identity as a life story. In A. Rabin, R. Zucker, R. Emmons, & S. Frank (Eds.), *Studying persons and lives* (pp. 148–200). New York: Springer.

McAdams, D. P., Lensky, D., Daple, S. A., & Allen, J. (1988). Depression and the organization of autobiographical memory. *Journal of Social and Clinical Psychology, 7,* 332–349.

McCullough, L., Winston, A., Laikin, M., & Vitolo, A. (1989, June). *The effect of robustness of interpretation on patient affective and defensive responding and therapy outcome.* Paper presented at the annual meeting of the Society for Psychotherapy Research, Toronto, Ontario, Canada.

Meichenbaum, D., & Gilmore, J. B. (1984). The nature of unconscious processes: A cognitive–behavioral perspective. In K. Bowers & D. Meichenbaum (Eds.), *The unconscious reconsidered* (pp. 273–298). New York: Wiley.

Messer, S. B. (1986). Behavioral and psychoanalytic perspectives at therapeutic choice points. *American Psychologist, 41,* 1261–1272.

Miller, G. A., Galanter, E., & Pribram, K. (1960). *Plans and structure of behavior.* New York: Holt, Rinehart & Winston.

Mitchell, S. A. (1984). Object relations theory and the developmental tilt. *Contemporary Psychoanalysis, 20,* 473–499.

Mitchell, S. A. (1989). *Relational concepts in psychoanalysis.* Cambridge, MA: Harvard University Press.

Moore, R. G., Watts, F. N., & Williams, J. M. G. (1988). The specificity of personal memories in depression. *British Journal of Clinical Psychology, 27,* 275–276.

Ogden, T. (1982). *Projective identification and psychotherapeutic technique.* Northvale, NJ: Jason Aronson.

Piaget, J. (1955). *The language and thought of the child.* Cleveland, OH: Worth. (Original work published 1926)

Piaget, J. (1962). *Play, dreams and imitation in childhood.* New York: Norton.

Piper, W., Debbane, E., Bienvenu, J., deCarufel, F., & Garanti, J. (1986). Relations between the object of focus of therapist interpretations and outcome in short-term psychotherapy. *British Journal of Medical Psychology, 59,* 1–11.

Racker, H. (1988). The meaning and uses of countertransference. In B. Wolstein (Ed.), *Essential papers on countertransference.* New York: New York University Press.

Reiser, B. J. (1983). *Contexts and indices in autobiographical memory* (Tech. Rep. No. 24). New Haven, CT: Yale University, Cognitive Science Program.

Reiser, B. J., Black, J. B., & Kalamarides, P. (1986). Strategic memory search processes. In D. C. Rubin (Ed.), *Autobiographical memory* (pp. 100–121). New York: Cambridge University Press.

Robinson, J. A., & Swanson, K. L. (1990). Autobiographical memory: The next phase. *Applied Cognitive Psychology, 4,* 321–335.

Roediger, H. L. (1990). Implicit memory: Retention without remembering. *American Psychologist, 45,* 1042–1056.

Rogers, C. R. (1951). *Client-centered therapy: Its current practice, implication, and theory.* Boston, MA: Houghton Mifflin.

Rosch, E., & Mervis, C. (1975). Family resemblances: Studies in the internal structures of categories. *Cognitive Psychology, 7,* 573–605.

Ruesch, J. (1961). *Therapeutic communication.* New York: Norton.

Rumelhart, D. E. (1980). Schemata: The building blocks for cognition. In R. Spiro, B. Bruce, & W. Brewer (Eds.), *Theoretical issues in reading comprehension* (pp. 35–58). Hillsdale, NJ: Erlbaum.

Rumelhart, D. E., McClelland, J. L., & the PDP Research Group. (1987). *Parallel distributed processing: Explorations in the microstructure of cognition.* . Cambridge, MA: MIT Press.

Rumelhart, D. E., & Ortony, A. (1977). The representation of knowledge in memory. In R. C. Anderson, R. J. Spiro, & W. E. Montague (Eds.), *Schooling and the acquisition of knowledge.* Hillsdale, NJ: Erlbaum.

Salovey, P., & Singer, J. A. (1989). Mood congruency effects in childhood versus recent autobiographical memories. *Journal of Social Behavior and Personality, 4,* 99–120.

Salovey, P., & Singer, J. A. (1991). Cognitive behavior modification. In F. H. Kanfer & A. P. Goldstein (Eds.), *Helping people change* (4th ed., pp. 361–395). New York: Pergamon Press.

Schafer, R. (1977). The interpretation of transference and the conditions for loving. *Journal of the American Psychoanalytic Association, 25,* 471–490.

Schafer, R. (1983). *The analytic attitude.* New York: Basic Books.

Schank, R. C. (1982). *Dynamic memory: A theory of reminding and learning in computers and people.* New York: Cambridge University Press.

Schank, R. C., & Abelson, R. P. (1977). *Scripts, plans, goals, and understanding.* Hillsdale, NJ: Erlbaum.

Schimek, J. G. (1983). The construction of the transference: The relativity of the "here and now" and the "there and then." *Psychoanalysis and Contemporary Thought, 6,* 435–456.

Schneider, W., & Shiffrin, R. M. (1977). Controlled and automatic information processing. Vol. 1. Detection, search, and attention. *Psychological Review, 84,* 1–66.

Shapiro, D. (1965). *Neurotic styles.* New York: Basic Books.

Showers, C., & Cantor, N. (1985). Social cognition: A look at motivated strategies. *Annual Review of Psychology, 36,* 275–306.

Silberschatz, G., Fretter, P., & Curtis, J. (1986). How do interpretations influence the process of psychotherapy? *Journal of Clinical and Consulting Psychology, 54,* 646–652.

Singer, D. G., & Singer, J. L. (1990). *The house of make-believe: Children's play and the developing imagination.* Cambridge, MA: Harvard University Press.

Singer, J. A. (1988). *Autobiographical memory instrument (AMI): A method for scoring memories reported in psychotherapy.* Prepared for the MacArthur Foundation Sponsored Program on Conscious and Unconscious Mental Processes, University of California, San Francisco, School of Medicine.

Singer, J. A. (1990). Affective responses to autobiographical memories and their relationship to long-term goals. *Journal of Personality, 58,* 535–563.

Singer, J. A., & Moffitt, K. H. (1991–1992). An experimental investigation of specificity and generality in memory narratives. *Imagination, Cognition, and Personality, 11,* 233–257..

Singer, J. L. (1974). *Imagery and daydream methods in psychotherapy and behavior modification.* New York: Academic Press.

Singer, J. L. (1985). Transference and the human condition: A cognitive-affective perspective. *Psychoanalytic Psychology, 2*(3), 189–219.

Singer, J. L., & Bonanno, G. (1990). Personality and private experience; Individual variations in consciousness and in attention to subjective phenomena. In L. Pervin (Ed.), *Handbook of personality, theory, and research* (pp. 419–444). New York: Guilford Press.

Singer, J. L., & Salovey, P. (1991). Organized knowledge structures and personality. In M. J. Horowitz (Ed.), *Person schemas and maladaptive interpersonal patterns* (pp. 33–81). Chicago: University of Chicago Press.

Singer, J. L., Sincoff, J. B., & Kolligian, J. Jr. (1989). Countertransference and cognition: Studying the psychotherapists' distortions as consequences of normal information-processing. *Psychotherapy, 26,* 344–355.

Strauman, T. J., & Higgins, E. T. (1987). Automatic activation of self-discrepancies and emotional syndrome: When cognitive structures influence affect. *Journal of Personality and Social Psychology, 53,* 1004–1014.

Sullivan, H. S. (1953). *The interpersonal theory of psychiatry.* New York: Norton.

Sullivan, H. S. (1956). *Clinical studies in psychiatry.* New York: Norton.

Taylor, S. E., & Crocker, J. (1981). Schematic basis of social information processing. In E. T. Higgins, C. P. Herman, & M. P. Zanna (Eds.), *Social cognition: The Ontario Symposium on Personality and Social Psychology* (pp. 89–134). Hillsdale, NJ: Erlbaum.

Tomkins, S. (1962). *Affect, imagery, consciousness* (Vol. 1). New York: Springer.

Tomkins, S. (1963). *Affect, imagery, consciousness* (Vol. 2). New York: Springer.

Tomkins, S. S. (1970). A theory of memory. In J. S. Antrobus (Ed.), *Cognition and affect* (pp. 59–130). New York: Little, Brown.

Tomkins, S. S. (1979). Script theory: Differential magnification of affects. In H. E. Howe, Jr. & M. M. Page (Eds.), *Nebraska Symposium on Motivation* (Vol. 27, pp. 201–236). Lincoln: University of Nebraska Press.

Tomkins, S. S. (1987). Script theory. In J. Aronoff, A. I. Rabin, & R. A. Zucker (Eds.), *The emergence of personality* (pp. 147–216). New York: Springer.

Tomkins, S. S. (1991). *Affect, imagery, consciousness* (Vol. 3). New York: Springer.

Tulving, E. (1972). Episodic and semantic memory. In E. Tulving & W. Donaldson (Eds.), *Organization of memory* (pp. 381–403). New York: Academic Press.

Tulving, E. (1983). *Elements of episodic memory*. New York: Oxford University Press.

Weiss, J., & Sampson, N. (1986). *The psychoanalytic process: Theory, clinical observations, and empirical research*. New York: Guilford Press.

White, R. W. (1960). Competence and the psychosexual stages of development. In M. R. Jones (Ed.), *Nebraska Symposium on Motivation* (Vol. 8, pp. 97–141). Lincoln: University of Nebraska Press.

Williams, J. M. G., & Broadbent, K. (1986). Autobiographical memory in suicide attempters. *Journal of Abnormal Psychology, 95*, 144–149.

Williams, J. M. G., & Dritschel, B. H. (1988). Emotional disturbance and the specificity of autobiographical memory. *Cognition and Emotion, 2*, 221–234.

24

COUNTERTRANSFERENCE THEORY, QUANTITATIVE RESEARCH, AND THE PROBLEM OF THERAPIST–PATIENT SEXUAL ABUSE

MICHAEL J. TANSEY

I begin with an admission. The overwhelming majority of contributors to this book have achieved eminence as empirical researchers. Not only am I not an empirical researcher, I have until now been singularly uninterested in, if not contemptuous of, anything that the "number crunchers" have had to say. I have been a hardened example of the very type of practicing psychoanalytic psychologist whom this volume is intended to reach. Although I am an avid consumer of the theoretical literature, I have spent my entire career seeing patients in virtually complete isolation from what has been learned through quantitative research. My selection as a contributor to this volume was prompted by a recent book (Tansey & Burke, 1989) on the subject of countertransference which contains less than a handful of references to quantitative research, all of which were brought into the fold by my coauthor, Walter Burke.

I had intended to approach this chapter waving the banner of the hermeneutic approach. Psychoanalytic therapy is about searching for underlying meaning that must be interpreted, experienced, and understood only from the inside by the participants themselves—this was to have been my platform. What could possibly be learned from a group of natural scientists with their crude measures, fallacious "objectivity," oversimplified designs, and—worst of all—statistics! One could prove anything with statistics. The phrase "meaningful statistical data" was, to me, an oxymoron of hilarious proportions.

The author gratefully acknowledges the comments and suggestions of Merton Gill, Walter Burke, James Barron, and Robert Marshall.

I came away from my library research with a more positive view of the high level of sophistication and complexity that characterizes the work of a number of clinical investigators. But, at the same time, it must be confessed that although there were some discrepancies and surprises, the results of this research tended largely to support much of what I had come to believe. Had it been otherwise, this chapter undoubtedly would have been written along the skeptical lines that I had originally intended. I should emphasize that I continue to retain a healthy measure of skepticism, albeit diminished in scope, and I continue to believe in the overriding value of the hermeneutic approach, which holds that each clinical encounter must be examined for its unique and multiple meanings.

In the material to follow, I hope to gain the attention of other clinicians who reflexively scoff at the quantitative literature. For those who consider my language too strong or my prior disdain exceptional, I refer you to the observation of Luborsky, Crits-Christoph, Mintz, and Auerbach (1988), who suggested that "in fact, when a clinician ventures to present data gathered by quantitative methods, he or she is at risk to forfeit clinician status" (p. 274).

I begin this chapter with a brief overview and synthesis of the theoretical literature pertaining to countertransference. This is followed by an exploration of important findings in quantitative research that directly bear on countertransference theory. Special attention is paid to an especially urgent area of countertransference disturbance, the alarming incidence of which demands the attention of us all, namely, the sexual abuse of patients by their therapists. I conclude with observations concerning the desirable mutual influence between clinical theory and practice, on the one hand, and quantitative clinical research on the other.

COUNTERTRANSFERENCE THEORY: AN OVERVIEW

It is not my intention to give an exhaustive review of the literature pertaining to countertransference theory because this has already been done elsewhere on numerous occasions (Epstein & Feiner, 1979; Gorkin, 1987; Kernberg, 1965; Tansey & Burke, 1989). My chapter is designed to provide the reader with an overview and synthesis of the literature, highlighting what I consider to be the major developments and turning points in the evolution of countertransference theory. This will establish a frame of reference from which to explore the quantitative literature.

The term countertransference was introduced into the psychoanalytic literature by Freud (1910/1953a) in the following famous passage:

> We have become aware of the "countertransference," which arises in the physician as a result
> of the patient's influence on his unconscious feelings, and we are almost inclined to insist
> that he shall recognize his countertransference in himself and overcome it. (p. 144)

There is some debate as to what Freud actually meant by *overcome* (Tansey & Burke, 1989, p. 11). There are also differences of opinion as to whether Freud considered countertransference not only a dangerous impediment but also a potentially useful source of information about the patient. Some of the differences are substantive, some a consequence of varying definitions of terms. At the very least, it is clear that Freud's dominant view of countertransference was that it constitutes an impediment emanating from the analyst's own unresolved conflicts and personal concerns that interfere with the necessary "evenly-hovering attention." Unlike transference, which Freud came to view as the greatest danger and the best tool for psychoanalytic treatment, he never fully extended his conceptualization of countertransference to give equal consideration to both aspects. He recommended that the analyst seek a psychoanalytic purification in order to emulate the surgeon who puts aside all his feelings. Only through such a position of "emotional coldness" did Freud (1912/1953b) believe that the analyst could competently function.

Unlike so many other important subjects on which Freud wrote prolifically, he had little else to say on the subject of countertransference. Some 25 years after he had introduced the term, near the end of his life, Freud (1937/1953c) returned implicitly to the subject of counter-transference by recommending that the analyst himself return to the couch every 5 years for additional treatment. With characteristic emphasis on countertransference as an impediment, he referred to the need for special precautions in order to avoid the negative effects of the x-ray-like bombardment of working with patients.

Freud's recommendations for analysts to emulate the surgeon in order to achieve optimal "emotional coldness" set the tone for four decades in which little was publicly presented or written about countertransference. Contributions by Deutsch (1926), Ferenczi (1919), and Reik (1937) stand out as noteworthy exceptions during this lengthy period of silence. It was not, however, until around 1950—fully 40 years after the term was introduced and half the time that has elapsed from 1910 until now—that a flurry of papers appeared (Berman, 1949; Heimann, 1950; Little, 1951; Racker, 1957; Reik, 1948; Tower, 1956; Winnicott, 1949). In various ways and with different emphases, the point was repeatedly made that there was good news and bad news concerning countertransference. The bad news was that analysts are all frequently stirred up in one way or another with their patients; the good news is that this is not necessarily bad news!

On the contrary, it was asserted by many that analysts' emotional reactions to patients could potentially provide them with cues as to what might be going on with their patients in a way that could escape their logical and rational methods of examination. Analysts were encour-aged to reject what Reik (1948) referred to as the "worship of the bitch-goddess objectivity" (p. 147) because objectivity had become, in his view, confused with inhumanness at the expense of human sensitivity. Analysts must therefore "listen with the third ear" in order to make the best use of subtle affective signals emanating from within themselves. Heimann (1950, p. 81) wrote that "the analyst's unconscious understands that of his patient" on a deeper level than his conscious reasoning, and maintained that countertransference feelings should be sustained in consciousness so as to "subordinate them to the analytic task" rather than simply "discharging them (as the patient does)." Extending Freud's observation about transference, Racker (1957) asserted that countertransference also represents "both the greatest danger and the best tool" (p. 303) for analytic work.

In his 1965 review of the countertransference literature, Kernberg referred to the more positive view of the countertransference as potentially useful as the "totalist" camp, so named because of its broadened definition to encompass the therapist's total response to the patient. By contrast, Kernberg referred to the "classical" camp that retained the narrow view of counter-transference as a pathological impediment. The classical school of thought was led by Reich (1951, 1960) and Fliess (1953). Especially in Reich's work came the important caveat of the dangerous tendency to conclude too readily that a given response to a patient necessarily means something about the patient rather than about the therapist. In summarizing the two camps, Burke and I (Tansey & Burke, 1989) stated the following:

> Whereas the classicist may be too quick to attribute an intense response to the therapist's exclusively private concerns, the totalist runs the risk of too readily concluding that the countertransference response to the patient constitutes a royal road to the patient's unconscious rather than a detour into his own. (p. 28)

We concluded with the obvious need for a validating procedure that would provide some guide-lines for attempting to ascertain both the sources and the meanings of a given countertransference response to a patient. We then attempted to map out such a framework (Tansey & Burke, 1989, pp. 111–131), which I do not summarize here.

Following the intense period of interest in the 1950s came a second hiatus for papers on countertransference during the 1960s in which very little was written. Interest once again flared up in the 1970s and continued throughout the 1980s. One common area of study was the attempt to articulate various categories of countertransference experience (Buie, 1981; Chediak, 1979; Kernberg, 1984; Lakovics, 1983; Langs, 1976; Liberman, 1978; Marshall & Marshall, 1988; Meissner, 1982; Roland, 1981; Spotnitz, 1985; Springman, 1986), which Burke and I referred to as the "specifist" movement (Tansey & Burke, 1989, p. 33). In addition, papers and books continued to surface that served to deepen the understanding of the manner in which even intensely negative countertransference emotions—hate, despair, rage, guilt, greed, and so on—could be used in the service of furthering empathic understanding of what it is like to enter into the patient's world (Bollas, 1983; Gill, 1983; Gorkin, 1987; Grotstein, 1981; Levenson, 1972; Ogden, 1979, 1982; Sandler, 1976, 1987), thereby opening up avenues of communication potentially much more powerful than words alone.

The inexorable movement during the past two decades, however, has been away from the narrow classical view of countertransference as a pathological impediment toward the totalist conception that even in powerful emotional responses to a patient, there is the possibility—but by no means the certainty—that something useful might be learned about the patient. Indeed, a recent paper by Abend (1989), a noted classical analyst, asserted that the controversy over definition has been "irreversibly settled" in favor of the totalist view. Abend stated further that the mention of countertransference in case presentations has become a "mark of analytic professionalism" (p. 388) whereas once it was a stigma.

A critical point has been reached in the evolution of countertransference theory, an area that has overwhelming and profound implications for the entire therapeutic process. No longer do analysts expect to be unmoved by their patients. Despite the inevitable lingering of terminological differences, there is broadbased acceptance of Reik's (1948) admonition against the caricature of the blank screen analyst who confuses "objectivity" with insensitivity:

> The psychoanalyst is a human being like any other and not a god. There is nothing superhuman about him. In fact, he has to be human. How else could he understand other human beings? . . . . If he were cold and unfeeling, a "stuffed shirt" as some plays portray him, he would be an analytic robot or a pompous, dignified ass who could not gain entry to the secrets of the human soul. (p. 154)

The theoretical tolerance that has been extended to psychotherapists has been enormously beneficial in promoting a professional climate that encourages analysts to look inward in order to make the best use of their emotional responses to their patients.

Yet, as I discuss in the section on therapists' sexual abuse of patients, analysts must all remain firmly aware that countertransference, in addition to being a potentially useful tool of the highest order, also represents "the greatest danger" (Racker, 1957, p. 303) to analytic work. In collaboration with Burke (Burke & Tansey, 1985; Tansey & Burke, 1985, 1989), I have attempted to examine the interrelationships between and among empathy, projective identification, and countertransference. We have devoted special attention to elucidating the process whereby a therapist strives to be receptive to a patient's interactional influence, then to recognize and understand induced countertransference as meaningful, and ultimately to make use of his or her understanding to intervene and interpret empathically with the patient.

Given that therapists are at a point in their history in which countertransference responsiveness is widely accepted as inevitable, the question of the potential usefulness of explicit, intentional countertransference disclosure is coming increasingly into the forefront, prompting

Mitchell (personal communication, 1989) to call it "one of the thorniest questions that faces psychoanalysis today." Although it is by no means a new debate, it remains an especially heated one that calls into play underlying fundamental assumptions regarding the nature of psychological disturbance and the manner in which change comes about. Burke and I (Burke & Tansey, 1991) have suggested that the therapist's "anxiety of influence"—a phrase borrowed by Feiner (1979) from the literary critic, Harold Bloom—by the patient may have been supplanted by anxiety of the exposure of influence. Analysts may now be comfortable with the notion of induced countertransference, but the blank screen ideal (Hoffman, 1983) may persist in their near phobic dread (Bollas, 1983) of exposing their reactions to patients in the form of explicit countertransference disclosure. The spectrum of opinions is indeed broad, ranging from those who feel disclosure should have no place in "proper psychoanalysis" (Sugarman, 1989) to those who advocate its centrality to the analytic process (Ehrenberg, 1974, 1982).

In summary, the term countertransference was introduced by Freud in 1910 largely as a pathological impediment to analytic work. This view remained dominant until 40 years of clinical work overcame analysts' resistances to acknowledging the ubiquity of countertransference responsiveness. The next 40 years, which brings one to the present, witnessed an ongoing debate between the totalist perspective of countertransference as potentially useful versus the classical view of countertransference as only an impediment. There is now overwhelming consensus in favor of the totalist view, even within conservative classical ranks. The salient question has evolved from whether analysts can expect to be moved by their patients to how their understanding of their countertransference influences their intervening. Along these lines, the question of explicit countertransference looms large.

COUNTERTRANSFERENCE IN LIGHT OF QUANTITATIVE RESEARCH

As mentioned earlier, I began to explore the quantitative research on countertransference as a virtual newcomer, harboring more than my share of skepticism. My opening foray, involving a computer search of journals and periodicals, did nothing to dispel my pessimism. It proved exceedingly difficult to find anything at all involving hard numbers and countertransference. Plugging in *study* as a key word invariably produced numerous case studies, not what I was looking for. Similarly, the word *empirical* triggered many anecdotal articles in which the term was used in its generic sense as synonymous with *observational* or *experiential*. The studies that did turn up with hard numbers tended to be characterized by small sample sizes, questionable validity (e.g., actresses used as patients), insufficient complexity, dubious generalizability, and various other methodological difficulties—in short, precisely what I expected. I smugly prepared to unfurl my hermeneutical banner, but decided that I should first have a look at some of the psychotherapy research books of which I was dimly aware.

I focus here on the research projects led by Strupp, Luborsky, Orlinsky and Howard, and Wallerstein. I present the material on a study-by-study basis. As will be seen, they are unanimous in their view that no factor is more important in the therapeutic process than the therapist's attitudes and feelings toward the patient. I do not dwell on descriptions of methodology or design. They have in common what seems to be a high level of methodological and clinical sophistication in extended examinations of actual psychotherapies. The surprising convergence of their results cannot be ignored, even by the most tendentious critic.

Some mention should also be made of the seminal research of Weiss and Sampson and the Mount Zion Psychotherapy Research Group (1986). Their work is exemplary in its presentation of theory in conjunction with state-of-the-art research efforts to test aspects of the theory. But, regrettably, the authors did not investigate countertransference phenomena. The only relevant finding pointed to the need for the therapist's "neutrality" in order to pass the "patient's tests" by not acceding to the patient's demands for "transference gratification." Weiss and Sampson (1986) interpreted their data to indicate that patients tended to respond to therapist "neutrality," defined in this manner, by becoming more relaxed, flexible, and spontaneous rather than by responding in frustration with "regressive and/or resistive reactions, and/or painful affects" (p. 276) as would be expected according to other psychoanalytic theories of clinical process. By implication, this finding has ramifications for the handling and technical management of countertransference, but no further study of countertransference was reported.

I begin with an examination of relevant highlights from the project led by Orlinsky and Howard (1975). In an elaborate design of ongoing psychodynamic psychotherapy cases, the authors attempted to investigate the experience of 60 patients matched with 17 therapists who had a median experience of 6 years of practicing. Over a 6-month period in an urban, outpatient psychotherapy clinic, both patient and therapist were required to respond to a questionnaire after each session. This allowed for an illumination of the subjective experience of each participant that could then be compared and contrasted with the experience of the other. The authors believed that, similar to various psychological tests, they had developed an instrument that would provide data, the interpretation of which could penetrate conscious and unconscious defensive tendencies, on both the patient and the therapist:

> The dimensions that were obtained, in fact, went far beyond what could possibly have been reported by either the patients or the therapists as present in awareness. The patterns that emerge through factor analysis must have included much that was unconscious to the participants, if our interpretations of them have been correct. (Orlinsky & Howard, 1975, pp. 31– 32)

From their vast pool of data, what is most interesting and relevant to countertransference theory are the conclusions the authors came to regarding the elements that are considered to be most helpful and curative in the treatment process. Orlinsky and Howard (1975) found that the therapist's "failures in object perception"—by which they mean accuracy of the therapist's evaluation of the patient's experience as opposed to the patient's self-report—were found to be the "rule rather than the exception" (p. 222). Nevertheless, these failures seemed not to make a difference in treatment outcome. This finding is surprising, even for the clinician who well understands that he or she is less than omniscient in powers of observation.

A closer examination, however, of the method by which Orlinsky and Howard (1975) came up with this finding appears vastly to undermine its credibility. They essentially measured the accuracy of the therapist's object perception based on level of agreement with the patient's self-report. The therapist who agreed with the patient's report scored high; he or she who disagreed scored low. *No provision was made for considerations pertaining to the patient's unconscious*, despite the investigators' claim, mentioned earlier, of instruments penetrating unconscious defenses. Thus, if a therapist reported that he or she perceived his or her patient to be angry as a defense against unconscious sadness and fear but the patient reported only anger, the therapist would have been rated as having failed on two of three counts. It is not surprising, therefore, that the therapist's "object perception" of both "dialogue" (explicit content of the session) and "session development" was found to be much more reliable than the "disappointing results" of the therapist's object perception of the patient's feelings, aims, and behavior. Clearly, the latter three dimensions of object perception much more heavily involve therapist judgments of the patient's unconscious than do the dimensions of dialogue and session development. Although Orlinsky and Howard discussed this issue (pp. 195–196), it did not stop them from proceeding along the lines they chose, defending their position by stating that they were looking only for comparisons of average ratings.

Yet, despite Orlinsky and Howard's (1975) awareness of taking into account only the patient's conscious self-report as the standard of accuracy, they reported their results in a manner that often omitted this *highly* significant qualification. At times, they did mention their method (e.g., "The main disappointment is that therapists' object perception of patients are not very accurate, or at least not very accurate as guides to what patients report about themselves," p. 211); at other times, their interpretation of their finding was discussed with no mention that the patient's unconscious was not taken into account, leading to a highly misleading representation (e.g., "His failures in object perception were found to be the rule rather than the exception, but somehow these failures must not be crucial," p. 222). I discuss this example at some length because I believe it is the sort of misleading interpretation and reporting of data that is exceedingly alienating to the clinician. It seems to me that the problem easily could have been avoided by directing the therapist to report only on perceptions of what he believed the patient was conscious of. Furthermore, this example also demonstrates that researchers are involved in *interpretation* of their raw data and in so doing, may be no less prone to problems with "true objectivity" than the clinician attempting to interpret the material of a therapy hour.

Orlinsky and Howard (1975) maintained that, whereas the therapist's failures in so-called object perception seemed not to make a difference in outcome of treatment, in sharp contrast, what was crucial to the progress of treatment was the therapist's "responsiveness," measured by levels of activity and affective involvement. Failures in responsiveness were "often found to be attributable to the difficulties and obstacles presented by patients" (Orlinsky & Howard, 1975, p. 222), a finding that is highly consistent with contemporary countertransference theory, which speaks of the power of patients to evoke or induce stormy reactions in the therapist. Also consistent with contemporary theory were the findings pertaining to "empathic induction," in which it was determined that the therapist's conscious, self-reported feeling state, when compared with the concurrent feeling state of his or her patient, often proved to be an "empathic indicator" of what the patient was feeling (Orlinsky & Howard, 1975, p. 211). This was true both for what contemporary theory would refer to as the therapist's concordant and complementary identifications with the patient.

On the final page of the main body of their text, Orlinsky and Howard (1975) stated that the single most important piece of advice to the therapist is to "connect" with the patient:

> The therapist must connect in two ways. He must stay responsive to his own experience—to the spontaneous flow of impulse, feeling, and fantasy that gives him a sense of his personal position in the therapeutic involvement. He must also remain in touch with that parallel thread of aliveness and continuity in the patient's experience, no matter what unexpected turns it takes or frightening places it leads, and no matter how the patient tries to protect it and conceal it from him. . . . He functions as a medium through which the response of each becomes available to the other. This does not mean that therapist must interpret the patient's experience, nor that he must always disclose his own experience to the patient—although timely interpretation and timely disclosure can work to enlarge and strengthen the vital experiential bond. . . . The therapist's responsibility *is* his responsiveness to his patient and to himself—a responsiveness that serves to connect the experiences of each to the other. (p. 223)

I quote from the original at some length because it may surprise the skeptical clinician to note the closeness of the passages themselves, both in language and in content, to recent major contributions to countertransference theory, as, for example, in the works of Bollas (1983) and Ehrenberg (1982). Orlinsky and Howard clearly came out in favor of judicious countertransference disclosure when it is in the service of establishing a responsive connection. The primary importance that the researchers attached to the need to remain aware of one's countertransference—broadly defined as the total experience of the patient—could not have been more clearly stated. In addition, they explicitly asserted that the therapist's ability to make use of his or her difficult responses to patients is often the crucial element in overcoming impasses in treatment (Orlinsky & Howard, 1975, pp. 216–222).

At the same time, one is left to wonder how therapists are able to "connect" with their patient when their apparent "failure in object perception" is the rule rather the exception. Orlinsky and Howard did not account for this, but as I have indicated, the finding itself is highly questionable.

One last highlight from the Orlinsky and Howard (1975) study. It is evident that they interpreted their data to support the primacy of new experience as opposed to insight as a curative factor. In addition, their data also appeared to drive yet another nail into the coffin of the "blank screen" conceptualization of the therapist's role (Hoffman, 1983) in their finding that "patients were as astute in perceiving their therapists' feelings as the therapists were in perceiving their patients' feelings" (Orlinsky & Howard, 1975, p. 56). But, again, the usefulness and validity of this finding is questionable. First, it involved a comparison with the misleading finding of the therapists' faulty object perceptions, discussed earlier. Second, it involved only therapists' conscious reports as the standard of accuracy, and it did not allow that patients could be accurately perceiving something in the therapists of which the therapists could be unaware. Even so, the finding suggests that patients may be aware of a good deal more about therapists than therapists realize they are revealing.

In summary, the clinician would not appear to learn much that is new from the Orlinsky and Howard (1975) research. The findings were generally consistent with much of contemporary countertransference theory; the only real surprise was indications of therapists' putative tendency to be more often wrong that right in their object perceptions. But, as I have pointed out, a close scrutiny of the manner in which the authors came up with this interpretation of their data reveals major questions as to the validity of this finding.

I turn now to the seminal research contributions of Strupp and his collaborators. In a 1960 study, Strupp used a film interview to which therapists responded as vicarious interviewers in an attempt to investigate their perceptions and resulting clinical judgments and treatment plans. Although the data were not conclusive, he did find statistical trends suggesting that therapists' personal contributions—such as their attitude toward their patients and ability to relate in a "warm, empathic manner"—was more important than their technical approaches or levels of skill and experience. Furthermore, Strupp's results pointed to the probability that the therapists' attitudes toward their patients could strongly influence outcome and efficacy by creating a "reciprocal" attitude in patients. Thus, the outcome of the treatment for patients could be

> less a function of the alleged "severity" of his disorder than a specific response to a specific therapist. The latter may remain unaware of the self-realizing character of his expectations, and in fact regard the patient's performance as confirmation for his expectations. (Strupp, 1960, p. 104)

Strupp's interpretation of his data comes very close to many contemporary theorists, such as the recent book by Stolorow, Brandchaft, and Atwood (1987). In addition to emphasizing the conventional recommendations for personal analysis and intensive supervision, Strupp (1960) also called for clinical demonstrations using audio or film recordings to impress on therapists the "serious pitfalls associated with subjective factors and forestall incipient narcissistic beliefs in true 'objectivity' or the infallibility of clinical judgments" (p. 105).

Strupp's early work served to anticipate a continuing emphasis on the therapist's response to the patient as a variable second to none in influencing the course and outcome of psychotherapy. Although Strupp (1960) retained the narrow definition of countertransference, he also spoke of responses induced by the patient's negative behavior, which most today would consider under the rubric of countertransference. From his Vanderbilt Study conducted in the 1970s, he found that therapists had little success in "confronting or resolving the markedly negative reactions of the more difficult patients" (Strupp & Binder, 1984, p. 275). The therapists tended to react negatively and countertherapeutically, leading to exacerbated negative attitudes from the patient, premature terminations, and poor therapeutic outcomes.

The team led by Strupp found that therapy tended to be successful if, by the third session, patients felt accepted, understood, and liked by their therapists (Strupp & Binder, 1984, p. 274). Calling for concerted efforts to help therapists learn to deal more effectively with negative responses engendered by patients, Strupp and Binder (1984) interpreted their data to indicate that the therapist must "take a personal interest in the patient as a person" because the therapeutic encounter is not "a set of techniques operating in a vacuum" (p. 278).

Just as the final page of the book by Orlinsky and Howard (1975) emphasized the importance of the relationship, the final page of Strupp's (Strupp & Binder, 1984) most recent book concluded with the following ominous caveat:

> Therapists' negative responses to difficult patients were far more common and far more intractable than has been generally recognized. . . . We are dealing with a ubiquitous human tendency that represents perhaps the single most important obstacle to successful psychotherapy, thus meriting much greater attention than it has been accorded. (pp. 300–301)

Strupp and Binder cited similar conclusions in studies by Luborsky and Spence (1978) and Vaillant (1977). In a 1989 article, Strupp argued that his research had led him to conclude that "therapists who meet the criterion of a 'good therapist' are by no means the norm; on the contrary, more or less serious deficiencies are common, even among experienced and respected professionals" (p. 723). Furthermore, he stated that "as a therapist, one cannot avoid becoming an unwitting coactor in the patient's interpersonal drama," and he described the therapist's skill at handling the patient's hostile, negative, evocative pressure as the "greatest challenge facing the therapist" (Strupp, 1989, p. 719). Strupp's position, forged through a distinguished career of quantitative research, is in perfect accord with much of contemporary psychoanalytic theorizing as exemplified by writers such as Mitchell (1988), Gill (1983), and Levenson (1972). The challenge of managing stormy countertransference responses, involving both the therapist's own tendencies and the patient's interactional pressure, was the primary focus of my collaboration with Burke (Tansey & Burke, 1989).

In summary, the research of Strupp and his collaborators is in accordance with contemporary countertransference theory. Perhaps most important from the viewpoint of countertransference, Strupp and Binder (1984) have warned that negative reactions to patients are far more widespread and serious than has been recognized. Strupp (1989) has concluded that the managing of stormy countertransference is "the greatest challenge facing the therapist" (p. 719). Clearly, considerable training, skill, and technical ability is required to meet this challenge. Thus, even though Strupp's position seems to support the human as opposed to the technical side of the relationship as being more important, in order for a warm, empathic relationship to emerge, substantial technical skill must often be brought to bear. In his writing, Strupp demonstrated a high level of clinical sensitivity. One wonders how much his interpretation of his raw quantitative data was influenced by his clinical understanding, such that his interpretation would have tilted in a different direction had his clinical understanding been of another nature. This is not to say by any means that one should dismiss the results of the research but only to emphasize that epistemological questions are involved for the researcher no less so than for the clinician.

In a recent book summarizing research from the Penn Psychotherapy Project, led by Luborsky and his collaborators, Luborsky et al. (1988) identified eight curative factors in psychoanalytic psychotherapy. The two most potent were the patient's experience of a helping relationship and the therapist's ability to understand and to respond. The patient's experience of a helping relationship is determined both by his or her "readiness," as well as by a "reality-based part rooted in the actual relationship" (Luborsky et al, 1988, p. 149), which, of course, is heavily influenced by the second curative factor, defined as the therapist listening, understanding, and responding in a manner that enhances the helping relationship and accurately makes sense of the patient's material. Furthermore, the therapist's interventions "should be calculated to try to avoid fitting into the negative part expected by or even stimulated by the patient" (Luborsky et al., 1988, p. 154). As with the Strupp (1989) and the Orlinsky and Howard (1979) studies, the relationship was seen to be far more important than "the therapist's ability to offer a technique that is clear, reasonable, and likely to be effective" (Luborsky et al., 1988, p. 162), which was ranked as eighth in significance among the eight curative factors. Citing studies that show that different types of therapies have not usually been shown to have different effects on the outcome of the treatment, Luborsky et al. asserted that any technique presented in a clear, reasonable, and convincing fashion would enhance the probability for successful outcome. The implications of these findings of the need for the therapist's proper handling of countertransference are obvious.

Luborsky et al. (1988) compared their own data with the findings from the entire quantitative literature in an effort to find trends. Several results were relevant to the subject of countertransference and the critical importance attached to its proper management. Positive correlations with successful treatment outcomes were ascertained across all studies with the following therapist "during-treatment" factors (ranked from highest to lowest mean correlations): supportiveness, focusing on transference, amount of experience, positive regard and warmth, prognostic expectations (creating potential for self-fulfilling prophesy), empathy, encouraging independence, genuineness, and liking the patient.

With regard to the accuracy of the therapist's interpretations, Luborsky et al. (1988) could locate only their own study, which, although positively correlated with outcome, was insufficient to establish a trend. Their finding appears to contradict the questionable finding by Orlinsky and Howard (1975), mentioned earlier, that shows that the therapist's "failures in object perception were found to be the rule rather than the the exception" (p. 222), although such failures were apparently not crucial to outcome. Similarly, Luborsky's team found only two studies examining therapist hostility and negative attitudes toward the patient, one of which was significantly associated with poor treatment outcome and the other showing no significance. Taken together, they were insufficient to establish a trend. Once again, the results appear to contradict the Strupp and Binder (1984) research, which, in what seems to be a second serious omission, was not mentioned.

In summary, despite apparent differences, which may themselves be attributable to differences in terminology and methodology, the Luborsky team concurred with the Strupp team and the Orlinsky and Howard study in emphasizing the significance of the relationship as opposed to technique. Clearly, the research findings support the view that the therapist's awareness of and ability to manage his or her countertransference is absolutely central to a productive therapeutic relationship. Even so, although the results tend to support those who believe in the primary importance of the potentially curative effects of the relationship as opposed to technical considerations, I believe it is fair to say that there were no real surprises for the clinician in the Luborsky-led research.

The last research project to be considered was headed by Wallerstein at the Menninger Foundation. In 1986, he published the final results of a study of 42 treatments begun in 1954 and including follow-up data through 1982. A primary impetus of this research was to examine differences between psychoanalysis and "various mixes of expressive–supportive" therapy. They found that treatment results between the two approaches tended to "converge rather than diverge," reflecting "greater-than-expected success" for supportive therapy and "lesser-than-expected success" of psychoanalytic approaches (Wallerstein, 1986, pp. 725–730). Insofar as "structural" changes in personality functioning were concerned, the two types of treatment were "indistinguishable" in outcomes. In almost every one of the 42 treatments, including the psychoanalyses, "the treatment carried more supportive elements than originally intended, and these supportive elements accounted for more of the changes achieved than had been originally anticipated" (Wallerstein, 1986, p. 730).

These surprising findings moved Wallerstein (1986) to conclude that "the supportive aspects of all psychotherapy . . . . deserve far more respectful specification in all its forms and variants than has usually been accorded in the psychodynamic literature" (p. 730). Wallerstein then cited Rangell (1981), who arrived at similar conclusions based on his own clinical experience of 40 years as a practicing analyst. Although the major findings from the Wallerstein research did not directly mention either countertransference or "the therapist's experience of the patient" as a parameter of study, the implications of the research for countertransference theory are substantial. Once again, therapists' supportiveness of their patients comes through as an undeniably major element of change. It is not possible for therapists to be supportive of their patients—especially those who characteristically elicit negative responses from significant others—unless therapists are able to manage their countertransference responsiveness in the service of the treatment rather than allowing it to become a disruptive impediment.

In contrast to the bulk of the other studies mentioned, Wallerstein's (1986) research does appear to contain findings that may surprise the clinician in pointing to the converging results of various types of treatments. This is especially noteworthy because it would appear that the Menninger team would have been biased in the direction of interpreting their data to support the greater efficacy of psychoanalytic treatments as opposed to those categorized as merely supportive. It is regrettable, however, that the meanings of "supportive" were not more clearly spelled out because there is ample room for confusion, disagreement, and faulty assumptions regarding the term. For example, was Wallerstein using the term in reference to all interventions other than interpretations? If so, does this mean that interpretations, by definition, are not ever to be considered supportive? Were there ever any ways in which the therapist's supportiveness was viewed as having unfavorable results? On the other hand, what was meant by psychoanalysis and how was this type of treatment defined? Greater clarity on matters of terminology might have enhanced what nevertheless seem to be intriguing findings.

The results of all four studies—each of which was psychoanalytically informed—also point to a need for greater freedom on the part of therapists to be more emotionally expressive and involved with their patients. Although it would be wrong to say that the quantitative research I have outlined supports an "anything goes" stance on the part of the therapist, there appears to be unequivocal support for the notion that, for example, one can greet a patient in a waiting room in a friendly and warm manner without necessarily being guilty of "acting out." The research cited seems to add empirical credibility to the theoretical position taken by writers such as Ehrenberg, who observed that

> too much of one's affective participation can destroy the integrity of the analytic relationship, as does too much caution. What is obviously needed is a delicate, judicious balance which establishes optimal distance. (1984, p. 565)

In addition, as Gill (1983) has insisted, I believe that a continuous effort to analyze and understand the patient's experience of the therapist's involvement (or lack of it) is also needed, although the quantitative results neither support nor convincingly refute this notion.

In light of the overwhelming emphasis from the quantitative data on the therapist's supportiveness and responsiveness, however, one must bear in mind Racker's (1957) caveat that countertransference—again broadly defined as the therapist's total response to the patient—represents not only the best tool but also the greatest danger to analytic work. Whereas the risks involved in having hostile or negative feelings toward a patient are obvious to all, I turn now to an alarming trend within the profession that may be conceptualized as "responsiveness" that tragically goes much too far. I am referring to the sobering incidence of sexual abuse of patients by therapists.

THE PROBLEM OF THERAPIST–PATIENT SEXUAL ABUSE

Who among us is not aware of instances in which a respected colleague has been shown to have engaged in sexual contact with one or more patients? It occurs with alarming frequency among psychotherapists of every persuasion at all levels of experience, ranging from beginning therapists to those who have achieved national prominence for their contributions. As Carotenuto (1990) pointed out, no less a figure than Jung is reported to have been sexually intimate with one of his first analytic patients, Sabina Spielrein. At the time, Jung was "about thirty and unsatisfied in his marriage" such that he found it "totally disarming to find himself confronted with a very young girl, scarcely more than fifteen, intelligent, passionate, in love and capable, furthermore, of seeing to the bottom of his soul" (Carotenuto, 1990, p. 14)

Both Jung and Spielrein confided in Freud as to their sexual intimacy. As I mentioned earlier, Freud first introduced the term countertransference into the scientific literature in 1910. But the first time he actually used the term in writing was in a letter to Jung in June, 1909, regarding his entanglement with Spielrein:

> Experiences of this kind, however painful, are necessary, and it is difficult to avoid them. Only after going through them do we know life and what it is we have to deal with. As far as I am concerned, I have never completely given way, but I have been very close a number of times and have had a narrow escape. . . . But it doesn't matter. In that way, one's skin thickens as it must, one dominates the countertransference that one gets involved in every time, and one learns to transfer one's feelings and place them opportunely. It is a blessing in disguise. (Carotenuto, 1990, p. 9)[1]

In the early days of psychoanalysis, it is well known that Jung was by no means alone in his struggles. As Penfold (1987) pointed out, Breuer's attraction to Anna O. is reported to have aroused jealousy and despondence in his wife, and Mesmer is reported to have become permanently estranged from his wife during the treatment of a blind pianist. Given that the problem of eroticized countertransference is as old as psychoanalysis itself, it is indeed curious that so little has been written about such an important and controversial subject, even in regard to fantasy activity or countertransference arousal that is not explicitly acted on or expressed. In the past four decades when attitudes toward countertransference turbulence have become vastly more accepting, extremely useful papers dealing openly with authors' own attempts to manage and make constructive use of their own countertransference hate, despair, rage, guilt, greed, fear, and the like have become commonplace. And although they may exist, *I am not familiar with one single paper in which the author elaborated with any depth or detail about his or her own experience with countertransference infatuation or sexual urges toward a patient.* One can understand why a therapist would not risk the public exposure of sexual activity with a patient, but the absence of

---

[1]Given Jung's problems with Spielrein, it is interesting to consider the rift that took place between him and Freud shortly thereafter. At the core of the conflict was Jung's disagreement with Freud's theories regarding the underlying sexual nature of all human behavior.

papers dealing with sexual fantasy and urges toward a patient that are *not* acted on and might even be put to constructive use in the service of understanding critical aspects of the interaction is indeed unfortunate. Therapists have seen the benefit of such studies of other varieties of disturbing countertransference states.

I am also well aware that anyone who has had to navigate these troubled waters—again, even at the level of fantasy activity alone—would understand the difficulties in openly presenting such emotionally charged and controversial material. It may be compared to parents who feel guilty about having become furious with their children. As difficult a subject as that may be to talk about with others, I would suggest that it is much less difficult than voicing even fleeting feelings of sexual arousal toward one's child, at whatever level. Similar incest taboos, even at the level of fantasy activity alone, seem to prevail for therapists in regard to their patients. In striking contrast, the psychoanalytic world accepts—if not expects—that sexual urges will exist in children toward parents and patients toward therapists.

The problem of eroticized countertransference is, of course, by no means limited to our early psychoanalytic history. Consider, for example, that 23 of the 89 formal complaints that were opened for investigation in 1989 by the Ethics Committee of the American Psychological Association involved "sexual intimacy with client, dual relationship, or exploitation and/or sexual harassment" (American Psychological Association, 1990). Although this yields a figure of 26% of all cases formally investigated, one may be certain that 23 instances of alleged sexual abuse annually among all psychologists—psychoanalytically oriented or otherwise—dramatically underestimates the actual rate of occurrence.

An excellent review of the literature by Carr and Robinson (1990) adduces data to paint a much more disquieting picture. Citing studies by Kardener, Fuller and Mensh (1973), Holroyd and Brodsky (1977), DeRosis, Hamilton, and Morrison (1980), and Gartrell, Herman, and Olarte (1986) involving various national surveys of psychologists, psychiatrists, and physicians, Carr and Robinson pointed to remarkably similar findings. The range of male and female therapists acknowledging erotic contact with patients varied from 7.1% to 10.9% for men and 1.9% to 3.5% for women. Approximately 5.5% of male therapists and 0.6% of female therapists acknowledged sexual intercourse with patients. An additional 2.6% of male therapists and 0.3% of female therapists admitted having sexual intercourse with patients within 3 months of termination. Most cases involved repeated intercourse, and no less than 80% of the offenders had intercourse with more than one client. Despite the anonymous nature of these studies, one is left to wonder whether even these figures may not understate the problem.

Personal therapy or analysis in no way provides an adequate safeguard because, as the study by Gartrell et al. (1986) showed, offending therapists were *more likely* to have undergone treatment than nonoffenders. In addition, several studies (Bouhoutsos, Holroyd & Lerman, 1983; Feldman-Summers & Jones, 1984; Sonne, Meyer, & Borys, 1985) showed the disastrous consequences to the vast majority of patients who had sexual contact with their therapists. It is especially interesting to note that other studies cited by Carr and Robinson (Butler & Zelen, 1977; Gartrell et al., 1986; Herman, Gartrell, & Olarte, 1987; Holroyd & Brodsky, 1977; Perry, 1976) indicate that offending therapists tended to believe that sexual contact with patients was generally not helpful but that somehow *theirs was a special case that was not harmful and possibly was even therapeutic to the patient.* This finding is especially cautionary because it speaks to the vulnerability that therapists all have with any given patient, despite convictions that erotic contact is to be strictly avoided. It is also a finding that must be sharply contrasted with the psychotherapy quantitative research that argues for supportiveness and responsiveness on the part of the therapist for his or her patient. How often does a confused therapist become sexually involved with a patient, motivated not by conscious intentions to exploit but by grossly misguided efforts to be responsive, supportive, and in some way affirming of the patient?

The tragic incidence of damaging sexual involvement with patients represents a compelling expression of the need for much greater theoretical clarity and attention to the nature and meanings of eroticized countertransference. Unlike other forms of disruptive countertransference that have received such widespread and in-depth attention in the theoretical literature, it seems quite plausible to conclude that the incidence of patient sexual abuse might well be diminished if more could be known and openly discussed about eroticized countertransference prior to its enactment.

CLOSING COMMENTS

I close with comments first on the impact that quantitative research might have on countertransference theory and clinical practice and second on the guidance that countertransference theory and clinical practice might provide for future directions in quantitative research. Far and away, the consistent and unanimous message across all four major studies I have cited is that the quality of the relationship reigns supreme as a curative factor. Features such as the therapist's supportiveness, responsiveness, genuine caring, warmth, empathy, ability to connect, and resilience to the patient's hostile provocation again and again were shown to outweigh the therapist's technical or theoretical orientation. Similarly, the absence of these qualities was shown not to augur well for any treatment.

By contrast, the quantitative results were inconclusive regarding the curative value of "accurate" interpretations. Whereas the Luborsky team showed that accurate interpretations did indeed correlate with positive outcome, the Orlinsky and Howard study—albeit with highly questionable methodology—concluded that the failure in object perception by the therapist was more the rule than the exception; even so, this failure did not seem to influence outcome one way or the other.

I personally welcome the support for the view that psychotherapy is, above all, a human relationship in which the therapist cannot and should not remain a truly detached observer in the name of "objectivity" or "neutrality." Because of the emphasis on the human side of treatment as opposed to technical considerations, the quantitative results support what Mitchell (1988) referred to as the developmental-arrest and the relational-conflict models of psychoanalysis, both of which stress new experience as an important curative feature, along with insight via interpretation. By contrast, quantitative studies tend to refute the overriding emphasis of classical psychoanalysis on the therapist's emotional abstinence and interpretation as against new experience as a curative factor.

The quantitative studies are entirely consistent with the totalist view of countertransference as a potentially useful tool, and they appear to encourage greater emotional contact and expressiveness. And yet, as the data on therapist–patient sex graphically illustrate, there are limits that must be observed. Therapists' countertransference responsiveness can also be the rocks on which any treatment may founder. This may be true not only for negative, hostile responses to a patient, but also for seemingly positive, warm responses. As I have mentioned, one must wonder how many therapists who become sexually active with their patients do so in the grossly misguided belief that they are being "responsive" to the patients' needs. The studies cited earlier demonstrate that this is very often the case. The quantitative studies would appear to grant therapists permission, if not encouragement, to greet a patient back from vacation, for example, with a warm handshake; yet, therapists must continue to ask themselves in each particular situation what the meanings of this might be, both for themselves and for their patients. This is where the hermeneutic approach to interpreting individual underlying meaning asserts its hegemony. Quantitative studies can only help to make one aware of trends that must be examined anew in every clinical encounter. Quantitative research is neither the only way to establish such trends, nor is it likely ever the most persuasive way to the practicing clinician. Ultimately, for each therapist, quantitative findings must pass muster with what seems to make the most sense in his or her experience with patients, both cumulatively and on a day-to-day and patient-to-patient basis. Whether or not this is reasonable or wise, it seems to be inescapable that however statistically convincing quantitative studies may be, those that fail to square with clinical experience will virtually always be summarily dismissed.

For more than a decade, I had the good fortune to participate in a weekly psychoanalytic study group with Merton Gill involving audiotapes of psychoanalytic psychotherapy sessions that were meticulously examined in their entirety. Our prevailing focus centered on unverbalized transference–countertransference interaction and meaning. At the conclusion of each evening presentation, the therapist would typically be swimming with input from the dozen or so participants who had all put in their two cents. With characteristic wit, Dr. Gill would often quip, "OK, now try to forget all of this and go listen to the patient." The caveat not to foist meaning on the patient to the detriment of collaborative inquiry always proved to be very useful to the therapist who would be inclined to bombard the patient with all of the clever interpretations that had emerged from the group. The same danger exists with compelling quantitative studies in that therapists, in their efforts to understand their patients, might be inclined to substitute empirical "facts" in place of an exploration of individual underlying meaning. A warm handshake cannot be assumed a priori to be constructive responsiveness on the part of the therapist, just as it cannot be assumed to be destructive acting-out of one sort or another.

What might countertransference theory and clinical practice have to say to future quantitative research endeavors? As a clinician interested in theory, I am not alone in being unprepared to give up on the value of interpretation and insight, which operate hand-in-hand with new experience as equally important curative factors. I believe these elements may be difficult to operationalize, but it could be very illuminating to see more sophisticated work done along these lines. Unlike what I consider to be the flawed methodology of the Orlinsky and Howard (1975) study on object perception, any such attempts would have to take into account the patient's defenses against unconscious contents.

Second, I strongly disagree with any suggestion that hostile or negative countertransference *necessarily* has to lead to disruption or poor outcome. Along similar lines, the emphasis in the quantitative studies on therapists' supportiveness and responsiveness would seem to imply that therapists who are working well must at all times maintain warm, benevolent feelings toward their patients. This has not been my experience in my own work, in my supervision, or in my exposure to the taped presentations of colleagues over extended periods. We are all familiar with cases in which therapists appear to be denying to themselves negative feelings toward a patient while struggling to maintain a forced demeanor of cordiality or neutrality because they view their negative countertransference as unacceptable. Greater tolerance is called for in order to assist therapists to bring such negative feelings into consciousness so that they may be scrutinized and understood. One may read the quantitative studies as fostering intolerance of negative countertransference responses. True empathy with a patient is both an achievement as well as a means to an end.

Although stormy countertransference can indeed represent what Strupp (1989) called the "greatest challenge" facing a psychotherapist, my collaboration with Burke (Tansey & Burke, 1989) represents a systematic attempt to understand the manner in which such difficult emotional experiences for the therapist can be understood and potentially put to good use. This is an area worthy of more careful quantitative examination. Beyond the schema that we provided, the work of Marshall and Marshall (1988) holds a great deal of promise in offering operational constructs for various classes of the "transference–countertransference matrix." Their system potentially could be applied to existing data that might circumvent the massive problems associated with initiating sophisticated new projects.

Third, in order for quantitative research to have substantial impact on the practicing clinician, the results need to address more complex clinical phenomena than, for example, the need for the therapist to be supportive. Supportive under what circumstances? What is really meant by *support* anyway? Can an interpretation or a confrontation ever be considered supportive? If so, when and under what circumstances? Is support measured only by the immediate impact of a given intervention on a patient? If so, are there not problems with such a limited view? Are there ever difficulties with a therapist's approach that seems manifestly supportive?

Just as quantitative researchers bemoan the fact that they do not have greater influence on clinicians who merely reject what does not fit with their pet theories, similarly, the researchers themselves must answer to searching epistemological questions. As one knows, the "results" of quantitative research are not purely determined by hard and fast numbers. The numbers must be interpreted in one way or another as meaningful by the researchers, who themselves are going to be influenced by preexisting notions and biases, in some cases no less so than the practicing clinician. At an even more basic level, how much is the research design and methodology itself influenced by "experimenter bias," which skews the numbers in a particular direction, even prior to their ultimate interpretation? It would appear that the Wallerstein (1986) research with the Menninger team is a notable exception because the results tended not to favor greater efficacy in psychoanalytic treatment as opposed to more "supportive" forms of treatment, although again, what was meant by supportive was not adequately specified. The quantitative researcher thus would appear to be presented with a dilemma: On the one hand, in order to minimize the procrustean effect on numerical data of preexisting bias, the variables measured would need to be simple and straightforward. On the other hand, however, in order to excite the clinician, it would appear that the parameters of study need to be complex and controversial in order for the results not to be dismissed as superficial.

As an example of the sort of complex and controversial questions that would excite many clinicians, the potential usefulness of explicit countertransference disclosure is at the forefront of the theoretical debate. Once again, this is an area that might be explored more carefully with existing data pools so as to obviate the difficulties associated with launching entirely new data-generating projects. But the question cannot be answered with a simple yes or no. What would be meant by "disclosure," or for that matter, "useful"? When, how, with whom, and under what circumstances is disclosure useful or not useful? Does the therapist have a higher probability of usefulness later in the treatment versus earlier in the treatment? Do diagnostic considerations seem to differentiate? What are the longer term effects on the patient versus the immediate impact? Would differences be found pertaining to therapist disclosure of details of his or her life as opposed to revelations of thoughts or feelings pertaining only to the therapeutic interaction? Persuasive results to questions such as these might well cause the clinician to sit up and take notice.

In closing, I would like to say that I am grateful for having been confronted with the task of comparing the universe of quantitative research with that of countertransference theory. I come away from it with an appreciation for what has been accomplished by dedicated researchers, despite enormous methodological barriers. My ardent skepticism has been replaced by a belief that hard-won empirical data have the potential, not to substitute for, but to augment sound, individualized clinical judgment in the area of understanding countertransference.

REFERENCES

Abend, S. (1989). Countertransference and psychoanalytic technique. *Psychoanalytic Quarterly, 58,* 374–395.

American Psychological Association. (1990). Report of the Ethics Committee: 1988. *American Psychologist, 47,* 873–874.

Berman, L. (1949). Countertransferences and attitudes of the analyst in the therapeutic process. *Psychiatry, 12,* 159–166.

Bollas, C. (1983). Expressive uses of the countertransference. *Contemporary Psychoanalysis, 19,* 1–34.

Bouhoutsos, J., Holroyd, J., & Lerman, H. (1983). Sexual intimacy between psychotherapists and patients. *Professional Psychology: Research and Practice, 14,* 185–196.

Buie, D. (1981). Empathy: Its nature and limitations. *Journal of the American Psychoanalytic Association, 29,* 281–307.

Burke, W., & Tansey, M. (1985). Projective identification and countertransference turmoil: Disruptions in the empathic process. *Contemporary Psychoanalysis, 21,* 372–402.

Burke, W., & Tansey, M. (1991). Countertransference disclosure and models of therapeutic action. *Contemporary Psychoanalysis, 27,* 351–384.

Butler, S., & Zelen, S. (1977). Sexual intimacies between therapists and patients. *Psychotherapy: Theory, Research, and Practice, 14,* 139–145.

Carotenuto, A. (1990). Jung's confrontation with Sabina Spielrein: Towards new territories, Part II. *Psychologist Psychoanalyst, 10*(3), 9–16.

Carr, M., & Robinson, G. (1990). Fatal attraction: The ethical and clinical dilemma of patient–therapist sex. *Canadian Journal of Psychiatry, 35,* 122–127.

Chediak, C. (1979). Counter-reactions and countertransference. *International Journal of Psychoanalysis, 60,* 117–129.

DeRosis, H., Hamilton, J., & Morrison, C. (1980). *Washington psychiatric survey on sexual contact with their patients.* Unpublished manuscript.

Deutsch, H. (1926). Occult processes occurring during psychoanalysis. In G. Devereaux (Ed.), *Psychoanalysis and the Occult* (pp. 133–146). Madison, CT: International Universities Press.

Ehrenberg, D. (1974). The intimate edge in therapeutic relatedness. *Contemporary Psychoanalysis, 10,* 423–437.

Ehrenberg, D. (1982). Psychoanalytic engagement: The transaction as primary data. *Contemporary Psychoanalysis, 18,* 535–555.

Ehrenberg, D. (1984). Psychoanalytic engagement: II. Affective considerations. *Contemporary Psychoanalysis, 20,* 560–599.

Epstein, L., & Feiner, A. (1979). *Countertransference.* Northvale, NJ: Jason Aronson.

Feiner, A. (1979). Countertransference and the anxiety of influence. In L. Epstein & A. Feiner (Eds.), *Countertransference: The Therapist's contribution to the therapeutic situation* (pp. 105–128). Northvale, NJ: Jason Aronson.

Feldman-Summers, S., & Jones, G. (1984). Psychological impacts of sexual contacts between therapists or other health care practitioners and their clients. *Journal of Consulting and Clinical Psychology, 52,* 1054–1061.

Ferenczi, S. (1919). On the technique of psychoanalysis. In *Further contributions to the technique of psychoanalysis* (pp. 177–188). London: Hogarth Press.

Fleiss, R. (1953). Countertransference and counteridentification. *Psychoanalytic Quarterly, 11,* 211–227.

Freud, S. (1953a). The future prospects of psychoanalytic therapy. In J. Strachey (Ed. and Trans.), *The standard edition of the complete psychological works of Sigmund Freud* (Vol. 11, pp. 141–151). London: Hogarth Press. (Original work published 1910)

Freud, S. (1953b). Recommendations to physicians practicing psychoanalysis. In J. Strachey (Ed. and Trans.), *The standard edition of the complete psychological works of Sigmund Freud* (Vol. 12, pp. 111–120). London: Hogarth Press. (Original work published 1912)

Freud, S. (1953c). Analysis terminable and interminable. In J. Strachey (Ed. and Trans.), *The standard edition of the complete psychological works of Sigmund Freud* (Vol. 23, pp. 209–253). London: Hogarth Press. (Original work published 1937)

Gartrell, N., Herman, J., & Olarte, S. (1986). Psychiatrist–patient sexual contact: Results of a national survey: I. Prevalence. *American Journal of Psychiatry, 143,* 1126–1131.

Gill, M. (1983). The interpersonal paradigm and the degree of the therapist's involvement. *Contemporary Psychoanalysis, 19,* 200–237.

Gorkin, M. (1987). *The uses of countertransference.* Northvale, NJ: Jason Aronson.

Grotstein, J. (1981). *Splitting and projective identification.* Northvale, NJ: Jason Aronson.

Heimann, P. (1950). On countertransference. *International Journal of Psychoanalysis, 31,* 81–84.

Herman, J., Gartrell, N., & Olarte, S. (1987). Psychiatrist–patient sexual contact: Results of a national survey, II: Psychiatrists' attitudes. *American Journal of Psychiatry, 144,* 164–169.

Hoffman, I. (1983). The patient as interpreter of the analyst's experience. *Contemporary Psychoanalysis, 19,* 389–422.

Holroyd, J., & Brodsky, A. (1977). Psychologists' attitudes and practices regarding erotic and non-erotic contact with patients. *American Psychologist, 32,* 843–849.

Kardener, S., Fuller, M., & Mensh, I. (1973). A survey of physicians' attitudes and practices regarding erotic and non-erotic contact with patients. *American Journal of Psychiatry, 130,* 1077–1081.

Kernberg, O. (1965). Notes on countertransference. *Journal of the American Psychoanalytic Association, 13,* 38–56.

Kernberg, O. (1984). Countertransferences, transference regression, and the incapacity to defend. In H. C. Hayes (Ed.), *Between analyst and patient: New dimensions in countertransference.* Hillsdale, NJ: Analytic Press.

Lakovics, M. (1983). Classification of countertransference for utilization in supervision. *American Journal of Psychotherapy, 37,* 245–257.

Langs, R. (1976). *The therapeutic interaction* (Vol. 2). Northvale, NJ: Jason Aronson.

Levenson, E. (1972). *The fallacy of understanding.* New York: Basic Books.

Liberman, D. (1978). Affective response of the analyst to the patient's communications. *International Journal of Psychoanalysis, 59,* 335–340.

Little, M. (1951). Countertransference and the patient's response to it. *International Journal of Psychoanalysis, 32,* 32–40.

Luborsky, L., Crits-Christoph, P., Mintz, J., & Auerbach, A. (1988). *Who will benefit from psychotherapy?* New York: Basic Books.

Luborsky, L., & Spence, D. (1978). Quantitative research on psychoanalytic therapy. In S. Garfield & A. Bergin (Eds.), *Handbook of psychotherapy and behavior change* (pp. 331–368). New York: Wiley.

Marshall, R., & Marshall, S. (1988). *The Transference–Countertransference Matrix.* New York: Columbia University Press.

Mitchell, S. (1988). *Relational concepts in psychoanalysis.* Cambridge, MA: Harvard University Press.

Meissner, W. (1982). Notes on countertransference in borderline conditions. *International Journal of Psychoanalytic Psychotherapy, 10,* 89–123.

Ogden, T. (1979). On projective identification. *International Journal of Psychoanalysis, 60,* 357–373.

Ogden, T. (1982). *Projective identification and psychotherapeutic technique.* New York: Aronson.

Orlinsky, D., & Howard, K. (1975). *Varieties of psychotherapeutic experience.* New York: Teachers College Press.

Penfold, S. (1987). Sexual abuse between therapist and woman patient. *Canadian Women Studies, 8*(4), 29–31.

Perry, J. (1976). Physicians' erotic and non-erotic physical involvement with patients. *American Journal of Psychiatry, 133,* 838–849.

Racker, H. (1957) The meanings and uses of countertransference. *Psychoanalytic Quarterly, 26,* 303–357.

Rangell, L. (1981). Some notes on the postanalytic phase. *International Journal of Psychoanalytic Psychotherapy, 8,* 165–170.

Reich, A. (1951). On countertransference. *International Journal of Psychoanalysis, 32,* 25–31.

Reich, A. (1960) Further remarks on countertransference. *International Journal of Psychoanalysis, 41,* 389–395.

Reik, T. (1937). *Surprise and the psychoanalyst.* New York: Dutton.

Reik, T. (1948). *Listening with the third ear.* New York: Farrar, Strauss & Young.

Roland, A. (1981). Induced emotional reactions and attitudes in the psychoanalyst as transference in actuality. *Psychoanalytic Review, 68,* 45–74.

Sandler, J. (1976). Countertransference and role-responsiveness. *International Review of Psychoanalysis, 3,* 43–47.

Sandler, J. (1987). *Projection, identification, projective identification.* Madison, CT: International Universities Press.

Sonne, J., Meyer, B., & Borys, D. (1985). Clients reactions to sexual intimacy in therapy. *American Journal of Orthopsychiatry, 55,* 183–189.

Spotnitz, H. (1985). *Modern psychoanalysis of the schizophrenic patient* (2nd ed.). Northvale, NJ: Jason Aronson.

Springman, R. (1986). Countertransference: Clarification in supervision. *Contemporary Psychoanalysis, 22,* 252–277.

Stolorow, R., Brandchaft, B., & Atwood, G. (1987). *Psychoanalytic treatment: An intersubjective approach.* Hillsdale, NJ: Analytic Press.

Strupp, H. (1960). *Psychotherapists in action: Explorations of the therapist's contribution to the treatment process.* New York: Grune & Stratton.

Strupp, H. (1989). Can the practitioner learn from the researcher? *American Psychologist, 44,* 717–724.

Strupp, H., & Binder, J. (1984). *Psychotherapy in a new key.* New York: Basic Books.

Sugarman, A. (1989, August). *Countertransference: A classical critique.* Paper presented at the annual meeting of the American Psychological Association, New Orleans.

Tansey, M., & Burke, W. (1985). Projective identification and the empathic process. *Contemporary Psychoanalysis, 21,* 42–69.

Tansey, M., & Burke, W. (1989). *Understanding countertransference: From projective identification to empathy.* Hillsdale, NJ: Analytic Press.

Tower, L. (1956). Countertransference. *Journal of the American Psychoanalytic Association, 4,* 224–255.

Vaillant, G. (1977). *Adaptation to Life.* Boston: Little, Brown.

Wallerstein, R. (1986). *Forty-two lives in treatment: A study of psychoanalysis and psychotherapy.* New York: Guilford Press.

Weiss, J., & Sampson, H. (1986). *The psychoanalytic process.* New York: Guilford Press.

Winnicott, D. (1949). Hate in the countertransference. *International Journal of Psychoanalysis, 30,* 69–75.

25

INTERPRETATION: A CRITICAL PERSPECTIVE

DONALD P. SPENCE

Much of our current thinking about the way in which interpretations function in the course of therapy was first outlined by Strachey in 1934 in his classic paper, *The Nature of the Therapeutic Action of Psychoanalysis*. He noted at the time that only a "relatively small proportion of the psychoanalytic literature . . . has been concerned with the mechanisms" (p. 127) by which the therapeutic action of interpretation are achieved. More than half a century later, we still celebrate Strachey's model, despite the absence of compelling clinical confirmation. And we would still agree with Strachey that even though little is known about interpretation, "it does not prevent an almost universal belief in its remarkable efficacy . . . [possessing] many of the qualities of a *magic* weapon" (p. 141). Some of this magic stems from the interpretation per se, but appreciably more stems from its medieval logic and from factors that coincide with the interpretation such as the state of the transference and the developmental phase being reenacted. We start with the medieval background of clinical reasoning.

THE DOCTRINE OF SIGNATURES

Pick up any book on hermeneutics and the chances are better than even that the author will, sooner or later, call attention to the fact that "hermeneutics" is named after Hermes, the messenger of the Greek gods, a representative of eloquence, cunning, trickery, and theft. It follows, by implication, that hermeneutics is a slippery and mischevious undertaking that conceals as much as it reveals. All interpretative disciplines are therefore flawed by this questionable ancestry, and, for obvious reasons, this example finds particular favor with enemies of hermeneutics.

But the argument falters because the derivation is false, and the mistake tells us something important about the interpretative process. Reference to any etymological dictionary (e.g.,

Onions, 1966) will show that hermeneutics stems from the Greek word "hermeneuein," or interpret, whereas Hermes, on the other hand, gave rise to "hermaphrodite" (the son of Hermes and Aphrodite) and "hermetic." But these etymological facts can do little to stave off the common assumption that Hermes must be related to "hermeneutics." In other words, what is plausible becomes possible, and, if repeated often enough, becomes true.

Interpretation, to paraphrase Pasteur, can too often favor the prepared mind. Interpretations in a clinical setting have an unfortunate tendency to reflect the therapist's expectations rather than the underlying facts of the matter. We are only beginning to discover the extent to which a therapist's values can be projected onto the clinical material to produce a falsehood that masquerades as a truism. In a high proportion of cases, an apparent pattern match, along the lines of Hermes/hermeneutics, is sufficient to trigger the interpretation. But this kind of reasoning is uncomfortably reminiscent of medieval thought and its dependence on the so-called doctrine of signatures: the belief that the "nature of things, their co-existence, the way in which they are linked together and communicate, is nothing other than their resemblance" (Foucault, 1973, p. 29).

The medieval scientist looked on the world as a system of signatures—outward signs of a buried similarity. The skilled investigator of the natural world was familiar with all forms of transformation and was practiced at discovering the signature even when it was heavily disguised. He postulated a correspondence between the natural landscape and the surrounding universe, and one authority taught that "every star in the sky is only the spiritual prefiguration of a plant . . . just as each herb or plant is a terrestrial star looking up at the sky" (Foucault, 1973, p. 20). A similar parallel was thought to link humanity and universe, and this implied resemblance was the foundation for a good part of medieval medicine. A case in point concerns the description of apoplexy. Thought to be the local equivalent of a thunderstorm, it was considered frightening but not serious, and of a self-terminating nature, leaving no permanent consequences. Foucault (1973) stated,

> The lightening flashes and the eyes glitter with a terrible brightness, the rain falls, the mouth foams, the thunderbolt is unleashed and the spirits burst open breaches in the skin; but then the sky becomes clear again, and in the sick man [or woman] reason regains ascendency. (p. 23).

The medieval thinker identified four types of resemblances or similitudes, and each of these has a parallel in current clinical practice. The first type, "convenientia," calls our attention to contiguity and teaches us that forms that appear in close proximity or succession share some feature or features in common (see Foucault, 1973, pp. 18–19). In clinical practice, this similitude is expressed by the belief that contiguous associations tend to be related; thus an association that follows a dream is assumed to be about the dream, whereas associations that follow an interpretation are taken as comments on, or reactions to, the interpretation.

The second similitude, "aemulatio," is defined as a relation between two objects that are separated in space. In his book, Foucault (1973) stated,

> The human face, from afar, emulates the sky, and just as man's [or woman's] intellect is an imperfect reflection of God's wisdom, so his [or her] two eyes, with their limited brightness, are a reflection of the vast illumination spread across the sky by the sun and the moon. (p. 19)

In a clinical setting, the analyst is trained to be particularly sensitive to resemblances between interactions within the hour and significant events in the outside world. The detection and interpretation of the transference can be described as an application of aemulatio, as can the detection of so-called derivatives. Suppose the patient is expecting to terminate therapy in three weeks and at the same time aggressively cleaning out, dusting, and repainting a walk-in closet. By use of the similitude aemulatio, the analyst is able to link the end of therapy to the vigorous house-cleaning. Both activities represent the end of one phase of life and the beginning of another, and additional links can be imagined between the form of the closet (which has no windows) and the patient's mind, or between psychoanalysis and house-cleaning (recall that Freud referred to free associations as "chimney-sweepings").

The third similitude, "analogy," combines the functions of contiguity and emulation. "Like the latter, it makes possible the marvellous confrontation of resemblances across space, but it also speaks, like the former, of adjacencies, of bonds and joints" (Foucault, 1973, p. 21). Analogy can also help us understand more clearly the last clinical example. To the extent that cleaning out the closet is a metaphor for free association, we have further reason to believe that the first activity stands for the second. Further parallels may be seen between the design of a walk-in closet and the inaccessible nature of the unconscious: both locations are characterized by darkness, disarray, and accumulations from the past. And it can be argued that cleaning out and repainting the closet are similiar to the goals of therapy: to restructure and refurbish the mind.

"Sympathy," the final similitude, is the least restrictive of the four types and, as a result, the most arbitrary (see Foucault, 1973, pp. 23–24). Sympathy explains why fire, because it is warm and light, rises in the air; it explains why the sunflower, which is yellow, turns toward the sun (which is also yellow). Sympathy also explains why the roses at a funeral will take on the mood of the mourners and lose their petals as a sign of grieving. The application of sympathy in a clinical setting is best established by the discovery of a pattern match that depends on neither contiguity, similarity, or analogy. These matches, although often arbitrary, can be justified by such terms as "empathy" or "intuition," but these descriptions are little more than rationalizations.

Access to the four similitudes gave the medieval scientist the key to understanding the world by going from surface to depth. The target object—a sunflower, a drooping rose, an attack of apoplexy, or some other unknown object—was first searched for the presence of a signature, the outward sign of a buried similarity. Once the appropriate signature had been identified, it was then possible to determine which of the four similitudes had been at work; by reasoning backwards, the scientist could then determine the essence of the target object.

Quaint and charmingly old-fashioned, one might respond—a clearly outdated piece of reasoning. But have times changed all that much? A high proportion of current clinical interpretations are grounded on one or more of the four classical similitudes. When analysts base interpretations on a sequence of associations, they are depending on *convenientia*; when they rest their argument on the similarity of two images, they are using *aemulatio*. In her recent review of Masson's *Final Analysis*, Tavris (1990) cites just such an instance:

> When a friend of mine, a family therapist who earned her doctorate at the University of California, Berkeley, arrived at her first job at a psychoanalytic institute, she asked to see the evaluation in her file. Her new employer obliged. "Dr. —— is clearly a skilled clinician," one colleague had written, "in spite of her unmistakable signs of penis envy." The unmistakable signs were . . . her dangling earrings. Why would a woman wear jewelry that dangles if she did not envy the one thing in nature that dangles naturally? (p. 7)

(In similar fashion, examples can also be found of interpretations that employ the two other similitudes).

The search for hidden signs has become an essential part of the current psychoanalytic approach to meanings. A budding Amarylis bulb, with its long stalk and emerging head, immediately strikes the psychoanalyst as phallic; the speaker who suddenly loses his or her voice is described as castrated. In both instances, the psychoanalyst is basing the interpretation on the similitude of aemulatio. The world of natural objects has become, once again, a world of hidden and not-so-hidden meanings, opaque to the naive but transparent to the initiated who can see below the surface into the depths of being. The spread of psychoanalytic theory has brought us back to the Middle Ages once again. The analyst scans the world (and the patients' free-associations) for resemblances that will tell the analyst what latent content lies beneath the surface appearance. The psychoanalyst may not believe (as did Paracelsus) that it is God's will to allow "nothing to remain without exterior and visible signs in the form of special marks—just as a man [or woman] who has buried a hoard of treasure marks the spot that he [or she] may find it again" (Foucault, 1973, p. 26)—but the analyst still believes that psychoanalysis has made him or her a better reader of the text of the world and that ever since Freud, the psychoanalyst can see farther and deeper.

But in adopting this approach, the analyst is using an outmoded form of reasoning that has come under increasing criticism in the past 400 years. Responding to a natural tendency to look on similar patterns as somehow related, the unhappy fate of the doctrine of signatures at the hands of Galilean science should warn us of its dangers. In the first place, we recognize that choice of similitude is always arbitrary and often rests on a matter of taste. In many of the clinical examples that are cited in the literature, the choice was made without benefit of the patient's associations; in other cases, it stemmed from a priori decisions about symbolic meanings. In the second place, clinical examples are almost always based on single cases, and the danger of reasoning from the single instance has come under more and more attack. If we base our conclusions on a single specimen, we take the chance that they are based largely on contingent, fortuitous associations which may never co-occur a second time, and thus cannot be generalized to a larger population.

Our knowledge of the doctrine of signatures allows us to better understand the widespread (and mistaken) tendency to derive hermeneutics from Hermes. All such derivations are based on the similitude of aemulatio that teaches us that surface similarity is a tell-tale clue to an underlying connection. Similar fallacies had plagued medieval science and medicine up to the time of the Renaissance, and the history of science during the past 1000 years reminds us that it required the Newtonian revolution to put that similitude to rest.

> For Aristotle, the immediate perceptible appearance, that which present-day biology terms the *phenotype*, was hardly distinguished from the properties that determine the object's dynamic relation. . . . With the differentiation of phenotype from genotype, many old class distinctions lost their significance. The orbits of the planets, the free falling of a stone, the movements of a body on an inclined plane, the oscillation of a pendulum . . . prove to be simply various expressions of the same laws. (Lewin, 1931, p. 149)

Galilean science has desensitized us to the surface attributes of the visible world and the implication that similarly appearing stimuli have something in common. The new science allowed the investigation of underlying connections between dissimilar objects, and it was this shift in emphasis that helped to bring about the rise of a single science of physics that could unite such disparate phenomena as billiard balls, planets, and black holes. A strict adherence to the doctrine of signatures would have made it impossible to even conceive of such connections.

But despite the rise of modern science and a general tendency to favor Galileo over Aristotle, the theory of signatures has not been completely silenced. Not only does it flourish in present-day clinical practice, but it can be demonstrated in more carefully controlled settings as well. In a well-known experiment, Chapman and Chapman (1969) presented a group of naive judges with a set of figure drawings, and each drawing was accompanied by several diagnostic statements. The set was carefully designed so that there was no relation between the content of the drawing and the accompanying statements. A face with shifty eyes, for example, might carry the statement, "is concerned about making mistakes," and a face with an open mouth might be accompanied by the sentence, "suspects that enemies are out to trick him or her." Despite the lack of expected correlation, the judges markedly overestimated the co-occurrence of drawings and related statements; in the example just given, they would remember the face with shifty eyes as being accompanied by the sentence describing suspicion of enemies. It will also be noticed that the tendency to discover a connection that was not present in fact made it impossible for the judges to form a clear picture of the actual data set. Once again, we see the power of one of the classic similitudes. Because shifty eyes provides a useful metaphor for paranoia, the judges concluded that the two events must co-occur to a significant degree.

This demonstration of what the Chapmans have called "illusory correlation" provides us with a metaphor for understanding the basis for many interpretations. The clinician may give lip-service to the rule of "evenly-hovering attention," but in fact, tends to listen to the clinical material with a favorite set of theoretical predispositions. Just as we tend to believe that shifty eyes are a sign of paranoia, so we may believe that splitting is a sign of borderline personality. If the patient being treated is a diagnosed borderline, it is almost inevitable that signs of splitting will also be observed and to a degree that goes beyond their actual occurrence. The odds are also high that such signs will be remembered in significantly greater frequency than they actually occurred. Once again, we see that interpretation favors the prepared mind.

For another demonstration of the way in which doctrine can influence observation, consider two studies in a series of memory experiments by Loftus (1979). In the first of these studies, a group of subjects was presented with a series of color slides showing people walking, talking, arguing, reading, or engaged in similar activites. One slide, which was the critical stimulus, showed a person reading a book with a *green* cover (the color is significant). The subject was next asked a series of questions that alluded to some other color not in the slide; thus, he might be asked whether the person reading the book with the *blue* cover was wearing a hat. Finally, the subjects were asked about the colors in the original slides. In cases in which the suggested color (e.g., blue) was different from the true color (e.g., green), 44% of the subjects believed that they had seen the suggested color in the original slide. Thus, the suggestion coming after the slide was presented and after its memory had been formed, seems to have revised the original memory (i.e., the new color, blue, has been incorporated in the old memory).

In a more dramatic experiment, subjects were presented with a film of a multiple-car accident in which one car fails to stop at a stop sign and makes a right-hand turn into the oncoming traffic. To avoid a collision, the cars in the traffic stream came to a sudden stop, resulting in a five-car accident. At the end of the film, the subjects were asked a series of ten questions. The first question was asked in two forms:

1. How fast was Car A going when it ran the stop sign?
2. How fast was Car A going when it turned right?

The last question in the series (Question 10) asked whether the subject had actually seen a stop sign in the film. If the first question had mentioned a stop sign (Form 1), 53% of the subjects answered yes to Question 10; if the first question did not mention a stop sign (Form 2), 35% answered yes to Question 10. In other words, the wording of the first question influenced the original memory of the film.

For an even more dramatic illustration of the way popular theory can influence memory, consider the way in which early childrearing practices are misremembered by parents only a few years after the fact (Robbins, 1963). Retrospective reports of standard childrearing events were compared with clinic records, and significant distortions were found in the recall of such items as (a) when the infant stopped using the bottle, (b) when bowel training was begun, (c) when bladder training was begun, and (d) when the 2 a.m. feeding was stopped. The errors, particularly those made by the mothers, tended to follow the advice of Benjamin Spock (1957) as presented in his best-selling book on childrearing, *Baby and Child Care*. The parallel between the expert's advice and the prevailing direction of distortion strongly suggests that the mothers' memories were influenced by a highly visible theory.

The tendency to "discover" illusory correlations and the tendency to remember what is emphasized by standard theory carries an important implication for the relation between theory and evidence. To the extent that case reports are based on casual process notes and anecdotal accounts, the tendency to make illusory correlations goes unchecked by the actual events. So long as the recollection cannot be checked against a systematic record, the therapist will tend to overestimate a co-occurrence predicted by theory and fail to discover the unexpected linkage that might cause theory to be overturned. The tendency to erroneously misremember evidence in accordance with standard theory may explain why Strachey's theory of mutative interpretation still stands in almost its original form, despite the lack of confirming evidence. From the standpoint of the individual clinician, it may seem as if the memory of his or her clinical experience matches Strachey's model even though the clinician may simply be distorting private experiences to mesh with standard theory. Against this strong inner conviction, the lack of published confirmation would seem to make little difference.

ONE THEORY—THREE THEORISTS

In his classic paper, Strachey (1934) outlined the following sequence of steps that make it possible for an interpretation to produce a clinical effect:

1. The analyst takes advantage of his or her role as an auxiliary, superego, and in effect, gives permission for the expression of a small amount of unconscious content.

2. This content is typically directed at the analyst (e.g., the patient might feel suddenly angry).

3. The patient's ego becomes aware of the discrepany between unleashed feelings and the true nature of the object; aware, in Strachey's words, "of a distinction between his [or her] archaic fantasy object and the real external object [the analyst]" (p. 143).

4. An interpretation made at this point is in the position to call attention to the discrepancy and produces a breach in the neurotic vicious circle.

5. The patient becomes aware of the inappropriate nature of an outburst and is in a position to reduce its strength.

6. In the process, the patient may also gain access to the infantile roots of the archaic rage and the archaic fantasy object. (The reader should consult Strachey, 1934, for a more complete discussion of these schematic points.)

It comes as somewhat of a surprise, after reading this carefully reasoned outline, to find that Strachey provides us with no illustrative clinical example. Even though his paper is still cited as a classic example of how interpretations "work," we now begin to wonder whether his explanation has any direct application to the clinical situation. Is it, rather, a largely empty theory that promises more than it can possibly deliver? Is it mainly a rhetorical device that keeps alive the belief that a well-crafted interpretation can, because of its form and content, bring about a significant clinical effect? A belief, unfortunately, that has never been validated.

The possibility that theory may have little to do with evidence gains further support when we jump ahead in time. Seven years after Strachey's paper was published, there appeared another landmark paper on the mechanisms of interpretation. It would seem to be a close cousin of Strachey's model, and the similarity of the two models would suggest either that little, if any, disconfirming evidence had become available in the intervening period, or—the more troubling possibility—that theory counted more than data, and that theory and evidence have become essentially uncoupled.

In answer to the question, "How does interpretation work?" Fenichel (1941) listed the following steps:

1. What is to be interpreted is first *isolated* from the experiencing part of the ego. This preliminary task drops out when the patient already has some critical attitude towards that which is to be interpreted.
2. The patient's attention is drawn to his own *activity: he himself* has been bringing about that which up to now he has thought he was experiencing passively.
3. He comprehends that he had motives for this activity which hitherto he did not know of.
4. He comes to note that *at some other point,* too, he harbors something similar, or something that is in some way associatively connected.
5. With the help of these observations he becomes able to produce less distorted "derivatives," and through these the *origins* of his behavior gradually becomes clear. (pp. 52–53)

We now skip forward to 1976 and find, in Schafer's well-known book on action language, that his chapter on claimed and disclaimed actions was inspired by the Fenichel formulation just quoted. Schafer (1976) summarizes the model in the following words:

In brief, the summary of interpretation is this: to identify a network of intelligible actions where none was thought to exist, thereby expanding the range of acknowledged activity in the analysand's experience of his or her life, and to develop a history of this life as intelligible activity. (p. 127)

He then presents a long clinical example, which includes a number of interpretations of disclaimed actions, but unfortunately for our purposes, we are not told how the patient responded to these remarks nor how they affected the nature of his primary symptom.

This brief review of the legacy of the Strachey model shows us that some 56 years after it was first published, we are still apparently unable to provide convincing clinical confirmation of its validity. Despite the fact that our collective experience has been enriched by additional tens of thousands of clinical hours, we are still woefully short of persuasive instantiations of Strachey's model. But this lack of a reinforcing data base does not prevent subsequent theorists, such as Fenichel and Schafer, from adopting the original model and presenting it as a useful and, by implication, definitive account of a central psychoanalytic process. The truth value of the model does not seem to depend on its success in the clinical arena, but rather on the opinion of previous authors of evident reputation. Repeated reinforcement from psychoanalytic authorities seems more important than the nature of the clinical evidence.

The low standing of clinical examples becomes even clearer when we look carefully at the few specimen interpretations that are available in the literature. Very few of these are sufficiently complete to allow the reader to determine whether the Strachey model is confirmed. Of those remaining, a large majority fail to provide a clear account of the patient's response. There remain a disturbing number of entirely hypothetical examples that are even further impaired by transparent accompanying excuses. We necessarily become dismayed when Freud tells us, in one of his last papers, that he will use an extra-analytic experience to make his point because a more relevant instance "would be easy to find but lengthy to describe" (Freud, 1937/1964, p. 263);

the sceptical reader may find this to be a barely concealed rationalization. In similar fashion, nearly everyone remembers Kris's penetrating discussion of the "good hour" but few readers will remember that the example is entirely hypothetical![1] In his introduction to the concept, Kris (1956) tells us that "though not frequent, [it] is familiar to all analysts. . . . Its course is varied, and I offer only an abstraction from experiences well advanced in analytic therapy" (p. 446). At subsequent points in the paper, Kris either describes his inability to present verbatim examples (e.g., "time does not permit a detailed illustration"; p. 447) or continues his abstract description ("clinical observation indicates . . . theoretical assumptions suggest"; p. 447); at no point in the paper does he give a single clinical example.

SPECIMEN INTERPRETATIONS

What are the characteristics of a specimen interpretation? We can begin with the condition that the ideal interpretation leads to therapeutic change; indeed, the fact that it can bring about this result is one of the distinguishing characteristics of psychoanalysis in contrast to other types of therapy (e.g., behavioral approaches).

One of the more clear-cut examples appears in Reiser (1985). Early in a female patient's analysis, she remembered a time when she was 13 and she and her brother were making tapioca pudding in the kitchen. Her brother was accidentally scalded; she was sent off to get some burn medicine; and next remembers waking up on a park bench, three hours later, with no idea of how she got there. She did not remember the name of the medicine she was supposed to buy, and the forgetting has persisted up to the present.

Toward the end of a 4-year analysis, she had a vivid, two-part dream. In the first part, she was planning a trip to Europe and to a certain city, in or near Germany, but could not remember the name. Then the scene shifted, and she was in the kitchen of her fiance's home. She was naked and her brother-in-law said, "That's a wonderful tan you have." She felt embarassed, asked for a robe, and replied, "Well, I am tan but not nearly as tan as Danny [her fiance]."

The analyst noted that the first part of the dream was about forgetting and he wondered whether the second part was about remembering—specifically, the name of the forgotten medicine. He wondered if she might now be able to recall the medicine. She did—it was *tannic acid*. (The reader should consult Reiser, 1985, pp. 20–24, for a more extensive account of the dream, its place in the treatment, and the implications of this amnesia and its recovery.)

The interpretation in this example attracts our notice because it was apparently validated by its result. It is patently evident that the first part of the dream is about forgetting and it is a clinical master-stroke to suggest that the second part is about remembering, for this theme is not obvious in the material. The ready response, tannic acid, fits with the patient's history and with a story that was first told some 4 years earlier in treatment. (It would, of course, be of more than passing interest to know in what session the burn story had last been repeated in the course of the analysis.)

Subsequent work (see Spence, 1987, p. 189) has shown that when groups of analytically trained judges are presented with the full text of this patient's dream and asked what medicine comes to mind, a large proportion, on three separate occasions, replied tannic acid. (This reponse is made even by those judges who, because of their age, are not familiar with the medicine.) These data suggest that the response is coded in the dream—probably in the two

---

[1]This kind of memory lapse can be seen as another example of an illusory correlation. Kris's "good hour" is exactly what we would like to find in our clinical work, and wishing it were true goes a long way towards making it true. As a result, the everhopeful clinician tends to "remember" Kris's paper as a collection of actual vignettes and not as a hypothetical exercise.

sentences: "That's a wonderful tan you have," and "Well, I am tan but not nearly as tan as Danny." But had the analyst responded to the dream in a somewhat different manner, the encoded medicine might easily not have been uncovered.

For a less convincing interpretation, we turn to the now-famous *aliquis* episode from Freud's *Psychopathology of Everyday Life* (1901). During one of his vacation trips, he tells us that he fell into conversation with another academic who also turned out to be Jewish. They were discussing their social position and the acquaintance—who goes unnamed—gloomily speculates on the likely chance that he and his people are doomed to extinction. "Let someone arise from my bones as an avenger," he proudly concludes in Latin, but he stumbles over the famous epigraph from Virgil and both changes the word order and omits the second word *aliquis* (someone). Freud first supplies the correct quotation and second—note the order—interprets the slip.

The gist of his interpretation traces the link between aliquis and such words as liquid and liquify. Freud then tells us that in a certain church in Naples, once a year on a certain holy day, a vial of blood mysteriously liquifies. The acquaintance, it now appears, has been preoccupied with the possibility that his lady friend may be pregnant, and uneasily awaiting the unwelcome news that she has stopped her periods—that her blood, in other words, has not liquified and that, as a consequence, she is pregnant. To omit aliquis, Freud informs him, is to avoid this uncomfortable reminder; hence the misquotation.

The interpretation is possible—even ingenious—but unconvincing. Multiple violations of the law of parsimony arouse our suspicion and in addition, as Grünbaum (1984, pp. 190–194) has made clear, it is fatally flawed by its post hoc status. Had Freud given his explanation first without supplying the correct quotation, he could have tested its validity by listening to the response. Had the explanation removed the anxiety surrounding the possible pregnancy, the Virgil quotation might well have appeared intact. Had it done so, we would have been greatly reassured that Freud's line of reasoning was, in fact, the correct explanation for the slip. (Notice that such a demonstration would have paralleled the recovery of tannic acid in the Reiser vignette.)

Without this kind of test, we have no guarantee that Freud's interpretation is not merely another clever rearrangement of the key items in the conversation to construct a plausible reason for the forgetting of aliquis. Ingenious explanations are easier to arrive at than might be supposed (see Spence, 1976). In a recent study by Dahl (personal communication, January 15, 1975) on hypothesis formation, a group of analysts listened to the early hours of a case while studying a set of possible hypotheses. They were instructed to interrupt the reading whenever any one of them decided that enough evidence had accumulated to support one of the hypotheses. Many interruptions took place, but few were supported by more than one or two of the listeners. This finding suggests that each judge tends to hear the material in his own way and that we must be cautious about assuming that there is a pattern in the material, waiting to be discovered.

The vast majority of published interpretations would seem to fall toward the aliquis end of the scale—possible, even probable, but neither inevitable nor persuasive. Very few come close to generating the same conviction conveyed by the tannic acid example. Put another way, it could be argued that the vast majority of published interpretations will appeal to a convinced Freudian but will not convince the generalist. Consider the following example from Sharpe (1937; italics added):

Feeling of Depression

I have a "feeling of depression" was a patient's opening remark lately. The hour's analysis was concerned with anxiety regarding the female genitals. I had no hesitation finally in saying that he was dealing with repressed emotion concerning an incident some time in childhood when he *literally* felt the "depression" of a little girl's genitals. (p. 32)

This is a possible interpretation but without more detailed evidence, we can hardly say whether it was justified by the clinical material. And without seeing the response from the patient, we have little way of judging its clinical effectiveness. The following is another example by Sharpe (1937):

Taking Silk

In the dream, "I take a piece of silk from a cupboard and destroy it," I found that silk as silk *per se* stimulated no important associations, while the phrase "take silk" brought real emotional understanding because "take silk" is the device of metonomy and means "to be called to the bar," i.e., to become a barrister. The first more superficial meaning of the dream was the hatred the dreamer had of his profession and on further analysis, the dream revealed hostile feelings toward the man's father who was himself a lawyer. (p. 23)

This example is somewhat more convincing because we are told something about the patient's reaction to the interpretation. But it can also be argued that "real emotional under-standing" can mean anything from an "ah-ha" experience to a mild conviction of correctness, and without the clinical detail, we are at a loss to know exactly how the interpretation was received, and therefore left in the dark concerning its validity. Once again, the verdict must be—possible but not persuasive.

The last example can be found in Greenson (1967):

Telling off Pappa

A male patient for many years struggled with his fear of expressing his anger and rage at me directly. Toward the end of one hour he begins to describe what he would say to me if he were drunk. He becomes more and more abusive verbally, begins to bang the wall with his fist, pounds the couch with his feet, and finally jumps off the couch. . . . I say nothing but as he was about to stomp out of the office, I call out to him: "How does it feel to finally tell Pappa he's not so great after all?" The patient stops still in his tracks at the word Pappa. He turns around and looks at me . . . Then he says slowly: "Well, I finally did it, finally, finally, finally, after all these years; I told you all off . . . I finally feel I'm a grown man and not just a little boy masquerading as a man." (pp. 328–329)

Here, at long last, is an interpretation that triggers a clear-cut emotional response and seems to make a clinical difference in the therapeutic process. The dramatic shift from anger to tears strongly suggests that the interpretation is correct; the emotional change is further supported by the patient's words. And because we are presented with an unusually detailed clinical vignette, we are in a much better position to judge for ourselves the validity of the intervention.

The fact that after almost 100 years of psychoanalytic practice we have so few specimens of interpretation that are either convincing or are clear instantiations of the Strachey model, coupled with the fact that theoretical models of interpretation outnumber convincing specimens by a very wide margin, tends to suggest that the concept of the mutative interpretation, achieved by language alone, is more rhetorical than we like to admit.

The failure to find convincing examples or instantiations of the more popular theories leads us to distinguish between two classes of interpretations. In the high proportion of published instances, an interpretation represents an attempt by the therapist to find an implicit meaning in the patient's associations, and as we have seen, most of these attempts are neither persuasive nor clinically significant. Nevertheless, they are clearly interpretations in the mind of the analyst, and this group will be labeled interpretation$_1$. In a much smaller set of instances, the interpretation is formulated in such a way that it will produce a visible clinical effect; this type will be labeled interpretation$_2$. Because evidence for the second set is largely absent in the clinical literature, we can conceptualize the standard interpretation, or interpretation$_1$, as a rhetorical device, similar to hyperbole or metaphor, which takes on certain distinguishing lexical characteristics and is intended to produce a certain response in the listener. It will be noted that when we read a clinical transcript, we can almost always identify the interpretations as they occur, just as we can identify such other figures of speech as metaphor, simile, and hyperbole. And just as the standing of the latter is not diminished when the listener fails to notice the figure, so the standing of interpretation₁ is not diminished when it fails to produce a significant clinical response.

A certain number of interpretations are probably based on the medieval similitudes. It is surface resemblance—unadorned or variously transformed—that triggers the pattern match and that gives rise to the sense that a meaning has been found that links the patterns. But because the pattern match rests on the outmoded doctrine of signatures, it is probably not a clue to an underlying similarity, and it is partly for this reason that these interpretations fail to produce a significant clinical reaction. When, on the other hand, we come across a rare example of interpretation₂, we usually find that it is not based on one of the similitudes, and it is tempting to believe that it is the avoidance of medieval logic that allows it to produce a significant clinical response (consider the Reiser example in this regard). Where the first type of interpretations can be viewed as a kind of rhetorical figure, it should be clear that interpretation₂ can be described as a useful and necessary clinical instrument.

DEVELOPMENTAL SURROUND AND TRANSFERENCE

The fact that many of the traditional interpretations seem clinically ineffective is closely coupled with a growing awareness, on the part of practicing therapists, that the standing of language in the clinical arena is no longer as privileged as we once liked to assume. At certain times in treatment, the patient may be in the position of the nonverbal child for whom words are merely noises uttered by adults and sensed as having no significant semantic content. The so-called preoedipal patient may frequently fall into this category. A growing awareness of different developmental stages and the ways in which they can be reenacted in treatment has led to the realization that some patients need months or even years of nonverbal support before they are in a position to listen to, much less understand, even the simplest interpretation. In a more general sense, this new sensitivity to the role of the patient as a preverbal infant has forced us to see the Strachey model (and Point 4 in particular) as unnecessarily grounded in an adult ego psychology that is simply out of touch with early childhood concerns. We begin to realize that the Strachey model may be an expression of an adultomorphic view of the developing infant (and the regressed patient) and as new findings from developmental studies continue to accumulate, we are beginning to see that this view is widely discordant with that emerging from infant studies. Consider, in this connection, the following vignette from Viederman (1991):

> The patient was a young lawyer who was unassertive, especially in his professional life, and markedly inhibited sexually. . . . During the first year and a half of analysis, *interpretations seemed to evoke little meaningful response as the patient seemed mired in inhibitions in both personal and professional areas.* He continued the only heterosexual relationship he had ever had with a woman who was equally inhibited. . . . During this first year it was the tone and quality of the relationship that was most important. In the context of the patient's experience of me as a person who encouraged him in his exploration of the world, and with the support of a pleasant comfort that had developed in our relationship that contrasted markedly with the hostile and denigrating behavior of his mother, he developed a passionate attachment to a woman. . . . *Protected by this developing relationship with the woman, significant analytic work began.* (pp. 456–457; italics added)

At other times in treatment, the patient's sense of an interpretation's meaning may depend on the state of the transference. Schafer (1985) has reminded us (following Freud) that "the analysand must already have developed a transference attachment to the analyst so that he [or she] will not flee from the analysis as the repressed material is brought to light" (p. 279). If the relationship is strongly positive, the voice of the analyst takes on an added significance that goes far beyond the utterances themselves, and endows whatever is expressed with a persuasive power that is something more than its semantic content alone. It is for this reason that many interpretations$_1$ can be clinically effective; even when their content fails to address a significant clinical issue, the healing power of the therapist can make up the difference. This power is grounded in such factors as the "shared expectancy" that the patient will be helped (Frank, 1961, p. 115); the professional standing of the therapist; the quasi-ritualistic nature of the analytic process with its fixed schedule of appointments, near-mystical use of the couch, and the proscription of doctor–patient contact outside of regular appointment hours; the technical, almost arcane language sometimes shared by doctor and patient; and finally, the secrecy surrounding the analytic process (see Frank, 1973, pp. 325–330).

We can now begin to identify at least two crucial omissions in the literature on interpretation. Because we usually have no information in the clinical specimen about which particular developmental phase is being reenacted, we are unable to determine whether an interpretation failed because the words were wrong or because the patient, as in the first 18 months of the Viederman case, was largely disconnected from the analyst and unable to process any verbal intervention. We are beginning to realize that every published specimen must also contain a brief description of the reenacted developmental period.

The same caution applies to the state of the transference. Because its nature is rarely indicated in the usual published specimen, we have no way of separating effects of content from the kind of transferential effects that may endow the therapist's every utterance with a significant power of persuasion. If such effects are operating, it follows that many interpretations$_1$, even though they are largely rhetorical and clinically irrelevant, can acquire a certain degree of healing power and can apparently produce a significant clinical difference. Even interpretations$_1$ that are based on the outmoded doctrine of signatures can have a mutative effect on the patient under the proper conditions. But it is important to realize that the source of this effect lies not in their content (which is, after all, based on a faulty and outmoded logic) but stems from the surrounding context. If the state of the transference is sufficiently positive, it can invest the most neutral utterance with a curative influence that goes far beyond its lexical content. (By the same token, an interpretation$_1$, given in the midst of a negative transference, will continue to have no clinical effect.)

We can now understand the basis for some of the misunderstanding in the clinical literature. When specific clinical specimens are published as illustrative examples, the focus is almost always laid on their lexical content and very little is said about the reenacted developmental period, the state of the transference, or other surrounding clinical features. Because these factors are usually left out of the discussion, the relation between interpretative content and clinical effect seems largely unexplained. Examples of interpretations$_1$ may sometimes bring about important clinical changes despite their faulty logic and unfortunate reliance on the doctrine of signatures, and the puzzled reader is left wondering whether the old doctrines may be true after all. But of course the content is usually irrelevant; positive effects in these cases are more likely due to nonverbal influences. Because the literature on interpretation is largely silent on the developmental surround or the state of the transference, we have tended to misconstrue the role of content and overplay its significance.

This line of reasoning would also suggest that there may be times when even interpretations$_2$ may fall on deaf ears. Suppose that Reiser's patient had reported the same dream that was quoted previously, but was in the midst of a long-lasting negative transference at the time. We can easily imagine that the (lexically correct) interpretation might have gone largely unheard and the reader of such an example would conclude that it produced no response because it was logically flawed. It can be seen that the developmental surround and transferential state must always be taken into account in evaluating an interpretive attempt.

CONCLUSIONS

The concept of the mutative interpretation holds a central place in psychoanalytic theory, but little confirming evidence has accumulated in its support since the time when it was first announced. Despite the lack of clinical support, its standing still remains high. We have argued that this apparent paradox is probably the result of the general tendency for memory to conform to received wisdom (the Robbins effect). Psychoanalysts would seem to misremember their clinical experience in a way that probably supports the Strachey model. For this reason, it is not surprising to find successive generations of analysts (e.g., Fenichel and Schafer) writing tributes in its behalf.

Repeated examination of actual interpretations as presented in the psychoanalytic literature would suggest that the Strachey/Fenichel/Schafer theory is significantly unrelated to clinical practice. In the vast majority of cases (interpretations$_1$), an interpretation is not mutative. Furthermore, it would seem to be little more than a rhetorical figure, similar to metaphor, simile, or hyperbole; invoked by the analyst to bring about a certain effect in the patient; and that can be readily identified by its form and content. These interpretations, as we have seen, are frequently grounded on the now-discredited doctrine of signatures. For that reason, they are unlikely to achieve any mutative effect unless—and this is a critical condition—they happen to coincide with a state of positive transference or an enabling therapeutic alliance. It goes without saying that mutative effects under these conditions are a consequence of the patient–doctor relationship and have nothing to do with the content of the interpretation.

We have also identified a small minority of interpretations$_2$ that appear to have mutative effects for reasons of content alone. These constructions are more than rhetorical; they are apparently not based on the doctrine of signatures; and it remains to be seen whether they conform to Strachey's explanation or to a new model, yet to be developed. But for all their advantages, interpretations$_2$ are still vulnerable to such extralexical features as the developmental surround of the clinical moment and the state of the transference. Interpretations, which may seem clinically relevant and lexically appropriate, may simply go unheard if the patient feels too distant from the analyst to listen to more than a few words at a time; even the most carefully crafted utterance quickly becomes an inexact interpretation (see Glover, 1931) under these conditions.

The vivid contrast between a popular theoretical model and the small number of confirming examples suggests that interpretative theory is seriously out of touch with clinical practice. Classical theories of interpretation are apt to be constructed in a top-down manner, derived from abstract metapsychological postulates and received tradition, and as a result, are more or less unrelated to clinical findings. The Strachey model is further handicapped by an excessive reliance on lexical factors and a corresponding underestimation of the degree to which a patient may take on the role of the nonverbal or preverbal child.

The clinical data, on the other hand, are largely unavilable because of the absence of a public database, a tradition of using unsystematic process notes instead of sustained recording, and a widespread concern about protecting the privacy of both patient and analyst. Because the lion's share of clinical data gathered today are stored in the memories of practicing analysts, they are particularly vulnerable to the Robbins effect, and tend to be selectively misremembered in a way that can easily support standard theory. It is partly for this reason that theory has become decoupled from practice, and why Strachey's model continues to be celebrated, even in the face of a pitifully small amount of confirming evidence.

Our review of the clinical specimens would seem to suggest that verbal interpretations are significantly overrated as a therapeutic tool. Their effect, if positive, may stem largely from the nature of the developmental surround and the background doctor–patient relationship, which, if appropriate, gives a persuasive coloring to just about any utterance by the analyst. It is largely for this reason that interpretations based on an outmoded and erroneous logic (the medieval doctrine of signatures) can still seem to have an occasional mutative effect. A new model of interpretation is needed using available clinical examples, is constructed bottom-up (as opposed to top-down), and finds a way of taking both content and context into account. In support of this model, we need to develop a new mode of clinical reporting that will accompany the specific lexical utterance with specific markers for developmental surround and state of the transference.

If the Strachey model is oriented too strongly in a verbal and cognitive direction, what kind of model should take its place? We are only beginning to become aware of the complicated manner in which young children come to know that people have minds and the way in which much of our knowledge of the world is acquired through observation of, and experience with, interacting adults (see Hobson, 1991). Long before language is understood, infants learn certain meanings of danger and safety by studying the mother's reaction; mother's expression tells them, for example, that the "visual cliff" is not dangerous and may be crawled across (see Sorce, Emde, Campos, & Klinnert, 1985). The appropriate preoedipal, nonverbal interpretative model must find ways of translating these findings from the child development literature into the appropriate psychoanalytic strategies. The ideal interpretative model, when fully developed, will indicate how the classic forms of mother–infant sharing can be simulated in language when the patient is on the couch. But the model will also indicate points at which lexical interpretation may not be sufficient and when access to eye contact, body language, and other nonlexical cues may be a necessary prerequisite to any kind of shared understanding. When the ideal model has been developed, we may find that certain kinds of preoedipal information can only be transmitted in a face-to-face setting, and that a certain minimal amount of social referencing in the analytic setting is necessary before the more traditional interpretative work can begin.

REFERENCES

Chapman, L. J., & Chapman, J. P. (1969). Illusory correlation as an obstacle to the use of valid psycho-diagnostic signs. *Journal of Abnormal Psychology, 74,* 271–280.

Fenichel, O. (1941). *Problems of psychoanalytic technique.* Albany, NY: Psychoanalytic Quarterly.

Foucault, M. (1973). *The order of things.* New York: Vintage Books.

Frank, J. (1961). *Persuasion and healing.* Baltimore: Johns Hopkins University Press.

Freud, S. (1960). The psychopathology of everyday life. In J. Strachey (Ed. and Trans.), *The standard edition of the complete psychological works of Sigmund Freud* (Vol. 6, pp. 1–310). London: Hogarth Press. (Original work published 1901)

Freud, S. (1964). Constructions in analysis. In J. Strachey (Ed. and Trans.), *The standard edition of the complete psychological works of Sigmund Freud* (Vol. 23, pp. 257–269). London: Hogarth Press. (Original work published 1937)

Glover, E. (1931). The therapeutic effect of inexact interpretation. *International Journal of Psychoanalysis, 12,* 397–411.

Greenson, R. (1967). *The technique and practice of psychoanalysis.* Madison, CT: International Universities Press.

Grünbaum, A. (1984). *The foundations of psychoanalysis.* Berkeley: University of California Press.

Hobson, R. P. (1991). Against the theory of "Theory of Mind." *British Journal of Developmental Psychology, 9,* 33–51.

Kris, E. (1956). On some vicissitudes of insight. *International Journal of Psycho-Analysis, 37,* 445–455.

Lewin, K. (1931). The conflict between Aristotelian and Galilean modes of thought in contemporary psychology. *Journal of General Psychology, 5,* 141–177.

Loftus, E. (1979). *Eyewitness testimony.* Cambridge, MA: Harvard University Press.

Onions, C. T. (Ed.). (1966). *The Oxford dictionary of English etymology.* New York: Oxford University Press.

Reiser, M. (1985). Converging sectors of psychoanalysis and neurobiology: Mutual challenges and opportunities. *Journal of the American Psychoanalytic Association, 33,* 11–34.

Robbins, L. C. (1963). The accuracy of parental recall of aspects of child development and child rearing practices. *Journal of Abnormal and Social Psychology, 66,* 261–270.

Schafer, R. (1976). *A new language for psychoanalysis.* New Haven, CT: Yale University Press.

Schafer, R. (1985). Wild analysis. *Journal of the American Psychoanalytic Association, 33,* 275–299.

Sharpe, E. F. (1937). *Dream Analysis.* London: Hogarth Press.

Sorce, J. F., Emde, R. N., Campos, J., & Klinnert, M. D. (1985). Maternal emotional signaling: Its effect on the visual cliff behavior of 1-year-olds. *Developmental Psychology, 17,* 737–745.

Spence, D. P. (1976). Clinical interpretation: Some comments on the nature of the evidence. In T. Shapiro (Ed.), *Psychoanalysis and contemporary science* (Vol. 5, pp. 367–388). Madison, CT: International Universities Press.

Spence, D. P. (1987). *The Freudian metaphor.* New York: Norton.

Spock, B. (1957). *Baby and child care* (rev. ed.). New York: Pocket Books.

Strachey, J. (1934). The nature of the therapeutic action of psychoanalysis. *International Journal of Psycho-Analysis, 15,* 127–159.

Tavris, C. (1990, October 21). [Review of *Final analysis*]. *New York Times Book Review,* p. 7.

Viederman, M. (1991). The real person of the analyst and his role in the process of psychoanalytic cure. *Journal of the American Psychoanalytic Association, 39,* 451–489.

26

TESTING PSYCHOANALYTIC PROPOSITIONS ABOUT PERSONALITY CHANGE IN PSYCHOTHERAPY

LESTER LUBORSKY, JACQUES BARBER, AND PAUL CRITS-CHRISTOPH

In this chapter we review both the central theoretical propositions about change in psychoanalytic psychotherapy and the recent formal research on them. That combination of the rigorous clinical and the empirical is rare but is becoming less so. During the past 2 decades theory-based research on dynamic psychotherapy (as we call the psychoanalytically oriented psychotherapies) has begun to prosper. Before that time, most of the literature was either of a theoretical nature without explicit attention to systematic empirical support or was based on clinical observations from a few patients. Moreover, few of the systematic efforts at developing methods to measure and test the theories have been reported, and this research is barely known even to its numerous practitioners. We hope that our review can begin to fill this information gap.

The essential hallmark of dynamic psychotherapy is simply summed up by G. Klein (1970) as entailing a focus on achieving the understanding of *intentionality* (motivation) from the viewpoint of the patient. Beyond this definition, there is some diversity among psychodynamic theorists. We have, therefore, relied for our assemblage of the central theoretical propositions on a representative sample of writers on the techniques of dynamic therapy. Luborsky (1984) cited these sources and gave a fuller statement of these theoretical propositions. For all of these theorists

This chapter is an adaptation and update of the article, "Theory-Based Research for Understanding the Process of Dynamic Psychotherapy" in the *Journal of Consulting and Clinical Psychology* (Vol. 58, pp. 281–287). Copyright © 1990 by the American Psychological Association. Used by permission.

Preparation of this article was supported in part by National Institute of Mental Health Grants MH-39673 and MH-40472 to Lester Luborsky and Paul Crits-Christoph, respectively; Research Scientist Award MH-40710 to Lester Luborsky; Career Development Award MH-00756 to Paul Crits-Christoph; and NIMH Clinical Research Center grant P50-MH45178.

as well as for ourselves, the prime source of these propositions has been Freud's six papers on technique (Freud, 1911/1988b, 1912a/1988a, 1912/1961, 1913/1958b, 1914/1958c, 1915/1958a). Thus, our review focuses on mainstream theoretical propositions about dynamic therapy, not on the more specific theoretical ideas that distinguish the different theories from each other. Measures drawn from nondynamic theories are referred to when they are related to the dynamic theories, but we do not review the excellent process research on personality change in other psychotherapies, such as client-centered (Rogers & Dymond, 1954) and cognitive–behavioral (Barber & DeRubeis, in press; Hollon & Kriss, 1984).

THEORETICAL PROPOSITIONS

Compared with other reviews, ours is organized around theoretical propositions and studies of their operational measures. The six propositions we present are operationalizations of hypotheses within most accounts of dynamic therapy. Some of the research is new; some draws on or is related to these earlier reviews: Luborsky and Spence (1971, 1978); Orlinsky and Howard (1986); Luborsky, Crits-Christoph, Mintz, and Auerbach (1988); Dahl, Kachele, and Thomae (1988); Crits-Christoph, Barber, and Beebe (in press); Crits-Christoph, Barber, and Cooper (in press); and Miller, Luborsky, Barber, and Docherty (in press).

We have included theoretical propositions that are associated with two major classes of techniques of dynamic psychotherapy: the supportive and the expressive, often called the interpretative (Luborsky, 1984; Wallerstein, Robbins, Sargent, & Luborsky, 1956). Supportive techniques are designed to maintain or strengthen the existing defenses and level of functioning; expressive techniques are designed to foster increases in self-understanding through the patient's revelations and the therapist's interpretations of what has been revealed. The first theoretical proposition on forming an alliance is part of the supportive aspects of the relationship; the subsequent five propositions are related primarily to the expressive techniques.

For each theoretical proposition in our review, we first state the proposition, then give its sources (without going into an exhaustive review), and then describe some of the relevant research. After this exposition of the six propositions in this format, we conclude by pointing the way to the future of the field.

1. *A therapeutic alliance must develop if the patient is to benefit from dynamic psychotherapy.*

Sources. Freud (1913/1958b), in his recommendations for the technique of psychoanalysis, stressed the necessity for rapport between patient and therapist and for the therapist to listen with sympathetic understanding in order for a good relationship to develop. When this occurs, the therapist is providing a basic contribution to a supportive relationship. When the patient feels supported then the patient is empowered by the alliance to persevere in making efforts to deal with the symptoms that brought the patient to treatment.

Research. The concept of the therapeutic alliance had to be translated into an operational measure in order to test its implied theoretical proposition. The earliest operational translation (Luborsky, 1976) was built on Bordin's (1979) theoretical division of the alliance into "the goals, techniques and bonds." There are three types of therapeutic alliance measures: (a) counting of signs systems (Luborsky, 1976); (b) global rating systems, such as the California Psychotherapy Alliance Scales (CALPAS), with Therapist and Rater Versions (Marmer & Gaston, 1988); the Vanderbilt Therapeutic Alliance scale (Hartley & Strupp, 1983); the Penn Helping Alliance Rating Method (Luborsky, Crits-Christoph, Alexander, Margolis, & Cohen, 1983; Morgan, Luborsky, Crits-Christoph, Curtis, & Solomon, 1982); and the Therapeutic Alliance Rating System (Marmer, Horowitz, Weiss, & Marziali, 1986); and (c) patient questionnaires, such as the CALPAS-Patient Version (Marmar & Gaston, 1988), the Helping Alliance Questionnaire (Luborsky, McLellan, Woody, O'Brien, & Auerbach, 1985) and the Working Alliance Inventory (Horvath & Greenberg, 1986). For a comparison of some of these measures, see Tichenor and Hill (1986).

The therapeutic alliance measures have shown significant predictions of outcome in many studies. For example, Hartley and Strupp (1983) showed that higher scores on therapeutic alliance measures related to better outcome. After 25% of the treatment sessions had been completed, the total scale and the patient and therapist scales discriminated good from poor outcome groups. Similarly, Marmar, Gaston, Gallagher, and Thompson (1989) showed that the alliance factors of Patient Commitment and Patient Working Capacity from the CALPAS–Therapist Version were related to outcome, across three treatments (behavioral, cognitive, and brief dynamic), as was Patient Commitment from the CALPAS–Patient Version. The Penn Helping Alliance scales, applied only on the third and fifth session, have been found to significantly predict the outcome of psychodynamic psychotherapy (Morgan et al., 1982). In a review of eight studies predicting outcome from the alliance measures, Luborsky et al. (1988) reported that all had significant predictions of outcome with a mean correlation of .5. In a more detailed review Orlinsky and Howard (1986) found the same trend. DeRubeis and Feeley (in press), however, did not find significant prediction of outcome from the alliance in cognitive therapy for depression using the Penn Helping Alliance Rating Method. By far the most comprehensive review, by Horvath, Gaston, and Luborsky (in press), reported that the overwhelming majority of about 30 studies with correlations between alliance measures and outcome measures were significant (with a mean correlation around .3).

From a broader perspective the concept of the alliance is a facet of a more general concept, that of attachment. This term, and much of the early research using it, derives from Bowlby (1973). This work has been continued in a series of studies by Sroufe and Waters (1977) and Sroufe (1983). Later developments came about through the findings of Main and Goldwyn (1985) using the Adult Attachment Interview. The results of the research on attachment imply that it would be valuable to study psychotherapy data using some of the fruitful dimensions from the attachment literature, such as the intensity of attachments and the breadth versus restriction of attachments.

2. *Patients display a central relationship theme (the transference pattern).*

Sources. Freud (1905/1953, 1912/1988a) put forward this proposition almost from the start of psychoanalysis, and dynamic therapists have been relying on the concept ever since. Various authors differ in how much should be encompassed in the concept of transference (for a review, see Sandler, Holder, Kawenoka, Kennedy, & Neurath, 1969). On the one hand, some theorists (e.g., Waelder, 1956) restrict the use of the term "transference" to the description of the intense relationship with the therapist that evolves during treatment and that represents a reenactment of past relationships ("transference neurosis"). Others (Sandler et al., 1969) view transference as a broader concept that includes similar aspects of the patient's relationships with a variety of people including the therapist ("character transference").

We follow Freud (1905/1953, 1912/1988a) who generally used the broader concept. In fact the transference concept is intricately multifaceted. Through a reading of all that Freud wrote on transference, a collection can be assembled of 22 different observations about his concept (Luborsky, 1990). These observations fall into several types: the stimuli that set off the transference, the origins of transference, and the degree to which it is conscious or unconscious. Most of the observations do not appear to be theoretically based but rather they appear to be derived from his own experience with patients.

Research. Although the use of the concept was widespread, research methods were not available to assess transference reliably. Seitz (1966) was the first to conclude that the concept could not be judged reliably. But an alternative conclusion could have been that each clinician's idiosyncratic method of conceptualizing and assessing the transference made it difficult to assess reliably. In order to resolve the problem of reliability, a new method was created: the Core Conflictual Relationship Theme (CCRT) method (Luborsky, 1976). The method (Luborsky & Crits-Christoph, 1990) uses as its data base narratives from psychotherapy about interactions with other people, including the therapist. The method identifies the pattern and the relationship conflicts in these interactions in terms of three components: the wishes toward the others, the responses of the others, and the responses of the self. The combination of the most frequent types of each of these components across the narratives is designated the CCRT. From an orthodox psychoanalytic viewpoint, the CCRT and other similar methods are measures of character transference. The CCRT has been shown to be judged reliable on a moderate-sized sample (Crits-Christoph, Luborsky, Dahl, Popp, Mellon, & Mark, 1988).

A series of studies of the CCRT indicate that, the observations that Freud made about the nature of the transference template were generally similar to the observations made about the nature of the CCRT (Luborsky & Crits-Christoph, 1990). For 7 of Freud's 22 observations about transference, congruent evidence has been found in empirical studies with the CCRT. These 7 studies have shown that there is a parallel between the pattern in relation to the therapist and to other people; that wishes toward other people exist in every pattern; that the wishes tend to conflict with the expected responses from others; that the pattern is largely consistent over time; that some changes in the pattern occur over time; that accurate interpretations lead to more benefits from treatment; and that the pattern can be judged to be positive or negative. Preliminary results on smaller samples appear to be positive for 8 more of Freud's 22 observations. Operational measures have not yet been constructed that would make possible the study of the remaining seven observations.

In addition to the CCRT, 14 alternative central relationship pattern measures have been developed (Luborsky & Crits-Christoph, 1990), including configurational analysis (M. Horowitz, 1979), idiographic conflict summary (Perry, Augusto, & Cooper, 1989), and the frame method Teller & Dahl, 1981). The methods have these characteristics in common: (a) the database is a sample of relationship interactions, either narratives about them or observed samples of interactions; (b) the formulation focuses on the most frequent pattern; and (c) the formulation of the pattern is based in part on clinical judgment.

The alternative measures, besides the CCRT, that are the most psychometrically developed are (a) Benjamin's (1986) Structural Analysis of Social Behavior (SASB), in which a therapy session is divided into single thought units, and three types of judgments of each unit are made: the focus of the message, the degree to which the message is friendly versus hostile, and the degree of interdependence. These judgments are combined to form the SASB classification. (b) Another measure, the Consensual Response Formulation (L. Horowitz, Rosenberg, Ureno, Mertz, & O'Halloran, 1989), is based on a videotape of an evaluation interview presented to a group of clinicians, each of whom writes a dynamic formulation. The formulations are divided into thought units, and the most frequent thought units across clinicians are collected into a main consensual formulation. (c) Another method, the Plan Diagnosis method, grew out of a special and elaborate psychoanalytic theory of therapy developed and tested by Weiss, Sampson, and the Mount Zion Psychotherapy Group (1986). The patient's plan refers to the strategies devised by the patient to disconfirm his or her pathogenic beliefs. The components of the measure include the patient's goals, the inner obstructions, the ways the patient is likely to test the therapist, and the insights that will be helpful.

Beyond the psychoanalytic perspective, the transference pattern can be thought of as a version of a relationship schema. The concept of relationship schema has a long history in psychology. The classic memory research of Bartlett (1932) extended by Erdelyi (1985) relied on this concept. Considerable recent research has been devoted to the central relationship pattern and its parallels from psychodynamic and from cognitive psychology viewpoints (M. Horowitz, 1991; Kihlstrom, 1984). The relevance of the research in cognitive psychology to research on central relationship patterns in psychoanalysis is illustrated by the work of Fiske and Dyer (1985). They found, for example, that once a schema has been laid down the intake of new information is shaped by the preexisting schema.

3. *The therapist's interpretations of the relationship pattern with the therapist will be especially beneficial.*

Sources. Freud recommended that the patient's communications be permitted to run on until transference becomes a resistance. Then the transference should be interpreted, even though such interpretation might stir up resistance from time to time (Freud, 1913/1958b, p. 139).

Other theorists have emphasized the therapist's role in connecting the patient's pattern of interpersonal relationships as experienced with the therapist (the transference), to previous relationships with parental figures ("parent link") and to relationships with other people (e.g., Davanloo, 1980; Malan, 1976).

Research. Studies by Malan (1976) and Marziali (1984) suggested that the frequency of use of transference interpretations is related to better outcomes. Another version of transference interpretation, the linkage in a triangle of the therapist with past and current persons, correlated significantly with outcomes ($r = .57$; McCullough, Winston, Laikin, & Vitolo, 1989). Such results, however, were not replicated by Piper, Debbane, Bienvenu, de Carufel, and Garant (1986). Nor did Silberschatz, Fretter, and Curtis (1986) find differences in the patients' immediate benefits following transference versus nontransference interpretations.

Following Davanloo (1980), McCullough (1987) suggested a factor that might mediate the relation between interpretations and the treatment outcome: whether the interpretation leads to affective versus defensive responses. She found that interpretations followed by affect tended to be associated with better outcome, whereas interventions followed by defensiveness tended to be associated with poorer outcome. Such results raise the further question of whether a patient's defensive response is a traitlike characteristic or is due to the appropriateness of the interpretation. In favor of the first possibility is Azim, Piper, McCallum, and Joyce's (1988) finding that the patient's response to interpretation depends on the quality of the patient's object relations. Studies are needed to examine the complex interactions among the object of an interpretation, its appropriateness, the patient's immediate emotional versus defensive reaction, the patient's capacity for object relations, the alliance and end-of-treatment outcome measures.

4. *The patient will benefit more from more accurate interpretations.*

Sources. Freud (1912/1988a) recommended that interpretations be accurate. He illustrated this principle by extensive marshaling of evidence for his interpretations. Dynamic psychotherapists also implicitly share this opinion in their emphasis on the development of a dynamic formulation of the patient's problems. Despite the importance of accurate interpretations, few well-articulated guidelines are found in the literature. French (1954) is one of the few who further specified a principle for achieving such accuracy. He recommended that the therapist first identify the central relationship pattern, which he called the *nuclear conflict*, and then select interpretations that address this conflict.

Research. An early format for an operational measure of the quality of the therapist's interventions was contained in Auerbach and Luborsky's (1968) variable, *therapist responds effectively to patient's main communications.* For each session, the judge described first the patient's main communications, and second, the content of the therapist's responses, including interpretations, and then rated the degree of effectiveness of the second as a response to the first. The variable had moderate reliability and significantly distinguished better from poorer sessions.

Studies inspired by the Weiss et al. (1986) theory of therapy have assessed the relation between patients' progress and a theory-derived measure of accuracy of interpretation (Silberschatz et al., 1986). One pair of judges formulated the plan used by patients to try to disconfirm their pathogenic beliefs (the plan diagnosis formulation), and another pair of judges rated the compatibility of the therapists' interpretations with the patients' plan. These investigators reported that, for three patients, the degree of compatibility of the interpretations with the patient's plan was significantly correlated with patient's immediate positive responses in the session as measured by greater "*experiencing*," a term that refers to the capacity to both examine and be aware of the experience. The reliability (four to six judges pooled) for the Plan Compatibility of Intervention scales ranged from .85 to .89.

Another operationalization of this theoretical proposition was constructed using the patient's CCRT as a criterion (Crits-Christoph, Cooper, & Luborsky, 1988). One independent set of judges identified the CCRT, and the other set identified the degree of accuracy in terms of convergence with the therapist's interpretations. The reliabilities (three judges pooled) were high: .84 for wishes, .76 for responses from other, and .83 for responses of self. For 43 patients, the correlation between accuracy on the wish plus response-from-other components of the CCRT with outcome (a composite measure of ratings of change by therapist and patient) was .44 ($p < .01$). Accuracy on the response-of-self component of the CCRT was not related to outcome, suggesting that it is the focus on the interpersonal aspects of the theme (wish and response from other) that is most important. The results remained in force even after partialing out the effects of general errors in technique and the quality of the therapeutic alliance. This study also examined whether accurate interpretations had their greatest impact in the context of a positive therapeutic alliance, but no evidence for this appealing proposition was found.

Another study with a similar basic focus (Piper, Azim, Joyce, & McCallum, 1991) examined the convergence of the therapist's interpretations with the therapist's early session formulations of the main theme, in relation to the outcome of psychotherapy. The use of the therapist's formulations rather than those of independent judges is problematic, but it is still of value to see that the correspondence has a positive impact in relation to the outcome of the therapy.

Within client-centered therapy, the therapist's empathy for the patient is theoretically important, and many studies have been done on its predictive capacity for the outcomes of psychotherapy. Empathy in client-centered therapy tends to refer to the quality of the therapist's reflection of the patient's conscious feelings. In dynamic therapy, empathy is not the usual explanatory concept, nevertheless, it is probably related to accuracy of interpretation. In a recent review of research on empathy, Luborsky et al. (1988) reported that of 13 studies examining the relation between empathy and outcome, 8 were significant. For the 9 studies of the 13 that reported results in correlational form, the mean correlation was .26.

5. *Patients gain understanding about themselves and their relationships with others during psychodynamic treatment, which then leads to better outcome.*

Sources. The best known summation of this hypothesis is Freud's (1933/1964) aphoristic one: "Where Id was there shall Ego be" (p. 80), that is, knowledge is added to the ego through greater awareness of the forces of the id. It is a generally accepted tenet of technique in dynamic therapy that the therapist should strive to help the patient gain an understanding of what had been only partly or entirely unconscious, especially aspects of the transference pattern (Freud, 1914/1958c; Luborsky, 1984; Malan, 1976).

Research. Ways of measuring self-understanding (also called "insight") in psychotherapy are still much needed. Broitman (1984) studied the impact of interpretations that were compatible with the patient's unconscious plan. Results indicated that for each of three patients, interpretations that were plan compatible were followed by increases in insight. The measure of insight (derived from Morgan et al., 1982), however, was found to be highly related to the experiencing scale and therefore the findings for insight are likely to be redundant with the correlations reported between plan compatibility and experiencing (Silberschatz et al., 1986).

In our own research (Crits-Christoph, 1984; Crits-Christoph & Luborsky, 1990b), we operationalized a measure of self-understanding as the convergence of the patients' statements in the session about themselves with their independently established CCRTs. The patient's level of self-understanding of the CCRT about the therapist and about people, measured in early sessions of treatment, was significantly associated with outcome, but self-understanding about the CCRT in general and in relation to parents was not. We have not yet examined, however, the proposition that gains on our measure of self-understanding over the course of therapy would occur when patients improve.

The measure of experiencing developed by the client-centered researchers appears to be partly a measure of self-understanding. Experiencing is defined as a capacity with two facets: it is both the capacity to experience and the capacity to become aware of the experience (M. H. Klein, Mathieu-Coughlan, & Kiesler, 1986). Of 11 studies using the experiencing measure as a predictor (Luborsky et al., 1988), 4 were significantly positive, 2 were significantly negative, and 5 were nonsignificant, with a mean correlation of .38 for 3 studies that gave a correlational result. These studies showed a moderately positive relation between experiencing and outcome.

Further measures of self-understanding are needed that might capture evidence bearing on the hypothesis that greater self-understanding serves to help the patient benefit from psychotherapy. Among the measures that should be tried are the conventional rating method such as Morgan et al. (1982).

6. *Improved patients will show a greater change in their transference patterns than unimproved patients.*

Sources. This proposition is consistent with Freud's views about the purpose of transference interpretations. In the account of Dora's treatment, for example, Freud (1905/1953) is critical of himself for not having interpreted the transference that led Dora to leave treatment prematurely. The same proposition also appears throughout the clinical literature (e.g., Davanloo, 1980).

Research. This hypothesis was examined in a study of the changes in pervasiveness of the CCRT from early to late in therapy in 33 patients who received psychodynamic therapy (Crits-Christoph & Luborsky, 1990a). Pervasiveness of the CCRT was defined as the frequency of the repetition of similar components of the CCRT across the relationship episodes: The higher the pervasiveness score, the more relationship episodes contained the same CCRT components. We found that (a) the pervasiveness scores showed high agreement among judges; (b) these scores remained consistent from early to late in therapy, a finding that was in agreement with Freud's (1912/1988a) observation; (c) the pervasiveness of the patient's wishes remained consistent during treatment; (d) the patient's expectations of how others would respond to them were less negative, and similarly the negative responses from self decreased with treatment; and (e) at the same time positive responses from others increased.

Change in the CCRT's pervasiveness was found to be significantly correlated with change in the patient's level of distress and change in overall mental health. For example, the more negative expectation of responses from others decreased, the more mental health improved.

The conclusions from these findings are still limited because the CCRT is scored on a limited number (10) of narratives told by the patient early in treatment versus late in treatment. In addition, we have not yet examined whether changes in the CCRT from early to late are related to changes in the types of other people in the narratives.

Despite these limitations, however, we still succumb to the temptation to speculate on the implications of the findings on change in the CCRT for two alternative clinical theories of change in dynamic therapies. One theory holds that the transference is resolved in successful psychotherapy, the other theory holds that the transference is still evident but under better control and mastery. The results from this study are more consistent with the latter. This is especially true for the wishes, which remain consistent over time, whereas the responses from others and from self tend to change more with therapy.

FUTURE RESEARCH ON PSYCHOANALYTIC PROPOSITIONS

We have concentrated on research that tests the six most essential propositions about curative factors in dynamic psychotherapy. More work is needed on other crucial aspects of the general theory of change in dynamic psychotherapy beyond the propositions we have reviewed. Internalization, for example, is an important construct that has often been posited as a required capacity of a patient for being able to maintain the gains of psychotherapy (Kernberg, 1975). Unfortunately, few theoretical articles and even fewer empirical studies have addressed this concept. Future work on this construct, however, can build on Geller (1987) and on Orlinsky and Geller's (in press) examination of different facets of the concept. Other important psychoanalytic constructs for which additional theoretical and empirical work is desirable are resistance and working through.

Much more work is needed on Proposition 5 about the way dynamic therapy achieves its benefits through greater understanding of thoughts that were partly or entirely unconscious, especially aspects of the central relationship pattern. Methods to measure the level of awareness of conflictual material are much needed. The first attempts (Crits-Christoph & Luborsky, 1990b) indicated that the level of self-understanding at the beginning of treatment was significantly related to the outcomes of the treatment. Although the hypothesis concerning gains in self-understanding has not yet been even nearly adequately tested, there are strong theoretical reasons to persist with research on this topic.

A further proposition of dynamic psychotherapy holds that the therapist's adherence to the recommendations for techniques of dynamic psychotherapy should produce benefits for the patient. The mere existence of many guides to techniques, beginning with Freud's (1913/1958b, 1914/1958c, 1912/1988a) recommendations, implies that the writers and users of the manuals believe that adherence should be beneficial to the patient. These recommendations have been widely accepted, although a few have remained controversial. One of these recommendations deals with the degree to which it is permissible for the therapist to directly foster the therapeutic alliance through techniques other than just letting it develop naturally, in a generally accepting atmosphere of sympathetic understanding.

Studies addressing this issue can now be more rigorously performed because of the emergence of specific treatment manuals for dynamic psychotherapy (Luborsky, 1984; Kernberg, Selzer, Koenigsberg, Carr, & Appelbaum, 1989; Strupp & Binder, 1984). We (Barber, Crits-Christoph, & Luborsky, 1989) are engaged in developing an adherence and competence scale to the manual for supportive–expressive psychotherapy (Luborsky, 1984) and examining a sample of depressed patients to determine whether greater adherence is associated with greater benefits to the patient.

An issue related to adherence is the role of differences in the level of each therapist's skillfulness. It is important not only to know what therapists do (adherence) but also to know how well they do what they are supposed to do (competence or skillfulness). Sloane, Staples, Cristol, Yorkston, and Whipple (1975) reported that their improved patients viewed their therapist's skills as contributing to the treatment outcome. Sachs (1983) showed that the more the therapists made errors in technique, as rated on the Vanderbilt Negative Indicators Scale, the poorer the outcome, although her finding did not replicate in Crits-Christoph, Cooper, and Luborsky (1988).

Methods that provide data relevant to other theories, such as in the task-focused approach (Rice & Greenberg, 1984), should be tried in dynamic therapy. This approach allows for the testing of clinical microtheories of change by focusing on points in sessions at which clients are struggling to resolve problems. Hypotheses are tested about the types of therapists' interventions at those points that facilitate change. This approach has been applied, for example, to the analysis of change events in client-centered therapy (Wiseman & Rice, 1989).

PSYCHOANALYSIS AND PSYCHOLOGY: RAPPROCHEMENT

Almost from the beginning of psychoanalysis Freud (1895/1950) dreamed of and began shaping psychoanalysis into a general psychology. That agenda was continued by Rapaport (1961) in a series of theoretical papers, supported by some empirical research, but not empirical research on psychoanalytic or psychotherapeutic treatment. Our return to empirical studies on dynamic psychotherapies is a good basis for rapprochement between psychoanalysis and psychology. After all it was the milieu of treatment sessions that generated Freud's propositions about personality change in psychotherapy.

Research on several of these psychoanalytic propositions shows the mutual influence of psychoanalysis and psychology most clearly. For example, the research on the therapeutic alliance can be seen as part of a broader area of research on attachment behavior in children that has more recently been extended to attachment behavior in adults (Bowlby, 1973; Main & Goldwyn, 1985).

What has become an especially active field since about 1976 is the research on patterns or schemata derived from relationship interactions in psychotherapy. The interactions of this work in relation to cognitive psychology has become much more prominent (Fiske & Dyer, 1985; M. Horowitz, 1991; Luborsky, 1988; Luborsky, Crits-Christoph, Friedman, Mark, & Schaffler, 1991).

As another example, the research on accuracy of interpretation (Crits-Christoph, Cooper, & Luborsky, 1988) has as a future agenda an examination of correspondence of its findings with that from a variety of research studies on the sources of empathy in children and in adults.

As a whole our overview of the domains of psychoanalysis and psychology, through a review of research testing psychoanalytic propositions, reflects a mutually beneficial interaction that is being accomplished nowadays, more empirically than solely theoretically.

REFERENCES

Auerbach, A. H., & Luborsky, L. (1968). Accuracy of judgments of psychotherapy and the nature of the "good hour." In J. Schlien, H. Hunt, J. Matarazzo, & C. Savage (Eds.), *Research in psychotherapy* (Vol. 3, pp. 155–168). Washington, DC: American Psychological Association.

Azim, H., Piper, W., McCallum, M., & Joyce, A. (1988, June). *Antecedents and consequences of transference interpretations in short-term psychotherapy.* Paper presented at the Society for Psychotherapy Research, Santa Fe, NM.

Barber, J. P., Crits-Christoph, P., & Luborsky, L. (1989). *The Penn Adherence Scale for Supportive–Expressive Therapy (PAS-SE).* Unpublished manuscript.

Barber, J. P., & DeRubeis, R. J. (in press). On second thought: Where the action is in cognitive therapy for depression. *Cognitive Therapy and Research, 13,* 441–457.

Bartlett, F. C. (1932). *Remembering.* Cambridge, England: Cambridge University Press.

Benjamin, L. S. (1986). Operational definition and measure of dynamics shown in the stream of free associations. *Psychiatry, 49,* 104–129.

Bordin, E. (1979). The generalizability of the psychoanalytic concept of the working alliance. *Psychotherapy: Theory, Research and Practice, 16,* 252–260.

Bowlby, J. (1973). *Attachment and loss* (Vol. 2). New York: Basic Books.

Broitman, J. (1984). *Insight, the mind's eye.* Unpublished doctoral dissertation, Wright Institute, Berkeley, CA.

Crits-Christoph, P. (1984, May). *The development of a measure of self-understanding of core relationship themes.* Paper presented at the National Institute of Mental Health workshop on Methodological Challenges in Psychodynamic Research, Washington, DC.

Crits-Christoph, P., Barber, J. P., & Beebe, K. (in press). Psychodynamic research on insight and self-understanding. In N. Miller, L. Luborsky, & J. Docherty (Eds.), *A guide to psychodynamic treatment research.* New York: Basic Books.

Crits-Christoph, P., Barber, J. P., & Cooper, A. (in press). Clinical and research perspectives on interpretation in psychoanalysis and dynamic psychotherapy. In N. Miller, L. Luborsky, & J. Docherty (Eds.), *A guide to psychodynamic treatment research.* New York: Basic Books.

Crits-Christoph, P., Cooper, A., & Luborsky, L. (1988). The accuracy of therapists' interpretations and the outcome of dynamic psychotherapy. *Journal of Consulting and Clinical Psychology, 56,* 490–495.

Crits-Christoph, P., & Luborsky, L. (1990a). Changes in CCRT pervasiveness during psychotherapy. In L. Luborsky & P. Crits-Christoph (Eds.), *Understanding transference: The CCRT method* (pp. 133–146). New York: Basic Books.

Crits-Christoph, P., & Luborsky, L. (1990b). The measurement of self-understanding. In L.. Luborsky & P. Crits-Christoph (Eds.) *Understanding transference: The CCRT method* (pp. 189–196). New York: Basic Books.

Crits-Christoph, P., Luborsky, L., Dahl, L., Popp, C., Mellon, J., & Mark D. (1988). Clinicians can agree in assessing relationship patterns in psychotherapy. *Archives of General Psychiatry, 45,* 1001–1004.

Dahl, H., Kachele, H., & Thomae, T. (Eds.). (1988). *Psychoanalytic process research strategies.* New York: Springer-Verlag.

Davanloo, H. (1980). *Short-term dynamic psychiatry.* Northvale, NJ: Jason Aronson.

DeRubeis, R. J., & Feeley, M. (in press). Determinants of change in cognitive therapy for depression. *Cognitive Therapy and Research.*

Erdelyi, M. (1985). *Psychoanalysis: Freud's cognitive psychology.* New York: Freeman.

Fiske, S., & Dyer, L. (1985). Structure and development of social schemata: Evidence for positive and negative transference effects. *Journal of Personality and Social Psychology, 48,* 839–852.

French, T. M. (1954). *The integration of behavior* (Vol. 2). Chicago: University of Chicago Press.

Freud, S. (1950). Project for a scientific psychology. In J. Strachey (Ed. and Trans.), *The standard edition of the complete psychological works of Sigmund Freud* (Vol. 1, pp. 285–343). London: Hogarth Press. (Original work published 1895)

Freud, S. (1953). Fragment of an analysis of a case of hysteria. In J. Strachey (Ed. and Trans.), *The standard edition of the complete psychological works of Sigmund Freud* (Vol. 7, pp. 15–22). London: Hogarth Press. (Original work published 1905)

Freud, S. (1958a). Observations on transference-love (further recommendations on the technique of psychoanalysis). In J. Strachey (Ed. and Trans.), *The standard edition of the complete psychological works of Sigmund Freud* (Vol. 12, pp. 157–171). London: Hogarth Press. (Original work published 1915)

Freud, S. (1958b). On beginning the treatment (further recommendations on the technique of psychoanalysis). In J. Strachey (Ed. and Trans.), *The standard edition of the complete psychological works of Sigmund Freud* (Vol. 12, pp. 123–144). London: Hogarth Press. (Original work published 1913)

Freud, S. (1958c). Remembering, repeating and working through (further recommendations on the technique of psychoanalysis). In J. Strachey (Ed. and Trans.), *The standard edition of the complete psychological works of Sigmund Freud* (Vol. 12, pp. 145–156). London: Hogarth Press. (Original work published 1914)

Freud, S. (1961). Recommendations to physicians practicing psychoanalysis. In J. Strachey (Ed. and Trans.), *The standard edition of the complete psychological works of Sigmund Freud* (Vol. 12, pp. 109–120). London: Hogarth Press. (Original work published 1912)

Freud, S. (1964). New introductory lectures in psychoanalysis. In J. Strachey (Ed. and Trans.), *The standard edition of the complete psychological works of Sigmund Freud* (Vol. 22, pp. 7–184). London: Hogarth Press. (Original work published 1933)

Freud, S. (1988a). The dynamics of transference. In J. Strachey (Ed. and Trans.), *The standard edition of the complete psychological works of Sigmund Freud* (Vol. 12, pp. 97–108). London: Hogarth Press. (Original work published 1912)

Freud, S. (1988b). The handling of dream interpretation in psychoanalysis. In J. Strachey (Ed. and Trans.), *The standard edition of the complete psychological works of Sigmund Freud* (Vol. 12, pp. 89–96). London: Hogarth Press. (Original work published 1911)

Geller, J. (1987). The process of psychotherapy: Separation and the complex interplay among empathy, insight and internalization. In J. Bloom-Feshbach & S. Bloom-Feshbach (Eds.), *The psychology of separation through the life span* (pp. 459–514). San Francisco: Jossey-Bass.

Hartley, D., & Strupp, H. (1983). The therapeutic alliance: Its relationship to outcome in brief psychotherapy. In J. Masling (Ed.), *Empirical studies of psychoanalytic theory* (Vol. 1, pp. 1–38). Hillsdale, NJ: Erlbaum.

Hollon, S. D., & Kriss, M. R. (1984). Cognitive factors in clinical research and practice. *Clinical Psychology Review, 4*, 35–76.

Horowitz, L., Rosenberg, S., Ureno, G., Mertz, M., & O'Halloran, P. (1989). *The psychodynamic formulation, the modal response method and interpersonal problems.* Unpublished manuscript.

Horowitz, M. J. (1979). *States of mind.* New York: Plenum Press.

Horowitz, M. J. (1991). *Person schemas and maladaptive interpersonal patterns.* Chicago: University of Chicago Press.

Horvath, A., Gaston, L., & Luborsky, L. (in press). The relation between alliance measures and outline in psychotherapy: A meta-analysis. In N. Miller, L. Luborsky, J. Barber, & J. Docherty (Eds.), *Handbook of dynamic psychotherapy research and practice: A how-to-do-them guide.* New York: Basic Books.

Horvath, A. O., & Greenberg, L. S. (1986). The development of the Working Alliance Inventory. In L. S. Greenberg & W. M. Pinsof (Eds.), *The psychotherapeutic process: A research handbook* (pp. 529–556). New York: Guilford Press.

Kernberg, O. (1975). *Borderline conditions and pathological narcissism.* Northvale, NJ: Jason Aronson.

Kernberg, O., Selzer, M. A., Koenigsberg, H. W., Carr, A. C., & Appelbaum, A. H. (1989). *Psychodynamic psychotherapy of borderline patients.* New York: Basic Books.

Kihlstrom, J. (1984). Conscious, subconscious, unconscious: A cognitive perspective. In K. S. Bowers & D. Meichenbaum (Eds.), *The unconscious reconsidered.* New York: Wiley.

Klein, G. (1970). *Perception, motives and personality.* New York: Knopf.

Klein, M. H., Mathieu-Coughlan, P., & Keisler, D. (1986). The Experiencing Scale. In L. S. Greenberg & W. M. Pinsof (Eds.), *The psychotherapeutic process: A research handbook* (pp. 21–71). New York: Guilford Press.

Luborsky, L. (1976). Helping alliances in psychotherapy: The groundwork for a study of their relationship to its outcome. In J. L. Claghorn (Ed.), *Successful psychotherapy* (pp. 92–116). New York: Brunner/Mazel.

Luborsky, L. (1984). *Principles of psychoanalytic psychotherapy: A manual for supportive–expressive (SE) treatment.* New York: Basic Books.

Luborsky, L. (1988). Recurrent momentary forgetting: Its content and context. In M. Horowitz (Ed.), *Psychodynamics and cognition* (pp. 223–251). Chicago: University of Chicago Press.

Luborsky, L. (1990). The convergence of Freud's observations about transference with CCRT evidence. In L. Luborsky & P. Crits-Christoph (Eds.), *Understanding transference: The CCRT method* (pp. 251–266). New York: Basic Books

Luborsky, L. & Crits-Christoph, P. (1990). *Understanding transference: The CCRT method.* New York: Basic Books.

Luborsky, L., & Crits-Christoph, P., Alexander, L., Margolis, M., & Cohen, M. (1983). Two helping alliance methods for predicting outcomes of psychotherapy: A counting signs versus a global rating method. *Journal of Nervous and Mental Disease, 171,* 480–492.

Luborsky, L., Crits-Christoph, P., Mintz, J., & Auerbach, A. (1988). *Who will benefit from psychotherapy? Predicting therapeutic outcomes.* New York: Basic Books.

Luborsky, L., Crits-Christoph, P., Friedman, S., Mark, D., & Schaffler, P. (1991). Freud's concept of a transference template and vicissitudes of the core conflictual relationship theme illustrated on two specimen cases. In M. Horowitz (Ed.), *Person, schemas and maladaptive interpersonal behavior* (pp. 1–433). Chicago: University of Chicago Press.

Luborsky, L., McLellan, A. T., Woody, G. E., O'Brien, C. P., & Auerbach, A. (1985). Therapist success and its determinants. *Archives of General Psychiatry, 42,* 602–611.

Luborsky, L., & Spence, D. (1971). Quantitative research on psychoanalytic therapy. In A. E. Bergin & S. L. Garfield (Eds.), *Handbook of psychotherapy and behavior change* (pp. 408–437). New York: Wiley.

Luborsky, L., & Spence, D. (1978). Quantitative research on psychoanalytic therapy. In S. L. Garfield & A. E. Bergin (Eds.), *Handbook of psychotherapy and behavior change* (rev. ed., pp. 331–368). New York: Wiley.

Main, M., & Goldwyn, R. (1985). *Adult attachment classification system.* Unpublished manuscript, University of California, Berkeley.

Malan, D. M. (1976). *Toward the validation of dynamic psychotherapy.* New York: Plenum Press.

Marmar, C. R., & Gaston, L. (1988). *California Psychotherapy Alliance Scales (CALPAS) manual.* Unpublished manuscript, University of California, San Francisco.

Marmar, C. R., Gaston, L., Gallagher, D., & Thompson, L. W. (1989). Alliance and outcome in late-life depression. *Journal of Nervous and Mental Disease, 177,* 464–472.

Marmar, C. R., Horowitz, M. J., Weiss, D. S., & Marziali, E. (1986). Development of the Therapeutic Alliance Rating System. In L. S. Greenberg & W. M. Pinsof (Eds.), *The psychotherapeutic process: A research handbook* (pp. 367–390). New York: Guilford Press.

Marziali, E. (1984). Prediction of outcome of brief psychotherapy from therapist interpretive interventions. *Archives of General Psychiatry, 41,* 301–304.

McCullough, L. (1987, July). *The effects of therapist interventions combined with different patient responses and correlated with outcome at termination of treatment.* Paper presented at the Society for Psychotherapy Research, Ulm, Germany.

McCullough, L., Winston, A., Liskin, M., & Vitolo, A. (1989, June). *The effect of robustness of interpretation on patient affective and defensive responding and therapy outcome.* Paper presented at the annual meeting of the Society for Psychotherapy Research, Toronto, Ontario, Canada.

Miller, N., Luborsky, L., Barber, J., & Docherty, J. (in press). *Handbook of dynamic psychotherapy research and practice: A how-to-do-them guide.* New York: Basic Books.

Morgan, R., Luborsky, L., Crits-Christoph, P., Curtis, H., & Solomon, J. (1982). Predicting the outcomes of psychotherapy by the Penn Helping Alliance Rating Method. *Archives of General Psychiatry, 39,* 397–402.

Orlinsky, D., & Geller, J. (in press). Patients' representations of their therapist and therapy: A new focus of research. In N. Miller, L. Luborsky, & J. Docherty (Eds.), *A guide to psychodynamic treatment research*. New York: Basic Books.

Orlinsky, D., & Howard, K. (1986). Process and outcome of psychotherapy. In S. Garfield & A. Bergin (Eds.), *Handbook of psychotherapy and behavior change: An empirical analysis* (3rd ed., pp. 321–384). New York: Wiley

Perry, J. C., Augusto, F., & Cooper, S. H. (1989). The assessment of psychodynamic conflicts: 1. Reliability of an idiographic method. *Psychiatry, 52,* 289–301.

Piper, W., Azim, H., Joyce, A., & McCallum, M. (1991). Transference interpretations, therapeutic alliance and outcome in short-term individual psychotherapy. *Archives of General Psychiatry, 48,* 946–953.

Piper, W., Debbane, E., Bienvenu, J., de Carufel, F., & Garant, J. (1986). Relationships between the object of focus of therapist interpretations and outcome in short-term individual psychotherapy. *British Journal of Medical Psychology, 59,* 1–11.

Rapaport, D. (1961). On the psychoanalytic theory of motivation. In M. Jones (Ed.), *Nebraska Symposium on Motivation* (pp. 173–247) Omaha: University of Nebraska Press.

Rice, L., & Greenberg, L. (Eds.). (1984). *Pattern of change: Intensive analysis of psychotherapy process.* New York: Guilford Press.

Rogers, C., & Dymond, R. (1954). *Psychotherapy and personality change.* Chicago: University of Chicago Press.

Sachs, J. (1983). Negative factors in brief psychotherapy: An important assessment. *Journal of Consulting Clinical Psychology, 51,* 557–564.

Sandler, J., Holder, A., Kawenoka, M., Kennedy, H. E., & Neurath, L. (1969). Notes on some theoretical and clinical aspects of transference. *International Journal of Psychoanalysis, 50,* 633–645.

Seitz, P. F. D. (1966). The consensus problem in psychoanalytic research. In L. Gottschalk & A. Auerbach (Eds.), *Methods of research in psychotherapy* (pp. 209–225). New York: Appleton-Century-Crofts.

Silberschatz, G., Fretter, P., & Curtis, J. (1986). How do interpretations influence the process of psychotherapy? *Journal of Consulting and Clinical Psychology, 54,* 646–652.

Sloane, R. B., Staples, F. R., Cristol, A. H., Yorkston, N. J., & Whipple, K. (1975). *Psychotherapy versus behavior therapy.* Cambridge, MA: Harvard University Press.

Sroufe, L. A. (1983). Infant–caregiver attachment and patterns of adaptation in pre-school: The roots of maladaption and competence. In M. Perlmutter (Ed.), *Minnesota Symposium on Child Psychology* (Vol. 16, pp. 41–81). Hillsdale, NJ: Erlbaum.

Sroufe, L. A., & Waters, E. (1977). Attachment as an organizational construct. *Child Development, 48,* 1184–1199.

Strupp, H. S., & Binder, J. L. (1984). *Psychotherapy in a new key: A guide to time-limited dynamic psychotherapy.* New York: Basic Books.

Teller, V., & Dahl, H. (1981). The framework for a model of psychoanalytic inference. *Proceedings of the Seventh International Joint Conference on Artificial Intelligence, 1,* 394–400.

Tichenor, V., & Hill, C. E. (1989). A comparison of six measures of working alliance. *Psychotherapy, 26,* 195–199.

Waelder, R. (1956). Introduction to the discussion on problems of transference. *International Journal of Psychoanalysis, 37,* 367–368.

Wallerstein, R., Robbins, L., Sargent, H., & Luborsky, L. (1956). The psychotherapy research project of the Menninger Foundation: Rationale, method and sample use. *Bulletin of the Menninger Foundation, 20,* 221–280.

Weiss, J., Sampson, H., & the Mount Zion Psychotherapy Group (1986). *The psychoanalytic process: Theory, clinical observation and empirical research.* New York: Guilford Press.

Wiseman, H., & Rice, L. N. (1989). Sequential analysis of therapist–client interaction during change events. A task-focused approach. *Journal of Consulting and Clinical Psychology, 57,* 281–286.

27

A NEW PSYCHOANALYTIC THEORY AND ITS TESTING IN RESEARCH

HAROLD SAMPSON

I present an overview of the research program of the Mt. Zion Psychotherapy Research Group[1] and of the new psychoanalytic theory, developed by Weiss, on which that research is based (Weiss, Sampson, & the Mt. Zion Psychotherapy Research Group, 1986). This work is relevant to the unifying theme of this book—the relation between psychoanalysis and the rest of psychology—in two ways.

First, my colleagues and I have demonstrated that rigorous empirical research using ordinary scientific methods may be carried out systematically on broad, fundamental psychoanalytic hypotheses about unconscious mental functioning, psychopathology, and the treatment process. It can be carried out using the data of the psychoanalytic situation as well as of other psychotherapies. It can yield findings that disclose lawful relationships, challenge some long-established beliefs, and have implications for both theory and practice. In these ways, the work I report helps to make psychoanalysis less of a separate discipline based exclusively on a unique methodology.

Second, my and my colleagues' work suggests that unconscious mental life is much more similar to conscious mental life than has been generally recognized. Unconscious mental life is guided by adaptive considerations, including continuous appraisals of danger and safety, and it is regulated by higher mental functions such as thoughts, anticipations, beliefs, judgments, decisions, and plans. These characteristics of unconscious mental life apply not only to a conflict-free sphere (Hartmann, 1939/1958) but to central domains of psychoanalytic interest: repressed strivings, unconscious conflicts, psychopathology, and the treatment process. In these ways, also, this work provides a bridge linking psychoanalysis to the rest of psychology.

---

[1]Now known as the San Francisco Psychotherapy Research Group.

BACKGROUND

In 1958, Weiss began to study the process notes of psychoanalyses. His approach to this material was empirical. He focused his attention on indications of significant therapeutic changes in patients' behavior. He noticed, for example, when a patient brought important new material into the analytic work, such as reporting a childhood memory that had been long forgotten, experiencing a feeling that had previously been inaccessible, or exhibiting some new capacity in his or her behavior. Weiss (1971) referred to such changes as "the emergence of new themes" (p. 459).

Weiss (1971) made an important observation about these changes: Patients often made significant progress on their own, that is, without the help of interpretations by the analyst. New themes frequently emerged spontaneously. In addition, when patients became conscious of previously inaccessible (and presumably repressed) ideas, memories, fantasies, and feelings, they often did not seem to experience conflict in relation to the new material. They were calm as they presented it and did not struggle against it but instead worked with it to increase their understanding of their mental lives.

Weiss (1971) attempted to explain these observations by the familiar psychoanalytic hypotheses he had been taught. These hypotheses could not explain the timing of the spontaneous emergence of new themes or the patients' lack of conflict regarding emerging material that seemed to have been previously repressed. Weiss began to develop new hypotheses to account for his observations. He proposed that patients have some unconscious control over their repressions and that this control is regulated by unconscious appraisals of danger and safety. Patients maintain their repressions against a mental content when they believe, unconsciously, that it would endanger them to experience it. They are able to lift their repressions and experience the content when they believe unconsciously that they can experience it safely. This hypothesis is compatible with Freud's (1926/1959) revised theory of anxiety and defense and is similar to ideas proposed by Rangell (1969) and Sandler (1960).

Over a period of years, Weiss developed a comprehensive new theory of mental functioning, psychopathology, and treatment (see the next section) in which patients are seen to have more motivation to solve their problems, unconsciously as well as consciously, than had been generally assumed. Patients also are seen to have more capability of doing so than generally recognized. They work throughout therapy, unconsciously as well as consciously, to solve their problems with the help of the therapist. Weiss's new theory did not diminish the role of the therapist but, by elaborating on the patient's unconscious therapeutic work, provided a different understanding of how the therapist helps the patient.

Weiss and I began to discuss these hypotheses on a daily basis in the mid-1960s. We assumed that these hypotheses could be tested by rigorous research methods because they specified the conditions under which certain observable changes should take place. Moreover, the use of these hypotheses in our clinical work had convinced us of their considerable explanatory and predictive power. These convictions led us to undertake the arduous path of subjecting Weiss's hypotheses, along with competing hypotheses, to systematic empirical investigation.

AN OUTLINE OF WEISS'S THEORY

According to Weiss, people are powerfully motivated from infancy on to understand their world and to adapt to it (Stern, 1985; Weiss, 1990; Weiss et al., 1986). In attempting to adapt, they seek reliable knowledge about themselves, their relationship to others, and their interpersonal world. They organize this knowledge intrapsychically as a system of beliefs, unconscious as well as conscious, about their reality. These beliefs are an indispensable guide to adaptation and self-preservation. They organize perceptions of self and others, and "it is in accordance with his beliefs about reality that a person shapes his inborn strivings and by so doing evolves his personality" (Weiss, 1990, p. 660). People's emotions are also shaped by their beliefs about themselves and their situations; for example, people who believe that they are endangered are likely to feel anxious, or people who believe that they are unworthy of love may feel depressed (Silberschatz & Sampson, 1991).

Infants and children form some beliefs that may be called "pathogenic" because they impair functioning. People believe that the pursuit of certain goals will disrupt their all-important ties to their parents and will cause them to suffer from fear, anxiety, guilt, or shame. For example, a young man in analysis had formed the belief in childhood that if he made friends he would cause his mother, whom he perceived to be possessive, to become depressed. Therefore, if he were to form friendships, he would threaten his tie to his mother and also cause himself to suffer from intolerable guilt. In obedience to this belief and the dangers it predicted, he relinquished his desire to have friends and remained instead in a close, infantile relationship to his mother. This patient's early relationship to the analyst was guided by the unconscious belief that the analyst, like his mother, would be hurt if he were to have important relationships with anyone else.

People construct beliefs by inference from experience. Pathogenic beliefs are usually acquired in childhood from traumatic experiences with family members. They may, however, be acquired at any time of life and in relation to nonfamily members from powerful experiences. People's beliefs are subjective: Their construction is influenced by their age, life situation, and motivation. In the case of children, their construction is also greatly influenced by their inexperience and by overgeneralization from a small sample of people or instances. Although beliefs are subjective, their construction is also powerfully influenced by actual experiences. For example, a young girl whose parents complain or act hurt when she behaves independently is more likely to develop a strong conviction (belief) that her independence is harmful to her parents than a young girl whose parents seem cheerful about her independence. Or, a young boy who is ignored by his parents is more likely to develop the unconscious conviction that he is uninteresting and unimportant than a young boy whose parents display more interest in his activities. The child's inferences may be inaccurate from the viewpoint of an outside observer, but they are usually reasonable inferences in terms of the child's life situation and limited experience.

Any motive, goal, or psychic state (e.g., to feel happy or confident) may become linked, by inference from experience, to a dangerous consequence. For this reason, pathogenic beliefs are specific to the individual and are quite varied. For example, a young boy may form the belief that if he misbehaves he will burden his tired and overwhelmed parents, or that if he misbehaves he will be punished by rejection, or that if he misbehaves he can restore a parent's sense of confidence and authority by giving the parent an opportunity to scold or punish him. Or, a young girl may come to believe that if she is sexual toward her father he will be disgusted with her, or that if she is sexual he will lose control, or that if she is sexual toward him he will perk up and become less depressed. Or, a young boy may acquire the belief that if he is happy he will reassure his worried parents, or that if he is happy he will be acting cruelly to his miserably unhappy parents, or that if he is happy he will provoke rivalry from his easily threatened parents.

Psychopathology, according to Weiss (1990; Weiss et al., 1986) stems ultimately from pathogenic beliefs. It is in obedience to pathogenic beliefs that individuals institute repressions and develop symptoms, inhibitions, and character problems. People's affect and impulses, as well as their control or lack of control over them, are also shaped by their pathogenic beliefs (Weiss, 1990).

Because patients' problems stem from pathogenic beliefs, the central task of therapy is to disconfirm these beliefs. A therapeutic process is a process that disconfirms pathogenic beliefs.

How does this take place? Patients are highly motivated unconsciously to disconfirm their pathogenic beliefs because these beliefs are grim, impede the pursuit of highly desired goals, and cause great suffering. Patients work throughout therapy, unconsciously as well as consciously, to disconfirm these beliefs with the help of the therapist. Their work is guided by general plans about what they will attempt to accomplish first and what they will attempt to defer until later. These plans, which are always at least partly unconscious, indicate what pathogenic beliefs they will initially attempt to disconfirm, and how they will work to do so. In devising their plans, patients are guided by considerations of safety and danger.

Patients work in therapy in two general ways: by testing pathogenic beliefs in their relation to the therapist in the hope of disconfirming them and by thinking about their problems and acquiring greater insight into their pathogenic beliefs. In testing a belief, patients carry out a trial action in the hope that the therapist will not react as the beliefs predict. For example, Mr. D., the young man who isolated himself because he unconsciously believed that he would harm his possessive mother (and, by transference, other significant persons) if he formed friendships, tested this belief in relation to the analyst. He mentioned a college classmate with whom he had begun to have casual conversations about a shared course, and he implied that the classmate had a bad character and probably would not be good for him. The analyst mildly questioned this idea. The patient, encouraged by the analyst's comment, then noted various good traits about his potential friend. In the next session he recalled an incident from childhood in which his mother had criticized a playmate with whom he had just begun to form a friendship. He remembered that he had assumed that his mother did not want him to have friends and that he therefore gave up the new friendship.

This sequence illustrates one way in which a patient may unconsciously carry out a test of a pathogenic belief in relationship to the analyst. It also illustrates how, if the analyst's response tends to disconfirm the belief, the patient may feel safe enough to make immediate progress. The patient may begin to lift a defense, and new themes may become conscious.

Patients also work in therapy by thinking about their problems and their origins. They may be helped by the analyst's interpretations to understand their pathogenic beliefs and how they are related to their problems. Interpretations that help patients to understand and disconfirm their pathogenic beliefs lead to therapeutic progress (see the section on how patients respond to interpretations). Interpretations that tend to confirm patients' pathogenic beliefs may set patients back.

In order to help patients, the therapist "should infer the patient's conscious and unconscious beliefs about himself and his interpersonal world. The therapist may then perceive the patient's situation (with its dangers and opportunities) as the patient himself perceives it" (Weiss, 1990, p. 660). The therapist should also infer patients' unconscious plans to overcome their problems in therapy; that is, what beliefs patients are attempting to disconfirm and how they are working to disconfirm them. This understanding will enable the therapist to respond appropriately to patients' unconscious tests, thereby providing patients with experiences that serve to disconfirm powerfully the pathogenic belief that is being tested. It also enables the therapist to make interpretations that facilitate patients' plans.

Weiss's (1986) theory is about unconscious mental functioning as well as about psychopathology and treatment. It proposes that people have considerable unconscious control over their repressions and behavior. People may do unconsciously many of the things they do consciously: they may think, anticipate, assess potential consequences of a course of action, including whether to maintain a repression, or to defend against or make manifest a transference. People may compare the present to the past, form judgments, make decisions, and devise and carry out plans.[2] They may carry out these activities not only preconsciously, in relation to conflict-free issues, but unconsciously in relation to the central conflictual issues in their mental lives.

THE FIRST RESEARCH PARADIGM:
SAFETY AND THE EMERGENCE OF NEW THEMES

Weiss's (1971) crucial observation in his first process note studies was that patients may—and frequently do—become aware spontaneously of previously inaccessible mental contents, contents that the analyst would have assumed to have been repressed. They may become aware of these contents calmly and without conflict; they may use awareness of these contents to gain further understanding of their mental lives. This observation may have been known, more or less implicitly, by other psychoanalytic clinicians, but the theoretical issues posed by it had not been recognized. Therefore, the observation was never considered to require explanation, nor was it discussed in psychoanalytic theories of therapy and of technique. Weiss, however, recognized that the observation posed a problem, for traditional psychoanalytic hypotheses could not explain the *timing* of the emergence of the repressed material, its emergence without conflict, or its almost effortless utilization by the patient for therapeutic purposes.

The initial clinical paradigm for this phenomenon was referred to by Weiss (1952, 1971; Weiss et al., 1986) as "crying at the happy ending." It may be illustrated by a brief clinical example:

> Dr. H., in his first session back following the analyst's two month summer vacation, began to describe his own busy, active, and productive summer. He noted that he had not missed the analyst during the break from treatment. He was aware, however, that he enjoyed being back. A little later in the session, without interpretation, Dr. H. became aware of intense feelings of sadness about the separation. He proceeded, without anxiety, to discuss his feelings, and to connect them to childhood memories of separations from his mother. (Weiss, 1971)

It is essential that we closely examine the problem such an observation poses for certain familiar psychoanalytic explanations. In Freud's (1905/1953a) early theory, patients cannot lift their defenses on their own because their defenses are regulated automatically by the pleasure principle: "The process of bringing . . . unconscious material to light is associated with unpleasure, and because of this the patient rejects it again and again" (p. 266). Therefore, according to traditional theory, a repressed content such as a wish cannot ordinarily become conscious without interpretative help from the analyst unless it is intensified, or the defenses against it are weakened. In either of those situations, the repressed content may press toward consciousness. This, in turn, evokes intensified defensive efforts. If the repressed content is powerful enough, it may nonetheless push its way to consciousness without disguise. In this unusual circumstance, patients will continue to be in conflict with the content, will feel anxious about it, and will attempt to re-repress it. More commonly, the content becomes conscious in a compromise

---

[2] A person's judgments, decisions, and plans—whether conscious or unconscious, and whether based on pathogenic or normal beliefs about self and others—may of course lead to unanticipated, undesired, and maladaptive consequences. Error, failure, and even maladaptation do not result from only psychopathology. However, in the case of psychopathology, problems and maladaptations may arise because a person's pathogenic beliefs provide a grossly inadequate guide to the contemporary situation, or because the person's pathogenic beliefs compel the person to fail in certain ways, to lose control in certain ways, to punish self in certain ways, and so forth.

formation that, if successful, may enable the content to emerge without producing anxiety or conflict. In this situation, patients will not experience conflict with the emerging content because its importance is hidden. Patients will not understand the true significance of the emerging content and will be unable to use it progressively in their treatment until its significance has been interpreted to them.

This theory does not explain the timing of the emergence of sadness. Dr. H.'s sadness could not have become conscious because it had been intensified, for his sadness would in that case have been the most intense during the summer separation. It became conscious, however, only after he regained, during the first session following the separation, a sense of being reunited with the analyst. At that point, the cause for sadness was eliminated. Thus, the patient experienced his sadness precisely when there was no longer a reason to feel sad.

Moreover, if the sadness had become conscious because of its intensity, in spite of Dr. H.'s efforts to defend against it, he would have become anxious at its emergence and would have remained in conflict with it. Instead, the sadness emerged without manifest anxiety or conflict and the patient, instead of struggling against it, retained it in consciousness, worked on its meanings, and linked it to childhood memories.

If the sadness emerged in a well-disguised compromise formation, the patient would have been calm when it emerged, but he could not have understood its importance without interpretative help and would have been unable to work with it. The hypothesis that the sadness emerged as a compromise formation (or because of some subtle shift in the dynamic equilibrium of defense and impulse) cannot explain either the timing of the emergence or the fact that the patient used the emerging content almost effortlessly to deepen his understanding of his mental life.

In addition, the sadness could not have emerged as a gratification because sadness is not intrinsically gratifying. The patient's becoming aware of his sadness is instead an example of the kind of process that, according to Freud, contradicts his earlier assumption that unconscious mental life is regulated exclusively by the search for pleasure (1920/1955, p. 32). He was referring to processes in which people repeat experiences that cannot at any time have been pleasurable (Weiss et al., 1986, p. 10).

The emergence of the sadness cannot be explained as primarily a defense against some other content (e.g., as a defense against anger at the analyst/mother for abandoning him). This explanation is not based on any direct clinical evidence. In fact, the patient had in earlier work been conscious of anger toward his mother for leaving him but had not previously been able to face his sadness. The defense hypothesis also cannot explain the *timing* of the emergence or the observation that the patient did useful therapeutic work with the now-conscious sadness.

Weiss's (1971) explanation of the phenomenon was that the patient had repressed his sadness about the separation while the analyst was away because it would have endangered him to experience it then. The patient lifted his repression and began to face his sadness only after reestablishing his feeling of having a relationship with the analyst. This made it safe for him to experience his sadness. He brought it to consciousness not for gratification or for defense, but in order to master it. This explanation accounts for the timing of the emergence of the sadness, for the patient's lack of anxiety about it as he became aware of it, and for his lack of conflict with it afterward. It accounts for his continuing to work with his sadness therapeutically and his motivation and capability in linking it to childhood memories and thus expanding his self-knowledge.

Weiss's (1971) hypothesis about safety and the emergence of new themes has another virtue that will only become apparent in lines of research to be discussed in later sections: It has predictive power. It enables therapists, by specifying conditions that are likely to increase the patient's sense of safety, to predict that the presence of these conditions is likely to be followed by immediate therapeutic progress.

Weiss, and later others of us, confirmed this hypothesis repeatedly in our clinical work. We recognized, however, the need to go beyond exclusively clinical methods of testing hypotheses. We knew that only carefully designed studies, with controls for various sources of bias and error, could lend strong support—or alternatively, disconfirm—the hypothesis. We also recognized that formal research had contributed greatly to scientific advances in other fields, and we assumed it might have equally significant long term effects in psychoanalysis.

Sampson, Weiss, Mlodnosky, and Hause (1972) conducted a preliminary pilot study of the safety hypothesis. They studied an analytic patient, Mr. A., who was almost devoid of affect at the beginning of treatment. They were able to demonstrate by reliable measures and statistical tests of significance that as Mr. A. began to feel able to control his emotions and therefore to regulate their intensity safely, he then became able to experience more intense feelings. This study did not, however, compare Weiss's (1971) hypothesis directly with competing psychoanalytic hypotheses; therefore, a new method was developed and pilot-tested (Horowitz, Sampson, Siegelman, Wolfson, & Weiss, 1975). An improved version of the new methodology was then developed by Gassner, Sampson, Weiss, and Brumer (1982), and applied to a new case. I summarize their study in broad outline.

The purpose of the Gassner et al. (1982) study was to determine whether, as the hypothesis would lead one to anticipate, a patient may become conscious during analysis of previously unconscious contents that have not been interpreted, do so without anxiety or coming into conflict with the new content, and use the content to advance his or her therapeutic work. This combination of findings, as discussed earlier, cannot be explained adequately by alternative psychoanalytic hypotheses.

The study was carried out on the first 100 sessions of an audio-recorded psychoanalysis that had been conducted by an analyst in another city. The analyst was unfamiliar, at the time he treated the patient, with the Gassner et al. (1982) hypotheses.

The first step in their study (Gassner et al., 1982) was to identify a series of *new* contents or themes in the later hours within the 100 sessions (i.e., contents that had not been described by the patient earlier). In carrying out this step, Gassner et al. first identified new themes appearing in hours 41–100. The second step required psychoanalytic clinicians to judge, on the basis of their own individual case formulations derived from reading the process notes of the first 10 sessions, which of this pool of new themes would have been repressed at the beginning of the analysis. Nineteen psychoanalytic clinicians made this judgment independently. Gassner et al. accepted as previously unconscious content *only* those new themes that psychoanalytic clinicians *agreed highly* had been warded off earlier by defenses.

In order to avoid problems of circularity, the statements of new themes that were presented to the judges (for judgment as to whether these themes had been warded off earlier) omitted any cues as to whether the patient was anxious or conflicted when the themes first emerged. The judges rated each new theme on a 5-point scale. A rating of 5 reflected the judges' strong belief that the new theme had previously been unconscious.

The 19 judges made ratings on 100 randomly selected new themes. They did so, as I noted, on the basis of their own case formulation derived from reading the process notes of the first 10 sessions. Thirteen of the 100 statements received a mean scale score of 4 or greater. These statements, on which there was substantial agreement between judges that they had been previously unconscious, were designated as "judged previously warded off" themes.

Did the Gassner et al. (1982) methods *actually* yield *clinically meaningful* unconscious contents? They believe so. The patient herself, the treating analyst, and finally, a research group working independently from the judges, all provided evidence that the statements judges rated as warded off had been previously warded off and were of central significance to the patient.

There were seven new themes that the patient had *prefaced* with phrases acknowledging the patient's own awareness of facing a previously unconscious content. An example is "I've never let myself before think or feel such and such." These prefatory comments were deleted so as not to provide the judges with these clues. Nonetheless, the judges gave these seven statements—which the patient's comments identified as previously warded off—a mean rating of 4.

The treating analyst independently completed the same judgment task as the 19 judges. He rated as 4 or greater 11 of the 13 statements that they had identified as warded off. Moreover, he considered the statements to which the judges gave the highest ratings as so revealing that he asked that their contents in publications be disguised.

Finally, the research group, working independently of the judges, made their own case formulation and then evaluated the statements identified by the 19 judges as previously unconscious. The research group agreed that these new themes expressed significant, previously unconscious contents.

These three converging lines of evidence gave Gassner et al. (1982) confidence that their method—which is, after all, a formal research variant of the usual clinical method of identifying unconscious contents—*did identify clinically meaningful and significant previously unconscious contents.*

The next finding was that the analyst had not made any prior interpretations that related to the ideas expressed in 12 of the 13 themes judged as highly warded off.

Thus, a number of clinically meaningful unconscious contents became conscious in the latter part of the first 100 hours of Mrs. C.'s analysis, and they did so without prior interpretation.

Did the patient experience much anxiety or conflict as these contents emerged? Gassner et al. (1982) used three different measures of anxiety or conflict: Mahl's speech disturbance ratio; the Gottschalk-Gleser anxiety scale; and clinical ratings of anxiety by experienced clinicians. They compared the anxiety level on each of these measures when highly warded off contents emerged with the anxiety level accompanying the appearance of randomly selected patient statements. The patient was *significantly less anxious* on the Mahl scale when warded-off contents emerged than when random statements emerged. The other two measures showed no differences in anxiety level in the two circumstances.

Gassner et al. (1982) concluded that the patient became conscious of clinically meaningful unconscious contents regularly, without interpretation, and without evidence of intensified anxiety or conflict.

Finally, they used the Experiencing Scale to determine whether the patient worked progressively with the material as she became conscious of unconscious contents. This scale measures the patient's involvement with progressive therapeutic work, vividness of experiencing, and nondefensiveness. The patient's speech segments when previously unconscious contents emerged were rated significantly higher on the Experiencing Scale than randomly selected speech segments. This means that the patient was actually more involved with reflecting on her feelings when she expressed previously unconscious contents, and more involved in therapeutic work when these contents emerged, than she was at other randomly selected times.

This combination of findings supports Weiss's (1971) hypothesis that patients exercise some unconscious control over their defenses and that they may bring unconscious contents to awareness on their own, unaided by interpretation. They may do so on the basis of an unconscious appraisal that they may now experience the content safely.

The Gassner et al. (1982) study does not, however, explain just how patients may develop, through therapy, an increased sense of safety so that they may bring warded-off contents to consciousness. To answer this question empirically, I must turn to the next two lines of investigation.

THE PATIENT'S WORK: TESTING PATHOGENIC BELIEFS

Patients work to disconfirm pathogenic beliefs by testing these beliefs in their relation to the therapist. They do so throughout treatment. In testing, patients unconsciously carry out trial actions that invite the therapist to respond in ways that tend to confirm or disconfirm the belief. The patient unconsciously hopes that the analyst's response will tend to disconfirm the belief. For example, a young man who unconsciously believed that he would be in danger of castration if he expressed sexual interest in women tested the analyst by mentioning tentatively that a woman at work had given some hints of possible interest in him. He perceived the analyst's response of friendly interest as mildly encouraging. The patient became slightly more relaxed because the danger predicted by his belief had begun to be disconfirmed by the analyst's response. He mentioned that he found this woman somewhat attractive. After a long series of such tests, the patient became aware, without interpretation, that he had anticipated the analyst's disapproval of his interest in women. He recalled, somewhat vaguely, that as a 4-year-old child, he had felt close to his mother. When his father came home from work, he recalled that he felt anxious around him. In brief, the patient began to make progress, by testing the pathogenic belief, in understanding his unconscious sexual conflicts.

Patients' testing of pathogenic beliefs is a part of their reality-testing. In reality-testing, people distinguish a percept originating from within from a percept originating in the external world. According to Freud (1917/1957a), people may make this distinction on the basis of an action (e.g., they may move their heads to see whether the percept then disappears). In testing a pathogenic belief, people attempt to distinguish between a danger situation originating from within and based on an infantile trauma from a danger situation present in the external world. This attempt is made by carrying out a trial action and observing the consequences. Testing takes place in all relationships, but it is particularly prominent in therapy because patients' unconscious purpose in therapy is to disconfirm their pathogenic beliefs.

The hypothesis that patients test the therapist to disconfirm pathogenic beliefs leads to specific and testable predictions. If the therapist, in response to a test, responds in one way, the patient's belief may tend to be disconfirmed and he or she is likely to become less anxious and more productive in the therapy. If the therapist responds in another way, the patient's belief may not be disconfirmed and he or she will not show these improvements. The therapist's response to the patient's test is, from a research standpoint, the independent variable. One can determine the relationship between variations in therapist behavior, in response to a test, to certain specific and predictable consequences (e.g., reduced anxiety, increased therapeutic productivity). Several studies were conducted to test this hypothesis.

Study 1

Silberschatz (1986) carried out a study on the first 100 sessions of the analysis of Mrs. C. (This is the audio-recorded and transcribed case mentioned in the Gassner et al., 1982, study). The study involved the following three steps and subsequent statistical analysis of findings:

Step 1: Key tests (i.e., tests central to the patient's pathogenic beliefs) were reliably selected from transcripts of the 100 sessions by three analytic judges working independently of each other. The reliability of ratings of key tests by the judges was $r_{ll} = .63$, $r_{kk} = .82$. Forty-six key tests were identified.

Step 2: Four psychoanalysts familiar with the clinical application of the testing concept rated on a 7-point scale the degree to which the treating analyst "passed" each test (i.e., responded in a way likely to disconfirm the pathogenic belief being tested). The reliability of their ratings was $r_{ll} = .58$, $r_{kk} = .89$.

Step 3: Mrs. C.'s behavior immediately before and after each test was assessed on several patient measures. Each measure was scored by a different group of judges. Patient speech segments were approximately 6 minutes long and were presented to the raters in random order and without any context. The raters were unaware whether the segment occurred before or after the testing segment. They were also unaware of the aims of the research. The measures of patient behavior included the Experiencing Scale; a boldness scale (developed by Caston, 1986, to assess the degree to which the patient is able to confront or elaborate nontrivial material); an anxiety scale (categorized according to an affect scale developed by Dahl, 1979); and a relaxation scale (developed by Mayer, Bronstein, & F. Sampson to assess the patient's apparent relaxation during a speech segment [in Weiss et. al, 1986, pp. 200–202, p. 263]). Reliabilities (r_{kk}) ranged from .64 to .94 on these measures.

Silberschatz (1986) then correlated the degree to which the analyst passed the patient's key tests with changes in the patient's behavior, as measured by each of the aforementioned four scales. Each correlation was in the predicted direction and was statistically significant. The findings indicate that the patient, immediately following a passed test, tended to become less anxious, more relaxed, more involved in therapeutic work and more productive, and showed more boldness in tackling problems. These findings support the testing hypothesis and provide evidence of its predictive power.

Study 2

Silberschatz (1986) undertook a second study on the case of Mrs. C. to test the relative predictive power of two alternative psychoanalytic hypotheses about the same event. This study was possible because some of the patient's key tests (from my and my colleagues' viewpoint) were, from an alternative psychoanalytic perspective, instances of the patient making a transference demand on the analyst (e.g., for love, special treatment, guidance, praise). In some of these instances, the therapist response that was designated as "passing the patient's test" might be understood by other analysts as frustrating the patient's unconscious wishes as expressed in the transference demand.

The two psychoanalytic hypotheses make different predictions about how the patient will respond to the identical behavior by the analyst. According to the testing hypothesis, the patient is not seeking to gratify an unconscious wish but to test an unconscious pathogenic belief in relation to the analyst. Therefore, if the analyst "passes the test," the patient should feel reassured, less anxious, and bolder and freer in tackling problems. By contrast, if the patient is seeking to gratify an unconscious wish in the transference and the analyst does not gratify the wish, the patient will feel frustrated. The predicted behavior of the patient in this situation was specified by the investigators in the Menninger Psychotherapy Research Project: "Patients whose neurotic needs are not gratified within the transference respond to this frustration with regressive and/or resistive reactions, and/or painful affects" (Sargent, Horwitz, Wallerstein, & Appelbaum, 1968, p. 85).

Because the two hypotheses predict different behavior by the patient in the identical situation, one may determine empirically which hypothesis provides a better fit to the data. This was the study that Silberschatz (1986) carried out.

Step 1: Judges who believed in the traditional psychoanalytic hypothesis identified instances in the first 100 sessions of the case of Mrs. C. in which the patient was attempting to gratify an unconscious wish in relation to the analyst. Judges who believed in the testing hypothesis had previously selected instances of key tests. Silberschatz then identified only those instances that both groups of judges selected as examples fitting their theory. There were 34 such overlapping instances.

Step 2: Analytic judges who believed in the traditional hypothesis rated the therapist's response to each of the 34 overlapping instances for how well the analyst, by remaining appropriately neutral, had not gratified the patient's unconscious transference wish. These ratings were reliable (r_{kk} = .74). Analytic judges who believed in the testing hypothesis rated each of the 34 instances for how well the analyst had "passed the test." These ratings were also reliable (r_{kk} = .78).

Step 3: Silberschatz correlated ratings of the analyst's behavior by the two groups of judges. This correlation was .81 ($p < .001$). This means that the same behavior that one group of judges saw as testing, the other group saw as frustrating an unconscious wish by appropriate neutrality.

Step 4: Ratings of the patient's behavior on several variables before and after the analyst's response to the test had been obtained in the first study, described earlier.

Silberschatz then analyzed the data in the 34 overlapping instances to determine the relations between predictions and observations for each hypothesis. The major predictions of each theory are shown in the following display:

	Analyst passes test	Analyst frustrates wish
Patient anxiety	Decreases	Increases
Patient boldness	Increases	Decreases
Patient experiencing	Increases	Decreases
Patient relaxation	Increases	Decreases

The predictions of the testing hypothesis were consistent with observation. Specifically, statistically significant changes in the direction predicted by the testing hypothesis were found for anxiety (decreased), boldness (increased), and relaxation (increased) ratings. The Experiencing Scale scores changed nonsignificantly in the predicted direction (increased). Correspondingly, all predictions based on the wish-frustration hypothesis were unsupported by observation.

Data from this study, as well as from Study 1, lend support to the idea of testing. It thereby supports a set of related ideas: (a) that analytic patients work unconsciously to disconfirm pathogenic beliefs; (b) that this work involves higher mental functions (e.g., unconscious planning, unconscious carrying out of trial actions, unconscious assessment of the therapist's behavior in terms of whether it confirms anticipations of danger); (c) that the behavior of the patient is motivated by unconscious attempts to solve his or her problems rather than by the dynamic interaction of impulses and defenses; and (d) that the patient's behavior is guided by unconscious thoughts and assessments rather than by automatic dynamic interactions of forces.

Further Studies of Testing

Further studies of testing have been carried out by other investigators under the direction of Silberschatz and Curtis. These studies have been conducted on brief psychotherapies and have included some additional dependent variables. Significant correlations have been found between passing a patient's test and immediate increases in the patient's level of experiencing (Silberschatz & Curtis, 1991), immediate decreases in the patient's anxiety as measured by a new physiological measure of voice stress (Kelly, 1989), and immediate increases in the patient's level of adaptive regression (Bugas, 1986).

These successful replications using different patients, different psychotherapies (brief psychotherapy rather than psychoanalysis), and some different measures of patient change lend further support to the hypothesis that testing pathogenic beliefs is an important patient activity and that "passing" the patient's tests is an important factor determining therapeutic progress.

THE PATIENT'S WORK: HOW THE PATIENT RESPONDS TO INTERPRETATIONS

Interpretations also play a crucial role in psychoanalysis and psychoanalytic psychotherapies. Weiss et al. (1986) proposed that patients respond to interpretations differentially as a function of how useful the interpretation is to them in understanding and disconfirming their pathogenic beliefs and in pursuing their conscious and unconscious goals and plans. This hypothesis leads to testable predictions. The therapist's interpretations may be classified in accord with the extent to which the interpretations should enable a particular patient to carry out his or her plans for disconfirming pathogenic beliefs. It is then possible to analyze the relation between the plan compatibility (pro-planfulness) of the interpretation and immediate patient progress.

Caston (1986) pioneered an ingenious method for obtaining a reliable formulation of an individual patient's plan. His method has been further developed by other research group members (Curtis, Silberschatz, Sampson, Weiss, & Rosenberg, 1988; Rosenberg, Silberschatz, Curtis, Sampson, & Weiss, 1986). A useful way to analyze a patient's plan is in terms of (a) his or her inferred goals; (b) the inferred inner obstacles to attainment of his or her goals (i.e., pathogenic beliefs); (c) the inferred ways in which the patient is likely to test the therapist; and (d) the inferred insights that would help the patient carry out his or her plan and move toward his or her goals. For each of these four categories, plausible but not necessarily correct statements are generated independently by three or four judges who read transcripts of a patient's intake interview and of the opening sessions of the treatment. (If one is studying an analysis, the judge reads transcripts of the first 10 treatment sessions; if one is studying a brief psychotherapy, he or she reads transcripts of only the intake and first 2 treatment sessions.) The pooled items of all of the judges are then re-presented to them. The judges are then asked to rate each item for its pertinence to and priority in the patient's plan. Items that command high interjudge agreement are then included in what is called the *plan formulation* for that patient.

Caston (1986) also pioneered the first pilot studies of Weiss's (1986) hypothesis about the plan compatibility of interpretations and immediate patient progress. His findings were generally supportive of the hypothesis but inconclusive. Bush and Gassner (1986), using an improved methodology, carried out a pilot study on interpretations during the termination phase of the analysis of Mrs. C. They found that the plan compatibility of the analyst's interpretations was correlated significantly with the patient's acceptance of termination. On the basis of these preliminary studies, Fretter (1984) undertook a carefully designed study of the immediate effects of interpretations in three brief psychotherapies. I describe a portion of this study and its findings (Fretter, 1984; Silberschatz, Fretter, & Curtis, 1986).

Fretter (1984) used a single case-repeat design; that is, she carried out her procedures and analyzed her data on one case and then replicated the process on additional cases studied one at a time. The data were analyzed separately for each case because goals, pathogenic beliefs, and so forth, differed for each case. Therefore, the standards for assessing whether an interpretation was "pro-plan" differed for each case.

Fretter's (1984) sample consisted of three cases randomly selected from a larger sample of recorded and transcribed 16-session brief psychotherapies. The three cases were each diagnosed as suffering from chronic, neurotic depression. Six months after therapy, Case 1 showed an excellent outcome, Case 2 a good outcome, and Case 3 a poor outcome.

The therapists for the larger sample of cases were psychologists or psychiatrists with at least 3 years of private practice experience after completion of training. Some therapists were psychoanalysts; all had received specialized training in brief psychoanalytically oriented psychotherapy. The therapists held differing psychodynamic orientations. Patients were assigned to therapists in random order.

Fretter (1984) had all verbal comments made by the therapist over the course of the treatment classified independently by several judges as "interpretations" or "noninterpretations." This was done with near-perfect agreement between independent judges and yielded a list of all interpretations for each case.

Fretter (1984) then used new judges (four to six judges for each case) to rate each interpretation for its plan compatibility. She presented each judge with a very brief summary case history (from the intake and first 2 sessions). She also provided them with the plan formulation of that case. (The reliability of the plan formulation was obtained by the method described earlier.) This enabled the judge to evaluate in a case-specific way whether an interpretation would, for this patient, be "pro-plan." Ratings were made on a 7-point Likert scale ranging from -3 (*strongly anti-plan*) to $+3$ (*strongly pro-plan*).

Interpretations were removed from the transcript and presented to judges in random order. The judges were kept blind to the patient's response to the interpretation, to when the interpretations were given, and to the outcome of the case.

Reliabilities of ratings were good in each of the three cases (r_{kk} of .89, .88, and .85, respectively). Fretter (1984) used the mean of the judges' ratings for statistical analyses.

In order to measure the patient's immediate response to interpretations, Fretter used the Experiencing Scale (described earlier). The patient's experiencing was measured on approximately 3-minute patient speech segments immediately before and immediately after each interpretation. These segments were removed from the transcripts, typed on individual cards, and presented to judges in random order. Therefore, judges of these segments did not see the interpretation, did not know when the segment occurred in the therapy, and did not know whether the segment occurred before or after the interpretation. They were also blind to the outcome of treatment. Fretter used a residualized gain score to analyze the direction and degree of change in experiencing from before to after interpretation.

Findings

Fretter (1984) found a statistically significant positive correlation (ranging from .25 to .58) in each of the three cases between the plan compatibility of interpretations and changes in experiencing. Statistically significant correlations were also obtained in later work on these same cases for two other dependent variables: Pro-planfulness of interpretation was also associated significantly with *increased insight* (Broitman, 1985), and with *increased referential activity* (Bucci, 1988; Fretter, Bucci, Broitman, Silberschatz, & Curtis, 1988). The Referential Activity Scale rates speech for richness of sensory detail, imagery, specificity, and clarity. Language that is high on this scale has a quality of immediacy and liveness for the listener. Language that is low on this scale will sound abstract, general and vague, and lacking in specific and concrete detail.

In order to capture the cumulative impact of the plan compatibility of interpretations over the course of a session, Fretter (1984) took the mean score for plan compatibility for each hour and correlated it with the mean shift in the experiencing score for that hour. She found large and statistically significant correlations between plan compatibility and shifts in experiencing: The correlations were .54 in one case, .57 in a second, and .78 in a third. Figure 1 (in Silberschatz, Sampson, & Weiss, 1986) illustrates this relationship and shows visually the striking correspondence in each case between the plan compatibility of interpretations and the patient's immediate progress.

Fretter (1984) also decided to check on whether there was a relation between the plan compatibility of interpretations over the course of the therapy and how well the therapy turned out. In the case with the highest proportion of plan-compatible interpretations, there was an excellent outcome; in the case with the lowest proportion of plan-compatible interpretations, there was the poorest outcome; and the other case was in between on both plan compatibility and outcome. This finding means little in itself but encouraged me and my colleagues to undertake further research. In a subsequent study carried out by Norville (1989) on seven cases, strong positive correlations (approaching .70) were found between the overall plan compatibility of interpretations and the overall favorableness of outcome. The correlations were not statistically significant for this sample of seven cases, but they were sufficiently promising to encourage replication of Norville's study on a large sample.

Implications

Fretter's (1984) findings, combined with those of Broitman (1985) and Bucci (1988), have several implications: First, they indicate that what the therapist tells the patient—the content of interpretations—determined whether the interpretations were helpful. This finding indicates that the interpretations did not work primarily by providing patients with any one of a number of possible coherent frameworks or narratives for understanding their problems, for it demonstrates that different interpretive frameworks lead to significantly different results.

Second, the interpretations do not work simply by suggestion. The cure appears to be based in part on the specific medicine dispensed rather than on only the doctor.

Third, these findings also challenge any simple relational theory, that is, any theory that therapy works by providing the patient a benign and supportive relationship independent of what the therapist communicates to the patient.

Fourth, consistent with the findings of Silberschatz (1986) on testing, these results show that the therapist's interventions have an *immediate effect* on patient progress. This supports the idea that patients always unconsciously monitor the treatment environment for indications as to whether the infantile danger situations they unconsciously fear are real and present in the therapeutic situation. This means that the behavior of patients is regulated continuously by appraisals of their immediate reality.

These findings also lend further support to Weiss's (1986) plan concept by demonstrating once again the explanatory and predictive power of hypotheses derived from it. The plan concept predicts a certain order in nature, and my colleagues and I have found that order in several research studies.

PSYCHOANALYSIS AND PSYCHOLOGY

I would like to comment further on the relevance of this work to the relationship between psychoanalysis and the rest of psychology. Psychoanalysis developed independently from the rest of psychology, and it has for the most part remained a separate discipline. It arose in clinical practice, in the institutional setting of the private consulting room rather than the university. It developed a distinctive subject matter (unconscious conflict and unconscious mental life), a distinctive set of explanatory concepts, its own method of investigation, and its own research traditions.

The new science of psychoanalysis addressed important and fascinating problems in human life. Its concepts were revolutionary, and they concerned, and offered compelling explanations of, phenomena that had scarcely been touched by serious scientific inquiry. Not surprisingly, psychoanalysis influenced many areas of human thought, including other areas of psychology.

This influence was for the most part one way. Psychoanalysis itself remained relatively insulated from the research methods and findings in other areas of psychology. Until very recently, this has continued to be the case.

There have been, in addition to institutional and historic factors, significant scientific and theoretical reasons why psychoanalysis has remained mostly a separate science. One reason has been its research tradition, which has relied almost exclusively on a relatively informal case study method in which the treating analyst, in the course of his or her work, makes observations and inferences, develops familiar or new explanatory hypotheses, and tests these hypotheses against other observations in the same case or in other cases. The informal case study method is well suited to investigation of the subtle, complex, and often puzzling phenomena of mental life. It was essential to Freud's development of the field. It has enabled generations of analysts and analytically influenced clinicians—approaching the study of mental life with differing experiences, gifts, and theoretical perspectives—to create an extraordinarily rich and diverse body of clinical observations and lore, and to formulate hypotheses that have supplemented, extended, clarified, challenged, and even contradicted Freud's early theory.

Nonetheless, the traditional research method of psychoanalysis is subject to many serious and intrinsic problems and limitations (see, e.g., Bellak, 1961; Benjamin, 1950; Edelson, 1977, 1984; Escalona, 1952; Glover, 1952; Grunbaum, 1979; Lustman, 1963; Shakow, 1960; Silverman & Wolitzky, 1982; Wallerstein & Sampson, 1971). In brief, the method does not provide an investigator other than the treating analyst access to unselected, unbiased, relatively complete data from which he or she can form conclusions. Moreover, the very data produced in the analytic situation are shaped to some extent by the patient's compliances with the analyst, thereby making it suspect as proof of the analyst's theories. In addition, the methods of analyzing the data and drawing conclusions are more or less private and implicit, and they do not lead to univocal conclusions, even by trained, well-qualified observers. Because of these and other problems, the traditional method does not provide for rigorous testing of hypotheses or for a definitive way of choosing between competing hypotheses.

Exclusive reliance on this method, without *also* developing a substantial base of systematic, formal research, reflects a gross underestimation of the intensive, sustained, and specialized effort required to validate or disconfirm hypotheses, or to choose between competing hypotheses (Wallerstein & Sampson, 1971). The task of testing hypotheses cannot be carried out adequately as an aspect of ordinary clinical work, for it requires its own logic, procedures, controls, and standards. It also places special demands on the investigator's time and commitment.

The research tradition of psychoanalysis, with its uniqueness and its limitations, has contributed to the relative insulation of psychoanalysis from other sciences, including psychology. It has limited the interest of psychoanalysts in findings obtained by other methods; such findings are often considered irrelevant almost by definition because they do not provide data from the psychoanalytic situation. This research tradition has also limited the informed interest in psychoanalysis of many psychologists other than clinicians. The uniqueness and inaccessibility of the psychoanalytic research method has made it difficult for many psychological scientists to evaluate the credibility of psychoanalytic findings or to apply psychoanalytic findings readily to their own research problems.

The research discussed in this chapter has shown that alternative fundamental psychoanalytic hypotheses about the unconscious, psychopathology, and therapy may be tested systematically by ordinary research methods. Verbatim transcripts from the psychoanalytic situation as well as from other psychotherapies are used. Hypotheses are tested by research designs planned in advance to control for potential sources of bias and error; quantitative measures of pertinent variables and of relationships between variables are used; and statistical tests to determine the significance of the findings applied. The findings, if replicated independently, have important implications for theory and practice. Therefore, this work challenges the idea that psychoanalysis must remain a separate science based exclusively on a unique methodology. It helps, along with other work described in this book, to bring psychoanalysis into the mainstream of contemporary science, making it a part of a larger scientific enterprise.

A number of Freud's early concepts also contributed to the insulation of psychoanalysis from the rest of psychology. Freud (1905/1953b, 1915/1957b) assumed that unconscious mental life—the central domain of psychoanalytic interest—operated by entirely different rules than conscious or preconscious mental life. It was regulated exclusively by the pleasure principle. Its processes were not concerned with adaptation or with reality. Its processes automatically strove for immediate gratification without thought, anticipation, planning, judgments, or assessments of risk and evaluation of consequences. Similarly, unconscious thought automatically turned away from unpleasure, even as the infant automatically turns away physically from a noxious external stimulus. These hypotheses made traditional psychology—based for the most part on the study of higher mental functions or of behavior guided by adaptive considerations—applicable only to what Hartmann (1939/1958) referred to as the conflict-free sphere of the ego. Research concerned with higher mental functions or with adaptation appeared to be irrelevant to the main domains of psychoanalytic interest: unconscious mental life, unconscious conflict, psychopathology, and therapy.

Freud's early theory of unconscious mental functioning and of adaptation was modified in Freud's own ego psychology, in the work of Hartmann (1939/1958) and other ego psychologists, in the interpersonal theory of Harry Stack Sullivan (1953), in the work of some of the British object-relations theorists, in the contributions of the new students of infant development (see, e.g., Lichtenberg, 1983, 1989; Silverman, 1986; Stern, 1985), as well as in the work of many contemporary analytic writers (e.g., Rangell, 1968, 1969; Sandler, 1960). These modifications have gone in the direction of recognizing that adaptation to reality is a primary and central psychic concern from the beginnings of life; that the pleasure principle does not have exclusive sway over unconscious mental life; that the pleasure principle subserves adaptation; and that psychopathology may arise not because of the dominance of the pleasure principle over unconscious mental life but out of efforts at adaptation to reality. I have described these trends in some detail elsewhere (Sampson, 1990).

Weiss's (1986) theory and my and my colleagues' research has taken us still further in modifying Freud's early theory that unconscious (repressed) mental life is regulated exclusively by the pleasure principle and functions without regard to reality and adaptation. Weiss has proposed that a person may unconsciously do many of the same things he or she does consciously. The person can unconsciously think, anticipate, make discriminations, judgments, and decisions, form beliefs about the self and the world in which he or she lives, plan, compare past experiences to current situations, and assess risks and evaluate the realistic internal and external consequences of a course of action. These higher mental functions are used not only in preconscious thought but in thought about repressed strivings, unconscious conflicts, and unconscious beliefs about danger. Moreover, the patient's behavior in treatment is guided by adaptive considerations such as danger and safety, and is regulated by unconscious plans, anticipations, beliefs, and decisions. This research has supported these ideas and has suggested that a patient's behavior is more accurately predicted from his or her inferred unconscious goals, plans, and beliefs about reality than from his or her inferred drives and defenses.

In this way, too, this work makes psychoanalysis a less separate science. It makes psychoanalytic concerns and hypotheses more relevant to the core biological concept of adaptation, as well as to familiar topics within psychology bearing on thinking, planning, decision making, and belief systems. It also makes these fields of academic study and research more relevant to psychoanalysis.

REFERENCES

Bellak, L. (1961). Research in psychoanalysis. *Psychoanalytic Quarterly, 30,* 519–548.

Benjamin, J. D. (1950). Methodological considerations in the validation and elaboration of psychoanalytical personality theory. *American Journal of Orthopsychiatry, 20,* 139–156.

Broitman, J. (1985). Insight, the mind's eye: An exploration of three patients' processes of becoming insightful. *Dissertation Abstracts International, 46(8).* (University Microfilms No. 85-20,425)

Bucci, W. (1988). Linguistic evidence for emotional structures: Manuals and methods. In H. Dahl, H. Kachele, & H. Thoma (Eds.), *Psychoanalytic process research strategies* (pp. 29–49). New York: Springer.

Bugas, J. S. (1986). Adaptive regression and the therapeutic change process. Unpublished doctoral dissertation, Pacific Graduate School of Psychology, Menlo Park, CA.

Bush, M., & Gassner, S. (1986). The immediate effect of the analyst's termination interventions on the patient's resistance to termination. In J. Weiss, H. Sampson, & The Mount Zion Psychotherapy Research Group (Eds.), *The psychoanalytic process: Theory, clinical observations, and empirical research* (pp. 299–320). New York: Guilford Press.

Caston, J. (1986). The reliability of the diagnosis of the patient's unconscious plan. In J. Weiss, H. Sampson, & The Mount Zion Psychotherapy Research Group (Eds.), *The psychoanalytic process: Theory, clinical observations, and empirical research* (pp. 241–255). New York: Guilford Press.

Curtis, J., Silberschatz, G., Sampson, H., Weiss, J., & Rosenberg, S. (1988). Developing reliable psychodynamic case formulations: An illustration of the plan diagnosis method. *Psychotherapy, 25,* 256–265.

Dahl, H. (1979). The appetite hypothesis of emotions: A new psychoanalytic model of motivation. In C. E. Izard (Ed.), *Emotions in personality and psychopathology* (pp. 201–23). New York: Plenum Press.

Edelson, M. (1977). Psychoanalysis as science. *Journal of Nervous and Mental Disease, 165,* 1–28.

Edelson, M. (1984). Hypothesis and evidence in psychoanalysis. Chicago: University of Chicago Press.

Escalona, S. (1952). Problems in psycho-analytic research. *International Journal of Psycho-Analysis, 33,* 11–21.

Fretter, P. (1984). The immediate effects of transference interpretations on patients' progress in brief, psychodynamic psychotherapy. *Dissertation Abstracts International, 46(6).* (University Microfilms No. 85-12, 112)

Fretter, P. B., Bucci, W., Broitman, J., Silberschatz, G., & Curtis, J. T. (1988). *How the patient's plan relates to the concept of transference.* Unpublished manuscript.

Freud, S. (1953a). On psychotherapy. In J. Strachey (Ed. and Trans.), *The standard edition of the complete psychological works of Sigmund Freud* (Vol. 7, pp. 257–268). London: Hogarth Press. (Original work published 1905)

Freud, S. (1953b). The interpretation of dreams. In J. Strachey (Ed. and Trans.), *The standard edition of the complete psychological works of Sigmund Freud* (Vol. 5, pp. 588–604). London: Hogarth Press. (Original work published 1900)

Freud, S. (1955). Beyond the pleasure principle. In J. Strachey (Ed. and Trans.), *The standard edition of the complete psychological works of Sigmund Freud* (Vol. 18, pp. 3–64). London: Hogarth Press. (Original work published 1920)

Freud, S. (1957a). A metapsychological supplement to the theory of dreams. In J. Strachey (Ed. and Trans.), *The standard edition of the complete psychological works of Sigmund Freud* (Vol. 14, p. 232). London: Hogarth Press. (Original work published 1917)

Freud, S. (1957b). The unconscious. In J. Strachey (Ed. and Trans.), *The standard edition of the complete psychological works of Sigmund Freud* (Vol. 14, pp. 186–189). London: Hogarth Press. (Original work published 1915)

Freud, S. (1959). Inhibitions, symptoms and anxiety. In J. Strachey (Ed. and Trans.), *The standard edition of the complete psychological works of Sigmund Freud* (Vol. 20, pp. 77–175). London: Hogarth Press. (Original work published 1926)

Gassner, S., Sampson, H., Weiss, J., & Brumer, S. (1982). The emergence of warded-off contents. *Psychoanalysis and Contemporary Thought, 5(1)*, 55–75.

Glover, E. (1952). Research methods in psychoanalysis. *International Journal of Psycho-Analysis, 33*, 403–409.

Grünbaum, A. (1979). Epistemological liabilities of the clinical appraisal of psychoanalytic theory. *Psychoanalysis and Contemporary Thought, 2*, 451–526.

Hartmann, H. (1939). *Ego psychology and the problem of adaptation*. New York: International Universities Press. (Original work published 1958)

Horowitz, L. M., Sampson, H., Siegelman, E. Y., Wolfson, A. W., & Weiss, J. (1975). On the identification of warded-off mental contents. *Journal of Abnormal Psychology, 84*, 545–558.

Kelly, T. (1989). *Do therapist's interventions matter?* Unpublished doctoral dissertation, New York University, New York.

Lichtenberg, J. (1983). *Psychoanalysis and infant research*. Hillsdale, NJ: Analytic Press.

Lichtenberg, J. (1989). *Psychoanalysis and motivation*. Hillsdale, NJ: Analytic Press.

Lustman, S. L. (1963). Some issues in contemporary psychoanalytic research. *Psychoanalytic Study of the Child, 18*.

Norville, R. (1989). Plan compatibility of interpretations and brief psychotherapy outcome. *Dissertation Abstracts International, 50*, 5888. (University Microfilms No. 90-12770)

Rangell, L. (1968). The psychoanalytic process. *International Journal of Psycho-Analysis, 49*, 19–26.

Rangell, L. (1969). The intrapsychic process and its analysis: A recent line of thought and its current implications. *International Journal of Psycho-Analysis, 50*, 65–77.

Rosenberg, S., Silberschatz, G., Curtis, J., Sampson, H., & Weiss, J. (1986). The plan diagnosis method: A new approach to establishing reliability for psychodynamic formulations. *American Journal of Psychiatry, 143*, 1454–1456.

Sampson, H. (1990). The problem of adaptation to reality in psychoanalytic theory. *Contemporary Psychoanalysis, 26*, 677–691.

Sampson, H., Weiss, J., Mlodnosky, L., & Hause, E. (1972). Defense analysis and the emergence of warded-off mental contents: An empirical study. *Archives of General Psychiatry, 26*, 524–532.

Sandler, J. (1960). The background of safety. *International Journal of Psycho-Analysis, 41*, 352–356.

Sargent, H. D., Horowitz, L., Wallerstein, R., & Appelbaum, A. (1968). Prediction in psychotherapy research: A method for the transformation of clinical judgments into testable hypotheses. *Psychological Issues, 4(1, Serial No. 21)*.

Shakow, D. (1960). The recorded psychoanalytic interview as an objective approach to research in psychoanalysis. *Psychoanalytic Quarterly, 29*, 82–97.

Silberschatz, G. (1986). Testing pathogenic beliefs. In J. Weiss, H. Sampson, & The Mount Zion Psychotherapy Research Group (Eds.), *The psychoanalytic process: Theory, clinical observations, and empirical research* (pp. 256–266). New York: Guilford Press.

Silberschatz, G., & Curtis, J. (1991). *Measuring the therapist's impact on the patient's therapeutic progress*. Manuscript submitted for publication.

Silberschatz, G., Fretter, P., & Curtis, J. (1986). How do interpretations influence the process of psychotherapy? *Journal of Consulting and Clinical Psychology, 54*, 646–652.

Silberschatz, G., & Sampson, H. (1991). Affects in psychopathology and psychotherapy. In J. D. Safran & J. S. Greenberg (Eds.), *Emotion, psychotherapy, and change* (pp. 113–129). New York: Guilford Press.

Silberschatz, G., Sampson, H., & Weiss, J. (1986). Testing pathogenic beliefs versus seeking transference gratifications. In J. Weiss, H. Sampson, & The Mount Zion Psychotherapy Research Group (Eds.), *The psychoanalytic process: Theory, clinical observations, and empirical research* (pp. 267–276). New York: Guilford Press.

Silverman, D. (1986). Some proposed modifications to psychoanalytic theories of early childhood development. In J. Masling (Ed.), *Empirical studies of psychoanalytic theories* (Vol. 2, pp. 449–472). Hillsdale, NJ: Analytic Press.

Silverman, L. H., & Wolitzky, D. (1982). Towards the resolution of controversial issues in psychoanalytic treatment. In S. Slip (Ed.), *Curative factors in dynamic psychotherapy* (pp. 321–348). New York: McGraw-Hill.

Sullivan, H. S. (1953). *The interpersonal theory of psychiatry.* New York: Norton.

Stern, D. N. (1985). *The interpersonal world of the infant.* New York: Basic Books.

Wallerstein, R. S., & Sampson, H. (1971). Issues in research on the psychoanalytic process. *International Journal of Psycho-Analysis, 52,* 11–50.

Weiss, J. (1952). Crying at the happy ending. *Psychoanalytic Review, 39,* 338.

Weiss, J. (1971). The emergence of new themes: A contribution to the psychoanalytic theory of therapy. *International Journal of Psychoanalysis, 52,* 459–467.

Weiss, J. (1990). The centrality of adaptation. *Contemporary Psychoanalysis, 26,* 660–676.

Weiss, J., Sampson, H., & The Mount Zion Psychotherapy Research Group. (1986). *The psychoanalytic process: Theory, clinical observations, and empirical research.* New York: Guilford Press.

28

A PROPOSAL FOR IMPROVING THE PSYCHOANALYTIC THEORY OF TECHNIQUE

JEFFREY L. BINDER, HANS H. STRUPP, AND DANIEL L. ROCK

While the particular conceptual framework that guides [the therapist] creates the basis for his understanding of his patients and for the development of his techniques, this same theoretical structure at times constitutes the very blind which he cannot remove in order to see possible new solutions. (Ekstein & Wallerstein, 1972, p. 53)

Fifty years ago, Otto Fenichel (1941) found it "astonishing" that such a small proportion of the psychoanalytic literature was devoted to explicit discussions of therapy technique. Three decades later, Menninger and Holzman (1973) saw little change in this state of affairs. Today, regardless of the large amount of accumulated writings explicitly about technique, we believe that the *practical utility* of this literature is questionable. It appears that there always have been difficulties associated with articulating psychoanalytic technique. Strachey (1958) observed that Freud was reluctant to publish on the topic. The reasons given by Freud included (a) uneasiness about patients acquiring knowledge about the details of the technique and (b) skepticism about the value of didactic exercises in the training of novice analysts. Freud assumed that if analysts understood his theory of mental functioning, they could account for the actions of patients and thereby judge the therapeutic merits of using any particular technique.

We contend that the persistent influence of this assumption about the relationship of theory to practice has had detrimental effects on conceptions of psychoanalytic technique, on the understanding of therapist expertise, and on the training of psychoanalytic therapists. There is a greater congruence between the psychoanalytic theories of mental functioning and of therapeutic change than between either of these theories and a theory of technique (Menninger & Holzman, 1973). For example, the concept of the dynamic unconscious has as a corollary that unconscious material must be lifted from repression; similarly, the concept of defenses against unpleasant affects has a corollary that states that defenses must be removed or modified. However, the implications of these concepts for a theory of technique are limited to broad, strategic guidelines, such as that derivatives of unconscious material should be identified or resistances should be confronted and interpreted.

We believe that such broad therapeutic strategies reflect only a nascent theory of technique that lacks *specific* guidelines for the implementation of these strategies. Furthermore, there does not appear to be a consistent process whereby the evolution of theories of mental functioning and change lead to modifications of technique (Alexander, 1963). Instead, there is often a discrepancy between clinical theories and technique: Advances in clinical theory often do not produce corresponding technical developments, technical innovations occur in the absence of theoretical modifications or as a result of theoretical departures that have not been made explicit, or technical innovations and modifications may simply not follow from theory (Richards, 1984).[1]

In this chapter, we provide an overview of the evolution of psychoanalytic theories of mental functioning and therapeutic change, as well as implications for technique. These overviews are brief, but we believe that they capture the essence of the theories and provide a sufficient background for a more detailed examination of technical concepts.[2] We also offer the caveat that the subject of psychoanalytic technique contains vast diversity regarding terms and procedures (Kanzer, 1979). Therefore, the published conceptions regarding technique that we scrutinize do not represent all viewpoints but, nevertheless, are widely accepted.

We argue that the psychoanalytic theories of mental functioning and change do not yield a specification of therapeutic tactics that can serve as effective guidelines for practice. Furthermore, these conceptual frameworks do not account for the therapeutic skills required to implement techniques, nor do they explain the development of a psychoanalytic therapist from novice to expert. Furthermore, the training of psychoanalytic therapists is limited by the theoretical concepts of technique that guide clinical training.

We offer a proposal for improving this theory by incorporating relevant concepts from cognitive psychology. This area of psychological research is aimed at understanding the nature, acquisition, and development of skills within and across knowledge domains. Our working assumption is that selected principles, concepts, and methods from cognitive psychology can be adapted and incorporated into psychoanalytic theory, thereby improving our ability to describe therapeutic techniques and advance our understanding of the skills associated with effective technical performance.

THEORIES OF MENTAL FUNCTIONING AND CHANGE

Our aim is to determine how psychoanalytic theories of mental functioning and change have influenced conceptions of technique. Accordingly, within the vast corpus on these subjects, we selected for review widely cited texts on technique as well as articles explicitly devoted to the topic. We have attempted to choose representative works from the various epochs representing the evolution of psychoanalytic theory.

---

[1]Strupp (1969) has proposed that theoretical formulations follow, rather than precede, technical modifications. Therapists first experiment with innovative techniques, often in purely empirical fashion, and subsequently modify theory to fit technical procedures that demonstrate therapeutic benefit.

[2]It should be noted that we focus on "classical" theory, which is the parent theory from which such contemporary developments as object relations theory, interpersonal theory, and self psychology have been derived. We are confident that our observations about primarily the parent are valid for the children, although the latter is discussed.

The Early Theory

Early psychoanalytic theories of mental functioning and change represented the topographic, economic, and dynamic perspectives. Emphasis was on the dichotomy between dammed up, unconscious instinctual impulses and the countercathexes—or resistances—to their emergence into conscious awareness. Transference was considered the "most powerful" resistance because it was such an effective means for avoiding awareness of warded-off experiences. The corresponding theory of change emphasized releasing the dammed-up impulses by recognizing their derivatives in the form of wishes expressed primarily through the transference (Freud, 1912/1958a). Even with the advent of the structural hypotheses (Freud, 1923/1961), early textbooks tended to emphasize the recovery of warded-off instincts and their associated anxieties. This goal was to be achieved by doing away with defenses against instinctual impulses or replacing them with ones that were less susceptible to ego-dystonic symptom formation (Fenichel, 1941).

Technical concepts were aimed at rapid removal of resistances to the interpretation of unconscious material. Resistances tended to be viewed as impediments to gaining access to the important unconscious impulses. Accordingly, the earliest technical recommendations concerned interventions that encouraged the patient to overcome any impediment to free association (Freud, 1912/1958a, 1913/1958c, 1914/1958d). As the important role of ego resistances in the organization of dynamic conflict achieved greater recognition, more extensive recommendations for dealing with them were put forth (Fenichel, 1941). The analyst's "neutrality," anonymity, and "mirror" functions vis-à-vis the transference provided guidelines for relating to patients whose behavior toward the analyst was governed by resistances. Somewhat more detailed guidelines for interpreting resistances were recommended (e.g., the injunction to interpret defenses before impulses and to analyze defenses historically). A more general recommendation was always to interpret defenses and instinctual derivatives from surface to depth (Fenichel, 1941). The focus, however, remained on expeditiously removing resistances to gain access to the all-important unconscious impulses.

The Structural Theory

The advent of the structural model of the mind reflected increasing appreciation of the importance of ego defenses in the development, maintenance, and adaptation to psychic conflict (Brenner, 1976; Greenson, 1967; Menninger & Holzman, 1973). The corresponding theory of change continued to give primacy to uncovering unconscious impulses and their mental representations. However, increasing importance was also being placed on bringing to conscious awareness the functioning and purposes of unconscious ego defenses and their associated unpleasant affects. Management of transference and countertransference phenomena was necessary to induce a "transference neurosis," which set the stage for curative ego modifications through resolution of the core neurosis. The original therapeutic goal of psychoanalysis was simple recovery of unconscious material. This goal was superceded by the strategy of strengthening the ego's adaptive and defensive resources by means of working through (Brenner, 1976; Greenson, 1967; Menninger & Holzman, 1973). In addition, attention to the regressive transference neurosis reflected a growing emphasis on the interpersonal correlates of psychic conflict and their role in promoting therapeutic change. The explicit and implicit reciprocal expectations between patient and therapist (Menninger & Holzman, 1973) and the more general issue of the "working alliance" (Greenson, 1967) assumed greater importance in technical discussions.

Technical implications of the structural model of mental functioning inaugurated the contemporary version of classical psychoanalytic technique (Brenner, 1976). Greater importance was now being assigned to consistent and systematic analysis of resistances. Thus, resistances are pointed out, followed by examination of their modes, purposes, and histories (Greenson, 1967; Menninger & Holzman, 1973). More specific modifications in technique were also suggested. For example, the notion that all conscious mental activity contains facets of the three structures of the mind (i.e., id, ego, and superego) resulted in the advice to replace the sequencing of interpretations from defense to impulse and from surface to depth, with the formulation of interpretations around the order in which new or confirming information appears in associations (Brenner, 1976). Other elaborations of technique involved clarification of types of interventions (Greenson, 1967) and of the ideal sequencing of content areas toward which interpretations were directed (e.g., the "triangle of insight" of Menninger & Holzman, 1973). Increased appreciation of the interpersonal nature of the analytic process led to more extensive descriptions of the therapeutic relationship and of the analyst's "ideal" manner of relating to the patient. It was clearly understood that patients are influenced not only by the content of interventions, but also by the analyst's interpersonal manner (Greenson, 1967; Menninger & Holzman, 1973).

Contemporary Influences

A unique perspective of psychoanalytic theory has always been attention to the patient's "inner world" of subjective experiences (Gabbard, 1990). Today, object relations, self psychology, and interpersonal theories focus directly on subjective experiences of internalized self–other relationships. Kernberg (1984; Kernberg, Seltzer, Koenigsberg, Carr, & Appelbaum, 1989) has played a dominant role in bridging classic ego psychology and object relations theories that were formulated primarily in Great Britain (Fairbairn, 1954; Klein, 1963). He developed explanatory formulations of the consequences to ego structure of early difficulties in integrating internalized pleasurable and unpleasurable interpersonal experiences. The technical implications of formulations about mental functioning included a continued reliance on "standard analytic principles" (e.g., technical neutrality, interpreting from surface to depth, consistent transference analysis) with the addition of certain strategic emphases, particularly the resolution of fragmented ego states through confrontation and interpretation of contradictory modes of relating.

The attention to subjective experiences of self and others has been further extended by self psychology, which advocates as the primary technical strategy the analyst's sustained empathic inquiry. This intimate involvement in the patient's subjective world is presumed to facilitate the correction of deficits in his or her capacity to sustain a sense of well-being and to form mature, loving relationships with others (Kohut, 1971; Stolorow, 1990). Interpersonal theory has stressed the interrelatedness of the available repertoire of internal object relationships and the capacity to relate productively with others. Of particular importance for technique is the focus on the dyadic character of the patient–therapist relationship, in which the therapist is viewed as a "participant observer" (Havens, 1976; Levenson, 1972; Sullivan, 1953). The growing integration between classical and interpersonal theories has resulted in proposals to reconceptualize the therapist's role in the therapeutic relationship. Rather than being seen as a detached observer who presents a "mirror" for the patient's transference projections, patient and therapist interact and influence each other (Epstein & Feiner, 1979; Strupp & Binder, 1984). This changing view has also led to reformulations of transference and countertransference that assign greater weight to the contemporary transactions between patient and therapist (Gill, 1982).

THE ACTUAL RELATIONSHIP OF THEORY TO PRACTICE

As already stated, it is widely assumed that a theory of technique to guide practice can be derived from psychoanalytic theories of mental functioning and change (Brenner, 1976; Fenichel,

1941; Greenson, 1967; Menninger & Holzman, 1973; Richards, 1984; Strachey, 1958). Yet, the authors of books about psychoanalytic technique typically disclaim that their works are comprehensive treatments of the topic. Although some have argued that clinical theory has not developed sufficient specificity to serve as a consistent guide to technique (e.g., Brenner, 1976; Fenichel, 1941), other influential authors have questioned the capacity of psychoanalytic clinical theory ever to serve this purpose (e.g., Menninger & Holzman, 1973; Richards, 1984).

A lack of congruence between the psychoanalytic clinical theories and technical concepts has been a recurrent source of concern among analytic teachers. In a rare admission among analytic authors, Menninger (Menninger & Holzman, 1973) cited the discrepancy between procedural technical rules in his teaching and writing and his own "intuitive" practice style. He suggested that the source of this discrepancy was the lack of a systematic conceptual model of the treatment process (Menninger & Holzman, 1973). In his classic work on technique, Greenson (1967) criticized the standard works for providing broad technical principles without sufficient details of what analysts actually *do*. He gave as an example the procedure for analyzing resistances, which can mean one thing to one analyst and something "astonishingly" different to another. Yet, each believes that he or she is acting according to standard psychoanalytic principles.[3] In a panel discussion on technique, Robert Wallerstein was pointedly critical of the presumed relationship of clinical theory to technique:

> Analysts take almost as an article of faith that theory is . . . closely linked to technique and that change in theory will be directly translated into change or modification in technique. (cited in Richards, 1984, p. 587)

He proceeded to argue that changes in theory have not produced corresponding alterations in technique and that there is less conceptual articulation of the relationship between clinical theory and technical concepts than is commonly assumed (see also Alexander, 1963).

There are also recurrent concerns about the *discrepancy* between what is written about technique and what is actually taught as well as practiced (e.g., Greenson, 1967; Lipton, 1983; Strupp, 1969). For example, Levy (1987) argued that there is "a disparity between what is written about psychoanalytic technique and what is practiced by experienced clinicians" (p. 447). He pointed to the common recommendation for the analyst to allow the organization and content of the patient's unfolding material to dictate the formulation of interventions. In contrast, he cited technical "strategies" and "tactics" that are routinely taught by experienced clinicians to novices in clinical supervision. These include the sequence in which topics are taken up; variations in emphasis on interpreting transference and extratransference phenomena, as well as manifest versus latent content; delays in interpreting certain defenses while others are being explored; and "supportive" strategies with certain personality disorders that are used even in classical analysis (Wallerstein, 1989). Levy (1987) suggested that in clinical supervision, an "unofficial theory of technique" (p. 450) may be taught that fills the vacuum created by the inadequacies of the formal writings on technique.

In our view, the problem is that the "theory" of psychoanalytic technique primarily articulates broad and often abstract therapeutic strategies but that on the whole, it does not provide therapists with sufficiently specific recommendations for the moment-to-moment conduct of psychoanalytic therapy. Menninger (Menninger & Holzman, 1973) spoke about the "torturing problems" of novice therapists in the face of routine therapeutic decisions and actions. He also admitted his own bewilderment as a novice exposed to concepts and explanations that still left him unsure of where his therapies were headed. Menninger assumed that these problems would "melt" if the therapist was provided with a comprehensive theory of technique, which would

---

[3]This problem was already noted by Glover (1955).

serve as a "map" of the therapeutic terrain (Menninger & Holzman, 1973). However, Menninger's text, like many before and after, is akin to a map of the United States that indicates state boundaries but fails to show existing roads. It provides a broad overview of where one is and where one wants to end up, but once one sets out, the terrain often turns out to be more confusing than it appeared on the "map."

As previously stated, the representative works on technique that we reviewed tended to offer broad—and often vague—strategies, together with the understanding that these strategies would suffice to guide the practicing therapist. When illustrations of these principles in action are presented, they typically consist of short vignettes that condense entire sessions—or entire weeks or months of work—into a few sentences or at best a few paragraphs. What the therapist actually *did* was typically shrouded in mystery; general descriptions and summaries of many interventions were given, but when specific interventions were described, they were out of context so that the process of their development as well as their immediate purposes were unclear.

Two examples from Brenner (1976) are representative of these deficiencies. In the first example, the author is demonstrating how an understanding of the concept of "compromise formation" can effectively guide the handling of suicide ideation: "When we understand [compromise formation] *it is obvious how we should proceed technically.* . . .One should induce the patient to report [the suicide thoughts] as fully as possible and then to associate to them as freely as he can" (p. 15, italics added). The illustrative case vignette provides no useful picture of *how* the analyst proceeded: "Much time was spent during the early *months* (italics added) of this patient's analysis in analyzing his defenses" (p. 16). Interpretations are alluded to without any description of what actually transpired. Brenner ends the vignette by stating: "One can understand from this report, then, how important it is to be consistent in applying one's knowledge of psychic conflict and its consequences" (p. 20). At another point, the author sought to demonstrate the principle of concurrently examining defenses and warded-off derivatives: "the conjecture that [the patient] was defending against or warding off his anger in these various ways was repeatedly conveyed to him in interpretations during a period of several months" (p. 61). The reader has no idea whatsoever how or when these interpretations were conveyed.

In psychoanalytic therapy, "interpretation" is considered the premier technical tool. Yet, to our knowledge, there are no clearly articulated published guidelines for when and how to implement this type of intervention (Luborsky, Barber, & Crits-Christoph, 1990). Freud (1912/1958a, 1913/1958c) inaugurated the literature on technique with general "recommendations" to intervene when patient communication is "blocked" by transference resistances. However, he provided no examples of blocked communications or of resistances. Subsequent advice for the correct timing of interpretations has repeated the combination of vague rules with insufficient illustration. For example, interpretations are to be advanced when resistances appear on the "surface" of the mind (Fenichel, 1941; Freud, 1914/1958d); when the patient's frustration tension is too painful (Menninger & Holzman, 1973); not long before or long after the patient is "ready" (Brenner, 1976); when resistances are "demonstrable" (Greenson, 1967); and when affect and object relations themes are implicit in either verbal or nonverbal communication and are congruent with the themes evident in other modes of communication (Kernberg, 1984; Kernberg et al., 1989).

The same criticisms could be leveled at other discussions of psychoanalytic technique. This is not to deny that progress has been made, but it has primarily involved increasing the clarity and specificity of broad, strategic principles. For example, the concept of the "triangle of insight" (Menninger & Holzman, 1973) recommends a particular sequence of content areas for formulating interpretations that link conflictual themes enacted in transference with extratransference enactments. Types of interventions and their purposes have also received improved clarification (Greenson, 1967). Transference and countertransference problems associated with particular personality disorders have likewise undergone significant clarification (Kernberg, 1984; Kernberg et al., 1989).

Following Freud's (1913/1958c) famous chess metaphor, numerous authors have refrained from giving comprehensive expositions of psychoanalytic technique (e.g., Brenner, 1976; Fenichel, 1941; Luborsky, 1984). Freud had proposed that technical rules could be enumerated only for the beginning and end phases of treatment and, like chess, the intermediary moves were considered too numerous to be encompassed by systematic rules. Notwithstanding this limitation, it has been optimistically assumed that advances in psychoanalytic clinical theory would result in increased specificity of technical concepts (Brenner, 1976; Fenichel, 1941; Schaffer, 1982, 1983). Recent attempts to achieve this goal have taken the form of "treatment manuals," which were developed initially in response to the need for psychotherapy researchers to control the "therapist variable" (i.e., internal validity) in process–outcome studies (Klerman, Rounsaville, Chevron, Neu, & Weissman, 1984; Orlinsky & Howard, 1986; Strupp & Bergin, 1969). These manuals are now widely used as textbooks on technique. To examine the yield of manuals for practice, we focus on the two widely used approaches of Luborsky (1984) and Strupp and Binder (1984).

PSYCHOANALYTIC TREATMENT MANUALS

Manuals aim to develop (a) definitive descriptions of techniques, (b) detailed guides to the use of the techniques, and (c) therapist rating scales to measure the degree of adherence to the recommended techniques. The two manuals under discussion reflect somewhat different views of the relationship between clinical theory and technical concepts. Whereas Luborsky (1984) assumed a "loose" relationship between classic psychoanalytic clinical theory and his set of technical recommendations, Strupp and Binder (1984) searched for psychoanalytic concepts that appeared to involve minimal inference and were closely anchored to clinical data. They chose a combination of contemporary modifications of classic theory (e.g., Gill, 1982; Schlesinger, 1982) and selections from object relations theory (e.g., Sandler & Sandler, 1978) and interpersonal theory (e.g., Epstein & Feiner, 1979).

Both manuals discuss essentially the same techniques that are found in earlier analytic texts, but they consistently emphasize systematic analysis of transference phenomena.[4] Following the work of Menninger (Menninger & Holzman, 1973), Luborsky (1984) stressed interpretative links among transference enactments and evidence of the same conflicts in the patient's current and past relationships. From a more interpersonal theoretical orientation, Strupp and Binder (1984) stressed thorough examination of here-and-now transference–countertransference enactments. Both manuals represent significant improvements over previous texts in providing conceptual models for organizing clinical material into salient, conflictual interpersonal themes around which to focus the therapeutic work. Perhaps their most important contribution consisted of extensive annotated verbatim transcripts of treatment sessions, sometimes virtually of entire sessions, which gives the reader more meaningful illustrations of the techniques being discussed, including the rationale for specific interventions at a particular point in the unfolding process of a session.

In summary, the manuals for psychoanalytic psychotherapy improved the theory of technique in the following ways: (a) They describe technical concepts in a language closer to the experiences of actual practice; (b) they provide specific and concrete models for organizing clinical

---

[4]The priority accorded to systematic transference analysis has been a subject of debate among analytic clinicians. For a representative discussion, see Rangell (1980).

material around a focal theme; (c) they specifically define the therapeutic process; (d) they provide extensive descriptions of the therapist's role; and (e) they provide extensive, verbatim illustrations of the therapist at work.

Treatment manuals have been used in psychotherapy process–outcome studies that have demonstrated that technical adherence can be improved (Luborsky, McClellan, Woody, O'Brien, & Auerbach, 1985; Rounsaville, O'Malley, Foley, & Weissman, 1988). However, studies have also shown variations in ratings of therapeutic skill and effectiveness both across patients for a given therapist and across therapists (Lambert, 1989; Luborsky et al., 1986; O'Malley et al., 1988). Furthermore, our own detailed direct observations of experienced therapists who were trained with our manual (Strupp & Binder, 1984) support these findings. Although treatment manuals have elucidated technical concepts more effectively than previous texts, they still have not captured conceptually the blending of technical adherence and other skills that constitute therapeutic expertise or even good therapeutic practice. However, they have highlighted the problem of conceptualizing therapist skillfulness (Schaffer, 1982, 1983). Let us take a closer look at how the psychoanalytic texts and manuals have dealt with the issue of therapeutic skills.

THE PSYCHOANALYTIC VIEW OF THERAPIST SKILLS

In addition to being a method of investigating and treating mental disorders, psychoanalysis refers to a general theory of the mind (Richards, 1984). To some extent, this is too lofty a designation. Psychoanalytic theory is best suited to serve as a conceptual framework for understanding the development and nature of psychopathological functioning. However, authors of textbooks on technique have strained the theory's explanatory power when they have attempted to deal with the highly complex cognitive activities associated with therapists' technical performance. To illustrate this problem, we now examine how psychoanalytic theory has been used to explain several commonly recognized facets of therapeutic skill: (a) how clinical data are comprehended and organized; (b) how intellectual understanding and empathy are used in combination; (c) how thematic patterns, including resistances, are recognized; (d) the application of theoretical knowledge to clinical work; and (e) implications for clinical supervision.

Comprehending and Organizing Clinical Data

Early in the history of psychoanalytic treatment, Freud (1912/1958b) recognized a particularly difficult task for the therapist, namely, keeping in mind all of the facts and "psychological products" of the patient over the course of a treatment, as well as not confusing them with other patients. Others also have commented on the difficulty of identifying conflict themes, when the "clues" are so numerous, varied, and separated from one another in time (Brenner, 1976). Freud (1912/1958b) used the concept of "unconscious memory" to explain how this task was accomplished. He made the implicit assumption that the unconscious is capable of spontaneously organizing information and that this organizing process is particularly suited to identifying the conflictual themes of patients. Thus came into being the basic technical rule of maintaining "evenly suspended attention." Freud (1912/1958b) advised the analyst to "simply listen, and not bother about whether he is keeping anything in mind"(p. 112). Most likely drawing on his own subjective experiences (i.e., the experiences of an expert therapist), Freud (1912/1958b) described the result of this mindset: "Those elements of the material which already form a connected context will be at the doctor's conscious disposal; the rest, as yet unconnected and in chaotic disorder, seems first to be submerged, but *rises readily into recollection* (italics added) as soon as the patient brings up something new to which it can be related" (p. 112).

Freud's (1912/1958b) concept of "unconscious memory" does not meaningfully describe or explain the perceptual and cognitive processes involved in the interdependent tasks of identification, memory, and association to which he was referring. Nevertheless, over time, this concept has been elaborated and used as the primary explanation for the therapist's ability to understand the conscious and unconscious experiences of his or her patient. The analyst's unconscious is the "tool" with which he or she grasps the unconscious meanings of the patient's material and reconstructs it (Fenichel, 1941; Greenson, 1967; Menninger & Holzman, 1973). Likewise, the analyst's ability to formulate interpretations is presumed to be associated with the unconscious mind's organizing processes (Brenner, 1976).

The utility of these concepts for explaining the mental processes by which the therapist achieves understanding of his or her patients has been questioned. For example, during a panel discussion on technique (Richards, 1984), Paul Ornstein asserted that the notion of unconscious memory does not adequately describe the modes of observation and cognition involved in understanding patients. As an alternative, he advocated the concepts of intuition and empathy. However, his elaboration of these concepts—using terms such as "vicarious introjection," "trial identification," and "transient merger"—do not really add to our understanding of the components of the therapist's mental functioning. Likewise, such descriptions of therapists' comprehension as "to fuse primary- and secondary-process receptors into their 'analyzing instruments' " (Rangell, 1980, p. 97) are not enlightening. These descriptions are insufficient because they use relatively vague clinical terms ill-suited to describing or explaining the cognitive processes involved in skillful therapist performance.

Combining Intellectual Understanding and Empathy

Attempts to explain the manner in which therapists combine their intellectual knowledge (both of theory and about the individual patient) with their intuition and empathy are essentially uninformative. The therapist is viewed as "oscillating" between intuition/empathy and intellectual constructions (Fenichel, 1941; Greenson, 1967). However, elucidation of each pole of this oscillation, as well as the process of oscillating, is constrained by psychoanalytic theory, which stresses pathology and, therefore, offers no guidelines for teaching psychotherapists how to perform. The psychoanalytic treatment manuals we have discussed offer more useful guidelines for attending to the patient's communications. Each manual offers its version of a schematic framework for organizing clinical material into a therapeutic focus (Luborsky's, 1984, "core conflict relationship theme" and Strupp & Binder's, 1984, "cyclical maladaptive pattern"). However, these manuals do not shed any additional light on the cognitive processes with which the therapist goes about identifying and organizing material into the recommended framework. Consequently, their effectiveness as teaching aids remains limited.

Recognizing Thematic Patterns Including Resistances

Examination of a more specific (and basic) technical rule in psychoanalytic therapy further illustrates the limited descriptive and explanatory utility of analytic theory with regard to therapist performance. The primary aim of interpretation is to point out resistances (Freud, 1940/1964). The problem is that resistances can take any form; the term does not describe behavior but explains the purpose of behavior in a particular context (Fenichel, 1941; Schlesinger, 1982). Consequently, in order to identify and interpret resistances, the therapist must be adroit at identifying the meanings, purposes, and implications of actions in connection with other actions. In other words, he or she must be skilled at recognizing recurrent *patterns* of affect, cognition, and behavior.

There are, in fact, at least several different types of clinically meaningful patterns that may reflect the operation of resistance. First, there is the relatively straightforward pattern represented by conflict themes manifested in a patient's verbal and nonverbal communications. Second is the pattern represented by the transferential meanings of the patient's verbal communications and behavior. Because of the attention given to transference analysis in the theory of technique, it is assumed that analysts are always keenly attentive to this form of interpersonal pattern. For example, in their text, Menninger and Holzman (1973) made the following assumption: "Most analysts are constantly aware of the transference aspect of interpretation and make use of it specifically only when it is conspicuously present in an episode or phase of treatment" (p. 143). However, more recent observations by clinical teachers who have intensively studied the work of both novices and experienced therapists suggest that the typical analytic therapist's skill in consistently recognizing and interpreting subtle transference patterns (i.e., "disguised allusions to the transference") is greatly overestimated (Binder & Strupp, 1991; Gill, 1982; Strupp & Binder, 1984). A third form of interpersonal pattern is represented by transference enactments in which both patient and therapist are jointly participating. The influence of this transference manifestation has been emphasized by interpersonal theory (e.g., Levenson, 1972). The recognition skill that is required here involves identifying a pattern while one is immersed in enacting it.

Although the notion of "patterns" has become a familiar concept in psychoanalytic theory, stemming from the influence of the object relations and interpersonal perspectives, the mental processes involved in the therapist's ability to discern patterns is not a phenomenon clearly encompassed by the theory and therefore is not directly addressed in texts on technique or in the training of therapists. Yet, pattern recognition is considered a core component of skill in any knowledge domain (Glaser, 1990), as we elaborate now.

Application of Theoretical Knowledge to Clinical Work

We have previously discussed the concerns expressed by some psychoanalytic authors and teachers about the discrepancy between formal clinical theory and technical concepts on the one hand and the knowledge that is actually taught and implemented in practice (Levy, 1987; Lipton, 1983; Menninger & Holzman, 1973) on the other. There also has been a related concern about the inconsistency with which clinical and technical theories are applied in practice (Brenner, 1976; Fenichel, 1941). This concern most often has been directed at inexperienced therapists. For example, Fenichel (1941) observed that with inexperienced analysts, theoretical and practical knowledge "to a certain extent remain isolated from each other" (p. 2). He further observed that "it is difficult for them to recognize again the well understood theoretical concepts in what they see and experience in the patient, and still more in what they themselves say and do during the analytic hour" (p. 2). One frequently cited explanation for this discrepancy is the lack of sufficiently developed clinical theory and theory of technique (Fenichel, 1941; Schaffer, 1982, 1983). We have already discussed the problems associated with anticipating improvements in performance as a function of improved clinical theory.

Another often-cited explanation of the inconsistency in applying theoretical knowledge in practice involves pathologizing deficiencies in technical skill. It is generally assumed that skillful therapeutic performance is based on theoretical knowledge combined with intuition and empathy. Because these latter two components are considered talents that can be actualized through personal analysis, inconsistent applications of theory to practice are the result of "blind spots" or countertransference associated with unresolved conflicts in the therapist (Brenner, 1976; Fenichel, 1941; Greenson, 1967; Kanzer, 1979; Menninger & Holzman, 1973; Strachey, 1958).

This explanation greatly oversimplifies the perceptual and cognitive processes involved in the therapist's technical work. Similarly, it glosses over the formidable problems associated with imparting conceptual knowledge that can be accessed at appropriate times in practice (Bransford, Franks, Vye, & Sherwood, 1989). Thus, difficulties encountered by novice therapists—and probably to a greater extent than is realized, by more experienced therapists—in applying at appropriate times knowledge of theory and technique to practice may be due primarily to deficiencies in the writings and methods used to teach therapists. Countertransference as well as other personality issues may contribute to the problem, but they may not be the major contributors. In our discussion of cognitive psychology, we elaborate on how teaching methods influence the subsequent use of theoretical knowledge.

Implications for Supervision

The limitations inherent in psychoanalytic theory for dealing with the acquisition and implementation of technical skills are evident in other ways. Because the experienced therapist may underestimate the number and interdependence of learning processes that are associated with the acquisition of performance skills, as a clinical supervisor he or she may have unrealistic expectations of the novice's performance. Freud's (1912/1958b) therapeutic expertise was exemplified by his ability to "readily" retrieve from memory information about a patient at relevant moments, as well as to automatically integrate this material into a dynamic view of the patient. However, this level of technical performance is the product of various perceptual and cognitive skills smoothly operating in unison. Textbooks on analytic technique prescribe rules and recommendations that tacitly expect such a level of performance regardless of amount of experience. For example, clinical vignettes of specific technical mistakes are presented. The explanations for such delimited lapses in performance are identical to those given to account for broader misapplications of theory; technical mistakes are presumed to reflect either lack of theoretical knowledge or unresolved conflict in the therapist, such as identification with the patient's avoidance of unpleasant emotions (e.g., Brenner, 1976). This neglects the possibility of deficits in the process of acquiring conceptual knowledge about technique, which could lead to difficulties in consistently applying this knowledge in practice. Another example that is often cited is novice therapists' (or experienced therapists learning new techniques) tendency to rigidly overrely on technical rules and to be preoccupied with what is the "right thing to do," which can result in inattentiveness toward the patient. This problem has been explained as a manifestation of anxiety and defensiveness toward the unconscious conflicts with which the patient is struggling (e.g., Fenichel, 1941). Although unresolved conflict may contribute to the problem, the acquisition of any new skill may involve an extended period of disorganization and awkwardness.

Because experienced analytic teachers typically lack a clear theoretical framework for understanding and explaining the cognitive processes involved in their performance, they inadvertently tend to provide students with the *products* of their expertise. For example, experienced supervisors are prone to suggesting dynamic formulations that may dazzle the student and lead him or her to despair of ever becoming a good therapist or technical recommendations that the student may follow without a clear understanding of why or how the recommendations are to be carried out. In spite of these obstacles, experienced therapists do pass on their knowledge. However, this is probably done through a gradual process of internalization by the student of the teacher's implicitly communicated knowledge (Bransford & Vye, 1988). Because this form of mentoring is a gradual process requiring a good deal of time, only relatively few therapists may have sufficient opportunity during their training to take full advantage of this form of learning.

Although we assume that the training of most psychoanalytic therapists has resulted in a reasonable level of competence, there is a lack of empirical evidence to support this assumption.

In fact, during the course of training, the clinical performance of students is rarely observed directly by their teachers (Binder, Najavits, Strupp, & Rock, 1990). Furthermore, practicing psychoanalytic therapists have typically been reluctant to expose their work to peers (Greenson, 1967), a fact that has been the cause of some concern. For example, the renowned psychoanalytic teacher, Robert Waelder, made the following observation:

> [psychoanalytic practice is] . . . an occupation in which practitioners work alone with nobody observing them and without controls . . . there is always the danger of deterioration in the work of people who do not have the benefit of comparisons with the work of others and who are in no way supervised . . . [this may lead to deterioration] in a subtle sense. An analyst knows what he has seen in a patient but he cannot know what he has not seen but might have seen, and he may get an exaggerated idea of the completeness of his observations and the adequacy of his interpretations. (cited in Menninger & Holzman, 1973, p. 94)

More efficient training methods must be developed to maximize the performance levels of students. This is a particularly urgent need as long as practicing therapists are working under the constraints described by Waelder. Therefore, an improved understanding of the nature of therapist skills is needed. With this goal in mind, we turn to an area of psychological research—cognitive psychology—that may offer resources by which to develop a truly effective theory of psychoanalytic technique.

WHAT COGNITIVE PSYCHOLOGY CAN OFFER PSYCHOANALYTIC THEORY

Within cognitive psychology, there have been investigations of the cognitive and perceptual processes associated with expert performance in various knowledge domains, such as computer programming, medicine, mathematics, political science, and chess (Chase & Simon, 1973; Chi, Glaser, & Farr, 1988; deGroot, 1965; Lesgold et al., 1988; Soloway, Adelson, & Ehrlich, 1988). There are also studies that have attempted to elucidate the development of cognitive processes and structures associated with achieving skills and competence in a particular knowledge domain, as well as instructional methods that facilitate such cognitive development (Glaser, 1982, 1990). Related studies have investigated the contrasts among novices, less skilled performers, and experts in a particular knowledge domain (Charness, 1988; Chi et al., 1988). This area of cognitive psychology seeks to understand the nature and development of expertise from three perspectives: (a) the structures and processes that characterize skillful performance; (b) the initial state of the learner (i.e, the novice); and (c) the transformation processes involved in acquiring competence as well as the conditions for learning that can be implemented to foster this achievement (Glaser, 1982). We briefly examine each of these perspectives in terms of their potential for improving the psychoanalytic theory of technique and therapist training methods.

The Nature of Expertise

The most distinctive characteristic of expert performance in any knowledge domain that has been studied is the skill of *pattern recognition*. The "preeminence" of this skill in an expert is such that he or she virtually sees patterns different from the ones that are perceived by those with lesser skills (Glaser, 1990). Pattern recognition by experts is extraordinarily fast and accurate, and the patterns they perceive are broad, rich with detail, and organized around meaningful principles derived from core concepts in their knowledge domain. By contrast, novices (and those who are less skilled) perceive patterns that are constrained by concrete surface features of the situation (Chi et al., 1988; Glaser, 1990; Rock, 1990).

The superior pattern recognition skills of the expert does not reflect superior perceptual abilities. Indeed, experts typically excel only in their own domains, where they have accumulated extensive domain-relevant experience and knowledge. Of particular importance is the manner in which this knowledge has been stored in memory. The expert has a highly organized knowledge base that is structured around abstract principles that are linked to experiences with applying these principles in various practice situations. Through experience, components of the knowledge base become interconnected into coherent "chunks" of information, and newly acquired information is integrated into the existing structure of knowledge (Chi et al., 1988; Glaser, 1982, 1990). The speed, degree of automaticity, and quality of pattern recognition are primarily dependent on the organization of relevant knowledge possessed by the individual.

Empirical studies of the way an expert's domain relevant knowledge is mentally organized, and how this knowledge organization facilitates recognition of patterns in a practice situation, may help improve understanding of how expert psychotherapists organize and comprehend clinical material. Recall that Freud and others (Brenner, 1976; Freud, 1912/1958b) posed the question of how therapists remember and make sense of all of the "psychological products" to which they are exposed. Calling on his own subjective experiences of relevant patterns of data spontaneously coming to mind, Freud (1912/1958b) assumed that his unconscious memory was responsible. However, this explanation provides no useful heuristic for identifying the skills associated with understanding clinical material and for facilitating development of these skills. It can be argued that the conditions within which Freud constructed his theories of mental functioning and therapy technique resulted in his developing a structured knowledge base organized around interconnections among theoretical concepts and principles as well as innumerable clinical experiences. Such a knowledge base may have accounted for his ability to sort clinical material into meaningful patterns depicting dynamic conflict themes. Freud may have responded to perceptions in a clinical situation by *automatically* accessing from memory relevant prior experiences with the current patient and other patients as well as relevant concepts and principles, all of which aided him in organizing and giving meaning to his observations. We say more later about the conditions that foster development of such a knowledge base as well as implications for training.

A more circumscribed clinical example of the difference between the way expert and novice therapists recognize patterns involves the manner in which transference manifestations are viewed. The expert psychotherapist will typically experience a manifestation of transference as a vividly perceived interpersonal transaction that he or she spontaneously compares with memories of similar transactions with the same and other patients and that he or she automatically embeds in a conceptual network of psychodynamic principles. These principles might include the superimposition on current interpersonal situations of scenarios from childhood, the defensive function of action substituted for remembering, and the interpretative linking of transference to other similarly enacted transactions in other relationships. By extrapolating from explanations of experts' mental functioning in other knowledge domains (Glaser, 1990), we can hypothesize that the expert therapist's recognition of patterns is enhanced by the automatic retrieval from memory of structured, relevant "chunks" of interconnected concepts and clinical experiences. By contrast, the novice psychotherapist will tend to have much more circumscribed and fuzzy experiences of transference manifestations, and he or she will often describe these experiences in concrete terms such as the "amount" of transference that was evident in a session (personal experiences of the first two authors during the training of psychotherapists).

The decisions and resultant actions of experts tend to be superior to those of less proficiency; however, this superiority holds only within the specific domain of expertise (Chi et al., 1988).

The study of chess masters illustrates this phenomenon. In preparing for a move, chess masters do not consider a greater number of alternatives than do less skilled players, nor do they anticipate more subsequent moves. Rather, for them, only relatively good alternatives come spontaneously to mind (Chase & Simon, 1973; deGroot, 1965). Chess masters appear to have an "intuitive feel" for the right moves. As Bransford and Vye (1988) pointed out, "this provides a label for a phenomenon but it hardly helps clarify why the masters have 'better intuitions' " (p. 5).

A more enlightening explanation once again involves the organized structure of the expert's knowledge base. As a result of innumerable hours viewing configurations on a chess board, it has been estimated that a chess master can recognize approximately 50,000 different configurations (Posner, 1988). Furthermore, through experience he or she has stored in memory innumerable networks of configurations–moves–consequences. Consequently, the chess master's knowledge base is structured around interconnections among "declarative" knowledge (i.e., principles, concepts, and actual configurations) and "procedural" knowledge (i.e., the decisions and actions that result in successful performance). With cumulative experience, these interconnections become chunked into increasingly larger units (Chase & Simon, 1973; Chi et al., 1988).

For the expert, the mental processes of automatically combining declarative and procedural knowledge that are relevant to a practice situation are experienced as a smoothly spontaneous activity. This may help explain why psychoanalytic clinician–theorists assume that simply a (declarative) knowledge of personality theory and technical concepts will suffice to guide competent therapist performance (Brenner, 1976; Menninger & Holzman, 1973; Strachey, 1958). Yet, experienced therapists cannot precisely describe or explain their moment-to-moment performance with existent psychoanalytic technical concepts. They must rely on vague recommendations such as timing an interpretation by assessing how "ready" the patient is to receive it (Brenner, 1976). Furthermore, experienced therapists rely on the vague concept of "intuition" to explain their decision making (Greenson, 1967). It is assumed that intuition will be free to operate if the therapist has been well analyzed. However, it can now be seen that intuition refers to a complex array of skills—particularly pattern recognition—associated with a type of organized knowledge base. Declarative knowledge provides a guide for *what* is important to know, but such knowledge is insufficient without the procedural knowledge that serves as a guide (i.e., cognitive strategies) for *when* and *how* to act (Bransford & Vye, 1988). Although freedom from significant psychological conflict may be necessary for intuitive performance, we suggest that training experiences that facilitate the type of knowledge base that has been described is at least equally important.

Another distinctive characteristic of the expert is the capacity for self-monitoring and self-regulating during the course of performing. Experts are more aware than novices of when they have erred, when they have failed to comprehend, and when they need to modify their actions (Chi et al., 1988). These skills are attainable when sufficient cognitive processing resources are available during performance, which requires a certain degree of automaticity of pattern recognition and procedural skills (Chi et al., 1988). From a psychoanalytic perspective, self-monitoring and self-regulating skills are associated with freedom from the influence of countertransference. However, the relative absence of "blind spots" associated with unresolved emotional conflict is insufficient for the operation of these skills without the presence of automatized pattern recognition and procedural skills. This would explain why novices tend to be more susceptible than more experienced therapists to being provoked by their patients (i.e., more susceptible to countertransference).

We have discussed several of the characteristics of expertise that are particularly relevant to the practice of psychotherapy. We now take a brief look at the initial state of the learner, where psychoanalytic theory has something to offer to cognitive psychology.

The Initial State of the Learner

From a cognitive psychology perspective, an effective learning environment should combine a carefully planned structure with sufficient flexibility for adapting to the specific needs of individual learners. Glaser (1982) proposed that a "diagnostic" assessment of each learner's learning characteristics should be undertaken. Factors to be assessed would include initial knowledge and skills in the domain, initial skill related strengths and weaknesses, and skills associated with knowing how to learn. Cognitive psychology focuses primarily on cognitive skills and skill-learning histories. However, it also has been suggested that feelings and attitudes associated with learning are important. In fact, Posner (1988) claimed that producing an expert is not so much a matter of selecting someone with special capability as creating and maintaining the *motivation* for a long period of learning in a given knowledge domain.

The rich knowledge about unconscious processes and the products of dynamic conflict contained in psychoanalytic theory can potentially expand the cognitive psychology perspective on vicissitudes in learning. For example, psychoanalytic teachers have identified the influence of maladaptive (characterological) interpersonal patterns that tend to emerge in learning contexts. Ekstein and Wallerstein (1972) identified "problems about learning" of the novice therapist that involve the enactment of his or her maladaptive learning patterns concurrently in "practice" learning situations (supervised psychotherapy) and in the novice's relationship with his or her supervisor. Ekstein and Wallerstein coined the term *parallel process* to refer to these interpersonal patterns that interfere with learning about psychotherapy and described a supervisory process to deal with this phenomenon.

The Problem of "Inert" Knowledge

The third perspective from cognitive psychology refers to the transformation processes associated with development from novice to competent performer. This development is characterized by the transformation of factual or declarative knowledge into procedural or "use-oriented" knowledge (Bransford & Vye, 1988). Competent performance requires knowledge that is automatically accessible at appropriate times. This knowledge must combine comprehension of the immediate situation, based on relevant principles and concepts, with guidelines for action based on past experiences with the same or similar situations. Novices—as well as less skilled performers—can know a principle, a rule, or a specialized vocabulary without being able to identify the conditions for effective application (Glaser, 1990). From the investigations of the nature of expertise in various domains of knowledge, the concept of *inert knowledge* has been formulated by cogntive psychologists to explain the problem of applying knowledge in practice. Inert knowledge refers to facts, concepts, and theories that have been learned but are *not* spontaneously accessible to the learner at appropriate times because of deficiencies in the methods through which the knowledge was acquired (Bransford, et al., 1989; Rock & Bransford, in press).

Cognitive psychology research has provided evidence of inert knowledge in educational settings at all levels (e.g., Perfetto, Bransford, & Franks, 1983; Rock & Bransford, in press; Simon & Hayes, 1976). Although not identified as a problem of inert knowledge, possibly relevant evidence can be found in some studies of clinical performance. In analogue studies of clinical judgment, clinical psychologists and psychiatrists—regardless of experience level—often make highly inaccurate judgments (Faust & Ziskin, 1988). We have previously alluded to the presence of inert knowledge as an explanation for the observed inconsistency of inexperienced therapists in applying psychoanalytic concepts and principles in practice (Brenner, 1976; Fenichel, 1941). We have also alluded to its presence as an explanation for the inconsistency of therapists regardless of experience in applying principles that require relatively complex cognitive performances, such as identifying "disguised allusions to the transference" (Gill, 1982).

There appears to be a clear relationship between instructional techniques and a learner's ability to subsequently access information. For example, knowledge initially acquired solely through memorization will often not be used in new situations in which it is applicable (Bransford, Sherwood, Kinzer, & Hasselbring, 1987; Rock & Bransford, in press). It appears that three conditions exert primary influence on the depth of comprehension and accessibility of acquired knowledge:

1. The knowledge to be learned must be explicitly linked or made relevant to a to-be-solved problem in a specific domain (Chi et al., 1988).

2. The knowledge must be acquired through *active* involvement of the learner in a manner that encourages both memorization and comprehension of the material. Learners must be encouraged to view the material from a variety of perspectives and develop meaningful elaborations about it. In addition, the material must be presented in a manner that elicits a process of linking the new material with prior knowledge (Bransford et al., 1982).

3. The knowledge must be acquired in a context as similar as possible to the conditions of actual practice so that the learner learns to recognize features of problems as they appear in reality. The learner is also encouraged to practice selecting relevant from irrelevant material in the context of problem solving (Rock & Bransford, in press).

A structured teaching format that is designed around these three conditions is called "anchored instruction" (Bransford et al., 1989; Michaels, 1989; Risko et al., 1989; Rock, 1990; Rock & Williams, 1991). Material is presented in narrative form on videorecordings (tape or disk formats). Anchored instruction provides the opportunity to actively engage in solving authentic problems in a realistic context. It facilitates learning not only facts and procedures but also the conditions in which they are useful. Learners have the opportunity to practice separating relevant and irrelevant information, and formulating relevant information into a problem statement. After the recorded material is viewed, the learner is presented a problem that involves a principle or concept to be learned. The learner must combine reading about the to-be-learned material with searching the video material for relevant information. This process is iterated for learning new principles and concepts, often with the same video material.

The first expert psychoanalytic therapist may have inadvertently developed his or her expertise through a form of anchored instruction. Freud (1940/1964) generated the principles and concepts of psychoanalysis in the context of seeking to understand and treat the problems his patients brought to him. He borrowed and often modified concepts and methods from the fields of natural science, philosophy, and art when they appeared relevant to the problems he encountered, and when required by his clinical experiences, Freud formulated original ideas. Furthermore, his ideas and methods were continually put to the test of actual practice and repeatedly modified as a result of his experiences. In other words, Freud acquired his declarative and procedural knowledge through the process of active coping with real problems encountered in clinical practice.

Today, novice therapists are trained under conditions that may inadvertently promote the acquisition of inert knowledge. In graduate training programs, the student is usually introduced to psychoanalytic theory in didactic courses that are entirely separate from actual practice experience (Garfield, 1977). It is assumed that knowledge about technique can be adequately imparted in this fashion and that competent performance will inevitably come with supervised practice and personal therapy (Dewald, 1987; Ekstein & Wallerstein, 1972). As we have shown, textbooks on technique traditionally present clinical illustrations in the form of condensed vignettes that do not provide the reader with opportunities to practice selecting relevant from irrelevant material with regard to therapeutic problems or issues. When video illustrations of psychotherapy are used, the viewers may comment on the material but are not afforded the opportunity to actively work with the illustrated problem as they would in actual practice. Supervised clinical practice is considered to be the "cornerstone" of psychotherapy training (Dewald, 1987), but clinical psychology graduate students typically receive merely 1 year of supervision while on internship.[5] This is not much time in which to practice psychoanalytic principles, concepts, and methods in contexts relevant to their application. Furthermore, training programs tend to delegate supervisory responsibilities with the tacit assumption that supervisory skills develop "automatically" or are a function of psychotherapeutic skills. Supervision as a specific set of skills is rarely taught; instead, major criteria for selecting supervisors are often based on the availability of personnel (Matarazzo & Patterson, 1986). Furthermore, supervisors themselves are often relatively inexperienced therapists who are still early in the learning process (Ekstein & Wallerstein, 1972).

DIRECTIONS FOR IMPROVING THE THEORY AND TEACHING OF TECHNIQUE

The current psychoanalytic theory of technique is actually a relatively loose assortment of principles and concepts that span different levels of abstraction. For example, clarifying a conscious mood state refers to a more specific and behaviorally anchored technical recommendation than one that advises the "loosening" of unconscious ego defenses through interpretation. This example also illustrates how the theory's technical principles encompass specific techniques and broad strategies, with little explicit differentiation between the two. Furthermore, in the psychoanalytic technical literature, the term *skill* has been indiscriminately used in reference to almost any therapist activity, without systematic attempts to define the concept within a theory of technique (Binder et al., 1990).

Our selective review of cognitive psychology concepts suggests a structure for a more coherently organized theory of psychoanalytic technique. This theory would have three components:

1. The first component consists of generic cognitive and perceptual functions that must operate proficiently in order to achieve competent performance in any knowledge domain. These functions include, for example, pattern recognition; the ability to spontaneously recall procedural knowledge (i.e., memorized principles and concepts combined with guidelines for when and how to apply them) appropriate to the immediate situation; and self-monitoring and self-regulating activities. It is hypothesized that a psychoanalytic technical act consists of some subset of these generic functions operating to achieve a particular therapeutic objective. It is further hypothesized that when these generic cognitive and perceptual functions are performed smoothly in unison, they produce a *skillful* technical act.

2. These technical acts are a part of the second component of a theory of psychoanalytic technique. They are discrete techniques or tactics, such as interpretations; reflections and clarifications of feelings; "tracking" of conflict themes; avoidance of pejorative comments; and identifying a "disguised allusion to the transference." The implementation of these techniques is guided by procedural rules such as the following: (a) Interpretations should be clear and succinct. (b) Interventions should be timed so as to encourage further patient communications. (c) Re-

---

[5]Psychiatry residents receive more than 1 year of clinical practice but may not receive much more than 1 year of supervised psychotherapy experience.

flections and clarifications should accurately capture the patient's subjective experience as well as expanding it. (d) Focusing on conflict themes should be consistent. (e) The therapist should consistently maintain an attitude toward the patient that is neither indulgent nor critical. (f) Commenting on a "disguised allusion to the transference" should occur when, to the patient, it would be a plausible interpretation of recent events. It has been hypothesized that the smooth operation of a specific subset of generic cognitive and perceptual functions—particularly the spontaneous recall of procedural rules that are relevant to the immediate situation—results in the skillful implementation of a technique. It is further hypothesized that automatic and smooth technical performance allows the therapist to attend to the affective quality of his or her interactions with a patient. Of particular importance is the therapist's ability to monitor his or her reactions to provocative patient behavior. The therapist is able to maintain more consistent sensitivity to the patient's interpersonal needs and is, likewise, able to relate in a more relaxed and flexible manner. The interpersonal skills that are associated with developing and maintaining a "therapeutic alliance" are also a part of the second component of a theory of technique.

3. The third component of a theory of psychoanalytic technique consists of strategies for implementing combinations of discrete techniques in sequences that are aimed at achieving a particular effect. These strategies are governed by the principles composing the psychoanalytic theories of mental functioning (e.g., the dynamic unconscious, psychic determinism, compromise formation, internally structured self–object patterns, transference) and of change (e.g., resolving resistances, integrating unconscious feelings into conscious experience, modifying internalized maladaptive interpersonal patterns, developing a realistic and flexible self-image). Acquiring an understanding of these principles and of corollary technical strategies is part of one's declarative knowledge; that is, facts and concepts. However, in order for these strategies to provide effective guidelines for therapist actions, they must be transformed into procedural knowledge; that is, the therapist must have ample practice in using them under appropriate conditions so that a particular type of situation in the therapeutic process spontaneously evokes recollection of an appropriate technical strategy. It is hypothesized that technical strategies must be stored in memory as procedural knowledge in order for them to contribute to skillful technical performance.

SUMMARY

In the theory we are proposing, skillful technical performance is conceptually articulated as being the joint product of basic generic skills that form part of discrete technical acts and strategies that govern when and in what combination technical acts will be implemented. Although it is in preliminary form, we believe that the theory may serve as a useful heuristic for improving the organization, specificity, and clarity of existing psychoanalytic technical concepts. It may also encourage much needed empirical investigations of therapeutic skills. The proposed theory can also serve as a heuristic for evaluating and improving methods of teaching psychoanalytic technique. Although there is extensive literature on psychoanalytic training and supervision that is rich in clinical insights, this literature contains little evidence of systematic study and empirical evidence regarding training effectiveness (Strupp, Butler, & Rosser, 1988).

It can be said that the primary aim of any training program for psychodynamic therapy is to ensure the acquisition of a psychoanalytic knowledge base that effectively guides skillful technical performance. We have argued that in the traditional educational format—consisting of the triad of didactic courses, clinical supervision, and personal therapy—the novice therapist acquires theoretical concepts and technical rules in a form that renders this knowledge inconsistently available under relevant practice conditions. In other words, the traditional educational format encourages the acquisition of inert knowledge. The novice therapist may have memorized extensive theoretical and technical knowledge about therapy, but he or she does not necessarily know the appropriate conditions and means for applying them.

The proposed theory of technique could serve as a framework for defining techniques and strategies and for conceptually differentiating these two levels of intervention. This understanding could contribute to the development of a coherent sequence for learning progressively more complex techniques and strategies. Such efforts would be part of designing a psychodynamic therapy training program with an anchored instructional format. We have argued that this instructional format is particularly effective at imparting knowledge that is available for practical use; it is more efficient than traditional educational methods at facilitating the development of competent performance. Students would be exposed to segments of psychoanalytic theories along with relevant technical concepts under conditions in which they are required to identify and cope with clinical problems in learning contexts that simulate clinical practice (e.g., videotaped therapy vignettes). Furthermore, these learning experiences would be sequenced so as to facilitate progressive acquisition of increasingly more complex theoretical knowledge and technical skills. The student would have to demonstrate a criterion level of knowledge and applied performance in these simulated practice experiences prior to being given the responsibility of actually conducting psychotherapy with supervision. An improved theory of technique and anchored instructional methods could also provide guidelines for developing a more coherently structured approach to clinical supervision.

It goes without saying that we have not offered a finished theory of psychoanalytic technique or a ready-to-use training program. We hope that what has been offered is a conceptual model that will encourage significant advances in both psychoanalytic theory and training.

REFERENCES

Alexander, F. (1963). The dynamics of psychotherapy in the light of learning theory. *American Journal of Psychiatry, 120,* 440–448.

Binder, J. L., & Strupp, H. H. (1991). The Vanderbilt approach to time-limited dynamic psychotherapy. In P. Crits-Christoph & J. Barber (Eds.), *Handbook of short-term dynamic therapy* (pp. 137–165). New York: Basic Books.

Binder, J. L., Najavits, L. M., Strupp, H. H., & Rock, D. L. (1990). *How psychotherapists view their skills: A survey.* Unpublished manuscript.

Bransford, J. D., Franks, J. J., Vye, N. J., & Sherwood, R. D. (1989). New approaches to instruction: Because wisdom can't be told. In S. Vosniadou & A. Ortony (Eds.), *Similarity and analogical reasoning* (pp. 470–497). New York: Cambridge University Press.

Bransford, J. D., Sherwood, R. D., Kinzer, C. K., & Hasselbring, T. S. (1987). Macro-contexts for learning: Initial findings and issues. *Applied Cognitive Psychology, 1,* 93–108.

Bransford, J. D., Stein, B. S., Vye, N. J., Franks, J. J., Auble, P. M., Mezyniski, K. J., & Perfetto, G. A. (1982). Differences in approaches to learning: An overview. *Journal of Experimental Psychology: General, 11,* 390–398.

Bransford, J. D., & Vye, N. J. (1988). *Research on cognition and its implications for instruction: An overview.* Unpublished manuscript.

Brenner, C. (1976). *Psychoanalytic technique and psychic conflict.* New York: International Universities Press.

Charness, N. (1988). Expertise in chess and bridge. In D. Klahr & K. Kotovsky (Eds.), *Complex information processing: The impact of Herbert Simon* (pp. 183–208). Hillsdale, NJ: Erlbaum.

Chase, W. G., & Simon, H. A. (1973). Perception in chess. *Cognitive Psychology, 4,* 55–81.

Chi, M. T. H., Glaser, R., & Farr, M. J. (Eds.). (1988). *The nature of expertise.* Hillsdale, NJ: Erlbaum.

deGroot, A. D. (1965). *Thought and choice in chess*. The Hague, The Netherlands: Mouton.

Dewald, P. A. (1987). *Learning process in psychoanalytic supervision: Complexities and challenges*. New York: International Universities Press.

Ekstein, R., & Wallerstein, R. S. (1972). *The teaching and learning of psychotherapy* (2nd ed.). New York: International Universities Press.

Epstein, L., & Feiner, A. H. (Eds.). (1979). *Countertransference*. Northvale, NJ: Jason Aronson.

Fairbairn, W. (1954). *An object-relations theory of the personality*. New York: Basic Books.

Faust, D., & Ziskin J. (1988). The expert witness in psychology and psychiatry. *Science, 241,* 31–35.

Fenichel, O. (1941). *Problems of psychoanalytic technique*. Albany, NY: The Psychoanalytic Quarterly.

Freud, S. (1958a). The dynamics of transference. In J. Strachey (Ed. and Trans.), *The standard edition of the complete psychological works of Sigmund Freud* (Vol. 12, pp. 97–108). (Original work published 1912)

Freud, S. (1958b). Recommendations to physicians practicing psychoanalysis. In J. Strachey (Ed. and Trans.), *The standard edition of the complete psychological works of Sigmund Freud* (Vol. 12, pp. 111–120). (Original work published 1912)

Freud, S. (1958c). On beginning the treatment (further recommendations on the technique of psychoanalysis, I). In J. Strachey (Ed. and Trans.), *The standard edition of the complete psychological works of Sigmund Freud* (Vol. 12, pp. 121–144). (Original work published 1913)

Freud, S. (1958d). Remembering, repeating, and working-through (further recommendations on the technique of psychoanalysis, III). In J. Strachey (Ed. and Trans.), *The standard edition of the complete psychological works of Sigmund Freud* (Vol. 12, pp. 157–221). (Original work published 1914)

Freud, S. (1961). The ego and the id. In J. Strachey (Ed. and Trans.), *The standard edition of the complete psychological works of Sigmund Freud* (Vol. 19, pp. 3–66). (Original work published 1923)

Freud, S. (1964). An outline of psychoanalysis. In J. Strachey (Ed. and Trans.), *The standard edition of the complete psychological works of Sigmund Freud* (Vol. 23, pp. 144–215). (Original work published 1940)

Gabbard, G. O. (1990). *Psychoanalytic psychiatry in clinical practice*. Washington, DC: American Psychiatric Press.

Garfield, S. L. (1977). Research on the training of professional psychotherapists. In A. S. Gurman & A. Razin (Eds.), *The therapist's contribution to efffective psychotherapy: Empirical assessment* (pp. 63–83). New York: Pergamon Press.

Gill, M. M. (1982). *Analysis of transference I: Theory and technique*. New York: International Universities Press.

Glaser, R. (1982). Instructional psychology: Past, present, and future. *American Psychologist, 37,* 292–305.

Glaser, R. (1990). The reemergence of learning theory within instructional research. *American Psychologist, 45,* 29–39.

Glover, E. (1955). *The technique of psychoanalysis*. New York: International Universities Press.

Greenson, R. R. (1967). *The technique and practice of psychoanalysis*. London: Hogarth Press.

Havens, L. (1976). *Participant observation*. Northvale, NJ: Jason Aronson.

Kanzer, M. (1979). Developments in psychoanalytic technique. *Journal of the American Psychoanalytic Association, 27,* 327–375.

Kernberg, O. F. (1984). *Severe personality disorders: Psychotherapeutic strategies*. New Haven, CT: Yale University Press.

Kernberg, O. F., Seltzer, M. A., Koenigsberg, H. W., Carr, A. C., & Appelbaum, A. (1989). *Psychodynamic psychotherapy of borderline patients*. New York: Basic Books.

Klein, M. (1963). *Our adult world*. New York: Basic Books.

Klerman, G. L., Rounsaville, B., Chevron, E., Neu, C., & Weissman, M. M. (1984). *Interpersonal psychotherapy of depression*. New York: Basic Books.

Kohut, H. (1971). *The analysis of the self.* New York: International Universities Press.

Lambert, M. J. (1989). The individual therapist's contribution to psychotherapy process and outcome. *Clinical Psychology Review, 9,* 469–485.

Lesgold, A., Rubinson, H., Feltovich, P., Glaser, R., Klopfer, D., & Wang, Y. (1988). Expertise in a complex skill: Diagnosing X-ray pictures. In M. T. H. Chi, R. Glaser, & M. J. Farr (Eds.), *The nature of expertise* (pp. 311–342). Hillsdale, NJ: Erlbaum.

Levenson, E. A. (1972). *The fallacy of understanding: An inquiry into the changing structure of psychoanalysis.* New York: Basic Books.

Levy, S. T. (1987). Therapeutic strategy and psychoanalytic technique. *Journal of the American Psychoanalytic Association, 35,* 447–466.

Lipton, S. (1983). A critique of so-called standard psychoanalytic technique. *Contemporary Psychoanalysis, 19,* 35–46.

Luborsky, L. (1984). *Principles of psychoanalytic psychotherapy: A manual for supportive/expressive treatment.* New York: Basic Books.

Luborsky, L., Barber, J. P., & Crits-Christoph, P. (1990). Theory-based research for understanding the process of dynamic psychotherapy. *Journal of Consulting and Clinical Psychology, 58,* 281–287.

Luborsky, L., Crits-Christoph, P., McClellan, A. T., Woody, G., Piper, W., Liberman, B., Imber, S., & Pilkonis, P. (1986). Do therapists vary much in their sucess? Findings from four studies. *American Journal of Orthopsychiatry, 56,* 501–512.

Luborsky, L., McClellan, A. T., Woody, G. E., O'Brien, C. P., & Auerbach, A. (1985). Therapist success and its determinants. *Archives of General Psychiatry, 42,* 602–611.

Matarazzo, R. G., & Patterson, D. R. (1986). Methods of teaching therapeutic skill. In S. L. Garfield & A. E. Bergin (Eds.), *Handbook of psychotherapy and behavior change* (3rd ed., pp. 821–843). New York: Wiley.

Menninger, K. A., & Holzman, P. S. (1973). *Theory of psychoanalytic technique* (2nd ed.). New York: Basic Books.

Michaels, A. L. (1989). *The transition from language theory to therapy: Test of two instructional models.* Unpublished doctoral dissertation, Vanderbilt University, Nashville, TN.

O'Malley, S. S., Foley, S. H., Watkins, S. D., Imber, S., Sotsky, S. M., & Elkins, I. (1988). Therapist competence and patient outcome in interpersonal psychotherapy of depression. *Journal of Consulting and Clinical Psychology, 56,* 496–501.

Orlinsky, D. E., & Howard, K. I. (1986). Process and outcome in psychotherapy. In S. L. Garfield & A. E. Bergin (Eds.), *Handbook of psychotherapy and behavior change* (3rd ed., pp. 311–381). New York: Wiley.

Perfetto, G., Bransford, J. D., & Franks, J. J. (1983). Constraints on access in a problem solving context. *Memory and Cognition, 11,* 24–31.

Posner, M. I. (1988). Introduction: What is it to be an expert? In M. T. H. Chi, R. Glaser, & M. J. Farr (Eds.), *The nature of expertise* (pp. xxiv–xxxvi). Hillsdale, NJ: Erlbaum.

Rangell, L. (1980). Contemporary issues in the theory of therapy. In H. P. Blum (Ed.), *Psychoanalytic explorations of technique: Discourse on the theory of therapy* (pp. 81–112). New York: International Universities Press.

Richards, A. (1984). The relation between psychoanalytic theory and psychoanalytic technique. *Journal of the American Psychoanalytic Association, 32,* 587–602.

Risko, V. J., Kinzer, C. K., Goodman, J., McLarty, K., Dupree, A., & Martin, H. (1989). *Effects of macrocontexts on reading comprehension, composition of stories, and vocabulary development.* Paper presented at the meeting of the American Educational Research Association, San Francisco.

Rock, D. L. (1990). *Pattern recognition in psychological assessment: Nature of differences between novice, intermediate, and expert psychotherapists.* Unpublished manuscript.

Rock, D. L., & Bransford, J. D. (in press). An empirical evaluation of three components of the tetrahedon model of clinical judgment. *Journal of Nervous and Mental Disease.*

Rock, D. L., & Williams, S. M. (1991). *Anchored instruction: Suggestions for research on therapist learning.* Manuscript submitted for publication.

Rounsaville, B. J., O'Malley, S., Foley, S., & Weissman, M. M. (1988). Role of manual-guided training in the conduct and efficacy of interpersonal psychotherapy for depression. *Journal of Consulting and Clinical Psychology, 56,* 681–688.

Sandler, J., & Sandler, A. M. (1978). On the development of object relations and affects. *International Journal of Psychoanalysis, 59,* 285–296.

Schaffer, N. D. (1982). Multidimensional measures of therapist behavior as predictors of outcome. *Psychological Bulletin, 92,* 670–681.

Schaffer, N. D. (1983). Methodological issues of measuring the skillfulness of therapeutic techniques. *Psychotherapy: Theory, Research and Practice, 20,* 486–493.

Schlesinger, H. (1982). Resistance as a process. In P. Wachtel (Ed.), *Resistance: Psychodynamic and behavioral approaches* (pp. 25–44). New York: Plenum Press.

Simon, H. A., & Hayes, J. R. (1976). The understanding process: Problem isomorphs. *Cognitive Psychology, 8,* 165–190.

Soloway, E., Adelson, B., & Ehrlich, K. (1988). Knowledge and processes in the comprehension of computer programs. In M. T. H. Chi, R. Glaser, & M. J. Farr (Eds.), *The nature of expertise* (pp. 129–152). Hillsdale, NJ: Erlbaum.

Stolorow, R. D. (1990). Converting psychotherapy to psychoanalysis: A critique of the underlying assumptions. *Psychoanalytic Inquiry, 10,* 119–130.

Strachey, J. (1958). Editor's introduction to papers on technique. In J. Strachey (Ed. and Trans.), *The standard edition of the complete psychological works of Sigmund Freud* (Vol. 12, pp. 85–88). London: Hogarth Press.

Strupp, H. H. (1969). Toward a specification of teaching and learning in psychotherapy. *Archives of General Psychiatry, 21,* 203–212.

Strupp, H. H., & Bergin, A. E. (1969). Some empirical and conceptual bases for coordinated research in psychotherapy. *International Journal of Psychiatry, 7,* 18–90.

Strupp, H. H., & Binder, J. L. (1984). *Psychotherapy in a new key: A guide to time-limited dynamic psychotherapy.* New York: Basic Books.

Strupp, H. H., Butler, S. F., & Rosser, C. L. (1988). Training in psychodynamic therapy. *Journal of Consulting and Clinical Psychology, 56,* 689–695.

Sullivan, H. S. (1953). *The interpersonal theory of psychiatry.* New York: Norton.

Wallerstein, R. S. (1989). The psychotherapy research project of the Menninger Foundation: An overview. *Journal of Consulting and Clinical Psychology, 57,* 195–205.

INDEX

Bahnson, J., 335
Bahnson, T., 335
Baillargeon, R., 212
Bakan, D., 400, 405
Balint, M., 401
Baltes, P. B., 272, 275
Barber, J., 504, 510–511, 530
Bargh, J. A., 380, 382
Barsalou, L. W., 525
Bartlett, F. C., 520
Barton, M., 165
Basch, M., 436, 443
Bates, J. E., 250–251
Baxter, J., 335
Beardslee, W., 341
Beck, A., 420–421, 507, 531
Becker, J., 335
Beebe, B., 129, 136, 239
Behaviorism
    development of, 18
    instincts in, 18
    integrated with psychoanalytic theory, x
    and study of consciousness, 202
    in treating gender identity disorder, 262
Bellak, L., 332, 336
Bemporad, J., 419
Benedek, T., 170, 236
Benoit, D., 165
Bergman, A., 240, 376
Bergmann, B., 361
Berkman, L. F., 478
Berkson, G., 468
Bettelheim, B., 431
Binder, J. L., 504, 508–509, 611–612
Biofeedback, 479
Biological factors. See also Evolutionary theory;
        Psychosomatic research and theory
    adolescence and kinship relations, 58–59
    in adolescent development, 268–270
    in attachment theory, 178–179
    in defenses, 340
    in dreaming, 33, 349–355
    in emotions theory, 234
    in experiencing, 306, 320–323
    fidelity in sexual behavior, 17–18
    in Freud's formulations, 37–38, 300
    in gender identity disorder, 246–247, 249,
        251, 253–254

in infant capacity for experience, 205–206
in infant development, 130, 221–223
innate needs, 19–20
in instinct and stimuli, 17, 25
instrumental competencies in infant
        development, 221–223
in intentionality, 321–322
in language acquisition, 63–64
in late-onset disorders, 292–293
in memory, 351–352
motivation and altered states, 30
in motivational model, 94
in panic disorder, 478
in personality research, 91–94
regulatory behaviors in mother–infant
        development, 468–470
REM sleep/deprivation, 306–306, 359–361
in self–other distinction, 50–51
separation reactions, 468–470
of sleep, 347–348
in theories of psychopathology, 392
Bion, W. R., 241
Blass, R. B., 394–396
Blatt, S., 394–396, 415, 419–420, 424
Blinder, B., 336
Bliss, T. V. P., 351
Bloch, D., 246
Blos, P., 131, 267, 269–271, 273–274, 402
Bollas, C., 545
Bond, M., 334–335
Borderline disorders
    and defenses, 329, 336–339, 456
    depressive affects in, 458
    developmental etiology, 376–379
    ego weaknesses in, 394, 455–456
    in Kernberg's diagnostic scheme, 454–455
    object relations in, 457
    psychoanalytic conceptions of, 453–455
    review of research, 394, 455–458
    severity, and reality testing, 457
    thought disorders and, 456
    treatment, 460
Bower, T. G. R., 212–213
Bowlby, J., 42, 70, 129, 154–156, 169, 234–235,
        442, 506. See also Attachment theory
    on affective development, 230
    on attachment needs, 15
    on attachment–separation, 401, 404
    clinical work, 168
    ethological perspective, 42, 376
    and evolutionary thought, 70–71

research on depression, 419–420
Brandchaft, B., 239
Brazelton, T. B., 240–241, 365
Brazelton Neonatal Behavioral Assessment Scale, 213
Brenner, C., 168, 328, 610
Brentano, F., 80–82
Bretherton, I., 156, 165, 175
Brewer, W. F., 525
Bruer, J., 490
Burke, W., 542

California Psychological Inventory, 331
California Psychotherapy Alliance Scales, 574–575
Camerino, M., 467
Carlson, G., 338
Carlson, L., 521
Carlson, R., 521
Carnap, R., 3
Carr, M., 551
Carstens, A. A., 206–207, 214
Cartwright, R., 354
Case study, transference phenomenon, 517–520
Cassidy, J., 170
Caston, J., 597
Cathexis, 88, 323–324, 327
Chapman, J. P., 561–562
Chapman, L. J., 561–562
Charles, E., 338
Child abuse, attachment research, 166
Child Behavioral Checklist, 251
Child–caregiver relations. See also Attachment theory; Development, psychic
    affective development and, 130, 234–241
    animal research, 467–469
    attachment in, 20–21
    and aversive needs motivation, 22–23
    body–mind duality in interpretation of needs, 20
    childhood sexual trauma, 497–498
    classical vs. relational perspectives, 48
    conflict theory in, 50–54
    decontextualization of infant experience and knowledge, 224–225
    development as negotiation, 5, 58–59
    developmental aspects, 218–221
    essentials of early interaction, 240–241

and gender identity disorder, 247–252
and infant development of self, 140–141, 367–368
interactions and structure formation, 146–148
and late-onset disorders, 287–288
misinterpretation in, 23
mother's childhood experience and, 154, 170–171, 235
motivational theory, 12
in object relations theory, 468
organization of experience by infants, 211–212
in psychoanalytic theory, 173–174, 235, 391, 401–402
regulatory behaviors in, 468–470
regulatory system disturbances, 472–473
and REM sleep, 364, 366–367
role of repression in, 57–58
self-interest in, 51
in self psychology, 436, 471
and sensuality and sexuality, 24
and transitional objects, 471–472
Chomsky, N., 63–64
Chronobiology, 473
Cicchetti, D., 159
Clark, R. D., 213, 216
Coates, S., 130–131, 246, 249–251, 254
Cognitive–behavioral theory
    integrative aspects, 531–532
    and unconscious pathogenic beliefs, 507–508, 531
Cognitive psychology. See also Social cognitive theory
    in assessing defenses, 333
    cogntive styles and controls, 301–302, 336
    concept of preconscious in, 323–325
    consciousness in, 302–303, 381–382, 489–490
    defenses in, 8, 95
    desire in, 87
    development of, 82, 300–301
    ego defenses in, 304
    emotion in, 89–91, 122
    evocation of unconscious fantasy, 108
    motivational theory, 8, 86–89, 301, 383
    narrative construction in, 111
    primary–secondary process thinking, 303
    related to psychoanalytic techniques, 616–618
    related to psychoanalytic theory, 7–8, 78, 376–377

representations in, 79
self-monitoring techniques in managing
   countertransference, 618
supervision and training issues, 619–622
terminology, 315–320
theories on emotion, 89–91
unconscious in, 81–82, 305–306, 314
Cohen, D., 213
Cohler, B. J., 393
Cole, S. W., 527
Communication. *See also* Language
   and affective development, 474–475
   deception in, 56
   developmental considerations, 56, 404
   in higher primates, 21–22, 32
   in mother–infant regulatory system,
      474–475
   self-reflectiveness as human need, 24
   sign–signal, in infants, 21
Concept of the Object Scale, 457
Consciousness
   in cognitive science, 381–382
   defining, 203, 306, 316–317
   role of, 319–323
   states of, 95, 302–303, 489–490
Consensual Response Formulation, 576
Constructivism
   in developmental theories, 129
   in object relations theory, 188–189
   in psychoanalysis, 4
   representations in, 191
   in theories of mental structure, 187
Control–mastery theory
   emergence of repressed material in, 591–592
   empirical testing of, 592–599
   etiology in, 588–589
   interpretations in, 597
   origins of, 587
   pathogenic beliefs in, 6, 507, 531, 587–588,
      594
   therapeutic process in, 589–590, 601
Coonerty, S., 458
Cooper, S., 333, 335–338, 456–457
Core conflictual relationship themes, 6, 122,
   508, 511, 530, 576, 578–579
Countertransference
   concepts, 540–543
   disclosure, 554
   one-person and two-person psychologies,
      134–135, 143
   quantitative research, 543–550, 552–554

research needs, 553–554
role of, 510
self-monitoring techniques, from cognitive
   psychology, 618
in self psychology, 441–442
therapist–patient sexual abuse, 350–352
Cramer, B. G., 240–241, 365
Crick, F., 349–350, 355, 364
Crits-Christoph, P., 6, 121–122, 504, 510–511,
   530
Cybernetic systems theory, 476–477

Dahl, A., 338
Daple, S. A., 524
Darwin, C., 233
Davidson, D., 86
de Sousa, R., 122
DeCasper, A. J., 206–207, 214
Deception, in communication, 56
Defense Mechanism Rating Inventory, 334–335,
   340
Defense Style Questionnaire, 334–335
Defenses
   assessment of, 308–309, 327–328, 331–337,
      341, 356, 422
   in attachment theory, 178
   in borderline disorders, 329, 336–337,
      456–457
   in classical psychoanalytic theory, 60, 459,
      590–591
   classical vs. relational perspectives, 47
   in cognitive psychology, 8, 95
   conceptions of, 178, 308, 328–330,
      340–341
   developmental aspects, 332–333, 339–341,
      367–369
   and diagnoses, 337–339, 341–342
   and *DSM–III* and *DSM–IV*, 309, 332, 342
   early experimental research, 330–331
   and endogenous stimulation, 367–369
   in evolutionary theory, 60
   Freud, S., on, 327–328
   hierarchy of, 331–333, 341
   and intentionality, 8
   layering of, 92
   levels of personality organization, 454
   longitudinal studies, 331, 333
   in object relations theory, 328–329
   perceptual, 14, 302
   physiological factors, 322–323, 340
   research on, 304, 308, 333–334

Rorschach manifestations, 335–337, 422
in self psychology, 329
self-report instruments, 334–335
in social–cognitive theory, 383
in structure of unconscious, 31

Dement, W. C., 357–358, 361, 364

Demos, E. V., 130

Depression. *See also* Affective disorders
anaclitic vs. introjective, 420–422
associated with Alzheimer's disease, 444
gender as predisposing factor, 421
research on self-definition vs. relatedness, 419–421
in script theory, 524–525

Deprivation research, 26

Deutsch, H., 453, 465, 541

Development, psychic. *See also* Adolescence; Affective development; Attachment theory; Event theory; Geropsychology; Personality theory and research
adult, in self psychology, 443–444
and adult psychopathology, 137–138, 391–392, 416–419
animal research, 467–470
arrest model, 138
attachment in, 20–21, 42
attachment theory of, 129, 177–179
biological factors in, 178–179, 396
child–caregiver response patterns, 12, 32, 367–369
childhood sexual trauma, 497–498
childhood sexuality, 180
and clinical interpretation, 513
conflict in, 195–196
decontextualization by infants, 223–228
defenses in, 178, 332–333, 339–341, 367–369
and diagnosis, 179
dream research, 33
and drive–discharge–conflict model, 134
early patterns of interaction, research in, 135
essentials of early interaction, 240–241
and evolutionary theory, 56–57
exploration in, 21–22, 139–140, 156
feminist theory in, 408, 413–414
and gender identity, 24, 130–131
and gender identity disorder, 252–253
gerontological, 131–132
infant affective capacity, 210–212, 216
infant awareness in, 194–195
infant cognitive–perceptual ability, 212–213

infant endogenous stimulation, 367–360
infant experience, 205–209, 213, 367
infant misinterpretation in, 23
infant motivational organization, 219–221
infant organizational capabilities, 214–215, 217
infant research, 128, 130, 139–140, 208–209, 442–443
infant's external–internal discrimination, 136–137, 215–216
infant's integration of representations, 137
innate aggression and, 22
instrumental competencies and, 221–223
language in, 187–188, 228
and late-onset disorders, 287–288
learning research, 303
longitudinal research, 159–160, 162
motivational systems theory in, 12, 219–221
as negotiation process, 5, 58–59
in object relations theory, 129–130, 186–189
objective self and psyche, 202
organizational deficits in, 138–139
and personality organization, 454–455
personality research, 26
provisional identity in, 58–59
and psychic structure, 135, 367–369
in psychoanalytic theory, 45–48, 134, 176–177, 391–392
psychosexual phases of, 176
in relational matrix, 128
and REM sleep, 354, 364–369
of representations, 205, 377
repression in, 46–47, 57–58
role of prolonged childhood, 56–57
script and metascript in, 505
self-identity as goal of, 410
in self psychology, 394, 433, 436–437, 442–445
selfobject needs in, 137–138, 144–145, 240, 443–444
sense of self and, 16, 377–378
separation–individuation, 135–136, 176, 270
in social cognitive theory, 522
specialization in infants, 217–219
stage theory, 176–177, 222, 228
and storytelling in psychoanalysis, 106
symbiotic longings in, 135–136
and transference linkage, 135–136, 144–145
and transference patterns, 568–570
transformational perspective, 129, 135–136, 144–145, 147–149
transitional objects in, 471–472

and unconscious, 25, 28

Diagnosis. *See* Assessment and diagnosis

Diagnostic and Statistical Manual of Mental Disorders (DSM–III, DSM–III–R, DSM–IV)
    defenses in, 309, 332, 342
    posttraumatic stress disorder in, 397, 491

Dilthey, W., 3

Displacement, concept of, 25–26

Dissociation, 86

Dollard, J., 17

Donaldson, M., 223

Doob, L. W., 17

Dostrovsky, J., 352

Douvan, E., 271

Drake, R., 334–335, 338

Dreams
    constructivist view, 191
    current conceptions of, 33
    and endogenous drives, 358–359
    in evolutionary theory, 307–308, 353–354, 371
    Freud, S., on, 349
    narrative in, 355
    neurophysiological research, 349–350
    psychological content, 354
    and REM sleep research, 306–307, 350–353, 362–364
    representation of self in, 372
    representing drive behavior, 371–372
    as reverse learning, 349–350, 355
    in self psychology, 444–445

Dreyer, P. H., 272

Drive–discharge–conflict model, 134

Drives. *See also* Instincts
    accommodative structures and, 14
    in attachment theory, 172–175
    and dreams, 358–359, 371
    endogenous, 62–63
    ethological model, 42
    in evolutionary theory, 41, 70
    in Freudian theory, 127
    in humanistic psychology, 13
    and identity formation, 5, 45, 62–63
    and motivation, 62–63
    in object relations theory, 128
    in psychoanalytic theory, 172–175
    psychosocial model (Erikson), 42–43
    and REM sleep, 307
    self-actualization as goal of, 13, 19

vs. emotion, in development, 236
vs. relational model, 4–5, 65–70

DSM. *See Diagnostic and Statistical Manual of Mental Disorders (DSM–III, DSM–III–R, DSM–IV)*

Dunwiddie, T. V., 352

Dupkin, C., 246, 249–250

Dyk, R. B., 14

Dysfunctional Attitude Scale, 420

Eagle, M., 504

Eating disorders, 474

Edelson, M., 5–6, 8

Ego Function Assessment Scales, 332, 338

Ego Profile Scale, 332, 338

Ehrenberg, D., 545, 549

Eichberg, C. G., 163

Ekman, P., 210

Ellman, S., 306–307

Ellsworth, G., 340

Emde, R. B., 187, 234, 237, 407–408

Emmons, R. A., 527

Empathy, 578

Engel, G., 330, 466

Ensembled individualism, 414

Erhardt, A. A., 246

Erikson, E., 25, 42–43, 131, 236, 267, 270, 287, 408–413, 434

Esman, A. H., 273

Event theory
    body-bound experience and mental structure, 193–194
    defining event in, 190
    differentiation–integration processes, in development, 195–196
    interaction schemes, 189–190
    psychic change in, 191–193
    psychic conflict, in development, 195–196
    representations in, 191
    summary of, 197
    therapeutic goals, 196

Evolutionary theory
    adaptation in, 5, 40–43, 48–50, 56–57, 318
    capabilities of newborns, 213
    dreams in, 307, 353–354
    emergence of consciousness, 202–203
    endogenous drives and identity, 62–63
    fitness in, 48–50, 63
    Freud's interpretation, 38–40

Karp, S. A., 14
Katan, A., 270–271
Kegan, R., 190
Keller, S. E., 467
Kelly, G. A., 517, 531
Keniston, K., 271
Kernberg, O., 136, 189, 191, 329, 332, 336, 394, 431, 438, 453–455, 541
Kihlstrom, J. F., 305
King, B. E., 25
Kinsey, A. B., 269
Kinship theory, 50–51, 64–65
Klein, G.
    on clinical vs. theoretical research, 431
    cognitive styles, 14, 301–302, 336
    concept of self, 201, 406, 432
    motivational theory, 9, 27–28, 573
Klein, M., 169, 172, 368
Kleitman, N., 357–358
Knight, R., 453
Kobak, R., 163, 170, 178
Kobassa, S. C., 405
Kohlberg, L., 266–267, 273
Kohut, H., 392–394, 433–442
    concept of self, 128, 201, 471
    defenses, 329–330
    developmental theory, 136–138
    and evolutionary psychology, 64–65
    infant internalizations, 171
    maternal empathy, 169–170, 241
    selfobject needs, 144–145, 240
Kriegman, D., 4–5, 9
Kris, A., 103
Kris, E., 328, 330, 565
Kuhn, T. S., 186
Kwawer, J., 458

Lacan, J., 240
Lachmann, F., 61, 129, 136, 143, 145, 330
Lakoff, G., 111, 122, 187
Lampl-de Groot, J., 266
Lane, R. D., 475
Langs, R., 517
Language. *See also* Communication
    in Adult Attachment Interview, 162
    and assessing defenses, 335–336
    as biological process, 477
    as continuous process, 228

    developmental considerations in transference patterns, 568–569
    in developmental model, 187
    and infant research, 208–209
    innate capacity for, 63–64
    meaning distinct from essence, 83–85
    unconscious information processing, 380–381
LaPlanche, J., 431
Larsen, J., 352
Laufer, M., 269, 272
Laufer, M. E., 269
Laynch, G., 352
Lazarus, R., 90, 494
Learning. *See also* Memory
    and cognitive development, 303
    conditioning as, 18
    and discrete affects in infants, 211
    fetal capacity for, 207
    infant capacity for, 206–207, 365
    language, 63–64
    REM augmentation and, 370
    reverse learning theory of dreams, 349–350, 355
    role of play in, 21
    and set, in stimulus–response model, 13–14, 26
Legal issues, in stress disorder diagnoses, 495–496
Lensky, D., 524
Lerner, H., 308–309, 336–337, 452, 456–457
Lerner, P., 308–309, 336, 394, 456
Lerner Defense Scales, 336–337, 456
Levansen, R. W., 210
Levine, M., 335
Levy-Warren, M., 131
Lewin, K., 26–27, 276
Libet, B., 306, 321–323
Lichtenberg, J., 6–7, 9, 12, 21, 31, 139–140, 407
Lieberman, A., 178
Lindemann, E., 490
Linton, H., 336
Loewald, H. W., 61, 168, 190, 400–401
Loftus, E., 562
Lomo, T., 351
Long-term potentiation, 351–352
Lorenz, K., 17
Lowenstein, R. M., 328

Luborsky, L., 6, 121–122, 336, 504, 510–511, 530, 547–548, 552, 611–612
Lykes, M. B., 414

MacAlpine, I., 465
Mack, L., 25
Mack, R., 25
Mahler, M., 140, 169–172, 207–208, 379, 442
   caregiver role, 169–170, 240
   concept of self, 432
   infant development, 169–172, 208, 376
   separation–individuation, 401–402, 458, 471
   transference patterns, 133
Main, M., 161–163, 167, 170, 172–175, 177–178, 235
Mandler, G., 319
Marantz, S., 251
Marshall, R., 554
Marshall, S., 554
Martin, C. E., 269
Martin, G. B., 213, 216
Maslow, A., 13, 18–19
Mason, J. W., 467
Mason, M. A., 468
Master story concept, 5–6, 104–107, 113, 118–120
McAdams, D. P., 401, 405, 524
McCarley, R. W., 349, 355
McClelland, J. L., 523
McCullough, L., 577
McDougall, W., 13, 17
Medalie, J. H., 478–479
Meichenbaum, D., 531
Meissner, W., 430
Memory. *See also* Learning
   Alzheimer's disease, 444
   and control processes, 526
   influencing, research on, 562–563
   neural research, 351–352
   research on repression, 331
   role of REM sleep in, 353–355
   schemas in, 520–522
   and schematic change, 493
   script theory and, 521–522
   and set, in stimulus–response model, 13–14, 26
   and transference, 525–526
   traumatic, 491–492, 494

Menninger, K., 330, 609–610
Menninger Psychotherapy Research Project, 336, 422, 548
Messer, S. B., 531
Meyer, J., 246, 249–250
Michaels, R., 460
Miller, N. E., 17
Minnesota Multiphasic Personality Inventory, 331
Mirroring, 240
Mitchell, S., 4, 65, 128, 351, 543, 547
Mitchison, G., 350, 355, 364
Modell, A., 329, 405, 459
Moffitt, K. H., 525
Money, J., 246
Moral development in adolescence, 273
Motivation. *See also* Intentionality
   and altered states, 30
   assessment of state perspective, 30
   and attachment and affiliation needs, 15, 20–21, 140
   and aversive response needs, 15–16, 22–23, 30, 140
   in behaviorism, 18
   and cognition, 301
   in cognitive psychology, 8, 86–89
   concepts of self and, 16, 24–25, 432
   endogenous drives, 62–63
   in evolutionary theory, 40–43, 69–70
   and exploration and assertion needs, 15, 21–22, 139–140, 156
   functional autonomy concept, 26
   in humanistic psychology, 19
   in infants, 139–140, 219–221
   and instincts, 17
   interdisciplinary research on, 11
   intersubjective perspective, 30
   intrapsychic perspective, 29–30, 63
   Klein, G., on, 27–28
   and mind–body duality, 19–20
   modeled on biological functions, 94
   in object relations theory, 20–21
   physiological needs in, 12, 14–15
   psychoanalysis as theory of, 6–7, 9
   REM sleep and, 358–361
   repetition compulsion, 59
   and repression, 27
   research terminology, 13–14, 32
   in self psychology, 70
   selfobject needs in human development, 137–138, 240

on interpretation, 511, 563–565
Menninger Psychotherapy Outcome Study, 336
Menninger Psychotherapy Research Project, 422
on psychoanalytic technique, 511–512
psychobiological model, 466–467
psychosomatic factors, 478–479
rating therapeutic alliance, 575
rating transference patterns, 579–580
sociocultural factors, 478
therapeutic interpretations, 530–531, 548, 577–578
therapeutic relationship, 510
therapeutic technique, 509, 548–549

Paranoia, etiology, 417
Paul, J., 178
Paulhaus, D., 331
Pavlides, C., 352
Pavlov, I. P., 18
Penn Helping Alliance Rating Method, 574–575
Penn Psychotherapy Project, 547–548
Perception
    and cognitive styles and controls, 301–302
    conscious by nature, 90
    and defensive styles, 336
    in event theory, 190
    infant capacity, 212–213
    and intentionality, 80
    and motivation, 27, 301
    New Look studies, 301
    research on repression, 330–331, 336
    role in mental organization, 187
    Rorschach manifestations of defenses, 335–337
    and set, in stimulus–response model, 13–14, 26
    in sleep, in animals, 22
    subliminal, 8, 305–306
Perry, J., 333, 335, 337–338, 456
Personality theory and research
    anaclitic personality, 415
    developmental, 26, 270, 395, 399–408, 412–413
    emphasis on relatedness, vs. self-definition, 414–415
    emphasis on self-definition, vs. relatedness, 415
    in etiology of depression, 419–421
    evolutionary biology in, 91–94
    Freud, S., on, 400–401

intentional states, 91–93
introjective personality, 415
and psychopathology, 414–419
REM sleep research, 308
self-definition and relatedness, integration of, 395–396, 405–414
trait theorists, 92–93
and transference, 525–527
Piaget, J., 25, 130, 187, 190–192, 195, 212, 221, 273, 505, 522
Pine, F., 177, 240, 368, 376
Plan Compatibility of Intervention, 578
Play, role of, 21, 139, 364
Pleasure principle, 206
    and natural selection, 41–42
Poetzl, O., 302
Pollock, C., 335
Pomeroy, W. B., 269
Pontalis, J. B., 431
Popper, K. R., 3
Posner, M., 319
Posttraumatic stress disorder. See Trauma, psychic
Preconscious, defining, 316–317
Psychic structure. See also Unconscious
    actions vs. objects in, 187
    affect mechanisms in, 209–210
    body-bound experience in event theory, 193–194
    and borderline research, 455–456
    consciousness in, 202–204
    control processes in, 494
    deficit in, vs. organizational deficit, 138–139
    and early development, 135, 367–369
    in ego-psychology, 430
    infant's intrinsic capacities, 139–140, 213–217, 228–229
    models of, 145
    in object relations theory, 189
    organization of experience, 317–318
    psychic integration in, 204–205
    in psychoanalytic theory, 607–608
    schemas in, 505, 520–524
    scripts in, 521–522, 523–524
    theories of, 186–189
    and transference, 134–135
    transformational model, 146–147
    vs. psyche as dynamic system, 202
Psychoanalytic technique. See also Control-mastery theory; Defenses; Psychoanalytic theory; Repression; Therapeutic relationship; Transference; Treatment

analyst's unconscious memory, 612–613, 617
assessing source of psychopathology, 112
and cognitive psychology techniques, 616–618
derived from theory, 608–610, 612, 614–615
dream work, 33, 444–445
empirical claims about stories, 105–107
empirical research in, 508–509
evaluating clinical stories, 116–119
evocation of unconscious fantasy, 111–112
exploring painful fantasy, 109
extra-analytic material, 114–116
goals of, 6, 573, 607–608
identifying motivational systems, 28–31
identifying transference, 614, 617
integrative aspects, 512
interpeting manner of storytelling, 119
interpretation, 511–512, 530, 570–571, 577–578
interpretation, and medieval science, 559–563
interpretation followed by affect, 577
lack of technical literature on, 610–611
managing resistances, 613–614
outcome research, 511–512, 548–549
promoting insight, 578–579
representation-oriented brief psychotherapy with mother–infant dyads, 241
research needs, 512, 571, 580–581
as research subject, 605–606
role of regression, 61, 459
role of storytelling in, 99–100
role of transference, 61–62, 434
as science, 235–236, 599–601
sources of professional disagreement, 119–120
with storytelling and enactment, 114–115
supervision issues, 615–616, 619
supportive, defined, 574
therapeutic action, 113, 506–507
therapeutic relationship, 503–504, 510, 574–575
training in, 509, 620–623
treatment manuals in, 611–612
types of stories and enactments, 100–105
unconscious fantasy in, 5–6
unconscious pathogenic beliefs in, 507, 590–591, 594
understanding patient intentionality, 573
working through, 114
Psychoanalytic theory. *See also* Cognitive psychology; Evolutionary theory; Freud,

S.; Psychoanalytic technique; Self psychology
adolescent development in, 131, 269–272, 275–276, 402
affective development in, 175, 240, 270–272, 459, 474–475
assessment of state perspective on motivation, 30
and attachment theory, 129, 155, 159–160, 169–180
borderline concept in, 453–455, 458–460
child–caregiver relations in, 173–174, 235, 391, 401–402
classical–relational convergence, 43–44, 71
classical–relational dichotomies, 44–48
cognition in, 303
cognitive–behavioral integration in, 531–532
as cognitive discipline, 95
and cognitive psychology, 7–8, 78, 323–325, 375–376
concept of self in, 429–435
constructivism in, 4
defenses in, 60, 308, 327–328, 330, 459
developmental theories, 25, 134, 138, 176–177, 378–780, 391–392
displacement, and biological instinct, 25–26
divergence within schools of, 168, 172, 391–392
dreams in, 349–350
drive–discharge–conflict model, 134
early formulations, 607
empirical research in, 506–507
ethological influences in, 42, 376
evolutionary concepts in, 40–43, 70–71
and evolutionary psychology, 64–65
gender identity disorder in, 131, 260–261
goals of, 299
as hermeneutic discipline, 4, 6, 79, 122, 430, 539
historical relations with psychological science, ix–xii
infant development in, 136–137, 205–208, 470–473
influences on psychology research, 300–301
intentionality in, 78–81
interpersonal theories in, 379–380
layering of defenses, 92
memory systems, drive- or affect-organized, 111
metapsychology, 4, 77–78, 120–121, 299, 430–431
motivational theory, 6–7, 9, 29–30, 63

and motivation, 27, 31
neurophysiological research, 322–323
perceptual research, 330–331
and repetition compulsion, 59–60
role of, 5, 60–61
as self-manipulation of cognitions, 95
Research Center for Mental Health, xi
Reverse learning theory, 349–350, 355
Robinson, G., 551
Robinson, J. A., 525
Rock, D. L., 504, 508–509
Roffwarg, H., 364
Rogers, C., 13, 19
Rorschach methods, 308–309, 328, 335–337,
422, 456–458, 479
in borderline research, 456–458
related to psychoanalytic theory, 456
Rorty, R., 4
Rose, G. M., 352
Rosenberg, F., 272
Rosenberg, H., 272
Rovee-Collier, C., 224
Ruesch, J., 517
Rumelhart, D. E., 523

Safran, J., 508
Sampson, E. E., 408, 413–414, 504, 506, 531,
543–544
Sampson, H., 6, 121
Sander, L., 206, 238, 433
Sandler, A., 205, 376
Sandler, J., 205
Sanville, J., 401
Sceery, A., 163
Schachter, S., 89–90
Schafer, R., 6, 121, 328, 335, 394, 405, 431, 517,
564
Schank, R., 108, 122, 190, 521
Schemas
defining, 520–522, 576–577
developmental aspects, 522–526
in psychic structure, 505
Schilder, P., 188
Schimek, J., 189–190, 336
Schizophrenia
and defenses, 332, 336
sleep patterns, 361–362
Schleifer, S. L., 467

Schlesinger, H. J., 301–302
Schmale, A. H., 466
Schonbar, R. A., 6–7, 9
Schwartz, G. E., 475
Schwilk, C., 340
Scientific method
defense rating scales, 331–332
doctrine of signatures, and therapeutic
interpretation, 559–563
falsification criterion, 3
field theory, 276
meaning vs. essence in language of, 83
in proof of unconscious, 85–86
and psychoanalysis, 235–236, 314, 586,
599–601
in social cognitive research, 383–384
studying adolescent socialization, 276
theoretical preconceptions affecting,
512–513, 563
verification criterion, 3
Script theory
defining scripts, 521–522
developmental aspects, 522–524
mechanisms, 524–525
stages of memory transition, 525–526
and therapeutic relationship, 529
and transference interpretation, 524
Sears, R. R., 17
Self. See also Identity; Personality theory and
research; Self psychology
adolescent development, 270–271, 274
in attachment theory, 161
childhood trauma and development of, 498
concept of state in organization of, 30
concepts of, and transference phenomenon,
527
defining, 201
development of, and infant REM
stimulation, 367–368
in event theory, 194
infant capacity to form, 140–141
interaction structures in development of, 187
and motivation, 16, 24–25, 432
in object relations theory, 129–130
phenotypic–genotypic perspectives, 50–51
in psychoanalytic theory, 429–435
as representation, 188–189, 191
representations of, 372, 377–379
repression of, in child development, 60
subjective, 140, 202, 432
transformational perspective of development,
135–136

ABOUT THE EDITORS

James W. Barron, PhD, is the editor of the *Psychologist Psychoanalyst*. He is a founding member of the Massachusetts Institute for Psychoanalysis and the past-president of the Massachusetts Association for Psychoanalytic Psychology. Currently, Dr. Barron is an instructor in the Department of Psychiatry at Harvard Medical School. He is a graduate and faculty member of the Psychoanalytic Institute of New England, East. His special areas of interest include self analysis and psychoanalytic views of the creative process.

Morris N. Eagle, PhD, is a professor of psychology at the Ontario Institute for Studies in Education, University of Toronto. He has also been chairman of the psychology department and director of clinical training at York University in Toronto and at Yeshiva University in New York City. In addition, he has been on the faculty at the New School for Social Research and New York University and is currently on the faculty at New York University's postdoctoral program in psychoanalysis and psychotherapy. Other academic activities include appointments as Senior Fellow, Center for Philosophy of Science at the University of Pittsburgh; Visiting Scholar at the University of California, Berkeley, and University of Cambridge; and Distinguished Visiting Scholar at St. Andrews University in Scotland. Dr. Eagle is the author of *Recent Developments in Psychoanalysis: A Critical Evaluation* (1987) and has written more than 80 journal articles and chapters on psychology and psychoanalysis. He received the 1992 award for distinguished scientific contribution from the Division of Psychoanalysis of the American Psychological Association. He is also in part-time psychoanalytically oriented private practice.

David L. Wolitzky, PhD, is currently director of the New York University Psychology Clinic and associate professor of psychology, Department of Psychology, New York University. He is also a supervising analyst of the faculty of the New York University Postdoctoral Program in Psychotherapy and Psychoanalysis. He is a graduate of the New York Psychoanalytic Institute and a former director of doctoral and postdoctoral training in clinical psychology at New York University.

U